2013/14

THE GUIDE TO

UK COMPANY GIVING

NINTH EDITION

Denise Lillya & Tom Traynor

Additional research by:
Emma Weston

DIRECTORY OF SOCIAL CHANGE

Published by the Directory of Social Change (registered Charity no. 80051)

Head office: 24 Stephenson Way, London NW1 2DP

Northern office: Federation House, Hope Street, Liverpool L1 9BW
Tel: 08450 77 77 07

Visit www.dsc.org.uk to find out more about our books, subscription funding websites and training events. You can also sign up for e-newsletters so that you're always the first to hear about what's new.

The publisher welcomes suggestions and comments that will help to inform and improve future versions of this and all of our titles. Please give us your feedback by emailing publications@dsc.org.uk.

First published 1998
Second edition 1999
Third edition 2000
Fourth edition 2002
Fifth edition 2004
Sixth edition 2007
Seventh edition 2009
Eighth edition 2011
Ninth edition 2013

ISBN 978 1 906294 66 3

British Library Cataloguing in Publication Data
A catalogue record for this book is available from the British Library

Cover and text design by Kate Bass
Typeset by Marlinzo Services, Frome
Printed and bound by Page Bros, Norwich

FSC www.fsc.org
MIX
Paper from responsible sources
FSC® C023114

Contents

Foreword	iv
Introduction	v
About the Directory of Social Change	x
Charity of the Year and Smaller Organisations	xi
Facts and figures	xv
Matched funding	xvii
Applying to companies	xx
Aphabetical listing of companies	xxxii
How to use this guide	xxxiv
Alphabetical listing of company entries	1
Member organisations	
Arts & Business	343
Business in the Community	345
Scottish BITC	351
CommunityMark	353
ProHelp	354
Company activity listing	355
Geographical listing of head offices	360
Useful contacts	364
Index	367

Foreword

Half a billion poor children have been vaccinated in a programme by GAVI (the Global Alliance on Vaccines and Immunisations), made vastly more efficient through work by Goldman Sachs, an investment bank. Fully three million of those lives have been saved entirely by Goldman Sachs' work. Yet the bank didn't contribute a penny in cash.

The best philanthropy is when the donors use their resources in clever and unique ways to serve a cause. Goldman Sachs did that with GAVI, using some of its bond-structuring wizardry to reduce fluctuations in its income stream and hence enable that income to achieve more. The resources available to corporates are usually more sophisticated and bigger than those of other donors – PR teams, delivery fleets, offices, procurement experts, customer reach – which the best charity partnerships use well. The worst charity partnerships use just cash. 'Money is the least valuable social change asset', says Kurt Hoffman, former Director of the Shell Foundation and Director of the Institute for Philanthropy.

For fundraisers, this creates a conundrum. On one hand, companies can be fantastically valuable partners. But on the other, unlike grant-making foundations, they weren't set up to distribute money or support charitable causes, they're not obliged to do so, they're not specialised in it. Their primary responsibilities are to customers and shareholders, which any sensible company will insist and ensure that its charity partnerships support.

The wrong approach, then, is to treat them as cash machines. Somewhat better is to find how they can help *your organisation* – perhaps by donating product; by including you in large discounted purchasing arrangements; by letting you use office space or meeting rooms; by giving you access to their experts in HR, PR or property management. However, the best approach is to find how they can help *your beneficiaries.*

For instance, if in the UK you search on Google for 'suicide', ahead of the results is this:

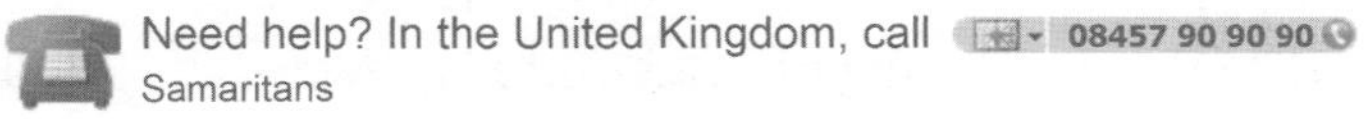

Need help? In the United Kingdom, call 08457 90 90 90
Samaritans

This probably cost Google very little to arrange, yet probably has a huge impact – and in a way which Google alone could generate. Does that generate money for the Samaritans? No. Does it nonetheless help its beneficiaries? You bet. Equally, The Coca-Cola Company in Africa used the trucks and network which form its legendary logistical operation to combat the spread of HIV and AIDS. It distributed condoms and attractive informational materials to all those dusty villages in the back of beyond where, astonishingly, you can always get a Coke.

In both examples – and many others like them – the 'donation' doesn't appear on a charity's income statement. Both achieved far more than if the company had given to a charity the money it spent, because the company already has the infrastructure.

The trick – with any donor, and most valuably with companies – is to find things which are cheap for the donor to give but valuable for you (and your beneficiaries) to receive. This valuable guide indicates which companies are open to helping and in what areas, and the onus is on charities to get creative in maximising the difference that makes.

Caroline Fiennes

Director, Giving Evidence (giving-evidence.com)

Author, *It Ain't What You Give, It's the Way that You Give It*

www.twitter.com/carolinefiennes

Introduction

Welcome to the ninth edition of *The Guide to UK Company Giving* which continues to provide relevant, updated policy information and commentary on the current state of corporate community involvement in the UK.

This edition features more than 550 companies, which together gave around £598.5 million (eighth edition: £762 million) in community support, including £470.1 million in cash donations (eighth edition: £512 million), mostly in the financial years 2010/11 or 2011 (or the latest available figures at the time of writing, occasionally 2011/12). There is a significant reduction in the amounts given in community contributions and cash donations on the previous edition, which taken at face value could be seen as reflecting the current economic climate; however, total pre-tax profit for all of the companies featured here increased by 55%. There are also fewer companies represented in this edition, as a number have ceased to exist, been taken over or merged with other companies or suspended their charitable giving. In the case of the latter, where no evidence of cash donations or significant community contributions could be found, companies have been omitted.

Each company entry provides essential information for accessing funding and resources. The entries for the larger givers are divided into separate sections, which usually reflects the increased availability of information on the community and charitable activities of those companies – there are around 100 of these fuller, more comprehensive entries. The remainder are more concise, again usually reflecting the availability of information, but summarised in the 'further information' field.

Most of the guide consists of individual company entries, but it contains additional sections offering advice and information for fundraisers, voluntary organisations, community groups, companies and individuals.

Company information

Our basic criteria for inclusion are that the company has made either: cash donations; gifts in kind such as equipment, volunteering, mentoring or secondment of its staff; and/or provided sponsorship or established partnerships in support of the community.

Wherever possible, we have quoted the UK charitable donations figure declared by the company in its annual report and accounts, as this continues to provide a tangible and unambiguous indicator of its commitment to the community. Failing this, we quote the worldwide donations figure, whilst making it clear that this is the case. We acknowledge, however, that cash donations are not the only way in which a company can provide support for charities and community groups. In many instances, and increasingly, the support given by companies in resources far outweighs their cash donations.

Where made available to us, we have included an additional figure for total community contributions. However, the means of measuring the value of these contributions, and even what should be included under this heading, are open to debate. In our view, the term should cover a company's charitable donations, plus support such as good-cause sponsorship and the value of gifts in kind such as equipment, pro bono work, secondments and employee volunteering during company time.

At the time of writing there is much debate about the future of company giving. There is a definite narrative developing around the notion that traditional corporate cash donations and gifts in kind are on the way out, and that more companies are moving towards partnerships and relationships with voluntary sector organisations based on shared social objectives. The most powerful (and most often) cited example of such a partnership is that between Samaritans and Network Rail. By sharing knowledge, training staff and campaigning together, they are both working to the same end of reducing suicide on the railways in a way that is far more productive and transformative than if Network Rail 'just' gave Samaritans a cash donation to do its own thing.

Although much of this discussion focuses on the largest companies supporting some of the largest charities, it is easy to see how this model of support could form the basis of relationships on a more local level. For example, a local youth charity could seek corporate sponsorship to run a local road awareness campaign, with the aim of reducing road traffic accidents involving young people. Or it could meet and speak with all the businesses within a two-mile radius of the local school and convince them to change the timings and routes of their deliveries so that they reduce traffic at the times and places where young people are most likely to be injured. The first option is quite transactional, but it is easy to see how the second is more engaging, makes the local companies a part of the solution, and potentially requires no direct funding to implement.

The theory is a good one, and placing charities' objectives at the heart of the relationship rather than cash opens up a whole range of possibilities for connecting companies to the visions, missions and objectives of charities in a way that is potentially more appealing, particularly in the current financial climate. It may also have the benefit of making some corporate social responsibility policies worth the paper they are printed on.

Aside from the theory and a few isolated examples, however, there is no reliable evidence to suggest a trend towards this kind of company giving, or that any companies are actively replacing other methods of support with this approach. For many charities, cash will be the best tool for the job, and for many companies, cash will be the most available and appropriate resource to meet what they see as their social obligations.

One of the determining factors in whether we see a shift in how companies give in future editions may well be the extent to which charities themselves instigate such relationships. For now, though, cash and giving in kind from companies remain a crucial part of the funding environment.

The term 'gifts in kind' can be misleading – it can include anything from the 'gift' of an old computer or a group of willing but unfocused volunteers with little to offer practically, to the really worthwhile contribution of pro bono legal or accountancy work provided by some private, professional firms or the secondment of a key member of staff to achieve a significant target or restructure a charity.

The term would have originally referred to goods, pieces of furniture or items of equipment (nearly always second-hand), whereas now, in the current economic climate, companies are increasingly offering staff time and skills as gifts in kind, which can be a very valuable asset for a charity. However, the term is often used in relation to articles alone without reference to professional or support services, and this can cause confusion.

If calculated and provided by the company, we quote management costs separately, as we do not consider it valid to include this as part of total community contributions. Obviously, companies incur certain costs in running their community investment programmes, but inclusion in the overall figure gives the impression of the available funding being greater than it actually is.

Finally, if possible, we give a figure for any cause-related marketing initiatives that a company may have undertaken. Again, we do not include this in the total community contributions figure because of its obvious commercial benefit to the company concerned.

Entry layout

The layouts used for the entries in this guide are described in the breakdown of the 'Fictitious Company' entry on page xxxiv. We hope that this will enable users to access the information they require on the various types of support that each company may offer more readily.

Geographical and activity indexes

Most companies state that a link between the company and the charity must exist for any appeal to be considered. The most obvious links are geographical, business activity or employee involvement. To help you prepare a preliminary list of companies to look at further, we have included a head office location index (see page 360) and a company activity listing (see page 355). Although the head office index is geographically biased towards London, it provides a useful starting point.

Comprehensive search facilities are available at DSC's subscription-based website: www.companygiving.org.uk, which also lists the directors and subsidiaries of each company.

Company listings

Our research accounts for about 80% to 90% of all giving by companies. However, there are companies which, by virtue of membership of one or more specific organisations, have declared an interest in supporting the community. So, even though the companies concerned do not necessarily have an entry in this guide, we have listed all current corporate members of Arts & Business, Business in the Community (BITC), Scottish Business in the Community and LBC (formerly known as the London Benchmarking Group). We have also listed those companies which have achieved BITC's Community Mark status which recognises companies that take an active and more holistic approach to community investment.

Details of ProHelp are also included as potentially a very useful source of support for charities. ProHelp is made up of a group of professional practices (including surveyors, architects, accountants and solicitors), each of which has offered to provide their professional services free of charge (or at minimal cost) to voluntary and community groups in their area. Rather than provide a list of ProHelp members, we have given the regional office contacts, as they are best able to provide up-to-date information on what is happening in their area and explain how you can access their services. These sections begin on page 343.

Company comparisons

The level of giving by companies in this guide varies greatly (from staff volunteering days with minimal or no cash donations given by the company, to tens of millions of pounds). Perhaps because of this, we tend to equate 'big giver' with 'most generous', but this may not be the case. Whilst very large companies may be applauded for giving, say, £4 million in donations, smaller companies giving a few hundred thousand pounds may actually be contributing a far greater proportion of their profits to charity. In this way, taken at face value, figures can be misleading with regard to judging who is making the greater gift to the community.

Although many companies' level of donations remains fairly constant year on year, others fluctuate significantly, and this is particularly the case in the recent recession where we have seen a reduction in company cash giving (and in community contributions).

There are fluctuations for a variety of reasons – a poor year for the company in terms of profits, a change in its community giving policy, a cutting down on cash donations and giving gifts in kind instead, or simply because in one year the company decided to substantially boost the free reserves of its associated charitable trust, thereby skewing its giving figures in that particular year. A company may not have become particularly parsimonious, but rather has been astute and forward thinking in its giving the year before.

Predicting and analysing company trends and making comparisons year on year can be a difficult task – there are so many variables to take into account – and this is further exacerbated by the unwillingness of many companies to declare UK-specific donations.

Total cash donations made by the companies detailed in this edition of the guide amounted to £470.1 million, a decrease of around 8.9% on the previous edition.

Total community contributions amount to £698.5 million, which shows a fall since the previous edition of 27.3% (8th edition: £762 million).

The table shows that around 68% of cash contributions came from the 25 companies in this edition, compared to 62% in the previous edition. The minimum figure required to gain entry into the top 25 is now at £4.3 million.

The top 25 companies

The Top 25 Companies (UK cash donations)

No.	Name	UK cash donations
1	Lloyds Banking Group	£43.8 million
2	Goldman Sachs International	£40.1 million
3	Tesco plc	£25.6 million
4	Barclays plc	£22.6 million
5	Vodafone Group plc	£21 million
6	BHP Billiton plc	£19.3 million
7	Santander UK	£14 million
8	Ecclesiastical Insurance Group plc	£11.7 million
9	HSBC Holdings plc	£10.6 million
10	Diageo plc	£10.5 million
11	Fidelity Investment Management Limited	£10.2 million
12	HESCO Bastion Limited	£10 million
13	British Sky Broadcasting Group plc	£9.1 million
14	Co-operative Group Limited	£8.8 million
15	Marks and Spencer Group plc	£6.9 million
16	Deutsche Bank	£6.8 million
17	Shell	£6.8 million
18	Scottish and Southern Energy plc (SSE)	£6.1 million
19	Virgin Atlantic Limited	£5.8 million
20	John Lewis Partnership plc	£5.6 million
21	Royal Mail Group plc	£5.2 million
22	ICAP plc	£4.9 million
23	WPP Group plc	£4.8 million
24	BP plc	£4.5 million
25	Thomson Reuters plc	£4.3 million
	Total	**£319 million**

The reluctance of the majority of companies to be truly transparent – that is, to state their contribution in each country rather than an overall global figure, or to declare in real terms what they have given to the community by way of their social investment – leads to confusion over not only who gave most but also what they gave and what it is that applicants should be applying for.

If companies state that funding or support is part of their commitment to their communities and they reap the benefits that this brings, then it is not unreasonable to ask the following questions? How much was given in volunteer time, mentoring hours, equipment, secondments etc.? What is the breakdown of the contribution given? And where did the cash contributions go, what good did they do and how were the successful applicants selected?

Corporate social responsibility

Corporate social responsibility (CSR), also known as corporate responsibility, corporate citizenship or sustainable responsible business (SRB), is a much-used term which seeks to define what an increasing number of people and groups believe the wider role of business in society should be.

Ideally, a CSR model should provide for the self-regulation of a company's impact on society and how to address that with measurable targets where possible. It should include the monitoring and review of its ethical policies and procedures, its environmental policy, its health and safety procedures, its employees' welfare, and the effect the company's business has on its customers, suppliers, communities and stakeholders.

The adoption of a CSR programme by an increasing number of companies stems, we believe, from both a recognition of the need to demonstrate (where they can) a commitment to the community, and (perhaps more likely) legislation which has forced companies to consider and calculate the damage caused by them to the environment, and to attempt to redress this where possible. The legislation has an impact on businesses by requiring them to improve in areas such as cutting carbon emissions. For example, the UK's Climate Change Bill commits the UK to an 80% reduction in carbon emissions by the year 2050.

Some companies, while addressing the environmental effect that they have on society and their more immediate communities, also engage with the communities in which they operate as part of their CSR programme. In many cases, this has resulted in companies recognising the work of voluntary organisations and the needs which they meet and also in the realisation there is a benefit to be gained in supporting them. These benefits include:

- getting good publicity and building brand awareness through association with an organisation or cause;
- gaining a deeper understanding of their own customer base;
- in the case of staff volunteering (mentoring or providing pro bono work), reaping a real staff development benefit with opportunities for skill and leadership development and even the improvement of financial performance (*The Value of Corporate Governance: The positive return of responsible business*, BITC, 2008).

Working in partnership can be of mutual benefit to both sides – companies bring their core business skills, including financial or logistical expertise, and access to supply chains and high-level contacts. Charities can provide their knowledge of what is needed on the ground and what approaches will be most effective.

There will always be those companies which meet their social responsibility obligations by simply going through the motions of signing up to any one of a number of CSR membership bodies, or by declaring their community contribution to be 'providing employment within our areas of operation', rather than taking real and positive community action. By having to take their statutory corporate responsibility requirements in other areas seriously, it is to be hoped that community engagement and obligation will be given the serious consideration it deserves too.

Measuring corporate support

The methods we use to gather information on companies' charitable support are relatively straightforward. Basic financial details and the level of cash donations for a particular year are obtained from published annual reports and accounts or information lodged at Companies House. For other support in addition to cash donations (gifts in kind such as pro bono work, employee volunteering and so on) and the specifics of a company's charitable support policy, we have spoken to the relevant person. With many companies nowadays, such information is increasingly to be found on their websites, which can sometimes be very helpful and informative: often giving advice on how to apply for funding, the company's criteria, what good causes they favour and sometimes case studies of previous beneficiaries.

The inclusion of policy details within a company entry is a very important aspect of our work as it provides fundraisers with the information necessary to make an informed decision about which companies to target. We do not recommend the scattershot approach, believing this to be not particularly successful, a waste of time for the parties concerned and potentially damaging to other, more qualified applicants.

For those without the necessary matching profile or fundraising resources, this guide, with its focus on cash donations and resources, provides straightforward evidence of the level of corporate community support for any listed company and points the way for small and medium-sized organisations to make informed decisions about which companies to approach.

Transparency

DSC has always maintained that it is in the public and the voluntary sector's interest to know about individual company policies so that a clearer picture of what support is available, where and for what purposes may be seen.

Companies, unlike grant-making charities, are clearly not primarily established to support good causes and they have neither the same practices and policies in place as grant-making charities nor perhaps, the inclination to sort through many applications looking for the most appropriate or worthwhile. For this reason it is important for the company to make clear and publicise its criteria for giving and for the potential applicants to see if they have a match or link, in order to save time and other resources for both parties.

We know from our research for this guide that some companies are gradually recognising and acting on the moral requirement to publish their policies on community/charitable giving, their targets, performance and the delivery of those targets, and who they have benefited in a particular financial year. However, a glossy brochure or section in the annual report with a myriad of statistics is not always transparent in a way that is useful to potential applicants. Very often the information given is emotive rather than substantial, avoids actual money spent, and/or concentrates on its employees' contributions, not distinguishing between the efforts of staff and the actual resources donated by the company in cash or in kind. It can also be seen in many instances that staff volunteering, while accredited to the company in what it has contributed to the community, is also accredited to the company in its contribution to staff development, thereby possibly avoiding costs for itself.

Companies which are truly transparent in any meaningful way with all that they do as regards community involvement are still, unfortunately, in the minority.

Caution

We are told that companies continue to receive many unsolicited or inappropriate appeals for support. While many bring this upon themselves due to a lack of clear guidelines for potential applicants, this should not be seen as an excuse to conduct blanket mailings. It is vitally important to do your research thoroughly.

Further information on how to approach businesses for support successfully is given in the 'Applying to companies' section on page xx. In general, however, before approaching any company in this guide, its entry should be read carefully. As we have stated previously, unless there is some clear link with a company, or your project is clearly within its defined areas of support, you should not be applying.

We also recommend that you download a copy of *Charities Working with Business Code of Fundraising Practice*, published by the Institute of Fundraising. This gives a good overview of the issues involved in undertaking a relationship with a company and is available at: www.institute-of-fundraising.org.uk.

DSC campaigns and the current environment

DSC believes that companies are capable of giving more to the sector than they do at present, and that they have an obligation to do so. We feel that there are unanswered questions around not just the amount that companies give, but also the effectiveness of the ways in which they do give and the extent to which large proportions of what is labelled 'company giving' should actually be considered giving at all.

Conclusion

The recent recession has clearly triggered an overall reduction in financial support to charities, but companies are still giving, and as their support often depends on an individual company's profits, a minority have actually increased their community contribution.

Our research for this edition suggests that companies are increasingly aware of the advantages of adopting and publicising clearer social responsibility policies; transparency in this area saves time and resources for all concerned. A company with clear guidelines and stated criteria for community giving will attract those charities that fit the bill and reduce the number of ineligible applications made to them, while at the same time charities will target those companies that are most likely to contribute to their cause.

Despite this awareness, it is apparent that many charities are still unclear about the most effective techniques to employ to secure contributions from the private sector.

Fundraisers should dedicate time when applying to companies, as they do in their applications to other funders. Companies' contributions, whether cash or in kind can be significant and, in the case of sponsorships or cause-related marketing, long lasting.

The aim of this guide is to provide the knowledge necessary to obtain company support through the provision of profile information on individual companies, identifying the kind of support available and how to access this effectively. We hope the use of it will help charities to secure company backing for the good causes they champion and support.

Acknowledgements

We would like to thank all the companies that have helped to compile this guide: both those which we have contacted directly and those which have made their annual reports and accounts and/or their websites informative and accessible. Notwithstanding this, the text and any mistakes within the guide remain ours rather than theirs.

We would also like to thank Caroline Fiennes for writing the foreword to this edition. She is Director of Giving Evidence (giving-evidence.com), a company which specialises in 'advice on giving, based on evidence'. She frequently speaks and writes in the press on a range of voluntary sector issues.

And finally . . .

If you have any comments about the guide, positive or negative, please get in touch with us at the Research Department, Directory of Social Change, Federation House, Hope Street, Liverpool, L1 9BW; tel: 0151 708 0136; email: research@dsc.org.uk

About the Directory of Social Change

DSC has a vision of an independent voluntary sector at the heart of social change. The activities of independent charities, voluntary organisations and community groups are fundamental to achieve social change. We exist to help these organisations and the people who support them to achieve their goals.

We do this by:

- providing practical tools that organisations and activists need, including online and printed publications, training courses, and conferences on a huge range of topics
- acting as a 'concerned citizen' in public policy debates, often on behalf of smaller charities, voluntary organisations and community groups
- leading campaigns and stimulating debate on key policy issues that affect those groups
- carrying out research and providing information to influence policymakers.

DSC is the leading provider of information and training for the voluntary sector and publishes an extensive range of guides and handbooks covering subjects such as fundraising, management, communication, finance and law. We have a range of subscription-based websites containing a wealth of information on funding from trusts, companies and government sources. We run more than 300 training courses each year, including bespoke in-house training provided at the client's location. DSC conferences, many of which run on an annual basis, include the Charity Management Conference, the Charity Accountants' Conference and the Charity Law Conference. DSC's major annual event is Charityfair, which provides low-cost training on a wide variety of subjects.

For details of all our activities, and to order publications and book courses, go to

www.dsc.org.uk, call 08450 777707 or email publications@dsc.org.uk.

Charity of the Year and smaller organisations

Del Redvers

This article was included in the last three editions of the guide; subsequently Business Community Connections has ceased operating. Nevertheless, we think the content of the article will still be of interest and use to certain readers.

Charity of the Year is a label increasingly applied to all manner of partnerships, but what does it really mean? Business Community Connections (BCConnections) researched how different charities and businesses use the Charity of the Year concept and in doing so identified several critical factors for success.

There are many forms of Charity of the Year partnership but with certain common themes. Most obviously and significantly they are time limited relationships although certainly not always one year in duration. The most widespread understanding of the term is a partnership in which the staff from a business undertake a range of activities to raise money for the identified charity. At the end of the year businesses often feel the need to replace the charity they support in order to prevent fundraising fatigue, and to ensure wider appeal to staff and customers as no one charity will be relevant to all stakeholders. This also gives the business the opportunity to support another charity.

Increasingly, however, other elements are added to the staff fundraising concept, such as cash donations, employee volunteering or other in kind donations, sponsorship, cause related marketing or lobbying and campaigning. Sometimes these partnerships involve very little or no staff fundraising at all. Many businesses involved in these other types of Charity of the Year relationship would not be able to support a staff fundraising partnership, perhaps because they have smaller numbers of higher paid staff with less free time. Similarly, it makes sense for companies with relevant goods or services to donate them in-kind to the charity as part of their contribution. The term Charity of the Year is used to brand a relationship, because although it can be misleading, it is a widely understood and accepted term.

For smaller organisations

Traditionally Charity of the Year relationships have been the preserve of large charities, frequently those able to offer national exposure to large corporate partners. There is, however, evidence to suggest a growing trend in the number of smaller charities seeking and successfully establishing Charity of the Year partnerships. The BCConnections research shows no reason why Charity of the Year should be out of bounds to small or medium sized charities and by the same token to Small and Medium Enterprises (SMEs). There are however a number of risks which can offset the many benefits available to both charities and businesses and which need to be weighed very carefully irrespective of the size of the organisation.

The advantages . . .

The research suggests that in general Charity of the Year partnerships do work for both partners. On the whole charities tend to put a financial value on the relationship of six or seven times the cost of establishing and managing the partnership. Whilst larger charities frequently net income in excess of £100,000 through these relationships, smaller charities also tend to consider them worthwhile activities even if they are very unlikely to achieve a six-figure financial contribution. A Charity of the Year partnership can . . .

1. Provide a reasonably predictable and often large income stream over a fixed period of time.
2. Provide an excellent opportunity to significantly increase the profile and reputation of the charity.
3. Create a track record of working with the corporate sector.
4. Lever support from other businesses and customers.

5 Increase fundraising activity from existing supporters.
6 Educate the workforce and customers of the business about the charity or its cause.
7 Offer access to employees as a new market of potential supporters.
8 Last longer than one year. There is a growing trend towards the 'Charity of 2 or 3 years' giving the security of a longer-term income stream.
9 Generate unrestricted income, although there is a developing trend towards restricted funds in these relationships.
10 Increase the morale at the charity, especially amongst the fundraising team.

And pitfalls . . .

There are many issues for a charity to consider before deciding whether or not to pursue a Charity of the Year relationship.

These partnerships can be resource intensive to manage, most significantly in terms of staff time. The cost benefit analysis section of the BCConnections research reveals that managing a small Charity of the Year partnership often takes at least 10% of one person's time. A large partnership can occupy from one to three employees on a full-time basis. There may also be costs associated with legal agreements for joint promotions, licencing and sponsorship arrangements.

Pitching for major Charity of the Year partnerships can be a significant undertaking in itself, requiring the investment of resources at an early stage, with no promise of a return. Once a partnership is agreed there is often a lengthy planning period before it is launched. Consequently, there exists a time lag between investing resources to develop the partnership and receiving the support. This can create a cashflow problem, particularly for smaller charities but also where a charity is expected to cover early costs such as producing badges and promotional material. Despite what can amount to considerable set-up costs, these partnerships will always be time limited and therefore, for most charities, cannot be considered a sustainable source of income.

Frequently, businesses use voting schemes to engage staff in selecting the Charity of the Year. This often results in the exclusion of many types of charities from the selection process as in an unrestricted ballot, staff have a tendency to vote for charities such as children, cancer and other health related charities with poignant issues.

There is always an element of risk on both sides in any corporate community relationship as a link is forged between the reputations of the two partners. With Charity of the Year this link is likely to be well publicised and consequently the relationship can backfire if it is considered to be unethical.

Getting a Charity of the Year partnership

If your organisation is seeking a Charity of the Year partnership, there are some things you should bear in mind . . .

1 Be strategic in your approach. Focus on the good fit between your charity and your target companies. Start building relationships with these businesses and try to grow the company contacts you already have. Think ahead and plan which business may adopt you next year or the year after that.
2 Decide on the cost benefit ratio you are prepared to accept. This is usually not just a financial exercise as it may involve judgements about intangible benefits and the potential worth of a partnership with the company in the longer term.
3 Be prepared to walk away. One of the most important messages to come out of the research is that charities need to assess at an early stage the potential value of the partnership, and then negotiate and decide whether or not it is worthwhile pursuing.
4 Consider approaching new businesses not previously involved in Charity of the Year partnerships.
5 Consider the benefits and drawbacks of a Charity of the Year partnership from the business point of view. Try to gain an understanding of why your target business might want a Charity of the Year partnership and more specifically with your organisation. This can help you to value your charity's worth and feel more confident about negotiating with the business.
6 If possible seek advice from a previous Charity of the Year of your target business. This should increase your understanding of the company, how they work and what they may want out of the partnership. This should be supplemented by in-depth research on the company from published sources.
7 Ask the business for a meeting at an early stage. This will give you more guidance about what they want from the partnership, before you invest significant resources. It will also help start to develop a relationship.
8 Be flexible about including other types of involvement for the partnership, apart from staff fundraising.
9 Consider at the outset how you could monitor the impact of your proposed Charity of the Year partnership on the wider community.

The pitch

When pitching for a Charity of the Year partnership, a key consideration is how the charity will be selected. If it is a management decision, there needs to be a focus on benefits to the business whilst for a staff ballot the proposal should be more emotive.

Where possible engage the beneficiaries of the charity in the process.

Proposals should be tailored specifically to the business you are approaching and stick to any brief given. Should the pitch fail, always ask for feedback and if appropriate a contribution; it is worth asking if the business can compensate you in any way for the time and resources invested. However, always be mindful of possible future relationships with that business.

For smaller Charity of the Year partnerships there is often no formal pitch process. Businesses that already engage in small scale Charity of the Year partnerships are more likely to use existing contacts or staff recommendations to identify future partners. Smaller businesses that have never had a Charity of the Year may need some guidance from the charity to help them appreciate the potential of the relationship.

Setting up the partnership

Planning

The importance of development time prior to publicising the partnership cannot be underestimated. In the BCConnections research over a quarter of the organisations did not plan the partnerships. Many larger businesses now select their Charity of the Year six months to one year before the publicised partnership year begins. For smaller partnerships, however, one or two months can provide ample planning time.

Agreement

A written agreement outlining the parameters of the relationships (objectives, targets, timeframes and budgets) plays an important role in managing the expectations of your partner. Clearly allocate responsibility for tasks and costs.

Seek to maximise the mutual benefit of the partnership. The greater the benefit for your business partner, the more seriously they will take the relationship and the greater the likelihood they will invest in Charity of the Year partnerships in the future.

Develop a plan of events, and a process for regular communication and review. Use the expertise of charity fundraisers to generate ideas for activities. Most charities find it easier to have a phased programme of fundraising events rather than doing everything at once.

Financial return

Consider whether there should be a minimum guaranteed return to the charity from the partnership. Some charities recommended including minimum guarantees in any documentation to protect against risk such as a minimum amount of cash to be raised. In addition agree what percentage of money raised will be restricted. Some charities will ask for a percentage of funding to be unrestricted to cover the costs of running the partnership. Also establish the timings of payments to the charity throughout the year and consider the impact on cashflow.

Whilst a single large cheque handed over at the end of the year may look impressive, it is often not a practical option, particularly for smaller charities.

Communications

Establish who will be responsible for the overall publicity of the partnership. If a logo is to be designed for the new partnership who will pay for it? Ensure that use of logos is agreed in advance.

There is also the issue of internal communication with the company's employees. Several charities have commented that it takes time to motivate and inspire staff to get involved in a programme of fundraising or other activities and the timetable should allow for this. The appointment of charity champions amongst the staff of the business can help to co-ordinate activity and provides a communication channel, particularly for multi-site operations.

Thinking ahead

Discuss the sustainability of the partnership and develop an exit strategy early on in the relationship. During review meetings consider whether it is beneficial to both partners to keep the relationship going beyond the year. Even if the charity is not designated Charity of the Year going forward, it may be possible to maintain and develop specific elements of the relationship, such as relationships with suppliers and payroll giving.

Measuring and monitoring

There has been an increasing emphasis on measuring the impact and benefits of Charity of the Year partnerships as with all other aspects of corporate community involvement. Like other types of relationship, there need to be mechanisms for measuring the social impact, benefits to the business and benefits to the charity. Significantly, Charity of the Year partnerships require careful measurement of the relationship itself as it is often more involved than other types of corporate community partnership.

Critically both parties need to know if there was a positive benefit compared to the cost of their involvement. Effective measurement of the partnership enables both parties to decide whether to undertake similar ventures in the future and identifies areas for improvement. Knowing what you want to measure at the outset allows for the correct accounting procedures to be put in place. For instance, without prior planning it may be easy for a company to breakdown staff fundraising by office or team but not by individual activities. This would make it impossible to measure the effectiveness of each activity.

The following represent some of the measures used by the businesses and charities we interviewed during the course of the research to assess the success of the partnership.

- Targets met or exceeded in planning and preparation.
- Financial target met or exceeded.
- % of company branches involved.

- Outcome of the partnership for charity beneficiaries; e.g. number of individuals helped as a
- result, or number of pieces of equipment purchased, amount of research time enabled etc.
- Positive PR; e.g. the number of articles/column cms or amount of television time.
- Number of contacts the charity has developed.
- Staff and customer surveys; e.g. awareness and perceptions of business and charity.
- Feel good factor; e.g. for business – number of letters, comments received in chat room, etc.
- Number of charity champions that come forward in the business.

Conclusions

Charity of the Year relationships are a popular and highly visible way for charities and businesses to work together for mutual benefit and to target the social impact of corporate support for the voluntary sector. Whilst there are no hard and fast rules about establishing and managing Charity of the Year partnerships, a considered and strategic approach will help to maximise the many advantages offered by this type of relationship whilst minimising the risk.

Smaller charities should be encouraged to consider how they can adapt the models developed by larger organisations. Although there is definitely the opportunity for charities of all sizes to benefit from Charity of the Year relationships, they are not necessarily appropriate for all organisations and represent just one of several types of relationship that can form between the voluntary and corporate sector.

Del Redvers, formerly Head of Sustainability for BMT Group Ltd.

Facts and figures

How much do companies give?

There is a statutory obligation for companies to record their charitable donations where the total exceeds £2,000 in any one year, and this will be declared in the company's annual accounts. The figure for their community contributions, however, is more difficult to obtain and often is not calculated at all.

Some companies (the global figure is currently 120) are members of LBG and, using its model, make available a clear breakdown of their community giving. LBG companies work together to measure corporate community investment. The LBG model provides a comprehensive and consistent set of measures against which companies can determine their contribution to the community, including cash, time and in kind donations, and management costs. The model also captures the outputs and longer-term impacts of the company's community investment projects on society and the business itself, and is widely regarded as the international standard for measuring such investment.

Unfortunately, the adoption of this methodology by companies is the exception rather than the rule, and the absence of any sort of breakdown by most companies makes comparisons and analysis of total community contributions all the more difficult.

Although many companies' levels of donations remains fairly constant year on year, others fluctuate significantly and for no apparent reason, which can also make predicting trends in company giving difficult. Furthermore, in trying to provide an accurate picture of the level of company support in the UK, we have been hindered by a significant number of the biggest givers failing to provide UK-specific figures.

Total cash donations made by the 551 companies in this guide amounted to £470.1 million (8th edition: £512 million), with a total community contributions figure of £598.5 million compared to £762 million in the previous edition. These figures show that the level of cash donations has decreased by 8.9%; total contributions have decreased by around 27.3%.

It is difficult to say if this represents a trend towards a reduction in cash donations and total contributions to the charitable sector, although part of this apparent decrease in support may be accounted for by a lack of information regarding the full extent of in kind support in the UK and its value, as explained above.

Charitable donations

What we can see from table 1 is that 68% of cash contributions came from the top 25 companies in the years 2010/11 and 2011, compared with 62% in 2009/10 and 2010. The minimum figure required to gain entry into the top 25 this time around was £4.3 million.

Table 1

The top 25 companies (UK cash donations)

No.	Name	UK cash donations
1	Lloyds Banking Group	£43.8 million
2	Goldman Sachs International	£40.1 million
3	Tesco plc	£25.6 million
4	Barclays PLC	£22.6 million
5	Vodafone Group plc	£21 million
6	BHP Billiton Plc	£19.3 million
7	Santander UK	£14 million
8	Ecclesiastical Insurance Group plc	£11.7 million
9	HSBC Holdings plc	£10.6 million
10	Diageo plc	£10.5 million
11	Fidelity Investment Management Limited	£10.2 million
12	HESCO Bastion Limited	£10 million
13	British Sky Broadcasting Group plc	£9.1 million
14	Co-operative Group Limited	£8.8 million
15	Marks and Spencer Group plc	£6.9 million
16	Deutsche Bank	£6.8 million
17	Shell	£6.8 million
18	Scottish and Southern Energy plc (SSE)	£6.1 million
19	Virgin Atlantic Limited	£5.8 million
20	John Lewis Partnership plc	£5.6 million
21	Royal Mail Group plc	£5.2 million
22	ICAP plc	£4.9 million
23	WPP Group plc	£4.8 million
24	BP Plc	£4.5 million
25	Thomson Reuters PLC	£4.3 million
	Total	**£319 million**

Donations as a percentage of profit

Combined pre-tax profits for all of the companies in this guide totalled £245.8 billion (8th edition: £158.7 billion). Total cash donations stood at 0.19% of pre-tax profit, compared to around 0.32% in the previous edition. As we can see, the reason for the reduction in the overall percentage of pre-tax profit given in cash donations is that, while the total cash donations figure is at a similar level to the previous edition of this guide, total pre-tax profit has increased by around 55%.

Community contributions

From table 2 we can see that the top 25 companies' community contributions represented over 67.1% of the total. The minimum entry figure for the top 25 is £5.2 million.

Table 2

The Top 25 Companies (UK community contributions)

No.	Name	UK contributions
1	Lloyds Banking Group	£85 million
2	Goldman Sachs International	£40.1 million
3	Barclays PLC	£30.3 million
4	Tesco plc	£25.6 million
5	Vodafone Group plc	£21 million
6	BHP Billiton Plc	£19.4 million
7	WPP Group plc	£15.3 million
8	Santander UK	£14 million
9	Co-operative Group Limited	£11.8 million
10	Ecclesiastical Insurance Group plc	£11.7 million
11	HSBC Holdings plc	£11.6 million
12	Marks and Spencer Group plc	£11.4 million
13	Diageo plc	£10.5 million
14	PricewaterhouseCoopers LLP	£10.3 million
15	British Sky Broadcasting Group plc	£10.2 million
16	Fidelity Investment Management Limited	£10.2 million
17	HESCO Bastion Limited	£10 million
18	National Grid Holdings One plc	£8.3 million
19	John Lewis Partnership plc	£7.8 million
20	Deutsche Bank	£7.6 million
21	Shell	£6.8 million
22	Scottish and Southern Energy plc (SSE)	£6.1 million
23	Virgin Atlantic Limited	£6.1 million
24	Thomson Reuters PLC	£5.2 million
25	Royal Mail Group plc	£5.2 million
	Total	**£401.6 million**

Contributions as a percentage of profit

As a percentage of pre-tax profits, community contributions for the companies listed in the guide stood at 0.24%, a decrease of 0.19% on last edition's figure (0.43%).

Matched funding

Corporate social responsibility (CSR) is no longer perceived as just making financial contributions to charities. Many companies now have seen the benefits of adopting a positive CSR/community-giving plan for themselves, and of their staff being proactive in the communities in which the company operates, or in society at large. At its best, CSR includes companies looking at their resources and their employees' core skills, and working out how they can contribute to society in a more sustainable way.

The growing trend towards larger companies becoming more proactive in their community giving – for example, choosing partnerships which complement their business, and being more focused in their approach – does not bode well for most voluntary organisations. This is particularly true for those that are smaller, and cannot give the same publicity to a company's contribution as the larger ones, or the less popular organisations such as those charities supporting ex-offenders or people dealing with drug addiction.

One way in which this can be balanced is by encouraging companies to adopt match funding schemes whereby they match the funds of those raised by their employees. This allows staff to choose causes for which they have an affinity, without considering what fits in with the company's particular business, or what the charity can give in return.

Our research for the ninth edition found that around a quarter of companies provide staff with matched funding schemes. There is an opportunity here for fundraisers to approach both those companies with an existing scheme with a request to address staff on behalf of their own charity and those companies who do not at present have a scheme in place.

The following article by Belinda Hunt of TrustCSR details the positive aspects of matched funding and encourages fundraisers to approach companies with this potential resource in mind.

TrustCSR, which is part of The Trust Partnership, specialises in CSR consultancy and the delivery of employee engagement and community investment programmes. Within employee engagement the main areas of expertise are the design, implementation, reporting and day-to-day management of programmes for a range of large corporate organisations.

The following information relates to TrustCSR's experience, its clients' views and statistics relating to their matched funding programmes, and is not necessarily indicative of the entire market place. However, we consider that the information provided will be both informative and useful for our readers.

Belinda Hunt writes:

What is matched funding?

Matched Funding, Matched Giving, Charity Top Up, or Booster Funding – no matter what name the scheme goes by, they all have the same fundamental goal for the corporate organisations offering them – to increase employee engagement amongst their workforce, build motivation and commitment, and develop their corporate reputation, both as a good employer, and also in the communities in which they work. These simple mechanisms, which allow employees to raise funds for their chosen charities and gain support from their employer, can be a powerful fundraising tool.

How does matched funding work?

In the majority of cases, the schemes are open to employees at every level of the organisation who participate in fundraising events or volunteering activity. Some organisations will consider personal donations for matched funding and some will make a financial contribution towards their employees' volunteering hours, even when they are undertaken within working hours.

What varies considerably from company to company is the amount they will donate per employee per year. Schemes start from £250 and go up to £5,000 per employee per financial year. Some organisations will allow their employees to apply as many times as they like, up to the stipulated limits, while others will only allow their employees to apply once per financial year, whether they apply for their total annual allocation or not.

Many companies also structure their matched funding programme around their Community Investment strategy, giving higher annual limits if employees choose to support charities whose objects fit within their own focus areas. For example, if their focus is on medicine and health, then charities falling within that arena may receive up to 100% of what the employee has raised, but if the charity's objects fall outside medicine and health, they may receive as little as 25%.

What's been happening recently?

With CSR moving up the corporate agenda, companies are concentrating their efforts on aligning their charitable giving more closely with their operations and development strategies. Rather than making ad hoc donations and responding to unsolicited funding requests, they are actively seeking ways to increase the impact their donations have on the wider community and the success of their operations. One of the ways they are achieving this is through more refined employee engagement schemes.

By running schemes which are easily accessible, have clear and concise guidelines and are actively promoted within the organisation, clients have all seen an increase in employee participation in recent years.

Our statistics show that during the peak of the economic downturn in 2010, the number of employees submitting matched funding applications fell by 32.84% against 2009. However, this trend is reversing and in 2011, the number of applications was up by 49.8%. We have seen this trend continue into 2012 with 33.73% more successful applications being processed than in 2011.

Whilst the number of applications has increased significantly, the amounts raised by employees, and therefore donated to charities, have not seen the same rate of growth. The increase in the value of donations was 8% in 2011 and a further 2.43% in 2012.

Overall, clients' donations equated to 57.29% to the value of their employees' fundraising totals in 2011 and 59.72% during 2012. The upward trend is continuing to have a positive impact on charitable income.

Which types of charities are benefiting most?

Although the majority of charities being supported are still the major national and international charities who hold annual campaigns and are in the forefront of people's minds, there is increasing support for smaller organisations.

A study of a cross section of TrustCSR clients has revealed that a rising number of employees support smaller charities (with an income of less than £250,000 per annum), and also charitable organisations within their local communities such as parent teacher associations, sports clubs and local guide or scout groups.

In 2011, 25% of all applications made were for smaller charitable organisations and although not a significant increase, this rose to 27% in 2012. In financial terms this equated to 30.43% of matched funding donations. When considering the size of these organisations' income, this could have a considerable bearing on their operations.

What can charities do to maximise the benefits of matched funding?

As the success of these matching schemes strengthens and companies increase the budgets dedicated to them, it is likely that fewer corporate organisations will want to make ad hoc donations at their current level. The implication of building close relationships with individual donors, and making them aware of matching schemes and other support that their employers might offer, will become increasingly important to fundraising strategies.

Tell your fundraisers about matched funding

Something as simple as reminding donors to ask their employer about matched funding could significantly boost a charity's annual income. Gift Aid information is included in most fundraising packs so why not matched funding information too?

Smaller organisations can use notice boards, circulars and newsletters to communicate the information.

Receipting

Every corporate organisation requires some form of proof of funds raised, whether this is a link to an online giving page, a formal receipt from the charity, or a letter of acknowledgement of the amount raised. Make it easy for your fundraiser to obtain this information in the format they require, publicise contact details and respond to requests for information.

Acknowledge corporate payments

Acknowledging the corporate donation, either through the employee or directly to the company helps to build better relationships and increases your charity's profile within the organisation. Many clients we speak to are frustrated by how few charities thank them for their matched funding and donations. As soon as you've cashed that corporate cheque, a letter of thanks, possibly including some detail about the community impacts achieved (or even photographs), makes it more likely that the company will run a story in an internal publication, in turn inspiring more employees to fundraise for that organisation and using their matched funding. It really is worth the effort.

Make corporate support easy

TrustCSR carries out due diligence checks on the majority of charities being supported by its client's employees. This includes money laundering, anti-terrorism and bank account verification checks.

By responding quickly and efficiently to requests for verification documents, your charity will be added to 'approved lists', receive prompt payment and develop a good reputation.

What about non-registered charities?

Some companies will support non-registered charitable organisations, but will often require a copy of their constitution. Make sure your fundraisers have access to a signed, up-to-date copy which they can supply upon request.

What is the future of matched funding?

With the increase in participation, higher budgets and stronger focus on employee engagement, matching funding is likely to become increasingly important as a source of funding for charities.

Companies are investing more time, strategic thought and money in making their schemes more user-friendly. The majority of our clients are in the process of adopting electronic platforms from which to run their matched funding, give as you earn and volunteering schemes, giving their employees greater power to choose which charities are supported and how.

Some companies are now rolling their matched funding schemes out across their global operations, giving each of their employees the same experience no matter where in world they are based. The impact of this is that more charities will be included in approved lists, making competition for this type of funding fiercer.

It is important therefore that, no matter what size your charity is, you take every opportunity to get your fundraisers to participate in their employers' schemes and show how you value the contribution corporate organisations make through this channel.

TrustCSR

TrustCSR is part of The Trust Partnership

Tel: 01285 841 900; email: info@TheTrustPartnership.com

TrustCSR, 6 Trull Farm Buildings, Tetbury, Gloucestershire GL8 8SQ

www.TrustCSR.com

Applying to companies

This section gives basic information on identifying potential companies to approach, how to establish contact with them and how to put together a proposal for them to consider.

Corporate social responsibility

This guide deals with one aspect of CSR which, broadly speaking, is the philanthropic, usually referred to as its charitable or community investment. Despite the increasing use of CSR by companies, it should be remembered that company giving is way below that of the general public and, to a lesser extent, grant-making charities.

According to recent research by DSC and the Centre for Charitable Giving and Philanthropy (CGAP), less than 5% of the voluntary sector's income comes from the private sector (*UK Corporate Citizenship in the 21st Century*, DSC and CGAP, 2012). Nevertheless, companies remain an important target for local, regional and national fundraisers.

Why apply to companies?

Company boards are ultimately responsible to their shareholders and answer to them as to how they use their profits. They will not be motivated primarily by philanthropy or by a desire to see new and pioneering voluntary activity. In many cases, companies will be looking to improve their image and their economic position in relation to their competitors, whether at a local, regional or national level.

There is, however, among some businesses, a desire to be seen to be giving something back to their community or society in general, and it is important for charities to have a strategy for applying to companies. It must be kept in mind that they are a different animal to grant-making charities and require a different approach.

Some companies, however, have now set up their own charities which, while having close ties to and receiving assets from the company, are separate legal entities. Whether these foundations are truly independent of the company in their giving is a matter of debate but they are nominally self- governing and set up for charitable purposes for the benefit of the public. In this respect, they should be applied to in the same way that you would make an application to any other grant- making charity.

The relationship you have with any company which donates to your cause, whether by cash, gifts in kind, staff time or other resources, is a two-way association. While you will be pleased to receive funding, the company will also benefit from the good publicity, awareness of local issues which they may not have previously had and a boost in morale for their staff. As with any relationship, your organisation needs to be selective about who it approaches, you need to be comfortable with the association you are about to establish. Research their website, or any other information, with this in mind.

Why companies give

To make an effective appeal to industry you must have a basic understanding of why firms give. This will enable you to put forward good reasons why they should support your work. Many companies, especially the larger, higher profile ones, receive hundreds, if not thousands, of requests for support from charities, voluntary sector organisations and local community groups each year. For your appeal to be successful it needs to be more than a general plea to 'put something back into the community'.

You can help a company justify its charitable support by telling them not just why you want the money, but why giving you support should be of interest to them. You can also tell them about any benefits they will get in return for their money and about the impact their donation will have on your work. At the very least you should be able to demonstrate a clear link with the company through a geographical, product, or employee contact or some other relevant connection.

Most companies give out of enlightened self-interest rather than for pure altruistic or philanthropic reasons, and see their giving in terms of 'community involvement' or 'community investment'. The main reasons why companies give are:

- To create goodwill. Companies like to be seen as good citizens in the communities in which they operate and as a caring company by their employees and society at large.
- To be associated with causes that relate to their business. Mining or extraction companies often like to support environmental projects, for example.
- To build good relations with employees. Support for employee volunteering is a growing area of company giving, creating a 'feel good' factor among employees and a sense of loyalty to their socially responsible employer. It can also be an excellent staff-development resource. Increasingly some preference is given to those charities for which staff are raising money or doing volunteer work. Funds raised may be matched (usually up to a set limit) and/or employees given work time off in which to volunteer.
- Because they are asked or it is expected of them.
- They also don't want to be seen as mean in relation to other rival companies in their particular business sector. They are concerned that the quantity and quality of their giving is appropriate to their status as a company.
- Because the chair/senior directors are interested in a particular cause (and perhaps support it personally). This is quite often the case with smaller companies where, as a result, it can be difficult to get a donation for causes outside of this criterion. Unless you know a friend of the managing director who will plead your case, success is unlikely.
- Because they have always given. Some companies never review their donations policy. They see donations more as an annual subscription to a list of charities they wish to support each year. Your aim should be to get your charity's name on to such a list, where it exists.
- Because the charity persists in its approach to the company and the company does not want to keep refusing a worthwhile cause. Persistence can pay, although if you are turned down you should consider whether you can improve your application, ask through another method, or ask for something else.
- For tax reasons. Giving to a charity can be done tax effectively. This will be an added benefit for the company, but seldom a determining factor.

Tax and company giving

The 2000 Finance Act made tax-effective giving straightforward for companies.

1 Donations: the company simply pays the full donation to the charity under Gift Aid and then deducts the total amount of its charitable donations from its pre-tax profit calculations at the end of the year. The level of benefit a company can receive in return is restricted on a sliding scale according to the amount of the donation, up to a maximum of £250 in benefits.

2 Business expenditure: any expenditure by a company which is wholly and exclusively for business purposes is also deductible against corporation tax liability. This will cover most sponsorship and advertising payments to charity.

3 Shares: companies are able to get tax relief for gifts of certain shares and securities to charity. See the HM Revenue & Customs website www.hmrc.gov.uk for more information.

It is worth pointing out that there is relatively little consistency in company giving. Outside the largest givers, few companies have any real policy for their charitable/ community involvement. Mostly they cover a wide range of causes, or attempt to deal with each appeal on its merits. For privately owned or family- controlled companies their giving is often little different from personal giving. For public companies, where it is the shareholders' funds that are being given away, there is pressure to dress up what they are doing, perhaps by claiming to give according to some well-defined criteria.

However, some companies do have clear policies. Where such policies are printed, please respect them. Dealing with a mass of clearly inappropriate applications is time-wasting for the corporate giver, and has caused some to consider winding-up their charitable support programme altogether.

What companies give

There are a variety of ways in which companies can support charities:

- A cash donation (usually a one-off grant).
- Pro bono (without charge) professional or technical work.
- Sponsorship of an event or activity.
- Sponsorship of promotional and educational materials.
- Sponsorship of an award scheme.
- Cause-related marketing, where the company contributes a donation to the charity in return for each product sold in order to encourage sales.
- Gifts in kind, which includes: giving company products or surplus office equipment; making company facilities available, including meeting rooms, printing or design facilities; help with mailings.
- Secondment of a member of staff to work with the charity, where a member of the company's staff helps on an agreed basis while remaining employed (and paid) by the company.
- Offering internships or work experience toa charity beneficiary or student at an educational institution.
- Offering a senior member of staff to the charity's management board.
- Providing expertise and advice or training.
- Encouraging and making it easy for employees to volunteer.

- Organising a fundraising campaign amongst employees, including encouraging employees to give through payroll giving.
- Advertising in charity brochures and publications.

Companies will always receive more applications than they will have the budget to meet. Community involvement budgets have not expanded in line with demands for support, and many companies now focus their grantmaking quite narrowly.

Some larger companies set up small grants schemes in regions or towns where they have a major factory or business presence. Others have matching schemes, where they match money collected or donated by employees. Some develop special grants programmes, while others have a Charity of the Year for their major donation and as a focus for encouraging staff involvement.

Cash donations

This is the most obvious way that a company can be asked to support your organisation and is probably the help you would most like to receive. Most cash donations are small (under £250), although some companies will match their employees' fundraising, which results in much larger total sums. You are more likely to be successful if you offer a 'shopping list' detailing the cost of specific items, rather than a vague request for general support.

In the entries at the end of this section we try to give an idea of the range of grants available from the large companies and what they like to support. This varies greatly from company to company. Some will have well-defined policies which work in a similar way to grant-making charities. They know to what they want and do not want to give. Guidelines are often publicised and applications may be handled by staff with job titles such as corporate affairs director or head of external affairs.

However, the majority of companies – especially the smaller ones – will have an informal approach. Here, any applications will be looked at by anyone from the personnel officer to the managing director, or their PA. They will not necessarily have any special insight into the voluntary sector and they will be doing the community support task on top of their work, and so may have to fit it into the odd Friday afternoon a month. They do not have the time to work through piles of paper or attend lengthy meetings to get to know the issues you are facing and the work you are doing.

A good number of companies will operate on the basis of the chair's six favourite charities and if you are not on the list you will have to find a way in, as the company giving policy will already be fixed. Inevitably, if you are successful with this sort of company, you may be successful with others, as part of company giving works on recommendation.

You might stand more chance of success if you can tie your application in with an event or celebration.

Anniversaries are useful: you may be able to find a company to tie in with your 50th year or your 500th member, for example. It will be particularly attractive if you have a time limit to your fundraising – this gives those working in the supporting company a definite target to work for.

Gifts in kind

Giving items or services rather than money can often be easier for a company. The value of the gift to the charity may be much more than the cost to the company. Companies might give:

- products for use by the charity;
- pro bono professional and technical advice;
- staff time;
- products as prizes or as lots to be auctioned;
- old stock and ends of lines for resale in charity shops;
- facilities such as meeting rooms, conference facilities or training.

If a company donates items that it makes or sells in the course of its trade, or an article that it has used in its trade (such as computers and furniture), then this can be treated as a tax-deductible business expense. The 'book value' of donated items (value as given in the accounts) is written off before the donation is made (unsaleable or damaged stock, ends of lines, etc.) and attracts full tax relief. There are organisations which act as clearing houses for gifts in kind, such as Kind Direct (formerly Gifts in Kind UK).

What kind of gift is a gift in kind?

Gifts in kind are donations of items or services, rather than the money to buy them. You might consider approaching specific companies for one of the following gifts:

- Secondment of staff with key skills to train or mentor your employees or volunteers.
- Donation of coach, train, airline or ferry tickets.
- Advertising on company websites.
- Use of surplus storage or sports facilities.
- Donation of hotel accommodation.
- Use of telephones for helplines.
- Design and printing of leaflets or posters.
- Donation of surplus food or drinks.
- Access to information on customer demography, attitudes or preferences.
- Vacant sites for recreation projects.
- Free loan of equipment, scaffolding, marquees, portaloos, etc.
- Free advertising space on temporarily unused sites.
- Insertion of a charity leaflet or appeal in a regular business or customer mailshot.
- Free servicing of vehicles.

Some practical tips on how to set about getting support in kind

1 Make a list of everything you need – a 'wish list'. This can include services as well as products (such as the design for a leaflet you plan to produce).

2 Go through the list and try to identify companies that might have what you require. Personal knowledge is

useful but you might also want to use business directories as well to widen your choice.

3 Make contact. Writing a letter can act as an introduction but you will probably need to follow it up with a phone call or personal visit. State your request, saying that it is for a charity and indicating how well used it will be and how important it is to your organisation's future. If the company does not want to donate, it might be able to give you a discount.
4 Be positive and enthusiastic. It can be very difficult for the company to refuse if it knows what you want and how important it is for you and the local community. It will always cost the company far less to donate the item than it would cost you to purchase it.
5 Say thank you. Report back subsequently on the difference the donation has made. Send them your annual report and later, perhaps try to recruit the company as a cash donor.

Employee volunteering/secondments/pro bono work

A major resource that companies can offer is their staff time and this can be provided in a number of ways:

- Employee volunteering: many of the large companies encourage their staff to volunteer, in or out of office hours, on the basis that this enhances the skills of their employees and promotes good community relations. Some companies match the amount an employee has raised for a chosen project.
- Professional skills: banks, law firms, accountants, advertising and PR companies can all encourage staff to give their professional skills free of charge or to become trustees.
- Secondment: This is where the company loans you a member of staff full time for an extended period. There needs to be a good reason why the company would do this, as it is an expensive form of support.

Employee volunteering is not only valuable in itself, it is also strategically important since you will be building a relationship with a member of staff who can then act as an intermediary in asking the company for other forms of support at a later date, including cash donations.

Advertising

Companies will sometimes take an advertisement in a publication. Possibilities include:

- your annual report
- programmes produced specifically for fundraising events
- conference folders, pads and pens
- leaflets aimed at your service users and others
- posters, including educational wall charts.

However, you do need to think through whether you actually want an advertisement or company logo to appear prominently on your materials.

Advertising can be broken down into two categories:

1 Goodwill advertising: where the primary purpose of the advertiser is to support a charity and to be seen supporting a good cause; this creates goodwill for the company rather than selling its products.
2 Commercial advertising: where the advertiser wishes to reach the audience that the charity's publication goes to, and the decision is made for purely financial considerations.

What are you offering to advertisers?

Before trying to sell the advertising, you need to recognise what you are offering. If it is goodwill advertising, then the prestige of the event, the nature of the audience, the location and any celebrities who will be present will be major incentives. Price is less of an issue than the work of the charity, although the advertiser will want to know the circulation and readership of the publication, any special characteristics of that readership and any particular connection between it and their product. If it is commercial advertising, these details become much more significant.

Pricing the advertising

The first consideration when pricing the advertising is the format of the publication. A lavish souvenir brochure is different from an annual report, and this in turn is very different from a single colour newsletter produced on your computer. There are two factors to consider when deciding the cost of the advertising.

1 How much do you want to raise? Divide this target by the number of pages of advertising to get a page rate.
2 How much are advertisers prepared to pay? For commercial advertising this is especially important. Try to define the value of your audience to them.

Once you have decided a page rate, then you can then set prices for smaller spaces that are slightly higher than pro rata. For example, if the page rate is £250, then a half page might be priced at £150, a quarter page at £85, and eighth page at £50. You can ask for higher sums for special positions, such as the back cover, the inside front cover and facing the contents page. For a regular publication, you could offer a series discount for taking space in several issues.

You might consider producing a rate card which contains all the information that the advertiser needs to know, including:

- a deadline for agreeing to take space
- a deadline for receipt of artwork and address where it is to be sent
- publication size
- print run
- use of colour on cover and inside pages
- page rates, including special positions, size of advertising space, and whether VAT is chargeable
- payment details.

A simple brochure or covering letter which sets out the reasons for advertising is useful, but posting copies out will generate little response. The way to sell advertising is on the telephone, where you make a call to follow up a letter you have sent. For larger advertisers, you might try to arrange a personal visit. The majority of people you approach will probably say 'no' but your job is to persuade a significant proportion to buy a space.

Business sponsorship

Sponsorship needs to be carefully defined. It is not a donation and the fact that you are a charity is largely irrelevant: it is a business arrangement. The charity is looking to raise funds for its work and the company wants to improve its image, promote and sell its products or entertain its customers.

The sponsor's contribution is usually money, although it could be a gift of goods such as football kits, services such as free transport, professional expertise such as promotion or marketing consultancy, the use of buildings such as an exhibition centre, or free promotion such as media coverage in a newspaper.

Many companies will provide much more in sponsorship than they would as a donation, but only so long as the commercial benefits warrant it. Developing links with the major national and local corporate sponsors could be an investment in your future that is well worth making now.

Most sponsors are commercial companies. There are four main options for sponsorship:

1 Businesses wanting to promote themselves, to create a better image or generate awareness in the local communities where they operate. This includes those companies with an 'image problem' – for example, mining and extraction companies associated with the destruction of the environment who want to project a cleaner image by being associated with a conservationist cause.

2 Businesses wanting to introduce or promote a product or service. This could include a new brand of trainers or shampoo, or a supermarket opening in the area. Public awareness is important if a product or service is to get accepted, so companies may be open to proposals that give a product or service more exposure.

3 Companies looking for entertainment opportunities to influence customers, suppliers, regulators, the media and other opinion formers. They may be interested in sponsoring a concert, a theatrical event, an art exhibition or a sporting event which would provide them with an appropriate entertainment opportunity and the opportunity to meet and mingle.

4 Companies that are committed supporters of your organisation. You may be able to offer them something that they would like to sponsor, even if it is partly for philanthropic reasons.

What are companies looking for?

Organisations looking for sponsorship should be able to offer at least some of the following things.

- A respectable partner (with the right image).
- A real partnership. What involvement is the sponsor looking for and how well does this opportunity meet its needs?
- A proven track record (preferably in securing and delivering sponsorships) and a professional approach. Has the applicant approached the business of getting sponsorship in a professional way, and can they demonstrate a similar professionalism in the running of their organisation?
- An interesting project (at least to the company management and possibly also company staff) and initiative. Does the sponsorship represent a new initiative, something that would not happen without the company's support? Is it interesting and lively?
- Continuity. Is there scope for a continuing relationship (over the next few years), or is the activity or event just a one-off?
- Genuine value for money. What are the benefits and how much money is the sponsor asking for? How does this rate compared with other possible sponsorships that the company might consider? The relationship of cost to return and the importance of the return to the company are the dominant factors affecting the decision to sponsor.
- Visibility. How 'visible' will the event be, and what specific publicity and PR benefits will accrue to the sponsor? Will the company name be given a high profile?
- Appropriateness. Is the activity or event appropriate to the sponsor? (Are you approaching the right company?)
- Targeted audience (possibly leading to direct marketing, such as providing the company's fair trade coffee at a reception for young entrepreneurs).
- Other tangible benefits (for example: good publicity, media coverage, link with brand advertising, entertainment opportunities for company directors and staff, access to VIPs, involvement of company employees or retirees, training or experience for employees, etc.)

Why companies like sponsorship

- It helps them get their message across.
- It can enhance or change their image.
- It can reach a target audience very precisely.
- It can be very cost-effective advertising or product promotion.
- Further marketing opportunities may develop from the sponsorship.
- It generates good publicity for the sponsor, often of a kind that money can't buy.
- It generates an awareness of the company within the local community in which the company operates and from where it draws its workforce and customers.
- Sponsors can entertain important clients at the events they sponsor.

What can be sponsored?

There is an extremely wide range of things that can be sponsored, including:

- cultural and sporting events;
- mass participation fundraising events, such as a marathon or fun run;
- the publication of a report or a book, with an attendant launch;
- the production of fundraising materials, leaflets and posters, or the sponsorship of a complete fundraising campaign;

- conferences and seminars, especially to specialist audiences (such as doctors) where promotional material can be displayed;
- vehicles, where the acknowledgement can be painted on the side;
- equipment such as cars or computers produced by the company;
- competitions, awards and prizes;
- scholarships, bursaries, travel grants.

The bulk of corporate sponsorship money goes to sport, with motor racing, golf, tennis, athletics, football and cricket all receiving huge amounts. These offer extensive media coverage, good opportunities for corporate entertainment and an association with a popular activity.

The arts is another big recipient of sponsorship – business support for the arts runs at around £133.2 million a year (*Private Investment in Culture 2010/11*, Arts & Business, 2013). Arts sponsorship is promoted by Arts & Business, which describes itself as acting 'as a crucible where businesses and arts organisations come together to create partnerships to benefit themselves and the community at large'.

Social sponsorship is much smaller by comparison, the 'market' is less crowded and there are all sorts of imaginative ways in which companies can sponsor events and activities run by charities.

Getting sponsorship: 10 practical tips

1. Before you begin, think about an ethical code. Are there some companies you wouldn't wish to be associated with?
2. Identify the right person in the company to contact. You need their name and job title. This will often be the marketing manager.
3. Stress the benefits of the sponsorship to the potential sponsor. This should be done often and as clearly as possible and backed up with statistics or other supporting information.
4. The size of the payment will be dependent upon the value of the sponsorship to the sponsor, not the cost of the work for you.
5. Help companies use their own resources to make the sponsorship work. Suggest, for instance, that they might like a picture story in their house magazine or in the trade press. Most are very keen to impress their colleagues and their rivals, but few think of this without prompting.
6. Sponsorship, especially long-term deals, is all about working together. Promise only what you know you can deliver, and always try to deliver a little bit more than you promised.
7. Remember that most sponsorship money comes in sums of under £10,000 and it is a local event you are planning, not Live Aid.
8. Get into the habit of reading adverts. Look particularly at local papers and trade press. Who has got money to spend on promotion? What kind of image are they trying to promote? Who are they trying to reach? How can you help them?
9. Mention another company that supports you. One satisfied sponsor can help you to get another.
10. Keep trying. It is hard work but sponsorships can be really valuable.

There may be an advertising agency or marketing consultant that can introduce sponsorship opportunities to sponsors. They will sometimes charge you a fee; more usually they will receive a commission from the sponsor. It depends who retains them, and in whose interests they are acting.

Your sponsorship package

It is not enough to offer 1,000 contacts to a company if they sponsor your event. Most of them may be irrelevant to the company. You need to say which 1,000 people will be involved and how.

Think of each group that you reach in one way or another. Estimate an annual number for each. The following are general groups of people to get the process started but there may be more specialised areas that you are in contact with. Some groups will overlap. The more you can define your different groups of contacts, and the more information you can give about them, the more help it will be to you and potential sponsors.

Group	Number
Adults	....
Men	....
Women	....
Young adults	....
Teenagers	....
Children	....
Consumers	....
(what, how and where people buy – drinks, clothes, transport, which shops, areas etc.)	
Businesses	....
(who do you use for products, services etc.)	
Schools	....
Clubs	....
Employed	....
Unemployed	....
Trainees	....
Agencies	....
Local authority	....
Central government departments	....
Quangos	....
Health authority	....
Other	....

Contractual issues

Sponsorship involves giving something in return for the money you are receiving, so you need to agree terms through a contract. This can be set out in a legal agreement (for larger sponsorships) or in the form of a letter. You need to be clear about the following:

- How long the arrangement will run. Is it for one year, which would require you to find a new sponsor next year, or can you get a commitment for several years? What happens at the end of this period – does the sponsor have a first refusal on the following year's event? Most successful sponsorships last for several years, and the benefit builds up over the sponsorship period. However, companies don't like being tied to sponsoring something indefinitely – their sponsorship programme would begin to look stale.
- The fee to be paid, and when the instalments are due. What benefits are to be delivered in return for the fee? These should be specified as clearly as possible, so that you know precisely what you are contracted to deliver.
- Whether VAT is chargeable. This will depend on whether your organisation is registered for VAT and the extent of the benefits offered to the sponsor. If VAT is chargeable, this should be discussed at the outset, and the fee agreed should be exclusive of VAT.
- Who will pay for what costs? Who pays for the additional publicity the sponsor requires is something that is often forgotten. There needs to be a clear agreement as to who is responsible for what, so you can ensure that everything is covered and there are no misunderstandings later on.
- Who is responsible for doing what? You will need to clarify who will do the public relations, who will handle the bookings, who will invite the guests, whose staff will receive the guests and so on.
- Any termination arrangements in the event of the activity having to be cancelled.
- Who is responsible for managing the sponsorship?
- You will need a named person on both sides.
- Whether the sponsor is a 'commercial participator' under the terms of the Charities Act 2006, when the requirements of the Charities Act will apply.

If everything is written down and agreed, there will be fewer problems later and it ensures that everything has been properly thought through at the outset. This list is not exhaustive and you should contact the Charity Commission for further information or advice: www.charitycommission.gov.uk

Joint promotions and cause-related marketing

Many larger charities are involved in promotional activity to help market a commercial product – this is often known as cause-related marketing. This can bring in large amounts of money and expose the name of the charity (and sponsor) to literally millions of people. The same idea on a smaller scale can also be adapted for use by local charities through local promotions.

Commercial promotions can include on-pack and licensing promotional deals, affinity credit cards, competitions and awards, the use of phone lines, etc. What they have in common is that they present an opportunity to raise money for your cause and to project your charity to new audiences, but they require that you work with the company and on its terms to achieve this.

This arrangement benefits both the charity and the commercial partner. It differs from sponsorship in that you are promoting the company's product or service (in return for a payment) as the primary purpose of the arrangement. But as with sponsorship, you will need to make a business case for it.

Getting started with promotions

Joint promotions are quite difficult to arrange and you must first talk about the possibility of your developing promotional links with companies with someone who has experience of this or with a marketing or advertising agency (but these can be costly).

You need to decide whether your charity is the type which can expect a commercial link of this sort. It has been generally accepted that national household- name charities and those addressing popular causes (such as helping children) are more likely to benefit from this area of fundraising than the less well- known charities or those addressing less 'popular' causes.

You should take the initiative yourself by contacting companies that might be interested in your work. You can also contact promotion agencies (that are not retained by you) to make them aware of the opportunities you are offering which they could include when appropriate in their sales pitch to companies.

If you are approached by a promotional agency pitching for business, this does not mean that anything is certain. It may be working independently, hoping that a good idea that involves your charity can then be sold to a company. In nine out of ten situations, these ideas come to nothing, and you may find you have put in considerable effort without getting any return.

Issues with sponsorships and joint promotions

Sponsorship involves a close working relationship with a company. Therefore you will need to be sure when you enter into any sponsorship agreement that this relationship will benefit your organisation and will not damage your charity's reputation. With commercial promotions the relationship is even closer. The charity is actively promoting the products of the company, so it is important that the product you are associated with is good value and good quality. With both arrangements it is important that you have no ethical problems in associating with that company. You should develop an ethical donations policy before you apply for any sponsorship or suggest a joint promotion – agreeing in advance which types of company you are happy to work with and which you are not. (See 'Ethical issues' on page xxx)

There is also the question of who will benefit most from the arrangement. How much you should expect to receive from a sponsorship or commercial promotion is also a difficult question. It may be worth a great deal to them to be linked with you. Any negotiation should start from what you think the association is worth to them. Your need for money should not dim the value of your commercial worth.

Finally, there are important legal issues arising from the 1992 Charities Act (and still applicable following the Charities Act 2006 and Charities Act 2011). The 1992 Act defines a 'commercial participator' as 'any person who carries on for gain a business which is not a fundraising business but who in the course of that business engages in any promotional venture in the course of which it is represented that contributions are to be given to or applied for the benefit of a charity'. In other words, high street shops often promote products on the understanding that part of the sale price will go to charity – for example charity Christmas cards published commercially state explicitly that for each pack sold a certain sum will go to charity. The Act also covers advertising and sales campaigns or other joint promotions by companies with charities. If the activity falls within the provisions of the Act, this then requires:

- a written agreement in a prescribed form between the charity and the commercial participator
- the public to be informed how the charity will benefit from its involvement, which shows what part of the proceeds or profits are to be given to the charity. This is a matter for professional advice.

The Charity Commission also suggests that trustees should consider the following points before allowing the charity's name to be associated with a particular business or product.

- The relationship is appropriate and will not damage the particular charity or the good name of charity as a whole.
- The proposed fundraising venture is a more effective way of raising money than others that might be considered, and that the terms of the arrangement are generally advantageous to the charity.
- The arrangement is set out in some detail and kept under review, such that the charity's name is not misused or improperly exploited, and the charity has the right to prevent future use of its name if the arrangement proves unsatisfactory. It may be worth taking legal advice in drawing up the terms of the arrangement.

The types of companies that give

Multinational companies

Most multinational companies have global giving programmes, generally tied to areas where they have or are developing business interests. Some multinational companies have an international structure for managing their giving, with budgets set for each area and a common policy regarding what they wish to support. With others, community investment remains at the discretion of local company management in the country concerned.

Geographically speaking, the further out from the centre (i.e. the company's headquarters) you are, the less you can expect to get. This can be broken down as follows: (i) most money is spent in the headquarters' town or region; (ii) most money is spent in the home country of the company; (iii) more money is spent in developed countries than developing ones.

Leading national companies

These are most likely to support large national charities, have their own sponsorship schemes and make smaller donations to local charities in the area in which they are headquartered or have a major business presence. Numerous national companies make grants through regional offices, while retail stores such as B&Q might use the local store manager to give advice on a local application. Such stores may also provide the manager with a small budget to spend at their discretion.

Larger local companies

In any city or region there are large companies which are important to the local economy. They will often feel a responsibility to support voluntary action and community initiatives in those areas, and value the good publicity this provides.

There are also companies with a regional remit. The water, electricity and independent television companies all have a specific geographical area within which they operate, even if they are part of a multinational company.

Smaller local companies

There are a myriad of companies that make up the local business community. Referred to as small and medium enterprises (SMEs), they are often overlooked in the rush to target the large companies on which good information is generally available. However, from manufacturers on trading estates to accountants and solicitors in the high street, the majority of SMEs claim to be involved with their local community. Many of these companies are privately owned, so the best approach will often be through the managing director or senior partner.

The best sources of information on what companies exist in your area are:

- The local Chamber of Commerce, where most of the more prominent local companies will be members.
- The Kompass directory of companies, which is regionally organised and can be searched online (gb.kompass.com).
- The local council: the business department might produce a list of major business ratepayers. The economic development section may have a list of major employers.
- The local newspaper, which will carry stories from time to time that mention local companies, and may provide information on new companies planning to set up in the area.
- You – by keeping your eyes open you can often identify local companies that it could just be worth approaching.

It is likely that most of the smaller companies you approach will not have a donations policy in place (if they give at all), and may well make their decisions on the basis of the personal interests of their managing director or senior partners. Some may never have made a charitable donation before and may not know about the related tax advantages available to them, so be prepared to tell them about these opportunities.

Some of these companies may prefer to give in kind – for example, a prize for a raffle or advertising in a souvenir brochure for a fundraising event. It might be easier to approach these companies for this sort of support in the first instance, and later on, once they have given something, persuade them to make a cash donation.

Small and medium-sized businesses will react quickly to economic conditions. When business is falling, their concerns will be for their staff, and not giving money to charities.

Staff time is also at a premium as numbers are small and people are usually stretched with their workload. Staff volunteering schemes are therefore unlikely to be entered into.

Charitable giving is far more likely to be led by the enthusiasms of the partners or directors, but is also likely to be responsive to causes where staff are involved. One local business gives the following advice:

- Match your request to what the business can afford. If a project is too large and the business can only give a small donation they will see their contribution as being swallowed up and not making any difference at all.
- Lengthy letters take up too much time to consider. It's much better if they're simple, succinct and concise.
- Letters should be typed rather than hand-written.
- A good track record gives the appeal credence.
- Corporate giving is not just about money – partners tend to give their time and skills through involvement, more so than cash.
- Telephone to make things happen. If this is daunting, either delegate the contact work to someone else (perhaps someone on your management committee who already has links with business people) or try to increase your confidence in some way.

Who to approach

Key factors in approaching companies

Research

Research is very important, not only into companies but also into personal contacts. When planning an appeal, an important first step is to find which of the people associated with your charity have influence or know people who have. If you can find a link between one of your supporters and a particular company – use it.

You should try to find out as much as you can about the companies you have identified as potential donors. But, remember:

- Companies generally have less well-defined policies than grant-making charities, although you can often determine a pattern in their giving.
- The chance of an application made 'out of the blue' getting substantial support is low.
- Appeals made towards the end of a company's financial year are less likely to succeed.
- Companies are more conservative in their giving and are less likely to support innovative projects (at least until they are established) or anything that is risky or controversial.
- Companies' policies change more frequently than those of grantmakers, because of mergers, takeovers, or a fall or rise in profits, so ensure your research is up to date. Consulting a copy of the company's latest annual report and accounts is not necessarily enough; they may have been taken over since then. Check the company's website, if they have one, the financial press on a regular basis, or make a quick telephone call to see if anything has changed such as company name, address or your contact.

The company

The firms to approach will depend on the nature of your organisation. If you are a national organisation then an appeal to the country's leading companies is appropriate. Local groups should approach local firms and local branches of national companies which have a presence in their area. Organisations can approach companies in allied fields: for example, theatres can appeal to fabric companies. Be imaginative when looking for a connection.

As outlined in the 'Smaller local companies' section, most local companies have no donations policy and you may have to explain the advantages to giving and approach them for in kind support in the first instance.

Larger companies might have a manager who is responsible for dealing with charitable appeals, although a donations committee (which includes senior management) may have the final say. The largest companies might also employ specialist staff to assess the applications and make recommendations.

You need to be selective when you decide on which companies to approach and then find out who you should contact within the company. The choice of company will depend upon what connection you have with them.

- Identify and match possible companies with various aspects of your work. In particular, try to find any local companies that are known for their generosity or who might want to support your particular beneficiary group.
- Contact BITC to find out about its membership or to help you identify local companies through its regional network.
- Has the company supported you before?
- Does it have a stated interest in your project such as the environmental initiative that you are promoting?
- Is the company local to your community?
- Are you consumers of its service or product?

- Does the company need better publicity in the community and could you offer that with a link?
- Do your activities contribute to improving the business environment?
- Is the company a large employer in the area with an interest in the current and future workforce?

Lastly, one big problem you may face involves the ownership of seemingly independent companies. Many companies are in fact part of much larger concerns. In recent years there has been a substantial number of mergers and takeovers, plus the buying and selling of business between corporations. A useful, although expensive, source of information is the directory *Who Owns Whom* (published by Gap Books), which has a subsidiary index listing most subsidiaries of companies included in this guide. Check your main library to see if they have a copy.

You can also use company annual reports, which (for most companies) can be obtained on request. These reports provide good background information on the company concerned, and occasionally information on its corporate support programme. Some private (and occasionally public) companies will not send out annual reports except to shareholders; in such cases you can go to Companies House to get hold of a copy. Offices are situated in Cardiff, Edinburgh, Belfast and London and the website address is: www.companieshouse.gov.uk

The person

Once you have decided on the company, you will need to find out how it is organised and who makes any decisions about charitable giving. Where a company has a number of branches or operating units throughout the country these may have some autonomy in grant decisions. There is usually a maximum amount that they can decide, over which the application will be passed to the next level: regional or national. If you can find this out beforehand it will save time in the long run.

You need to tailor your request to the level at which you are asking and to which budget it might come from; it may not necessarily be from the company's charitable giving budget but possibly marketing or personnel. Once you have established the budget source and level, you will then need to find the right person to talk and write to. Here are a few tips:

1 Find out what, if any, previous contact you or your group has had with companies: any previous fundraising approaches that have been made, and with what success.

2 Find out whether any of your management committee, volunteers or supporters have any personal contact with the companies you plan to approach – and whether they know people who have credibility in the business world who can help you do the asking. It may be appropriate for one of these contacts to sign the appeal letter.

3 Look into whether one of your volunteers or supporters is an employee of the company.

4 Find out if any of your clients or users work for the company.

5 Alternatively, you might be able to tie your appeal in to a known personal interest of a director.

6 Enlist a senior business leader to assist you with your fundraising. This can be someone to serve as chair of a development or fundraising committee, or just to contact a few colleagues and sign a few letters.

Generally an appeal through a personal contact will work the best. But if you don't have a contact and can see no way of developing one, then you will have to come up with another link.

As a first step you might contact the company to find out:

- who is responsible for dealing with charitable appeals and their name and job title
- what information they can send regarding their company
- any procedure or timetable for submitting applications
- whether they might be interested in coming to see your organisation at work. Visits are useful when discussing bigger donations with the larger companies, but are difficult to arrange for anything small.

Unfortunately, there is no short cut if you have no inside knowledge of the company. Be prepared to spend time on the company's website or the telephone, particularly if the company has no decided policy on giving.

Almost certainly your appeal will be in the form of a letter. Make this as personal as you can. Circular letters are likely to end up in the bin and many companies will not consider circular appeals as a point of policy. Make the letter professional but motivating, and short and to the point.

Be specific in your approach

Rather than sending out a circular mailing to 100 or1,000 companies, you will be more successful if you select a few companies you believe will be particularly interested in your project, and target your application to them and their policy.

Find a good reason why you believe the company should support you and include this prominently in your letter. You may be able to relate what you are doing as a charity to companies which have some relevance to your work: for example, a children's charity can appeal to companies making children's products; a housing charity to construction companies, building societies, etc. Any relationship, however tenuous, creates a point of contact on which you can build a good case for obtaining the company's support. If there is no relationship, should you be approaching that company at all?

There may be occasions when a charity will not want to accept money from a company in a related industry (see the environmental/youth group examples in 'Ethical issues' below). Similarly, a local charity might not want money from a company that has made people in the area redundant. Each charity has to judge where it draws the line.

Be clear about why you need the money

You must be clear about the objectives of the work for which you are raising money, particularly its timescale and how it relates to your overall programme of work. Try to think in project terms rather than seeking money to cover basic administration costs. This can be difficult, because most people spend most of their money on administration in one form or another, so you need to develop projects out of your current activities to present to potential donors. You can build a percentage of administration costs into the costs of a project. If you relate what you are doing to a specific timescale, this again makes what you are applying for appear more of a project than a contribution to your year-on-year core costs.

Be persistent

Do not underestimate the persistence factor. If you do not receive a donation in the first year, do not assume that the company will never support you. Go back a second and even a third time.

If you are going back, mention the fact that you have applied to the company previously, perhaps saying that you are now presenting something different which may be (you hope) of more interest.

If the company gives you reasons for refusing support, use these to help you put in more appropriate applications in the future. If the response is that the company does not give to your particular type of activity, then you know that it is no use you going back. If the company said its funds were fully committed, you can try to find out when would be a better time to apply (although this might only have been a convenient excuse because the company did not want to give to you).

Note the response to your appeal and use any information you can glean to improve your chances the next time.

Ethical issues

Receiving support from companies can be problematic if the business values or practice of the company conflict with what your organisation stands for. There are two approaches:

1. Some organisations will accept money from anyone, on the basis that the money can be used to do good.
2. Others define certain types of company that they will not accept support from. Tobacco, alcohol, gambling, armaments, mining/oil industries, polluters and companies operating overseas that underpay their workforce are all areas of business activity that can cause problems.

An ethical stance is of particular importance where the work of the charity is directly connected with the issue or where the relationship is high profile.

Decide your ethical policy before approaching companies. It should be agreed by the management committee and minuted. You might want to define and agree a policy in consultation with everyone in your organisation, although sometimes this can be contentious and create divisions. If you think this is likely, it might be better to treat each decision on an ad hoc basis whilst moving towards some sort of consensus on policy.

Sometimes the issues are clear cut. It is relatively easy, for example, for an environmental group to decide whether to accept money from a nuclear power company, or a youth charity from a tobacco or alcohol company. The product relationship with the cause is clear, and all the charity has to do is agree a position on the issue.

Three organisations that chart the ethical behaviour of companies and which can provide you with the information you need to formulate an ethical donations policy:

1. EIRIS (Ethical Investment Research Services) researches companies on the FT All-Share Index. Its main aim is to advise on socially responsible investment. A charge is made for its services.
2. Ethical Consumer Research Association produces *Corporate Critic*, which rates more than 25,000 companies on their ethical performance at: www.corporatecritic.org.
3. Ethical Corporation provides 'business intelligence for sustainability', mainly aimed at big business but it also provides information which charities may find useful. It is a subscription service, although some free information is available: www.ethicalcorp.com.

Writing an appeal letter

Put yourself in the position of the company. Why should they want to give their shareholders' funds to you? Why should they choose your charity's appeal ahead of any others they might receive? Think about the benefits they will get from supporting you and mention these in your letter (for sponsorship proposals these benefits will be central to your success or failure). Then consider the following important points:

- Think of a project or aspect of your work that the business sector might like to support. Generally, do not appeal for administration costs or a contribution to an endowment fund. Recognise that companies are likely to be interested in some ideas and not others. For example, a drugs charity would be more likely to get money for education than rehabilitation. An appreciation of the kind of projects that companies like to support will be very helpful to you.
- Your letter should be clear and concise. Try to get it all on one side of A4. You can always supply other information as attachments. It should be written clearly and be free from jargon. Someone not familiar with what you are doing should be able to read and understand it and be persuaded to act on it. Give your letter in draft to someone outside your charity to read and comment on before finalising it and sending it out.

- You should state why you need the money and exactly how it will be spent. The letter itself should be straightforward. It should include the following information (not necessarily in this order): what the organisation does and some background on how it was set up; whom the organisation serves; why the organisation needs funds; how the donation would be spent if it were to be forthcoming; and why you think the company might be interested in supporting you.
- You should attempt to communicate the urgency of your appeal. Fundraising is an intensively competitive business; there is a limited amount of money to give away, and you have to ensure that some of it comes your way. If it appears that although you would like the money now it would not matter terribly much if you got it next year, this will put people off. But don't give the impression you are fundraising at the last minute. Show them you are professional and you have carefully planned your fundraising appeal. You should also try to show that your charity is well- run, efficient and cost-effective in how it operates.
- You should mention why you think the company should support your cause. This could range from rather generalised notions of corporate responsibility and the creation of goodwill in the local community, to more specific advantages such as improved customer relations and the good publicity company will get from supporting your cause. If the firm's generosity is to be made public, for example through advertising or any publicity arising from the gift, then emphasise the goodwill which will accrue to the company.
- Ask for something specific. Many companies, having been persuaded to give, are not sure how much to give. You can ask a firm to give a donation of a specific amount (matched to what you believe its ability to contribute to be), or to contribute the cost of a particular item. You can suggest a figure by mentioning what other companies are giving. You can mention a total and say how many donations you will need to achieve this. Don't be unreasonable in your expectations. Just because a company is large and rich, it doesn't mean that it makes big grants.
- If you can demonstrate some form of 'leverage' this will be an added attraction. Company donations on the whole are quite modest, but companies like to feel they are having a substantial impact with the money they spend. If you can show that a small amount of money will enable a much larger project to go ahead, or will release further funds, say, on a matching basis from another source, this will definitely be an advantage.
- Having written a short appeal letter, you can append some background support literature. This should not be a 50-page treatise outlining your latest policies but, like your letter, it should be concise and to the point: a record of your achievements, your latest annual report, press cuttings, or even a specially produced brochure to accompany your appeal.
- Make sure that the letter is addressed to the correct person at the correct address. It pays to do this background research. Keep all the information on file as it will make your job much easier next time.
- Don't assume that every company will give. Make parallel approaches to a number of companies.
- Consider who might be the best person to make the approach or sign the letter. It may not be you but could be a senior business executive from another company which has already supported your organisation. Their endorsement of your work can provide reassurance to other companies.
- Every time you buy from a company, ask for a discount. This will save you money, but is also a way of getting them to support you.
- Check if the company is registered for payroll giving and, if it is, ask if you can promote your cause to its employees.
- If you are successful, remember to say thank you; this is an elementary courtesy which is too often forgotten. If the company gives you any substantial amount of money, then you should try to keep it in touch with the achievements related to its donation (such as a brief progress report or copies of your annual report or latest publications).
- If you do not succeed, go back again next year (unless the company says that it is not its policy to support your type of organisation or to give to charity at all). Persistence can pay. If you have received a donation, go back again next year. The company has demonstrated that it is interested in what you are doing and in supporting you. It may well do it again next year, especially if you have thanked it for the donation and kept it in touch with how the project developed.

How companies reply to you

Many companies will not even reply to your appeal. A few may acknowledge receipt of your letter, and occasionally you will get thanked for your request and be told that it is being considered and you will only hear the outcome if you are successful. Up to half of the companies you approach will write back, depending on the spread of the companies you approach. Larger companies have a system for dealing with charity mail, and most will see it as good PR to give a reply.

Smaller companies which do not give much charitable support will not have the time or the resources to do anything but scan the mail and discard most of it.

What sort of reply should you expect? If you do an extensive appeal, you will inevitably get a lot of refusals. These will normally be generic letters apologising and saying that they can't support you; occasionally you may get a letter sent to you personally. You might also get a cheque.

Good luck!

Alphabetical listing of companies

This section gives information on more than 550 companies from all sectors of industry, gathered from a combination of annual reports and company websites, and supplemented by our own research.

Types of company

A company may be: a public limited company (designated plc), normally a company with shares quoted on the stock exchange; a privately owned company; or a subsidiary company. If it is a subsidiary it may have retained its own identity for charitable donations and we would include an entry in this guide. Other subsidiaries included are British-based subsidiaries of an overseas-based company.

Where a company has been recently acquired it may not yet have decided whether it will continue to manage its own donations budget.

Through acquisitions and mergers, companies may now be owned by a holding company, a conglomerate, or a transnational company. We usually only give the name of the holding company. You may have to do your own research to link local companies and plants with the head office that may have ultimate control over their donations. The company annual report, usually available free on request, lists subsidiary and associate (less than 50% owned) companies and reports on the activity of the company during the year. We have included the main subsidiaries of each company within the entry. However, for many companies this is taken from the latest annual report, which can be several months out of date. The *Who Owns Whom* directory (published by GAP Books) also lists subsidiaries of UK companies, and more up-to-date information can often be found on company websites.

Interpreting financial information

The charitable donations figure given is that published by the company in the 'Director's Report'

section of its annual report and accounts. As far as we know, legally this should relate only to cash donations. However, companies are increasingly including the value of secondments, gifts in kind, advertising or sponsorship which, customarily, are included in the total contributions figure. Furthermore, a company's present level of donations does not necessarily indicate future commitments. Sending an appeal to less generous companies may actually persuade them to increase their donations. Certainly if they never receive appeals there will be no outside pressure on them to change their policy, although in general if a company is only giving a little your chances of success are reduced.

Normally a coordinated company donor will budget a certain sum for its charitable donations and stick within this amount. Some allocate their entire budget at an annual meeting; others spread donations throughout the year. Some give to causes they wish to support until the budget is used up and then stop; others continue to give even after the budget is spent if an appeal takes their fancy. If they reply to your appeal, many will write and say that their budget is 'fully committed'. Often this is simply a polite way of refusing support.

The year-end is important in that if you get your appeal in soon afterwards the company will not have spent its charitable budget for the coming year. However, if a company allocates its budget evenly throughout the year and receives a flood of applications at the start of its new financial year, some which would have been supported later in the year now miss out. There is no fail-safe answer to this problem. However, your chances of success are usually improved by sending the application earlier rather than later in the company's financial year.

How to interpret the donations policy

There are certain standard phrases that appear in the policy of the company entries.

No response to circular appeals

This means that 'Dear Sir/Madam' letters, whether they are hand-signed or use photocopied signatures, are probably not even read, let alone replied to.

Preference for local charities in areas of company presence / Preference for appeals relevant to company business / Preference for charities where a member of staff is involved

These are self-explanatory. Local charities should check whether appeals can be made locally or must be sent to head office. Any link with the company should be highlighted.

Preferred areas of support are . . .

We asked companies to tick preferred areas of support to indicate the sort of appeals most likely to interest them.

Exclusions (no grants for . . .)

The same list was used as for the preferred areas, with common exclusions being: fundraising events, advertising in charity brochures, appeals from individuals, denominational (religious) appeals, political/campaigning activity, and bricks and mortar appeals.

Before applying, potential applicants should always consider whether there is a particular reason why the company might want to support them.

How to use this guide

Below is a typical company entry, showing the format we have used to present the information obtained from each of the companies. Remember to always check the company's website for information before making an application. You should submit your request in writing, but may wish to ask for details of the grants procedure, check the contact for charitable donations or request a copy of the latest annual report. The latter, along with community support information, may also be obtained via the quoted website address.

Fictitious Productions plc

Spin

Correspondent: A Grant, CSR Manager, 68 Nowhere Street, Anytown AN6 2LM (tel: 01510 000000; fax: 01511 000000; website: www.fictprod.co.uk)

Directors: Terence Story, Chair; Shelley Yarn, Chief Executive; Luther Tale (women: 1; men: 2)

Year end	31/03/2011
Turnover	£837,300,000
Pre-tax profit	£292,000,000

Nature of business: The company is involved in the production of fictitious information.

Company registration number: 116565

Subsidiaries include: Cashflow Industries, False Publications, Sundry Matters, and Wage Packet Co.

Brands include: Storytime; Truth Ltd; Dizzy Media; and Blank Page.

Main locations: Grimsby, Liverpool, Bristol, Perth

UK employees: 3,872

Total employees: 7,689

Membership: Arts & Business, BITC, LBG

Charitable donations

UK cash (latest declared):	2011	£420,000
	2010	£350,000
	2009	£225,000
	2008	£184,000
	2007	£243,000
Total UK:	2011	£575,000
Total worldwide:	2011	£7,868,000
Cash worldwide:	2011	£1,234,000

Community involvement

The company supports local enterprise agencies and considers secondment of employees to local economic development initiatives.

Corporate giving

The company's community contributions totalled £575,000 in 2011. This included in kind giving, the cost of secondments and arts sponsorship, and charitable donations of £420,000. National grants range from £250 to £5,000. Local grants range from £25 to £500.

Major grant recipients in 2011 included Any Town LGBT Network (for information leaflets), Perth Parent & Toddler Association (towards play equipment) and the local wildlife trust.

The full name of the company is given with the companies listed in alphabetical order.

Only the large corporate givers have specialist staff dealing with appeals (a direct line number may be given in such instances). However, the company secretary, public relations or marketing departments will deal with appeals to many companies. Unless otherwise stated, the address is for the head office, to which appeals should be sent.

We give all available names of the directors and include the ratio of women to men on the board, where known.

Financial statistics: The year-end, turnover and pre-tax profit (a figure in brackets denotes a loss). Most relate to 2011. The figures give an indication of the scale of the company's giving relative to its size.

The main area of company activity. This can be useful if you are looking for a product link.

The registration number at Companies House, or in the case of a financial institution such as a Building Society, its FSA number, is also included.

A sample of the company's subsidiaries is listed here. Full details are usually given within the company's annual accounts.

A sample of the company's brands is given here. Full details are available on company websites.

The main locations are useful if you are looking for a geographical link.

The number of total employees and UK employees, where information is available.

Indicates whether the company is a member of Arts & Business, Business in the Community and LBG.

Figures for the last five years available are given. Also, figures for total UK and total worldwide contributions are given and these include the value of in kind giving, good-cause sponsorship, secondments, etc., where available.

This provides an overview of the company's community support, detailing preferred causes and any geographical areas that are favoured.

Quotes total cash donations made and, if available, total community contributions.

Examples of grants and their size, where known, are listed. Large grants are often a good indicator of the company's priorities.

In kind support

The company donates surplus or used furniture/equipment to local causes.

Some companies give gifts in kind, which can be anything from used stock to valuable pro bono work.

Employee-led support

A charity is selected each year to benefit from employee fundraising, with the company making a contribution by way of matched funding.

Payroll giving: A scheme is operated by the company.

Many company employees give time and money to local causes, including fundraising and expertise. If a payroll giving scheme is operated, we state so.

Commercially-led support

Sponsorship: The arts – The typical sponsorship range is from £1,000 to £25,000. It sponsors Southport Sinfonietta and supported music festivals in Grimsby and Perth.

Covers good-cause sponsorship, if undertaken, and will include a contact, if different from the main correspondent. Provides information on cause-related marketing promotions, if applicable.

Corporate social responsibility

CSR committee: There company has a separate CSR committee.

CSR policy: All charitable contributions are made through the Fictitious Productions Foundation, which is funded by donations of bonuses from employees and matched funding by the company.

CSR report: A CSR report is available on the company's website.

Here we give details of the structure of any designated CSR committee and when it meets; the company's CSR policy (if one exists and is published), with details of its approach to community giving if known; and information on if and when a CSR/sustainability report is published and where it is available.

Exclusions

No response to circular appeals. No grants for fundraising events, purely denominational religious appeals, local appeals not in areas of company presence, large national appeals, overseas projects, political activities or individuals. Non-commercial advertising is not supported. It does not sponsor individuals or travel.

Lists any areas, subjects or types of grants the company will not consider. **Check here first.**

Applications

In writing to the correspondent. Applications are considered by a donations committee which meets three times a year.

Includes how to apply and when to submit an application. We also state whether there is further information available from the company.

3i Group plc

Financial services

Correspondent: Patrick Dunne, Group Communications Director, 16 Palace Street, London SW1E 5JD (tel: 020 7928 3131; fax: 020 7928 0058; email: KevinDunnCR@3i.com; website: www.3i.com)

Directors: Adrian Montague, Chair; Michael Queen, Chief Executive; Julia Wilson, Group Finance Director; Jonathan Asquith; Alistair Cox; Richard Meddings; Willem Mesdag; Christine Morin-Postel (women: 2; men: 7)

Year end	31/03/2011
Pre-tax profit	£324,000,000

Nature of business: 3i is an international investor focusing on private equity, infrastructure and debt management.

Company registration number: 1142830

UK employees: 450

Total employees: 450

Membership: BITC

Charitable donations

UK cash (latest declared):	2011	£408,600
	2010	£407,490
	2009	£483,750
	2008	£454,130
	2007	£429,409
Total UK:	2011	£408,600
Total worldwide:	2011	£408,600
Cash worldwide:	2011	£408,600

Corporate social responsibility

CSR committee: The CSR Committee consists of six members. However the board as a whole is responsible for corporate responsibility – the executive directors are responsible for ensuring compliance with 3i's corporate values and standards. 3i's Corporate Responsibility Committee considers and reviews environmental, ethical and social issues relevant to 3i's business and reports regularly to the board.

CSR policy: The following information is taken from the company's website:

> 3i has been active for many years in a range of charitable and social enterprise activities. The concept of social enterprise is a natural fit with 3i's approach to supporting businesses.
>
> Our charitable activities are concentrated on young people, education and the disadvantaged in the communities where we have offices. Charities are supported on the basis of their effectiveness and impact. We are supportive of employees who volunteer for charitable work or become trustees of charities.

CSR report: A CSR report was last published in 2009.

Exclusions

No support for political appeals or individuals.

Applications

In writing to the correspondent.

Other information

The company's charitable giving for the year to 31 March 2011 totalled £408,566 (2010: £407,490).

3i's charitable activities are concentrated on young people, education and the disadvantaged in the communities where their offices are based.

Beneficiaries of 3i's charitable contributions include: The Passage; GOONJ; Community Links; Education at Historic Royal Palaces; Enterprise Education Trust; Bridges Ventures.

3M United Kingdom plc

Chemicals and plastics

Correspondent: Company Secretary, 3M United Kingdom plc, 3M Centre, Cain Road, Bracknell RG12 8HT (tel: 0870 536 0036; website: www.3M.com/uk)

Directors: Z. Dickson; D. Gray; P. Williams; J. McSheffrey

Year end	31/12/2010
Turnover	£492,000,000
Pre-tax profit	£526,000,000

Nature of business: The principal activity of the company is the manufacture and marketing of a range of coated materials and other related products and services. These include abrasives, adhesives, cleaning materials, tapes, reflective materials and office stationery products.

Company registration number: 1123045

Main locations: Bangor, Bedford, Aycliffe, Atherstone, Bracknell, Manchester, Clitheroe, Hillington, Gorseinon, Bridgend, Runcorn, Northallerton

Membership: BITC

Charitable donations

UK cash (latest declared):	2010	£239,000
	2008	£423,000
	2007	£412,000
Total UK:	2010	£239,000
Total worldwide:	2010	£239,000
Cash worldwide:	2010	£239,000

Corporate social responsibility

CSR committee: There was no evidence of a separate CSR Committee.

> **CSR policy:** The group plays a strong role in the communities in which they are based.

We were unable to determine the ratio of women to men on the board.

CSR report: There was no evidence of a separate CSR report.

Exclusions

No support for appeals from individuals, third party fundraisers, local appeals not in areas of company presence, large national appeals or overseas projects.

Applications

In writing to the correspondent. To be considered for support, local projects must fall within one or both of the topic areas (education and the environment) and relate to a community in which 3M has a site presence. Additionally, proposals must fulfil one or more of the following criteria:

- Be from a registered UK charitable concern
- Address a specific identified local community need
- Involve 3M volunteers
- On completion, show measurable results

Other information

3M in the UK focuses its community giving, nationally, around road safety programmes for children and, at a local level, on organisations serving the communities where 3M operates. Support for the latter concentrates on two areas – education and the environment – although grants are also given for relief of suffering.

In 2010, the company made cash donations in the UK and Ireland totalling £239,000. There appeared to be little information available on specific donations. However, the group did stipulate where the charitable donations were made and how much was donated for each of the following categories: environment (£10,000); education (£178,000); relief of suffering (£4,000); and 'other' (£47,000).

In aiming to help the communities closest to its UK and Ireland sites, 3M provides support in a number of ways including:

- Financial donations/grants
- In kind gifts of 3M products and services
- Volunteer services from employees and retirees
- Use of 3M facilities

Information taken from the latest accounts available at the time of writing.

Abbott Mead Vickers – BBDO Ltd

Advertising/marketing

Correspondent: Company Secretary, 151 Marylebone Road, London NW1 5QE (tel: 020 7616 3500; fax: 020 7616 3600; website: www.amvbbdo.com)

Directors: Colin Fleming; Farah Golant; Priscilla Snowball; Ian Pearman (women: 2; men: 2)

Year end	31/12/2011
Turnover	£57,700,000
Pre-tax profit	£12,700,000

Nature of business: Advertising agency.

Company registration number: 1935786

Main locations: London

Total employees: 392

Membership: BITC

Charitable donations

UK cash (latest declared):	2011	£67,000
	2009	£62,000
	2008	£69,000
	2006	£59,000
	2005	£64,000
Total UK:	2011	£67,000
Total worldwide:	2011	£67,000
Cash worldwide:	2011	£67,000

Corporate social responsibility

CSR committee: No information appeared to be available.

CSR policy: No information appeared to be available.

CSR report: No information appeared to be available.

Applications

In writing to the correspondent.

Other information

In 2011 the company donated £67,000 (2010: £77,000). A list of beneficiaries was unavailable.

Aberdeen Asset Management

Financial services

Correspondent: Corporate Social Responsibility Committee, 10 Queen's Terrace, Aberdeen AB10 1YG (tel: 01224 631999; fax: 01224 647010; website: www.aberdeen-asset.co.uk)

Directors: R. C. Cornick, Chair; Martin Gilbert, Chief Executive; Andrew Laing; Bill Rattray; Anne Richards; Hugh Young; Anita Frew; Julie Chakraverty; Gerhard Fusenig; Kenichi Miyanaga; Jim Pettigrew; Simon Troughton; Giles Weaver (women: 2; men: 11)

Year end	30/09/2011
Turnover	£784,000,000
Pre-tax profit	£301,900,000

Nature of business: Aberdeen Asset Management is an independent asset management group, which has been listed on the London Stock Exchange since 1991 and is today a FTSE 250 company.

Company registration number: 82015

Total employees: 1,851

Membership: BITC

Charitable donations

UK cash (latest declared):	2009	£202,000
	2008	£172,000
Total worldwide:	2011	£953,000
Cash worldwide:	2011	£953,000

Corporate social responsibility

CSR committee: Primary responsibility for these matters rests with Andrew Laing, chairman of the corporate social responsibility steering committee.

CSR policy: The company's charitable giving policy is made up of three parts: to support causes local to its offices, national causes in the countries in which it operates and internationally. The over-arching strategy on charitable giving is with a focus on community groups, health, children and older people.

CSR report: There was no evidence of a separate CSR report.

Applications

In writing to the correspondent.

Other information

During the year, the group made various charitable contributions totalling £953,000 (2009: £202,000). Donations included: Maggie's Cancer Caring Centres; Parkinson's UK; Women's Aid and EveryChild.

The company is currently working with the Charities Aid Foundation to expand payroll giving across the group and a new employee volunteering programme is scheduled to be rolled out to offer employees the opportunity to volunteer to assist a favoured local charity for up to two days per annum.

The company gives financial support to charities and various activities, and offers assistance in kind, such as printing services, auction prizes and the use of offices for fundraising events and other meetings. It also donates computer equipment to the Strongbones Children's Charitable Trust.

The company is now in year three of a five year commitment to support the first Information and Support Worker for North East Scotland for the Parkinson's Disease Society (PDS).

ABPA Holdings Ltd

Transport and shipping services

Correspondent: Corporate Communications Manager, Aldwych House, 71–91 Aldwych, London WC2B 4HN (tel: 020 7430 1177; fax: 020 7430 1384; email: csr@abports.co.uk; website: www.abports.co.uk)

Directors: Doug Morrison, Director; K. E. Bradbury; P. Busslinger; P. L. H. Camu; J. N. S. Cooper; G. P. R. Kay; D. W. Kerr; P. R. Lyneham; J. M. McManus; J. M. Rolland

Year end	31/12/2011
Turnover	£423,400,000
Pre-tax profit	(£562,900,000)

Nature of business: The provision of port and transport-related services to ship and cargo owners and other users of seaports in the UK, and the ownership and development of properties at port locations.

The company was incorporated on 14 November 2011 as an intermediate holding company within the group of companies owned by the ultimate parent undertaking ABP (Jersey) Ltd.

Company registration number: 7847153

Main locations: Barrow, Barry, Ayr, Swansea, Teignmouth, Troon, Southampton, Plymouth, Port Talbot, Silloth, Newport, Lowestoft, Ipswich, King's Lynn, Immingham, Hull, Fleetwood, Garston, Grimsby, Goole, Cardiff

Total employees: 1,927

Charitable donations

UK cash (latest declared):	2011	£100,300
	2009	£90,000
	2008	£140,000
	2007	£91,000
	2006	£40,000
Total UK:	2011	£278,400
Total worldwide:	2011	£278,400
Cash worldwide:	2011	£100,300

Corporate social responsibility

CSR committee: Information taken from the company's 2011 CSR report:

> The chief executive has overall responsibility for the group's performance and strategy on CR issues. The board receives regular updates on key CR issues and bi-annual updates on the group's overall progress on CR matters.
>
> Responsibility for the implementation of CR strategy and the management of day-to-day issues is delegated to a multi-disciplinary CR Steering Committee that includes representatives from the group's personnel, communities, health and safety, environment, internal audit and risk management functions. The terms of reference for this committee include implementation of new initiatives, monitoring of performance, the provision of updates to the board and reporting of performance to external stakeholders. The committee meets once a quarter and is chaired by the Commercial Director.
>
> At regional level, the local port director has overall responsibility for management of CR issues. Each region has local managers whose responsibility it is to address key CR issues such as community relations, health and safety, employee relations and environmental management.
>
> In addition, multi-disciplinary resource efficiency groups meet regularly to review and improve the environmental efficiency of our operations. These groups are designed to encourage the flow of ideas from our employees and report regularly to the CR Steering Committee.

CSR policy: Statement taken from the 2011 CSR report:

We understand that our daily operations can have an impact on our local communities and we work hard to ensure that, where we do affect our neighbours, the effects are positive rather than detrimental. We also appreciate that our business has the potential to make a positive contribution to local communities and that we cannot operate successfully in isolation from them.

We therefore endeavour to foster harmonious and mutually beneficial relationships with this important stakeholder group.

We were unable to determine the ratio of women to men on the board.

CSR report: Published annually.

Exclusions

There are no definite exclusions; instead the company will consider all appeals individually.

Applications

In writing to the correspondent. Applications are sorted and likely candidates referred to the Group Chief Executive.

Other information

Information taken from the CSR report for 2011:

Our total community investment in 2011, including contributions in kind, amounted to £278,400. Our total cash contributions amounted to £100,300 (2010: £94,900).

The group's charitable donations in 2011, comprising cash, gifts in kind, the cost of services and facilities used for charitable purposes, and the cost of employee involvement in charitable endeavours during office hours, totalled £125,400 (2010: £143,700). Charities that benefited from donations in 2011 included national and international organisations such as the NSPCC and the Disasters Emergency Committee (DEC), as well as local clubs and societies including the Ipswich Maritime Trust and various branches of the Sea Cadets.

Our ports' community investment policy is to direct our cash and in kind contributions primarily towards education, medical and maritime charities, arts sponsorship, civic organisations, and local partnerships. At our small corporate head office in Aldwych, London, our policy is to support charities local to our premises, maritime charities, and charities that have a personal connection to head office employees.

In 2011, and for the third year running, ABP took part in the 24 Peaks Challenge organised by Seafarers UK. This exercise involved a number of our employees walking up 24 peaks in the Lake District, each over 2,400 feet in 24 hours. The challenge, as well as helping to highlight the importance of team work, also raised £14,906 for Seafarers UK.

Give As You Earn (GAYE): Through the scheme ABP continues to match employee donations and meet the administration costs. The average monthly donation per employee has risen to £25 during 2011 (2010: £22). Currently 5.9% of employees participate in the scheme and the company is looking at ways to promote further uptake. In 2011 employees donated approximately £35,180 (2010: £30,100) to good causes through the Give As You Earn scheme during the year, which was matched by ABP.

Sponsorship: The group has continued its sponsorship of the Welsh National Opera (WNO), bringing it to its 25th year of continuous support.

Accenture UK Ltd

Accountants

Correspondent: Mary-Jane Smith, The Accenture Foundation, 60 Queen Victoria Street, London EC4N 4TW (tel: 020 7844 4000/020 7844 5387; fax: 020 7844 4444; email: corpcitizenship@accenture.com; website: www.accenture.com)

Directors: Pierre Nanterme, Chief Executive Officer and Chair; Pamela J. Craig, Chief Financial Officer; Mark Moody-Stuart; Dina Dublon; Charles Giancarlo; Nobuyuki Idei; William L. Kimsey; Robert I. Lipp; Marjorie Magner; Blythe J. McGarvie; Gilles C. Pélisson; Wulf von Schimmelmann (women: 3; men: 9)

Year end	31/08/2012
Turnover	£17,380,100,000

Nature of business: Accenture is a global management consulting, technology services and outsourcing company. Accenture (UK) Ltd is a wholly owned subsidiary of the Accenture group and the main trading entity for Accenture in the United. Kingdom.

Company registration number: 4757301

Main locations: Newcastle upon Tyne, Manchester, London, Aberdeen, Edinburgh

Total employees: 177,000

Membership: BITC, LBG

Charitable donations

UK cash (latest declared):	2012	£118,250
	2009	£733,000
	2008	£182,000
	2007	£433,000
	2006	£603,000
Total UK:	2012	£118,250
Total worldwide:	2012	£27,585,600

Corporate social responsibility

CSR committee: No details found.

CSR policy: Taken from the 2011/12 CSR Report:

Accenture's long-standing involvement in corporate citizenship means that, as we help our clients achieve high performance, we also focus on our people and the communities in which we live and work.

CSR report: A CSR report was available from the company's website.

Exclusions

No support for political appeals or religious appeals.

Applications

Proposals are generally invited by the trustees or initiated at their request. Unsolicited applications are discouraged and are unlikely to be successful, even if they fall within the areas in which the trustees are interested.

The UK Foundation trustees have agreed criteria under the overarching theme of 'Building Skills for Better Futures'. This covers registered charities working within the areas of employability and enterprise.

Other information

Accenture have developed a corporate citizenship initiative, Skills to Succeed, which focuses on building skills that enable people around the world to participate in and contribute to the economy.

We remain highly committed to the communities in which we live and work through our corporate citizenship efforts. Most notable is our Skills to Succeed initiative, through which we aim to equip 250,000 people worldwide with skills to get jobs or start businesses. Additionally, Accenture and the Accenture Foundations will contribute more than $100 million by the end of 2013 to support our corporate citizenship efforts through global and local giving as well as pro bono services by Accenture employees. Today we have more than 200 initiatives that are making a real impact on the economic vitality of individuals, families and communities around the world.

In 2011/12 the company spent over £27 million in cash donations, volunteer time, sponsorship and in kind donations to charitable causes worldwide. No separate cash donation figure was available, nor what was given in the UK. However, the company donated £118,250 to its foundation and we have used this as the UK cash giving figure although it is likely that the company gave substantially more.

The Accenture Foundation (Charity Commission no: 1057696) The Accenture Foundation supports registered or exempt charities working in education and training and disadvantaged communities, especially when on behalf of children/young people and in areas local to Accenture offices.

In 2010/11, the Accenture Foundation had an income of just over £220,000 and made grants totalling £2.6 million. Beneficiaries included: VSO (£514,000); Leonard Cheshire Disability (£410,000);

Oxfam (281,000); Youth Enterprise (£140,000); Depaul UK (£85,000). Smaller grants were also made totalling £311,000.

Accenture actively seeks opportunities that will allow it to best utilise its key skills and so have the most beneficial impact on society and its people. It does this through enabling its employees to engage in pro bono programmes, voluntary service overseas placements, projects conducted with Accenture Development Partnerships, three day community allowance and secondments.

Sponsorship: Accenture has sponsored numerous high profile community events and institutions over the past few years. The organisation claims that these associations help promote their business, while allowing them to enjoy the benefits of supporting worthwhile organisations that a make a positive impact on local culture and community. Accenture is the exclusive High Performance Business Partner of the world-renowned Royal Shakespeare Company (RSC).

Payroll giving: *Give As You Earn* – Employees are able to sign up to donate to charities of their choice through tax effective payroll giving.

Addleshaw Goddard

Legal

Correspondent: Karen Sinclair, Milton Gate, 60 Chiswell Street, London EC1Y 4AG (tel: 020 7606 8855/020 7788 5504; fax: 020 7606 4390; email: karen.sinclair@addleshawgoddard.com; website: www.addleshawgoddard.com)

Directors: Paul Devitt; Monica Burch; Adam Bennett; Adrian Collins; John Joyce; Simon Kamstra; Michael Leftley; Richard Papworth (women: 1; men: 7)

Year end	30/04/2011
Turnover	£160,610,000

Nature of business: Legal firm.

Company registration number: 4673315

Total employees: 1,017

Membership: BITC

Charitable donations

UK cash (latest declared):	2011	£220,700
	2009	£150,000
	2008	£150,000
	2007	£75,000
	2006	£66,000
Total UK:	2011	£220,700

Corporate social responsibility

CSR committee: The CSR Committee can be contacted by the email address provided.

CSR policy: The firm is recognised as being an excellent place to work and the CSR programme is designed to create and develop opportunities for our people to realise their potential.

This information was obtained from the company's website:

> The firm's charitable trust has been established since 2003, during which time it has made donations of over £350,000. The trust is funded entirely by the partners of the firm, who each make an annual contribution.
>
> The trust supplements the work of the CSR programme, through the financial support of good causes and CSR related projects at a local office level.

CSR report: The CSR report was available from the company's website.

Exclusions

No support for general or circular appeals, local appeals not in the areas of company presence, animal welfare, individuals or political/religious appeals.

Applications

In writing to the correspondent.

Other information

In 2011, the company raised £220,700. This money was raised as a combination of employee fundraising efforts and also contributions from the firm's charitable trust.

Donations can be broken down as follows:

- Candlelighters, Leeds – £42,683
- GOSH, London – £59,017
- St Ann's Hospice, Manchester – £120,000

Current projects include:

- SKILL! – workshops designed to bring about entrepreneurship amongst teenagers
- Leeds Wise, Open and Trusted (WOT) – an initiative which provides mentoring for young people who have come from a care background, making the transition to higher education
- International Enterprise Challenge – the company sponsors an essay writing competition (about enterprise and the developing world)
- The Passage – employees volunteer to help with the Monday breakfast service at a day centre for the homeless in Victoria

adidas (UK) Ltd

Sports clothing

Correspondent: Company Secretary, The adidas Centre, Pepper Road, Hazel Grove, Stockport SK7 5SD (tel: 01614 192500; fax: 01614 192603; website: www.adidas.com/home/uk)

Directors: R. H. Auschel; G. A. C. R. Steyaert; P. A. Suchoparek; K. L. Smith; A. R. Hackett

Year end	31/12/2011
Turnover	£487,860,000
Pre-tax profit	£23,394,000

Nature of business: The distribution and retail of sports goods to the sports trade in the UK.

Company registration number: 1075951

Main locations: Stockport, Bolton, Basingstoke, Chelmsford

UK employees: 1,104

Total employees: 1,104

Charitable donations

UK cash (latest declared):	2011	£36,500
	2010	£18,600
	2009	£43,000
	2008	£54,000
	2006	£18,000
Total UK:	2011	£36,500
Total worldwide:	2011	£36,500
Cash worldwide:	2011	£36,500

Corporate social responsibility

CSR committee: The group's Social and Environmental Affairs team was set up in the late 1990s to help select and govern projects.

CSR policy: This information was obtained from the company's website:

> To help select projects that respond to local needs we have set up an efficient network made up of local businesses to exchange best practice and ensure mutual support.

Unable to determine the ratio of women to men on the board.

CSR report: There is no evidence of a separate CSR report.

Applications

Applications are accepted and reviewed throughout the year in the order in which they are received. Requests must be submitted in writing. The request should be sent to the company's closest subsidiary or liaison office.

Other information

In 2011, Adidas (UK) donated £36,500 to charities within the UK. Previous beneficiaries included: Save the Children; Score; Right to Play; Operation Breakthrough.

Admiral Group plc

Insurance

Correspondent: Communications Manager, Capital Towers, Greyfriars Road, Cardiff CF10 3AZ (tel: 08718828282; website: www.admiralgroup.co.uk)

Directors: Alistair Lyons, Chair; Henry Engelhardt, Chief Executive Officer; Andrew Probert; David Stevens; Manfred Aldag; Martin Jackson; Keith James; John Sussens; Kevin Chadwick; Lucy Kellaway; Margaret Johnson; Colin Holmes (women: 2; men: 10)

Year end		31/12/2011
Turnover		£2,190,300,000
Pre-tax profit		£317,400,000

Nature of business: The company is the holding company for the Admiral Group of companies. The group sells, administers and underwrite private car insurance in the UK through six brands – Admiral, Bell, Diamond and elephant.co.uk, Gladiator Commercial and Confused.com.

Company registration number: 3849958

Brands include: Admiral, Bell, Diamond, elephant.co.uk, Gladiator Commercial, Confused.com, Balumba.es, AdmiralDirekt.de, Conte.it, Rastreator.com, Elephant Auto, Le Lynx, Chiarezza, Inspop Technologies.

Main locations: Swansea, Cardiff

Total employees: 5,324

Charitable donations

UK cash (latest declared):	2011	£178,000
	2009	£100,000
	2008	£106,000
	2007	£87,000
	2006	£38,000
Total UK:	2011	£178,000
Total worldwide:	2011	£178,000
Cash worldwide:	2011	£178,000

Corporate social responsibility

CSR committee: There is no evidence of a separate CSR committee.

CSR policy: The group has supported and continues to support a number of charities including Samaritans and Great Ormond Street Hospital Charity.

> Admiral plays a positive role in the community through charitable fund raising and encouraging staff to engage with local community partners. We promote payroll giving and provide matched funding for eligible staff initiatives.
>
> Our charity and community programme focuses on serving the communities near our office locations in Cardiff, Swansea and Newport and since 2007 our overseas locations.

Admiral Community Chest was set up in 1998 to help staff and their families who are involved with local charities, clubs and organisations.

CSR report: The CSR report is available from the company's website.

Exclusions

No support for local appeals not in areas of company presence or political appeals.

Applications

In writing to the correspondent. Note, however, that local support tends to be directed towards organisations involved with Admiral employees or their immediate family.

Other information

In 2011 Admiral gave £178,000 (2010: £168,000) in charitable donations. The following information is provided by the company:

> Admiral plays a positive role in the community through charitable fund raising and encouraging staff to engage with local community partners. We promote payroll giving and provide matched funding for eligible staff initiatives.
>
> Our charity and community programme focuses on serving the communities near our office locations in Cardiff, Swansea and Newport and since 2007 our overseas locations. Admiral Community Chest is a fund set up by the Company to provide financial support to staff and their families directly involved with local charities and organisations. The chest has been running for over 7 years and in that time we have been able to contribute to over 500 charities and organisations.
>
> *Festival of Sport*
>
> For the last 6 years Admiral has supported the Neath Port Talbot Festival of Sport for children with disabilities in Margam Park, South Wales. In 2011, 129 members of Admiral staff volunteered to attend the week-long event and support children in taking part in the activities which they otherwise may not have had the confidence or ability to do. Neath Port Talbot's Disability Sport Development Officer and festival organiser Vicky Radmore said, 'We're very grateful for the continued support from Admiral. Without their support we would not be able to accommodate as many young people, let alone provide the diversity of activities.
>
> *Balumba – Apadrina Un Poblado*
>
> Balumba, our direct insurer in Spain which launched in October 2006 has also embraced the company culture of giving back to the local and international community. Balumba runs a corporate volunteering program whereby employees work together to improve an impoverished community. Balumba have chosen to 'adopt' Mariankiari village, in Junin, Peru. This will result in Balumba and its staff providing a helping hand to bring about sustainable improvements that meet basic human needs and improve the quality of life in the village. One visit was made during 2011, and a group of employees will be visiting the village in 2012 to further relationships with the villagers and establish the donation options which would be of most benefit to the community.
>
> *UK Community Chest*
>
> Admiral's Community Chest is a scheme set up to enable staff to have a very direct say in where our charitable budget is spent. If a member of staff or their family has involvement in an organisation, charity, school or local sports club and that group needs funding for something, then a member of staff can apply to the Community Chest for the funding. Since its launch in 1998, over £500,000 has been donated to organisations in the local area (with over 1000 successful applicants). In 2011 alone, the entire budget of £178,000 of the Community Chest has been given as donations.

Adnams plc

Hotels, brewers/distillers

Correspondent: Rebecca Abrahall, Charity Administrator, Sole Bay Brewery, Southwold, Suffolk IP18 6JW (tel: 01502 727200; fax: 01502 727201; email: charity@adnams.co.uk; website: www.adnams.co.uk)

Directors: Jonathan Adnams, Chair; Andy Wood, Chief Executive; Stephen Pugh; Simon Loftus; William Kendall; Steven Sharp (women: 0; men: 6)

Year end		31/12/2010
Turnover		£50,912,000
Pre-tax profit		£2,818,000

Nature of business: The principal activities of the company are brewing, retailing and wholesaling beer, wines, spirits and minerals, property ownership and hotel management.

Company registration number: 31114

UK employees: 402

Total employees: 402

Membership: BITC

Charitable donations

UK cash (latest declared):	2010	£32,000
	2009	£34,000
	2008	£15,000
	2007	£40,000
	2006	£39,000
Total UK:	2010	£32,000
Total worldwide:	2010	£32,000
Cash worldwide:	2010	£32,000

Corporate social responsibility

CSR committee: There is no evidence of a CSR committee.

CSR policy: This information was obtained from the company's website:

> The Adnams Charity was founded in 1990 to celebrate Adnams centenary as a public company. It is funded by a percentage of Adnams annual profits, mandated dividends, donations and legacies.
>
> The Adnams Charity awards grants to worthy causes within 25 miles of Southwold or, in the case of national charities, exclusively for the benefit of those living within 25 miles of Southwold. Grants normally range from £100 to £2,500 and the trustees expect to see the results of their donations within six months.

CSR report: A separate CSR report available from the company's website.

Exclusions

The Adnams Charity does not normally make grants to religious organisations or private clubs unless these can demonstrate that the purpose of the grant is for something of clear public benefit, accessible to all. No grants to individuals, although public bodies and charities may apply on behalf of individuals.

Applications

An application form is available from the Charity Administrator by emailing charity@adnams.co.uk, telephoning 01502 727200 or writing to the Charity Administrator.

The applicant organisation will be asked to provide information on:

- What the grant is for
- Who will benefit
- How much the item(s) will cost – provide a detailed quotation
- Other fundraising activities being undertaken and amount raised so far
- To whom cheques should be made payable in the event of a grant being made

In addition, where possible, the most recent set of audited accounts should be enclosed with the application. A copy of your 'reserves policy' if you are applying from a registered charity is also required. The trustees meet quarterly, normally in January, April, July and October. Applications should be submitted early to ensure they are placed on the review list.

Other information

During the year 2010, Adnams gave £32,000 in donations. '1% of company operating profits are donated annually to the Adnams Charity (Charity Commission no. 1000203). The charity has been giving grants within 25 miles of Southwold (in Waveney, Suffolk) since 1990.'

Adobe Systems Europe Ltd

Computer software

Correspondent: Company Secretary, 151 Vincent Street, Glasgow G2 5NJ (website: www.adobe.com)

Directors: J. Nemeth; R. Rowley; S. Van Herck

Year end	30/11/2011
Turnover	£62,117,000
Pre-tax profit	(£2,607,000)

Nature of business: The marketing of Adobe products on behalf of other group companies.

Company registration number: SC101089

Main locations: Uxbridge, London, Edinburgh, Glasgow

Total employees: 359

Charitable donations

UK cash (latest declared):	2007	£54,000
Total worldwide:	2011	£1,800,000

Corporate social responsibility

CSR committee: No relevant UK details found.

CSR policy: Statement taken from Adobe's Corporate Responsibility website:

> Adobe is deeply committed to helping transform the world through digital experiences. Equally strong is our dedication to improving the world through responsible, global corporate citizenship. We believe that acting responsibly and giving back provides long-term, sustainable benefits to our communities, our employees, and our business. Read the following reports for details on Adobe's Corporate Social Responsibility programs and progress.

We were unable to determine the ratio of women to men on the board of directors.

CSR report: There is an annual CSR report published.

Applications

In writing to the correspondent.

Other information

Information is taken from the annual report and accounts for Adobe Systems Europe Ltd. In 2011 the European company did not declare any charitable contributions, however, this entry has been retained to provide information on the American company's Youth Voices programme which provides support in London schools. According to the CSR report for 2010, Adobe donated a total of $3 million (£1.8 million) in community giving, including matching gifts, 'dollars for doers' and sponsorships. It is unknown how much of this was donated within the UK. Grants from the Adobe Foundation (US) have not been included as it is not clear how the foundation is funded.

Adobe's UK support is focused on its Youth Voices initiative which 'provides youth in underserved communities with the critical skills they need to become active and engaged members of their communities and the world at-large'. The Adobe Youth Voices global network currently includes more than 557 sites, grantees, and organisations, such as the Intel Computer Clubhouse and iEARN, in 32 countries, engaging youth and educators in schools and out-of-school programmes. Participating sites in the UK for 2010 included:

- Dagenham Park Community School, London Borough of Barking and Dagenham
- Dunraven School, London Borough of Lambeth
- Kid's Company, London Borough of Southwark
- Plashet School, London Borough of Newham
- St Marylebone CE School, London Borough of Westminster
- St Charles Catholic Six Form College, London Borough of Kensington and Chelsea
- Mulberry School, London Borough of Tower Hamlets
- Mile End Community Project, London Borough of Tower Hamlets
- Body and Soul Project, London Borough of Ealing
- Westminster Kingsway, London Borough of Camden
- Crown Woods, London Borough of Greenwich
- Urban Hope, London Borough of Islington

Employee volunteering: Every year Adobe celebrates its commitment to community involvement during its 'Community Action Week'. In 2010, 877 volunteers donated 2,436 hours.

Payroll giving: Adobe matches employee donations to schools on non-profit organisations.

AEA Technology plc

Consultancy

Correspondent: Jenny Owen, Company Secretary, AEA Technology Group plc, 6 New Street Square, London EC4A 3BF (tel: 0870 190 8322; fax: 0870 190 8109; email: jenny.owen@aeat.co.uk; website: www.aeat.co.uk)

Directors: Andrew McCree, Chief Executive; Dr Paul Golby, Chair; Rodney Westhead; Kevin Higginson; Tim Robinson; Bernard Lord (women: 0; men: 6)

Year end	31/03/2011
Turnover	£113,700,000
Pre-tax profit	£7,000,000

Nature of business: AEA is an energy and climate change consultancy, offering integrated environmental solutions worldwide. It assists government with evidence based policy development and solves environmental challenges to improve organisational performance.

Company registration number: 3095862

Main locations: Derby, Harlow, Harwell, Glengarnock, Risley, London, Winfrith, Barnsley

UK employees: 938

Total employees: 938

Charitable donations

UK cash (latest declared):	2009	£38,300
	2008	£8,957
	2007	£25,483
	2006	£28,380
	2005	£48,942

Corporate social responsibility

CSR committee: No evidence of a separate CSR Committee.

CSR policy: This information was available from the company's website:

> We believe it is important to make a contribution towards our local and global community, not only through our advice,

services and products but also through our own actions.

From advising local SMEs on sustainability to supporting local schools to reduce carbon, our Community Investment Programme ensures we are continually identifying opportunities to support worthy causes.

CSR report: Information available from the company's website.

Exclusions

Previously no support for advertising in charity brochures, animal welfare, appeals from individuals, elderly people, fundraising events, medical research, overseas projects, political appeals, religious appeals, sickness/disability, social welfare or sport.

Other information

During the year 2010/11 there was no figure for charitable donations. However, community contributions were listed on the company's website and were as follows:

- **Renewable World:** The company made a donation to Renewable World instead of sending traditional Christmas cards
- **WaterAid 200 Mountain Challenge:** AEA's Scottish office will be taking part in this event in order to raise money that will go towards providing water and sanitation to communities in Nepal
- **Antarctica 2041 Ltd:** The company made charitable donations to this charity, which is dedicated to the preservation of Antarctica by the promotion of recycling, renewable energy and sustainability to combat the effects of climate change
- The company also supported: Jeans For Genes; Children 1st; Helen and Douglas House; Motor Neurone Disease Association and BBC Children in Need

Aegis Group plc

Media

Correspondent: Emma Thomas, Company Secretary, 180 Great Portland Street, London W1W 5QZ (tel: 020 7070 7700; fax: 020 7070 7800; website: www.aegismedia.com)

Directors: John Napier, Chair; Jerry Buhlmann, Chief Executive; Charles Strauss; Mark Jamison; Nigel Morris; Simon Francis; Patrick Stahle; Nigel Sharrocks; Andreas Bolte; Mark Cranmer; Martyn Rattle; Nick Waters; Annie Rickard; Valerie Scoular (women: 2; men: 12)

Year end	31/12/2011
Turnover	£11,854,700,000
Pre-tax profit	£147,800,000

Nature of business: Aegis Group plc is one of the world's leading media and digital marketing communications groups. Aegis is made up of two operating businesses, Aegis Media (Carat, Vizeum, Posterscope, Isobar and iProspect) and Aztec, the scan-based market and consumer insights company.

The principal activity of the group is the provision of a wide range of services in the areas of media communications and market research.

Company registration number: 1403668

Main locations: London

UK employees: 7,246

Total employees: 16,578

Membership: LBG

Charitable donations

UK cash (latest declared):	2009	£310,000
	2007	£200,000
	2006	£300,000
	2005	£400,000
Total worldwide:	2011	£5,480,000

Corporate social responsibility

CSR committee: The CR Department oversees the minimum standards and reporting for community involvement. A champion network has been established to implement engaging CR initiatives.

CSR policy: In response to community issues, Aegis developed a network of community champions which are responsible for monitoring and reporting community data, as well as delivering engaging locally relevant community initiatives in the form of fundraising, volunteering or pro bono projects. There was also the initiation of a partnership with GlobalGiving UK to develop a global community imitative.

CSR report: The CSR report is contained within the annual accounts. Several paragraphs were dedicated to the community.

Exclusions

No support for local appeals not in areas of company presence.

Applications

In writing to the correspondent.

Other information

In 2011, the company made charitable donations of £5.48 million; however this includes fundraising by staff and in kind donations.

The estimated total value of community initiatives in 2011 was the 'equivalent to 3.4% of the company's pre-tax profit.'

The top three charitable causes across the company's global network were Education and Young People, Social Welfare and Health. An example of this was Aegis Media Switzerland's launch of the 'Kanzlei Kinder' project, focused on cleaning up the local square for children to use. The company saw a shift from one-off donations to more strategic and longer term engagements.

In 2011, 346 charities were helped in 210 activities, with a total of 4,777 beneficiaries.

Aegon (Scottish Equitable plc)

Insurance

Correspondent: Company Secretary, Lochside House, Edinburgh Park, Edinburgh EH12 9SE (tel: 01313 399191; website: www.aegon.co.uk)

Directors: Adrian Grace, Chief Executive; Tommy Young; Charles Garthwaite; Clare Bousfield, Chief Financial Officer; Duncan Jarrett; Jim Ewing; Rob Waller; Richard Dallas (women: 1; men: 7)

Year end	31/12/2011
Turnover	£7,247,800,000

Nature of business: The transaction of life assurance, pensions and other long-term insurance business in the UK.

Company registration number: 144517

Brands include: Aegon

Main locations: Lytham St Annes, Edinburgh

Total employees: 3,000

Charitable donations

UK cash (latest declared):	2011	£153,000
Total UK:	2011	£153,000
Total worldwide:	2011	£153,000
Cash worldwide:	2011	£153,000

Corporate social responsibility

CSR committee: No details found.

CSR policy: CSR information taken from Ageon's website: 'We're committed to making a positive contribution to the society and environment we work in. Of course, profitable and sustainable growth is important to us, but so is helping to make a brighter future for our customers, communities and environment we work in.'

CSR report: Annual Sustainability report published on Aegon's website.

Applications

In writing to the correspondent.

Other information

In 2011 the company Scottish Equitable plc donated £153,000 to charitable causes nominated by its employees. Of this, £65,000 was donated to: Down's Syndrome Scotland, Kindred, Macmillan Cancer Support, Blue Skies Hospital Fund, Cystic Fibrosis Trust and North West Air Ambulance.

The company's Community Involvement Programme focuses on three main areas:

- Projects in the community
- Employee volunteering

- Sharing resources and skills

In 2007 the company established the AEGON Breakfast Club in Edinburgh, in partnership with the Heart of Midlothian Education and Community Trust and the City of Edinburgh Council. The initiative aims to fund breakfast clubs at every primary school in the city, where there is an identified need, giving children a free, healthy, nutritional start to the day. More information can be found on the Breakfast Club website www.aegonbreakfastclub.org.

The following information is taken from Aegon's website:

> In the UK, our corporate responsibility initiatives impact on the local environment, a range of charities, school children and improving access to tennis. Our recent corporate social responsibility highlights include:
>
> - 2,000 breakfasts served to school children
> - Almost £150,000 donated to our charity partners and good causes last year
> - Over two million school kids reached through the AEGON Schools Tennis programme
> - Over 200 parks offering communities improved access to tennis
> - 80% of our waste is recycled
>
> We also support our employees in their efforts to raise money for a wide variety of other charities and good causes. Each Christmas, for example, employees donate presents to children being supported in Women's Aid refuges in their local area, through the AEGON Giving Tree.
>
> And our voluntary hours programme provides the chance to take 12 hours a year of paid leave each year to work for registered charities or non-profit organisations.

Ageas Insurance Ltd (formerly Fortis Insurance Ltd)

Insurance

Correspondent: Company Secretary, Ageas House, Tollgate, Eastleigh, Hampshire SO53 3YA (tel: 02380 644455; website: www.ageas.co.uk)

Directors: A. J. Clarke; B. D. Smith; C. Dobson; H. A. Pickford; J. O. Grosvenor; J. C. Hance; M. N. Urmston; L. G. Nicholls; M. Cliff; R. J. Smale (women: 2; men: 8)

Year end	31/12/2010
Turnover	£865,500,000
Pre-tax profit	(£14,600,000)

Nature of business: Principally motor, travel and household insurance, and small commercial lines business.

Company registration number: 354568

Main locations: Eastleigh, Gloucester

UK employees: 1,542

Total employees: 1,542

Charitable donations

UK cash (latest declared):	2010	£9,000
	2009	£35,000
	2008	£40,000
	2007	£48,000
	2006	£43,000
Total UK:	2010	£9,000
Total worldwide:	2010	£9,000
Cash worldwide:	2010	£9,000

Corporate social responsibility

CSR committee: There was no evidence of a separate CSR Committee.

CSR policy: No CSR policy published.

CSR report: There was no evidence of a separate CSR report.

Applications

In writing to the correspondent.

Other information

In 2010, the company made charitable donations in the UK totalling £9,000. Details of beneficiaries were not available.

Aggregate Industries Ltd

Building materials, quarrying

Correspondent: Company Secretary, Bardon Hall, Copt Oak Road, Markfield, Leicestershire, United Kingdom LE67 9PJ (tel: 01530 816600; fax: 01530 816666; website: www.aggregate.com)

Directors: Roland Köhler; George Bolsover; Alain Bourguignon; John Bowater; Angela Yeoman; Benoît-Henri Koch; Christopher Garnett; James Davis; Norman Fowler (women: 1; men: 8)

Year end	31/12/2010
Turnover	£49,428,000
Pre-tax profit	£49,428,000

Nature of business: Aggregate Industries and its subsidiaries are engaged in the exploitation of land and mineral reserves principally for the supply of heavy building materials for construction activities.

The company became part of the Holcim Group in 2005.

Company registration number: 5655952

Main locations: Coalville

Total employees: 0

Charitable donations

UK cash (latest declared):	2010	£294,700
	2009	£138,500
	2007	£63,000
	2006	£55,000
	2005	£112,000
Total UK:	2010	£445,100
Total worldwide:	2010	£445,100
Cash worldwide:	2010	£294,700

Corporate social responsibility

CSR committee: No specific details found.

CSR policy: Information taken from the group's website:

> People play a valuable part in sustainable construction. The people who live and work around us influence what we do and how we do it; they are fundamental to the maintenance of our licence to operate.
>
> Our community plan was developed as a result of numerous conversations with our neighbours over many years. Our expectation is that this plan will provide a simple framework to improve our support for those around us which in turn will allow us to build stronger connections with our communities.

CSR report: There is a Sustainability section on the group's website and a Sustainability report is produced annually. A Community Plan document is also available.

Exclusions

No support for political or religious appeals.

Applications

In writing to the correspondent.

Other information

During 2010, financial support by the group to projects of £294,700 was given, and donated materials were valued at £150,400. In line with the group's community plan, efforts are becoming more targeted towards in kind donations; volunteering employee hours and expertise. Over the year 1,473 hours were given to the communities in which the group operates. Previous beneficiaries include: Oban Sea Cadets; Lismore Heritage Centre for development; Riding for the Disabled Association; Oban Lifeboat Fund.

Aggreko plc

Engineering, services

Correspondent: Company Secretary, 120 Bothwell Street, Glasgow G2 7JS (tel: 01412 255900; fax: 01412 255949; email: investors@aggreko.com; website: www.aggreko.co.uk)

Directors: P. Rogerson, Chair; Rupert Soames; Angus Cockburn; George Walker; Bill Caplan; Kash Pandya; David Hamill; Robert MacLeod; Russell King; Ken Hanna; Peter Kennerley (women: 0; men: 11)

Year end	31/12/2011
Turnover	£1,229,900,000
Pre-tax profit	£304,400,000

Nature of business: Rent civil engineering machinery.

Company registration number: SC177553

Total employees: 4,262

Charitable donations

UK cash (latest declared):	2011	£43,400
	2009	£49,000
	2008	£76,000
Total UK:	2011	£43,400
Total worldwide:	2011	£157,000
Cash worldwide:	2011	£157,000

Corporate social responsibility

CSR committee: The CSR Committee is partnered with the Ethics Committee.

CSR policy: This information was obtained from the company's website:

> Aggreko has a policy of encouraging local teams to engage with the communities in which they work, and each year they undertake innumerable initiatives to help the disadvantaged or those affected by natural disasters.
>
> We have a policy of giving little donations to many organisations which are involved with the communities in which we work, rather than giving a lot of money to a few.

CSR report: The CSR report is published annually.

Applications

In writing to the correspondent.

Other information

In 2011 the group made donations of £157,000 (2010: £300,000) in cash, employees' time and other services to a range of charitable, community and disaster relief organisations. Of this total £43,400 (2010: £43,300) was given to UK charities. A list of beneficiaries was not available.

'Aggreko has a policy of encouraging local teams to engage with the communities in which they work and each year they undertake innumerable initiatives to help the disadvantaged or those affected by natural disasters.'

Aggreko has a policy of giving little donations to many organisations which are involved with the communities in which we work, rather giving a lot of money to only a few. The company's largest single donation goes to Book Aid International, a charity promoting literacy in Africa, with whom the company has been working with since 2006.

Agilent Technologies UK Ltd

Information technology

Correspondent: Company Secretary, 610 Wharfedale Road, Winnersh Triangle, Wokingham, Berkshire RG41 5TP (tel: 01314 520200; fax: 01314 520419; email: arlene_dickson@agilent.com; website: www.agilent.com)

Directors: P. Gourlay; N. Johnson; Y. Mackie

Year end	31/10/2011
Turnover	£120,043,000
Pre-tax profit	£7,417,000

Nature of business: The design, manufacture, marketing and servicing of products and system for measurement, communication and chemical analysis.

Company registration number: 3809903

Main locations: Winnersh, Queensferry

Total employees: 18,500

Charitable donations

UK cash (latest declared):	2011	£10,200
	2009	£23,000
	2008	£45,000
	2007	£54,000
Total UK:	2011	£10,200
Total worldwide:	2011	£10,200
Cash worldwide:	2011	£10,200

Corporate social responsibility

CSR committee: No dedicated CSR committee.

CSR policy: Agilent's CSR policies do not relate to this UK company. Information obtained from the company's website stated that:

> Agilent's worldwide community programs tangibly demonstrate the company's values and commitment to corporate citizenship. In communities where we operate, we contribute through foundation and company grants, employee volunteerism, public policy and community partnerships in the areas of science education, and workplace giving campaigns.

Unable to determine ratio of women to men on the board.

CSR report: Information available on the company's website. CSR report on the company's US contribution is updated annually.

Applications

Local appeals should be made in writing to the correspondent.

For information about the Agilent Foundation (US philanthropic organisation) see company website.

Other information

The company supports science and mathematics in line with its overall objectives. In 2010/11 the company made charitable donations of £10,200. We have no details of the beneficiaries.

This information was obtained from the company's annual report:

> Through grants and donations, Agilent supports programs designed to increase student interest and achievement in science education, with an emphasis on populations underrepresented in the technology industry. Each year Agilent employees throughout the world devote thousands of volunteer hours to increasing student interest in science and other community activities.
>
> Agilent supports essential programs that deliver respect, hope and solutions to communities around the world where Agilent has a presence. In addition to making donations, Agilent volunteers aid scores of non profit agencies each year during community service events.
>
> Agilent Technologies and its Foundation are focused primarily on science education in communities worldwide where Agilent has a presence. In addition, Agilent supports a broad range of nonprofit programs through its annual giving campaign in the United States and Canada, and to designated community organisations in other areas of the world.

Air Products Group Ltd

Oil and gas/fuel

Correspondent: Company Secretary, Hersham Place Technology Park, Molesey Road, Walton-on-Thames, Surrey KT12 4RZ (tel: 01932 249200; fax: 01932 258565; website: www.airproducts.co.uk)

Directors: P. M. Neligan; D. Sheridan; G. M. Rhodes

Year end	30/09/2011
Turnover	£563,459,000
Pre-tax profit	£124,756,000

Nature of business: The manufacture and sale of industrial gases, the design and construction of equipment for the production and use of industrial gases, and the manufacture and sale of speciality chemicals.

Company registration number: 3101747

Main locations: Crewe, Walton-on-Thames

Total employees: 1,920

Charitable donations

UK cash (latest declared):	2011	£65,500
	2009	£110,000
	2008	£110,000
	2007	£154,000
	2006	£89,000
Total UK:	2011	£65,500
Total worldwide:	2011	£65,500
Cash worldwide:	2011	£65,500

Corporate social responsibility

CSR policy: No CSR information available.

We were unable to determine the ratio of women to men on the board.

Applications

In writing to the correspondent.

Other information

During the year the company's donations to UK charities totalled £65,500. We have no details of beneficiaries but previous projects/ organisations supported by the company include: Rydens School, Surrey – Young Apprentice competition; London Schools Hydrogen Challenge; Wildlife Aid – Surrey; Manchester Camerata; The Police Community Clubs of Great Britain;

Overton Rugby Festival; and, Elmbridge Sports Awards.

Akzo Nobel UK Ltd

Chemicals and plastics

Correspondent: Company Secretary, 28th Floor Portland House, Bressenden Place, London SW1E 5BG (tel: 020 7932 9800; fax: 020 7932 9932; website: www.akzonobel.com/uk)

Directors: Leif Darner; Tex Gunning; Hans Wijers; Keith Nichols; Rob Frohn (women: 0; men: 5)

Year end	31/12/2011
Turnover	£1,200,000,000
Pre-tax profit	£570,000,000

Nature of business: The group is an industrial materials company involved in polymer technology and surface science. Business areas are: pharmaceuticals; coatings; and chemicals. With the acquisition of ICI, AkzoNobel became the largest supplier of decorative paints.

Company registration number: 128124

Main locations: London, Newhouse, Gateshead, Southampton, Plymouth, Brentwood, Buckhaven, Milton Keynes, Cambridge, Beith, Henley-on-Thames, Congresbury, Blackburn

Total employees: 57,240

Charitable donations

UK cash (latest declared):	2009	£6,000
	2006	£6,000

Corporate social responsibility

CSR committee: There was no evidence of a separate CSR Committee.

CSR policy: According to the company's website its community programme is a worldwide initiative that encourages employees to get involved within their local communities. Although there are numerous examples of successful projects from around the world, none of them are from the UK, and unfortunately, we have been unable to obtain full community investment figures for Akzo Nobel businesses in the UK.

CSR report: Information available from the company's website.

Exclusions

The company provides no support for political parties, their institutions, agencies or representatives.

Applications

In writing to the correspondent.

Other information

There was no information regarding cash donations for 2011. However, we can surmise that the company gave at least £47,000 through its Project of the Year programme.

The company started its Education-Industry Partnership Programme in 1991. This aims to interest young students in science and technology through a closer collaboration between the company's sites and the educational system.

From the contents of the company's website it is clear that Akzo Nobel acknowledges its wider responsibilities to society, though there is little specific reference to its UK programme.

The focus of the company's community programme for sponsorship and donations is to stimulate young talent.

Support through sponsorship and donations are given to selected activities in the fields such as education, sports, science, healthcare, culture and the arts. Beneficiaries have included The Coulthard Institute of Art, Museum of the Chemical Industry, The Royal Society, The National Museum of Science and Industry, The Museum of Film, Photography and Television and The National Railway Museum.

Project of the Year: Around 3,550 AkzoNobel employees voted in the 2011 Best Practices Competition to choose last year's best Community Program project in the company. Decorative Paints Mumbai was selected from the 15 finalists for their community project. The first prize winning project was entitled: 'Fruitful way to offer poor farmers a sustainable future.' Company volunteers helped set up a 'model' farm by transforming a half-acre plot of arid land into a lush, green site in one of Mumbai's poorest areas. Their initiative set in motion similar projects, which resulted in 150 acres of land being converted into productive farms.

Marine and Protective Coatings in Shanghai, China, won the Second Prize for their 'The world is water' project. A detailed program was developed to stimulate children's interest in water and issues surrounding it, educating them on how important water is to the environment.

The Third Prize was awarded to Pulp and Paper Chemicals in Bahia, Brazil, for their 'Keeping poor youngsters on the right track' project. The volunteering employees committed to making life better for some young children living in poor circumstances in Bahia who were at risk for getting into dangerous or unhealthy situations after school.

The three winners receive cash prizes of €30,000, €20,000 and €10,000, respectively, to be spent by employees involved in the winning projects on good causes in their own countries, in the spirit of the Community Program.

Alcoa UK Holdings Ltd

Metals

Correspondent: Company Secretary, 1 Park Row, Leeds LS1 5AB (email: Nicola.Acton@alcoa.com; website: www.alcoa.com/united_kingdom/en/home.asp)

Directors: L. M. Fargas Mas; J. R. Camino

Year end	31/12/2010
Pre-tax profit	(£2,608,000)

Nature of business: Alcoa is a world leading producer of primary aluminium, fabricated aluminium, and alumina. Active in all major aspects of the industry.

Company registration number: 499001

Subsidiaries include: Howmet Ltd

Main locations: Telford, Runcorn, London, Laindon, Exeter, Coalville, Birmingham

Charitable donations

UK cash (latest declared):	2010	£0
	2008	£42,000
	2007	£34,000
	2006	£55,000
	2005	£39,000
Total UK:	2010	£0
Total worldwide:	2010	£0
Cash worldwide:	2010	£0

Corporate social responsibility

CSR committee: There is no evidence of a separate CSR Committee.

CSR policy: The company's main support for local voluntary and community groups in England is via the Alcoa Foundation; although a small amount comes from within the UK.

Unable to determine the ratio of women to men on the Board.

CSR report: There is no evidence of a separate CSR report.

Applications

In writing to your local foundation contact (situated at each Alcoa site), who will then make recommendations to the Alcoa Foundation for grant awards.

Full details of grant giving guidelines and procedures are available at: www.alcoa.com/global/en/community/info_page/Request_grant_community-based.asp.

Other information

Since 2009, the UK based company has made donations totalling £394,400. Recent beneficiaries have included Bromford Bridge daycare Centre, Birmingham. Alcoa's grantmaking is focused around four key objectives: Building Tomorrow's Workforce and Leaders; Community Capacity and Resilience; Health and Safety and Sustainable Development. Priority is given to projects and organisations in or near communities where Alcoa offices or plants are located, currently: Birmingham, Coalville, Exeter, Laindon. London, Runcorn and Telford.

Since 2002 the Alcoa Foundation, based in the United States, has made grants totalling $1.9 million worldwide. Its website provides a comprehensive breakdown of its grantmaking.

Allen and Overy LLP

Legal

Correspondent: Susan Hazledine, Head of Social Investment, Bishops Square, One Bishops Square, London, E1 6AD, United Kingdom (tel: 020 3088 0000/020 3088 3729; fax: 020 3088 0088; email: susan.hazledine@allenovery.com; website: www.allenovery.com)

Directors: David Morley; Wim Dejonghe; Ian Dinwiddie; Cath Bell-Walker; Tim House; Helge Schaefer; Alan Paul; Jane Townsend; Boyan Wells; Jason Haines; Genevieve Tennant (women: 4; men: 7)

Year end	30/04/2011
Turnover	£1,050,100,000
Pre-tax profit	£428,800,000

Nature of business: International law firm.

Company registration number: OC306763

Main locations: London

Total employees: 4,289

Membership: BITC

Charitable donations

UK cash (latest declared):	2009	£367,500
	2008	£365,000

Corporate social responsibility

CSR committee: There is no evidence of a separate CSR Committee.

CSR policy: Information was obtained from the company's website

> Allen & Overy's extensive global pro bono and community affairs programme is an important part of who we are and the values on which we build our business. As one of the emerging global elite of law firms, with broad international cover and deep local roots, Allen & Overy is in a unique position to impact on the communities in which we live and work and to help those in need in the wider world.

CSR report: There is no CSR report, however there is great deal of information available from the company's website.

Applications

Charitable giving (London)

If your organisation falls within the guidelines given and you wish an application to be considered, send a letter and supporting documents to the correspondent.

Set out details of your organisation, the project for which sponsorship is required, the amount being requested and the charitable registration number. Short listed requests are considered by the Allen and Overy Charities Committee in their quarterly meetings.

Outside of London each Allen and Overy office has a community programme contact and partner who are responsible for their local initiatives.

Charity or Community Partner of the Year

If you would like to nominate a charity or community organisation, send a note addressed to the Head of Social Affairs, setting out the following:

- How the organisation meets the criteria
- Potential volunteering opportunities with the organisation for our staff
- Suggested ways in which Allen and Overy could support the organisation

As in previous years, Allen and Overy's Charities Committee will make the final decision. Applications are considered in February/March of each year.

For funding from The Allen and Overy Foundation, address your application to: R Crane, First Combined Trust, The Allen and Overy Foundation at the company's address.

Information available: The firm have produced two excellent reports on its work with its local communities; these are 'Pro Bono and Community Affairs Report 2009, which details its significant work in these areas, and 'Artbeat' which covers its community arts initiative. Both are downloadable from the firm's website.

Other information

Allen and Overy are an international law firm with an extensive pro bono community affairs programme. Some of the organisations to benefit from pro bono work have included: Advocates for International Development (A4D); Battersea Legal Advice Centre; Interrights; Liberty; Crisis; and, Toynbee Hall.

The firm's global and local programmes are structured around themes that are relevant to its business – Global Firm, Global Responses, Access to Justice, Access to Education and Employment and Communities. The community affairs work in London is mainly centred on the Tower Hamlets area and includes a clear strategy linked to its staff's aspirations to help children and young people through educational and regeneration projects. Young people's basic skills are enhanced, their self-confidence and self-esteem is raised, and they have a better chance of breaking the cycle of poverty and unemployment.

Allen and Overy work with local organisations and local schools including St John's Primary School, Bethnal Green Technology College, School Governors, CityGateway and The Brokerage CityLink.

The Allen and Overy Foundation

(Charity Commission no: 803071) is administered by the London Charities Committee which is comprised of partners within the firm.

In 2010/11 there appeared to be no information of donations given by the company. However, in 2008/09 the foundation received £367,000 in voluntary income which we have attributed to the firm. Grants totalling almost £369,000 were made. Beneficiaries included: Educational Charity of the City of London Solicitors (£60,000); British Red Cross (£57,000); The Sutton Trust and South West London Law Centre (£20,000 each); Toynbee Hall and Crisis UK (£15,000 each) and Whitechapel Mission (£10,000).

The charities committee will make donations to charities that:

- Are law related
- Are based in our neighbouring boroughs of Tower Hamlets and Hackney
- Have Allen and Overy volunteers participating in their activities

The committee has recently given greater emphasis to the third option, to recognise the dedication of staff to the firm's pro bono and community activities.

Allen and Overy Global Foundation

In 2010 the firm launched the Allen and Overy Global Foundation, replicating the Allen and Overy Foundation based in London. The global foundation will make charitable donations to communities around the world. The majority of the Global Foundation's funds will be distributed by individual offices to local charities and causes, but there will also be a global fund that will allow the trustees to respond to international causes and appeals.

The following is taken from the company's website:

> We seek out innovative opportunities to make the best use of the skills, resources, time and energy we have to share with those who will most benefit from it. Getting involved in pro bono and community work also provides our staff with a valuable opportunity for personal and professional development.
>
> Our global and local programmes are structured around themes that are relevant to us as a business:
>
> - Global Firm, Global Responses
> - Access to Justice
> - Access to Education and Employment

- Helping our Local Communities
- Charitable Giving
- Global Charity Partner – Red Cross

If you have a specific query or you would like to find out about volunteering opportunities, please email: probonoteam@allenovery.com

Allianz Insurance plc

Insurance

Correspondent: HR Director, 57 Ladymead, Guildford, Surrey GU1 1DB (tel: 01483 568161; fax: 01483 300952; email: sian.glennane@allianz.co.uk; website: www.allianz.co.uk)

Directors: C. B. Booth, Chair; D. A. Torrance, Chief Executive; Baron C. von Bechtolsheim; B. Bovermann; T. D. Kingston; M. J. Churchlow; J. M. Dye; P. J. Gennoy; G. A. Gibson; C. D. Hanks; D. J. Knowles; K. Willis

Year end	31/12/2010
Turnover	£1,652,000,000
Pre-tax profit	£156,600,000

Nature of business: The group undertakes all classes of insurance business.

Company registration number: 84638

Main locations: Brentford, Liphook, Guildford, Tunbridge Wells

UK employees: 4,300

Total employees: 5,016

Membership: BITC, LBG

Charitable donations

UK cash (latest declared):	2010	£221,300
	2009	£367,452
	2008	£238,618
	2007	£146,095
	2006	£132,048
Total UK:	2010	£221,300
Total worldwide:	2010	£478,000
Cash worldwide:	2010	£478,000

Corporate social responsibility

CSR committee: CSR policy is dealt with by the HR department.

CSR policy: Allianz supports communities through direct and financial contributions. This information was obtained from the company's website:

> Our mission is to be the 'outstanding competitor in our chosen markets'- operating responsibly and managing our social and environmental risks is essential if we are to meet this goal.

Unable to determine the ratio of women to men on the board.

CSR report: The CSR report was available from the company's website and is produced annually.

Exclusions

No support for political appeals or organisations whose activities are not aligned with the themes of the company.

Applications

For further details contact the correspondent.

Other information

In 2010 the company has made charitable donations of £221,300. The company supports organisations/ community groups that are aligned with their themes. Themes include: financial security, health and welfare, animal welfare, environment, equality and education.

In 2009 the company launched a new long-term (minimum of three years) partnership with *Help the Hospices*, the leading charity supporting hospice care throughout the UK. In 2010, the company raised £160,000 for Help the Hospices as well as providing training courses for staff and management. Other beneficiaries include: The Prince's Trust (Allianz has given £125,000 to the Prince's Trust since 2006 to support its work); Chance to Shine; Jubilee Sailing Trust.

Payroll Giving: The company operates a Payroll Giving Scheme which offers employees the chance to make regular donations to a charity of their choice. The company also takes part in various fundraising events. In 2010 Allianz employees had raised £39,000 for their nominated charity, Help the Hospices, which the company then added 10% to.

AMEC plc

Building/construction, engineering, property

Correspondent: Charities Committee, 76–78 Old Street, London EC1V 9RU (tel: 020 7539 5800; fax: 020 7539 5900; email: frank.stokes@amec.com; website: www.amec.com)

Directors: John Connolly, Chair; Samir Brikho, Chief Executive; Ian McHoul; Neil Bruce; Neil Carson; Colin Day; Tim Faithfull; Simon Thompson (women: 0; men: 8)

Year end	31/12/2010
Turnover	£2,950,600,000
Pre-tax profit	£272,500,000

Nature of business: AMEC's provides a broad range of services to the oil and gas industry worldwide. The company has regional; offices throughout England, Scotland and Wales.

Company registration number: 1675285

Main locations: Aberdeen, Ashford, London, Birchwood, Birmingham, Manchester

Total employees: 21,907

Membership: LBG

Charitable donations

UK cash (latest declared):	2010	£295,000
	2009	£549,000
	2007	£188,000
	2006	£186,000
	2005	£108,000
Total UK:	2010	£295,000
Total worldwide:	2010	£553,000
Cash worldwide:	2010	£553,000

Corporate social responsibility

CSR committee: There is a separate 'Charities Committee'.

CSR policy: Information was obtained from the company's website:

> AMEC is committed to supporting the communities in which we operate and to society in general, acting with integrity and adhering to the highest ethical standards, promoting respect and diversity in our workforce and ensuring a safe and health workplace. Our responsibility to the wider social environment is more than that and includes promoting sustainable development, encouraging volunteering by our employees and strict compliance with applicable laws.

CSR report: The CSR report was obtained from the company's website and is produced annually. The company's latest sustainability report is available online at: www.amec.com.

Exclusions

Non-charitable grants cannot be considered.

Applications

In writing to the correspondent.

Other information

In 2010 AMEC gave £553,000 in charitable donations which was match funding for staff fundraising initiatives in their local communities – £295,000 was donated to UK organisations. We do not have details of beneficiary organisations. Previous information indicates support for education, enterprise, environment and health. Almost £100,000 was donated to SOS Children to help Haiti.

During 2010, AMEC employees volunteered for 3,304 hours and donated over £460,000.

Amey UK plc

Miscellaneous

Correspondent: Wayne Robertson, Company Secretary, Sherard Building, Edmund Halley Road, Oxford OX4 4DQ (tel: 01865 713100; website: www.amey.co.uk)

Directors: Richard Mottram, Chair; Santiago Olivares, Vice Chair; Mel Ewell; Andrew Nelson; Jaime Aguirre; Nicolas Villen; Alfredo Garcia; Inigo Jodra (women: 1; men: 7)

Year end		31/12/2010
Turnover		£1,013,000,000
Pre-tax profit		£87,201,000

Nature of business: A leading provider of support services in the UK, ranging from transportation and education, to defence and health.

Company registration number: 4736639

Main locations: Birmingham, Belfast, Preston, Manchester, Newport, Glasgow, Edinburgh, Bristol

Total employees: 10,456

Membership: BITC

Charitable donations

UK cash (latest declared):	2010	£74,000
	2009	£96,468
	2008	£96,468
	2007	£60,783
	2006	£46,070
Total UK:	2010	£74,000
Total worldwide:	2010	£74,000
Cash worldwide:	2010	£74,000

Corporate social responsibility

CSR committee: There was no evidence of a separate CSR Committee.

CSR policy: This information was obtained from the company's website:

> Amey aims to meet the challenge of sustainable development by managing social, environmental and wider economic impacts arising from our business activity with the intention of making a meaningful contribution to a more sustainable future.
>
> We engage with local residents to make a positive, sustainable impact in areas of social and economic concern such as long-term unemployment, crime and deprivation.

CSR report: There was no evidence of a separate CSR report.

Exclusions

No provision for funding or other support to political organisations of any sort, and only exceptionally to provide funding or support to religious organisations as part of an initiative to the general benefit of a community. No funding or support will be given to individuals outside the business.

Applications

In writing to the correspondent.

Other information

In 2010, the company donated £74,000 to local organisations. The company focuses it charitable contributions on areas of social and economic concern such as long-term unemployment, crime and deprivation. The company runs back-to-work programmes; support local youth sports teams and develops relationships with citizen organisations. Past beneficiaries include: The Duke of Edinburgh's Award; Wooden Spoon.

Amlin plc

Insurance

Correspondent: Charities and Community Panel, St Helen's, 1 Undershaft, London EC3A 8ND (tel: 020 7746 1000; fax: 020 7746 1696; website: www.amlin.co.uk)

Directors: Roger Taylor, Chair; Charles Philipps; Christine Bosse; Marty Feinstein; Richard Davey; Brian Carpenter; Nigel Buchanan; Richard Hextall; Tony Holt; Sir Mark Wrightson (women: 1; men: 9)

Year end		31/12/2010
Turnover		£1,748,100,000
Pre-tax profit		£259,200,000

Nature of business: Amlin is a leading insurance group operating in the Lloyd's, UK, Continental European and Bermudian markets. It specialises in providing insurance cover to commercial enterprises and reinsurance protection to other insurance companies around the world.

Company registration number: 2854310

Total employees: 1,100

Charitable donations

UK cash (latest declared):	2010	£147,300
	2009	£134,000
	2008	£81,000
Total UK:	2010	£147,300
Total worldwide:	2010	£147,300
Cash worldwide:	2010	£147,300

Corporate social responsibility

> **CSR committee:** The charities budget in the UK is managed by a Community and Charities Panel chaired by a senior underwriter. Non-UK subsidiaries' community and charities budgets are managed locally under the direction of their boards.

CSR policy: This information was obtained from the company's website:

> Amlin aims to build a sustainable business through the consistent application of our values in relationships with shareholders, employees, clients and other stakeholders. We seek to make a positive contribution to the communities in which we operate, placing integrity and professional excellence at the heart of our business practice.

CSR report: The CSR report is located within the annual report.

Applications

In writing to the correspondent.

Other information

In 2010 Amlin's cash contribution was £147,300. Amlin's UK charity and community activities are guided and facilitated by a panel, chaired by the Group Finance Director, which meets at least quarterly and comprises senior representatives from each UK business area. Amlin delivered a second successful Community Action Learning project at Newlands Bishop Farm, near Solihull.

Staff raised over £20,000 for Farleigh Hospice, a local adult hospice with centres in Chelmsford, Maldon and Braintree, Essex.

Amlin sponsored Art for Youth London for a second year. The three-day sale in the Royal College of Art made a profit of £83,000 for the charity, UK Youth.

Charity of the Year: Macmillan Cancer Support (2011). This relationship may be continuing, however more recent information was unavailable.

Anglesey Aluminium Metals Ltd

Metals

Correspondent: Community Relations Officer, Penrhos Works, PO Box 4, Holyhead, Gwynedd LL65 2JJ (tel: 01407 725000; fax: 01407 725001; email: AAM_CommunitiesRelations@riotinto.com; website: www.angleseyaluminium.co.uk)

Directors: T. Blondel; J. Barneson; S. Bolduc, Chair; J. M. Donnan; B. J. King; M. Foucault

Year end		31/12/2010
Turnover		£135,859,000
Pre-tax profit		(£17,936,000)

Nature of business: The company owns and operates an aluminium smelter.

Company registration number: 909645

UK employees: 100

Total employees: 100

Charitable donations

UK cash (latest declared):	2010	£1,350
	2009	£8,000
	2008	£25,000
	2007	£21,000
	2006	£15,000
Total UK:	2010	£1,350
Total worldwide:	2010	£1,350
Cash worldwide:	2010	£1,350

Corporate social responsibility

> **CSR committee:** As part of the community relations programme, the board has agreed to the financial allocation for the Donations and Sponsorship Committee. The committee administrate the fund allocated by the board.

CSR policy: This information was obtained from the company's website:

> As an organisation we are committed to open, transparent communication with our local community and stakeholders. Over the last 2 years AAM have been keen to develop a sustainable legacy for the local community and have been working with the Welsh Government and the Isle of Anglesey County Council to create employment and generate economic activity in the area.

Unable to determine the ratio of women to men on the Board.

CSR report: There appeared to be no CSR report but information was available from the company's website.

Exclusions

No support for individuals, political or religious appeals, or local appeals not in areas of company presence.

Applications

In writing to the correspondent.

Other information

In 2010, the company made donations of £1,350 (2009: £8,000). At the time of writing (January 2013), the latest accounts available were for 2010, however given the information from 2009 below it is unlikely that donations to charitable causes will have increased significantly in recent years.

In the notes to the financial statements 30 September 2009 the company stated:

> Anglesey Aluminium Metal Ltd has been unable to secure an affordable supply of electricity post September 2009. From October 2009 Anglesey Aluminium Metal Ltd will continue operations as a secondary aluminium remelt facility. The change in the primary business of Anglesey Aluminium Metal Ltd has resulted in a reduction in the number of employees from 577 to around 100. This reduction will be by a mixture of voluntary and compulsory redundancies.
>
> AAM has funded the maintenance and development of the coastal park near to the headquarters and has allowed the public to use the land as part of their Community Relations programmes since 1969.

Anglia Regional Co-operative Society Ltd

Retail – department and variety stores, supermarkets

Correspondent: David Strode-Willis, Company Secretary and HR Group Manager, Westgate House, Park Road, Peterborough PE1 2TA (tel: 01733 225300; fax: 01733 313078; email: executive.office@arcs.co.uk; website: www.arcs.co.uk)

Directors: Harry Whitelock, Chair; John Brewer; Jean Humphreys; Roger Newton; Pam Baker; Douglas Boyall; Andy Arbon; Graeme Watkins; Hugh Bennett; Neil Mackie; Vince Moon (women: 2; men: 9)

Year end	03/09/2011
Turnover	£182,121,000
Pre-tax profit	£5,992,000

Nature of business: Co-operative society trading in food, household goods, furniture and funerals.

Company registration number: IP08644R

Main locations: Peterborough

UK employees: 2,785

Total employees: 2,785

Charitable donations

UK cash (latest declared):	2011	£27,000
	2009	£30,000
	2008	£30,000
	2007	£67,000
	2005	£75,000
Total UK:	2011	£27,000
Total worldwide:	2011	£27,000
Cash worldwide:	2011	£27,000

Corporate social responsibility

CSR committee: All applications are evaluated by the ACCF Committee using a set criteria, and all applications elected for support are presented for approval to our board of directors.

CSR policy: The society has a separate fund for community giving. This information was obtained from the company's website:

> Previously known as Share 600, the key objective of the Anglia Co-operative Community Fund is to support as much as possible charitable community activities organised by individuals, voluntary organisations or charities.

CSR report: There was no evidence of a separate CSR report, however information was available from the company's website.

Exclusions

No grants for: running costs; causes deemed to promote a particular religious viewpoint; statutory services, party political causes; or causes they believe conflict with the ethos of the co-operative movement. No support for animal welfare, the arts, enterprise/training, heritage, overseas projects, religious appeals, science/technology, sickness/disability, social welfare or sport.

The society does not consider 'Charity of the Year' applications.

Applications

In writing to the correspondent.

Other information

The Anglia Co-operative Community Fund

The society gave the following information on its community fund:

> The ACCF was able to support many applications received from local charities and worthy causes during the year. The main charities supported through 2011 were SENSE and Action for Children each receiving a share from £24,000. Other organisations and charities supported in 2010/11 were: BLESMA; All Hallows Nursing Home, Bungay; Peterborough & District Deaf Children's Society; Halesworth Town Centre Group; National Autistic Society.
>
> The Society also supports the Retail Trust which is a charity specifically for retail employees. Community efforts cover initiatives such as honey bees through 'Plan Bee'. The Society has supported efforts to raise awareness of the threat to the honey bee by setting up working hives at the Headquarters, providing educational visits for schools to see the bees at work.
>
> With organisations and charities facing difficult times, the number of requests for support increased significantly, so much so that the decision was reached that requests for Raffle Prizes to assist with fundraising activities would be assessed and processed immediately on receipt. The awards made by the ACCF were not always financial. In this year alone 78 raffle prize awards were made. The charities and local good causes supported throughout the year have been very diverse.

Anglian Water

Water

Correspondent: Sustainable Development Department, Anglian House, Ambury Road, Huntingdon, Cambridgeshire PE29 3NZ (tel: 01480 323000; fax: 01480 323115; website: www.awg.com)

Directors: Andre Bourbonnais; Daniel Fetter; Cressida Hogg; Manoj Mehta; Niall Mills; Christine O'Reilly; Christian Seymour; Philip White; Adrian Montague, Chair; Peter Simpson, Managing Director, Anglian Water Services; Scott Longhurst, Managing Director, Finance and Non Reg Business (women: 2; men: 9)

Year end	31/03/2011
Turnover	£1,412,000,000
Pre-tax profit	(£12,400,000)

Nature of business: The group's business is: Water supply and distribution, waste water collection and treatment, providing social housing repairs and property development. The group is registered under the Companies (Jersey) Law 1991.

Company registration number: 2366656

Subsidiaries include: Maintenance and Property Care Ltd, Power Services HVDE Ltd, Ambury Developments Ltd, PURAC Ltd, Rutland Insurance Ltd, Alpheus Environmental Ltd, Morrison International Ltd, MVM Holdings Ltd

Main locations: Peterborough, Huntingdon

Total employees: 6,898

Membership: Arts & Business, BITC

Charitable donations

UK cash (latest declared):	2011	£790,000
	2010	£790,000
	2009	£790,000
	2008	£1,040,000
	2007	£1,040,000
Total UK:	2011	£790,000
Total worldwide:	2011	£790,000
Cash worldwide:	2011	£790,000

Community involvement

Anglian Water is the principal subsidiary of Anglian Water Group Ltd (AWG). Anglian Water Group Ltd., is owned and controlled by a consortium of investors consisting of the Canada Pension Plan Investment Board, Colonial First State Global Assessment Management, Industry Funds Management and 3i. The company has stated that it is the group's policy that it has adopted a co-ordinated approach to the management of its community investment throughout the group businesses. The community programme is predominantly based on employee involvement at all levels throughout the business with some financial support for special projects.

Corporate giving

Financial information is taken from the Anglian Water Group's annual report and accounts. In 2010/11, the group 'made available' £750,000 (2010: £750,000) to the Anglian Water Assistance Fund, (this fund is not registered with the Charity Commission), which paid a total of around £600,000 (2010: £400,000) directly to customers who qualified for assistance. 'That amount is included as an operating cost in the statutory and regulatory accounts.'

In addition to its donation to the trust fund, the company also gave £40,000 (2010: £40,000) in support of WaterAid, its nominated charity.

No figure was available with regard to the company's in kind support.

In kind support

On occasion the company, due to upgrades on IT systems, has redundant computer hardware which it is no longer able to use. In support of its re-use/ recycle ethos it can usually offer this equipment to charity/community organisations in the vicinity of its local offices. Equally, in some cases where office upgrades are necessary, some furniture (e.g. desks, chairs, filing cabinets) become surplus to requirement and are therefore offered to the local community rather than simply disposed of. To find out if there is a current recycling programme running in your area, contact the sustainable development department.

Employee-led support

The Anglian Water Group Community Investment Scheme, Give me Five, has been under review and a new scheme, Love To Help, has replaced this community programme. Local good causes are supported by staff and the company then pledges to match up to 30 hours per year of work time to help staff do more volunteering. Volunteer activities include:

River Care: This is a company driven initiative run in conjunction with the charity Keep Britain Tidy and Water Aid: The project supports volunteers to improve their local river environment by helping them with the removal of litter, fly-tipped debris and non-native species. This is the company's industry charity and Anglian Water is a supporter and fundraiser. Employees volunteer to help at regional or national events.

Many employees give active support to a lot of good causes in the community which can range from volunteering with local scouts, through to being a school governor.

Payroll giving: The company operates the Give As You Earn scheme.

Commercially-led support

Sponsorship: *WaterAid.* The group sponsors, undertakes fundraising activities, offers payroll giving and volunteer company time to support this charity's international aid work. Employees themselves have raised £183,000 (2010: £275,000) for WaterAid this year.

Corporate social responsibility

CSR committee: There is a Sustainable Development department.

CSR policy: The website states: 'AWG believes that corporate responsibility (CR) is about supporting and actively encouraging strategies and behaviours that demonstrate our commitment to the long-term viability of the business.'

The company's key issue is sustainability through improving water quality, the environment, climate change and reducing waste.

There are community pages on the website but this again involves in the main protecting and improving the environment.

CSR report: There is no CSR report published.

Exclusions

No support for advertising in charity brochures, appeals from individuals, political appeals or sport (unless at educational level), animal welfare, medical research or religious appeals.

Applications

In writing to the correspondent.

Note: The group's 2010/11 annual report states: 'Individual requests for sponsorship were declined on the basis that the company's policy is to encourage community involvement rather than charitable donations.'

Anglo American plc

Mining

Correspondent: Anji Hunter, Group Head of Government and Social Affairs, 20 Carlton House Terrace, London SW1Y 5AN (tel: 020 7968 8888; website: www.angloamerican.com)

Directors: David Challen; C. K. Chow; Rene Medori, Finance Director; Phuthuma Nhleko; Jack Thompson; Mamplele Ramphele; Peter Woicke; Philip Hampton; Ray O'Rourke; John Parker, Chair; Cynthia Carroll, Chief Executive (women: 2; men: 9)

Year end	31/12/2011
Turnover	£19,071,972,000
Pre-tax profit	£6,724,460,000

Company registration number: 3564138

Subsidiaries include: Mondi Packaging (UK) Ltd, Cleveland Potash Ltd, Tarmac Group Ltd

Main locations: London

Total employees: 100,000

Membership: BITC

Charitable donations

UK cash (latest declared):	2011	£1,430,000
	2009	£1,608,000
	2007	£1,545,000
	2005	£824,402
Total UK:	2011	£1,430,000
Total worldwide:	2011	£76,088,000
Cash worldwide:	2011	£1,430,000

Community involvement

The company's charitable donations in the UK are primarily made through the **Anglo American Foundation** (Charity Commission no. 1111719). The foundation welcomes applications from organisations involved with the following areas: education; international development; health/HIV; environment; and, London-based community development.

Corporate giving

The following statement is taken from the group's annual report for 2012:

> During the year, Anglo American, its subsidiaries and the Anglo American Group Foundation made donations for charitable purposes or wider social investments amounting to $122 million (£76.1 million) (1.27% of operating profit from subsidiaries and joint ventures).
>
> Charitable donations of $1 million were made in the UK, of which the main categories were: education and training (42%) and health and welfare (12%). These figures were compiled with reference to the London Benchmarking Group model for defining and measuring social investment spending. A fuller analysis of the Group's social investment activities can be found in the Sustainable Development Report 2011.

Unfortunately, we have been unable to determine the worldwide figure for charitable giving and have used the UK figure as is our practice.

Anglo American Group Foundation
In 2011, the foundation's accounts state that it received over £1.4 million from Anglo American Services and other related companies within the group (we have used this figure for the UK cash contribution). This is likely to remain the foundation's major source of income in the future. Beneficiaries included: CARE International – Brazil £119,350); Leonard Cheshire Disability (£78,500); Engineers Without Borders (£60,000); Centrepoint (£54,500); Samaritans (£23,000); Sightsavers International (£20,000).

In kind support

The company may, from time to time, provide additional support through gifts in kind.

Partners
Partners include: CARE International; Fauna and Flora International; Natural History Museum and Women in Mining.

Employee-led support

The company has an employee volunteering scheme and allows company time off for community support activities to take place. Employee fundraising is matched by the company up to a maximum of £500 per employee.

Payroll giving: A scheme is operated by the company on behalf of its employees.

Commercially-led support

Sponsorship: Arts and good-cause sponsorship is undertaken.

Corporate social responsibility

CSR committee: No details found. There is a Social Affairs department.

CSR policy: Taken from the Sustainability section on the group's website:

> *Society*
> For Anglo American, society is an inclusive concept. It embraces our workforce, the communities in which they live, the citizens of host countries and the implications of what we do for the wider population for generations to come.

CSR report: An annual Sustainability report is published and available from the website.

Exclusions

No support for appeals from individuals, medical research, political appeals, religious appeals or sport.

Applications

Applications to the company should be made to the correspondent and to the foundation to: Miss Catherine Louise Marshall, Anglo American Group Foundation, 20 Carlton House Terrace, London SW1Y 5AN.

AOL UK Ltd

Information technology, media

Correspondent: Head of Corporate Responsibility, 62 Hammersmith Road, London W14 8YW (tel: 020 7348 8000; fax: 020 7348 8002; email: ukcharity@aol.com; website: www.corp.aol.com)

Directors: N. Patel; K. Tabb; A. Werner

Year end	31/12/2010
Turnover	£65,610,000
Pre-tax profit	(£21,028,000)

Nature of business: Launched in the UK in 1996, AOL UK is an interactive service company and a division of AOL Europe – the internet, online and e-commerce services company.

Company registration number: 3462696

Total employees: 5,660

Charitable donations

UK cash (latest declared):	2010	£0
	2009	£5,000
	2008	£64,000

Corporate social responsibility

CSR committee: There was no evidence of a dedicated CSR Committee.

CSR policy: This information was obtained from the company's website:

> AOL UK has longstanding relationships with a number of UK charities in order to extend the benefits of the internet to their users. Our priority areas are young people and people with disabilities.
>
> The community investment programme at AOL seeks to extend the benefits of the internet to those who would most benefit from the medium but are often the least likely to obtain access through traditional means. This is often addressed by providing direct funding, advice and support in kind to charities and community groups going online to demonstrate innovative use of the medium.

Unable to determine the ratio of women to men on the board.

CSR report: There was no evidence of a separate CSR report, however information was available from the company's website.

Exclusions

No funding or support for individuals (including, for example, overseas events and marathons), advertising or sponsorship in charity brochures (including calendars and ball programmes).

Applications

AOL UK does not accept unsolicited applications.

Other information

In 2010 the company donated £0 (2009: £5,000).

AOL UK offers each employee up to two days paid leave per year to volunteer for good causes, be it AOL's partner charities or their own chosen charity. There is also an annual Time Warner Volunteer Day (Time Warner own AOL) with past projects including planting trees, painting playgrounds, and working on a city farm.

AOL UK also helps employees to raise funds for their chosen charities by offering matched funding for individuals and teams.

Payroll giving: The Give As You Earn scheme is offered by the company, enabling employees to donate to good causes directly from their salary, before tax is deducted.

AOL supports GiveNow.org which is hosted by CAF (Charities Aid Foundation) and the Time Warner Foundation. GivenNow.org is the UK's first website to enable donors to give both their time and money to the charities of their choice.

Apax Partners LLP

Financial services

Correspondent: David Marks, Trustee, Apax Foundation, 33 Jermyn Street, London Sw1Y 6DN (tel: 020 7872 6300; fax: 020 7666 6441; email: foundation@apax.com; website: www.apax.com)

Directors: Martin Halusa; John Mergrue; Michael Phillips; Andrew Sillitoe; Christian Stahl (women: 0; men: 5)

Year end	31/03/2011

Nature of business: Apax Partners is an independent global private equity advisory firm.

Company registration number: OC303117

Total employees: 300

Charitable donations

UK cash (latest declared):	2011	£3,453,800
	2008	£2,800,000
Total UK:	2011	£3,453,800
Total worldwide:	2011	£3,453,800
Cash worldwide:	2011	£3,453,800

Community involvement

The partnership's values are set out on its website:

> *Community*
> Act with respect and consideration for the communities in which we operate. Apax is committed to engaging constructively with the communities in which its funds invest. It has policies in place for corporate giving and encouraging individual employees in their personal charitable endeavours.
>
> The Apax Foundation is the channel for Apax's corporate giving and community engagement globally. The Foundation concentrates its major grant-giving on the

area of social entrepreneurship. Social entrepreneurship is a natural fit with what Apax does commercially and is also an area where several of our team, including some of the foundation's trustees, have significant experience.

In order to encourage the personal charitable and philanthropic activities of its staff, the foundation also commits to projects in which Apax staff take an active role.

Established in 2006, **The Apax Foundation** (Charity Commission no. 1112845) is the formal channel for Apax Partners' charitable giving and receives a percentage of the firm's profits and carried interest.

Apax Partners has a history of support for social enterprise and the firm is continuing this tradition with social enterprise chosen as the area on which the Apax Foundation will mainly focus. This encompasses charities working for the relief of financial hardship and the advancement of education in the United Kingdom and overseas.

One of the primary goals of the foundation is to support the range and diversity of the personal charitable efforts of the Apax Partners team. The Apax Foundation supports their endeavours by making grants to all of the charitable organisations that benefit from the active involvement of a member of the Apax Partners team.

Corporate giving

The foundation's wholly owned subsidiary, Apax E Member Ltd, received profit share of £3.45 million from Apax Partners LLP during the year (2010: £3.18 million). The foundation made total donations of £1.07 million. Beneficiaries included: Private Equity Foundation (£177,000); Social Finance (£150,000); International Bridges to Justice (£127,000); Mosaic Business in the Community (£95,350); Shivia Microfinance (£80,000); London Business School (£70,000); Non Profit Incubator and Bromley by Bow Centre (£50,000 each); Enterprise Education Trust (£47,500); Royal Free Hospital (£15,000); Crisis UK (£13,300); Marathon Trust (£12,500); and National Gallery Trust (£12,000).

Employee-led support

Matched funding

The foundation supports the fundraising and volunteering activities of Apax Partners staff. The matching scheme is designed to encourage and support the team's personal involvement with charities close to their hearts. The foundation makes a 'matching' donation to any charity which benefits from the significant, active, ongoing involvement of any member of the team in any of its regions. Donations in the year 2010/11 totalled £200,000.

Corporate social responsibility

CSR committee: The partnership's main channel of funding is its foundation which has independent trustees.

CSR policy: The partnership's website with regard to community responsibility states:

Act with respect and consideration for the communities in which we operate.

Apax is committed to engaging constructively with the communities in which its funds invest. It has policies in place for corporate giving and encouraging individual employees in their personal charitable endeavours.

The Apax Foundation is the channel for Apax's corporate giving and community engagement globally.

The Foundation concentrates its major grant-giving on the area of social entrepreneurship. Social entrepreneurship is a natural fit with what Apax does commercially and is also an area where several of our team, including some of the Foundation's Trustees, have significant experience.

In order to encourage the personal charitable and philanthropic activities of its staff, the Foundation also commits to projects in which Apax staff take an active role.

CSR report: Information on the 'Wider Community' including details of the Apax Foundation is included in the annual report and accounts.

Applications

In writing to the correspondent.

ARAMARK Ltd

Catering services

Correspondent: Mark Faulkner, UK Communications Manager, Millbank Tower, 21–24 Millbank, London SW1P 4QP (tel: 020 7963 0000; fax: 020 7963 0500; website: www.aramark.co.uk)

Directors: Robbie Wheeler; Andrew Main; D. Doyle

Year end	30/09/2011
Turnover	£341,447,000
Pre-tax profit	£16,502,000

Nature of business: The management and provision of a range of food, vending and refreshment services to industry and commerce.

Company registration number: 983951

Main locations: Leeds, Aberdeen

Total employees: 10,983

Membership: BITC

Charitable donations

UK cash (latest declared): 2009	£72,000

Corporate social responsibility

CSR committee: Each of our directors has a key sponsorship role for each aspect of CR:

- Community – Andrew Main
- Environment – Clive Cooper
- Human Rights – Robbie Wheeler
- Marketplace: Supply Chain – Clive Cooper
- Marketplace: Customers and Consumers – Morag McCay
- Workplace: Health, Safety and Wellbeing – Robbie Wheeler
- Workplace: Employees – Robbie Wheeler

CSR policy: Extract taken from the company's website:

Our strategy is based on a deeper, broader and wider approach. To be done properly, we have to go further than just scratching the surface. We believe that every element of the CR agenda is important. While there is always a need to prioritise, we are committed to reviewing all of our impact areas and developing plans to enhance our performance.

We are building on a great platform. Around our business, excellent examples of working in communities, sustainable procurement, healthy eating strategies and employee welfare activities are evident. The CR strategy brings all that great work together and builds upon it.

To be successful, CR has to be embedded into the core of the way we do business. The start of this was the buy in from ARAMARK Corporation and the UK Management Committee to the importance of a clear focus on CR throughout our business. This culminated in the appointment of a CR Director, Val Carter, and CR Implementation Manager, Sue Lightfoot. To ensure the message gets down to every member of our team, our award-winning CR Training and Awareness Pack has been rolled out to all contracts and support teams.

The key stakeholders in ARAMARK's Corporate Responsibility programme are:

- Our employees
- Supply Chain
- Health & Safety
- Legal
- Marketing and Communications
- Human Resources
- Clients
- Customers
- Government
- NGOs
- Charities

We could not determine the ratio of women to men on the board.

Applications

In writing to the correspondent.

Other information

From the information that is available, it appears that most of the company's support is in kind in nature and/or directed through its employees. Unfortunately, we were unable to obtain a community contributions figure for 2010 and no cash donations were declared in the annual report and accounts for that year.

The following information was taken from the company's website:

Community activity is led by our Star Teams, which work in conjunction with Business in the Community. Star Teams provide the framework for ARAMARK employees to make a real difference to their local area with its goal to make a positive impact on the communities in which the organisation operates.

ARAMARK also encourages teams and individuals to take part in their own choice of activities and these are publicised both internally, in our employee magazine, The Mark, and externally, often through the local press.

Charity of the Year: ARAMARK also supports nominated charities across the company. At present these are *ChildLine, Macmillan Cancer Support, the RLNI, SSAFA Forces Help,* and *Hospitality Action.*

Payroll giving: Through the 'Pennies from Heaven' scheme employees are able to donate to the company's chosen charities by giving the odd pennies from their monthly pay.

Archant

Media

Correspondent: Company Secretary, Prospect House, Rouen Road, Norwich NR1 1RE (tel: 01603 772772; email: company.secretary@archant.co.uk; website: www.archant.co.uk)

Directors: Richard Jewson, Chair; Adrian Jeakings, Chief Executive; Brian McCarthy; Simon Copeman; Johnny Hustler; Richard Wyatt; Mike Walsh; June de Moller; Peter Troughton; John Ellison (women: 1; men: 9)

Year end	31/12/2010
Turnover	£139,253,000
Pre-tax profit	£5,726,000

Nature of business: Archant is a privately-owned company with around 1500 shareholders.

Company registration number: 4126997

Main locations: Barnstaple, Ilford, Dereham, Diss, Exeter, Ely, Felixstowe, Harlow, Hitchin, Huntingdon, Ipswich, Sudbury, Weston-super-Mare, Welwyn Garden City, Bury St Edmunds, Colchester, Cheltenham, Cromer, Maidstone, Lowestoft, London, Norwich, Wimbledon, Preston, Reigate, St Albans, Southampton

Total employees: 1,929

Membership: BITC

Charitable donations

UK cash (latest declared):	2010	£73,000
	2009	£81,000
	2007	£102,000
	2005	£103,000
Total UK:	2010	£73,000
Total worldwide:	2010	£73,000
Cash worldwide:	2010	£73,000

Corporate social responsibility

CSR committee: No details published.

CSR policy: No information was available regarding the company's CSR policy.

CSR report: No information found.

Exclusions

No support for advertising in charity brochures, appeals from individuals, fundraising events, overseas projects, political appeals or religious appeals.

Applications

In writing to the correspondent.

Other information

In 2010 the company gave £73,000 in charitable donations. In addition to making direct donations, Archant supports charitable fundraising by its staff through the Archant Gold scheme, a programme of matched funding, and by part-matching staff charitable donations through the payroll Give As You Earn scheme.

Arla Foods Ltd

Food manufacture

Correspondent: Company Secretary, Arla House, 4 Savannah Way, Leeds Valley Park, Leeds LS10 1AB (tel: 01133 827000; fax: 01133 827030; website: www.arlafoods.co.uk)

Directors: S. D. Stevens; J. E. Pederson; L. E. Dalsgaard Hoff; P. Lauritzen; A. Amirahmadi

Year end	31/12/2011
Turnover	£1,587,176,000
Pre-tax profit	£31,058,000

Nature of business: Arla Foods UK plc, through its subsidiary companies, is a leading supplier of milk and dairy products in the UK market. The group supplies liquid milk, cream, butter, spreads, cheeses, fresh dairy products, yoghurts and desserts to the major supermarkets.

Company registration number: 2143253

Subsidiaries include: Claymore Dairies Ltd, Blakes Chilled Distribution Ltd

Main locations: Manchester, Naim, Northallerton, Newcastle, Oakthorpe, Ruislip, Sheffield, Settle, Hatfield Peverel, Leeds, Ashby de la Zouch

Total employees: 2,843

Charitable donations

UK cash (latest declared):	2011	£46,000
	2009	£33,000
	2008	£36,000
	2007	£24,000
	2006	£34,000
Total UK:	2011	£46,000
Total worldwide:	2011	£46,000
Cash worldwide:	2011	£46,000

Corporate social responsibility

CSR committee: No details found.

CSR policy: The following heads the Sustainability pages of the company's website:

> At Arla we believe that milk is nature's best food product. We are proud to process milk to make yoghurt, cheese, butter, milk powder and many other dairy products to the benefit and delight of people all over the world.
>
> Most of our products are as natural as they can be and we have long maintained high food safety and environmental standards, so a commitment to getting even Closer to Nature is a natural choice for us. We combine traditional craftsmanship and world-class technologies, making sure we think about nature in every aspect of our supply chain, right from the cow until our products reach your home.

It was not possible to determine the ratio of women to men on the board.

CSR report: No report published.

Applications

In writing to the correspondent.

Other information

In 2011 the company made donations to UK charitable organisations of £46,000. A list of beneficiaries was not available. The following extract is taken from the Sustainability pages of the company's website:

> *Kids Closer to Nature*
>
> As part of Arla's Closer to Nature ambitions a campaign, aimed at encouraging more children to enjoy the great outdoors, launched in January 2011. Kids Closer to Nature is a programme that will see Arla develop a range of activities throughout 2011 and is designed to encourage children of all backgrounds and locations to experience the great outdoors and take them Closer to Nature on a daily basis.
>
> As part of the campaign, a grant scheme for members of the public to create natural spaces is also being launched. Alongside all of this activity, Arla has developed a Kids Closer to Nature online adventure club, which is being supported by television celebrities Chris Packham and Philippa Forrester. The Nature Adventure Club provides parents, teachers and children with exciting incentives to go outside and learn about all aspects of nature throughout the seasons whether it's in their back garden, local park, or school playing fields.
>
> To ensure as many children as possible benefit from these initiatives, Arla is also working with the National Schools Partnership on a range of resources for primary school teachers to encourage pupils to explore and understand nature through links to the national curriculum.
>
> Through Closer to Nature Arla has identified the opportunity to raise awareness of the increasing number of children who are not playing outside or

interacting with nature and its aim is to turn this trend around.

The company has been involved in a scheme called Community Challenge since 1998, which makes contributions to local communities in which the company has operations. Employees can access Community Challenge funding by raising money for a cause which Arla matches or they can apply for a grant if they volunteer for ten hours a month or more outside work hours.

Arriva plc

Motors and accessories

Correspondent: Community Relations Support, 1 Admiral Way, Doxford International Business Park, Sunderland SR3 3XP (tel: 01915 204000; fax: 01915 204001; email: corporateresponsibility@arriva.co.uk; website: www.arriva.co.uk)

Directors: David Martin, Chief Executive; Martin Hibbert; Alison O'Connor; Mike Cooper; Bob Holland; David Evans (women: 1; men: 5)

Year end	31/12/2010
Turnover	-£47,413,000
Pre-tax profit	(£47,413,000)

Nature of business: The principal activities of the group are the operation of bus and train services in the UK and nine countries in mainland Europe.

Company registration number: 347103

UK employees: 30,250

Total employees: 47,500

Charitable donations

UK cash (latest declared):	2010	£17,250
	2009	£66,000
	2008	£97,000
	2007	£112,000
	2006	£149,000
Total UK:	2010	£17,250
Total worldwide:	2010	£17,250
Cash worldwide:	2010	£17,250

Corporate social responsibility

CSR committee: There are no details of a separate CSR Committee.

CSR policy: Much of Arriva's charitable giving is in the form of in kind donations.

CSR report: The CSR report is available from the company's website.

Applications

The company website states: 'Unfortunately we cannot support all the requests for support that we receive. If you are a charitable organisation or community group who would like our support, read our community relations policy before contacting us'.

Requests for support for community partnerships should be sent to corporateresponsibility@arriva.co.uk or in writing to the correspondent.

Other information

In 2010 the group made charitable donations of £17,250 (2009: £66,000).

> **Development and working in partnership:** Partnership working with suitable organisations is a feature of Arriva's community relations programme. We aim to build long-term relationships with community partners, not just for the benefit of the charity or community organisation, but also for the benefit of the company. Our support may be financial or practical, and sometimes involves the direct support of our employees.
>
> **Employees in the community**: Many of our employees give their time to local community groups and projects. We recognise these efforts through our Arriva Community Action Awards initiative, which makes cash awards available to employees for their community organisations.

Arup Group Ltd

Consulting engineers

Correspondent: Peter Klyhn, 13 Fitzroy Street, London W1T 4BQ (tel: 020 7636 1531; fax: 020 7580 3924; email: ovafound@arup.com; website: www.arup.com)

Directors: J. Baster; M. D. Bear; A. J. Belfield; R. F. Care; T. G. A. Carfrae; A. K. C. Chan; P. G. Dilley, Chair; G. S. Hodkinson; L. M. Lui; J. C. Miles; M. Raman; D. J. Singleton; D. A. Whittleton (women: 2; men: 11)

Year end	31/03/2011
Turnover	£966,427,000
Pre-tax profit	£46,011,000

Nature of business: The company and its subsidiaries practice in the field of consulting engineering services, in architecture and other related professional skills.

Arup is a wholly-independent organisation, and is owned in trust for the benefit of its employees and their dependents. Each of Arup's employees receives a share of the firm's operating profit each year.

Company registration number: 1312454

Main locations: Edinburgh, Dundee, Southampton, Glasgow, Bristol, Cardiff, Cambridge, Newcastle upon Tyne, Liverpool, London, Manchester, Nottingham, Leeds, Solihull, Sheffield, Wrexham, Winchester, Belfast

Total employees: 9,934

Charitable donations

UK cash (latest declared):	2011	£219,000
	2009	£551,000
	2008	£281,000
	2007	£66,000
	2006	£36,000
Total UK:	2011	£219,000
Total worldwide:	2011	£688,000
Cash worldwide:	2011	£688,000

Corporate social responsibility

CSR committee: There appeared to be no separate CSR Committee.

CSR policy: Information was obtained from the 2009 Corporate Governance Report:

> At Arup, our progress towards being a truly sustainable firm is a journey of improvement, where each step along the way informs the next. With each step comes greater clarity and insight, such that our exploration of sustainability now touches everything that we do, including the way we approach sustainability on behalf of our clients.

CSR report: CSR reports were available for previous years but not for 2010/11.

Applications

In writing to the correspondent, with brief supporting financial information. Trustees meet quarterly to consider applications (March, June, September and December) which are first sifted by the Chair and Secretary.

Further information is available at the foundation's website: www.ovearupfoundation.org.

Other information

In 2010/11, the Arup Group Ltd gave charitable donations in the UK of £219,000 (2008/09: £551,000), of which almost £140,000 appears to have been donated to its associated trust.

The Ove Arup Foundation

Established to commemorate the life of the late Sir Ove Arup, The Ove Arup Foundation (Charity Commission no. 328138) is an educational trust supporting initiatives related to the built environment. Endowed by the partnership for the first seven years of its existence (1989–1995) through an annual gift, the trustees decided in 2000 to provide further funding over the next five years and to increase the scope of the foundation internationally.

Around one-third of the foundation's funds are available each year for major projects. It gives grants for research and projects, including start-up and feasibility costs. Further information is available on the foundation's website (www.theovearupfoundation.org).

The top ten donations in 2010/11 were: The Ove Arup Foundation (£95,400); Engineers Without Borders (£43,650); RedR (£24,580); The Smith Family (£24,240); Sports Aid (£21,200); Lincoln Centre for the Performing Arts

(£20,940); Red Cross (£18,130); The Royal Academy of Engineering (£14,100); and the Australian Natural Disaster Appeal and Save the Children – Japanese Earthquake Appeal (£12,000 each).

ASDA Stores Ltd

Retail – supermarkets

Correspondent: Julie Ward, The ASDA Foundation Administrator, ASDA House, Southbank, Great Wilson Street, Leeds LS11 5AD (tel: 01132 435435; fax: 01132 418666; website: www.ASDA.co.uk)

Directors: J. McKenna; A. Clarke; R. Bendel; A. Moore; C. Redfield; S. King; E. Doohan; K. Hubbard; H. Tatum; S. Smith

Year end	31/12/2011
Turnover	£21,661,000,000
Pre-tax profit	£506,900,000

Nature of business: Principal activities: the operation of food, clothing, home and leisure superstores throughout Great Britain. In 1999 ASDA became part of Wal-Mart Stores Inc., based in Arkansas.

Company registration number: 464777

Brands include: George; Smart Price; Extra Special; Good for You!; ASDA Brand; ASDA Organics; ASDA Great Stuff.

UK employees: 176,453

Total employees: 176,453

Membership: BITC

Charitable donations

UK cash (latest declared):	2011	£2,200,000
	2009	£1,600,000
	2008	£600,000
	2007	£600,000
	2006	£600,000
Total UK:	2011	£2,200,000
Total worldwide:	2011	£2,200,000
Cash worldwide:	2011	£2,200,000

Community involvement

ASDA's charitable giving is made mainly through its charity, **The ASDA Foundation** (Charity Commission no. 1124268) where the trustees will distribute the funds to charities nominated by store colleagues.

The ASDA Foundation is ASDA's charitable trust. The objectives of the foundation are:

- To provide financial support to the local good causes that have the direct support and involvement of our colleagues (in stores, depots, George House and ASDA House
- To support local sustainable projects, as agreed by the trustees
- To administer funds raised for Tickled Pink (Breast Cancer Care and Breast Cancer Campaign), Children in Need, Tommy's, Sporting Chance, Everyman, Text Santa, Fields In Trust and Pedal Power, which are ASDA's national campaigns; and
- When overseas disasters occur, ASDA customers and colleagues support the appeal and coordinate the Disaster Emergency Committee. In 2011, the earthquake in Japan and the flood in East Africa all funds raised were co-ordinated through the foundation

Funding guidelines are available from the foundation's annual report and accounts.

The following information is taken from the community pages of the company's website:

> ***ASDA in the local community***
> We're really keen that every ASDA store plays an active role in the life of their local community. From raising money for local charities to volunteering, our colleagues take their responsibilities towards their local communities very seriously.

Community Life

In 2012 ASDA launched a new initiative called Community Life. Each store will have a Community Life Champion to work one day a week with community groups and local organisations. They will arrange events in store and inspire colleagues and customers to get involved in local community work.

Local heroes

ASDA has been taking the opportunity to recognise 'local heroes' by inviting them to the opening ceremonies of ASDA Supermarkets – smaller, local stores, many of them converted from former Netto stores.

ASDA Athletes

Every ASDA store has partnered with a local athlete to support their development and raise their profile in the community. In return the athletes give something back by getting involved in activities such as visiting local schools, clubs and groups.

You can find information for your local area on community initiatives, your local community champion and the opportunity to nominate an organisation by visiting the 'Find your nearest ASDA' facility on the community webpage.

Corporate giving

ASDA Stores Ltd provides funding to ASDA Foundation through profit made on sales of the mid-week National Lottery. ASDA Foundation then distributes these funds to charitable good causes and sustainable projects. The foundation supplements the good causes that colleagues support locally, as well as a number of bigger ad-hoc projects that make a real difference to local communities. It also manages all funds raised for national charities and monies raised in ASDA House.

In 2011, there was an unrestricted donation from the company, ASDA Stores Ltd of £2.2 million which was spent on supporting fundraising activities out in the stores with promotional materials and marketing. We have taken this figure to represent the company's 2011 cash contribution. Whilst the money was spent on supporting fundraising activities out in the stores with promotional materials, mailing, point of sale and marketing, this cash amount was donated by the company to the foundation to use at its discretion.

From the unrestricted funds of the foundation, beneficiary organisations included: Mobile Youth Provision (£160,000); Rolling Sound Ltd (£81,600); Your Square Mile (£72,500); Young People Cornwall (£43,600); Sparks – Children's Health Charity and Wishes for Kids (£31,500 each); Wellbeing of Women (£25,000); Anton Junior School (£20,000); Civil Unrest – Riots of 2011, Lynn Athletic Club and Simon on the Streets (£15,000 each); East Durham Heritage Group and Seashell Centre (£10,000 each); Wetheringsett Community Trust (£5,000); Canolfan Nefyn and Teen Cancer (£4,000 each); Wakefield Hospice (£2,000); and Business in the Community and Worsley Menses Community Association (£1,000 each).

Of the restricted funds, money raised by ASDA stores colleagues was: Breast Cancer Care (£1.3 million); Children In Need (£1 million); Tommy's (£589,000); Everyman (£241,400); Text Santa (£64,800); Sporting Chance (£49,000); National Disasters (£36,000); and Pedal Power (£3,700). As this is money raised by staff and customers and not given by the company out of profits, we have not included this in the cash UK contributions.

Employee-led support

Employee and customer fundraising

ASDA colleagues can choose the charity (or charities) to which they and their team wish to donate their fundraising monies. If there is no preference as to the good cause, the money should be donated to one of ASDA's national charities:

- Children in Need
- Tommy's
- Tickled Pink
- Sporting Chance
- Everyman
- Fields in Trust
- Pedal Power
- Text Santa

In 2011, ASDA staff and customers raised £3.4 million in total for the company's national charities.

Details of all ASDA's national charities and examples of staff's fundraising activities and achievements can be found at: charities.ASDA.com.

Corporate social responsibility

CSR committee: There is no evidence of a separate CSR Committee.

CSR policy: This information was obtained from the company's website:

> **The ASDA Foundation** (Charity Commission no. 1124268) is our charitable trust which was set up in 1988 to support local good causes chosen by our colleagues, and is funded by profits from the mid-week national lottery.
>
> We see the foundation as one of the many ways to give something back to the communities that support us. That's why we lend a hand to the wide range of good causes with which our colleagues are involved including everything from local charities and playgroups to football teams.
>
> The ASDA Foundation is primarily for colleagues who have already raised money for their chosen cause through their store or depot, and require additional support.
>
> Under the Foundation's terms, we will assist any charity in the UK, as well as people and projects that require financial assistance, providing they have the support of local ASDA colleagues.
>
> Because we receive thousands of applications each year, we are not able to support every cause, and cannot consider applications where the donation will be used to pay salaries or where it will be added to general funds.
>
> We will always look at each application based on these criteria and on the individual merits of the cause, and its potential benefits to the local community.
>
> For further information see the foundation's website: charities.ASDA.com/ASDA-foundation and for a copy of the latest accounts, visit: www.charity-commission.gov.uk

Unable to determine the ratio of women to men on the board.

CSR report: There appears to be no evidence of a separate CSR report, however there is a great deal of information available from the company's website.

Exclusions

No response to circular appeals. No support for advertising in charity brochures, appeals from individuals, overseas projects, political appeals, expeditions, or local appeals not in areas of company presence. It neither sponsors charitable activities by people other than ASDA colleagues.

Applications

In writing to the correspondent for applications to The ASDA Foundation.

The trustees of The ASDA Foundation will look at each application based on criteria and merit and applicants should provide as much information as possible as to how the funding will benefit the local community.

Applications for the various initiatives taken by local stores such as ASDA Athletes, ASDA Community Life Champions, you should apply to your local store, or to nominate a cause that you would like to see ASDA support in your local community, apply online at: charities.ASDA.com/.

Ashmore Group plc

Business services

Correspondent: Juliet Phommahaxay, The Ashmore Foundation, 5th Floor, 61 Aldwych, London WC2B 4AE (tel: 020 3077 6000/020 3077 6153; email: foundation@ashmoregroup.com; website: www.ashmoregroup.com)

Directors: Michael Benson; Mark Coombs, Chief Executive Officer; Graeme Dell; Nick Land; Jonathan Asquith; Melda Donnelly (women: 1; men: 5)

Year end	31/12/2011
Turnover	£281,400,000
Pre-tax profit	£217,200,000

Nature of business: Ashmore Group is a specialist emerging markets fund manager across six core investment themes: external debt, local currency, special situations, equity, corporate high yield and multi-strategy.

Company registration number: 3675683

Total employees: 152

Charitable donations

UK cash (latest declared):	2011	£177,500
	2010	£175,000
	2009	£139,000
	2008	£30,000
Total UK:	2011	£177,500
Total worldwide:	2011	£177,500
Cash worldwide:	2011	£177,500

Corporate social responsibility

CSR committee: There is no evidence of a separate CSR Committee.

CSR policy: All charitable contributions are currently made through The Ashmore Foundation set up in 2008 and funded by 'bonus sacrifices' from employees and matched funding by the company.

CSR report: A CSR report is available on the company's website.

Applications

In writing to the correspondent.

Other information

The Ashmore Foundation (Charity Commission no. 1122351)

In 2011, the Ashmore Foundation's income was £355,000. We have used 50% of this figure as the company's UK cash contribution as the foundation was initially set up with 50% matched funding and this appears to be the way the foundation has been funded since then.

The foundation's grantmaking policy is wide ranging but has a particular focus on education and healthcare, the former in particular seen as the best way to help the long-term self-development of emerging market countries.

The Chief Executive Officer of Ashmore is a trustee of the foundation, supported by two other employee trustees. Grantmaking has initially focused on building relationships with existing established charities within the emerging market world, and also supporting proposals emanating from employees' suggestions.

The foundation channels financial support through two schemes:

1. a small grants scheme, providing grants of up to £5,000 to a range of eligible charities
2. a partnership scheme for larger grants and longer-term relationships with strong organisations where their missions are clearly aligned and where there is demonstrable evidence of an effective approach.

The foundation is particularly interested in supporting innovative local organisations which display a knowledge of the local context and culture, demonstrable involvement of and commitment to the community served, ability to measure results and cost-effectiveness.

Ashtead Group plc

Industrial products/services

Correspondent: Company Secretary, King's House, 36–37 King Street, London EC2V 8BB (tel: 020 7726 9700; fax: 020 7726 9705; website: www.ashtead-group.com)

Directors: Chris Cole, Chair; Geoff Drabble; Ian Robson; Brendan Horgan; Sat Dhaiwal; Hugh Etheridge; Michael Burrow; Bruce Edwards; Ian Sutcliffe (women: 0; men: 9)

Year end	30/04/2011
Turnover	£846,500,000
Pre-tax profit	£31,000,000

Nature of business: Equipment rental company with stores throughout England, Scotland and Wales.

Company registration number: 1807982

UK employees: 1,921

Total employees: 7,521

Charitable donations

UK cash (latest declared):	2009	£139,000
	2008	£55,000
Total worldwide:	2011	£50,000
Cash worldwide:	2011	£50,000

Corporate social responsibility

CSR committee: There is no evidence of a separate CSR Committee.

CSR policy: Information was obtained from the company's website:

> At Ashtead we are committed to running our business in a responsible and sustainable way. We recognise the importance of giving back to the communities where we do business. We have a number of community programmes across the US and the UK as well as individual initiatives at a number of our profit centres.

Although the company stated that it was committed to the community, there appeared to be little evidence of this in the annual report.

CSR report: The CSR report was contained within the annual accounts, however there was no information dedicated to the community.

Applications

In writing to the correspondent.

Other information

In 2010/11 the company gave £50,000 in charitable contributions (2009: £139,000). We have no details of beneficiary groups.

Associated British Foods plc

Food manufacture

Correspondent: Assistant Company Secretary, Weston Centre, 10 Grosvenor Street, London W1K 4QY (tel: 020 7399 6500; fax: 020 7399 6580; website: www.abf.co.uk)

Directors: Peter Smith; Timothy Clarke; Lord Jay of Ewelme; Javier Farran; Charles Sinclair, Chair; George Weston, Chief Executive; John Bason; Emma Adams (women: 1; men: 7)

Year end	17/09/2011
Turnover	£11,065,000,000
Pre-tax profit	£757,000,000

Nature of business: The activities of the group principally concern the processing and manufacture of food worldwide and textile retailing in the UK and continental Europe. ABF has five key business areas: Sugar, Agriculture, Retail, Grocery and Ingredients. The ultimate holding company is Wittington Investments Ltd.

Company registration number: 293262

Subsidiaries include: Food Investments Ltd, The Ryvita Co. Ltd, British Sugar plc, Jacksons of Piccadilly Ltd, AB Agri Ltd, ABF Grain Products Ltd, Jordan's (NI) Ltd, R Twining and Co. Ltd, Mauri Products Ltd, Patak's Foods Ltd, Patak's Breads Ltd, The Billington Food Group Ltd, ABF Investments plc, Abitec Ltd, Cereform Ltd, Primark Stores Ltd, Nambarrie Tea Co. Ltd, G Costa and Co. Ltd, British Sugar (Overseas) Ltd

Brands include: Allinson; Argo; Askeys; Baking Mad; Billington's; Blue Dragon; Burgen; Crusha; Don; Jacksons of Piccadilly; Jordans; Karo; Kingsmill; La Tisaniere; Mazola; Ovaltine; Patak's, Ryvita, Silver Spoon, Speedibake; Spice Islands; Sunblest; Tip Top; Tone's; Twinings.

Main locations: London

UK employees: 36,330

Total employees: 102,253

Membership: BITC

Charitable donations

UK cash (latest declared):	2009	£2,400,000
	2008	£1,600,000
	2007	£1,600,000
	2006	£400,000
	2005	£300,000
Total worldwide:	2011	£2,700,000

Community involvement

We consider it appropriate to draw readers' attention to the following:

In addition to the company's substantial worldwide charitable/community contributions, The Garfield Weston Foundation (Charity Commission no: 230260) receives a substantial proportion of its income from its holding in Wittington Investments Ltd (the holding company of Associated British Foods plc) which, although administered from the same address, is operated entirely independently of the company.

ABF's annual accounts for 2010/11 state:

> The Garfield Weston Foundation is an English charitable trust, established in 1958 by the late W Garfield Weston. The foundation has no direct interest in the company, but as at 17 September 2011 was the beneficial owner of 683,073 shares (2010 – 683,073 shares) in Wittington Investments Ltd representing 79.2% (2010 – 79.2%) of that company's issued share capital and is, therefore, the company's ultimate controlling party. At 17 September 2011 trustees of the Foundation comprised two children and two grandchildren of the late W Garfield Weston and five children of the late Garry H Weston.

As one of the largest grantmaking trusts in the UK, details of the work of the Garfield Weston Foundation can be found in *The Guide to Major Trusts Volume 1*, published by the Directory of Social Change.

In addition to the above, the company states in its annual report and accounts, that it actively encourages its operating companies to 'engage with the local community in the areas of operation'. Examples of this include the community activities given in the 'In kind support' section.

Corporate giving

For year ended 17 September 2011 the company declared worldwide charitable contributions of £2.7 million (2010 – £2.8 million). The following statement is taken from an email received from the Assistant Company Secretary in response to our enquiry regarding charitable donations in the UK:

> The £2.7 million figure given in the 2011 accounts for Associated British Foods plc ('ABF' plc') represents the collective figure of cash donations, local community projects and donations in kind (e.g. food donations) made during the financial year by the various business throughout the ABF group on a world-wide basis. Each business submits its figure, where relevant, to the ABF centre which collates the information into one overall figure for the purposes of including it in the consolidated accounts for ABF plc.
>
> The Garfield Weston Foundation does not have a direct interest in ABF plc but it is the beneficial owner of a substantial proportion of Wittington Investments Ltd. WIL in turn owns 54.5% of the issued share capital of ABF plc. No direct cash donations are made by ABF to the foundation but WIL and the foundation each derive income from the dividend payments from their respective investments.

Garfield Weston Foundation

For year ended 5 April 2011, the Garfield Weston Foundation received £18.3 million comprising dividends received from Whittington Investments Ltd., and distributed £40.5 million supporting 1,781 appeals (from a total of 3,304 received. 2010: 3,183).

The grants made support a wide range of charitable activities and the trustees have been able to increase the overall percentage of appeals supported and the overall amount donated, in the case of donations by over 18%. There were two grants of £3 million, and four of £1 million.

Arts	129	£10.68 million
Education	171	£9.56 million
Health	122	£6.48 million
Religion	508	£4.16 million
Welfare	234	£3.17 million
Youth	260	£2.96 million
Community	287	£1.6 million
Environment	57	£1.59 million
Other	13	£288,000

In kind support

The company's Responsibility section on its website states:

> British Sugar, UK British Sugar has played an instrumental role in supporting the Snibston Discovery Museum in the East Midlands to preserve ancient timbers that once spanned the River Trent. Rescue excavations at Hemington Quarry, Leicestershire, between 1993 and 1998 revealed three successive medieval bridges preserved beneath gravel bar deposits and alluvium. The timbers include the only surviving example of an

11th century bridge across a major river and the most complete Norman timber structure in Britain. Following their excavation, the timbers have been undergoing an innovative conservation process. Over the past 14 years, the bridge timbers have been immersed in a sucrose solution supplied by British Sugar. Excited by the technical challenge of preserving these rare medieval timbers, since 1996 British Sugar has donated around 70 tonnes of liquid sugar to Leicestershire County Council to undertake this process.

Vivergo, UK has invested substantial time in a number of local community projects: e.g. several contractors on a project donated time and materials to build a conservatory at a local respite home and a Vivergo team spent a day doing a makeover of the garden. Vivergo is also spending £25,000 planting trees in the local area and has established a community forum to engage the local town and village councils in what it is doing and help them to understand what is being built by Vivergo and why.

Employee-led support

Vivergo, UK – £20,000 was raised through a number of employee-organised fundraising initiatives for the KIDS charity which provides support to families with children who have learning difficulties. £5,000 of this was donated by the company.

Corporate social responsibility

CSR committee: There is a CSR Committee and Team.

CSR policy: The company states in the Corporate Responsibility section of its annual report for 2010/11 that with regard to communities, it recognises its responsibilities as a member of the communities in which it operates and encourages its businesses to engage with them as and how they wish.

In addition, a substantial 'contribution' is received by the Garfield Weston Foundation – see 'Community Contributions' for details.

In the chair's statement given in the 2011 annual report the subject of diversity is highlighted. The chair states:

> We very much welcome the publication, in February, of the Davies Review of Women on Boards. We recognise the benefits of diversity throughout the business, including gender diversity, and we employ many senior female managers across the group including, importantly, in operational areas. The issue of gender diversity at board level is of unanimous concern and was a specific issue considered during this year's board evaluation process. Both as a business and a board, we will continue to appoint on merit but it has now been agreed with the Nominations committee that we will ask executive search agencies to ensure that half of the candidates they put forward are women. We have a gender diversity task force with representation from across the group's businesses, the aims of which are to increase the visibility of, and opportunities for, women at all levels of seniority, and to encourage them in their development.

CSR report: The company has a comprehensive Corporate Responsibility report covering: environment, people, suppliers, products and customers and communities. The annual report and accounts for 2010/11 state that the company has a commitment to producing a CSR report within every three years and to maintaining information on its website. The latest available report at the time of writing was for the year 2010 (the first such report).

Exclusions

Sponsorship is not undertaken.

Applications

Any appeals addressed to the UK head office are forwarded to the administrator of the Garfield Weston Foundation (Tel: 020 7399 6565; Fax: 020 7399 6584). Only registered charities are considered.

With regard to subsidiary companies, we have been unable to find out what they hold as independent budgets for giving at a local level. We do know that individual companies support local communities with in kind donations – see 'in kind support'.

AstraZeneca

Pharmaceuticals

Correspondent: Charitable Appeals Department, 15 Stanhope Gate, London W1K 1LN (tel: 020 7304 5000; fax: 020 7304 5151; website: www.astrazeneca.com)

Directors: Louis Schweitzer, Chair; David Brennan, Chief Executive; Simon Lowth; Michele Hooper; Bruce Burlington; Jean-Philippe Courtois; Rudy Markham; Dame Nancy Rothwell; Shriti Vadera; John Varley; Marcus Wallenberg (women: 3; men: 8)

Year end	31/12/2011
Turnover	£33,600,000,000
Pre-tax profit	£12,400,000,000

Nature of business: The group's principal activities are the research, development and marketing of medicines for serious health conditions.

Company registration number: 2723534

Main locations: Alderley Edge, Cambridge, Macclesfield, Loughborough, Luton, London, Stonehouse, Tytherington, Wilmslow, Chorlton-cum-Hardy, Brixham, Bristol, Edinburgh

UK employees: 8,700

Total employees: 57,200

Membership: LBG

Charitable donations

UK cash (latest declared):	2011	£333,000
	2009	£100,000
Total UK:	2011	£333,000
Total worldwide:	2011	£789,559,000

Corporate social responsibility

CSR committee: There was no evidence of a CSR Committee. There is a Charitable Appeals Department.

CSR policy: This information was obtained from the company's annual report:

> Wherever AstraZeneca operates worldwide, we aim to make a positive contribution to our local communities through partnerships, charitable donations and other initiatives that help to make a sustainable difference. Our investment is focused on improving health and promoting science skills.

CSR report: There was no evidence of a CSR report.

Exclusions

No support for circulars, advertising in charity brochures, individuals, older people, fundraising events, political/discriminatory groups, religious appeals, sport, anything contrary to company business, capital projects or building appeals.

Applications

In writing to the correspondent at the head office address.

Other information

The company's 'Community investment' section on its website states:

> In 2011, we spent a total of $1.27 billion [£789.5 million] (2010: $1.41 billion [£876.6 million]) on community sponsorships, partnerships and charitable donations worldwide, including our product donation and patient assistance programmes which make our medicines available free of charge or at reduced prices. Through our three patient assistance programmes in the US we donated products valued at an average wholesale price of over $938 million [£583.1 million] (2010: $1.38 billion [£857.9 million]). We also donated products worth $8.2 million, valued at average wholesale price, to the charitable organisations: Americares and Direct Relief International.

The group supports the work of the Brightside Trust, a charity that aims to help underprivileged young people to enter the medical and healthcare professions. Support included a two year secondment to the charity as well as an ongoing contribution in cash (around £100,000 over three years). We have used this figure as the company's cash UK cash contribution over three years as we have no other UK cash figure.

Through its 'Inspiring Science' programme, run in conjunction with the CREST awards scheme in the UK, a programme of project work relevant to the secondary education science curriculum is undertaken. Schools of the students judged to have delivered the best projects receive a cash prize. Further information is available at: www.inspiringscience.co.uk

AstraZeneca Science Teaching Trust
The AstraZeneca Science Teaching Trust (Charity Commission no. 1064864), an independent charity with a total trust fund of around £21 million provided by the company, supports a programme of projects designed to help build the knowledge, skills and understanding required to lead and teach science effectively and confidently in primary schools. For the past two years the trust has had almost no income (around £200) although annual expenditure remains high at over £1 million in 2011 and £736,000 in 2010.

> Employees are encouraged to become involved in community-based charitable activities through a matched funding scheme, whereby individuals' efforts in fundraising may be matched by a company donation.
>
> We focus our support in the UK on charitable and not-for-profit organisations based near, or operating close to, AstraZeneca's key sites (Alderley Park, Avlon, Brixham, London, Luton, and Macclesfield).

AT&T (UK) Ltd

Telecommunications

Correspondent: Media Relations Director, Highfield House, Headless Cross Drive, Redditch B97 5EQ (tel: 01527 518181; website: www.att.com)

Directors: Randall Stephenson; Jon Madonna; Gilbert Amelio; Reuben Anderson; James Blanchard; John McCoy; Lynn Martin; James Kelly; Jaime Chico Pardo; Joyce Roche; Matthew Rose; Laura D'Andrea Tyson; Patricia Upton (women: 4; men: 8)

Year end	31/12/2010
Turnover	£124,280,000,000
Pre-tax profit	£18,238,000,000

Nature of business: Telecommunications and networking company.

Company registration number: 1765868

Main locations: London

Total employees: 267,000

Charitable donations

Total worldwide:	2010	£148,200,000

Corporate social responsibility

CSR committee: There is evidence of a Corporate Governance and Nominating Committee.

CSR policy: AT&T were committed to much philanthropic work during 2010. Educational programmes included job shadowing; grants to high schools with proven track records of success and research into the US' dropout crisis.

In 2010, AT&T donated 9 million hours of employee and retiree time through volunteer programmes. The equivalent in dollars calculated by AT&T totalled $192 million. More than $31 million was donated through employee giving.

CSR report: A separate CSR report was available from the company's website.

Exclusions

The foundation does not support the following categories:

- Individuals
- Organisations whose chief purpose is to influence legislation or to participate or intervene in political campaigns on behalf of or against any candidate for public office
- Endowments or memorials
- Construction or renovation projects
- Sports teams or any sports-related activity or competition, even if it addresses our program interests
- Fundraising events or advertising

Applications

In writing to the correspondent.

Other information

There was no information about UK community giving or donations for 2010.

The company has stated that it has always taken a proactive approach when it comes to funding and areas of interest include education, underserved communities and arts and culture, especially where these are linked to broadening access to technology.

W. S. Atkins plc

Information technology

Correspondent: Richard Webster, Company Secretary, Woodcote Grove, Ashley Road, Epsom, Surrey KT18 5BW (tel: 01372 726140; fax: 01372 740055; website: www.atkinsglobal.com)

Directors: Allan Cook, Chair; Uwe Krueger, Chief Executive Officer; Heath Drewitt, Chief Financial Officer; Alun Griffiths; Admiral the Lord Boyce; Fiona Clutterbuck; Joanne Curin; Raj Rajagopal; Rodney Slater (women: 2; men: 7)

Year end	31/03/2012
Turnover	£1,711,100,000
Pre-tax profit	£135,500,000

Nature of business: The group operates primarily as a multi-discipline design and engineering consultants with a focus on engineering and appropriate building design. The company's operations are based in over 70 offices throughout the UK.

Company registration number: 1885586

Main locations: Epsom

UK employees: 8,654

Total employees: 16,453

Charitable donations

UK cash (latest declared):	2010	£93,054
	2009	£187,757
	2008	£191,527
	2007	£205,813
	2006	£97,534
Total UK:	2010	£93,054
Total worldwide:	2012	£99,000
Cash worldwide:	2012	£99,000

Corporate social responsibility

CSR committee: No details found.

CSR policy: Most of the company's community giving appears to be outside of the UK. The website states: 'Atkins is committed to positive stakeholder engagement in the communities in which we operate, with a particular focus on supporting local education initiatives by deploying our broad range of skills and expertise as appropriate.'

CSR report: CSR review published annually.

Exclusions

No support for political appeals.

Applications

In writing to the correspondent.

Other information

During the year 2011/12, the Group made charitable donations of almost £99,000 (2010/11: £135,000). The beneficiaries of these donations were local charities serving the communities in which the Group operates or charities working in areas relevant to the Group's activities. The Group intends to continue its focus on local charities in the current financial year. We have no details of the organisations supported or whether they were in the UK or overseas. Although the group appears to give substantial support in kind, we have no details of the value of this.

The company actively engages in a range of educational initiatives from primary schools through to universities and is known to offer a number of undergraduate prizes at universities.

Aurum Funds Ltd

Financial services

Correspondent: J L Weingartner, Company Secretary, Ixworth House, 37 Ixworth Place, London SW3 3QH (tel: 020 7589 1130; fax: 020 7581 1780; email: clientservices@aurumfunds.com; website: www.aurum.com)

Directors: K. R. Gundle; D. A. Mark; A. Sweidan; J. L. Weingartner

Year end	31/12/2010
Turnover	£1,830,190
Pre-tax profit	£161,585

Nature of business: Specialist investment manager of hedge funds.

Company registration number: 3007670

Total employees: 1,756

Corporate social responsibility

CSR committee: There was no evidence of a separate CSR Committee.

CSR policy: From the information displayed on the website it appeared that the company supported five charities, however there was limited information available.

Unable to determine the ratio of women to men on the board.

CSR report: There was no evidence of a separate CSR report.

Applications

In writing to the correspondent.

Other information

We could not find information on the company's charitable UK giving, however, we know from its website that Aurum supports five charities. We do not know if this support is in kind or cash. The five charities given support are: ARK – established to transform the lives of children who have disabilities or who have suffered abuse, illness or poverty; Synchronicity Foundation – supporting globally, education, environment and healthcare; PATA – providing support for HIV/AIDS children, their families and communities throughout Africa; One to One Children's Fund – providing support for children throughout the world who have suffered as a result of disasters, the trauma of war and prejudice; and Norwood – the major UK charity providing children and family services.

Autonomous Research LLP

Business services

Correspondent: Keith Lawrence, Autonomous Research Charitable Trust, Moore Stephens, 150 Aldersgate Street, London EC1A 4AP (tel: 020 7334 9191; email: keith.lawrence@moorestephens.com).

Company address: 11 Ironmonger Lane, London EC2V 8JN (tel: 020 7776 3400; fax: 020 7776 3401; email: info@autonomous-research.com; website: www.autonomous-research.com)

Directors: Stuart Graham; Edward Allchin; Jacques Henri Gaulard; Manus Costello; Andrew Crean; Andrew Ritchie; Kim Shapiro; Giovanni Carriere; Corrine Cunningham; Geoff Elliott; Jonathan Firkins; Jacob Kruse; Farquhar Murray; Giulia Raffo; Britta Schmidt; Andreas Vollmer; Jason Robins; Richard Smalley; Lord Myners (women: 3; men: 15)

Year end	31/03/2011
Turnover	£14,262,021

Nature of business: Independent research provider on banking and insurance companies.

Company registration number: OC343985

UK employees: 8

Total employees: 8

Charitable donations

UK cash (latest declared):	2011	£183,000
Total UK:	2011	£183,000

Corporate social responsibility

CSR committee: There was no evidence of a separate CSR Committee.

CSR policy: This information was obtained from the company's website:

> An important part of the Autonomous culture is to give something back. We allocate 5% of annual profits linked to partner shares to charitable causes. The funds are administered by the Autonomous Research Charitable Trust (Charity Commission no. 1137503). The ARCT has been established in accordance with industry best practice, with both an external independent trustee on the board and a formal conflicts of interest policy (available upon request).
>
> The ARCT's core aims are as follows:
>
> - To help disadvantaged people get a step up in life. Our focus is therefore upon people rather than wildlife conservation or ecology
> - To empower people to improve the quality of their lives. We are therefore naturally drawn to projects based around education opportunities or helping with start-up business ventures
> - To focus our resources upon a small number of key partner charities – both in London and abroad – where we feel we can make a difference and establish long-term relationships
> - Our involvement is not simply about giving money. The partners of Autonomous will also be active in mentoring, providing business and career advice and in a variety of other hands-on roles

CSR report: There was no evidence of a separate CSR report but there was information available on the company's website.

Applications

In writing to the correspondent.

Autonomy Corporation plc

Information technology

Correspondent: Company Secretary, Cambridge Business Park, Cowley Rd, Cambridge, Cambridgeshire CB4 0WZ (tel: 01223 448000; fax: 01223 448001; email: autonomy@autonomy.com; website: www.autonomy.com)

Directors: Robert Webb, Chair; Jonathan Bloomer; Richard Gaunt; Sushovan Hussain; Frank Kelly; Dr Michael Lynch; John McMonigall (women: 0; men: 7)

Year end	31/12/2010
Turnover	£870,336,000
Pre-tax profit	£282,194,000

Nature of business: A global leader in infrastructure software.

Company registration number: 3175909

Total employees: 1,900

Charitable donations

UK cash (latest declared):	2009	£70,000
	2008	£96,700
Total worldwide:	2010	£57,900
Cash worldwide:	2010	£57,900

Corporate social responsibility

CSR committee: There appeared to be no evidence of a CSR Committee.

CSR policy: This information was obtained from the company's website: 'Autonomy is committed to supporting the principles of economic success, environmental stewardship and social responsibility.'

CSR report: There appears to be no evidence of a separate CSR report; however, one paragraph explained charitable donations in the annual report.

Applications

In writing to the correspondent.

Other information

The group made $92,000 (nearly £60,000), in charitable donations during 2010 to a variety of charities including the Prince's Trust and the University of Calgary (2008: $110,000 – £70,000).

The group mainly supports education. It also budgets annually for specific charitable requests from individual staff members, in areas where there is an opportunity to make a significant and measurable impact in the non-profit sector.

> The company's matching gift programme matches employee donations to non-profit organisations meeting the company's requirements for charitable donations. Finally, the company permits employees to volunteer a certain number of hours of paid time per year to the charity of their choice subject to company criteria.

Aveva Group plc

Information technology

Correspondent: Corporate Responsibility Team, High Cross, Madingley Road, Cambridge CB3 0HB (tel: 01223 556655; fax: 01223 556666; website: www.aveva.com)

Directors: Nick Prest, Chair; Richard Langdon, Chief Executive; Philip Dayer; Jonathan Brooks; Herve Couturier; James Kidd (women: 0; men: 6)

Year end	31/03/2011
Turnover	£173,988,000
Pre-tax profit	£49,795,000

Nature of business: The principal activities of the group are the marketing and development of computer software and services for engineering and related solutions. The company is a holding company.

Company registration number: 2937296

UK employees: 472

Total employees: 972

Charitable donations

UK cash (latest declared):	2011	£36,000
	2010	£36,000
Total UK:	2011	£36,000
Total worldwide:	2011	£49,600
Cash worldwide:	2011	£49,600

Corporate social responsibility

CSR committee: The chief executive has board responsibilities for matters relating to the group's culture and ethical policies, environmental matters and customer and employee issues.

CSR policy: This information was obtained from the company's website:

> As a Group we seek to operate responsibly and ethically in all areas of our business. We have a strong ethical belief in the way business should be conducted and how employees should be treated. We have integrated social, environmental and ethical policies into the way we do business and how we interact with our stakeholders including our shareholders, employees, customers, suppliers and local communities.

CSR report: There was no evidence of a CSR report; however information was available from the company's website.

Applications

In writing to the correspondent.

Other information

During the past year Aveva donated almost £50,000 to a range of organisations. Beneficiary groups included:

East Anglian Air Ambulance; East Anglian Children's Hospice (EACH); Mid-Anglia General Practitioner Accident Service (MAGPAS); Arthur Rank Hospice; Headway; Macmillan Cancer Support; International Committee of the Red Cross; The Prince's Trust; The Outward Bound Trust; Help for Heroes; and Marie Curie Cancer Care.

The Group's policy was to continue to support local charities in the areas in which they operate as well as a number of national and international charities.

Matched funding: The efforts of employees who took part in the Chariots of Fire Charity Marathon, the Oxford to Cambridge Bike Ride and Red Nose Day have been matched funded by the group.

In kind contributions: The group provides both software and training support to enable engineering students to gain hands-on experience of the latest technologies and use these to undertake a variety of academic and practical projects directly applicable to the industries in which they will work.

Aviva plc

Insurance

Correspondent: Corporate Responsibility Specialists Team, St Helen's, 1 Undershaft, London EC3P 3DQ (tel: 020 7283 2000; fax: 020 7662 8182; website: www.aviva.com)

Directors: Patrick Regan, Chief Financial Officer; Mary Francis; Russell Walls; Euleen Goh; Scott Wheway; Richard Karl Goeltz; Leslie Van de Walle; Lord Sharman of Redlynch, Chair; Andrew Moss, Group Chief Executive; John McFarlane; Trevor Matthews; Igal Mayer; Glyn Barber; Gay Huey Evans; Michael Hawker (women: 3; men: 12)

Year end	31/12/2011
Turnover	£30,000,000,000
Pre-tax profit	£635,000,000

Nature of business: The company transacts life assurance and long-term savings business, fund management, and all classes of general insurance through its subsidiaries, associates and branches in the UK, Continental Europe, North America, Asia, Australia and other countries throughout the world.

Company registration number: 2468686

Subsidiaries include: Norwich Union Wealth Management Ltd, Norwich Union Trust Managers Ltd, CGU Bonus Ltd, Commercial Union Life Assurance Co. Ltd, Norwich Union Life Holdings Ltd, London and Edinburgh Insurance Group Ltd, Norwich Union Annuity Ltd, CGU Insurance plc, General Accident plc, Norwich Union Healthcare Ltd, CGU Underwriting Ltd, Norwich Union Life and Pensions Ltd, Morley Properties Ltd, Morley Fund Management Ltd, Morley Pooled Pensions Ltd, CGNU Life Assurance Ltd, Northern Assurance Co. Ltd, Norwich Union Insurance Ltd, CGU International Insurance Ltd, Norwich Union Portfolio Services Ltd, your-move.co.uk Ltd, Norwich Union Investment Funds Ltd, Norwich Union Linked Life Assurance Ltd

Main locations: Croydon, Bristol, Cheadle, Eastleigh, Exeter, Glasgow, York, Southampton, Sheffield, Romford, Stevenage, Norwich, Newcastle

UK employees: 17,620

Total employees: 36,562

Membership: BITC, LBG

Charitable donations

UK cash (latest declared):	2011	£2,800,000
	2009	£1,300,000
	2008	£2,200,000
	2007	£1,400,000
	2006	£1,400,000
Total UK:	2011	£2,800,000
Total worldwide:	2011	£11,635,300
Cash worldwide:	2011	£8,287,000

Community involvement

The following information is taken from the UK CR report:

> Working closely with national and regional partners and through our own employees, we work hard to have a long-term impact on our communities.
>
> Nationally, we partner with Railway Children to raise awareness of and support vulnerable children who are alone and at risk on our streets, as part of our global Street to School programme. Through our work, we currently support all of the refuge beds in the UK.
>
> We also invest in our potential customers and employees of the future. We have a national programme to improve economic literacy in secondary schools. It's delivered by Aviva volunteers alongside our long-term partner, Citizenship Foundation – who also help us run the innovative 'Chance to be the Chancellor' competition to uncover tomorrow's financial leaders.
>
> Our national sports sponsorships include a premier league football club, the Rugby Premiership and 60 UK athletes. They have also provided training to over 2,000 teachers and engaged with over 500,000 young people across the UK as part of the Grass Roots Sports programme.
>
> Locally, we have enhanced our corporate responsibility networks at Aviva's 10 main sites across the UK by recruiting additional volunteers, empowering CR network leaders to make local charity grant awards from the central CR budget, and facilitating the appointment of 10 new local charity partners.
>
> Employee participation is integral to our approach. We offer three days' paid leave to volunteer, the opportunity to nominate and vote for local charities to benefit from Aviva funding, we operate an employee CR awards programme, and we contribute to the fundraising our employees do through our £Plus scheme.

Street to School

Aviva's Street to School programme around the world recognises that every child living or working on the street should have the opportunity to fulfil their potential. The UK's partner is **Railway Children**, a charity which fights for vulnerable children who are alone and at risk on the streets. In its second year, the programme continued to build momentum and deliver against its three core objectives: employee engagement, customer and brand, and the cause.

Grass Roots Sports
Through sponsorship of Premiership Rugby, UK Athletics and Norwich City Football Club Aviva in the UK aims to:

- Make a difference beyond elite sport and direct a significant proportion of investment at grassroots level
- Help children get active and play a role in positively impacting the trend for childhood obesity
- Help children build self-esteem through participation in sport
- Leave a legacy by growing the sport for the children of the future
- Allow employees to feel the benefits of the sponsorship programmes by the participation of their children, parents getting involved in coaching and this positively impacting on how staff feel about working for Aviva

Through UK Athletics, Aviva is the first financial services company to become a partner to the Department of Health's **Change4Life** campaign, which aims to significantly reduce the nation's obesity levels by encouraging adoption of healthy behaviours. Aviva directly support up to 60 young athletes across the UK though the **On Camp With Kelly** programme, each benefiting from unique training and development experiences. By the end of the 2011/12 school year, 80,000 children will have participated in the Aviva Premiership Rugby Schools programme since it launched in 2010.

In 2011, the clubs worked with 650 primary schools, trained 1,300 teachers and engaged with 40,000 young people. Aviva has long been a supporter of the community programmes at Norwich City Football club (NCFC). Its unique **Footy Finance** programme uses the medium of football to help young people become more financially aware.

The **Ability Counts** programme uses a range of sporting activities to build confidence amongst disabled children and adults.

The **Aviva Summer Cup** is the largest junior football tournament in the region, run over two days by Community Sports Foundation, and engages with around 5,000 members of the local community.

Financial capability
Aviva is actively engaged in supporting people at different stages in their lives to help them make informed decisions about their future. It has partnered for four years with Citizenship Foundation to deliver **Paying for It**, a schools programme covering financial education.

Corporate giving

In 2011, the group made total community contributions, including management costs, of £12.4 million (2010: £11.4 million) in line with the company's strategic focus to support community and charitable initiatives in education, life trauma and financial literacy. The charitable spend was £8.2 million, gifts in kind £111,000 and the cost of volunteering is given as £779,700. We were unable to discover the UK only figures. We do know that £2.8 million was invested in the Grass Roots Sports Programmes which appear to be UK based. We have therefore used this figure for the UK cash contribution although in reality it is likely to be significantly more.

In 2009, Aviva launched 'Street to School', a five-year global charitable initiative, which aims to get children and young people off the street and into education. Working with leading charities and experts, and supported by employees and customers, the company aims to champion the needs of street children in the communities in which it has a presence. The 'Street to School' programme accounts for over 50% of the group's charitable donations and will gradually be adopted in every country in which Aviva operates.

Employee-led support

Staff are encouraged to take part in community-related projects through various initiatives, such as, staff volunteering, mentoring and fundraising activities, which the company matches. This is seen by the company as part of staff's personal development and employees can apply for up to three paid volunteering days per year. In 2011, staff in the UK contributed 30,000 volunteering hours and raised over £700,000 for charitable causes.

One initiative is the company's programme, **Paying for It** (www.payingforit.org.uk) launched by Aviva in 2007, which, in 2011, continued to take economic citizenship teaching into schools up and down the country with the help of over 70 specially trained Aviva volunteers. Using specially tailored resources available online for all schools to access, classes address issues of financial and social importance, such as housing, the environment and health.

The **Chance to be Chancellor** competition was run in conjunction with The Times as part of the Paying for It programme. It offers engaging activities to help young people find out more about the current economic challenges facing the country and act out the role of the Chancellor in delivering their vision for the economy.

The UK **Street to School** programme commits the company to raise awareness of the 100,000 young people under the age of 16 who run away from home every year. The UK partner is Railway Children, a charity dedicated to supporting vulnerable children living alone and at risk on the streets. In 2011, more than 14% of UK employees were actively involved in Street to School through volunteering, fundraising or donating. Over 4.6 million customers were reached with Street to School messaging and donated over £69,000 to Railway Children through '£ per policy' customer incentives.

Payroll giving: The Give As You Earn scheme is in operation and in 2011 the total global contribution was £874,400.

Commercially-led support

Sponsorship: Each individual business in the group is responsible for its own sponsorship and community support programmes, developed to meet their local market needs. Aviva, for example, will consider sponsoring good causes, education, music and sport projects.

Charity partners: Organisations the group works with include:

- Office of the High Commissioner for Human Rights
- Oxfam – a partner since 2006 providing immediate help to international communities suffering life trauma
- Save the Children and the Consortium for Street Children – the major Street to School partners
- CSR Asia's Community Investment Roundtable and Qi Global – encouraging community investment in Asia Pacific
- Railway Children, Barnardo's, CRY (Child Rights and You), Covenant house, China Youth Federation, SHÇEK and HOPE Worldwide – a few of the Street to School partners from around the world
- Schools Business Partnership, Business in the Community, Free the Children, UK Athletics, Citizenship Foundation, City of York Council – some of the partners the group are working with to support education and financial literacy

Corporate social responsibility

CSR committee: The company's CR section on its website states:

> Our programme covers all our business operations worldwide. It is overseen at group level by the group CR team, led by Marie Sigsworth, group CR director. Appointed managers in the businesses are responsible for managing the CR programme locally. We also have a dedicated board CR committee which is responsible for CR strategy and policy,

and for reviewing the progress of our CR programme. The committee comprises three non-executive directors, Aviva's chairman and the group's chief executive.

CSR policy: Statement taken from the company's website:

At Aviva we believe that corporate responsibility means taking positive action, treating our colleagues, customers and suppliers with respect, applying consistently high standards in everything we do and having a constructive role in the communities in which we operate. Our vision and strategy for CR is aligned to the company strategy and informed by stakeholder analysis, to make sure that we meet their needs, from our employees and customers to our shareholders and investors.

CSR report: A CR report is published annually and available from the company's website. There are downloads available for individual areas of operation e.g. UK, Continental Europe.

Exclusions

At group level, Aviva will not normally consider supporting:

- Individuals looking for sponsorship or charity fundraising donations either on their own behalf or that of a charity (staff excluded)
- Political organisations
- Extreme 'high risk' or 'free sports'
- Organisations or issues already supported by Norwich Union in the UK
- Charities already receiving long-term support around the world, either from Norwich Union or an Aviva company
- A staff Charity of the Year (on a separate basis)
- Paid advertisements in charity brochures or events programmes

Applications

In writing to the correspondent.

Avon Cosmetics Ltd

Health/beauty products

Correspondent: Donations Dept., Nunn Mills Road, Northampton NN1 5PA (tel: 01604 232425; fax: 01604 232444; website: www.avon.uk.com)

Directors: D. Afonso; N. Clark; A. Gallagher; L. M. Garley Evans; A. Judge; S. McArdle; A. A. Russell; S. Schlackman; A. Tucker (women: 5; men: 5)

Year end	31/12/2010
Turnover	£328,879,000
Pre-tax profit	£4,000,000

Nature of business: The principal activities of the company are the distribution and sale of beauty products and the sale and distribution of gift and decorative products.

Company registration number: 592235

Main locations: Northampton

Total employees: 42,000

Membership: BITC

Charitable donations

UK cash (latest declared):	2010	£643,000
	2009	£53,300
Total UK:	2010	£1,029,000
Total worldwide:	2010	£1,029,000
Cash worldwide:	2010	£643,000

Community involvement

The Avon Foundation

In 1955 the company formalised philanthropic efforts with the creation of the Avon Foundation, which advances the mission to improve the lives of women and their families.

The foundation's main efforts are today focused on the critical issues of breast cancer and domestic violence, and Avon global philanthropy is advancing these causes in more than 50 countries. Avon and the Avon Foundation also support emergency and disaster relief, while a scholarship program for Avon associates and sales representatives maintains the tradition of supporting education.

The latest Avon Foundation Impact Report and details on mission programs, grants, educational materials and financial reports can be found on the Avon Foundation website.

Corporate giving

In 2010 the company made charitable donations amounting to £643,000 supporting the breast cancer cause and the fight to end violence against women. The company spent an additional £386,000 on other charitable activities.

Employee-led support

Support is given to employees' volunteering/charitable activities through financial help, matching employee fundraising and giving, and allowing company time off to volunteer.

Payroll giving: Avon operates the Give As You Earn scheme.

Commercially-led support

Cause-related marketing: Avon Breast Cancer Crusade raises funds through the sale of promotional pin badges and jewellery.

Corporate social responsibility

CSR committee: There was no evidence of a separate CSR Committee.

CSR policy: This information was obtained from the company's website:

Avon Cosmetics has long been associated with the fight against breast cancer and is the world's largest corporate supporter of the cause. The Avon Breast Cancer Crusade was launched in the UK in 1992 to raise funds for and awareness of breast cancer. Since then Avon has worked in partnership with charities including Breakthrough Breast Cancer, Macmillan Cancer Support and Breast Cancer Care. Avon's activities have supported research, awareness raising, lobbying and care and support services.

CSR report: There was no evidence of a separate CSR report.

Exclusions

No support for advertising in charity brochures, animal welfare charities, appeals from individuals, the arts, overseas projects, political appeals, religious appeals, science/technology or sport.

Applications

In writing to the correspondent.

Avon Rubber plc

Defence, motors and accessories

Correspondent: Miles Ingrey-Counter, Company Secretary, Hampton Park West, Melksham, Wiltshire SN12 6NB (tel: 01225 896800; fax: 01225 896899; email: enquiries@avon-rubber.com; website: www.avon-rubber.com)

Directors: Richard Needham, Chair; Stella Pirie; David Evans; Peter Slabbert, Chief Executive; Andrew Lewis (women: 1; men: 4)

Year end	30/09/2011
Turnover	£107,600,000
Pre-tax profit	£10,212,000

Nature of business: The principal activities of the group are the design and manufacture of respiratory protection products for defence, police, fire and other emergency services, together with the design and manufacture of a range of polymer based products for the dairy, defence and aerosol industries.

Company registration number: 32965

Main locations: Westbury, Trowbridge, Melksham

Total employees: 679

Charitable donations

UK cash (latest declared):	2009	£9,839
	2008	£18,883
	2007	£13,257
	2006	£22,787
	2005	£26,000
Total worldwide:	2011	£15,380
Cash worldwide:	2011	£15,380

Corporate social responsibility

CSR committee: There was no evidence of a separate CSR Committee.

CSR policy: This information was obtained from the group's annual report:

The group maintains a fund with the Community Foundation for Wiltshire and Swindon, a charity dedicated to strengthening local communities in West Wiltshire by targeting its grants to make a genuine difference to the lives of local people.

CSR report: There was no evidence of a separate CSR report, however there were two pages dedicated to the community within the group's annual report.

Exclusions

No support for animal welfare charities, circular appeals, appeals from individuals, local appeals not in areas of company presence, large national appeals or overseas projects.

Applications

All applications are dealt with by the Wiltshire and Swindon Community Foundation, 48 New Park Street, Devizes, Wiltshire SN10 1DS (Tel: 01380 729284. Fax: 01380 729772; website: www.wscf.org.uk; email: info@wscf.org.uk).

Other information

Contributions for charitable purposes amounted to £15,300 consisting exclusively of numerous small donations to various community charities in Wiltshire, Michigan, Wisconsin, Georgia and Mississippi.

In the UK the Group maintains a fund with the Community Foundation for Wiltshire and Swindon, a charity dedicated to strengthening local communities. The Group Director of Human Resources is a trustee of the Foundation, which targets its grants to make a genuine difference to the lives of local people.

The Community Foundation celebrated 20 years of supporting the voluntary sector this year and Avon's fund provided grants to: HELP Counselling; Westbury Rugby Football Club; Wiltshire Music Centre; ASK; Trowbridge Rangers FC.

AXA UK plc

Healthcare, insurance

Correspondent: J P Small, Company Secretary, 5 Old Broad Street, London EC2N 1AD (website: www.axa.co.uk)

Directors: A. J. Hamilton, Chair; P. J. Evans, Chief Executive; J. P. Asquith; A. J. Blanc; I. Brimecome; H. de Castries; R. G. Dench; J. P. Drouffe; D. Duverne; K. G. Gibbs; S. N. Hardy; M. J. Kellard; A. R. Monro-Davies; J. O'Neill

Year end	31/12/2010
Turnover	£569,000,000
Pre-tax profit	£442,000,000

Nature of business: Following the disposal of its traditional life and pensions, protection and group pensions business, AXA UK now has a focus on three key areas of growth:

- Wealth management
- Insurance
- Healthcare

Company registration number: 2937724

UK employees: 111,738

Total employees: 111,738

Membership: BITC, LBG

Charitable donations

UK cash (latest declared):	2010	£702,300
	2009	£149,000
	2008	£137,000
Total UK:	2010	£702,300

Community involvement

Community activities

2011 community activities across the UK and Ireland included:

- Support for the Junior Achievers programme – empowering youth and preparing them for a financially independent life
- Providing a contact centre of 100 lines for the Children in Need appeal
- Supporting students in a Bolton school with CV writing, work experience and careers advice
- Raising £22,600 for Macmillan Cancer Support
- Raising £11,000 for the East Africa Crisis Appeal

The following information is from the company's CR section on its website:

> In 2008, AXA established the **AXA Research Fund** to support scientific research that would contribute to understanding and preventing environmental, life and socio-economic risks. The purpose of the Fund is to:
>
> - Contribute to scientific breakthroughs
> - Help reframe public debate on global risks-related issues
> - Develop our own expertise in cutting-edge science
>
> Since 2008 the Fund has committed €76 million globally to 308 projects. We have recently committed a further €100 million to be invested between 2013 and 2018. In the UK we are supporting over 60 projects.

The company also supports CARE, a global humanitarian organisation which aims to address the underlying causes of poverty and move towards sustainable development. Most of its programmes are based on microfinance, education, AIDS relief, food security and drinking water.

Corporate giving

In 2010, the AXA UK group made contributions totalling £702,000. £350,000 was donated to the French Education Trust; £175,000 for Mesothelioma research and £177,000 for other charitable purposes.

In kind support

In addition to local and employee-specific fundraising campaigns, the company supports national campaigns with employee fundraising and in kind donations.

Employee-led support

The company's CR section on its website states:

> We want to be a good neighbour in the communities where we operate. So we work with community groups to address specific local needs and provide our people with personal development opportunities.
>
> We do this through the *Hearts in Action* volunteering scheme, fundraising for local charities and emergency relief. In 2011 we launched The AXA Ambition awards. The awards support talented young people in our local communities to fulfil their dreams and ambitions in the fields of science, community, sports and the arts.
>
> Hearts in Action is AXA's global community partnership programme. It provides volunteer and charity fundraising opportunities for employees and is designed to build links between our business, our people and our local communities. It acts as a guideline for community involvement but allows local offices to develop programmes that are suitable for their employees and local community needs.

Corporate social responsibility

CSR committee: There was no evidence of a separate CSR Committee.

CSR policy: Information taken from the company's website:

> In many ways, being 'responsible' is our business. Our products and services give support, reassurance and security to our customers.
>
> Corporate Responsibility at AXA means working to reduce our environmental impact, supporting local communities and working with stakeholders. It plays an important part in helping us achieve our vision and ensures that AXA contributes to society.

AXA UK's corporate responsibility strategy is organised around four pillars: marketplace, workplace, community and environment.

Unable to determine the ratio of women to men on the Board.

CSR report: There was no evidence of a CSR report.

Applications

In writing to the correspondent.

Babcock International Group plc

Marine, transportation

Correspondent: Albert Dungate, Group Company Secretary and General Counsel, 33 Wigmore Street, London W1U 1QX (tel: 020 7355 5300; fax: 020 7355 5360; website: www.babcockinternational.com)

Directors: Mike Turner, Chair; Peter Rogers, Chief Executive; Bill Tame, Group Finance Director; Archie Bethel; Kevin Thomas; David Omand; Justin Crookenden; Ian Duncan; Nigel Essenhigh; Kate Swann; Albert Dungate (women: 1; men: 10)

Year end	31/03/2012
Turnover	£3,070,400,000
Pre-tax profit	£173,000,000

Nature of business: Support services in telecommunications, transport and education. Services are underpinned by three core capabilities:

- Managing assets and infrastructure
- Delivering projects and programmes
- Integrating engineering expertise

Company registration number: 2342138

Main locations: Bournemouth, Chichester, Bordon, Watford, Portsmouth, Reading, Southampton, London, Hove, Leatherhead

Total employees: 27,000

Charitable donations

UK cash (latest declared):	2012	£272,000
	2011	£236,000
	2009	£281,000
	2008	£212,000
	2007	£93,000
Total UK:	2012	£272,000
Total worldwide:	2012	£272,000
Cash worldwide:	2012	£272,000

Corporate social responsibility

CSR committee: No details found.

CSR policy: The following information is taken from the Responsibilities section of the group's website:

> In many places, we are the largest employer in the region. We seek to engage with the communities around our sites and operations and to provide opportunities for employees to assist with local initiatives and support local charities that are important to them. We have group-wide guidelines setting out our approach to charitable donations, our commitment to the communities in which we operate and the broader interests of our customers. As well as ensuring financial donations are appropriately targeted, they also encourage active engagement with the communities in which we operate through local community support programmes.

CSR report: No report available. There is a Sustainability section in the annual report and accounts which mentions community giving. This information can be found in 'Other information'.

Exclusions

No support for advertising in charity brochures, animal welfare, appeals from individuals, the arts, enterprise/training, environment/heritage, overseas projects, political appeals, social welfare or sport.

Applications

In writing to the correspondent.

Other information

Across the Babcock group, donations to charitable causes in 2011/12 amounted to £272,000 (2010/11: £236,000). The group continues to support SSAFA – the forces charity for supporting service families in times of need.

The company also provides community support by way of employee volunteering, fundraising, mentoring and pro bono work as well as Give as you Earn and matched giving.

BAE Systems

Defence, aerospace

Correspondent: Subscriptions and Donations Committee, Warwick House, PO Box 87, Farnborough Aerospace Centre, Farnborough, Hampshire GU14 6YU (tel: 01252 373232; email: community@baesystems.com; website: www.baesystems.com)

Directors: Linda Hudson; Paul Anderson; Michael Hartnall; Peter Mason; Nick Rose; Carl Symon; Dick Olver, Chair; Ian King, Chief Executive; Peter Lynas, Group Finance Director; Harriet Green; Lee McIntire; Paula Rosput Reynolds (women: 3; men: 9)

Year end	31/12/2011
Turnover	£19,154,000,000
Pre-tax profit	£1,027,000,000

Nature of business: The main activity of the Group is Defence – comprising the design and manufacture of civil and military aircraft, surface ships, submarines, space systems, radar, avionics, communications, electronics and guided weapon systems.

Company registration number: 1470151

Subsidiaries include: Spectrum Technologies plc, Future Naval Systems, IFS Defence Ltd, Innovation Partnerships Worldwide Ltd, Gripen International, RG Ammunition, Airbus UK, Avionics Group, AMS Integrated Systems

Main locations: Strathclyde, Prestwick, Somerset, London, Northamptonshire, Wiltshire, Yorkshire, Surrey, Cumbria, Cwmbran, County Durham, Cheshire, Buckinghamshire, Bristol, Cambridgeshire, Bridgend, Lancashire, Leicestershire, Kent, Isle of Wight, Hertfordshire, Hampshire, Greater Manchester, Gloucestershire, Glascoed, Glasgow, Essex, Edinburgh, Dunfermline, Dorset

Total employees: 13,400

Membership: BITC, LBG

Charitable donations

UK cash (latest declared):	2011	£1,400,000
	2009	£1,600,000
	2008	£3,400,000
	2007	£1,400,000
	2005	£1,200,000
Total UK:	2011	£1,400,000
Total worldwide:	2011	£4,000,000
Cash worldwide:	2011	£4,000,000

Community involvement

The company's focus is on issues connected to its business, such as the armed forces and their families and science, technology, engineering and mathematics education.

As well as one-off support the company undertakes longer projects that help charities plan their work further in advance. This includes its Relationship Charity Awards (in the UK) that fund specific projects for up to five years.

The company states that its community investment benefits charities and its business by helping build good relationships with local communities and by contributing to employee development and job satisfaction.

Corporate giving

During 2011, the amount donated for charitable purposes in the UK was £1.4 million (2010 £1.5 million). In line with the Company Giving strategy, this included:

£911,000 given to armed forces charities, with major donations being made to ABF The Soldiers' Charity, Combat Stress, Erskine Hospital, Soldiers, Sailors, Airmen and Families Association (SSAFA) Forces Help, and The Royal British Legion; £461,000 donated to education charities, including donations to Arkwright Scholarships Trust, Engineering Development Trust, Furness Academy, Smallpeice Trust, Enthuse Charitable Trust and The Prince's Trust; with the remaining £71,000 donated for other charitable purposes, including the advance of health and culture/heritage.

Employee-led support

Where possible, volunteering is integrated into formal career development programmes. Examples include, running a careers advice session at a local school or providing health and safety training for a local charity. Employees are also regularly involved in a range of individual or team volunteering projects such as helping out in local schools and packing Christmas boxes for injured armed forces personnel and their families.

A number of staff give time and energy to support local community programmes involving education and training (such as job shadowing/work experience and mentoring schemes), and the development of local business enterprise initiatives. Staff are also seconded to charities and enterprise projects, through the individual business units rather than head office.

Matched funding: The company matches employee fundraising and has a matching scheme for hours spent by employees volunteering (up to an allocated amount).

Education: The company is involved in a range of projects to promote better understanding between industry and education at national and local level. It aims to strengthen its links with a number of schools, technology colleges and universities.

Payroll giving: Various payroll deduction schemes are operated in some parts of the business.

Commercially-led support

Sponsorship: Sponsorship is undertaken; contact the community team for information.

Corporate social responsibility

CSR committee: There is a Subscriptions and Donations Committee.

CSR policy: The following statement is taken from the company's website:

> *Supporting communities*
> Charities, schools and not-for-profit organisations make a hugely valuable contribution to society. We support their work through donations and sponsorships, by encouraging employees to share their time and expertise as volunteers and by supporting employee fundraising.

CSR report: CSR report is published within the annual report and accounts.

Applications

In writing to the correspondent. The committee meets quarterly. Local appeals are handled by the regional site managers.

Bain and Company Inc. United Kingdom

Business services, financial services, healthcare, industrial products/services, media, metals, mining, oil and gas/ fuel, aviation, property, telecommunications

Correspondent: Company Secretary, 40 Strand, London WC2N 5RW (tel: 020 7969 6000; fax: 020 7969 6666; website: www.bain.com)

Director: S. Min, Director

Year end	31/12/2011

Nature of business: Bain and Company is one of the world's leading global strategy consulting firms, serving clients across six continents.

Company registration number: FC014328

Main locations: London

Membership: BITC

Applications

In writing to the correspondent.

Other information

Although Bain do not give grants, the level of in kind support is significant and warrants inclusion here.

Employee Challenge Fund

This has been established to enable one-off activities to be sponsored through the participation of London 'Bainies' in team-based challenges.

- *Education*: This involves employees in a variety of programmes including in-depth mentoring of secondary students, and one-on-one reading programmes with primary schoolchildren and mentoring through the Princes' Youth Trust
- *Homelessness*: The company has had an ongoing working relationship with Business Action on Homelessness for a number of years. A recent example of this involved small teams of Bain volunteers creating a website
- *Capital Cares*: Bain is a founder member of the organisation which aims 'to create a step change in quantity and quality of employee volunteering in the UK'. This initiative has enabled employees to volunteer to undertake activities such as cleaning up the Thames or gardening at homeless shelters
- *Pro Bono Consulting*: Bain aims to make a significant case team investment (on average every two years) on important social issues. Work has been carried out alongside Business Action on Homelessness, and the World Faiths Development Dialogue
- *Not for profit capacity building: Sounding Board, London* – This innovative program teams the company's partners and managers with CEOs of UK charities to provide an informal channel for expert input into their toughest challenges. In addition, it offers seminars. The company currently works with nearly 20 of the leading charities in the UK from sectors as diverse as health, poverty relief, homelessness and education
- *Support*: Bain also provides support – financial, marketing, advisory – to foundations such as Fulbright, the Voices Foundation and the Wellbeing Trust

Bain Cares

Bain's London office encourages and facilitates its employees to contribute their time and skills to community work through the 'Bain Cares' community involvement programme. This has three key areas:

- Education
- Homelessness
- High impact volunteering

Further significant in kind investment is made through pro bono consulting on important social issues. Over 70% of the employees in Bain's London office are included in the community programme.

Payroll giving: The firm operate a payroll giving scheme through which small charities with which Bain employees are affiliated are supported.

Balfour Beatty plc

Business services

Correspondent: Corporate Communications Department, Cavendish House, Cross Street, Sale, Manchester M33 7BU (tel: 01619 727500/020 7216 6800; email: bbfutures@balfourbeatty.com; website: www.bbfutures.org)

Directors: Steve Marshall, Chair; Ian Tyler, Chief Executive; Anthony Rabin; Duncan McGrath, Chief Finance Officer; Andrew McNaughton; Peter Zinkin (women: 0; men: 6)

Year end	31/12/2011
Turnover	£11,035,000,000
Pre-tax profit	£246,000,000

Nature of business: Provider of services to infrastructure owners operating in professional services, construction services, support services and infrastructure investments.

Company registration number: 2818602

Total employees: 50,195

Membership: BITC

Charitable donations

UK cash (latest declared):	2011	£500,000
	2009	£2,500,000
Total UK:	2011	£500,000
Total worldwide:	2011	£500,000
Cash worldwide:	2011	£500,000

Community involvement

The following information is taken from the 2011 Sustainability Report:

> *Corporate Community Policy and Theme:*
> In recent years, our plc community and charity programmes have focused entirely on helping young people, particularly those suffering from some form of disadvantage, to raise their aspirations, achievement levels and quality of life. These objectives have been expressed in a number of ways.
>
> Balfour Beatty has been lead sponsor and corporate partner to the London Youth Games since 2008. During that time participation levels in the multi-sport programme have more than tripled and the participation of young disabled people

and of those from ethnic minorities has risen by a factor of five.

The Company has operated in partnership with The Prince's Trust for over five years in their Get Into Construction scheme to offer disadvantage young people training and jobs in the infrastructure sector. In this period over 200 courses have been run and some 3,000 young people have been given the basic skills to take up training or jobs in the industry.

In late 2008, the Company formed its own charitable trust, 'Building Better Futures', through which it has donated over £1.5 million to young people's charities over the last three years. Among the causes supported in this time has been the installation of specialist play equipment in homes for disabled children; grants for tools, clothes and equipment to help young people find work; cash awards for groups of young people with good ideas to help the workings of their local community, practical help for 18-year-olds leaving long-term institutional care and support for adoption services for 'hard-to-place' children in need of a new family.

2011 Review

A major review of our Group-wide policies and practices was carried out and a new structure for corporate policy and purpose has been developed to take account of the Group's increasing size and geographical spread and to fulfil our desire to align our community programmes more closely with key social issues and our core business activities.

Our plans for 2012

Following our strategic review in 2011 we will launch Balfour Beatty Building Better Futures in 2012. This will integrate common themes across the business in terms of:

- Employability and employment of young people
- Helping the most disadvantaged young people in society
- Health, sport and wellbeing

Balfour Beatty Charitable Trust

(Charity Commission no. 1127453) was established in the company's centenary year (2009), to advance in life and relieve the needs of young people suffering from disadvantage by assisting with the provision of advice, training and education and other activities. The trust can also support general charitable purposes.

'Through the trust, branded Building Better Futures, the company has worked principally in partnership with Action for Children, and The Prince's Trust to deliver a series of programmes aimed at helping disadvantaged young people.

The 2011 Sustainability Report provides the following information:

Beatty has built a long-term partnership with Action for Children and provides funding and volunteering support to young carers, enabling them to take well-earned breaks from the enormous day-to-day responsibilities they face in caring for relatives at home. We also support the care leavers' programme which provides practical support in helping young people through a very difficult phase in their lives, when they move away from home into their own independent accommodation.

During 2011, 97 trips were organised for young carers, with over 2,000 children and young people participating and, in the year, 140 care leavers were provided with essential tools to help them move successfully into independent living.

Balfour Beatty part funds the services provided by Coram, the UK's most successful charity adoption service. Coram consistently has an almost perfect success rate in finding permanent, loving homes for children who prove to be particularly hard to place. Critical to the programme's success is the emphasis on post-adoption support and care, ensuring families have what they need to help their families thrive.

Charity of the Year: Action for Children

Corporate giving

No figure could be found for corporate giving in 2011/12, however, we know that £1.5 million has been donated to young people's charities over the last three years through its charitable trust. We have therefore taken the figure of £500,000 as the company's cash donation in this financial year.

Employee-led support

The company has stated that in 2012 it will also be focusing on building a volunteering culture and will be conducting a group-wide review to help achieve this.

Commercially-led support

Sponsorship: Balfour Beatty continues to sponsor the London Youth Games, Europe's largest youth sports programme.

Corporate social responsibility

CSR committee: No specific details found.

CSR policy: Taken from the Sustainability Report 2011:

We launched our 2020 sustainability vision in 2009. It identifies three broad areas for co-ordinated action: profitable markets, healthy communities and environmental limits. We believe that a truly sustainable way of conducting our business will:

- Help our customers reach their own sustainability goals
- Increase returns for shareholders through profitable growth in the green economy
- Create a better place for our employees to develop and prosper, and
- Provide infrastructure which benefits the wider community and the environment.

CSR report: A Sustainability report is published annually.

Applications

In writing to the Corporate Communications department.

J. C. Bamford Excavators Ltd

Plant equipment

Correspondent: Company Secretary, Lakeside Works, Denstone Road, Rocester, Uttoxeter, Staffordshire ST14 5JP (tel: 01889 590312; website: www.jcb.com)

Directors: Sir Anthony Bamford; Lady Bamford; A. R. Blake; J. C. E. Bamford; G. A. Macdonald (women: 1; men: 4)

Year end	31/12/2010
Turnover	£371,800,000
Pre-tax profit	(£5,600,000)

Nature of business: The company manufactures heavy construction and agricultural equipment.

Company registration number: 561597

Total employees: 1,139

Charitable donations

UK cash (latest declared):	2009	£100,000
	2008	£400,000
	2006	£200,000
	2005	£200,000
	2004	£2,000,000
Total worldwide:	2010	£400,000
Cash worldwide:	2010	£400,000

Corporate social responsibility

CSR committee: No specific committee.

CSR policy: None published.

CSR report: None published.

Applications

For the company: to the Company Secretary: For the Foundation: to the Foundation's Administrator, The Bamford Charitable Foundation at the company's address. Trustees meet informally on a regular basis. Requests for assistance are considered by the trustees and grants are approved where necessary. One formal trustees' meeting is held each year.

Other information

In 2010 the company made charitable donations of £400,000 (2009: £100,000). We have no details of beneficiary organisations.

The Bamford Charitable Foundation

The Bamford Charitable Foundation (Charity Commission no. 279848), aims to make grants to applicants whose activities are charitable, in particular those within a 40 mile radius of Rocester, Staffordshire. The foundation's principal source of income is generated from its endowment fund.

In 2009/10 income was £44,000 and grants committed were £244,000. Grants were made to 26 organisations, with 20 of these being for amounts over £1,000. Beneficiaries included: Denstone Foundation (£60,000); Louis Dundas Centre (£50,000); The Stroke Association (£15,000); English National Ballet School (£10,000); and Society for Welfare of Horses and Ponies (£1,000).

Bank of England

Banking

Correspondent: Linda Barnard, Community Relations Manager, Threadneedle Street, London EC2R 8AH (tel: 020 7601 4444/020 7601 4329; email: charity@bankofengland.co.uk; website: www.bankofengland.co.uk)

Directors: Mervyn King; Charlie Bean; Paul Tucker; David Lees; Brendan Barber; Roger Carr; Lady Susan Rice; Adair Turner; Mark Tucker; Harrison Young; John Stewart (women: 1; men: 10)

Year end	28/02/2011
Turnover	£547,000,000
Pre-tax profit	£132,000,000

Nature of business: The Bank of England is the central bank of the United Kingdom. The bank is based in London and has agencies in Belfast, Birmingham, Bristol, Cambridge, Exeter, Glasgow, Leeds, Liverpool, Manchester, Newcastle, Nottingham, Southampton, and Greater London.

Company registration number: RC000042

Main locations: Belfast, Birmingham, Leeds, Cardiff, Cambridge, Bristol, Exeter, Gloucester, Glasgow, Southampton, Newcastle-on-Tyne, Loughton, Manchester, Liverpool, London, Nottingham

UK employees: 1,839

Total employees: 1,839

Charitable donations

UK cash (latest declared):	2011	£352,000
	2010	£384,000
	2009	£331,000
	2008	£343,000
	2007	£410,000
Total UK:	2011	£670,000
Total worldwide:	2011	£670,000
Cash worldwide:	2011	£352,000

Corporate social responsibility

CSR committee: The Community Relations team focuses on programmes aimed at overcoming social disadvantage and diversity issues.

CSR policy: This information was obtained from the company's CSR report:

> The Bank of England aims to be a socially responsible employer through encouraging its staff to be involved in community initiatives and be recognising their involvement. We aim to achieve this by:
>
> - Encouraging staff to become involved in community initiatives both through their own efforts and through a range of programmes managed by the bank;
> - Focusing donations on organisations that are supported by staff;
> - Supporting the local community links of the bank's regional agencies;
> - Providing benefits in kind to the voluntary sector.

CSR report: A full CSR report is available from the company's website.

Exclusions

No support is given towards expeditions, holidays, orchestras, conferences, overseas work, organisations of a political nature, religious activities (unless they benefit the wider community), appeals from individuals, choirs, theatres, churches, animals or third-party fundraising.

Applications

Donations can be made locally at the discretion of the branch agent and subject to a limited budget. Otherwise, appeals should be addressed to the correspondent.

Other information

During 2010/11 the bank contributed an estimated total of £670,000 in support of its community programme (2009/10: £640,000). Cash donations totalled £352,000 (2009/10: £384,000), including: £32,000 donated to 66 charities via the **payroll giving scheme**.

Arthritis Research Campaign and the Still Death and Neonatal Death Society received £33,640 from fundraising activities (the bank matched to the tune of £20,000).

The bank may grant staff paid leave to perform voluntary duties in the community.

Bank of Ireland UK Financial Services Ltd

Financial services

Correspondent: Corporate Responsibility Officer, PO Box 27, Temple Quay, Bristol BS99 7AX (tel: 01179 437207; email: PCB@boi.com; website: www.bank-of-ireland.co.uk)

Directors: Patrick Molloy; Dennis Holt; Richie Boucher, Group Chief Executive; Des Crowley, Chief Executive Officer; Denis Donovan, Chief Executive; John O'Donovan; Tom Considine; Paul Haran; Rose Hynes; Jerome Kennedy; Patrick Kennedy; Heather Ann McSharry; Patrick O'Sullivan; Joe Walsh (women: 2; men: 12)

Year end	31/12/2010
Turnover	£786,200,000

Nature of business: Financial services.

Company registration number: 2124201

Main locations: Bristol

Total employees: 14,284

Membership: BITC

Charitable donations

Total UK:		£3,625,000
Total worldwide:	2010	£3,625,000

Corporate social responsibility

CSR committee: There was no evidence of a separate CSR committee.

CSR policy: The information available from the annual report mentioned the Give Together scheme but did not stipulate any specific charitable figures for 2010.

CSR report: There was no evidence of a CSR report.

Exclusions

No support is given to appeals from individuals, general appeals, religious appeals, overseas travel, arts and sports projects with no community or charitable element, or medical research, equipment or treatment.

Applications

In writing to the correspondent. As part of the Give Together initiative, the bank is operating a database of organisations that are interested making volunteering opportunities known to Bank of Ireland employees. If you would like opportunities for your organisation to be included, send the details by post-to: The Give Together Initiative, Bank of Ireland Group, 5th Floor, Baggot Street, Dublin 2, or email to givetogether@boimail.com.

Other information

In March 2007 Bank of Ireland Group introduced a new community initiative, which has changed the way they contribute to charitable organisations and community groups. The concept was developed following a detailed review of Bank of Ireland's community investment, where one of the main findings was that valuable work being done by employees could be enhanced if encouraged and supported by the bank.

As a result, the bank decided to channel the community investment into facilitating and supporting employee activities through a new initiative called Give Together. The Give Together initiative was established to support employees who wish to volunteer their time and support causes which are important to them. It involves a commitment by the Bank of Ireland to give each employee one day's leave per year to volunteer their time to a cause of their choice. The bank has also put in place a fund for materials and equipment to support these endeavours and which allows the Bank of Ireland to contribute to employees fundraising achievements.

Since 2007 with the support of Give Together, over £14.5 million has invested in more than 1,300 community organisations, including over 700 in 2010. We have divided this investment amount by the number of years the initiative has been running to give an overall community contribution figure for 2010.

'Many of the bank's previous methods of corporate giving are now incorporated into the Give Together initiative.'

The UK Financial Services Division incorporates Business Banking in Great Britain and Northern Ireland, the branch network in Northern Ireland, the UK residential mortgage business and the joint ventures with the Post-Office, namely Post-Office Financial and Travel Services. Financial figures given here relate to the UK Financial Services only, contained within the accounts of the Bank of Ireland which are for a nine month period.

The Banks Group

Mining

Correspondent: Grants and Development Manager, Banks Community Fund, West Cornforth, Ferryhill, Durham DL17 9EU (tel: 0844 209 1515; fax: 0844 209 1565; website: www.hjbanks.com)

Directors: H. J. Banks; R. J. Dunkley; N. A. Brown; G. A. Styles; S. R. Tonks

Year end	30/09/2011
Turnover	£54,604,000
Pre-tax profit	£2,099,000

Nature of business: Opencast coal mining and the development of interests in land.

Company registration number: 2267400

UK employees: 364

Total employees: 364

Charitable donations

UK cash (latest declared):	2011	£14,200
	2009	£21,000
	2007	£22,000
Total UK:	2011	£14,200
Total worldwide:	2011	£14,200
Cash worldwide:	2011	£14,200

Corporate social responsibility

CSR committee: The Banks Group has a dedicated community team working within the communities closest to its sites providing information to local people, and identifying community projects that may benefit from The Banks Community Fund.

CSR policy: The following is taken from the group's website and mainly refers to liaison with the community over the group's property development proposals:

> Development with care is central to the aims and objectives of our business. The phrase ideally describes how we interact with people inside and outside our company and it is the guiding principle of the way we carry out our business at all times.
>
> - To inform the local community or its representatives of our intentions to ensure they have an opportunity to respond to our proposals
> - For our schemes to provide tangible benefits to local people, maximising both community and environmental benefits
> - To encourage open channels of communication with the community throughout the life of the scheme
> - To be transparent with regard to environmental and planning issues
> - To involve the community in the design stages of our proposals where possible

We were unable to determine the ratio of women to men on the Board.

CSR report: Some information regarding Banks Community Fund is given on the website.

Exclusions

No support for individuals, political or religious appeals.

Applications

In writing to the correspondent.

Further information is available at: www.bankscommunityfund.org.uk

Please note that County Durham Foundation administers the Landfill Communities Fund on behalf of the Banks Community Fund.

Other information

In the 2010/11 annual report and accounts, £14,200 was declared as the group's cash charitable donations.

The Banks Group supports local community groups, sports clubs and voluntary organisations, offering practical advice and assistance where possible. It also provides a range of educational opportunities to local schools, colleges and universities. The Banks Group has a community team working within the communities closest to the company's sites. Part of its role is to identify community projects that may benefit from Banks' site specific community benefits funds. In addition to the above, there is also the Banks Community Fund which supports local environmental and community improvement projects in the areas surrounding Banks Group's operations. Monies for this come via the Landfill Communities Fund, wind farm developments and property developments.

Barclays plc

Banking

Correspondent: Board Citizenship Committee, Community Affairs, 1 Churchill Place, Canary Wharf, London E14 5HP (tel: 020 7116 1000; website: www.barclays.com)

Directors: Andrew Likierman; John Sunderland; Fulvio Conti; David Booth; Reuben Jeffery III; Simon Fraser; Chris Lucas; Marcus Agius; Alison Carnwarth; Dambisa Moyo; Michael Rake; David Walker, Chair; Antony Jenkins, Chief Executive (women: 2; men: 10)

Year end	31/12/2011
Turnover	£20,589,000,000
Pre-tax profit	£5,879,000,000

Nature of business: Barclays plc is a UK-based financial services group engaged primarily in the banking and investment banking businesses. In terms of assets employed, Barclays is one of the biggest financial service groups in the UK. The group also operates in many other countries around the world.

Company registration number: 48839

Subsidiaries include: FIRSTPLUS Financial Group plc, Charles Schwab Europe, Woolwich plc, Gerrard Management Services Ltd

Brands include: Barclaycard, FirstPlus, Woolwich

Main locations: London

Total employees: 34,100

Membership: BITC, LBG

Charitable donations

UK cash (latest declared):	2011	£22,600,000
	2009	£19,300,000
	2008	£19,600,000
	2007	£30,400,000
	2006	£35,200,000
Total UK:	2011	£30,300,000
Total worldwide:	2011	£63,500,000
Cash worldwide:	2011	£58,200,000

Community involvement

Barclays provides funding and support to over 8,000 charities and voluntary organisations, ranging from small, local charities, to international organisations.

The following information is taken from the 2011 annual report and accounts:

> *Supporting our communities*
>
> Our role in the communities goes far beyond what we deliver through our core business activities. The future success of communities and economies is reliant on the next generation having the right skills. We focus on empowering young people with the necessary financial, entrepreneurial and life skills to achieve financial independence and security. In 2011, we invested £63.5 million in community programmes which reached over two million people. These activities were supported by 73,000 colleagues who

donated their time, skills and money to support community causes.

Two million people in 33 countries were supported through Barclays community investment activities, of which: 745,000 benefited from financial capability programmes; over 43,000 received employability skills training and over 4,300 benefited from work experience placements.

Our programmes aim to empower disadvantaged young people with the skills they need to achieve financial independence, security for themselves and their families and the ability to contribute positively to the economy. They fall into three categories:

- Financial skills help young people manage their money more effectively to avoid unmanageable debt and have the confidence to plan for the future
- Enterprise skills help young people set up their own business to provide for themselves, and support the growth of the wider economy
- Life skills such as literacy, numeracy, communications and team-working skills enable young people to improve their prospects for employment and play a full role in society

Barclays has an excellent website where its community programmes are described giving detailed information regarding its charitable giving and staff contributions.

Corporate giving

In 2011, the group committed £30.3 million in support of the community in the UK (2010: £28.6 million), including donations of £22.6 million (2010: £22.9 million). £63.6 million was invested globally in community programmes which reached over two million people.

Some of the projects/organisations to benefit from the bank's support were: Bikeworks, Bromley by Bow Centre, CARE International UK, Spaces for Sports, Unicef and You Can B.

In kind support

Community Placements: This scheme introduces former Barclays employees (who have recently left the bank either through retirement or a redundancy package) to voluntary organisations which would benefit from the individual's financial skills and knowledge, and which fit within the focus of the bank's community programme.

Employee-led support

In 2011, 73,000 colleagues – nearly half the workforce – supported community activity through volunteering, fundraising and regular giving.

Barclays states that because of the wide range of organisations (national and local) its employees want to support, its approach has always been not to limit help to a single 'adopted' charity. Employees are therefore supported in their choices in a variety of ways.

Volunteering: Staff wishing to provide practical help to charities and community groups can apply for grants through its employee volunteering scheme. Additionally, the 'Volunteer 2day scheme' allows staff at least two days of Barclays time each year in which to volunteer. In 2011, 418,000 hours were given in support of volunteering activities.

Charities or community groups which think they would benefit from Barclays volunteer support through the 'Make a Difference Day' are encouraged to email the bank's local community team. Organised by Community Service Volunteers (CSV), a leading volunteering charity, it encourages people to give their time and skills, not their money, to play an active role in community life. Barclays has been one of the largest corporate contributors of volunteers and in 2011, 20,620 colleagues from 32 countries took part.

In addition, the Barclays Citizenship Awards recognise those who have made an outstanding contribution to their communities. The Awards recognise and celebrate employees' activities to support their communities.

Matched funding

Barclays matched fundraising scheme allows thousands of Barclays colleagues across the globe to raise money for their favourite charities and have their fundraising total matched by Barclays up to £750 (or local equivalent). Barclays will match the fundraising efforts of colleagues up to three times per year. In 2011, £24 million was raised through our matched fundraising programme, with over 21,000 employees taking part in fundraising events.

Colleagues who gather a group of five or more volunteers can apply for a grant of up to £500 to go towards materials and expenses for their project.

Payroll giving: Barclays operates the Pennies from Heaven payroll giving scheme.

Give As You Earn is also in operation for employees. 15,000 employees were involved in regular payroll giving throughout 2011, donating over £4 million to charities (including Barclays matching).

Commercially-led support

Sponsorship: – Arts and good-cause sponsorship is ONLY undertaken at regional level.

Sport – Barclays Spaces for Sports is a global programme bringing sports sites and projects to disadvantaged communities. It focuses on regeneration and sports, creating sustainable sports sites for people to engage in sport and physical activities in areas without such facilities. In the UK, 200 community sports sites have been created in partnership with the Football Foundation, supporting more than 40 different sports. For full information visit: www.barclays.com/community/spacesforsports

Corporate social responsibility

CSR committee: Board Citizenship Committee:

> In 2011, we strengthened our governance framework by creating a Board Citizenship Committee as a formal sub-committee of our Board of Directors. The committee is chaired by Group Chairman Marcus Agius and includes two non-executive Directors.
>
> Progress against our priorities is reviewed regularly and will be formally assessed at least twice yearly by the Board Citizenship Committee and the Executive Committee. A range of management committees are responsible for specific aspects of Citizenship performance.

CSR policy: CSR information taken from the 2011 annual report and accounts:

> Citizenship is one of Barclays four execution priorities and is integral to our business. In the first instance, Citizenship is about contributing to growth in the real economy, creating jobs and supporting sustainable growth. Second, it is about the way we do business: putting our customers' interests at the heart of what we do, and managing our impact responsibly. Third, it is about supporting our communities through investment programmes and the direct efforts of our employees.

CSR report: There is a citizenship report published within the annual report and accounts.

Exclusions

Barclays will not support the following:

- Political parties or bodies
- Promotion of religious beliefs
- Sponsorship of individuals
- Rotary, Lion Clubs and other third-party giving organisations
- Hospital costs for individuals
- Medical treatment and medical research
- Capital appeals (for example, for buildings)
- The arts (unless the donation provides direct support to a disadvantaged group)
- Micro-finance loan fund capital (donations can be used to support the establishment and operation of community motivated micro-finance programmes, but cannot be used as capital for on-lending direct to clients)

Applications

Enquiries/appeals to head office should be sent to the correspondent.

A. G. Barr plc

Drinks manufacture

Correspondent: Marie Holcroft, 2nd Floor Mansell House, Aspinall Close, Middlebrook, Horwich, Bolton BL6 6QQ (tel: 01236 852400; fax: 01236 852477; website: www.agbarr.co.uk)

Directors: Ronald G. Hanna, Chair; Roger A. White, Chief Executive; Martin Griffiths; Alex Short; Andrew Memmott; Jonathan Kemp; W. Robin G. Barr; Jonathan Warburton (women: 0; men: 8)

Year end	20/01/2011
Turnover	£222,000,000
Pre-tax profit	£31,600,000

Nature of business: The group trades principally as a manufacturer, distributor and seller of soft drinks.

Company registration number: SC005653

Brands include: IRN-BRU; KA; Orangina; Rubicon; Strathmore Water; Tizer

Main locations: Cumbernauld, Moston, Pitcox, Bolton, Mansfield, Newcastle, Wembley, Tredegar, Sheffield, Forfar, Walthamstow, Wednesbury

Charitable donations

UK cash (latest declared):	2011	£225,850
	2010	£170,000
	2009	£113,000
Total UK:	2011	£225,850
Total worldwide:	2011	£225,850
Cash worldwide:	2011	£225,850

Corporate social responsibility

CSR committee: There was no evidence of a separate CSR Committee.

CSR policy: The following information is taken from the CSR section of the website:

> We are committed to playing both a supportive and an active role in the community by providing financial, in kind, practical and staff volunteering support to charitable organisations, good causes and community groups at both a local and national level.
>
> 1% of our profits are utilised in supporting charities, good causes and community activities.
>
> Corporate responsibility at Barr is neither a new thing nor a separate programme of activity – it is part of what we believe makes good business sense.
>
> Corporate Responsibility is an integral part of our overall business and remains one of the 7 core areas of our strategic focus.

CSR report: There was no evidence of a separate CSR report.

Applications

In writing to the correspondent.

Community in kind donations: The following statement is taken from the company's website:

> Over the years we have assisted many thousands of community groups, charities and good causes with donations of Barr Soft drinks products and merchandise in order to help them raise much needed funds. If you would like to approach us for a product or merchandise (subject to availability) donation then can you please send us your request in writing detailing some background information on your group, what event or activity you would like us to support, when the event or activity is happening and exactly what level of support you are looking for. Due to the high number of requests that we receive can you please allow 4 to 6 weeks for us to respond on whether or not we will be able to assist you. It is our intention always to respond with an answer to every request for assistance that we receive.

Email marieholcroft@agbarr.co.uk or send a written request to: Marie Holcroft, A. G. Barr plc, 2nd Floor Mansell House, Aspinall Close, Middlebrook, Horwich, Bolton BL6 6QQ.

Other information

In 2010/11 there appears to be no record of donations to charitable causes (2009/10: £170,000). However, we have estimated that the company gives 1% of after-tax profit to charitable causes as this is what the company suggests they give annually. With this in mind, we can estimate that the company made donations of £225,850 in this financial year.

In 2010/11, beneficiaries of the company's support included: The Prince's Trust, Lenzie Academy – East Dunbartonshire, Sporting Heroes for the Future, Westfield Primary School – Cumbernauld and TAUT 100. The company also provided funding for kits and equipment to six cycling and four swimming clubs throughout Scotland.

Barratt Developments plc

Building/construction

Correspondent: See 'Applications', Barratt Developments plc, Barratt House, Cartwright Way, Forest Business Park, Bardon Hill, Coalville (tel: 01530 278278; fax: 01530 278279; website: www.barrattdevelopments.co.uk)

Directors: Robert Lawson, Chair; Mark Clare, Group Chief Executive; Robert Davies; Tessa Bamford; David Thomas; Steven Boyes; Clive Fenton; Roderick MacEachrane; Mark Rolfe (women: 1; men: 8)

Year end	30/06/2011
Turnover	£2,035,400,000
Pre-tax profit	£42,700,000

Nature of business: The group's principal activities comprise house building and commercial development.

Company registration number: 5688068

UK employees: 4,405

Total employees: 4,405

Charitable donations

UK cash (latest declared):	2011	£45,700
	2009	£28,300
	2008	£53,300
	2007	£22,900
Total UK:	2011	£45,700
Total worldwide:	2011	£45,700
Cash worldwide:	2011	£45,700

Corporate social responsibility

CSR committee: There was no evidence of a separate CSR Committee.

CSR policy: Previous CSR reports have noted that a charitable giving charter has been established which:

- Links charitable giving to major developments and nearby local charities
- Supports employees who engage in charitable and voluntary work
- Has embedded community activity in its graduate development programmes

However, there is no CSR report available for this financial year and no evidence of the charitable giving charter.

CSR report: CSR information was found within the company's annual report.

Applications

National charities should contact the marketing department at: Barrett Developments plc, Kent House, 1st Floor, 14–17 Market Place, London W1W 8AJ. (Tel: 020 7299 4898).

Local charities should contact the nearest regional office.

Other information

During the year the group made charitable donations of £45,700 (2010: £36,100). Of the donations in the current year £5,000 was to the University College London Hospitals Charitable Foundation and the remainder was to local and good causes.

BASF plc

Chemicals and plastics

Correspondent: Company Secretary, PO Box 4, Earl Road, Cheadle Hulme, Cheshire SK8 6QG (tel: 01614 856222; fax: 01614 860891; website: www.basf.co.uk)

Directors: T. B. Jensen; S. Hatton; G. A. Thomson; G. M. Mackey; T. Urwin; J. Delmiotiez

Year end	31/12/2011
Turnover	£571,342,000
Pre-tax profit	£6,503,000

Nature of business: Chemicals, paints, plastics, pharmaceuticals.

Company registration number: 667980

Subsidiaries include: Elastogram UK Ltd

Main locations: Wantage, Cheadle, Deeside, Manchester, Woolpit, Middlesbrough, Ruddington, Cinderford, London, Nottingham, Alfreton

Total employees: 391

Charitable donations

UK cash (latest declared):	2011	£220,500
	2009	£51,000
	2008	£91,000
Total UK:	2011	£220,500
Total worldwide:	2011	£220,500
Cash worldwide:	2011	£220,500

Corporate social responsibility

CSR policy: No CSR details available for this company.

We were unable to determine the ratio of women to men on the board.

Applications

In writing to the correspondent for national appeals. For local appeals contact the nearest relevant site.

Other information

In 2011, BASF made charitable donations in the UK of £220,500 (2010: £37,000). We have no details of the beneficiaries.

Baxter Healthcare Ltd

Healthcare

Correspondent: The Company Secretary, Wallington, Compton, Newbury, Berkshire RG20 7QW (tel: 01635 206000; fax: 01635 206115; website: www.baxterhealthcare.co.uk)

Directors: G. E. Braham; H. P. Keenan

Year end	31/12/2010
Turnover	£138,172,000
Pre-tax profit	£15,241,000

Nature of business: Technologies related to the blood and circulatory system.

Company registration number: 461365

Main locations: Thetford, Stockport, Liverpool, Northampton, Newbury, Oxford

Total employees: 1,193

Charitable donations

UK cash (latest declared):	2010	£16,000
	2009	£15,000
	2008	£29,000
Total UK:	2010	£16,000
Total worldwide:	2010	£16,000
Cash worldwide:	2010	£16,000

Corporate social responsibility

CSR committee: Not known.

CSR policy: Taken from the Baxter International Inc. website: 'We define sustainability as a long-term approach to including our social, economic and environmental responsibilities among our business priorities. Baxter's efforts in this area align with and support our mission of saving and sustaining lives.'

The ratio of women to men on the board is not known.

CSR report: None for this UK company.

Applications

To be considered for support from the foundation, registered charities must be nominated by a Baxter employee, not via unsolicited applications, and be eligible under the foundations guidelines. Details of the latter can be found at www.baxter.com.

Other information

In 2010 the UK company made charitable donations totalling £16,000 of which £3,600 was given to Comic Relief.

Support is only given to registered charities. Charities are sometimes nominated by a Baxter employee, especially if they operate in an area where there is a Baxter facility, or where a large number of Baxter employees live. In the UK, assistance is only given in the areas where the company operates. Currently, these are Liverpool, Newbury, Northampton, Oxford, Stockport and Thetford.

Baxters Food Group Ltd

Food manufacture

Correspondent: Peter McLuckie, Secretary, Highfield House, Fochabers, Moray, Scotland IV32 7LD (tel: 01343 820393; email: info@baxters.co.uk; website: www.baxters.com)

Directors: Audrey Baxter, Executive Chair; William King, Chief Executive; Andrew Baxter; Nicholas Wheater (women: 1; men: 3)

Year end	28/05/2011
Turnover	£125,844,000
Pre-tax profit	£7,066,000

Nature of business: The manufacture of high quality, ambient, chilled and frozen food, supply retail and foodservice customers in the UK and key overseas markets.

Company registration number: SC23572

UK employees: 925

Total employees: 925

Charitable donations

UK cash (latest declared):	2011	£15,360
	2009	£6,000
	2007	£128,000
	2006	£174,000
Total UK:	2011	£15,360
Total worldwide:	2011	£15,360
Cash worldwide:	2011	£15,360

Corporate social responsibility

CSR committee: There was no evidence of a separate CSR Committee.

CSR policy: Information relating to CSR was difficult to obtain from the company's website. Previous entries from the database noted that charitable donations had been previously made to The Baxters Foundation.

The foundation's interests are in the relief of poverty, health, education, citizenship, community, development, the arts, heritage, culture, science, sports and recreation, and the environment.

The foundation benefits children and young people, older people, and people with disabilities or health problems.

CSR report: There was no evidence of a separate CSR report.

Applications

In writing to the trustees of The Baxters Foundation at the company's address.

Other information

In 2010/11, the company made charitable donations of £15,400 which went to the Baxters Foundation (Scottish Charity No. SC033432). No further information was available. The majority of the company's charitable support is directed through foundation which is based at the same address as the company. Support is given to both organisations and individuals. Although support is primarily given in Scotland, other areas of the UK may be considered.

Bayer plc

Chemicals and plastics

Correspondent: CSR Committee, Bayer House, Strawberry Hill, Newbury, Berkshire RG14 1JA (tel: 01635 563000; fax: 01635 563513; email: corporate.communications@bayer.co.uk; website: www.bayer.co.uk)

Directors: M. S. Dawkins; I. Paterson

Year end	31/12/2010
Turnover	£374,567,000
Pre-tax profit	£39,311,000

Nature of business: Marketing of healthcare and polymer products manufactured by Bayer Group companies, and the provision of administration services to group companies as well as their parties.

Company registration number: 935048

UK employees: 668

Total employees: 668

Charitable donations

UK cash (latest declared):	2010	£40,300
	2009	£11,000
Total UK:	2010	£40,300
Total worldwide:	2010	£40,300
Cash worldwide:	2010	£40,300

Corporate social responsibility

CSR committee: This information was obtained from the company's website:

> Our community support programme is overseen by a committee which aims to be professional, sympathetic, impartial and systematic. That must include a firm and clear statement of what we can and cannot support, subject to available funds and the balance of our existing community work.

CSR policy: This information was obtained from the company's website:

> Bayer has many responsibilities – one of which is to generate benefits for the communities in which we operate. This may happen through support at a national or international level, usually business linked and often driven by the needs of the community itself. Here in the UK/ Ireland, we also believe in the importance of local community support.

Unable to determine the ratio of women to men on the board.

CSR report: There was no evidence of a CSR report; however information was available from the company's website.

Exclusions

Bayer is unable to support:

- Individuals rather than group activities
- Religious, political or racially aligned movements
- Projects or activities bridging a gap in government or local authority funding
- Sporting or recreational activities unless closely associated to Bayer
- Entries in log books, year books or support advertising
- Projects of a local nature which are outside key locations of Newbury, Cambridge, Norwich and Dublin
- Conferences, lectures, trips, respite breaks or holidays
- National initiatives

Applications

Given that you meet Bayer's criteria, you will then need to complete the 'CSR Request Form' (available from their website). The information you provide will supply Bayer with the key details they require to make an informed decision regarding your proposal.

Post-your completed CSR Request Form and supporting materials to the correspondent. Alternatively, you can send it by email: corporate.communications@bayer.co.uk or by fax: 01635 563513.

Note that Bayer only accept postal, email or faxed requests and are unable to take telephone calls to discuss individual requests.

Bayer's committee reviews applications received on a monthly basis throughout the year. Bayer will contact you by email or letter to let you know if they are able to support you or not.

Other information

In 2010, Bayer gave £40,300 (2009: £11,000) in cash charitable donations. All community support is given through the Bayer Foundation, which donates primarily to healthcare related organisations.

The company's CR section on its website states:

> Bayer supports activities that are local to us and are:
>
> - Linked to our employees' own community activities
> - Linked to one of Bayer's 5,000 products or services
> - Specifically benefiting from Bayer's involvement
> - Beneficial to numbers or groups of people
>
> We support activities which enhance local quality of life through:
>
> - The environment
> - Community care
> - Culture and the arts
> - Education
> - Projects in line with our Mission Statement
> - Projects benefiting groups and not individuals
>
> While activities meeting the above criteria will be considered, they do not automatically qualify for support, as other factors (such as budget already committed) must be taken into account.

BBA Aviation plc

Engineering, transport and communications

Correspondent: Community Involvement and Charitable Giving, 20 Balderton Street, London W1K 6TL (tel: 020 7514 3999; fax: 020 7408 2318; email: info@bbaaviation.com; website: www.bbaaviation.com)

Directors: Michael Harper, Chair; Simon Pryce, Chief Executive; Mark Hoad; Nick Land; Mark Harper; Peter Ratcliffe; Hansel Tookes (women: 0; men: 7)

Year end	31/12/2010
Turnover	£1,183,000,000
Pre-tax profit	£95,400,000

Nature of business: At a glance:

> BBA Aviation maintains a balanced portfolio of aviation services and aftermarket businesses serving markets with attractive long-term growth opportunities. The business and general aviation (B&GA) market accounts for around two thirds of BBA Aviation's revenue, commercial aviation around one quarter of revenue, with the remainder coming from the military market.

Company registration number: 53688

Total employees: 10,049

Charitable donations

UK cash (latest declared):	2010	£76,000
	2009	£30,000
	2008	£26,000
Total UK:	2010	£76,000
Total worldwide:	2010	£371,000
Cash worldwide:	2010	£371,000

Corporate social responsibility

CSR committee: There was no evidence of a separate CSR Committee.

CSR policy: This information was obtained from the company's website:

> As well as supporting communities by encouraging local employment and careers and by using local facilities, all BBA Aviation businesses – through employees and on a more formal basis – play an active role in a variety of local, regional and national organisations and charities.

CSR report: There was no evidence of a separate CSR report, however there was one page dedicated to the community within the company's annual accounts.

Applications

In writing to the correspondent.

Other information

During the year 2010, group donations to charities worldwide were £371,000 (2009: £149,000) with UK charities receiving £76,000 (2009: £30,000).

The group's annual report for 2010 makes the following statement:

> Each of our sites and businesses recognises the importance of being a good neighbour and contributing to the community in which it operates. BBA Aviation's businesses play an active role in supporting a variety of local, regional and national organisations and charities. Local businesses identify charities and community projects in which they would like to be involved and, where appropriate, efforts are co-ordinated at a local or business level to deliver more meaningful support to a chosen activity. We are proud to play an active role in a variety of local activities and charities.

Shareholders with a small number of shares, the value of which makes it uneconomical to sell, may wish to consider donating them to charity through ShareGift, a registered charity.

The Group also launched its new parent company charitable giving programme during the year. BBA Aviation employees, on behalf of a charity, apply for a cash donation. During the year donations totalling £150,000 have been made via this programme.

Beneficiaries included: Princess Alice Hospice (£8,250), which will fund 95 visits of a community nurse to patients in the area, and Off the Record, which is an outreach and drop-in organisation with two centres supporting disadvantaged young people in the Portsmouth area. £15,000 was donated to provide further training and support for volunteers.

BC Partners Ltd

Financial services

Correspondent: Secretary, BCP Foundation, 40 Portman Square, London W1H 6DA (tel: 020 7009 4800/020 7009 4800; fax: 020 7009 4899; email: bcpfoundation@bcpartners.com; website: www.bcpartners.com)

Directors: S. Quadrio Curzio, Chair; R. Svider; M. A. Twinning

Year end	31/12/2010
Turnover	£88,355,085
Pre-tax profit	£9,606,580

Nature of business: Investment advisors to the managers of offshore funds for investment in principally unquoted companies.

Company registration number: 2020410

Total employees: 104

Charitable donations

UK cash (latest declared):	2010	£138,000
	2009	£136,000
	2008	£132,250
Total UK:	2010	£138,000
Total worldwide:	2010	£138,000
Cash worldwide:	2010	£138,000

Corporate social responsibility

CSR committee: There was no evidence of a CSR Committee.

CSR policy: There was no information available regarding CSR Policy.

Unable to determine the ratio of women to men on the board.

CSR report: There was no evidence of a CSR report.

Applications

In writing to the correspondent.

Other information

In 2010, BC Partners Ltd donated £138,000 (2009: £136,000) for charitable purposes. We have no information regarding the beneficiary groups. The company has established a foundation through which we believe it will channel its community investment.

BCP Foundation: Established in 2010 for general charitable purposes, the BCP Foundation (Charity Commission no. 1136956) is funded by the private equity firm BC Partners Ltd. The foundation's first accounts from 2010/11 show an income of £147,000, all of which came from the company.

Beazley plc

Insurance

Correspondent: PA to, Jonathan Gray, Plantation Place South, 60 Great Tower Street, London EC3R 5AD (tel: 020 7667 0623; fax: 020 7674 7100; email: info@beazley.ie; website: www.beazley.com)

Directors: Andrew Horton; Martin Bride; Adrian Cox; Jonathan Gray; Neil Maidment; Clive Washbourn; Jonathan Agnew; George Blunden; Gordon Hamilton; Padraic O'Connor; Vincent Sheridan; Ken Sroka (women: 0; men: 12)

Year end	31/12/2011
Turnover	£1,452,400,000
Pre-tax profit	£62,700,000

Nature of business: Beazley plc is a specialist underwriting business. Specialist areas include; professional indemnity, property, marine, reinsurance, accident and life, and political risks and contingency business.

Company registration number: 102680

Total employees: 805

Charitable donations

UK cash (latest declared):	2011	£57,500
	2010	£56,265
	2009	£53,000
	2008	£67,000
Total UK:	2011	£57,500
Total worldwide:	2011	£163,300
Cash worldwide:	2011	£105,800

Corporate social responsibility

CSR committee: The UK charity budget is managed by a charity committee chaired by Jonathan Gray and consideration is given to a wide range of activities, particularly where members of staff are engaged in fundraising activities.

CSR policy: This information was obtained from the company's annual report:

> Intrinsic to our culture is an ethical approach to business conducted by and towards all our stakeholders. The values that form the essence of our brand and our working culture are professionalism, integrity, effectiveness and dynamism.

CSR report: There was not a separate CSR report but there was a great deal of information available contained in the annual report.

Applications

In writing to the correspondent.

Other information

In 2011, the group made charitable donations in the UK of £57,500 (2010: £56,265). The group supports three chosen charities to which the committee donates an annual payment, Rwanda Aid (international), Concordia (local), Trees for Cities (ecological); as well as supporting staff in fundraising for their chosen charities.

> We encourage employee involvement in a range of community programmes across the group and each employee can take up to two days per year to participate in charitable and local community initiatives.
>
> Programmes for 2011 have mainly focused on voluntary schemes involving schools from East London. Beazley is involved in two schemes on a weekly basis. In 2012, a financial literacy workshop will be held at one of the participating schools, Canon Barnett in Tower Hamlets.

Payroll giving: The group runs a payroll-giving scheme in the UK in association with the Charities Aid Foundation. In 2011, 27 employees took part, donating £42,500 to 33 charities.

Bellway plc

Building/construction

Correspondent: G Kevin Wrightson, Company Secretary, Seaton Burn House, Dudley Lane, Seaton Burn, Newcastle upon Tyne NE13 6BE (tel: 01912 170717; fax: 01912 366230; email: julian.kenyon@bellway.co.uk; website: www.bellway.co.uk)

Directors: John K. Watson, Chair; Howard C. Dawe; Alistair M. Leitch; Edward (Ted) F. Ayres; Peter M. Johnson; Mike R. Toms; John A. Cuthbert (women: 0; men: 7)

Year end	31/07/2011
Turnover	£886,000,000
Pre-tax profit	£67,000,000

Nature of business: The company's main activity is house building.

Company registration number: 1372603

Main locations: Bedworth, Altrincham, Wetherby, Tamworth, Uxbridge, Wakefield, Ringwood, Merstham, Newcastle upon Tyne, Glasgow, Eastcote, Chadderton, Chelmsford, Cardiff

Total employees: 1,496

Charitable donations

UK cash (latest declared):	2011	£20,700
	2009	£11,300
	2008	£22,000
	2007	£96,000
	2006	£87,300
Total UK:	2011	£20,700
Total worldwide:	2011	£20,700
Cash worldwide:	2011	£20,700

Corporate social responsibility

CSR committee: There was no evidence of a separate CSR Committee.

CSR policy: This information was obtained from the company's website:

> We support a number of charitable initiatives throughout the country and we are frequently involved in a number of community activities and sponsorships. During the year we have hosted visits

from local schools, donated goods and services and sponsored exhibitions and local sporting events.

CSR report: There was no evidence of a separate CSR report; however two pages were dedicated to CSR within the annual report.

Exclusions

No support for advertising in charity brochures, appeals from individuals, animal welfare, fundraising events, overseas projects, political appeals, or religious appeals.

Applications

In writing to the correspondent.

Other information

During 2010/11, the group made charitable donations of £21,000 (2009: £11,300).

This information was obtained from the company's Annual Report:

> Bellway employees make a very real difference to the communities in which they work and we are proud of the contribution our own staff make to many voluntary organisations around the country. Regular initiatives such as dress down days, raffles and staff sponsorships result in valuable funding for a variety of charitable causes throughout the country.
>
> £505 was raised for Make-A-Wish Foundation in the company's Yorkshire division; £1,400 was raised by employees in the West Midlands for the Cancer Ward at Birmingham's Queen Elizabeth Hospital; and £8,000 was raised by a Welsh team to support a school that takes care of autistic children.

Berkeley Group plc

Building/construction, property

Correspondent: R J Stearn, Company Secretary, Berkeley House, 19 Portsmouth Road, Cobham, Surrey KT11 1GD (tel: 01932 868555; fax: 01932 868667; website: www.berkeleygroup.com)

Directors: Tony Pidgley, Chair; Rob Perrins; Nick Simpkin; Karl Whiteman; Sean Ellis; David Howell; Alan Coppin; John Armitt; Victoria Mitchell (women: 1; men: 8)

Year end	30/04/2011
Turnover	£740,000,000
Pre-tax profit	£140,000,000

Nature of business: Principal activity: residential house building and commercial property investment and development.

Company registration number: 1454064

Main locations: Edgbaston, Twickenham, Cobham, Potters Bar, Portsmouth

Charitable donations

UK cash (latest declared):	2011	£800,000
	2009	£127,599
	2008	£268,286
	2007	£171,973
	2006	£190,977
Total UK:	2011	£800,000
Total worldwide:	2011	£800,000
Cash worldwide:	2011	£800,000

Community involvement

> Launched in 2011, the **Berkeley Foundation** (Charity Commission no: 268369) is designed to capture, co-ordinate and drive forward the group's corporate social responsibility activities. The objective of the foundation is to 'improve the lives of young people, their families and communities'. The main strategic focus is on supporting young people in London and the South East, particularly those not in education, employment or training. We believe there is a direct connection between their fortunes and the success of the places and communities in which Berkeley works.

The Berkeley Foundation intends to work with organisations that can model new ways of supporting young people, as well as funding projects and services that have already proven their worth.

Charity partnerships: Shelter and The Lord's Taverner's. It also supported three Olympians and Paralympians at the London 2012 Games.

Corporate giving

In 2010/11, the company's charitable donations totalled £800,000 (2009: £127,500).

Corporate social responsibility

CSR committee: There was no evidence of a separate CSR Committee.

CSR policy: In 2010, the group set up the Berkeley Foundation. The Berkeley Foundation is designed to capture, coordinate and drive forward the Group's corporate social responsibility activities.

Employee numbers could not be found.

CSR report: There was no evidence of a separate CSR report; however information regarding donations and the establishment of the Berkeley Foundation was widely available both on the website and in the annual report.

Exclusions

No support for political appeals.

Applications

In writing to the correspondent.

Bestway (Holdings) Ltd

Cash 'n' carry

Correspondent: Mohammed Younus Sheikh, Secretary to the Foundation, Abbey Road, Park Royal, London NW10 7BW (tel: 020 8453 1234; fax: 020 8965 0359; email: zulfikaur.wajid-hasan@bestway.co.uk; website: www.bestway.co.uk)

Directors: Sir Anwar Pervez, Chair; Zameer Choudrey; Younus Sheikh; Abdul Khalique Bhatti; Adalat Khan Chaudhary, Arshad Chaudhary; Rizwan Pervez; Dawood Pervez

Year end	30/06/2011
Turnover	£1,841,294,000
Pre-tax profit	£102,717,000

Nature of business: The principal activity of the group is the operation of cash and carry warehouses in the UK supplying groceries, tobacco, wines and spirits, beers and other household goods, together with property investment.

Company registration number: 1392861

Main locations: Bolton, Birmingham, Oldbury, Luton, London, Liverpool, Manchester, Northampton, Newcastle-under-Lyme, Peterborough, Plymouth, Romford, Swansea, Croydon, Bristol, Cardiff, Gateshead, Exeter, Leicester, Leeds

Total employees: 4,724

Charitable donations

UK cash (latest declared):	2011	£723,000
	2009	£869,000
	2007	£680,000
	2006	£787,000
	2005	£684,000
Total UK:	2011	£723,000
Total worldwide:	2011	£723,000
Cash worldwide:	2011	£723,000

Corporate giving

The company donates a percentage of its yearly profits to charitable causes. During the year 2010/11 the group donated £723,000 to the **Bestway Foundation** (registered charity no. 297178). The foundation provides scholarships/grants to university students of South Asian origin, both in the UK and overseas. The foundation also relieves sickness and preserves good health, both in the UK and South Asia, by giving grants to organisations including hospitals and medical research establishments. The foundation also supports UK charities that provide relief in suffering of the 'old, disabled and needy'.

In 2010/11 the foundation gave £486,000 in grants which included: £68,000 to Crimestoppers; £60,000 to the National Hospital Development Fund and £20,000 to Imran Khan Flood Relief. 97 grants were made to individuals.

Corporate social responsibility

CSR committee: None for the company.

CSR policy: The group's CR policy concentrates on the environment.

Unable to determine the ratio of women to men on the board.

CSR report: None for the company.

Applications

In writing to the correspondent, enclosing an sae. Applications are considered in March/April. Telephone calls are not welcome.

Betfair Group Ltd

Gaming

Correspondent: Administrator, Waterfront, Hammersmith Embankment, Chancellors Road (access on Winslow Road), London, England W6 9HP (tel: 020 8834 8000; email: corporate@betfair.com; website: corporate.betfair.com)

Directors: Edward Wray, Chair; David Yu, Chief Executive; Stephen Morana; Mike McTighe; Ian Dyson; Josh Hannah; Fru Hazlitt; Baroness Denise Kingsmill (women: 2; men: 6)

Year end	30/04/2011
Turnover	£393,311,000
Pre-tax profit	£26,617,000

Nature of business: The provision of betting services and online gaming products.

Company registration number: 6489716

Main locations: Hammersmith, Stevenage

UK employees: 2,038

Total employees: 2,038

Charitable donations

UK cash (latest declared):	2011	£560,000
	2009	£250,000
	2008	£331,000
	2007	£290,000
Total UK:	2011	£560,000
Total worldwide:	2011	£560,000
Cash worldwide:	2011	£560,000

Community involvement

Charity partners include Charlton Athletic Community Trust, which supports a community football programme in South Africa and St Andrews Resource Centre in Dublin. The company also supported racing charities including the British Racing School and Moorcroft Racehorse Welfare Centre. Long-standing support continued for the Injured Jockeys Fund.

Corporate giving

The company donated £560,000 to over 110 causes, including £134,000 to the GREaT Foundation.

Employee-led support

Matched funding: Employees play a pivotal role in fundraising for the company's Charity of the Year. In 2011, Betfair raised £145,000 for *The Anthony Nolan Trust* and staff are currently raising £75,000 for the *Prostate Cancer Charity*, which will be matched by Betfair.

> We are proud of the number of local initiatives where we get our employees involved directly by using their two days' volunteering leave. We aim to use peoples' skills to make a real impact wherever possible.

Corporate social responsibility

CSR committee: Non-executive board member Fru Hazlitt chairs the CR Committee, which met four times in 2011. This committee ensures executive ownership of CR issues. A central CR department manages a day-to-day performance, interacting with small CR teams which have responsibility for community and environmental initiatives in all our main offices.

CSR policy: This information was taken from the company's Annual Report:

> Taking pride in the communities in which we live and work is at the heart of how we do business, illustrated by our wide-ranging community investment.

CSR report: There was no evidence of a separate CSR report; however two pages were dedicated to the community in the annual report.

Applications

In writing to the correspondent.

BGC International LP

Financial services, securities/ shares

Correspondent: The Secretary, Annual Charity Day, One Churchill Place, Canary Wharf, London E14 5RD (tel: 020 7894 7700; fax: 020 7894 7669; email: charity@bgcpartners.com; website: www.bgcpartners.com)

Directors: Howard W. Lutnick, Chair; Shaun D. Lynn; Stephen M. Merkel; Anthony Graham Sadler; Sean A. Windeatt; Stephen T. Curwood; John H. Dalton; Barry R. Sloane; Albert M. Weis (women: 0; men: 9)

Year end	31/12/2010
Turnover	£85,500,000
Pre-tax profit	£51,500,000

Nature of business: An inter-dealer broker and clearer in securities and derivatives.

Company registration number: 1976691

Total employees: 2,743

Charitable donations

UK cash (latest declared):	2008	£313,000
	2007	£127,000
Total worldwide:	2010	£7,710,000
Cash worldwide:	2010	£7,710,000

Corporate social responsibility

CSR committee: A separate CSR Committee was present.

CSR policy: This information was obtained from the company's website:

> We believe that the pursuit of excellence should extend beyond the boardroom. We're keen to support promising athletes whose commitment, tenacity and daring reflect our own values. Through our sponsorship we also hope to reinvigorate sport in the community, encouraging children and young people to rediscover their confidence through the challenge of physical activity.
>
> BGC selects a number of charities to support each year.

CSR report: There was no evidence of a separate CSR report.

Applications

BGC selects a number of charities to support each year on their Annual Charity Day. Applications should be submitted in writing to: charity@bgcpartners.com.

Other information

BGC has held an annual global charity day since 2006. Each year the global revenues generated by the firm's brokers from the designated day's trading are donated to selected charities. In 2010, the company donated £7.7 million. UK beneficiaries included: Barnardo's; Children in Crisis; Lowe Syndrome Trust; Scope; and The Dispossessed Fund.

BHP Billiton plc

Mining

Correspondent: (see 'Applications'), Neathouse Place, London SW1V 1BH (tel: 020 7802 4000; fax: 020 7802 4111; website: www.bhpbilliton.com)

Directors: Carlos Cordeiro; David Crawford; Jacques Nasser, Chair; Keith Rumble; John Schubert; John Buchanan; Wayne Murdy; Marius Kloppers, Chief Executive; Malcolm Broomhead; Carol Hewson; Lindsay Maxsted; Shriti Vadera; Jane McAloon (women: 3; men: 10)

Year end	30/06/2011
Turnover	£46,092,307,500
Pre-tax profit	£13,938,475,200

Nature of business: BHP Billiton plc operates solely as a holding company for the BHP Billiton Group plc. The principal activities of the group are mineral and hydrocarbon exploration and production, metals production, marketing, and research and development.

Company registration number: 3196209

Main locations: Liverpool, London

Total employees: 40,757

Membership: BITC

Charitable donations

UK cash (latest declared):	2011	£19,290,000
	2009	£39,000,000
	2008	£723,000
	2007	£375,000
	2006	£632,772
Total UK:	2011	£19,414,600
Total worldwide:	2011	£125,667,400
Cash worldwide:	2011	£115,161,300

Community involvement

Extract taken from the 2010/11 annual report:

> *Community development*
>
> Our community development programs are driven by our desire to improve the quality of life of people in our host communities. Our operations implement their programs using community development plans that have been developed in consultation with local stakeholders. The plans are formulated from data gathered from an impacts and opportunities assessment and a baseline social study that includes education, health and environment quality of life indicators. The requirement that this occurs in all our operations is part of the implementation of GLDs.
>
> Community development projects are selected on the basis of their capacity to impact positively on the quality of life indicators. We monitor progress by tracking changes in these indicators every three years. All community projects are assessed in relation to anti-corruption requirements prior to approval and are implemented in accordance with the ethical requirements in the Code of Business Conduct. This approach is mandated under the Community GLD.

Corporate giving

In 2010/11 community investment totalled US$195.5 million (£125.7 million), comprising cash, in kind support and administrative costs and included a US$30 million (£19.3 million), contribution to the company's UK-based charitable company, BHP Billiton Sustainable Communities.

The annual report states:

> The cash component of our FY2011 community investment comprises:
>
> - Direct investment in community programs made from BHP Billiton companies on an equity share basis
> - Contributions to the Group's charitable foundations, *excluding BHP Billiton Sustainable Communities
> - The Enterprise Development and Socio-economic Development components of our Broad-Based Black Economic Empowerment programs in South Africa

* This has been added to the figure we give for worldwide cash contributions.

Employee-led support

BHP Billiton has established a Matched Giving Programme through which the company will match the community contributions made by employees. Every employee (including full and part time) is entitled each year to match their contributions to not-for-profit organisations that benefit the community. These contributions can be employee volunteering, fundraising or cash donations (including pay-roll donations).

Corporate social responsibility

CSR committee: Line managers have ultimate accountability for ensuring our businesses contribute to sustainable development.

CSR policy: Extract taken from the 2011 Sustainability Report:

> Our Sustainable Development Policy is one of five BHP Billiton policies. The Policy defines our commitments to environmental and social responsibility.
>
> Community – engaging with those affected by our operations, including employees, contractors and communities; and respecting fundamental human rights.

CSR report: There is an annual Sustainability report.

Applications

Applications to the registered charity: BHP Billiton Sustainable Communities (Charity Commission no. 1131066) should be made in writing to the correspondent after checking the website for information regarding grants from the charity.

Write to: BHP Billiton Sustainable Communities, 1 Neathouse Place, Westminster, London SW1V 1BH; tel: 020 7802 4000; email: hsec@bhpbilliton.com.

Big Yellow Group plc

Services

Correspondent: Paul Donnelly, Corporate Social Responsibility Manager, 2 The Deans, Bridge Road, Bagshot, Surrey GU19 5AT (tel: 01276 470190; fax: 01276 470191; email: mcole@bigyellow.co.uk; website: bigyellow.hemscottir.com)

Directors: Nicholas Vetch, Chair; James Gibson, Chief Executive Officer; Adrian Lee; John Trotman; Tim Clark; Jonathan Short; Philip Burks; Mark Richardson; Steve Johnson (women: 0; men: 9)

Year end	31/03/2011
Turnover	£42,558,000
Pre-tax profit	£20,200,000

Nature of business: Provision of self-storage and related services.

Company registration number: 3625199

Total employees: 301

Charitable donations

UK cash (latest declared):	2010	£17,000
	2009	£28,000
Total UK:	2010	£17,000

Corporate social responsibility

CSR committee: There is no evidence of a separate CSR committee.

CSR policy: This information was obtained from the company's annual report:

> Big Yellow's CSR policy aims to strike the balance between its social, economic and environmental responsibilities as an owner, operator and developer of self storage buildings. In order to maintain a sustainable business for its customers, staff and investors, the Board has committed significant resources to the social and environmental aspects of its operations.

CSR report: There was a section of the annual report devoted to Corporate Social Responsibility, however there was no information relating to community contributions.

Applications

In writing to the correspondent, or to the manager of the local outlet. Big Yellow Group plc has 72 stores in the UK – visit the company's website for details.

Other information

In 2011 storage space has been provided free of charge or at reduced rates to local community groups within the catchment area of its stores, and charities. Big Yellow Group encourages employee involvement in charitable giving and 'frequently matches any amounts made by individuals'. No figures were available.

Birmingham International Airport Ltd

Airport operators

Correspondent: Community Team, Birmingham B26 3QJ (tel: 01217 677448/ 01217 677448; fax: 01217 677065; email: community@birmirminghamairport.co.uk; website: www.birminghamairport.co.uk)

Directors: J. L. Hudson, Chair; P. Kehoe, Chief Executive Officer; M. J. Kelly; W. Heynes; M. Lloyd; E. Clarke; J. Morris; J. Lloyd

Year end	31/03/2011
Turnover	£103,000,000
Pre-tax profit	£10,000,000

Nature of business: The principal activity is the operation and management of Birmingham International Airport and the provision of associated facilities and services.

Company registration number: 3312673

Main locations: Birmingham

UK employees: 566

Total employees: 566

Membership: BITC

Charitable donations

UK cash (latest declared):	2011	£50,000
	2008	£52,000
	2007	£52,000
	2006	£50,000
	2005	£50,000
Total UK:	2011	£50,000
Total worldwide:	2011	£50,000
Cash worldwide:	2011	£50,000

Corporate social responsibility

CSR committee: There was no evidence of a separate CSR Committee.

CSR policy: This information was obtained from the company's website:

> Charitable giving is important to us and is a key part of our community programme. Each year we receive dozens of requests for support and while we can't meet everyone's expectations, we're able to help raise significant sums for local good causes.

Unable to determine the ratio of women to men on the board.

There was no evidence of a separate CSR Report; however information was available from the company's website.

CSR report: There was no evidence of a separate CSR report; however information was available from the company's website.

Exclusions

No grants for individuals, sports kits, trips or projects resulting in short-term benefit e.g. events, performances or visits, commercial organisations, or those working for profit, projects which have already been carried out or paid for, organisations which have statutory responsibilities such as hospitals or schools, unless the project is clearly not a statutory responsibility. Grants are not normally given towards the purchase of land or buildings or general repair and maintenance – requests for equipment, fixtures and fittings may be supported. Grants will also not normally be recurrent

Support will not be considered for advertising in charity brochures, animal welfare, overseas projects, religious appeals, medical purposes, or science/ technology.

Applications

On a form available from the correspondent. Applicants will be advised when the next grant allocation meeting is being held. The trust may want to visit the project.

Applications can be submitted at any time, with grants awarded twice a year in April and October. Successful applicants are required to submit a progress report after six months, and again after 12 for longer projects. Grants will not be awarded to the same organisation in consecutive years. Applicants must wait at least three years before applying for another grant.

Information Available: The company produces further information in its application guidelines.

Other information

The Birmingham International Airport Community Trust Fund: The company set up a trust to fund a wide range of community-based projects which will benefit the community and environment around Birmingham Airport. The Community Trust Fund (Charity Commission no. 1071176) receives £50,000 each year from the airport, topped up by fines imposed on airlines for exceeding the airport's noise violation levels. Geographically, the trust supports a very defined area which, broadly speaking, is that bounded by Grove End, Berkswell, Honiley and Washwood Heath. Projects outside of this region cannot be funded, even if the communities feel they are affected by the disruption caused by the airport. The trust acts independently of the airport management.

Areas of work the trust supports are:

- Environment improvement and heritage conservation
- Bringing the community closer together through facilities for sport, recreation and other leisure-time activities
- Improving awareness of environmental issues or environmental education and training activities
- Encouraging and protecting wildlife

It describes the types of projects it wishes to support as including community centres, community groups, sports, playgroups, schools, youth clubs, scouts, gardens/parks, environment, music and churches. Work should benefit a substantial section of the community rather than less inclusive groups, although work with older people or people with special needs is positively encouraged.

The maximum grant made is for £3,000, and grants tend to go to community groups with low incomes; organisations with large turnovers are rarely supported. Grants may be for capital or revenue projects, although the trust will not commit to recurrent or running costs, such as salaries.

> Our Nominated Charity is Acorns Children's Hospice Trust, one of the best-known charities in the region. Acorns provides care and support for children and young people who have life limiting or life threatening conditions. They currently support nearly 600 children and 800 families, including those who are bereaved. Their specialist nursing and support services provide a vital lifeline for these families who would face a much tougher challenge coping alone. Since our partnership with Acorns began, our staff have raised £22,500.

On the last Friday of each month, non-uniformed staff take advantage of 'Dress Down Friday' where, for a small donation, they are able to wear casual clothes to work. The proceeds are donated to a different local charity each month, nominated by the staff themselves. Beneficiaries for 2011 were: SANDS; Rotary's End Polio Now Campaign and Donna Louise Hospice Trust.

Biwater Holdings Ltd

Engineering, waste management

Correspondent: J S Lamb, Company Secretary, Biwater House, Station Approach, Dorking RH4 1TZ (tel: 01306 740740; fax: 01306 885233; website: www.biwater.com)

Directors: A. E. White, Chair; C. A. White; D. F. W. White; J. J. Jones

Year end	31/03/2011
Turnover	£173,300,000
Pre-tax profit	£22,500,000

Nature of business: Principal activities: contracting, manufacturing and the provision of services to the water industry worldwide.

Company registration number: 929686

Main locations: Dorking, Heywood, Bournemouth

UK employees: 574

Total employees: 1,821

Charitable donations

UK cash (latest declared):	2011	£25,600
	2008	£79,000
	2007	£55,000
	2006	£52,000
	2005	£37,000
Total UK:	2011	£25,600
Total worldwide:	2011	£30,000
Cash worldwide:	2011	£30,000

Corporate social responsibility

CSR committee: No dedicated CSR committee.

CSR policy: Taken from the company's website:

> At Biwater we take our corporate and social responsibilities very seriously. This code is a fundamental element of our business practice. With it, we are fully engaged with our employees, our customers, our suppliers, and investors and government agencies with whom we inter relate both in the UK and abroad. We employ this code in the workplaces where Biwater is operating, in protecting the environment around us, and in supporting the communities in which we live and work.
>
> In communities with:

- Interaction with local populations, respecting established customs and priorities
- Sponsorship and charitable support for communal activity
- Social and sports commitments to the wider society.

It is not clear from the annual report and accounts what the ratio of women to men is on the board.

CSR report: No CSR report published.

Applications

In writing to the correspondent.

Other information

In 2010/11, the company and its subsidiary undertakings made donations for charitable purposes of £30,000 of which £25,600 was in the UK and £4,300 abroad mainly for education, community support and medical purposes.

Previous research suggested that the company supports mainly Dorking charities.

BlackRock Investment Management (UK) Ltd

Financial services

Correspondent: Adrian Dyke, Charity Administrator, 33 King William Street, London EC4R 9AS (tel: 020 7743 3000; fax: 020 7743 1000; website: www.blackrock.co.uk/index.htm)

Directors: Robert S. Kapito, President; Laurence D. Fink, Chair and Chief Executive; Kenneth B. Dunn; Ivan G. Seidenberg; William S. Demchak; Thomas H. O'Brien; Mathis Cabiallavetta; James Grosfeld; Murry S. Gerber; John Varley; Linda Gosden Robinson; David H. Komansky; Sir Deryck Maughan; James E. Rohr; Abdlatif Y. Al-Hamad; Dennis D. Dammerman; Robert E. Diamond Jr; Thomas K. Montag (women: 1; men: 17)

Year end	31/12/2010
Turnover	£8,600,000,000

Nature of business: BlackRock is a provider of global investment management, risk management and advisory services to institutional and retail clients around the world.

Company registration number: 2020394

Total employees: 9,100

Charitable donations

UK cash (latest declared):	2010	£118,000
	2009	£146,500
	2008	£179,500
	2007	£150,000
	2006	£230,000
Total UK:	2010	£118,000
Total worldwide:	2010	£7,000,000
Cash worldwide:	2010	£7,000,000

Corporate social responsibility

CSR committee: There was no evidence of a CSR Committee.

CSR policy: The firm donates to its charitable foundation, which then distributes the money accordingly.

CSR report: There was no evidence of a CSR report.

Applications

The trustees invite staff, clients and business associates of the firm to submit applications on behalf of a registered charity of their choice. Unsolicited letters of application are therefore unlikely to be successful.

Other information

The company donated £118,000 to the BlackRock (UK) Charitable Trust in 2010. The company is wholly-owned subsidiary of BlackRock Group Ltd (formerly Merrill Lynch Investment Managers Ltd) and directs its community support through the BlackRock (UK) Charitable Trust (Charity Commission no. 1065447).

The BlackRock (UK) Charitable Trust
In 2010, the trust received a donation of £118,000 from BlackRock Investments (2009: £146,500) from the firm. Grants were made during the year totalling £184,000 (2009: £207,000). Grants of £1,000 or more included those to: The Prostate Cancer Charity (£31,000); BlackRock Community Action Team (£26,400); The Burnaby Blue Foundation and Ovarian Cancer Action (£7,000 each).

Bloomsbury Publishing plc

Media

Correspondent: Ian Portal, Company Secretary, 36 Soho Square, London W1D 3QY (tel: 020 7494 2111; fax: 020 7434 0151; email: csm@bloomsbury.com; website: www.bloomsbury.com)

Directors: Nigel Newton, Chief Executive; Wendy Pallot; Richard Charkin; Jeremy Wilson, Non-Executive Chair; Ian Cormack; Sarah Jane Thomson (women: 2; men: 4)

Year end	28/02/2011
Turnover	£103,398,000
Pre-tax profit	£4,220,000

Nature of business: The principal activities of the group are the publication of books and the development of electronic reference databases.

Company registration number: 1984336

Total employees: 355

Charitable donations

UK cash (latest declared):	2011	£10,000
	2009	£100
	2008	£3,500
	2007	£3,000
	2006	£34,000
Total UK:	2011	£10,000
Total worldwide:	2011	£10,000
Cash worldwide:	2011	£10,000

Corporate social responsibility

CSR committee: There was no evidence of a separate CSR Committee.

CSR policy: The group makes minor cash donations that support literary art, education and literacy which included Book Aid International, The Charleston Trust and other charities that meet its specific criteria.

CSR report: There was no evidence of a separate CSR report and information on community contributions is somewhat limited in the annual report.

Exclusions

No support for individuals, religious or political appeals.

Applications

In writing to the correspondent.

Other information

During 2010/11 the Group gave £10,000 in community contributions (2010: £100).

With its focus on promoting literacy, Bloomsbury actively supports Booktrust (which has the objective of promoting and celebrating books and reading among children and adults), Oxfam and Barnardo's, as well as schools and libraries. Bloomsbury donates over 100,000 books annually which include both overseas and UK donations. The group also donated signed copies of books by leading authors for charity auctions and support the Booktrust 'Booked Up' scheme to give every child a book.

BlueBay Asset Management plc

Business services

Correspondent: Company Secretary, 77 Grosvenor Street, London W1K 3JR (tel: 020 7389 3700; fax: 020 7389 3499; email: marketing@bluebayinvest.com; website: www.bluebayinvest.com)

Directors: John Roberts, Chair; Hugh Willis; Mark Poole; Nick Williams; Alex Khein; Alan Gibbins; John Montalbano; Dan Chornous; Frank Lippa; Katherine Gibson; Graeme Hepworth (women: 1; men: 10)

Year end	31/10/2011
Turnover	£231,138,000
Pre-tax profit	£24,872,000

Nature of business: The principal activity of the group is the provision of investment management services.

Company registration number: 3262598

Total employees: 228

Charitable donations

UK cash (latest declared):	2011	£5,000
	2009	£2,000
	2008	£52,000
Total UK:	2011	£5,000
Total worldwide:	2011	£5,000
Cash worldwide:	2011	£5,000

Corporate social responsibility

CSR committee: There was no evidence of a CSR Committee.

CSR policy: There was no evidence of a CSR Policy.

CSR report: There was no evidence of a CSR report.

Applications

In writing to the correspondent.

Other information

In 2010/11 the company made charitable donations of £5,000 (2009: £2,000). No further information was available.

BMW UK Ltd

Motors and accessories

Correspondent: The Company Secretary, Ellesfield Avenue, Bracknell, Berkshire RG12 8TA (tel: 01344 426565; fax: 01344 480203; website: www.bmw.co.uk)

Directors: T. Abbott; P. Picker; L. Willisch

Year end	31/12/2010
Turnover	£3,228,443,000
Pre-tax profit	£39,308,000

Nature of business: The principal activity is the importation, storage and distribution of BMW products in the UK.

Company registration number: 1378137

Main locations: Birmingham, Swindon, Hook, Thorne, Coleshill, Oxford, Goodwood, Bracknell

UK employees: 8,000

Total employees: 8,000

Charitable donations

UK cash (latest declared):	2010	£121,000
	2009	£25,000
	2006	£25,000
	2005	£25,000
Total UK:	2010	£121,000
Total worldwide:	2010	£121,000
Cash worldwide:	2010	£121,000

Corporate social responsibility

CSR committee: There was no evidence of a separate CSR Committee.

CSR policy: This information was obtained from the company's website:

> Corporate Social Responsibility is an area that BMW Group in the UK takes very seriously. Since 2001 BMW Group has established a significant presence in the UK. Engaging with the communities in which it operates has been fundamental to BMW, and it has successfully made a contribution to society over and above an economic one.

Unable to determine the ratio of women to men on the board.

CSR report: A CSR report was available, however it was out of date at the time of writing (2008).

Exclusions

No response to circular appeals.

Other information

During the year the company made charitable donations of £121,000. Donations over £2,000 were as follows: BEN – Motor and Allied Trades Benevolent Fund (£97,000); The Newspaper Press Fund (£13,000) and Air Ambulance (£2,500).

The Body Shop International plc

Retail – miscellaneous

Correspondent: Lisa Jackson, Chief Executive – Body Shop Foundation, Watersmead, Littlehampton, West Sussex BN17 6LS (tel: 01903 731500/01903 844039; fax: 01903 726250; website: www.thebodyshopfoundation.org)

Directors: Sylvia Jay; Christian Mulliez; Geoff Skingsley; Frederic Ennabli, Chief Executive Officer; Sophie Gasperment, Executive Chair (women: 2; men: 3)

Year end	31/12/2011
Turnover	£420,500,000
Pre-tax profit	£49,300,000

Nature of business: The Body Shop is a multi-local, values-led, global retailer. The group sells skin and hair care products through its own shops and franchised outlets.

The Body Shop became part of the L'Oréal Group in 2006 and de-listed from the London Stock Exchange on 12 July of that year. 'It retains its unique identity and values and continues to be based in the United Kingdom. It operates independently within the L'Oréal Group and is led by the current management team of The Body Shop reporting directly to the CEO of L'Oréal.'

Company registration number: 1284170

Subsidiaries include: Soapworks Ltd

Main locations: Glasgow, Littlehampton

Total employees: 2,965

Membership: BITC

Charitable donations

UK cash (latest declared):	2011	£700,000
	2009	£1,900,000
	2008	£1,500,000
	2007	£1,700,000
	2006	£1,000,000
Total UK:	2011	£700,000
Total worldwide:	2011	£1,000,000
Cash worldwide:	2011	£1,000,000

Community involvement

Founder of The Body Shop, Dame Anita Roddick, stated: 'The business of business should not just be about money, it should be about responsibility. It should be about public good, not private greed.'

The majority of the company's corporate donations are made through its charitable foundation.

The Body Shop Foundation (Charity Commission no. 802757)

The foundation is funded by annual donations from the company and through various fundraising initiatives. The foundation's approach to funding is to actively seek out groups working towards social and environmental change and who might not otherwise attract funding.

The foundation supports three main areas, namely, animal protection, social justice and environmental protection. Its aim is to:

- Support organisations at the forefront of social and environmental change
- Support groups with little hope of conventional funding
- Support projects working to increase public awareness

The foundation is currently running the following grants programmes:

- Global grants programme
- Zone funding programmes: Asia Pacific; Europe, Middle East and Africa; and, The Americas
- Local community grants programme – Littlehampton and Southwark areas

Global Grants Programme

The programme aims to fund issues across the foundation's overall mission statement of human and civil rights, environmental and animal protection and during this financial year has operated to the following structure:

- Long-term funding relationships of two to three years, with funding of up to £820,000 per year, to groups to help with core funding or long-term projects working in the areas of Access to Education for women and girls and Water
- One off grants of up to £10,000 supporting issues addressing de-forestation

Zone Funding Programmes (formerly Regional Funding Programmes)

The Zone Funding Programmes were set up in 2005 to ensure that the foundation's global remit was being met and that input from The Body Shop International's global markets was developed in terms of project identification.

The Programmes in this financial year (2011/12), operated across the three operational zones of The Body Shop International. These were the Asia Pacific Zone, the Europe, Middle East and Africa Zone, and the Americas Zone.

Each Zone has a panel with representatives from The Body Shop's employees, franchisees and consultants from within that Zone. Permanent members of each Panel are the Values Representative from each TBS Zone and the Grants Manager of The Body Shop Foundation. These members ensure continuity of administration and control. As is normal, the trustees of the foundation have final sign off for all grants.

Each Zone meets annually to decide on their individual funding focuses and strategies, dependent on that Zone's social and cultural needs. Panel members bring their skills and local knowledge to the meetings in order to best reflect the needs of those communities. All Zones invite The Body Shop employees, consultants and franchisees to nominate projects for potential funding and these nominations are shortlisted and presented to the Zone panels for consideration.

Local Community Grants Programme
The Local Community Grants Programme aims to fund projects in the geographical areas local to The Body Shop International's head offices in Littlehampton, West Sussex and Southwark, London. Money available for this programme is £50,000 during the year. A committee of employees of The Body Shop International service centres in Littlehampton and London meet annually to decide on grant recipients and levels of funding from a shortlist of grant applications made from head office staff nominations.

Corporate giving

In 2011, the company made charitable donations of £1 million of which £700,000 went to the company's foundation. We have no information about which organisations benefited from the remaining £300,000 made directly by the company, or where they were based.

The Body Shop Foundation
The company's annual review for 2011/12 provides detailed information on the work undertaken by the foundation. 117 grants were awarded totalling over £694,000 and were categorised as follows: Human Rights – £447,000; Environmental Protection (£138,000); and Animal Protection (£109,000). Unusually, there did not appear to be a list of individual beneficiary organisations.

Global grants programme
A total value of grants of £249,000 has been made in this year to 22 organisations under this programme. Previous beneficiary organisations included: End Child Prostitution and Trafficking; Good Earth Trust; Environmental Justice Foundation; National Association for People Abused in Childhood; In-Kind Direct; RugMark and Forest Stewardship Council UK; Born Free, Malawi; British Union for the Abolition of Vivisection; Together for Sudan.

Zone Funding Programmes (formerly Regional Funding Programmes)

The following grants, excluding additional support costs, have been made this year:

Asia Pacific Zone Funding Programme has granted £113,500 to 21 organisations within the focus areas of:

- Family Protection covering domestic violence, child abuse, street children, trafficking, neglect, child labour
- Poverty covering education, microcredit schemes, life-skills training, child labour
- Environmental Sustainability covering wildlife conservation, forest animals, forest preservation/conservation, access to water, alternative technologies

Europe, Middle East and Africa Zone Funding Programme has granted £154,500 to 32 organisations within the focus areas of:

- Domestic Violence
- Animal Rights
- Social and Environmental Development

The Americas Zone Funding Programme has granted £127,000 to 30 organisations within the focus areas of:

- Human Rights women and girls' empowerment. This may include education, civil rights, domestic violence, income generation, self-esteem
- Animal Protection this may include rescue centres (no kill policies), wildlife conservation, anti-vivisection projects, endangered species
- Planet Preservation this may include sustainable farming practices, elimination of chemical poisoning, waste reduction and recycling

Local Community Grants Programme
Grants available through the local community programme totalled almost £50,000 and were awarded to 12 organisations.

In kind support

Fundraising initiatives, including charity shops and product sales are carried out by the company's foundation and form part of its income.

Employee-led support

Employees are encouraged to take an active role in their local communities. At the UK global head office, employees are entitled to six days of volunteer time, supporting local projects and causes as individuals and as business teams.

Commercially-led support

Campaigning: The Body Shop has a long history of campaigning including issues fundamental to its values such as being actively against animal testing and sponsoring posters for Greenpeace.

Corporate social responsibility

CSR committee: No details found.

CSR policy: There is no specific CSR information given for the company. However, the website gives full details of the company's campaigns, ethics and fair trading initiatives.

The following information is taken from the 'Our Company' section of the website:

> *Our five core values*
> The Body Shop is a leader in promoting greater corporate transparency, and we have been a force for positive social and environmental change through our campaigns around our five core Values: Support Community Fair Trade, Defend Human Rights, Against Animal Testing, Activate Self-Esteem, and Protect Our Planet.
>
> We source some of the finest raw ingredients from the four corners of the globe. We harness the skills of artisan farmers and add our expertise to create effective products . . . . . .
>
> We trade fairly so communities benefit as well as you. We never test on animals, and all our products are 100% vegetarian. We campaign with passion on issues close to our heart, because activism is in our blood. We always keep people, animals and the planet in mind.

CSR report: There is an annual Values report published available from the website.

Exclusions

The foundation does not sponsor individuals, fund sporting activities or the arts or sponsor or support fundraising events, receptions or conferences. In addition, no donations can be made to promote religious causes or political campaign causes, although the foundation may work with religious or political organisations on partnership projects and fundraise with organisations that have a political or religious foundation for causes that support its values and principles.

No donations can be made to, nor funds raised for organisations linked to animal testing, organisations advocating violence or discrimination or in other ways promoting behaviour not in keeping with the foundation's principles.

Applications

The Body Shop International and The Body Shop Foundation no longer accept unsolicited applications for funding.

However, in exceptional circumstances the company may respond to a humanitarian emergency and make a special donation to a public appeal, but such a donation must have the approval of the CEO.

Bodycote plc

Engineering

Correspondent: U.S Ball, Company Secretary, Springwood Court, Springwood Close, Tytherington Business Park, Macclesfield, Cheshire SK10 2XF (tel: 01625 505300; fax: 01625 505313; email: info@bodycote.com; website: www.bodycote.com)

Directors: AM. Thomson, Chair; SC. Harris, Chief Executive; DF. Landless; J. Vogelsang; JA. Biles; K. Rajagopal

Year end	31/12/2011
Turnover	£570,700,000
Pre-tax profit	£75,800,000

Nature of business: Operating an international network of facilities, Bodycote is a provider of thermal processing services for every market sector including aerospace and defence, automotive, power generation, oil and gas, construction, medical and transportation.

Company registration number: 519057

Total employees: 5,533

Charitable donations

UK cash (latest declared):	2011	£9,000
	2010	£3,000
	2009	£3,000
	2008	£11,000
Total UK:	2011	£9,000
Total worldwide:	2011	£9,000
Cash worldwide:	2011	£9,000

Corporate social responsibility

CSR committee: There appeared to be no evidence of a CSR Report, however information was available from the company's website but it was somewhat limited.

CSR policy: This information was obtained from the company's website:

> As a group, Bodycote is committed to acting responsibly as a good corporate citizen. Bodycote's policies are implemented across the group and cover subjects including: people; ethical standards; conflicts of interest and politics.

Unable to determine the ratio of women to men on the board.

CSR report: There appeared to be no evidence of a separate CSR Committee.

Applications

In writing to the correspondent.

Other information

Charitable donations during the year amounted to £9,000 (2010: £3,000). We have no information regarding beneficiary groups, or the company's policy with regard to charitable giving. In the past the company has donated to UK charities and we have used this figure as the UK cash contribution.

Boodle and Dunthorne Ltd

Retail – miscellaneous

Correspondent: N A Wainwright, Trustee, The Boodle and Dunthorne Charitable Trust, Boodles House, Lord Street, Liverpool L2 9SQ (tel: 01512 272525/01512 240580; fax: 01512 551070; email: beamorrison@boodles.com; website: www.boodles.com)

Directors: N. A. Wainwright; F. J. Wainwright; M. J. Wainwright; E. A. Wainwright; J. A. Wainwright; J. B. Wainwright

Year end	28/02/2011
Turnover	£41,890,800
Pre-tax profit	£4,079,000

Nature of business: Designer jewellers and silversmiths.

Company registration number: 472968

UK employees: 90

Total employees: 90

Charitable donations

UK cash (latest declared):	2011	£142,300
	2009	£112,600
	2008	£184,000
	2007	£195,500
Total UK:	2011	£142,300
Total worldwide:	2011	£142,300
Cash worldwide:	2011	£142,300

Corporate social responsibility

CSR committee: There is no evidence of a separate CSR committee.

CSR policy: Boodle and Dunthorne has a specific interest in UK based charities, especially those that work with young people and children.

Unable to determine ratio of women to men on the board.

CSR report: There is no evidence of a separate CSR report.

Exclusions

Not known.

Applications

In writing to the correspondent.

Other information

In 2010, Boodle and Dunthorne made donations of £142,000 (2009: £152,000) to charities in the UK. A list of beneficiaries was available from the company's website and were as follows:

- Only Connect, a creative arts company that guides and teaches prisoners, ex-offenders and young people in London through the arts
- Rainbow Trust Children's Charity, which provides emotional and practical support to families who have a child with a life threatening or terminal illness
- Shining Faces, a UK registered charity providing aid to a Christian orphanage in southern India
- Alder Hey Children's Hospital 'Imagine Appeal', which is a fundraising initiative that aims to develop and enrich the health care of around 250,000 children and young people every year

It is unclear as to whether this money was donated through the Boodle Charitable Foundation (Charity Commission no. 1077748), or distributed by the company itself. The foundation made grants in 2011 totalling £129,000.

Booker Group plc

Cash 'n' carry, wholesale

Correspondent: Mark Chilton, Company Secretary, Equity House, Irthlingborough Road, Wellingborough, Northamptonshire NN8 1LT (tel: 01933 371000; fax: 01933 371010; email: info@bookergroup.com; website: www.bookergroup.com)

Directors: Richard Rose, Chair; Charles Wilson, Chief Executive; Jonathan Prentis; Mark Aylwin; Guy Farrant; Bryn Satherley; Lord Bilimoria; Andrew Cripps; Stewart Gilliland; Karen Jones (women: 1; men: 9)

Year end	25/03/2011
Turnover	£3,595,800,000
Pre-tax profit	£71,400,000

Nature of business: The company is the UK's largest cash and carry operator, supplying approximately 305,000 catering businesses and 73,000 independent retailers.

Company registration number: 5145685

Total employees: 9,063

Charitable donations

UK cash (latest declared):	2011	£22,000
	2010	£20,000
Total UK:	2011	£22,000
Total worldwide:	2011	£22,000
Cash worldwide:	2011	£22,000

Corporate social responsibility

CSR committee: There was no evidence of a separate CSR Committee.

CSR policy: For the past two years the group has made donations to the Caravan and Sweet Charity. Both of these charities support those who work in food manufacturing. There was little information available on the group's website and in the annual report.

CSR report: There was no evidence of a separate CSR report.

Applications

In writing to the correspondent or to the local outlet.

Other information

In 2010/11, staff and directors raised £53,300 (2009: £51,000) for 132 charities across the country. A list of beneficiaries was unavailable. The group donated £11,000 each to Caravan and Sweet Charity (2009: £10,000 each). In addition donations totalling £59,000 (2009: £55,500) were made to charities by colleagues through the 'Give As You Earn' scheme.

Boots

Healthcare, pharmaceuticals

Correspondent: Hayleigh Sleigh, Charity and Community General Enquiries, D90 Building West G14, Nottingham, NG90 1BS, (For Sat Nav purposes use NG7 2TG) (tel: 01159 687242; email: hayley.sleigh@boots.co.uk; website: www.boots-uk.com/csr)

Directors: Ornella Barra; Alex Gourlay; George Fairweather; Marco Pagni; Dominic Murphy; Mattia Caprioli; Sergio D'Angelo; Chris Britton; Tony De Nunzio; Nick Land; Etienne Jornod; Stefano Pessina, Chair (women: 1; men: 11)

Year end	31/03/2011
Turnover	£20,218,000,000
Pre-tax profit	£637,000,000

Nature of business: The group's principal activities are: retailing of chemists' merchandise; the development, manufacture and marketing of healthcare and consumer products; the provision of opticians and other healthcare services.

Company registration number: 4452715

Brands include: Almus, Alvita, Boots Pharmaceuticals, Boots Laboratories, Botanics, No7, Serum7, Solei SP, Soltan.

Main locations: Nottingham

Total employees: 1,056

Membership: BITC, LBG

Charitable donations

UK cash (latest declared):	2011	£1,360,000
	2010	£1,300,000
	2009	£1,500,000
	2008	£2,620,330
	2007	£1,458,000
Total UK:	2011	£3,648,000
Total worldwide:	2011	£5,500,000
Cash worldwide:	2011	£1,800,000

Community involvement

Note: All of the information contained herein, except the year-end financial figures, refers to Boots UK.

The company's priority is to contribute positively to the communities that it serves. Community health is at the centre of this activity and the focus is on building active partnerships that will produce projects and initiatives with real health benefits.

Ornella Barra, Chair of the social responsibilities committee states in the 2010/11 CSR Report:

> Partnerships are key to the way we operate and in September 2010, we launched an ambitious new charity partnership between Boots UK and Macmillan Cancer Support to offer a new level of support to people living with cancer. Together we are developing a range of initiatives, including volunteering and fundraising, with the ambition that within three years, everyone in the UK will have access to the best cancer information and support in their community.

In the UK Boots is working with two key charity partners – Macmillan Cancer Support and BBC Children in Need (which they have supported for a number of years). In addition, it works with other charities including Action for Blind People. The UK wholesale business has a number of charity partners including The Prostate Cancer Charity, Leonard Cheshire Disability and CLIC Sargent.

Employees are encouraged to share their expertise to help people lead healthier lifestyles and are provided with opportunities to devote their time and energy to supporting causes that matter. Employees' fundraising efforts are also supported and the company provides a matched giving scheme to staff, enabling them to claim up to £500 to match their own funds raised. The company also offers the 'Give As You Earn' payroll giving facility.

Community Targets for 2011/12

- Continue to deliver our strategic partnership with Macmillan Cancer Support, providing accessible cancer information and advice to our customers, increasing customer recognition and raising £2 million
- Develop our 'Miles for Macmillan' colleague campaign increasing colleague participation to 15,000. Work with Macmillan Cancer Support to develop the 'Miles for Macmillan' customer offer, increasing customer participation and fundraising levels
- Deliver Pharmacist, healthcare team and general colleague engagement for Macmillan Cancer Support through increased participation in e-learning, CPD and volunteering programmes
- Provide £250,000 financial support to Nottinghamshire charities and voluntary organisations through the Boots Charitable Trust. Aim to continue to support 50 organisations, building on our 40th anniversary year
- Deliver our 8th year of support for BBC Children in Need raising £500,000 through colleague and customer fundraising

The Boots Charitable Trust is an independent grantmaking trust established in the 1970's and wholly funded by the company. Currently the trust's giving is focused in the county of Nottinghamshire, in recognition of Boots' long history with the area.

The trust's priorities for donations are:

Health

Community Healthcare – community healthcare services; homecare; after care; sufferers of medical conditions and people with disabilities; continuing care.

Health Education and Prevention – promoting knowledge and awareness of specific diseases or medical conditions.

Life-long Learning

Helping people of any age to achieve their educational potential through supplementary schooling, literacy and numeracy projects, community education, vocational/restart education for the unemployed or alternative education for excluded school pupils.

Community Development

Helping groups to organise and respond to problems and needs in their communities or networks. This would include organisations such as Councils for Voluntary Services and self-help groups.

Social Care

Personal Social Services – organisations assisting individuals or families to overcome social deprivation (e.g. people who are homeless or who have disabilities (and their carers), lone parents and childcare groups and other family support groups).

Social Preventive Schemes – activities preventing crime, dropping out and general delinquency and providing other social care outreach work, social health and safety awareness schemes etc.

Community Social Activities – activities to promote social engagement for vulnerable people mitigating against isolation and loneliness.

On average the trust gives around 50 grants per year to charities and voluntary organisations with a preference for people living in Nottingham and Nottinghamshire. Trustees are especially keen on projects with the capacity to deliver significant impact and which reach the greatest number of people.

Boots Benevolent Fund

The Boots Benevolent Fund (The Benny Fund) is a registered charity which provides financial help and support to serving and retired colleagues who are unexpectedly experiencing financial hardship. The Benny Fund is open to all Boots' colleagues in the UK. It aims to help when unexpected events happen and staff are faced with homelessness, debts involving bailiffs, large utility bill arrears or essential living requirements where they are facing financial hardship. The Benny Fund annually supports about 600–800 people with grants and loans.

Corporate giving

In 2010/11, the company's UK contributions were £4 million through charitable donations, gifts in kind, management costs and employee time. The worldwide community contributions totalled (including the UK contribution) £5.1 million compared to £4.9 million in the previous year. These contributions are made up of cash donations (charitable and other donations) and non-cash donations, which include employee time, in kind donations and also management costs.

We have been able to give figures, provided by Boots in its annual report 2010/11, which exclude management costs from its community contributions in the UK (which is our policy). However, we have not been able to extricate these costs from *where* the money was given. Consequently, the total UK and worldwide figures include the management costs.

A large proportion of the contributions made are to healthcare related projects reflecting its focus on pharmacy. Donations are usually made either at a national or a local level within the countries that the company operates.

The Boots Charitable Trust

During the year to March 2010/11 the company donated £250,000 to the trust. 146 applications and almost 600 telephone calls were received by the trust which made donations of £260,000.

Beneficiaries included: Ashfield Citizens Advice, Family Care, Friary Drop In and Prostitute Outreach Workers (£10,000 each); Headway Nottingham (£8,000); and Broxtowe Women's Project, Charis Life Church and Disability Nottinghamshire (£5,000 each).

The Boots Benevolent Fund (The Benny Fund): In 2010/11 the fund supported between 600–800 people in 2010/11 which amounted to £147,500. Email: btc.cshelpdesk_team@boots.co.uk

In kind support

Unwanted products such as damaged or end of line stock have been donated to charities as gifts in kind. As well as being of benefit to the voluntary sector this reduces the amount of waste sent to landfill. National and international charities providing humanitarian aid and medical assistance are supported in this way.

In June 2011 the company announced a new pan-European partnership with the European Organisation for Research and Treatment of Cancer (EORTC) Charitable Trust. Together they aim to support the creation and funding of a 'biobank' for colorectal cancer and later a platform for blood sampling to enable genetic profiling. This directly complements the ongoing partnership with Macmillan Cancer Support in the UK.

Employee-led support

Volunteering programmes enable Boots' employees to participate in a range of community activities in company time, sharing their skills and expertise with schools, hospitals and voluntary organisations. The company encourages employee commitment to its corporate and social responsibility activities by providing volunteering opportunities and supporting fundraising efforts.

In December 2009 Boots announced a new charity partnership between Boots UK and Macmillan Cancer Support which now offers a new level of support to people living with cancer. A range of initiatives is being developed, including volunteering and fundraising, with the ambition that everyone in the UK will have access to the best cancer information and support in their community. One fundraising initiative for example is Boots' colleagues are making a commitment to raising funds for Macmillan with the company-wide fundraising initiative 'Miles for Macmillan'. Boots employees all over the UK are aiming to clock up 290,000 miles – 290,000 is the number of people being diagnosed with cancer every year in the UK – in a variety of ways; cycling, rowing, jogging and even stilt walking.

The CSR section of the Boots website gives the following information:

> Our No7 consultants use their time and expertise to support Look Good . . . Feel Better beauty workshops for women with cancer, an initiative sponsored by the cosmetics industry.
>
> The free sessions take place in hospitals across the UK. Many of our No7 Consultants regularly volunteer at these sessions, providing morale-boosting makeovers and advice on skin care and make-up. By the end of 2010/11, workshops were taking place in 60 hospitals, with around 120 No7 consultants volunteering. Boots UK also donated over 40,000 No7 products during 2010/11 to support these workshops.
>
> No7 consultants were provided with training on giving advice to people experiencing the visual side effects of cancer treatments including how to draw on eyebrows and make eyelashes appear thicker for people who have undergone chemotherapy as well as advice on skin changes.
>
> From voluntary work with the Nottingham Hospice back in 2007 to improve their retail design, that resulted in the charity opening a 'flagship' store in Ruddington in 2008, our people rose to the challenge from the national body, 'Help the Hospices' by sharing their expertise to a much wider group of charity shop owners. A range of disciplines came together to deliver both a valuable resource and informative conference for twenty two local charities.
>
> Team challenges give our people the opportunity to spend a day in the local community sharing their skills with schools, charities and community groups. Challenges have included helping to plant new gardens, revamp meeting rooms, organise birthday parties and renovate community benches and gardens. During 2010/11, 485 colleagues from Boots UK's support office delivered 36 projects and donated over 3,700 hours to the community.

The Boots UK 'Make The Difference' initiative encourages employees who have raised money for charity to apply for matched funding from Boots UK up to a maximum of £500. During 2010/11 approximately 470 employees benefited from a 'Matched Giving Scheme', where the company made contributions of £167,000.

Further information on in kind giving can be found in Boots' Corporate Responsibility Report 2010/11.

Payroll giving: The company offers the Give As You Earn payroll giving facility. At the end of 2010/11, over 2,500 colleagues were giving regularly to a charity of their choice in this way.

Commercially-led support

The **Boots Learning Store** website, www.bootslearningstore.com, provides educational support for children, teachers and parents. This is an interactive educational resource for all ages addressing issues of health, science and well-being. It includes a comprehensive set of teachers' notes which are available to download. The site also has a dedicated parents' section providing health advice and links to other health related sites. See: www.bootslearningstore.com

Cares for Kids is a partnership of businesses, schools and volunteers that is changing children's lives and raising their aspirations. Business funding, volunteers, parents and teachers have come together to create breakfast clubs which give children the best start to the day.

Boots UK continued to support the national **Eisteddfod of Wales**, one of Europe's largest and oldest annual cultural festivals, which attracts over 150,000 visitors a year. To mark a decade of support, a Boots on-site shop was set up, as well as a stand promoting health and wellbeing. Boots UK Welsh speaking pharmacists conducted over 1,000 blood pressure checks and Body Mass Index checks throughout the week as well as providing over 300 No7 customer makeovers.

Corporate social responsibility

CSR committee: This consists of four board directors. Each principal business has a corporate social responsibility 'action group', with a 'champion' who has overall responsibility for the day-to-day running of the corporate social responsibility agenda, and for delivering against locally set targets. Guidance and additional expertise are available if required from a member of the corporate social responsibility team within the group.

CSR policy: The following information is taken from the 2010/11 CSR Report:

> We ensure robust governance and operational management of our Corporate Social Responsibility (CSR) agenda, which is fully aligned with our overall business strategy, values and goals.
>
> In 2004, we formally adopted a framework and governance process for managing and reporting our wide-ranging CSR activities. Underpinned by ongoing consultation and dialogue with internal and external stakeholders, our strategy was shaped under four key CSR areas; Community, Environment, Marketplace and Workplace. Each element has a long-term objective or ambition, the names of those accountable and responsible for delivery, together with detailed targets and milestones against which performance is monitored and reported. Each year we review the elements of our CSR order to ensure it best reflects the concerns of stakeholders. Every year, after consultation with our stakeholders, we review the Group's priorities in each of these four areas and, where appropriate, set new revised priorities within which targets can be set for the year ahead. For example in 2010/11, our priorities focused on community healthcare (community); carbon management (environment); product sustainability (marketplace); and healthy workplaces (workplace).
>
> Our CSR mission and purpose for Boots UK emerged from a comprehensive baseline review of our CSR strategy in the latter part of 2008/09:
>
> To be the UK's most socially responsible retailer in the health and beauty market.
>
> We will do this by:
> - Improving the health of our customers and their communities
> - Protecting the environment
> - Leading the development of sustainable products, and
> - Placing our customers and colleagues at the heart of our business

CSR report: Published annually.

Exclusions

The Boots Charitable Trust will not support the following:

- Projects benefiting people outside Nottinghamshire
- Individuals
- Organisations that are not registered charities and have income or expenditure of more than £5,000 per year
- Charities seeking funds to redistribute to other charities
- Projects for which there is a legal statutory obligation

Applications

Boots Charitable Trust

Applications to the trust are only accepted on the official application form which must be accompanied by your latest annual report and detailed accounts, constitution and policy documents. Letters of support from partnership and statutory organisations, local CVS's and so on will go to support your application, as will statistics on the numbers of people benefiting from your activities.

The application form can be downloaded as a Word document, or it can be posted out to you by the correspondent, to whom it should be returned once completed. All applications are responded to.

For amounts under £2,000 there is no deadline for applications and the decision period is one to two months.

For amounts over £2,000 the trustee meetings are held bi-monthly in January, March, May, July, September and November. The deadline for receipt of applications is the 7th of the month preceding the meeting i.e. 7 February for the March meeting, 7 April for the May meeting and so on. The decision period is two to four months.

Contact: Julie Lawrence, Boots Charitable Trust. Email: btc.cshelpdesk_team@boots.co.uk.

Boyer Allan Investment Investment Management LLP

Financial services

Correspondent: See 'Applications', Boyer Allan Investment Management LLP, 12–18 Grosvenor Gardens, London SW1W 0DH, United Kingdom (tel: 020 7881 8100; fax: 020 7881 8200; website: www.boyerallan.com)

Directors: J. E. K. Booker; J. M. E. Boyer; A. H. S. Tay; N. T. Allan; A. D. Callendar; C. R. Erith; G. S. L. Granville; T. G. Orchard; N. J. Tregear; S. M. Woolfe

Year end	31/03/2011
Turnover	£8,726,782
Pre-tax profit	£4,721,365

Nature of business: Provision of fund management services.

Company registration number: OC304444

Charitable donations

UK cash (latest declared):	2011	£201,500
	2009	£800,000
	2007	£500,000
	2006	£871,828
Total UK:	2011	£201,500
Total worldwide:	2011	£201,500
Cash worldwide:	2011	£201,500

Community involvement

Boyer Allan Investment Managements (BAIM) charitable support in the UK is channelled through **The Queen Anne's Gate Foundation** (Charity Commission no. 1108903) of which BAIM is the major benefactor. The foundation was established as a charitable trust in March 2005.

The following information is taken from the foundation's 2011 accounts:

> The aim of the benefactors is to contribute funds annually to the foundation, but the amounts contributed will depend in part on the somewhat volatile earnings of BAIM, and indeed in the long term on the ownership structure of BAIM. The foundation seeks to support projects and charities within the following broad criteria. It seeks to make a contribution that is meaningful in the context of the project/charity with which it is working. It tries to focus in particular on projects which might be said to make potentially unproductive lives productive. This tends to mean a bias towards educational and rehabilitative charities and those that work with underprivileged areas of society.
>
> There is an attempt to focus a significant proportion of donations on the UK and Asia. In principle and increasingly, there is a willingness to commit or soft commit funding for three years if it enables the chosen charity or project to plan more effectively. The foundation also supports

one-off appropriate causes, as they become available.

Corporate giving

The net income of the foundation, including the gifts from the benefactors for the year ended 30 April 2011 amounted to £201,500 (2010: £102,000) and donations were made totalling £673,000 (2010: £809,000).

Corporate social responsibility

CSR committee: None.

CSR policy: None published.

We were unable to determine the ratio of women to men on the board of directors.

CSR report: None.

Applications

In writing to: The Trustees, The Queen Anne's Gate Foundation, Wilcox and Lewis, Lincoln House, 1 Berrycroft, Willingham, Cambridge CB4 5JX.

BP plc

Oil and gas/fuel

Correspondent: Company Secretary, International Headquarters, 1 St James's Square, London SW1Y 4PD (tel: 020 7496 4000; fax: 020 7496 4630; website: www.bp.com)

Directors: Carl-Henric Svanberg, Chair; Bob Dudley, Chief Executive; Professor Dame Ann Dowling; Frank Bowman; Brendan Nelson; Phuthuma Nhleko; William Castell; Iain Conn; Dr Brian Gilvary; George David; Paul Anderson; Dr Byron Grote; Andrew Shilston; Ian Davis; Antony Burgmans; Cynthia Carroll (women: 2; men: 14)

Year end	31/12/2011
Turnover	£2,367,000,000
Pre-tax profit	£24,480,000

Nature of business: The group's principal activities comprise of exploration and production of crude oil and natural gas; refining, marketing, supply and transportation; and the manufacturing and marketing of petrochemicals. BP has major operations in Europe, North and South America, Asia, Australasia and parts of Africa.

Company registration number: 102498

Main locations: London

Total employees: 83,400

Membership: Arts & Business, BITC

Charitable donations

UK cash (latest declared):	2011	£4,500,000
	2009	£850,000
Total UK:	2011	£4,500,000
Total worldwide:	2011	£65,350,000
Cash worldwide:	2011	£65,350,000

Community involvement

Information taken from the company's 2011 annual report:

> Our strategy focuses on long-term partnerships with a small number of internationally renowned institutions: the British Museum, the National Portrait Gallery, the Royal Opera House and Tate Britain. In 2011, BP's partnerships were renewed and extended with all four institutions. BP will invest almost £10 million over the next five years.
>
> *Education programme*
>
> For over 40 years, BP has implemented a nationwide education programme for young people aged between 5–19 years. There are three main strands to the company's educational support:
>
> - Strategic partnerships with the Science Museum and the Natural History Museum
> - The BP Educational Service; and
> - The Schools Links programme
>
> The **Scottish Forest Alliance**, a partnership between BP, Forest Enterprise, RSPB Scotland and the Woodland Trust Scotland was launched in 2001. BP has made a funding pledge of £10 million over 10 years.

Corporate giving

In 2011, BP donated £17 million to UK organisations of which £4.5 million went directly to UK charities.

The 2011 annual report states:

> our direct spending on community programmes in 2011 was $103.7 million, (£65.2 million), which included contributions of: $37.5 million in the US (£23.6 million); $27.0 million in the UK (£17 million), including $7.2 million [£4.5 million] to UK charities, of which $2.5 million (£1.57 million) was for arts and culture, $2.8 million (£1.76 million), for enterprise development, and $1.6 million (£1 million) for education; $2.6 million in other European countries; and $36.6 million in the rest of the world.

Employee-led support

The **London 2012 Young Leaders Programme**, supported by BP and working in partnership with charities, is designed to give a group of disadvantaged young people the chance to make a positive change to their lives. This will be achieved by participation in a number of volunteering opportunities between April 2010 and the end of the Olympic and Paralympic Games in September 2012. BP employees are coaching 100 young people from communities around the UK, helping them organise community programmes, take a high-profile role in the Games and build skills they will need to be the leaders in their communities after the Games have ended.

Through the **BP Foundation**, employees are able to access matching funds for time spent on charitable activities and for donations and gifts to good causes. As a result of this employee match-giving programme, charitable organisations in the UK benefited from around £2.6 million and over 33,500 hours of volunteering time in 2010.

Commercially-led support

BP is a Principal member of Arts and Business.

Corporate social responsibility

CSR committee: There is a Community Outreach Team and a Safety, Ethics and Environment Assurance Committee.

CSR policy: This information was obtained from the company's Annual Report: 'We use our technical knowledge and global reach where relevant to support national and regional governments in their efforts to develop their economies' sustainability and provide public resources such as education and health.'

CSR report: Information was available from the Annual report, the Sustainability report and the company's website.

Applications

In writing to the correspondent.

BP Educational Services (BPES) can be contacted by writing to: PO Box 105, Rochester, Kent ME2 4BE (Email: bpes@bp.com; Tel: 08714723020).

Bradford and Bingley plc

Building society

Correspondent: Michael Hammond, Head of Corporate Responsibility, PO Box 88, Croft Road, Crossflatts, Bingley BD16 2UA (tel: 01274 555555/ 01216 338143; email: csr@bbg.co.uk; website: www.bbg.co.uk)

Directors: Richard Pym, Chair; Kent Atkinson; Richard Banks; Michael Buckley; Sue Langley; Philip McLelland; Keith Morgan; Louise Patten; John Tattershall (women: 2; men: 7)

Year end	31/12/2011
Turnover	£476,000,000
Pre-tax profit	£434,500,000

Nature of business: On 29 September 2008, all of B&B's retail branches and its savings accounts were transferred to Abbey. These were rebranded Santander in January 2010. The remainder of the business, including the mortgage books of B&B and specialist lending arm Mortgage Express were nationalised and taken into public ownership by the Government. B&B is permanently closed to new lending, but continues to provide services to existing borrowers.

UK Asset Resolution Ltd (UKAR) is the holding company established on 1 October 2010 to bring together the government-owned businesses of Bradford and Bingley plc (B&B) and Northern Rock (Asset Management) plc

(NRAM). The management and control of B&B was integrated with NRAM under UKAR on 1 October 2010.

B&B is permanently closed to new lending, but continues to provide services to existing mortgage borrowers, with mortgage accounts.

For company information about Bradford and Bingley and Mortgage Express, or for information supporting customers and mortgage intermediaries visit the Bradford and Bingley website.

Company registration number: 2269202

Membership: Arts & Business

Charitable donations

UK cash (latest declared):	2011	£13,150
	2009	£1,000,000
	2008	£1,400,000
Total UK:	2011	£13,150
Total worldwide:	2011	£13,150
Cash worldwide:	2011	£13,150

Corporate social responsibility

CSR committee: No details found.

CSR policy: Information taken from the UKAR website:

> UKAR aims to conduct its business in a socially responsible manner in respect of our customers, the environment, the communities we operate in and the workplace.

CSR report: None found.

Applications

In writing to the correspondent.

Other information

Statement taken from the 2011 annual report:

> Bradford & Bingley supports fundraising activities by matching the first £250 of funds raised per employee during the year, and by matching employee donations through a payroll-giving programme. During the year, B&B matched employee fundraising to the total of £6,370 (2010: £7,310) and payroll-giving totalled £13,540 (2010: £7,320).

UKAR colleagues raised £80,300 for 'corporate charities'. Donations were given to Business Action on Homeless, Samaritans, Shelter, Sue Ryder Manorlands, St Benedict's and Cystic Fibrosis Trust.

Total giving by the company/group appears to be £6,370 plus matched payroll giving of £6,775 totalling £13,145.

Information taken from the UKAR website:

> *Community*
>
> Our focus in 2012 is to support a charity for young people through the NSPCC.
>
> At each site we also have a local charity chosen by our colleagues. These are Sue Ryder – Manorlands in Crossflatts (West Yorkshire), Tiny Lives Special Babies in Doxford (Sunderland) and the Sir Bobby Robson Foundation in Gosforth (Newcastle upon Tyne)
>
> We are committed to:
>
> - Using the skills of the business to support education in our communities
> - Building the skills of our colleagues through community engagement
> - Supporting colleagues with their own community and charity initiatives

Bristol-Myers Squibb Pharmaceuticals Ltd

Pharmaceuticals

Correspondent: Fred Egenholf, Community Affairs, Philanthropy and Responsibility, BMS House, Uxbridge Business Park, Sanderson Road, Uxbridge UB8 1DH (tel: 01895 523000; fax: 01895 523010; website: www.b-ms.co.uk)

Directors: S. P. Allaker; A. Diarra

Year end	31/12/2010
Turnover	£158,145,000
Pre-tax profit	(£15,532,000)

Nature of business: The selling, distribution and development of ethical pharmaceutical products.

Company registration number: 2487574

Main locations: Moreton, Uxbridge, Chester

UK employees: 547

Charitable donations

UK cash (latest declared):	2010	£0
	2009	£10,000
	2008	£5,000
	2007	£2,000
	2006	£82,000
Total UK:	2010	£0

Corporate social responsibility

CSR committee: There was no evidence of a CSR Committee.

CSR policy: This information was obtained from the company's website:

> Our commitment to corporate social responsibility has remained consistently strong since the establishment of the Bristol-Myers Squibb Foundation. The mission of the foundation is to help reduce health disparities by strengthening community-based health care worker capacity, integrating medical care and community-based supportive services, and mobilising communities in the fight against disease.

Unable to determine the ratio of women to men on the Board.

CSR report: There was no evidence of a CSR report.

Exclusions

Bristol-Myers Squibb does not make grants in support of non-scientific or non-educational programs and there is no support for individuals, political appeals, religious appeals, local appeals not in areas of company presence, fundraising events or advertising in charity brochures.

Applications

Application should be made in writing to the correspondent, the Grants and Donations Administrator at the Uxbridge office.

Other information

Charitable donations by this company were nil in 2010.

Bristol-Myers Squibb supports strategic initiatives that help address health disparities in four key areas: HIV/AIDS in Africa, hepatitis in Asia, serious mental illness in the United States and cancer in central and eastern Europe. The company provides sponsorships, corporate memberships, and other kinds of support.

Bristol-Myers Squibb's grants and charitable programme supports local and national organisations whose purposes are compatible with the principal activity of the company.

At a local level, grants may also be given for community projects around the company's main sites, which are in Chester, Moreton (Wirral), and Uxbridge. Bristol-Myers Squibb does not make grants in support of non-scientific or non-educational programmes and there is no support for individuals, political appeals, religious appeals, local appeals not in areas of company presence, fundraising events or advertising in charity brochures.

Brit Insurance Holdings plc

Insurance

Correspondent: Company Secretary, 55 Bishopsgate, London EC2N 3AS (tel: 020 7984 8500; fax: 020 7984 8501; website: www.britinsurance.com)

Directors: Robert Barton, Chair; Dane Douetil, Chief Executive; Joseph MacHale; Peter Hazell; Cornelis Schrauwers; Willem Stevens; Maarten Hulshoff (women: 1; men: 6)

Year end	31/12/2010
Turnover	£1,442,700,000
Pre-tax profit	£116,400,000

Nature of business: A major UK-domiciled general insurance and reinsurance group writing both UK and international business.

Company registration number: 3121594

Charitable donations

UK cash (latest declared):	2011	£0
	2010	£582,000
	2009	£303,000
Total UK:	2011	£0

Corporate social responsibility

CSR committee: There was no evidence of a CSR committee.

CSR policy: This information was obtained from the company's website:

> We are committed to supporting local communities. Our strategy is to select charitable giving and community projects based on three criteria:
> - Projects should be for a good cause and operate in an area relevant to us
> - Financial involvement should be able to be leveraged for the benefit of the good cause, such as sponsored charity cricket matches
> - Projects should, where possible, offer alignment with the group's vision

CSR report: There was no evidence of a CSR report.

Applications

In writing to the correspondent.

Other information

In 2011, the company made no charitable donations (2010: £582,000).

In 2010, the Group entered a long-term partnership with Chance to Shine: an initiative run by the Cricket Foundation. The programme draws together people from all cultures and backgrounds and gives children including those with special educational needs the chance to acquire important skills, values and attitudes.

A day of play at the Brit Insurance Oval was again donated to the Lloyd's Community Programme to enable 190 children from Tower Hamlets to enjoy cricket coaching and a tournament.

We have no figures relating to the value of these activities.

British Airways plc

Aviation

Correspondent: Community Relations, HBBG, Waterside, Harmondsworth, Middlesex UB7 0GB (tel: 0870 850 9850; email: community.branch@britishairways.com; website: www.ba.com)

Directors: Martin Broughton, Chair; Keith Williams, Chief Executive Officer; Alison Reed; Nick Swift, Chief Financial Officer; Andrew Crawley; Frank van der Post; Rafael Sánchez-Lozano Turmo; Enrique Dupuy de Lôme; Ken Smart; Gavin Patterson (women: 1; men: 9)

Year end	31/12/2011
Turnover	£9,987,000,000
Pre-tax profit	£679,000,000

Nature of business: Principal activities: the operation of international and domestic scheduled and charter air services for the carriage of passengers, freight and mail and the provision of ancillary airline and travel services.

Company registration number: 1777777

Main locations: Harmondsworth

Total employees: 39,295

Membership: BITC, LBG

Charitable donations

UK cash (latest declared):	2011	£170,000
	2010	£190,000
	2009	£444,000
	2008	£398,000
	2007	£120,000
Total UK:	2011	£170,000
Total worldwide:	2011	£9,100,000
Cash worldwide:	2011	£170,000

Corporate social responsibility

CSR committee: Taken from the 2011/12 CSR report:

> One Destination, our Corporate Responsibility programme, is managed by our Environment team. We have recently enhanced the governance of the programme and it is now overseen by the British Airways Leadership Team chaired by our CEO, Keith Williams. In addition we have established a Corporate Responsibility Board chaired by Gavin Patterson, a British Airways non-executive director. The One Destination team reports to the British Airways Leadership Team on a quarterly basis and to the Corporate Responsibility Board on a six monthly basis.

CSR policy: Statement taken from the company's website:

> British Airways and Iberia place corporate responsibility at the heart of their business. They run comprehensive programmes which are geared towards managing and minimising the environmental impact, supporting the communities, conservation projects and charities in the countries they fly to, encouraging their customers and suppliers to act responsibly and providing a working environment that motivates, develops and supports their colleagues.

CSR report: Published annually.

Exclusions

No support for appeals from individuals, political appeals or religious appeals. Advertising in charity brochures is rarely undertaken.

Applications

All requests must be made in writing and sent on charity headed paper by fax to 020 8738 9848 or by post-to the address given above.

Other information

Total direct and in kind donations for 2011 were £9.1 million (2010: £8 million). Of these, direct charitable donations amounted to £170,000. A comprehensive review of the company's charitable and community contributions is given in its CSR report for 2011/12, from which the following statements and examples are taken:

> We continue to support communities in the countries where we operate through our partnerships with a network of UK charities. In 2011 we worked with 56 community and conservation organisations who have benefited from flight bursaries, excess baggage, merchandise, cargo space and fundraising events.
>
> We continue to be members of both the London Benchmarking Group (LBG) and Business in the Community. LBG's benchmarking model is used to assess our total contribution to the community. Business in the Community reported that our total direct and in kind donations for 2011 amounted to £9.1 million, £170,000 of which was direct charitable donations.
>
> ***The British Airways Community Learning Centre***
>
> The Centre (CLC) was opened in 1999 with a goal to share the talent and expertise of British Airways with students and teachers from local and UK schools and colleges. Six specialist trainers deliver regular one-day workshops for primary and secondary schools, giving an insight into the world of work. The programmes include information and communication technology (ICT), customer service, languages, global and environmental education. British Airways' corporate work experience scheme is also run from the CLC. In 2011, 7,953 young learners and teachers benefited from working with the team both at the CLC and in their schools, taking the total from 1999 to 69,343.
>
> ***Emergency relief flights***
>
> British Airways provides assistance to official disaster emergency appeals. An example is its most recent response in East Africa. In August 2011 we provided a freighter service to Addis Ababa which carried 110 tonnes of aid for Oxfam and UNICEF, and we continue to provide cargo space on scheduled Nairobi services to support the relief effort. We have also supported Oxfam, Save the Children and UNICEF with 50 complimentary flights. In addition, our passengers also contributed £136,000 during the two week onboard appeal in August.
>
> ***Environmental education***
>
> Our environmental education programmes give young people access to the natural world, offering learning experiences within the rich resource of nearby Harmondsworth Moor. We work in partnership with a number of external organisations such as the Wildfowl and Wetlands Trust, whose expertise helps us add depth and richness to our environmental programmes. In 2011, 1,126 young people participated in the programme.
>
> ***Language programmes***
>
> Our award-winning language programmes have continued to thrive with 1,037 young learners participating in either primary or secondary school language workshops at the CLC in 2011. Presentations about the importance of having a language in business have also proved to be very popular with 1,227 young learners having benefited from a school visit from the team in 2011.

The British Airways Language Flag Award (BALFA)
BALFA is a vocational language speaking test aimed at increasing linguistic accuracy and confidence. The scheme is open to any UK school. 89 schools and 210 teachers currently take part.

> ***Volunteering awards***
> In December 2011 thirteen colleagues from across British Airways were awarded Olympic tickets for their work and contribution to many charities across the UK and overseas. Colleagues who have worked tirelessly to fundraise for Flying Start were also recognised.

Charity Partner: Comic Relief

Flying Start
In 2011 Flying Start, the corporate partnership with Comic Relief raised £1,946,600 taking the total to almost £2.3 million since the partnership began in June 2010.

> ***Payroll giving***
> As many as 3,138 current and retired colleagues donate to charity through our payroll giving scheme, raising over £582,000 for their chosen charities. The top three charities are Highflight, which is a charity for young people with disabilities who want to learn to fly or have a flight experience, Cancer Research UK and Sreepur Village, Bangladesh, a project for abandoned women and children who design cards and other goods for sale in the UK.

British American Tobacco plc

Tobacco

Correspondent: UK Social Reporting Manager, Globe House, 4 Temple Place, London WC2R 2PG (tel: 020 7845 1000; fax: 020 7240 0555; website: www.bat.com)

Directors: Christine Morin-Postel; Robert Lerwill; Sir Nicholas Scheele; Karen de Segundo; Dr Gerard Murphy; Anthony Ruys; Richard Burrows, Chair; Nicandro Durante, Chief Executive; Ben Stevens, Finance Director and Chief Information Officer; John Daly; Ann Godbehere; Kieran Poynter (women: 3; men: 9)

Year end	31/12/2011
Turnover	£46,123,000,000
Pre-tax profit	£4,931,000,000

Nature of business: Principal activities: the manufacture, market and sale of cigarettes and other tobacco products.

Company registration number: 3407696

Subsidiaries include: Rothmans Finance plc, Tobacco Insurance Co. Ltd, Weston Investment Co. Ltd, Rothmans International Tobacco (UK) Ltd

Brands include: Benson and Hedges, Dunhill, Lucky Strike, Rothmans

Main locations: London, Southampton, Aylesbury

Total employees: 87,813

Membership: BITC, LBG

Charitable donations

UK cash (latest declared):	2011	£1,900,000
	2009	£2,000,000
	2008	£2,000,000
	2007	£2,200,000
	2006	£3,000,000
Total UK:	2011	£1,900,000
Total worldwide:	2011	£13,700,000
Cash worldwide:	2011	£13,700,000

Community involvement

Social investment activities include a range of community and charitable projects, centred on empowerment (giving people training, education and opportunities to help them develop), civic life (activities that aim to enrich public and community life) and sustainable agriculture and environment (contributions to local agriculture).

Corporate giving

In 2011, total community contributions amounted to £13.7 million (2010: £15.4 million) worldwide. Charitable donations in the UK accounted for £1.9 million (2010: £2 million). We could find no information regarding the distribution of these amounts. The Sustainability Report for 2011 states that reporting on community programmes is not given as it is considered that this information is more relevant locally and therefore global data is not collected.

Corporate social responsibility

CSR committee: There is a CSR committee comprising four board members. This is supported at regional and local levels through combined audit and CSR committees. The regional audit and CSR committees meet three times a year and feeds in to board level discussions.

CSR policy: The CSR committee reviews CSR and makes recommendations to the board as regards the company's management of its CSR and the conduct of business in accordance with the Statement of Business Principles; monitors and reviews the effectiveness of social, environmental and reputational issues, the group's plans for and progress of business sustainability; and the effectiveness of the CSR governance process.

CSR report: There is an annual Sustainability report. The report does not contain information on community programmes as it is considered that this information is more relevant locally and global data is not collected.

Exclusions

No support for causes outside the company's areas of focus.

Applications

In writing to the correspondent.

The British Land Company plc

Financial services, property

Correspondent: Anthony Braine, Group Secretary, York House, 45 Seymour Street, London W1H 7LX, Telephone, Fax +4 (tel: 020 7486 4466; fax: 020 7935 5552; email: info@britishland.com; website: www.britishland.com)

Directors: Dr Chris Gibson-Smith, Chair; Chris Grigg, Chief Executive; Lucinda Bell; Tim Roberts; Stephen Smith; Charles Maudsley; John Gildersleeve; Lord Turnbull; Aubrey Adams; Dido Harding; Richard Pym; Simon Borrows; William Jackson (women: 2; men: 13)

Year end	31/03/2011
Turnover	£310,000,000
Pre-tax profit	£830,000,000

Nature of business: Property investment and development, finance and investment.

Company registration number: 621920

Main locations: London

Total employees: 734

Membership: BITC, LBG

Charitable donations

UK cash (latest declared):	2011	£38,590
	2009	£92,400
	2008	£36,000
	2007	£177,093
	2006	£67,640
Total UK:	2011	£38,590
Total worldwide:	2011	£38,590
Cash worldwide:	2011	£38,590

Corporate social responsibility

CSR committee: There was evidence of a CSR Committee.

CSR policy: This information was obtained from the company's website:

> British Land builds constructive relationships with the communities in which it operates. It does this by supporting selected local initiatives through staff volunteering, skills mentoring and financial assistance. Larger national programmes may also be supported where they benefit communities neighbouring British Land's investments.
>
> British Land is strongly committed to investing in the future through education, the arts and sport, with particular emphasis on helping young people.

CSR report: A full CSR report was available from the company's website.

Exclusions

The company will not provide support for political purposes.

Applications

In writing to the correspondent.

Information available: The company's 2010/11 Corporate Social Responsibility Report is available online.

Other information

£38,590 (2010: £92,420) was donated during the year to a range of charities including those connected with education, the performing arts and charities local to where the company has property interests.

> Thanks to the generosity of staff, occupiers, suppliers, shoppers and other visitors to British Land properties, the company raised £771,000 for good causes, up from £492,000 last year, benefiting charities such as the British Heart Foundation, Fairbridge, Help for Heroes, Marie Curie Cancer Care and the Poppy Appeal.

Sponsorship: British Land undertakes extensive good cause sponsorship of organisations involved in arts, education and sport. These included British Land's national charity Fairbridge, Capital Kids Cricket, arts charity Create, the East London Business Alliance (ELBA), Habitat Heroes, LandAid, and The Prince's Regeneration Trust.

British Sky Broadcasting Group plc

Media

Correspondent: Donations and Sponsorships Team, Corporate Responsibility, Grant Way, Isleworth, Middlesex TW7 5QD (tel: 020 7705 3000; fax: 020 7705 3030; email: corp.responsibility@bskyb.com; website: corporate.sky.com)

Directors: Allan Leighton; Arthur Siskind; Tom Mockridge; David DeVoe; David Evans; Gail Rebuck; Jacques Nasser; Lord Wilson of Dinton; Nicholas Ferguson; Andrew Higginson; Andrew Griffith; Daniel Rimer; James Murdoch, Chair; Jeremy Darroch, Chief Executive Officer (women: 1; men: 14)

Year end	30/06/2011
Turnover	£6,597,000,000
Pre-tax profit	£1,014,000,000

Nature of business: Satellite pay television operator, BSkyB launched its digital television services in the UK on 1 October 1998.

Company registration number: 2247735

Subsidiaries include: BSkyB Finance Ltd, Sky Subscribers Services Ltd, Sky Ventures Ltd, Sky In-Home Service Ltd, Sky Television Ltd

Main locations: Leeds, Manchester, Harrogate, Livingstone, Dunfermline, Isleworth

Total employees: 16,006

Membership: Arts & Business, BITC, LBG

Charitable donations

UK cash (latest declared):	2011	£9,119,000
	2010	£9,160,000
	2008	£5,195,000
	2006	£3,825,000
	2004	£1,050,061
Total UK:	2011	£10,226,500
Total worldwide:	2011	£10,226,500
Cash worldwide:	2011	£9,119,000

Community involvement

Sky's 'The Bigger Picture' is the company's community programme focusing on the arts, education, environment, sport, health and taking social responsibility for its activities. Sky continues to align its community investment to the wider goals of the business and its customers and utilises its brand, platform and technology in community investment.

Current initiatives include: Sky Sports ECB Coach Education Programme, Living for Sport, Project Green Sky, Karma Life, Joining In and Accessibility. For more detailed information on Sky's substantial environmental, community and charitable contribution, go to: www.jointhebiggerpicture.com.

Corporate giving

The following information is taken from the company's Bigger Picture Review for 2011:

> In 2010/11, Sky made total community contributions in the UK and Ireland of £11.3 million (including management costs). This was broken down as follows (amount in brackets):
>
> - Cash 80.6% (£9.1 million)
> - Time 5.9% (£662,500)
> - In kind 3.9% (£445,000)
> - Management costs 9.6% (£1.1 million)
>
> The following areas were supported:
>
> - Health 30%
> - Art and culture 21%
> - Education and young people 19%
> - Environment 16%
> - Social welfare 10%
> - Other 5%
> - Emergency relief 0.1%

In kind support

(See also 'Commercially led support')

Sport: Over 25,000 young people have benefited from **Sky Sports Living for Sport**, a grassroots sports initiative run by the **Youth Sport Trust**.

This programme aims to support teachers working with young people between the ages of 11 and 16 who may be finding school life difficult for one reason or another. It can be used in different ways, e.g. to help meet behaviour improvement targets, or to support attendance strategies. The programme is about 'using sport as a starting point to motivate and inspire young people back into school life.'

For nine years, Sky has been working with *Youth Sport Trust* to use sport to inspire young people. *Sky Sports Living for Sport* is available to all secondary schools in the UK. So far over a third of the UK's secondary schools have joined in, with over 25,000 young people benefiting with improved self-confidence and self-esteem.

The initiative involves teachers working with a group of 11–16 year olds within the school to identify a sports activity they're interested in. Through taking part in a series of lessons and organising their own sports event at the end, the project is designed to inspire and support every participant in areas relevant to them, whether it's improving confidence, attainment at school, or leading a healthier lifestyle.

Teachers submit their plans for their bespoke project online, and in return Sky provides a starter pack and sports kit for all young people to help get the project underway. As each school project progresses, a mentoring visit is arranged from one of Sky's team of past and present sports stars, to offer inspiration and motivation to the group. Sky's 17 athlete mentors, led by its ambassador, Olympic sprinter Darren Campbell, have life stories that highlight the rewards and challenges of being an athlete, and aim to show participants that anything is possible. They cover a whole host of sports from wheelchair basketball and rugby to judo and sailing.

Sky Sports ECB Coach Education programme has trained over 23,000 grassroots coaches, helping the ECB (England and Wales Cricket Board) to provide more coaching courses and deliver better quality coaching resources.

The programme offers training at four levels, beginning with 14–18 year olds who want to get involved in leading cricket activities at school or a club. It goes right through to training at Head Coach level, equipping coaches with the skills to enable the development of players' technical, tactical, mental, physical and lifestyle requirements, at club, district or county level.

For more details visit the website: www.livingforsport.skysports.com.

Employee-led support

Information taken from the Bigger Picture Review 2011:

> ***Community***
>
> We believe that our 16,500 people can help us make a real difference in our local communities and reap benefits at the same time, so we try to make it easy for them to get involved. We give them two days of paid time off each year to volunteer, and create engaging Environment, Sport and Arts initiatives for them to get involved with. We are

generous with our contributions to their payroll giving and fundraising efforts.

Our employees can make tax-free donations to a charity of their choice directly from their salary and we give an extra 50p for every £1 given. We also support employee fundraising with pound-for-pound matching, up to £300 if fundraising as an individual, or £1,000 if fundraising as part of a team of two or more Sky people. Our people have generously donated £350,000 through Payroll Giving and one-off donations to a variety of UK registered charities over the course of the past year, which Sky has matched with a further £150,000.

Payroll giving: Employees can participate in a Give As You Earn scheme.

Commercially-led support

Sponsorship: ***The arts*** – BSkyB is a Principal member of Arts and Business.

Information taken from the 2011 Bigger Picture Review:

One of the biggest challenges in the arts world is securing funding to support innovative and new works of art. That's why, in April 2011, Sky Arts launched the Sky Arts Ignition Series. The Sky Arts Ignition Series will collaborate with six arts organisations over three years to create brand new works. For each chosen project, Sky Arts will provide a cash investment of up to £200,000 and work with the arts partners to bring their projects to a wider audience on screen and on the ground. Sky Arts will also provide marketing, publicity and new media support.

We also launched the Sky Arts Ignition: Futures Fund which is designed to help young talent working in visual art, theatre, performance art, music, dance or literature to bridge the development gap from school or college to becoming a working artist. The fund will support five individuals aged 18 – 30 with a bursary of £30,000 each and provide each artist with a mentor from Sky, who will help develop their commercial skills and knowledge.

We continued to support some of the most prestigious arts festivals and events both by investing in the organisation's growth and sustainability, and by bringing the festival experience to those who couldn't attend through our programming. Between October 2010 and May 2011 we took The Book Show on the road to leading literary festivals. We also broadcast from and supported a number of music festivals across the country including Isle of Wight, Latitude and the Cambridge Folk Festival. Sky is now the largest broadcaster of music festivals in the UK and Ireland.

Through our Sky Arts At... programme we partnered with 18 regional arts organisations across the UK and Ireland, bringing the best regional arts content to our viewers, and supporting local arts communities by raising their profile. Our partnerships this year have included the Dublin Theatre Festival, Frank Zappa festival at The Roundhouse, The Royal Court, Rambert Dance Company and Museums at Night.

Sport

Sky Sports Living for Sport

Our successful Sky Sports Living for Sport initiative uses sport to make a difference to young people's lives. The initiative provides secondary schools with sports star mentor visits and resources to motivate and inspire young people through sport and help them gain the academic and life skills they need. Teachers work with a group of pupils to identify a sports activity they're interested in. By taking part in a series of lessons and organising their own celebration event at the end, the project is designed to inspire and support every participant in areas relevant to them, whether it's improving confidence, attainment at school, or leading a healthier lifestyle.

Our team of 23 athlete mentors comes from a whole range of backgrounds and sports and they visit participating schools to share their life-changing stories. This year, Ryder Cup winning captain Colin Montgomerie, footballers Jamie Redknapp and Ruud Gullit and many others took time out to coach and inspire local school pupils. The programme has shown tremendous results in terms of changing behaviour and improving academic grades amongst the students participating. Participants achieved 14% higher than the national average in their English exams, and 4% higher than the national average in maths. A huge number also showed improvement in confidence, attitudes to learning, and health and wellbeing. So far 1,650 secondary schools have joined in. This equates to more than a third of all UK secondary schools and is on the way to our target of 2,000 schools by 2012. Over 33,000 young people have benefited from Sky Sports Living for Sport over the last eight years.

Cricket: Sky has teamed up with the England and Wales Cricket Board (ECB) to 'make sure future generations get the opportunity to experience the game'. The Sky Sports ECB Coach Education programme equips coaches with the necessary skills to deliver high quality coaching at all levels of the game – from coaching assistant to county head coach.

Over the past year, [2011], we've worked with the England and Wales Cricket Board to bring through over 10,000 more cricket coaches. And through Sky Sports Living for Sport, we've worked with the Youth Sport Trust to engage and inspire another 7,500 young people.

Cycling: Cycling is one of Britain's most successful sports, and through our five-year partnership with British Cycling, we want to encourage more people to get involved – our aim is to get a million more people on their bikes by 2013. our Sky Ride campaign, with free events, activities information and support to inspire and help people of all ages or abilities to get on their bikes and have fun. And we support the elite through our partnership with British Cycling and creation of Team Sky, a professional British road racing team.

This, our second year of Sky Ride mass participation cycling events, saw us holding 12 events in 10 cities. Working with British Cycling and partner councils we open up the streets of major cities across Britain to bikes, giving people the opportunity to ride around the traffic free streets of their city with family and friends, for free. Over 200,000 cyclists of all ages and abilities took part this year, including 85,000 at the Mayor of London's Sky Ride event through central London. In each Sky Ride city we also delivered a programme of Sky Ride Locals – free, weekly led cycle rides by British Cycling trained ride leaders. The rides capture the enthusiasm created by the city events and offer a way for people to keep cycling. Riders can pick a level to suit their age and ability giving them a chance to improve confidence levels.

In 2010, over 500 rides took place, attracting 11,000 participants. 84% of Sky Ride Local attendees said they would definitely cycle more regularly as a result of taking part.

Corporate social responsibility

CSR committee: There is a CSR committee.

CSR policy: Taken from the 2010/11 annual report and accounts:

Contributing positively to our communities

Sky's recognisable brand, and our presence in over 10 million homes, provides us with a unique opportunity and responsibility to make a positive contribution to the communities in which we live and work.

We focus our efforts in three areas where we believe we can make the most difference: environment; sport; and arts. We regularly scrutinise our strategy to ensure our activities continue to be appropriate.

CSR report: Bigger Picture Review is a comprehensive annual report on the company's CSR activities.

Exclusions

No support for animal welfare charities, appeals from individuals, elderly people, heritage, medical research, overseas projects, political or religious appeals.

Applications

Refer to the company's website for further information on the company's corporate responsibility programme – 'The Bigger Picture'.

British Sugar plc

Sugar refiners

Correspondent: R S Schofield, Company Secretary, Sugar Way, Peterborough PE2 9AY (tel: 01733 563171; fax: 01733 563068; website: www.britishsugar.co.uk)

Directors: M. I. Carr; K. L. Carter; G. De Jaegher; T. Dornan; M. Rowlands; S. D. Moon; R. N. Pike; P. Frampton

Year end	17/09/2011
Turnover	£777,600,000
Pre-tax profit	£123,100,000

Nature of business: British Sugar Group is a wholly owned subsidiary of international food, ingredients and retail group, Associated British Foods plc (ABF) for which there is a separate listing. It operates from locations in East Anglia and the East Midlands (Bury St Edmunds, Cantley, Newark, Peterborough, and Wissington).

Company registration number: 315158

Main locations: Wissington, Newark, Peterborough, Bury St Edmunds, Cantley

UK employees: 2,117

Total employees: 2,117

Charitable donations

UK cash (latest declared):	2011	£33,000
	2009	£48,000
	2008	£34,000
	2007	£100,000
	2006	£100,000
Total UK:	2011	£33,000
Total worldwide:	2011	£33,000
Cash worldwide:	2011	£33,000

Corporate social responsibility

CSR committee: There was no evidence of a separate CSR Committee.

CSR policy: British Sugar has particular interests in projects in the areas of health and healthcare, education, environment and enterprise, with employee inspired community projects receiving special attention.

The company encourages its sites to play an active role in local communities through media visits, school activities, agricultural and environmental events.

Unable to determine the ratio of women to men on the board.

CSR report: There was no evidence of a separate CSR report; however information was available from the company's website.

Exclusions

No support for individuals or political purposes.

Applications

In writing to the correspondent.

Other information

Donations to UK charities are made on a money match basis matching employees' efforts pound for pound. In 2010 donations amounted to £33,000 (2009: £48,000).

Charitable donations used to be made through the company's charity, British Sugar Foundation. The trustees' report contained in the accounts for 2007 states:

> At a board meeting on 24 January 2008 the trustees resolved to wind up the charity. The decision was made as there are no longer any advantages to making charitable donations via the charitable company. The contribution that British Sugar plc would have donated to the charity each period will continue to be distributed directly by British Sugar plc and will be administered with regard to the objectives of the charitable company. The overheads of running the scheme will continue to be funded by British Sugar plc and not deducted from the amount available for donations. The reserves of £8,555 were distributed prior to the application to wind up the charitable company.

Britvic Soft Drinks plc

Drinks manufacture

Correspondent: Corporate Responsibility Committee, Britvic House, Broomfield Road, Chelmsford, Essex CM1 1TU (tel: 01245 261871; fax: 01245 261871; email: info@britvic.co.uk; website: www.britvic.co.uk)

Directors: Gerald Corbett, Chair; Paul Moody, Chief Executive; John Gibney; Ben Gordon; Joanne Averiss; Michael Shallow; Bob Ivell (women: 1; men: 6)

Year end	02/10/2011
Turnover	£1,290,400,000
Pre-tax profit	£105,100,000

Nature of business: Britvic plc is one of Europe's leading soft drinks companies. Current operations comprise Britvic GB, Britvic Ireland, and Britvic France. The group is completed by Britvic International which manages the export and franchise of many of the group's brands across more than 50 countries.

Company registration number: 5604923

Main locations: Ballygowan, Beckton, Huddersfield, Leeds, Norwich, Rugby, Widford

Total employees: 3,532

Membership: BITC, LBG

Charitable donations

UK cash (latest declared):	2011	£581,300
	2009	£242,000
	2008	£83,000
Total UK:	2011	£581,300
Total worldwide:	2011	£581,300
Cash worldwide:	2011	£581,300

Community involvement

Britvic continued to support local groups through the **Britvic Community Fund** held at the Essex Community Foundation. Grassroots projects, such as local breakfast clubs and local charities received funding.

The company decided to support a water project in Ethiopia for its global community initiative for 2010/11. Britvic also continues to support UNICEF.

Charity partner: Barnardo's is Britvic GB's company charity. Alongside the company's usual donation, Britvic also organised a month-long 'Big Britvic Barnardo's Raffle', offering staff the chance to win prizes donated by the company.

This year saw the development of a programme to help Barnardo's target youngsters who are experiencing problems due to not being in education, employment or training. Barnardo's has now received government funding to deliver a pilot of this programme in North London. Britvic's own programmes will serve as an induction to their own workshops for this identified group

Corporate giving

In 2010/11 the group gave charitable donations of £581,300 (2009: £242,000).

Employee-led support

Learning for Life

A long-term community investment strategy has been launched – 'Learning for Life'. Community investment and volunteering policies underpin the programme and these policies encourage employees to play their part in the community and support their chosen charities.

Britvic employees are given two paid days a year to use for volunteering opportunities, either individually or as part of a team. 2010/11 saw 50 employees from the Beckton site rejuvenate the outside area of a local school.

Commercially-led support

Charity partner: This year Britvic and PepsiCo brands have partnered with Groundwork (a leading environmental regeneration charity) to start a movement to transform outdoor spaces all over the country. Every drink represents one square centimetre of real land transformed in either a park, playground, skate park or 5-a-side football pitch.

Corporate social responsibility

CSR committee: There was no evidence of a separate CSR Committee.

CSR policy: Britvic believes in being an active member of the communities in which we operate. We support those communities through schemes such as matched funding, training, and employee volunteering.

CSR report: A CSR report was available from the company's website.

Applications

In writing to the correspondent.

Broadland Properties Ltd

Property

Correspondent: The Company Secretary, 137 Scalby Road, Scarborough, North Yorkshire YO12 6TB (tel: 01723 373461; fax: 01723 500021)

Directors: J. Guthrie, Chair; P. J. Guthrie; R. Guthrie; M. Robson; M. J. Harrison; R. G. Urquhart; J. M. Hill

Year end	30/09/2011
Turnover	£30,968,000
Pre-tax profit	£6,119,000

Nature of business: Property dealers.

Company registration number: 483844

Main locations: Scarborough

UK employees: 284

Total employees: 284

Charitable donations

UK cash (latest declared):	2011	£49,300
	2009	£10,700
	2008	£684,500
	2007	£288,500
	2006	£115,700
Total UK:	2011	£49,300
Total worldwide:	2011	£49,300
Cash worldwide:	2011	£49,300

Corporate social responsibility

CSR policy: There was no information regarding CSR.

Unable to determine the ratio of women to men on the board.

Exclusions

Generally no support for local appeals outside of the Scarborough area. No support for advertising in charity brochures, animal welfare, appeals from individuals, overseas projects, political appeals or religious appeals.

Applications

In writing to the correspondent. The company's UK giving, in the main supports groups with a Scarborough postcode.

Other information

During the year the group made charitable donations totalling £49,300. Beneficiaries included: Scarborough Cricket Club (£8,000); Scarborough Rugby Union Football Club (£7,500); Scarborough Symphony Orchestra (£2,500) and Spifox (£2,000). Numerous smaller donations were made to a wide variety of charities and local causes including £21,500 in Poland by the Polish subsidiaries.

N Brown Group plc

Retail – miscellaneous

Correspondent: Philip Harland, Company Secretary, Griffin House, 40 Lever Street, Manchester M60 6ES (tel: 01612 368256; fax: 01612 382662; email: enquiries@nbrown.co.uk; website: www.nbrown.co.uk)

Directors: Lord Alliance of Manchester, Chair; Alan White, Chief Executive; Anna Ford; Nigel Alliance; Dean Moore, Group Finance Director; Ivan Fallon; Lord Stone of Blackheath; John McGuire (women: 1; men: 7)

Year end	26/02/2011
Turnover	£718,800,000
Pre-tax profit	£94,500,000

Nature of business: Provider of direct home shopping.

Company registration number: 814103

Brands include: Brands include: Ambrose Wilson, Fifty Plus, High and Mighty, Marisota, Simply Be and J D Williams.

Main locations: Manchester

Total employees: 3,256

Charitable donations

UK cash (latest declared):	2011	£71,000
	2010	£70,569
	2009	£85,211
	2008	£114,392
	2007	£52,371
Total UK:	2011	£71,000
Total worldwide:	2011	£71,000
Cash worldwide:	2011	£71,000

Corporate social responsibility

CSR committee: No information available.

CSR policy: The Group is committed to investment in, and support of, the communities in which it operates.

CSR report: CSR reporting is contained within the annual report and accounts and on the company's website.

Exclusions

No support for political appeals.

Applications

In writing to the correspondent.

Other information

During 2010/11, the company made charitable donations totalling £71,000 (2009/10: £70,500). Information taken from the annual report and accounts:

> The group maintains its close links with the Christie Hospital in Manchester and the Retail Trust. It also regularly encourages employees to participate in fundraising activities for these, and other worthwhile causes. These events can be anything from national support such as Children in Need and the Alzheimer's Society to very local causes for hospices and children's hospitals in and around Greater Manchester. The group maximises the potential donation by matching the level of money raised by employees to double the size of the donation.
>
> In the last financial year, money was raised for a number of noteworthy causes, such as £21,000 for Access and 180 employees taking part in the Manchester Bupa 10k run. The group once again supported the Canal Boat adventure charity where employees paid for more than 100 deprived and disabled children to enjoy a holiday. In addition the group's employees have organised fundraising activities to assist the following good causes: Barnardo's; Christies; Help for Heroes; Crossroads Care Association; MacMillan Cancer Care; Beechwood Cancer Care; Children in Need; FACT (Families for Autistic Children); When You Wish Upon a Star; and Cheetham's School of Music.
>
> Numerous separate charitable fundraising events were held by employees and sponsored, or participated in, by the group, raising more than £60,000.

The company has in the past made in kind contributions, for example during 2009/10 it donated a considerable quantity of clothing stock to Wood Street Mission in Manchester, a charity established to help poor families and children. We have no information regarding in kind contributions for this financial year.

Bruntwood Ltd

Property

Correspondent: Kate Vokes, Company Secretary, City Tower, Piccadilly Plaza, Manchester, Greater Manchester M1 4BT (tel: 01612 361647; email: info@bruntwood.co.uk; website: www.bruntwood.co.uk)

Directors: Michael Oglesby, Chair; Chris Oglesby, Chief Executive; Rowena Burns; Kate Vokes; Kevin Crotty; Andrew Butterworth; Kate Harrison; Peter Crowther; Chris Roberts; Rob Yates; Iain Grant; John Marland; Colin Sinclair; David Guest; Craig Burrow; Richard Burgess (women: 3; men: 13)

Year end	30/09/2011
Turnover	£99,049,000
Pre-tax profit	£11,204,000

Nature of business: Property Investment Company.

Company registration number: 2825044

Main locations: Leeds, Liverpool

UK employees: 431

Total employees: 431

Membership: Arts & Business, BITC

Charitable donations

UK cash (latest declared):	2011	£1,200,000
	2009	£690,000
	2007	£500,000
Total UK:	2011	£1,200,000
Total worldwide:	2011	£1,200,000
Cash worldwide:	2011	£1,200,000

Community involvement

The Oglesby Charitable Trust (Charity Commission no. 1026669)

The trustees support a variety of charitable causes including artistic development, both at an individual and a group level, educational grants and building projects, environmental improvement projects, medical aid and research and improving the lives and welfare of the underprivileged, where possible, by the encouragement of self-help. Their policy is primarily, but not exclusively, to support local charities in the Greater Manchester Area and the North West of England. They have recently widened their geographical support to make donations to charities involved in projects of which the trustees have become aware in East Africa and Northern India.

Acorn Fund (smaller donations):

The Oglesby Charitable Trust has a fund set aside each year for smaller donations and these range between £200 and £1,000.

Corporate giving

10% of the company's profit was given to good causes in 2010/11. This figure amounted to £1.2 million, £955,000 of which was donated to The Oglesby Charitable Trust. The trust's income is currently around £955,000 per annum and grants in the year 2010/11 totalled £760,000. Beneficiaries of the trust have included: National Asthma Campaign, Deaf Blind Society and the Community Foundation for Greater Manchester.

Employee-led support

The company supports a wide variety of charitable causes with one charity becoming the main focus for staff fundraising every few years. These projects are selected on the basis of the difference they can make to local communities. Since 2010, staff fundraising efforts have been focused on OnSide and the Factory Youth Zone in North Manchester. Bruntwood staff have pledged to raise £300,000 over the next three years.

Corporate social responsibility

CSR committee: There was no evidence of a separate CSR Committee.

CSR policy: This information was obtained from the company's CSR Report:

> Bruntwood's work in its communities covers a very broad canvas, from working to take care of the environment to improving people's quality of life through charitable and cultural support. We are committed to spend 10% of our annual profits on charitable activity, as well as the additional contributions made by our staff in volunteering and fundraising and the personal contribution of the family through the Oglesby Charitable Trust.

CSR report: A full and detailed CSR report is available on the company's website.

Exclusions

A list of exclusions can be found on: www.oglesbycharitabletrust.co.uk.

Applications

In writing to the correspondent.

Applications to the Oglesby Charitable Trust should be made using the form downloadable from the trust's website (www.oglesbycharitabletrust.co.uk) and returned to: The Oglesby Charitable Trust, PO Box 336, Altrincham, Cheshire WA14 3XD.

BT Group plc

Telecommunications

Correspondent: Steve Kelly, Corporate Responsibility Team, BT Group Communications, 81 Newgate Street, London EC1A 7AJ (tel: 020 7356 5000/ 020 7356 6678; fax: 020 7356 5520; website: www.btplc.com)

Directors: Michael Rake, Chair; Gavin Patterson; Tony Chanmugam, Group Finance Director; Tony Ball; Phil Hodkinson; Eric Daniels; Patricia Hewitt; Ian Livingston, Chief Executive; Karen Richardson; Jasmine Whitbread; Nicholas Rose (women: 3; men: 8)

Year end	31/03/2012
Turnover	£18,897,000,000
Pre-tax profit	£2,445,000,000

Nature of business: The provision of fixed lines, broadband, mobile and TV products and services and networked IT services.

Company registration number: 4190816

Subsidiaries include: Cellnet Group Ltd, Martin Dawes Telecommunications Ltd, Telecom Securicor Cellular Radio Ltd

Main locations: London

UK employees: 73,900

Total employees: 89,000

Membership: BITC, LBG

Charitable donations

UK cash (latest declared):	2010	£2,500,000
	2009	£2,500,000
	2008	£2,500,000
	2007	£3,000,000
	2006	£2,500,000
Total UK:	2010	£2,500,000
Total worldwide:	2012	£29,900,000

Community involvement

BT's website states:

> We want to make a positive contribution to society. We recognise by investing in and supporting our communities, we can help to build a more economically sustainable, educated and socially-inclusive society. That's why we invest one per cent of our annual pre-tax profits into programmes which benefit communities and the environment.
>
> We focus our investment on areas related to our core business, using information and communications technology (ICT) to build stronger communities. The time, expertise and money that we give, supports our work with community partners, helps motivate our people and enhances our reputation.

Charity Partners: BT works with a number of strategic charity partners helping people benefit from improved communications skills and technology.

> We work in close partnership with many charities and place value in maintaining strong, long-term relationships. At the end of March 2012 our customers and employees helped raise over £1 million for *ChildLine* and *Cancer Research UK*.
>
> We work in partnership with many charities, but here we focus on relationships with the British Red Cross, who we support with direct funding, ChildLine and Cancer Research UK both of whom our employees and customers raise funds for.

British Red Cross is supported with its global disaster management programme. BT's involvement in 2012 provided funding for IT and communications kits to help vulnerable global communities prepare for, respond to, and recover from natural disasters.

ChildLine is the organisation that provides support for children and young people, including a 24 hour helpline. BT has worked with ChildLine since its inception 25 years ago.

Cancer Research UK, the UK's leading cancer charity, has been supported through the year by BT employees through various fundraising events.

London 2012 Olympic Games and Paralympic Games:

BT is investing in education programmes that help young people across the UK engage with the Games at the same time as developing their communication skills. With the company's support a Legacy Centre has been built just outside the Olympic Park as a resource for young people in the area.

BT Paralympic World Cup is supported by BT with a four year commitment to disability sport and working in collaboration with The Lord's Taverners. BT will build 12 sensory rooms across the country for young people with disabilities and communication challenges.

MyDonate was launched by BT in 2011. This giving platform, which doesn't have a service or commission is now used by more than 3,000 charities, with around 100 new charities joining us every week.

Country Charity Partnership Programme was launched by BT Global Services to support communities across the world. To date, projects in the Unites States, France, Spain, Germany, Benelux and India have been funded.

Learning and skills: This programme involves BT working with a number of partners on projects that grow young people's communication and collaboration skills, and supports them in the transition from learning to the world of work. BT has also developed learning and skills projects for young people as part of 'Get Set', the London 2012 Olympic and Paralympic Games' official education programme.

Telethons:

> BT people and our technology support the largest telethons in the UK. This year we got behind BBC Children in Need and Sport Relief, helping raise the money needed to support people in need around the world. For Sport Relief alone, our network handled up to 134 calls per second.

Corporate giving

In the 2012 annual report and accounts, BT states: 'Our investment in society is made through time, cash and in kind contributions – and totalled just over £31.9 million in 2012.' Investment has three strategic priorities set out in the 2011 Sustainability Report: building stronger communities; reducing carbon emissions and the company's impacts on the environment and behaving responsibly – towards customers, people and suppliers (figures include cash, time and in kind)]. 'Of this, in 2012, £29.9 million (94%) was focused on community investment.'

> Overall we invested £31.9 million in 2012, which at 1.5% was well above our target of a minimum investment of 1% of the prior year's adjusted profit before taxation. In 2012 the calculation methodology was changed in order to create a stronger link to current performance. In 2011 and 2010 the calculation was based on adjusted profit before taxation from two years previously.

Unfortunately we have been unable to determine BT's UK only cash or in kind contributions and have therefore given the global figure of £29.9 million as its worldwide contribution.

In kind support:

BT gives in kind support to charities such as ChildLine, and since 1986 has provided a Freephone number (08001111), office space and technical expertise. Since its inception the charity has answered more than three million calls.

Employee-led support

Information taken from the 2012 annual report and accounts:

> We are committed to investing in the communities that we live and work in and our people are encouraged to participate in their local communities. We run a formal volunteering programme to help them do this. In 2012 11% of our people volunteered some 50,000 volunteer days with an estimated value of £15.6 million to our communities.

BT Community Champions awards scheme is a global programme giving grants to community and voluntary organisations BT employees volunteer with. The awards recognise employees who participate in voluntary work within their communities either in BT time, or in their own time. Anyone who has been involved with a community organisation or charity for more than a year can apply for a cash grant of up to £500 or branded sports clothing for their group.

Country Charity Partnerships programme, launched in the 2010, encourages employees globally to propose partnerships between BT and community and environmental organisations that benefit the communities where the company operates. Through this programme BT is providing the charity One Economy with support over the next two years to fund the development of an online platform for young people to teach adults how to use the internet. The project will target low-income communities and is designed to help young people and adults learn ICT skills and improve their employment prospects. BT employees will also volunteer their time to help One Economy provide digital literacy training.

In 2009/10, BT's **Volunteer Programme** has provided more than 28,000 employee days to local communities and a range of charities and social enterprises. Each employee can volunteer up to three days of work time at a charity they are passionate about. Examples include schools and youth groups, organisations supporting the elderly or disadvantaged groups, and environmental programmes to help make communities cleaner and greener.

BT also sponsors a number of specific programmes to increase skills through volunteering. One supports young people moving from education into work, while another places skilled BT people on secondment to its charitable partners.

London 2012 Volunteering Week London 2012 Olympic Games and Paralympic Games: BT employees were involved as volunteers during the Games and participated in projects in the run up to the Olympic Games and Paralympic Games, including a programme to improve the canals and walkways near the Olympic Park.

Payroll giving: The following statements are taken from the company's website:

> Over 10 per cent of our UK employees donate regularly through our Give As You Earn (GAYE) scheme – making it one of the largest of its kind in the UK.
>
> By March 2012 over £2.5 million was donated by employees in the UK alone. with an additional £1 million in matched contributions donated by BT.

Commercially-led support

The arts – Through a pioneering partnership with the UK's leading modern art gallery, Tate, BT sponsors its website Tate Online.

The BT Series allows visitors to the site to explore works by selected artists and ask about their work. This series has been developed with BT's creative design and film-making team. BT provides Tate with technological support, online broadcasting and hosting and develops innovative projects such as this. Support is also given to the preservation of the UK's telecommunications heritage.

Corporate social responsibility

CSR committee: Information taken from the 2012 annual report and accounts:

> The Committee for Sustainable and Responsible Business oversees our corporate responsibility, environment and community activities, including charitable expenditure and the Better Future strategy for maximising our contribution to society.
>
> The committee has a diverse membership, which is designed to bring as wide a range of views as possible to the review of corporate responsibility and sustainable business within BT. We also interact with the independent Leadership Advisory Panel chaired by Jonathon Porritt. The panel provides advice on corporate responsibility issues, and the panel chair attends one CSRB meeting per year.
>
> The panel produces an annual statement which is set out in our Better Future report. The CSRB met four times in 2012. We have overseen and approved investment in projects which make a difference for the communities in which we operate and our environment with a focus on building stronger communities both through the use of technology and supporting volunteering activities of employees.

CSR policy: The company's Sustainability Report for 2012 states:

> We make many positive contributions to society, the economy and the environment that we operate in through our people, products and services, and using resources responsibly. We know that there is more to do to help meet the challenges that society faces, and that we

> need to step up to deliver on our leadership ambition.
>
> Our Better Future strategy sets out how we will become a responsible and sustainable business leader. Our strategy evolves in response to changes in our operating environment and stakeholder views.

For more information visit:

www.btplc.com/Responsiblebusiness

CSR report: Better Future report published annually, covers progress against BT's goal to be a responsible and sustainable business leader.

Exclusions

No response to circular appeals or generic applications. No denominational appeals, political appeals, appeals from individuals or brochure advertising.

Applications

BT state that they are proactive in their charitable giving and give significant support to various programmes which are BT led. They are also involved with specific charity partners and encourage employees worldwide to donate time, skills and expertise to charitable/good causes.

BTG International Ltd

Pharmaceuticals

Correspondent: Corporate Responsibility Dept., 5 Fleet Place, London EC4M 7RD (tel: 020 7575 0000; fax: 020 7575 0010; email: info@btgplc.com; website: www.btgplc.com)

Directors: Garry Watts, Chair; Louise Makin, Chief Executive; Rolf Soderstrom; Peter Chambre; Giles Kerr; Melanie G. Lee; Ian F. R. Much; Jim O'Shea (women: 2; men: 6)

Year end	30/09/2011
Turnover	£110,600,000
Pre-tax profit	£19,500,000

Nature of business: BTG is an international specialty pharmaceuticals company that is developing and commercialising products targeting critical care, cancer, neurological and other disorders.

Company registration number: 2670500

Main locations: Ceredigion

UK employees: 525

Charitable donations

UK cash (latest declared):	2011	£12,900
	2010	£6,200
	2009	£6,000
Total UK:	2011	£12,900
Total worldwide:	2011	£12,900
Cash worldwide:	2011	£12,900

Corporate social responsibility

CSR committee: BTG's website states: 'Our Corporate Responsibility Committee comprises employees from all the main areas of the business, as we recognise that this breadth of knowledge helps us to understand all of our environmental impacts.'

CSR policy: This information was obtained from the company's Annual Report:

> We principally give to charities which either support diseases or conditions in which we are therapeutically focused or that benefit the local communities in which we operate. We encourage employees to support charitable events to raise money for their chosen charities and in most locations we match individual donations up to a designed cap.

CSR report: A CSR report was available from the company's website.

Applications

In writing to the correspondent.

Other information

In 2010/11, the company gave £12,900 in cash donations to charitable causes.

The following local charities received donations:

- Cancer Research UK
- The MS Society, UK
- Marie Curie Cancer Care, UK
- Wales Air Ambulance, Wales
- Christian Lewis Children's Cancer Charity, Wales
- Ty Hafan- palliative care for children, Wales

In its manufacturing plant in Wales, the company periodically organises educational open days for local schools.

Give As You Earn (GAYE): is in operation for employees to give to a charity of their choice.

Bunzl plc

Distribution, print/paper/packaging

Correspondent: P N Hussey, Company Secretary, York House, 45 Seymour Street, London W1H 7JT (tel: 020 7725 5000; fax: 020 7725 5001; website: www.bunzl.com)

Directors: Philip Rogerson, Chair; Michael Roney, Chief Executive; Ulrich Wolters; Patrick Larmon; David Sleath; Brian May; Peter Johnson; Eugenia Ulasewicz (women: 1; men: 7)

Year end	31/12/2011
Turnover	£5,109,500,000
Pre-tax profit	£193,700,000

Nature of business: Providing outsourcing solutions and customer service orientated distribution and light manufacture, primarily of plastic and paper based products.

Company registration number: 358948

Main locations: London

UK employees: 3,934

Total employees: 11,956

Charitable donations

UK cash (latest declared):	2011	£220,000
	2009	£210,000
	2007	£200,000
	2005	£201,000
Total UK:	2011	£220,000
Total worldwide:	2011	£440,000
Cash worldwide:	2011	£440,000

Corporate social responsibility

CSR committee: The Board governs CSR matters within a policy framework however there is no evidence of a separate CSR Committee.

CSR policy: This information was obtained from the company's CSR Report:

> Although Bunzl's operations are international, our strength is in the local nature of our businesses. In keeping with this ethos, we particularly support the fund raising activities championed by our employees locally. This is supplemented by donations made at Group level to charities predominantly in the fields of healthcare, disability and the environment.

CSR report: An up to date CSR report is available from the company's website.

Exclusions

No support for political and religious appeals.

Applications

In writing to the Celia Baxter, Director of Group Human Resources.

Other information

During 2011, Bunzl made charitable donations totalling £220,000 (2009: £210,000).

Employees have raised funds through taking part in sponsored runs and walks for Macmillan Cancer Support, Cancer Research, Brain Research Trust and Birmingham Children's Hospital.

Bupa Ltd

Healthcare, insurance

Correspondent: (See 'Applications' below), Bupa House, 15–19 Bloomsbury Way, London WC1A 2BA (tel: 0800 600 500; website: www.bupa.co.uk)

Directors: Baroness Bottomley; Peter Crawdon; George Mitchell; Neil Taylor; Lawrence Churchill; Prof. Sir John Tooke; Lord Leitch, Chair; Ray King, Chief Executive; Rita Clifton; John Lorimer (women: 2; men: 8)

Year end	31/12/2011
Turnover	£8,018,100,000
Pre-tax profit	£220,000,000

Nature of business: Principal activities: operation of health insurance funds and the provision of healthcare facilities and services, including ownership and management of hospitals, care homes, children's nurseries, homecare health screening services and occupational health services.

Company registration number: 2306135

Subsidiaries include: Care First Group plc

Main locations: London

Total employees: 42,488

Membership: BITC, LBG

Charitable donations

UK cash (latest declared):	2011	£3,100,000
	2009	£3,700,000
	2008	£4,900,000
	2007	£5,700,000
	2006	£5,300,000
Total UK:	2011	£3,100,000
Total worldwide:	2011	£7,300,000
Cash worldwide:	2011	£7,300,000

Community involvement

The company's giving is channelled mainly through its associated charity:

The Bupa Foundation (Charity Commission no. 277598)

The foundation's objectives are: 'To prevent, relieve and cure sickness, ill-health and infirmity of every kind (including physical injuries) and to preserve and safeguard health by conducting and commissioning research (the results of such research to be disseminated to the public) for the purpose of the preservation and safeguarding of health and in addition by the award of grants to individuals to undertake such research in furtherance of the Objects.'

Corporate giving

According to the annual accounts, during 2011, Bupa made charitable donations totalling £7.3 million (2010: £5.5 million). This included payments to The Bupa Foundation of £2.6 million (2010: £2.6 million), the Sanitas Foundation of £800,000 (2010: £400,000), the Bupa Health Foundation in Australia of £3.4 million (2010: £1.8 million) and UK registered charities of £500,000 (2010: £600,000). The Bupa Foundation's accounts however show this amount as being received in 2010 with income for the foundation in 2011 recorded as £115,000. We have taken our information from the 2010 accounts.

The Bupa Foundation

The foundation continued its policy of donating grants and during 2010 awarded £2.25 million to medical research projects.

Employee-led support

Volunteering by staff is actively encouraged through the provision of a wide range of volunteering opportunities in specialist areas such as children and young people, education, homelessness, and older people.

In June 2011, Bupa Global Challenge engaged 60,000 people to get moving. Employees and local communities took part in 444 events in 15 countries. From dancing in New Zealand care homes and a walking challenge in Hong Kong to a cycling fund-raiser in Bolivia, participants discovered the health benefits of physical activity. Nearly 26,000 staff volunteered in 2011.

Matched funding: Bupa also matches the money that its employees raises for charity, and donated £500,000 to charities in 2011 to support its volunteer efforts.

Payroll giving: The company operates the Give As You Earn Scheme.

Commercially-led support

Sponsorship:

The Bupa Great North Run is the premier event in the Great Run series and firmly established as Britain's biggest participation event. From just 12,000 runners at the very first staging in 1981, the event has now grown to a record 55,000 accepted entrants from over 100,000 applicants in 2012. Starting in Newcastle, the course takes in the iconic Tyne Bridge, goes through Gateshead passing the famous international athletics stadium and finishes in the coastal town of South Shields.

Sponsorship is undertaken with health charities such as the Alzheimer's Society.

> *Partnerships*
> Start to Move, a Bupa partnership with Youth Sport Trust, will transform the way physical education is taught in UK schools to 4–7 year olds. By equipping teachers to teach skills fundamental to physical activity, children will learn the ABCs of movement – stability, locomotion and object control. In the 2011/12 academic year, 180,000 children took part.

Corporate social responsibility

CSR committee: The Group Sustainability Committee meets quarterly to support and influence progress. A network of Sustainability Champions is responsible for implementing the commitments in each business unit.

CSR policy: No specific policy details found.

CSR report: There is a Sustainability report published within the annual report and accounts.

Exclusions

The company does not support appeals from individuals, political appeals or religious appeals.

Applications

Bupa Foundation: The foundation's website (www.bupafoundation.com) provides detailed information regarding applications, eligibility and closing dates for awards. Any initial enquiries should be addressed to Teresa Morris – email: bupafoundation@bupa.com).

bwin.party

Gaming

Correspondent: The Ethics Committee, 711 Europort Ave, Gibraltar (tel: 0035020078700; website: www.bwinparty.com)

Directors: Simon Duffy, Chair; Norbert Teufelberger, Co-Chief Executive Officer; Jim Ryan, Co-Chief Executive Officer; Joachim Baca; Martin Weigold, Chief Finance Officer; Rod Perry; Per Afrell; Geoff Baldwin; Manfred Bodner; Tim Bristow; Helmut Kern; Lord Moonie; Georg Riedl (women: 0; men: 13)

Year end	31/12/2011
Turnover	£540,436,260
Pre-tax profit	£338,844,300

Nature of business: Digital gaming.

Following the merger of bwin and PartyGaming that completed in March 2011, bwin.party is listed on the London Stock Exchange under the ticker: BPTY and a member of the FTSE250 Index. The group is incorporated and licensed in Gibraltar and operates across Europe, India, Israel and the US.

Company registration number: 91225 (Gibraltar)

Total employees: 2,481

Charitable donations

UK cash (latest declared):	2011	£145,000
	2009	£187,600
	2008	£101,700
Total UK:	2011	£145,000
Total worldwide:	2011	£145,000
Cash worldwide:	2011	£145,000

Corporate social responsibility

CSR committee: The Ethics Committee is responsible for community involvement and charitable giving.

CSR policy: CSR information taken from the group's website:

> As a new company our collective policies for sustainability and responsibility have yet to be formalised, but the historic approach taken by both bwin and PartyGaming will ensure that we continue to raise the standards of consumer protection and responsible eCommerce practices.

CSR report: Published within the annual report and accounts.

Applications

In writing to the correspondent.

Other information

The following information is taken from the group's website:

> In addition to the efforts of our employees though pro bono activities, both bwin and PartyGaming have a history of offering financial support to a number of worthy

causes. In the past this has tended to focus on supporting gambling-related charities, but not exclusively. We have also made contributions to a number of other important initiatives such as Great Ormond Street Hospital, Disaster Relief Fund of Red Cross, the 'Pioneers for Change' course for social entrepreneurs, Children's Cancer Research and Children's Cancer Aid.

Employee volunteering:

Through a formal *pro bono* scheme we hope to encourage our employees to spend between 4–8 hours of their time on charitable, community or environmental projects. This will allow them to enhance their personal development and broaden their personal perspective whilst returning something to their local communities.

Previous initiatives that our staff have been involved with include supporting the homeless in east London, a women's refuge in Gibraltar, orphans in Sofia, children's hostels in Tel Aviv and centres for the elderly in Hyderabad.

The CSR report published within the annual report for 2011 refers to charitable giving but no actual figure could be found. We have estimated a figure based on previous years' giving. The following information is taken from the report:

We plan that a greater allocation of our contribution to charities and good causes will be made available to the pro bono scheme that we plan to roll-out to former bwin offices in 2012. In aggregate we target approximately 0.2% to 0.25% of the prior year's Clean EBITDA to be allocated for charitable and responsible gaming causes. At least 60% of which is earmarked for gambling-related charities such as the Gambling Research Education and Treatment Foundation in the UK and the establishment of the international healthcare network.

CA plc

Computer software, information technology

Correspondent: Community Team, Ditton Park, Riding Court Road, Datchet, Slough, Berkshire SL3 9LL (tel: 01753 577733; fax: 01753 825464; email: lisa.stassoulli@ca.com; website: www.ca.com)

Directors: Arthur F. Welnbach, Chair; William E. McCracken, Chief Executive; Raymond J. Bromark; Gary J. Fernandes; Rohit Kapoor; Kay Koplovitz; Christopher B. Lofgren; Richard Sulplzio; Laura S. Unger; Ron Zambonini (women: 2; men: 8)

Year end	31/03/2011
Turnover	£2,900,000,000
Pre-tax profit	£760,000,000

Nature of business: Management software company, delivering software and services across operations, security, storage, and life cycle management for performance and reliability of IT environments.

Company registration number: 1282495

Main locations: Edinburgh, Taunton, Nottingham, Datchet, London, Altrincham

Total employees: 14,000

Membership: BITC

Charitable donations

UK cash (latest declared):	2009	£500,000
	2006	£500,000
	2005	£500,000

Corporate social responsibility

CSR committee: There was no evidence of a separate CSR Committee.

CSR policy: This information was obtained from the company's website:

CA Technologies is a global corporation with a local commitment. We work to improve the quality of life in communities where we live and work worldwide and are fully committed to advancing social environmental and economic sustainability.

CA Technologies supports programmes around the world that promote social services, encourage health and wellness, and deliver relief and response during times of crisis. The goal is to support people dealing with a range of challenges, from the family stresses of military life to disease, poverty and unexpected disasters.

CSR report: An interactive CSR report was available on the company's website.

Applications

In writing to the correspondent.

Other information

We were unable to determine the amount of cash donations made by the group during 2010/11. Historically, this company does not give every year.

Cable and Wireless Worldwide plc

Telecommunications

Correspondent: Ms Tracy O'Brien, Worldwide House, Western Road, Bracknell, Berkshire RG12 1RW (tel: 01908 845000/01344 713000; email: foundation@cw.com; website: www.vodafone.com)

Directors: John Barton, Chair; Gavin Darby, Chief Executive Officer; Clive Butler; Penny Hughes; Ian Gibson, Chief Financial Officer; David Lowden (women: 1; men: 5)

Year end	31/03/2012
Turnover	£2,149,000,000
Pre-tax profit	(£392,000,000)

Nature of business: Communications company specialising in providing mission critical communication services.

Company registration number: 238525

Total employees: 6,510

Charitable donations

UK cash (latest declared):	2010	£136,000
Total UK:	2010	£136,000
Total worldwide:	2012	£509,000
Cash worldwide:	2012	£509,000

Corporate social responsibility

CSR committee: No details found.

CSR policy: Statement taken from the company's website:

Cable&Wireless Worldwide is committed to maintaining a sustainable business. We recognise that:

- Many of the potential solutions to climate change lie with the development of products and services in our sector
- Sustainable partnerships give us the transparency and opportunity to manage risk effectively and safely
- Our resources can have a positive impact on the communities in which we do business
- An ethical business provides the foundation for a compliant and governed operation, underpinning all our working relationships

CSR report: Annual CR report available online.

Applications

In writing to the correspondent.

Other information

During the year ended 31 March 2012, the Group made charitable donations totalling £509,000. The Company established the **Cable&Wireless Worldwide Foundation** (Charity Commission no. 1144008) during the year, the primary aim of which is to enhance the lives of those with special needs through its expertise in mission critical communications. The foundation's strategy is to partner and build relationships with institutions that support, research, develop or implement the appropriate, specialist communication requirements for those with special needs.

A newly registered charity, accounts for the foundation were neither due nor received at the Charity Commission at the time of writing (September 2012). Further information on the foundation and the company's corporate responsibility arrangements can be found on the company's website.

Employee-led support

Every year, people from Cable&Wireless Worldwide get involved in a range of local initiatives where appropriate, using their skills to train people in their local communities. We have a colleague top up scheme and more than 80 colleagues have taken advantage of the scheme, raising money for 29 charities of their choice in 2010/11.

We also support payroll giving and are currently awarded a bronze certificate for 4% of colleagues donating through **Give As You Earn** (GAYE).

Partnerships

We work in partnership with several local, national and international charities to help address the social and environmental needs of the communities where we operate. We do this through sharing our communications and technological expertise, resources – including colleague volunteering – and funding.

Cable and Wireless plc

Telecommunications

Correspondent: Head of Public Affairs, 3rd Floor, 26 Red Lion Square, London WC1R 4HQ (tel: 020 7315 4000; email: investor.relations@cwc.com; website: www.cwc.com)

Directors: Richard Lapthorne, Chair; Tony Rice, Chief Executive; Tim Pennington; Nick Cooper; Simon Ball; Mary Francis; Kate Nealon; Ian Tyler (women: 2; men: 6)

Year end	31/03/2011
Turnover	£2,346,000,000
Pre-tax profit	£456,000,000

Nature of business: The company's principal activity is the provision of telecommunication services. While its headquarters are in London, the company has a presence in 38 countries, managed through four business units in the Caribbean, Panama, Monaco and Macau.

Until 26 March 2010 Cable and Wireless plc comprised two standalone business units: Cable and Wireless Communications and Cable and Wireless Worldwide. Cable and Wireless Worldwide separated from Cable and Wireless Communications by way of a demerger on 26 March and is now a separately listed company.

Company registration number: 238525

Main locations: Coventry, London, Swindon, Southampton, Wokingham, Birmingham, Bracknell

UK employees: 153

Total employees: 7,213

Charitable donations

UK cash (latest declared):	2011	£120,000
	2010	£1,100,000
	2008	£1,500,000
	2007	£1,400,000
	2006	£200,000
Total UK:	2011	£120,000
Total worldwide:	2011	£10,700,000
Cash worldwide:	2011	£10,700,000

Community involvement

The company aims to contribute positively to the social and economic development of the communities in which it operates. Various international charitable activities are described in the company's annual report for 2009/10 including initiatives concerning child protection, prevention of crime, reaching older people, training, education and apprenticeships.

Corporate giving

In 2010/11, the company made worldwide community contributions of £1.1 million. It has not been possible to determine how much of this went to UK charities/community organisations, however we do know that a contribution of £120,000 went to the Porthcurno Trust in the UK.

In kind support

Free internet access is provided to schools in Dominica and in Jamaica through the LIME Foundation, 1,090 computers have been given to 110 schools on the island since 2007.

Commercially-led support

Sponsorship: *Education* The company sponsors the Porthcurno Telegraph Museum in Cornwall which tells the story of global communications from the first use of electricity to how we communicate today.

Corporate social responsibility

CSR committee: There was no evidence of a CSR committee.

CSR policy: Taken from the company's website:

1. Contribute positively to the social and economic development of the communities in which the group operates
2. Respect cultures, values and human rights throughout its operations
3. Nurture best practice in the group's activities
4. Seek continuous improvement in environmental performance

CSR report: report available from the website.

Exclusions

The company only supports proposals that match its policy and does not offer support for advertising. No support for individuals other than employees. Proposals must relate to locations where the company does business or potentially has global scope. No support for political or religious causes or UK-centric projects.

Applications

In writing to the correspondent.

Cadbury plc (now Kraft)

Confectionery

Correspondent: Louise Ayling, Cadbury Foundation, Cadbury House, Uxbridge Business Park, Uxbridge, Middlesex UB8 1DH (tel: 01895 615000; fax: 01895 615001; website: www.cadbury.co.uk/contact/faq.aspx)

Year end	31/12/2010

Nature of business: Principal activities: the manufacture and marketing of confectionery.

On 2 February, 2010, Cadbury became part of Kraft Foods which has a separate DSC listing. Cadbury no longer has a community investment team at its offices in Uxbridge and neither does it produce its own accounts. The Cadbury Foundation is still in existence.

Company registration number: 52457

Subsidiaries include: Reading Scientific Services Ltd, Connaught Investments plc, Berkeley Square Investments Ltd, Trebor Bassett Ltd

Brands include: Creme Egg; Dairy Milk; Dentyne; Flake; Green and Blacks; Halls; Stomorol; Trident.

Main locations: Bournville, Maple Cross, Hertfordshire

Charitable donations

UK cash (latest declared):	2009	£750,000
	2008	£507,391
	2007	£750,000
	2006	£750,000
	2005	£750,000

Community involvement

Most requests for charitable donations in the UK are channelled through the **Cadbury Foundation** (Charity Commission no. 1050482) – the company's charitable trust which has no endowment but is funded by grants from the company each year.

Grants are given mainly in support of organisations working with education and enterprise, health, welfare or the environment. National charities and local groups around its sites (in Birmingham, Bristol, London (Hackney) and Sheffield) may be assisted.

On 2 February 2010, Cadbury became part of Kraft Foods Inc. The foundation's accounts for 2010 provide confirmation by Kraft to the trustees of their commitment of honouring the existing current three year funding plan due to expire in 2012.

Corporate giving

Cadbury Foundation

In 2010, the foundation received a donation of £750,000 from the company (now Kraft) plus £30,500 in donated services such as seconded staff and auditor's fees. The foundation in turn made grants totalling just over £703,500, with beneficiaries in the UK including the Confectioners' Benevolent Trust, Young Enterprise, Sheffield City Council, Achimota Trust, London Wildlife Trust and Hackney Business Partnership.

Exclusions

The company's website states:

> In view of the policy of concentrating grants behind selected projects, most ad hoc appeals have to be declined and are therefore not encouraged.
>
> The foundation does not support: requests for commercial sponsorship; help with funding of individuals' education and training programmes; purchase of advertising space; involvement in fundraising projects; travel or leisure projects; donation of gifts in kind (including company products); regional projects unless in the locality of company operations.
>
> Normally support has not been given for projects outside the UK since it is policy to provide support through local businesses in the many countries around the world where Cadbury has operations.

Applications

Appeals outside the criteria defined are not encouraged, as most grants are committed in advance on an ongoing basis.

However, if you are able to answer 'Yes' to all the below, then it may be possible for the foundation to consider your organisation for funding:

- Is the project promoting education, enterprise or employability within a group or groups of people?
- Would your client base be considered 'at risk' or 'socially excluded'?
- Are you located in geographical proximity to one of our major UK operations (e.g., Birmingham, Sheffield, Bristol, London (Hackney))?
- Are some of our employees already involved?

Write to the correspondent at: Cadbury Foundation, Cadbury House, Uxbridge Business Park, Uxbridge, Middlesex UB8 1DH.

Cadogan Group Ltd

Furniture manufacture, property

Correspondent: Paul Loutit, Correspondent to the Trustees, 18 Cadogan Gardens, London SW3 2RP (tel: 020 7730 4567; fax: 020 7881 2300; website: www.cadogan.co.uk)

Directors: Viscount Chelsea; J. H. M. Bruce; H. R. Seaborn; R. J. Grant; C. V. Ellingworth; J. D. Gordon; J. A. de Havilland

Year end	31/12/2011
Turnover	£105,924,000
Pre-tax profit	£71,581,000

Nature of business: The principal activity of the group is property investment.

Cadogan Group Ltd is the holding company for the UK property investment business of the family of Earl Cadogan. The company is ultimately owned by a number of charitable and family trusts.

Company registration number: 2997357

Main locations: London

Total employees: 110

Charitable donations

UK cash (latest declared):	2011	£1,380,220
	2008	£821,000
	2007	£178,000
	2006	£88,000
	2005	£50,000
Total UK:	2011	£1,380,220
Total worldwide:	2011	£1,380,220
Cash worldwide:	2011	£1,380,220

Community involvement

The group makes most of its charitable donations through the **Cadogan Charity** (Charity Commission no: 247773). Particular reference is given to those based, or operating in, London and Scotland.

Corporate giving

The group's charitable contributions for the year were £45,000 (2010: £46,000). In addition, the Cadogan Charity, a shareholder in the company, makes donations to a variety of local and national charities.

The Cadogan Charity

The charity supports organisations involved in: community/social welfare; medical research; education; the environment; animal welfare; and military charities.

During 2010/11 the charity received an income of £1.3 million from Cadogan Group Ltd and made contributions amounting to £1.6 million. Beneficiaries included: NSPCC – Full Stop Campaign (£400,000); St George's Cathedral, Perth (£367,000); In-Pensioners Mobility Fund (£100,000); St Wilfred's (£85,000); Awareness Foundation and Home of Horseracing Trust (£25,000 each); Corum – Life Education Centres (£15,000); Anchor House, Diabetes UK, Game and Wildlife Conservation Trust and Right to Play (£10,000 each); and Battersea Dogs and Cats Home (£2,000).

Corporate social responsibility

CSR policy: No CSR information was available.

We were unable to determine the ratio of women to men on the board.

Exclusions

No grants to individuals.

Applications

In writing to the correspondent.

Caledonia Investments

Accountants, financial services, leisure, property

Correspondent: Company Secretary, Cayzer House, 30 Buckingham Gate, London SW1E 6NN (tel: 020 7802 8080; fax: 020 7802 8090; email: enquiries@caledonia.com; website: www.caledonia.com)

Directors: James Loudon, Chair; Will Wyatt, Chief Executive; Stephen King; The Hon Charles Cayzer; Jamie Cayzer-Colvin; John May; Charles Allen-Jones; Mark Davies; Richard Goblet d'Alviella; Charles Gregson; David Thompson (women: 0; men: 11)

Year end	31/03/2011
Turnover	£33,200,000
Pre-tax profit	£24,300,000

Nature of business: Caledonia is a UK investment trust company, listed on the London Stock Exchange.

Company registration number: 3142560

Main locations: London

UK employees: 797

Total employees: 797

Charitable donations

UK cash (latest declared):	2011	£60,800
	2008	£110,000
Total UK:	2011	£60,800
Total worldwide:	2011	£60,800
Cash worldwide:	2011	£60,800

Corporate social responsibility

CSR committee: There was no evidence of a separate CSR Committee.

CSR policy: This information was obtained from the company's website:

> Caledonia encourages employees to support local voluntary organisation and charitable causes and provides matched sponsorship to their fundraising activities.

CSR report: There was no evidence of a separate CSR report.

Applications

In writing to the correspondent.

Other information

In 2010/11, the company donated a total of £60,800 to charities. We have no details of the beneficiaries. Grants to national organisations have previously ranged from £200 to £2,000.

The company supports the work of the Royal Horticultural Society.

Calor Gas Ltd

Oil and gas/fuel

Correspondent: Communications Manager, Athena Drive, Tachbrook Park, Warwick CV34 6RL (tel: 01926 330088; website: www.calor.co.uk)

Directors: J. M. Kearney; S. Rennie; J. Wakkerman; S. Kinnaird

Year end	01/01/2011
Turnover	£480,100,000
Pre-tax profit	£42,500,000

Nature of business: The principal activity of the company is the processing, marketing and distribution of liquefied petroleum gas.

Company registration number: 303703

Main locations: Warwick

UK employees: 1255

Total employees: 1255

Membership: BITC

Charitable donations

UK cash (latest declared):	2010	£34,000
	2009	£14,000
	2008	£29,000
Total UK:	2010	£34,000
Total worldwide:	2011	£34,000
Cash worldwide:	2011	£34,000

Corporate social responsibility

CSR committee: No details available.

CSR policy: Taken from the company's website:

> A sustainable approach is central to Calor's culture, focusing on a balanced consideration of economic, social and environmental aspects in all our activities.
>
> Calor has a long history of supporting not only the local areas in which we work, but also the rural communities we serve.

Unable to determine the ratio of women to men on the Board.

CSR report: None published.

Applications

In writing to the correspondent.

Other information

In 2010, the company gave £34,000 to charitable organisations (2009: £14,000). £15,000 was donated to Cardiac Risk in the Young, £10,000 was given to Leamington Football Club and the remaining £9,000 was distributed to local charities.

The company's website gives the following information:

> Calor has found it more valuable and effective to focus our support on the work of one charity at a national level as a means of engaging staff around one central cause. As such Calor adopts a national corporate charity, typically for a 3 year duration, for whom the majority of corporate fundraising efforts are undertaken.

National corporate charity

Calor's national corporate charity is chosen by an all-staff voting process as outlined below:

1 All staff are given the opportunity to nominate a national charity of their choice.
2 The 5 charities with the most nominations are then put to an all-staff vote.
3 The charity that receives the most votes during a set period of time is adopted as Calor's new national charity.

Calor will agree with the new charity a fundraising target (usually £100,000) and a timeframe for the partnership to last (usually a maximum of 3 years). Calor will then support the national charity until either the target is reached or the duration of the agreement is completed.

Gift of the gas

'Gift of the Gas' is Calor's cylinder retrieval scheme whereby a £5 donation is made to the national corporate charity for every Calor cylinder returned to a Calor Centre or participating outlet, and the owner is not in possession of their cylinder refill authority agreement form. All monies raised by Calor's 'Gift of the Gas' scheme will be donated to the national corporate charity, as well as monies raised by other ad-hoc activities.

Other charitable donations

Charities outside of the national corporate charity will be supported using central funding in the following situations:

1 Individual Employee Support–Employees who undertake an individual activity for a registered charity will be offered a £50 donation. Larger amounts can be awarded at senior management discretion.
2 Customer Support–The Sales Manager responsible for the individual customer will be asked for their opinion on each request. The guideline donation range will be £50-£500, depending upon circumstances.
3 Calor Location Support–The Site Manager responsible for the location will be asked for their opinion on each request. The guideline donation range will be £50-£500, depending upon circumstances.

Ad-hoc charitable donations

In addition to the above, management may use their discretion to support registered charities using local budgets.

Payments

Following the decision to award a payment to a charity, a cheque request will be completed and the payment sent to the endorsing manager to hand the cheque to the charity. Publicity associated with any payment should be generally welcomed and agreed with the Corporate Affairs Manager beforehand.

LPG Appliances (i.e. BBQs or portable heaters) or gas may be offered as alternative to cash donations. This is to be agreed in advance with the Corporate Affairs Manager.

Volunteering: All Calor staff are entitled to one day paid leave each year to give something back to their local community – from volunteering in their local charity shop, to helping re-decorate their local school.

Charity of the Year: In 2010, a new charity partnership was formed with Cardiac Risk in the Young (CRY). CRY is a national charity which works to raise awareness of, and support those affected by, sudden cardiac death.

Camelot Group plc

Gaming

Correspondent: Community Investment Department, Magdalen House, Tolpits Lane, Watford, Herts WD18 9RN (tel: 01923 425000; fax: 01923 425050; website: www.camelotgroup.co.uk)

Directors: Wayne Kozun; Julie Baddeley; Lee Sienna, Chair; Diane Thompson, Chief Executive; Patrick Brown; Tony Illesley; Gerry Archer; Louise Botting (women: 3; men: 5)

Year end	31/03/2011
Turnover	£5,822,400,000
Pre-tax profit	£40,100,000

Nature of business: Camelot is the operator of The UK National Lottery.

On 8 July 2010, the group was acquired by Premier Lotteries UK Ltd, a subsidiary of Ontario Teachers' Pension Plan. The company changed its status during 2011, from a public limited company to a private limited company.

Company registration number: 2822203

Main locations: London, Liverpool, Cardiff, Glasgow, Belfast

Total employees: 783

Membership: BITC, LBG

Charitable donations

UK cash (latest declared):	2011	£300,000
	2009	£900,000
	2008	£1,900,000
	2007	£3,100,000
	2005	£2,000,000
Total UK:	2011	£300,000
Total worldwide:	2011	£300,000
Cash worldwide:	2011	£300,000

Community involvement

The company has created a community investment framework that gives employees support in their contributions outside the workplace. However, there is very little information on what the company gives its annual charitable donation to. This appears to be declining (in 2009 it was £900,000, in 2008, £1.9 million).

The geographical areas given preference are near to the company's headquarters in Watford, its call centre in Aintree near Liverpool, Glasgow, Cardiff and Belfast.

Charity of the Year: Marie Curie Cancer Care

Corporate giving

During the year, the group made donations to charitable organisations of £300,000 (2010: £300,000) and in addition made some contributions in kind by way of an employee volunteering scheme. As all organisations associated with the group's giving are registered UK charities, we have used this as the UK cash figure.

Organisations that Camelot has worked with include: Media Trust, Common Purpose, Education Extra and GamCare.

In kind support

This is provided through gifts in kind and staff secondments.

Employee-led support

Employees are entitled to four hours a month of volunteering in their local community and the chance to double funds they raise for charities by way of match funding by the company.

An initiative called Team Camelot was launched in 2010 which helps employees get involved in community activities. Team Camelot has its own forum on the corporate intranet which profiles employee community investment and engagement activities, provides a calendar of events and celebrates employee achievements.

Match Funding is given to all employees who take part in a sponsored event to raise money for a charitable cause of their choice. Camelot will match fund up to £750 per person a year, or £4,500 for a group event with six employees or more.

Corporate social responsibility

CSR committee: No details found.

CSR policy: Statement taken from the company's website:

> Camelot is now one of the world's most successful lottery operators and corporate responsibility is firmly embedded into the way it works. Consumer protection, stakeholder engagement, community investment, and managing our impact on the environment touch every aspect of the way we do business.

CSR report: No specific report found but a responsibility section on the website refers to staff fundraising and volunteering.

Exclusions

Activity outside of the community involvement policy; overseas appeals/sponsorship; individuals; advertisements in charity brochures/programmes; general appeals.

Applications

In writing to the correspondent.

Canary Wharf Group plc

Property

Correspondent: Howard Dowter, One Canada Square, Canary Wharf, London E14 5AB (tel: 020 7418 2000; fax: 020 7418 2222; website: www.canarywharf.com)

Directors: Sir George Iacobescu, Chair and Chief Executive; Peter Anderson II; Ahmad Mohamed Al-Sayed; Robert Falls; Collin Lau; Sam Levinson; Alex Midgen; Brian Niles (women: 0; men: 8)

Year end	31/12/2010
Turnover	£287,500,000
Pre-tax profit	£219,700,000

Nature of business: Property development, investment, and management.

Company registration number: 3114622

Main locations: London

Membership: BITC

Charitable donations

UK cash (latest declared):	2010	£550,000
	2009	£687,000
	2008	£1,000,000
	2007	£394,500
	2006	£208,800
Total UK:	2010	£550,000
Total worldwide:	2010	£550,000
Cash worldwide:	2010	£550,000

Community involvement

The group primarily supports local community initiatives in and around the East Docklands and Tower Hamlets areas. In 2010, the group provided enough funding to employ an outreach worker on behalf of the charity, SPLASH.

Canary Wharf plc has also set up the **Isle of Dogs Community Foundation – IDCF** (Charity Commission no. 802942) – a trust set up to ensure that local people have a permanent endowment to support local community groups and to help people into work.

Charitable donations and funding have been made to all ages and all denominations since its establishment. Beneficiaries of small, one-off donations have included: Teachfirst; Careers Academies UK; and University of East London Art School Travel Bursaries.

Corporate giving

We could find no stated total figure for the amount donated by the group in 2010. We do know that £250,000 was donated to the **IDCF** in 2010. The same amount was donated to the Tower Hamlets and Canary Wharf Further Education Trust and £50,000 was granted to the Canary Wharf Achievement Fund.

In kind support

The group provides free office space for charities.

Corporate social responsibility

CSR committee: There was no evidence of a separate CSR Committee.

CSR policy: This information was obtained from the company's website:

> Canary Wharf Group works with the local community both to consult and inform local people about our development and operation, and to support projects for local people.
>
> Our primary activity is to provide engagement, and a point of contact, rather than to provide funding, although we have a limited programme of small grants to local charities and groups. We are particularly proud of the way in which our team has been able to help local small groups identify public, private and charitable sources of funding and support for projects and in this way we have been instrumental in some very large and successful programmes.

CSR report: A CSR report was available from the company's website.

Exclusions

No support for advertising in charity brochures, animal welfare, appeals from individuals, local appeals not in areas of company presence or potential 'Charity of the Year' partners.

Applications

In writing to the correspondent.

Canon UK Ltd

Business services

Correspondent: Lisa Attfield, Public Relations Corporate Executive, Cockshot Hill, Woodhatch, Reigate, Surrey RH2 8BF (tel: 01737 220000; fax: 01737 220022; email: lisa.attfiled@cuk.cannon.co.uk; website: www.canon.co.uk)

Directors: H. Iwarsson; L. Holmes; A. Recio

Year end	31/12/2010
Turnover	£278,193,000
Pre-tax profit	£12,753,000

Nature of business: The principal activity of the company is digital imaging.

Company registration number: 1264300

Main locations: Reigate

UK employees: 1,444

Total employees: 1,444

Charitable donations

UK cash (latest declared):	2008	£9,000
	2006	£41,600
	2005	£46,300

Corporate social responsibility

CSR committee: No details found.

CSR policy: This information was obtained from the company's annual report:

> The Canon Group shall endeavour to make a positive contribution to people, communities and societies throughout the world.
>
> We engage with organisations, individuals and communities where we operate; helping tackle social and health issues and promoting wealth and income creation. We invest in regional and local projects and bring our corporate social responsibility activities to life in the communities we depend on.

Unable to determine the gender of the Board.

Exclusions

No support for overseas projects, religious or political appeals.

Applications

In writing to the correspondent who is a member of the CARE Committee. The committee meets regularly to assess requests for support.

Before submitting a request, ensure you read the 'Canon CARE Scheme – Request for Support Guidelines' on Canon's website – www.canon.co.uk/About_Us/About_Canon/Sponsorship/Canon_CARE_Guidelines.aspx

All charitable requests should be sent to Canon UK Ltd, Woodhatch, Reigate, Surrey RH2 8BF for the attention of Lisa Attfield.

'Canon regrets that, due to the very large number of enquiries received on a weekly basis, we are not always able to respond personally to all requests. If your enquiry is successful, you will be contacted within 14 days of receipt of your application with details of the help that we are able to offer.'

Other information

In 2010 the group made no charitable donations although the company clearly have involvement in good causes in their communities. Unfortunately, it is not possible to calculate the cost of its contribution.

> ***The Canon CARE Scheme***
>
> The Canon CARE scheme was established in 1990 when its founding members identified the fact that Corporate Social Responsibility (CSR) would continue to be an important topic and feature highly on business agendas into the future. The company's motivation and dedication in this area has encouraged new CARE Committee members to continue driving initiatives forward and the scheme is still driven by a team which meets regularly throughout the year.
>
> In the course of an average week, the company receives around 50 requests from charitable or community organisations asking for cash donations, products to assist with fundraising events and print requests. These desires are submitted by humanitarian charities for the disadvantaged or ill, organisations and individuals working in the field of education, employment/business enterprise developments, the arts, environmental programmes and many more. Canon identified the need to have a clear set of guidelines and established a working Committee to oversee all its charitable donations and activities.
>
> The CARE scheme looks to support charitable and community projects or initiatives in the following five areas:
>
> *Business & Community* – is aimed at building relationships with local businesses and organisations thus encouraging job creation and community interaction.
>
> *Education* – directed to supporting schools, colleges, and extra curricular activity.
>
> *Arts & Culture* – benefits creative initiatives and programmes which encourage community interest and participation.
>
> *Humanitarian* – designed to provide assistance and support to a variety of health related causes.
>
> *Environment* – aimed at supporting community and environmental organisations to assist with improving the environment in which we all live and operate.

Caparo Group Ltd

Manufacturing

Correspondent: Company Secretary, Caparo House, 103 Baker Street, London W1U 6LN (tel: 020 7486 1417; fax: 020 7224 4109; website: www.caparo.com/en-gb)

Directors: Hon Lord Paul of Marylebone, Chair; Hon Anjili Paul; Hon Akash Paul; Hon Angad Paul (women: 1; men: 3)

Year end	31/12/2010
Turnover	£435,400,000
Pre-tax profit	(£14,300,000)

Nature of business: Specialists in the manufacture and supply of steel and engineering products.

Company registration number: 1387694

Main locations: London

UK employees: 2,782

Total employees: 2,782

Charitable donations

UK cash (latest declared):	2010	£213,000
	2008	£500,000
	2007	£1,042,510
	2006	£522,000
	2005	£500,000
Total UK:	2010	£213,000
Total worldwide:	2010	£213,000
Cash worldwide:	2010	£213,000

Corporate social responsibility

CSR committee: There is no evidence of a separate CSR committee.

CSR policy: This information was obtained from the company's website:

> At Caparo, Corporate Social Responsibility and concern for environment, health and safety are the intrinsic elements of the company's long-term strategy. Caparo's CSR commitment is a manifestation of its determination to improve quality of life not only for its employees, but the society at large.

CSR report: There is no evidence of a separate CSR report, however CSR information was available on the company's website.

Exclusions

Will not offer support for political appeals or fundraising events.

Applications

In writing to:

Trustees of The Ambika Paul Foundation, 103 Baker Street, London W1U 6LN

Other information

During 2010 Caparo donated £213,000 (2009: £500,000) to the Ambika Paul Foundation (Charity Commission no. 276127). The foundation focuses its charitable contributions on education/training, medical/health/sickness, overseas famine relief and arts and culture. It specifically wishes to benefit children/young people and people of a particular ethnic or racial origin.

Capita Group plc

Professional support services

Correspondent: Maggi Bell, Business Development Dir. – Community Engagement, 71 Victoria Street, Westminster, London SW1H 0XA (tel: 020 7799 1525; fax: 020 7799 1526; email: corporate@capita.co.uk; website: www.capita.co.uk)

Directors: Martin Bolland, Chair; Paul Pindar, Chief Executive; Gordon Hurst; Andy Parker; Vic Gysin; Maggi Bell; Nigel Wilson; Paddy Doyle; Martina King; Paul Bowtell (women: 2; men: 8)

Year end	31/12/2010
Turnover	£2,744,000,000
Pre-tax profit	£309,800,000

Nature of business: The group provides a range of white-collar integrated professional support services to clients in local and central government, education, and the private sector. Services include: administrative services; consultancy; IT and software services; and human resource provision.

Company registration number: 2081330

Main locations: London

Total employees: 35,415

Membership: BITC, LBG

Charitable donations

UK cash (latest declared):	2009	£500,000
	2008	£600,000
	2007	£500,000
	2006	£500,000
	2005	£400,000
Total worldwide:	2010	£1,650,000
Cash worldwide:	2010	£700,000

Corporate social responsibility

CSR committee: The Corporate Responsibility working group, which includes senior representatives from across the business, meets four times a year. The CR report for 2010 states: 'We are currently looking at setting up a more formal CR committee including external representatives, which will discuss and challenge our work, providing further input into and development of our CR activities.'

CSR policy: The following is taken from the company's Sustainability Report 2010:

> Our approach to Corporate Responsibility is straightforward:
>
> - We identify the key social and environmental impacts of our work
> - We set objectives to reduce these impacts and improve our performance
> - We monitor and measure our progress towards these targets
> - We report on our performance, so that stakeholders, both inside and outside the Company can review our progress and make informed decisions about the company
>
> Paul Pindar, our Chief Executive, has overall responsibility for our charitable support and Maggi Bell, our Business Development Director, has responsibility for our community engagement. Through our 'Capita Commit' programmes – which include our community investment programme and our charity partnerships – we aim to tackle exclusion of all kinds. The programme is applied centrally at a Group level and also by individual businesses, to address specific local needs.

CSR report: The company produces an annual Sustainability report available online.

Exclusions

No support outside that being given to Capita's chosen charities.

Applications

In writing to the correspondent.

Other information

In 2010, the company made charitable donations of £700,000 (2009: £500,000) and supported organisations involved in education, social exclusion and health. Total corporate donations include support for the charity partner and matched funding scheme, other CR initiatives and disaster appeals. The company states in its 2010 annual report that it estimates total community investment was £1.65 million (2009: £1.4 million). However, although it is not possible to determine whether all of this was of a charitable nature, we have used the figure as the total worldwide community contribution. Money raised by employees totalled £600,000. We have been unable to discover what part of the total cash and community figures was applied in the UK.

The group has an active charity programme 'Helping Hands', and supports employees in raising funds for charity. A central charity team organises a number of group-wide activities throughout the year and are supported by a network of charity champions across operations.

Payroll giving: There is a payroll giving scheme in operation and in 2010, 1,400 employees donated to over 219 charities through this.

Matched funding: There is also a matched funding scheme supporting employees in their individual charitable efforts, the company donating £88,000 in matched funding in 2010.

Charity Partner: One corporate charity partner is chosen by employees, with the relationship lasting up to two years. During 2011 and 2012 the charity partner was *Alzheimer's Society*. The following information is taken from the company's website:

> We will begin working with a new charity partner at the start of 2013. The first stage of the selection process is to ask our employees to nominate charities that they would like to support. We will then contact the top 10 charities nominated by the most employees and begin the next stage of the selection process.

Capital One Holdings Ltd

Financial services

Correspondent: Community Relations, Trent House, Station Street, Nottingham NG2 3HX (website: www.capitalone.co.uk)

Directors: B. T. Cole, Managing Director; Steve Hulme, UK. Chief Financial Officer; Victoria Mitchell, Chief Risk Officer; Michael Woodburn, Vice President and UK. Chief Operating Officer (women: 1; men: 3)

Year end	31/12/2010
Turnover	£624,260,000
Pre-tax profit	£218,981,000

Nature of business: A holding company whose subsidiaries provide a range of banking, financial and related services.

Company registration number: 3861423

Main locations: Nottingham, London

UK employees: 626

Total employees: 626

Membership: BITC

Charitable donations

UK cash (latest declared):	2010	£330,200
	2009	£430,550
	2008	£335,300
	2006	£159,000
	2005	£125,000
Total UK:	2010	£330,200
Total worldwide:	2010	£330,200
Cash worldwide:	2010	£330,200

Corporate social responsibility

CSR committee: No specific details of a CSR Committee or team.

CSR policy: The following is taken from the company's website:

> As a mark of our commitment to CSR, we have a number of policies and practices and we are always looking at how we can improve our current position.
>
> I hope that you find the CSR information in the areas of Market place and our customers, Community, and Environment open and helpful and that it provides an insight into the challenges that we face as well as the achievements that we are proud of.

CSR report: No CSR report published on website.

Applications

In writing to the correspondent.

Other information

In 2010 the company donated £330,200 in the UK to charitable causes.

The company supports the following organisations bringing sports opportunities to children in Nottingham: Nottingham Rugby Football Club; National Ice Centre; Nottinghamshire County Cricket Club; Nottingham Forest Football Club; Football In The Community programme (Notts County); St Ann's and Sneinton Education Partnership; Scope; and Children In Need.

Employees have been taking their skills into local schools since 1997, helping children to build their confidence with key curriculum subjects. The company runs the **Right to Read** and **Number Partners** schemes to help local schoolchildren improve their numeracy and literacy skills. Also, **E-volve**, where employees can become an online mentor to a local secondary school pupil, providing support to help them build their skills, plan their careers and prepare for exams.

Employees spend a day every year getting involved with the community supporting schools, nurseries, playgroups and youth centres. They have also created business plans, websites, databases and provided financial consultancy to community groups.

The company operates several donation schemes:

- Our employees can ask us to match (or part-match) the amount they raise for charity in their own time
- If our employees give more than 50 hours of their own time to voluntary service in a year, we have a Community Investment Grant to give to their charity of choice
- Our 'pennies from heaven' scheme helps employees automatically donate the pennies in their salaries to Macmillan Cancer Support
- 'Give as you earn' gives employees a tax efficient way of donating to their favourite charity straight from their salary

Partners include: Capital One continues to financially support the *Money Advice Trust* each year to support its valuable work of free, independent financial advice for those with debt problems.

Capital Shopping Centres Group plc

Financial services

Correspondent: Alexander Nicoll, Director of Corporate Responsibility, 40 Broadway, London SW1H 0BT (tel: 020 7887 4220; email: alexander-nicoll@capshop.co.uk; website: www.intugroup.co.uk)

Directors: Kay Chaldecott; John Abel; Ian Durant; P. Burgess, Chair; D. Fischel, Chief Executive; R. Gordon; I. Henderson; A. Huntley; R. Rowley; Neil Sachdev; A. Strang; J. Whittaker (women: 1; men: 11)

Year end	31/12/2011
Turnover	£516,100,000
Pre-tax profit	£27,200,000

Nature of business: The principal activity is that of a property investment company. It is the leading company in the UK regional shopping centre industry. Formerly Liberty International plc, the company was renamed Capital Shopping Centres Group plc 2010 upon the demerger of its central London business into a separate listed company, Capital and Counties.

Company registration number: 1503621

Main locations: London

Total employees: 628

Membership: BITC, LBG

Charitable donations

UK cash (latest declared):	2011	£332,000
	2009	£309,000
	2008	£290,000
	2007	£271,000
	2006	£931,000
Total UK:	2011	£2,132,000
Total worldwide:	2011	£2,132,000
Cash worldwide:	2011	£332,000

Corporate social responsibility

CSR committee: The board takes direct responsibility for determining policy and strategic direction on CR matters. Our broad strategic direction is disseminated through the CR Board Committee and progress against our operational objectives is delegated to the CR Management Committee. Delivery of the agreed action plans, targets and objectives is the responsibility of executive management reporting to the CR Management Committee, as appropriate.

CSR policy: The following quotes are taken from the company's CSR policy:

> We have long recognised the mutual benefits of incorporating the principles of sustainability into our business. For Capital Shopping Centres, Corporate Responsibility (CR) is our contribution towards sustainable development by considering environment, social and stakeholder issues in formulating our business objectives.
>
> *Communities*
>
> Our strategy is to enhance the quality of life of those communities where we operate and where we are an employer. This means developing a constructive partnership approach with local, county and regional authorities, supporting where practical their sustainable development objectives and complying with applicable regulations.

CSR report: The company produces an annual CSR report.

Applications

In writing to the correspondent.

Other information

The following information was provided by the company and is taken from the 2011 CR Report:

> During the year 2011, the group made charitable donations amounting to £332,000 (2010: £233,000). In addition, the directly managed shopping centres provided the equivalent of £1.4 million in support, including staff time working in the community and the provision of free mall space and services. They facilitated a further £406,000 through collections by charities in the malls. The total cash equivalent community support for the year was £2.1 million (2010: £1.9 million). The company further reports that 6,597 hours were spent on community engagement during 2011.

Cargill plc

Commodity traders, distribution, food services, shipping

Correspondent: See 'Applications', Knowle Hill Park, Fairmile Lane, Cobham, Surrey KT11 2PD (tel: 01932 861000; fax: 01932 861200; website: cargill.com)

Directors: C. W. Oliver; P. de Braal; M. R. Douglas; R. I. Nield; J. C. Reynolds; R. D. Thurston (women: 0; men: 6)

Year end	31/05/2011
Turnover	£1,134,416,000
Pre-tax profit	£82,737,000

Nature of business: Cargill is an international provider of food, agricultural and risk management products and services.

Company registration number: 1387437

Main locations: London, Wolverhampton, York, Worksop, Manchester, Liverpool, Hereford, Hull, Cobham, Within St Hughes

UK employees: 3,300

Total employees: 142,000

Charitable donations

UK cash (latest declared):	2011	£231,500
	2009	£39,800
	2008	£115,500
	2007	£49,000
	2006	£66,200
Total UK:	2011	£363,500
Total worldwide:	2011	£37,839,000

Corporate social responsibility

CSR committee: In the UK, there are five Cares Councils which support a number of initiatives and projects across the UK.

CSR policy: The following is taken from the company's UK website:

> Corporate responsibility is part of everything we do. It is a company-wide commitment to apply our global knowledge and experience to help meet complex economic, environmental and social challenges wherever we do business. It is a process of continually improving our standards, our actions and our processes. Corporate responsibility extends not only to our own operations but to our wider communities and is based on four commitments:
>
> - We will conduct our business with high levels of integrity, accountability and responsibility
> - We will develop ways of reducing our environmental impact and help conserve natural resources
> - We will treat people with dignity and respect
> - We will invest in and engage with communities where we live and work
>
> We recognize our continued success depends on the growth and health of our communities and partners, as well as the vitality and conservation of our natural resources. We are working with a diverse group of global, national and local organisations to support responsible economic development, help protect the environment and improve communities.

CSR report: report on global corporate responsibility actions is published annually.

Exclusions

Grants are not given to:

- Organisations that do not serve communities where Cargill has a business presence
- Individuals or groups seeking support for research, planning, personal needs or travel
- Public service or political campaigns
- Lobbying, political or fraternal activities
- Benefit dinners, fundraising events or tickets to the same
- Fundraising campaigns, walk-a-thons, or promotions to eliminate or control specific diseases
- Athletic scholarships
- Advertising sponsorships
- Religious groups for religious purposes
- Publications, audio-visual productions or special broadcasts
- Lobbying, political or fraternal activities
- Medical equipment (ambulances, defibrillators)

Applications

Cargill businesses and facilities and their employees give through 300 employee-led, worldwide Cargill Cares Councils. The councils provide support for local charitable and civic organisations and programs such as food relief agencies, schools and youth programs, and local environmental projects.

The following information is taken from Cargill's website:

> Cargill businesses and facilities and their employees also give through 300 employee-led, worldwide Cargill Cares Councils. The councils provide support for local charitable and civic organizations and programs such as food relief agencies, schools and youth programs, and local environmental projects.
>
> *How to apply*
>
> Cargill managers or Cargill Cares Councils are typically responsible for reviewing local grant requests and making funding decisions.
>
> *Partnerships:*
>
> How we select our partners:
>
> We seek partnerships with established, credible global, national and local organisations that are in the communities we have a business presence in. Our partners:
>
> - Align with our purpose of nourishing people
> - Serve within our focus areas
> - Have a presence in or make an impact to the communities we do business in
>
> We typically identify partner organisations that:
>
> - Our involvement can make a distinct contribution and help to create solutions
> - Align with our business interests
> - Solve real and underlying problems
> - Engage our employees and leverage their expertise
> - Provide collaboration opportunities with others including customers and non-governmental organisations (NGOs)

Other information

In 2010/11, Cargill plc declared cash donations in the UK of £231,520. We have no information relating to the beneficiaries. Total contributions in the UK were £363,500 and worldwide (£3.8 million).

The following information was provided by the company:

> Cargill invests in its communities through supporting programmes that focus on improving nutrition and health, education and environmental stewardship. Corporate contributions are supplemented by individual businesses and employee-led fundraising and volunteer efforts through more than 250 Cargill Cares Councils around the world.
>
> In the UK, we have five Cares Councils who support a number of initiatives and projects across the UK, some of these include:
>
> *Health and Nutrition*
>
> - Provided funds to local school in Leatherhead in Surrey, to build an outdoor eating area enabling every student to have access to a healthy nutritious meal
> - Supporting Lincolnshire Businesses for Breakfast programme which enables 16 local schools to provide healthy breakfasts and advice on health and nutrition
> - Employee volunteers helped to establish vegetable gardens at a local homeless shelter in Manchester. These vegetables allow the shelter to provide home-grown healthy meals to those who use their service
>
> *Education*
>
> - Working with the Salford Education Business Partnership to run food science workshops for local school students
> - A group of volunteers provide one-to-one reading sessions with local schools in Manchester
>
> *Environment*
>
> - Partnering with the Surrey Cares Trust in order to protect and enhance Surrey waterways
> - Funding and creating a wildlife garden for a local school in Witham St Hugh's
> - In Hereford we partnered with Concern Universal to highlight the importance of water conservation
>
> ***FareShare***
>
> FareShare, a national food charity in the UK, aims to relieve food poverty and find a solution to environmental problems of surplus but still edible food, promoting the message that 'no good food should be wasted.
>
> As part of Cargill's commitment to providing safe, nutritious and accessible food supplies, Cargill's grain and oilseed and refined oil businesses have been supporting FareShare since 2009 and provided a two-year financial commitment to the charity in order to open a new depot in Liverpool, UK.
>
> This depot, which was officially opened in September 2010, is the 13th FareShare depot in the UK and will support in excess of 100 community groups in Liverpool distributing 'fit for purpose' food to those most in need.
>
> The proximity of the depot to Cargill's Liverpool operations will also enable employees to get involved either through volunteering or sharing their expertise in areas such as logistics, planning, health and safety and food safety to the organisation.
>
> In addition to the investment in Liverpool, Cargill also raised funds in Manchester to support Emerge, the North West franchise partner of FareShare, which relies on local funding to support its vital services.
>
> ***Children's Adventure Farm Trust (CAFT)***
>
> Cargill has partnered with CAFT, a local charity that provides holidays for disabled, disadvantaged and terminally ill children and their carers from across the North West Region, since 2006. In addition to funding raised by Cargill and its employees since the partnership began, Cargill volunteers have helped CAFT improve the farm environment for the children and their families.
>
> Every year Cargill hosts a family fun day at CAFT, inviting employees and their families to spend the day participating in a variety of events and challenges designed to raise much needed funds for CAFT's vital work.

Worldwide Giving: The following statement appears on the company's website – 'Cargill's charitable giving efforts reached US $61.1 million [£3.8 million] for fiscal year 2011.' We have no breakdown of what this figure includes.

Carillion plc

Building/construction

Correspondent: Richard Tapp, Dir. Legal Services and Chair to the Appeals Committee, 24 Birch Street, Wolverhampton WV1 4HY (tel: 01902 422431; fax: 01902 316165; website: www.carillionplc.com)

Directors: Philip Rogerson, Chair; John McDonough, Chief Executive; Richard Adam; David Garman; Richard Howson; David Maloney; Steve Mogford; Vanda Murray (women: 1; men: 7)

Year end	28/12/2010
Turnover	£5,139,000,000
Pre-tax profit	£167,900,000

Nature of business: Providing expertise in commercial and industrial building, refurbishment, civil engineering, road and rail construction and maintenance, mechanical and electrical services, facilities management and PFI Solutions

Company registration number: 3782379

Main locations: Wolverhampton, Leeds, Manchester, Liverpool, London, Bristol, Brentford, Glasgow

UK employees: 19,476

Total employees: 30,056

Membership: BITC

Charitable donations

UK cash (latest declared):	2010	£200,000
	2009	£200,000
	2008	£129,000
	2007	£150,000
	2006	£145,000
Total UK:	2010	£200,000
Total worldwide:	2010	£1,489,500
Cash worldwide:	2010	£611,200

Corporate social responsibility

CSR committee: Carillion delivers its policy through its stakeholder engagement process, sustainability targets and community activities. The group's Business Units implement plans to ensure this policy will be delivered.

CSR policy: The group's policy states:

> To achieve our policy we will focus our efforts on 5 key elements:
>
> - Engaging with the workforce of the future
> - Engagement to support community improvement
> - Engagement focused on employment and training
> - Engagement to enhance employee morale
> - Engagement as a good neighbour

CSR report: An annual Sustainability report is published.

Applications

In writing to the correspondent.

Other information

Payments for charitable purposes made by the group during the year ended 31 December 2010 amounted to £200,000 (2009: £200,000). The primary beneficiaries of these charitable donations were: The Transformation Trust; The Wildlife Trust; the British Occupational Health Research Foundation; Business in the Community; CRASH; RedR; and, Walking with Wounded.

Further performance detail can be viewed at: sustainability11.carillionplc.com/communities/performance-data. While the annual accounts give a figure of £200,000, the performance data given on the website shows different figures. We have taken the website figures to be worldwide. As is our policy, we have excluded management costs from the total figure.

The following extract is from the group's annual report:

> The Carillion Group also contributes more than one per cent of profits per annum in cash or in kind (staff time on community projects) to community activities and is a corporate member of Business in the Community.
>
> Over the past ten years Carillion has supported the Wildlife Trusts through voluntary work by employees and annual donations to the Natural Habitats Funds. To date over £300,000 has been donated to this fund which has supported 48 projects.
>
> In 2006 Carillion joined the Business in the Community's Business Action on Homelessness (BAOH) campaign to help homeless people throughout the UK get off the streets and back into work. BAOH is one of many campaigns organised through Business in the Community (BITC). It is the most successful programme to get long-term unemployed people into work. Carillion as an employer has a prime role to support the BAOH programme and get individuals 'Ready to work'. Our commitment is to be the crucial link that provides two-week work placements opportunities for homeless clients to help them re-enter the job market. Carillion supports clients by giving them a 'work buddy' during the placement and throughout their journey. Candidates are now being placed in roles across the group.

Payroll giving: The company operates a payroll giving scheme.

Sponsorship: The company undertakes good-cause sponsorship. Address any proposals to the correspondent.

The Carphone Warehouse Group plc

Retail – miscellaneous, telecommunications

Correspondent: Corporate Responsibility Team, 1 Portal Way, London, W3 6RS, United Kingdom (tel: 020 8896 5000; fax: 020 8896 5005; website: www.cpwplc.com)

Directors: Charles Dunstone, Chair; Roger Taylor, Chief Executive Officer; Nigel Langstaff, Chief Financial Officer; John Gildersleeve; Baroness Morgan of Huyton; John Allwood (women: 1; men: 5)

Year end	31/03/2012
Turnover	£6,400,000
Pre-tax profit	£762,200,000

Nature of business: Independent retailer of mobile phones and services.

Company registration number: 3253714

Total employees: 18

Charitable donations

UK cash (latest declared):	2009	£217,000
	2008	£220,000
	2007	£117,000
Total worldwide:	2012	£284,000
Cash worldwide:	2012	£284,000

Corporate social responsibility

CSR committee: There appears to be a Corporate Responsibility Team but no member details were available.

CSR policy: Taken from the company's website:

> The Board is committed to high standards of corporate and social responsibility and expects the same from the investments of the Group. Whilst all businesses of the Group seek to operate in a socially responsible way, given its relative size, this effort is focused especially within CPW Europe.

CSR areas covered are: community and charity; environment; people and public concerns.

CSR report: Contained within the annual report and accounts.

Applications

The company selects its own charitable partners. Unsolicited appeals are unlikely to succeed.

However, through employees fundraising efforts it may possible to get additional support from The Carphone Warehouse Foundation.

Other information

The following is taken from the company's website:

> Carphone Warehouse supports its charity partner Get Connected. The company chose to support a charity that is involved in communication, so that it can help with more practical and technical support in addition to fundraising. Get Connected is a registered charity that offers a free, confidential helpline for children and young people under the age of 25. Using technology such as phone, text or webmail, young people who are struggling to cope with the pressures of modern day life can speak with trained volunteers and be put in touch with the specific support they need.

The following statements are taken from the annual report and accounts for 2012:

> Last year we worked with Get Connected to raise approximately £390,000 through activities such as a week-long national fundraising event, a quiz night and by offering intrepid employees the chance to raise funds by trekking or skydiving. The majority was raised through our flagship fundraising event, the charity auction, which raised a record-breaking £250,000. We also generated approximately £45,000 for Get Connected through our 'Take Back' handset recycling scheme.
>
> In 2011/12, CPW Europe contributed £179,000 to the running costs of Get Connected and committed £105,000 to improve their office space and upgrade their telecommunication systems to cope with increasing demand. During the next financial year our in-house corporate responsibility function will focus on developing the charity partnership and will aim to increase the public profile of Get Connected.

The Carphone Warehouse Foundation
The Carphone Warehouse Foundation (not registered with the Charity Commission) was set up over eight years ago to support employees with their own fundraising initiatives. Small grants are awarded to charities nominated by employees. The foundation will match the amount an employee has raised for their chosen charity by up to £200, or £500 for a team fundraising for the same event. Last year the foundation sponsored 21 employees and donated £4,200.

Catlin Group Ltd

Insurance

Correspondent: Vanya Howard, Corporate Responsibility Officer, 3 Minster Court, Mincing Lane, London EC3R 7DD (tel: 020 7626 0486; fax: 020 7623 9101; email: info@catlin.com; website: www.catlin.com)

Directors: Sir Graham Hearne, Chair; Stephen Catlin, Chief Executive; Benjamin Meull; Guy Beringer; Alan Bossin; Bruce Carnegie-Brown; Michael Crall; Jean Claude Damerval; Kenneth Goldstein; Robert Gowdy; Nicholas Lyons (women: 0; men: 11)

Year end	31/12/2010
Turnover	£2,589,104,700

Nature of business: Catlin Group Ltd is an international specialist property and casualty insurer and reinsurer.

Company registration number: 3114348

Main locations: Birmingham, Glasgow, Ipswich, Kent, Leeds

UK employees: 795

Total employees: 1,602

Membership: BITC

Charitable donations

UK cash (latest declared):	2009	£460,000
	2008	£458,500
	2007	£116,500
Total worldwide:	2010	£516,000
Cash worldwide:	2010	£516,000

Corporate social responsibility

CSR committee: There is a Community Committee and a dedicated CSR Officer – Vanya Howard. Catlin's community involvement efforts are co-ordinated by a Community Committee, which includes members from across the group globally. The committee meets frequently to manage charitable contributions centrally and to discuss programmes to encourage employee charitable giving and involvement in community schemes.

CSR policy: The following statement is taken from the CSR Report 2010.

> We have a responsibility to the communities in which are offices are located. We attempt to 'give back' to these communities through both charitable donations and employee involvement. We believe that it is extremely important for a business such as Catlin to encourage employees to work to make communities better places to live.

CSR report: Published annually.

Applications

In writing to the correspondent.

Other information

The group made total charitable donations of £516,000 during 2010 (2008: £460,000). Catlin's charitable and community activities are concentrated in Bermuda, the group's headquarters, and in the United Kingdom, where the majority of the group's employees are based. It is not clear how much in cash donations was donated to the UK. Every two years, UK employees select two partner charities, which receive donations from Catlin and its employees as well as volunteering support. In 2010 the chosen charities were the **Alzheimer's Society** and the **Dame Vera Lynn Trust**, which provides support to children with cerebral palsy and their parents and carers.

The following information is taken from the group's annual report and accounts for 2010 and its website:

> We focus on initiatives that relate to youth and education, although all worthy causes will be considered. The group's community involvement strategy consists of two primary strands:
>
> *Charitable contributions* – Catlin makes monetary contributions to a variety of charities and good causes around the world.
>
> *Community involvement* – Catlin encourages employees to become involved in activities whose goal is to improve the communities in which they live and work. For its own part, Catlin as a company also participates in community oriented initiatives.
>
> Catlin also maintains a long-standing sponsorship of the *Sick Children's Trust*, a UK-based charity which provides support and accommodation to the families of children undergoing hospital treatment.
>
> Since 2009, Catlin has been a trustee and partner of *St Paul's Way*, a secondary school in the London borough of Tower Hamlets located near the Group's London office.
>
> *The Lloyd's Community Programme*'s mission is to improve the opportunities for and environment of the people of Tower Hamlets and neighbouring East London boroughs by mobilising the support and involvement of individuals and companies in the Lloyd's market. Catlin has worked with the LCP for many years and is actively involved in a number of projects.
>
> ***Matched Funding:***
> The group operates a Fund Matching Scheme which acknowledges the voluntary work and fundraising efforts of its employees. The scheme is designed to recognise money raised through employees' personal endeavours such as running in marathons or organising special events. Under the scheme the company will donate, usually up to a maximum of £500 or $1,000 per employee per annum, in support of any fundraising activities and in recognition of volunteering commitments.
>
> ***Give As You Earn:***
> In the United Kingdom Catlin offers employees a 'Give As You Earn' scheme, under which employees authorise the Group to deduct from their monthly salaries contributions to their chosen charity, which are matched by the group up to a maximum of £600 per employee per annum.
>
> ***Sponsorships:***
> *Art Catlin* is a programme set-up, managed and funded by Catlin and its art team, which helps young graduate artists get a foothold in the industry and offers a single touch-point for the art industry as a whole. The highlight of the programme is the Catlin Art Prize, which has been unearthing and rewarding new talent since its inception in 2007. Each year Art Catlin curator Justin Hammond scours graduate art shows around the UK for the best emerging artists, 40 of whom are selected to appear in the exclusive Catlin Guide – a limited edition collection of artist profiles.

Cattles plc

Financial services

Correspondent: Community Investment Officer, Kingston House, Centre 27 Business Park, Woodhead Road, Birstall, Batley WF17 9TD (tel: 01924 444466; fax: 01924 442255; email: cr@cattles.co.uk; website: www.cattles.co.uk)

Directors: M. A. Young; R. D. East; J. M. Briggs; J. R. Drummond-Smith

Year end	31/12/2010
Turnover	£285,000,000
Pre-tax profit	(£246,900,000)

Nature of business: Provision of financial services such as secured and unsecured personal loans, hire purchase credit facilities and merchandise.

Company registration number: 543610

Main locations: Oxford, Manchester, Leeds, Hull, Glasgow, Nottingham, Cleckheaton, Birstall

Total employees: 2,495

Charitable donations

UK cash (latest declared):	2010	£0
	2009	£1,000,000
	2008	£400,000
	2007	£300,000
	2006	£434,000
Total UK:	2010	£0
Total worldwide:	2010	£0
Cash worldwide:	2010	£0

Corporate social responsibility

CSR committee: No details published of CSR Committee.

CSR policy: No specific CSR policy published.

Unable to determine the ratio of women to men on the board.

CSR report: There appears to be no published information.

Exclusions

No support for general appeals, fundraising events or individuals.

Applications

In writing to the correspondent.

Other information

There were no charitable donations made in 2010 (2009: £100,000). In the past, charitable donations have been made to organisations seeking to improve the financial skills and general welfare of young people and organisations addressing the issues of social disadvantage in the communities served by the group's businesses.

CEF Holdings Ltd

Electronics/computers

Correspondent: Company Secretary, 141 Farmer Ward Road, Kenilworth, Warwickshire CV8 2SU (tel: 01926 514380; website: www.cef.co.uk)

Directors: R. H. Thorn; T. B. Yallop; A. Jackson; M. S. Jacobs; K. A. D. Barnett; G. L. Hartland; T. A. Hartland; J. A. Mackie; C. H. Beddows (women: 0; men: 9)

Year end	30/04/2011
Turnover	£38,323,000
Pre-tax profit	£4,742,000

Nature of business: Principal activity: electrical wholesalers and manufacturers.

Company registration number: 316018

Total employees: 3,533

Charitable donations

UK cash (latest declared):	2011	£454,000
	2009	£467,000
	2008	£490,000
	2007	£438,000
	2006	£353,000
Total UK:	2011	£454,000
Total worldwide:	2011	£454,000
Cash worldwide:	2011	£454,000

Corporate social responsibility

CSR policy: No CSR details published.

Exclusions

No support for advertising in charity brochures, animal welfare, appeals from individuals, fundraising events, overseas projects, political appeals, religious appeals or local appeals not in areas of company presence.

Applications

All potential beneficiaries are identified personally by the trustees. Unsolicited applications are not, therefore, acknowledged.

Other information

In 2010/11, the company made charitable donations of £454,000 (2010: £378,000). This was the amount received by the Janet Nash Charitable Trust (Charity Commission no. 326880), which historically, the company covenants its donations to.

The Janet Nash Charitable Trust

In 2010/11, the trust had an income of £454,000 and charitable expenditure was £433,000. Seven organisations and 35 individuals received donations from the trust. The trust usually prefers to support a number of the same organisations each year, particularly 'medical and hardship' causes and individuals in need. Benefiting organisations in 2010/11 included: Acorns; Aide Au Pere Pedro Opeka Association; The Get A-Head Charitable Trust; Dyslexia institute; Shirley Medical Centre; and the Alzheimer's Society.

Celtic Energy Ltd

Mining

Correspondent: Managing Director, 9 Beddau Way, Castlegate Business Park, Caerphilly CF83 2AX (tel: 02920 760990; email: info@coal.com; website: www.coal.com)

Directors: L. Humphreys; Richard Walters; R. Thompson; DHM. Consultancy Ltd

Year end	31/03/2011
Turnover	£68,447,000
Pre-tax profit	£29,022,000

Nature of business: Celtic Energy Ltd operates opencast coal mining sites in South Wales. The company currently operates three coaling sites. An extension to the key high volatility coking coal site at Margam is currently under planning review by the Welsh Assembly Government. The company is a wholly owned subsidiary of Celtic Group Holdings. The ultimate parent undertaking is Celtic Mining Group Ltd.

Company registration number: 2997376

Main locations: Aberdare

UK employees: 317

Total employees: 317

Charitable donations

UK cash (latest declared):	2011	£73,000
	2009	£28,000
	2008	£17,000
	2007	£24,000
	2006	£26,000
Total UK:	2011	£73,000
Total worldwide:	2011	£73,000
Cash worldwide:	2011	£73,000

Corporate social responsibility

CSR policy: No CSR details published.

Unable to determine the ratio of women to men on the board.

Exclusions

No support for political or religious appeals. Local appeals not in areas of company presence.

Applications

In writing to the correspondent.

Other information

In 2011 the company gave £73,000 in charitable cash donations. The following information is taken from its website and details the company's community contributions and involvement:

> To promote good relations, each site has a community liaison committee which comprises local councillors and residents. Their role is to act as a point of contact between the community and the company. Meeting on a regular basis, the committee is kept fully up to date on the site's progress, and each member has the opportunity to air their views.
>
> The site community liaison committee is also responsible for administering a significant community donations budget throughout the life of the site. This is in addition to the community benefit package provided by the company.
>
> Schools, charities, sporting groups and local organisations throughout South Wales have benefited from donations from Celtic Energy. The company is committed to supporting local good causes for the long-term benefit of both the young and old alike.
>
> Celtic Energy sites are visited regularly by local school children of all ages. The company offers assistance with school projects by providing schools with on site and classroom support. Needless to say, the children love to see the big machines.
>
> With the majority of the company's employees living within the local communities, they, as residents, play an active role in community life. Be it at rugby matches, school plays, fun days or concerts, Celtic Energy has a presence throughout the community.
>
> With an open door policy, visitors are welcome to visit any of Celtic Energy's operating sites and see for themselves the work that is undertaken on site and the work that goes on in the community. Occasionally, the sites hold open days to encourage local residents and visitors to South Wales to view and discuss the operations of a surface coal mine. This is of course, particularly important for the

education of children who are also encouraged to accompany their parents.

Just call your local Mine Manager or the Head Office at Caerphilly to arrange a visit.

However, should you have any concerns with regard to our operations in your area please do not hesitate to telephone 0845678943 or email: enquiries@coal.com.

CEMEX UK Operations

Building/construction

Correspondent: Company Secretary, CEMEX House, Coldharbour Lane, Thorpe, Egham, Surrey TW20 8TD (tel: 01932 568833; fax: 01932 568933; website: www.cemex.co.uk)

Directors: L. H. Russell; C. A. Leese; L. Zea; I. Madridejos; J. Gonsalez; D. K. J. O'Donnell; C. Uruchurtu; L. Zea (women: 0; men: 8)

Year end	31/12/2010
Turnover	£744,653,000
Pre-tax profit	(£64,067,000)

Nature of business: Principal activities: production and supply of materials for use in the construction industry.

Company registration number: 249776

Main locations: Rugby, Barrington, South Ferriby, Rochester, Egham

UK employees: 3,531

Total employees: 3,531

Membership: BITC

Charitable donations

UK cash (latest declared):	2010	£27,000
	2009	£72,309
	2008	£130,614
	2007	£202,105
	2006	£14,567
Total UK:	2010	£27,000
Total worldwide:	2010	£27,000
Cash worldwide:	2010	£27,000

Corporate social responsibility

CSR committee: No details of a CSR committee could be found.

CSR policy: The company channels its charitable contribution through the CEMEX UK Foundation but there appears to be no written policy with regard to its charitable and community giving.

CSR report: No recent CSR report for the company available on its website.

Exclusions

No support for political appeals.

Applications

In writing to the correspondent. Applicants wishing to establish if they meet the company's proximity criteria can now visit: cemexlocations.co.uk.

Other information

During 2010, the company made charitable donations totalling £27,000 (2009: £72,000). The company channels its charitable contribution through the CEMEX UK Foundation (not a registered charity). We have no information regarding the value of any in kind contributions made.

CEMEX UK Foundation

The activities of the foundation cover a number of key areas including the company's charity of the year, supporting employees volunteering and matched funding of employees fundraising efforts. The foundation will also consider applications for financial and in kind support for community activities in the vicinity of company operations. However, these small scale donations still require approval by the foundation. Projects supported include schemes which improve local air, land and water quality.

The *Cemex Community Fund* was created to administer a proportion of the landfill tax receipts paid to the government by the company in support of environmental and community projects. The fund likes to support individual projects of an approximate value of £15,000. To date the fund has supported over 170 projects with a total value in excess of £10 million. The fund is able to support a wide range of community projects. The criteria for qualifying projects can be found on the fund's website: www.cemexcf.org.uk

Rugby Group Benevolent Fund was established over 50 years ago by the then chair of Rugby Cement, Sir Halford Reddish and has supported a range of community projects over that period. Recent projects include a community minibus for the Rugby Volunteer Centre and roof repairs to Barrington Village Hall.

For further information see the foundation's website.

Matched Funding: Employees involved in raising money for charities and their communities have their efforts matched by the company up to a maximum of £250.

Charity of the Year: Butterfly Conservation – there appears to be a long-standing and continuing relationship with this charity.

Center Parcs Ltd

Leisure

Correspondent: Chief Executive Officer, One Edison Rise, New Ollerton, Newark, Nottinghamshire NG22 9DP (website: www.centerparcs.co.uk)

Directors: D. Camilleri; M. P. Dalby; P. Kent; J. Leavor; A. M. Robinson; C. Whaley; G. White; P. Inglett

Year end	28/04/2011
Turnover	£126,100,000
Pre-tax profit	£26,800,000

Nature of business: Agent to manage the development of the four UK Center Parcs villages. The company is a wholly owned subsidiary of another company incorporated in the EEA and has chosen not to prepare its own group accounts under section 400 of the Companies Act 2006.

Company registration number: 1908230

Main locations: Penrith, Newark, Brandon, Warminster

Total employees: 5,329

Charitable donations

UK cash (latest declared):	2011	£90,000
	2009	£15,000
Total UK:	2011	£90,000

Corporate social responsibility

CSR committee: No dedicated CSR Committee or Team.

CSR policy: There appears to be no published policy.

Unable to determine the ratio of women to men on the Board.

CSR report: The group's CSR report is given in its annual review which covers: our people, nature and biodiversity, sustainability and charity.

Applications

In writing to the correspondent.

Other information

No charitable cash donations are declared in the company's 2010/11 accounts but we know that the company itself-donated £90,000 to Great Ormond Street in match funding. The figures for cash generated income from operations and pre-tax profit are taken from the Group's financial review of the same year.

Center Parcs contributes in other ways to its communities and national charities with in kind contributions. Unfortunately, we have no figure for this.

The company has a number of initiatives benefitting charities and good causes:

- The Center Parcs villages support local schools through donations, work experience and skills development
- Less fortunate families are assisted and the company donates breaks to charities supporting terminally ill children
- Center Parcs supports Beds for Bedz, run by Great Ormond Street Hospital, by inviting guests to opt-in and make a donation when booking their short break holiday. The company then matches the donations made by guests. So far £217,000 has been raised through guest donations, Center Parcs match-funding and fundraising events at Center Parcs locations. £90,000 was donated under the match funding scheme

Center Parcs is accredited with the Wildlife Trusts' Biodiversity Benchmark for Land Management. This is a nationally recognised standard for commitment to biodiversity, demonstrating responsible land management.

Sponsorship: In July, 2008, Center Parcs and Badminton England announced the start of a five year partnership working together beyond the London 2012 Olympic and Paralympic Games.

Center Parcs is the official partner of Team England. Team England comprises of the elite English badminton players from junior to senior levels. Key tournaments for Team England are the World Championships, Commonwealth Games and European Championships. As the official partner of Team England, Center Parcs' logo appears on the team's shirts when they compete in major team tournaments and international matches.

Center Parcs National Schools Championships is England's largest schools participation event with over 22,000 children representing 1,600 schools taking part in the championship and ultimately 164 children from 36 schools contesting the National Final at Center Parcs.

Workplace Giving Scheme: The company covers the cost of administering this scheme to allow an individual's entire donation to go to their chosen charity.

Charity of the Year: Great Ormond Street Children's Hospital Charity is the corporate Charity of the Year.

Centrica plc

Oil and gas/fuel

Correspondent: Community Relations, Millstream, Maidenhead Road, Windsor, Berkshire SL4 5GD (tel: 01753 494000; fax: 01753 494001; email: community@centrica.com; website: www.centrica.com)

Directors: Helen Alexander; Mary Francis; Mark Hanafin; Paul Rayner; Philip Bentley; Andrew Mackenzie; Chris Weston; Nick Luff; Roger Carr, Chair; Sam Laidlaw, Chief Executive; Margherita Della Valle; Lesley Knox; Ian Meakins (women: 4; men: 9)

Year end	31/12/2011
Turnover	£22,824,000,000
Pre-tax profit	£1,268,000,000

Nature of business: Centrica's principal activities are the provision of gas, electricity and energy related products and services. The group also operates gas fields and power stations and provides roadside assistance and other motoring services.

Company registration number: 3033654

Subsidiaries include: British Gas Trading Ltd, Dyno Holdings Ltd, Accord Energy Ltd, British Gas Services Ltd, GB Gas Holdings Ltd, Hydrocarbon Resources Ltd

Brands include: British Gas, Scottish Gas, Dyno.

Main locations: Windsor

Total employees: 39,432

Membership: BITC, LBG

Charitable donations

UK cash (latest declared):	2009	£4,800,000
	2008	£5,900,000
	2007	£4,065,000
	2005	£6,700,000
	2004	£5,800,000
Total worldwide:	2011	£37,000,000
Cash worldwide:	2011	£1,790,000

Community involvement

The following information is taken from Centrica's website:

Investing in Communities

Our eighth Business Principle, 'Investing in communities,' describes our aim to develop enduring relationships based on mutual trust, respect and an understanding of our impact. We focus our resources where we can make an effective contribution and enable our employees to get involved in community activities. To make a real difference, we focus on five areas that are closely aligned with our business:

- Climate change and the environment: we are committed to playing an active role to reduce the effects of climate change by championing energy efficiency, investing in renewable power, and reducing our own carbon footprint
- Fuel poverty and social inclusion: we are committed to working with public and voluntary sector partners to support our most vulnerable customers particularly those affected by fuel poverty
- Health and safety: we focus on the health and safety of our employees, customers and others who could be affected by our activities
- Education, skills and employability: we invest in education to promote learning about energy-related issues and deliver programmes to support training and skills development
- Employee involvement: we enable and encourage our employees to get involved in their communities through charitable giving and volunteering

Our approach involves:

- Systematic management based on clearly identified objectives
- Long-term partnerships with community organisations and charities
- Ongoing evaluation of our contributions and impacts they achieve

Supporting communities

Our businesses support the communities where they operate by investing in social projects that enhance community relationships and relate to our core business activities, as outlined in our Group Community and Local Impact Policy. Whether we are working to build skills, regenerate communities or combat fuel poverty, the overall aim is to tailor solutions for optimal long-term impact. We work through our charity partners and other programmes to deliver locally-tailored support.

Corporate giving

The group's accounts state that during the year, the group made cash charitable donations to support the community of £1.8 million (2010: £21.1 million) and total community contributions and related activities on community support are valued at £67.7 million (2010: £105.3 million). However, we have used the figures given in the group's data centre and based on the LBG model as this gives a better breakdown of where the monies were spent. These are as follows:

Total community contributions £67.66 million includes 'LBG contributions' and 'mandatory contributions' (given as £26.64 million). Voluntary contributions made by the group are valued at £37 million (this is the cost of voluntary programmes to support vulnerable customers in the UK and North America). There is a further breakdown of contributions by the LBG group of cash donations – £1.79 million, cost of volunteering time of £1.16 million, in kind donations of £200,000, commercial initiatives of £570,000 and management costs of £1.06 million. This gives a total community contribution (minus management costs) of £2.97 million and a cash contribution figure of £1.79 million.

Beneficiaries supported were in the following categories:

- Education and young people
- Health
- Environment
- Social welfare
- Other

In kind support

Centrica provides in kind support from computers and IT equipment to office furniture and stationery.

Employee-led support

Employees are encouraged and enabled to 'make a positive impact' on their local communities. Time off is provided for volunteering to support employees to develop their skills and apply their expertise. The range of volunteering opportunities is available to employees through the UK 'Get Involved' programme.

Other community initiatives are designed to allow employees to support organisations to which they have a personal connection and which match their skills and needs. Employees are encouraged to contribute financially to local and national charities through payroll giving, matched funding and the employee lottery. Employees are supported in these initiatives as well as other causes they care about. The group enables staff to do this by facilitating donations, offering volunteering and fundraising opportunities and giving them time off to volunteer. This enhances the group's community impact and promotes employee engagement. Almost 82,000 hours were volunteered by employees in 2011.

Payroll giving: Employees can donate through payroll giving, apply for matched funding and use other giving services directly through the company's intranet.

Commercially-led support

Sponsorship: This form of support is only considered if it forms part of a specific project with which the company is already involved.

Corporate social responsibility

CSR committee: The General Counsel and company secretary are responsible for the implementation of this policy. The Corporate Responsibility team manages group wide community investments while business units oversee brand community initiatives and business sites coordinate local engagement.

The following information is taken from Centrica's website:

> We will communicate this policy to each Centrica business unit to facilitate the implementation of this policy across the group. The policy will be fully disclosed, available online, and communicated to interested parties. The success of the policy will be reviewed as appropriate by the Corporate Responsibility Committee.
>
> **CSR policy:** We have a direct impact on local communities through our gas and power assets, our offices and call centres and through the 10 million visits our engineers make to homes in the UK and North America every year. We recognise that good relations with local communities are fundamental to our sustained success.
>
> We believe that working in partnership with communities over a sustained period of time is the most effective way to achieve real results and lasting change. Our approach is to engage with our neighbours, community leaders, non-governmental organisations and charities to understand the implications of our activities and changes in industry and wider society.

CSR report: Annual CR Performance Review sets out progress during the year.

See also the Group Community and Local Impact Policy available from the group's website.

Exclusions

Since Centrica focuses its investments in areas aligned with its business and strives to avoid any conflicts of interest, it does not offer support to individuals, animal welfare organisations, building projects, political or denominational groups, arts bodies or sports groups.

Applications

In writing to the correspondent.

Channel 4 Television Corporation

Telecommunications

Correspondent: Corporate Responsibility Dept., 124 Horseferry Road, London SW1P 2TX (website: www.channel4.com)

Directors: Lord Burns, Chair; David Abraham, Chief Executive (women: 0; men: 2)

Year end	31/12/2011
Turnover	£941,400,000
Pre-tax profit	£44,000,000

Nature of business: Broadcasting company.

Company registration number: 1533774

Main locations: Belfast, Glasgow, Edinburgh, Manchester

Total employees: 763

Membership: BITC

Charitable donations

UK cash (latest declared):	2011	£1,500,000
	2009	£1,000,000
	2008	£1,100,000
Total UK:	2011	£1,500,000
Total worldwide:	2011	£1,500,000
Cash worldwide:	2011	£1,500,000

Community involvement

Taken from the 2010 CSR report:

> We continue to play a responsible role in the community. In addition to the community engagements achieved through our diversity programmes, we also work in partnership with our suppliers and a variety of charitable organisations to play a responsible role in the community. To formalise our approach, we are currently developing a charitable strategy.

Channel 4 is a member of the Media CSR Forum (mediacsrforum.org), Business in the Community (bitc.org.uk) and the Corporate Responsibility Group (crguk.org).

Corporate giving

During 2011, the group donated £1.5 million to charities (2010: £1.4 million). All of the £1.5 million (2010: £1.1 million) was paid to charities to provide training to improve the overall expertise of television staff in the industry.

In kind support

Disaster Emergency Committee: Channel 4, working in partnership with the Independent Television Network (ITN), is a broadcast partner for the DEC. When a large-scale international crisis strikes, Channel 4 broadcasts a two to three-minute national television appeal, to publicise the situation and raise funds. In 2011, the company continued with its support for the DEC by broadcasting the East Africa famine appeal.

Channel 4 has formed links with several local charities and community groups and provides support in terms of meeting room space, building tours and donations of surplus office furniture and technical equipment. Office supplies such as toners and ink cartridges are donated to charity for recycling and cooking oil is donated as green fuel.

Employee-led support

Volunteering: Channel 4 recognises that volunteering can have a meaningful, positive impact on both our staff and community, and we support this by having a Volunteering Policy. 2011 was the European Year of Volunteering and to celebrate this, in September we held an Open Day for 12 charities, in order that they could showcase their volunteering opportunities. In 2012, we will continue to identify opportunities and promote them as part of staff personal development.

Matched Funding: The company matches funding pound-for-pound up to £2,500 if teams of two or more staff team up to support a good cause.

Payroll Giving: There is a scheme in operation.

Commercially-led support

Big4 art project: The Big 4 is a 50-foot-high metal '4' outside the company's London headquarters. Since its inception in 2007, a variety of artists, both internationally renowned and emerging talent, have created 'skins' for the 4. The project has evolved into a regular competition for art and design students and recent graduates, with the winning design chosen by a panel of art and design experts. The 2010 'skin' was created by Stephanie Imbeau and was entitled Shelter. The Big 4's 2011 skin has been awarded to Hannah Gourley, a Fashion and Textile Graduate, for Time to Breathe.

Corporate social responsibility

CSR committee: No details found.

CSR policy: The following statement is taken from the company's website:

> *Corporate Responsibility*
> Channel 4's role goes beyond creating powerful television. Our operating model has always required us to strike a balance

> between public service and commercial content.
>
> The aim of our Corporate Responsibility (CR) strategy is to fulfil our public service remit in a responsible manner.
>
> To this end, our mission is to promote social, environmental and personal change.
>
> In order to achieve our mission, we continue to develop our strategy around the following 5 impact areas:
>
> *Accountability*
> We aim to promote responsible behaviour.
>
> *Community*
> We aim to continue to play a responsible role in the community.
>
> *Environment*
> We are committed to minimising any adverse effects of our operations on the natural environment and finite resources.
>
> *People*
> Our belief is that diversity contributes to the fulfilment of our public service remit and to being the best that we can creatively be. We aim to nurture and develop talent within our business and across the media industry in order to work with the most diverse range of people across the UK.
>
> *Suppliers*
> Where applicable, we aim to promote responsible behaviour in the supply chain.

CSR report: Published annually and available from the annual report and accounts and the company's website.

Applications

In writing to the correspondent.

Chelsea Building Society

Building society

Correspondent: Sally Davies, CR and Community Support Consultant, Thirlestaine Hall, Thirlestaine Road, Cheltenham, Gloucestershire GL53 7AL (tel: 01242 271526; fax: 01242 271222; email: sally.davies@thechelsea.co.uk; website: www.thechelsea.co.uk)

Directors: Ed Anderson, Chair; Chris Pilling, Chief Executive; Kate Barker; Roger Burden; Lynne Charlesworth; Richard Davey; Philip Johnson; David Paige; Simon Turner; Ian Bullock; Andy Caton; Robin Churchouse (women: 2; men: 10)

Year end	31/12/2011
Turnover	£520,000,000
Pre-tax profit	£130,000,000

Nature of business: Building society.

FSA registration number: 106085

Main locations: Bournemouth, Reading, Worthing, London, Maidstone, Oxford, Norwich, Chatham, Cheltenham, Brighton, Bristol, Watford, Ipswich, Leicester, Guildford, Birmingham, Exeter, Plymouth, Southampton

Total employees: 3,266

Charitable donations

UK cash (latest declared):	2011	£462,000
	2009	£75,000
	2007	£142,000
	2006	£173,000
	2005	£73,000
Total UK:	2011	£462,000
Total worldwide:	2011	£462,000
Cash worldwide:	2011	£462,000

Community involvement

The merger of the Yorkshire and Chelsea building societies completed on 1 April 2010. The enlarged society is known as Yorkshire Building Society, with the Chelsea Building Society name being retained and operated as a separate and distinct brand within the Yorkshire Group.

The company helps to support worthwhile causes, concentrating on the causes it considers its members think are important by actively seeking to obtain recommendations for suitable charities to support from all members. The main focus for the society's charitable giving is the **Yorkshire Building Society Charitable Foundation** (Charity Commission no. 1069082).

The foundation is a registered charity which provides financial assistance to local charities and good causes, and acts as a focus for the company's charitable giving. It concentrates on helping the elderly, vulnerable people, including children and those with special needs and suffering hardship.

Corporate giving

The group donated £462,000 to more than 2,000 UK charities in 2011, of which 90% were member nominated.

Employee-led support:

Charity of the Year: Staff raised over £85,000 for the Alzheimer's Society. The group made an additional £90,000 to the organisation.

Corporate social responsibility

CSR committee: There was no evidence of a separate CSR Committee.

CSR policy: This information was obtained from the company's website:

> Chelsea Building Society is determined to be a valuable part of the community by helping members to buy and own their own homes and encouraging others to save. But our commitment goes further than this.
>
> We also help to support worthwhile causes, concentrating on the causes our members think are important. The main focus for the society's charitable giving is the Yorkshire Building Society Charitable Foundation

CSR report: There was no evidence of a separate CSR report.

Exclusions

The trustees of the foundation will not usually consider grants for the following:

- Activities which are mainly/usually the statutory responsibility of central or local government, or some other responsible body (except proposals for added support service)
- Schools, universities and colleges (except for projects which will specifically benefit disabled students and are additional to statutory responsibilities)
- Hospitals, medical centres, medical treatment research (except projects extra to statutory responsibilities)
- Collecting funds for later distribution to other charities or individuals
- Political or pressure groups
- Profit distributing organisations
- Individuals or individual fundraising efforts, including expeditions or overseas travel
- General fundraising events, activities or appeals
- Fabric appeals for places of worship and the promotion of religion
- Animal welfare or wildlife
- Charities which have substantial reserves (in excess of 12 months expenditure) or in serious deficit
- The purchase of minibuses or other vehicles
- The acquisition, renovation and refurbishment of buildings

No support for applications from outside of the society's areas of operation within the UK.

Applications

Yorkshire Building Society Charitable Foundation.

Cheshire Building Society

Building society

Correspondent: Jean Trace, CR Assistant, Castle Street, Macclesfield, Cheshire SK11 6AF (tel: 01625 613612/ 01793 656145; fax: 01625 617246; email: corporate.responsibility@nationwide.co.uk; website: www.thecheshire.co.uk)

Nature of business: Building society provider of competitive investments, mortgages, and complementary financial services. For company accounts, see the Nationwide website.

FSA registration number: 106078

Charitable donations

UK cash (latest declared):	2010	£1,000
	2009	£1,000
	2007	£196,000
	2005	£268,000

Applications

Grants are only made to local groups. You should contact your local branch before preparing an application letter.

Other information

Following the merger of the Cheshire Building Society with the Nationwide, charitable giving is almost negligible as Nationwide grants awards on behalf of its merged companies. See separate listing for the Nationwide which makes significant charitable contributions.

Giving by the Cheshire will now be restricted to a £1,000 a year budget to be distributed to very local groups with grants of around £50.

Chrysalis Group Ltd

Media

Correspondent: Company Secretary, The Chrysalis Building, Bramley Road, London W10 6SP (tel: 020 7221 2213; fax: 020 7221 6455; email: enquiries@chrysalis.com; website: www.bmg.com)

Directors: J. Lascelles; A. Mollett; P. Lassman; M. Ranyard; H. Masuch; M. Dressendoerfer; J. Dobinson

Year end	30/09/2010
Pre-tax profit	(£7,155,000)

Nature of business: Provision of management and administration services to members of the Chrysalis Group of companies and acting as an investment holding company.

Company registration number: 946978

Total employees: 27

Charitable donations

UK cash (latest declared):	2010	£0
	2009	£5,000
	2008	£16,400
	2007	£21,800
Total UK:	2010	£0
Total worldwide:	2010	£0
Cash worldwide:	2010	£0

Corporate social responsibility

CSR committee: No evidence of a CSR committee.

CSR policy: None.

We do not know the ratio of women to men on the board.

CSR report: None.

Exclusions

No support for religious or political activities.

Applications

In writing to the correspondent.

Other information

In 2009/10 the group made no charitable donations and this may be because the company made a loss. We know that previously the group have supported the music charity Nordoff Robbins, which provides music therapy services to adults and children who are affected by illness, disability, trauma or isolation.

Chrysalis's website contains the following statement regarding its community support in the UK: 'We recognise the benefit we can bring to the communities where we operate and to the wider world through charitable activities. We will make a positive contribution to the lives of the people around us, and facilitate our staff in contributing to worthwhile causes.' Unfortunately, no information regarding what these benefits might be, or for whom, was available.

CIBC World Markets plc

Banking

Correspondent: Mr Angus Scott, Trustee, The CIBC World Markets Children's Foundation, Canadian Imperial Bank of Commerce, 150 Cheapside, London EC2V 6ET (tel: 020 7234 6000; fax: 020 7234 6691; email: ukchildren'smiracle@cibc.co.uk; website: www.cibcwm.com)

Directors: Gerald T. McGaughey, President and Chief Executive Officer; Michael Capatides; Victor Dodig; Kevin Glass; Richard Nesbitt; Jim Prentice; Richard Venn; David Williamson; Tom Woods (women: 0; men: 9)

Year end	31/10/2011
Turnover	£7,823,243,870
Pre-tax profit	£2,591,780,850

Nature of business: Investment bank.

Company registration number: 2733036

Main locations: London

Total employees: 42,000

Charitable donations

UK cash (latest declared):	2011	£102,000
	2009	£36,000
	2008	£216,600
	2007	£125,000
	2006	£213,000
Total UK:	2011	£102,000
Total worldwide:	2011	£2,618,600
Cash worldwide:	2011	£2,618,600

Corporate social responsibility

CSR committee: No specific details found.

CSR policy: Statements taken from the 2010/11 annual report and accounts:

> Our commitment to corporate responsibility extends from our vision, mission and values and is integrated into our operations and business practices. We recognise that the long-term success and viability of our business is closely linked to the confidence and trust our clients and stakeholders have in our organisation.
>
> We are committed to causes that matter to our clients, employees and communities. Our goal is to make a difference through corporate donations, sponsorships and the volunteer spirit of our employees.

CSR report: Information on CSR published in the annual report and accounts.

Applications

In writing to the correspondent.

Other information

CIBC World Markets Children's Miracle Foundation

The company's charitable fundraising is mainly focused on 'Miracle Day', which occurs on the first Wednesday of December each year. All commission generated on that day is donated to children's charities via the CIBC World Markets Children's Miracle Foundation (Charity Commission no. 1105094). Further funds are raised at a number of events hosted by CIBC World Markets for clients and staff.

The key objectives of Miracle Day include:

- To raise the quality of life for children in the communities served by CIBC World Markets
- To demonstrate our dedication in helping to prepare children for future success
- To encourage volunteerism and foster community involvement on the part of our employees

To be eligible to apply for funds groups must be UK/European registered charities which are well-administered, with a record of achievement and the potential for success which will bring a tangible benefit to children in the communities where they live within Europe.

In 2010/11 the foundation received £99,000 from Miracle Day, plus £3,000 to pay for audit fees. The foundation gave £100,000 in grants to children's charities. CIBC Miracle Day raised in total a record $4.1 million (£2.6 million) in 2010.

Citibank International plc

Financial services

Correspondent: See 'Applications', Citigroup Centre, 33 Canada Street, Canary Wharf, London E14 5LB (tel: 020 7986 4000; fax: 020 7986 2266; website: www.citigroup.com)

Directors: D. J. Challen; D. Taylor; M. L. Corbat; A. M. Duffell; L. M. Pigorini

Year end	31/12/2011
Turnover	£432,000,000
Pre-tax profit	£59,000,000

Nature of business: Provider of financial services.

Company registration number: 1088249

Main locations: London

Total employees: 60,000

Membership: BITC, LBG

Charitable donations

UK cash (latest declared):	2009	£979,000
	2008	£979,000
	2007	£1,177,607
	2005	£964,000
	2004	£895,000
Total worldwide:	2011	£75,300,000

Community involvement

Information taken from the Global Citizenship Report for 2011:

> Citi seeks to support organisations and causes that are important to our employees and to the communities in which we operate. Where possible and appropriate, we also seek to ensure consistency between our community giving and our business goals and operations. This means that we look to support programs that fulfil Citi's legal or regulatory requirements or public policy objectives, and/or programs that align with our business objectives, corporate culture, and strategic philanthropic goals.
>
> While we financially support organisations in a wide range of areas, a significant amount of our giving assists partners and programs working to expand financial inclusion and economic empowerment in underserved communities.
>
> ***Youth Education and Livelihoods outside the U.S.***
>
> We support educational and training opportunities that lead to improved employment prospects, increasing young people's ability to contribute to the economy.
>
> In countries where completing secondary school is the critical milestone, we focus on efforts to help students develop the knowledge, skills and attitudes to earn a living wage, start their own business or pursue further education and training. In countries where obtaining a degree is critical, we focus on increasing the number of low-income students who enrol in and complete post-secondary education.
>
> ***Citi Foundation***
>
> The Citi Foundation, based in the U.S., supports the economic empowerment and financial inclusion of low – to moderate income people in communities where Citi operates. We work collaboratively with a range of partners to design and test financial inclusion innovations with potential to achieve scale, and we support thought leadership and knowledge-building activities. Through a 'More than Philanthropy' approach, we put the strength of Citi's business resources and people to work to enhance our philanthropic investments and generate measurable positive impact.
>
> The Citi Foundation uses a results-oriented measurement framework, outlined in the Citi Foundation Grant Guidelines that informs the way we assess the impact of programs we fund. Our approach, and the way we measure success, emphasize results for participants rather than the grantees' completion of funded activities. Every grant is tracked to identify ways to ensure success and understand what works and why.
>
> In 2011, 96 percent of the Citi Foundation's investments were within our mission and focus. Through these efforts, we reached 1.6 million individuals working toward specific financial inclusion and economic empowerment goals. Of these, 30 percent fully achieved their financial inclusion goals in 2011 while the remainder will make significant strides toward improving their financial prospects. In addition, approximately 40 percent of all investments are aligned with our goal to support research and thought leadership efforts that encourage practitioner innovation, shape the industry dialogue, and promote public policy development.

Disaster Response

> As a global bank, Citi recognizes the positive impact we can have on individuals and communities struck by unexpected hardships. Citi and the Citi Foundation have a long and proud tradition of providing support to communities affected by disasters. In 2011, we re-examined our disaster response strategy in order to use resources to generate measurable impact and align investments with our mission and focus. Our new strategy employs a holistic approach to disaster response: supporting preparedness, immediate response, and rebuilding efforts that all contribute to the long-term economic recovery of communities.

Corporate giving

In 2011, *Citibank International plc* declared charitable donations of £20,600 (2010: £58,500). However, the group's Global Citizenship Report for 2011 states: 'We make financial donations to non-profit organisations in a range of disciplines including community development, education, culture and the arts, and diversity. In 2011, Citi contributed $43 million (£26.8 million) in corporate giving, outside the Citi Foundation.'

The report further states that in 2011, Citi and the Citi Foundation gave more than $121 million (£75.3 million) to support non-profit organisations in communities where employees and customers live and work.

We know from previous research that the Citi Foundation makes grants to UK-based organisations and this year supported London's *Fair Finance*, an organisation focused on supporting financial services to the underserved community of East London. Previous UK beneficiaries include: Charities Aid Foundation America; National Citizens Advice, United Kingdom ($100,000/£63,750) and Young Enterprise London ($140,000/£89,000) – both under the financial education and asset building programme; and Teach First, United Kingdom – under the education programme ($100,000/£63,750).

Note that the grants to the Charities Aid Foundation were on behalf of the following: African Caribbean Diversity, Business in the Community, Bygrove Primary School, Create Arts Ltd, Greenwich and Lewisham Roots and Wings, Specialist Schools an Academies Trust, Speakers Trust, Teach First, Tower Hamlets Education Business Partnership, Toynbee Hall, UK Career Academy Foundation.

Employee-led support

In 2011, 789,000 employee hours were dedicated to volunteering and more than 40,000 Citi volunteers took part in nearly 1,100 local services projects in 78 countries during Citi's Global Community Day.

Commercially-led support

Citi-FT Financial Education Summit

The Citi Foundation has partnered with the Pearson Charitable Foundation and the Financial Times to develop and support this annual summit – an international forum on financial literacy. Now in its ninth year, (2012), the Summit has become the leading annual global forum on financial capability.

Corporate social responsibility

CSR committee: The Corporate Sustainability group and Community Development group manage communications with NGOs.

CSR policy: Statement taken from the Global Citizenship Report 2011:

> Citi's global presence provides the responsibility and the opportunity to contribute to solutions that help the environment, strengthen the financial system, and build a better future.
>
> Responsible finance is our focus – doing what's right for clients, for communities, and for the financial system. It is the key to restoring, and deserving, the trust of the people we serve.

CSR report: There is an annual Global Citizenship report published on the website.

Exclusions

The Citi Foundation does not provide funding related to:

- Advertising, special events, dinners, telethons, benefits, or fundraising activities
- Religious, veteran or fraternal organisations (unless they are engaged in a project benefiting an entire community)
- Individuals

- Political causes, campaigns, or candidates
- Memorials
- Private foundations
- Requests deemed as 'pass-through' funding
- Matched funds

Applications

To apply to the Citi Foundation, use the online contact form: https://www.citibank.com/citi/contact/foundation/who/contact.htm

For more information on the citizenship initiatives described in the 2011 Global Citizenship Report, visit Citi's website or contact:

Tyler Daluz
Corporate and Sustainability Communications
citizenship@citi.com
Citigroup Inc.
399 Park Avenue
New York, NY 10022.

Citroen UK Ltd

Motors and accessories

Correspondent: Human Resources Department, 221 Bath Road, Slough SL1 4BA (tel: 0844 463 0010; website: www.citroen.co.uk)

Directors: J-M. Gales; F. Banzet; N. Willetts; C. Carsalade; C. Musy; J. M. Gales; M. Lynch; L. Jackson

Year end	31/12/2010
Turnover	£974,416,000
Pre-tax profit	£5,196,000

Nature of business: The main activity of the company is the importing and the sale of Citroën cars, vans and replacement parts.

Company registration number: 191579

Main locations: Slough

UK employees: 553

Total employees: 553

Charitable donations

UK cash (latest declared):	2010	£78,000
	2009	£44,000
	2008	£81,000
	2006	£71,000
	2005	£69,000
Total UK:	2010	£78,000
Total worldwide:	2010	£78,000
Cash worldwide:	2010	£78,000

Corporate social responsibility

CSR policy: No CSR information available.

Exclusions

No support for individuals.

Applications

In writing to the correspondent.

Other information

In 2010, the company made contributions for charitable purposes of £78,000 (2009: £44,000) to BEN, the motor trade benevolent fund. Previously we were advised that, as general rule, it is better to apply for support through the individual dealerships.

Clinton Cards plc

Retail – miscellaneous

Correspondent: Paul Salador, CSR Committee, The Crystal Building, Langston Road, Loughton, Essex IG10 3TH (tel: 020 8502 3711; fax: 020 8502 0295; website: www.clintoncards.co.uk)

Directors: Darcy Willson-Rymer, Chief Executive Officer; Clinton Lewin; Stuart Houlston; Paul Salador; John Robinson; Debbie Darlington; Don Lewin, Chair; John Coleman; Brian Jackson; Robert Gunlack (women: 1; men: 9)

Year end	31/07/2011
Turnover	£364,218,000
Pre-tax profit	(£10,662,000)

Nature of business: The main activity is the specialist retailing of greeting cards and associated products.

Company registration number: 985739

Main locations: Loughton

UK employees: 8,350

Total employees: 8,350

Charitable donations

UK cash (latest declared):	2011	£361,000
	2009	£299,000
	2008	£390,000
	2007	£309,000
	2006	£360,000
Total UK:	2011	£361,000
Total worldwide:	2011	£361,000
Cash worldwide:	2011	£361,000

Corporate social responsibility

CSR committee: A CSR Committee headed by Paul Salador, Director, meets three times a year 'with other members of staff co-opted as necessary'.

CSR policy: No specific policy with regard to charitable/community giving. The CSR pages of the annual report contain three paragraphs on this which refer to creating local jobs, creating products and encouraging stores to 'sell products with charitable contributions'.

CSR report: Contained within the annual report and financial statements for 2010.

Applications

In writing to the correspondent.

Other information

During the period the group made charitable donations of £361,000 (2010: £389,000). The principal beneficiaries were: Barts and the London Charity HPB; Breast Cancer Care; and Marie Curie Cancer Care. In addition, there were numerous smaller payments to other charities.

Close Brothers Group plc

Financial services, banking

Correspondent: Corporate Social Responsibility Committee, 10 Crown Place, London EC2A 4FT (tel: 020 7655 3100; fax: 020 7655 8917; website: www.closebrothers.co.uk)

Directors: Strone Macpherson, Chair; Preben Prebensen, Chief Executive; Jonathan Howell, Finance Director; Bruce Carnegie-Brown; Ray Greenshields; Douglas Paterson; Jamie Cayzer-Colvin; Geoffrey Howe (women: 0; men: 8)

Year end	31/07/2011
Turnover	£360,500,000
Pre-tax profit	£78,500,000

Nature of business: Close Brothers is the parent company of a group of companies involved in merchant banking.

Company registration number: 520241

Main locations: London

Total employees: 2,500

Charitable donations

UK cash (latest declared):	2009	£154,000
	2008	£168,000
	2007	£186,000
	2006	£147,000
	2005	£323,000
Total worldwide:	2011	£228,500
Cash worldwide:	2011	£228,500

Corporate social responsibility

CSR committee: Taken from the annual report and accounts for 2010/11: 'A CR committee was established in 2010 and is chaired by a member of the executive committee. The committee includes representatives from across the divisions and provides a forum for sharing ideas and raising awareness of the group's CR objectives.'

CSR policy: The following statement has been taken from the group's website:

> Close Brothers Group plc is committed to high standards of corporate governance, corporate responsibility and risk management in directing and controlling its business. The UK Corporate Governance Code is the principal governance code applying to UK companies listed on the London Stock Exchange.
>
> It is the board's view that the company's governance regime has been fully compliant with the best practice set out in the code with effect from 4 January 2011, when Geoffrey Howe was appointed as an additional independent non-executive director. Prior to this date less than half the board of directors, excluding the chairman, were independent but the

company's governance regime was otherwise fully compliant.

CSR report: None published.

Exclusions

No support for political appeals.

Applications

In writing to the correspondent.

Other information

The company's charitable donations during 2010/11 amounted to £228,500 (2009/10: £281,000). Matched funding for employees participating in fundraising activity accounted for 25% with the remainder from direct company contributions to charities across the UK and Europe. Unfortunately there appears to be no information relating to the value of any community contributions the company has made in kind. We have used the cash contributions figure for the worldwide cash and contributions as we have no other information.

The 2010/11 annual report gives the following information under the heading 'Community':

> The group encourages all staff to participate in the community and support charitable causes and offers a number of opportunities for involvement. *Charitable donations:* During the year, the group has established a charitable partnership with The Prince's Trust and for the first time held a number of group wide fundraising events. *Volunteering:* The group encourages employees to volunteer in projects to help make a difference in local communities. The group will shortly be promoting staff participation in a school reading partnership project which is a ten week project where staff volunteer their time to read with children from a Tower Hamlets school in London. The group intends to continue promoting further opportunities for employee volunteering. *Work experience:* The group continues to offer two work experience programmes throughout the year. These provide young students and school children with the opportunity to work in various departments within the group, gaining practical experience of a financial services group.
>
> *Give As You Earn*
>
> The group continues to promote the GAYE scheme. Participation in the scheme has increased to 11% (2010: 10%) of all group employees, and the group achieved a Payroll Giving Quality Mark Gold Award in April 2011 in recognition of the strong participation rate.
>
> *Matched giving*
>
> In order to encourage both individual and team fundraising efforts, during the year the group has introduced a policy offering support for staff involved in fundraising. This matched giving policy offers employees the chance to have 30% of the raised amount, up to a maximum of £250, matched by the group.

Clydesdale Bank plc

Banking

Correspondent: Irene Swankie, Community Affairs Manager, 30 St Vincent Place, Glasgow G1 2HL (tel: 01412 487070; fax: 01412 040828; email: irene.swankie@nabgroup.com; website: www.cbonline.co.uk)

Directors: Jonathon Dawson; Cameron Clyne; John Hooper; David Fell; Richard Gregory; Roy Nicolson; Elizabeth Padmore; Malcolm Williamson, Chair; David Thorburn, Chief Executive (women: 1; men: 8)

Year end	30/09/2011
Turnover	£983,000,000
Pre-tax profit	£237,000,000

Nature of business: The Clydesdale Bank plc together with its subsidiary undertakings (which together comprise the Group) is the United Kingdom arm of the National Australia Bank Ltd.

Company registration number: SC001111

Brands include: Yorkshire Bank

Main locations: Glasgow, Edinburgh

UK employees: 5,589

Total employees: 5,589

Membership: BITC

Charitable donations

UK cash (latest declared):	2011	£808,000
	2010	£921,000
	2009	£842,000
	2008	£336,000
	2007	£280,000
Total UK:	2011	£808,000
Total worldwide:	2011	£808,000
Cash worldwide:	2011	£808,000

Community involvement

Since 2005, £400,000 has been invested in the Group's community programme 'Count Me In' which focuses on numeracy and is delivered through local libraries across 19 local authorities in England and Scotland.

Corporate giving

The bank channels its charitable donations through the *Yorkshire and Clydesdale Foundation*, a registered Scottish charity (No. SC039747) which was established during 2008. During the year 2011, the foundation has made donations to 650 charities totalling over £800,000. Since 2005, the Group has also invested £400,000 in its community programme 'Count Me In'. See 'Community Involvement.'

In kind support

Rental of office premises is provided to the Common Purpose and Home Start organisations in the UK.

Employee-led support

Charity Partner

On 1 February 2008 Clydesdale and Yorkshire Banks joined forces to announce the launch of a brand new charity partnership initiative with Help the Hospices. Help the Hospices is the leading charity supporting hospice care throughout the UK. The majority of hospice care in the UK is provided by Help the Hospices member hospices – local charities rooted in the communities they serve. Since the partnership began, the banks and employees have raised over £2 million for hospice care. Employees fundraising is matched pound for pound by the bank. The money raised supports 116 local hospices throughout the UK in their vital work.

Employees have also provided over 18,000 volunteering hours for their local hospice since the partnership was formed.

Payroll Giving

This scheme allows employees to make voluntary donations every month direct from their salary to a variety of causes close to their hearts. To date over 20% of employees are donating to charities and the company has been awarded H M Gold Quality Mark for Payroll Giving. Employees who choose to donate to the Bank's Charity Partner will have their donation matched pound for pound by the Bank.

Commercially-led support

Sponsorship

Current sponsorship properties include:

- Clydesdale Bank Premier League – Clydesdale Bank's sponsorship of the Scottish Premier League began in June 2007 and will continue through until the end of the 2012/2013 season. To find out more about how you can get involved visit the SPL sponsorship website: www.cbfootball.co.uk
- Clydesdale Bank 40 – Clydesdale Bank 40 is a family friendly format that includes children's activities and supports the development of UK cricket. 'This exciting three year partnership with the England and Wales Cricket Board is an excellent fit with our community based approach to sponsorship. Many of the matches took place on a Sunday with some being screened on Sky Sports and the final taking place at Lords.' For further information visit: www.ecb.co.uk/clydesdalebank40

Find out sponsorship requirements at: www.cbonline.co.uk/sponsorship/requirements.

Corporate social responsibility

CSR committee: There is a Community Affairs Manager – see 'Applications'.

CSR policy: The Community section of the National Australia Group Annual Review focuses on: community investment, disaster relief, reconciliation action and volunteering.

CSR report: The National Australia Bank Ltd produces annual reports combining Shareholder Review and Corporate Responsibility Review. The community section focuses on: community investment, disaster relief, reconciliation action and volunteering.

Exclusions

No response to circular appeals. No support for advertising in charity brochures, animal welfare, appeals from individuals, overseas projects, political appeals, religious appeals, capital projects or salary expenses, or local appeals not in areas of company presence.

Applications

If you wish to apply for an award from the **Yorkshire and Clydesdale Foundation**, refer to their criteria and details of application procedure: www.cbonline.co.uk/about-clydesdale-bank/community/charitable-donations-about-us

The website states that:

> Following a review in 2012 the Foundation Trustees launched an annual awards programme, The Yorkshire and Clydesdale Bank Foundation 'Spirit of the Community Awards'. These awards launched in February 2013 replaced the previous donation programme which closed in December 2012.
>
> The awards will support projects that advance financial education, improve employability and promote environmental protection or improvement.
>
> The 2013 Awards have now closed and information on the winners will be announced in due course. The 2014 Awards will open for applications in early 2014.
>
> *Community partnerships*
>
> Clydesdale Bank is one of many organisations that are committed to making a difference in the community. Through our Community Partnership programme, we work with a select number of groups to address shared issues of concern. Our current community investment priorities are numeracy and financial capability and we have two flag ship programmes; Count Me In and Count and Grow.
>
> We do not normally support:
>
> - Activities taking place outside Clydesdale Bank's operating area
> - Individuals and individual fundraisers
> - Capital projects
> - Salary expenses
> - Third party fundraising (i.e. advertising in charity programmes or gala fundraising events)political or religious organisations
>
> If your organisation satisfies these criteria and would like to consider a partnership there is no application form to complete. Send a proposal setting out the following:
>
> - A brief history of your organisation
> - Confirmation of charitable or not-for-profit status
> - How your organisation is funded, including details of any other corporate partners
> - A copy of your annual report/review and accounts
> - The sponsorship fee and project costs
> - Benefits to Clydesdale Bank as sponsor and an outline of how you plan to acknowledge support from the Bank
> - Supporting PR/Communications plan (outline only) – you may wish to include press cuttings of previous projects or partnerships
> - Details on how you plan to evaluate the impact of your project
>
> Completed proposals should be sent to: Irene Swankie, The Community Affairs Manager, Clydesdale Bank Exchange, Level 7, 20 Waterloo Street, GLASGOW G2 6DB.

Note that in view of the volume of proposals received, the bank is unable to enter into discussion by telephone or to meet with organisations prior to receiving a written proposal.

Coats plc

Textiles

Correspondent: Company Secretary, 1 The Square, Stockley Park, Uxbridge, Middlesex UB11 1TD (tel: 020 8210 5000; fax: 020 8210 5025; website: www.coats.com)

Directors: Gary Weiss, Chair; Paul Forman, Group Chief Executive; Blake Nixon; Rex Wood-Ward; Mike Allen (women: 0; men: 5)

Year end	31/12/2010
Turnover	£999,885,000
Pre-tax profit	£51,396,000

Nature of business: Principal activities: manufacture, processing and distribution of sewing thread for industrial and domestic use, homewares and fashionwares.

Company registration number: 104998

UK employees: 219

Total employees: 21,751

Charitable donations

UK cash (latest declared):	2010	£7,600
	2009	£21,300
	2008	£9,330
	2007	£14,000
	2006	£16,000
Total UK:	2010	£7,600
Total worldwide:	2010	£7,600
Cash worldwide:	2010	£7,600

Corporate social responsibility

CSR committee: The company's website states:

> A multi-functional team came together from across the business to identify the important CR issues for Coats.
>
> In November we appointed a global Head of CR to coordinate the programme and to make sure that we achieve our objectives.
>
> **CSR policy:** Over the past year we have reviewed our approach to Corporate Responsibility (CR), have identified what is important to us as a business and have set some global action plans and targets to support sustainability across our business. Full detail is provided in this section of our corporate website.
>
> We pride ourselves on being a part of the local communities in which we operate and our units are encouraged to develop close relationships with local people, business partners and community groups.
>
> In many locations around the world, we have a community programme in place and many of our employees volunteer to be part of these initiatives.
>
> We also aim to be a good corporate citizen and engage regularly with local authorities and other organisations in the community. It is important to us that we play a key role in local society, not least of which because that's where our employees come from. However, we have yet to globally align our community and charitable activities, which are currently handled at a local level.
>
> During 2012 we plan to develop a global policy to define our corporate approach to community investment. We will report on our progress next year.

CSR report: Information and data included in a separate section on the company's website.

Applications

In writing to the correspondent.

Other information

In 2010, the company made charitable donations of around £7,600 (2009: £14,000). We have no details of the beneficiaries.

Sponsorship: *Education* – The company supports several academic appointments in a number of educational centres.

The Coats Foundation Trust

Although historically associated with the company, the foundation's income is derived from investments and not currently funded by the company. However, the Coats Trustee Company Ltd, which administers the trust, includes directors from the company. The foundation is established for relief in need, the advancement of education and purposes beneficial to the community in the interests of social welfare.

Cobham plc

Aerospace, electronics/ computers

Correspondent: Eleanor Evans, Chief Legal Officer and Company Secretary, Brook Road, Wimborne, Dorset BH21 2BJ (tel: 01202 882020; fax: 01202 840523; website: www.cobham.com)

Directors: J. F. Devaney, Chair; A. J. Stevens, Chief Executive Officer; W. G. Tucker, Chief Financial Officer; M. Beresford; P. Hooley; J. S. Patterson; M. H. Ronald; M. W. Hagee (women: 0; men: 8)

Year end	31/12/2010
Turnover	£1,902,600,000
Pre-tax profit	£189,300,000

Nature of business: Design and manufacture of equipment, specialised systems and components used primarily in the aerospace, defence, energy and electronics industries and the operation and maintenance of aircraft, particularly in relation to special mission flight operations.

Company registration number: 30470

Main locations: Almondbank, Bournemouth, Southampton, Wimborne, Teesside, Kinloss

Total employees: 11,636

Membership: BITC

Charitable donations

UK cash (latest declared):	2010	£84,000
	2009	£85,000
	2008	£85,000
	2007	£68,000
	2006	£78,000
Total UK:	2010	£84,000
Total worldwide:	2010	£84,000
Cash worldwide:	2010	£84,000

Corporate social responsibility

CSR committee: The corporate responsibility and sustainability committee is supported by two subcommittees: the business ethics and compliance committee and the safety, health and environment committee.

CSR policy: The 2010 CRS Report states: 'Cobham recognises the need for business to contribute to wider society and our local communities in particular'. And: 'A strategic review of corporate philanthropy was undertaken during 2010. The findings of the review indicated that more activities and fundraising in local communities occurs than is always reported.'

CSR report: The report contains very little useful information on charitable giving or community contribution.

Exclusions

No support for animal welfare, individuals, the arts, elderly people, environment/heritage, overseas projects, political appeals, religious appeals, social welfare or sport.

Applications

In writing to the correspondent.

Other information

The company restricts its charitable support to causes in the Dorset area where it is based and to business-related national organisations. Within this area it will consider charities in the fields of children/youth, education, enterprise/ training, fundraising events, medical research, science/technology and sickness/disability. Advertising in charity brochures will also be considered, again if Dorset-based.

The following is taken from the annual report and accounts for 2010: 'The amount donated during the year for charitable purposes was £84,000 (2009: £85,420). Of this sum, individual donations in excess of £2,000 to UK charities were made to the value of £2,500 (2009: £10,000) to armed services charities, £15,000 (2009: £6,350) to business enterprise charities and £2,500 (2009: £nil) to other charities.'

In kind support can be provided to local initiatives in the form of the free use of meeting rooms and premises, the donation of surplus computer equipment and furniture, and the offer of places on in-house training courses. No breakdown is given of the value of any in kind support either in the UK or worldwide.

Cobham donated use of its rugged portable satellite communications systems to connect emergency services in the aftermath of the Haiti earthquake in 2010.

Coca-Cola Great Britain

Drinks manufacture

Correspondent: The Secretary, Consumer Information Centre, 1 Queen Caroline Street, Hammersmith, London W6 9HQ (tel: 020 8237 3000; fax: 020 8237 3700; email: corporateresponsibility@eur.ko.com; website: www.coca-cola.co.uk/ community)

Directors: S. Guha; I. Panizo; J. Woods; S. Roche; B. Gerber; D. Kearney

Year end	31/12/2010
Turnover	£170,000,000
Pre-tax profit	£25,900,000

Nature of business: Coca-Cola's business in Great Britain is made up of two separate companies with different roles. Together, these companies manufacture, distribute and market its range of drinks.

The companies are Coca-Cola Great Britain (CCGB), which is a wholly owned subsidiary of The Coca-Cola Company and Coca-Cola Enterprises Ltd (CCE), which is part of Coca-Cola Enterprises Inc. These two companies form the business in Great Britain. CCGB markets and develops new and existing brands.

CCE manufactures and distributes soft drinks for both The Coca-Cola Company and other brand owners.

Company registration number: 1724995

Main locations: East Kilbride, Aberdeen, Peterlee, Wakefield, Warrington, Nottingham, Coventry, Peterborough, Northampton, Milton Keynes, Bristol, Cardiff, Uxbridge, London

UK employees: 230

Total employees: 230

Membership: BITC

Charitable donations

UK cash (latest declared):	2010	£10,000
	2008	£151,000
Total UK:	2010	£10,000

Corporate social responsibility

CSR committee: There was no evidence of a separate CSR Committee.

CSR policy: This information was obtained from the company's website: 'Coca Cola Great Britain is an active member of the community. We support education programmes and encourage active lifestyles, in order to help teenagers achieve their personal best.'

Unable to determine the ratio of women to men on the board.

CSR report: A CSR report was available from the company's website.

Applications

In writing to the Consumer Information Centre at the company's address.

Other information

In 2010, Coca-Cola Holdings (United Kingdom) Ltd declared charitable contributions of £10,000 (2008: £151,000). Each year Coca-Cola contributes to the local communities in which it operates, both through its own community investment activities and through local community sponsorships, charitable donations, employee volunteering and the provision of in kind donations. One of the main aims of Coca-Cola in the community is to help young people achieve their best through education and sport.

Education

Thames21: This environmental charity aims to clean up London's waterside grot-spots, to remove graffiti and create new habitats for wildlife in the capital.

Encouraging active lifestyles

The company sees encouraging young people to be more physically active as an important part of its community work.

StreetGames
StreetGames aims to provide sporting opportunities to teens in disadvantaged communities across the country.

Colgate-Palmolive UK Ltd

Personal care products

Correspondent: General Manager, Guildford Business Park, Middleton Road, Guildford GU2 8JZ (tel: 01483 302222; fax: 01483 303003; website: www.colgate.co.uk)

Directors: L. Swayze; P. Graylin; G. Malcolm

Year end	31/12/2010
Turnover	£221,168,000
Pre-tax profit	£64,254,000

Nature of business: Producer of toothpastes, soaps, toiletries, detergents and similar products.

Company registration number: 178909

Main locations: Guildford

UK employees: 157

Total employees: 157

Charitable donations

UK cash (latest declared):	2010	£32,000
	2008	£5,000
	2007	£6,000
Total UK:	2010	£32,000
Total worldwide:	2010	£32,000
Cash worldwide:	2010	£32,000

Corporate social responsibility

CSR policy: No CSR information available for this company.

Unable to determine the ratio of women to men on the board.

Applications

In writing to the correspondent.

The global grants programme address is:
Colgate-Palmolive Company
Contributions Department
300 Park Avenue
New York, NY 10022
USA.

Other information

In 2010 the company gave £32,000 in cash charitable donations (2009: £17,000) principally by way of matched funding of money raised by employees. We have no details of beneficiaries.

The parent company in the United States supports children's causes across the world concerned with promoting the importance of oral health through education and prevention. The primary focus is to reach children in schools through videos, storybooks, songs, CD-ROMs and interactive activities.

Colt Group

Business services, information technology

Correspondent: Investor Relations, Beaufort House, 15 St Botolph Street, London EC3A 7QN (tel: 020 7390 3900; website: www.colt.net)

Directors: Ken Miller, Chair; Alan O'Hea, President; Antoine Ligtvoet, Group Chief Executive; Christophe Guillot; Michael Klincke; Simon O'Hea; Mike Ward-Penny; David Wesley-Yates (women: 0; men: 8)

Year end	31/12/2010
Turnover	£146,331,000
Pre-tax profit	£5,665,000

Nature of business: Providing business telephony, data networking services, IT managed services and consulting services to design, build and manage customer solutions.

Company registration number: 905918

UK employees: 947

Total employees: 947

Membership: BITC

Charitable donations

UK cash (latest declared):	2010	£670
	2009	£6,000
	2008	£26,000
Total UK:	2010	£670
Total worldwide:	2010	£5,000
Cash worldwide:	2010	£5,000

Corporate social responsibility

CSR policy: No CSR information available.

Applications

In writing to the correspondent.

Other information

During 2010 subsidiaries of the company donated £5,000 (2009: £4,000) to charitable organisations, of which £670 (2009: £275) was donated in the UK. We have no information regarding the value of any in kind giving.

The Colt Foundation (Charity Commission no. 277189)was established under a Trust Deed of 28 August 1978 by the O'Hea family with gifts of shares in Colt International and Associated Companies Ltd. This gift is now represented by 22% of Ordinary £1 shares in Colt Investments Ltd, which is the holding company for the Colt Group of Companies. The primary interest of the Colt Foundation is to promote and encourage research into social, medical and environmental problems created by commerce and industry. In its first 33 years of operation it has awarded more than £13.5 million in grants to over 200 projects and supported over 220 students studying some aspect of occupational health. Further information can be found on the foundation's website: www.coltfoundation.org.uk.

Charities of the year: Employees in each Colt country vote on a charity partner to support and work with over the next two years.

Communisis plc

Information management and communication

Correspondent: PA to Company Secretary, Wakefield Road, Leeds LS10 1DU (tel: 01132 770202; fax: 01132 713503; website: www.communisis.com)

Directors: P. Hickson, Chair; A. Blundell, Chief Executive; P. King; A. Blaxill; J. Wells; D. Rushton; N. Howes; M. Firth; R. Jennings (women: 0; men: 9)

Year end	31/12/2010
Turnover	£193,166,000
Pre-tax profit	£4,917,000

Nature of business: The principal activities of the group are the manufacture of printed products for direct marketing, forms, stationery and critical transactional products (such as statements and cheques) and the provision of print sourcing services.

Company registration number: 173691

Main locations: Liverpool, Leicester, Newcastle upon Tyne, London, Bath, Crewe, Manchester, Lisburn, Rickmansworth, Leeds

UK employees: 1,375

Total employees: 1,384

Charitable donations

UK cash (latest declared):	2009	£1,400
	2008	£21,600
	2007	£32,000
	2006	£31,000
	2005	£34,250

Corporate social responsibility

CSR committee: No information available.

CSR policy: No information available.

CSR report: Contained within the annual report and accounts.

Applications

The company does not provide support for advertising in charity brochures, the arts and political or religious appeals. No support is given towards appeals from individuals.

Other information

The following statement is taken from the annual report and accounts for 2010. 'During the year we made donations to the Scottish Community Foundation, Just Giving, the NSPCC and the World Food Programme.' No figures are given for company contribution either in cash or in kind value. There is some information given around employee-led initiatives and examples are:

> *Million Makers* is a scheme run by the Prince's Trust, in which teams of employees in businesses across the country are challenged to turn a £10,000 profit from seed funding of £1,500. the money is used by the trust to help underprivileged young people in the UK. The team has raised more than £26,000 for Million Makers to date and won Best Fundraising Book in the UK at the Gourmand World Cookbook Awards. *Action Aid:* On an employee's suggestion, we support this international charity by encouraging employees to make a payroll deduction each month. Employees contribute generously – about £80 per month. *Orchid:* This is the only UK charity to focus entirely on male-specific cancers. Communisis employees took part in several events during the year including the London Marathon in April 2010 to raise funds.

Compass Group plc

Retail – restaurants/fast food

Correspondent: Carol Wilkinson, Corporate Affairs, Rivermead, Oxford Road, Uxbridge, Middlesex UB9 4BF (tel: 01895 554554; fax: 01895 554555; email: ukcorporateresponsibility@compass-group.co.uk; website: www.compass-group.co.uk)

Directors: Gary R. Green; Andrew Martin; Susan Murray; Don Robert; Ian Robinson; James Crosby; John Bason; Gary Green; Roy Gardner, Chair; Richard Cousins, Chief Executive (women: 1; men: 9)

Year end	30/09/2011
Turnover	£15,833,000,000
Pre-tax profit	£958,000,000

Nature of business: The principal activity is the provision of contract food services to business and industrial organisations around the world.

Company registration number: 4083914

Subsidiaries include: Eurest, Select Service Partner Ltd, National Leisure Catering Ltd, Payne and Gunter Ltd, Select Service Partner Airport Restaurants Ltd, Letheby and Christopher Ltd

Brands include: Amigo/Outtakes; Caffè Liscio; Deli Marche/So Deli; Mama Leone's; PUUR; Steamplicity; Zona Mexicana. Franchises include: Burger King; Chick-Fil-A; Costa; Starbucks

Main locations: Uxbridge

UK employees: 62,967

Total employees: 471,108

Membership: BITC

Charitable donations

UK cash (latest declared):	2009	£5,600,000
	2008	£1,500,000
	2007	£1,162,000
	2006	£1,556,000
	2005	£1,340,000
Total worldwide:	2011	£5,900,000

Community involvement

Examples are given here of the company's community involvement schemes:

Junior Chefs' Academy

The academy is set up for children who show an interest in cooking and during 2009 over 47 ten-week courses were offered to schoolchildren. The programme teaches students vital skills about food safety, hygiene and preparation.

The programme is run at cookery schools in colleges throughout the UK, many of which are in locations that have traditionally high levels of unemployment – or people leaving school at sixteen.

Since the programme began in 2003, over 3,000 teenagers have graduated nationwide.

The following extract is from the group's CSR report:

> According to feedback from schools, the programme improves the students overall behaviour, concentration and self-esteem when back in school. Pupils are very excited about getting into the Junior Chefs' Academy. Those that haven't been successful in joining the first programmes are anxious to make sure they get in the next. It has given them a new insight when selecting their options and as a result some have now indicated catering as an option for GCSE's.'
>
> *ESS offenders rehabilitation project*
>
> ESS Support Services Worldwide has become a partner in a unique catering training scheme launched at HMP Drake Hall, Staffordshire. Launched four years ago, the initiative offers offenders from the all women's prison the opportunity to gain nationally-recognised catering qualifications by working alongside members of the ESS team at the nearby Swynnerton Army training camp. Successful candidates are employed by ESS for six to nine months on the same terms and conditions as other team members.
>
> Since the scheme started, many offenders have gained basic qualifications through the initiative, with many more planning to take part in the scheme. Post-release, a total of forty ex-offenders have been successfully employed in the catering and hospitality sector.

Corporate giving

In 2010/11, the company made worldwide community contributions of £5.9 million (2010: £5.8 million). We do not know what proportion of this was given in the UK, nor what was cash as opposed to in kind. Following an enquiry to the company regarding a breakdown of its charitable giving, we received the following statement from the Director of Health, Safety and Environment: 'I write to advise you that we are working with our countries (around 50) to breakdown the origins of their charitable contributions ahead of our 2012/13 reporting, however, currently we do not have this information available to publish.'

Employee-led support

Employees undertaking voluntary work in the community are recognised by the company through the presentation of awards and donations to their nominated charities. As a result of the combined efforts of UK based employees, this year over £800,000 has been raised for the company's partner – *Cancer Research UK*. Cancer Research UK will continue to be supported by the company's fundraising initiatives during 2012.

Payroll giving: Employees are encouraged to register and choose an amount they would like to contribute every month. The company then deducts this amount from their salaries and contributes an extra 10% towards the charity.

Corporate social responsibility

CSR committee: There is a CSR Committee – see 'CSR Policy'.

CSR policy: The company produces a CSR report from which the following statement is taken:

> Established in 2007, the Corporate Responsibility Committee continues to provide direction and guidance on all aspects of business practice and responsibility, ensuring consistent application wherever we operate. The committee's primary responsibilities include: endorsement of CR policies; overseeing occupational health and food safety performance; environmental practices; business conduct and the positive promotion of employee engagement, diversity and community investment.

CSR report: Published annually.

Exclusions

The company does not support advertising in charity brochures, animal welfare, individuals, the arts, elderly people, heritage, medical research, overseas projects, political or religious appeals and science/technology.

Applications

In writing to the correspondent.

Computacenter plc

Information technology

Correspondent: The Charity Committee, Computacenter House, 93–101 Blackfriars Road, London SE1 8HL (tel: 020 7620 2222; fax: 020 7593 4446; email: charity@computacenter.com; website: www.computacenter.com)

Directors: Mike Norris, Chief Executive; Tony Conophy, Chief Finance Officer; Greg Lock, Chair; Peter Ogden; Ian Lewis; John Ormerod; Brian McBride; Philip Hulme (women: 0; men: 8)

Year end	31/12/2011
Turnover	£2,852,303,000
Pre-tax profit	£72,101,000

Nature of business: Computacenter is a leading independent provider of IT infrastructure services.

Company registration number: 3110569

Main locations: Hatfield, Belfast, Birmingham, Bristol, Cardiff, Edinburgh, Manchester, Milton Keynes, Nottingham, Reading

UK employees: 4,958

Total employees: 11,013

Charitable donations

UK cash (latest declared):	2011	£83,000
	2009	£100,000
	2008	£87,000
Total UK:	2011	£83,000
Total worldwide:	2011	£83,000
Cash worldwide:	2011	£83,000

Corporate social responsibility

CSR committee: Charity Committee
Computacenter's charity programme is steered by the charity committee, which comprises a cross section of employees throughout the company. Any questions about the programme, fundraising activities or suggestions can be emailed to: charity@computacenter.com.

CSR policy: The following information is taken from the group's website:

> *Charity Policy*
> Computacenter's charity policy is to support three corporate charities for a two-year period. At the end of that period, staff are asked to select alternatives from a shortlist that includes the current charity partners. The charities are approved by the charity committee and are registered within the UK. Each of the charities will receive considerable support from Computacenter in this period. Funds collected via fundraising activities within the programme are in most instances matched by Computacenter. In working with these charities, we hope to achieve three main aims:
> - To demonstrate our commitment to the wider community
> - To motivate staff across the company by encouraging teambuilding activities in a worthwhile cause
> - To communicate Computacenter's core values to customers, staff and other stake-holders

CSR report: No specific report found but current information available from the company's website.

Applications

In writing to the correspondent.

Other information

In 2011 employees in the UK raised nearly £83,000 (2010: £115,000) for the chosen charity partners. Support for the Hertfordshire Fire and Rescue dogs continued as well as support for Kidsafe a road safety awareness campaign at local schools. The company's accounts do not declare a donation for charitable purposes from the company itself-but the website states that staff fundraising is matched. We have therefore taken the cash donation from the company to be £83,000.

Give As You Earn: A company-wide Give As You Earn (GAYE) scheme allows employees to make monthly contributions to any UK charity of their choice through automatic deduction from their salaries. This is tax deductible and attracts a 10% subsidy from the Inland Revenue. The full amount of the contribution goes to the charity because Computacenter handles all the administration at its own expense.

Sponsorship: Computacenter is the official IT supplier to the **RPA** – a non-profit making trade union dedicated to the welfare of all professional rugby players. The company also sponsors **Hertfordshire Fire and Rescue Service,** the Fire Investigation Dog Programme.

Charity Partners: Help for Heroes, Macmillan Cancer Support and The Great Ormond Street Children's Charity.

Congregational and General Insurance plc

Insurance

Correspondent: David John Collett, Secretary to the Trustees, Currer House, Currer Street, Bradford BD1 5BA (tel: 01274 700700; fax: 01274 370754; email: trust@congregational.co.uk; website: www.congregational.co.uk)

Directors: Carlo Cavaliere, Chief Executive; Ian Campbell, Finance Director; Martin Scott; David Collett, Chair; Harry Driver; Stephen Lockley; Barry Pollard (women: 0; men: 7)

Year end	31/03/2011

Nature of business: The transaction of general insurance business, in the form of the insurance for fire and other damage to property.

Company registration number: 93688

Main locations: Bradford

UK employees: 53

Total employees: 53

Charitable donations

UK cash (latest declared):	2011	£747,000
Total UK:	2011	£747,000
Total worldwide:	2011	£747,000
Cash worldwide:	2011	£747,000

Community involvement

The company is a wholly-owned subsidiary of **The Congregational and General Charitable Trust** (Charity Commission no. 297013). The trust was established to 'promote the Christian religion and in particular United Reformed Church and Congregational denominations and other churches which are of the protestant tradition'. It supports a wide range of churches, educational establishments, charitable organisations and community projects. Clear and helpful instructions on how to apply for a grant can be found on the company's website.

Corporate giving

The trust usually receives a proportion of company profits from the insurance company and in 2011 the trust had income from the trading subsidiary's profit of £747,000 (2010 £350,000). A council of members is responsible for the administration and management of the trust and all grants are made entirely on merit.

Corporate social responsibility

CSR policy: No CSR information available.

Applications

Applications to the associated trust should be made in writing to: David Collett, Secretary to the Trustees, Currer House, Currer Street, Bradford, West Yorkshire BD1 5BA.

Cookson Group plc

Manufacturing

Correspondent: Appeals Administrator, 165 Fleet Street, London EC4A 2AE (tel: 020 7822 0000; fax: 020 7822 0100; website: www.cooksongroup.co.uk)

Directors: Jeff Harris, Chair; Nick Salmon, Chief Executive; Mike Butterworth, Group Finance Director; François Wanecq; Dr Emma FitzGerald; Jeff Hewitt; Peter Hill, Director; Jan Oosterveld; John Sussens; Richard Malthouse (women: 2; men: 8)

Year end	31/12/2011
Turnover	£2,826,400,000
Pre-tax profit	£211,600,000

Nature of business: The Cookson Group is a holding company for an internationally-based group of companies principally engaged in the manufacture of specialist industrial materials, equipment, processes and services for use in industry. The group is divided into three divisions: electronics, ceramics and precious metals.

The group is located mainly in the UK, North America and Western Europe.

Company registration number: 251977

Main locations: London

Total employees: 34

Charitable donations

UK cash (latest declared):	2011	£0
	2009	£0
	2008	£0
	2007	£100,000
	2006	£100,000
Total UK:	2011	£0
Total worldwide:	2011	£0
Cash worldwide:	2011	£0

Corporate social responsibility

CSR committee: Health, safety and environmental matters are reviewed by the Board, there is no specific CSR committee.

CSR policy: The following policy statement is taken from the annual accounts, however, no mention is made of community involvement:

> Cookson recognises that its operations impact a wide community of stakeholders, including investors, employees, customers, business associates and local communities, and that appropriate attention to the fulfilment of its corporate responsibilities can enhance overall performance. In structuring its approach to the various aspects of corporate social responsibility, the company takes account of guidelines and statements issued by stakeholder representatives and other regulatory bodies from around the world. Social, environmental and ethical matters are reviewed by the board, including the impact such matters may have on the group's management of risk.

CSR report: CSR statements are contained within the annual report.

Exclusions

No support for appeals from individuals; the arts; enterprise/training; fundraising events; political appeals; religious appeals; science/technology; social welfare; or sport.

Applications

In writing to the correspondent. Telephone approaches are not welcomed.

Other information

In previous years the group has given cash donations to UK charities totalling around £100,000 and support has been given to Sight Savers International, The Bede Foundation, CBI Education Foundation, Council for Industry and Higher Education and Crisis. The company donates to both national and local charities, with a preference for those based in the City or its environs. Preferred areas of support have included: homelessness (especially regarding young people), advertising in charity brochures, animal welfare charities, children/youth, education, elderly people, environment/heritage, medical research, overseas projects, and sickness/disability charities.

The group recorded nil charitable donations for 2010/11 but the entry has been included because it is thought charitable giving might resume.

Cooper Gay (Holdings) Ltd

Insurance

Correspondent: Company Secretary, 52 Leadenhall Street, London EC3A 2EB (tel: 020 7480 7322; fax: 020 7481 4695; website: www.coopergay.com)

Directors: T. C. D. Esser, Chief Executive Officer; J. Flanagan; P. P. Rock (women: 0; men: 3)

Year end	31/12/2010
Turnover	£15,573,000
Pre-tax profit	£9,670,000

Nature of business: Holding company for insurance group.

Company registration number: 998625

Main locations: London

Total employees: 601

Charitable donations

UK cash (latest declared):	2009	£108,000
	2008	£6,000
	2006	£78,000
	2005	£230,000
Total worldwide:	2010	£30,000
Cash worldwide:	2010	£30,000

Corporate social responsibility

CSR policy: No CSR information.

Exclusions

Only registered charities are supported. No support for students.

Applications

In writing to the correspondent. Applications are considered twice a year.

Other information

In 2010 the company gave £30,000 in charitable donations. We could find no information on where the money was donated or which organisations/causes were supported. The Cooper Gay Charitable Trust to which the company has previously donated has ceased to exist.

Co-operative Group Ltd

Pharmaceuticals, retail – department and variety stores, banking, retail – supermarkets

Correspondent: Senior Community Manager, 8th Floor, New Century House, Corporation Street, Manchester M60 4ES (tel: 01618 341212/01618 275950; fax: 01618 331383; website: www.co-operative.coop/corporate)

Directors: Ursula Lidbetter; Steve Watts; Ben Reid; Duncan Bowdler; Marilynne Burbage; Chris Herries; David Pownall; Steven Bayes; Eric Calderwood; Paul Flowers; Stuart Ramsay; Herbert Daybell; Len Wardle, Group Chair; Jenny Barnes; Martyn Cheadle; Ray Henderson; Mark Smith; Liz Moyle; Patrick Grange (women: 5; men: 14)

Year end	31/12/2011
Turnover	£12,318,000,000
Pre-tax profit	£231,000,000

Nature of business: The Co-operative Group is the UK's largest mutual business, owned not by private shareholders but by over six million consumers. It is the UK's fifth biggest food retailer, the leading convenience store operator and a major financial services provider, operating The Co-operative Bank, Britannia and The Co-operative Insurance. Among its other businesses are the number one funeral services provider and Britain's largest farming operation.

Company registration number: 525R

Subsidiaries include: CIS Mortgage Maker Ltd, Millgate Insurance Brokers Ltd, Syncro Ltd, Farmcare Ltd, Hornby Road Investments Ltd, Goliath Footwear Ltd, CIS Policyholder Services Ltd, CRS (Properties) Ltd, Herbert Robinson Ltd, CIS Unit Managers Ltd

Brands include: CIS Co-operative Insurance, Co-operative Bank, Co-op e-store, smile, Shoefayre, Travelcare, Somerfield, Britannia.

Main locations: Manchester

Total employees: 102,007

Membership: Arts & Business, BITC, LBG

Charitable donations

UK cash (latest declared):	2011	£8,800,000
	2009	£7,000,000
	2007	£8,300,000
	2005	£4,400,000
	2004	£3,900,000
Total UK:	2011	£11,800,000
Total worldwide:	2011	£11,800,000
Cash worldwide:	2011	£8,800,000

Community involvement

Statement taken from the 2011 annual report and accounts:

In line with the co-operative principle of concern for community, The Co-operative operates an extensive programme of community investment, which embraces everything from small grants awarded by local member committees to international strategic alliances designed to tackle issues such as global poverty and climate change. With the launch in 2011 of the Ethical

Operating Plan, 'Keeping Communities Thriving ' has been accorded a central position in business strategy, and the community investment programme has been increasingly focused towards fulfilling this and the Plan's other objectives.

Community Map

Created in 2010, the Community Map is an interactive web tool that pinpoints the locations of thousands of schools, community groups and charities benefiting from the Cooperative's work in the UK. The map was updated and re-launched in early 2012 showcasing some 10,000 individual projects. www.co-operative.co.uk/communitymap

Programmes

The following list gives the group's top ten programmes:

- Inspiring Young People
  - Truth about Youth
  - Green Schools Revolution
  - Co-operative Schools
  - Co-operative StreetGames Young Volunteers
  - Co-operative British Youth Film Academy and Co-operative Film Festival
  - Co-operative Academies
  - The Britannia Foundation
  - Sponsorship
- Charity of the Year
- Co-operative Membership Community Fund
- Employee community engagement
- Co-operative Enterprise Hub
- Bank charity credit cards in support of UK communities
- Green Energy Revolution
- Consumer Credit Counselling Service 'fairshare contributions'
- Employee fundraising
- Drinkaware

The Co-operative Community Investment Foundation (known as the Community Fund)

The Community Fund supports community, voluntary and self-help organisations by awarding small grants of between £100 and £2,000. 2011 saw an increase in both the number of awards made and the amount donated, with £2.7\ million dispersed to 2,430 community groups. Decision-making on grant applications is undertaken by 48 area committees.

Awards are made to organisations that carry out positive work in the community, and to projects that meet all, or most, of the following criteria: addresses a community issue; provides a long-term benefit to the community; supports co-operative Values and Principles; and is innovative in its approach.

The Co-operative Foundation

The Co-operative Foundation is a charitable trust that was set up in 2000 (Charity Commission no. 1080834) and is funded by the Co-operative Group. The group has donated £14.7 million to the foundation to date (2011), £5 million of which has been invested to provide funding for the foundation's current grantmaking programme, Truth about Youth. The Truth about Youth grantmaking scheme was developed by the foundation to challenge and change negative perceptions of young people, by supporting projects that enable young people to work with adults, the media and the wider community.

Grants of £280,000 each have been awarded to charities in each of the Co-operative's seven democratic regions, who will work with the foundation for at least two years: Envision in Birmingham; Platform 51 (formerly YWCA) in Cardiff; Regional Youth Work Unit in Tyne and Wear; Prince's Trust in Bristol; Young Scot in Glasgow; Oval House in London; and the Royal Exchange Theatre in Manchester.

During 2011, Envision, Regional Youth Work Unit and Young Scot all successfully applied for and achieved a further year's funding. A new partner will be sought in Wales during 2012.

A youth advisory panel made up of young participant representatives from all the partners was established in 2011, the aim of which is to share best practice and facilitate collaborative working.

A new three-year strategy (2012–2014) will ensure Truth about Youth can continue to operate with the current partners in each region and will build on the solid foundations the partners have made in communities across the UK.

The Britannia Foundation and The Britannia Community Fund

The Britannia Foundation is supported by a £500,000 annual donation from The Co-operative Banking Group. The foundation offered grants of between £1,000 and £25,000 to schools and registered charities working within education, with a particular focus on supporting numeracy and financial literacy. In 2011, 47 awards were made totalling almost £426,000.

The Britannia Community Fund also supports schools and educational charities, and awarded smaller grants (up to £1,000) to 110 groups totalling almost £38,000 in 2011.

Note: In 2011, the Co-operative Foundation and the Co-operative Community Investment Foundation (CCIF) merged and the assets and liabilities of the former were transferred to CCIF. The cash balances are to be transferred over in 2012 and will show in that year's accounts.

The Britannia Foundation and Britannia Community Fund merged with the CCIF in 2012.

In kind support is also given by the group by way of a pro-active and significant volunteering programme.

Corporate giving

Community investment in the UK made by The Co-operative in 2011 was £11.8 million. This was broken down as: £8.8 million cash; £2.7 million employee time; and £300,000 in gifts in kind. We have not included the amounts given for 'leverage' or management costs.

Co-operative Foundation (Charity Commission no. 1080834)

The Co-operative Foundation was set up for general charitable purposes in 2000 and is funded by the Co-operative group. In 2010/11 the foundation received £1.1 million from the Co-operative group.

Truth about Youth

The foundation's main current programme, Truth about Youth, aims to challenge and change negative perceptions of young people. The objectives of the programme are:

- To support young people to deal positively with the challenge of growing up in a culture, which has a widespread negative perception of youth
- To increase levels of interaction between young people and adults to develop projects in which they all have an interest and for those projects to have a lasting benefit
- To engage young people in identifying and setting up their own co-operative projects which address their needs and demonstrate young people's value to society
- To successfully communicate the outputs and outcomes of the projects to as wide an audience as possible

During 2010/11, the foundation trustees continued to roll out the programme on a national scale.

For any enquiries regarding Truth about Youth contact Sarah Robinson, Foundation Manager, on 01612 463039 or email: srobinson@co-operative.coop

Environment Fund

The objective of this fund is to support one or two environmental projects each year in the North West of England. Projects should bring benefits to significant numbers of people, leave a lasting legacy, be innovative and provide clear cut environmental benefits. In 2010/11 the trustees awarded £10,000 to Mid-Antrim Beekeepers Association.

The Co-operative Community Investment Foundation

The key objective of the community fund is to support self-help voluntary and community groups. The fund is overseen by a group of trustees, with the group's 45 area committees having responsibility for allocating community fund awards and assessing applications within their areas. Applicants must demonstrate that their project carries out positive work in a local community in which at least one Co-operative group business trades, addresses a community issue; provides a good long-term benefit to the community; ideally is innovative in its approach, and is aligned to the group's values and principles.

In 2011, the CCIF received almost £3.3 million from the Co-operative group and the trustees awarded grants totalling nearly £2.7 million to 2,430 groups across the UK. The table shows how these awards were distributed.

The Co-operative Membership region	Awards 2011	Total 2011
South and West Region	431	£499,000
North West and North Midlands	381	£447,000
North	483	£434,000
South East	341	£422,000
Central and Eastern	359	£385,000
Scotland and Northern Ireland	374	£334,500
Cymru/Wales and Borders	215	£172,500
Total	2,584	**£2.7 million**

In kind support

In kind donations were made by the group to the value of £300,000 in 2011.

Staff volunteering – The number of employees involved in community activity in work time during 2011 was 13,397 and the number of days invested in community activity in work time was 27,760. Colleague volunteering included the Mencap Inspire Me programme. 'Through this programme, employees from across the UK became mentors for young people with learning disabilities, providing personal support, guidance, encouragement and inspiration.'

Charity of the Year – This initiative enables a selected national charity to benefit from employee fundraising, and volunteering for a dedicated 12-month term. Alongside fundraising, local communities are also engaged in the charitable aims of the nominated charity, to raise awareness and influence change.

In 2011, the partnership with Mencap and its sister charity, ENABLE Scotland, raised a record £7 million, which was the largest donation received by Mencap.

Employee-led support

Volunteering programme: Staff are actively encouraged to take part in the volunteering programme which supports and encourages their interest in community and charitable initiatives. Employees can take part in community volunteering in work time – providing benefits to the volunteers themselves and to the local community. Employees can volunteer for either individual opportunities, such as mentoring, or team challenges, such as creating a reading garden in a local primary school.

StreetGames Young Volunteers: Operating in some of the most deprived wards in England and Wales, this programme provides young people with the opportunity to develop their sports coaching and community leadership skills. For some, this can even provide a valuable route into paid employment or other youth work. Since it was launched in October 2007, the project has seen 1,150 young volunteers give 27,000 volunteering hours to help develop sport in their local communities. StreetGames is now a national partner of Sport England and is regarded as a national centre of expertise for developing doorstep sport in disadvantaged communities.

Grassroots programme: The Co-operative Insurance runs an extensive programme of grassroots initiatives throughout the UK, including football coaching and the provision of kits and equipment to junior teams. To date it has provided football kits to over 3,200 youth football teams and coaching for over 16,000 children.

2008 saw almost 6,000 members of staff volunteer and fundraise for their local communities, contributing over 45,000 hours of time and effort.

Matched giving: Colleagues choosing to support other charities can apply to The Co-operative Booster Fund, which supplements their fundraising activities. Fundraising efforts are topped-up by £100 for an individual and £400 for a team (subject to terms and conditions).

£3.7 million was raised for the 2009 **Charity of the Year**, the *Royal National Institute for the Deaf.*

Payroll giving: Staff are able to contribute to their chosen charity through the provision of a payroll giving scheme.

Commercially-led support

Cause-related marketing:

We continue to lead the way in our commitment to international development and human rights. The Co-operative Food is the leading UK supermarket for *Fairtrade* availability, and in 2011 we launched a partnership with *CARE International UK* to support lendwithcare.org – an innovative scheme to allow people in the UK to lend money directly to entrepreneurs in the developing world. Our leading stance on responsible finance was recognised with The Co-operative Bank named the most sustainable bank in Europe, for the third year running in 2012.

Charity credit cards – The bank offers a range of credit cards, each linked to one of 15 charity partners. A donation is made to the chosen charity when an account is opened and additional donations are made in proportion to the amount spent using the card. In 2011, a total of £1.38 million was raised for charity through affinity credit cards.

'Customers Who Care' – This scheme donates 1.25 pence for every £100 spent on credit and debit cards. Cumulatively, this fund has given over £4\ million in donations to over 80 charities and organisations since its launch in 1994.

The Co-operative Antibacterial Handwash – The Co-operative Pharmacy launched this new affinity product with UNICEF in early 2011. The Co-operative Antibacterial Handwash raises money to support a project in Togo – 15 pence is donated from every sale of handwash. £400,000 was pledged to the project in 2010 to deliver basic sanitation to 195,000 people in 390 villages.

The Global Development Co-operative (GDC) – This new initiative was unveiled at the New York launch of the United Nations International Year of Co-operatives in 2011. It aims to raise £20\ million from organisations that support international development and extend the reach of the co-operative model. These funds will then be used to provide low-cost loans for capital and infrastructure projects around the world.

Sponsorship: Britannia, which is a trading name used by The Co-operative Bank plc, is involved in football through its sponsorships of Stoke City, the Britannia Stadium and stand sponsorship at Port Vale.

To support our top level football sponsorships, we also have a grassroots football programme which includes initiatives to provide coaching, kits and equipment to junior teams to help increase participation in the sport in communities around the UK.

To find out more about the Co-operative Group's sponsorships, visit the group sponsorships website.

Charity partners include: RSPB, Oxfam, Amnesty International UK, Greenpeace, WaterAid, ActionAid, Help the Aged, Christian Aid.

The Co-operative is a Principal member of Arts and Business.

Corporate social responsibility

CSR committee: There is a Social Responsibility Team.

CSR policy: The following statement is taken from the group's Social Responsibility Report for 2011:

Social Responsibility – Our Approach

Taking a responsible approach to business has been a guiding principle of The Co-operative since its inception. Co-operative Values and Principles – such as concern for community and equality – date back to the 19th century, and also

> resonate with contemporary ideas of corporate responsibility. When considering these issues, the business is responsive to the views of its stakeholders, particularly members and customers.

To read the group's sustainability policy, visit: www.co-operative.coop/corporate/sustainability/overview/managing-sustainability/

CSR report: Comprehensive Social Responsibility report published annually.

Exclusions

The Co-operative Membership Community Fund excludes:

Groups other than community, self-help and voluntary groups; the core activities of auxiliary groups; non-charitable purposes (although a group does not have to be a registered charity); overseas activities; grant or loan schemes; religious worship; core activities of statutory services; improvements to property not owned by the applicant; party political activity; individual sponsorship; and cadets.

Applications

The Co-operative Membership Community Investment Foundation (Community Fund)

The Co-operative Membership Community Fund (Charity Commission no. 1093028) operates a grants scheme supporting local communities throughout the UK. The scheme is funded by Co-operative members donating some or all of their share of profits, which is then given away in the form of small grants in their local communities.

To be successful, a **group** must:

- Carry out positive work in the community

and a **project** must:

- Address a community issue
- Provide a good long-term benefit to the community
- Support co-operative values and principles
- Ideally be innovative in its approach

Application forms including an online facility, and details on applying to the fund can be found at: www.co-operative.coop/en/community-fund.

If you have any queries about applying or eligibility, please 'phone the help line on 01618 275879, or send an email to: community.fund@co-operative.coop

The Co-operative Foundation

The foundation's current grantmaking programme is *Truth about Youth* where the foundation is working with seven charities in seven cities across the UK delivering this programme over the next two to three years.

Any enquiries regarding Truth about Youth contact Sarah Robinson, Foundation Manager, on 01612 463039 or srobinson@co-operative.coop.

Cooper-Parry LLP

Accountants

Correspondent: Human Resource Dept, 3 Centro Place, Pride Park, Derby DE24 8RF (tel: 01332 295544; fax: 01332 295600; email: thought@cooperparry.com; website: www.cooperparry.com)

Directors: Colin Shaw, Chair; Jeremy Bowler, Chief Executive (women: 0; men: 2)

Year end	30/04/2011
Turnover	£14,475,000
Pre-tax profit	£3,990,000

Nature of business: Accountants and business advisors.

Company registration number: OC301728

Main locations: Nottingham, Leicester

Membership: BITC

Charitable donations

UK cash (latest declared):	2011	£1,150
	2010	£1,400
Total UK:	2011	£1,150
Total worldwide:	2011	£1,150
Cash worldwide:	2011	£1,150

Corporate social responsibility

CSR policy: No CSR information available.

Applications

In writing to the correspondent.

Other information

In 2010/11, Cooper-Parry declared just £1,150 in cash donations. However, the firm's community support, although in kind, has previously been valued at around £100,000 and does not appear to have decreased, even though we were unfortunately unable to find a calculated figure.

The firm's employees continue to support charities in their fundraising efforts. The firm's accounts for April 2011 state:

> We are committed to giving something back to the communities that we live in and work with. We have a strong sense of community involvement and are proud to participate in and lead local initiatives. We understand the importance of helping address social, economic and environmental needs and we are involved in a number of business initiatives in our local communities where we are demonstrating our willingness to donate time, resources, and expertise. Our Cooper Parry Corporate Challenge continues to be the largest single fundraiser across the entire Experian Robin Hood Marathon. In the last eight years we have raised over £210,000 for the Marathon's designated charities and in 2011 we will be supporting the Dame Kelly Holmes Legacy Trust.Over70 teams from the East Midlands entered the Cooper Parry 10k Business Team Challenge in Derby raising a further £15,000.

Costain Group plc

Building/construction

Correspondent: Tracey Wood, HR and Legal Director, Costain House, Vanwall Business Park, Maidenhead, Berkshire SL6 4UB (tel: 01628 842444; email: info@costain.com; website: costain.com)

Directors: Andrew Wyllie, Chief Executive; David Allvey, Chair; John Bryant; Tony Bickerstaff, Group Finance Director; James Morley; Michael Alexander; Samer G. Younis (women: 0; men: 7)

Year end	31/12/2011
Turnover	£986,300,000
Pre-tax profit	£25,500,000

Nature of business: Engineering and construction group.

Company registration number: 1393773

Total employees: 4,159

Membership: BITC

Charitable donations

UK cash (latest declared):	2009	£95,300
	2007	£35,533
	2006	£13,129
	2005	£21,121
Total worldwide:	2011	£135,000
Cash worldwide:	2011	£135,000

Corporate social responsibility

CSR committee: The company has a dedicated CR Director and monitors progress on a regular basis.

CSR policy: Taken from the company's annual report for 2011:

> We are committed to operating our business responsibly and sustainably, ensuring that we meet our customers' and society's needs while managing the social, environmental and economic impacts of our business. Our primary focus is to both understand and meet the needs of stakeholders.

CSR report: Section in annual report 'Performing Responsibly' which covers the environment, employees, the supply chain etc. There is very little information charitable giving.

Exclusions

No support for local appeals not in areas of company presence, general appeals or circulars.

Applications

In writing to the correspondent setting out briefly why your application should be eligible for a donation. Donations are normally for very small sums of money and are made to registered charities only.

Other information

Charitable donations of £135,000 (2010: £95,000) were made by the group during the year, principally to industry related charities serving the communities in which the group operates. Through an employee volunteering policy, the company provides employees with the opportunity to 'develop and share skills while making a visible and sustainable difference to local communities. In 2011, we saw an increase in the number of days our employees volunteered and we have set a target to increase this contribution by 10% in 2012.' Unfortunately there is no figure given for the number of volunteers or cost of volunteer time.

Costcutter Supermarkets Group Ltd

Retail – supermarkets

Correspondent: John Haigh, Charity Correspondent, Making A Difference Locally Ltd, Waldo Way, Normanby Enterprise Park, Scunthorpe DN15 9GE (tel: 01904 488663/01724 282028; website: www.costcutter.com)

Directors: C. J. Graves; N. Ivel; D. M. Thompson; A. M. Barber; J. R. Davison; A. P. King; I. Bishop

Year end	30/04/2011
Turnover	£632,493,000
Pre-tax profit	£10,344,000

Nature of business: The Costcutter Supermarkets Group is a franchise operation, with convenience stores throughout the UK.

Company registration number: 2059678

UK employees: 166

Total employees: 166

Charitable donations

UK cash (latest declared):	2011	£2,600
	2009	£218,000
Total UK:	2011	£2,600
Total worldwide:	2011	£2,600
Cash worldwide:	2011	£2,600

Corporate social responsibility

CSR policy: No CSR information available.

Unable to determine the ratio of women to men on the board.

Applications

In writing to your local store.

Enquiries regarding the charity, Making A Difference Locally Ltd., should be sent to the correspondent.

Other information

The company accounts state that in 2010/11 charitable donations of £2,625 were made mainly to sporting charities.

The following information regarding cause-related marketing, is taken from the company's website and relates to monies raised through the sale of specific goods in the group's convenience stores:

> Costcutter is proud to be local which is why our 'Local Pride' campaign is so important to us.
>
> Local Pride is a campaign dedicated to raising funds for good causes and charities across the UK by raising funds for Making A Difference Locally, a registered charity which in turn ensures that the money raised is spent on good causes in the local area in which they were raised.
>
> The Local Pride campaign does this by working with our suppliers to specially select products which when you the customer buys them a few pence from each sale goes to Making A Difference Locally.
>
> Making A Difference Locally then works with Local Pride and your local store to identify and distribute the money that's been raised by that store to good causes in its community, such as the local football team in need of a new kit.
>
> Stores taking part in Local Pride submit formal applications nominating their local good causes to Making A Difference Locally as the governing charity whose job it is to ensure that donations are properly made and that the recipients comply with strict guidelines. Making A Difference Locally will vet these good causes to make sure they are genuine beneficiaries. Only after a good cause has passed this process can they be eligible to receive donations from Making A Difference Locally.
>
> You the customer can therefore raise money for your local good causes by purchasing specific products, and the great thing is it doesn't cost you any more money!
>
> Making A Difference Locally Ltd (company number 6502266) is a registered charity, registered with the Charity Commission with number 1123800. It is governed by a board of directors who receive no remuneration from the charity and are in place to ensure nominated good causes are genuine and worthy beneficiaries.

Coutts and Co

Banking

Correspondent: Kay Boland, The Coutts Charitable Trust, 440 Strand, London WC2R 0QS (tel: 020 7753 1000/020 7957 2822; fax: 020 7753 1028; email: kay.boland@coutts.com; website: www.coutts.com)

Directors: The Earl of Home, Chair; Gordon Francis Pell; Michael John Morley, Chief Executive; James Hedley Rawlingson; Brian Hartzer; Rory Tapner (women: 0; men: 6)

Year end	31/12/2010
Turnover	£472,724,000
Pre-tax profit	£169,698,000

Nature of business: Banking and allied financial services. Coutts is the private banking arm of the Royal Bank of Scotland Group. The bank's main location is London, but there are 32 offices internationally.

Company registration number: 36695

Brands include: RBS Coutts

Main locations: Liverpool, Manchester, Newcastle upon Tyne, Oxford, Nottingham, Winchester, Tunbridge Wells, Bristol, Cardiff, Cambridge, Isle of Man, Jersey, Leeds, Eton, Guildford, Bath, Birmingham, Bournemouth

Membership: Arts & Business

Charitable donations

UK cash (latest declared):	2011	£750,590
	2009	£1,267,500
	2006	£832,956
	2005	£522,088
	2004	£405,195
Total UK:	2011	£750,590
Total worldwide:	2010	£750,590
Cash worldwide:	2010	£750,590

Community involvement

The Coutts Charitable Trust (Charity Commission no. 1000135) was set up in 1987 to formalise Coutts and Co.'s charitable giving and makes a large number of small donations to a wide range of charities each year. During 2010 over 1,500 grants of typically between £500 and £750 were awarded to UK registered charities. A portion of the charitable budget is used for larger donations and the trust also supports charities with longer term pledges, including the Peabody Trust, one of the oldest and largest social landlords in London, housing around 50,000 people in approximately 18,000 properties.

The trust's main source of funding is derived from a fixed percentage of the bank's pre-tax profits, which is distributed to selected causes.

Grants are given by the trust to UK organisations only and it prefers to support organisations in areas where the bank has a presence, mainly London. Charities supported include those involved with helping the homeless, rehabilitation and teaching self-help (drug; alcohol; young offenders), disadvantaged adults and children, youth organisations, the elderly, medical research, heritage, education and the relief of poverty.

> Many applications are supported by key clients and, in these circumstances, the criteria may be relaxed. Staff and pensioners of Coutts & Co., involved with charities in a personal capacity, are encouraged to apply to the trust and support is also given to members of staff who give their time voluntarily to raise funds for charities of their choice.

Corporate giving

The total amount given for charitable purposes by the company and its subsidiary undertakings during the year ended 31 December 2010 was £618,700 (2009: £976,000). The figure we have used for charitable contributions is that received by the Coutts Charitable Trust for the period 2010/11.

Coutts Charitable Trust

In 2010/11 the covenant income of £750,590 (2009/10: £1,269,000), was received from Coutts and Company. During the year approximately 1,750 applications (2009/10 – 1,600) for assistance were received and the trustees identified and made donations totalling over £1,197,000 (2009/10 -£863,700) to 1,502 charitable organisations (2009/10 – 1,199). Grants are generally in the region of £1,000 to £3,000, with an occasional larger grant. The trust benefits a very wide range of groups and a complete list of all donations (over £1,000), is given in its accounts filed with the Charity Commission.

A small selection of the trust's beneficiaries in 2010/11 is given here: St Mark's Hospital Foundation (£20,200); The No Way Trust (£15,000); Shelter (£10,000); Royal Albert Hall and UK Youth (£5,000 each); Abbeyfield (Reading) Society, Accessible Coach Holidays, Action on Addiction, Bianca Jagger Human Rights Foundation; Build Africa; East End CAB; Independence at Home; Islington Boys' Club; Lyric Hammersmith; Mind; National Society for Epilepsy; Neighbours In Poplar; One in Four; Royal Northern College of Music; Tantrum for Kids; Tenovus; The Living Room; University College London Hospital, Victims Support London; World Jewish Relief and Young Gloucestershire (£1,000 each).

Employee-led support

Volunteering

During 2010, employees have undertaken challenges to support the causes close to them. In October a team of four staff members raised over £19,000 trekking the Great Wall of China in aid of the Prince's Trust. A larger team of 30 bankers have fundraised to achieve their initial goal of raising £141,000 to fund a ChildLine supervisor role for three years. Having reached that target by £70,000 by the end of 2010, they have continued to hold events such as the 66 mile coast to coast walk, and bike rides from London to Reims in their aim to double their target, which they are on course to achieve by June 2011.

Payroll giving: The company operates the Give As You Earn scheme.

Commercially-led support

Sponsorship: *The arts* – support has been given to the Almeida Theatre, the Design Museum and the Royal Opera House, amongst others.

Corporate social responsibility

CSR policy: Taken from the Annual Review 2010:

> We have continually shaped our business to meet the changing needs and expectations of our clients and society. Today, this remains our modus operandi, along with seeking to build strong communities both within our business and between clients and Coutts staff, in the towns and cities where we work and live.

CSR report: Annual Review available online.

Exclusions

No response to circular appeals. No support for appeals from individuals or overseas projects.

Applications

Applications to the Coutts Charitable Trust should be addressed to the correspondent, at any time. Applications should include clear details of the purpose for which the grant is required. Grants are made regularly where amounts of £500 or less are felt to be appropriate. The trustees meet quarterly to consider larger donations.

Coventry Building Society

Building society

Correspondent: Ms Sarah Godderidge, Correspondent, Coventry BS Charitable Foundation, Oakfield House, PO Box 600, Binley, Coventry CV3 9YR (tel: 0845 766 5522/02476 653746; website: www.thecoventry.co.uk)

Directors: David Harding, Chair; David Stewart, Chief Executive; John Lowe, Finance Director; Colin Franklin; Roger Burnell; Ian Geden; Ian Pickering; Fiona Smith; Glyn Smith; Bridget Blow (women: 2; men: 8)

Year end	31/12/2011
Turnover	£730,000,000
Pre-tax profit	£59,500,000

Nature of business: Building Society

Company registration number: 5830727

UK employees: 1,847

Total employees: 1,847

Charitable donations

UK cash (latest declared):	2011	£1,100,000
	2009	£100,000
	2008	£200,000
	2007	£111,600
	2006	£78,000
Total UK:	2011	£1,100,000
Total worldwide:	2011	£1,100,000
Cash worldwide:	2011	£1,100,000

Community involvement

Coventry Building Society Charitable Foundation (Charity Commission no. 1072244) was launched in 1998, and since then has donated over £780,000 to local charities and community groups.

> The foundation, which is entirely funded by Coventry Building Society, is an independent entity with a board of trustees who determine the criteria by which grants are made.
>
> The grant process is administered on behalf of Coventry Building Society Charitable Foundation by Heart of England Community Foundation. This is a specialist independent grant provider which, in association with a network of local Community Foundations, takes responsibility for assessing grant requests in accordance with Coventry Building Society Charitable Foundation criteria.
>
> Small charities or community groups operating within reach of our branch network can apply. We do not donate to charities or community groups with an annual income in excess of £250,000.
>
> Priority is given to groups or activities aimed at improving the quality of life among groups who are disadvantaged or deprived, the consequence of which may otherwise lead to social exclusion.
>
> We welcome applications from small grass roots charities and community groups that focus on:
>
> - Young people, particularly those who are disadvantaged
> - Vulnerable groups such as the frail elderly, people with physical disability, people with learning difficulties or those who are mentally ill
> - Small neighbourhood groups in areas experiencing the greatest disadvantage
> - Supporting communities and voluntary organisations through assisting them in the achievement of social and community development
>
> We wish to support as many charities as possible and as such do not offer large sums. In exceptional circumstances, we may offer up to £3,000 however the grants will tend to be smaller than this.

For more information visit: www.coventrybuildingsociety.co.uk/your-society/tlc-for-charities/charitable-foundation.

Corporate giving

The Society provided for donations of £1.1 million (2010: £1.8 million) to charitable organisations during the year. During 2011 the Society has provided for a donation of £1 million (2010: £1.7 million) to the Poppy Appeal and £50,000 (2010: £50,000) to the Coventry Building Society Charitable Foundation.

In kind support

The Society is nearing the end of its three year programme of support for Age UK. During this time almost £150,000 has been raised, but of equal importance has been the opportunity to increase awareness amongst staff and members of the work undertaken by Age UK, and the issues faced by the UK's elderly.

Employee-led support

In 2011, the Society supported through its maturing programme of community activity, around 260 charities and community groups. Members of staff gave their time, expertise and enthusiasm in raising funds and directly volunteering for a wide variety of organisations ranging from local charities to raising over £40,000 for Children in Need.

Charity Partner: Royal British Legion

Corporate social responsibility

CSR committee: No designated committee.

CSR policy: Statement taken from the company's annual report:

> The Society has, over a number of years, developed an established programme of support that reflects the core competences of the organisation and the needs of local communities. Of particular note has been the ongoing work to enhance financial literacy, which now spans a range of initiatives from supporting numeracy and literacy in primary schools, to working with specialist finance academies and tackling personal debt issues amongst adults through partnerships with Citizens Advice Bureaus in Coventry and Stroud. These initiatives are well regarded by the organisations involved, in particular the consistency of the Society's support over a sustained period. The directors believe that the Society's links between its core business activities and supporting vulnerable people demonstrates the best of corporate responsibility in action.

CSR report: Information relating to community, environment and staff is contained within the company's annual report.

Exclusions

The society will not consider grants for the following:

- Large charities which enjoy national coverage
- Charities with no base within the branch area
- Charities with an annual donated income in excess of £250,000
- Charities with assets over £500,000
- Projects requiring an ongoing commitment
- Large capital projects
- Maintenance or building works for buildings, gardens or playgrounds
- Major fundraising
- Projects which are normally the responsibility of other organisations (such as the NHS, Education Department and local authorities)
- Sponsorship of individuals
- Requests from individuals
- Replacing funds that were the responsibility of another body
- Educational institutions unless for the relief of disadvantage
- Sporting clubs or organisations unless for the relief of disadvantage
- Medical research and equipment
- More than one donation for the same organisation in any one year – further applications will be considered after three years
- Animal welfare
- Promotion of religious political or military causes

Applications

To apply for a grant from the Coventry Building Society Charitable Trust, print off and fill in the application form from the company website. Send the completed application form accompanied with a copy of recent report and accounts to the correspondent.

The society states: 'it may not be always be possible to support all applications even if they fully meet the foundation's criteria. We reserve the right to support those charities we believe to be worthy of our support'.

Information available: Further information regarding the application form and policy guidelines is available at the society's website: www.thecoventry.co.uk.

Credit Suisse

Banking

Correspondent: Corporate Citizenship Dept., One Cabot Square, London EC14 4QJ (email: emea.philanthropy@credit-suisse.com; website: www.credit-suisse.com/uk/en)

Directors: Urs Rohner, Chair; Peter Brabeck-Letmathe, Vice Chair; Jassim Bin Hamad J. J. Al Thani; Robert Benmosche; Iris Bohnet; Noreen Doyle; Jean-Daniel Gerber; Walter B. Kielholz; Andreas N. Koopmann; Jean Lanier; Anton van Rossum; Aziz R. D. Syriani; David W. Syz; Richard E. Thornburgh; John Tiner (women: 2; men: 13)

Year end	31/12/2011
Turnover	£17,042,000,000
Pre-tax profit	£2,250,000,000

Nature of business: Banking.

Company registration number: 891554

Total employees: 49,700

Charitable donations

UK cash (latest declared):	2009	£110,000
Total worldwide:	2011	£8,500,000
Cash worldwide:	2011	£8,500,000

Corporate social responsibility

CSR committee: There was evidence of a separate CSR Committee.

CSR policy: This information was obtained from the company's website:

> Credit Suisse and its employees have been working with selected partner organisations around the world for many years to help address social challenges and improve the living standards of disadvantaged people.
>
> Credit Suisse partners with charities through direct financial donations as well as contributions of time and professional skills. Collaboratively, we are making a positive impact on individual lives resulting in stronger communities. We believe that forming long-term partnerships with a select group of charities allows us to make a meaningful impact in the community and we concentrate our grant making on organisations working to bridge the gap from education to employment. In addition to our corporate philanthropy, we also encourage our employees to become active volunteers and donors through a variety of schemes including our Charity of the Year program, the Professional Development in the Community programs and various tutoring and mentoring initiatives with local partner schools.

CSR report: An up to date CSR report was available from the company's website.

Applications

In writing to the correspondent.

Other information

The amount of charitable donations given to the UK in 2011 could unfortunately not be found and it has only been possible to determine the amount of money given on a Europe-wide basis, which was £8.5 million.

The following are examples of the company's community investment in the UK:

- Organisation of eight employability workshops to help young people to improve their employability in the labour market
- Credit Suisse endeavours to provide children and young people with the opportunity to experience classical music and art first hand. Together with the National Gallery in London, for example, it has developed special educational projects for local schools and social institutions that already receive support from Credit Suisse
- Credit Suisse supports a range of initiatives globally (including the UK), where it has business operations. Project support focuses on education and participation and is established through long-term partnerships

In 2011, the company took steps to increase employee volunteering. 71 Credit Suisse volunteers helped out in a pilot employability programme in conjunction with Scope for young people with disabilities in Tower Hamlets.

Crest Nicholson plc

Property

Correspondent: Company Secretary, Crest House, Rycroft Road, Chertsey, Surrey KT16 9GN (tel: 01932 580555; fax: 0870 336 3990; email: info@crestnicholson.com; website: www.crestnicholson.com)

Directors: Stephen Stone, Chief Executive; William Rucker, Chair; Malcolm McCaig; Pam Alexander; Patrick Bergin, Group Finance Director (women: 1; men: 4)

Year end	31/10/2010
Turnover	£284,400,000
Pre-tax profit	(£27,400,000)

Nature of business: Property developer.

Company registration number: 1040616

Main locations: Cardiff, Brentwood, Bristol, Hemel Hempstead, Weybridge, Tamworth, Westerham

UK employees: 464

Total employees: 464

Charitable donations

UK cash (latest declared):	2010	£2,000
	2009	£2,000
	2006	£46,000
	2005	£48,000
Total UK:	2010	£2,000
Total worldwide:	2010	£2,000
Cash worldwide:	2010	£2,000

Corporate social responsibility

CSR committee: No dedicated team responsible for charitable/community giving.

CSR policy: The company's website (with regard to charitable giving) focuses mainly on the fundraising activities of its staff.

CSR report: A Sustainability report is published annually.

Applications

In writing to the correspondent.

Other information

During the year the group made donations to charities of £2,000 (2009 £2,000). Employees have continued to support the Group's nominated charity, **The Variety Club** and raised £11,000 for this cause during the year.

Croda International plc

Chemicals and plastics

Correspondent: Corporate Social Responsibility Team, Cowick Hall, Snaith, Goole, East Yorkshire DN14 9AA (tel: 01405 860551; fax: 01405 861767; website: www.croda.com)

Directors: Martin Fowler, Chair; Steve Foots, Chief Executive; Sean Christie, Finance Director; Keith Layden; Stanley Musesengwa; Nigel Turner; Steve Williams; Alan Ferguson (women: 0; men: 8)

Year end	31/12/2011
Turnover	£574,300,000
Pre-tax profit	£242,200,000

Nature of business: Croda is a world leader in natural based speciality chemicals which are sold to virtually every type of industry. The company has approximately 3400 employees, working in 34 countries.

Company registration number: 206132

Total employees: 3,190

Membership: BITC

Charitable donations

UK cash (latest declared):	2009	£38,000
	2008	£57,000
Total worldwide:	2011	£2,000
Cash worldwide:	2011	£2,000

Corporate social responsibility

CSR committee: Croda's CSR Steering Committee is comprised of representatives from all regional business units and is responsible for the strategic management of CSR within the Group, as well as ensuring all reporting obligations can be satisfied through the effective collation of data.

CSR policy: The following policy statement is taken from the company's website:

> Our position as one of the world's leading speciality chemical manufacturers brings with it many responsibilities. We recognise that Croda is not just about products, or how they are made, or how they are used, but also the impact of our activities on: Marketplace – our partners; Environment – our world; employees – our people; Community – our neighbours.
>
> Sustainability and social responsibility have always been synonymous with Croda. Our emphasis on 'natural chemistry', using raw materials from renewable resources to make our products. Our ongoing drive to develop 'cleaner', safer processes and technology to make these products. Our quest to find the best people to join us, and then to train them and develop their skills. Our relationships with our neighbours in the community, and in schools and education.

CSR report: Details of the company's corporate responsibility initiatives and activities are set out in its annual report. The company also has a separate Sustainability report, available in print and online which expands on the core themes of sustainability within Croda as well as providing more quantitative information on performance against its CSR targets.

Applications

In writing to the correspondent.

Other information

Charitable donations made by the group in the year amounted to £11,000 (2010: £13,000). The company operates the '1% Club' which allows employees to take off 1% of their working time to volunteer in local community activities. The following statement is taken from the 2011 annual report:

> During 2011 all manufacturing sites and offices completed a stakeholder audit and developed at least one project as a result of community engagement. In 2011, our employees have spent 4,679 hours in their local community, significantly exceeding the 2,021 hours invested in 2010. The number of employees using four or more hours of 1% Club time was 488 (15.2% of Group).Even more satisfying is that a total of 684 (21.3% of Group) employees took part in 1% Club activities during 2011, compared to 9.3% in 2010.
>
> The 1% Club has proven to be extremely successful in allowing our employees to contribute to the community, and to express their passion for the good causes affecting the lives of those in the areas in which we live and work. In every measurement of performance, including breadth and quantity of involvement by our employees, the level of impact delivered by our personnel is fantastic. It is our belief that developing both the quality and quantity of this activity will continue to deliver benefits for our business in terms of staff motivation and personnel development, whilst developing quality links with our neighbours. As such we will continue to challenge our level of activity in terms of community engagement and will look to further increase activity levels against those delivered in 2011.

Unfortunately although the company's contribution is significant, we could find no financial calculation attributable to the 1% Club and have taken the company's donation as that quoted in its annual report.

Cummins Ltd

Engineering

Correspondent: Company Secretary, 49–51 Gresham Road, Staines, Middlesex TW18 2BD (website: www.cummins.com)

Directors: A. J. Robinson; I. M. Barrowman; R. J. Eyres; H. S. Foden; R. Somerville

Year end	31/12/2010
Turnover	£1,278,036,000
Pre-tax profit	£238,701,000

Nature of business: The principal activity is the manufacture, sale, distribution and servicing of diesel engines and components. The company is a subsidiary of Cummins Inc. (US).

Company registration number: 573951

Main locations: Ramsgate, Huddersfield, Daventry, Darlington, Stamford, Hinckley, Wellingborough, Cumbernauld, Stockton-on-Tees, Peterborough

Total employees: 3,310

Charitable donations

UK cash (latest declared):	2010	£54,000
	2008	£43,000
	2007	£19,300
	2006	£49,900
	2005	£38,300
Total UK:	2010	£54,000
Total worldwide:	2010	£54,000
Cash worldwide:	2010	£54,000

Corporate social responsibility

CSR policy: No CSR information available.

Unable to determine the ratio of women to men on the board.

Applications

In writing to the correspondent.

Other information

In 2010 the company made donations totalling £54,000 which was distributed to various charities. We have no information regarding the beneficiaries. The company accounts state that the company was involved in a wide range of community projects through the active participation of its employees.

Previously, we were advised that within the UK, the company prefers to support projects local to its manufacturing plants and offices. Organisations concerned with youth, education, the environment, and disadvantaged people are favoured.

P. Z. Cussons plc

Household, pharmaceuticals

Correspondent: Company Secretary, PZ Cussons House, Bird Hall Lane, Stockport SK3 0XN (tel: 01614 918000; fax: 01614 918191; email: pzweb.general@pzcussons.com; website: www.pzcussons.com)

Directors: Alex Kanellis, Chief Executive; Chris Davis; Brandon Leigh; John Pantelireis; Richard Harvey; Derek Lewis; Professor John Arnold; Simon Heale; James Steel; Ngozi Edozien; Helen Owers (women: 2; men: 9)

Year end	31/05/2011
Turnover	£820,000,000
Pre-tax profit	£109,000,000

Nature of business: Principal activities: manufacture and distribution of soaps, toiletries, cleaning agents, pharmaceuticals, refrigerators and air conditioners.

Company registration number: 19457

Brands include: 1001, Carex, Charles Worthington, Cussons, Freshness!, Imperial Leather, Morning Fresh, Pearl, Racasan

Main locations: Stockport

Total employees: 8,001

Membership: BITC

Charitable donations

UK cash (latest declared):	2011	£50,000
	2009	£343,000
	2008	£50,000
	2007	£50,000
	2006	£50,000
Total UK:	2011	£50,000
Total worldwide:	2011	£50,000
Cash worldwide:	2011	£50,000

Corporate social responsibility

CSR committee: There was evidence of a CSR Committee.

CSR policy: This information was obtained from the company's website:

> We recognise our responsibilities to society and, in particular, to the local communities in which we operate. We are committed to enriching the lives of our local communities. Wherever we operate, we ensure that our activities do not have any material adverse environmental or social impact upon local communities.

CSR report: There was no evidence of a separate CSR report.

Applications

In writing to the correspondent.

Other information

Past information has suggested the company donates around £50,000 each year to charities. We have no details of the beneficiaries. The company has a preference for local charities in areas of company presence, particularly projects involving children and youth, social welfare, medical, education, recreation and people with disabilities.

The associated **Zochonis Charitable Trust** (Charity Commission no. 274769) made grants of £2.6 million in 2010/11, for general charitable purposes. Its income is derived almost exclusively from shareholdings in the company but it acts independently.

Daejan Holdings plc

Property

Correspondent: M R M Jenner, Company Secretary, Freshwater House, 158–162 Shaftesbury Avenue, London WC2H 8HR (tel: 020 7836 1555; fax: 020 7497 8941; website: www.daejanholdings.com)

Directors: D. Davies; S. I. Freshwater; B. S. E. Freshwater; R. E. Freshwater; A. M. Freshwater (women: 0; men: 5)

Year end	31/03/2011
Turnover	£102,692,000
Pre-tax profit	£84,363,000

Nature of business: Property investment and trading, with some development. The major part of the group's property portfolio comprises commercial, industrial and residential premises throughout the UK and in the US.

Company registration number: 305105

Total employees: 141

Charitable donations

UK cash (latest declared):	2009	£120,000
	2008	£120,000
	2007	£120,000
	2006	£120,000
	2005	£120,000
Total worldwide:	2011	£150,000
Cash worldwide:	2011	£150,000

Corporate social responsibility

CSR policy: No information was available relating to CSR specifically.

Exclusions

Organisations dealing with professional fundraisers, large overhead expenses and expensive fundraising campaigns are avoided. Support is not given to the arts, enterprise or conservation.

Applications

In writing to the correspondent (who is also the correspondent for the payroll giving scheme). There is no donations committee.

Other information

Part of The Freshwater Group of companies, Daejan continues to support community activities, focusing principally on education. Donations this year totalled £150,000 (2010: £120,000). We have no information regarding where the money was given or which organisations received awards.

Some years ago shares representing 6.3% of the capital of the company were donated to charitable companies which, in consequence, received dividend payments in the year of £760,000 (2010: £750,000).

Payroll giving: The company operates the Give As You Earn Scheme.

Daily Mail and General Trust plc

Media

Correspondent: Charities Committee (see Applications), Northcliffe House, 2 Derry Street, London W8 5TT (tel: 020 7938 6349; fax: 020 7937 4625; website: www.dmgt.co.uk/cr)

Directors: Rt Hon Viscount Rothermere, Chair; M. W. H. Morgan, Chief Executive; S. W. Daintith; J. G. Hemingway; D. M. M. Dutton; P. M. Dacre; P. M. Fallon; C. W. Dunstone; F. P. Balsemão; T. S. Gillespie; D. J. Verey; K. J. Beatty; N. W. Berry; D. H. Nelson; D. Trempont; N. D. Jennings (women: 0; men: 16)

Year end	02/10/2011
Turnover	£1,989,800,000
Pre-tax profit	£124,500,000

Nature of business: Principal activity: publication and printing of newspapers and periodicals.

Company registration number: 184594

Subsidiaries include: Staffordshire Sentinel Newspapers Ltd, DMG Pinnacle Ltd, Northcliffe New Media Holdings plc, Euromoney Publications plc, The Publishing Co. Ltd, Hull Daily Mail Publications Ltd, W.H.Y Publications limited, Northcliffe Newspapers Group Ltd, Cornwall and Devon Media Ltd, Herald Express Ltd, Derby Daily Telegraph Ltd, Harmsworth Quays Printing Ltd, Leicester Mercury Group Ltd, DMG Trinity Ltd, The Journal Co. Ltd, Aberdeen Journals Ltd, DMG Home Interest Magazines Ltd, DMG Angex Ltd, Lincolnshire Publishing Co. Ltd, Bristol United Press plc, Armdag Newspapers Ltd, Northcliffe Retail Ltd, Gloucestershire Newspapers Ltd, Nottingham Post-Group Ltd, Essex Chronicle Series Ltd, Metropress Ltd, Harmsworth Quays Ltd, DMG Exhibition Group Ltd, The Western Morning News Co. Ltd, Express and Echo Publications Ltd, Alderton Ltd, DMG Business Media Ltd, Arts and Entertainment Programming Ltd, Grimsby and Scunthorpe Newspaper Ltd, Associated Newspapers Ltd, South West Wales Publications Ltd, New Era Television Ltd, DMG Antique Fairs Ltd, Central Independent Newspapers Ltd, Teletex Ltd, British Pathe plc, DMG Radio Ltd, Westcountry Publications Ltd, The Cheltenham Newspaper Co. Ltd, DMG Regional Radio Pty Ltd, The Printworks Ltd, The Courier Printing and Publishing Co. Ltd, Publications Ltd

Main locations: London

Total employees: 15,157

Charitable donations

UK cash (latest declared):	2009	£700,000
	2008	£946,000
	2007	£866,000
	2006	£809,000
	2005	£880,000
Total worldwide:	2011	£3,392,000
Cash worldwide:	2011	£1,392,000

Corporate social responsibility

CSR committee: CSR Committee reports directly to the board. The committee does not formulate CR policy and acts in an advisory rather than an executive capacity. Its remit is to monitor environmental, waste, sustainability, employee, customer, supplier and community practices across DMGT. Committee members include interested parties with relevant group-wide responsibilities and senior nominees from our five main business units.

CSR policy: The following is taken from the company's annual report:

> We manage a portfolio of very diverse businesses. As such, a one-size-fits-all CR policy would be counter-productive. Each of our businesses operates in particular conditions. They understand their own markets. They are best placed to define and promote their own CR objectives. We aim to equip our people with the knowledge, the resources, the training and, crucially, the permission to take effective action. We try not to be prescriptive in our approach. Our various businesses have evolved CR strategies to fit their distinct cultures and underlying objectives.

The company's website states: 'All our newspapers promote significant CR community activities'.

CSR report: Contained within the annual report of the company.

Exclusions

No support for: individuals looking for sponsorship; individuals, other than staff, who are looking for charity fundraising donations or sponsorship for fundraising activities; very large charities; paid tables at charity events.

Applications

At a corporate level the responsibility for charitable donations lies with the DMGT Charity Committee. Apply to the correspondent in writing. The responsibility for community involvement throughout our divisions resides with the managing director of each business.

Other information

Charitable donations made by the group in the year amounted to £1.4 million (2010: £860,000). We have no breakdown of this figure relating to where the money was donated or to which groups it was given. The amount excludes the cost of publicity, often provided free of charge by the Group's titles, and funds raised by them. The group estimates that over £2 million in free advertising space has been given by Associated Newspapers titles.

Staff are encouraged to engage with stakeholder communities and get involved with charitable projects. Each business approaches this in its own way. Some examples of support in the UK are given here:

> Jobsite UK is helping children locally. Employees give time to assist in schools close to its Havant headquarters. It also runs a football mentoring scheme alongside Portsmouth FC.
>
> Youth is also a priority at DMGT HQ. It supports the Prince's Trust, which last year helped 44,000 young people get back in work or education.
>
> Metro has built a 3.3 million readership by forging close links with the cities it serves. When riots erupted in England over the summer the paper wanted to reach out to affected companies. It offered them free advertising space and design services. The initiative soon extended to other titles. Associated Newspapers as a whole donated over £2 million worth of advertising space in the aftermath of the riots.
>
> A&N Media is proud to have made a donation to the Team 2012 Fundraising Appeal, supporting Britain's athletes on their journey to success. The company is also encouraging homegrown talent with journalism scholarships, an MA in journalism at the University of Kent, the Catch-22 internship scheme and with a Journalism Diversity Fund.

Daily Mail and General Trust's (DMGT) charitable donations are allocated by a charities committee at DMGT, as well as being made on a smaller scale by divisional and local managements. The committee prefers to make donations to media and local charities where there is an employee representative who will sponsor and report back on the impact the allocation has had.

In addition to the above, the group runs numerous fundraising campaigns through its newspapers, media subsidiaries and events.

Items left over from reader promotions have been donated to community groups. A children's library in an inner city housing estate in Glasgow was set up and has now tripled in size because of its popularity. It is stocked with classic novels, encyclopaedia and cartoon DVDs and provides these items free to local youngsters.

Comprehensive information regarding the group's charitable and community support is available on DMGT's corporate website under 'DMGT in the Community'. The Charity Committee Principles are contained in a useful policy document, visit: www.dmgt.co.uk.

Payroll giving: Associated Newspapers operates an on-line payroll giving scheme, working in partnership with Workplace Giving UK, which enables staff members to make more tax-efficient personal donations to their preferred charities.

Sponsorship: *The arts* – the company undertakes arts sponsorship (local to company headquarters). *Sport* – now in its 22nd year The Daily Mail Schools Rugby is the largest schools rugby tournament in the world.

Dairy Crest Group plc

Dairy products

Correspondent: Chair CR Committee, Claygate House, Littleworth Road, Esher, Surrey KT10 9PN (tel: 01372 472200; fax: 01372 472333; email: investorrelations@dairycrest.co.uk; website: www.dairycrest.co.uk)

Directors: Mark Allen, Chief Executive; Martyn Wilkes, Managing Director; Alastair Murray, Finance Director;

Anthony Fry, Chair; Stephen Alexander; Andrew Carr-Locke; Richard Macdonald; Howard Mann (women: 0; men: 8)

Year end	31/03/2011
Turnover	£1,604,500,000
Pre-tax profit	£77,800,000

Nature of business: Dairy Crest is the UK's leading dairy company, processing and selling fresh milk and branded dairy products in the UK and Europe.

Company registration number: 3162897

Brands include: Brands include: Cathedral City, Clover, Country Life.

Total employees: 6,539

Membership: BITC

Charitable donations

UK cash (latest declared):	2011	£100,000
	2010	£100,000
	2009	£100,000
Total UK:	2011	£100,000
Total worldwide:	2011	£100,000
Cash worldwide:	2011	£100,000

Corporate social responsibility

CSR committee: There is a CSR Committee.

CSR policy: Statement taken from the company's annual report:

> As a responsible business we are committed to fully integrating corporate responsibility into our business strategy. To ensure we are able to continuously improve our performance this year we participated in Business in the Community's index and following a rigorous assessment we were awarded 87%, which is at the higher end of their silver band. This is an encouraging result for us as we continue to try to do the right thing from both a moral point of view and from a commercial point of view.

CSR report: CSR reporting is contained within the company's annual report.

Applications

In writing to your local site, referenced, 'Local Community Committee', or to the correspondent for corporate CSR enquiries.

Other information

Charitable donations amounted to £100,000 (2009/10: £100,000). We have taken the contributions to be within the UK as the company appears not to support causes abroad. In kind contributions are not currently given a valuation, but data is being collated for future years.

The company supports the Prince's Countryside Fund and works alongside 15 other prominent UK businesses to provide grants to projects that help British farms and rural communities. One of the charities the company has chosen to support both through the fund and independently is 'Pub is the Hub' which helps pubs offer rural communities additional services like a shop, internet café or Citizens Advice.

The company's programme 'Keeping it Local' is run by community committees who have supported about 100 community projects ranging from school gardening projects through to after school clubs and projects that help clear polluted or overgrown public spaces. Other community projects include working with Greater Manchester police to help them reduce crime in the Salford area, and a music project, TUPUP which teaches children to learn a musical instrument – in this instance a home-made ukulele made from a tub.

Charity of the Year (2012): British Heart Foundation.

Dana Petroleum plc

Oil and gas/fuel

Correspondent: Chief Executive, 17 Carden Place, Aberdeen AB10 1UR (tel: 01224 652400; fax: 01224 652401; website: www.dana-petroleum.com)

Directors: Marcus T. Richards; Jin Seok Yi; David A. Crawford; Eugene Synn; Seong Hoon Kim; Chang Koo Kang (women: 0; men: 6)

Year end	18/12/2010
Turnover	£598,272,000
Pre-tax profit	£26,373,000

Nature of business: Dana Petroleum, acquired by the Korean National Oil Corporation in 2010, is an oil and gas business with operations in the UK, Egypt, Norway, The Netherlands and Africa.

Company registration number: 3456891

Total employees: 38

Charitable donations

UK cash (latest declared):	2009	£100,000
Total worldwide:	2010	£126,000
Cash worldwide:	2010	£126,000

Corporate social responsibility

CSR committee: No specific committee.

CSR policy: The following statements are taken from the company's website:

> As Dana grows and develops, the company and its employees recognise their collective and individual responsibilities as corporate citizens. This has created a strong corporate culture underpinned by ethical values which we apply wherever we operate and with whomever we meet. Dana now operates in seven countries, employing national staff and carrying out work activities close to local communities. The company recognises the potential impact of its presence and takes its responsibilities to people and their living environments very seriously.
>
> *Charity:* We believe in offering our time and expertise in addition to financial support, and hope to maintain meaningful partnerships with the charitable organisations with which we are involved.
>
> We are constantly researching new ways to become more proactively involved in the communities we are part of, and recognise that business and community are intrinsically connected.

CSR report: No CSR report published. CSR pages on website.

Applications

In writing to the correspondent.

Other information

In 2010 contributions totalling £126,000 (2009: £63,000) were made during the year to local charities and projects focused on communities and areas close to areas of operations. Specific examples of Dana's partnerships and contributions are:

- The company has for many years now supported The Aberdeen Foyer, a highly respected charity established in 1995 to prevent and alleviate homelessness amongst vulnerable 16 – 25 year olds in North East Scotland. Dana makes an annual donation to the organisation
- In 2010 the company was introduced to VSA Young Carers Project, a service aimed at supporting hugely deserving young people who, as a result of the dedication to the well being of family members, often miss out on the fun, excitement and learning curves of childhood. Dana fund week long respite adventure holidays for the young carers each summer, and hope to offer the personal and professional skill set of our staff as and when needed in the future
- Another recently formed partnership is with Transition Extreme, a Social Enterprise that doubles as a world class extreme sports facility. Transition boasts a climbing wall, BMX biking, skateboarding and in line skating park as well as space used for Martial Arts and a café. The value created from these activities is used to support the social enterprise, which aims to engage young people into maximising their potential with music, art and extreme sports. We worked closely with the team at Transition to come up with the idea for a Community Access Project, where young people from Aberdeen's seven most disadvantaged areas have the opportunity to use the facilities and have instruction free of charge. Dana and Sport Scotland fund the initiative entirely
- Financial support for local sporting clubs to encourage and facilitate healthy life choices for children and young adults as well as support for local residents seeking sponsorship for extremely challenging charitable activities
- Fielding of a team in the annual 'BG Egypt Challenge', organised by CARE. Not only did they enjoy a superb team-building experience, but they also raised $15,000 towards CARE's work in Upper Egypt
- Local support for NGOs and schools in the villages neighbouring the onshore drilling location in Morocco

- Following discovery of possible burial mounds along the transportation route to our onshore Taj-1 well at Bouanane, Morocco, Dana committed to support the archaeological mapping of those cultural sites
- Norway donations continued Dana's focus on healthy lifestyles for children, funding the purchase of musical instruments for local school bands, equipment for local football clubs, a bandy team and a water polo club. Donations also funded training for a local dance group, altogether engaging several hundred children
- The Company also continues to support staff who are actively involved in charitable organisations and activities including local football and swimming clubs, organising local fun runs and charity balls

Now that Dana is part of a wider organisation, the company hopes to expand upon their community involvement and corporate philanthropy to include more sustainable and innovative projects. It is a major priority going forward to conduct comprehensive research into the primary issues affecting the communities we are part of, and identify how we can interact with other public and private sector organisations to form a cohesive platform from which to address these issues. Some of the areas we will be focusing on over the coming year are sustainable communities, education and services aimed at people with disabilities.

Darty plc (formerly Kesa Electricals plc)

Retail – electrical

Correspondent: Chair of Corporate Responsibility Committee, The Company Secretary, 22–24 Ely Place, London EC1N 6TE (tel: 020 7269 1400; fax: 020 7269 1405; website: www.kesaelectricals.co.uk)

Directors: David Newlands, Chair; Thierry Falque-Pierrotin, Chief Executive; Dominic Platt, Finance Director; Peter Wilson; Michel Brossard; Bernard Dufau; Michel Léonard; Alan Parker; Andrew Robb (women: 0; men: 9)

Year end	30/04/2011
Turnover	£4,754,960,027
Pre-tax profit	£48,776,650

Nature of business: Electrical retailing group operating in ten countries.

Company registration number: 4232413

Total employees: 26,238

Charitable donations

UK cash (latest declared):	2010	£51,250
Total worldwide:	2011	£97,000
Cash worldwide:	2011	£97,000

Corporate social responsibility

CSR committee: There is a corporate responsibility team comprising senior managers from each of the businesses. Chaired by the Company Secretary, the team meets regularly to share best practices and develop practical performance measures that could be adopted across the group.

CSR policy: The group has a code of conduct which sets out the standards of behaviour expected in the group and of all who work for the group, in their relationships with employees, customers, suppliers, business partners, the community (including the environment), government and all other stakeholders in the business.

CSR report: Published in the annual report and accounts.

Applications

In writing to the correspondent.

Other information

The group's support for charitable causes is principally through the work done by the group's operating companies to the value of €121,000 (£97,125). The majority of the company's community activities are locally driven, reflecting customer demands and market sensitivities.

DDB UK Ltd

Advertising/marketing

Correspondent: Head of Human Resources, 12 Bishops Bridge Road, London W2 6AA (tel: 020 7258 3979; fax: 020 7402 4871; website: www.adamandeveddblondon.com)

Directors: S. Watson; Stephen Woodford, Managing Director

Year end	31/12/2011
Turnover	£104,013,000
Pre-tax profit	£10,303,000

Nature of business: The principal activity of the company is that of an advertising agency.

Company registration number: 933578

Main locations: London

Total employees: 419

Charitable donations

UK cash (latest declared):	2011	£36,000
	2009	£32,000
	2008	£23,000
Total UK:	2011	£36,000
Total worldwide:	2011	£36,000
Cash worldwide:	2011	£36,000

Corporate social responsibility

CSR committee: No details.

CSR policy: No CR details available.

We could not determine the ratio of women to men on the board.

CSR report: None published.

Applications

In writing to the correspondent.

Other information

In 2011, cash donations to charity totalled £36,000 (2010: £23,000). We do not have details of beneficiaries but previous recipient organisations have included: World Wildlife Fund; NABS; History of Advertising Trust; and, Brain Tumour UK.

DDB London is one of the companies in the Omnicom Group and is the trading name of DDB UK Ltd.

We were previously advised that the company supports national and international charities with direct donations. It normally supports the arts, children/youth, education, the elderly, enterprise/training, environment/heritage, fundraising events, medical research, political and religious appeals, science/technology, sickness/disability, social welfare, sport and advertising in charity brochures.

The company's Charity of the Year is chosen through staff nomination of a charity which is directly involved with any of the issues stated above.

The company has an employee volunteering scheme.

Payroll giving: The Give As You Earn and NABS schemes are in operation.

De La Rue plc

Print/paper/packaging

Correspondent: Chief Executive, De La Rue House, Jays Close, Viables, Basingstoke, Hampshire RG22 4BS (tel: 01256 605000; fax: 01256 605004; website: www.delarue.com)

Directors: Nicholas Brookes, Chair; Tim Cobbold, Chief Executive; Colin Child; Warren East; Sir Jeremy Greenstock; Sir Julian Horn-Smith; Victoria Jarman; Gill Rider; Edward Peppiatt (women: 2; men: 7)

Year end	26/03/2011
Turnover	£460,000,000
Pre-tax profit	£80,000,000

Nature of business: The company is a commercial security printer and papermaker, involved in the production of over 150 national currencies and a wide range of security documents. The company is also a leading provider of cash handling equipment and solutions to banks and retailers as well as a range of identity systems to governments worldwide.

Company registration number: 3834125

UK employees: 2061

Total employees: 3997

Charitable donations

UK cash (latest declared):	2009	£144,000
	2008	£79,000
	2007	£110,500
	2006	£97,000
	2005	£205,000
Total worldwide:	2011	£104,000
Cash worldwide:	2011	£104,000

Corporate social responsibility

CSR committee: There was no evidence of a separate CSR Committee.

CSR policy: No specific policy details published.

CSR report: There was a CSR report available within the group's annual report.

Exclusions

Generally no support for circular appeals, fundraising events, brochure advertising, individuals, purely denominational (religious) or political appeals, local appeals not in areas of company presence or large national appeals. No telephoned applications can be considered. Applications that do not fall within the prescribed categories will not be considered unless there are extenuating or emergency circumstances. Grant applications made by individuals either in the UK or abroad cannot be considered.

Applications

In writing to the correspondent. Registered charities only can apply.

Applications for the trust are considered at trustees meetings held in February and July.

Other information

In 2010/11 Group donations for charitable purposes amounted to £58,000 (2009/10: £96,000).

The De La Rue Charitable Trust (Charity Commission no: 274052), established by the company in 1977, aims to direct funds to appropriate causes in countries where De La Rue operates, emphasising educational projects promoting relevant skills, international understanding or relieving suffering. The trust depends on dividends from investments for its income. During 2010/11, the Trust distributed £46,000 (2009/10: £45,000).

During the year employees organised fundraising activities to benefit various charities, including the provision of 100 emergency ration packs for Sri Lankan flood victims, fundraising for various local hospices in the UK and gaining sponsorship for taking part in the Three Peaks Challenge in the summer of 2010 in aid of the Haiti earthquake appeal.

Payroll giving: The company operates the Give As You Earn scheme.

Debenhams plc

Retail – department and variety stores

Correspondent: Ms Sarah Carne, Correspondent to the Trustees, c/o Debenhams Foundation, 1 Welbeck Street, London W1G 0AA (020 7408 3231; website: www.debenhamsplc.com)

Directors: Nigel Northridge, Chair; Michael Sharp, Chief Executive; Chris Woodhouse, Finance Director; Dennis Millard; Martina King; Adam Crozier; Mark Rolfe; Sophie Turner Laing (women: 2; men: 6)

Year end	03/09/2011
Turnover	£2,209,800,000
Pre-tax profit	£160,300,000

Nature of business: Department store.

Company registration number: 5448421

Total employees: 30,624

Membership: BITC

Charitable donations

UK cash (latest declared):	2011	£1,100,000
	2009	£409,000
	2008	£293,000
Total UK:	2011	£1,100,000
Total worldwide:	2011	£1,100,000
Cash worldwide:	2011	£1,100,000

Community involvement

In 2011, following a charity audit by the company, the **Debenhams Foundation** (Charity Commission no. 1147682) was established through which all charitable giving will be channelled. The objects of the foundation are to preserve and protect health and relieve financial hardship and for general charitable purposes. These objects will be achieved primarily through grantmaking. The foundation operates worldwide. Accounts for the charity were neither due nor received at the Commission as this is a newly registered organisation, however, as the company has stated that their funding will be through the foundation, we have taken the £1.1 million as donations made in the UK.

A new community champion programme has also been launched which gives store managers and their teams a framework for building and growing their contribution to the communities in which they operate.

The following information is taken from the corporate responsibility section of the group's website:

Debenhams is a strong supporter of charities at both a national and local level.

Debenhams supports national charities including Breast Cancer Campaign and the NSPCC.

Many charities are supported by Debenhams at a local level including children's charities, schools, sports clubs, animal and wildlife charities, old people's homes, hospitals, hospices and medical charities. The Food Services division is a corporate member of the Anaphylaxis Campaign and fully supports the great work they do, helping people with severe allergens and persuading the food industry (including catering) of the need to provide detailed and accurate allergen information.

Charity Partner: The Breast Cancer Campaign has been supported by Debenhams for a number of years through the sale of special products and in-store events.

Corporate giving

During the year the group made charitable donations totalling £1.1 million (2010: £700,000). The company supports various charities. Key donations made during the year were £260,000 to the NSPCC, £249,000 to the Breast Cancer Campaign, £65,000 to the Estée Lauder MAC Aids campaign and £25,000 to the Marine Conservation Society.

Employee-led support

> Our key national charity is *Breast Cancer Campaign* which we have supported for ten years through the sale of special products and in-store events. Recent activities included 'Cycle To The Moon', which saw store employees and customers pedal the 225,622 miles distance to the moon in a sponsored cycle event, and 'Step On It', a series of walks 46,000 steps long – one for every person diagnosed with breast cancer in the UK each year.

Commercially-led support

> Our clothing brand Mantaray is a proud supporter of the Marine Conservation Society (MCS). Our support for the MCS's work for clean seas, sustainable fisheries and protected sea life is practical as well as financial. Our employees and customers take part in beach clean-ups and surveys, helping to clear the UK's beaches of the tide of litter currently endangering the life of coastal wildlife such as seabirds, dolphins, porpoises and marine turtles.

Corporate social responsibility

CSR committee: Martina King chairs the Sustainability Committee, formed in October 2010.

CSR policy: Statement from the chair of the Sustainability Committee taken from the 2011 annual report:

> The Debenhams' board is committed to living up to our responsibilities as a retailer, an employer, a business partner, a steward of the environment and a member of the community, in short to being a responsible business. We are also keenly aware of our role as the steward of Debenhams' shareholders' investments.

We firmly believe that these aims are entirely complementary and we cannot achieve one without the other. In short, our business strategy must reflect our broader responsibilities – and vice versa.

The community: we should be an active and responsible member of the communities in which we operate. As a business, we should support local and national charities and community groups, both through fundraising and volunteering, and we should encourage our employees to participate in local community activities.

CSR report: There are four sustainability committee work groups whose reports are published within the annual report and accounts.

Following review, the principal method of communication for sustainability issues will be online. The sustainability website can be found at: sustainability.debenhamsplc.com.

Applications

In writing to the correspondent for grant-giving or to the local store for community projects, gifts in kind etc.

Deep Sea Leisure plc

Leisure

Correspondent: Heather Taylor, Forthside Terrace, North Queensferry, Inverkeithing, Fife KY11 1JR (tel: 01383 411411; website: www.blueplanetaquarium.com)

Directors: S. J. Elaiho; A. Barrachina, Chair; J. Fernandes-Pinero; D. L. Soriano; G. O'Donnell

Year end	31/10/2011
Turnover	£12,461,000
Pre-tax profit	£2,105,000

Nature of business: Owner and operator of public aquarium visitor attractions.

Company registration number: SC135353

Main locations: Ellesmere Port

UK employees: 225

Total employees: 225

Charitable donations

UK cash (latest declared):	2011	£3,000
	2008	£6,800
	2007	£11,918
	2006	£9,730
Total UK:	2011	£3,000
Total worldwide:	2011	£3,000
Cash worldwide:	2011	£3,000

Corporate social responsibility

CSR policy: No CSR information available.

We were unable to determine the ratio of women to men on the board.

Applications

In writing to the correspondent. However, be aware that there is a limited budget and that many of the current grant recipients are supported regularly.

Other information

In 2010/11 grants were given to eight organisations totalling almost £3,000 (2009/10: £7,500). Beneficiaries included: Anthony Nolan Trust (£550); Ellesmere Port Scouts and North West Air Ambulance (£500 each); Youth Federation (£140); and Shark Trust (£120).

Deep Sea Leisure provides small scale support to charities working with children, people with disabilities, animal welfare and the environment. There is some preference for Scottish-based organisations.

Deloitte

Accountants

Correspondent: Director of Community Investment, Stonecutter Court, 1 Stonecutter Street, London EC4A 4TR (tel: 020 7936 3000; fax: 020 7583 1198; website: www.deloitte.co.uk)

Directors: Steve Almond; David Sproul, Senior Partner and Chief Executive; Sharon Fraser; Richard Punt; David Cruickshank, Chair; Margaret Ewing; Stephen Griggs; Heather Hancock; Andy Hodge; Panos Kakoullis; Timothy Mahapatra; Vince Niblett; Paul Robinson; Nick Sandall; Nick Shepherd (women: 3; men: 12)

Year end	31/05/2011
Turnover	£2,098,000,000
Pre-tax profit	£510,000,000

Nature of business: Audit, tax, corporate finance and management consultancy services.

Company registration number: 2400371

Main locations: Bristol, Cardiff, Leeds, Southampton, Reading, London

Membership: Arts & Business, BITC, LBG

Charitable donations

UK cash (latest declared):	2009	£2,022,000
	2008	£1,867,000
	2007	£1,139,908
	2006	£1,000,000
	2005	£400,000
Total worldwide:	2011	£9,152,000

Community involvement

Deloitte invests in excess of 1% of UK pre-tax profit towards its community involvement. It is committed to supporting the community at a national and local level through its network of offices throughout the UK.

Disability sport

Deloitte is committed to ensuring a positive legacy from the London 2012 Games and Deloitte Disability Sport remains the largest programme of its kind in the UK, driving participation at the grassroots and, developing the performance of talented athletes and supporting the ParalympicsGB team in achieving more at future Games. More than 1,700 disability sport clubs are listed on Deloitte Parasport (www.parasport.org.uk) and the firm has supported more than 300 talented athletes through the Talented Athlete Sponsorship Scheme run by SportsAid. The first corporate challenge raised in excess of £750,000.

Education and skills

In 2009, Deloitte made a £2.5 million investment over the following five years to develop a new generation of employability skills trainers in FE Colleges across the country. Over the course of the programme, the Deloitte initiative will train up to 800 new trainers. These trainers will teach employability skills classes to students on vocational courses, helping them to develop the skills, attitudes and behaviours that they need to secure and sustain employment.

To date more than 25,000 young people have completed Deloitte employability courses with nearly 90% going into higher education or straight into full-time employment.

The Deloitte Foundation (not a registered charity) supports a wide variety of charities, with a particular focus on causes supporting children and young people, health and the community. A significant portion of the foundation's budget is used to provide matched funding for staff contributions, payroll giving and charity fundraising.

Charities of the Year: National charity partners for 2010–2012 are **Cancer Research UK, Help for Heroes** and **Children with Leukaemia.** Deloitte has raised over £2 million since the start of the partnerships.

Corporate giving

In 2010/11 Deloitte made a total firm community contribution of £11.2 million. Of this, £2 million was given by staff (and which we do not include in our figures for giving). Although Deloitte's giving is clearly substantial, we have been unable to determine the amount given in cash contributions to charities and how much of the total figure was given in the UK.

In kind support

In kind support is given through the provision of volunteering activities and pro bono professional services. In 2010/11, staff gave 44,900 hours of professional time in this way.

Deloitte also operates a 'Computers for Charity' scheme, whereby each Christmas staff are invited to apply for a fully reconditioned laptop on behalf of any UK charity or community organisation that they currently support. Up to 100 laptops each year are provided, with more than 500 having been given away since the scheme began.

In addition to Deloitte's Charities of the Year, the company also has established relationships with ParalympicsGB and SportsAid through Deloitte Disability Sport, and the Serpentine Gallery.

Employee-led support

In 2010/11, the number of volunteers from Deloitte was 3,219, providing over 50,000 hours of voluntary work in the community.

Employee fundraising is matched by the company up to a maximum of £500 per person, while employee giving is matched up to a maximum of £100 per person, per month. Employees can also receive up to half-a-day per month off to volunteer for approved community projects.

The company provides professional and financial support to a wide variety of charities and community organisations, placing a special emphasis on supporting the young and disadvantaged. Staff are encouraged to become involved in charity and community projects with the full support of the firm. Activities include:

- Secondary school mentoring
- Prince's Trust business mentoring
- Volunteering in the firm's time
- Regional office fundraising
- The annual 'Computers for Charity' competition
- A highly successful Give As You Earn scheme

Payroll giving: The Give As You Earn scheme is in operation, managed through the Charities Aid Foundation. 24% of staff participate in the scheme. The charitable fund also matches the contributions made by the staff fund through this.

Commercially-led support

Deloitte has a broad range of sponsorship programmes that include supporting the arts, culture and sport. A key partnership has been made with the Royal Opera House. Deloitte was also a second tier sponsor of the 2012 Olympic and Paralympic Games.

Corporate social responsibility

CSR committee: There is an advisory panel on corporate responsibility.

CSR policy: Taken from the Responsibility Report for 2010/11: 'We believe passionately in the need to invest in the communities in which we live and work, and to achieve the maximum impact by focusing on the delivery of our cores skills and expertise.'

CSR report: Published within the annual report and accounts.

Exclusions

No support for advertising in charity brochures, appeals from individuals, overseas projects or political/religious appeals.

Applications

In writing to the correspondent. However, few ad hoc or unsolicited requests for funding are approved.

Derbyshire Building Society

Building society

Correspondent: Jeremy Hicks, Corporate Affairs Manager, PO Box 1, Duffield Hall, Duffield, Derby DE56 1AG (tel: 01332 841000; email: jeremy.hicks@nationwide.co.uk; website: www.thederbyshire.co.uk)

Nature of business: Core business activities are focused on: mortgage lending, personal savings and investment products, life and general insurance business, and personal financial advice.

FSA registration number: 106078

Charitable donations

UK cash (latest declared):	2009	£6,000
	2008	£5,000
	2007	£5,000

Corporate social responsibility

CSR committee: None.

CSR policy: Taken from the Derbyshire's website:

> Corporate Social Responsibility is much more than addressing environmental issues. For us at the Derbyshire, it gives us an opportunity to demonstrate to our communities that they are as important to us as we are to them. Our members have expressed a desire to want to make a difference within their communities and it is our intention to support that.

CSR report: None.

Exclusions

No support for advertising in charity brochures, animal welfare, appeals from individuals, overseas projects or political or religious appeals.

Applications

In writing to the correspondent.

Other information

Derbyshire Building Society, a trading division of Nationwide Building Society, states it is committed to supporting local charities, community groups, organisations and good causes. Unfortunately, we were unable to ascertain from the Derbyshire how much was given by them to the community in cash or other donations since the merger with Nationwide. The following information is taken from the 2011 annual report and accounts of the Nationwide:

> Since 2003, the Derbyshire Building Society has sponsored the annual Derby 10k run. The 2011 race had 3,500 entrants. As well as bringing together the local community, it is an essential fundraising activity for the charity organiser, Sporting Futures. They seek to reduce the risk of crime and antisocial behaviour in Derbyshire's communities by encouraging targeted young people to join in physical recreation.

Deutsche Bank

Banking

Correspondent: Kate Cavelle, Director, Deutsche Bank CSR UK, See 'Applications' (tel: 020 7545 8000; fax: 01133 361890; email: kate.cavelle@db.com; website: www.db.com/uk/socialresponsibility.html)

Directors: Dr Hugo Banziger; Stefan Krause; Herman-Josef Lamberti; Jürgen Fitschen; Anshuman Jain; Rainer Neske; Dr Joseph Ackermann, Chair; Kevin Parker; Werner Steinmuller; Seth Waugh; Robert Rankin; Pierre de Weck (women: 0; men: 12)

Year end	31/12/2011
Turnover	£26,792,179,000
Pre-tax profit	£4,346,028,800

Nature of business: Deutsche Bank is the holding company of a group providing international merchant banking and investment management services.

Company registration number: BR000005

Subsidiaries include: Morgan Grenfell

Main locations: Edinburgh, London

Total employees: 100,996

Membership: Arts & Business, LBG

Charitable donations

UK cash (latest declared):	2011	£6,842,000
	2009	£6,247,000
	2007	£4,800,000
	2006	£3,000,000
	2005	£4,500,000
Total UK:	2011	£7,564,000
Total worldwide:	2011	£79,063,580
Cash worldwide:	2011	£75,901,040

Community involvement

The company produce a very helpful guide detailing its UK charitable funding. The following are some of the programmes available:

> *Community Development Fund*
> Deutsche Bank's Community Development Fund, at its heart, aims to help disadvantaged people in the UK to thrive. We are focused on supporting those hardest to reach, whether through helping them to live independently and securely, encouraging aspirations or supporting the development of education and skills. Projects that we fund provide

access to exciting opportunities that give people the chance to succeed. Ultimately, we aim to create an educated, productive society that benefits the individual, the community and the economy as a whole. With this in mind, the Fund is focused on two broad themes:

Education – Enabling Talent
We initiate and support projects that maximise the potential of young people and ensure their educational journey is enjoyable and successful. We want to keep young people in school by enriching the system that exists and providing even more opportunities for them to attain and achieve both in and outside the classroom.

In addition we aim to encourage students to progress into further and higher education and expand their knowledge about careers and the workplace as a whole. Through this approach, we aim to create a well-educated, highly skilled and employable generation, with the ability to thrive independently. With this in mind, our Education projects focus on three main areas of activity:

- Retention: projects that ease the transition between primary and secondary schools, reduce absenteeism, and help prevent exclusion
- Achievement: projects that raise aspirations, achievements and attainment levels, with a particular focus on core curriculum subjects (English, Maths and Science), financial literacy and enterprise
- Progression: projects that educate, encourage, and prepare for progression into further and higher education, training and employment

Social Investments – Creating Opportunities
Reaching people and communities most in need and helping them to achieve economic independence and success are at the core of Deutsche Bank's Corporate Citizenship strategy. Social investment at Deutsche Bank takes many forms, including building the capacity of charities, supporting work at grassroots levels, providing finance for social enterprises and helping those hardest to reach and most in need with opportunities to succeed. To achieve this we focus on the following areas of social investments in the UK:

- Education Outreach: working with young people between the ages of 16–24 who have fallen through the cracks of mainstream education and help them back into education, employment or training
- Social Finance: providing investments into community vehicles that provide both social and economic returns
- Employment and Enterprise: providing employability training and support to re-enter the workplace for the long-term unemployed
- Homelessness: addressing the causes of homelessness and helping the homeless to re-integrate themselves back into society
- Activating Communities: supporting local neighbourhoods to create strong, thriving communities through the provision of small grants and investing our people. We do this through the Deutsche Bank Small Grants Fund

The Deutsche Bank Small Grants Fund
Deutsche Bank is committed to supporting the grassroots, local initiatives often overlooked by other funders. We recognise that these groups often provide an invaluable service within their communities, and they can be extremely efficient in their operations. Our small grants fund is administered by several intermediaries, who allow us to have significant impact in line with our Community Development Funding Guidelines. Priority areas and timescales vary and the funds are limited so on occasion they may not be available; please contact the partner operating in your area for more details:

- The London Community Foundation: please contact: enquiries@londoncf.org.uk
- Birmingham and Black Country Community Foundation: please contact Suzanne Randall: suzanne.randall@bbccf.org.uk
- Community Foundation for Merseyside: please contact Tina Kennedy: tina.kennedy@cfmerseyside.org.uk
- Scottish Community Foundation: please contact Annie Howie: annie@scottishcf.org

Art and Music – Fostering Creativity
With its engagement in art, Deutsche Bank contributes to the cultural development of society. Cultivating an environment that fosters creativity and innovation is a vital stimulus to growth and adds value to both art and business.

The Collection: In the UK the focus of our Art activities lies with the Deutsche Bank collection. With over 56,000 pieces globally of which 4,000 are in the UK alone, Deutsche Bank has one of the most significant and largest corporate contemporary art collections worldwide. The collection is managed by our in-house Art Department who curate and co-ordinate the collection which is on display in our buildings and our offices across the globe.

All requests relating to the collection should be directed to: Eleanor Blunden (Tel: 020 7547 6607; Fax: 020 7545 7181; email: eleanor.blunden@db.com. All requests relating to sponsorships should be directed to: email: sponsorship.uk@db.com.

Information taken from the company's website:

> Deutsche Bank Corporate Citizenship UK promotes and coordinates socially responsible activities on behalf of the bank and its employees in the UK. The Bank supports charities and community organisations within our key principles: Enabling Talent through Education, Creating Opportunities through Social Investments and Fostering Creativity through Art and Music. The underlying principle for all these themes however is our dedication to Committing Ourselves through Corporate Volunteering and Ensuring Viability through Sustainability. Each year, the bank invests millions in cash and time to support some of the UK's most deprived communities. Our ultimate goal globally is to build social capital; you can find out more about Deutsche Bank's CSR activities on our global website. www.db.com/csr.

Charities of the Year 2013: Elephant Family and Helen Bamber Foundation.

Corporate giving

In 2011, the bank made total community contributions in the UK of £7.56 million of which £6.84 million was in cash donations. This was broken down as follows:

- Education £1.7 million
- Social investment £1.6 million
- Donations direct from business areas £830,000
- Franchise funding £480,000
- Art and music £282,000
- Employee programmes: charities of the year (seed funding) £30,000 matched giving £1.6 million

Employee volunteering in working hours was valued at £190,000 and Gifts in kind at £126,000.

In kind support

The bank encourages its staff to provide their time, skills and energy on a voluntary basis to local education projects. Staff can apply for a grant of up to £300 from the bank to donate to the organisation with which they volunteer.

Gifts in Kind: In 2011 Deutsche Bank gave around £126,000 worth of gifts in kind for charitable purposes.

Employee-led support

Corporate volunteering programmes: In the UK, the bank's Corporate Citizenship team provides volunteer support to those individuals most in need in the communities local to the company's offices. All activities are geared towards raising aspirations, building confidence, creating opportunities and breaking down barriers for some of the most disadvantaged individuals. In 2011, 1,607 volunteers from the UK contributed to the corporate volunteering programmes.

Community Awards: Deutsche Bank values the time employees spend supporting their preferred causes and charities. Community Awards have been devised to recognise commitment of time by employees to these good causes, 'out of hours'. The awards are between £100 and £1,000 each to the benefiting cause. Each year there is also a 'Community Award of the Year', selected from all the year's community awards.

This award is worth up to £5,000 to the benefiting cause.

Note: the following information is taken from the booklet: 'Deutsche Bank Corporate Citizenship UK – A guide for charitable organisations', available from the company's website:

> Throughout all of our activities we underpin our financial support with the commitment of our talent. Corporate volunteering is an integral part of our programme both here in the UK as well as across the globe. As a policy, we do not provide volunteers to organisations outside of our existing community partners. This is to ensure we maintain focus and maximise the impact we can have with our partners. The exception to this rule is within the realm of Community Team Challenges.

All requests for Community Team Challenges should be directed to: Sarah Wyer, tel: 020 7547 0965; fax: 01133 361890; email: sarah.wyer@db.com.

Matched funding: The bank's matched giving scheme matches employee charitable donations like for like, (up to a maximum per person per year), no matter whether they donate through Give As You Earn, a one-off donation or through sponsorship. For the latter, there is no limit on how much an employee can fundraise within the bank.

Payroll giving: The bank offers its employees the Give As You Earn scheme and automatically matches employee donations.

Commercially-led support

Sponsorship: Sponsorship is undertaken. See 'Community Involvement'.

Corporate social responsibility

CSR committee: There is a UK Corporate Citizenship team. The following information is taken from the Corporate Citizenship UK CSR report for 2010:

> The UK Charities Committee plays a pivotal role in the bank's society related efforts. Every business unit within Deutsche Bank UK is represented on the Committee. At the beginning of each financial year, the committee members work together to plan how the bank's Corporate Citizenship strategy will be delivered in the UK. They ensure the programmes in which the bank is involved are correctly governed, and are relevant to interests of the various business areas.
>
> Committee members also provide leadership and champion the projects to others within the bank. Prior to programmes being funded and before yearly budgets are reassessed, the Corporate Citizenship UK team undertake due diligence on existing and proposed community partnerships. The team then presents the proposals to the Charities Committee, which approves the partnerships.

CSR policy: Statement taken from the report 'Pass on Your Passion' Corporate Responsibility report 2010 – the latest available relating to the UK at the time of writing (November 2012):

> Deutsche Bank regards corporate social responsibility (CSR) as an investment in society and in its own future. We consider our topmost social responsibility to be internationally competitive, to earn commensurate profits, and to grow as a company. Our second priority as a good corporate citizen is to earn money in a manner that is both socially and ecologically responsible. The third and most visible part of CSR is our support for socially beneficial activities.

CSR report: There is an annual global CSR report.

Exclusions

Deutsche Bank's community development programme does not support projects or organisations that deliver outside the three themes outlined above. It also does not as a bank support the following, although it may support individual employee efforts in respect of such donations including matched giving:

- Animal welfare projects
- Capital projects
- Drugs related projects
- Heritage projects
- Individual sponsorship
- Medical/medical research charities
- Charities or initiatives with religious/political objectives
- Sponsorship of events/tables for projects not associated with core community development activities

Applications

There is a helpful booklet 'Deutsche Bank Corporate Citizenship UK – A guide for charitable organisations' available from the company's UK website. This includes all current contacts for the company's various UK programmes.

Devro plc

Food manufacture

Correspondent: HR Manager, Gartferry Road, Moodiesburn, Chryston, Glasgow G69 0JE (tel: 01236 879191; fax: 01236 872557; website: www.devro.com)

Directors: Steve Hannam, Chair; Peter Page, Chief Executive; Peter Williams, Finance Director; Paul Neep; Stuart Paterson; Simon Webb (women: 0; men: 6)

Year end	31/12/2010
Turnover	£237,039,000
Pre-tax profit	£55,166,000

Nature of business: Devro is the worldwide leader in the provision of collagen products for food markets. Technical, manufacturing and R&D operations are located in four countries.

Company registration number: SC129785

Brands include: Cutisin; Coria; Edicol; Ralex; Select.

Main locations: Glasgow

UK employees: 506

Total employees: 1,483

Charitable donations

UK cash (latest declared):	2009	£42,000
	2008	£49,000
	2003	£37,000
Total worldwide:	2010	£54,000
Cash worldwide:	2010	£54,000

Corporate social responsibility

CSR committee: See – CSR Policy.

CSR policy: The company's 2010 annual CSR report states:

> The group takes its social responsibility obligations very seriously, with our intentions reflected in our group policies. Those on health and safety, the environment, quality and human resources are reviewed annually. To achieve this in 2010, the chief executive invited contributions from managers, safety committees and trade union and employee representatives, and the updated policies were then endorsed by the Board at the end of the year. They are available on our website: www.devro.com.

CSR report: Published annually.

Exclusions

No support for large national appeals or those through third party fundraisers, advertising in charity brochures, animal welfare charities, the arts, overseas projects, political appeals, religious appeals, science/technology or social welfare.

Applications

In writing to the correspondent.

Other information

The contributions made by the group during the year for charitable purposes amounted to £54,000 (2009: £42,000). The contributions were mainly made to charities where the group's operations are based and supported local community groups, schools and colleges and health care and medical research.

Dhamecha Holdings Ltd

Cash 'n' carry, property

Correspondent: P K Dhamecha, Trustee of Ladema Dhamecha Charitable Trust, Wembley Stadium Industrial Estate, First Way, Wembley, Middlesex HA9 0TU (tel: 020 8903 8181; fax: 020 8902 4420; website: www.dhamecha.com)

Directors: K. R. Dhamecha; S. R. Dhamecha; J. Patel

Year end	31/03/2011
Turnover	£527,240,000
Pre-tax profit	£8,313,000

Nature of business: The principal activities are wholesale food cash and carry, property dealings and the manufacture and sale of paper disposable products.

Company registration number: 6519903

Main locations: Wembley, Barking, Croydon, Enfield, Watford

Total employees: 414

Charitable donations

UK cash (latest declared):	2011	£200,000
	2009	£246,700
	2007	£225,000
	2006	£200,000
	2005	£200,000
Total UK:	2011	£200,000
Total worldwide:	2011	£200,000
Cash worldwide:	2011	£200,000

Corporate social responsibility

CSR committee: No information given.

CSR policy: The following statement is taken from the company's website:

> Over the years, The Dhamecha Group have developed a reputation for looking after the welfare of its people.
>
> They work hard to create a safe working environment for their staff and, as a consequence, that of their customers, through regular, up-to-date health and safety training, encouraging a positive attitude towards their environment and taking practical, preventative precautions on a daily basis.
>
> They also enhance, in a range of ways, the economic development of the communities in which they operate. When K.R., S.R. and J.R. Dhamecha started the business, they set up a charitable foundation in recognition of the important part that their mother, Laduma, had played in their personal development (their father died at an early age).
>
> Since that day, and through this trust, the Dhamecha Group have supported a large number of long-term good causes on a local, a national and a global basis. In addition, they also donate to an array of worthy charities.

There was no other CSR information available.

We were unable to determine the ratio of women to men on the board.

CSR report: None published.

Applications

In writing to the correspondent, who is a trustee of the Laduma Dhamecha Charitable Trust.

Other information

The company makes its charitable contributions through the Ladema Dhamecha Charitable Trust (Charity Commission no: 328678), and during 2010/11 donated £200,000. The trust made various donations to charities involved in the provision of medicine and medical research; education projects; cultural activities; relief of poverty; and community projects.

Diageo plc

Food manufacture, retail – restaurants/fast food, brewers/ distillers

Correspondent: Head of Corporate Citizenship, Lakeside Drive, Park Royal, London NW10 7HQ (tel: 020 8978 6000; email: csr@diageo.com; website: www.diageo.com/en-row/CSR)

Directors: Deirdre Mahlan; Paul A. Walker; Todd Stitzer; Paul Tunnacliffe; Lord Hollick of Notting Hill; Philip Scott; Laurence Danon; Peggy Bruzelius; Betsy Holden; Dr Franz Humer, Chair; P. S. Walsh, Chief Executive; Lord Davies of Abersoch (women: 4; men: 8)

Year end	30/06/2011
Turnover	£13,232,000,000
Pre-tax profit	£2,360,000,000

Nature of business: The group's principal activity is the manufacture and distribution of spirits, wines and beer.

Company registration number: 23307

Subsidiaries include: United Distillers and Vintners (HP) Ltd, Guinness Ltd, United Distillers and Vintners (ER) Ltd

Brands include: Baileys; Bell's; Blossom Hill; Buchanan's; Captain Morgan; Ciroc; Crown Royal; Gordon's; Guinness; J&B; Johnnie Walker; Jose Cuervo; Ketel One; Piat d'Or; Smirnoff; Tanqueray.

Main locations: London

Total employees: 23,786

Membership: BITC, LBG

Charitable donations

UK cash (latest declared):	2011	£10,500,000
	2009	£11,200,000
	2008	£10,700,000
	2007	£10,600,000
	2006	£11,800,000
Total UK:	2011	£10,500,000
Total worldwide:	2011	£25,609,000
Cash worldwide:	2011	£17,500,000

Community involvement

As well as the support given through the Diageo Foundation (Charity Commission no. 1014681), the company makes its own contributions to assist charitable and community activities in the communities it serves. Currently, besides its primary focus on responsible drinking, Diageo's other community activities fall into four further focus areas, chosen to reflect where its businesses have the greatest impact and where the company can make the most difference. These are:

- Skills for life – working with unemployed or disadvantaged young adults to become accepted, active citizens of their community
- Water of life – projects that protect the environment or improve access to safe drinking water in developing countries
- Local communities- supporting Diageo's employees in actively engaging in the community, by assessing community needs, harnessing employees' skills, and encouraging volunteering and fundraising
- Disaster relief – the provision of humanitarian aid in the form of emergency relief and supporting longer-term reparation projects while facilitating employee-led fundraising

The Diageo Foundation

The Diageo Foundation's aim is to create positive, long-term change in the community. It focuses on areas of humanitarian need, primarily in developing countries in Africa, Latin America, Asia and Eastern Europe, where it can make the most difference. The foundation provides kick-start funding and expertise in establishing local projects, some of which are run in partnership with local businesses.

The foundation makes charitable donations, matches employee fundraising in the UK and provides longer-term social investment in areas where it can make the most difference.

The foundation is funded entirely by Diageo. It makes grants in support of projects or causes proposed by Diageo businesses and externally.

To be eligible for funding from the Diageo Foundation, projects must fall within one of the four key focus areas listed above. They must also demonstrate the following:

- Addressing a community/social need, in particular excluded and disadvantaged people who, with support, can help themselves to transform their own lives
- Building partnerships with community groups and NGOs
- Helping build the skills-base of individuals or communities
- Maximising grants to make them as effective as possible
- Building the economic prosperity of a community
- Planning a clear exit strategy and appropriate mechanisms to ensure that the benefits derived from the project are sustainable
- Having clear, well-defined objectives in place, including planned outcomes, desired impact, measurement and evaluation

- Enhancing the project, if appropriate, by working in partnership with a local Diageo business

There is normally a three-year limit to any funding commitment.

The maximum funding available for any one project is £50,000. Payments are made normally over a maximum period of three years.

The Diageo Foundation encourages projects which obtain additional funding from external sources as this can lead to sustainability.

The main areas normally considered to be outside the foundation's guidelines are:

- Organisations which are not registered charities
- Individuals
- Loans, business finance or endowment funds
- Medical charities or hospitals
- Promotion of religion
- Animal welfare
- Expeditions or overseas travel
- Political organisations
- Advertising
- Product donations
- Capital projects (e.g. buildings)

Diageo in the UK is funding a training programme for midwives to help them educate expectant mothers about the risks of alcohol to their unborn child. Run by the National Organisation for Foetal Alcohol Syndrome, it is estimated it will each an estimated 10,000 midwives over the next three years.

Information provided for this company and its foundation has been taken from both the company's and foundation's websites with reference to the Annual Report for 2011 and the Sustainability and Responsibility Report for the same year.

Corporate giving

The following information is taken from the annual report and accounts for 2010/11. During the year, total charitable donations made by the group were £28 million (2010: £24.9 million). UK group companies made donations of £10.5 million (2010: £12.0 million) to charitable organisations including £1.1 million (2010: £1.1 million) to the Diageo Foundation and £7.7 million (2010: £7.4 million) to the Thalidomide Trust.

In the rest of the world, group companies made charitable donations of £17.5 million (2010: £12.9 million) including £3 million to the Thalidomide Foundation Ltd in Australia (2010: £nil). We have taken the figures to represent cash donations as they are referred to as 'donations' in the company's annual Sustainability and Responsibility Report for 2011. We do not have a figure for 'in kind' giving. Cause-related marketing figures and management costs have been deducted (as is our policy for all companies) from the overall worldwide total giving.

In kind support

The company acknowledges that whilst financial contributions are important, the giving of time and skill by its staff or surplus products and other in kind donations can often achieve more.

Employee-led support

Employee fundraising/giving receives match funding.

Payroll giving: The company operates the Give As You Earn scheme.

Commercially-led support

Sponsorship: The company undertakes good-cause sponsorship.

Corporate social responsibility

CSR committee: The Sustainability and Responsibility Report and the group's social, ethical and environmental policies are published on the Diageo website. Two executive working groups (one on alcohol in society, chaired by the corporate relations director, and one on environmental performance, chaired by the president, global supply), assist the committee with decisions on specific issues.

CSR policy: The following statement is taken from the annual report and accounts for 2010/11:

> Chaired by the chief executive and responsible for making decisions or, where appropriate, recommendations to the board or executive committee concerning policies, issues and measurement and reporting for the following impacts across Diageo's value chain: alcohol in society, water, broader environmental sustainability, community, our people and governance and ethics. Progress in these areas is reported periodically to the board and publicly through a separate Sustainability & Responsibility Report, selected aspects of which are subject to external assurance.

CSR report: Sustainability and Responsibility report: published annually. Much of the report focuses on responsible drinking and creating a 'more positive role for alcohol in society'.

> Water is separated out from the company's other environmental impacts in the report because of the 'global importance of water and its material impact on our business'. 'For Diageo the water challenge is most acute in Africa, where the UN predicts that 50% of the population will face water scarcity by 2025. We are proud of our strong presence in and commitment to Africa – which accounts for about 14% of our total net sales but 84% of our organic growth. We expect this growth to continue, but with the increased production comes increased demand on water management, an especially important problem in a region where we have identified that around half of our production sites are located in water-stressed areas.
>
> Community involvement takes up a small section of the report and focuses mainly on countries overseas in which the company is developing its brand. In the community investment section an example of giving in the UK is the Do-Be skills training for young people in Scotland where the company has collaborated with the charity Do-Be and a small business. This is a new learning programme designed to help young people develop fundamental skills such as IT, literacy and numeracy in three of Scotland's major cities.

Applications

Applications to the **Diageo Foundation** should be addressed to the Administrator at the above address. (Tel: 020 7927 5417; Email: diageofoundation@diageo.com).

Write providing details of the project, how it relates to the Diageo Foundation's focus areas and the amount of funding required – on no more than two sides of a sheet of paper. The foundation will contact you if it requires further details.

You will normally receive written notification of whether your application has been successful or not within six to eight weeks.

Domino Printing Sciences plc

Business services

Correspondent: Company Secretary, Trafalgar Way, Bar Hill, Cambridge CB23 8TU (website: www.domino-printing.com)

Directors: Peter Byrom, Chair; Nigel Bond, Group Managing Director; Gary Havens; Andrew Herbert, Group Finance Director; Philip Ruffles; Mark Wrightson; David Brown; Christopher Brimsmead (women: 0; men: 8)

Year end	31/10/2011
Turnover	£314,080,000
Pre-tax profit	£57,446,000

Nature of business: A global provider of total coding and printing solutions.

Company registration number: 1363137

Total employees: 2,241

Charitable donations

UK cash (latest declared):	2011	£24,000
	2009	£25,100
	2008	£35,600
Total UK:	2011	£24,000
Total worldwide:	2011	£24,000
Cash worldwide:	2011	£24,000

Corporate social responsibility

CSR committee: No committee set up.

CSR policy: The following statement is taken from the company's website:

> Domino firmly believes that corporate responsibility is integral to business success, and we are firmly committed to the welfare of our stakeholders including our communities, employees, environment, value chain, and shareholders. Domino expects every member of staff to take individual responsibility for their performance and to work together to achieve these goals.
>
> As well as creating jobs within the community and engaging with local government and educational bodies, we sponsor local philanthropic causes that promote science, technology, engineering, or mathematics (STEM) skills and STEM educational programmes. We also endeavour to support organisations neighbouring Domino facilities. It is company policy to make available work placement schemes for local students. We encourage staff to become involved in charitable activities and fundraising by matching their funds (up to a pre-set limit), and allowing them to nominate which organisations the company supports

CSR report: CSR report contained within the annual report but there is very little information on the community aspect.

Applications

In writing to the correspondent.

Other information

In 2011 the group made charitable donations to UK charities and other worthy causes amounting to £24,000. The annual report for 2011 states:

> Domino's ethics policy requires the company to make appropriate contributions to the local community's wellbeing. This is achieved by charitable donations, close involvement with local schools and colleges and provision of training and work experience including accommodating overseas students needing to use their English language skills in a business environment.

Matched Funding: Domino matches money raised by employees for worthy causes. Donations have been made to a broad range of organisations including Macmillan Cancer Support, Marie Curie Cancer Care and Guide Dogs for the Blind as well as local hospitals and youth organisations.

Doughty Hanson and Co. Managers Ltd

Financial services, property, information technology

Correspondent: Ms Julie Foreman, The Doughty Hanson Charitable Trust, PO Box 31064, LONDON SW1Y 5ZP (tel: 020 7663 9300; website: www.doughtyhanson.com)

Directors: Richard Hanson, Chair; Richard Lund; Stephen Marquardt; Graeme Stening (women: 0; men: 4)

Year end	31/12/2011
Turnover	£64,011,000
Pre-tax profit	£28,047,000

Nature of business: Doughty Hanson has three main businesses: Private Equity; Real Estate; and Technology Ventures.

Company registration number: 3015047

Total employees: 89

Charitable donations

UK cash (latest declared):	2011	£244,200
	2009	£245,000
	2008	£428,000
Total UK:	2011	£244,200
Total worldwide:	2011	£283,200
Cash worldwide:	2011	£283,200

Corporate social responsibility

CSR committee: No details found.

CSR policy: The following is taken from the company's website:

> Doughty Hanson and its portfolio companies are involved with a number of charities and social enterprises. The work we do in the CSR arena is primarily driven by the social, community and philanthropic impact it generates rather than any commercial imperative.

CSR report: There is an annual Sustainability report published and available online.

Applications

Applications should be made to the correspondent.

Other information

In 2011 the company gave £283,200 in cash donations (2010: £247,800), of which £244,200 (2010: £243,680) was donated to the company's charitable foundation. The bulk of Doughty Hanson's charitable giving is channelled through, and is the key donor of: **The Doughty Hanson Charitable Foundation**

The foundation, (Charity Commission no. 1080755) was established in 2000 for the relief of poverty, distress and suffering, to promote, develop and maintain public education and appreciation of the arts and science and to further religious work and education in any part of the world, and any other charitable purposes. The company states that many of the charities it supports receive more than one donation or annual support. The focus of the foundation's work currently is for smaller charities where a specific project has been identified, often requiring capital expenditure.

In 2011 the foundation committed £250,000 to 37 different causes in the UK and around the world. Grants range from around £30,000 – to under £100. Beneficiaries included: The Private Equity Foundation and Medicinema (£20,000 each); Parkinson's (£15,000); The Ireland Funds (£13,000); Switchback and The Centre for Social Justice (£10,000 each); Brainwave, Canine Partners and More than Gold (£5,000 each); Ayuda Directa (£3,000); British Red Cross (£2,500); and Sightsavers International.

Matched funding

The foundation will also match any amounts raised in sponsorship by an employee. The company encourages applications to be made by investors, business partners and portfolio companies.

To find out more about the activities of the foundation, email: dhcf@doughtyhanson.com.

Dow Chemical Company Ltd

Chemicals and plastics

Correspondent: Company Secretary, Diamond House, Lotus Park, Kingsbury Crescent, Staines, Middlesex TW18 3AG (tel: 020 3139 4000; fax: 020 3139 4004; website: www.dow.com)

Directors: Andrew N. Liveris, Chair and Chief Executive; Arnold A. Allemang; Jacqueline K. Barton; James A. Bell; Jeff M. Fettig; John B. Hess; Paul Polman; Dennis H. Reilley; James M. Ringler; Ruth G. Shaw (women: 2; men: 8)

Year end	31/12/2010
Turnover	£433,053,000
Pre-tax profit	£14,339,000

Nature of business: The company is a worldwide manufacturer and supplier of chemicals and performance products, plastics, hydrocarbons and energy, and consumer specialities including agricultural products, and consumer products.

Company registration number: 537161

Main locations: King's Lynn, Wilton, Sandbach, Seal Sands, Staines, Middlesbrough, Mirfield, Nuneaton, Billingham

UK employees: 231

Total employees: 231

Charitable donations

UK cash (latest declared):	2010	£29,000
Total UK:	2010	£29,000
Total worldwide:	2010	£29,000
Cash worldwide:	2010	£29,000

Corporate social responsibility

CSR policy: No CSR information available.

Applications

Previous research suggested that preferential consideration is given to requests for donations recommended by employees. Unsolicited applications/ blanket appeal letters are not therefore considered.

Other information

In 2010 this company gave £29,000 in charitable donations in the UK. No further information was available.

Dow Corning Ltd

Chemicals and plastics

Correspondent: Community Relations Co-ordinator, Cardiff Road, Barry, Vale of Glamorgan CF63 2YL (tel: 01446 732350; fax: 01446 747944; website: www.dowcorning.com/barry)

Directors: H. Davies; P. Cartwright; L. McInally; M. Matthews; J. Whitlock; I. Wilson; B. Tessin; K. Palumbo

Year end	31/12/2010
Turnover	£440,431,000
Pre-tax profit	£9,180,000

Nature of business: Manufacture and marketing of silicone and silicon-based products, technologies, and services.

Company registration number: 486170

Main locations: Barry

UK employees: 581

Membership: BITC

Charitable donations

UK cash (latest declared):	2010	£26,000
	2009	£17,000
	2008	£23,000
Total UK:	2010	£26,000
Total worldwide:	2010	£26,000
Cash worldwide:	2010	£26,000

Corporate social responsibility

CSR committee: There is a Corporate Responsibility Committee.

CSR policy: The following statement is taken from the group's website:

> *In our local communities*
> We want the communities where our facilities are located to be great places to live, work, grow and play. So we reach out to our neighbors and work with local educators, civic groups, charities and community leaders to advance education and improve the quality of life for all.
>
> *Investing and involved*
> With grants, donations, sponsorships, matching gifts, hands-on help and more, Dow Corning is improving lives today and investing in the well-being of future generations. Learn what we are doing to make a lasting difference in these key areas: education, community vitality, volunteering and community outreach.

CSR report: Sustainability report published annually.

Exclusions

No support for raffle prizes, for individuals (such as sponsorship for overseas travel or individual fundraising), donations to central funds of charities, political or religious groups, one-off events such as fetes, parades, shows, tournaments, concerts, group travel expenses for excursions or overseas adventures, medical research, general fundraising appeals where Dow Corning funding is not used on specific projects or purchases, uniforms or sports strips for sports teams, national or international appeals, or advertising.

Applications

In writing to the correspondent. Only written appeals will be considered.

The following is taken from the company's webpage: www.dowcorning.com/content/about/aboutcomm/Barry_Community_donations.asp

> Each year we receive many requests for support for local projects. Many organisations look for our help with donations of equipment, sponsorship or practical support from employees.

Other information

In 2010 the company gave £26,000 in charitable cash donations (2009: £17,000). This figure is not a reflection of the company's total contribution to its local community, however we could find no figures for 'in kind' giving.

Dow Corning targets investment in communities where its employees work and live. Its corporate giving programmes operate at major sites in Asia, Europe, and the Americas, with each site managing its own programme. In the UK the company operates from Barry, South Wales and has its own education centre on site. We have no figures for the Dow Corning Corporation's global giving.

Barry site Nature Centre

The following information is taken from the company's website:

> The Barry site has a fantastic 30 acre nature reserve with an education building suitable for school and group educational visits. This sits adjacent to our manufacturing areas showing that wildlife and industry can coexist side by side. The area offers some unique habitats for wildlife to flourish. Educational visits are encouraged and we can offer activities to support the sustainability curriculum that schools follow. The center is built overlooking the large fishing ponds and can be used by schools and local groups for environmental studies, field trips and science projects. With a commitment to sustainability, Dow Corning used materials from sustainable resources wherever possible when designing and constructing the education center. Environmental features were incorporated – for example ground source heating and solar panels provide heat and power for the center; while rainwater is harvested and recycled to provide a water source.

Dow Corning continues to focus on advancing science, technology, engineering and math education; community vitality and high tech employment opportunities. The company's website gives details of its programmes across its sites.

Regular communication with local people takes place through a number of channels, these include: the publication of a regular community newsletter – 'Dow Corning News'; the provision of a helpline for those concerned about environmental and health and safety issues; open house 'Forums for Neighbours'; and, a monthly Community Advisory Panel consisting of representatives from the Barry area.

Employees are encouraged to become involved in supporting their local communities through practical help. A major part of this is the active programme the company has in supporting students and teachers in local schools with science, maths and technology. Employee fundraising is matched by the company up to a maximum of £250.

The company's website gives the following guidelines:

> *Guidelines for grants:*
> A small team of employees meet monthly to discuss all the requests. Priority is given to requests from local groups and the team tries to make sure that any Dow Corning donation helps as many people as possible and has a long-term benefit.
>
> We will consider requests that meet the following criteria:
> - Projects that are local to the Barry, South Wales site and benefit people locally with preference given to requests from Barry and Sully areas and then the Vale of Glamorgan
> - We prefer to make donations to properly established organisations rather than to an informal group
> - Donations must have a wide benefit ensuring a good number of people can be impacted by the funding
>
> If the above broad criteria can be met then requests must meet the following more specific criteria:
> - Activities that will help young people learn more about science, math and technology, or skills that they will need in their future careers, or to make them better citizens
> - Ideas that will help organisations or communities to improve safety or the local environment
> - Activities or projects that help improve the local community's health and wellbeing
> - Projects that help improve the local biodiversity (nature, wildlife, etc)
> - projects that promote good citizenship
> - Projects that can help the elderly

There is a **Dow Corning Foundation** detailed on the company's website, however, projects must benefit the U.S. communities in which our employees live and work.

Drax Group plc

Electricity

Correspondent: Corporate and Social Responsibility Dept., Drax Power Station, Selby, North Yorkshire YO8 8PH (tel: 01757 618381; website: www.draxgroup.plc.uk)

Directors: Charles Berry, Chair; Dorothy Thompson, Chief Executive; Tony Quinlan, Finance Director; Peter Emery; Tim Cobbold; Tim Barker; Mike Grasby; David Lindsell; Tony Thorne (women: 1; men: 8)

Year end	31/12/2010
Turnover	£1,648,400,000
Pre-tax profit	£254,900,000

Nature of business: Drax Group plc is the holding company of the Drax group of companies. The principal activities of the Group are the generation

and sale of electricity at the Drax Power Station, Selby, North Yorkshire and the sale of by-products of the electricity generation

process. The Group also has an electricity supply business, Haven Power Ltd (Haven Power), which serves business customers.

Haven Power is a direct subsidiary of the Group's principal trading subsidiary, Drax Power Ltd.

Company registration number: 5562053

UK employees: 1,044

Total employees: 1,044

Membership: BITC

Charitable donations

UK cash (latest declared):	2010	£87,400
	2009	£96,000
Total UK:	2010	£87,400

Corporate social responsibility

CSR committee: The group's website states:

> The board has ultimate control of policies in respect of both the wider corporate responsibility, such as our Code of Business Ethics, and our environmental and health and safety programmes. The board's policies are implemented by dedicated specialists who make sure effective processes and procedures are in place to assure compliance and to identify and to report on risks and opportunities.

Donations are considered by the Sponsorship Team – see 'Other information'.

CSR policy: The following is taken from annual report and accounts 2010:

> We operate our business within a framework of increasingly stringent and challenging legislative and regulatory requirements. We are, however, mindful of the still tougher expectations held by our wider stakeholder group. For us, corporate and social responsibility is about achieving a balance between the commercial and regulatory rigours of the competitive sector within which we operate and our commitment to our stakeholders as a whole.
>
> *Community relations*
>
> We are committed to being a good neighbour to our local community and our 'caring for the community' philosophy involves being part of local and regional communities. Our involvement takes the form of sponsoring a variety of local charities and fund raising events, promoting our own campaigns which focus on the three themes of youth sport, education and the environment, and maintaining open communication channels and good working relationships with the region's key opinion formers.

CSR report: reporting on CSR is contained within the annual report and accounts.

Applications

In writing to the correspondent.

Other information

The following information is taken from the company's report and accounts for 2010:

> *Sponsorship and fundraising*
>
> During 2010, we gave financial support of £131,450 (2009: £139,000) in total across a range of charitable and non-charitable community causes. Of that total, charitable donations amounted to £87,500 (2009: £88,000).
>
> Some £18,000 of the total donations were made under the direction of our sponsorship team, across a range of activities within a 20-mile radius of the power station. Each month the team meets to consider requests received for charitable donations and community sponsorship and makes awards against our criteria of furthering community, environmental and sporting interests. Examples of the good causes supported through the sponsorship team in 2010 are donations to Camblesforth Community Primary School to enhance their existing music lessons through the provision of tuition to develop instrumental skills and to Vixen Radio to soundproof the radio station's new studio.
>
> Sponsorship monies have been used to help a variety of local causes from sponsoring a concert at Selby Abbey in aid of the Selby Abbey Appeal for restoration work to sponsoring new strips for junior football and rugby clubs.
>
> **Matched funding:** Drax also operates a '£ for £' and Give As You Earn matching scheme, under which we match any monies raised for, or donated to, charity by employees. During 2010, approximately £46,700 of the total donations made were through this scheme.

DSG International plc

Retail – electrical

Correspondent: PA to Helen Grantham, Corporate Responsibility Committee, Maylands Avenue, Hemel Hempstead, Hertfordshire HP2 7TG (tel: 0844 800 2030; website: www.dixonretail.com)

Directors: Nicholas Cadbury, Group Finance Director; John Allan, Chair; John Browett, Chief Executive; Rita Clifton; Andrew Lynch; Prof. Dr Utho Creusen; Tim How; Dharmash Mistry (women: 1; men: 7)

Year end	30/04/2011
Turnover	£8,341,800,000
Pre-tax profit	(£224,100,000)

Nature of business: The company's main activity is the retailing of high technology consumer electronics, personal computers, domestic appliances, photographic equipment, communication products and related financial and after sales services.

Company registration number: 333031

Brands include: Brands include: Currys/PC World; Dixons Travel; DSGI Business; KNOWHOW; Gigantti; Lefdal.

Main locations: Nottingham, Sheffield, Bury, Hemel Hempstead

UK employees: 23,091

Total employees: 39,733

Charitable donations

UK cash (latest declared):	2011	£0
	2010	£0
	2009	£200,000
	2008	£400,000
	2007	£875,000
Total UK:	2011	£0
Total worldwide:	2011	£0
Cash worldwide:	2011	£0

Corporate social responsibility

CSR committee: The Group Finance Director, Nicholas Cadbury, is the board member responsible for corporate responsibility matters at Dixons Retail. He is supported in this task by the Corporate Responsibility Committee, which comprises senior executives from key business areas and is chaired by Helen Grantham, the Company Secretary and General Counsel.

CSR policy: The following information is taken from the annual report and accounts for 2010/11:

> The Corporate Responsibility Committee has established the following key performance indicators, which enables it to monitor performance against the priorities that it has set:
>
> - Colleague diversity – age, gender and ethnicity of its employees
> - Health and Safety – employee and customer accidents and injuries
> - Ethical supply chain audits
> - Customer satisfaction

- Waste electrical equipment collected and recycled
- Business waste recycled
- Group carbon emissions
- Contributions to the community

CSR report: A CSR report is contained within the annual report and accounts.

Exclusions

No grants are made towards: third party fundraising activities; political or religious organisations; projects that should be funded from statutory sources, overseas appeals; community sponsorship of any kind; or animal charities.

Applications

Visit the company's website for current information before applying.

Other information

According to the company's accounts, during the period 2010/11 the company made no charitable donations.

Most of the company's charitable contribution appears to be supporting its staff in volunteering and fundraising activities; we have no information of the cost of this to the company, if any. The following is taken from the company's 2010/11 annual report and accounts:

> Given the difficult economic environment experienced across Europe, the charitable activities in the UK were refocused in 2009 to reflect lower levels of fund raising activity. The programme continues the theme of improving access to technology for disadvantaged and disabled children, while encouraging colleagues to engage with their local communities by supporting local charities. While colleagues can support a charity of their choice, the Group has selected two national charities that colleagues can choose to support, Lifelites and the e-Learning Foundation, who are working locally with colleagues to support their fundraising efforts. Under the new programme our colleagues have participated in many local and national activities, including the Phone Pledge Evening for Red Nose Day at our KNOWHOW Customer Contact Centre at Sheffield where over 100 colleagues took part in raising over £118,000.
>
> Colleagues are also invited to apply for a grant from the **DSG international Foundation,** (Charity Commission no. 1053215, the group's charitable trust, to support their fundraising activities, subject to certain criteria.

The company is the sole benefactor of the foundation, the beneficiaries of which are supported in education, community affairs, health and disabilities, heritage and the environment. There has been no contribution made by the company to the foundation for the past two accounting years. This lack of contribution is thought to be due to the current economic downturn. The foundation itself-had outgoings of £6,000 in 2010/11.

Du Pont (UK) Ltd

Industrial products/services

Correspondent: Company Secretary, Wedgwood Way, Stevenage, Hertfordshire SG1 4QN (tel: 01438 734000; fax: 01438 734836; website: www2.dupont.com/Social_Commitment/en_US)

Directors: A. Baker; A. Gough

Year end	31/12/2010
Turnover	£370,073,000
Pre-tax profit	£45,635,000

Nature of business: The group's principal business is the manufacture, sale and distribution of chemical products (fibres, polymers, chemicals and specialities, and electronics).

Company registration number: 4556216

Main locations: Londonderry, East Kilbride, Maydown, Ruabon, Corby, Stevenage, Sudbury, Bristol, Darlington, Romiley

UK employees: 313

Corporate social responsibility

CSR committee: Not specified.

CSR policy: The following is taken from the company's website:

> *Community involvement*
>
> To thrive, healthy businesses need healthy communities. DuPont improves the quality of life and enhances the vitality of the communities in which we operate by supporting community sustainability efforts. Sustainable communities recognise the interdependence of social progress, economic success and environmental excellence. Through financial contributions and the active volunteer participation of employees, DuPont provides support to programs and non-profit organisations that address one or more components of community sustainability.

Unable to determine the ratio of women to men on the board.

CSR report: None published on website.

Exclusions

No grants are made to: non-registered charities; disease-specific organisations; endowment funds; service organisations; individuals; political causes; sectarian groups whose work is only available to members of one religious community; or organisations without good equal opportunity processes.

Applications

As each DuPont site in the UK is responsible for its own community contributions, contact the most appropriate one.

The DuPont Contributions and Memberships Team is responsible for non-education-related financial contributions. Most corporate grants involve programmes in the DuPont headquarters community of Wilmington, Delaware, and other communities where the company has a major presence. We do not know how successful UK applicants have been.

The committee reviews requests in the spring and autumn (usually May and September).

Requests must be submitted in writing and include a one- to two-page description of the organisation and the programme to be funded, as well as an explanation of how the program relates to the DuPont philosophy of community sustainability. Include an email address for the organisation, if possible.

Send non education-related requests to:

Corporate Contributions Office
DuPont
1007 Market Street
Wilmington, DE 19898

Applicants will be notified in writing of grant review results. 'Organisations should not make plans based only on verbal conversations.'

Other information

As each DuPont site in the UK is responsible for its own community contributions, no community contributions figure was available from the company's accounts. The company website suggests that in kind support, e.g. the donation of land to a conservation group, may be made in cases where the organisations programmes and activities relate to the company's goals.

The company's website states that:

> DuPont is committed to improving the quality of life and enhancing the vitality of communities in which it operates throughout the world. Through financial contribution and the volunteer efforts of its employees, DuPont supports programmes that address social progress, economic success and environmental excellence – all vital components of community sustainability.
>
> Each year, DuPont contributes to numerous efforts that meet the needs of various groups and global communities where the company operates. Areas of support include:
>
> - Educational programmes
> - Culture and the arts
> - Environmental initiatives
> - Human and health service organisations
> - Civic and community activities
>
> Within these criteria support may be available from three sources. Firstly, from the individual DuPont business units in the UK; secondly, from the Corporate Contributions Office in the USA; and thirdly, from the DuPont Centre for

Collaborative Research and Education, also in the USA.

Duchy Originals Ltd

Food manufacture

Correspondent: See 'Applications', The Old Ryde House, 393 Richmond Road, East Twickenham TW1 2EF (tel: 020 8831 6800; website: www.duchyoriginals.com)

Directors: Michael Jary, Chair; Leslie Ferrar; Stephen Nelson; Craig Sams (women: 0; men: 4)

Year end	31/03/2011
Turnover	£2,365,400
Pre-tax profit	£2,237,800

Nature of business: The ownership and management of a range of premium organic food and drink products under the 'Duchy Originals' brand.

Company registration number: 2478770

UK employees: 1

Total employees: 1

Membership: BITC

Charitable donations

UK cash (latest declared):	2011	£625,000
	2009	£0
	2008	£0
	2007	£743,000
	2006	£1,291,000
Total UK:	2011	£625,000
Total worldwide:	2011	£625,000
Cash worldwide:	2011	£625,000

Community involvement

Duchy Originals was launched in 1990 by HRH The Prince of Wales with an aim that every product 'is good, does good and tastes good'. 2010/11 was the first full financial year in which Duchy Originals worked in partnership with Waitrose. Waitrose has the exclusive right to originate, promote and distribute Duchy Originals products in the UK. The new licensing and distribution agreement has significantly increased the charitable donations made by Duchy Originals and next year's (first full year of) trading is expected to generate in excess of £1 million for charity.

The following information is taken from the company's website:

> We donate our profits to The Prince's Charities Foundation, which was founded by HRH The Prince of Wales in 1979. The Prince established the foundation to enable him to help support a variety of charitable causes and projects. The Prince's Charities Foundation is a grant-making charity which supports a wide range of causes and projects by making charitable donations. Profits from Duchy Originals, the Highgrove shops and other social enterprises within The Prince's Charities are donated to the foundation.
>
> The foundation receives an ever-increasing number of requests for assistance. Donations are made to an extensive variety of causes working with environmental issues, health and hospices, community and welfare, education, heritage, the built environment and charities supporting servicemen and women.

Corporate giving

According to the annual report and accounts for the company, in 2010/11, £625,000 was donated to The Prince of Wales's Charitable Foundation (Charity Commission no. 1127255). In total £1.6 million was paid to the foundation but a substantial part of this was a loan repayment used to restructure the company in a previous year. It was the directors' intention to donate all taxable profits in 2011/12 to charity.

In 2010/11 the foundation donated over £1.5 million in grants to charities and £3.2 million in directly funded charitable activities supporting various causes including: children and young people; culture; education; environment; medical welfare and overseas aid. These figures exclude support costs.

Corporate social responsibility

CSR policy: No specific policy, report or team given by the company – its only contribution is given directly to The Prince of Wales Charitable Foundation, a registered charity.

Applications

In writing to: The Trustees, The Prince's Charities Foundation, Clarence House, St James's, London SW1A 1BA (Tel: 020 7930 4832).

Dunelm Group plc

Retail – clothing and footwear, retail – department and variety stores

Correspondent: Chief Executive, Fosse Way, Syston, Leics LE7 1NF (tel: 0845 165 6565; email: customerservices@dunelm-mill.co.uk; website: www.dunelm-mill.com)

Directors: Bill Adderley, Founder and Life President; Geoff Cooper, Chair; Nick Wharton, Chief Executive; Marion Sears; David Stead, Company Secretary; Simon Emeny; Will Adderley (women: 1; men: 6)

Year end	02/07/2011
Turnover	£538,474,000
Pre-tax profit	£83,649,000

Nature of business: Specialist out-of-town homewares retailer providing a comprehensive range of products to a wide customer base, under the brand name Dunelm Mill.

Company registration number: 4708277

Total employees: 6,600

Charitable donations

UK cash (latest declared):	2011	£56,000
	2009	£49,000
	2008	£46,000
Total UK:	2011	£56,000
Total worldwide:	2011	£56,000
Cash worldwide:	2011	£56,000

Corporate social responsibility

CSR committee: No specific committee. 'The chief executive reports regularly to the board on all CSR matters.'

CSR policy: The following is taken from the company's website:

> Dunelm Group plc recognises its duty to behave responsibly to all parties affected by its business operations and to minimise its business related social, ethical and environmental impacts. As part of this commitment we have focused on reducing key impacts in many significant areas such as waste management, energy reduction and carbon emissions.
>
> The board places particular emphasis on maintaining good relationships with its customers, employees and suppliers; on health and safety and ethical sourcing; on environmental issues; and charitable contributions.

The company has a commitment to nominate a Charity of the Year and to support it through collections in stores and various employee events throughout the year, matched by donations from the group.

CSR report: Contained within the annual report and accounts.

Applications

In writing to the correspondent.

Other information

The total value of donations made by the group in the year 2010/11 was £56,000 (2009/10: £60,000). In addition, £84,000 was raised by staff.

Charity of the Year: Wallace and Gromit's Children's Foundation (2011/12). Collections are made in stores for the nominated charity throughout the financial year, specific fundraising events are organised and the group makes its own donations.

Dŵr Cymru Welsh Water

Water

Correspondent: Richard Curtis, Company Secretary, Pentwyn Road, Nelson, Treharris CF46 6LY (tel: 01443 452300; fax: 01443 452323; website: www.dwrcymru.com)

Directors: Robert Ayling, Chair; Nigel Annett, Managing Director; Chris Jones, Finance Director; Peter Perry; John Bryant; Tony Hobson; James Strachan; Stephen Palmer; Menna Richards; Anna Walker (women: 2; men: 8)

Year end		31/03/2011
Turnover		£676,700,000
Pre-tax profit		£63,200,000

Nature of business: Provision of water services.

Company registration number: 2366777

Main locations: Treharris

UK employees: 1,727

Total employees: 1,727

Membership: BITC

Charitable donations

UK cash (latest declared):	2011	£8,000
	2009	£44,000
	2008	£18,500
	2007	£32,874
	2006	£33,395
Total UK:	2011	£8,000
Total worldwide:	2011	£8,000
Cash worldwide:	2011	£8,000

Corporate social responsibility

CSR policy: No CSR information available.

Applications

Note: As a not-for-profit company operating for the benefit of its customers, any donations that are made by Welsh Water are done so in support of employees fundraising efforts. Applications outside of this are not, therefore, accepted or acknowledged.

Other information

In 2010/11 the company made charitable cash donations totalling over £8,000. Beneficiaries included: Wales Air Ambulance (£500); Water Aid (£750); Hope House Children's Hospice and Milford Haven Port Authority (£1,500 each). The company does not engage in sponsorship but instead supports its staff in community schemes by providing their business/management expertise, mentoring or other skills. The company supports and provides resources for advancing education in conservation issues, particularly that of teaching schoolchildren the value of water and how to conserve it, and is also a supporter of the international charity Water Aid.

Dyson Ltd

Domestic appliances, engineering

Correspondent: Alan Briggs, Trustee, The James Dyson Foundation, Tetbury Hill, Malmesbury, Wiltshire NS16 0RP (tel: 01666 827200/01666 827205; email: jamesdysonfoundation@dyson.com; website: www.dyson.co.uk)

Directors: Max Conze; James Shipsey (women: 0; men: 2)

Year end		31/12/2011
Turnover		£219,900,000
Pre-tax profit		£45,000,000

Nature of business: Manufacture of domestic appliances.

Company registration number: 2627406

Charitable donations

UK cash (latest declared):	2011	£200,000
	2008	£3,092,000
	2007	£3,525,000
	2006	£2,140,000
	2005	£2,885,000
Total UK:	2011	£200,000
Total worldwide:	2011	£200,000
Cash worldwide:	2011	£200,000

Community involvement

Community involvement:

The company's support is channelled through the **James Dyson Foundation** (Charity Commission no. 1099709). Established in 2002, the foundation promotes charitable giving, especially to charities working in the fields of science, engineering, medicine, education and social and community welfare, particularly in the area of Malmesbury. With a committee to manage giving, and registered charity status, it is intended that the James Dyson Foundation will assist educational institutions working in the field of design, technology and engineering, as well as charities carrying out medical or scientific research. Locally, the foundation seeks to support charitable projects in or nearby Malmesbury, the town where Dyson is based.

Dyson's own employees also contribute to the foundation and are encouraged to take an active role in selecting projects and fundraising, especially for **Dyson's charity partnerships** (CLIC – Cancer and Leukaemia in Childhood, Meningitis Research Foundation and Breakthrough Breast Cancer).

Occasionally small grants are granted to charitable projects that fall within the foundation's criteria.

Corporate giving

Charitable donations are channelled through the James Dyson Foundation and in 2011 the company declared £200,000 (2010: £4.2 million).

In 2010/11 the foundation's income was £186,000 (2009/10: £545,000) the majority of which came from Dyson Ltd.

During the year, the foundation made grants totalling £584,800 which was broken down as follows: education and training (£496,600); science and medical research (£72,100) and social and community welfare (£14,000).

Beneficiaries for the year included:

- *Education* – James Dyson Awards (£101,500), Royal College of Art (£100,000), Pompidou Project (£29,800) and Japan Educational Project (£5,900)
- *Science* – Dyson Centre for Neo-natal Care (£55,500), and Sparks (£2,280)
- *Social* – Awards of less than £1,000 totalling £7,400

In kind support

Design engineers from Dyson host workshops at schools and universities throughout the country and the foundation provides free resources to Design and Technology teachers throughout the UK.

The company provides an information pack for teachers and lecturers which can be used in conjunction with the Dyson Education Box and both are free of charge.

Each year, the company donates a number of Dyson vacuum cleaners to charitable causes within the James Dyson Foundation's objectives.

Employee-led support

Dyson workers in Malmesbury, Wiltshire, also contribute to the foundation and are encouraged to take an active role in selecting projects and fundraising, especially for Dyson's charity partnerships.

Commercially-led support

A special edition Dyson vacuum helped raise £1.7 million, funding the Dyson Microarray Laboratory at the Royal Marsden in London. This state-of-the-art facility helps scientists study thousands of genes at a time, identifying patterns relevant to breast cancer and its treatment. 'Having lost both his parents to cancer, the charity holds special relevance to James Dyson.'

The annual *James Dyson Award* inspires students from around the world to engineer a solution to an everyday problem and elevates their work on a global platform. Contenders have included folding plugs, sprinkler taps, emergency rescue devices, water purifiers and airless tyres. The international winner gets a £10,000 towards the development of their idea. A further £10,000 goes to their university department. Some of the winners have gone on to join the Dyson team.

Corporate social responsibility

CSR policy: No specific CSR information could be found except for that found on the charitable ventures pages on the company's website.

Exclusions

The foundation does not provide support for political purposes and local appeals not in areas of company presence.

Applications

In writing to the correspondent.

E.ON UK plc

Electricity, oil and gas/fuel

Correspondent: Chair and Chief Executive, Westwood Way, Westwood Business Park, Coventry CV4 8LG (tel: 02476 424000; fax: 02476 425432; website: www.eon-uk.com)

Directors: Paul Golby, Chair and Chief Executive; Graham Bartlett; Brian Tear; Maria Antoniou (women: 1; men: 3)

Year end	31/12/2010
Turnover	£9,241,000,000
Pre-tax profit	£808,000,000

Nature of business: E.ON UK is part of the E.ON IT Group which provides IT Services to the whole of E.ON within Europe. Business Services and UK Centre provide key services for the whole of E.ON UK, delivering cost effective processes and vital functional support.

Company registration number: 2366970

Main locations: Nottingham, Coventry

UK employees: 12,000

Total employees: 79,000

Membership: BITC

Charitable donations

UK cash (latest declared):	2010	£345,000
	2009	£162,000
	2008	£141,000
	2007	£130,000
	2006	£29,000
Total UK:	2010	£345,000
Total worldwide:	2010	£407,500
Cash worldwide:	2010	£407,500

Corporate social responsibility

CSR committee: No details of committee on website.

CSR policy: Dr Paul Golby, E.ON UK Chief Executive, states:

> Taking actions on our six responsibilities is key to our business and we continued to make great progress in 2010. However, the challenges facing the energy industry show no signs of abating. We must continue our efforts to ensure the energy we supply and solutions we provide make the world of energy cleaner and offer our customers a better energy experience.

The six responsibilities referred to focus on environmental issues.

CSR report: Performance report produced annually.

Exclusions

No support for: advertising in charity brochures; animal welfare; appeals from individuals; enterprise/training; fundraising events; medical research; political appeals; religious appeals; or sickness/disability charities.

Applications

In writing to the correspondent.

Other information

Donations to charitable organisations during the financial year by the group amounted to £407,500 (2009: £169,000). Donations to charitable organisations during the financial year by the Company amounted to £345,000 (2008: £162,000).

The company encourages employees to get involved in its employee volunteering programme and also matches funds raised by employees for charitable/good causes.

Other initiatives exist to support employee fundraising activities, such as providing maths and IT support for schoolchildren.

E.ON UK's community support is focused on areas relevant to the company's business activities – where it is based and where its employees live and work, i.e. predominantly in and around its offices, call centres and power station sites.

As well as a regional focus, community activities are targeted on areas relevant to the business and where maximum benefit can be brought. Community investment strategy is based on three key areas – education, supporting vulnerable consumers and working with communities close to its sites. Charitable organisations are also supported through the Employee Community Fund, Charity of the Year and payroll giving initiatives.

Payroll giving: The company has established an employee payroll giving scheme.

Eaga plc

Miscellaneous, services

Correspondent: Dr Naomi Brown, eaga Charitable Trust, Dr Naomi Brown, eaga Charitable Trust, PO Box 225, Kendal LA9 9DR (tel: 01912 458501/01539 736477; fax: 01912 458560; email: eagact@aol.com; website: www.carillion.com)

Directors: Drew Johnson, Chief Executive; Ian McLeod, Chief Financial Officer; David Routledge; William MacDiarmid; Giles Sharp; Charles Berry, Chair; Malcolm Simpson; Quintin Oliver; Tracy Clarke; Roger Aylard (women: 1; men: 9)

Year end	31/05/2010
Turnover	£762,179,000
Pre-tax profit	£41,471,000

Nature of business: The group is a 'green support services company' engaged in the provision of outsourced services and products that address a wide range of environmental and social challenges.

Company registration number: 3858865

Main locations: Cardiff, Birmingham, Belfast, Birkenhead, Knowsley

Total employees: 4,684

Membership: BITC

Charitable donations

UK cash (latest declared):	2010	£201,000
	2009	£245,000
	2008	£135,000
	2007	£250,000
Total UK:	2010	£201,000
Total worldwide:	2010	£201,000
Cash worldwide:	2010	£201,000

Corporate social responsibility

CSR committee: No details found.

CSR policy: Statement taken from the 2010 annual report and accounts:

> Eaga's commitment to social responsibility is driven by our core values; to care for our partners, customers and communities.
>
> Corporate social responsibility sits at the core of the business and complements our business objectives. Eaga's innovative and holistic approach to social responsibility ensures that we adopt a creative approach to the social and environmental needs of the communities that we serve.

CSR report: The 2010 Corporate Social Responsibility report is available both as a hard copy and in an interactive online format at www.Eaga.com.

Applications

Applications to the charitable trust should be made in writing to the correspondent; current details of the bid deadlines and other information relating to grants can be found on the company's website.

Other information

During the year 2010 the company and the group made charitable donations of £201,000 (2009: £245,000) principally to the independent eaga Charitable Trust and the eaga Community Fund managed for eaga by the Community Foundation. The following information is taken from the company's website:

> The independent eaga Charitable Trust (eaga-CT) is a grant-giving trust that currently supports projects and research in two main areas: the relief of fuel poverty and the promotion of energy efficiency; and vulnerable consumers – multiple needs and preferences.
>
> The trust was founded by eaga Partnership Ltd in 1993. Since the inception of eaga Charitable Trust, eaga has donated over £3.1 million to the trust, which the trust has used to give grants for action and research projects into the causes of fuel poverty and its impacts on health.
>
> Although eaga continues to be its sole funder, eaga Charitable Trust is an independent body which exists separately from eaga. eaga-CT has no involvement with the operations of eaga or any other eaga companies.

East Midlands Airport

Airport operators

Correspondent: Administrator, Community Fund, Building 34, Nottingham East Midlands Airport, Castle Donnington, Derby DE74 2SA (tel: 01332 852801/01332 818414; fax: 01332 852959; email: community@eastmidlandsairport.com; website: www.eastmidlandsairport.com)

Directors: Mike Davies, Chair; Charlie Cornish, Group Chief Executive; Penny Coates; Mike Hancox; Richard Leese; David Partridge; Angela Spindler; Stuart Chambers; James Wallace; Neil Thompson; Dave Goddard (women: 2; men: 11)

Year end	31/03/2011
Turnover	£350,200,000
Pre-tax profit	£80,600,000

Nature of business: Airport operator.

Company registration number: 5150652

Main locations: Derby

UK employees: 2,591

Total employees: 2,591

Membership: LBG

Charitable donations

UK cash (latest declared):	2011	£100,000
	2009	£18,000
	2007	£50,000
	2006	£50,000
	2005	£40,000
Total UK:	2011	£100,000

Corporate social responsibility

CSR committee: There was no evidence of a separate CSR Committee.

CSR policy: Taken from the CR report for 2011:

> Investing in our local communities is a vital part of our sustainability strategy. We do this in many ways, from community funding programmes and initiatives, to investment in terms of time and resource. This year, we have particularly focused on volunteering programmes, offering colleagues up to two working days per year to dedicate to community activities.

CSR report: Published within the annual report and accounts.

Exclusions

No support for local appeals not within ten miles of the airport boundary.

Applications

Guidance notes and an application form are downloadable from EMA's website. Completed applications should be returned to the correspondent.

Other information

The Manchester Airports Group (MAG) is the UK's largest British-owned airport operator. Its four airports – Manchester, **East Midlands**, Bournemouth and Humberside – currently serve around 24 million passengers every year.

The group and its subsidiaries during the year gave donations which totalled £100,000 (2010: £100,000). The donations were all made to recognised local and national charities for a variety of purposes. Group contributions are recorded in the Manchester Airports Group entry.

The following information is taken from the company's (**East Midlands Airport**) website:

> East Midlands Airport supports a number of local charities and organisations through a variety of methods.
>
> *Community Fund*
>
> The East Midlands Airport Community Fund was established in April 2002 and since then over £600,500 has been pledged to a whole range of initiatives which aim to bring lasting benefit to the communities around the airport.
>
> The Community Fund is managed independently by a Community Fund Management Committee that meets six times a year, and is open to community groups within a defined 'area of benefit' that meet certain criteria. See a map of the area of benefit.
>
> The Fund is supported by an annual donation of £50,000 from the airport and through the fines imposed when aircraft exceed our strict noise limits. The Community Fund awards grants to support eligible projects that have a long-lasting community and/or environmental benefit.
>
> *Fund objectives*
>
> In order for an application to be successful it must meet at least one of the following objectives:
>
> - To bring the community closer together through facilities for sport, recreation and other leisure time activities
> - Offer environmental improvement and/or heritage conservation
> - Improve awareness of environmental issues through environmental education
> - Encourage and/or protect wildlife
>
> *Local community sponsorship*
>
> We are aware that there are many worthwhile community groups and projects that provide a lasting benefit to their local area. At East Midlands Airport we are committed to supporting as many of these as possible and working alongside groups to provide a positive influence to those areas around the airport site.
>
> We receive a large number of requests for help every week, and we try to help as many groups and projects as possible.
>
> Support for local initiatives has long been a feature of our work and every year a range of local groups benefit from an airport grant. The aim of these grants is to contribute to the success of areas most heavily affected by our operations, for example by supporting local village fetes, art groups, local museums, sporting initiatives and many others besides.

See the company's website for information on how to apply.

> *Charity collections*
>
> To show our support to any local fundraising group we offer space in our Departures hall to enable charities to collect from passengers. Groups must supply a copy of their public liability insurance and a risk assessment.
>
> *Coins for causes*
>
> In 2009, East Midlands Airport launched a new scheme with the aim of collecting any unwanted foreign currency or any sterling donations for a local charity, by placing collection boxes in the arrivals hall. The charity chosen by airport colleagues for 2010/11 was Rainbows Children's Hospice, who received over £2,600. Colleagues have voted again for their chosen charity for 2011/12, and this year we will be collecting for the Derbyshire, Leicestershire and Rutland Air Ambulance.

easyJet plc

Aviation

Correspondent: Corporate Responsibility Dept., Hangar 89, London Luton Airport, Luton, Bedfordshire LU2 9PF (email: easyjet@mailnj.custhelp.com; website: www.easyjet.com)

Directors: Sir Michael Rake, Chair; Charles Gurassa; Carolyn McCall, Chief Executive; Chris Kennedy, Chief Financial Officer; Adèle Anderson; David Bennett; John Browett; Rigas Doganis; Keith Hammill; Andy Martin (women: 2; men: 8)

Year end	30/09/2011
Turnover	£2,733,000,000
Pre-tax profit	£248,000,000

Nature of business: Airline operators.

Company registration number: 3034606

UK employees: 5,116

Total employees: 8,288

Charitable donations

UK cash (latest declared):	2011	£0
	2009	£50,000
Total UK:	2011	£0
Total worldwide:	2011	£0
Cash worldwide:	2011	£0

Corporate social responsibility

CSR committee: No details published.

CSR policy: Taken from the annual report and accounts 2011:

> The safety of our customers and staff is easyJet's number one priority; it remains a core part of our DNA. From all across the business, the boardroom to the flight deck and the check-in desk to the maintenance bay, safety informs everything we do and is the starting point for every decision, at all times. The evolution of our open and just culture continues with easyJet being at the

> forefront of promoting open reporting of all safety-related incidents, no matter how minor they may appear at first glance. At easyJet, we aim to maintain processes and structures to monitor and manage safety related risk throughout the business.

CSR report: Contained within the annual report and accounts.

Applications

In writing to the correspondent.

Other information

The 2011 annual report states:

> easyJet has continued to support the Alzheimer's Society as its European charity partner. Through onboard collections we have managed to raise over £800,000 for this charity. Our charitable support also focuses on our employees and their efforts to raise funds for local charities across our pan-European bases. This has involved raising funds for a number of different charities and has seen our staff undertake numerous activities including, the London and Paris marathons, and the Three Peaks challenge to name a few.

easyJet's contributions would appear to come solely from staff fundraising and therefore their contribution has been listed as nil.

Ecclesiastical Insurance Group plc

Insurance

Correspondent: Mrs R J Hall, Allchurches Trust Ltd, Beaufort House, Brunswick Road, Gloucester GL1 1JZ (tel: 01452 528533; fax: 01452 423557; website: www.ecclesiastical.com)

Directors: The Ven N. Peyton; M. D. Couve; J. F. Hylands; A. P. Latham; Philip Mawer; W. M. Samuel, Chair; M. C. J. Hews, Chief Financial Officer; M. H. Tripp, Group Chief Executive; Ms D. P. Wilson; S. A. Wood, Managing Director UK; D. Christie (women: 1; men: 10)

Year end	31/12/2011
Turnover	£484,205,000
Pre-tax profit	(£7,671,000)

Nature of business: Principal activity: general and long-term insurance.

Company registration number: 1718196

Subsidiaries include: Crusade Services Ltd, Ansvar Insurance Co. Ltd, Gerling Global London Market Ltd, Ansvar Conference Services Ltd, Hinton and Wild (Home Plans) Ltd, The Churches Purchasing Scheme Ltd, Blaisdon Properties Ltd, Ansvar Pensions Ltd, Allchurches Investment Management Services Ltd, Eccint Ltd, Allchurches Life Assurance Ltd

Main locations: Gloucester

UK employees: 763

Total employees: 1,025

Membership: BITC

Charitable donations

UK cash (latest declared):	2011	£11,700,000
	2008	£7,000,000
	2007	£14,100,000
	2006	£10,700,000
	2005	£5,350,000
Total UK:	2011	£11,700,000
Total worldwide:	2011	£11,700,000
Cash worldwide:	2011	£11,700,000

Community involvement

The 2011 annual report states:

> We intend to establish a clearer approach to measuring our community impact and to put in place a mechanism for community partners to provide feedback. We can then raise our game, expect more of ourselves and others, and support our business partners, staff and customers to deliver to a better standard too.

The company is owned by the **Allchurches Trust** (Charity Commission no. 263960) to which all charitable grants made by the company are given. The object of the Trust is to promote the Christian religion and to contribute to the funds of any charitable institutions, associations, funds or objects and to carry out any charitable purpose.

The trust has adopted the following priorities:

- Supporting the mission and work of the dioceses and cathedrals of the Church of England by the distribution of annual grants
- Supporting requests for financial assistance from Anglican churches, Churches of other denominations and Christian communities and organisations in accordance with its grantmaking policy
- Maintaining a special project fund to support substantial projects which may have a broad impact on the Christian community in the UK
- Maintaining an overseas project fund to support the church and Christian community overseas in accordance with its grantmaking policy

There is a preference for charities working within Gloucestershire.

The trustees regularly review the grantmaking policy of the Trust 'to ensure it remains appropriate to the strategic direction of the charity and its objects'. A copy of the grantmaking policy is available from the company secretary at the registered office.

Applicants are advised to visit the website: www.allchurches.co.uk

In addition to the above, the group has partnerships 'with a number of organisations that share our social conscience and values' and to which it gives support. Staff are also encouraged to volunteer for local community-minded charities.

Corporate giving

In 2011, the company made charitable donations totalling £11.7 million which was donated to Allchurches Trust (see Community Involvement section).

Allchurches Trust (Charity Commission no. 263960)

During 2010, (the latest accounts available at the time of writing – August 2012), the trust allocated charitable distributions amounting to over £8.3 million. A breakdown of these grants is as follows: Diocesan grants (almost £6 million); Cathedral Grants (£1.1 million); and other grants including churches, other religious institutions, community appeals and hospitals and hospices (£1.4 million).

In addition to the above the group also supported eighteen partnerships.

Employee-led support

30% of the group's staff volunteer and supported local community-minded charities including English Heritage and The Children's Society. Good causes local to the company's offices are also supported. In 2011, employee time donated (during normal working hours) was 1,376 hours, £56,000 was raised through payroll giving and the employee fundraising total was over £100,000.

Commercially-led support

Cause-related marketing: The company has launched an ISA charitable giving scheme; or the 'nicer ISA' as they have termed it. Under the scheme, every Ecclesiastical ISA investor has the opportunity to select a charity from a carefully chosen list. If this option is taken up, the equivalent of 0.25% of an individual's savings will be donated to their selected charity on an annual basis.

Corporate social responsibility

CSR committee: The board reports on and is responsible for CSR matters. No details of any subcommittees found.

CSR policy: Extract taken from the publication 'Stronger Communities Plan':

> The current economic and social climate makes what we stand for and what we believe in more important than ever.
>
> Our Stronger Communities Plan is a way for us to address our responsibilities in the communities we care about, providing everyone with a way to get involved and continue making a real and lasting difference.
>
> A sense of community is central to who we are. Our Stronger Communities Plan has four elements: local communities; environment; suppliers; and workplace. Combined, they will make what we do for our communities – and our customers – even better.

These four elements fundamentally support how we treat our customers and how they experience us. It means we can build even more confidence, understanding and empathy through continued good practice; whether that's the environmental policy we're so proud of, or the standards we demand of our suppliers.

Ultimately, it means we can continue to build a strong relationship with our customers, delivering exemplary service now, and well into the future.

CSR report: Published within the annual report and accounts.

Exclusions

The trustees do not make grants to charities with political associations. Support is not normally given for advertising in charity brochures, animal welfare charities, individuals, fundraising events, medical research, or sport.

Applications

Applications are not considered by the company but by the trustees of the Allchurches Trust Ltd., which owns the group. Applications should be submitted in writing in the form prescribed, detailing charity number, the objectives of the charity, the appeal target, how the funds are to be utilised, funds raised to date and previous support received from the trust. If available, the application should be accompanied by supporting literature and annual report/accounts. Grants are awarded to a range of purposes including: children's welfare, Christian values, medical research, social wellbeing and wildlife preservation.

Further details about the work of Allchurches Trust Ltd or advice on how to apply for financial assistance can be obtained by contacting the Company Secretary, Beaufort House, Brunswick Road, Gloucester GL1 1JZ or email: atl@eigmail.com.

Economist Newspaper Ltd

Business services, media

Correspondent: Georgina Saad, Charities Liaison Officer, 25 St James's Street, London SW1A 1HG (tel: 020 7830 7000; fax: 020 7839 2968/9; website: www.economist.com)

Directors: Andrew Rashbash, Chief Executive; Rupert Pennant-Rea, Chair; Rona Fairhead; Lynn Forester de Rothschild; Philip Mengel; Lord Stevenson of Coddenham; David Bell; John Elkann; John Micklethwait; Chris Stibbs; Simon Robertson (women: 2; men: 9)

Year end	31/03/2011
Turnover	£347,000,000
Pre-tax profit	£60,000,000

Nature of business: Principal activities: publication of The Economist and specialist publications including European Voice and, in the United States, CFO, Journal of Commerce, and Roll Call; supply of business information (Economist Intelligence Unit).

Company registration number: 236383

Main locations: London

UK employees: 162

Total employees: 1,371

Charitable donations

UK cash (latest declared):	2011	£129,000
	2009	£132,000
	2008	£151,000
	2007	£125,000
	2006	£88,000
Total UK:	2011	£129,000
Total worldwide:	2011	£579,000
Cash worldwide:	2011	£42,000

Corporate social responsibility

CSR policy: No CSR information available.

Exclusions

The Economist Charitable Trust does not support appeals from non-charities, circular appeals, applications of a chain-letter type, gala charity events, advertising in charity brochures, appeals from individuals, larger national appeals, church restoration appeals, politically sensitive organisations, organisations of a religious or denominational nature, single service (among forces) charities, arts sponsorship (see above) or appeals from ordinary educational establishments (e.g. schools, university building funds). *Special schools or projects for disabled students are the exception to this rule.*

Animal welfare appeals are supported via staff matching only. Fundraising events are only supported by gifts in kind, and these are usually bought from other (e.g. disabled) voluntary organisations. Sport appeals are only supported if for people with disabilities.

Applications

Applications to the trust should be addressed to: Georgina Saad, The Economist Group, 26 Red Lion Square, London WC1R 4HQ.

A simple letter plus latest report and accounts is preferred – a telephone call to clarify specific queries is welcomed (ring: 020 7576 8061). The Economist Charitable Trust is run by a small team of staff volunteers. Applications can be made at any time.

Advice to applicants: The company states that multiple approaches are wasteful and counter-productive, particularly when they are addressed to directors who retired some time ago, indicating use of out-of-date lists. A few applications each year are rejected simply because they are badly presented. Many more fail because their deadlines for events are far too close when they apply. Applicants are also advised that if they are asked for additional information, this is a sign of interest in the project and not the opposite.

Unsigned, circular appeals will not receive a response.

Other information

Information taken from the group's annual report and accounts for 2010/11 states:

During the financial year, the Group made donations to charities amounting to £170,896 (2010: £163,671), and also provided services in kind (free advertising, for example) worth £408,053 (2010: £479,215).

As an international company, we conduct business in many different markets round the world. In the countries in which we operate, we abide by local laws and regulations. We make an active contribution to local charities by charitable giving. We encourage our people to participate in charitable and community activities and we permit them to take time off for this purpose.

The company's main area of non-cash support is gifts in kind. For example, the Economist supports the visual arts by allowing its premises to be used for exhibitions. There are frequent events throughout the year, allowing up and coming artists to display their work to the general public. A wide range of causes are supported via staff matched fundraising.

Cash donations are largely made through The Economist Charitable Trust (Charity Commission no. 293709). The principal activity of the trust is the disbursement of monies received from The Economist Newspaper Ltd to various charities. 50–60% of the trust's donations go to charities in the fields of communication, education, literacy and retraining for individuals and groups who are disadvantaged in some way.

Payroll giving: The company operates the Give As You Earn scheme.

Sponsorship: Arts sponsorship may be undertaken.

EDF Energy plc

Electricity

Correspondent: Community Involvement Team, 40 Grosvenor Place, Victoria, London SW1X 7EN (tel: 020 7242 9050; email: corporate.responsibility@edfenergy.com; website: www.edfenergy.com)

Directors: Simone Rossi; Vincent de Rivaz, Chief Executive (women: 1; men: 1)

Year end		31/12/2010
Turnover		£6,421,100,000
Pre-tax profit		(£342,900,000)

Nature of business: Providers and suppliers of electricity and gas to commercial, residential and industrial customers and the provision of services relating to energy, including purchasing of fuel for power generation and the generation of electricity.

Company registration number: 2366852

Main locations: Sunderland, London

Total employees: 14,858

Membership: BITC

Charitable donations

UK cash (latest declared):	2010	£3,230,900
	2009	£3,386,000
	2008	£2,799,000
	2007	£2,724,824
	2006	£2,370,505
Total UK:	2010	£3,230,900
Total worldwide:	2010	£3,230,900
Cash worldwide:	2010	£3,230,900

Community involvement

The company is interested in causes concerned with education, youth, community development, environment and sport. Support is given in the area the company operates which covers London, the south east and the south west of England, as well as around its customer services centre in Sunderland.

EDF Energy Trust

The company recognises the financial problems some customers face and helps those in need through the EDF Energy Trust (Charity Commission no. 1099446) which was the first energy trust to be established in the UK. Grants are awarded by the trust to vulnerable domestic customers of EDF Energy who are in debt with or struggling to pay their gas/electricity charges, and/or need help with other essential household debts or essential household items.

Receiving donations from EDF Energy since 2003, the trust is independent of its donor company and is governed by the usual board of trustees. However, the administration of the trust is undertaken by Charis Grants Ltd (Charis) on their behalf.

Charis exists to facilitate charitable and corporate giving by designing, developing and managing a range of services in support of vulnerable members of society. Grant management is undertaken by Charis awarding grants to its beneficiary group for utility debt and other essential household bills and costs.

The EDF Trust, through Charis, actively encourages applications from customers for grants and the following is taken from the Charis website:

Current *domestic customers* of any of the following companies can apply for financial help. *Money advice agencies* can apply for special funding by visiting the EDF Energy Trust or British Gas Energy Trust websites. Alternatively contact: admin@charisgrants.com for further information.

British Gas and Scottish Gas: contact the British Gas Energy Trust.

EDF Energy: contact the EDF Energy Trust.

Anglian Water and Hartlepool Water: contact the Anglian Water Assistance Fund.

Veolia Water Central, Veolia Water East and Veolia Water Southeast: contact the Veolia Water Trust.

South East Water's Helping Hand: this new fund makes provisional awards against water and sewerage debts, which will be confirmed if the applicant makes ongoing payments against current bills for six months. Application forms are available on the web site: www. southeastwater.co.uk/helpinghand

To request an application form for any of the above contact Charis Grants on: 01733 421060. Application forms are also available on The Charis 'Publicity' webpage or alternatively visit the appropriate website.

Note: Applicants submitting one application form will be automatically considered for any other funds for which they are eligible.

The EDF Trust also provides grants to organisations. Money is awarded to:

- Increase the availability of independent money/debt advice services in communities to resolve energy debt problems and support applications to the trust
- Provide education to organisations and individuals on awareness and prevention of fuel debt
- Provide appropriate signposting information where appropriate to ensure that customers of EDF Energy are able to access energy efficiency advice and measures

Grants are also available for community-based renewable energy projects through the Green Energy Fund (see 'Commercially-led support' for details).

Charity Partners: Global Action Plan and the MS Society.

Corporate giving

In 2010, the company made total cash donations in the UK of over £3.05 million to the EDF Energy Trust. In turn, the trust made grants to organisations, individuals and families of £2.9 million. Support costs were £423,000. In 2010, the trust received and assessed a total of 6,390 applications. In total, 3,755 awards were made with a value of £2 million. Awards can be broken down as follows: 3,406 to clear gas and electricity debts with a value of £1.9 million and 349 Further Assistance Payments with a value of £116,300. The trust can also, in exceptional circumstances, clear other household debts and purchase essential household items.

In addition to clearing gas and electricity debts, 14 charitable money advice organisations were awarded grants to provide debt and energy advice within their local communities and raise awareness of the help available from the trust. A further 45 charitable organisations were awarded one-off grants for small capital items/activities to assist in the provision of energy debt advice and the submission of online applications to the trust.

Training events were held in May and October for organisations funded by the trust and the trust developed an online application form to increase access and ease the process of applying.

For full information on the trusts activities see its annual report and accounts available from the Charity Commission website.

In kind support

Education: A range of educational programmes supports the company's climate and social commitments:

The Pod – Programme for greener schools

The Pod was launched in September 2008 and was developed to help EDF Energy meet its social commitment of engaging with 2.5 million children by 2012. Since its launch more than 15,800 schools and over 20,500 teachers have registered to the programme which due to popular demand has expanded to cover the topics of water, waste, transport, biodiversity and climate science in addition to its core topic of energy. It has free teaching materials e.g. lesson plans, resource packs, information and games as well as providing a place for children to blog and to share pictures and films of the great work that they have been doing in school. The Pod helps teachers prepare for and run lessons and green projects in schools. Each school gets its own homepage which can be customised with details about the school building and its eco-code, etc. The teaching materials on the Pod were written with the help of teachers and EDF partner, the Eden Project. Activities have been endorsed by Eco-Schools, the largest environmental schools programme in the world, and completing these activities on the Pod will help schools achieve eco-schools bronze, silver and green flag awards as well as earning Pod medals.

The programme aims to make real and measurable difference to the energy efficiency and carbon output of schools and is the sustainability and regeneration strand of the London 2012 education programme 'Get Set'. Visit www.jointhepod.org for more information.

Safety in Education – Power up
Within the Networks business unit, there is a team of education advisors that work with schools across South and East England to help children learn about the dangers of electricity. EDF has pledged to reach at least one million young people with this message by 2012.

The Power Up website supports this programme and provides lesson plans with supporting information for teachers and parents, as well as educational games and interactive quizzes for children. By focusing on electricity and safety, students learn where electricity comes from; how it gets to homes; and, most importantly, how to stay safe. You can visit Powerup at www.edfenergy.com/powerup

Power Academy: bridging the skills gap
To address the challenge of the 'skills gap', where fewer young people are entering careers in engineering, EDF is supporting university students on engineering degree courses through the Power Academy. This is an initiative backed by 17 UK companies and six universities; run by the Institute of Electrical Engineering and Technology to ensure a steady stream of talent for the future.

Students are offered scholarships, help with fees, cash for living expenses, paid holiday placements and long-term career prospects.

Engineering Development Trust
Within the company's nuclear business, young people across the country are encouraged to develop skills in Science, Technology, Engineering and Mathematics ('STEM') by working with schools in the communities that are local to company sites.

EDF works with the Engineering Development Trust on projects such as GO4SET, sending trained STEM 'ambassadors' to mentor teams of Year 9/S2 (Scotland) in exciting projects, with the aim of stimulating interest and highlighting the opportunities for young people in science, technology and engineering. For more information visit: www.go4set.org.uk.

The Industrial Trust
The Industrial Trust is the leading national provider of focused out-of-school and in-company educational experiences for young people. The aim of the Industrial Trust is to give every young person the opportunity to pursue a career that will excite and fulfil them and which will contribute to the UK economy.

EDF has been working with the Trust since 2004. The main focus of the partnership is to create interest among young people in the energy and utility industry sectors.

Employee-led support

The company has a 'Helping Hands' scheme which allows all employees to spend two days performing voluntary work on normal pay if they match these two days of work in their own time. By donating their time and energy, employees are encouraged to build relationships with community groups and charities.

Charity Partners: Employees are encouraged to support the company's national charity partners and it has committed to match the money raised by up to £100,000 for both Global Action Plan and ParalympicsGB.

Global Action Plan
Through the partnership with Global Action Plan, many employees participate in the charity's EcoTeams programme. EcoTeams are groups of people – work colleagues, neighbours, friends – who work together to make positive changes; from minimising the energy they use to cutting down on the stuff they throw away. With the support of a trained team leader, team members agree their own goals and how to achieve them.

ParalympicsGB
Money donated through employee fundraising will enable ParalympicsGB to take a bigger, better prepared team to compete and EDF will be working with the ParalympicsGB team to support and raise awareness of the need for a diverse workforce and what this means.

Payroll giving: Over 900 EDF Energy employees make regular charitable donations through a payroll giving scheme, supporting more than 156 charities.

Commercially-led support

Cause-related marketing: EDF Green Tariff customers pay an additional 0.42 pence per kWh (inc. VAT) on top of standard rates. This amount is matched by the company and placed into a Green Energy Fund which is used to support the installation of renewable generation equipment for community-based and educational projects.

Sponsorship: *Sport* – 'The programme is one of the most comprehensive schools programmes in world rugby. Community coaches work with primary school teachers and children – boys and girls aged eight to ten, and EDF Energy make sure schools have the right equipment to go on and play the game for years to come.'

Corporate social responsibility

CSR committee: There is a Community Involvement Team.

CSR policy: The group's CSR focuses on sustainability. The following is taken from the group's website:

> We're certain that sustainability must be at the heart of any energy company's long-term strategy. We want to lead the way in tackling the biggest environmental and social issues facing our industry and we've clearly defined our agenda through sustainability commitments.

CSR report: A Sustainability Commitments Performance Update is published annually.

Applications

Organisations wishing to apply to the trust should address their letter to: Charis Grants Ltd, EDF Energy Trust, 3rd Floor, Midgate House, Midgate, Peterborough PE1 1TN (Tel: 01733 421021; email: edfet@charisgrants.org.uk).

Further information about the trust is available at: www.edfenergytrust.org.uk.

Electrocomponents plc

Distribution

Correspondent: Corporate Responsibility Dept., International Management Centre, 8050 Oxford Business Park North, Oxford OX4 2HW (tel: 01865 204000; fax: 01865 207400; email: queries@electrocomponents.com; website: www.electrocomponents.com)

Directors: Ian Mason, Group Chief Executive; Peter Johnson, Chair; Simon Brodie, Group Finance Officer; Adrian Auer; Paul Hollingworth; Rupert Soames; Ian Haslegrave (women: 0; men: 7)

Year end	31/03/2011
Turnover	£1,182,200,000
Pre-tax profit	£114,000,000

Nature of business: Founded in 1937, the company is a global distributor of electronics and maintenance products operating in 80 countries.

Company registration number: 647788

Total employees: 5,784

Charitable donations

UK cash (latest declared):	2011	£10,000
	2010	£9,000
	2009	£172,000
Total UK:	2011	£10,000
Total worldwide:	2011	£44,000
Cash worldwide:	2011	£44,000

Corporate social responsibility

CSR committee: The group chief executive is the director responsible for CSR, environment and health and safety across the business.

CSR policy: The following statement is taken from the company's website:

> We believe that the progressive alignment of our core values and strategy with responsible and ethical business policies and practices helps enhance employee engagement and competitiveness, and is also for sustainable growth and success.
>
> Our board takes account of CSR matters in our business operations. Our group chief executive is the director responsible for CSR, environment and health and safety across the business.
>
> Our core values and principles and the standards of behaviour to which every employee is expected to work are set out in a policy manual, 'Our Standards'. We apply these values and principles to dealings with our customers, suppliers and other stakeholders

CSR report: Annual CSR report contained within the annual report and accounts.

Applications

In writing to the correspondent.

Other information

In 2010/11 the company gave £10,000 (2009/10: £9,000) in charitable donations in the UK. Outside the UK donations were £34,000.

Supporting education is a key theme for the UK business. It is a sponsor of the local Business Academy and an active participant in the Young Enterprise Scheme and Enterprise in Action. It also supports a 'Mentor' programme for teenage children in local schools.

In 2010/11, UK based employees raised over £50,000 for various charities, including: the Lakelands Day Care Hospice, Help for Heroes, the Riding School for the Disabled, Warwickshire and Northamptonshire Air Ambulance, Rosie Weaver Campaign and George Eliot School.

The following statement is taken from the company's website:

> We positively encourage our employees to be involved with charitable activities. We support their efforts to raise funds and increase the awareness of personal worthy causes, as well as organising events for national charities.
>
> In the UK our business has been granted patron status of the children's charity, the NSPCC.
>
> The emphasis is on local focus as opposed to a central or corporate policy, consequently there are many smaller activities conducted locally rather than one or two large global initiatives.
>
> Examples of these local initiatives include:
>
> - Our UK business's call centre supporting the UK's Comic Relief charity as part of the donation network across the country
> - Our Allied business in North America actively participating in a number of community initiatives, such as the United Way and the Battered Women's Foundation
> - Our Asia Pacific management team donating to charities in the wake of the 2011 earthquake and tsunami in Japan

We have no valuation for the in kind support given.

Elementis plc

Chemicals and plastics

Correspondent: Company Secretary, 10 Albemarle Street, London W1S 4HH (tel: 020 7408 9300; fax: 020 7493 2194; email: elementis.info@elementis-eu.com; website: www.elementis.com)

Directors: David Dutro, Chief Executive Officer; Robert Beeston, Chair; Brian Taylorson, Finance Director; Ian Brindle; Andrew Christie; Chris Girling; Kevin Matthews (women: 0; men: 7)

Year end	31/12/2010
Turnover	£445,847,820
Pre-tax profit	£61,334,400

Nature of business: A leading global specialty chemicals company.

Company registration number: 3299608

Total employees: 1,200

Charitable donations

UK cash (latest declared):	2010	£8,230
	2009	£7,200
	2008	£2,200
Total UK:	2010	£8,230
Total worldwide:	2010	£35,800
Cash worldwide:	2010	£35,800

Corporate social responsibility

CSR committee: No specific committee details.

CSR policy: The following information is taken from the company's website:

> *Community Values*: It is Elementis policy to actively promote the safety and well-being of the communities in which we operate and to ensure that we conduct our business in a way that is open and transparent to our neighbours.
>
> We seek to engage positively with our local communities. It is our policy to operate as a 'good neighbour' and we encourage and facilitate employees volunteering or fund raising in support of local community organisations.
>
> Elementis takes a decentralised approach to working with the communities in which we operate. The company sets guidelines but does not dictate any specific areas or priority for corporate support, since we are aware that needs and priorities vary from community to community.
>
> This bottom up approach is designed to encourage management and employees at individual sites to focus on local issues and to take full responsibility for implementation of local programmes.

CSR report: Annual CSR report contained within the annual report and accounts.

Applications

In writing to the correspondent.

Other information

The following information is taken from the CSR Report contained within the annual report and accounts for 2010/11:

> During the year the Group donated $56,040 [£35,800] for charitable purposes of which $12,872 [£8,230] was made in the UK. The preference is to support the areas and causes in which our employees participate. Examples of corporate support include: sponsoring an employee who participated in the London Marathon to raise funds for the Alzheimer's Society; matching donations raised by a group of employees from our Livingston plant, who participated in a fundraising walk to Ben Nevis, in order to help fund home care to a young girl who has a serious medical condition; and sponsoring a child from Belarus, organised by the Friends of Chernobyl's Children UK registered charity. As well as the specific examples given, organisations and groups supported last year include the global Red Cross relief effort for the earthquake in Haiti, local youth and sports clubs, schools, arts groups, hospice and other welfare related groups, a drought relief and education initiative, and medical research and health related charities.

Payroll Giving: The company operates a payroll giving programme in the UK.

Eli Lilly and Company Ltd

Pharmaceuticals

Correspondent: Chair of the Grants and Donations Committee, Lilly House, Priestley Road, Basingstoke RG24 9NL (tel: 01256 315000/01256 315000; fax: 01256 315412; website: www.lilly.co.uk)

Directors: R. Sequeira; S. Harper; R. Ascroft; L. Bickle; S. Chatham; P. Troutt; J. Brown; E. Zinn

Year end	31/12/2010
Turnover	£812,113,000
Pre-tax profit	£497,008,000

Nature of business: Eli Lilly and Company Ltd is a research-based corporation that develops, manufactures and markets human medicines, medical instruments, diagnostic products and animal health products. Corporate headquarters are located in Indianapolis, USA.

Company registration number: 284385

Main locations: Basingstoke

Total employees: 1,391

Charitable donations

UK cash (latest declared):	2009	£0
	2007	£314,000
Total worldwide:	2010	£233,013,100
Cash worldwide:	2010	£35,607,900

Corporate social responsibility

CSR committee: Taken from the 2010 CSR report:

> As a global company, Lilly governs corporate responsibility issues through our global corporate affairs leadership. The senior vice president of corporate affairs and communications (SVPCAC) reports directly to the chief executive officer and sits on the corporation's executive committee, which facilitates direct engagement with other senior Lilly executives on corporate responsibility priorities, actions, and outcomes. The SVPCAC also reports regularly to the public policy and compliance committee of the board of directors, providing a link to the corporation's highest governing body. At the operational level, the senior director of corporate responsibility (SDCR) reports directly to the SVPCAC and also sits on the global corporate affairs leadership team.

The UK has a grants and donations committee.

CSR policy: CSR information is taken from the company's website:

> Our long-established core values guide us in all that we do:
>
> - Respect for people, which includes our concern for the interests of all people worldwide who touch, or are touched by, our company: healthcare providers, patients, employees, shareholders, partners, suppliers and communities
> - Integrity that embraces the very highest standards of honesty and ethical behaviour
> - Excellence that is reflected in our continuous search for new ways to improve the performance of our business to become the best at what we do

We were unable to determine the ratio of women to men on the board.

CSR report: An annual CSR report is available from the global website.

Applications

In writing to the correspondent, or by phone to discuss the suitability of the application.

Other information

We have no information regarding the amount given in the UK by the company but the CSR report for 2010 states that worldwide product and other in kind donations were $373 million [£233 million] and cash contributions were $57 million [£35.6 million].

In the UK, each site operates a local grants and donations programme to benefit the local community.

> *Grants and donations*
>
> Lilly is committed to supporting projects which improve patient care and provide educational information to the medical community and which support initiatives in the local community in the area surrounding Lilly sites. The following are examples of grants that the Lilly UK Grants and Donations Committee will consider for funding:
>
> - Charitable donations
> - Healthcare professional education (not travel grant requests for support to attend scientific conferences. These are dealt with separately, please go to Travel Request)
> - Patient advocacy
> - Patient education programmes
> - Local activities in the areas of health, science and children/youth

Visit: www.lilly.co.uk/our-responsibilities/grants-programme for detailed information on the company's grants programme and how to apply.

> *Partnerships with patient organisations*
>
> Lilly UK is committed to partnering with patient advocacy organisations for the benefit of patients and in a way that is true to the ABPI Code of Practice and Lilly's integrity in business policy. The company has agreed with patient advocacy organisations that it will make public the scope of our partnerships with them in the UK in order to increase transparency. This includes stating the amount of funding that Lilly provides.

Matched funding and Payroll giving

Lilly UK has an established Employee Programme that supports employee's fundraising activities by providing a company donation to their beneficiary charity. Lilly also provides company contributions through payroll giving schemes.

EMI Group Ltd

Music

Correspondent: See 'Applications'.
Company address: 27 Wrights Lane, London W8 5SW (tel: 020 7795 7000; fax: 020 7795 7296; website: www.emimusic.com)

Directors: Fraser Duncan; Julie Williamson; Arjan Breure; Ruth Prior; Roger Faxon, Chief Executive; Andre Bourbonnais; Stephen Alexander (women: 2; men: 5)

Year end	31/03/2010
Turnover	£1,651,000,000
Pre-tax profit	(£624,000,000)

Nature of business: EMI covers all aspects of the music industry from music recording and publishing through to manufacture, marketing and distribution.

Company registration number: 229231

Main locations: London

Total employees: 3,380

Charitable donations

UK cash (latest declared):	2010	£162,000
	2008	£400,000
	2007	£200,000
	2006	£300,000
	2005	£300,000
Total UK:	2010	£162,000
Total worldwide:	2010	£488,000
Cash worldwide:	2010	£488,000

Corporate social responsibility

CSR committee: No details found.

CSR policy: The following extract is taken from the company's website:

Community Giving

Within EMI's framework for community giving we often focus on the issues of youth and music as we believe sharing our knowledge and skills can make a meaningful difference to young people. One of our best known initiatives in this area is the EMI Music Sound Foundation (EMI MSF) which was established by EMI in 1997 and has since become the largest single sponsor of specialist performing arts colleges.

CSR report: No report published.

Exclusions

Emi Group will not support political appeals.

The EMI Music Sound Foundation will not support applications from outside the United Kingdom, non-school based community groups, music therapy centres, and so on, applications over £2,500.

Applications

Applications to the EMI Music Foundation should be made using the form downloadable from its site (www.musicsoundfoundation.com). Guidance notes are provided with the form.

Completed applications should be returned to: Janie Orr, Chief Executive, EMI Music Sound Foundation, 27 Wrights Lane, London W8 5SW.

Other information

The company, during 2009/10, made charitable donations of £488,000. Limited details of the beneficiaries were available but at least £162,000 of this appears to have been donated to the EMI Music Sound Foundation, established in 1997 to support music education.

EMI Music Sound Foundation (Charity Commission no: 1104027)

EMI continues to cover virtually all of the foundation's administration costs, which enables the charity to spend close to 100% of its investment income on supporting schools, teachers and students in the UK and Ireland. In 2011, EMI MSF has awarded grants totalling £283,600. Beneficiaries of the foundation's charitable donations include: Springwood High School (£10,000); University of Limerick

(£7,300); and Royal Academy of Music (5,000).

Funds are distributed in the following ways: bursaries for music students in chosen colleges; and individual grants (not exceeding £2,000).

In the UK EMI is also supporting the A&R Music Business Apprenticeship run by BIMM, the country's leading rock 'n' roll college. The BIMM and EMI Apprenticeship is designed to develop abilities in specific A&R practices along with the history of A&R and an understanding and overview of the music industry.

EMI business units around the world are free to make their own community investment decisions so that company resources can be appropriately matched with the local need. In the UK employees are encouraged to participate in volunteer roles with the company's charity partners on the ground, while also making in kind donations – often merchandise – when and where appropriate.

2009/10 annual report and accounts were the latest available at the time of writing (September 2012).

ERM Group Holdings Ltd

Business services

Correspondent: Louise Cameron, ERM Foundation UK, At the company's address (tel: 020 3206 5200; fax: 020 3206 5440; email: louise.cameron@erm.com; website: www.erm.com/foundation)

Directors: John Alexander, Chief Executive; Andrew Silverbeck, Finance Director; John Simonson; Mike Hauck; David McArthur; Chris Busby; James Kelly; Philip Gore-Randall, Chair; Robin Bidwell; Kevin Reynolds (women: 0; men: 10)

Year end	31/03/2011
Turnover	£434,248,000
Pre-tax profit	(£16,120,118)

Nature of business: The principal activities of the group are the provision of environmental, social, risk and health and safety consulting services.

Company registration number: 5593398

Total employees: 3,397

Charitable donations

UK cash (latest declared):	2011	£62,600
	2008	£111,000
	2007	£138,000
Total UK:	2011	£62,600
Total worldwide:	2011	£78,000
Cash worldwide:	2011	£78,000

Corporate social responsibility

CSR policy: No CSR information available

Applications

In writing to the correspondent.

Other information

In 2010/11, the group made donations to charity of £78,000, of which £62,600 went to The ERM Foundation UK.

ERM (Environmental Resources Management) was established in the UK in 1971. In order to help the company and its staff support and contribute to environmental projects at home and in the developing world, the **ERM Foundation** UK (Charity Commission no. 1113415) was established in March 2006. The company state that:

> The ERM Foundation UK supports environmental and community projects near each of our offices ensuring ERMers are able to participate in projects. ERMers are encouraged to nominate charities and projects that they feel would benefit from both our professional expertise and the support the ERM Foundation can bring.

Support for these causes is given through appropriate charitable, educational and scientific means and can include pro bono as well as financial assistance. Projects have ranged from programmes to help inner city teenagers experience life in the national forest to promoting household resource conservation.

Ernst and Young LLP

Financial services

Correspondent: Nicky Major, Head of Corporate Responsibility, 1 More London Place, London SE1 2AF (tel: 020 7951 2000; fax: 020 7951 1345; email: nmajor@uk.ey.com; website: www.ey.com/uk)

Directors: Robin Heath; Steve Varley; Andy Baldwin; Hywel Ball; Lisa Cameron; Ailsdair Mann; Andrew McIntyre; Robert Overend; Robin Tye

Year end	29/06/2012
Turnover	£1,631,000,000
Pre-tax profit	£358,000,000

Nature of business: Financial and professional services provider.

Company registration number: OC300001

Main locations: Reading, Southampton, Liverpool, London, Luton, Manchester, Newcastle, Nottingham, Cambridge, Bristol, Hull, Inverness, Leeds, Glasgow, Edinburgh, Exeter, Birmingham, Belfast, Aberdeen

Membership: Arts & Business, BITC, LBG

Charitable donations

UK cash (latest declared):	2010	£314,100
Total worldwide:	2012	£5,159,000

Corporate social responsibility

CSR committee: No specific details found.

CSR policy: Statement taken from the website:

> At Ernst & Young, we ask ourselves what we can do to make a difference – not just for our clients and for our own business and profession, but for our communities, for the greater good of society everywhere and for the sustainability of our planet. We believe that one of the best ways to build a better business is by building a better world. To do this we:
>
> - Pursue a business strategy that is responsible in both the short and the long-term
> - Take action to increase the well-being of society while adding value to the business
> - Focus on all of the impacts made by the organisation
>
> Responsibility and sustainability are integral to our business strategy, our values and our day-to-day operations. It's how we understand our impact on the world around us and the sum total of our actions. It means considering all of our key stakeholders in relation to our marketplace, our workplace, our environmental impact and our communities

CSR report: No report published but the firm's website has useful information regarding performance targets and achievements.

Exclusions

The firm does not support staff involvement with charitable organisations which are:

- Politically focused or biased groups
- Religious groups

Applications

Unfortunately, Ernst and Young does not respond to or take unsolicited requests for support.

Other information

In 2011/12 Ernst and Young contributed almost £5.16 million to charitable and community causes. Unfortunately, there appears to be no breakdown of how much of this amount was given within the UK and what part of it was made in cash donations.

The following information is taken from the firm's website which includes very detailed and helpful information regarding its community investment programme:

> ***Achieving potential in our communities***
>
> Being a responsible and sustainable business isn't just about being economically successful. It's about thinking carefully about how to invest in

society today to make sure there will be a business context where both we and society can thrive tomorrow. Globally, we support and invest in the grass roots of the world's economies as well as working with some of the biggest and most successful companies. In the UK and Ireland this means investing in the education of tomorrow's workforce and entrepreneurs, and in small businesses, social enterprises and entrepreneurs that can help restore and create economic and social wellbeing.

This approach:

- Addresses real and pressing issues that are important to our business, our people and society
- Fits our business strategy and, therefore, leverages opportunities to use our professional skills to make the greatest difference possible
- Allows us to focus on how we invest our time and resources

Working with community organisations

Working with our community partners ensures we can offer all of our people a diverse range of opportunities throughout our UK locations. It allows us to build long-term sustainable relationships with our partners, enabling us to provide high value support. Significant community partnerships are with:

- The Prince's Trust
- Education Partnerships
- Private Equity Foundation
- Comic Relief
- UnLtd
- Bright Ideas Trust

Key 2011 – 12 community outcomes

- We contributed the cash equivalent of £5.159 million to charitable causes and our communities
- 28% of our people volunteered 43,539 hours
- We provided 8,720 hours of pro bono support
- Our people raised over £1.4 million for charitable causes (including matched funding from Ernst & Young)
- Our community investment programme achieved a top rated 'Platinum' score in BITC's Corporate Responsibility Index
- As the honorary account for Comic Relief we have counted over £5.5 million in public donations
- We raised £297,500 for The Prince's Trust (target: £125,000)
- We launched the Accelerate Network in London, which provides workshops and mentorship to budding and established entrepreneurs to support them to grow their business
- We launched and delivered Smart Futures, which is aimed at helping young people (16–17 years old) from underprivileged backgrounds to unlock their work potential
- As founding partner, we continue to support the development of ThinkForward. ThinkForward focuses on identifying young people (aged 12) at risk of becoming NEET and provides a range of interventions over a number of years to ensure a smooth transition from education to work, training or FE

Sponsorships:

Over the past 17 years we have sponsored some of the most successful art exhibitions ever held in the UK and this has given us an opportunity to contribute to the cultural life of the country. We're extending that commitment to include sporting excellence, through our sponsorship of the Glasgow 2014 Commonwealth Games – one of world's most exciting sports events.

Current sponsorships

- Glasgow 2014 Commonwealth Games – we're proud to be the Official Professional Advisor to the Glasgow 2014 Commonwealth Games

Past sponsorships include:

- CBI Conference 2012: We're proud to have been headline sponsors of the CBI Conference 2012
- British Design 1948–2012: Innovation in the Modern Age, at the V&A, London, from 31 March – 12 August 2012
- Maharaja: The Splendour of India's Royal Courts, at the V&A, London, from 10 October 2009 to 17 January 2010

We continued our long-term involvement with the Tate with sponsorship of the temporary Visitor Centre at Bankside Power Station before the opening of the new Tate Gallery of Modern Art in May 2000. In addition, our support helped to make possible the opening of Lambeth Palace to the public for the first time, together with an arts-based project bringing together local school children, the Tate's education department and Lambeth Palace.

We won the prestigious Association for Business Sponsorship of the Arts (ABSA) award for the Best First Sponsorship and Best Single Project for Picasso and Cezanne respectively.

Business sponsorship of the arts allows works to be shown to a wider audience than would otherwise have the chance to see them. Many of the paintings in the exhibitions we have sponsored have never been shown together. Over the years, our clients and staff, along with the general public, have gained a lot of enjoyment from exhibitions we have supported.

Ernst and Young is a Principal member of Arts and Business.

Esh Group

Building/construction

Correspondent: Andy Radcliffe, Bowburn North Industrial Estate, Bowburn, County Durham DH6 5PF (tel: 01913 774570; fax: 01913 774571; email: enquiries@eshcharitabletrust.org.uk; website: www.eshgroup.co.uk/corporate-responsibility)

Directors: Austin Donohoe, Chair; Brian Manning, Chief Executive; Andy Radcliffe, Finance Director and Company Secretary; John Davies; Freddie Fletcher; Michael Hogan (women: 0; men: 6)

Year end	31/12/2010
Turnover	£169,266,000
Pre-tax profit	£450,000

Nature of business: The principal activities of the group during the year were building, construction, civil engineering and property refurbishment.

Company registration number: 3724890

Total employees: 952

Membership: BITC

Charitable donations

UK cash (latest declared):	2010	£107,000
	2008	£215,000
	2007	£221,177
	2006	£201,660
Total UK:	2010	£107,000
Total worldwide:	2010	£107,000
Cash worldwide:	2010	£107,000

Corporate social responsibility

CSR committee: No details published.

CSR policy: Taken from the group's annual report and accounts:

> ***Investing in the Community***
>
> We are committed to the communities from which we draw our direct workforce and we recognise the impact we have on the local economy and on those communities. As a result, Esh Group and its staff are involved in numerous community projects and many local charities benefit from our support.

CSR report: Published within the annual report and accounts of the group.

Exclusions

No support for political appeals.

Applications

Further details of how to apply to the trust, eligibility criteria and so on, are available at: www.eshcharitabletrust.org.uk.

Other information

The group's cash support for charitable and community organisations are primarily made via the Esh Group Foundation, referred to by the company as the Esh Group Charitable Trust (Charity Commission no. 1112040). The foundation aims mainly to help young people, the disadvantaged, the environment and communities within the North East of England.

During 2010, the foundation's income was only £1,000. Expenditure was £64,250. In January 2013 the foundation's website (www.eshcharitabletrust.co.uk) stated that funding was temporarily suspended and will be reviewed in January 2012 (sic).

Previous beneficiaries include: Sports Recycler Ltd (granted £9,000); Pensbury Street Group (granted £3,500).

Grow with Esh

Now in its fourth year, 'Grow with Esh' has involved 80 schools, thousands of children, their friends, families and communities, in creating some remarkable gardening projects many of which are sustainable. Working with 20 primary schools each year, the scheme helps young people across the region to develop horticultural projects in or near their school grounds by providing a 'seed funding' grant. Each year additional prizes are announced which reward exceptional projects which have engaged pupils and the wider community, provided excellent classroom learning and highlighted issues such as healthy eating and entrepreneurship.

Partnership: Durham County Cricket Club Foundation

Earlier in 2010, Durham County Cricket Club launched the Durham County Cricket Foundation with Esh Charitable Trust as its main community partner. The Foundation aims to inspire and motivate. On an individual basis this involves building self-esteem, raising aspirations and encouraging people to become fitter, healthier and more active. In communities, the Foundation helps to tackle racism, bullying, anti-social behaviour and encourages more to commit to further education.

Sponsorship:

The group sponsors various organisations including: Newcastle Eagles Basketball Team; Esh Winning Football Club.

Esso UK Group Ltd

Oil and gas/fuel

Correspondent: Community Affairs Assistant, UK Community Affairs, ExxonMobil House, Mailpoint 8, Ermyn Way, Leatherhead, Surrey KT22 8UX (tel: 01372 222000; fax: 01372 223222; website: www.exxonmobil.co.uk)

Directors: J. Blowers; K. T. Biddle; B. W. Corson; K. J. Dickens; L. D. DuCharme; J. Selzer

Year end	31/12/2011
Turnover	£22,337,000,000
Pre-tax profit	£1,833,000,000

Nature of business: Principal activities: the exploration for, production, transportation and sale of crude oil, natural gas and natural gas liquids; the refining, distribution and marketing of petroleum products within the UK.

The immediate parent company is Esso Holding Company UK Inc. The ultimate parent company and controlling party is Exxon Mobil Corporation, incorporated in New Jersey, USA.

Company registration number: 1589650

Main locations: Leatherhead, Fawley, Fife, Aberdeen

Total employees: 6,387

Charitable donations

UK cash (latest declared):	2011	£1,000,000
	2009	£600,000
	2008	£600,000
	2007	£500,000
	2006	£400,000
Total UK:	2011	£1,000,000
Total worldwide:	2011	£1,000,000
Cash worldwide:	2011	£1,000,000

Corporate social responsibility

CSR committee: Taken from the 2011 Corporate Citizen Report:

> The Public Issues and Contributions Committee reviews and provides advisory guidance on publicly significant policies, programs, and practices, including corporate citizenship topics. According to PICC chairman, Edward Whitacre Jr: 'the PICC's charter is to advise the corporation on public issues, especially those relating to safety, health, and the environment, and on overall contributions objectives, policies, and programs. This role allows us to assess these activities, monitor performance and action plans to improve performance, and make site visits to ensure adherence to company policies and procedures.

CSR policy: CSR information is taken from the Exxon Mobil Corporation's website but there is very little information on UK giving.

Community Development

As we invest in communities, we pursue long-term projects with strategic goals that are aligned with global and social priorities as well as our business strengths. We seek to have a more meaningful impact by focusing the majority of our spending on significant challenges in the regions where we operate.

We were unable to determine the ratio of women to men on the board.

CSR report: There is an annual Corporate Citizen report available from the group's website.

Exclusions

No response to circular appeals. No grant support for advertising in charity brochures, animal welfare, appeals from individuals, medical research, overseas projects, political appeals, religious appeals, or sport.

Applications

The company responds to all appeals received, but unsolicited appeals are very rarely successful.

Other information

In 2011, Esso UK Ltd made charitable donations of £1 million in support of community projects and initiatives. We do not have any information on specific beneficiary groups.

The 2011 Corporate Citizen Report for the parent company **Exxon Mobil** states that $278 million [£174.8 million], was given in combined corporate and employee giving in the form of cash, goods, and services worldwide. The majority of this seems to have been given outside the UK.

> Employees and retirees donated $44 million [£27.7 million], through ExxonMobil's matching gift, disaster relief, and employee giving programs. This includes more than $3.6 million [£2.3 million], donated by ExxonMobil employees, retirees, dealers, and distributors to support disaster-relief efforts in response to the magnitude 9.0 earthquake that hit Japan in 2011. When combined with corporate donations, ExxonMobil together with our employees and retirees contributed $278 million to community investments worldwide.

Unfortunately we have not been able to separate corporate giving from employee fundraising.

Employee volunteering: Through company-sponsored volunteer programs, more than 23,000 ExxonMobil employees, retirees, and their families donated more than 728,900 volunteer hours to 5,300 charitable organisations in 43 countries in 2011. Of this, 11,000 participants donated more than 168,100 hours to more than 1100 organisations in countries outside the United States.

Euro Packaging Ltd

Manufacturing

Correspondent: Nasir Awan, 20 Brickfield Road, Yardley, Birmingham B25 8HE (tel: 01217 066181; fax: 01217 066514; email: info@eurocharity.org.uk; website: www.europackaging.co.uk)

Directors: D. Mosley; S. Flaherty; P. Windle; J. Green

Year end	31/12/2010
Turnover	£126,472,000
Pre-tax profit	£980,000

Nature of business: Manufacturer and consolidator of packaging products. The company is now wholly owned by the Majid family who acquired its assets, along with Border Convertors Ltd in September 2009.

Company registration number: 1328600

UK employees: 293

Charitable donations

UK cash (latest declared):	2010	£2,800,000
	2009	£122,000
	2008	£0
Total UK:	2010	£2,800,000
Total worldwide:	2010	£2,800,000
Cash worldwide:	2010	£2,800,000

Community involvement

The company makes its charitable donations through the **Euro Charity Trust** (Charity Commission no.1058460). The mission of the trust is: 'To assist the underprivileged to improve their lives, who in turn can assist their families and communities and live a healthy and dignified way of life'. This mission is met in the main by relieving poverty, providing education and forming partnerships to deliver and sustain projects.

Corporate giving

The 2010 annual report and accounts for the Euro Charity Trust state: Donations received from companies within the group headed Euro Packaging UK Ltd were £2.8 million (2009 – £1.3 million).

In 2010 the trust had assets of £1.67 million, an income of £5.67 million and made donations totalling £3.8 million. ECT has moved away from one-off grants to multi-year commitments and focuses increasingly on projects in India and Malawi. However, because the company donation was made to a UK registered charity, we have used this figure as the amount of cash given in the UK.

Corporate social responsibility

CSR committee: No committee.

CSR policy: No details found.

We were unable to determine the ratio of women to men on the board.

CSR report: No published report.

Applications

In writing to the correspondent.

Evans Property Group Ltd

Property

Correspondent: Administrator, Millshaw, Ring Road, Beeston, Leeds LS11 8EG (tel: 01132 711888; fax: 01132 718487; website: www.evanspropertygroup.com)

Directors: Ian Marcus, Managing Director; Paul Millington, Financial Director; Alan Syers; Simon Bottomley; James Pitt (women: 0; men: 5)

Year end	31/03/2011
Pre-tax profit	£989,787

Nature of business: Property investment and development.

Company registration number: 4422612

Charitable donations

UK cash (latest declared):	2009	£120,000

Corporate social responsibility

CSR committee: No committee details published.

CSR policy: Taken from the company's website:

> Evans Property Group corporate responsibility encompasses the way we do business, our people, our clients, our community and charitable support; and the environment around us and sustainability issues.
>
> Evans Property Group is keenly aware of its responsibilities to the communities in which it operates and we strive to ensure that all of our operations and business practices are at all times conducted responsibly and ethically

CSR report: No CSR report available.

Exclusions

No support for local appeals not in areas of company presence, appeals from individuals, animal welfare, overseas projects, and political or religious appeals.

Applications

In writing to the correspondent.

Information available: The company produces a social responsibility report.

Other information

Information taken from the company's website:

> Evans Property Group is proud to support a wide variety of local and national charities including Outward Bound, Variety Club, Breast Cancer Haven and many more.
>
> ARISE (the Alliance to Reward Initiatives and Social Enterprise) was established in 2005 by Land Securities Group plc, Evans Property Group and Munroe K, as a source of funding for groups and organisations seeking support to wholly or part fund community-based initiatives and activities in South Leeds. Further details about the ARISE initiative can be obtained from administrator: Tim Flanagan c/o Polo PR Partnership, Tel. 01423 870134.

An employee volunteering scheme is in operation and the company matches employee fundraising. The company provides support through gifts in kind and joint promotions.

Unfortunately we could find no reference to the actual amount given in charitable donations or contributions by the company.

Sponsorship: The company undertakes arts and good-cause sponsorship. Contact the correspondent for further information.

Everything Everywhere Ltd (formerly T-Mobile (UK) Ltd)

Telecommunications

Correspondent: J Blendis, Company Secretary, Hatfield Business Park, Hatfield AL10 9BW (tel: 01707 315000; fax: 01707 319001; website: explore.ee.co.uk/our-company)

Directors: Olaf Swantee, Chief Executive Officer; Neal Milsom; Timotheus Hottges; Gervais Pellissier; Benoit Scheen; Claudia Nemat (women: 1; men: 5)

Year end	31/12/2011
Turnover	£6,784,000,000
Pre-tax profit	(£113,000,000)

Nature of business: UK mobile communications provider. The group, which operates exclusively in the UK, runs Orange and T-Mobile and was formed in April 2010 when France Telecom S.A. and Deutsche Telekom A.G. combined their respective UK mobile businesses as a joint venture.

Company registration number: 2382161

Brands include: Orange; T-Mobile.

UK employees: 14,604

Total employees: 14,604

Membership: BITC, LBG

Charitable donations

UK cash (latest declared):	2011	£45,700
	2009	£189,000
	2006	£30,000
Total UK:	2011	£45,700
Total worldwide:	2011	£45,700
Cash worldwide:	2011	£45,700

Corporate social responsibility

CSR committee: There is a Responsibility Team. Strategy is signed off by the CEO, and the Head of Responsibility is Chief of Staff, Stephen Harris.

CSR policy: Statement taken from the group's website:

> We developed our strategy through a detailed assessment of our business, our potential risks and our performance in the responsibility space.
>
> Our strategy addresses our most important issues and outlines what we want to stand for.

The group aims to achieve 20% involvement of employees in community programmes, including volunteering and fundraising by 2015.

CSR report: No report published for 2011. The group intends to report on its 2011 CSR targets in 2015.

Applications

In writing to the correspondent.

Other information

In 2011 the company made charitable contributions of £44,700. We have no details of grantees, but previous beneficiaries have included: Disaster Emergency Committee (£45,000); The Trust Partnership (£35,000); The Red Cross (£28,500); The British Heart Foundation, Macmillan Cancer Support and Cancer Research UK (£20,500 each); and RED (£19,000).

Execution Ltd

Financial services

Correspondent: Cheryl Mustapha-Whyte, Correspondent, 10 Paternoster Square, London EC4M 7AL (tel: 020 7456 9191; fax: 020 7375 2007; email: info@executionlimited.com; website: www.espiritosantoib.co.uk)

Directors: Damien Devine; Nick Finegold; Luis Luna Vaz; Angus Macpherson; Charles Ashton; Dipesh Patel; Paulo Araujo; Tara Cemlyn-Jones (women: 1; men: 7)

Year end	31/12/2010
Turnover	£40,746,804
Pre-tax profit	(£4,653,295)

Nature of business: Institutional stock broking firm.

Company registration number: 4058971

Total employees: 127

Charitable donations

UK cash (latest declared):	2010	£850,100
	2009	£13,000,000
	2007	£1,550,000
	2006	£945,000
Total UK:	2010	£850,100
Total worldwide:	2010	£850,100
Cash worldwide:	2010	£850,100

Community involvement

The firm states that:

> Execution Ltd has developed a philanthropic programme to tackle poverty and disadvantage in the UK. To achieve this, in July 2003 the firm formed the **Execution Charitable Trust** (ECT) (Charity Commission no. 1099097). Funding for ECT is generated through Execution Ltd's annual charity trading days through which the gross commissions earned by Execution Ltd are given to ECT.
>
> The responsibility of ECT is to allocate and administer the charitable funds raised by Execution Ltd. This funding has been donated to local community organisations throughout the UK. The allocation of ECT funding to effective charities is undertaken with the advice of New Philanthropy Capital

The criteria by which NPC selects charities are determined by the trust which describes its aim as being 'an entrepreneurial and progressive funder of effective charities that tackle the causes and symptoms of poverty and disadvantage.' The criteria are listed below.

To tackle poverty and disadvantage, the ECT has chosen to support multi-purpose community organisations that:

- Are based in deprived communities in the UK
- Are led by passionate members of the local community
- Provide a wide range of activities and opportunities for people of all ages and backgrounds
- Enhance the social and economic well-being of the community
- Enhance people's self-confidence, skills and employment prospects
- Reduce feelings of loneliness and isolation
- Strengthen citizen engagement in decision-making processes
- Campaign for better government or corporate policies and public services

ECT is willing to award unrestricted grants to the charities it supports. ECT believes that this type of funding gives effective charities the flexibility necessary to achieve their goals.

In addition to providing financial support, ECT can also provide other types of assistance to help strengthen and sustain the work of the charities it funds including consultancy support.

Corporate giving

In 2010 the company's annual Charity Trading Day raised £850,000 which was donated to the Execution Charitable Trust. The trust in turn spent almost £959,000 on charitable activities. Major grant recipients listed in the trust's 2011 accounts were: ARK; Myeloma UK; Peace One Day – Surrey; The Tullochan Trust – Dunbartonshire; Bryncynon Community Revival Strategy Ltd – Wales; Family Action – London; and South Side Family – Bedford.

In kind support

ECT can also provide other types of assistance to help strengthen and sustain the work of the charities it funds. Moreover, ECT undertakes a workshop every year for charities funded to facilitate the exchange of lessons learned.

Corporate social responsibility

CSR committee: No details published.

CSR policy: None published.

CSR report: None published. Charitable donation is detailed in the Execution Trust's charitable accounts.

Applications

Charities are asked not to approach Execution Charitable Trust with funding proposals as the trust has appointed New Philanthropy Capital (NPC) to proactively identify effective organisations on its behalf. However, if you wish to alert NPC to the work of your charity, complete the online form at www.executioncharitabletrust.org to submit basic information. This information will be added to NPC's database.

F&C Asset Management plc

Financial services

Correspondent: David Logan, Chair, CR Committee, Exchange House, Primrose Street, London EC2A 2NY (tel: 020 7628 8000; fax: 020 7628 8188; website: fandc.com/corporate/corporate-responsibility)

Directors: Edward Bramson, Executive Chair; Alain Grisay, Chief Executive; David Logan, Chief Financial Officer; Jeremy Charles; Charlie Porter; Richard Wilson (women: 0; men: 6)

Year end	31/12/2011
Turnover	£267,000,000
Pre-tax profit	£47,000,000

Nature of business: The group's business is asset management.

Company registration number: SC073508

Main locations: London, Edinburgh

Total employees: 952

Membership: BITC

Charitable donations

UK cash (latest declared):	2009	£86,000
	2008	£139,000
	2007	£117,000
	2006	£94,000
	2005	£75,000
Total worldwide:	2011	£274,000
Cash worldwide:	2011	£274,000

Corporate social responsibility

CSR committee: The board is ultimately responsible for CR within the group. Development of F&C's policies on CR and their implementation throughout the group are co-ordinated by the CR Committee, chaired by David Logan.

CSR policy: Statement taken from the company's website:

> F&C has two overarching strategic ambitions:
>
> - To enable our clients to respond effectively to changing dynamics in the world economy through our products and by influencing companies to improve business performance; and
> - To ensure that F&C meets the highest practicable standards of corporate responsibility in our own operations.
>
> The company remains committed to meeting these ambitions in 2012.

The company have identified four areas for their CR commitment: marketplace; environment; workplace and community.

CSR report: An annual report is available from the company's website.

Exclusions

No support for political or religious appeals.

Applications

In writing to the correspondent.

Other information

In 2011, the group made contributions to charity of £274,000 (2010: £211,000).

The following is taken from the company's website:

> F&C is committed to achieving top quartile status amongst UK companies in terms of CR. We do this by:
> - Introducing financial support and wherever practical offering time off work to support employees involved in charitable activities.
> - Target 15% of employees participating in the Give as You Earn Scheme and will match employee GAYE contributions up to a monthly level
> - Target 365 staff days per year to a charitable or community programme.

The company will offer support to charities who meet at least one of the following criteria: Education and Young People; Health and Healthcare; Sustainability and Environment; Community.

The company operates a Give As You Earn (GAYE) scheme.

During 2011, the company matched employee Give As You Earn contributions totalling £22,000 and 90 volunteering days were recorded. In 2012 F&C targeted 365 staff days of community work.

Family Assurance Friendly Society Ltd

Financial services

Correspondent: Community Programme Manager, 16–17 West Street, Brighton, East Sussex BN1 2RL (tel: 01273 725272/ 01273 725272; fax: 01273 736958; website: www.familyinvestments.co.uk)

Directors: Robert Weir, Chair; Norman Riddell; Peter Box; Veronica France; John Reeve, Chief Executive; Rob Edwards; John Adams, Finance Director; Keith Meeres; Miles Bingham; Ian Buckley (women: 1; men: 8)

Year end	31/12/2011
Turnover	£45,441,000
Pre-tax profit	£6,961,000

Nature of business: Provision of financial services (life assurance, savings and protection schemes).

Company registration number: 110067

Main locations: Brighton

Total employees: 393

Charitable donations

UK cash (latest declared):	2011	£19,000
	2009	£13,000
	2007	£19,000
	2005	£7,000
Total UK:	2011	£19,000
Total worldwide:	2011	£19,000
Cash worldwide:	2011	£19,000

Corporate social responsibility

CSR committee: No details found.

CSR policy: Taken from the 2011 annual report:

> *Our work in the community*
>
> At Family our desire to do the right thing for our customers, employees and local community has always been central to our ethos. Our award-winning Community Programme, which has been running for 20 years, has always taken a different approach to working with the local community by the creation of mutually beneficial relationships and activities, where there is not only benefit for the local community, but also a benefit to Family – mainly in the development and motivation of our employees.

CSR report: Contained within the annual report and accounts.

Exclusions

The society does not normally support advertising in charity brochures, appeals from individuals, enterprise/training, heritage, overseas projects, political/ religious appeals, science/technology or social welfare.

Applications

In writing to the correspondent.

Other information

During 2011 the society contributed £19,000 in community support. No figure was calculated as to their total contribution although we know they have given support in kind from the 2011 annual report which states:

> *Working in the Community*
>
> 2011 has been an excellent year with 100 employees giving more than 880 hours in support of the programme. Included in these figures are our core activities, which can be broadly broken down into two categories: education and community challenges.
>
> *Education* has been a major part of our community programme. We support all age groups, from nurseries through to sixth form students. Activities range from Family employees running regular maths clubs at a local primary school, through to running work orientation and interview skills days for a local sixth form college.
>
> Our *community challenges* are an opportunity to get employees out into the community to provide hands-on assistance to local charities and other nonprofit organisations. This is a great way of providing team and relationship building opportunities for employees whilst helping local causes.

Fenner plc

Chemicals and plastics

Correspondent: Corporate Responsibility Team, Hesslewood Country Office Park, Ferriby Road, Hessle, East Yorkshire HU13 0PW (tel: 01482 626500; fax: 01482 626502; website: www.fenner.com)

Directors: Mark Abrahams, Chair; Nicholas Hobson, Chief Executive Officer; Richard Perry, Group Finance Director; David Buttfield; John Sheldrick; Alan Wood; Debra Bradbury, Company Secretary (women: 6; men: 6)

Year end	31/08/2011
Turnover	£718,300,000
Pre-tax profit	£69,600,000

Nature of business: Manufacturer and distributor of conveyor belting and reinforced precision polymer products.

Company registration number: 329377

Total employees: 4,548

Charitable donations

UK cash (latest declared):	2011	£151,000
	2009	£10,000
	2008	£10,000
Total UK:	2011	£151,000
Total worldwide:	2011	£151,000
Cash worldwide:	2011	£151,000

Corporate social responsibility

CSR committee: Taken from the annual report and accounts for 2010/11:

> The board sets the strategy and has overall responsibility for the development and monitoring of the group's policies related to Corporate Responsibility. The task of ensuring that these policies are communicated and applied at a divisional and operating unit level is delegated through the senior managing directors to each operating unit's senior management. All policies and associated management systems are reviewed at least annually and at any time when significant changes in the business, legislation or industry standard demand. Each division is encouraged to reflect good practice within the group.

CSR policy: The CSR report states with regard to Community Involvement:

> Fenner believes that good relations and longterm partnerships with the communities in which it works are fundamental to its success. Fenner always considers the potential social and environmental impacts that its business activities may have on those communities and such considerations are embedded within the group's decision making processes. The group's support for the communities it operates in is driven at a local, rather than corporate level. The approach, adopted across the globe, is to support and enhance employee efforts in their communities through the application of the group's resources.

CSR report: Published within the annual report and accounts.

Applications

In writing to the correspondent.

Other information

During the year, the group donated £151,000 (2010: £84,000) to charitable, social and community-related organisations.

The annual report for 2010/11 states:

> Fenner Dunlop Europe in the UK continued to support Hull Compact, a charitable organisation that helps children develop their academic potential by providing a university bursary to a Hull student on a financial needs basis. It also offers work experience placements for pupils at local schools.
>
> James Dawson in the UK sponsored a local girls' school netball team who embarked on a trip to Kenya and also sponsored the local under-eights football kit.
>
> Employees and operating units have given their time and helped raise funds for a variety of charities and projects over the past year.

Fenwick Ltd

Retail – department and variety stores

Correspondent: Company Secretary, Elswick Court, 39 Northumberland Street, Newcastle upon Tyne NE99 1AR (tel: 01912 325100; fax: 01912 396621; website: www.fenwick.co.uk)

Directors: M. A. Fenwick, Chair; J. J. Fenwick; N. A. H. Fenwick, Group Managing Director; J. F. Fenwick; J. A. Fenwick; H. M. Fenwick; J. F. C. Overtoom

Year end	28/01/2011
Turnover	£433,516,000
Pre-tax profit	£36,701,000

Nature of business: Department stores.

Company registration number: 52411

Main locations: Canterbury, Brent Cross, Leicester, Kingston, Newcastle, London, York, Windsor, Tunbridge Wells

UK employees: 2,391

Total employees: 2,391

Charitable donations

UK cash (latest declared):	2011	£106,000
	2009	£142,700
	2007	£116,000
Total UK:	2011	£106,000
Total worldwide:	2011	£106,000
Cash worldwide:	2011	£106,000

Corporate social responsibility

CSR policy: No CSR information available. We were unable to determine the ratio of women to men on the board.

Exclusions

No support for circular appeals, advertising in charity brochures, political appeals, overseas projects or small purely local appeals not in areas of company presence.

Applications

In writing to the correspondent. Local stores have an independent budget for appeals.

Other information

In 2010/11 the company made charitable donations of £106,000 in support of causes local to its stores. We have no information regarding the particular beneficiary groups.

Fidelity Investment Management Ltd

Financial services

Correspondent: Sian Parry, Fidelity UK Foundation, Oakhill House, 130 Tonbridge Road, Hildenborough, Kent TN11 9DZ (01732 777364; website: www.fidelityukfoundation.org)

Directors: B. R. J. Bateman; S. M. Haslam; C. J. Rimmer

Year end	30/06/2011
Turnover	£461,771,000
Pre-tax profit	£169,898,000

Nature of business: The management and distribution of unit trusts and the management of pension funds.

Company registration number: 2349713

Total employees: 2,002

Charitable donations

UK cash (latest declared):	2011	£10,161,205
	2009	£3,975,000
	2008	£5,942,000
	2007	£11,759,000
	2006	£11,210,000
Total UK:	2011	£10,161,205
Total worldwide:	2011	£10,161,205
Cash worldwide:	2011	£10,161,205

Community involvement

Fidelity Investments' community involvement and charitable giving falls into one of four categories:

- A community sponsorship programme (Fidelity Cares), which supports small fundraising and community events local to its offices. Full criteria are given on the company's website at: www.fidelity.co.uk
- Employee activities, e.g. volunteering, charity days and a matched funding scheme
- Educational initiatives – supporting initiatives linked to the business, such as financial capability and enterprise education
- The Fidelity UK Foundation (Charity Commission no. 327899)

The foundation currently directs the majority of its grants to locations where the company has an office, i.e. Kent, Surrey and London. Support is focused on arts and culture, community development, education, and health.

Charity Partners

> Fidelity Worldwide Investment's approach to Corporate Citizenship has been demonstrated over the years through its active support for the underprivileged and needy. Our vision is to support the local community through our Community Sponsorship Programme around our offices. Our employees are active in raising funds for charity and they can apply for matching grants from the company, thereby significantly increasing the sums raised. Over the years, Fidelity staff have also raised many thousands of pounds for a number of worthy causes through the in-house collections for charities chosen by employees.

A full list of current and former charity partners is given at: www.fidelity.co.uk/investor/about/corporate-citizenship/charity-partners.page

Corporate giving

In 2011, FIL Investment Management Ltd made no cash donations (2010: £12 million) to the Fidelity UK Foundation (Charity Commission no. 327899), but a donation was made by the parent company FHL. We have taken this figure to be the voluntary income of £10 million received by the foundation for that financial year. The company gave £161,000 to a wide variety of charities including supporting a substantial number of donations for local children's charities, schools and hospitals.

Fidelity UK Foundation

The foundation's assets in 2011 stood at £121 million. It had a total income of almost £11.4 million and made grants totalling over £4.4 million. This figure was broken down as follows:

Arts and culture	£1.7 million
Education	£1.2 million
Health	£990,000
Community	£509,000

Beneficiaries included: *Arts and Culture* – The British Museum (£260,000) and Painshill Park Trust Ltd (£100,000); *Health* – The UCL Hospitals Charitable Foundation (£330,000) and Anthony Nolan Trust (£100,000); *Community* – Kent Community Foundation (£200,000); In Kind Direct (£50,000); The Place to Be (£25,000) and Leap Confronting Conflict (£20,000); and *Education* – Teach First (£360,000) and The Dickens House and The Dickens House Fund (£50,000).

In kind support

Education

Fidelity aims to provide younger people with the skills and confidence they need to develop into responsible and individual corporate citizens, and help them make informed choices about their future.

Support is therefore given to initiatives that reflect the company's values and areas of expertise:

- Financial education – projects that reflect its expertise, encouraging greater knowledge and understanding

about longer term financial planning and investments
- Enterprise education – projects that enable young people to have a greater knowledge and understanding about the world of business
- Literacy – initiatives that aim to improve literacy levels. Fidelity works closely with local schools through its reading partner schemes
- Arts and culture – through its outreach programme, Fidelity are committed to providing access for the local community to arts and culture, particularly for young people who might otherwise not have the opportunity

Other areas of interest include projects that enhance young people's understanding of technology and support them in planning their careers and developing future aspirations.

Note: The company does not make cash donations to individual schools, instead preferring to fund projects that benefit several schools or to offer employees' time and skills.

Employee-led support

Fidelity supports and encourages its employees to be active members of their communities. They do this through the schemes listed below.

Grant matching: Through the employee grant-matching programme, funds raised for charitable or not for profit organisations are matched by the company.

Volunteering: Fidelity provides its employees with access to potential volunteering opportunities and some direct funding to cover costs.

Payroll giving: Through Give As You Earn, Fidelity facilitates regular giving by providing this scheme for all employees and covering all administration costs.

Corporate social responsibility

CSR committee: No details found.

CSR policy: We play an active part in making a difference to our communities, especially in the areas where we have offices or our employees live. We provide sponsorship for local charity events that give us an opportunity to help them raise further funds.

The Corporate Citizenship Programme concentrates on three main areas:
- **Employees** – supporting employees to be active members of their communities through direct cash support and provision of volunteering and fundraising opportunities
- **Communities** – supporting the communities local to offices by sponsoring charity fundraising events and providing small grants to local charities
- **Volunteering** – supporting a favourite charity or a Fidelity selected charity by giving up time

We were unable to determine the ratio of women to men on the board.

CSR report: No report published but helpful website section on Corporate Citizenship.

Exclusions

Fidelity (the company) will not support the following:
- Religious, political and animal-support charities
- Individuals
- Individual schools
- Events for exclusive audiences such as black tie events
- High-risk activities, such as parachute jumps, motor racing and abseiling

In addition, it does not usually support sports events, clubs and teams, nor advertise in charity event programmes, diaries or directories.

The **Fidelity Foundation** applies the restrictions listed below.

Grants are not generally made to:
- Start-up, sectarian, or political organisations
- Private schools, and colleges or universities
- Individuals

Grants are not made for:
- Sponsorships or benefit events
- Scholarships
- Corporate memberships
- Advertising and promotional projects
- Exhibitions

Generally grants are not made for running costs, but may be considered on an individual basis; grants will not normally cover the entire cost of a project; and grants will not normally be awarded to an organisation in successive years.

Applications

In writing to the correspondent, including a copy of the foundation's summary form, downloadable from www.fidelityukfoundation.org/apply.html

The foundation currently directs the majority of its grants to locations in which FIL has offices, mainly in Kent, Surrey and London. Applications are considered from other locations on a selective basis. Beneficiaries are mostly UK registered charities operating in the UK, primarily in the fields of arts and culture, community development, education and health.

The foundation seeks to add lasting, measureable value to the recipient charities. With a view to the recipient charities achieving long-term self-sufficiency, the grants are typically for projects such as capital improvements, technology upgrades, organisational development and planning initiatives.

Each grant application is considered on an individual basis against the grantmaking criteria. Site visits are made by foundation staff (and from time to time by trustees) to establish a fuller understanding of the applicant and their needs. Foundation staff will keep in contact with potential beneficiaries to understand trends and changes in need which might inform the trustees in their grantmaking.

Beyond the basic guidelines, foundation staff review an organisation to determine whether collaboration and investment can add value. Among the factors considered are an organisation's financial health, strength of its management team and board and overall strategic plan.

Foundation staff also analyse the size and the scope of an organisation by evaluating its position within the charity sector and assessing the needs of its beneficiaries. This helps to evaluate whether a grant has the potential to measurably improve a charitable organisation's impact.

Although there are no deadlines for submitting grant proposals, final decisions can take between three and six months, with an initial response being given to all applicants within three months.

Fidessa Group plc

Business services

Correspondent: Company Secretary, One Old Jewry, London EC2R 8DN (tel: 020 7105 1000; fax: 020 7105 1001; email: eu.info@fidessa.com; website: www.fidessa.com)

Directors: John Hamer, Chair; Chris Aspinwall, Chief Executive; Andy Malpass, Finance Director; Ron Mackintosh; Philip Hardaker; Elizabeth Lake (women: 1; men: 5)

Year end	31/12/2011
Turnover	£278,300,000
Pre-tax profit	£42,500,000

Nature of business: Fidessa group is a leading supplier of multi-asset trading, portfolio analysis, decision support, compliance, market data and connectivity solutions for firms involved in trading the world's financial markets.

Company registration number: 3234176

Total employees: 1,681

Charitable donations

UK cash (latest declared):	2011	£44,000
	2009	£27,000
	2008	£37,000
Total UK:	2011	£44,000
Total worldwide:	2011	£44,000
Cash worldwide:	2011	£44,000

Corporate social responsibility

CSR committee: No committee.

CSR policy: The following statement is taken from the company's annual report for 2011:

> *Corporate social responsibility*
> Employees are encouraged to follow good principles of social behaviour which are reflected in the group's social and ethics policy. This policy is regularly updated and communicated to staff via the intranet. The board believes the group has a relatively low social impact but nevertheless sees the value that can be added through corporate social responsibility. Participation in activities with local communities where it carries out its business helps to integrate the group with local communities.

CSR report: No report published.

Applications

In writing to the correspondent.

Other information

The total amount of charitable donations made by the group during 2011 was £44,000 (2010: £29,000). Donations were made to various charities but the names of those benefitting have not been published by the company.

The following is taken from the company's 2011 annual report:

> Employees are encouraged to nominate charities they would like to raise funds for and to participate actively in raising money for these charities through internal fundraising events, several of which are typically held each year. In addition, the Group sponsors charity events, such as for example charity runs or bicycle rides, and also gives sponsorship to individual staff who undertake activities for charity.

Filtronic plc

Electronics/computers

Correspondent: HR Manager, Unit 2, Acorn Park, Charlestown, Shipley, West Yorkshire BD17 7SW (tel: 01274 535610; fax: 01274 598263; website: www.filtronic.co.uk)

Directors: Hermant Mardia; Michael Brennan; Howard Ford; Graham Meek; Reginald Gott; Alan Needle (women: 0; men: 6)

Year end	31/05/2011
Turnover	£15,500,000
Pre-tax profit	(£7,000,000)

Nature of business: The principal activity is the design and manufacture of microwave products for wireless telecommunications systems and defence applications.

Company registration number: 2891064

Main locations: Newton Aycliffe, Shipley, East Kilbride, Wolverhampton

Total employees: 159

Charitable donations

UK cash (latest declared):	2011	£450
	2009	£0
	2008	£6,000
	2007	£6,000
	2006	£27,000
Total UK:	2011	£450
Total worldwide:	2011	£450
Cash worldwide:	2011	£450

Corporate social responsibility

CSR committee: There is no CSR committee.

CSR policy: The group's approach to CSR is detailed within the CSR section of the annual report and accounts.

CSR report: There is a CSR section within the annual report and accounts.

Exclusions

The company will not support any political purposes.

Applications

In writing to the correspondent.

Other information

In 2011 the company gave £450 in donations 'to various charities'. In 2010 there were no donations at all and so at least this year's figures are an improvement on that.

Financial Services Authority

Financial services

Correspondent: Susan Oliver, Health, Safety and Corporate Responsibility Advisor, 25 The North Colonnade, Canary Wharf, London E14 5HS (tel: 020 7066 5976; fax: 020 7066 5977; email: susan.oliver@fsa.gov.uk; website: www.fsa.gov.uk)

Directors: Adair Lord Turner, Chair; Margaret Cole; James Strachan; Iain Brown, Company Secretary; Amanda Davidson; Andrew Scott; Sandra Dawson; Paul Tucker (women: 3; men: 5)

Year end	31/03/2011
Turnover	£16,600,000
Pre-tax profit	£30,300,000

Nature of business: Regulator for the financial services industry.

Company registration number: 1920623

Main locations: London, Edinburgh

UK employees: 3,291

Total employees: 3,291

Membership: BITC

Charitable donations

UK cash (latest declared):	2010	£0
	2009	£8,300
	2007	£18,000
	2006	£200,000
	2005	£100,000
Total UK:	2010	£42,000
Total worldwide:	2011	£42,000

Corporate social responsibility

CSR committee: Taken from the CSR report for 2010/11:

> The Corporate Responsibility Action Group (CRAG) is chaired by our CR Advisor, Susan Oliver, and comprises members who hold direct responsibility for key aspects of our social and environmental performance. These are: Central Procurement, Company Secretariat, HR, Community Affairs, Internal Communications, Facilities, the Staff Consultative Committee, Risk and Direct Reports. This group drives the implementation of CR activities and other relevant actions in line with stakeholder expectations. It also ensures that social and environmental issues are integrated into our everyday activities.

CSR policy: The following policy is taken from the authority's website:

> Our Community Affairs programme has been running since 1999, following our move to Canary Wharf. It was formed to meet these business objectives:
> - To help staff from different business units to meet each other
> - To facilitate the integration of staff into a new workplace
> - To support the FSA's learning and development strategy
> - To enable the FSA to develop closer links with the local community in which it operates
>
> The programme gives staff 20 hours per year to engage in volunteering activities. We focus on three issues:
> - Education
> - Employability
> - Regeneration
>
> These issues were identified with the support of local partners, such as the East London Business Alliance.

CSR report: There is an annual CSR report published.

Applications

In writing to the correspondent.

Other information

No charitable cash contributions for the year 2010/11 although we hope this is due to the economic climate and not a permanent situation.

The following extracts are taken from the FSA annual report for 2010/11:

> Following the termination of the lease agreement at 25 Bank Street, the FSA (in partnership with its service providers) made a voluntary gift of furniture which was no longer required by the FSA to a registered charity. This furniture, when purchased as new furniture four years ago, cost the FSA £70,000 and at the time of the donation had an estimated value of £42,000.
>
> ***Community***
> The FSA strives to have a positive impact on society. It encourages, supports and enables staff to play an active role in the local community near its headquarters. Key performance indicators assess the numbers of employees involved in

volunteering and the number of community recipients of the FSA's various projects. Staff are encouraged to view volunteering as a part of their personal development, and, to facilitate that, all applications for volunteering are now put through the FSA's internal learning and development booking system.

Findel plc

Catalogue shopping

Correspondent: Company Secretary, 2 Gregory Street, Hyde, Cheshire SK14 4TH (tel: 01943 864686; fax: 01943 864986)

Directors: D. A. Sugden; R. W. J. Siddle; T. J. Kowalski; P. B. Maudsley; E. F. Tracey; M. L. Hawker; L. C. Powers-Freeling; S. S. McKay (women: 1; men: 7)

Year end	01/04/2011
Turnover	£540,749,000
Pre-tax profit	£3,577,000

Nature of business: Principal activities: the sale of greeting cards, paper products, gifts and educational supplies through mail order catalogues and the provision of e-commerce and mail order services to third parties.

Company registration number: 549034

Brands include: Brands include: Davies Sports; Kleeneze.

Total employees: 3,160

Charitable donations

UK cash (latest declared):	2011	£16,000
	2009	£75,000
	2008	£73,000
	2007	£333,000
	2006	£79,000
Total UK:	2011	£16,000
Total worldwide:	2011	£16,000
Cash worldwide:	2011	£16,000

Corporate social responsibility

CSR committee: There does not appear to be a dedicated CSR committee.

CSR policy: The following statement is taken from the company's website:

> The success of the group is firmly linked to its actions in respect of its Corporate Social Responsibilities. As well as remaining fully compliant with all relevant legislation, the group is determined to continually evaluate and enhance its performance in this area.

CSR report: There is a CSR report contained within the annual report and accounts but with little information on community support. There are also pages on the website.

Exclusions

The company does not normally support appeals from individuals, animal welfare, the arts, enterprise/training, environment/heritage, science/technology, social welfare, sport, political or religious appeals or overseas projects.

Applications

In writing to the correspondent.

Other information

In 2010/11, the company made cash donations of £16,000. We have no details of the beneficiaries.

The following is taken from the company's website:

> Community involvement – Both the company and its employees work to support local communities, predominantly in the areas where we have group facilities. Our Home Shopping and Educational Supplies products are also much in demand for donating to less privileged schools, good causes and establishments, both in the UK and abroad.

First plc

Transport and communications

Correspondent: The Charity and Sponsorships Committee, 395 King Street, Aberdeen AB24 5RP (tel: 01224 650100; fax: 01224 650140; email: csapplications@firstgroup.com; website: www.firstgroup.com)

Directors: Martin Gilbert, Chair; Tim O'Toole, Chief Executive; Nick Chevis; David Begg; Colin Hood; John Sievwright; Martyn Williams (women: 0; men: 7)

Year end	31/03/2012
Turnover	£6,678,700,000
Pre-tax profit	£279,900,000

Nature of business: The provision of passenger transport services primarily through provision of local bus and coach services and passenger railways. The company operates in the UK and North America.

Company registration number: SC157176

Main locations: London, Aberdeen

Total employees: 124,705

Membership: BITC, LBG

Charitable donations

UK cash (latest declared):	2012	£254,000
	2011	£260,000
	2009	£107,000
	2008	£120,000
	2007	£100,000
Total UK:	2012	£254,000
Total worldwide:	2012	£1,542,400
Cash worldwide:	2012	£509,400

Corporate social responsibility

CSR committee: See 'Applications'.

CSR policy: Community: 'We are committed to making a real difference to the communities in which we operate by supporting a wide range of charitable causes and community organisations.'

CSR report: Published annually.

Exclusions

Initiatives and causes that First plc does not fund include:

- Political parties or bodies
- Promotion of religious beliefs
- Third-party giving organisations
- Projects funded from local or central government
- The arts (unless the donation provides direct support to one of our criteria)
- Animal welfare
- Research projects that are not directly associated with the needs of the business

Applications

Charity and sponsorship

First plc has a charity and sponsorship committee which comprises 12 staff members who are geographically spread across the UK to encompass all operating areas. The committee considers and decides upon requests for funding and gifts in kind based on its charitable criteria, which includes:

- Young people
- Health
- The environment

Applications which fall outside these charitable criteria will not be considered for funding. **External applications must be supported in the form of a letter from a FirstGroup employee.** This applies to external individuals, charities and community organisations. External applications which fail to provide a supporting letter will not be considered for funding. Also note the supporting letter must be submitted at the same time as the application.

However, if you meet the necessary funding criteria and would like to apply for charity or sponsorship support from First plc, download and complete the application form available from the company's website.

When completed the form should be emailed to: cscapplications@firstgroup.com Alternatively, you may post-it to the correspondent.

Local partnerships

If you would like First plc to consider a proposal for your area, contact:

Annalise Tyrie, Group Community Relations Manager, FirstGroup plc, 131–151 Great Titchfield Street, London W1W 5BB. (Tel: 020 3008 7504; Email: annalise.tyrie@firstgroup.com).

Other information

During 2011/12, the group made various cash donations to UK charities totalling approximately £254,000 (2010/11: £260,000). Based on the London Benchmarking Group model, £1.65 million (2010/11: £2.45 million) was contributed to the communities in which the group operates. We have no separate UK figure for community contributions and have deducted the amount given from commercially led activities as is our usual practice. Total worldwide contributions are therefore £1.54 million – that is, the total of charitable gifts and community investments, see below for details.

The group's website states:

> Our community strategy focuses on three key areas:
> - Community Partnerships:
> - Charitable Giving; and
> - Employee Volunteering
>
> In each of these areas we will be seeking to improve co-ordination and strengthen current activity. In particular, we will be seeking ways in which our community activity can provide learning and development opportunities by actively engaging our employees.
>
> *Community Partnerships*
>
> Through the community strategy we will be seeking to build on these partnerships. This will include looking at ways to add value and opportunities to extend initiatives across regions or to other companies with the potential to develop nationwide programmes where appropriate.
>
> *Charitable Giving*
>
> A wide range of charitable giving takes place across First, through both the local operating companies and at group level. This includes monetary donations but also extensive donations in kind such as the provision of buses free of charge for charitable events and initiatives. Through the community strategy we will be seeking to strengthen our management of charitable giving. A starting point has been the establishment of a national charity partnership with **Save the Children** which we will support through activity at both operating company and Group level. This will bring our employees together in a common cause and provide a greater focus to our charitable giving activities.
>
> Through the Group national charity we will set fundraising targets and support the annual fund raising initiative.
>
> This will be supported by ongoing activity at local level in support of a range of organisations which we will seek to monitor and co-ordinate more systematically through the community strategy
>
> *Employee Volunteering*
>
> Through the community strategy we will be seeking to extend the opportunities available to our employees to participate in volunteering schemes. We will seek to achieve this by building further on our relationship with Business in the Community. Previously through our relationship with Business in the Community we established an ongoing programme of community challenges as part of our supervisory training NVQ. This programme has been highly successful and has clearly demonstrated the positive benefits to our employees from volunteering. We will also be seeking to strengthen the link between our volunteering activity and our environmental conservation and biodiversity programme to strengthen the impacts of these initiatives

Sponsorship: *Sport* – First plc have been a major supporter of the Paul Lawrie Junior Golf Development Programme for several years.

> The programme involves training teachers at participating primary schools to give lessons during PE periods for pupils from P4 upwards, using plastic clubs and sponge balls. It proceeds with support for coaching and the organisation of flag days and local tournaments throughout primary and secondary schools until the young golfer is ready to become a fully-fledged member of a golf club.

Employees' volunteering/charitable activities receive financial support from the company, which also matches their fundraising and giving.

First has provided the Archie branded bus which was key in promoting the Archie Foundation's message and brand.

Besides supporting its Charity of the Year (Save the Children), through group partnerships help was also given to Outward Bound and UCAN. In addition, by emailing season's greetings to contacts and posting a seasonal message on its website, the savings made enabled about £12,000 to be set aside to support six staff nominated charities to the sum of £2,000 each. The charities were:

- Save the Children
- Girl Guiding Association – South Lanarkshire
- Excellent Development
- Royal National Lifeboat Institution (RNLI)
- Royal Society for the Prevention of Cruelty to Animals (RSPCA)
- Chavey Down Project (Part of Quarriers)

The following information is taken from the 'Data' webpage on the company's website:

> For the first time this year we have used participant feedback and the LBG model to measure the benefits of our community investment delivered through our long-term partnerships. We can now record the tangible impacts of our contributions.
>
> Community contributions £1.65 million
>
> LBG breakdown:
> - Charitable gifts: £509,409
> - Community investments: £1 million
> - Commercial initiatives: £106,000
> - Number of staff involved in voluntary projects during company time: 1,172
> - Total amount of Payroll Giving contributions: £23,000
> - Total amount raised by staff for charitable causes: £53,549
> - Number of beneficiaries experiencing a direct positive impact on their quality of life as a direct result of our support: 558
> - Total number of direct beneficiaries: 2,935
> - Amount of cash donated through our Charity and Sponsorship Committee: £72,576 supporting 106 charitable organisations

Charity of the Year 2010/11: Save the Children

Ford Motor Company Ltd

Motors and accessories

Correspondent: Andy Taylor, Director, Ford Britain Trust, Room 1/447, Eagle Way, Brentwood, Essex CM13 3BW (tel: 01277 252551; fax: 01277 251439; website: www.ford.co.uk/fbtrust)

Directors: Stephen Butler; Kimberly Caslano; Anthony Earley; Edsel Ford; William Clay Ford; Richard Gephardt; James Hance; William Helman; Irvine Hockaday, Jr; Jon Huntsman; Richard Manooglan; Ellen Marram; Alan Mulally; Homer Neal; Gerald Shaheen; John Thornton (women: 2; men: 14)

Year end	31/12/2011
Turnover	£88,000,000,000
Pre-tax profit	£5,600,000,000

Nature of business: The Ford Motor Company Ltd is a wholly owned subsidiary of the Ford Motor Company of Dearborn, Michigan, USA.

Principal activity: the manufacture of motor cars and commercial vehicles, component manufacture and associated leasing and hire purchase activities.

The company and its subsidiaries operate principally in the UK and the Republic of Ireland. It is part of an integrated vehicle manufacturing group of Ford companies throughout Europe.

Company registration number: 235446

Total employees: 164,000

Membership: BITC

Charitable donations

UK cash (latest declared):	2011	£167,000
	2009	£313,000
	2008	£317,000
	2006	£828,000
Total UK:	2011	£167,000

Corporate social responsibility

CSR committee: There was no evidence of a separate CSR Committee.

CSR policy: This information was obtained from the company's website:

> We define corporate social responsibility as being willing to help others, being environmentally conscious and socially tolerant. With those guiding principles in mind, we've designed a special programme to promote tolerance and equal opportunities, and actively support social and environmental protection

programmes. Through our Ford Britain Trust, we provide grants to fund local education and other not-for-profit projects.

CSR report: There was no evidence of a separate CSR report.

Exclusions

Ford Britain Trust: National charities are rarely supported, except for specific local projects in Ford areas. Applications in respect of sponsorship, individuals, research, overseas projects, travel, religious or political projects are not eligible. Applications for core funding and/or salaries, revenue expenses, and major building projects are rarely considered. Generally: no support for circulars, fundraising events, brochure advertising, individuals, purely denominational appeals, political appeals, local appeals not in areas of company presence or overseas projects.

Applications

Applications to the Ford Britain Trust are by application form available on their website – www.ford.co.uk/fbtrust

The trustees meet in July and November each year. Applications are considered in order of receipt and it may take several months for an application to be considered.

Although each application is carefully considered, the number of applications the trust receives far outstrips its resources and regretfully, therefore, the number of applicants it is able to help is limited.

Information available: Guidelines for applicants are given on the company's website at www.ford.co.uk/ie/fobtrust.

Other information

In 2011, the company made donations of £167,000 (2009: £313,000). The company donates money through the Ford Britain Trust (Charity Commission no: 269410). Major beneficiaries were: BEN, Lord's Taverners, Walk the Walk and Wooden Spoon.

> We pay special attention to projects focusing on education, environment, children, the disabled, youth activities and projects that provide clear benefits to the local communities close to our UK locations. The Ford Britain Trust particularly encourages applications from Ford employees, but is open to all, provided that the qualifying organisations meet our selection criteria.

Small Grant (up to £250) beneficiaries for 2011 included: Cancer Research UK; Castle Point Sports Club for the Disabled; Little Havens Children's Hospice; Ilford East District Scout Council; Dunton Community Association and Tigers JFC.

Forth Ports plc

Marine

Correspondent: Company Secretary, 1 Prince of Wales Dock, Edinburgh EH6 7DX (tel: 01315 558700; fax: 01315 537462; website: www.forthports.co.uk)

Directors: D. H. Richardson, Chair; C. G. Hammon; W. W. Murray; S. R. Paterson; E. G. F. Brown; D. D. S. Robertson; J. L. Tuckey; M. L. Clayton

Year end	31/12/2010
Turnover	£181,900,000
Pre-tax profit	£56,300,000

Nature of business: Forth Ports plc (Forth Ports) provides handling and logistic-related services. It operates seven ports – Dundee on the River Tay, Tilbury on the River Thames and five ports on the Firth of Forth – Leith, Grangemouth, Methil, Burntisland and Rosyth.

Company registration number: SC134741

Main locations: Tilbury, Leith, Dundee

UK employees: 977

Total employees: 138

Charitable donations

UK cash (latest declared):	2010	£21,000
	2009	£20,000
Total UK:	2010	£21,000
Total worldwide:	2010	£21,000
Cash worldwide:	2010	£21,000

Corporate social responsibility

CSR committee: There would seem to be no dedicated CSR Committee.

CSR policy: Taken from the company's website: 'We aim to provide excellent service to our customers, to provide a safe working environment for our employees and to create sustainable communities through long-term investment.'

Unable to determine the ratio of women to men on the board.

CSR report: A CSR report is contained within the annual report and accounts.

Applications

In writing to the correspondent.

Other information

In 2010 Forth Ports plc gave £21,000 in cash charitable donations. The following is taken from the company's website:

> Our involvement varies from donations, through activities to raise funds to the provision of services, time and support. The Company donated land to The Merchant Navy Memorial Trust for the erection of a monument in memory of merchant seamen who have lost their lives in conflict. The memorial was unveiled by HRH The Princess Royal in November. One of the figures in the 6 Times multi-part sculpture work by Antony Gormley sits on one of our piers beside Ocean Terminal. There have been fund raising events such as the two teams from the Marine Department in Scotland that went white water rafting on the River Tummel – raising £3,000 for Seafarers UK. Ocean Terminal supports a number of charities by allowing them space in the Centre to promote the work they do and collect vital funds.

Freshfields Bruuckhaus Deringer LLP

Legal

Correspondent: Simon Hall, Global CR and Community Investment Partner, 65 Fleet Street, London EC4Y 1HS (tel: 020 7936 4000; fax: 020 7832 7001; website: www.freshfields.com)

Directors: Konstantin Mettenheimer, Joint Senior Partner; William Lawes, Senior Partner; Ted Burke, Managing Partner; Stephen Eilers, Executive Partner (women: 0; men: 4)

Year end	30/04/2011
Turnover	£1,115,700,000
Pre-tax profit	£416,900,000

Nature of business: International law firm.

Company registration number: GE000156

Main locations: London

Total employees: 4,409

Membership: BITC, LBG

Charitable donations

UK cash (latest declared):	2008	£540,000
	2007	£490,447
	2006	£481,994
	2005	£245,949
Total worldwide:	2011	£8,790,000
Cash worldwide:	2011	£1,139,000

Corporate social responsibility

CSR committee: CR and Community Investment.

CSR policy: The following statement is taken from the firm's 2010/11 CSR report:

> *Supporting our communities*
> We feel a responsibility to make a positive impact on the communities in which we operate and beyond not only because it's the right thing to do but also because it's good for business. Our aim is to maximize the value we add to our communities through our pro bono and community investment programmes tailored to the interest and expertise of everyone working for us.

CSR report: Online CSR report published annually.

Applications

In writing to the correspondent.

Other information

During 2010/11 the firm made charitable contributions of over £8.79 million worldwide. Cash donations amounted to £1.14 million (figures include management costs). The total hours contributed to pro bono and volunteering was nearly 50,000.

The company's contributions are broken down into:

- Cash contributions to community organisations
- Time spent by their volunteers giving pro bono legal advice (providing professional legal services to people and organisations in need at no cost)
- Time spent by volunteers on community activities (including mentoring programmes, reading initiatives, work experience placements, charity trustees and team challenges); and
- In kind giving including providing design and prints services and office space to community partners at no cost

Most of Freshfields' worldwide community investment and pro bono legal advice contribution is focused on four themes: improving access to justice for individuals and acting for not-for-profit organisations pro bono; reducing homelessness and tackling wider social exclusion; promoting human rights; and raising the levels of achievement and aspirations of young people from disadvantaged backgrounds, and improving their skills.

Beneficiaries include: Shelter, Crisis, StreetShine and REDRESS.

Sponsorship: London 2012 Olympic and Paralympic Games.

Friends Life FPL Ltd

Insurance

Correspondent: Corporate Responsibility Manager, Pixham End, Dorking, Surrey RH4 1QA (tel: 0870 608 3678; fax: 01306 654991; website: www.friendslife.com)

Directors: E. B. Bourke; D. E. Hynam

Year end	31/12/2011
Turnover	£808,335,000
Pre-tax profit	£716,695,000

Nature of business: The company's ultimate parent and controlling company is Resolution Ltd. The Group's principal activities comprise manufacturing and administering life and pensions products in the UK and related international markets. This encompasses the UK protection market, UK group pensions and vesting annuity market and international savings and investments, pensions and protection markets.

Company registration number: 4113107

Main locations: Dorking, Exeter, Salisbury, Manchester

Membership: BITC, LBG

Charitable donations

UK cash (latest declared):	2009	£180,000
	2008	£55,000
	2007	£83,000
Total worldwide:	2011	£1,480,000

Corporate social responsibility

CSR committee: Information taken from the CSR report for 2012:

> Resolution Ltd has created a Corporate Responsibility Committee to oversee CR at the highest level. The committee leads the development of our CR vision, policy and strategy, and has three core members: the senior Independent Director of Resolution Operations, the company secretary and the CR director (for both Resolution Ltd and Friends Life Group).
>
> The chief executive of Friends Life is responsible for implementing the CR strategy through his senior executive team, supported by the Friends Life Corporate Responsibility team.

CSR policy: Taken from the company's website:

> Friends Life believes that building and maintaining relationships of trust in the local community is vital to the sustainable future of its business. Our community investment programme is centred around our employees, enabling them to support the communities in which they live and work. We also have a number of strategic partnerships, such as Global Action Plan and Macmillan Cancer Support, that link to other aspects of our corporate responsibility programme.

We were unable to determine the ratio of women to men on the board.

CSR report: Published annually and available from the website.

Exclusions

Note the company does not support:

- Individuals conducting their own fundraising for charity
- Political or religious organisations, including local churches
- Overseas trips and travel expenses
- Applications for specialist school status or school building projects

Applications

Enquiries regarding corporate support at a local level should be addressed to the appropriate person at the relevant site.

The contact for the foundation is: The Secretary to the Friends Provident Foundation at the above address. Alternatively you can send an email to: foundation.enquiroes@friendsprovident.-co.uk

Full details about how to apply to the foundation are available at: www.friendsprovident.com/foundation/.

Other information

In 2011, Friends Life Group calculates that its total worldwide community investment was £1.48 million. Unfortunately we have no breakdown of where in the world specific amounts were invested nor any distinction between cash donations and in kind contributions.

The following is taken from the CSR report for 2012:

> In 2011, the Friends Life Group invested more than £1.48 million in community investment activities. We revamped our Community Programme, moving away from smaller local donations towards more strategic charity partnerships. We now focus our energy and resources on large-scale charity partnerships that make a significant difference to people's lives. Selected through a company-wide vote, we support causes that are relevant to our business and to which we can offer meaningful, long-term strategic involvement.
>
> In 2011, Macmillan Cancer Support was chosen by Friends Life employees as our first official charity partner and the decision has been taken to continue the partnership for 2012.
>
> For the first time this year, we introduced match funding from Friends Life through our 'Give as you earn' scheme. Rather than matching the more ad hoc employee fundraising activities we have supported in the past, we now match employee contributions through this formal scheme. A key part of our community programme, the scheme supports taxfree giving and Friends Life matches employee donations by up to £20 per month or £240 in a full year. Employees are able to choose which charity they wish to support. During this first year, 409 employees (7.9%) signed up and donated nearly £139,000 to charity. Including match funding, our total donations through the scheme amounted to over £198,000. We aim to increase the number of employees involved in 2012.
>
> We moved our focus this year away from literacy mentoring towards encouraging employees to volunteer as School Governors through a poster and intranet recruitment campaign. School governance is one of the most important volunteering roles in education. Governors support school staff and enable them to provide the best possible standards of education. At any one time there will be around 40,000 vacancies for School Governors across the country.
>
> In 2011, over 1,000 Friends Life employees based around the world took part in fundraising, volunteering or giving to support social and environmental causes, investing more than 6,000 hours of company paid time and taking part in 35 community challenges with our partner, Community Service Volunteers (CSV). 18 employees regularly undertook school governor duties and 6 continue to be engaged in literacy mentoring.

Friends Provident Foundation (Charity Commission no. 1087053)

The foundation was established in 2001 for general charitable purposes. Its main focus is to provide improved access to appropriate financial services to those who are currently excluded.

Further information on the foundation's giving can be found in the DSC publication: *The Guide to Major Trusts Volume 2.*

Fujitsu Services Holdings plc

Information technology

Correspondent: Juliet Silvester, Head of Corporate Social Responsibility, Observatory House, Windsor Road, Slough, Berkshire SL1 2EY (tel: 0870 234 5555; email: askfujitsu@uk.fujitsu.com; website: www.fujitsu.com/uk)

Directors: Duncan Tait; Roger Gilbert; Stephen Clayton; Ella Bennett; David Roberts; Akihisa Kamata (women: 1; men: 5)

Year end	31/03/2011
Turnover	£1,630,200,000
Pre-tax profit	(£36,400,000)

Nature of business: Holding company of an IT services group.

Company registration number: 142200

Main locations: Slough

UK employees: 10,700

Total employees: 170,000

Membership: BITC

Charitable donations

UK cash (latest declared):	2011	£149,500
	2009	£126,000
	2008	£107,000
	2007	£85,000
	2006	£178,000
Total UK:	2011	£149,500

Corporate social responsibility

CSR committee: Fujitsu has an established CSR Board that shapes how their CSR programme should be delivered throughout the UK and Ireland. The board meets regularly to discuss the way forward for the various areas that are incorporated within Fujitsu UK and Ireland CSR programme. Its members include members of the executive team as well as key stakeholders, senior members of the CSR team and an external advisor.

CSR policy: This information was obtained from the company's website:

> As an organisation, we are committed, both locally and globally, to the continued development of the societies in which we operate. Our approach to CSR spans five complementary areas: Environment, Social Action, Inclusion, Wellbeing and Safety.
>
> We seek to work collaboratively with strategic charity partners to deliver mutually beneficial programmes that have a positive impact on society. We continue to fund regional Impact on Society groups, which support charitable causes within local communities.

CSR report: Fujitsu has published a CSR Principles report, available from its website.

Applications

In writing to the correspondent.

Other information

In 2010/11 the company made donations in the UK totalling £149,500 (2009: £126,000). No further details on beneficiaries were available.

Fujitsu UK and Ireland puts responsible business practice at the heart of our organisation. Working with community and charitable causes forms a major part of our commitment to have a positive impact on society and contribute to a sustainable, prosperous future.

As an IT services company, Fujitsu is committed to leveraging ICT to confront the growing number of issues that impact our communities. We use our core strengths and technologies to make positive differences to communities and society at large. This is demonstrated through a range of activities including our key charity partner relationship with Shelter, the 'Shaping Tomorrow With Fujitsu' scheme that provides ICT into local communities to help improve young people's skills and chances for future employment, and our support of BITC Connectors scheme for which Fujitsu has delivered a specifically designed social networking platform called BITC Connect hosted in the Cloud.

Fujitsu also has a commitment to supporting young people in the UK. Fujitsu is a patron of the Prince's Trust and has a long standing and established partnership with the charity, supporting the trust in various ways from volunteering to fundraising projects. More recently Fujitsu has also supported Children in Need; fundraising annually for the charity.

Through regionally managed Impact on Society groups Fujitsu also contributes to local communities by supporting charitable and not-for-profit organisations that our employees are involved with or that are close to their hearts. The groups provide both financial and non-financial support to causes.

Future plc

Media

Correspondent: Human Resources Dept, 30 Monmouth Street, Bath BA1 2BW (tel: 01225 442244; fax: 01225 822836; email: graham.harding@futurenet.com; website: www.futureplc.com)

Directors: Peter Allen, Chair; Mark Wood, Chief Executive; Graham Harding; Manjit Wolstenholme; Seb Bishop; Mark Whiteling; Mark Millar (women: 1; men: 6)

Year end	30/09/2011
Turnover	£141,700,000
Pre-tax profit	(£19,300,000)

Nature of business: Future plc produces magazines, websites, events and a range of multi-media services for commercial partners.

Company registration number: 3757874

Total employees: 1,182

Charitable donations

UK cash (latest declared):	2011	£37,000
	2009	£55,000
	2008	£24,000
	2007	£49,000
Total UK:	2011	£37,000
Total worldwide:	2011	£37,000
Cash worldwide:	2011	£37,000

Corporate social responsibility

CSR committee: There was no evidence of a separate CSR Committee.

CSR policy: Future actively supports the communities in which it operates through charitable donations and by encouraging people to get involved in community initiatives.

CSR report: There was no evidence of a separate CSR report; however, two pages were dedicated to CSR within the company's annual report.

Exclusions

No donations to individuals, political or religious organisations.

Applications

In writing to the correspondent.

Other information

The total amount of charitable donations made by the group in 2010/11 was £37,000 (2009: 55,000). Future's charitable donation policy provides for a matched contribution scheme. Employees raise money for their chosen charity and Future matches this amount, subject to a reasonable limit and to qualification under the rules of the scheme. During the year £13,000 was paid under the charitable match scheme (2009: £16,000).

As well as the charity matching scheme, Future makes local charitable donations in the cities where it has offices. In the UK, Future continued its partnership with Bath based charitable foundation, Quartet, who makes donations to local charities on the company's behalf.

G4S plc

Transport and communications

Correspondent: Group Communications Executive, The Manor, Manor Royal, Crawley, West Sussex RH10 9UN (tel: 020 8770 7000; fax: 020 8772 2000; email: investor@g4s.com; website: www.g4s.com)

Directors: John Connolly, Chair; Mark Seligman, Deputy Chair; Nick Buckles, Chief Executive; Trevor Dighton; Grahame Gibson; Lord Condon; Adam Crozier; Mark Elliott; Winnie Kin Wah Fok; Bo Lerenius; Paul Spence; Clare Spottiswoode; Tim Weller (women: 2; men: 11)

Year end	31/12/2010
Turnover	£7,397,000,000
Pre-tax profit	£435,000,000

Nature of business: G4S plc provides security services, cash services and justice services internationally.

Company registration number: 4992207

Main locations: Sutton

Total employees: 650,000

Membership: BITC

Charitable donations

UK cash (latest declared):	2010	£63,000
	2009	£311,000
	2008	£313,000
	2007	£311,000
	2006	£94,000
Total UK:	2010	£63,000
Total worldwide:	2010	£375,000
Cash worldwide:	2010	£375,000

Corporate social responsibility

CSR committee: The CSR Committee was established in 2010. The committee has ensured that CSR issues remain a core part of the group's strategy and has enabled the Board to have greater visibility of the key CSR issues affecting the group.

CSR policy: G4S seeks to make a positive impact on local communities. The group encourages investment in community projects, whether directly through cash or through staff volunteering, and fundraising. The majority of the group's investment focuses on the health, education, welfare and support of children and young people.

CSR report: A CSR report was available from the company's website.

Exclusions

The group will not give political contributions. It is not known if there are any other exclusions.

Applications

Applications to the group communications executive.

Other information

Charitable contributions made by the group during the year amounted to £375,000 (2009: £311,000). Charitable contributions made by the group in the UK, amounted to £63,000. The purposes of which such contributions were made and the amount donated to each purpose were: child welfare: £20,000; health and medical: £22,000; local communities: £16,000; NGOs: £2,000; poverty relief: £1,000; and sports: £2,000.

The group remains committed to the support of the charities, the community, job creation and training.

G4S runs a sponsorship matching programme where payments totalling £40,000 of employee fundraising, including £12,000 paid to children's groups and clubs and £19,500 to hospitals, hospices and healthcare.

G4S also supported the delivery of 13 evolution programmes in conjunction with HMP Wold Prison. The programme aims to deter young people involved in anti-social or criminal behaviour from their current lifestyle. The five week programme aims to give young people a platform to achieve while empowering them to do so. Over the last two years, the programme has engaged with over 100 young people of whom 92 have re-entered school or education, employment or training on completion of the programme.

The Game Group plc

Computer software

Correspondent: Corporate Responsibility Committee, Unity House, Telford Road, Basingstoke, Hampshire RG21 6YJ (tel: 01256 784000; website: www.game.co.uk)

Directors: Ian Shepherd, Chief Executive; Peter Lewis, Chair; Ben White, Group Finance Director; Christopher Bell; Dana Dunne; Ishbel Macpherson; David Mansfield (women: 1; men: 6)

Year end	31/01/2011
Turnover	£1,625,000,000
Pre-tax profit	£23,100,000

Nature of business: The group is Europe's leading specialist pc and video games retailer trading via retail outlets and ecommerce sites. The parent company, The GAME Group plc, is an investment holding company.

Company registration number: 875835

Total employees: 10,218

Charitable donations

UK cash (latest declared):	2011	£173,000
	2010	£160,000
Total UK:	2011	£173,000
Total worldwide:	2011	£173,000
Cash worldwide:	2011	£173,000

Corporate social responsibility

CSR committee: The group's CR Committee is dedicated and fully-empowered to improve the way we incorporate our CR principles and practices into our everyday business. Each member represents key stakeholders. 'GAME Group's CR Committee reports to the board via group finance director, Ben White. Quarterly reports to the board help to ensure that CR remains integral to the way we do business.'

CSR policy: Information taken from the group's website:

> At GAME Group, we recognise that we have a responsibility to understand and endeavour to meet the needs of everyone involved in our business.
>
> We count among our stakeholders the Group's suppliers, customers, employees, bankers and lenders, shareholders and the people in the communities in which we live and operate. Throughout our work with all these parties, we endeavour to have a positive impact in UK society and on the environment whilst striving to achieve our commercial objectives.

CSR report: The website has a separate CSR section. Information also published within the annual report and accounts.

Applications

In writing to the correspondent.

Other information

During 2010/11 the group made charitable donations of £173,000 including £168,000 to the group's UK charity partner, Children's Hospices UK and £5,000 to Children's Sunshine Hospices in Ireland. The group also donated computer games and software to charities and community groups across the UK. We have no figures for the value/cost of in kind giving by the company.

Activities within the community have included:

- In Kenilworth, a team of 20 contributed to the John Waterhouse Project, a residential centre that provides short breaks for young people with severe learning or physical disabilities. The GAME volunteers redecorated bedrooms and bathrooms, and donated a range of consoles and software
- A team of 20 staff transforming a run down bungalow into a multipurpose warm and welcoming Family Centre. Game also donated games and consoles. The West Midlands based centre managed by national children's

charity, Action for Children, provides counselling and recreational facilities to vulnerable young people

- Supporting the May Place Hostel which works with vulnerable local homeless people and provides accommodation, emotional support, help with returning to education or work and also a drop-in service for practical items such as blankets. The company's support will include help with refurbishment projects and skill development initiatives through staff volunteering and organising donations of essential items like clothing and cups
- Game is also a founding member of the Basingstoke Community Foundation and will be working with the foundation to provide donations to grass roots community projects based locally to Basingstoke

Charity of the Year: Children's Hospices UK

GAP (UK) Ltd

Clothing manufacture, retail – clothing and footwear

Correspondent: Company Secretary, Castle Mound Way, Rugby, Warwickshire CV23 0WA (tel: 01788 818300; website: www.gapinc.com)

Directors: Glenn Murphy, Chair and Chief Executive; Sabrina Simmons; Adrian Bellamy; Domenico de Sole; Robert Fisher; William Fisher; Isabella Goren; Bob Martin; Jorge Montoya; Mayo Shattuck III; Katherine Tsang; Kneeland Youngblood (women: 3; men: 9)

Year end	28/01/2012

Nature of business: Clothing supplier and manufacturer.

Company registration number: 3918195

Main locations: London, Coventry, Rugby

Total employees: 132000

Charitable donations

UK cash (latest declared):	2011	£110,000
	2009	£110,000
	2008	£110,000
	2007	£108,000
	2005	£575,100
Total UK:	2011	£110,000
Total worldwide:	2012	£110,000
Cash worldwide:	2012	£110,000

Applications

The company's website gives the following information:

> Gap Foundation does not accept unsolicited proposals or requests for sponsorships. Our strategy is to seek out and build strong partnerships with a limited number of national, regional and local community organisations in line with our target causes, underserved youth in the developed world and women in the developing world. We sponsor a select, limited number of events in our headquarters' communities where we have high employee participation.
>
> Gap Foundation typically does not make merchandise donations by request. We do, however, partner with Gifts In Kind International (GIKI) to process all merchandise donations that become available. Interested nonprofit organisations may sign up with GIKI to potentially receive donations from Gap Inc. and all of GIKI's other clients.

Other information

UK giving is through the **Gap Foundation** and average around £110,000. Previous beneficiaries have included: Prince's Trust (£45,000); NCH Children's Charity (£25,000); Centrepoint (£25,000); Coventry and Warwickshire YMCA (£8,000); and Bradby Club – Rugby (£6,000).

The foundation also matches funds raised by employees for qualifying charitable organisations as well as providing in kind support, it is therefore possible that the total amount distributed to charitable organisations by Gap in the UK is higher than that quoted.

Whilst the company provides much information on its grantmaking activities in the USA, little is available on its work in the UK except for a list of grant beneficiaries. However, as all funding appears to come via the Gap Foundation, it can be assumed that the main areas of work supported here are as in the USA. These areas are: community investment; empowering youth; advancing women; and global investment. The geographical focus of its UK support is Warwickshire and the surrounding areas. There also some support for charities based in London, where the company has an office.

GE Healthcare

Healthcare

Correspondent: PA to the Company Secretary, Pollard's Wood, Nightingale Lane, Chalfont St Giles, Buckinghamshire HP8 4SP (tel: 01494 545200; email: gefoundation@ge.com; website: www3.gehealthcare.co.uk)

Directors: P. Grenouillet; M. Murphy; K. O'Neill; R. A. Cornell Jr (women: 0; men: 5)

Year end	31/12/2011
Turnover	£183,000,000
Pre-tax profit	(£38,000,000)

Nature of business: Principal activities are the development, manufacture and sale of specialised products for research-based biotechnology supply and for the diagnosis and treatment of disease. Major UK locations are Slough, Amersham, Bedford and Hatfield.

Company registration number: 1002610

Main locations: Amersham, Aberdeen, Cardiff, Chalfont St Giles, Little Chalfont, Gloucester

UK employees: 1,408

Total employees: 301,000

Charitable donations

UK cash (latest declared):	2011	£57,000
	2009	£63,000
	2008	£90,000
	2006	£23,000
	2005	£35,000
Total UK:	2011	£57,000

Corporate social responsibility

CSR committee: There was no evidence of a separate CSR Committee.

CSR policy: This information was obtained from the company's website:

> While GE is dedicated to solving some of the world's biggest challenges, the company recognises that such work cannot be accomplished through large-scale commercial means alone. From education and community development to health and the environment, the GE family also invests time and energy in addressing these issues on a community level.
>
> Philanthropic efforts, including donations made by GE Foundation and GE employees and retirees, are one important way to support a range of such activities. Volunteerism is another, as the GE Volunteers network facilitates the donation of time and talent to develop and foster communities. In broader endeavors, GE addresses disaster relief in an equally focused manner, combining volunteerism and product donation to help communities in need.

CSR Committee: There was no evidence of a CSR Committee.

CSR Report: There was no evidence of a CSR Report for 2011.

CSR report: There was no evidence of a separate CSR report.

Applications

For local, small scale UK support, apply in writing to the correspondent.

GE Foundation

The GE Foundation does not encourage unsolicited proposals. Through ongoing research in the field, the GE Foundation develops targeted initiatives and invites specific institutions and organisations to apply within those initiatives. Its capacity to review unsolicited proposals is extremely limited.

Other information

The company donated £57,000 to UK charities in 2011.

Previous research identified that the company, primarily through its philanthropic arm the GE Foundation (US charity), develops and supports various programmes in its communities. This can be through either financial support or employee volunteering.

Examples of previous organisations in the UK supported by the foundation include:

Sandfields School – GE is supporting a Neath Port Talbot Council project at Sandfields School, Port Talbot which aims to get at risk youngsters back into school.

Bristol Education Action Zone – GE is supporting an innovative project to develop the skills and confidence of children in four of Bristol's inner city schools.

SETNET – GE is a major supporter of SETNET – the Science, Engineering, Technology and Mathematics Network.

General Motors UK Ltd

Motors and accessories

Correspondent: Cherie Denton, Charity Department, Griffin House, Osborne Road, Luton LU1 3YT (tel: 01582 721122; email: cherie.denton@vauxhall.co.uk; website: www.vauxhall.co.uk)

Year end	31/12/2011
Turnover	£4,184,500,000
Pre-tax profit	(£78,200,000)

Nature of business: The company manufactures, markets and branded services passenger cars and light vans.

Company registration number: 135767

Main locations: Ellesmere Port, Luton

UK employees: 3,016

Charitable donations

UK cash (latest declared):	2011	£278,000
	2009	£101,000
	2007	£231,000
	2006	£218,000
Total UK:	2011	£278,000

Corporate social responsibility

CSR committee: No mention of a CSR committee.

CSR policy: Unable to determine the ratio of women to men on the board.

CSR report: The company has a CSR report available from its website.

Exclusions

No grants for circular appeals, advertising in charity brochures, appeals from individuals, fundraising events, medical research, overseas projects, political appeals, religious appeals, science/technology, or local appeals not in areas of company presence. The company does not give raffle prizes or vehicle donations.

Other information

In 2011, General Motors UK donated a total of £278,000 to charities in the UK. The company regularly supports BEN – the automotive industry charity, Help for Heroes, WOMAC (Women on the Move Against Cancer) and local charities around the company's sites. Employees regularly raise funds for Macmillan Cancer Support, The Vauxhall Employee Charity Fund and organise the London to Brighton Bike Ride which benefits the British Heart Foundation, raising £160,000 over the past five years.

Genting UK plc

Gaming

Correspondent: Company Secretary, Circus Casino Star City, Watson Road, Birmingham B7 55A (website: www.gentingcasinos.co.uk)

Directors: Tan Sri Lim Kok Thay; P. M. Brooks

Year end	31/12/2011
Turnover	£227,400,000
Pre-tax profit	£26,100,000

Nature of business: The main activity of the company is that of casino operators.

Company registration number: 1519749

Main locations: Liverpool

Total employees: 3,428

Charitable donations

UK cash (latest declared):	2011	£205,500
	2009	£122,000
	2008	£90,000
	2007	£277,000
	2006	£300,000
Total UK:	2011	£205,500
Total worldwide:	2011	£205,500
Cash worldwide:	2011	£205,500

Corporate social responsibility

CSR committee: There was no evidence of a separate CSR Committee.

CSR policy: The company has attempted to remain an integral part of the local communities in which it operates through supporting local initiatives and causes.

Unable to determine the ratio of women to men on the board.

CSR report: There was no evidence of a separate CSR report.

Exclusions

No support for appeals from individuals; the arts; environment/heritage; fundraising events; overseas projects; political appeals; religious appeals; or science/technology.

Applications

In writing to the correspondent.

Other information

The company made a donation of £178,000 in the year to the Gambling, Education and Treatment Foundation (2010: £166,500). £27,500 was paid to local charities (2010: £35,500).

In the UK, the group is committed to contribute to public education on responsible gaming, research into the prevention and treatment of problem gambling and the identification and treatment of problem gamblers. Its voluntary contribution to the Gambling Research, Education and Treatment Foundation (now operating as 'The GREaT Foundation') supports these commitments by helping to fund research works by UK universities, education initiatives and registered charities. Genting UK is accredited by GamCare for high standards of socially responsible practices. Apart from charitable donations to GREaT, Genting UK also supports fundraising for national charities and various charitable events.

Geopost-UK Ltd

Logistics

Correspondent: The Company Secretary, Roebuck Lane, Smethwick, West Midlands B66 1BY (tel: 01215 002500; email: marketing.dept@geopostuk.com; website: www.geopostuk.com)

Directors: D. McDonald; D. L. Adams; C. Sheils; P. M. Chavanne

Year end	02/01/2011
Turnover	£282,203,000
Pre-tax profit	£35,040,000

Nature of business: Part of La Poste (The French Post-Office), the company is engaged in the provision of transport related services, which include the collection and delivery of parcels, distribution and logistics management.

Company registration number: 732993

Total employees: 4,197

Charitable donations

UK cash (latest declared):	2008	£101,000
	2007	£72,500
	2006	£57,600
	2005	£67,000
Total worldwide:	2011	£93,500
Cash worldwide:	2011	£93,500

Corporate social responsibility

CSR committee: No information available.

CSR policy: None published.

Ratio of women to men on board not known.

CSR report: None published.

Applications

In writing to the correspondent.

Other information

In 2010 the company made charitable donations of £93,500. We have no details of the beneficiaries.

GKN plc

Engineering

Correspondent: Simon Hardaker, Corporate Social Responsibility Dept., PO Box 55, Ipsley House, Ipsley Church Lane, Redditch, Worcestershire B98 0TL (tel: 01527 517715; fax: 01527 517700; email: cr@gkn.com; website: www.gkn.com)

Directors: Roy Brown, Chair; Nigel Stein, Chief Executive; Marcus Bryson; William Seeger; John Sheldrick; Michael Turner; Shonaid Jemmett-Page; Richard Parry-Jones; Andrew Reynolds Smith; Tufan Erginbilgic (women: 1; men: 9)

Year end	31/12/2011
Turnover	£5,746,000,000
Pre-tax profit	£351,000,000

Nature of business: An international company involved in the automotive and aerospace industries.

Company registration number: 4191106

Main locations: Birmingham, London, Weston super Mare, West Bromwich, Sutton Coalfield, Walsall, Telford, Portsmouth, Redditch, Yeovil, Edgware, Eastleigh, Chesterfield, Lichfield, Leek, Isle of Wight

UK employees: 5800

Total employees: 36925

Charitable donations

UK cash (latest declared):	2011	£34,300
	2009	£191,400
	2007	£166,800
	2005	£236,900
Total UK:	2011	£34,300
Total worldwide:	2011	£747,800
Cash worldwide:	2011	£747,800

Corporate social responsibility

CSR committee: There was no evidence of a separate CSR Committee.

> **CSR policy:** The company not only strives to support projects and activities in local areas, it also seeks to minimise any negative impact on local communities. The company supports charities and community organisations, as well as providing opportunities for employees to volunteer and fundraise.
>
> We support charities and community organisations, as well as provide opportunities for employees to volunteer and fundraise, in a variety of ways, including:
>
> - Providing paid time off for employees involved in community activities
> - Fundraising for local causes
> - Operating a charitable giving scheme
> - Providing volunteer support for community projects
> - Building links with local education establishments
> - Offering work experience placements

CSR report: There was no evidence of a separate CSR report.

Exclusions

No support for political appeals.

Applications

Appeals, in writing, should be addressed to the Company Secretary.

Other information

Charitable donations made by group companies around the world totalled £747,800, of which £34,340 was to UK registered charities. In addition, the GKN Millennium Trust (Charity Commission no. 1051266), a UK charitable trust established in 1995, donated a total of £137,000 to the Engineering Development Trust and Young Enterprise in 2011. The trust also provided funding totalling £108,000 for the winning projects of the group's 2009 Evolve competition, designed to foster long-term sustainable links in local educational establishments.

Gladedale Group Holdings Ltd

Building/construction, property

Correspondent: David Scott, Group Corporate Responsibility Director, Ashley House, Ashley Road, Epsom, Surrey KT18 5AZ (tel: 01372 846000; website: www.gladedale.com)

Directors: Alan Bowkett, Chair; Neil Fitzsimmons, Group Chief Executive; Colin Lewis, Group Chief Operating Officer; Liz Catchpole, Group Finance Director; Joanne Massey, Group Company Secretary and General Counsel (women: 2; men: 3)

Year end	31/12/2010
Turnover	£341,344,000
Pre-tax profit	(£86,141,000)

Nature of business: Gladedale is a privately owned, investment holding company for a group of businesses principally engaged in housebuilding and property development.

Company registration number: 6986776

Total employees: 834

Charitable donations

UK cash (latest declared):	2010	£29,000
	2009	£0
	2008	£0
	2006	£100,000
	2005	£24,000
Total UK:	2010	£29,000
Total worldwide:	2010	£29,000
Cash worldwide:	2010	£29,000

Corporate social responsibility

CSR committee: No details of a committee available, although there is a CSR Director.

CSR policy: Information taken from the company's website:

> As a leading residential and commercial developer, we recognise that it is our duty to act as a responsible business and a good neighbour in the communities in which we work.
>
> We endeavour to conduct our business with integrity and openness, delivering optimum economic value and ensuring the observance of environmental and community issues.
>
> We embrace our responsibilities towards our employees, investors, customers, clients, stakeholders and the wider communities in which we work.

CSR report: No report published.

Applications

In writing to the correspondent.

Other information

During 2010 the company made charitable donations of £29,000 to community projects.

The following information was taken from the company's website:

> Gladedale Group are proud sponsors of the Robert Burns World Federation Schools Festivals 2011. This sponsorship facilitates the involvement of 160,000 Scottish/adopted Scottish school pupils into a variety of competitions aimed at promoting Scottish Music, Poetry, Language and Dialect and the Arts predominantly but not exclusively through the works of Robert Burns Scotland's national Bard. This is Gladedale's fourth year as Corporate Sponsors and David Scott, Gladedale's Corporate Responsibility Director states ' seldom does sponsorship of a single organisation bring with it an opportunity to influence a whole generation, yet our ongoing Partnership with the Burns Federation has gone some way to future-proofing Scotland's cultural heritage.

GlaxoSmithKline plc

Healthcare, pharmaceuticals

Correspondent: Katie Pinnock, UK Corporate Contributions, GSK House, 980 Great West Road, Brentford, Middlesex TW6 9GS (tel: 020 8047 5000/020 8047 5000; email: katie.apinnock@gsk.com; website: www.gsk.com)

Directors: Sir Christopher Gent, Chair; Sir Andrew Witty, Chief Executive; Sir Crispin Davis; Dr Stephanie Burns; Prof. Sir Roy Anderson; Sir Deryck Maughan; Dr Daniel Podolsky; Tom de Swann; Dr Moncef Siaoui; Stacey Cartwright; Simon Dingemans; Lynn Elsenhans; Judy Lewent; Jing Ulrich; Sir Robert Wilson (women: 5; men: 10)

Year end	31/12/2011
Turnover	£27,400,000,000
Pre-tax profit	£7,698,000,000

Nature of business: The group's principal activities are the creation and discovery, development, manufacture and marketing of pharmaceutical products, including vaccines, over-the-counter medicines and health-related consumer products.

Company registration number: 1047315

Subsidiaries include: Wellcome Ltd, Stafford-Miller Ltd, The Wellcome Foundation Ltd

Brands include: Aquafresh, Beechams, Horlicks, Lucozade, Macleans, Niquitan, Ribena

Main locations: Stevenage, Hertfordshire, Stockley Park, Middlesex, Ulverston, Cumbria, Ware, Hertfordshire, Montrose, Tayside, Greenford, Middlesex, Dartford, Kent, Barnard Castle, County Durham, Beckenham, Kent

Total employees: 97,389

Membership: Arts & Business, BITC, LBG

Charitable donations

UK cash (latest declared):	2011	£1,400,000
	2009	£5,600,000
	2007	£6,000,000
	2005	£4,000,000
	2004	£4,000,000
Total UK:	2011	£1,400,000
Total worldwide:	2011	£204,000,000
Cash worldwide:	2011	£57,000,000

Community involvement

The company's community investment 'aims to improve health and increase access to medicines and healthcare services'.

'We are transparent about our charitable giving with data being published in our Annual Report and Corporate Responsibility Report in March each year. We are further increasing transparency by publishing details of our individual charitable grants over £10,000 ($15,000).' Details of GSK's grants awarded can be found on the company's website: www.gsk.com/responsibility/our-people-and-communities/charitable-grants

Corporate giving

In 2011 in the UK, GlaxoSmithKline made donations of £10,000 or more directly to charitable organisations totalling £1.4 million, helping over 50 organisations in health, medical research, science education, the arts and the environment. The company also makes smaller grants, although these are as yet unreported, so the figure we quote here is likely to be higher. No figure was available this year for in kind support in the UK. Potential applicants should note that the company's website states that: 'GlaxoSmithKline supports community initiatives in both the developed and the developing world. Identifying the right projects is an important responsibility, and that's why the company takes a strategic, proactive approach and **does not generally support unsolicited requests for funding.'**

Beneficiaries of grants in the UK during 2011 included: British Lung Foundation (£165,000); Access Sport (£120,000); Understanding Animal Research (£100,000); Epilepsy Action (£76,000); Prostate Action (£50,000); Heritage Care Ltd (£36,000); Medical Research Council (£25,000); Dartford Grammar School (£20,000); Skin Care Campaign (£17,000); YMCA Dartford (£15,000); and Arrow Riding Centre for the Disabled (£10,000).

Healthcare

The annual GlaxoSmithKline IMPACT Awards are run in partnership with the King's Fund to recognise and promote excellence in community healthcare. To be eligible for a GSK IMPACT Award, organisations must have an annual income of less than £1.5 million, and must have been operating in the UK for at least three years:

- Up to ten winners receive £30,000 plus the overall winner will receive an extra £10,000
- Up to ten runners-up receive £3,000
- Organisations do not need to present a new project, and winners decide how to spend the award money

For further details, visit the King's Fund's website: www.kingsfund.org.uk.

The company works with charities, including Crisis, WellChild, Scope and Help for Heroes, to help to deliver healthcare-related programmes and services.

Education

In the UK, GSK supports a range of programmes, activities and resources designed to make science more relevant to young people and support professional development for science teachers.

Examples include *Project Enthuse* – half of secondary school science teachers in the UK have had no subject training within the past five years. Project Enthuse was launched in 2008 to improve continuing professional development (CPD) of science teachers and to provide them with the latest techniques to rekindle interest in science.

Teachers, assistants and technicians can apply for an Enthuse Award to help them study at the National Science Learning Centre at the University of York. The award will cover course fees, replacement teachers to cover their absence, travel and accommodations for 2,200 teachers each year. The schools will also receive a small amount of money to help implement ideas back in the classroom.

£30 million pounds has been generated to fund the project, coming from the UK government, Wellcome Trust and industry organisations including GlaxoSmithKline, which donated £1 million.

'Over 4,000 science teachers from around the UK have taken the opportunity to use the amazing facilities and world class teaching at the National Science Learning Centre. The £30 million funding being provided by project Enthuse will allow many state schools throughout the UK to engage with resources they wouldn't normally have access to.'

The Environment

GSK currently supports the Royal Botanical Gardens at Kew with the following projects: The Millennium Seed Bank Partnership; and the Bursaries for Schools education programme.

Global community investment was £204 million in 2011. Product donations globally were £126 million. GSK values its product donations at cost (average cost of goods) rather than wholesale acquisition cost, as it believes it is a more accurate reflection of the true cost to the company.

In kind support

The company values its worldwide in kind support at £4 million, including the cost of employees' salaries while they are volunteering.

Employee-led support

The company supports employees in the UK that work with their local communities through the PULSE programme. The following information is taken from the company's CSR report:

> PULSE gives employees the chance to join a non-profit or non-governmental organisation (NGO) for a three or six-month, full-time placement. It enables employees with leadership potential to develop professional skills in new and challenging environments while helping partner organisations to develop and implement strategic plans, improve their processes and operations, and enhance their communications and marketing.

Payroll giving: The company operates the Give As You Earn scheme

Commercially-led support

In 2011 the company reported a worldwide figure of £9 million worth of cash donations to support the arts and culture. The company's website invites individuals, most likely from a healthcare, educational or environmental background, to contact its UK office with enquiries about potential sponsorship requests.

The company is a Principal member of Arts and Business.

Corporate social responsibility

CSR committee: There is a Corporate Responsibility Committee, which consists of members of the board of directors, namely Sir Christopher Gent,

Dr Stephanie Burns, Lynn Elsenhans and Dr Daniel Podolsky. The committee meets three times per year, or more frequently if necessary.

The Corporate Responsibility Committee provides a Board-level forum for the review of external issues that could potentially impact upon our business and reputation. The committee is also responsible for overseeing our worldwide charitable donations and community support. The committee consists of Independent Non-Executive Directors and the Chair.

CSR policy: The following is taken from GSK's CR Principles document, available from the company's website:

Our Corporate Responsibility Principles

Our CR Principles are underpinned by our values and identify our key responsibility issues.

They provide guidance on the standards to which GSK is committed and the CR Committee review our progress on meeting these commitments. Each of our Principles maps to one of the four key themes which we see as the most important for responsible and sustainable business growth.

Health for all

- Access to medicines: we will continue to research and develop medicines to treat diseases of the developing world. We will find sustainable ways to improve access to medicines for disadvantaged people, and will seek partnerships to support this activity
- Research and innovation: in undertaking our research and in innovating we may explore and apply new technologies and will constructively engage stakeholders on any concerns that may arise. We will ensure that our products are subject to rigorous scientific evaluation and testing for safety, effectiveness and quality. We will comply with or exceed all regulations and legal standards applicable to the research and development of our products

Our people and communities

- Employment practices: we will treat our employees with respect and dignity, encourage diversity and ensure fair treatment through all phases of employment. We will provide a safe and healthy working environment, support employees to perform to their full potential and take responsibility for the performance and reputation of the business
- Community investment: we will make a positive contribution to the communities in which we operate, and will invest in health and education programmes and partnerships that aim to bring sustainable improvements to underserved people in the developed and developing world

Our behaviour

- Standards of ethical conduct: we expect employees to meet high ethical standards in all aspects of our business by conducting our activities with honesty and integrity, adhering to our CR principles, and complying with applicable laws and regulations
- Products and customers: we will promote our products in line with high ethical, medical and scientific standards and will comply with all applicable laws and regulations
- Leadership and advocacy: we will establish our own challenging standards in corporate responsibility, appropriate to the complexities and specific needs of our business, building on external guidelines and experience. We will share best practice and seek to influence others, while remaining competitive in order to sustain our business
- Human rights: we are committed to upholding the UN Universal Declaration of Human Rights, the OECD guidelines for Multi-national Enterprises and the core labour standards set out by the International Labour organisation. We expect the same standards of our suppliers, contractors and business partners working on GSK's behalf
- Engagement with stakeholders: we want to understand the concerns of those with an interest in corporate responsibility issues. We will engage with a range of stakeholders and will communicate openly about how we are addressing CR issues, in ways that aim to meet the needs of different groups while allowing us to pursue legitimate business goals

Our planet

- Caring for the environment: we will operate in an environmentally responsible manner through systematic management of our environmental impacts, measurement of our performance and setting challenging performance targets. We will improve the efficiency of all our activities to minimise material and energy use and waste generated. We aim to find opportunities to use renewable materials and to recycle our waste

CSR report: A detailed CSR report is available on the company's website.

Exclusions

No support for appeals from individuals. For example, the company is unable to provide support for individual students or Raleigh International applicants, but does support organisations such as the British Medical Association Charity Trust, which in turn provides financial assistance to medical students. No support for fundraising events, advertising in charity brochures, purely denominational (religious) appeals, political appeals or sport.

Applications

Appeals for charitable support on a national scale should be addressed in writing to the correspondent.

Organisations seeking support for community projects within the locality or region of GSK sites should contact the relevant site to request the correct company contact.

Applicants are asked to supply a concise summary of their aims, objectives and funding requirements together with a copy of their most up-to-date audited accounts.

Glencore UK Ltd

Commodity traders

Correspondent: Company Secretary, 50 Berkley Street, London W1H 0LU (tel: 020 7629 3800; fax: 020 7499 5555; email: info@glencore.com; website: www.glencore.com)

Directors: Simon Murray, Chair; Ivan Glasenberg, Chief Executive; Steven Kalmin; Peter Coates; Leonhard Fischer; Anthony Hayward; William Macaulay; Li Ning (women: 0; men: 8)

Year end	31/12/2010
Turnover	£144,978,000
Pre-tax profit	£4,340,000

Nature of business: International commodity traders. The company is a wholly owned subsidiary of Glencore International AG, a company incorporated in Switzerland.

Company registration number: 1170825

Charitable donations

UK cash (latest declared):	2008	£268,000
	2007	£2,084,000
	2006	£1,400,000

Corporate social responsibility

CSR policy: There was no information regarding CSR available at the time of writing.

Exclusions

No support for circular appeals, fundraising events, advertising in charity brochures, appeals from individuals, culture and recreation, research, environment and heritage, local appeals not in areas of company presence or overseas projects.

Applications

In writing to the correspondent.

Other information

There was no information regarding charitable contributions or activity.

The Go Ahead Group plc

Transport and communications

Correspondent: Samantha Hodder, Group Corporate Affairs Director, 3rd Floor, 41–55 Grey Street, Newcastle upon Tyne NE1 6EE (tel: 01912 323123/ +44(0)2078213928; fax: 01912 210315;

email: samantha.hodder@go-ahead.com; website: www.go-ahead.com)

Directors: Patrick Brown, Chair; Rupert Pennant-Rea; Andrew Allner; Katherine Innes Ker; Nick Horler; David Brown; Keith Down; Carolyn Sephton (women: 2; men: 6)

Year end	31/03/2011
Turnover	£2,297,000,000
Pre-tax profit	£84,800,000

Nature of business: The principal activities of the group are the provision of integrated public transport – through its aviation, bus, parking and rail operations. Its subsidiaries provide transport solutions across London, the Home Counties, the North East and the South East of England.

Company registration number: 2100855

Main locations: Brighton and Hove, Newcastle upon Tyne, London, North Eastern England, Oxford, Wiltshire, Dorset, Blackburn, Glasgow, Cardiff

Total employees: 22,201

Charitable donations

UK cash (latest declared):	2011	£182,000
	2009	£270,000
	2008	£302,000
	2007	£100,000
	2006	£400,000
Total UK:	2011	£349,000
Total worldwide:	2011	£349,000
Cash worldwide:	2011	£182,000

Corporate social responsibility

CSR committee: There was no evidence of a separate CSR Committee.

CSR policy: This information was obtained from the company's CSR Report:

> Good relationships with our local communities are essential to our businesses. We engage with them through local authorities, schools and colleges, local businesses, charities and passenger user groups. We actively work with local groups to enhance community programmes and local facilities.

CSR report: A full CSR report was available from the company's website.

Exclusions

No support for advertising in charity brochures, animal welfare, appeals from individuals, environment/heritage, overseas projects, political appeals or religious appeals.

Applications

In writing to the correspondent.

Other information

In 2010/11 the company provided charitable donations, sponsorship and community support in the UK totalling nearly £349,000. Cash donations amounted to £182,000.

The company assists employees' volunteering/charitable activities through financial support.

In kind support includes providing bus services to charities, the donation of advertising space, and the development and delivery of programmes on safer bus travel for schoolchildren.

Goldman Sachs International

Banking, securities/shares

Correspondent: Mike Housden, Correspondent to the Trustees, Peterborough Court, 133 Fleet Street, London EC4A 2BB (tel: 020 7774 1000/ 020 7774 1000; website: www.goldmansachs.com)

Directors: P. D. Sutherland, Chair; R. J. Gnodde; Lord Griffiths of Fforestfach; M. S. Sherwood; R. A. Vince

Year end	31/12/2011
Turnover	£3,188,737,700
Pre-tax profit	£1,932,156,920

Nature of business: Provision of investment banking, trading, asset management and securities to corporations, financial institutions, governments and wealthy individuals.

Company registration number: 2263951

Main locations: London

Total employees: 33,300

Membership: BITC

Charitable donations

UK cash (latest declared):	2011	£40,100,000
	2009	£1,986,000
	2008	£16,904,300
	2007	£1,940,000
Total UK:	2011	£40,100,000
Total worldwide:	2011	£101,500,000
Cash worldwide:	2011	£64,000,000

Community involvement

In the UK Goldman Sachs has established two registered charities:

The Goldman Sachs Foundation Charitable Gift Fund (UK) (Charity Commission no. 1120148) – set up for the advancement of education, the relief of poverty, the advancement of religion and any other purposes charitable in both English and American law; and

Goldman Sachs Gives UK (Charity Commission no. 1123956) – established for the advancement of education, the relief of poverty, the advancement of religion and any other charitable purposes. The ongoing strategy of the fund is to make grants pursuant to its objects.

Corporate giving

The firm's annual report and accounts for 2011 stated:

> Charitable contributions were $163 million [£101.5 million] during 2011, primarily including $78 million to Goldman Sachs Gives, our donor-advised fund, and $25 million [£15.5 million] to The Goldman Sachs Foundation. Compensation was reduced to fund the charitable contribution to Goldman Sachs Gives. The $78 million contribution is in addition to prior year contributions made to Goldman Sachs Gives. The firm asks its participating managing directors to make recommendations regarding potential charitable recipients for this contribution.

Cash and investment donations were made to its two UK registered foundations, information for which was taken from the Summary Information Return for 2011 submitted to the Charity Commission by Miss Hannah Wilby, on behalf of both sets of trustees:

> ***The Goldman Sachs Foundation Charitable Gift Fund (UK)***
> The charity is a grant-funder with wide charitable objects and funds a broad range of charities and charitable projects in the UK and abroad. In the last year grants were made to support charities that build and stabilise communities, increase educational opportunities, advance health, relieve poverty, promote the arts and culture and to further other exclusively charitable purposes under English and American law.
>
> The ongoing strategy of the charity is to make grants pursuant to its objects from **donated funds solicited from subsidiary companies of the partners and managing directors of The Goldman Sachs Group Inc. and its affiliates and subsidiaries.* The charity operates as a 'donor advised fund' whereby the charity establishes accounts for individual donors and nominees of corporate donors who may then make recommendations on how the donations should be granted to beneficiary charities. The trustees of the charity maintain ultimate discretion over grants and pursue a broad strategy of ensuring proper due diligence in the assessment of grant applications and the public benefit offered by grant recipients.

**Charitable contributions of $163 million (£101.5 million) given in total during 2011 are not broken down into UK/ worldwide figures. Nor is there a breakdown of what was given by the firm as opposed to those monies raised/donated by employees and former employees.*

We have taken the figures of £37.8 million and £2.34 million donated to the two charitable organisations as representing the company's UK cash figure as these charities are registered here with the Charity Commission. This will include monies donated/raised by employees etc., which is not our standard practice, but it simply is not possible to calculate a totally accurate figure and we consider it is necessary for our readers to have an indication of the amounts available to them from the company via the two charitable organisations.

During the year 2010/11 the fund had voluntary income and donated investments of US$3.2 million (£2.32 million) received from Goldman

Sachs and its subsidiaries. In turn, the trustees made grants totalling US$3.69 million (£2.2 million).

151 grants were made during the financial year in the following categories:

- Education – £1.58 million
- Humanitarian- £369,680
- Community – £201,500
- Medical – £71,000
- Arts and culture – £62,400
- Other – £9,680

Grants were made to support charities that build and stabilise communities, increase educational opportunities, advance health, relieve poverty, promote the arts and culture and to further other exclusively charitable purposes under English and American law.

Beneficiaries included: Trustees of Princeton University, Cambridge Foundation, President and Fellows of Harvard College, St Andrews Church and iPartner India.

> ***Goldman Sachs Gives UK***
> The charity is a grant-funder with wide charitable objects and funds a broad range of charities and charitable projects in the UK and abroad. In the last year grants were made to support charities that build and stabilise communities, increase educational opportunities, advance health, relieve poverty, promote the arts and culture and to further other exclusively charitable purposes under English law.
>
> The ongoing strategy of the charity is to make grants pursuant to its objects *from donated funds solicited from subsidiary companies of The Goldman Sachs Groups Inc., and from current and former employees, partners and managing directors of The Goldman Sachs Group Inc. and its affiliates and subsidiaries.* The charity operates as a 'donor advised fund' whereby the charity establishes accounts for individual donors and nominees of corporate donors who may then make recommendations on how the donations should be granted to beneficiary charities. The trustees of the charity maintain ultimate discretion over grants and pursue a broad strategy of ensuring proper due diligence in the assessment of grant applications and the public benefit offered by grant recipients.

Income from Goldman Sachs International received in 2010/11 was over £37.8 million. 391 grants were awarded during the financial period amounted to £16.2 million and were for the following charitable causes:

- Education – £4.9 million
- Community – £3.6 million
- Humanitarian – £3.2 million
- Medical – £2.3 million
- Arts and Culture – £1.3 million
- Other – £615,250

Beneficiaries included: Opportunity International United Kingdom (£1 million); and University of Oxford Balliol College (£850,000).

Note that the company's year end differs from that of its two associated charities and so outgoing company figures will differ from that declared in the charities' accounts as income.

In kind support

As 'part of a long tradition of public service and socially responsible business practice', Goldman Sachs has established the Community Capital Group to promote public awareness and understanding of the role played by the modern market system in local communities around the world. 'Through the sharing of its financial expertise and supporting innovative community projects it seeks to promote how use of efficient capital markets tools can increase local economic opportunity.'

Employee-led support

Community TeamWorks is the group's global volunteer initiative that allows staff to take a day out of the office and spend it volunteering with local nonprofit organisations. In 2012, more than 25,000 Goldman Sachs people from 48 offices around the world partnered with more than 950 non-profit organisations on a diverse array of community service projects.

Public Service Programme: This programme is a global initiative which provides the company's top performing staff with a unique opportunity to serve the public and develop leadership skills in an environment away from Goldman Sachs. PSP 'Fellows' are selected and given one year's paid leave to serve with organisations aligned with the firm's corporate initiatives. An example of this is a Fellow who has been seconded to Save the Children in order to strengthen its campaign to achieve a two-thirds reduction in under-5 mortality by 2015.

Matching Gift Programme: The programme encourages employees to support their chosen charitable organisations. Giving is matched by the company on a 1:1 basis to eligible organisations.

Commercially-led support

Citizenship programmes

10,000 Women

The Goldman Sachs *10,000 Women* initiative is a five-year investment to provide underserved female entrepreneurs around the world with a business and management education.

The Goldman Sachs *10,000 Women* initiative operates through a network of more than 80 academic and nonprofit institutions. These partnerships help develop locally relevant coursework and improve the quality and capacity of business education worldwide.

The women selected for the program enrol in customised certificate programs ranging from five weeks to six months. Topics covered include marketing, accounting, writing business plans and accessing capital.

Students are offered mentoring and postgraduate support by partner institutions, local businesses and the people of Goldman Sachs.

> Investing in women is one of the most effective ways to reduce inequality and facilitate inclusive economic growth. Research conducted by Goldman Sachs over several years has shown that investing in education for women has a significant multiplier effect, leading to more productive workers, healthier and better-educated families, and ultimately to more prosperous communities.
>
> Funding for *10,000 Women* is provided by Goldman Sachs and The Goldman Sachs Foundation. Our people from offices around the world contribute their time as mentors, selection-committee participants and guest lecturers in the classrooms of global academic partners.

10,000 Small Businesses

Goldman Sachs *10,000 Small Businesses* is an investment to help entrepreneurs create jobs and economic opportunity by providing greater access to education, capital and business support services. 10,000 Small Businesses is funded by Goldman Sachs and the Goldman Sachs Foundation.

Sponsorship

British Museum: Goldman Sachs is partnering with the British Museum, one of the world's leading cultural institutions, to sponsor its major 2013 exhibition: Life and death in Pompeii and Herculaneum.

Financial Times and Goldman Sachs Business Book of the Year Award: This annual award was in 2012, a prize of £30,000 prize to 'go to the book that is judged to have provided the most compelling and enjoyable insight into modern business issues'. There was £10,000 awarded to each runner-up.

Corporate social responsibility

CSR committee: No relevant UK details found.

CSR policy: Statement taken from the 2011 group annual report:

> Goldman Sachs is committed to driving economic growth. In 2011, we made significant progress in corporate engagement expanding our support of education and small business, extending our global network of academic and non-profit partners and encouraging our people to give and participate in volunteer programs that have an impact on the communities in which we work and live.

We could not determine the ratio of women to men on the board.

CSR report: There is an annual global Environmental, Social and Governance report published on the group's website.

Exclusions

Grants will not be made to individuals; fraternal organisations; political causes, campaigns or candidates; or fundraising events.

Applications

For company applications contact the Charitable Services Team at the company's address.

For both **The Goldman Sachs Foundation Charitable Gift Fund (UK)** and **Goldman Sachs Gives UK:**

Charities Aid Foundation ('CAF') and CAF America, and Ayco Company L.P. review grant eligibility applications and other requests for grant funding on behalf of the directors. Subject to the express approval of each grant application by one of the directors on behalf of the directors, CAF and CAF America then distribute funds in furtherance of the fund's objects.

In the first instance, address applications to Mike Housden, a trustee of both charities.

Note: CAF's contact details are:

Charities Aid Foundation
25 Kings Hill Avenue
Kings Hill
West Malling
Kent ME19 4TA
T: 03000 123 000
F: 03000 123 001
E: enquiries@cafonline.org.

Grainger plc

Property

Correspondent: Dave Butler, Director of Corporate Affairs, 161 Brompton Road, Knightsbridge, London SW3 1QP (tel: 01912 611819/020 7795 4700; fax: 01912 695901; email: dbutler@graingerplc.co.uk; website: www.graingerplc.co.uk)

Directors: Robin Broadhurst, Chair; Andrew R. Cunningham, Chief Executive; Mark Greenwood; Robert R. S. Hiscox; John Barnsley; Henry Pitman; Nick Jopling; Peter Couch; Baroness Margaret Ford; Belinda Richards; Tony Wray (women: 2; men: 9)

Year end	30/09/2010
Turnover	£296,200,000
Pre-tax profit	£26,100,000

Nature of business: The Group owns, acquires and trades regulated and market-let tenanted properties

Company registration number: 125575

UK employees: 258

Total employees: 274

Charitable donations

UK cash (latest declared):	2010	£17,500
	2009	£12,600
	2008	£18,900
	2007	£36,800
Total UK:	2010	£17,500
Total worldwide:	2010	£17,500
Cash worldwide:	2010	£17,500

Corporate social responsibility

CSR committee: There was no evidence of a CSR Committee.

CSR policy: Grainger seeks to demonstrate its long-term commitment to the communities in which it operates by improving the economic, social and environmental quality of these environments.

CSR report: A CSR report was available from the company's website.

Applications

In writing to the correspondent.

Other information

In 2010, the company gave £17,500 (2009: £12,600) in cash donations to charitable causes. Grainger is the Foundation Partner member of LandAid and have committed £10,000 per annum for a period of three years. The company have also adopted the employee matching fund and make occasional causes to specific causes.

Great Portland Estates plc

Property

Correspondent: P A to the Chair, 33 Cavendish Square, London W1G 0PW (tel: 020 7647 3000; fax: 020 7016 5500; website: www.gpe.co.uk)

Directors: Martin Scicluna, Chair; Toby Courtauld, Chief Executive; Timon Drakesmith; Neil Thompson; Charles Irby; Jonathan Nicholls; Phillip Rose; Jonathan Short (women: 0; men: 8)

Year end	31/03/2012
Turnover	£57,900,000

Nature of business: The main activity of the company is property development and investment.

Company registration number: 596137

Main locations: London

UK employees: 77

Total employees: 77

Charitable donations

UK cash (latest declared):	2012	£52,339
	2011	£48,036
	2009	£47,500
	2008	£45,000
	2007	£45,350
Total UK:	2012	£52,339
Total worldwide:	2012	£52,339
Cash worldwide:	2012	£52,339

Exclusions

No support for political appeals or appeals in an area where the company has no presence.

Applications

In writing to the correspondent.

Other information

During the year ending 31 March 2012, the Company made donations for charitable purposes amounting to £52,339. The group encourages its staff to be involved in charitable activities. In particular, the group targets charities involved in health, the homeless and the community, and, where practicable, allows temporarily vacant buildings to be occupied, at no cost, by charities seeking premises. In partnership with Westminster Education Authority, through a Primary School Volunteer scheme, 18% of the group's employees have participated for a fourth year in helping pupils at St Vincent's school in Marylebone to improve their reading.

Subsidiaries:

The Company owns, directly or through subsidiary undertakings, all of the ordinary issued share capital of the following principal subsidiary undertakings, all of which are incorporated in England and operate in the United Kingdom:

B & H S Management Ltd; G.P.E. (Hanover Square) Ltd; Collin Estates Ltd; G.P.E. (New Bond Street) LLP; Courtana Investments Ltd; G.P.E. (61 St Mary Axe) Ltd; G.P.E. (Bermondsey Street) Ltd; G.P.E. (St Thomas Street) Ltd; G.P.E. (80 Bishopsgate) Ltd; Ilex Ltd; G.P.E. (88/104 Bishopsgate) Ltd; J.L.P. Investment Company Ltd; G.P.E. Construction Ltd; Knighton Estates Ltd; Foley Street Ltd; Pontsarn Investments Ltd.

Greencore Group UK

Food manufacture

Correspondent: Conor O'Leary, Company Secretary, UK Centre, Midland Way, Barlborough Links Business Park, Barlborough, Chesterfield S43 4XA (tel: 01909 545900; fax: 01909 545950; website: www.greencore.com)

Directors: Ned Sullivan, Chair; Patrick Coveney, Chief Executive; Alan Williams; Diane Walker; John Herlihy; Gary Kennedy; Patrick McCann; Eric Nicoli; David Simons (women: 1; men: 8)

Year end	30/09/2011
Turnover	£804,210,000
Pre-tax profit	£11,170,000

Nature of business: Manufacturer and supplier of convenience foods and ingredients to consumer, industrial and food service markets.

Company registration number: 372396

Main locations: Deeside, Hunslet, Kiveton, Lisburn, Runcorn, Worksop, Lydney

Total employees: 6,703

Charitable donations

UK cash (latest declared):	2009	£60,000
	2008	£60,000

Corporate social responsibility

CSR committee: There was no evidence of a separate CSR Committee.

CSR policy: This information was obtained from the company's annual report:

> Greencore is aware of the positive impact that it can have within the local communities in which its sites operate and actively encourages its people to engage in local community projects. The types of activities vary across the sites and include participation in local school activities and donation of products.

CSR report: There was no evidence of a separate CSR report.

Exclusions

No support for worthy local causes/ projects unless within the immediate area (circa ten mile radius) of an operating site.

Applications

Small local organisations seeking support will normally be aware of Greencore manufacturing facilities close to them. However, if you are unsure about this first check on the company's web site (www.greencore.com) to see if there is one close by. If so, there exists the means to log a request for support through the 'Contact Us' facility.

Greencore asked it be made clear that: 'Requests that ignore our clearly stated guidelines will not receive a response, but those with genuine enquiries will be assisted to discuss their projects with the appropriate contact'.'

Other information

The following information is taken from the group's website:

> The majority of Greencore sites have developed close relationships with local schools and colleges. We support a number of our employees in serving as school governors and have helped a number of primary schools achieve the status of 'Healthy School' under the UK's National Healthy Schools Programme. Help is also provided to a number of school sports teams to promote exercise as a key element of a healthy lifestyle. Our sites share best practice in promoting these relationships. The group has established learning centres at some of its larger Convenience Foods sites. These offer training in key skills, such as English and computer-based skills. For example, our Sandwiches facility at Manton Wood has established partnerships with local colleges running specialist language courses to support the integration of a multicultural workforce into the community. Greencore is proud to support colleagues in their fundraising efforts for charities and other good causes. The group also supports the UK's food trade charity, Caravan, which helps those suffering hardship in retirement, as well as encouraging better pension provision across the food industry as a whole.
>
> Greencore's partnership with FareShare helps provide meals for those in need. FareShare works with a number of food manufacturers and retailers in the UK collecting food that would otherwise have gone to waste. Every pallet of surplus food can contribute to 1,400 meals. Greencore [rolled] this activity out across more sites in 2012.

Greene King plc

Brewers/distillers

Correspondent: Corporate Social Responsibility Dept., Westgate Brewery, Bury St Edmunds, Suffolk IP33 1QT (tel: 01284 763222; website: www.greeneking.co.uk)

Directors: Rooney Anand, Chief Executive; Tim Bridge, Chair; Matthew Fearn, Finance Director; John Brady; Ian Durant; Norman Murray (women: 0; men: 6)

Year end	01/05/2011
Turnover	£1,042,700,000
Pre-tax profit	£116,800,000

Nature of business: Greene King is a leading pub retailer and brewer, running pubs, restaurants and hotels.

Company registration number: 24511

Total employees: 20,218

Charitable donations

UK cash (latest declared):	2011	£25,800
	2010	£18,400
	2009	£18,700
Total UK:	2011	£25,800
Total worldwide:	2011	£25,800
Cash worldwide:	2011	£25,800

Corporate social responsibility

CSR committee: No mention of a specific committee found.

CSR policy: Taken from the company's website:

> As a leading pub retailer and brewer in the UK we have a responsibility to ensure that we conduct our business in an ethical and responsible manner.
>
> We are committed to building a sustainable business and our corporate responsibility initiatives focus around a number of key areas, including food safety and supply, the environment and responsible retailing.

CSR report: Published annually.

Applications

In writing to the correspondent.

Other information

Donations by the company for charitable purposes made during the period amounted to £25,800 (2010: £18,400). The company contributes further by, for example:

Sponsoring, in partnership with The East Anglian Daily Times, the Suffolk Community Awards. The awards are designed to celebrate the success of local people, community groups and organisations that have made a difference in their community.

Working in partnership with a number of charitable organisations offering a mix of financial support, time, skills and gifts in kind. To help either good local, national or international causes, many employees, licensees and customers across the UK get involved in raising money through a varied range of activities such as sports events, quizzes, raffles, auctions, and karaoke. The following is taken from the 2011 CSR report:

> Last year our managed pubs, hotels and restaurants supported their local communities in a range of fundraising activities raising over £280,000 for various local and national charities and appeals. Our Loch Fyne Restaurants raised an additional £4,600 during 2010 for their national charity, the RNLI. Our Brewing and Brands division held their first charity ball back in May 2010 as part of Greene King's Real Food and Beer Festival in Bury St Edmunds. The event, which celebrated community heroes, raised over £12,000 for EACH (East Anglia Children's Hospices) and Focus 12. Last year we donated £14,161 to The GREaT Foundation. Formerly known as the Responsibility in Gambling Trust, the GREaT Foundation was established as a charity in 2002 as Britain's largest funding body responsible for tackling problem gambling through the funding of research, education and treatment from voluntary donations.

An interesting and no doubt much appreciated example of the group's community contribution was 'Beer for the Boys', in support of servicemen and women on their flight back from active service in Afghanistan. This initiative saw that service personnel were treated to a well-deserved taste of home when thousands of cans and bottles of Old Speckled Hen were donated to Brize Norton and to local barracks in Dalton.

Greggs plc

Food manufacture, retail – miscellaneous

Correspondent: The Trust Manager, Greggs Trust, Fernwood House, Clayton Road, Jesmond, Newcastle upon Tyne NE2 1TL (tel: 01912 817721/01912 127626; email: greggstrust@greggs.co.uk; website: www.greggs.co.uk)

Directors: Derek Netherton, Chair; Kennedy McMeikan, Chief Executive; Raymond Reynolds; Richard Hutton; Bob Bennett; Iain Ferguson; Julie Baddeley; Ian Durant; Roger Whiteside (women: 1; men: 8)

Year end	01/01/2011
Turnover	£662,326,000
Pre-tax profit	£52,523,000

Nature of business: The principal activity of the group is the retailing of sandwiches, savouries and other bakery related products with a particular focus on takeaway food and catering. The majority of products sold are manufactured in house.

Company registration number: 502851

Main locations: Newcastle upon Tyne

UK employees: 19,504

Total employees: 19,504

Membership: BITC

Charitable donations

UK cash (latest declared):	2010	£1,400,000
	2009	£300,000
	2007	£730,000
	2006	£548,000
	2005	£609,000
Total UK:	2010	£1,400,000
Total worldwide:	2011	£1,400,000
Cash worldwide:	2011	£1,400,000

Community involvement

The following statement is taken from the company's website:

> Greggs plc is committed to being socially responsible in the way that we run our business and giving something back to those communities in which we operate. We believe that, as a growing and profitable business, we have a responsibility to help those less fortunate than ourselves. We also want to ensure that we progressively work to minimise the impact our business has on the environment.

In support of this the company gives 1% of pre-tax profits in charitable donations, mainly through the **Greggs Foundation** (Charity Commission no. 296590) and the Greggs Breakfast Club scheme. The main objective of the trust is the alleviation of the effects of poverty and social deprivation in the areas where the company trades. Projects in the fields of the arts, the environment, conservation, education and health will be considered, so long as they have a social welfare focus and/or are located in areas of deprivation.

The company shared 10% of profits, a record £5.8 million, through the national profit share scheme.

Greggs launched two major initiatives in conjunction with other businesses, to help break the cycle of unemployment for marginalised groups- a work placement scheme for homeless people and a training course for women offenders in prison.

The Greggs Foundation is an independent charity. It was established in 1987 by Ian Gregg, founder of the Greggs bakery chain and continues to have a very close association to bakery firm Greggs plc. For information on the Greggs Foundation, see the *Guide to the Major Trusts Volume 1,* published by the Directory of Social Change. The Foundation's 4 initiatives are as follows:

Breakfast Clubs- Helping over 8,000 primary school pupils get a healthy start to the school day. The Greggs Breakfast Club scheme was awarded Gold Status by the Food and Drink Federation Community Awards.

Major Grants- Providing grants to charitable organisations in the North East of England to help support key salary positions.

Hardship Fund- Helping families in the North East of England who are in extreme financial hardship with grants made through relevant social organisations.

Regional Grants- Supporting charities around Great Britain with grants for projects and activities.

Corporate giving

In 2010, the company made charitable cash donations of £1.4 million, although considerably more was raised by its staff and customers.

Employee-led support

Payroll giving: The company operates the Give As You Earn scheme, money from which is contributed to the Greggs Foundation.

Corporate social responsibility

CSR committee: There was a CSR Committee present.

> **CSR policy:** Greggs is a growing company that has always cared about 'doing the right thing' for our local communities, our people, our customers and for our environment. Our values underpin our approach to social responsibility and help us run our business in a safe and responsible way.

CSR report: Information regarding CSR was available from the company's annual report.

Exclusions

Major grants:

- Animal welfare
- Capital projects (including purchase, construction and refurbishment of buildings)
- Events such as Conferences, Seminars and Exhibitions
- Expeditions and Overseas Travel
- Fee-charging residential homes, nurseries and care facilities
- Festivals, performances and other arts and entertainment activities
- Fundraising events
- Holidays and outings
- Hospitals, Health Service Trusts, medically related appeals and medical equipment
- Individuals other than through the Hardship Fund
- Large, well-staffed organisations with a greater fundraising capacity
- Loans or repayment of loans
- National organisations and their regional branches
- Mini-buses other than community transport schemes
- Research – academic and medical
- Religious promotion
- Replacement of statutory funds
- Retrospective grants
- Schools other than for pre-school and after school clubs and activities promoting parental and community involvement
- Sponsorship – organisations and individuals
- Sports kit and equipment
- Uniformed organisations e.g. scouts, guides and sea cadets

Hardship fund:

- Payment of debts
- Computer equipment
- Sponsorship
- Overseas expeditions

Applications

The following outline regarding applications to the Greggs Trust is taken from its website (www.greggstrust.org.uk) where fuller information is available.

> Applications are welcomed from all sections of the community. Your organisation does not have to be a registered but it must have charitable objectives.
>
> We make donations under our 'Major Grants' programme to local, community-based projects.
>
> We also make grants through approved agencies to families and individuals under our 'Hardship Fund' programme.
>
> We don't consider applications for amounts below £1,000. However, divisional charity committees in Greggs plc's regional divisions make grants up to that level and applications received at this office may be passed on to them for their consideration.

Grosvenor Group

Property

Correspondent: Virginia Parish, The Grosvenor Office, 70 Grosvenor Street, London W1K 3JP (tel: 020 7408 0988; fax: 020 7629 9115; email: virginia.parish@grosvenor.com; website: www.grosvenor.com)

Directors: Lesley Knox, Chair; Mark Preston, Group Chief Executive; Nicholas Scarles, Group Finance Director; Alasdair Morrison; Jeremy Newsum; Peter Vernon; Rod Kent; Nicholas Loup; Domenico Siniscalco; Andrew Bibby; Michael McLintock; Owen Thomas; Jeffrey Weingarten (women: 1; men: 12)

Year end	31/12/2011
Turnover	£195,200,000
Pre-tax profit	£315,000,000

Nature of business: The group's principal activities are property investment, development and fund management in Britain and Ireland, North America, Continental Europe, Australia and Asia Pacific.

Company registration number: 3219943

Main locations: Liverpool, Edinburgh

UK employees: 242

Total employees: 545

Membership: BITC

Charitable donations

UK cash (latest declared):	2011	£1,500,000
	2009	£1,800,000
	2008	£1,700,000
	2007	£2,000,000
	2006	£1,500,000
Total UK:	2011	£1,500,000
Total worldwide:	2011	£1,800,000
Cash worldwide:	2011	£1,800,000

Community involvement

The group's community support is, in the main, routed through **The Westminster Foundation** (Charity Commission no. 267618) which was established in 1974 as the Grosvenor family's charitable foundation and supports a wide range of charitable causes.

The group also established **The Liverpool One Foundation** (Charity Commission no. 1112697) in connection with the group's development of a 42-acre retail site ('Liverpool One') situated in the centre of Liverpool.

The **Community Foundation for Greater Manchester** is also supported.

The Westminster Foundation

Grants are targeted at communities local to businesses and land owned by the Grosvenor Estate. In the UK this means areas such as London W1 & SW1, the North West of England (specifically Chester and the surrounding area and rural Lancashire), the Sutherland and Edinburgh areas of Scotland and any areas where the property company 'Grosvenor' is undertaking large development projects.

In the UK the foundation only gives grants to groups and organisations that are registered with the Charity Commission, or where the grant is for an exclusively charitable purpose.

The foundation does not give grants to individuals, holiday charities, animal charities, medical research or for building conservation.

Fuller details are given in *The Guide to the Major Trusts Vol. 1*, also published by the Directory of Social Change.

The Liverpool One Foundation

The Liverpool ONE Foundation was formally established in 2005 by the private sector partners involved in delivering the Paradise Project that were committed to supporting the local community. Funding for this Foundation comes from a group of companies working on, or otherwise involved in the redevelopment of the centre of the City of Liverpool (the 'Liverpool One' project). This, includes the Grosvenor Group which along with its fellow corporate founders have pledged, in total, to donate £250,000 a year to the foundation.

From the outset, the Directors of the Liverpool One Foundation anticipated that it would continue after the development process had run its course. In September 2009 they, and the trustees of the Westminster Foundation agreed to pass the management of the Liverpool ONE Foundation across to the **Community Foundation for Merseyside** (CFM).

CFM is one of the largest community foundations in the UK and has extensive relationships with charities local to Liverpool ONE. It is hoped that working with them will ensure that grants from the Liverpool ONE Foundation make a difference to the lives of people across Merseyside both now and in the future.

Projects should meet one or more of the following themes;

- The prevention or relief of poverty
- Education and skills – especially for young people
- Social and community advancement
- Health

In addition, local priorities have been set for each borough of Merseyside. Groups applying to the fund should ensure that their proposed project meets the local priorities which relate to their area as follows:

- Knowsley – Health
- Liverpool – Children and young people's diversionary activities
- Sefton – Older people and intergenerational projects; children and young people's diversionary activities; improvements to the local environment
- St Helens – Health; children and young people
- Wirral – Community capacity building for children and young people in particular

For more information about the grants available from the Liverpool ONE Foundation visit www.cfmerseyside.org.uk.

The Duke of Westminster has been a supporter of the **Manchester Community Foundation** since 1990.

Since then it has gone from strength to strength and now comprises a substantial community of donors committed to improving the quality of life across Greater Manchester and helping to build stronger communities within the city.

Grants are directed towards geographical areas in which the Grosvenor Family and Grosvenor Group have a particular connection. Each operating company within the Grosvenor Group has its own charity committee and they put forward recommendations for grants for consideration at the quarterly foundation meetings.

Corporate giving

Charitable contributions during the year amounted to £1.8 million (2010: £1.7 million). £1.5 million was donated to the Westminster Foundation (2010: £1.4 million), the grantmaking foundation for the Grosvenor family and business interests. As a registered charity, the Westminster Foundation focuses on social care and education, military welfare, and environment and conservation, and also provides subsidised office accommodation on Grosvenor's London estate to over 30 registered charities.

Employee-led support

Staff are encouraged to undertake their own fundraising for charities by the active promotion of Give As You Earn within the UK, as well as by the matched funding of employees' charitable fundraising across all our Operating Companies. The group is developing a policy on pro–bono activity, to reflect the widespread involvement of staff in giving time and expertise to support their communities in other ways.

Corporate social responsibility

CSR committee: No specific CSR committee details found.

CSR policy: Extract from the annual report and accounts for 2011: 'We are broadening the scope of our focus on the environment to include wider sustainability issues in response to the desire of our trustees, our board, and our staff to take Grosvenor's commitment to social responsibility a stage further.'

CSR report: There is a published Environment Review. Currently focused on environmental issues, the report is available from the website.

Exclusions

The group will not fund individuals or organisations which are not registered charities.

Applications

Applications should be made in writing to the correspondent who will ensure that they are dealt with appropriately, i.e. passed on to the relevant foundation.

Guardian Media Group plc

Media

Correspondent: Phil Boardman, Company Secretary, PO Box 68164, Kings Place, 90 York Way, London N1P 2AP (tel: 020 3353 2000; fax: 01612 112042; website: www.gmgplc.co.uk)

Directors: Amelia Fawcett, Chair; Andrew Miller, Chief Executive; Nick Backhouse; Neil Berkett; Stuart Taylor; Alan Rusbridger; Simon Fox; Judy Gibbons; Darren Singer; Phil Boardman (women: 2; men: 8)

Year end	03/04/2011
Turnover	£466,100,000
Pre-tax profit	£9,000,000

Nature of business: Newspaper and magazine publishing. The group has national newspapers as well as regional evening and weekly papers in the North West, Berkshire and Surrey.

Company registration number: 94531

Main locations: Manchester, London

Total employees: 2113

Charitable donations

UK cash (latest declared):	2011	£370,000
	2010	£370,000
	2009	£472,000
	2007	£503,731
	2006	£351,261
Total UK:	2011	£370,000
Total worldwide:	2011	£370,000
Cash worldwide:	2011	£370,000

Corporate social responsibility

CSR committee: A CSR steering committee has been created and is chaired by the chief executive officer.

CSR policy: This information was obtained from the company's website:

> At GMG an awareness of the wider responsibilities of business has always been at the heart of what we do. The Manchester Guardian was founded to promote liberal interest and the ethos of public service has long been part of the group's DNA.
>
> The Scott Trust Foundation and GMG's subsidiaries are involved in a range of activities designed to support the wider community, manage environmental impacts and promote press freedom in the UK and abroad.

CSR report: An interactive CSR report was available from the company's website.

Exclusions

The company will not support political appeals.

Applications

In writing to the correspondent. Appeals sent directly to individual papers are dealt with separately.

Other information

Charitable donations during the year totalled £370,000 (2010: £370,000), of which £284,000 was paid to national charities, £53,000 to local charities and £33,000 to overseas charities. Charitable donations of £235,000 was paid to the Scott Trust Foundation (Charity Commission no. 1027893).

The Guardian Media Group plc is wholly-owned by The Scott Trust. It has a board of 12 members who are chosen from areas of the media industry that reflect GMG's business interests. The Scott Trust Charitable Fund was set up to support projects associated with independent journalism, journalist ethics, media literacy and journalist training in the UK and abroad. Its main aim is to ensure the commercial success of the group and to uphold the trust's values. While each division of Guardian Media Group chooses to support its own charitable ventures, a more strategic focus has been placed at the centre of the group with the creation of the Scott Trust Foundation. Its remit reflects one of the trust's key objectives of 'promoting the causes of freedom of the press and liberal journalism both in Britain and elsewhere'. (The foundation's main purpose, however, is the training of journalists primarily in Eastern Europe and Africa.)

GNM works with its local communities to address their social and environmental needs, from education and mentoring to conservation. It also works with organisations that use journalism as a training tool to support disadvantaged communities.

The group works with its local communities to address their social and environmental needs, from education and mentoring to conservation. It also works with organisations that use journalism as a training tool to support disadvantaged communities.

Halfords Group plc

Retail – miscellaneous

Correspondent: David Sawday, Icknield Street Drive, Washford West, Redditch, Worcestershire B98 0DE (tel: 01527 517601/01527 513571; fax: 01527 513201; email: david.sawday@halfords.co.uk; website: www.halfordscompany.com)

Directors: Dennis Millard, Chair; David Wild, Chief Executive; Paul McClenaghan; Keith Harris; Bill Ronald; Claudia Arney; Andrew Findlay; David Adams (women: 1; men: 7)

Year end	01/04/2011
Turnover	£869,700,000
Pre-tax profit	£125,600,000

Nature of business: The principal activity of the group is the retailing of auto, leisure and cycling products.

Company registration number: 4457314

Main locations: Manchester, Brighton, London, Glasgow, Berwick on Tweed, Workington

UK employees: 11,000

Total employees: 11,000

Membership: BITC

Charitable donations

UK cash (latest declared):	2011	£73,000
	2009	£26,000
	2008	£30,000
	2007	£40,000
	2006	£20,000
Total UK:	2011	£73,000
Total worldwide:	2011	£73,000
Cash worldwide:	2011	£73,000

Corporate social responsibility

CSR committee: There was no evidence of a CSR Committee.

CSR policy: This information was obtained from the company's CSR Report:

> We see CSR as a core business consideration as it derives strategic, commercial and reputational benefits. We aim to achieve standards of responsible care across a number of key areas, including: customers, trading, health & safety, the environment, employee welfare and the community.

CSR report: A section of the annual report was devoted to CSR.

Exclusions

The group will not fund appeals from individuals, applicants on behalf of individuals, private fundraising groups or organisations not registered with the Charity Commission.

Applications

In writing to the correspondent.

Other information

During the year the group contributed £73,000 to charities in the UK, including donations to BEN, a charity supporting individuals and families linked to the motor industry and associated trades.

Charity of the Year: In total during the 18 month partnership with **Macmillan Cancer Support** the group raised in excess of £134,000. Fundraising activities included: the Macmillan Coffee Morning and the Macmillan Big Picnic. The biggest event was a Halfords/Macmillan Cycle challenge, which saw 400 employees take part in a Cycle Relay raising £45,000.

From April 2011 the group entered into a new partnership with *Cancer Research* which will span two years.

The company holds an apprenticeship scheme to combat unemployment.

Halma plc

Business services

Correspondent: PA to the Company Secretary, Misbourne Court, Rectory Way, Amersham, Buckinghamshire HP7 0DE (tel: 01494 721111; fax: 01494 728032; email: halma@halma.com; website: www.halma.com)

Directors: Geoff Unwin, Chair; Andrew Williams, Chief Executive; Kevin Thompson; Jane Aikman; Norman Blackwell; Steve Marshall; Neil Quinn; Adam Meyers; Stephen Pettit; Richard Stone; Carol Chesney (women: 2; men: 9)

Year end	02/04/2011
Turnover	£518,428,000
Pre-tax profit	£104,551,000

Nature of business: Halma makes products for hazard detection and life protection.

Company registration number: 40932

UK employees: 1,705

Total employees: 3,875

Charitable donations

UK cash (latest declared):	2010	£4,400
	2009	£15,300
Total UK:	2010	£4,400
Total worldwide:	2011	£4,400
Cash worldwide:	2011	£2,500

Corporate social responsibility

CSR committee: There was no evidence of a separate CSR Committee.

CSR policy: This information was obtained from the company's website:

> In line with our decentralised structure, social and community activities are sponsored and undertaken at the direction of subsidiary management. Each subsidiary has the freedom to implement its own initiatives.

CSR report: There was no evidence of a separate CSR report.

Applications

In writing to the correspondent.

Other information

In 2010/11, group companies made charitable donations amounting to £2,500 (2010: £4,400). We have no details of recipient organisations.

Hammerson plc

Property

Correspondent: Stuart Haydon, Company Secretary, 10 Grosvenor Street, London W1K 4BJ (tel: 020 7887 1000; fax: 020 7887 1010; email: HumanResources@hammerson.com; website: www.hammerson.com)

Directors: John Nelson, Chair; David Atkins, Chief Executive; Peter Cole; Timon Drakesmith; Terry Duddy; Jacques Espinasse; Anthony Watson; John Hirst; Judy Gibbons (women: 1; men: 8)

Year end	31/12/2011
Turnover	£458,900,000
Pre-tax profit	£346,300,000

Nature of business: Owner-manager and developer of retail and office property in the UK and France.

Company registration number: 360632

Main locations: Aberdeen, Birmingham, Brent Cross, Bristol, Leicester, Peterborough, Reading, Southampton, London

Total employees: 380

Membership: BITC, LBG

Charitable donations

UK cash (latest declared):	2011	£145,000
	2009	£135,000
	2008	£140,000
	2007	£91,000
	2006	£118,000
Total UK:	2011	£145,000

Corporate social responsibility

CSR committee: There was no evidence of a separate CSR Committee.

CSR policy: The company continues to measure its community investment through its community investment tool. This helps to quantify the socio economic impacts that the company has upon a developed area and focus on long-term priorities. The company's ongoing community initiatives include cash, time and in kind donations.

CSR report: A full CSR report was available from the company's website.

Exclusions

No support for political appeals.

Applications

In writing to the correspondent. Each application is considered on its merits, but about 95% of applications will be unsuccessful.

Information available: The company produces a Corporate Social Responsibility Report which can be accessed via their website www.hammerson.com.

Other information

During the year 2011 Hammerson made charitable donations in the UK of £145,000 (2009: £135,000). Under the company's charitable donations policy, donations are made to a variety of children's, medical, music and arts charities and to charities connected to localities in which the company is represented. In addition to these charitable donations, the company provides financial assistance to other projects of benefit to the community.

The company implemented a co-ordinated response to manage both the immediate and long-term impacts in the areas where it operates that were affected by the civil unrest in 2011. The company provided finance, skills and expertise to support local businesses and communities.

Hasbro UK Ltd

Toy manufacture and distribution

Correspondent: CSR Committee, 2 Roundwood Avenue, Stockley Park, Uxbridge, Middlesex UB11 1AZ (tel: 020 8569 1234; email: helen.dunlop@hasbro.co.uk; website: www.hasbro.co.uk)

Directors: D. Ferry; J. Harper; R. Hutton

Year end	27/12/2011
Turnover	£132,435,000
Pre-tax profit	£6,311,000

Nature of business: Toy and game manufacturer.

Company registration number: 1981543

Brands include: Action Man, K'Nex, Monopoly, Mr Potato Head, My Little Pony, Pokemon, Transformers, Tweenies, Weebles, Wizards of the Coast

Main locations: Uxbridge, Newport

UK employees: 185

Total employees: 185

Charitable donations

UK cash (latest declared):	2011	£47,200
	2010	£36,000
	2009	£34,000
	2008	£47,000
	2006	£52,000
Total UK:	2011	£47,200
Total worldwide:	2011	£47,200
Cash worldwide:	2011	£47,200

Corporate social responsibility

CSR committee: There was evidence of a separate CSR Committee.

CSR policy: The company supports communities worldwide by partnering with charities, providing financial and product donations and encouraging employees to volunteer.

Unable to determine the ratio of women to men on the board.

CSR report: A CSR report was available from the company's website.

Applications

Refer to the company website for more information.

Product donations: No applications will be accepted in writing as all requests need to go via Hasbro's online system. If you have a question about how to complete the online form see the FAQ section on the company's website.

Other information

In 2010/11 the company made donations to UK charities totalling £47,200 (2009/10: £36,000). A list of specific beneficiaries was not available.

Hasbro provides comprehensive information on its website about the different types of support it provides to charitable and community organisations, along with details of how to apply.

Hasbro's criteria for donations are as follows:

- Priority is given to charitable and community organisations that work with children and families
- For schools – Hasbro prioritise schools in the Hillingdon Borough (where its Stockley Park offices are based), or schools close to its Newport warehouse. The same applies to playgroups and pre-school nurseries
- The majority of donations take the form of toys and games donations
- Cash donations/sponsorship are usually only given to its nominated charities of the year

Staff take part in 'Team Hasbro' volunteering activities through a programme of regular and one-off events and a Give As You Earn scheme allows them to make tax free donations to the charity of their choice directly from their salaries.

Heathrow Airport Holdings Ltd (formerly BAA Ltd)

Airport operators

Correspondent: Caroline Nicholls, Director BAA Communities Trust, The Compass Centre, Nelson Road, Hounslow, Middlesex TW6 2GW (tel: 020 8745 9800/07836 342495; email: caroline_nicholls@baa.com; website: www.heathrowairport.com)

Directors: Nigel Rudd, Chair; Colin Matthews, Chief Executive; Jose Leo; Richard Druin; Renaud Faucher; Nichoals Vilien; Wilfried Kaffenberger; Ernesto Lopez; Stuart Baldwin; Santiago Olivares; David Begg; Richard Lomax; Christopher Beale (women: 0; men: 13)

Year end	31/12/2011
Turnover	£2,414,000,000
Pre-tax profit	(£206,000,000)

Nature of business: BAA plc owns and operates seven UK airports: Heathrow, Gatwick, Stansted, Aberdeen, Edinburgh, Glasgow and Southampton. Each airport is run by a separate operating company.

The following statement was taken from the company's website:

> Our business is changing its name to reflect changes within the company, and we're now no longer known as BAA.
>
> Heathrow, Glasgow, Aberdeen and Southampton airports now operate under their stand-alone brands. BAA (SP) Ltd has changed its name to Heathrow (SP) Ltd and BAA Funding Ltd is now Heathrow Funding Ltd.
>
> What this means is:
>
> - Over time the name BAA will disappear and the relevant airport name will take its place
> - As now, the relevant registered company number and name will appear on documents and correspondence
> - The services provided, and all usual contacts, will remain the same
> - Over time, the BAA.com website will be archived and replaced by pages on the relevant airport websites

Company registration number: 1970855

Subsidiaries include: Aberdeen Airport Ltd, Edinburgh Airport Ltd, World Duty Free plc, Southampton International Airport Ltd, Heathrow Airport Ltd, Gatwick Airport Ltd, Glasgow Airport Ltd, Stansted Airport Ltd

Brands include: BAA, Heathrow Express, World Duty Free

Main locations: Heathrow, Gatwick, Edinburgh, Glasgow, Southampton, Stansted, Aberdeen

UK employees: 8,583

Total employees: 8,583

Membership: BITC

Charitable donations

UK cash (latest declared):	2011	£1,000,000
	2009	£1,000,000
	2008	£1,300,000
	2007	£1,376,238
	2006	£1,313,000
Total UK:	2011	£1,000,000
Total worldwide:	2011	£1,000,000
Cash worldwide:	2011	£1,000,000

Community involvement

The company has its own charitable trust, **The BAA 21st Century Communities Trust** (Charity Commission no.1058617). This provides grants in the areas surrounding its airports. The trust has set a vision to 'Work with communities, to create significant and positive social change'. Its objectives are:

- To create learning opportunities for young people and so raise their aspirations
- To break down barriers to employment through skills development
- To help protect the environment
- To support staff active in the community

The aim is to help them create significant and positive social change. Support is concentrated on projects which will be of community benefit in the areas of education, the environment and economic regeneration. Applications should be made to the airport nearest the project and details for each of the five airports can be found on the company's website under the Communities Trust section.

In 2011 the trust:

- Donated nearly £700,000
- Awarded more than 350 grants
- Unlocked £100,000 in matched donations
- Donated more than £80,000 towards fundraising by airport staff

The trust works closely with the communities the airports serve, to try and make sure that grants go where they are most needed – there is a dedicated local community fund and a local grants panel at each airport to support trustees with their decisions about the donations being considered.

Check out our local airport community funds at Aberdeen, Glasgow, Heathrow, Southampton, Stansted.

There are also a couple of charitable trusts connected to Gatwick Airport. Gatwick Airport Community Trust (Charity Commission no. 1089683) which supports welfare causes, community facilities and development, the arts, cultural, sports and environmental and conservation schemes. Applications should be made to: Gatwick Airport Community Trust, c/o Public Affairs, 7th Floor Destinations Place, Gatwick Airport, West Sussex RH6 ONP (Tel. 01892 826088).

Gatwick Airport Pantomime Society (Charity Commission no. 1090214) supports a wide range of causes in West Sussex, including help for people who are sick, have disabilities, need medical treatment or have housing difficulties, community development and animal charities. Applications should be made to: Barry Charles Lloyd, 14 Lambourn Close, East Grinstead, West Sussex RH19 2DP (01342 315991).

Corporate giving

In October 2012 the Group changed the name of some of the companies within the group. The main changes from a reporting perspective are listed below:

- BAA Ltd was renamed to Heathrow Airport Holdings Ltd
- BAA Airports Ltd was renamed to LHR Airports Ltd

- BAA (NDH1) Ltd was renamed to Airport Holdings NDH1 Ltd
- BAA (SH) plc was renamed to Heathrow Finance plc
- BAA (SP) Ltd was renamed to Heathrow (SP) Ltd
- BAA Funding Ltd was renamed to Heathrow Funding Ltd

The 2011 accounts for the group were still in the name of BAA Ltd and it is from these accounts that we have taken our information for the purposes of this entry.

The accounts state that the group's charitable donations for the year amounted to £1 million (2010: £1 million). The main beneficiaries of charitable donations, the relevant amounts donated and the main activity of these beneficiaries were:

BAA Communities Trust – providing support for local community projects close to BAA's airports – £620,500. Heathrow Travelcare – £152,000 which provides counselling or assistance to passengers and airport staff.

Heathrow Airport Ltd gave £13,000 to Groundwork Thames Valley which promotes conservation, protection and improvement of the physical/natural environment.

The BAA Communities Trust gave £700 in grants in 2011. The trust's accounts are detailed and informative and obtainable from the Charity Commission. Beneficiaries included: Celtic Football Club, Hatfield Broad Oak Parish Council and Science Alive (£50,000 each); Green Corridor and Haybrook College (£40,000 each); Groundwork Thames Valley (£30,000); VSO (£20,000); Catch 22 (£10,000); Birchanger Wood Trust, Edinburgh Science Foundation and Link Community Development (£5,000 each); Cazfest Ltd (£3,500); Marie Curie Hospice and Saints Foundation (£2,000 each); and Drumchapel High School and Youth Outreach Bus (£1,250).

In kind support

The group also provides support in the form of resources such as, the sharing of professional skills and expertise, or the use of equipment and premises.

Employee-led support

Airport staff are supported with grants to support their volunteering and fundraising activity. The company matches employee giving on a pound for pound basis, and employee fundraising to a maximum of £250. Staff are also given time off to volunteer.

Payroll giving: The company operates the Payroll Giving in Action and the Give As You Earn schemes.

Charity of the Year: Whizz-Kidz (2012/13).

Corporate social responsibility

CSR committee: No designated committee for CSR could be found.

CSR policy: The following information is taken from the company's website:

> We manage our business in a way that has a positive effect across economic, social and environmental areas.
>
> We believe that it is possible for aviation to develop sustainably, enhancing the economic and social benefits while managing the environmental and community impacts.
>
> Corporate responsibility is an integral part of BAA's way of doing business. Each BAA-owned airport has a managing director responsible for identifying the sustainability impacts relevant to its operations and for developing and implementing a corporate responsibility policy to manage these impacts. Please see the links below for further information on the community and environment around your local airport.

There are links on the website to take you to each individual airport's CSR policy.

CSR report: There are links on the website to the various airports and their initiatives with regard to sustainability, the environment and community involvement.

Exclusions

No support is given to circular appeals, advertising in charity brochures, animal welfare, appeals from individuals, the arts, elderly people, fundraising events, heritage, medical research, overseas projects, political appeals, religious appeals, science/technology, sickness/disability, or sport.

Applications

Applicants are advised to contact the community relations manager at their local airport. For enquiries regarding the Communities Trust, contact Caroline Nicholls at the address provided.

Heineken UK Ltd

Brewers/distillers

Correspondent: See 'Sponsorship', 2–4 Broadway Park, South Gyle, Edinburgh EH12 9JZ (tel: 01315 281000; email: corporate.responsibility@s-n.com; website: www.heineken.co.uk)

Directors: A. J. den Elzen; P. N. Hoffman; L. J. W. Mountstevens; S. Orlowski; R. Pring; M. D. Porter

Year end	31/12/2010
Turnover	£1,660,000,000
Pre-tax profit	£730,000,000

Nature of business: The group's principal activity is the operation of breweries in the United Kingdom and Europe.

Company registration number: SC065527

Main locations: Tadcaster, Manchester, Reading, Hereford, Avonmouth, Dunston

Total employees: 2,220

Membership: BITC

Charitable donations

UK cash (latest declared):	2010	£0
	2009	£0
	2008	£1,200,000
	2007	£1,300,000
	2006	£1,400,000
Total UK:	2010	£0
Total worldwide:	2010	£0
Cash worldwide:	2010	£0

Corporate social responsibility

CSR committee: There is evidence of a CSR advisory board.

CSR policy: Unable to determine the ratio of women to men on the board.

CSR report: There is no evidence of a CSR report for this year, however previous reports indicate that Heineken is active within the community.

Exclusions

Previously, no grants for advertising in charity brochures, appeals from individuals, under-18 age group, fundraising events, medical research, political appeals, religious appeals, or local appeals not in areas of company presence.

Sponsorship of individuals, other than company employees, is not undertaken.

Applications

When telephoning the corporate responsibility team, it is company policy to require a named person. For this reason applicants are advised to use the email address.

Other information

The 2011 company accounts for Heineken UK Ltd declared no charitable cash donations. We have also been unable to determine an amount from the company's website. However, we consider that Heineken's community investment must be fairly substantial as it achieved the BITC Community Mark in 2011.

H. J. Heinz Co. Ltd

Food manufacture

Correspondent: Liz Keane, Trust Secretary, Hayes Park South Building, Hayes, Middlesex UB4 8AL (tel: 020 8573 7757/020 8848 2223; fax: 020 8848 2325; email: charitable.trust@uk.hjheinz.com; website: www.heinz.co.uk)

Directors: M. Mazzitelli; N. Perry; C. Page; D. Woodward; G. Price; M. A. Hill

Year end	27/04/2011
Turnover	£778,700,000
Pre-tax profit	£15,700,000

Nature of business: Principal activities: the manufacture, processing, growing and distribution of food.

Company registration number: 147624

Main locations: Worcester, Hayes, Kitt Green, Leamington, Kendal, Grimsby, Westwick, Okehampton, Telford

Total employees: 2,150

Charitable donations

UK cash (latest declared):	2011	£85,000
	2008	£85,500
	2007	£180,000
	2006	£136,000
	2005	£144,000
Total UK:	2011	£85,000
Total worldwide:	2011	£118,100

Corporate social responsibility

CSR committee: There was no evidence of a separate CSR Committee.

CSR policy: 'The company has been committed to providing support to promote the quality of life among the communities in which it operates for many years through the establishment of the Heinz Charitable Trust.'

Unable to determine the ratio of women to men on the board.

CSR report: There was no evidence of a separate CSR report however information was available from the company's website.

Exclusions

The Heinz Charitable Trust does not:

- Support politically oriented causes in any way
- Consider religious appeals if the object is to promote denominational principles
- Take advertising space in charity programmes/brochures
- Support individuals undertaking educational/vocational studies
- Consider unsolicited research projects
- Directly support individuals or groups undertaking sponsored events
- Accept commercial sponsorship

Applications

In writing to the correspondent or by using the online application form.

Note that, generally, only organisations registered as national charity organisations will be considered.

The trustees meet once a year, usually in July or August to consider major appeals for donations. However, a subcommittee, which is authorised to make grants of up to £10,000, meets more frequently. This committee also selects applications to be considered by the trustees at their annual meeting.

Other information

Donations of £85,000 were made in 2011 with £80,000 of this total being given to the Heinz Charitable Trust.

The following information is taken from the company's website:

Heinz Charitable Trust

The Heinz Charitable Trust (Charity Commission no. 326254) has long been committed to providing support to promote the quality of life among the communities in which we are present. The trust is overseen by a group of appointed trustees, drawn from all areas of our company.

The HCT has guidelines that charities it supports should be from one of the following areas:

Nutrition – Promoting improvements in and a better understanding of good nutrition, and contributing to the health and well-being of people and communities.

Healthy Children and Families – Improving the overall well-being of people by ensuring children and families have the resources and services necessary to help them live healthy and happy lives.

Education: The company is involved in local education/business partnerships and provides educational materials for schools.

The company also gives goods to raise money for local charities.

Helical bar plc

Property

Correspondent: Company Secretary, 11–15 Farm Street, London W1J 5RS (tel: 020 7629 0113; fax: 020 7408 1666; website: www.helical.co.uk)

Directors: Giles Weaver, Chair; Michael Slade, Chief Executive Officer; Nigel McNair Scott, Finance Director; Tim Murphy, Deputy Finance Director and Company Secretary; Gerald Kaye; Matthew Bonning-Snook; Antony Beevor; Wilf Weeks; Andrew Gulliford (women: 0; men: 9)

Year end	31/03/2011
Turnover	£119,059,000
Pre-tax profit	(£6,280,000)

Nature of business: Helical Bar is a property development and investment company.

Company registration number: 156663

UK employees: 25

Total employees: 34

Charitable donations

UK cash (latest declared):	2011	£13,000
	2010	£13,000
Total UK:	2011	£13,000
Total worldwide:	2011	£13,000
Cash worldwide:	2011	£13,000

Corporate social responsibility

CSR committee: The Board of Directors has responsibility for CSR.

CSR policy: Extract from the 2010/11 CSR report:

> Helical recognises that our business activities impact on the environment and the wider communities in which we operate. As our business involves working with joint ventures partners and outsourcing partners, our direct impacts as a business are relatively small. However, we are aware of the influence we can exert through the implementation of responsible environmental and social practices via our partners, contractors and suppliers.
>
> An endorsement of Helical's commitment to managing environment and social impacts is our continued listing in the FTSE4Good Index. The FTSE4Good Index measures the performance of companies that meet globally recognised corporate responsibility standards and facilitates investment in those companies. Maintaining listed status on this Index remains a key priority for Helical, and informs our evolving approach to Corporate Responsibility.

Employee figures are for administration and management staff.

CSR report: Published in the annual report and accounts.

Applications

In writing to the correspondent.

Other information

In 2010/11 the company contributed £13,000 to charitable causes, including donations to King Sturge Charitable Trust, Land Aid and the sponsorship of an Under 13 football team. The company has also made a number of in kind contributions (use of space etc.) but we have no costings for these.

Henderson Group plc

Financial services

Correspondent: Director of Corporate Affairs, 201 Bishopsgate, London EC2M 3AE (tel: 020 7818 1818; fax: 020 7818 1820; email: info@henderson-group.com; website: www.henderson.com)

Directors: Rupert Pennant Rea, Chair; Andrew Formica, Chief Executive; Shirley Garrood; David Jacob; James Darkins; Gerald Aherne; Duncan Ferguson; Tim How; Robert Jeens; Kevin Dolan (women: 1; men: 9)

Year end		31/12/2011
Turnover		£682,800,000
Pre-tax profit		£82,200,000

Nature of business: The principal activities of the group are the provision of investment management services and the transaction of various classes of insurance business. The group has businesses in the UK, Europe and the US.

Company registration number: 2072534

Total employees: 1,043

Membership: BITC

Charitable donations

UK cash (latest declared):	2011	£149,500
	2009	£53,000
	2008	£59,000
	2007	£55,000
	2006	£71,000
Total UK:	2011	£149,500
Total worldwide:	2011	£149,500
Cash worldwide:	2011	£149,500

Corporate social responsibility

CSR committee: There was no evidence of a CSR Committee.

CSR policy: This information was obtained from the company's website:

> The group recognises its impact on the local London community in which it operates and is committed to building partnerships within this community.

CSR report: A CSR report was available from the company's website.

Exclusions

No response to circular appeals or to sponsorship requests for individuals. No support for: fundraising events; advertising in charity brochures; religious appeals; or overseas projects.

Applications

In writing to the correspondent.

Other information

£149,500 was donated to the community and charities during 2011 (2010: £53,000). The following information is taken from the company website:

> Our preferred charity since 1987 has been Community Links, the inner city charity running community-based projects in East London. Founded in 1977, the charity helps thousands of vulnerable children, young people and adults every year. Most of its work is delivered in Newham, a borough which ranks highly on the index of deprivation.
>
> In addition to staff related fundraising of £74,500, we donated £50,000 to the Isaac Newton institute and £25,000 to The Carers Resource.

Herbert Smith Freehills LLP

Legal

Correspondent: Company Secretary, Exchange House, Primrose Street, London EC2A 2HS (tel: 020 7374 8000; email: corporateresponsibility@hsf.com; website: www.herbertsmithfreehills.com)

Directors: Jonathan Scott; David Willis; Kevin Lloyd; David Reston; Scott Cochrane; Alex Bafi (women: 0; men: 6)

Year end		30/04/2011
Turnover		£136,067,000
Pre-tax profit		£132,527,000

Nature of business: International law firm.

Company registration number: OC310989

Main locations: London

Total employees: 2,281

Membership: Arts & Business, LBG

Charitable donations

UK cash (latest declared):	2009	£106,000

Corporate social responsibility

CSR committee: There was no evidence of a separate CSR Committee.

CSR policy: This information was obtained from the company's website:

> In addition to our growing programme of legal and non-legal volunteering and in kind support, we also support charities financially through employee sponsorship, employee-selected charity of the year and through direct funding from the firm. Herbert Smith Freehills directly funds charities that are delivering local impact consistent with our wider community investment programme, or who are working in the fields of access to justice and legal advice and educational support for young people.

CSR report: There was no evidence of a separate CSR report.

Applications

In writing to the correspondent.

Other information

Neither the company website nor its annual accounts provided a definitive figure for its charitable giving.

Charity of the Year:

The company website states the following: 'Our charity of the year partnerships take place every two years. Only charities that have been nominated by partners or members of staff may be considered for charity of the year selection. We are delighted to announce that *WaterAid* are our chosen charity of the year for 2011.'

Other beneficiaries the firm has supported recently include: London Legal Support Trust, Hackney Business Venture, Personal Support Unit at the Royal Courts of Justice, Inquest and Free Representation Unit.

Support for Refuge: Herbert Smith Freehills has a long standing relationship with **Refuge** – the UK's leading charity working to address issue of domestic violence.

> Our relationship with Refuge has developed over a period of about ten years, in which time we have supported the charity in a variety of ways – through employee volunteering, legal pro bono advice on a range of matters, and charitable and in kind giving.
>
> **Centrepoint:** A number of our people participate in the annual Centrepoint 'sleep out'. Centrepoint is one of the UK's leading homelessness charities. This event is designed to highlight the issue of street homelessness by challenging volunteers to spend a night sleeping outside and raise money for the charity through sponsorship.
>
> **Sponsorship:** *Spitalfields Festival* – Sponsorship will build on an extensive programme of community investment by directly supporting Spitalfields Festival outreach with local schools. In addition to our core sponsorship activities the firm regularly works with the *National Portrait Gallery* to provide arts workshops and careers sessions to the schools it supports in the communities near to its London office.

Payroll giving: Herbert Smith Freehills also operates a payroll giving programme and pays all of the administration charges to ensure that all employee contributions goes direct to the charity. In addition, the firm makes numerous donations to charity as sponsorship for employees carrying out charitable fundraising activities.

HESCO Bastion Ltd

Defence

Correspondent: See 'Applications', Knowsthorpe Gate, Cross Green Industrial Estate, Leeds LS9 0Np (tel: 01132 486633; fax: 01132 483501; email: info@hesco.com; website: www.hesco.com)

Directors: B. Heselden; J. A. Heselden; M. Hughes (women: 2; men: 1)

Year end		31/01/2011
Turnover		£120,431,609
Pre-tax profit		£22,420,909

Nature of business: The company develops and manufactures defence wall systems under the name of Concertainer. Used for the purpose of force protection, flood protection and erosion control; the units are used within the military as a means of protecting personnel and facilities against secondary fragmentation.

Company registration number: 2600319

Total employees: 202

Charitable donations

UK cash (latest declared):	2011	£10,044,600
	2009	£3,050,000
	2007	£11,455,520
	2005	£305,850
Total UK:	2011	£10,044,600
Total worldwide:	2011	£10,044,600
Cash worldwide:	2011	£10,044,600

Community involvement

The company has a preference for supporting organisations based in West Yorkshire, especially the Leeds area, working in health/ill health, respite care, medical research, children and young people or conservation.

Corporate giving

In 2007/08, the company established the HESCO Bastion Fund with an exceptional donation of £10 million to the Leeds Community Foundation which is responsible for running it.

In 2010/11 also, the company gave £10 million to the Leeds Community Foundation for the purposes of the HESCO Bastion Fund, now known as Jimbo's Fund having been renamed after the death of J W Heselden. It continues to support projects/groups benefiting people living in LS9 LS14 and LS15. Deadlines for receipt of applications are published on the Leeds Community Foundation website as are guidelines and criteria for applying. Groups can apply for between £250 and £20,000 and applications can be made online.

Previous beneficiaries include: Bridge Street Church – youth centre; Caring for Life – education block; FDM – community transport; Friends of Middleton Park – community activities; Leeds Mencap – activities for young children; People in Action – general activities; Sheffield Children's Hospital – general activities; Sick Children's Trust – home from home centre; Soccerworks – football coaching; St Cyprians – holiday scheme; St Philip's Osmondthorpe – roof appeal; Sue Ryder Care Wheatfields – general contribution; Unicef – general contribution; Martin House Children's Hospice – general contribution; St Gemma's hospice – general contribution.

Corporate social responsibility

CSR committee: No details found.

CSR policy: None published.

CSR report: None published.

Exclusions

Jimbo's Fund will not support:

- General appeals and contributions to large scale projects
- Applications from individuals
- Trips abroad or overseas projects
- Organisations raising funds to redistribute to other causes, sponsorship for events or activities, advertising in charity or other brochures
- Project from organisations that are in poor financial health or those that have had a previous grant from us which has not been managed satisfactorily
- Projects offering very limited local benefit
- Organisations seeking to move into the area because they think funding is available, without any local connections or demonstration of need for their work

Applications

For further information and details of how to apply, contact:

Leeds Community Foundation, Ground Floor 51a St Paul's Street, Leeds LS1 2TE

Tel (0113) 2422426. Fax (0113) 242 2432 or email: info@leedscommunity foundation.org.uk

The foundation suggests that would be applicants initially complete the 'Expression of Interest' form on its website.

Hess Ltd

Oil and gas/fuel

Correspondent: Andy Mitchell, Communications Manager, Level 9, The Adelphi Building, 1–11 John Adam Street, London EC2N 6AG (tel: 020 7331 3000; email: andy.mitchell@hess.com; website: www.hess.com)

Directors: John B. Hess, Chair and Chief Executive; Samuel W. Bodman; Nicholas F. Brady; Gregory P. Hill; Edith E. Holiday; Thomas H. Kean; Risa Lavizzo-Mourey; Craig G. Matthews; John H. Mullin III; Frank A. Olson; Ernst H. von Metzsch; F. Borden Walker; Robert N. Wilson (women: 2; men: 11)

Year end	31/12/2011
Turnover	£23,000,000,000
Pre-tax profit	£2,500,200,000

Nature of business: The exploration and production of oil and gas. The ultimate holding company is the Hess Corporation based in the USA.

Company registration number: 807346

Main locations: London, Aberdeen

Total employees: 14,350

Charitable donations

UK cash (latest declared):	2009	£0
	2007	£73,000
	2006	£54,000

Corporate social responsibility

CSR committee: A CSR Committee was in operation.

CSR policy: This information was obtained from the company's website:

At Hess, we believe that a world-class company achieves both a high standard of operating performance and acts with a social conscience. The company partners with host government, community groups and other stakeholders to develop programmes that can make a measurable and sustainable difference.

Hess Corporation's support for community programmes and partnerships includes social initiatives in the Americas, Europe, Southeast Asia and Africa. Company-sponsored activities range from helping victims of disasters, providing humanitarian relief, supporting education and improving community infrastructure, including roads, schools and hospitals.

CSR report: An up to date CSR report was unavailable.

Exclusions

No support is given for advertising in charity brochures, animal welfare, appeals from individuals, purely denominational (religious) appeals, local appeals not in areas of company presence, overseas projects or political events.

Applications

Appeals from national charities should be addressed in writing to the correspondent. The Aberdeen office (1 Berry Street, Aberdeen AB25 1HS tel. 01224 841330) deals with appeals relevant to that region.

Other information

We were unable to find the figure for charitable giving by the company in the UK or details of the recipient groups/ organisations.

The company undertakes a range of activities in support of the communities in which it operates. The centrepiece of the company's programme is a large-scale effort to transform primary education in the West African nation of Equatorial Guinea.

Teacher fellowships in the UK: Partnering with Earthwatch, Hess created 30 fellowships to enable secondary school teachers to take part in environmental research projects and take their learning back into their class rooms and local communities.

Every year since 2001, Hess has collected donations at the company's retail locations to benefit the March of Dimes, an organisation dedicated to preventing birth defects, premature birth and infant mortality.

Hess employees across the world are encouraged to lend time, energy and expertise to community-based organisations.

Hewlett-Packard Ltd

Electronics/computers

Correspondent: The Corporate Social Responsibility Committee, Cain Road, Bracknell RG12 1HN (email: hp.philanthropy@porternovelli.co.uk; website: www.hp.com/uk)

Directors: Margaret C. Whitman, President and Chief Executive; Marc L. Andreessen; Shumeet Banerji; Rajiv L. Gupta; John H. Hammergren; Raymond J. Lane; Ann M. Livermore; Gary M. Reiner; Patricia F. Russo; G. Kennedy Thompson; Ralph V. Whitworth (women: 3; men: 8)

Year end	31/10/2011
Turnover	£127,245,000
Pre-tax profit	£3,214,000

Nature of business: Hewlett-Packard Ltd is a subsidiary of the Hewlett-Packard Company incorporated in the USA. The principal activities of the group are the design, manufacture and marketing of measurement and computation products and systems.

Company registration number: 690597

Main locations: Bracknell, Bristol, Erskine (Glasgow)

Total employees: 349,600

Membership: BITC

Charitable donations

UK cash (latest declared):	2009	£170,000
	2008	£170,000
	2007	£138,000
	2006	£209,000

Corporate social responsibility

CSR committee: There was evidence of a separate CSR Committee.

CSR policy: This information was obtained from the company's website:

> Social innovation at HP centres on the belief that the same passion, energy, and culture of innovation that make HP a successful company can also be used to make a profound and positive social impact in the world. HP's Office of Global Innovation helps share HP talent and technology where they are needed most.

CSR report: There was evidence of a separate CSR report however it was not up to date.

Exclusions

HP does not consider the following types of grant requests:

- Requests from individuals
- Requests for grants for religious activities, churches
- Requests for sponsorships or grants for conferences, seminars, contests, fundraising activities, promotional items, sports events, marketing, TV and video production, research or feasibility studies
- Requests from individual schools (unless through one of our grant initiatives)
- For-profit ventures
- Requests from programs that discriminate on the basis of race, creed, colour, religion, gender, national origin, sexual orientation, age, disability or veteran status
- Requests for used or obsolete equipment
- Discounted purchases
- Requests from organisations that provide support or resources to any individual or entity that advocates, plans, sponsors, engages in, or has engaged in terrorist activity; or to anyone who acts as an agent for such an individual or entity. Support or resources include currency or other financial instruments, financial services, lodging, training, safe houses, false documentation or identification, communication equipment, facilities, weapons, lethal substances, explosives, personnel, transportation, and any other services or physical assets. Any violation of this certification is grounds for return to the **donor** of all funds advanced to **grantee**

Applications

HP EMEA (Europe, Middle East, Africa) does not accept unsolicited requests for grants.

Other information

Previously cash donations in the UK have totalled between £140,000 – £200,000 and we have used a mid-way figure as a guide as unfortunately we were unable to find the actual cash donations given in the UK in 2011. In the past the company has supported National Children's Home and the Prince's Trust.

HP also supports schools in their efforts to increase computer literacy. and has a long-established, strong relationship with Kelvin School in Glasgow, a school for children who have multiple disabilities, including visual impairments.

HP encourages employees and retirees to apply their abilities and expertise to volunteer efforts to improve local communities. This is done through pro bono work and general volunteering.

HFC Bank Ltd

Banking

Correspondent: Teresa Howlett, Community Affairs Executive, HFC Bank, Camden House West, The Parade, Birmingham B1 3PY (01344 892462; website: www.hfcbank.co.uk)

Directors: C. M. Armstrong; I. C. McKenzie; I. S. Jenkins; M. J. Thundercliffe

Year end	31/12/2011
Turnover	-£21,226,000
Pre-tax profit	(£13,533,000)

Nature of business: The principal activity of the company comprises banking services.

Company registration number: 1117305

Main locations: Winkfield, Birmingham, Bracknell

Total employees: 354

Charitable donations

UK cash (latest declared):	2011	£0
	2009	£25,700
	2007	£30,000
Total UK:	2011	£0
Total worldwide:	2011	£0
Cash worldwide:	2011	£0

Corporate social responsibility

CSR committee: There was no evidence of a separate CSR Committee.

CSR policy: This information was obtained from the company's website:

> At HFC Bank, we actively support the communities in which we operate and are proud of the work we do in raising money for both national charities and local initiatives.
>
> Our major charity partners are Macmillan Cancer Support and St Basil's, a West Midlands-based charity to prevent youth homelessness. In addition to corporate donations, employees are actively involved in their own fundraising projects and HFC supports these efforts through a matching programme.

Unable to determine the ratio of women to men on the board.

CSR report: There was no evidence of a separate CSR report.

Exclusions

No support for advertising in publications and associated materials, appeals from individuals, the arts, heritage, medical research, overseas projects, political appeals, religious appeals, science/technology, social welfare or sport. 'Charity of the Year' proposals are not accepted.

Applications

In writing to the correspondent. Potential applicants can obtain guidelines from the company.

Other information

The company made no charitable donations this year.

HFC Bank supports the communities in which it operates and raises money for both national charities and local initiatives in the areas of youth, education and economic development. Major charity partners are Macmillan Cancer Support, Acorns Children's Hospice and RSPCA. Fundraising activities in Winkfield and Birmingham also benefit local schools and organisations, such as Garth Hill College.

Employees are actively involved in their own fundraising projects and HFC Bank supports these efforts through a matching programme where employees' fundraising efforts are matched up to a maximum of £500 per year. Employees are also actively involved in their own fundraising and are given company time off in which to volunteer.

Payroll giving: The Hands on Helping scheme is in operation.

Hibu (formerly Yell Group plc)

Business services, advertising/ marketing

Correspondent: Company Secretary, One Reading Central, Forbury Rd, Reading, Berkshire RG1 3YL (tel: 0845 603 7109; website: www.yellgroup.com)

Directors: Bob Wigley, Chair; Mike Pocock, Group Chief Executive Officer; Tony Bates, Group Chief Finance Officer; Elizabeth Chambers; John Coghlan; Toby Coppel; Carlos Espinosa de los Monteros; Kathleen Flaherty; Richard Hooper (women: 2; men: 7)

Year end	31/03/2012
Turnover	£1,609,900,000
Pre-tax profit	(£1,417,100,000)

Nature of business: An international directories business operating in the classified advertising market in the United Kingdom, United States, Spain and Latin America.

Company registration number: 4180320

Brands include: Brands include: Yellow Pages.

UK employees: 5,614

Total employees: 12,931

Membership: BITC, LBG

Charitable donations

UK cash (latest declared):	2010	£675,000
	2009	£1,100,000
Total worldwide:	2012	£217,000
Cash worldwide:	2012	£217,000

Corporate social responsibility

CSR committee: No details found.

CSR policy: Statement taken from the 2011/12 CSR report:

> Our vision remains for corporate responsibility to provide our shareholders and other stakeholders with confidence that Yell is a well-managed and responsible company. Our corporate responsibility strategy will concentrate on three areas:
> - Being a responsible, sustainable business
> - Championing local businesses
> - Helping local communities to thrive

CSR report: Published within the annual report and accounts.

Applications

In writing to the correspondent.

Other information

During 2011/12, Hibu (formerly Yell Group plc), made charitable donations totalling £217,000 supporting various community related charities and projects. It is not clear where the money was given and we have used this figure as the worldwide cash contribution.

In the UK, the group has a network of 'Community Champions' – volunteers based at offices across the UK who arrange support for local charities through fundraising and in kind support.

> In 2011, our US people contributed more than $250,000 to their charity partner, United Way. United Way of America works with more than 1,250 local United Way offices throughout the country in a coalition of charitable organisations to pool efforts in fundraising and support, focusing mainly on education, income and health.
>
> In Spain our aim is to give visibility to charities by promoting their fundraising campaigns on paginasamarilas.es as well as designing and developing emails to send to our extensive database of clients, customers and employees, with excellent results.

Give As You Earn is in operation at the company's offices. In 2010, Yell UK people donated £30,000 through their salaries, to charities of their choice. Yell covers the cost of administering the programme.

National charity partners: The Red Balloon Learner Centres and The Woodland Trust

Hikma Pharmaceuticals plc

Pharmaceuticals

Correspondent: Corporate Responsibility Dept., 13 Hanover Square, London W1S 1HL (tel: 020 7399 2760; fax: 020 7399 2761; email: media@hikma.com; website: www.hikma.com)

Directors: Samih Darwazah, Chair; Said Darwazah, Chief Executive; Mazen Darwazah; Sir David Rowe-Ham; Ali Al-Husry; Michael Ashton; Breffni Byrne; Dr Ronald Goode; Robert Pickering (women: 0; men: 9)

Year end	31/12/2011
Turnover	£566,800,000
Pre-tax profit	£58,000,000

Nature of business: The principal activities of the group are the development, manufacture and marketing of a broad range of generic and in-licensed pharmaceutical products in solid, semi-solid, liquid and injectable final dosage forms. The majority of Hikma's operations are in the MENA region, the United States and Europe.

Company registration number: 5557934

Total employees: 6,165

Charitable donations

UK cash (latest declared):	2009	£689,700
	2008	£1,515,800
Total worldwide:	2011	£1,976,000
Cash worldwide:	2011	£1,976,000

Corporate social responsibility

CSR committee: There was evidence of a Responsibility and Ethics Committee.

CSR policy: This information was obtained from the company's website:

> Through charitable contributions, we are also looking to help prevent and treat some of the world's most challenging health issues. Since 2010 we have contributed to the Global Fund to fight AIDS, Tuberculosis and Malaria, which works to fight these diseases.
>
> We collaborate with community groups to support public policies that promote economic and social development, within the context of each of the local cultures in which we operate.

CSR report: A CSR report was available from the company's website.

Applications

In writing to the correspondent.

Other information

During the year the group made charitable donations of £1.9 million (2009: £1.7 million), principally to local charities serving the communities in which the group operates.

Across the group, support was given to local causes, donating medicines to NGOs and communities in crisis.

> The Hikma Global Volunteering Day, held in April each year, aims to encourage employees to invest time in their local communities. Aligned with our business objectives, the Volunteering Day aims to support better health in local communities.
>
> This year the company has:
> - Donated medicines to Libya and the Gaza strip including anti-infective, cardiovascular and diabetes products
> - Raised awareness by sponsoring anti-obesity and breast cancer campaigns
> - Raised money to fund breast cancer treatment and research in the US

William Hill plc

Gaming, leisure

Correspondent: Thomas Murphy, CRRI Committee, Greenside House, 50 Station Road, Wood Green, London N22 7TP (tel: 020 8918 3600; fax: 020 8918 3775; website: www.williamhillplc.com)

Directors: Gareth Davis, Chair; Ralph Topping, Chief Executive; Neil Cooper, Group Finance Director; David Edmonds; Ashley Highfield; David Lowden; Georgina Harvey; Imelda Walsh; Thomas Murphy (women: 2; men: 7)

Year end	27/12/2011
Turnover	£17,911,400,000
Pre-tax profit	£187,400,000

Nature of business: The principal activities of the group during the period continue to be the operation of licensed betting offices and the provision of telephone and internet betting and online casino and poker services.

Company registration number: 4212563

Main locations: Haringey

Total employees: 15,000

Charitable donations

UK cash (latest declared):	2011	£986,000
	2009	£920,000
	2008	£773,000
	2007	£581,000
	2006	£423,000
Total UK:	2011	£986,000
Total worldwide:	2011	£986,000
Cash worldwide:	2011	£986,000

Community involvement

We seek to support the communities in which we operate through charitable donations and other relevant payments.

Corporate giving

In 2011 the company gave £986,000 in charitable donations, the largest proportion of which was £703,000 paid to the Responsibility in Gambling Trust (now the GREaT Foundation).

The company's charitable donations are mainly focused on organisations involved in areas of greatest relevance to its business and include contributions to those involved in:

- Promoting a responsible approach to gambling; undertaking research into problem gambling; and providing information, advice and help to those who are at risk or are experiencing difficulties with their gambling
- Greyhound and racehorse welfare
- Support to disadvantaged individuals in horse and greyhound racing

In kind support

The company engages with local communities to combat crime. In December 2011, it launched an anti-robbery Crimestoppers campaign in conjunction with the launch of a Safe Bet Alliance initiative in Merseyside. Campaign literature was sent to postcode districts and posters were displayed in the company's shops and distributed by local Police Community Support Officers.

Employee-led support

Matched giving:
Employees' fundraising efforts are supported by matching the funds they raise. Donations totalling £74,250 were made in 2010/11 in support of employees' fundraising activities.

Payroll giving
During the year, the company introduced a payroll giving scheme that allows employees to make donations directly to charities they choose.

Corporate social responsibility

CSR committee: The Corporate Responsibility and Regulated Issues (CRRI) Committee oversees all regulatory and compliance issues relating to the business and advises the board on environmental, social and ethical matters. It is assisted by the Corporate Responsibility Working Group, which consists of management representatives involved in embedding and implementing corporate responsibility activities in day-to-day operations in each business function. The Working Group is overseen by Thomas Murphy, a member of the CRRI Committee and the Company's General Counsel and Company Secretary.

CSR policy: Information taken from the company's website:

> *Wider Communities*
> We seek to support the communities in which we operate through charitable donations and employee activities. Our group policy on charitable donations aims to support groups close to our business and to encourage employees' fundraising efforts through a matching scheme.

From the 2011 CR report:

> During 2011, we made good progress against our objectives. Looking ahead, we are in the process of building a corporate responsibility strategy that encompasses both the regulatory and sustainability matters. We aim to integrate further the corporate responsibility issues into our business operations, thereby improving the sustainability of the business for the long-term.

CSR report: Published annually.

Exclusions

William Hill does not make donations to political parties.

Applications

In writing to the correspondent.

Hiscox plc

Insurance

Correspondent: Alexander Neil Foster, Trustee, Hiscox Foundation, 1 Great St Helen's, London EC3A 6HX (tel: 020 7448 6000; fax: 020 7448 6900; email: enquiry@hiscox.com; website: www.hiscox.com/responsibility.aspx)

Directors: Robert Hiscox, Chair; Bronislaw Masojada, Chief Executive; Stuart Bridges; Robert Childs; Daniel Healy; Ernst Jansen; Dr James King; Robert Macmillan; Gunnar Stokholm (women: 0; men: 9)

Year end	31/12/2011
Turnover	£1,186,824,000
Pre-tax profit	£17,271,000

Nature of business: Insurance.

Company registration number: 2837811

Total employees: 1,254

Charitable donations

Total worldwide:	2011	£533,000
Cash worldwide:	2011	£533,000

Corporate social responsibility

CSR committee: There was no evidence of a separate CSR Committee.

CSR policy: This information was obtained from the company's website:

> We believe that our company can help the communities of which it is part, beyond simply providing jobs. To that end we support a range of social initiatives through the Hiscox Foundation. Since our expansion to the US, there is now also a Hiscox Foundation USA.
>
> The foundation's policy is to contribute principally to activities in areas that are close to our hearts: education; science; the arts; and helping the elderly and the most disadvantaged and vulnerable members of our society to live independently and with dignity.

CSR report: There was no evidence of a separate CSR report.

Applications

In writing to the correspondent.

Other information

Hiscox donated £533,000 to charities in 2011. The group has maintained its involvement in its local communities with the strong support of its employees.

The Hiscox Foundation (Charity Commission no, 327635):

> The Hiscox Foundation is a charity funded by an annual contribution from Hiscox to give donations to deserving causes. It gives priority to any charity in which a member of staff is involved, with the aim of encouraging and developing employees to become involved in charitable work. Hiscox staff continued their support of the Richard House Hospice and during 2011 raised over £28,500. The foundation has supported HART (Humanitarian Aid Relief Trust) with a further £30,000 during 2011.

HART helps some of the poorest and most abused people in the world.

Mentoring: 'Hiscox is a member of the Lloyd's Community programme, which supports local initiatives concerning education, training, enterprise and regeneration. In London for example, the Reading Partners scheme has continued, through which staff assist pupils at the Elizabeth Selby Infants School in Tower Hamlets.'

In Bermuda, Hiscox supports the Centre Against Abuse which provides shelter, support and tools to those involved in relationship abuse. Hiscox also supports The Women's Resource Centre by funding the centre's 24 hour hotline. Other support was provided to the Bermuda Senior Islanders' Centre, and Big Brothers and Big Sisters of Bermuda. The group continues to support the Bermuda Masterworks Foundation, which aims to repatriate artworks by Bermudian artists or featuring Bermuda landscapes/seascapes. Hiscox has also renewed a three-year commitment to support the Whitechapel Art Gallery.

Julian Hodge Bank Ltd

Banking

Correspondent: PA to the Company Secretary, 30–31 Windsor Place, Cardiff CF10 3UR (tel: 02920 220800; fax: 02920 230516; website: www.julianhodgebank.com)

Directors: John Mitchell, Chair; Jonathan Hodge; David Austin; David Landen; Keith James; Hywel Jones; Adrian Piper (women: 0; men: 7)

Year end	31/10/2011
Turnover	£9,027,000,000
Pre-tax profit	£2,559,000,000

Nature of business: Provision of a wide range of personal and business banking services and independent financial advice.

Company registration number: 743437

Main locations: Cardiff, Nantwich

UK employees: 64

Total employees: 64

Corporate social responsibility

CSR committee: There was no evidence of a separate CSR Committee.

CSR policy: This information was obtained from the company's website:

> Apart from its business objectives, the group also recognises a social responsibility to the community and will continue to provide financial support for welfare, medical, academic (Julian Hodge Institute of Applied Macroeconomics) and educational concerns. Usually, this is through the medium of The Jane Hodge Foundation or the Sir Julian Hodge Charitable Trust, charities which together own nearly 80% of the ordinary share capital of the bank's parent company, The Carlyle Trust Ltd.

CSR report: There was no evidence of a separate CSR report.

Applications

Applications for both The Sir Julian Hodge Charitable Trust and The Jane Hodge Foundation should be addressed to the Secretary to the Trustees:

Ty Gwyn, Lisvane Road, Lisvane, Cardiff CF14 0SG. Telephone: 02920 766521 Email: dianne.lydiard@janehodgefoundation.co.uk

Other information

Although we have been unable to obtain a figure regarding the bank's level of support via the company's associated trusts, full details of the trusts' support criteria and application procedure can be found in the Directory of Social Change publications *The Guide to Major Trusts* volumes 1 and 2.

HomeServe plc

Services

Correspondent: Corporate Responsibility Dept. (Community), Cable Drive, Walsall, West Midlands WS2 7BN (tel: 01922 426262; email: media@homeserve.com; website: www.homeserveplc.com)

Directors: Barry Gibson, Chair; Richard Harpin, Chief Executive; Martin Bennett; Stella David; Mark Morris; Andrew Sibbald; Jon Florsheim; Jonathan King; Ian Chippendale; Anna Maughan; Rachael Hughes (women: 3; men: 8)

Year end	31/03/2011
Turnover	£467,117,000
Pre-tax profit	£117,051,000

Nature of business: Provides home maintenance services to over 4.5 million homes in the UK, France, Spain and the USA.

Company registration number: 2648297

Charitable donations

UK cash (latest declared):	2010	£23,000
	2009	£43,000

Corporate social responsibility

CSR committee: There was no evidence of a separate CSR Committee.

CSR policy: This information was obtained from the company's website:

> HomeServe is committed to developing and implementing a successful Corporate Responsibility programme that benefits key stakeholders and utilises HomeServe's core skills to make a sustainable difference to its communities. We believe that a successful business must also be a responsible business.
>
> We aim to:
>
> - Use our core skills to give something back to the community, specifically in people's homes
> - Support more vulnerable members of the community by helping them in their homes
> - Develop partnerships with charitable and other organisations which are closely aligned to our business activities and therefore maximise our contribution
> - Support and encourage employee involvement in charitable giving and volunteering, using relevant employee skills to support the community

CSR report: There was no evidence of a CSR report although there was detailed information regarding CSR available on the company's website.

Applications

In writing to the correspondent.

Other information

The amount of donations made by the company could not be found.

> This year the business has increased its focus on the community and has formed its first national community partnership in the UK with *Marie Curie Cancer Care*.
>
> HomeServe chose Marie Curie as our first national charity partner because, in addition to the traditional fundraising channels, we are in a unique position to help Marie Curie patients in their own homes. Utilising our network of tradesmen and engineers, we plan to undertake emergency and repair work in patients' homes to provide support to them during their illness.
>
> HomeServe has pledged to donate £1 million to Marie Curie over three years to March 2013. This target comprises employee fundraising and volunteering, customer donations, sponsorship and gift-in kind contributions.
>
> The company sponsored Marie Curie's first ever Walk Ten in 2010 and has renewed this deal for 2011. Homeserve's sponsorship money helped Marie Curie with its advertising budget. £250,000 was raised.
>
> Employees have been raising money through sponsored marathons, fun runs, sky dives, cycling trips, cake bakes and dress-down days.
>
> **Pennies for Patients Scheme:** This enables many Home Serve employees to donate odd pennies from their monthly pay, (up to 99p a month) directly to Marie Curie.
>
> HomeServe supports Comic Relief each year by opening donation lines in their call centres. More than 200 volunteers answered 3,050 donation calls on Red Nose Day, raising over £100,000 to help vulnerable people in both the UK and Africa.
>
> The company continues to run an annual Youth Team Sponsorship Scheme and during the year awarded 24 grants to local youth teams linked to Home Serve employees.

HomeServe has also provided ad-hoc support to other charities throughout the year (in 2010/11 this included the Pakistani Flood Appeal and the Royal British Legion Poppy Appeal).

Honda of the UK Manufacturing Ltd

Motors and accessories

Correspondent: I Howells, Company Secretary, Highworth Road, South Marston, Swindon SN3 4TZ (tel: 01793 831183; fax: 01793 831177; website: world.honda.com/community)

Directors: M. Nishimae, Chair; S. Takizawa

Year end	31/03/2011
Turnover	£1,980,848,000
Pre-tax profit	£7,201,000

Nature of business: The principal activity of the company is the manufacture of motor vehicles, including the manufacture of motor engines and other vehicle parts.

Company registration number: 1887872

Main locations: Slough, Swindon

Total employees: 3,149

Charitable donations

UK cash (latest declared):	2011	£29,000
	2009	£13,000
	2008	£110,000
	2007	£33,000
	2006	£69,000
Total UK:	2011	£29,000
Total worldwide:	2011	£29,000
Cash worldwide:	2011	£29,000

Corporate social responsibility

CSR committee: No relevant details found.

CSR policy: Taken from the 2012 CSR report:

> Honda is striving to be a company that society wants to exist by pursuing CSR initiatives based on the Honda philosophy and sharing joy with people worldwide.

We were unable to determine the ratio of women to men on the board.

CSR report: Annual CSR report mainly focusing on areas outside the UK.

Applications

In writing to the correspondent.

Other information

In 2010/11, cash donations in the UK totalled £29,000 (2009/10: £6,000).

The company is also involved in local community campaigning:

Safe Drive, Stay Alive programme – uses impactful visual presentations and moving personal testimonies to teach young people the importance of safe driving before they become drivers. Since 2005, Honda of the UK Manufacturing has contributed £85,000 to the program, each year sponsoring an education officer in the local fire brigade who coordinates the program in local schools. In 2009, Honda of the UK Manufacturing helped bring Safe Drive, Stay Alive to over 8,000 teenagers from 56 schools and colleges in Swindon and Wiltshire.

Swindon Academy – in the five-year period 2006 to 2011, Honda of the UK Manufacturing has committed to investing £1 million in Swindon Academy, which has a specialism in Science with Business and Enterprise. In addition to financial support, Honda offers students of the academy a wide variety of innovative programs, in which associate volunteers play an essential role. In Honda's Prepare for Work workshops, students go through a practice recruitment process from initial application to mock selection tests and learn about the rigors of the modern hiring process. Honda also provides extensive support to the scientific curriculum of the school and is involved in science fairs on an ongoing basis.

Hoover Ltd

Domestic appliances

Correspondent: Miss M Rowlands, Hoover Foundation, Pentrebach Factory, Pentrebach, Merthyr Tydfil CF48 4TU (tel: 01685 721222/01685 721222; website: www.hoover.co.uk)

Directors: A. Bertali, Chair; D. J. Lunt; R. B. Mudie; G. Palma; D. Meyerowitz; M. Osguthorpe; M. Severgnini; A. H. Bokhari

Year end	31/12/2010
Turnover	£215,181,000
Pre-tax profit	£12,781,000

Nature of business: Manufacture of domestic laundry, refrigeration, and vacuuming appliances.

Company registration number: 2521528

Total employees: 471

Charitable donations

UK cash (latest declared):	2010	£6,200
	2009	£84,000
Total UK:	2010	£6,200
Total worldwide:	2010	£6,200
Cash worldwide:	2010	£6,200

Corporate social responsibility

CSR committee: There was no evidence of a separate CSR Committee.

CSR policy: The company directs charitable donations through The Hoover Foundation.

Unable to determine the ratio of women to men on the board.

CSR report: There was no evidence of a separate CSR report.

Exclusions

No grants to individuals, including students.

Applications

In writing to the correspondent.

Other information

The company appears to direct its grant giving through the Hoover Foundation (Charity Commission no. 200274).

Hoover Foundation

In 2010, the foundation had an income of £6,200 and a total expenditure of £50,500. Although fuller details were unavailable, the company's website states:

> The foundation's managing trustees have established sustained relationships with a number of charities. As well as national causes, organisations close to our UK business locations (South Wales, Glasgow and Bolton) have received particular attention. Strategic financial assistance given by Hoover has helped *Childline* create the National Childline charity shops, and we regularly assist with funds for ongoing activities. The Hoover Foundation is also a major sponsor of the Welsh Young Consumer of the Year.

House of Fraser (Stores) Ltd

Retail – department and variety stores

Correspondent: Peter Hearsey, Company Secretary, Granite House, 4th Floor, 31 Stockwell Street, Glasgow G1 4RZ (website: www.houseoffraser.co.uk)

Directors: Don McCarthy, Chair; John King, Chief Executive; Mark Gifford; Jonathan Byrne; Jim McMahon; Mike Pacitti; Steffan Cassar; Stuart Rose; Einar Jonsson (women: 2; men: 8)

Year end	29/01/2011
Turnover	£669,200,000
Pre-tax profit	£19,900,000

Nature of business: Department store operators.

Company registration number: SC021928

Brands include: Army and Navy, Arnotts, Barkers, Binns, Cavendish House, D H Evans, David Evans, Dickins and Jones, Dingles, Frasers, Hammonds, Howells, Jolly's, Kendals, Rackhams, Schofields

Main locations: Glasgow, Swindon

UK employees: 5,241

Total employees: 5,241

Charitable donations

UK cash (latest declared):	2011	£161,400
	2009	£245,000
	2008	£41,000
	2007	£31,000
	2006	£47,337
Total UK:	2011	£161,400
Total worldwide:	2011	£161,400
Cash worldwide:	2011	£161,400

Corporate social responsibility

CSR committee: There was no evidence of a separate CSR Committee.

CSR policy: This information was obtained from the company's website:

> We make charitable donations wherever possible and, along with our nominated charity of the year, the stores are encouraged to undertake their own fundraising events and activities for local charities.

CSR report: There was no evidence of a separate CSR report.

Exclusions

Support is not generally given to circular appeals, appeals from individuals, purely denominational (religious or political) appeals, local appeals not in areas of company presence or overseas projects.

Applications

In writing to the correspondent. Local charities are supported at the discretion of the store managers in their region.

Other information

In 2010/11 the company gave £161,400 in charitable donations. The accounts do not give details of the beneficiary groups to which the money was given.

The following current information relating to House of Fraser's supported charities is taken from the company's website: 'The group supports the Royal Marsden Cancer Campaign and has raised over £500,000. The group also supports Sparks.'

House of Fraser has recently launched 'Change for Life'; a concept where customers are encouraged to donate their spare change to The Royal Marsden Cancer Campaign. Change bags are available in all House of Fraser stores; you can fill the bags with £1 of change and make a donation while in store, or fill them at home and bring them back at a later date.

The company holds a 'Charity Golf Day' which has supported numerous charities over the last ten years. Since 2004, around £244,000 (including this year's donation) has been given to various charities. This year's donation was split equally between Walk the Walk and Retail Trust.

Locally: Contact your local store if you wish to know about the charities they support. Individual stores are encouraged by the group to raise money for national and local charities.

Howden Joinery Group plc

Furniture manufacture, retail – DIY/furniture

Correspondent: Head of Marketing and Advertising, International House, 1st Floor, 66 Chiltern Street, London W1U 4JT (website: www.howdenjoinerygroupplc.com)

Directors: Will Samuel, Chair; Mark Allen; Michael Wemms; Matthew Ingle, Chief Executive; Angus Cockburn; Tiffany Hall; Mark Robson, Chief Financial Officer (women: 1; men: 6)

Year end	26/12/2011
Turnover	£853,800,000
Pre-tax profit	£110,000,000

Nature of business: Manufacture, distribution and retail sale of kitchen cabinetry and related products.

Company registration number: 2128710

Main locations: London

Total employees: 6,276

Charitable donations

UK cash (latest declared):	2009	£599,000
	2008	£425,000
	2007	£410,000
	2006	£376,000
	2005	£515,000
Total UK:	2009	£814,000
Total worldwide:	2011	£814,000

Corporate social responsibility

CSR committee: No specific details found.

CSR policy: The following statement is taken from the annual report and accounts:

> Responsibility to local communities – each of our sites is an integral part of the community in which it operates, and helping those communities to flourish is important to everyone who lives and works in them.

CSR report: Published within the annual report and accounts.

Exclusions

No grants for overseas projects, political or religious appeals, science/technology or local appeals not in areas of company presence.

Applications

In writing to the correspondent.

Other information

Charitable donations, including kitchen and joinery products and services donated to various charities, made during the period amounted to £814,000 (2010: £793,000). It has not been possible to separate the group's cash charitable contribution from its in kind donations and employees' contributions.

Cash and stock donations, together with employee fundraising activities, typically supported local schools, village halls, care homes, hospices, sports clubs, youth groups and many other community activities.

As well as donating discontinued products on which students can practise, many depots also sponsor end of year awards and prizes at local schools and colleges and are working with ConstructionSkills, the Sector Skills Council and Industry Training Board for the construction industry, to put in place a bursary scheme for new apprentice joiners.

Over seven years ago a partnership was formed with Leonard Cheshire Disability, a locally focused organisation. For the past five years Howden Joinery Group has funded many areas of Leonard Cheshire Disability's volunteer recruitment and training programme, including the 'Can Do' Initiative.

Payroll giving: A scheme is in operation.

HP Enterprise Services UK Ltd

Information technology

Correspondent: Company Secretary, Amen Corner, Cain Road, Bracknell, Berkshire RG12 1HN (website: h21007.www.hp.com/uk)

Directors: M. Birch; S. Burr; S. Grayson; M. Lewthwaite; T. Perkins; J. Shaikhali; N. Wilson (women: 1; men: 6)

Year end	30/10/2010
Turnover	£2,570,000,000
Pre-tax profit	£2,400,000,000

Nature of business: A leading technology services company delivering a broad portfolio of information technology and business outsourcing services.

Company registration number: 53419

Main locations: London, Luton, Uxbridge

UK employees: 12,469

Charitable donations

UK cash (latest declared):	2010	£9,400
	2009	£15,400
	2008	£61,700
	2006	£37,700
	2005	£67,900
Total UK:	2010	£9,400

Corporate social responsibility

CSR committee: There was no evidence of a separate CSR Committee.

CSR policy: There was no information available regarding CSR.

CSR report: There was no evidence of a separate CSR report.

Applications

In writing to the correspondent.

Other information

In 2009/10 the company donated £9,400. A list of beneficiaries was not available.

HSBC Holdings plc

Financial services, banking

Correspondent: HSBC in the Community, Level 36, 8 Canada Square, London EC3R 6AE (tel: 020 7991 8888; fax: 020 7992 4880; email: communityaffairs@hsbc.com; website: www.hsbc.com)

Directors: S. T. Gulliver, Group Chief Executive; D. J. Flint, Group Chair; S. A. Catz; M. K. T. Cheung; L. M. L. Cha; J. D. Coombe; R. A. Fairhead; J. Faber; A. A. Flockhart; J. W. J. Hughes-Hallett; J. P. Lipsky; W. S. H. Laidlaw; J. R. Lomax; I. J. Mackay, Group Finance Director; N. R. N. Murthy; Simon Robertson; J. L. Thornton

Year end	31/12/2011
Turnover	£51,813,421,096
Pre-tax profit	£13,578,355,713

Nature of business: Retail banking and wealth management, commercial banking, global banking and markets, and global private banking. The network covers 84 countries and territories in Europe, the Asia-Pacific region, the Middle East, Africa, North America and Latin America.

Company registration number: 617987

Subsidiaries include: The British Bank of the Middle East, First Direct, Midland Life Ltd, Midland Bank Ltd, East River Savings Bank, Eversholt Holdings Ltd, Samuel Montagu and Co. Ltd, HFC Bank, Forward Trust Ltd, James Capel and Co. Ltd

Main locations: Leeds, London

UK employees: 51,000

Total employees: 298,000

Membership: Arts & Business, BITC

Charitable donations

UK cash (latest declared):	2011	£10,600,000
	2009	£6,500,000
	2007	£18,400,000
	2006	£16,400,000
	2005	£15,800,000
Total UK:	2011	£11,600,000
Total worldwide:	2011	£64,936,700
Cash worldwide:	2011	£59,659,800

Community involvement

The following statement is taken from the Sustainability Report for 2011:

> We invest in community projects on behalf of our owners, our shareholders. A broad set of principles is used to guide our donations, based on our approach to philanthropy, our business, and our desire to maximise our impact. In 2011, a panel of non-executive Board Directors, investors and representatives from NGOs, education, social consultancies and business reviewed these principles to ensure they fit with HSBC's values and reflect the needs of our external stakeholders. Their feedback helped us refine our approach to philanthropy. These principles guide the evaluation of the suitability and sustainability of the projects in which we invest:
>
> - Community programmes should follow themes which are both globally significant and locally relevant. This enables the Group to connect across international boundaries, but also allows flexibility for regions and countries to address their own issues
> - Our approach to philanthropy should be business-like. We should be proactive and make a difference, entering into long-term commitments (typically three to five years) with specific objectives
> - We should use our skills as well as our money. This means becoming an active contributor to social investment; for instance, considering debt and equity investments with a social purpose
> - Our community investment programmes should use and engage our people. We want our employees to take their skills into the NGOs and the communities we work with and to learn from them
>
> HSBC supports the communities in which it operates both through the involvement of employees and through donations. Policy is to focus effort on education – particularly for young people – and on the environment. 75 per cent of the company's community giving is targeted towards these two areas.
>
> Our approach is to partner with world-class charities that are making a difference, and we remain involved in the decisions about how the money is spent. We encourage our employees to get involved in their local communities, and we know that this motivates and engages our people.
>
> HSBC believes that support for primary and secondary education, in particular for the underprivileged, is crucial to the future development and prosperity of every country.
>
> In addition to funding original education initiatives around the world, HSBC is keen to involve its experienced and supportive staff in building and developing mentoring programmes, and offering career guidance and job internships for talented young people.

Charity partners: SOS Children's Villages, Junior Achievement, the Foundation for Environmental Education, the Climate Group, Earthwatch Institute, Smithsonian Tropical Research Institute and WWF.

Corporate giving

In 2011, the bank donated £10.6 million in the UK to community projects on education, the environment and other local causes. HSBC employees raised £5.1 million for charities, of which £2.5 million was match funding provided by HSBC through their employee 'pound for pound' scheme. Fifteen thousand HSBC employees have volunteered 80,000 hours of their own time in the community. In 2011, HSBC states that it spent US$96.1 million (£59.6 million) cash on community investment activities. Total investment excluding management costs was US$104.6 million (£64.9 million).

Employee-led support

Employee volunteering: During 2011, employees volunteered almost 465,000 hours supporting the community in their own time and 271,600 in the group's time.

In education

HSBC in the UK runs a £3.4 million partnership with the financial education charity pfeg (Personal Finance Education Group). Called 'What Money Means', this partnership is increasing the quality and quantity of financial capability education in UK primary schools. The programme brings pfeg, local authorities and educationalists together to develop resources and approaches that are helping primary school teachers feel more confident in teaching money skills to younger children.

The environment

Employees are also involved in a variety of projects related to environmental sustainability and climate change. In 2007, HSBC launched a ground-breaking five-year partnership (the HSBC Climate Partnership) between HSBC and four environmental charities – The Climate Group, Earthwatch, Smithsonian Tropical Research Institute and WWF – to tackle climate change. 'The partnership aims to create cleaner, greener cities across the world; create individual HSBC climate champions worldwide; help protect some of the world's major rivers; and conduct the world's largest ever field experiment on the long-term effects of climate change on the world's forests.

> *Local projects*
>
> We believe it's important to support employees working on local grassroots programmes and projects. Any staff engaged in a local project that supports young people or the environment and which utilises bank volunteers, is able to apply for funding for their chosen charity to help run the project. Past projects have included creating sensory gardens in schools, taking children from inner-city areas to the pantomime and supporting local city farms.
>
> In 2011, 112 local projects were approved for funding, donating a total of £491,000 and involving 2,849 volunteers over 22,520 hours.
>
> All our employees are entitled to one day's paid leave each year to participate in a volunteering activity with a registered charity or community organisation.

Around 1,000 HSBC employees in the UK work on a voluntary basis with the charity Young Enterprise, advising and encouraging young people to set up their own businesses.

Matched funding: Employees are given time off in which to volunteer, with their fundraising efforts being matched by the bank up to a maximum of £500.

Payroll giving: The bank operates the Give As You Earn scheme.

HSBC is a Principal member of Arts and Business.

Commercially-led support

Sponsorship

The following information is taken from HSBC's website:

> At HSBC we view sponsorship both as an investment to help sustain and grow our business and as an opportunity to connect with customers and colleagues in the local communities in which we serve.
>
> At HSBC we know first-hand how important it is to understand and learn from different countries and people around the world, which is why the delivery of our sponsorships has a special focus on developing youth, furthering education and embracing different cultures.
>
> *Sports sponsorships*
>
> HSBC is a major sponsor of sport around the world – with a broad portfolio of sponsorships focusing on Rugby, Tennis, Golf and Eventing. HSBC's proud tradition of sponsoring sport dates back to 1980, with the Hong Kong Sevens Rugby Tournament. Running throughout all these associations is a major commitment to the development of sport for young people in the local community. Sport plays a major part in the development of life skills and values in society and HSBC is proud to support a wide range of programmes locally that bring opportunities and learning to young people around the world.
>
> *Cultural sponsorships*
>
> HSBC believes that Cultural Exchange has important business benefits, and knows first-hand how vital it is to appreciate and understand different values in order to build successful relationships and do business internationally.
>
> HSBC's global Cultural Exchange programme seeks to increase understanding and interaction among cultures around the world through the exploration of culture in all its varied forms – including fine art, cuisine, music, language and literature.
>
> Each cultural project is chosen for its ability to enhance cultural awareness and provide tangible benefits for the brand and the business.

To apply for sponsorship, complete and submit the online form: www.hsbc.com/1/2/about/sponsorship.

Corporate social responsibility

CSR committee: Heads of Corporate Sustainability in each of the HSBC's main regions have joint reporting lines to their local chair or chief executive, and to the group Head of Corporate Sustainability. The group head of human resources is responsible for sustainability on behalf of the group chief executive and the HSBC Holdings board.

CSR policy: The following statement is taken from the group's website:

> For HSBC, being sustainable means managing our business across the world for the long-term. That means achieving sustainable profits for our shareholders, building long-lasting relationships with customers, valuing our highly committed employees, respecting environmental limits and investing in communities.

We were unable to determine the ratio of women to men on the board from the information given in the annual report and accounts.

CSR report: There is a comprehensive Sustainability report published annually.

Exclusions

No support for advertising in charity brochures, animal welfare, appeals from individuals, the arts, elderly people, fundraising events, political appeals, religious appeals, science/technology, sickness/disability, or sport.

Applications

In writing to the correspondent.

Alan Hudson Ltd

Agriculture

Correspondent: D W Ball, Trustee, 1–3, York Row, Wisbech, Cambs PE13 1EA (tel: 01945 583087/01945 461456)

Director: Alan Hudson

Year end	31/10/2010
Turnover	£1,712,061

Nature of business: Fruit growers.

Company registration number: 613979

Charitable donations

UK cash (latest declared):	2010	£21,000
	2008	£218,000
	2007	£141,000
	2006	£117,500
Total UK:	2010	£138,000
Total worldwide:	2010	£138,000
Cash worldwide:	2010	£21,000

Corporate social responsibility

CSR policy: There was no information found in the company's accounts. No website was available.

Applications

In writing to the correspondent at: The Hudson Foundation, 1–3 York Row, Wisbech Cambs PE13 1EA.

Other information

The company is wholly owned by The Hudson Foundation (Charity Commission no.280332) and donates its taxable profits for the year to the charity by way of Gift Aid. In 2010, the company paid the charity the rent of £21,000. The company has since donated a further £117,000 by way of gift aid to the Hudson Foundation.

The Hudson Foundation

The object of the foundation is the relief of infirm and/or older people, in particular the establishment and maintenance of residential accommodation for relief of infirm and/or older people and to make donations to other charitable purposes with a preference for the Wisbech area. The accounts state that 'whilst the trustees do make contributions to revenue expenditure of charitable organisations, they prefer to assist in the funding of capital projects for the advancement of the community of Wisbech and district.'

Hunting plc

Exploration services

Correspondent: Ms Anna Blundell-Williams, Public Relations Co-ordinator, 3 Cockspur Street, London SW1Y 5BQ (tel: 020 7321 0123; fax: 020 7839 2072; email: anna.bw@hunting.plc.uk; website: www.hunting.plc.uk)

Directors: Richard Hunting, Chair; Dennis Proctor, Chief Executive; John Hofmeister; John Nicholas; Andrew Szescila (women: 0; men: 5)

Year end	31/12/2011
Turnover	£608,800,000
Pre-tax profit	£79,800,000

Nature of business: The principal activity of the company is oil services.

Company registration number: 974568

Main locations: London

Total employees: 3,453

Charitable donations

UK cash (latest declared):	2009	£56,000
	2008	£51,000
	2007	£57,000
	2006	£49,000
	2005	£49,000

Corporate social responsibility

CSR committee: There was no evidence of a separate CSR Committee.

CSR policy: This information was obtained from the company's website:

> The company acknowledges and is committed to its social responsibilities within the area in which it operates. Its contribution and involvement is determined by regional custom and best practice in those locations and is subject to regular monitoring and review by the board and divisional management.

> In this way subsidiaries support a range of charitable and community projects in their local areas. Community support is delivered in many different ways, from corporate sponsorship to individual employees being encouraged and supported to participate in charitable events.

CSR report: There was no evidence of a separate CSR report.

Exclusions

The company does not make political donations.

Applications

In writing to the correspondent. The trustees of the Hunting Charitable Trust meet once a year, generally in November.

Other information

There was no information regarding charitable donations for 2011.

The following information is taken from Hunting's 2011 annual accounts:

> Of particular note is the annual Hunting Art Prize which, after a quarter of a century of supporting British art, was relaunched in Houston, Texas in 2006. The Hunting Art Prize is among the largest art awards in the US and is the largest award in North America for painting and drawing.

Huntsman/Tioxide Europe Ltd

Chemicals and plastics

Correspondent: PA to the Company Secretary, Haverton Hill Road, Billingham TS23 1PS (tel: 01642 370300; fax: 01642 370290; website: www.huntsman.com)

Directors: Jon M. Huntsman, Chair; Peter R. Huntsman, Chief Executive; Jon M. Huntsman Jr; Nolan D. Archibald; Dr Mary C. Beckerle; M. Anthony Burns; Dr Patrick T. Harker; Sir Robert J. Margetts; Wayne A. Reaud; Alvin V. Shoemaker (women: 1; men: 9)

Year end	31/12/2011
Turnover	£11,221,000,000
Pre-tax profit	£360,000,000

Nature of business: The manufacture of titanium oxide and titanium compounds.

Company registration number: 249759

Main locations: Adlington, Billingham, Duxford, Grimsby, Hartlepool, Llanelli, Redcar, Shepton Mallet

Charitable donations

UK cash (latest declared):	2009	£0
	2006	£18,000
	2005	£25,000

Corporate social responsibility

CSR committee: There was evidence of a separate Corporate Governance Committee.

CSR policy: The company directs charitable donations to The Huntsman Foundation (US based).

CSR report: An up to date CSR report was unavailable although previous years were.

Applications

The company has factories in Adlington, Billingham (International Headquarters), Duxford, Grimsby, Hartlepool, Llanelli, Redcar and Shepton Mallet. Support is focused on charities local to these sites.

Other information

Previous research suggested in 2006 the company made charitable donations totalling £18,000 (2005: £25,000). We have no information regarding more recent donations.

> Our founder and chairman, Jon M. Huntsman, oversees charitable foundations with a view to making life better for families around the world. Combating Cancer Jon Huntsman – whose parents both died of cancer and who is a cancer survivor himself – is personally waging the battle against this killer disease. Jon and Karen have donated and raised more than $350 million to establish and fund the Huntsman Cancer Institute and Hospitals. The Institute's team of internationally renowned specialists and researchers are working in diverse fields to reduce the rate of cancer deaths and to ease the burden of the disease.
>
> Huntsman is committed to long-term relief effort for the country of Armenia. Since this former Soviet republic was ravaged by an earthquake in 1988, Huntsman has donated an estimated $20 million to rebuild the country.

IBM United Kingdom Ltd

Electronics/computers

Correspondent: Mark Wakefield, Corporate Community Relations Manager, PO Box 41, North Harbour, Portsmouth, Hampshire PO6 3AU (tel: 0870 542 6426; fax: 0870 542 6329; email: wakefim@uk.ibm.com; website: www.ibm.com/uk/en)

Directors: W. Chrystie; C. Wyatt; S. Leonard

Year end	31/12/2011
Turnover	£3,974,300,000
Pre-tax profit	£327,500,000

Nature of business: IBM United Kingdom Ltd is the UK subsidiary of IBM Corporation. It is involved in the provision of information technology services and solutions, and the development, production and supply of advanced information technology products.

Company registration number: 741598

Main locations: London, Portsmouth, Glasgow

Total employees: 16,075

Membership: BITC

Charitable donations

UK cash (latest declared):	2011	£3,700,000
	2008	£800,000
	2007	£800,000
	2006	£800,000
	2005	£800,000
Total UK:	2011	£3,700,000
Total worldwide:	2011	£3,700,000
Cash worldwide:	2011	£3,700,000

Community involvement

IBM UK's support for charitable and community organisations is directed through its associated charity, **IBM United Kingdom Trust** (Charity Commission no. 290462).

The trust primarily achieves its aims by supporting the development and delivery of IBM's own community involvement programmes where these meet the charitable objectives of the trust. Effectively, support is provided for the majority of IBM's community involvement programmes in the UK, as well as for IBM's pan-European corporate social responsibility programmes within Europe, the Middle East and Africa.

Most of the trust's income comes from the IBM International Foundation or the IBM Corporation and its subsidiaries.

The following initiatives are supported by the trust:

Promoting volunteering

On Demand Community – The UK community grants programme is designed to support IBM employees who have registered as volunteers for the on demand community programme. The scheme provides money or IBM products to eligible community organisations and schools where IBM employees and retirees are actively volunteering, and in support of specific projects. In 2010, 363 grants were made in 21 countries to organisations where volunteers contribute time on a regular basis.

To be eligible an organisation must be a registered charity or other not-for-profit community organisation that offers assistance in areas such as education, the environment, arts/cultural activities, health and human services and so on. It must also be located in the community where the volunteer activity takes place.

Charities and schools may also be eligible for 'technology discounts'. IBM offers substantial discounts on many hardware and software products for schools and voluntary (not-for-profit) organisations supported by IBM volunteers.

MentorPlace – In 2010, successful MentorPlace programmes were run in France, Ireland, Poland, Spain, Sweden and the UK where IBM mentors worked on a one to one basis with over 350 disadvantaged young people.

Increasing the use of technology in education

KidSmart – Since 1999 the trust has supported a major IBM global programme called KidSmart to provide nursery schools in areas of significant disadvantage with computers in purpose designed plastic units. During 2010, a total of 1,976 KidSmart 'Young Explorer' units were shipped to 29 countries. Over 120,000 children have benefitted from these and 4,000 teachers have been trained to use KidSmart effectively for teaching and learning.

Reading Companion – IBM has developed a programme to support the development of literacy skills in both children and adults, through an innovative web based programme that 'listens' to readers and provides feedback on their progress to both the reader and their teacher. The software is based on IBM's voice recognition technology. There are now 12,904 active users of Reading Companion.

Support for research

The trust makes grants that enable the IBM Corporation both to share its technical expertise and to provide support for students and academics engaged in leading programmes related to computer sciences with universities in Europe.

Science and technology

IBM's wide range of science and technology programmes are delivered by IBM volunteers, in partnership with educational institutions. In addition, IBM has initiated 'Science in Schools' collaborative networks in 13 countries.

Aiding the disadvantaged

Two principal grants were made in this category during 2010. They were to *Emmaus Hampshire* which provides formerly homeless people with a supportive environment and *AbilityNet* to support work with people with disabilities.

Comprehensive information regarding the above support, eligibility and how to apply are provided on the company's website at: www-05.ibm.com/uk/news/ondemandcommunity/index or, should this link change, go to IBM UK's homepage > About Us > On Demand Community.

Corporate giving

In 2011, IBM UK made cash donations to UK not for profit organisations of £200,000 (2010: £200,000) for educational, cultural and social welfare activities. Grants are made to organisations where IBM employees volunteer. We understand that the majority of this is disbursed through the company's trust, IBM United Kingdom Trust (Charity Commission no. 290462).

At the time of writing the latest accounts available for the IBM United Kingdom Trust were for 2010, when it had an income of just over £3.7 million. The majority of the trust's income is provided by the IBM International Foundation or the IBM Corporation and its subsidiaries. Grants were made totalling £3.7 million and went towards increasing the use of IT in education, educational research, improving the life of people with disabilities and disadvantaged people, promoting volunteering, and health, environment and poverty.

Employee-led support

Through its On Demand Community initiative, IBM encourages and supports employees and retirees to undertake voluntary work, organising its community involvement policies to motivate people to volunteer. The company's intranet site has a database of volunteer opportunities which allows staff to find a good cause which matches their interests.

Payroll giving: The company operates the Give As You Earn scheme.

Corporate social responsibility

CSR policy: No specific CSR information for the UK company.

We were unable to determine the ratio of women to men on the board.

Exclusions

IBM will not support organisations which advocate, support, or practice activities inconsistent with IBM's non-discrimination policies, whether based on race, colour, religion, gender, gender identity or expression, sexual orientation, national origin, disability or age. Documentation (in the form of an Equality of Opportunity statement) demonstrating that organisations comply with the above statement will be required.

IBM reserves the right to determine which organisations are eligible for grants.

Applications

All requests for funding need to be requested by the employee rather than the recipient organisation, as organisations without an IBM employee volunteering cannot be supported. It might, however, be worth charitable and community groups based around company sites advertising voluntary positions on its intranet site to open up this avenue of funding.

The trust's strategy for grantmaking falls into three key areas:

- The provision of grants that advance the aims of the trust and support IBM programmes
- The provision of small grants in support of charitable organisations in the communities surrounding IBM sites; and
- The provision of grants that support and encourage employee volunteering by IBM staff

For applications to the IBM UK Trust contact Mark Wakefield, Corporate Community Relations Manager, IBM UK Trust, Mail Point 1PG1, 76 Upper Ground, London SE1 9PZ, telephone no. 020 7202 3608 or email – wakefim@uk.ibm.com

Note: Unsolicited applications from organisations are not considered by the trust.

ICAP plc

Financial services

Correspondent: The Charity Day Team, 2 Broadgate, London EC2M 7UR (tel: 020 7000 5000/020 7000 5000; fax: 020 7000 5975; email: charity.day@icap.com; website: www.icapcharityday.com)

Directors: John Nixon; John Slevwright; Charles Gregson, Chair; Michael Spencer, Group Chief Executive Officer; Iain Torrens, Group Finance Director; Robert Standing; Diane Schueneman; Hsieh Fu Hua (women: 1; men: 7)

Year end	31/03/2012
Turnover	£1,681,000,000
Pre-tax profit	£217,000,000

Nature of business: The company is the world's largest interdealer broker and is active in the wholesale markets for OTC derivatives, fixed income securities, money market products, foreign exchange, energy, credit and equity derivatives.

Company registration number: 3611426

Subsidiaries include: BrokerTec Europe Ltd, Exotix Investments Ltd, Garban-Intercapital Systems Ltd, Guy Butler Ltd, Harlow (London) Ltd, T&M Securities Ltd

Main locations: London

Total employees: 5,100

Charitable donations

UK cash (latest declared):	2012	£4,900,000
	2010	£5,000,000
	2009	£5,000,000
	2007	£9,200,000
	2005	£2,100,000
Total UK:	2012	£4,900,000
Total worldwide:	2012	£12,750,000
Cash worldwide:	2012	£12,750,000

Community involvement

The company donates to charitable causes the money raised each year during its 'Charity Day', launched in 1993. On this day each year, the group donates its entire revenue, without any cost reductions, to various charities selected by local offices. This unique event includes the commission made by brokers as well as the company's revenue. The company recognises this as also having the benefit of motivating employees.

There is significant staff, customer and supplier involvement in Charity Day and the charities are selected by ICAP's staff in each region in which it operates.

The revenue would otherwise contribute directly to the broker commission pool and, as such, staff also contribute directly in a personal financial way to the good causes supported.

The following statement is taken from the company's website:

> Charity Day has made such a big impact on the charities we support around the world because giving away one day's revenue and commissions every year has enabled us to fund entire projects – such as a badly-needed clinic in a remote part of Kenya, a science laboratory in a rural school in India or research into conditions such as cystic fibrosis which has progressed as far as clinical trials] over 1000 projects worldwide. We have been following up on some of these projects and you can read about them in the 'Success Stories' section of the website.

Corporate giving

In 2011 ICAP's Charity Day raised £12.75 million for more than 200 charitable organisations. Of this, £4.9 million was donated to UK charities. Recipient organisations included: Cure Parkinson's Trust, Debbie Fund, Face Africa, Fauna and Flora International, Fight for Peace, Maggie's, Reed's School, The Kevin Spacey Foundation, War Child, Women for Women, World Child Cancer.

Employee-led support

The firm matches employees charitable fundraising and giving to a maximum of £250 per person, per year.

Payroll giving: The company operates the Give As You Earn scheme.

Corporate social responsibility

CSR committee: There is a dedicated Charity Day Team (See Contact details).

CSR policy: Taken from the annual report and accounts 2011/12:

> ICAP Charity Day came into being in 1993 as a unique way of making a significant difference to charities by giving away all of our revenue and commissions on one day each year.

CSR report: A CSR report is published within the annual report and accounts.

Applications

In writing to the correspondent.

IG Group Holdings plc

Gaming

Correspondent: Corporate Responsibility Dept., Cannon Bridge House, 25 Dowgate Hill, London EC4R 2YA (tel: 020 7896 0011; email: info@igindex.co.uk; website: www.iggroup.com)

Directors: Jonathan Davie, Chair; Tim Howkins, Chief Executive; Peter Hetherington; Christopher Hill; Andrew MacKay; Nat le Roux; Roger Yates; David Currie; Stephen Hill; Martin Jackson (women: 0; men: 10)

Year end	31/05/2011
Turnover	£320,392,000
Pre-tax profit	£163,000,000

Nature of business: IG Group is a provider of financial spread betting and CFDs. An established member of the FTSE 250 and offices across Europe, the US, Japan, Singapore and Australia.

Company registration number: 4677092

UK employees: 100

Total employees: 952

Charitable donations

UK cash (latest declared):	2010	£52,400
	2009	£50,000
Total worldwide:	2011	£119,000
Cash worldwide:	2011	£119,000

Corporate social responsibility

CSR committee: There was no evidence of a separate CSR Committee.

CSR policy: This information was obtained from the company's website:

> IG Group is committed to ensuring that its interactions with employees, clients, suppliers, shareholders, society and the wider environment are managed responsibly. A sense of responsibility underlies all our businesses and is manifested in everything from our dealings with clients to conscientiousness about the environmental impact we make.

CSR report: There was no evidence of a separate CSR report.

Applications

In writing to the correspondent.

Other information

In 2010/11 the I G Group made charitable donations of £119,000 (2010: £40,000) as follows: Japanese earthquake relief fund (£37,290); The Gambling Trust (£26,290); The Entrepreneurs Foundation (£20,000); Employee-matched giving (£11,750); Specialist schools (£10,500); Cricket Foundation (£5,000); and 'other' (£8,212).

The company grants additional leave for employees for voluntary work on a like-for-like basis up to a maximum of five matched days per annual leave year.

Matched funding: The company encourages employees to engage in activities that help their development and support local communities. Employees raised money for the Bobby Moore Fund for Cancer Research UK by entering the Three Peaks Challenge where they raised £8,000. The company matched funding of almost £12,000 in 2011.

The IG Group also runs a volunteering scheme with Volunteer Reading Help (VRH) where employees can volunteer as a reading helper in a local primary school. Reading helpers volunteer once a week for an hour and commit for a minimum of one year to work with the same children each week. IG employees typically work in Islington.

Imagination Technologies Group plc

Manufacturing

Correspondent: Company Secretary, Imagination House, Home Park Estate, Kings Langley, Hertfordshire WD4 8LZ (tel: 01923 260511; fax: 01923 268969; email: info@imgtec.com; website: www.imgtec.com)

Directors: Geoff Shingles, Chair; Hossein Yassale, Chief Executive; Richard Smith; David Hurst-Brown; Ian Pearson; David Anderson (women: 0; men: 6)

Year end	30/04/2011
Turnover	£98,045,000
Pre-tax profit	£16,360,000

Nature of business: Imagination Technologies Group plc is an international leader in the creation and licensing of semiconductor System-on-Chip Intellectual Property (SoC IP) and in the development and manufacture of DAB digital and connected radios.

Company registration number: 2920061

Total employees: 725

Charitable donations

UK cash (latest declared):	2011	£1,200
	2010	£16,000
	2009	£800
Total UK:	2011	£1,200
Total worldwide:	2011	£1,200
Cash worldwide:	2011	£1,200

Corporate social responsibility

CSR committee: There was no evidence of a separate CSR Committee.

CSR policy: There was no information regarding CSR Policy.

CSR report: There was no evidence of a separate CSR report.

Applications

In writing to the correspondent.

Other information

In 2010/11 the group gave £1,200 in cash donations. A list of beneficiaries was unavailable.

IMI plc

Engineering

Correspondent: John O'Shea, Company Secretary, Lakeside Solihull Parkway, Birmingham Business Park, Birmingham B37 7XZ (tel: 01217 173700; email: info@imiplc.com; website: www.imiplc.com)

Directors: Roberto Quarta, Chair; Robert Lamb, Chief Executive; Terry Gateley; Kevin Beeston; Anita Frew; Bob Stack; Douglas Hurt; Roy Twite; Ian Whiting; Sean Toomes (women: 1; men: 9)

Year end	31/12/2010
Turnover	£2,131,000,000
Pre-tax profit	£301,400,000

Nature of business: IMI is a diversified engineering group operating in two main areas: Fluid controls and Retail dispense. It manufactures and sells internationally.

Company registration number: 714275

Main locations: Birmingham, Manchester, Liverpool, Yorkshire

Total employees: 14,403

Charitable donations

UK cash (latest declared):	2010	£214,000
	2009	£233,000
	2007	£205,000
	2006	£235,000
	2005	£298,000
Total UK:	2010	£214,000
Total worldwide:	2010	£214,000
Cash worldwide:	2010	£214,000

Corporate social responsibility

CSR committee: There was no evidence of a CSR Report.

CSR policy: This information was obtained from the group's annual report:

> The communities where we operate are crucial to the success of IMI. We have a duty to be a responsible business citizen and to meet our commitments to these communities. Although our projects and facilities can bring benefits to local communities by creating jobs and investment in the surrounding area, they can also give rise to concerns.

CSR report: There was no evidence of a CSR committee.

Exclusions

No support for political appeals.

Applications

In writing to the correspondent. Grant decisions are made by an appeals committee which meets on an ad hoc basis. Local appeals should be sent to the relevant local plant or branch.

Other information

£214,000 was given during 2010 (2010: £233,000), by the company, for community and similar purposes. The group supports a range of selected national charities and smaller charitable organisations operating in communities where the group has a presence. The group will support charities/organisations involved in the community; education; children/young people; health/ill health; and overseas projects.

Imperial Tobacco Group plc

Tobacco

Correspondent: Kirsty Mann, Senior CR Engagement Manager, PO Box 244, Upton Road, Southville, Bristol BS99 7UJ (tel: 01179 636636; email: cr@uk.imptob.com; website: www.imperial-tobacco.com)

Directors: Robert Dyrbus; Pierre Jungels; Ken Burnett; Michael Herlihy; Susan Murray; Berge Setrakian; Mark Williamson; Malcolm Wyman; Matthew Phillips; Iain Nappier, Chair; Alison Cooper, Chief Executive (women: 2; men: 9)

Year end	30/09/2011
Turnover	£29,223,000,000
Pre-tax profit	£2,153,000,000

Nature of business: Tobacco manufacturer.

Company registration number: 3236483

Brands include: Davidoff; Drum; Ducados; Fine; Fortuna; Gauloises; Golden Virginia; JPS; Lambert and Butler; Nobel; Rizla; Style; West; Windsor Blue.

Main locations: Bristol, Nottingham

Total employees: 38,200

Membership: BITC, LBG

Charitable donations

UK cash (latest declared):	2011	£1,800,000
	2009	£1,900,000
	2007	£200,000
	2006	£700,000
	2005	£984,000
Total UK:	2011	£1,800,000
Total worldwide:	2011	£3,000,000
Cash worldwide:	2011	£1,800,000

Community involvement

The following statement is taken from the company's annual report for 2011:

> We have revised our approach to community investment to better focus on supporting countries of need and those which are most important in terms of tobacco supply and our business presence. We allocated around £3 million to partnership investment in 2011 as well as the management time involved to maximise the benefits from our involvement.

The following guidelines were published in the Group's CSR report 2011:

> *Community investment guidelines*
> We are pleased to support a wide variety of charities and not-for-profit organisations around the world, in order to invest in the communities in which our employees live. The following guidelines for these donations apply throughout the Group. To administer them we have a number of Regional Community Investment Committees that apply the following criteria and decide whether or not to make donations from their budgetary allocations. The criteria on which funds are allocated are:
>
> - We will seek to ensure allocation of funds to worthy causes aligned with the direction of our broader corporate strategy for business sustainability
> - We will not make political donations
> - We will give preference to charities or not-for-profit organisations operating in the geographical areas of our own operations, thus benefiting the communities in which our employees live
> - We will give preference to charities in which our employees are actively involved? in particular, we prefer to match funds raised by employees' own activities
> - We will give preference to officially recognised or registered charities
> - Qualifying donations will be supported on merit, subject to budgetary considerations
>
> We will not seek publicity for the individual donations we make? however, we will account for donations by broad category only. We may agree to the use of the Company name on occasions where it may increase the opportunity for the charity, or not-for-profit organisation, to generate additional contributions. We would like to publicise success stories internally, or on our website – in such cases text would be agreed in advance by both parties. We will not fund projects if we feel it might be potentially disadvantageous to the Group, or to the charity or not-for-profit organisation concerned.
>
> Since we cannot support all appeals, we will not normally give financial support to individuals, research projects, expeditions or trips.
>
> We do not use our community investment for advertising purposes or for promoting our products.

Charities and not-for-profit organisations receiving substantial funds from governments will be given a lower priority.

We support a limited number of large international partnerships. Proposals for such projects should address issues of international concern.

Prospective funding partners must be willing to communicate regularly, and work closely with our employees. Our aim is to work together to maximise community benefit.

Funding decisions are taken after careful consideration and discussion by our International Community Investment Committee.

Corporate giving

The group's annual report for 2011 states that it supports the communities in which it operates by allocating £3 million (2010: £3 million) to *partnership investment.* From this figure, £200,000 (2010: £200,000) was donated to UK registered charities operating in the UK, £300,000 (2010: £300,000) to UK registered charities operating abroad and £1.3 million (2010: £1.3 million) through the UK Charities Aid Foundation to charities based overseas. The company is a member of the London Benchmarking Group but the breakdown of cash donations/ contributions in kind (which LBG recommends) does not appear to have been published. A request for a breakdown of these figures was sent in February 2012.

In line with our usual practice, we have taken all these donations as the UK cash contribution as they were donated to UK registered charities.

Employee-led support

The group states that:

During the year our employees also gave their time during normal working hours to contribute to local community programmes in a number of countries. Imperial Tobacco in Bristol In August this year litter was collected from the streets by a team of around 60 Imperial Tobacco employees in Bristol. The litter-picking exercise underlined Imperial Tobacco's ongoing support for the 'Love Where You Live' campaign operated by the UK charity Keep Britain Tidy. The campaign, backed by a number of high-profile FMCG companies, highlights the litter problem as one we have a collective responsibility to address.

Corporate social responsibility

CSR committee: The group gives the following information:

Our chief executive is responsible for recommending to the board and communicating policy, standards and direction for community investment and charitable activity in the group. The central financial allocation is administered by a number of Community Investment Committees made up of senior employees and the Altadis Foundation. The Altadis Foundation was created in 1992 and is registered with the Spanish Ministry of Culture.

Central Corporate Responsibility along with the Committees and Altadis Foundation, oversee significant international projects, following an approval process for funding; monitoring the expenditure and reporting annually on project activity and disbursements.

CSR policy: The company's annual accounts for 2011 state: 'Our responsibility strategy focuses on four areas: making and selling responsibly, enabling our people, respecting natural resources and partnering with and contributing to society.'

CSR report: This is produced annually and has a section on 'Partnering and Contributing in Society' from which the following quote is taken (2011):

Partnership Projects

We address long-term challenges in our supply chain through partnership programmes with our suppliers and with nongovernmental organisations (NGOs). This includes various ongoing programmes to find solutions to issues such as climate change, environmental protection, forestry protection, child labour, sustainable development and poverty alleviation.

Exclusions

The group gives the following information:

The nature of our product, combined with our own International Marketing Standards, means that we are unwilling to make donations to charities or not-for-profit organisations involving young people, where there is a chance that our motives may be misconstrued. However, we recognise that some young people are amongst the most disadvantaged and deserving of charitable support. We therefore consider carefully potential exceptions to this norm. For example, one of our important partnerships is with the Elimination of Child Labour in Tobacco (ECLT) Foundation. Details of exclusions can be found on the company's website.

Applications

The following information is taken from the Group's CSR Report 2011:

Applicants must complete an online form found on the company's website under 'Corporate Responsibility'. We prefer to support charities and not-for-profit organisations which our employees already support by their own activities. Our own employees can apply for support through the Company Intranet.

If you wish to enter into a partnership with us at a regional or international level please complete the online form. If you have any supporting documentation, leaflets or other information about the organisation on whose behalf you are seeking our assistance, please make a note of this on your application form so you may be contacted with details of where to send the material.

Inchcape plc

Motors and accessories

Correspondent: Company Secretary, 22a St James's Square, London SW1Y 5LP (tel: 020 7546 0022; fax: 020 7546 0010; email: contact@inchcape.com; website: www.inchcape.com)

Directors: Ken Hanna, Chair; Andre Lacroix, Chief Executive; Will Samuel; John McConnell; Alison Cooper; David Scotland; Michael Wemms; Nigel Northridge; Simon Borrows (women: 1; men: 8)

Year end	31/12/2010
Turnover	£5,885,400,000
Pre-tax profit	£223,800,000

Nature of business: Inchcape is a scale automotive retail group operating in Australia, Belgium, Greece, Hong Kong, Singapore and the UK. The group also has operations in a number of other global markets. It represents leading automotive brands and operates either a retail, or a vertically integrated retail model (i.e. exclusive distribution and retail), depending on the market.

Company registration number: 609782

Main locations: London, Watford

UK employees: 5,106

Total employees: 14,068

Charitable donations

UK cash (latest declared):	2009	£0
	2007	£100,000
	2006	£100,000
	2005	£100,000
Total worldwide:	2010	£11,800
Cash worldwide:	2010	£11,800

Corporate social responsibility

CSR committee: To emphasise the importance of CR, the company established a Board CR Committee which met four times in 2010.

CSR policy: This information was obtained from the company's annual report: 'At Inchcape, we recognise that corporate responsibility is a long-term programme. Our approach is to ensure that we make responsible, economic, environmental and social behaviour intrinsic to the way we work.'

CSR report: There was no separate CSR report; however five pages were devoted to CSR in the company's annual report.

Applications

In writing to the correspondent.

Other information

In 2010 the company made charitable donations totalling £11,800.

Inchcape's extensive international interests allows the group to support many different communities and cultures, often through sponsorship and support of local charities for local people.

This year Inchcape has sponsored a children's soccer school in Hong Kong; supported the Mother and Child Rehabilitation Centre in Ethiopia and supported UK road safety charity, Brake, in the UK.

Informa plc

Business services, information management and communication

Correspondent: John Burton, Company Secretary, 4th Floor, 27 Mortimer Street, London W1T 3JF (tel: 020 7017 5000; email: headoffice@informa.com; website: www.informa.com)

Directors: Derek Mapp, Chair; Peter Rigby, Chief Executive; Adam Walker; Dr Pamela Kirby; John Davis; Stephen A. Carter; Dr Brendan O'Neill; Rupert Hopley (women: 1; men: 7)

Year end	31/12/2011
Turnover	£1,275,300,000
Pre-tax profit	£295,900,000

Nature of business: Informa is an international provider of specialist information and services for the academic and scientific, professional and commercial business communities across 40 countries.

Company registration number: 3099067

Main locations: Tunbridge Wells, Colchester, Ashford, Richmond, Byfleet, Victoria, London

Total employees: 8,275

Charitable donations

UK cash (latest declared):	2011	£300,000
	2009	£200,000
	2008	£200,000
	2007	£208,464
	2005	£143,000
Total UK:	2011	£300,000
Total worldwide:	2011	£300,000
Cash worldwide:	2011	£300,000

Corporate social responsibility

CSR committee: There was no evidence of a separate CSR Committee.

CSR policy: This information was obtained from the company's website:

> There are three elements to Informa's Community Strategy:
>
> 1 The first is our global fundraising, spearheaded by our annual flagship event 'Go Bananas' for the World Cancer Research Fund. This involves a day of fun runs and other activities across all of our businesses globally
> 2 The second is our community partnership programme, which encourages each of our businesses in their key locations to set up long-term relationships with community partners that have a local or strategic link to their business
> 3 The third is our employee volunteering policy. Under this policy, every member of staff is entitled to take a day's leave each year to volunteer with an organisation of their choice

CSR report: A CSR report was available from the company's website.

Exclusions

No support for political appeals.

Applications

In writing to the correspondent.

Other information

During 2011, the company donated £300,000 to charitable organisations.

Since July 2011, Informa has pledged its support to the Prince's Trust financially through corporate donation and fundraising.

Employees in South Africa have supported Ekukhanyeni, which works with two socially deprived communities in Johannesburg since 2007.

Innocent Drinks

Drinks manufacture

Correspondent: Alan Gerbi, Innocent Foundation, 51 Stourhead Gardens, London SW2 00UL (tel: 020 8600 3993; email: hello@innocentdrinks.com; website: www.innocentfoundation.org)

Directors: Alan Gerbi, Trustee; Christina Archer, Trustee; Adam Balon, Trustee; Richard Reed, Trustee; Jon Wright, Trustee

Year end	31/12/2010

Nature of business: Production of natural fruit drinks.

Company registration number: 5054312

Charitable donations

UK cash (latest declared):	2008	£17,000
	2007	£663,000
	2006	£595,000
	2005	£397,000

Corporate social responsibility

CSR committee: No details published.

CSR policy: The company's website provides the following statement on sustainability:

> It might make us sound like a Miss World contestant, but here at Innocent, we want to leave things a little bit better than we find them. We strive to do business in a more enlightened way, where we take responsibility for the impact of our business on society and the environment, aiming to move these impacts from negative to neutral or (better still) positive. It's part of our quest to become a truly sustainable business where we have a net positive effect on the wonderful world around us.

CSR report: None published.

Applications

Contact the foundation before making a detailed proposal by filling in the short online form.

Other information

Accounts could not be found for the company at Companies House. From the details given on the website, we understand that the majority of the foundation's giving is outside the UK.

The company's foundation webpage states:

> We are a grant giving organisation that works with NGOs to deliver our vision of sustainable farming for a secure future.
>
> We are currently supporting 16 partner projects primarily in countries where innocent drinks sources its fruit. We have an agricultural focus, because we believe it is essential for communities to get the most out of the natural resources available to enable a sustainable and improved future.
>
> The employees, shareholders, EBT and company of innocent drinks give 10% of profits to charity, the majority of which goes to the innocent foundation.

The foundation's accounts for 2010 state that £520,000 is owed by the company to the foundation on which interest of 2.5% is being charged.

Intercontinental Hotels Group plc

Drinks manufacture, hotels

Correspondent: Jade Adnett, Charity Sponsorships, Broadwater Park, North Orbital Road, Denham, near Uxbridge, Buckinghamshire UB9 5HR (tel: 01895 512000; email: companysecretariat@ihg.com; website: www.ihg.com)

Directors: David Webster, Chair; Richard Solomons, Chief Executive; Thomas Singer; Kirk Kinsell; Tracy Robbins; David Kappler; Graham Allan; Jennifer Laing; Jonathan Linen; Luke Mayhew; Dale Morrison; Ying Yeh (women: 3; men: 9)

Year end	31/12/2011
Turnover	£1,102,904,000
Pre-tax profit	£310,020,300

Nature of business: Hospitality chain of hotels, soft drinks and public houses.

Company registration number: 3203484

Main locations: Windsor

Total employees: 7,956

Membership: BITC

Charitable donations

UK cash (latest declared):	2009	£519,000
	2007	£626,000
	2005	£800,000
Total worldwide:	2011	£961,000
Cash worldwide:	2011	£961,000

Corporate social responsibility

CSR committee: No details found.

CSR policy: This information was obtained from the company's website:

> We are committed to active involvement in the local communities around our hotels and corporate offices. Ultimately that means being a valued, responsible community partner by ensuring that our business objectives make a positive difference to the communities in which we operate.
>
> The aim of our charitable endeavours is to support global efforts that represent the business goals of IHG and which make a positive difference to the communities in which we operate
>
> We support charities which:
> - Operate or have needs in one of our areas of focus; environmental sustainability, creating local economic opportunity or providing disaster relief
> - Are open to innovative approaches to tackling the need
> - Are operationally efficient and can demonstrate their ability to follow through on a proposal
> - Explain clearly the benefits to IHG and our hotel communities.

CSR report: An interactive CSR report was available from the company's website.

Exclusions

The group states that it has the following restrictions on giving:

- Contributions are only made to organisations with verifiable charity status and those whose ethical principles are consistent with our Code of Ethics
- IHG does not support organisations that discriminate on the basis of race, religion, creed, gender, age, physical challenge or national origin. In addition, contributions generally are not provided to:
  - Individuals
  - Religious organisations
  - General operating support for hospitals and health care institutions
  - Capital campaigns
  - Endowment funds
  - Conferences, workshops or seminars not directly related to IHG's business interests

> IHG generally does not commit to multi-year grants; only the first year of multi-year requests will be assured, but subsequent years will be dependent upon annual evaluation for future support
>
> IHG does not make political donations of any kind

Applications

In writing to the correspondent.

Note that organisations to which the company is asked to contribute must be registered charities. Donations must be used for the sole benefit of the eligible organisations and are restricted to the use of the project for which the donation is being made.

Other information

During the year, the group donated £961,000 (2010: £519,000) in support of community initiatives and charitable causes.

IHG will also be working with the London Organising Committee of the Olympic and Paralympic Games to support the sustainability goals of London 2012.

The company has formalised its partnership with CARE International to help provide strategic advice and guidance to our hotels in times of crisis.

International Personal Finance

Financial services

Correspondent: Corporate Responsibility Dept., Number Three, Leeds City Office Park, Meadow Lane, Leeds LS11 5BD (tel: 01132 856700; fax: 01132 451675; email: enquiries@ipfin.co.uk; website: www.ipfin.co.uk)

Directors: Christopher Rodrigues, Chair; John Harnett, Chief Executive Officer; Gerard Ryan; David Broadbent, Finance Director; Tony Hales; Charles Gregson; Edyta Kurek; John Lorimer; Nicholas Page (women: 1; men: 8)

Year end	31/12/2011
Turnover	£649,500,000
Pre-tax profit	£100,500,000

Nature of business: 'A leading provider of simple financial products and services to people of modest means.'

Company registration number: 6018973

Total employees: 9,156

Membership: LBG

Charitable donations

UK cash (latest declared):	2011	£56,000
	2009	£750,000
Total UK:	2011	£100,000
Total worldwide:	2011	£1,170,000
Cash worldwide:	2011	£600,000

Community involvement

Information is taken from the group's website:

> We're committed to developing community initiatives that make a positive, long-term impact. The key aim of our group community investment policy is to balance the needs of the community with strategic business concerns, the issues our customers and agents find important and the aspirations of our employees.
>
> We set broad community-investment objectives for the group, but have a regional approach to the delivery of specific programmes to ensure specific needs are met. For this reason we have community investment specialists in all markets and wherever possible we work with external specialists from the charity, community and/or consumer protection sector.
>
> The key area of focus is financial education. This is because we want to empower consumers to make informed choices and create a market of well-informed consumers. Some of our local programmes have been the first of their kind and we have some great examples where our programmes are starting to mature.
>
> Our community investment strategy has three strands:
>
> *Improving financial education*
> Financial literacy is our main area of focus. We recognise the importance of supporting education on money management and using credit wisely.
>
> *Social inclusion*
> We support local social inclusion and education programmes that aim to improve the lives of people excluded from society – whether through poverty, lack of education or physical or mental impairment.
>
> *Volunteering*
> Employee involvement is an important aspect of how we invest in our communities. Most of our businesses facilitate and encourage employee volunteering where we look to link volunteering with skill development or use it as a way of bringing our values to life.

Corporate giving

In 2011, a total of £1.17 million (£740,000 excluding management/staff costs) was given in community investment; this represents 1.2% of pre-tax profit (the same level as 2010, despite a substantially reduced profit figure). This benefitted 446 charities and not-for-profit organisations and over 65,000 direct beneficiaries. 'We feel our community activities provide great benefits for our business too, with projects found to increase employee satisfaction, contribute to skill development and generate positive press coverage as well as raising the profile of the company.'

Employee-led support

IFP staff carry out a significant amount of volunteering in support of community causes and in 2011, 2,800 employees across the group volunteered over 11,500 hours in company time. Employees also contributed a further 11,500 hours of their time outside business hours.

£100,000 has been leveraged through activities such as payroll giving and fundraising.

Corporate social responsibility

CSR committee: For sustainability governance, visit: www.ipfin.co.uk/sustainability/governance.aspx

CSR policy: Information taken from the group's website:

We have a proactive community investment programme which focuses on social inclusion and financial literacy, addressing a real business risk by helping to create a market of well-informed consumers.

CSR report: reporting on non-financial performance across customers, people, community investment and environment can be found in the specific sections of sustainability in practice. Full details of these measures (i.e. scope, definitions and how we've decided what to report) are included in our Basis of reporting.

Applications

In writing to the correspondence.

Invensys plc

Instrumentation

Correspondent: PA to the Company Secretary, 3rd Floor, 40 Grosvenor Place, London SW1X 7AW (tel: 020 3155 1200; website: www.invensys.com/en/corporateresponsibility)

Directors: Sir Nigel Rudd, Chair; Wayne Edmunds, Chief Executive; David Thomas; Bay Green; Deena Mattar; Michael Parker; Pat Zito; Dr Martin Read; Paul Lester; Victoria Hull; Francesco Caio

Year end	31/03/2011
Turnover	£2,486,000,000
Pre-tax profit	£222,000,000

Nature of business: A leading provider of automation and controls for use in homes, offices and industry.

Company registration number: 166023

Total employees: 20,341

Charitable donations

UK cash (latest declared):	2011	£0
	2010	£15,000
	2008	£200,000
	2007	£300,000
Total UK:	2011	£0
Total worldwide:	2011	£300,000
Cash worldwide:	2011	£300,000

Corporate social responsibility

CSR committee: There was no evidence of a separate CSR Committee.

CSR policy: This information was obtained from the company's website:

Invensys is committed to supporting the principles of economic success, environmental stewardship, diversity and social responsibility. We believe that by acting as a responsible global citizen, we will not only minimize business risk but also enhance our reputation as a business partner.

CSR report: A full CSR report was available from the company's website.

Applications

In writing to the correspondent.

Other information

The 2011 accounts state the following:

During the year group donations to charities and community causes worldwide were £300,000 (2010: £200,000), with UK charities receiving £nil (2010: £nil).

Community involvement: Our businesses provide a variety of programmes such as matching gifts, sponsorship of activities and paid volunteer time to allow our employees to participate actively in community events.

The company is recognised as one of the top ten supporters of the Blood Transfusion Service in the South West of the UK.

Investec plc

Financial services, banking

Correspondent: Alison Gardner, Sustainability Department, 100 Grayston Drive, Sandown, Sandton 2196, South Africa (tel: 020 7597 4000; fax: 020 7597 4070; email: ourbusinessresponsibility@investec.co.za; website: www.investec.co.uk)

Directors: Bernand Kantor, Managing Director; S. Koseff, Chief Executive Officer; HJ. du Toit; G. R. Burger (women: 0; men: 4)

Year end	31/03/2011
Turnover	£2,238,783,000
Pre-tax profit	£466,378,000

Nature of business: Specialist bank and asset manager.

Company registration number: 3633621

Total employees: 7,237

Membership: LBG

Charitable donations

UK cash (latest declared):	2010	£1,300,000
Total worldwide:	2011	£5,000,000
Cash worldwide:	2011	£4,500,000

Community involvement

Community involvement

The following information is taken from the company's 2010/11 annual report and accounts:

Corporate Governance

CSI in Europe and the UK

We have placed strong historical emphasis on education and entrepreneurship as key areas of active social investment focus, while also supporting other causes, albeit more passively. Empowering disadvantaged communities and facilitating socio-economic growth and upliftment remains our stated objective.

In keeping with our business model of independent, highly autonomous business units, supported by a strong centre, there is no single overriding approach to social investment within the group, although clear commonalities exist. Each of the regions has pursued social investment as deemed appropriate to their circumstances and where they are in the evolution of their business.

UK and Europe

The UK social investment programme plays a key role in the fulfilment of one of Investec's core values, that of making an unselfish contribution to society. It champions sustainable social investment by:

- Building dedicated charitable partnerships
- Engaging all Investec employees in making a positive difference
- Harnessing our diverse resources and collective talent

Key developments during the period:

- Investec was a finalist in the education category at the 2010 Lord Mayor's Dragon Awards. These awards recognise the contributions made by companies to their local communities
- We are currently undertaking a review of the progress we have made with our social development programme over the last two years. This will allow us to set targets for the next two years. We would like to achieve a 50% sign-up rate for volunteers by March 2012
- We are supporting three projects initiated by the Bromley by Bow Centre, an internationally renowned charity which has earned a reputation as a dynamic social business that has transformed its community in East London over the last 25 years
- We run a mentoring programme for 50 students from Morpeth school and have also funded their outward bound initiative
- Investec provided funding for the development of a new market garden enterprise at the Newham City farm, which will provide jobs and a stable income stream to many poverty stricken individuals. Our volunteers are involved in transforming the farm, as well as supporting a variety of other projects such as sports sessions for young people, and by hosting educational workshops and fun days

Corporate giving

Community contributions:

During the year, Investec plc made donations for charitable purposes, totalling £1.5 million (UK and Europe) and Investec Ltd made donations for charitable purposes, totalling R38.4 million (£3 million). Unfortunately we do not have a breakdown of which organisations were supported, nor the amount given specifically within the UK.

Investec's role in society and as a responsible citizen remains a key priority. To contribute to the upliftment and empowerment of the communities within which we operate, we engage in a number of ways. We strive to work with a particular focus on education and entrepreneurial projects. In 2011, our businesses committed over £5 million to a range of community initiatives around the world, an increase of 29% from the previous year.

Employee-led support

Volunteering opportunities are varied and range from coaching young people in success skills, to creating an eco-garden for a local primary school, to running a rugby workshop for young people and mentoring young people in literacy skills.

To encourage staff volunteering, each staff member is entitled to take one day per year to volunteer for the five charitable partners. 25% of staff have registered to volunteer. In 2010, 35 runners signed up to participate in the 2010 London marathon and raised a total of £57,300 for various charities.

Commercially-led support

Sponsorship: 'There are no hard and fast rules as to who or what we sponsor as we believe that opportunities come in different shapes and forms. We sponsor both individuals and teams from local to international levels.' Current sponsorships include support for English Test Cricket, Hockey, Tottenham Hotspur FC, Opera Holland Park, Liverpool Philharmonic Orchestra and The National Gardens Scheme. For full information visit the company's website.

Corporate social responsibility

CSR committee: Peter Thomas, a non-executive director on Investec's board, is responsible for all issues pertaining to sustainability. We also have sustainability representatives in each of the major geographies in which we operate. We have a global sustainability forum that meets quarterly to discuss any issues and developments related to sustainability in each of our areas of operation. The forum has representation from all business units including central functions as well as senior management. Feedback on relevant sustainability issues is also provided to board members at each board meeting.

CSR policy: Investec's chosen terminology for all areas of sustainability and corporate social investment and/or responsibility is Our Business Responsibility (OBR). The following information is taken from the company's website:

> In pursuit of sustainable profits we seek to be a positive influence in all our business activities, in each of the societies in which we operate. We do this by empowering communities through entrepreneurship and education, leveraging the value in our diversity, and addressing climate change and our use of natural resources.
>
> Investec's approach to sustainability is divided into the areas of profit, people and planet. Our endeavours to pursue sustainable profits include having a positive impact on each of the societies in which our business activities operate. We aim to do this by enriching communities through education and entrepreneurship and embracing diversity while constantly striving to reduce the overall size of our environmental footprint.
>
> **CSR report:** In 2011 we produced an integrated report which brings together the financial and non-financial aspects of our business which we believe will show a more complete and balanced picture of our business and performance. As a result, there is no separate sustainability report this year as our approach to the various aspects of sustainability has been documented throughout the integrated annual report. However, for review purposes, various elements of sustainability have been brought together in an online information document.

Applications

In writing to the correspondent.

IPC Media Ltd

Media

Correspondent: Corporate Responsibility Team, Blue Fin Building, 110 Southwark Street, London SE1 0SU (tel: 020 3148 5000; website: www.ipcmedia.com)

Directors: S. J. Auton; H. Averill; F. A. Dent; R. J. Evans; S. K. Evans; S. Hirst; D. H. Mair; C. L. Meredith; J. A. Newcombe; N. Robinson; P. R. Williams

Year end	31/12/2011
Turnover	£33,123,000
Pre-tax profit	£45,490,000

Nature of business: The publication of magazines.

Company registration number: 53626

Total employees: 1,755

Charitable donations

UK cash (latest declared):	2011	£5,120
	2008	£22,000
	2007	£24,000
	2006	£38,000
	2005	£13,000
Total UK:	2011	£5,120
Total worldwide:	2011	£5,120
Cash worldwide:	2011	£5,120

Corporate social responsibility

CSR committee: No details found.

CSR policy: Taken from the company's website: 'Corporate Responsibility (CR) at IPC focuses mainly on our impact on, and interaction with, the community, particularly in Southwark, our HQ's local borough, and on relevant environmental issues.'

We were unable to determine the ratio of women to men on the board from the company's accounts.

CSR report: No report published.

Applications

In writing to the correspondent.

Other information

In 2011 the company made charitable donations totalling £5,120. Although only this very small amount is declared in the company's accounts, it does offer support to the community by way of in kind donations including volunteering and staff fundraising.

IPC's corporate responsibility agenda currently focuses on three main areas – community and education, environment and the collective input and action from employees.

IPC is a member of The Media Trust, The Media CSR Forum, Heart of the City and Better Bankside.

> *Employee Volunteering*
>
> IPC's Employee Volunteering Policy enables employees to take up to two days' paid time per year to take part in voluntary activities in the community.
>
> Many IPC employees choose to use one of their volunteering days to take part in the annual Time Warner Volunteers' Day, working alongside employees from our sister companies in London. The day provides an opportunity to help out at a local community organisation; for example, lending physical labour to gardening projects, painting murals at a playground or running a children's activity day.
>
> Through IPC's membership of the Media Trust, increasing numbers of employees are also using their unique skills to assist a charity. This may take the form of advising a charity on its marketing strategy, assisting them in devising a communications campaign or helping to develop a website, and the employee's involvement may consist of a one-off meeting or an ongoing relationship over a number of months. In addition, two employees currently serve on the Media Trust Youth Advisory Board.
>
> Other current volunteering activities include mentoring, serving as trustees on charity boards and taking part in 'team challenge' events.

Support for charities

Alongside support for the Charity of the Year, the company provides ad hoc support to charities, either via a financial or an in kind donation. Support is typically given to organisations that are local to its offices and whose work is aligned with the company's key community priorities (young people, arts, education and literacy). Some IPC brands choose one or more charities to support on an ongoing basis. Among many examples, Woman and Home raised more than £2 million in recent years for Breast Cancer Care, primarily through events involving its readers and website users.

Payroll Giving

IPC supports its employees in donating to charity via its payroll giving scheme, 'Giving, etc.' Employees can either make regular contributions direct to their favourite charity or charities, or open a charity account that enables them to donate to any charity whenever they want.

Charity of the Year 2012
Following a company-wide vote in autumn 2011, IPC chose SHHiRT – Samuel Hardgrave Harlequin Ichthyosis Trust – as its Charity of the Year for 2012. SHHiRT is the only UK registered charity dedicated solely to researching Harlequin Ichthyosis – a very rare skin disease – and helping those affected by it.

ITV plc

Media

Correspondent: Responsibility Team, 104 ITV Yorkshire, Kirkstall Road, Leeds LS3 1JS (tel: 020 7156 6000; email: responsibility@itv.com; website: www.itvplc.com)

Directors: Andy Haste; John Ormerod; Archie Norman, Chair; Adam Crozier, Chief Executive; Ian Griffiths, Group Finance Director; Mike Clasper; Lucy Neville-Rolfe (women: 1; men: 6)

Year end	31/12/2011
Turnover	£2,140,000,000
Pre-tax profit	£327,000,000

Nature of business: Independent television company.

Company registration number: 4967001

Main locations: Aberdeen, Bristol, Carlisle, Cardiff, Leeds, Southampton, Plymouth, Glasgow, Norwich, Newcastle, London, Manchester, Birmingham

Total employees: 3,958

Membership: BITC

Charitable donations

UK cash (latest declared):	2011	£1,500,000
	2009	£1,710,000
	2008	£2,010,000
	2007	£1,380,000
	2006	£2,000,000
Total UK:	2011	£4,900,000
Total worldwide:	2011	£4,900,000
Cash worldwide:	2011	£1,500,000

Community involvement

ITV's giving is made of a range of activities, including air-time for appeals or charitable programming, show tickets and merchandise to auction off as charitable prizes, the use of facilities and expertise for projects and direct cash donations.

> It is essential that we have a framework around our charitable giving to ensure that any charities, campaigns, or causes we are endorsing as 'ITV' in a corporate, broadcasting or content making capacity are credible, that any charitable giving is lawful, and that anyone who has a vested interest in ITV can understand the value of our commitment.

Requests for charitable giving
If you are looking for charitable giving from ITV follow the guidelines below.

All individuals or organisations supported by ITV's charitable giving programme must be able to demonstrate the following:

- Have registered charitable status or equivalent
- Clear equality policy in relation to protected characteristics covered by the Equality Act 2010. Including age, gender, ethnicity, sexuality, disability, sexual orientation, religion or belief
- Defined target audience, reach and impact which aligns to ITV's Corporate Responsibility Strategy

Preference is given to organisations that are aligned to the company's strategy and are therefore dedicated to at least one of the following activities/goals (in no particular order):

- Supports the future and sustainability of drama and arts, with a particular preference for organisations working with their local communities and has some activity outside of London
- Supports and inspires the next generation of talent for the future (on and off screen)
- Makes a difference at grass-roots level within the communities they represent
- Helps to promote access to the industry through a diversity focused remit
- Has a direct purpose/remit that fits within:
  - The content or aim of a particular programme/show that ITV is broadcasting
  - One of the company's on-air or on-line charity campaigns
  - One of the company's chosen off-air Corporate Responsibility campaigns
- Offers expertise, guidance or assistance across an area that ITV has identified within its business operations that the company wants to improve or to make a positive change
- Supports the attraction, growth and retention of diverse and/or young talent
- Or, supports the local community and environment in which ITV operates

Information on programmes, appeals and campaigns coming up that are looking for partners will be visible on the itv.com website

The Granada Foundation, an independent charity (Charity Commission no. 241693), makes grants for arts, sciences, advancing education and for recreation and leisure time occupation in the interests of social welfare. The foundation is 'entirely reliant on the income and investment returns from its investments'.

Corporate giving

In 2011, ITV contributed cash and in kind support worth nearly £5 million. This equates to 1.7% of pre-profit tax. The company has contributed to £1.5 million in cash (2010: £1.5 million) and £3.4 million in kind (2010: £5.7 million). In addition, through campaigns such as Born to Shine, Malaria No More and Text Santa, £6.4 million has been raised through text and phone lines. Text Santa was a major new charity initiative, launched as a dedicated on-air appeal over the Christmas period, raising awareness and money for those most vulnerable during the festive period. In all, a total of £4.1 million was raised which was split between charities: Carers UK, Crisis, Help the Hospices, Samaritans and WRVS, as well as children's hospital charities Great Ormond Street Hospital Children's Charity, Noah's Ark Appeal, Helping Hand, and Yorkhill Children's Foundation.

The Granada Foundation
In 2010/11 the foundation made grants totalling £113,500 to organisations across the ITV Granada region. Beneficiaries included: Buxton Festival (£20,000); Liverpool Biennial of Contemporary Art (£15,000); Abbot Hall Gallery (£10,000); Greater Manchester Museum of Science and Industry Trust and Nowgen (£5,000 each); STEMNET (£4,000); University of Manchester School of Computer Science and Writing on the Wall (£2,000 each); and Waters Edge Arts Ltd (£1,000).

In kind support

The 'Community' section of ITV's Corporate Responsibility website (responsibility.itvplc.com) states:

> Our presence extends beyond newsworthy stories and campaigns. Our employees and onscreen talent within our ten regions play a substantial role within our communities. Volunteering, mentoring, training opportunities, donations, guest appearances, open days, access to our facilities – all of this activity adds up and makes a real difference to the people and communities where we are present.

Employee-led support

Staff are supported in taking one day's paid leave per year to devote to a cause they care about. Volunteering time that is undertaken during working hours is captured and monitored. This enables ITV to monitor the scheme and include within its in kind charitable giving contribution figure.

The 'Volunteering' section of ITV's Corporate Responsibility website states:

> We believe we can best serve our communities and colleagues by helping causes relevant to our expertise and knowledge. We target media and creative arts, education and conservation projects, and identify opportunities to use our

professional skills to make a difference. Projects also help develop volunteers' team working, leadership, creativity and communication skills. Our internal database of volunteering opportunities helps colleagues search for projects that suit them.

In 2011, we introduced our 'One in a Million' award to recognise the volunteering work of an individual from within ITV. Colleagues were able to nominate and the individual was selected by 'CR committee members'. We will be using our winners story in 2012 to encourage more people to get involved in volunteering.

Further to our main Volunteering Scheme, our in-house lawyers provide legal support free of charge to UK charities and disadvantaged people through the *ITV Legal Pro Bono Bank*, in partnership with law firm Hogan Lovells.

Launched in 2009, this service provides support free of charge to UK charities and disadvantaged people. The scheme overcomes insurance issues that often prevent in-house corporate lawyers from providing pro bono services.

ITV in-house lawyers now have the opportunity to provide support for Hogan Lovells' current pro bono clients, including Save the Children, Action for the Blind and social entrepreneurship charity UnLtd. The Bank has also created new initiatives, including a legal clinic for Body and Soul, a UK charity supporting children, teenagers and families affected by HIV. ITV and Hogan Lovells lawyers work side-by-side to offer legal advice to the charity and its members in individual and group sessions. See our volunteering video for more information.

We are dedicated to encouraging colleagues to take part in company-wide volunteering events each year. For example at the end of 2011, 1,562 colleagues came together, across 13 of our locations, to break a Guinness World Record for the largest secret Santa game ever, live on This Morning. Through colleagues getting involved and giving up their time we raised awareness of our new appeal Text Santa and also directly raised donations for the charities involved.

Commercially-led support

ITV's Corporate Responsibility website also gives the following information:

On our doorstep

We use the power of our brand to support local causes and champion local heroes. Our regional news teams use regional air-time and behind the scenes resources to champion local heroes and gain local support for campaigns that make a difference on a national level.

Examples include:

- The People's Millions
- Pride of Britain Awards
- Walk for Life

Reaching Communities

We often use the power of our well-known channels and programme brands to help raise awareness and donations for charities. They are chosen for their close link or association with the programme content. However, each year ITV selects a number of charities to be part of our annual festive fundraiser – *Text Santa*. The charities selected reflect ITV's own unique position of being a national organisation but have a strong presence across our regions.

Partnerships: The company develops relationships with other broadcasters, local organisations and knowledge specialists to 'make the most impact within our communities'. Examples of partnerships include: Business in the Community; Creative Diversity Network; Media Trust; Stonewall; and Working Families.

Corporate social responsibility

CSR committee: Strategy and objectives have been identified by a Corporate Responsibility Committee which was reviewed and restructured in 2011. The strategy and objectives are supported by the Management Board.

A new role of Head of Corporate Responsibility has been appointed to roll out the strategy across the company. The Head of CR is responsible for consolidating activity for maximum impact and managing policy around charitable giving, both on and off-screen. This role reports directly into the Group HR Director, who also chairs the Corporate Responsibility Committee, ensuring all activities are relevant and integrated into the business.

The current ITV Corporate Responsibility Committee members are listed at: responsibility.itvplc.com.

CSR policy: All CSR information is taken from the company's dedicated CSR website and financial information from the 2011 annual report and accounts: responsibility.itvplc.com/community-and-giving/charitable-giving

One of our Corporate Responsibility aims is to be recognised as a company that makes a real difference in the regions and communities it represents; and to be seen as a company that promotes accessibility to ITV by encouraging and developing new and diverse talent.

This includes:

- Supporting our regional news teams in community activity and raising awareness on a national level of the work they do
- Delivering a robust framework through our CR strategy and charitable giving policy, for our colleagues to 'do their bit' through initiatives such as volunteering, mentoring and fundraising
- Utilising our physical assets, expertise and charitable giving policy to support local community initiatives and projects
- Investing in our youth programmes. Supporting a minimum of 140 young, talented individuals from the age of 14 plus through our Work Inspiration scheme and our Modern Apprenticeship programme
- Formalising our partnerships and utilising our memberships effectively
- Continuing to grow our online communities – developing pride and loyalty in our brand

Exclusions

The company does not consider circular or general appeals.

Applications

Applications for support from the company should be made in writing to the correspondent. If you or your organisation meets the eligibility and strategic priorities outlined in the section 'Community Involvement', you can write or email. Ensure you highlight how you meet the set criteria and what support you are looking for to be included in ITV's review process.

The team endeavours to consider all legitimate requests and respond within a month.

Applications for support from the foundation should be made to: Irene Langford, PO Box 3430, Chester CH1 9BZ. Telephone: 01244 661867 or email: irene.langford@btconnect.com. For further information visit the website: granadafoundation.org.

Jaguar Cars Ltd

Motors and accessories

Correspondent: S L Pearson, Company Secretary, Abbey Road, Whitley, Coventry CV3 4LF (website: www.jaguar.com/gb)

Directors: P. W. Cope; K. D. M. Gregor; P. Hodgkinson; U. Menon; P. C. Popham; R. D. Speth; M. D. Wright

Year end	31/03/2012
Turnover	£3,862,500,000
Pre-tax profit	£208,100,000

Nature of business: The design, development, manufacture and marketing of high performance luxury saloons and specialist sports cars.

Company registration number: 1672070

Main locations: Birmingham, Halewood, Coventry, Gaydon

Total employees: 5,494

Membership: Arts & Business, BITC

Charitable donations

UK cash (latest declared):	2012	£42,450
	2009	£34,000
	2006	£103,000
	2005	£84,000
	2004	£120,000
Total UK:	2012	£42,450
Total worldwide:	2012	£42,450
Cash worldwide:	2012	£42,450

Corporate social responsibility

CSR committee: No details found.

CSR policy: No CSR information was found for Jaguar Cars Ltd.

We were unable to determine the ratio of women to men on the board.

CSR report: None published.

Applications

In writing to the correspondent.

Other information

In 2011/12 the company made donations to national charities totalling £42,450. A list of beneficiaries was not available. Previously, the company has supported the National Society for the Prevention of Cruelty to Children, the Juvenile Diabetes Research Foundation and BEN (Automotive Benevolent Fund).

Jardine Lloyd Thompson Group plc

Insurance

Correspondent: Group Charity Committee, 6 Crutched Friars, London EC3N 2HP (tel: 020 7528 4444; website: www.jltgroup.com)

Directors: Geoffrey Howe, Chair; Dominic Burke, Chief Executive; Lord Leach of Fairford; Mark Drummond Brady; Richard Harvey; Simon Keswick; Nick MacAndrew; Simon Mawson; John Paynter; Vyvienne Wade (women: 1; men: 9)

Year end	31/12/2011
Turnover	£818,764,000
Pre-tax profit	£134,479,000

Nature of business: The company is a holding company of an international group of insurance broking companies and a Lloyd's members' agency.

Company registration number: 1679424

Main locations: London

UK employees: 3,140

Total employees: 6,566

Charitable donations

UK cash (latest declared):	2009	£106,000
	2007	£267,000
	2006	£389,000
	2005	£462,000
Total worldwide:	2011	£407,900
Cash worldwide:	2011	£407,900

Corporate social responsibility

CSR committee: A CSR Committee was present.

CSR policy: This information was obtained from the company's website:

> Corporate Social Responsibility (CSR) is important to Jardine Lloyd Thompson. Increasingly, our employees are taking a keen interest in understanding what the company is doing to minimise its impact on the environment as well as the positive actions JLT is taking to put something back into the community.

CSR report: There was no evidence of a separate CSR report.

Exclusions

No grants for fundraising events, advertising in charity brochures, appeals from individuals or large national appeals.

Applications

In writing to the correspondent. The charity committee meets four times a year.

Other information

In 2011, the group donated £407,900 to charity. Its charity initiative, 'JLT Making a Difference' focuses efforts in three ways:

- All UK staff are able to take advantage of a 'Charity Day', this gives them one day every year when they can spend company time helping a charity or working in the local community. As a Lloyd's Community Programme partner, employees from the London offices are encouraged to give up their lunch hours twice a week to visit a school to help with IT training and support
- JLT will match pound for pound any amount raised by UK staff in fundraising activities they undertake up to a maximum of £5,000. Each year the group Charities Committee seeks to ensure that a large proportion of its annual budget supports these employee fundraising activities. In 2011, £113,000 was spent matching charity activities
- Thirdly, the group Charities Committee will consider the many requests received for donations from a wide variety of local and national charities. All requests are considered carefully on their merits, the group does however take a particular interest in charities connected to communities local to our offices. The Charities Committee also supports various employee charitable fundraising events which are designed to raise funds and encourage greater staff engagement, both in the UK and through the group's offices internationally

JD Sports Fashion plc

Retail – clothing and footwear

Correspondent: Investor Relations Dept., Hollinsbrook Way, Pilsworth, Bury, Lancashire BL9 8RR (tel: 01617 671000; email: investor.relations@jdplc.com; website: www.jdplc.com)

Directors: Peter Cowgill, Chair; Barry Brown, Chief Executive; Brian Small; Colin Archer; Chris Bird; Andrew Leslie (women: 0; men: 6)

Year end	29/01/2011
Turnover	£883,669,000
Pre-tax profit	£78,629,000

Nature of business: JD Sports Fashion plc is a retailer of sport inspired fashion apparel and footwear.

Company registration number: 1888425

Total employees: 11,231

Charitable donations

UK cash (latest declared):	2011	£39,000
	2010	£17,000
	2009	£29,500
Total UK:	2011	£39,000
Total worldwide:	2011	£39,000
Cash worldwide:	2011	£39,000

Corporate social responsibility

CSR committee: There was no evidence of a separate CSR Committee.

CSR policy: The group's main focus was upon cancer related charities in 2010/11.

CSR report: There was no evidence of a separate CSR report.

Applications

In writing to the correspondent.

Other information

During the financial year the group made charitable donations of £39,000 (2009/10: £54,000).

The following information relating to the group's community involvement is taken from the annual report 2010/11:

> The group seeks to be involved in the community where it can make an appropriate contribution from its resources and skills base. Examples of this include:
>
> - JD Sports Fashion plc sponsorship of the City of Salford 10k in September 2010
> - Donations to The Geoff Thomas Foundation which works closely with Leukemia & Lymphoma Research on raising funds to speed up the delivery of effective new treatments to patients with blood cancer
> - Donations to The Marina Dalglish Appeal to improve cancer treatment facilities in Liverpool
> - Donations to Boot out Breast Cancer which raises funds to provide equipment for as many breast cancer unit in the North West as possible
> - Donations to Cancer Research UK
> - Donations to The Elizabeth Hardie Ferguson Charitable Trust Fund which was founded by Sir Alex Ferguson

JJB Sports plc

Retail – clothing and footwear, sports clothing

Correspondent: Company Secretary, Martland Park, Challenge Way, Wigan, Lancashire WN5 0LD (tel: 01942 221400; fax: 01942 629809; email: customerservices@jjbsports.com; website: www.sportsdirectplc.com/corporate-responsibility.aspx)

Directors: Mike McTighe, Chair; Keith Jones, Chief Executive; David Williams;

Richard Manning; David Adams; Sir Matthew Pinsent; Alan Benzie; Richard Bernstein (women: 0; men: 8)

Year end	30/01/2011
Turnover	£362,894,000
Pre-tax profit	(£181,365,000)

Nature of business: The principal activity of the group is the retail of sportswear and sports equipment. The group also operates a separate leisure division which operates health clubs and indoor soccer centres.

Company registration number: 1024895

Main locations: Aberdeen, Luton, Milton Keynes, Wrexham, Blackburn, Truro

UK employees: 5,166

Total employees: 5,166

Charitable donations

UK cash (latest declared):	2009	£30,000
	2008	£32,700
	2007	£2,000
	2005	£26,000

Corporate social responsibility

CSR committee: There was evidence of a separate CSR Committee; details can be found on the company's website.

CSR policy: This information was obtained from the company's website:

> JJB recognises that it has a duty to ensure that its business is conducted in a socially responsible manner meeting high standards in both social and environmental behaviour. JJB values the relationships with both its customers and the wider community. The group provides a valuable service to the community by supplying a wide range of competitively priced sports clothing, footwear and accessories through its retail stores to enable the general public to take care in health, sporting activities.

CSR report: There was no evidence of a separate CSR report.

Applications

In writing to the contact.

Other information

The company's charitable donations and the value of its contributions is not known. The following is taken from the company's website:

> JJB continues to support local and national charities as well as supporting local sporting teams. Currently, we provide two of our sites rent free to registered charities.
>
> £3,792 was raised for Macmillan Cancer Relief through the sale of football badges and discounts on sporting leisurewear.
>
> £3,738 was raised for Breakthrough Breast Cancer through the sale of pin badges in the company's stores.
>
> A number of JJB colleagues ran in the London Marathon raising individual amounts for charity.
>
> JJB launched a shoe recycling programme. Customers receive a voucher redeemable against a new pair of sports shoes when they deposit an old pair in store. The money that JJB raises from this activity is donated to its chosen charity, Whizz-kidz.

S. C. Johnson Ltd

Household

Correspondent: Faye Gilbert, Trustee, Johnson Wax Ltd Charitable Trust, Frimley Green, Camberley, Surrey GU16 7AJ (tel: 01276 852000/01276 852000; fax: 01276 852412; email: givinguk@scj.com; website: www.scjohnson.co.uk)

Directors: S. C. Hampel; B. Goodwin

Year end	01/07/2011
Turnover	£131,688,000
Pre-tax profit	£4,763,000

Nature of business: The company manufactures and markets waxes, polishes and cleaning products for the consumer and industrial markets.

Company registration number: 4166155

Main locations: Frimley Green, Egham

UK employees: 45

Total employees: 45

Charitable donations

UK cash (latest declared):	2011	£66,000
	2009	£228,000
	2008	£313,000
	2007	£317,000
	2006	£320,000
Total UK:	2011	£66,000
Total worldwide:	2011	£66,000
Cash worldwide:	2011	£66,000

Corporate social responsibility

CSR committee: The company donates to its associated charitable trust and application should be made to the correspondent. No specific committee details found.

CSR policy: We were unable to determine the ratio of women to men on the board.

CSR report: No report published.

Exclusions

A request falls outside of our corporate guidelines if it:

- Benefits a single individual
- Is an individual raising money for a charity
- Is for another country
- Is for attendance at a charity dinner, conference and so on
- Is samples for gift bags or other marketing uses
- Is payroll giving
- Is in conflict with the interests of the company
- Duplicates the services of another organisation or project already existing in the community
- Duplicates a previous donation made within 12 months

Applications

In writing to the correspondent for applications to the Johnson Wax Charitable Trust. For sponsorship and company enquiries to the company secretary.

Other information

In 2010/11, contributions from S C Johnson Ltd totalling £66,000 were paid to the Johnson Wax Charitable Trust (Charity Commission no. 200332).

The Johnson Wax Ltd Charitable Trust

The trust is a grantmaking charity established for general charitable purposes. Donations made by the trust in 2010/11 totalled £335,000 and were broken down as follows: health related charities (£116,000); education (£91,000); June Community Day (£38,000); arts and sports (£27,300); environment (£19,500); local community (£19,000); and employee matching scheme (£8,000). Examples of the company's community involvement can be found on its website.

Sponsorship: *Arts/Sports* – SC Johnson has a long tradition in supporting arts and sports for people with disabilities in the UK. Alongside its support for national organisations, it also offers help to smaller organisations.

Community Day: Once a year, for a day in June, the company closes down as much of the business as possible to give its employees the opportunity to volunteer for work on local community projects.

Johnson Matthey plc

Metals

Correspondent: Corporate Communications Officer, 40–42 Hatton Garden, London EC1N 8EE (tel: 020 7269 8400; fax: 020 7269 8466; email: sustainability@matthey.com; website: www.matthey.com/sustainability)

Directors: Sir John Banham, Chair; N. A. P. Carson, Chief Executive; T. E. P. Stevenson; R. J. MacLeod; A. M. Thomson; R. J. W. Walvis; A. M. Ferguson; Sir Thomas Harris; M. J. Roney; D. C. Thompson; L. C. Pentz; W. F. Sandford (women: 1; men: 11)

Year end	31/03/2011
Turnover	£9,984,800,000
Pre-tax profit	£260,600,000

Nature of business: Johnson Matthey plc is a speciality chemicals company that focuses on its core skills in catalysis, precious metals, fine chemicals and process technology

Company registration number: 33774

Main locations: Enfield, Fenton, Hanley, Clitheroe, Cambridge, Newcastle upon Tyne, London, Heysham, Wallsend, Swindon, Royston, Sheffield, Reading

Total employees: 9,742

Membership: BITC, LBG

Charitable donations

UK cash (latest declared):	2011	£320,000
	2010	£298,000
	2009	£366,000
	2007	£282,000
	2006	£330,000
Total UK:	2011	£320,000
Total worldwide:	2011	£517,000
Cash worldwide:	2011	£517,000

Corporate social responsibility

CSR committee: There was a separate CSR Committee.

CSR policy: This information was obtained from the company's annual report:

> Johnson Matthey has a strong tradition for good community relations and the company and its employees are actively involved in programmes worldwide. We have an important contribution to make to economic development of our local communities, not only as an employer but also through collaboration and investment, both financial and in kind.

CSR report: There was a separate Sustainability report as well as information which was available from the company's website and the annual report.

Exclusions

No support for advertising in charity brochures, appeals from individuals, political appeals or religious appeals.

Applications

In writing to the correspondent. A donations committee meets quarterly.

Note: Charitable donating is reviewed in March each year to set the programme for the following financial year, beginning in April. Check for details of current areas of support.

Other information

During the year the group donated £517,000 (2010: £458,000) to charitable organisations worldwide, of which £320,000 (2010: £298,000) was in the UK. This figure only includes donations made by Johnson Matthey and does not include payroll giving, donations made by staff or employee time. In 2010/11, a total of 48 charitable causes received an annual donation through the company.

The company and its employees are actively involved in programmes worldwide and the company is a member of the London Benchmarking Group (LBG).

At a group level, Johnson Matthey operates a charitable donations programme which includes support for organisations working in the areas of environment, medical and health, science and education, social welfare and international development. There is an annual donations scheme where a number of charities are selected every three years and receive a donation from the company each year for that period.

Community activities are wide ranging and include charitable giving, support for educational projects, the advancement of science and economic regeneration projects.

Employees participate in activities or hold community related roles outside of the work environment. The company is supportive of this broader community engagement, allowing employees time off during working hours as appropriate. Due to the support, a group wide volunteering policy is being developed which will be issued during 2011/12. This forms part of a broader programme of work now underway to establish a more formal community investment strategy for the group. This will continue in 2011/12 with the aim of establishing a community investment strategy and policy during the year to support the company's operations in developing their community programmes.

Recent charity partners have included: British Heart Foundation; Alzheimer's Society; The International Red Cross and Red Crescent Movement and EveryChild.

Johnson Service Group plc

Miscellaneous

Correspondent: The Company Secretary, Johnson House, Abbots Park, Monks Way, Preston Brook, Cheshire WA7 3GH (tel: 01928 704600; fax: 01928 704620; email: enquiries@johnsonplc.com; website: www.jsg.com)

Directors: John Talbot, Chair; Yvonne Monaghan; Chris Sander; Kevin Elliott; Paul Ogle; Michael Del Mar; William Shannon; Paul Moody (women: 1; men: 7)

Year end	31/12/2011
Turnover	£240,000,000
Pre-tax profit	£14,000,000

Nature of business: The company is principally engaged in textile rental, dry cleaning and facilities management.

Company registration number: 523335

UK employees: 5,591

Total employees: 5,591

Charitable donations

UK cash (latest declared):	2011	£19,900
	2009	£31,000
	2008	£31,000
	2007	£75,000
	2006	£59,000
Total UK:	2011	£19,900
Total worldwide:	2011	£19,900
Cash worldwide:	2011	£19,900

Corporate social responsibility

CSR committee: There was no evidence of a separate CSR Committee.

CSR policy: This information was obtained from the company's website:

> The Johnson Service Group is acutely aware of its responsibilities to the communities in which it operates, and from which both its customers and employees are drawn. We are committed to progressively embedding CSR best practice into every aspect of our operations. We endeavour to manage these in a responsible manner, believing that sound and demonstrable performance in relation to CSR policies and practices is a fundamental part of business success.
>
> The group is committed to continuous improvement in its CSR program and encourages its operating businesses and partners to strive for heightened performance.

CSR report: There was no evidence of a separate CSR report.

Exclusions

No support for circular appeals, appeals from individuals, religious appeals, local appeals not in areas of company presence, large national appeals or overseas projects.

Applications

In writing to the correspondent.

Other information

In 2011 contributions by the group to charitable causes totalled £19,900 (2009: £31,000). A list of beneficiaries was unavailable.

> The group and its individual operating companies seek to be good neighbours, and work in partnership with our people to help their local communities. Major ongoing charitable initiatives include Johnson Cleaners' partnership with Macmillan Cancer Relief to encourage the return and re-use of hangers, and the Johnson Group Cleaners Charity's support for a range of local registered charities dedicated to helping the underprivileged

Johnston Press plc

Media

Correspondent: P A to the Chief Executive, 53 Manor Place, Edinburgh EH3 7EG (tel: 01312 253361; fax: 01312 254580; email: jpnm.coordinator@jpress.co.uk; website: www.johnstonpress.co.uk)

Directors: Ian Russell, Chair; Ashley Highfield, Chief Executive; Mark Pain; Ralph Marshall; Camilla Rhodes; Geoff Iddison; Kjell Aamot; Danny Cammiade; Grant Murray; Peter McCall (women: 1; men: 9)

Year end	01/01/2011
Turnover	£427,996,000
Pre-tax profit	(£113,775,000)

Nature of business: Newspaper publishers.

Company registration number: SC015382

Total employees: 5,502

Charitable donations

UK cash (latest declared):	2009	£29,000
	2008	£41,000
	2007	£136,000
	2006	£133,000
Total worldwide:	2011	£32,000
Cash worldwide:	2011	£32,000

Corporate social responsibility

CSR committee: There was no evidence of a separate CSR Committee.

CSR policy: This information was obtained from the company's website:

> Johnston Press is committed to operating all of the group's business activities to the highest standards of business ethics and integrity. The group is heavily involved with schools and encouraging young people to interact with their local newspapers through projects, visits and creating advertisements and pages for actual publication. The group provides people with a forum for airing their view, with opportunities to meet politicians and other decision-makers and with the chance to shape their own newspapers and websites through reader panels.

CSR report: The group's CSR report was available from the company's website.

Applications

In writing to the correspondent.

Other information

In 2010, the company made charitable donations of £32,000 (2009: £29,000). Although there were extensive examples in the annual report of various fundraising campaigns Johnston Press has been involved in promoting, there were no specific details of where the company's donations went.

Through its various newspapers the company provides free space and discounted advertising to charitable organisations. 'Our newspapers and websites were again at the forefront of a series of community campaigns and events – highlighting their close links with the areas they serve. They have also been responsible for fundraising for a wide variety of good causes.'

Jones Lang LaSalle Ltd

Property

Correspondent: PA to Company Secretary, 22 Hanover Square, London W1A 2BN (tel: 020 7493 6040; fax: 020 7408 0220; website: www.joneslanglasalle.co.uk)

Directors: Richard Batten, Chair; Andrew Gould; Neil Prime; Philip Marsden; Guy Grainger; Mark Stupples; Chris Ireland; Richard Howling (women: 0; men: 8)

Year end	31/12/2010
Turnover	£184,300
Pre-tax profit	£128,200

Nature of business: Provision of real estate consultancy services.

Company registration number: 1188567

Main locations: Edinburgh, Glasgow, Leeds, London, Manchester, Norwich, Birmingham

Total employees: 40,000

Membership: BITC

Charitable donations

UK cash (latest declared):	2009	£34,800
	2008	£48,500
	2006	£30,600
	2005	£5,800

Corporate social responsibility

CSR committee: There was no evidence of a separate CSR Committee.

CSR policy: This information was obtained from the company's annual report:

> We encourage and promote the principles of corporate social responsibility and sustainability everywhere we operate. Since our business operations span the globe, we seek to improve the communities in which our people work and live. We design our corporate policies to reflect the highest standards of corporate governance and transparency, and we hold ourselves responsible for our social, environmental and economic performance.

CSR report: A CSR report was available from the company's website. Five pages were dedicated to community involvement.

Applications

Contact your nearest office for further information.

Other information

Worldwide charitable donations exceeded £1.1 million.

Previous research suggested that the company had stated: 'Jones Lang LaSalle and its employees provide generous financial and other support to many worthwhile community programmes.' Areas of support included children's causes, education, older people's organisations, vocational training, environmental and heritage concerns, medical research, science, welfare, disability and sports. It has offices in Birmingham, Edinburgh, Glasgow, Leeds, Manchester, and Norwich and across London and it is likely that preference will be given to these areas.

The group's community strategy is intentionally decentralised so that it can address the local needs of communities.

Keepmoat Ltd

Building/construction

Correspondent: Secretary, Keepmoat Foundation, The Waterfront, Lakeside Boulevard, Doncaster DN4 5PL (tel: 01302 346620; fax: 01302 346621; email: foundation@keepmoat.com; website: www.keepmoat.com)

Directors: Tom Allison, Chair; David Blunt, Chief Executive; Chris Bovis; Allen Hickling; Peter Hindley; John Thirlwall; David Cowie; Richard Brandon (women: 0; men: 8)

Year end	31/03/2011
Turnover	£680,000,000
Pre-tax profit	£68,000,000

Nature of business: The Keepmoat group is principally engaged in the refurbishment and construction of residential dwellings.

Company registration number: 1998780

Main locations: Doncaster

Total employees: 2,917

Charitable donations

UK cash (latest declared):	2011	£84,000
	2009	£106,000
	2008	£75,000
Total UK:	2011	£84,000
Total worldwide:	2011	£84,000
Cash worldwide:	2011	£84,000

Corporate social responsibility

CSR committee: There was no evidence of a separate CSR Committee.

CSR policy: The Keepmoat group directs its community support through the Keepmoat Foundation which is described as: 'An independent 'Community Investment Programme' which helps transform lives by supporting local charities, community groups, schools and community-based initiatives [as well as] sustainable projects which can inspire and educate people in communities all over the UK.'

CSR report: There was no evidence of a CSR report.

Exclusions

The Keepmoat Foundation states that it does not fund the following:

- Groups that have substantial unrestricted funds
- National charities (unless identified as a strategic project with local and regional benefits)

- Activities promoting political or religious beliefs. Faith groups can apply, but they will need a separate set of rules ensuring that their project is open to all people in the community
- Statutory bodies e.g. schools, local councils colleges
- Endowments
- Small contributions to large projects
- Projects for personal profit or individual benefit
- Minibuses or other vehicle purchases
- Projects that have already happened
- Animals
- Sponsorship and fundraising events

Applications

The foundation gives the following information:

> **Community projects:** The Keepmoat Foundation partners with a national network of 10 community foundations in the areas in which we work. Each of the 10 is allocated money from the Keepmoat Foundation, to provide grants to smaller, less well-resourced groups in local communities.
>
> For further information, please contact us at foundation@keepmoat.com.
>
> **Youth projects:** The panel chooses projects by region, which meet foundation objectives and have been researched by the executive advisor.
>
> The panel does not accept unsolicited requests for support.

Other information

In 2010/11 the company made charitable donations of £84,000 (2009/10: £201,000). Grants for community projects range from £500 to £1,500 and are usually one-off.

Support is focused on youth and community projects, particularly those which:

- Support people in greatest need
- Are locally-led and run
- Involve people who face particular discrimination or disadvantage e.g. Black and Minority Ethnic Communities, young people, people with disabilities, carers, and people with mental health problems
- Respond to local community needs
- Work well with other local community initiatives
- Give real value for money

Grants can be awarded to meet capital costs (e.g. buying equipment) and/or to meet running costs (for example, room hire). Projects must benefit more than one person.

Kelda Group Ltd

Water

Correspondent: Ann Reed, Community Affairs Manager, Western House, Halifax Road, Bradford BD6 2SZ (tel: 01274 600111/01274 692515; email: ann.reed@yorkshirewater.co.uk; website: www.keldagroup.com)

Directors: Richard Flint; Kevin Whiteman; Stuart McFarlane; Liz Barber (women: 1; men: 3)

Year end	31/03/2012
Turnover	£961,800,000
Pre-tax profit	(£510,500,000)

Nature of business: Holding company for Kelda Group.

Company registration number: 2366682

UK employees: 3138

Total employees: 3138

Membership: BITC

Charitable donations

UK cash (latest declared):	2009	£0
	2007	£35,000
	2006	£500,000
	2005	£500,000
Total worldwide:	2012	£700,000
Cash worldwide:	2012	£700,000

Corporate social responsibility

CSR committee: There was no evidence of a separate CSR Committee.

CSR policy: This information was obtained from the company's website:

> The group contributes to the communities which it serves. It encourages and supports colleagues in volunteering, charitable giving and community involvement.
>
> We have an extensive engagement programme, providing support and help-in kind to a wide variety of different organisations across the communities we serve. These partnerships are of enormous important to us in terms of forging stronger links and by making a tangible and positive difference to the quality of people's lives.
>
> We provide this support in three key areas:
>
> - Education – through educating young people and local communities on the value of what we do
> - Environment – playing a key role as one of Yorkshire's largest land owners in enhancing the natural and build environment
> - Empowerment – providing opportunities for our colleagues to share skills with the local community through employee supported volunteering
>
> We aim to do this by:
>
> - Providing a range of educational visits into our industry, strongly aligned to the National Curriculum, through our education and outreach programme
> - Raising awareness of our capital investment programme through open days, customer events and community presentations
> - Educating customer groups through our campaign work on key issues relevant to the water industry
> - Supporting local communities through our employee supported volunteering programme
> - Providing financial support through our employee fundraising team to local and regional charities, and by offering Payroll Giving opportunities
> - Recognising vulnerable customers through our Helping Hands register, providing guidance and support in respect of bill payment, and raising awareness of bogus caller issues
> - Communicating widely, where possible, throughout the delivery of capital investment work to deliver the best possible solution whilst minimising disruption to customers
> - Managing our impact on the local environment through our investments to coastal and river water quality, by reducing our carbon footprint, creating more of our own energy and by developing a plan to manage water supplies in the event of a drought
> - By developing sustainable environmental and community partnerships and through regular liaison with key stakeholders throughout the region and industry

CSR report: There was no evidence of a separate CSR report.

Applications

No longer accepting applications.

Other information

In 2011/12 the company's accounts state charitable donations of £700,000, although there were no details on where this money went, and we have previously been informed that the company no longer makes cash donations.

Keller Group plc

Engineering

Correspondent: Social Responsibility Dept. (Community), Capital House, 25 Chapel Street, London NW1 5DH (tel: 020 7616 7575; email: j.holman@keller.co.uk; website: www.keller.co.uk)

Directors: Roy Franklin, Chair; Justin Atkinson, Chief Executive; James Hind; Bob Rubright; Dr Wolfgang Sondermann; Pedro Lopez Jimenez; Gerry Brown; Ruth Cairnie; Chris Girling; David Savage (women: 1; men: 9)

Year end	31/12/2011
Turnover	£1,154,300,000
Pre-tax profit	£21,900,000

Nature of business: International independent ground engineering specialists with unrivalled coverage in Europe, US and Australia and a growing presence in the Middle East and Asia.

Company registration number: 2442580

UK employees: 373

Total employees: 6757

Charitable donations

UK cash (latest declared):	2011	£300
	2009	£70,300
	2008	£2,000
Total UK:	2011	£300
Total worldwide:	2011	£106,000
Cash worldwide:	2011	£106,000

Corporate social responsibility

CSR committee: There was no evidence of a separate CSR Committee.

CSR policy: This information was obtained from the company's annual report: 'Our companies often play an important role in their communities, typically by supporting their employees when they engage with community groups and local charities.'

CSR report: There was no evidence of a separate CSR report.

Applications

In writing to the correspondent.

Other information

Donations made by the group in the UK for charitable purposes were £300 (2009: £70,000) with charitable donations of £106,000 (2009: £149,000) made by the group as a whole.

> Companies within the Keller Group often play an important role in their communities. While much of our work is undertaken in remote areas, away from local populations, our companies support their employees when they engage with community groups and local charities. This brings direct benefits to the business, in terms of employee satisfaction and development, as well as to the communities with which they work.
>
> In the UK, we operate a matching scheme, whereby donations made by employees to registered charities are matched by the company. We are also organising Work in the Community days, where employees can give up some of their working time to support worthwhile projects.

Kellogg Company of Great Britain Ltd

Food manufacture

Correspondent: Bruce Learner, Community Team, The Kellogg Building, Talbot Road, Manchester M16 0PU (tel: 01618 692000; email: Bruce.Learner@kellogg.com; website: www.kelloggs.co.uk)

Directors: J. Gregory; N. Jaynes; F. Roquet-Jalmar; A. O'Brien; S. Hopwood

Year end	01/01/2011
Turnover	£109,568,000
Pre-tax profit	£7,885,000

Nature of business: The principal activity of the group is the manufacture, marketing and sale of cereal-based food products.

Company registration number: 199171

Main locations: Wrexham, Manchester

Total employees: 1,071

Charitable donations

UK cash (latest declared):	2009	£450,000
	2008	£450,000
	2005	£548,000
Total worldwide:	2011	£20,201,600

Corporate social responsibility

CSR committee: Taken from the CSR 2011 report:

> At the Board of Directors level, we have a Social Responsibility Committee composed of four members, all of whom are independent. The committee, which has been in existence since 1979, met twice in 2010 and oversees all aspects of our corporate responsibility approach.
>
> Other committees of the Board address corporate responsibility issues as well. For example, the Audit Committee reviews environmental performance. The Board as a whole also addresses key issues discussed in this report, including many relating to health and nutrition.
>
> At the senior executive level, our chief sustainability officer reports directly to the chief executive officer. Our corporate responsibility strategy has been fully integrated into our business, with subject-matter experts for each pillar area who report on progress to the heads of their business units.

CSR policy: The following extract is taken from the 2011 CSR report:

> *Community Ambition*
>
> Contributing to the communities in which we operate will remain an important element of our corporate responsibility strategy. We will seek to concentrate on nutrition (including malnutrition) and physical fitness through product donations for the hungry, as well as programs that educate children and parents about good nutrition and help families stay active.

We were unable to determine the ratio of women to men on the board.

CSR report: Published annually.

Applications

Kellogg's is now pro-active in its charitable giving and does not consider unsolicited applications. Its focus is on activities/groups that have a connection with the company's business, i.e. health and sport.

Other information

Information given here and relating to global philanthropic contributions is taken from Kellogg's website. Unfortunately we could find no UK specific figures for charitable giving.

Charitable donations are funded through the Kellogg Company and Kellogg's Corporate Citizenship Fund. The W K Kellogg Foundation, founded by Mr Kellogg is a separate and distinct entity, making its own social investments and governed by its own independent trustees. The following information is taken from the company's 2010 CSR report:

> In 2010, we focused on strategic charitable investments that mirror our objectives as a global food company. We also worked to make fewer, but more targeted, donations that have greater impact and broader reach. For example, we:
>
> - Donated $32 million [£20.2 million] in cash and products to charitable organisations worldwide
> - Continued to donate food to food banks and programs around the world
> - Contributed to breakfast programs that provided millions of morning meals to schoolchildren around the globe
> - Supported a downtown revitalisation project in our headquarters city of Battle Creek, Michigan
> - Provided cash and/or product donations to assist with disaster relief efforts in Japan, Haiti, Chile, Australia and other regions
>
> At Kellogg, we view nutrition, wellness and wellbeing as intertwined, and we seek to support charitable initiatives that promote a healthier world. For that reason, we focus our strategic philanthropy programs on nutrition and malnutrition, physical fitness, and community development. We also support initiatives that expand opportunities for people of diverse backgrounds.
>
> In 2010, we contributed more than $13 million in cash, including brand philanthropy, and $19 million in products to nonprofits and charitable organisations around the world. Our goal is to donate the equivalent of 2 to 2.5 percent of pre-tax, annual profits to worthy social causes. This includes cash donations equal to half a percent of pre-tax profits and in kind product donations equal to 1.5 to 2 percent of pre-tax profits.
>
> In addition, individual brands may support charitable initiatives that are of interest to consumers. Typically, a brand will make a financial contribution during a specified time period for an identified cause.
>
> *Hunger Relief*
>
> Each year, Kellogg donates millions of dollars worth of products to Feeding America, the leading hunger-relief organisation in the United States. Over the last five years, we have contributed more than 115 million pounds of food to the organisation. In Europe, we donate products to food banks in the United Kingdom, Germany, Spain, France and Holland.
>
> We also recently began donating products that were damaged during transit. These products, which we are providing to food banks, meet our exacting food-safety and quality-control standards, although the packaging is unfit for retail sales. Instead of sending the damaged products to landfills, we are sending them to food banks around the U.S., Mexico, and the UK. We continue to look for ways to donate good, nutritious products.

Kellogg in the UK

Kellogg's Swim Active

The Kellogg's Swim Active programme was launched in 2006 and funds over 50 community projects which aim to break down any barriers people may have that prevent them from participating in swimming. Examples of Swim Active projects include providing free swimming for children during the school holidays, providing transport to pools in rural locations and introducing special lessons for children with disabilities.

Kellogg's Breakfast Clubs

Set up in 1998, breakfast clubs provide a healthy meal at the start of the day in a fun and friendly environment.

> They provide a great opportunity for kids to play, learn and socialise with classmates. Breakfast clubs are proven to improve children's behaviour, punctuality and attendance rates at school. They also increase concentration levels throughout the morning and can often improve relationships between teachers and children so everyone's happy.
>
> Working together with our charity ContinYou, we have helped develop breakfast club services at over 500 schools in the UK which deliver around 2 million breakfasts each year.

As Kellogg in the UK has decided to be pro-active in their charitable giving and focus on two programmes, breakfast clubs and swimming, community group funding appears to be no longer available.

Matched funding

A scheme is in operation matching employees' fundraising efforts pound for pound.

Kier Group plc

Building/construction

Correspondent: Corporate Responsibility Dept., Tempsford Hall, Sandy, Bedfordshire SG19 2BD (tel: 01767 640111; fax: 01767 640002; email: info@kier.co.uk; website: www.kier.co.uk)

Directors: Phil White, Chair; Paul Sheffield, Chief Executive; Hugh Raven; Richard Bailey; Haydn Mursell; Steve Bowcott; Ian Lawton; Chris Geoghegan; Nick Winser (women: 0; men: 9)

Year end	30/06/2011
Turnover	£2,056,000,000
Pre-tax profit	£57,700,000

Nature of business: Activities span building, civil engineering, opencast mining, facilities management, residential and commercial property investment and PFI project investment.

Company registration number: 2708030

UK employees: 10,128

Total employees: 10,685

Membership: BITC

Charitable donations

UK cash (latest declared):	2011	£64,000
	2009	£354,000
	2008	£252,000
Total UK:	2011	£64,000
Total worldwide:	2011	£64,000
Cash worldwide:	2011	£64,000

Corporate social responsibility

CSR committee: The CR Steering Committee is determined to improve the focus and management of its Group community engagement without in any way compromising the ongoing good work undertaken locally by our businesses wherever they operate among their closest communities.

CSR policy: This information was obtained from the company's CSR report:

> Community engagement is much more than just supporting charities and sponsoring football teams; it is about having social and economic impact on local communities and we tailor our CR activities to suit the needs of the local community. It is our intention that the activities, programmes and initiatives that we deliver are designed to support local priorities and make a real difference to people's lives.
>
> Our CR vision is to 'deliver a brighter future for our communities.

CSR report: A full CSR report was available from the company's website.

Applications

In writing to the correspondent.

Other information

During 2010/11, the group companies donated £64,000 (2009: £354,000) to a wide variety of charities and other organisations across the UK and overseas. A list of beneficiaries was unavailable.

> The Kier Foundation is in the process of being created as a registered charity established and funded by the company and through which much of the group's community engagement will be channelled and supported in the future. As part of the foundation initiative, the board will establish a formal relationship with a national charity on an annual or two-year basis through which the foundation can channel and share resources, as well as helping deliver tangible projects and activities by group employees and businesses nationwide.

Kier has entered into a partnership with ConstructionSkills to develop a programme which will deliver 100 construction team leader apprentices per annum across all disciplines.

154,000 hours of time was given for community engagement activities.

Kingfisher plc

Property, retail – DIY/furniture

Correspondent: Nick Folland, Legal and Corporate Responsibility Director, 3 Sheldon Square, Paddington, London W2 6PX (tel: 020 7372 8008; fax: 020 7644 1001; email: corporateresponsibility@kingfisher.com; website: www.kingfisher.co.uk)

Directors: Daniel Bernard, Chair; Ian Cheshire, Chief Executive; Andrew Bonfield; Pascal Cagni; Clare Chapman; Anders Dahlvig; Janis Kong; John Nelson; Kevin O'Byrne; Phil Bentley; Michael Hepher (women: 2; men: 9)

Year end	29/01/2011
Pre-tax profit	£10,506,000,000

Nature of business: Home improvement retail group.

Company registration number: 1664812

Main locations: Middlesex, London, Croydon, Eastleigh, Harrow, Hull, Hayes, Leeds

Total employees: 78,000

Membership: BITC

Charitable donations

UK cash (latest declared):	2010	£417,000
	2007	£300,000
	2006	£300,000
	2005	£300,000
Total worldwide:	2011	£1,598,000
Cash worldwide:	2011	£952,000

Corporate social responsibility

CSR committee: There was no evidence of a separate CSR Committee.

CSR policy: This information was available from the company's website:

> We want to help create lasting improvements and benefits in the communities we serve. Helping to create sustainable communities is one of the key priority areas where we can make a difference- focusing on community projects and the broader role we can play in working with governments, local authorities and other stakeholders to help create more sustainable communities.

CSR report: There was no evidence of a separate CSR report however one page was dedicated to CSR in the company's annual reports as well as information being available from the company's website.

Applications

In writing to the correspondent.

Other information

Kingfisher and its subsidiaries made contributions to charity/community projects worth an estimated £1.6 million. This included cash donations (£952,000) and gifts-in kind (£443,000 – retail cost). Support was also given through the donation of time by employees

(£203,000). 26,000 works hours were spent on volunteering activities.

The company is currently working to develop a new community strategy as part of its 2020 CR vision.

In 2011, community investment increased by 70% mainly due to a significant increase at B&Q UK.

This year's charity partners are: Save the Children; HIV/AIDS Partnership; Action for Blind People; and Community Payback.

Kodak Ltd

Chemicals and plastics

Correspondent: Kodak Sponsorship Department, Corporate Public Relations, Hemel One, Boundary Way, Hemel Hempstead, Hertfordshire HP2 7YU (tel: 01442 261122; fax: 01442 240609; email: gb-sponsorship@kodak.com; website: www.kodak.co.uk)

Directors: J. Butler; M. Harding; P. Gibbons; H. Isaacs; D. Lambert; B. McGowan; D. Webb; J. Wildman

Year end	31/12/2010
Turnover	£100,400,000
Pre-tax profit	£6,700,000

Nature of business: Principal activities are the manufacture, supply and distribution of photographic film, paper, chemicals, digital imaging equipment, together with services associated with these activities. The company is a wholly owned subsidiary of the Eastman Kodak Company.

Company registration number: 59535

Main locations: Hemel Hempstead, Harrow

Total employees: 1,256

Charitable donations

UK cash (latest declared):	2010	£1,000
	2009	£91,200
	2008	£392,100
	2006	£73,000
	2005	£142,000
Total UK:	2010	£1,000
Total worldwide:	2010	£1,000
Cash worldwide:	2010	£1,000

Corporate social responsibility

CSR committee: No details found.

CSR policy: The 2010 annual report states:

Corporate Social Responsibility: 'Throughout its 100-year history, Kodak has been committed to act in a responsible manner towards all of its respective stakeholders, be they employees, shareholders, customers, suppliers, and also the local communities in which it operates.'

We were unable to determine the ratio of women to men on the board.

CSR report: No report available. The group website, www.kodak.com provides information on Global Sustainability.

Exclusions

Kodak does not support advertising in charity brochures, purely denominational appeals, large national appeals, purely local appeals not in areas of company presence, appeals from individuals, overseas projects or circulars.

Applications

All appeals (charity, education or sponsorship) should be addressed to the correspondent.

Advice to applicants: The company welcomes appeals from charities, but receives a large amount of mail. Applicants should therefore take note of the main areas of interest – science education and research.

Other information

Charitable donations including those for scientific educational and research purposes in the UK in 2010 were £1,000 (2009: £91,200). We have no details of beneficiary groups but in the past organisations supported by Kodak include: UNICEF; national Museum of Photography, Film and Television; Royal Photographic Society; Breakthrough Breast Cancer; Hope for Children; and, The Prince's Trust.

Kodak may donate products for raffle prizes, provide the use of premises for meetings, or help with graphic reproduction.

Sponsorship

Through Asthma UK, Kodak has sponsored the children's interactive website 'Kick-A' and the launch of the Asthma UK Youth Conferences. In 2011, Kodak is supporting an initiative to connect 17–23 year olds with our consumer products, so they can use images to promote living a full life with asthma.

The company has sponsored Breakthrough Breast Cancer's Breakthrough £1,000 Challenge for a number of years. The event challenges individuals, groups and teams to raise £1,000 for the organisation's work a challenge which has been accepted by many of the company's employees.

KPMG LLP

Accountants

Correspondent: See 'Applications', Salisbury Square House, 8 Salisbury Square, London EC4Y 8BB (tel: 020 7311 1000; fax: 020 7311 3311; website: www.kpmg.co.uk)

Directors: John Griffith-Jones, Joint Chair; Prof. Dr Rolf Nonnenmacher, Joint Chair; Richard Bennison; Hubert Achermann; Abdullah Al Fozan; Mike Ashley; Guy Bainbridge; Klaus Becker; Aidan Brennan; Simon Collins; Andrew Cranston; Herman Dijkhuizen; Ernst Grobl; Harald von Heynitz; Mathieu Meyer; Iain Moffatt; Stein-Ragnar Noreng; Johann Pastor; Tim Payne; Karin Riehl; Graeme Ross; Carsten Schiewe; Joachim Schindler; John M. Scott; Patrick Simons; Jurgen van Breukelen; Jaap van Everdingen; Jack van Rooijen; Stefan Zwicker (women: 1; men: 28)

Year end	30/09/2011
Turnover	£3,800,000,000
Pre-tax profit	£746,000,000

Nature of business: The provision of professional services through the core functions of assurance, tax, consulting and financial advisory services (covering transaction services, corporate finance, corporate recovery and forensic). Legal services are provided by Klegal, an independent law firm associated with KPMG.

The KPMG Europe LLP board has the ultimate responsibility for ensuring that an appropriate system of risk management and internal quality control operates throughout the group – covering all enterprise risks.

Company registration number: 3513178

Main locations: Birmingham, Bristol, Cardiff, Cambridge, Edinburgh, Gatwick, Glasgow, Ipswich, Leeds, Leicester, Milton Keynes, Newcastle upon Tyne, Liverpool, Manchester, Nottingham, Preston, Plymouth, Reading, St Albans, Southampton, Stoke on Trent, Watford, St Helens, St Asaph, Kings Norton, Aberdeen

Total employees: 29,845

Membership: BITC, LBG

Charitable donations

UK cash (latest declared):	2009	£12,275,000
	2007	£1,000,000
	2006	£813,000
Total worldwide:	2011	£16,300,000

Corporate social responsibility

CSR committee: There was no evidence of a separate CSR Committee.

CSR policy: This information was obtained from the company's website: 'Corporate Social Responsibility is woven deeply into our business strategy. It allows us to lead by example, make a real difference in communities, employ the best people, connect with our clients and cut our costs and environmental impact.'

CSR report: There was no evidence of a separate CSR report however four pages were dedicated to CSR in the company's annual report, as well as information which was available via the company's website.

Exclusions

Assistance to private educational establishments, political parties, or primarily evangelical causes and campaigns is not given.

Applications

Charity partners

The following information is given by Mona Bitar, partner at KPMG, on Howard Lake's fundraising.co.uk.

> ***How we choose charity partners***
>
> You may be interested in knowing how we as a firm go about selecting the charities that we work with.
>
> This time around in fact marked a new departure for us. Any charity is open to apply to us and we usually receive around 50 applications or more. We have a charity steering group, drawn from the workforce at all levels across the firm, who meet and agree a shortlist from the applications received usually five or six charities. In the past, we have then had a whole staff vote and quite simply whichever charity got the most votes would be chosen.
>
> Whilst this has worked really well, this time around we wanted to be absolutely sure that the charities we work with share something of our own core interests and issues. That there is a strategic fit, in business speak. So rather than have a staff vote, the charity steering group invited the shortlist of half a dozen to come in and meet us. From that, the two charities that we have selected really stood out: literacy has been a longstanding focus for much of our community work, while homelessness links very well to our growing interest in social inclusion and social mobility enabling people, from all walks of life, to unlock their own potential. So Action for Literacy and Shelter shone through and we're really excited about the choices that we have made.

To contact the CSR department you can email CSR@kpmg.co.uk; the direct email address given on fundraising.co.uk for Mona Bitar is ukfmaskmona@kpmg.co.uk.

The KPMG Foundation UK: Note that the foundation is pro active in seeking projects to fund and regrets that it is not in a position to respond to unsolicited grant applications.

Only registered charities are funded.

Other information

There are two strands to KPMG's community involvement activity, namely, employee volunteering and a programme of charitable giving. KPMG's charitable giving policy states:

> KPMG's donation policy focuses on community and environment, particularly through education, to help enhance social inclusion for individuals and communities and to support charities that maintain and enhance biodiversity. Our donations budgets are to support the volunteering of our people.

The company has contributed more than 2,400 pro bono hours worth more than £400,000 across seven African countries.

Support is also available from the **KPMG Foundation** (Charity Commission no. 1086518) which was established in October 2001 with a capital sum of £10 million from KPMG. The foundation states that it is a completely separate entity to KPMG LLP but, nevertheless, does have representatives from the firm on its board of trustees. The foundation's support costs are covered by the firm.

The focus of the KPMG Foundation is on education and social projects for the disadvantaged and under privileged, with particular emphasis on unlocking the potential of children and young people, up to 30 years of age, who for primarily social reasons have not fulfiled their educational potential.

The foundation maintains its focus in England, Scotland and Wales and states that the 'key driver' will be the quality of projects rather than where a project is geographically.

In particular, the trustees have chosen to support four very distinct groups within this broad umbrella of 'disadvantage'. Those groups are:

- Refugees
- Young offenders
- Children and young people who have been in care
- Children and young people with dyslexia/literacy difficulties

KPMG Foundation

In 2010, the foundation had an income of £564,000 and made grants totalling nearly £642,000. This was broken down as follows:

- Refugees (£32,000)
- Young offenders (£126,000)
- Young people who have been in care (£62,500)
- Young people with educational needs (£485,000)

> ***Employee volunteering/giving***
>
> Community and environmental projects are an exciting way for our people to broaden their skills. KPMG the UK firm provides the following opportunities:
>
> - Everyone has 3.5 hours of firm time each month to volunteer
> - We have donation budgets to support volunteering
> - We run a Give As You Earn Scheme, with all donations made to our Staff Selected Charity, matched pound for pound up to the value of £100,000
> - Each of our offices has a CSR forum which decides its local priorities within a clearly defined national framework
>
> Our annual 'Make a Difference Day' provides our people with an opportunity to get involved in numerous projects. In the combined group a record 4,000 people participated in Make a Difference Day and team challenges supporting more than 300 projects within their local communities.

The firm donates computers and other IT equipment through the national Tools for Schools programme.

From time to time, furniture and other office equipment that is surplus to requirements are made available to community organisations.

Under an innovative new agreement, KPMG staff in the UK who use the firm's Corporate Card to pay for their business expenses will be helping to raise funds for KPMG's Charity of the Year. KPMG hopes to raise at least £100,000 for charity through the scheme.

Payroll giving: Give As You Earn is available nationally and is supported by the firm.

Charity Partners: Action for Literacy and Shelter (2012–14).

Kraft Foods UK Ltd

Food manufacture

Correspondent: Corporate Affairs Team, St George's House, Bayshill Road, Cheltenham, Gloucester GL50 3AE (tel: 01242 236101; fax: 01242 512084; website: www.kraftfoodscompany.com/eu)

Directors: Irene Rosenfield, Chair and Chief Executive; Ajaypal S. Banga, President; Myra M. Hart; Peter B. Henry; Lois D. Juliber; Mark D. Ketchum; Richard A. Lerner; Mackey J. McDonald; John C. Pope; Fredric G. Reynolds; Jean-Francois M. L. Van Boxmeer (women: 3; men: 9)

Year end	31/12/2010
Turnover	£33,853,085,500

Nature of business: The principal activity of the company is food manufacture.

Company registration number: 203663

Main locations: Cheltenham, Banbury

Total employees: 126,000

Membership: BITC, LBG

Charitable donations

UK cash (latest declared):	2010	£750,000
	2008	£99,000
	2007	£94,000
	2006	£191,000
	2005	£97,500
Total UK:	2010	£780,500
Total worldwide:	2010	£62,330,000
Cash worldwide:	2010	£750,000

Corporate giving

The company's Progress Report for 2011 states: 'In 2011 we donated $100 million (£62,330,000) in cash, food and time to nonprofit organisations around the world.' We were unable to find any breakdown of this amount, where it was spent and to which organisations it was given.

In 2010, the company made a donation of £750,000 to the Cadbury Foundation, plus £30,500 in donated services such as seconded staff and auditor's fees. The foundation in turn made grants totalling just over £703,500, with beneficiaries in the UK including the Confectioners' Benevolent Trust, Young Enterprise, Sheffield City Council, Achimota Trust, London Wildlife Trust and Hackney Business Partnership.

Employee-led support

Taken from the Progress Report 2011: 'Our robust volunteer program encourages employee contributions of time, money and skills where they are needed most in our communities around the globe. Fostering volunteerism is good for the community, our employees and our company.' There are 26,000 volunteers in 72 countries supporting 900 projects through 350 nonprofit organisations.

Corporate social responsibility

CSR committee: No information.

CSR policy: None published.

CSR report: None published.

Applications

If you wish to apply for support for a school or local community project that fits Kraft's categories, contact the corporate affairs team on 01242 284511 or email ukcorporate@krafteurope.com.

Kwik-Fit Group

Motors and accessories

Correspondent: Company Secretary, 3 Hardman Square, Spinningfields, Manchester M3 3EB (website: www.kwik-fit.com)

Directors: David Reid, Chair; Ian Fraser, Group Chief Executive Officer; Michael Healy, Group Finance Director; Eric Bouchez; Eleanor Chambers; Colm O'Sullivan; Michel Pans (women: 1; men: 6)

Year end	31/12/2010
Turnover	£874,800,000
Pre-tax profit	£92,300,000

Nature of business: Operation of automotive repair services in the UK, France and Holland and a financial services business in the UK.

Company registration number: 5452193

Main locations: Broxburn, Uddingston

Total employees: 8,287

Charitable donations

UK cash (latest declared):	2010	£100,000
	2009	£200,000
	2008	£100,000
	2007	£100,000
	2006	£100,000
Total UK:	2010	£100,000
Total worldwide:	2010	£100,000
Cash worldwide:	2010	£100,000

Corporate social responsibility

CSR policy: No specific CSR information found. There is information on the environment and recycling on the website.

Exclusions

No response to circular appeals. No grants for advertising in charity brochures or appeals from individuals.

Applications

It would appear that any unsolicited applications the company receives are unlikely to be successful and we would therefore advise you not to write.

Other information

The group contributed £100,000 to national and local charities during 2010 (2009: £200,000). The Kwik-Fit Group was acquired by PAI Partners, headquartered in France, in 2005 and is represented by four directors on the board of Speedy 1 Ltd. As the holding company of the Kwik-Fit Group, Speedy 1 Ltd's (2010) report and accounts are those we refer to here.

Previously, we have been advised that the group and its employees continue to support, financially and in kind, a wide range of charitable activities. In particular, there is an emphasis on initiatives that support children and young people, community development and road safety. We cannot find any information demonstrating that this has changed.

Sponsorship: The company undertakes good cause sponsorship of local community events and competitions for local schoolchildren.

Ladbrokes plc

Gaming, hotels, leisure

Correspondent: CSR Department, Imperial House, Imperial Drive, Rayners Lane, Harrow, Middlesex HA2 7JW (tel: 020 8868 8899; fax: 020 8868 8767; email: csr@ladbrokes.co.uk; website: www.ladbrokesplc.com)

Directors: Peter Erskine, Chair; Richard Glynn; Ian Bull; Richard J. Ames; John Kelly; John F. Jarvis CVO,; Christopher J. Rodrigues; Sly Bailey; Darren Shapland; Christine Hodgson; Richard Moross (women: 2; men: 9)

Year end	31/12/2011
Turnover	£976,100,000
Pre-tax profit	£187,700,000

Nature of business: The group's principal activity is the provision of a range of betting and gaming services.

Company registration number: 566221

Subsidiaries include: Inter-National Hotel Services Ltd, Ladbrokes Ltd, LivingWell Health and Leisure Ltd

Main locations: Watford, Harlow

UK employees: 13,170

Total employees: 15,512

Charitable donations

UK cash (latest declared):	2011	£630,000
	2009	£700,000
	2007	£720,000
	2005	£54,000
	2003	£152,000
Total UK:	2011	£630,000
Total worldwide:	2011	£630,000
Cash worldwide:	2011	£630,000

Community involvement

There is a trust associated with the company – **Ladbrokes in the Community Charitable Trust** (Charity Commission no. 1101804).

The trust seeks to support smaller local charities and groups through its countrywide network of betting shops. Its declared aims are to support causes concerned with education and training, medical/health/sickness issues, and sport and recreation.

The company was a founding member of the Responsibility in Gambling Trust (RIGT) and has a significant partnership with Crimestoppers.

Corporate giving

During 2011, the trust donated just under £630,000 to charitable and community causes across the UK, including £100,000 to Cancer Research UK; £80,000 to Age UK; £60,000 to CLIC Sargent; and £66,000 to Breast Cancer Campaign.

Employee-led support

The group actively encourages employees to undertake fundraising activities, particularly in support of Ladbrokes in the Community Charitable Trust. Employees raised over £515,000 during 2011.

Charity partners: Ladbrokes is the official partner of Race for Life, organised by Cancer Research UK, the Bobby Moore Fund and Crimestoppers.

Corporate social responsibility

CSR committee: There was no evidence of a separate CSR Committee.

CSR policy: This information was obtained from the company's website: 'We are committed to being a good corporate citizen and use our corporate resources in ways that benefit the social, economic and environmental conditions of the communities in which we operate.'

CSR report: There was evidence of a separate CSR report.

Exclusions

No support is given to appeals for advertising in charity brochures, the arts, appeals from individuals, circular appeals, fundraising events, overseas projects, political appeals, religious appeals, or small, purely local appeals not in an area of company presence.

Applications

For Ladbrokes in the Community Charitable Trust, the procedure is to secure the support of your local shop in raising funds on behalf of your cause. Any monies raised are then banked with the trust, with consideration of additional funds being added by Ladbrokes taken by the trust's grants committee which meets every five to six weeks.

Lafarge Aggregates Ltd

Quarrying

Correspondent: Charity Adviser, Communications Dept., PO Box 7388, Granite House, Watermead Business Park, Syston, Leicester LE7 1WA (tel: 0844 561 0037; fax: 0870 336 8602; website: www.lafarge.co.uk)

Directors: J. M. Greenwood; D. M. James; A. McRae; J. A. Verity; S. J. Wykes; S. Davidson; D. Grimason

Year end	31/12/2011
Turnover	£421,761,000
Pre-tax profit	(£3,760,000)

Nature of business: Supplier of asphalt, aggregate, concrete products and ready mixed.

Company registration number: 297905

Main locations: Leicester

Total employees: 1,556

Membership: BITC

Charitable donations

UK cash (latest declared):	2011	£21,700
	2009	£38,000
	2008	£820,000
	2007	£820,000
Total UK:	2011	£42,600
Total worldwide:	2011	£42,600
Cash worldwide:	2011	£21,700

Corporate social responsibility

CSR committee: No specific details found.

CSR policy: Statement taken from the company's website:

> We are committed to supporting the communities around our operations and recognise the importance of being a good neighbour and a trusted partner. Key achievements in this area include:
>
> - A unique partnership with the Prince's Trust
> - A 37% decrease in community complaints
> - All quarries have the opportunity to have an operational Liaison Committee

We were unable to determine the ratio of women to men on the board.

CSR report: The first Sustainability report covers the period 2007–2010 and is available from the company's website.

Exclusions

Local appeals not in areas of company presence.

Applications

Charitable donations programme

Charities and community organisations are encouraged to apply for a cash or materials donation. To be eligible for consideration, your organisation must be located within three miles of an operational Lafarge Aggregates and Concrete UK site or be otherwise affected by its operations – contact Lafarge's charity advisor for further information. To find out which Lafarge Aggregates and Concrete UK site is nearest you, refer to the 'Location finder' on their website.

All requests for cash or materials donations must be made in writing, with details of your organisation and/or project. If you are requesting a materials donation, indicate the type and quantity of material, when it is needed and if you require delivery or will be collecting the material.

Other information

In 2011 Lafarge Aggregates Ltd donated both monies and materials in kind to a variety of organisations throughout the UK to the value of £42,600 (2010: £11,600). Donations to registered charities were £21,700 (2010: £1,830).

The annual report for 2011 states:

> The company also encourages and supports local communities to utilise the opportunities presented by the Landfill Communities Fund (LCF), to receive grant funding for reclamation, public amenity, pollution reduction, biodiversity or historic buildings projects. Since 2005, the company has given £4.4 million to such projects through the LCF. The company works with Derbyshire Environmental Trust who administers the scheme throughout the UK on its behalf.
>
> *Partnerships*
>
> In 2009, the company embarked on a three year partnership with the Prince's Trust. As part of this partnership, the company has identified opportunities for the company to actively support the work the Prince's Trust does, helping disadvantaged young people.
>
> *Local liaison committees*
>
> All quarries are encouraged to put in place a local liaison committee, comprising of representatives from the local community including parish, district or county councillors, conservation organisations and authorities. The local liaison committee is critical to managing regular dialogue between our sites and the local community. These dynamic forums allow members to hear about quarry developments and operations, and have their questions answered by Lafarge representatives. Over 65 meetings were held at local liaison committees during 2010.

The Laird Group plc

Engineering

Correspondent: The Company Secretary, 100 Pall Mall, London SW1Y 5NQ (tel: 020 7468 4040; fax: 020 7839 2921; email: info@laird-plc.com; website: www.laird-plc.com)

Directors: Nigel Keen, Chair; Sir Christopher Hum; Professor Michael Kelly; Jonathan Silver; Andrew Robb; Dr William Spivey; Anthony Reading (women: 0; men: 7)

Year end	31/12/2011
Turnover	£59,000,000
Pre-tax profit	£53,000,000

Nature of business: Electronics and technology company.

Company registration number: 55513

Main locations: London

Total employees: 10,957

Charitable donations

UK cash (latest declared):	2011	£2,300
	2009	£9,200
	2008	£4,880
	2007	£35,000
	2006	£15,000
Total UK:	2011	£2,300
Total worldwide:	2011	£22,800
Cash worldwide:	2011	£22,800

Corporate social responsibility

CSR committee: There was no evidence of a separate CSR Committee.

CSR policy: This information was obtained from the company's annual report:

> Laird recognises the need to behave as a good corporate citizen and remains committed to a programme of continuous improvement in all areas of corporate responsibility.

CSR report: There was no evidence of a separate CSR report.

Exclusions

No support for political appeals.

Applications

In writing to the correspondent.

Other information

During the year Laird gave £2,300 to UK charities (2010, £5,460) and £22,770 to charities worldwide.

Examples of this include:

- Sponsored walks and holiday gift programmes
- Donation of funds to tornado relief efforts in Joplin, Missouri, USA and to earthquake relief efforts in Japan
- Local nature reserve conservancy efforts
- Support of educational projects

Lancashire Holdings Ltd

Insurance

Correspondent: Shavon Edwards, Corporate Responsibility Department, Lancashire Holdings Ltd, Power House, 7 Par-la-Ville Road, Hamilton HM 11, Bermuda (tel: 020 7264 4000/ +1(441)278–8950; fax: 020 7264 4077; email: shavon.edwards@lancashiregroup.com; website: www.lancashiregroup.com)

Directors: Richard Brindle, Chair and Chief Executive; Alex Maloney; Neil McConachie; Martin Thomas; John Bishop; Emma Duncan; Ralf Oelssner; Robert Spass; William Spiegel (women: 1; men: 8)

Year end	31/12/2011
Turnover	£393,600,000
Pre-tax profit	£139,400,000

Nature of business: Lancashire is a global provider of specialty insurance products operating in Bermuda, London and Dubai. Focusing on short-tail, specialty insurance risks, mostly on a direct basis, under four main classes: property, energy, marine and aviation.

Company registration number: 1477482

Charitable donations

UK cash (latest declared):	2009	£699,000
Total worldwide:	2011	£797,000
Cash worldwide:	2011	£1,250,000

Corporate social responsibility

CSR committee: There was evidence of a 'Donations Committee'.

CSR policy: This information was obtained from the company's website:

> At the Lancashire Group, our success is built on strong relationships with our people, clients and stakeholders. However many communities do not benefit from the success our relationships have created. War, famine, natural disaster, endemic poverty and a lack of opportunity are powerful inhibitors to development worldwide. That is why we established the Lancashire Foundation as the cornerstone to these commitments.

CSR report: A CSR report was available within the company's annual report.

Applications

In writing to the correspondent.

Other information

This year the company donated just under £800,000 to charity.

The following is taken from the company's website:

> We're personally involved with most of the charities we support. Our people contribute their time and expertise, as well as voting donations through the [Lancashire] Foundation. Examples of the charities we supported in 2010 were:
>
> - Vauxhall City Farm, *which* provides an opportunity for Londoners to encounter farm animals from around the world, face-to-face. It aims to provide an educational, recreational and therapeutic program for children and people of all ages, abilities and cultures, to contribute to community cohesion and regeneration, and to promote environmental awareness
> - Kids Company, which works to support over 17,000 marginalised and excluded children and young people every year in London

Other charities supported this year include: Coalition for the Protection of Children (based in Bermuda); International Care Ministries and Age Concern.

> ***Lancashire Foundation***
>
> Lancashire set up the Lancashire Foundation, a Bermuda charitable trust, in 2007 with the aim of creating a charitable trust for the benefit of charitable causes in Bermuda and elsewhere. The foundation's trustee is an independent third-party professional trust company that makes donations following recommendations made by the company's donations committee, which consists of Lancashire employees and independent members. Specific criteria have been set for the foundation's charitable giving. These criteria include causes where Lancashire staff or independent donations committee members have a close relationship with those who operate the charity and therefore have the ability to monitor and influence outcomes.

Land Securities Group plc

Property

Correspondent: P M Dudgeon, Company Secretary, 5 Strand, London WC2N 5AF (tel: 020 7413 9000; fax: 020 7925 0202; email: corporate.responsibility@landsecurities.com; website: www.landsecurities.com)

Directors: Alison Carnwath, Chair; Robert Noel, Chief Executive; Martin Greenslade; Richard Akers; David Rough; Sir Stuart Rose; Kevin O'Byrne; Chris Bartram; Simon Palley; Stacey Rauch (women: 2; men: 8)

Year end	31/03/2011
Turnover	£701,900,000
Pre-tax profit	£1,227,300,000

Nature of business: Land Securities is the largest UK property group, involved in both property development and investment, and property outsourcing.

Company registration number: 4369054

Main locations: Birmingham, London, Portsmouth, Sunderland, Cardiff, Gateshead, East Kilbride, Leeds, Glasgow

Total employees: 692

Membership: BITC, LBG

Charitable donations

UK cash (latest declared):	2010	£871,000
	2007	£487,600
	2006	£559,000
	2005	£580,000
Total worldwide:	2011	£829,000
Cash worldwide:	2011	£829,000

Corporate social responsibility

CSR committee: There was evidence of a separate CSR Committee.

CSR policy: This information was obtained from the company's annual report:

> We have a long tradition of working closely with local communities during the development stages of our sites. Wherever we have major property holdings, we invest in employment, education and enterprise opportunities to help create thriving and sustainable communities. Our approach also involves us in collaborating with partners to deliver training and employment opportunities and providing financial support to local community groups through grant giving and charity. We engage with schools, colleges and universities to provide education programmes that help to prepare young people for the world of work.

CSR report: There was evidence of a separate CSR report.

Exclusions

No support for political appeals.

Applications

In writing to the correspondent.

Other information

During 2010/11 the company's total community contribution, including charity committee funds, was £829,000 (2009: £871,000). The company also offers bursaries and each year employees can apply for a bursary, each up to the value of £500, to help the groups they support to contribute to the local community.

The company offers fifteen £500 bursaries for employees to support community groups they are involved in.

Over 10,194 hours was given in employee time. In monetary terms this would total £3.7 million.

Land Securities are involved in the **Give As You Earn** (GAYE) scheme.

Lazard and Co. Ltd

Banking

Correspondent: Charities Committee, 50 Stratton Street, London W1J 8LL (tel: 020 7187 2000; fax: 020 7072 6000; website: www.lazard.com)

Directors: Kenneth M. Jacobs; Ashish Bhutani; Steven J. Heyer; Sylvia Jay; Vernon E. Jordan, Jr; Philip A. Laskawy; Laurent Mignon; Gary W. Parr; Hal S. Scott; Michael J. Turner (women: 1; men: 9)

Year end	31/12/2011
Turnover	£1,829,512,000

Nature of business: Financial advisor and asset management services.

Company registration number: 162175

Main locations: London

Charitable donations

UK cash (latest declared):	2010	£0
	2005	£141,000

Corporate social responsibility

CSR policy: No information was available.

Applications

Unsolicited applications are unlikely to succeed. Applicant charities must have a direct link with a member of staff at Lazard's in order to be considered for support.

Other information

There was no information regarding charitable donations available.

Leeds Building Society

Building society

Correspondent: The Secretary, Leeds Building Society Charitable Foundation, 105 Albion Street, Leeds LS1 5AS (tel: 01132 167296; fax: 01132 257549; website: www.leedsbuildingsociety.co.uk)

Directors: Robin Smith, Chair; Peter Hill, Chief Executive; John Anderson; Robin Ashton; Carol Kavanagh; Robin Litten; Les Platts; Abhai Rajguru; Kim Rebecchi; Ian Robertson; Bob Stott (women: 2; men: 9)

Year end	31/12/2011
Pre-tax profit	£50,200,000

Nature of business: The provision, to existing and prospective members, of residential mortgages and retail saving products.

FSA registration number: 164992

Main locations: Leeds

UK employees: 926

Total employees: 926

Membership: BITC

Charitable donations

UK cash (latest declared):	2011	£219,000
	2009	£180,000
	2007	£94,000
	2006	£80,000
	2005	£60,000
Total UK:	2011	£219,000
Total worldwide:	2011	£219,000
Cash worldwide:	2011	£219,000

Exclusions

The Foundation is unlikely to make donations for:

- The restoration or upgrading of buildings, including churches
- Environmental charities (unless there is a benefit to a disadvantaged community)
- Administration equipment such as IT equipment for a charity's own use

The Foundation is unable to support:

- Projects with religious, political or military purposes
- Overseas charities or projects
- Individuals, including sponsorship of individuals
- Animal welfare projects
- Medical research

Applications

Apply in writing to the Secretary. There is no application form and you should simply apply to the contact in writing. Remember to include the following information:

- The name of your organisation
- The name of the project, and brief information about its work
- A contact name, address and phone number
- Your registered charity number
- Details of what the donation would be used for
- Who would benefit from the donation
- Your nearest Leeds Building Society branch

Generally, applications for community based projects which aim to provide relief of suffering, hardship or poverty, or their direct consequences will be considered.

Some examples of the areas in which donations have been made include:

Support to:

- Homeless people
- Adults and children with physical and mental disabilities
- Older people
- Underprivileged families
- Deaf, blind and partially sighted people; and
- Community projects benefiting local residents
- Victims of natural and civil disasters in the UK

The project must operate in the area of one of our 67 branches.

Donations are normally in the range of £250 to £1,000. The application must be for capital expenditure. Applications towards general running costs will not be considered. Your local branch can forward your application if that would be more convenient.

All applications will be acknowledged. The Trustees meet quarterly in March, June, September and November. Following the meeting you will receive notification of whether or not you have been successful.

Other information

In 2009, the group made a charitable donation of £76,000 to the Leeds Building Society Charitable Foundation (Charity Commission no. 1074429). The 'Caring Saver Account' enabled further donations of £44,000 to be made to charities. Other charitable donations in the year amounted to £58,000. Four main charities are supported: Save the Children, Marie Curie, Help the Aged and the Leeds Building Society Charitable Foundation.

Subsidiaries include: Leeds Financial Services Ltd; Leeds Mortgage Funding Ltd; Leeds Overseas (Isle of Man) Ltd; Headrow Commercial Property Services Ltd; Mercantile Asset Management Ltd; Countrywide Rentals 1 Ltd; Countrywide Rentals 2 Ltd; Countrywide Rentals 3 Ltd; Countrywide Rentals 4 Ltd; Countrywide Rentals 5 Ltd; Leeds Building Society Covered Bonds LLP.

Legal and General plc

Financial services

Correspondent: Tim Breedon, Group Chief Executive, The Charity Committee (tel: 020 3124 2000/020 3124 2091; fax: 020 3124 2500; website: www.legalandgeneralgroup.com)

Directors: John Stewart, Chair; Tim Breedon, Group Chief Executive; Nick Prettejohn; Stuart Popham; John Pollock; Henry Staunton; Rudy Markham; Julia Wilson; Mark Gregory; Clara Furse; Nigel Wilson, Group Chief Financial Officer; Mike Fairey (women: 2; men: 10)

Year end	31/12/2011
Turnover	£18,317,000,000
Pre-tax profit	£956,000,000

Nature of business: The group's principal activities are: the provision of long-term insurance, investment management and general insurance.

Company registration number: 1417162

Subsidiaries include: Arlington Business Parks Partnership, Gresham Insurance Company Ltd, Trident Components Group Ltd

Main locations: London, Brighton, Cardiff, Birmingham

Total employees: 8,058

Membership: BITC

Charitable donations

UK cash (latest declared):	2009	£2,800,000
	2008	£3,200,000
	2007	£1,860,000
	2006	£2,300,000
	2005	£2,279,000
Total UK:	2009	£2,884,900
Total worldwide:	2011	£3,563,200

Community involvement

The following statement is taken from the group's website:

> *Community Commitments:*
> To manage appropriate international CSR programmes to address the ESG (Environmental, Social and Governance) risks and reputation in those marketplaces.
>
> To support the community as a whole, especially on grass roots issues where we feel we can make a difference in key programmes.
>
> To partner with third sector organisations to campaign for the issues that matter to our markets and businesses. To support and encourage employee involvement in charitable giving, volunteering and in utilising the resources available to them.

Corporate giving

During 2011, charitable donations totalling over £3.4 million (2010: £3.2 million) were made by the company and by employees through approved schemes. We were unable to discover the amount given solely by the company as opposed to those monies raised by employees through fundraising.

Employee-led support

Community awards scheme: Employees are encouraged to support charitable activities in their local communities. A 'Community Awards' scheme exists to recognise the good work of its employees in the community. Six winners are chosen from a list of nominees, each of whom receive £1,000 on behalf of the charity or group supported.

Community Volunteering Projects
Charity initiatives benefiting from employee involvement included: Acorns Children's Hospice; Guide Dogs' Puppy in Training; The Suzy Lamplugh National Personal Safety Day; Shelter; West Midlands Wonderkids Awards.

Payroll giving: The company offer the Give As You Earn scheme. In 2011, 948 employees gave money to charity via Give As You Earn.

Matched funding: Employees are entitled to Legal and General's Employee Sponsorship Matching Scheme as part of their employment package. A total of £580,870 (including Legal and General matching) was donated to 357 charities in 2011.

Corporate social responsibility

CSR committee: Legal and General's CSR Committee is chaired by Tim Breedon, Group Chief Executive. The CSR Committee is supported by six subcommittees including a Group Charity Committee.

CSR policy: Statement taken from the 2011 annual report:

> We believe that we have a responsibility to help strengthen the communities and the environment in which we live and work. We do this by becoming involved in local projects and lending our support to initiatives where we can help to enrich the quality of life and increase opportunities for all. We have been leading the way in working with experts from the third sector about the changing needs of society, which increasingly impact our business. This can also help the third sector to operate in a more sustainable and commercially viable way, as traditional routes of funding become harder to source in the current economic climate.

CSR report: Published annually.

Exclusions

Legal and General does not support animal charities, overseas based charities or international projects, religious organisations (except where it can be proven that the project is undertaken on behalf of the community as a whole) or political organisations.

Applications

Information about national charities which meet the group's guidelines should be sent to the correspondent. Appropriate local appeals should be sent to the relevant local contact.

National decisions are made by the charity committee and approved by the group board on an annual basis; local appeals are considered by individual offices. Overseas grants are handled by the subsidiary company in each country.

John Lewis Partnership plc

Retail – department and variety stores, retail – supermarkets

Correspondent: Gemma Lacey, Head of CSR, Partnership House, Carlisle Place, London SW1P 1BX (tel: 020 7828 1000; email: gemma_lacey@johnlewis.co.uk; website: www.johnlewis.com)

Directors: Andy Street; Anne Buckley; Johnny Aisher; David Barclay; Marisa Cassoni; Tracey Killen; Kim Lowe; Mark Price; Patrick Lewis; David Anderson; Simon Fowler; Baroness Hogg; Tony Probert; Charles Mayfield, Chair (women: 5; men: 9)

Year end	29/01/2011
Turnover	£7,361,800,000
Pre-tax profit	£367,900,000

Nature of business: The company trades under the name of John Lewis (full line department stores and smaller 'at home' stores) and Waitrose (food shops, including supermarkets and convenience stores).

The partnership is a retail business run on co-operative principles. All the ordinary share capital is held by a trustee – John Lewis Partnership Trust Ltd – on partners' (employees') behalf. Under irrevocable trusts the balance of profits is available to be shared among all partners after provision for prudent reserves and for interest on loans and fixed dividends on shares held outside. Management is accountable to the general body of partners, in particular through elected councils and through the partnership's journalism.

Company registration number: 238937

Subsidiaries include: Findlater Mackie Todd and Co. Ltd, Herbert Parkinson Ltd, Waitrose Ltd, Stead, McAlpin and Co. Ltd, J H Birtwistle and Co. Ltd

Brands include: John Lewis, Waitrose.

UK employees: 76,500

Total employees: 76,500

Membership: BITC, LBG

Charitable donations

UK cash (latest declared):	2011	£5,654,000
	2010	£5,071,800
	2009	£4,009,490
	2008	£2,846,361
	2007	£2,599,163
Total UK:	2011	£7,800,000
Total worldwide:	2011	£7,800,000
Cash worldwide:	2011	£5,654,000

Community involvement

The following information has been provided by John Lewis:

> The Partnership is at the heart of many communities and believes it makes sense to act locally wherever they do business. Its partners are powerful advocates of their values and help to transform the communities in which they trade. The Partnership aims to be responsive to the needs of local communities and Partners are inspired to make a contribution. They support a diverse range of community initiatives and constantly appraise and prioritise how they can best serve the communities in which they operate. By advocating local focus, its Partners can develop closer relationships at a local level, leading to longer term commitments. John Lewis has Community Liaison Co-ordinators operating as a dedicated resource based within its stores nationwide and its Waitrose shops have appointed the Section Manager Personnel as the Community Lead. These Partners are responsible for community engagement in their location and they champion community issues. They are responsible for delivering:
>
> - Community Matters scheme. In 2010/11 Waitrose donated over £2.7 million to a wide range of charities and community groups. After a successful trial in 2011 this scheme is being extended to all John Lewis

stores from May 2012. The scheme has also been developed to allow flexibility for local organisations that would prefer to have a Partner volunteer or inn-kind donation rather than a financial contribution
- Community rooms – an initiative to provide space within a number of stores to local causes and charities
- Local Partner volunteering
- Local initiatives and tailored support to local communities
- Raise customer awareness of charitable organisations via in store community boards

Corporate giving

In 2010/11, the partnership made a total community contribution of £8.8 million, (equivalent to 2.4% of pre-tax profits). Included in this figure were: charitable donations: £5.6 million; the value of staff time: £1.5 million; in kind donations: £700,000; and management costs of £1 million. Excluding management costs, community contributions totalled £7.8 million. Causes supported were for welfare, music and arts, health, learning and the environment. In addition, substantial financial and practical support was given to causes in the communities where the company trades.

In kind support

In kind support includes the donation of products, gift vouchers and resources such as meeting room space. In 2011 a number of John Lewis and Waitrose shops began providing space for charities and community groups to use free of charge.

Employee-led support

The company sees a mutual benefit in encouraging its partners (staff) to get involved in community activities – it reinforces the company's commitment not just to its communities, but to staff as well. Partners develop their confidence, learn new skills, take on new responsibilities and become more motivated. The Partnership's company-wide volunteering programme is the Golden Jubilee Trust (GJT), established as a charity in 2000. Through the GJT, any Partner can apply for a full- or part-time volunteering secondment with a UK-registered charity for up to six months. In 2010 partners spent over 24,000 hours on GJT secondments. Building on the success of this scheme, the company is exploring new and more flexible ways of encouraging partners to be more active in their local communities. For example, in 2012 Waitrose launched a local delivery model enabling more opportunities for Partners to volunteer locally. Every Waitrose shop will volunteer for an average of 250 hours, with the flexibility for the number of hours to be scaled according to the store size.

Payroll giving: The Partnership has an established Give As You Earn scheme with Sharing the Caring, the fundraising arm of the Charities Aid Foundation (CAF), to enable partners to make tax-free charitable donations directly from their pay.

Commercially-led support

Sponsorship: Waitrose sponsors the **Royal Horticultural Society's Campaign for School Gardening**, which aims to have 80% of the UK's 21,500 primary schools actively using a garden by the end of 2012. In January 2011, 12,679 schools had already signed up.

Waitrose also sponsors the **Specialised Chefs Scholarship** at Bournemouth and Poole College, offers a wide variety of demonstrations and events in its own cookery studios, and continues to be a partner member of Farming and Countryside Education.

The stores also sell Christmas cards with a contribution made to charities.

Corporate social responsibility

CSR committee: Full details on the company's website at: www.johnlewispartnership.co.uk/csr/our-approach/governance.

CSR policy: The company has a strong commitment to corporate responsibility. The following extract is taken from the company's website:

> The Partnership has long believed that commercial success is directly linked to being a good corporate citizen and our founder's ideals continue to shape our approach to corporate social responsibility (CSR). To build a successful, sustainable business in today's competitive market, we must continue to develop long-term relationships with our customers and suppliers, and demonstrate our keen sense of civic responsibility.
>
> Being a responsible business is important to us. As co-owners of the business, our employees, known as Partners, work hard and have a shared passion for our approach to CSR. We are determined to embrace diversity and earn a reputation as an 'employer of distinction' by treating all our Partners with respect, honesty and fairness.
>
> We act with integrity and courtesy and share the rewards and responsibilities of co-ownership. These principles underpin our environmental policies, our involvement with local communities and our approach to responsible sourcing and trading.

CSR report: The Partnership produces a Corporate Social Responsibility report available on its website at: www.johnlewispartnership.co.uk/csrreports.

Exclusions

The company does not support: individuals; religious, ethnic or political groups; third party fundraising activities; projects overseas; or the purchase of advertising space.

Applications

As the Partnership's preference is now to support smaller, more local causes, qualifying applicants should contact the Community Liaison Coordinator at their nearest John Lewis shop, or the Waitrose champion for community giving at their nearest Waitrose.

It is also possible to enquire about receiving support from the company by using the online 'Charity Donation Request Contact Form'. this can be found under the 'Contact us' link on their website.

Linklaters

Legal

Correspondent: Ian Roe, Global Corporate Responsibility Manager, One Silk Street, London EC2Y 8HQ (tel: 020 7456 2000; email: ian.roe@linklaters.com; website: www.linklaters.com)

Directors: Robert Elliot, Senior Partner; Simon Davies, Firmwide Managing Partner

Year end	30/04/2011
Turnover	£1,200,000,000
Pre-tax profit	£514,800,000

Nature of business: International law firm.

Company registration number: OC326345

Main locations: Colchester, London

UK employees: 2,158

Total employees: 4,695

Membership: BITC, LBG

Charitable donations

UK cash (latest declared):	2010	£2,250,000
	2009	£847,000
	2008	£900,000
	2007	£850,000
Total UK:	2010	£3,500,000
Total worldwide:	2011	£3,500,000

Community involvement

Linklaters global charitable donations budget is based on 0.5% of its global profits. However, Linklaters contribute more than money to their community investment programme by providing pro bono (i.e. free) legal advice and representation to those unable to afford it. In addition staff volunteers are actively involved in many projects local to the firm's 26 offices around the world. In the UK Linklaters focus its efforts in Hackney and Colchester.

The following information is taken from BITC's website:

> The firm has integrated its approach to Corporate Responsibility throughout the business and recognises that, through its business activities, it has an impact on

society as an advisor, an employer and an enterprise. Accordingly, the global firm has developed a community strategy that aims to reflect their business, and make the best use of employee skills.

The global strategy focuses on promoting achievement, enterprise and access to justice but also allows each of its offices to tailor its support to address specific local needs. In the UK, a London Community Investment Committee exists to lead activity, and it is responsible for allocating budgets, monitoring impacts and championing participation.

Linklaters' longstanding and active community programme works with local community partners to address common challenges that have been identified through internal and external stakeholder engagement. Last year, in London, this included nearly 19,000 hours of pro bono legal advice to those otherwise unable to afford such support.

Linklaters supports and encourages employees to engage in community investment programmes, through volunteering, fundraising and pro bono work. The firm has made a strong commitment to measuring and evaluating performance of programmes, and is able to demonstrate the business and community win:win across its programmes.

Organisations working in the following areas are preferred: the Arts; Children/youth; Education; and, Enterprise/training. Support is also given to a 'charity of the year.

Corporate giving

In 2010//11, the firm's London office invested over £3.5 million in cash and volunteer time in this way. This included more than 12,000 hours of pro bono legal advice to those otherwise unable to afford such support. Linklaters' longstanding and active community programme works with local community partners to address common challenges that have been identified through internal and external stakeholder engagement.

We have been unable to find a cash only figure either for the UK or globally and have used the £3.5 million quoted by BITC on its website.

In kind support

Legal: *Pro bono clients* – this involves providing legal advice and legal services to a range of charities and voluntary organisations at no, or reduced, cost.

The firm's community programmes are designed to support non-profit groups, charities, law centres, advice agencies and small businesses in Hackney and, to a lesser extent, other east London boroughs. These range from local school literacy and maths programmes to giving legal advice at law centres, ethnic minority undergraduate mentoring and supporting initiatives to tackle homelessness. Individual, group and firm-wide involvement is encouraged and all of this work is carried out during the working week.

Linklaters' education programme 'Linking Work with Learning' was awarded a 'highly commended' ranking at the Business in the Community's Awards for Excellence, in July 2010. The scheme, which was launched in November 2007, is a ground-breaking volunteering initiative between the firm and every primary and secondary school in Hackney. It is designed to develop the employability skills and raise the aspirations of students across the borough.

Linklaters has also become the first Magic Circle law firm to hold Volunteering England's 'Investing in Volunteers' standard. In making the award, on Tuesday 6 July, Volunteering England highlighted the quality and consistency of the firm's volunteering programme, reporting that 'there is a clear and well-understood commitment to community investment and, in particular, employee volunteering across the firm'.

Whenever possible, the firm also makes available meeting rooms for those charities and organisations it supports which require the use of central London facilities.

The School for Social Entrepreneurs: an organisation established to encourage and develop entrepreneurs working for social benefit through a programme of personal development based on action learning. Linklaters provides bursaries for four students, supporting them with mentors from within the business. Linklaters' people gain inspiration from the participants whilst the entrepreneurs understand a little more of broader business challenges.

The 'Lawyers in Schools' twinning scheme: pioneered by Linklaters and the Citizenship Foundation, this scheme provides opportunities for lawyers to deepen students' understanding of legal issues. The aim of the programme has always been to encourage other firms to deliver the course in other places. To date, 19 firms have taken up this challenge across the country, ensuring the sustainability and success of this programme.

Employee-led support

In 2010/111, over 31,000 hours were spent volunteering by Linklaters' staff in the UK with 19,000 hours spent on pro bono legal advice. Globally, 43,660 hours were volunteered. All staff are given a minimum of a day a year to volunteer. Besides the structured in kind support provided through pro bono work and established volunteering options, staff have raised money for a range of charities. This is matched pound for pound by the firm's matched giving scheme, up to a maximum of £500 for individuals and £1,000 for teams. Volunteering for the same organisation above 26 hours per year is recognised in the same way.

Linklaters LinkAid (Charity Commission no.: 1076058) is administered by a special committee comprising representatives from across the firm and staff are actively encouraged to promote charities of particular interest to them.

In 2010, it had an income of £84,000 and gave grants totalling £192,000. Beneficiaries were: Camfed (£155,400); Contact the Elderly (£30,000); Raleigh International (£5,650); and Crisis (£1,000).

In addition, a large number of staff make monthly fixed amount donations to specific charities of their choice through direct debit arrangements, whilst others create their own personal charity account into which they can place funds and from which they can donate to charities of their choice at a time they consider appropriate. In 2009/10, 40% of staff globally volunteered, benefiting over 17,000 people through over 370 different organisations.

The 2011 Corporate Responsibility Report states that 40% of UK staff were involved in community volunteering programmes, with 123 community organisations benefitting 3,100 people.

Payroll giving: The Give As You Earn scheme is offered by the firm to enable employees to give tax effectively to a charity/charities of their choice or to the firm's Link Aid Fund.

Commercially-led support

Sponsorship: *The arts* – Around 20% of the firm's annual donations budget goes towards supporting concerts in the City of London and Spitalfields Festivals.

Corporate social responsibility

CSR committee: The global strategy focuses on promoting achievement, enterprise and access to justice but also allows each of its offices to tailor its support to address specific local needs. In the UK, a London Community Investment Committee exists to lead activity, and it is responsible for allocating budgets, monitoring impacts and championing participation.

CSR policy: Statement taken from the firm's website:

> *Corporate Responsibility*
> By far, the firm's greatest impact on the wider world is through the advice we provide our clients. In essence, our greatest responsibilities are to provide our clients with the highest quality advice and excellent service, to be judicious about who we act for and, above all, to act with

integrity in everything we do. All our responsibilities to our clients, to our colleagues and to wider society support the long-term, sustainable achievement of our vision.

25% of the London Partnership is female.

CSR report: Global and national CR reports published annually.

Exclusions

No support for appeals from individuals or local appeals not in areas of company presence. We have been informed by Linklaters that 'The firm is now almost always proactive in its community investment and rarely funds speculative applications.'

Applications

In writing to the correspondent.

LINPAC Group Ltd

Print/paper/packaging

Correspondent: Company Secretary, 3180 Park Square, Birmingham Business Park, Birmingham B37 7YN (tel: 01216 076700; fax: 01216 076767; website: linpacpackaging.com)

Directors: J. Darlington, Chair; N. Carr; J. Allkins; J. Durston

Year end	31/12/2010
Pre-tax profit	(£50,000)

Nature of business: The principle activities of the group are the manufacture and marketing of plastic and paper products for packaging. Based in the UK, LINPAC comprises four core divisions, offering tailored packaging and supply chain products and services worldwide. It has 83 locations across 29 countries.

Company registration number: 4792926

Main locations: Birmingham

Total employees: 0

Charitable donations

UK cash (latest declared):	2010	£0
	2008	£48,000
	2007	£43,000
	2006	£48,000
	2005	£58,000
Cash worldwide:	2010	£0

Corporate social responsibility

CSR committee: No evidence of a committee.

CSR policy: Taken from the company's website:

> At LINPAC we recognise our responsibility to give something back to the communities in which we operate and to act in a safe and environmentally aware manner. As a global manufacturing and services business, we know that it is only by looking beyond simple economic success that we can sustain long-term competitive advantage for ourselves and our customers.

We were unable to determine the ratio of women to men on the board.

CSR report: No report published.

Exclusions

No support for appeals from individuals. No support for local appeals not in areas of company presence.

Applications

In writing to the correspondent.

Other information

We could find no mention of the group making charitable donations in the year 2010. This may be due to the company incurring a loss and if so, we would expect charitable donations to be made if and when the company shows a profit.

The company's website contained the following information regarding its charitable support:

> The group actively supports many charitable activities. We believe we can make the most difference when we partner with local charities and initiatives, and involve our people. We encourage our divisions globally to support charities that really mean something to them and upon which their involvement can make a significant positive impact. In recent years, donations have been made around the world to educational facilities, children's homes and medical research, as well as to provide care and equipment for children with genetic disorders. We also host visits to our manufacturing sites for schools and community groups in many countries, to help create awareness and understanding of the packaging industry.

Littlewoods Shop Direct Home Shopping Ltd

Retail – department and variety stores

Correspondent: Head of Corporate Communications, Skyways House, Speke Road, Speke, Liverpool L70 1AB (website: www.shopdirect.com)

Directors: P. L. Peters; A. S. Barclay; H. M. Barclay; R. Faber; D. W. Kershaw; G. Monk; M. Seal

Year end	30/06/2011
Turnover	£2,569,700,000
Pre-tax profit	(£242,100,000)

Nature of business: Internet and catalogue home shopping.

Company registration number: 5059352

Main locations: Preston, Liverpool, Oldham, Sunderland

Total employees: 18,690

Charitable donations

UK cash (latest declared):	2011	£100,000
	2009	£300,000
	2008	£6,000,000
	2007	£600,000
	2006	£600,000
Total UK:	2011	£100,000
Total worldwide:	2011	£100,000
Cash worldwide:	2011	£100,000

Corporate social responsibility

CSR committee: There is a dedicated Corporate Responsibility Board chaired by the group CEO.

CSR policy: CSR information is taken from the group's website:

> At Shop Direct Group, we are determined to behave in a responsible way with strong ethical and environmental standards and to be a good citizen in the communities in which we operate.
>
> To help manage our corporate social responsibilities effectively, we divide our stakeholders into five key areas:
>
> - Our Customers
> - Our Community
> - Our Suppliers
> - Our People
> - Environment

We were unable to determine the ratio of women to men on the board.

CSR report: Published annually.

Exclusions

No support for advertising in charity brochures, animal welfare, appeals from individuals, children/youth, elderly people, fundraising events, medical research, overseas projects, political appeals, religious appeals, science/technology, sickness/disability, social welfare or sport.

Applications

In writing to the correspondent.

Other information

In 2010/11 the company made charitable donations of £100,000. The following information is taken from the group's website:

> Shop Direct Group is committed to making a positive impact on the communities in which we operate.
>
> As part of this commitment, we support a range of community and charitable organisations through a variety of activities. The focus for our activities is improving the lives of children and families. We do this through a variety of ways:
>
> - Charitable donations: cash and in kind
> - Employee volunteering
> - Partnering with our local high school
> - Matched-giving
> - Shop Direct Foundation

For further information visit: www.shopdirect.com.

Financial information has been taken from Shop Direct Ltd; the holding company for the Shop Direct group of companies.

Liverpool Victoria

Financial services, insurance

Correspondent: The Company Secretary, County Gates, Bournemouth, Dorset BH1 2NF (tel: 01202 292333; fax: 01802 292253; email: pressoffice@lv.com; website: www.lv.com)

Directors: Dennis Holt, Chair; Michael Rogers, Chief Executive; Richard Rowney; Philip Moore; John O'Roarke; Mark Austen; Ian Reynolds; John Edwards; Cath Keers; Caroline Burton (women: 2; men: 8)

Year end	31/12/2011
Turnover	£2,900,000,000
Pre-tax profit	(£16,900,000)

Nature of business: The society is an incorporated Friendly Society which carries on insurance and financial services business in the UK.

FSA registration number: 110035

Total employees: 4,782

Charitable donations

UK cash (latest declared):	2011	£212,000
	2009	£111,000
	2007	£70,000
	2005	£166,000
	2004	£38,400
Total UK:	2011	£212,000
Total worldwide:	2011	£212,000
Cash worldwide:	2011	£212,000

Corporate social responsibility

CSR committee: There was no evidence of a separate CSR Committee.

CSR policy: The group aims to help the local communities in which it operates, especially near its head offices which are located in Bournemouth. Previous initiatives have supported children, young people plus recreation and sports.

CSR report: There was no evidence of a separate CSR report.

Exclusions

Circulars, general appeals and individuals.

Applications

In writing to the correspondent.

Other information

In 2011, Liverpool Victoria donated £192,000 through the Charities Aid Foundation (CAF). The group also donated £20,000 to Great Ormond Street Hospital for Children.

The company sponsors sporting events such as the LV=County Championship, Britannia Rescue Bobsleigh Team and Rugby' Union's Anglo-Welsh tournament.

LV also encourages staff volunteering in their own time by matching up to 21/2 days' holiday for time spent on community based activities.

LV= Streetwise is an initiative between the emergency services, local authorities and the business community, and raises awareness of everyday safety and good citizenship.

LV= Kidzone is a scheme which works by giving children colour-coded wristbands that match-up with clearly marked sections of the beach. These bands help lost children get reunited with their family through a contact number on the wristband.

LV= SOS Kit Aid is a charity which collects donations of new and used rugby and cricket kit from individuals, schools, sports clubs and manufacturers. It then recycles the kit by passing it on to projects helping disadvantaged youngsters in the UK and overseas.

In 2011, LV's support meant that more than 20,000 young people who might not otherwise have been able to take part in sport were given kit so they could join in.

Lloyd's

Insurance

Correspondent: Miss Victoria Mirfin, Correspondent, Lloyd's Charities Trust, One Lime Street, London EC3M 7HA (tel: 020 7327 1000/020 7327 6075; email: communityaffairs@lloyds.com; website: www.lloyds.com)

Directors: John Nelson, Chair; Richard Ward, Chief Executive Officer; Paul Jardine; Andreas Prindl; Graham White; Lord Ashton of Hyde; Rupert Atkin; Simon Beale; Robert Childs; Michael Deeny; Robert Finch; Matthew Fosh; Christopher Harman; Reg Hinkley; Lawrence Holder; Alan Lovell; David Manning; Nicholas Marsh (women: 0; men: 18)

Year end	31/12/2011
Turnover	£316,899,000
Pre-tax profit	£117,845,000

Nature of business: Insurance underwriting market.

Company registration number: 3189123

UK employees: 746

Total employees: 909

Membership: Arts & Business, BITC, LBG

Charitable donations

UK cash (latest declared):	2011	£618,000
	2009	£352,000
Total UK:	2011	£618,000
Total worldwide:	2011	£618,000
Cash worldwide:	2011	£618,000

Community involvement

The following information is taken from the company's website:

Lloyd's is committed to giving charitable support, focusing on areas that reflect the market's unique character and business.

Lloyd's Charities Trust [Charity Commission no. 207232]

For over 50 years, Lloyds Charities Trust has been providing charitable support to a wide range of local, national and international charities on behalf of the Lloyd's market.

Clearer focus, greater impact

From 2010, Lloyd's Charities Trust aims to maximise the impact of Lloyd's charitable giving, by focusing on three key areas, each reflecting an aspect of this unique market's character and business:

- Making a great city greater: at home in London, we give to tackle disadvantage and foster opportunity
- Responding to disasters and emergencies: around the world, we give to relieve suffering and rebuild lives
- Preparing for the future: we give to equip individuals and communities with the resources and skills they need to meet the challenges of a rapidly changing world

Lloyd's Patriotic Fund works closely with armed forces charities to identify the individuals and their families who are in urgent need of support.

Lloyd's Benevolent Fund (Charity Commission no. 207231) assists those in need who work in or have worked within the Lloyd's community. Dependents are also eligible for assistance at the discretion of the trustees. Financial assistance is provided in the form of grants and practical help is also given for those unable to cope with everyday problems. Contact: Lloyd's Benevolent Fund, Lloyd's, One Lime Street, London EC3M 7HA.

Lloyd's Tercentenary Research Foundation since its establishment in 1988, has funded over 100 years of academic research in the fields of engineering, science, medicine, business and the environment through the provision of postdoctoral fellowships and business scholarships.

Today, through its partnership with the Insurance Intellectual Capital Initiative and UK Research Councils, Lloyd's Tercentenary Research Foundation continues its work of funding top flight academic research by supporting new programmes of research on insurance related issues.

When available, details of these projects will be posted on the website and will be circulated via the normal routes by the relevant Research Councils.

US Scholarships

In collaboration with the Fulbright Commission, Lloyd's Tercentenary Research Foundation will be funding scholarships for UK academics or professionals to undertake research in the US on a subject related to insurance. Application is via the Fulbright Commission website, where full details can be found.

Partner charities: Brighter Futures for Londoners

This is a three-year partnership between Lloyd's Charities Trust, Bromley by Bow Centre and Prince's Trust.

> Lloyd's is proud to have its home in an amazing city but we know that while London creates opportunities for many, huge disparities still exist. The aim of the partnership is simple – to provide advice, training and support to help disadvantaged Londoners overcome the challenges they face and seize the opportunities London offers.
>
> Over the course of the partnership Lloyd's Charities Trust plans to donate over £350,000 to these charities.

Corporate giving

In 2011 the company declared cash charitable donations of £618,000.

Only accounts for 2010 were available for the trust at the time of writing (August 2012). These show that donations, grants and bursaries totalled £379,000 with management costs of £5,280. Beneficiaries included: Prince's Trust (£66,000 in 2010 and £75,000 over the next two years; Bromley By Bow Centre (£50,000 a year for three years); DEC Haiti Earthquake Appeal, Chilean Red Cross Chile Earthquake Appeal and the DEC Pakistan Floods Appeal (donations of between £20,000 – £30,000); Maritime London Officer Cadet Scholarship, Reed's School and Mulberry School for Girls (three donations of between £5,000 – £15,000).

Employee-led support

Lloyd's Community Programme celebrated its 22nd year in 2011.

> The Lloyd's building is situated in a part of London where its neighbouring communities face significant challenges. The Lloyd's Community Programme (LCP) has always been keen to support its neighbours and our focus is to invest in the future of the next generation.
>
> LCP received an overwhelming level of support in 2011, with 1,514 people from the market volunteering through 16 schemes. In total, they contributed 13,858 hours and reached over 2,900 people. These volunteers carry out a wide range of activities, from reading schemes in schools to cooking meals for the vulnerable at shelters for the homeless. Last year over 1,460 people working in the Lloyd's Market shared their skills and enthusiasm in this way.

Corporate social responsibility

CSR committee: For useful CSR contacts visit: www.lloyds.com/Lloyds/Corporate-Responsibility/Contacts.

CSR policy: Lloyd's CSR focuses on the environment and the community.

CSR report: Separate website page giving full details of community giving and details of achievements published within the annual report and accounts.

Exclusions

No support for advertising in charity brochures, animal welfare, appeals from individuals, the arts, sponsorship, environment/heritage, fundraising events, medical research, political appeals, religious appeals, science/technology, sport or local appeals not in areas of company presence.

Applications

Lloyd's Charities Trust – Apply in writing to the correspondent.

Lloyd's Community Programme – Contact community affairs for further information.

Lloyds Banking Group

Financial services, banking

Correspondent: Community and Sustainable Business Dept, Group Corporate Affairs, Lloyds Banking Group (tel: 020 7626 1500; email: Responsible.business@lloydsbanking.com; website: www.lloydsbankinggroup.com)

Directors: Anthony Watson; Julian Horn-Smith; Lord Leitch; T. Timothy Ryan; Glen R. Moreno; Martin A. Scicluna; Winfried Bischoff, Chair; Anita M. Frew; David L. Roberts; António Horta-Osório; Sara V. Weller (women: 2; men: 9)

Year end	31/12/2011
Turnover	£21,466,000,000
Pre-tax profit	£2,685,000,000

Nature of business: Lloyds Banking Group is one of the largest financial services companies in the UK, covering retail banking, commercial and corporate banking, mortgages, life assurance and pensions, general insurance, asset management, leasing, treasury and foreign exchange dealing. (Lloyds TSB Group plc was renamed Lloyds Banking Group on 19 January 2009, following the acquisition of HBOS plc.)

Company registration number: 2065

Subsidiaries include: Abbey Life Assurance Co. Ltd, Scottish Widows Investment Partnership Group Ltd, Scottish Widows plc, Cheltenham and Gloucester plc, Black Horse Ltd, Scottish Widows Annuities Ltd, The Agricultural Mortgage Corporation plc

Brands include: Bank of Scotland; Halifax; Lloyds TSB; Scottish Widows.

Main locations: London

UK employees: 116,371

Total employees: 120,449

Membership: Arts & Business, BITC

Charitable donations

UK cash (latest declared):	2011	£43,800,000
	2009	£33,477,000
	2008	£29,603,000
	2007	£37,463,000
	2006	£37,335,000
Total UK:	2011	£85,000,000
Total worldwide:	2011	£85,000,000
Cash worldwide:	2011	£43,800,000

Community involvement

The group's Responsible Business Report 2011 states: 'In 2011 we increased our investment by over 10 per cent from 2010 when we were recognised by the London Benchmarking Group as the biggest corporate investor in UK communities.'

Lloyds Banking Group operates one of the largest community programmes in the UK. The majority of cash donations are made through the four independent Lloyds TSB Foundations, which are grantmaking trusts covering England and Wales, Northern Ireland and the Channel Islands and the Bank of Scotland Foundation.

Foundation funding supports charities working to meet social and community needs. The main grants programmes are designed to address essential community needs and in particular, to support small under-funded charities.

Additional and substantial in kind support is also provided by the Lloyds Banking Group.

Corporate Charity of the Year: Save the Children

The Charity of the Year for 2011 and continuing into 2012 was Save the Children. Staff from across the group have raised £1.4 million including matched giving in 2011, significantly exceeding the initial fundraising target of £1 million.

This is enough to support up to 46 FAST (Families and Schools Together) programmes in local communities. 'FAST is proven to support parents to engage in their child's education – 85% of a child's success at school depends on the type of support their parents/guardians provide at home.'

Corporate giving

The data table in the 2011 Responsible Business Report gives the following information:

Economic and social impact	2010	2011
Money contributed to the financial advice sector	£12.5 million	£14.8 million
Total amount invested in communities across the UK	£76 million	£85 million
Total amount donated to the group's charitable foundations	£29 million	£29 million
Funds raised by colleagues for the Charity of the Year	£1.3 million	£1.4 million

Note: We have combined the figures for money contributed to the financial advice sector and that donated to the group's charitable foundations to give the total UK cash contribution. Although we know that £85 million was invested in total, it is not clear how much of this was in kind and therefore have used the figure as the total contribution.

In 2011, over £85 million was invested in UK communities, including support for financial capability, higher education and sports for young people. A significant amount of this investment was directly to the Lloyds TSB Foundations and the Bank of Scotland Foundation where the group donated almost £30 million to support charities working in some of the most disadvantaged communities in the UK.

The Lloyds TSB Foundations and the Bank of Scotland Foundation
2011 was the 25th anniversary of the Lloyds TSB Foundations. Since their creation and the launch of the Bank of Scotland Foundation in 2010 more than £510 million has been provided by the group, enabling the independently run foundations to support thousands of charities across the UK. The foundations use their knowledge and expertise to direct funds where they are most needed, disbursing grants to local, regional and national charities that operate at the heart of communities.

The foundations focus their support on social and community needs and education and training. In particular, support is given to recognised charities helping disadvantaged people to play a fuller role in society. Within this general objective, each of the four foundations supports their own areas of special interest. Further details of the foundations' aims, grant-giving, proposed activities, case studies, etc., can be seen at: www.lloydstsbfoundations.org.uk

Funding
A new funding deal was reached by the Lloyds Banking Group with three of its foundations just before Christmas 2009. The Lloyds TSB Foundations for England and Wales, Northern Ireland and the Channel Islands will see their funding increase over the next four years under the new agreement. However their percentage entitlement to the group's profits will halve in the long term.

Under the previous arrangement, the foundations were legally entitled to 1% of the group's annual profits. Under the new covenant, the foundations will receive a fixed grant for the next four years, to cover the period when the group is expected to be unprofitable. After 2013 the foundations will receive 0.5% of the group's profits.

The Lloyds TSB Foundation for Scotland did not sign up to this agreement. Following legal action the court upheld the foundation's claim that it was due £3.5 million from the bank for 2010; however, in January 2013, following an appeal by the bank the Supreme Court reversed this decision and said the foundation was owed just £38,920. Funding from the bank to Lloyds TSB Foundation for Scotland will cease in 2019.

In kind support

The group has a large and dynamic property portfolio and surplus furniture is donated to local groups. Lloyds TSB also provides office space to the charity In kind Direct.

The group supports major charity appeals launched by the Disasters Emergency Committee, as well as certain sponsored appeals such as Children in Need, Comic Relief and the Royal British Legion.

Requests for local counter appeal support should be directed to the relevant branch. Note, however, that no more than one counter appeal will be possible in any branch at any one time.

Employee-led support

Information taken from the RB report 2011:

> *Staff volunteering*
> In 2011, over 16,000 colleagues volunteered. This more than doubled the number of volunteers from the previous year of 7,300. The increase was achieved by campaigns to raise awareness across the Group. Our target is to have 22,000 colleagues volunteering during 2012.
>
> *Money for Life programme*
> We already train teachers and community groups on financial education. Now, we are also training our colleagues to teach financial education. So far over one hundred bank managers have completed Teach Others and are volunteering in communities across the UK, equating to 2,000+ hours of engagement. We currently have a waiting list of over 150 colleagues looking to get involved in the next intake.
>
> *Lloyds Scholars*
> The success of the Lloyds Scholars programme owes a lot to the enthusiasm and support shown by our colleagues in endorsing and embracing the initiative. Employees have volunteered in their hundreds to become assessors at the recruitment stage, mentors throughout the scholars' time at the university and as line managers for summer internships.
>
> *Our Day to Make a Difference*
> This volunteering programme enables colleagues to spend one day a year volunteering for a charity or community project of their choice. With 103,000 colleagues in the Group, this programme can have a real impact among local communities across the UK. Colleagues are able to use their skills and enthusiasm for a good cause without losing a day's pay or holiday allowance.
>
> *Give & Gain Day*
> Business in the Community's Give & Gain Day is the UK's largest single day of volunteering. Over the last three years Lloyds Banking Group has been the largest company participant. In 2011 over 2,000 colleagues took part. We also announced our sponsorship of Give & Gain Day for the next three years.
>
> *National School Sport Week*
> In the build-up and excitement of the London 2012 Games we are encouraging young people to do more sport. Our community programme provides resources to schools to plan activities leading up to and during the week. In 2011, over 4 million young people and over 2,400 colleagues took part.

Coaches for Communities
Bank of Scotland partnered with the Scottish Football Association, the Scottish Government's 'cashback for communities' Scheme and the Scottish Sun newspaper in 2009 to launch 'Coaches for Communities'; an initiative which aims to get more people involved in youth football in Scotland by providing free football coaching.

'Coaches for Communities' provided training to 1,250 people, including 30 of the group's employees, leading to a Level One Early Touches qualification. Once qualified, the Scottish FA and the Scottish Schools' Football Association will link participants up with a local community group or team in their area. The initiative builds on Bank of Scotland's ongoing support for grassroots football in Scotland. Through a partnership with the Scottish FA, the bank supports programmes which operate in all 32 local authorities across Scotland to deliver football training and leagues involving over 300 schools and 10,000 young people.

Besides the foundations' support for local community causes, thousands of group employees volunteer to help in their communities, raise funds for the group's Charity of the Year and/or make direct donations to charity using the payroll giving system.

Payroll giving: The group operates the Give As You Earn scheme.

RB report 2011: **Matched giving:**

> The Foundations also operate a Matched Giving Scheme, allowing Group colleagues in the UK to claim up to £1,000, doubled from 2010, in matched giving each year. This funding provides much needed help for the charities they are supporting. Over 6,200 applications were made in 2011, totalling £2.3 million in matched giving for charity.
>
> We ran a series of events and activities to raise funds for our Charity of the Year, *Save the Children*. We raised £1.4 million

from the fundraising and generosity of our colleagues.

Commercially-led support

Sponsorship:

London 2012 Olympic and Paralympic Games. The group was the official banking and insurance partner of the 2012 Games and it encourages employees and individual branches to support its vision of 'inspiring and supporting young people, communities and businesses all over Britain on their journey to London 2012 and beyond'.

Lloyds TSB Local Heroes Programme provides funding to more than 250 emerging young athletes each year across Britain.

Lloyds TSB National School Sport Week is the biggest community sport programme in the UK and 'uses the power of the London 2012 Games to inspire young people to understand the benefits of sport and take part in more sporting activity'. The programme is delivered in partnership with the charity *Youth Sport Trust.*

Financial Capability Project is a partnership between Lloyds Banking Group, the Consumer Financial Education Body (CFEB) and HM Treasury and the Learning and Skills Improvement Service (LSIS). Funding provided will be put towards helping tutors and lecturers in the UK to improve the financial management skills of the young people and adults who attend their courses, making them confident and financially capable to enter further education or the world of work. Organisations wanting to apply for sponsorship by the group should note the following, taken from the group's 'Community Investment Policy' leaflet:

> Sponsorship requests are those that provide a commercial return through exposure of Lloyds TSB's company name or brand. 'You should forward any local requests for sponsorship to your branch who will liaise with their Local Director office where local priorities are determined.
>
> As a general guide we do not support individuals or overseas activity and would prefer local initiatives to follow the national programme.
>
> The Group Sponsorship department deals with the national sponsorship programme. Any requests for sponsorship that refers to a specific product should be forwarded to the relevant business unit within Lloyds TSB.

Lloyds TSB is a Principal member of Arts and Business.

Corporate social responsibility

CSR committee: A new Responsible Business Steering Group was established in 2011 to drive the group's new responsible business strategy. It comprises business leaders from across the group.

The steering group meets every two months and reports to the board and group executive committee twice a year. In 2012, an independent panel of experts and opinion formers is to be set up to provide 'thought leadership and challenge' to the group.

CSR policy: The group's strategy was reviewed in 2011, and focuses on:

- Putting customers first
- Investing in communities
- Becoming the best bank for colleagues
- Working responsibly with other stakeholders
- Reducing environmental impacts

CSR report: A detailed annual Responsible Business report is published.

Exclusions

For Lloyds TSB Foundations

The foundations do not fund the following types of organisations and work:

Organisations:

- Organisations that are **not** registered charities
- Second or third tier organisations (unless there is evidence of direct benefit to disadvantaged people)
- Charities that mainly work overseas
- Charities that mainly give funds to other charities, individuals or other organisations
- Hospitals, hospices or medical centres
- Rescue services
- Schools, colleges and universities

Types of work:

- Activities which a statutory body is responsible for
- Capital projects, appeals, refurbishments
- Environmental work, expeditions and overseas travel
- Funding to promote religion
- Holidays or trips
- Loans or business finance
- Medical research, funding for medical equipment or medical treatments
- Sponsorship or funding towards a marketing appeal or fundraising activities
- Work with animals or to promote animal welfare

Applications

For Lloyds TSB Foundations only:

Lloyds Banking Group has devised an online eligibility test. This consists of a process which, if your application meets all the criteria, leads on to an online eligibility questionnaire.

Further details of grant-giving policies and guidelines can be obtained by contacting the appropriate Lloyds TSB Foundation for your locality.

- Lloyds TSB Foundation for England and Wales, Pentagon House, 52–54 Southwark Street, London SE1 1UN; tel: 0870 411 1223; email: enquiries@lloydstsbfoundations.org.uk; website: www.lloydstsbfoundations.org.uk
- Lloyds TSB Foundation for Scotland, Riverside House, 502 Gorgie Road, Edinburgh EH11 3AF; tel: 01314 444020; email: enquiries@ltsbfoundationforscotland.org.uk; website: www.ltsbfoundationforscotland.org.uk
- Lloyds TSB Foundation for Northern Ireland, 2nd Floor, 14 Cromac Place, The Gasworks, Belfast BT7 2JB; tel: 02890 323000; email: info@lloydstsbfoundationni.org; website: www.lloydstsbfoundationni.org
- Lloyds TSB Foundation for the Channel Islands, Lloyds TSB House, 25 New Street, St Helier, Jersey, Channel Islands JE4 8RG; tel: 01534 845889; email: John.Hutchins@Lloydstsbfoundations.org.uk; website: www.ltsbfoundationci.org

Each of the foundations' websites provides detailed and very useful information on making an application for funding.

It should be noted that the foundations cannot fund all eligible applications even if they are of a high quality because each year the total amount requested by eligible charities exceeds budget. Other reasons for the foundations not being able to make a grant include:

- Charities' core work not being sufficiently focused on the foundations' mission
- Applications not falling within guidelines
- Applicants not filling in the application form properly
- Charities not having up to date annual returns or accounts filed with the Charity Commission or other relevant regulatory bodies

For Lloyds Banking Group plc only:

Contact: Richard Cooper, Head of Corporate Social Responsibility, 25 Gresham Street, London EC2V 7HN.

Lockheed Martin UK Ltd

Information technology

Correspondent: Melanie Coles, Hampshire Office, Manning House, 22 Carlisle Place, London SW1P 1JA (tel: 020 7798 2850/02392 443000; website: www.lockheedmartin.co.uk)

Directors: Robert J. Stevens, Chair and Chief Executive; Nolan D. Archibald; Rosalind G. Brewer; David B. Burritt; James O. Ellis, Jr; Thomas J. Falk; Gwendolyn S. King; James M. Loy; Douglas H. McCorkindale; Joseph

W. Ralston; Anne Stevens; Robert J. Stevens (women: 3; men: 9)

Year end	31/12/2011

Nature of business: Systems integrator and supplier of high technology systems and service to defence and government customers.

Company registration number: 2372738

Main locations: Farnham, Culdrose, Havant, Yeovil, Swindon, London, Malvern, Lincoln, Farnborough, Andover, Ampthill, Whiteley

Charitable donations

UK cash (latest declared):	2009	£18,000
	2008	£10,000

Applications

In writing to the correspondent.

Other information

In 2009 charitable contributions made by Lockheed Martin UK Ltd totalled £18,000 (2008: £10,000). The company's UK webpages provide the following information:

> Our employee volunteers assist in a variety of social, environmental and practical projects on behalf of the company. Our aim is to build close relationships with our community partners who surround the company's main operating sites across the country.
>
> LMUK holds a number of events per year in support of improving the local environment for the communities in which we live. The LMUK Volunteering Day is a company-wide event and tasks undertaken could include basic DIY, such as painting and decorating for less privileged establishments who have limited funding, to garden clearing and the development of sensory nature trails for special-needs schools.
>
> LMUK donates, per annum, approximately £40,000 for charitable organisations, including employee fundraising. Examples include; Help for Heroes, Jeans for Jeans, Comic Relief/Sport Relief, Fly Naval Heritage Trust, Children in Need, Macmillan Cancer Support, Cancer Research UK4U and the Poppy Appeal.
>
> Community outreach involvement for Lockheed Martin UK (LMUK) means balanced, focused and targeted benefit to worthwhile causes across the UK. Supporting environment conservation, providing activities and challenges to benefit education and raising funds for various charitable foundations, either directly or via our customer community, are all examples of how Lockheed Martin UK strives to contribute to society.
>
> From providing volunteers to help young people learn about technology and careers in engineering through to project based learning, and the provision of work placements and careers advice for teenagers, LMUK holds numerous education outreach activities to reach out to our communities. Lockheed Martin UK exhibit interactive demonstrations, host student open days and run engineering challenges at shows and events and provide mentoring to children at schools and colleges throughout the UK.

Lofthouse of Fleetwood Ltd

Confectionery

Correspondent: Mrs D W Lofthouse, Trustee, Lofthouse Foundation, Maritime Street, Fleetwood, Lancashire FY7 7LP (tel: 01253 872435/01253 872435; fax: 01253 778725)

Directors: D. W. Lofthouse; J. A. Lofthouse; D. C. Lofthouse (women: 1; men: 2)

Year end	31/12/2011
Turnover	£38,953,234
Pre-tax profit	£5,388,459

Nature of business: Manufacturers of medicated confectionery.

Company registration number: 781277

Main locations: Fleetwood

UK employees: 285

Total employees: 285

Charitable donations

UK cash (latest declared):	2011	£65,000
	2009	£65,500
	2008	£4,000
	2007	£113,000
	2006	£170
Total UK:	2011	£65,000
Total worldwide:	2011	£65,000
Cash worldwide:	2011	£65,000

Corporate social responsibility

CSR committee: No details found.

CSR policy: None published.

CSR report: None published.

Exclusions

The foundation does not support advertising in charity brochures, animal welfare, the arts, overseas projects, religious appeals, science/technology or social welfare.

Applications

In writing to the correspondent.

Other information

During the year 2011 the company made charitable donations of £65,000 to the Lofthouse Foundation.

Lofthouse Foundation

Manufacturers of the famous 'Fisherman's Friend', most of the company's charitable support is channelled through the Lofthouse Foundation (Charity Commission no. 1038728). The foundation was established in June 1994 with general charitable objects for the benefit of Fleetwood and its environs in particular by the provision of such amenities and facilities for the benefit of the public as are not provided from public funds.

There are three trustees, all of whom are members of the Lofthouse family.

In 2011 the foundation received £65,000 from the company and in turn donated £65,000 to the New Fleetwood Gym Club as part of a five-year commitment to the club.

Logica plc

Business services

Correspondent: CSR Dept. (Community and Charity), 250 Brook Drive, Green Park, Reading, Berkshire RG2 6UA (tel: 020 7637 9111; fax: 020 7468 7006; website: www.logica.com)

Directors: David Tyler, Chair; Andy Green, Chief Executive; Himanshu Raja; Sergio Giacoletto; Noel Harwerth; Wolfhart Hauser; Frederic Rose; Jan Babiak (women: 6; men: 2)

Year end	31/12/2011
Turnover	£3,921,300,000
Pre-tax profit	£32,700,000

Nature of business: A European business and technology service company integrating people, business and technology into effective, sustainable ecosystems.

Company registration number: 1631639

UK employees: 5,472

Total employees: 41,784

Charitable donations

UK cash (latest declared):	2011	£191,000
	2009	£92,000
	2008	£97,100
Total UK:	2011	£191,000
Total worldwide:	2011	£191,000
Cash worldwide:	2011	£191,000

Corporate social responsibility

CSR committee: There was no evidence of a separate CSR Committee.

CSR policy: The company is primarily focused on charitable efforts concerning environmental issues.

CSR report: A separate CSR report was available from the company's website.

Applications

In writing to the correspondent.

Other information

Total UK charitable donations in 2011 were £191,000 (2009: £92,000).

> Logica . . . encourages employees to support charities and participate in local charitable events and, where possible, donates surplus computers to local good causes. When making charitable donations, the strategy is to develop partnerships with national charities and non-governmental organisations in the countries in which the company operates. Logica also supports projects that actively involve employees and, where possible, make use of their technical knowledge and expertise.

Give As You Earn: The company supports Give As You Earn schemes to facilitate financial donations by employees via the payroll.

Lonmin plc

Mining

Correspondent: Corporate Responsibility Team (UK Giving), 4 Grosvenor Place, London SW1X 7YL (tel: 020 7201 6000; fax: 020 7201 6100; website: www.lonmin.com)

Directors: Roger Phillimore, Chair; Ian Farmer, Chief Executive; Simon Scott; Cyril Ramaphosa; Karen de Segundo; Jim Sutcliffe; David Munro; Len Konar; Michael Hartnall; Jonathan Leslie; Mahomed Seedat (women: 1; men: 10)

Year end	30/09/2011
Turnover	£1,259,143,200
Pre-tax profit	£185,205,300

Nature of business: Mining – producer of platinum group Metals.

Company registration number: 103002

Total employees: 25,097

Charitable donations

UK cash (latest declared):	2011	£2,700
	2010	£35,500
	2009	£35,000
	2008	£33,000
Total UK:	2011	£2,700
Total worldwide:	2011	£2,700
Cash worldwide:	2011	£2,700

Corporate social responsibility

CSR committee: CR Team in the UK. See Correspondent details.

CSR policy: Taken from the Sustainable Development Report 2011:

> A shortage of relevant and necessary skills in local communities where we operate presents a risk to our ability to follow through with our commitment to employing members of these communities. Our success is therefore directly linked to the educational and economic empowerment of communities as well as their health and ability to work.

CSR report: Published annually.

Applications

In writing to the correspondent.

Other information

Charitable donations made by the group during 2010/11 in the UK amounted to £2,700 (2009/10: £35,500). We have no details of beneficiary groups. The group appears to make significant contributions abroad though it is not possible to say what percentage of this goes to charities or for charitable purposes.

Community investment abroad – The following is taken from the company's website:

> Since 2006, we have focused our community development programmes on the commitments outlined in the Social and Labour Plans for Marikana. Our key focus areas are infrastructure development, educational support, health support and local business development, including commercial agriculture. These projects have been selected and developed in close collaboration with local authorities and government to ensure that we complement local development plans. We have a number of training programmes in place that affords the community with the opportunity to enhance their skills and knowledge. These training programmes encompass diversity training, ABET and project specific training, including school governance training and knowledge shared as part of the eco-schools curriculum.

Low and Bonar plc

Chemicals and plastics, print/ paper/packaging

Correspondent: Company Secretary, 9th Floor, Marble Arch Tower, Bryanston Street, London W1H 7AA (tel: 020 7535 3180; fax: 020 7535 3181; website: www.lowandbonar.com)

Directors: Martin Flower, Chair; Steve Good, Chief Executive; Mike Holt; Steve Hannam; Folkert Blalsse; Chris Littmoden; John Sheldrick (women: 0; men: 7)

Year end	30/11/2011
Turnover	£344,600,000
Pre-tax profit	£10,200,000

Nature of business: Plastics, packaging and specialist material manufacture.

Company registration number: SC008349

Main locations: Manchester, Bamber Bridge, Telford, Hull, Barnsley, Dundee, London

Total employees: 1,870

Charitable donations

UK cash (latest declared):	2009	£0
	2008	£15,000
	2007	£15,000
	2006	£15,000
	2005	£20,000
Total worldwide:	2011	£15,000
Cash worldwide:	2011	£15,000

Corporate social responsibility

CSR committee: There was no evidence of a separate CSR Committee.

CSR policy: The company is primarily concerned with environmental issues.

CSR report: There was no evidence of a separate CSR report.

Exclusions

No support for non-registered charities. No grants for local appeals not in areas of company presence; advertising in charity brochures; animal welfare; appeals from individuals; enterprise/ training; fundraising events; political or religious appeals; science/technology; overseas projects, or sport.

Applications

In writing to the correspondent.

Other information

The company made £15,000 worth of charitable donations in 2010/11 (2009: nil).

No other information was available.

Lush Cosmetics Ltd

Health/beauty products

Correspondent: Sophie Pritchard, Charitable Giving manager, 29 High Street, Poole, Dorset BH15 1AB (tel: 01202 667830; email: charitypot@lush.co.uk; website: www.lush.co.uk)

Directors: A. Gerrie; M. Constantine; Ms M. Constantine (women: 1; men: 2)

Year end	30/06/2011
Turnover	£272,202,000
Pre-tax profit	£21,321,000

Nature of business: The production and retail of cosmetic products.

Company registration number: 4162033

Total employees: 5,007

Charitable donations

UK cash (latest declared):	2011	£1,495,000
	2009	£836,000
	2008	£482,000
	2007	£160,000
	2006	£45,000
Total UK:	2011	£1,495,000
Total worldwide:	2011	£1,495,000
Cash worldwide:	2011	£1,495,000

Community involvement

Lush's 'Charity Pot' contains hand and body lotion produced from fairly traded cocoa butter and almond oil and is sold in its various retail outlets. This year (2010/11) the product was sold in twenty countries including Australia, New Zealand, Canada, Chile, France, Japan, Spain, Sweden, the USA and the UK.

The total amount that the consumer pays for the product (excluding the VAT which the UK government receives) goes into the Lush Charity Pot Fund which is then used to support a variety of charities, good causes and campaign groups.

The company also runs limited edition charity products to raise funds for specific causes. Two examples are a chameleon bath bomb which raised funds for a campaign group working to end the trading of reptiles and other exotic animals and a molasses based shampoo for anti-tar sands campaigners.

The company aims to support causes and organisations that are overlooked by others and also prioritise work to address the root causes of issues through campaigns, education and activism. Support is not limited to registered charities but is also given to campaign groups and other organisations which are not registered with the Charity Commission. Support ranges from a few hundred pounds to a maximum of £10,000 per project, the average grant is around £4,000.

In addition to Charity Pot and limited edition charity products, the UK also continued with the initiative known as the Carbon Tax Fund. This is a self-imposed tax charged on staff's international flights at a rate of £50 per tonne of carbon dioxide emitted and the funds raised are donated to environmental groups. A total of £109,000 was made from this fund this year.

The company also launched the Sustainable Lush Fund in the UK in 2010. A total of £118,000 was donated through the fund predominantly to permaculture farms and training conferences around the world, some of which are associated with the company's suppliers.

Corporate giving

During 2010/11, Lush Partners worldwide donated £1.58 million to charities and other good causes. Of this, £1.5 million was from Lush Group or Associate countries (7% of pre tax profits). Funds donated are mainly generated through the sales of Charity Pot body cream. Whilst we would not usually record market related giving, it was considered that as this amount was substantial and almost all of the company's giving, the information should be made available to readers.

Beneficiaries of the Charity Pot Fund have included: Coalition to Abolish the Fur Trade; The Fox Project; Earth Restoration Service; Rockpool Candy.

Corporate social responsibility

CSR committee: No committee details published.

CSR policy: No published policy.

We were unable to determine the ratio of women to men on the board.

CSR report: No specific report but information on Lush's charitable activities is given on its website.

Applications

To apply for a Charity Pot grant a funding application form will need to be completed. Guidelines can be found at: https://www.lush.co.uk/content/view/393. To request an application form, email charitypot@lush.co.uk.

Man Group plc

Financial services, agriculture

Correspondent: Lisa Clarke, Secretary to the Charitable Trust, Riverbank House, 2 Swan Lane, London EC4R 3AD (tel: 020 7144 1000/020 7144 1000; fax: 020 7144 1923; email: charitabletrust@mangroupplc.com; website: www.man.com/GB/man-charitable-trust)

Directors: John Aisbitt, Chair; Peter Clarke, Chief Executive; Alison Carnwath; Matthew Lester; Emmanuel Roman; Kevin Hayes, Finance Director; Phillip Colebatch; Patrick O'Sullivan; Frederic Jolly; Nina Shapiro (women: 2; men: 8)

Year end	31/03/2012
Turnover	£1,030,568,460
Pre-tax profit	£201,754,792

Nature of business: The company is a leading global provider of alternative investment products and solutions.

Company registration number: 2921462

Main locations: London

UK employees: 891

Total employees: 1,596

Membership: Arts & Business, LBG

Charitable donations

UK cash (latest declared):	2011	£1,571,650
	2008	£5,500,000
	2007	£3,105,000
	2006	£2,455,000
	2005	£1,724,596
Total UK:	2011	£1,834,550
Total worldwide:	2012	£4,360,300
Cash worldwide:	2012	£2,367,020

Community involvement

The majority of Man's giving is through its associated charity, the Man Group plc Charitable Trust (Charity Commission no. 275386)

The charity is funded by a proportion of Man Group plc profits and is established for general charitable purposes at the discretion of the trustees. In practice the trust focuses on 'empowering disadvantaged young people through education, the arts and sport; literacy and numeracy; vulnerable populations and disaster relief'.

> *Grant making policy*
>
> The charity prefers to concentrate its support on smaller charities where its donations make a material difference and where it can work in partnership with charities that are less likely to obtain support from the general public. The trust likes to focus on activities that offer assistance directly to individuals, families and communities as well as those that increase the capacity of organisations and individuals.
>
> The interest and involvement of Man Group plc employees is also considered. The trust is interested in finding out about volunteering opportunities, but will not give preferential considerations to organisations or projects providing such opportunities. The trustees also favour charities that are involved in the local community in the deprived areas of London.
>
> The recipient charities should be able to demonstrate sound financial management. The trust does not look favourably on those charities whose administration costs are excessive in relation to the service they provide.

Charity of the Year: Starlight Children's Foundation (2012).

Corporate giving

According to the company's annual report and accounts, Man's charitable contribution is based on the financial performance of the business.

> Man paid \$3.8 million (£2.4 million) to the Trust and charitable committees of our overseas offices and \$7 million (£4.4 million) was spent on charitable donations in FY 2011. With less funding available we narrowed our focus to support those charities working with the most excluded and disadvantaged, such as supporting the homeless or long-term unemployed into education, training or employment.

In 2010/11, the Man Group plc Charitable Trust received £1.9 million in donations of which £1.8 million was recorded as voluntary income from the company. Of this, £1.6 million was in cash and £262,900 was in kind. Total donations £2.2 million were awarded by the trust in the following amounts:

Disadvantaged youth
Promoting inclusion (£432,000); Education (£214,000); Arts and culture (£84,500); Sport (£62,500); A full list of beneficiaries is given in the annual report and helpful details of the project supported where the trust awarded upwards of £20,000.

Literacy and numeracy (£215,000).

Vulnerable populations
Homeless people (£234,500); Domestic violence (£100,000); Mental health (£80,000).

Disaster relief (£100,000).

Other support (£209,500).

Beneficiary organisations included: The Connection at St Marin-in-the-Fields (£90,000); Impetus Trust (£55,000); The Place2Be and Community Links (£50,000 each); UK Mathematics Trust and Volunteering Help (£25,000 each); Career Academies UK and London Playing Fields Association (£20,000 each); RNIB (£15,000); Charlie Waller Memorial Trust (£10,000); and Royal College of Art (£9,000).

The trust's administration and support costs are met by the company.

Employee-led support

The company's volunteering programme, ManKind, allows all employees two days paid leave per year to support either charities of their choice or one of the charities supported by the trust. Since the launch, staff have taken part in many activities including serving breakfast to the homeless, facilitating employability workshops for disaffected youth and reading to primary schoolchildren.

The trust has also supported an annual charity since 2004, selected by employees and this year's charity, The Place2Be, received £75,000 from the trust in the nine month period to December 2011, as well as being the focus of a number of events and volunteer support from employees.

The trust will match up to £100 per person per month, individual employee fundraising efforts. There are no constraints as to which charity may benefit from these donations.

Payroll giving: The Give As You Earn scheme is in operation. In 2011, the trust matched this giving with a donation of £60,000.

Commercially-led support

Sponsorship:

The arts – Man sponsors three major literary prizes – The Man Booker Prize for Fiction, the Man Booker International Prize and the Man Asian Literary Prize.

Corporate social responsibility

CSR committee: No dedicated committee details found.

CSR policy: The following statement is taken from the company's website:

> Our corporate responsibility strategy is to pursue high standards of behaviour, both corporate and individual, which underpin our reputation and maintain the trust and loyalty of all our key stakeholders. We focus on five key areas of corporate responsibility.
>
> - World class governance and risk management
> - Responsibilities to our marketplace and our clients
> - Attracting, motivating and developing the best people
> - Contributing to our communities
> - Protecting the environment

CSR report: Published within the annual report and accounts and a CSR section on website.

Exclusions

The Man Group plc Charitable Trust does not generally support: large national charities; charities which use external fundraising agencies; animal charities; charities primarily devoted to promoting religious beliefs; endowment funds; requests that directly replace statutory funding; individual beneficiaries; successful applicants from the previous twelve months.

Applications

In writing to the correspondent.

Manchester Airport Group plc

Airport operators

Correspondent: The Administrator, Manchester Airport Community Trust Fund, Wythenshawe, Manchester M90 1QX (tel: 08712710711; fax: 01614 893813; email: trust.fund@manairport.co.uk; website: www.manchesterairport.co.uk)

Directors: Mike Davies, Chair; Charlie Cornish, Chief Executive; Penny Coates; Stuart Chambers; Dave Goddard; Mike Hancox; Sir Richard Leese; Vanda Murray; David Partridge; Angela Spindler; James Wallace; Neil Thompson (women: 3; men: 9)

Year end	31/03/2011
Turnover	£350,200,000
Pre-tax profit	£80,600,000

Nature of business: The second largest airport group in the UK. The Group (MAG), comprises Manchester – the largest UK airport outside London, East Midlands – a major regional base for low cost, charter and cargo airlines, together with regional airports at Humberside and Bournemouth. MAG also runs airport related businesses engaged in the management and development of property, car parking and retail activities. Owned by the ten Greater Manchester Councils comprising the Council of the City of Manchester (55%) and the nine neighbouring local authorities: Bolton, Bury, Oldham, Rochdale, Salford, Stockport, Tameside, Trafford and Wigan (5% each).

Company registration number: 4330721

Membership: BITC

Charitable donations

UK cash (latest declared):	2011	£100,000
	2009	£150,000
	2008	£100,000
	2007	£189,000
	2006	£189,000
Total UK:	2011	£100,000
Total worldwide:	2011	£100,000
Cash worldwide:	2011	£100,000

Corporate social responsibility

CSR committee: There was no evidence of a separate CSR Committee.

CSR policy: This information was obtained from the company's website:

> Our Community Strategy works on the key themes that local people tell us are important and which benefit our business:
>
> - Education – equipping local people with the skills that they need to achieve the future that they desire and in particular work in our airport
> - Employment – inspiring local people to want to work on our site to create career paths to enter our business
> - Local Community – helping to create a thriving economically sound community
> - Airport Community – creating opportunities for colleagues to support the Community Strategy for the benefit of the community whilst building their own skills

CSR report: A CSR report was available from the company's website.

Exclusions

No support for appeals from individuals, commercial organisations, organisations which have statutory responsibilities such as hospitals or schools (unless the project is clearly not a statutory responsibility), those working for profit, or for organisations outside of the trust boundary.

Applications

Grant applications to the Manchester Airport Community Trust Fund should not be made without first reading the policy guidelines. These, along with an application form, are available upon request from the Fund Administrator. You can also get an application form and further information on-line from www.manchesterairport.co.uk

Charities and schools in communities in close proximity to Manchester airport which do not qualify for funding from the trust fund may apply for prizes for fundraising by contacting the correspondent.

Trustees meet quarterly. You should return your completed form to the administrator no later than the first Friday of March, June, September or December for consideration by the trustees the following month.

If you are successful you will usually receive a cheque a month after the trustees' meeting. You must send the trust fund original invoices/receipts for the works or goods you purchased within three months of receiving your grant cheque.

Other information

The group donated £100,000 in 2010/11 (2009/10: £150,000).

The following information is taken from the group's website:

> The **Manchester Airport Community Trust Fund** (Charity Commission no: 1071703) is a registered charity and was established to promote, enhance, improve and protect both the natural and built environment in our local community.
>
> In 2011/12, Manchester Airport will be contributing £100,000 which is further enhanced by income from fines imposed on airlines when their aircraft exceed our noise limits. These funds are then used to

support neighbourhood and community projects throughout the area.

Manchester Airport aims to maximise its impact within local communities by harnessing support from other companies. Three business support groups have been set up under the leadership of the Airport. These are as follows: *The Airport Community Network* (ACN); *Business Working with Wythenshawe*; *The Longridge and Shaw Heath.* All groups work to deliver projects to support social and economic regeneration through professional expertise and advice; equipment; volunteers and access to facilities and premises.

In 2010/11 the group supported the *Royal Horticultural Society* (RHS) to expand its network of *Regional Campaign for School Gardening Advisors* to help more than 300,000 schoolchildren in the North West to get gardening.

The company joined Manchester International Festival and invited parents and babies to a musical show written by the Scottish Opera.

The 'Adopt a Player' project was run once again with the Halle Orchestra and Bridgewater Hall. Musicians held interactive lessons for Year 6 and 7 pupils from the local area.

Marks and Spencer Group plc

Financial services, retail – clothing and footwear

Correspondent: Mike Barry, Corporate Social Responsibility, Waterside House, 35 North Wharf Street, London W2 1NW (tel: 020 7935 4422; fax: 020 7487 2679; website: corporate.marksandspencer.com)

Directors: Robert Swannell, Chair; Marc Bolland, Chief Executive; Steven Sharp; Kate Bostock; John Dixon; Jeremy Daroch; Steven Holliday; Alan Steward, Chief Finance Officer; Laura Wade-Gery; Martha Lane-Fox; Jan du Plessis; Miranda Curtis; Vindi Banga; Amanda Mellor (women: 4; men: 10)

Year end	31/03/2012
Turnover	£9,934,300,000
Pre-tax profit	£658,000,000

Nature of business: The principal activities are retailing clothes, beauty products, home products, food and the provision of financial services.

Company registration number: 214436

Subsidiaries include: St Michael Finance plc

Brands include: Simply Food, St Michael.

Main locations: London, Chester

Total employees: 57,054

Membership: BITC, LBG

Charitable donations

UK cash (latest declared):	2012	£6,900,000
	2010	£5,200,000
	2009	£5,200,000
	2008	£5,400,000
	2007	£3,800,000
Total UK:	2012	£11,400,000
Total worldwide:	2012	£11,400,000
Cash worldwide:	2012	£6,900,000

Community involvement

Marks and Spencer (M&S) makes donations to charitable organisations through its local stores. They each have a small, limited budget and focus their support towards issues that are important to their local community.

Through **Marks and Start,** its flagship community programme, the company helps people to prepare for the world of work. In particular it is aimed at: people who are homeless; people with disabilities; the young unemployed; schoolchildren, including those in deprived areas; students who are the first in their family to aim for higher education; and parents wanting to return to work.

In addition to the above, in kind support is given through the donation of food and clothing.

Corporate giving

During the year 2011/12, the group made charitable donations to support the community of £11.4 million (2010/11: £12.3 million), excluding management costs and memberships. This figure would appear to include the figures calculated for employee time and stock donations. Contributions were principally total cash donations of £6.9 million (last year £6.9 million) which included those to: Breakthrough Breast Cancer, Macmillan Cancer Support, Great Ormond Street Hospital, UNICEF, Groundwork, WWF, MCS, the Marks and Start programme and the local community.

In kind support

The group has reduced its waste in the last five years and now does not send anything to landfill. This reduction in waste is reflected in the overall reduction in waste stock donations to a variety of charities, £3.2 million (last year £4.1 million) including Oxfam, the Newlife Foundation and Shelter.

Employee-led support

Employees are encouraged to give up their spare time to raise cash and volunteer for a wide range of charities and organisations. Each year, in support of this, M&S sets aside funds to match the charitable fundraising that its people do out of working hours. M&S encourages teamwork between colleagues through the programme's criteria which requires a minimum of five employees to be fundraising together for the same organisation.

During 2011/12, the group also donated £1.3 million (2010/11: £1.3 million) of employee time, principally on fundraising and volunteering, Marks and Start and school work experience programmes.

In addition, the group supported a number of charity partners in raising funds of £8.5 million (2010/11: £10.9 million). This principally consisted of funds raised from customer clothing donations to Oxfam through The Clothing Exchange, funds raised by Groundwork as a result of M&S support and employee and customer donations.

Payroll giving: The Give As You Earn scheme is in operation. Sharing the Caring, the payroll giving arm of the Charities Aid Foundation, is now visiting each of M&S's stores and head office locations annually, in order to promote the scheme.

Commercially-led support

The following information is taken from M&S's Plan A website (plana.marksandspencer.com):

> *Cause-related marketing:*
> *Breakthrough Breast Cancer*
> M&S raises money through donations on sales of specially designed products during Breast Cancer Awareness month in October, and as part of the Fashion Targets Breast Cancer campaign in April-May.
>
> Breakthrough Breast Cancer also benefits from a donation on the post surgery lingerie range which is sold all year round.
>
> *Groundwork* – M&S is donating all the profits (1.85p per bag) from our 5p food carrier bag charging scheme to environmental charity Groundwork; to invest in projects that will improve parks, play areas and public gardens in neighbourhoods around the UK.

Corporate social responsibility

CSR committee: There is a dedicated CSR committee.

CSR policy: Statement taken from the 'How We Do Business Report' for 2012:

> During 2011/12 we've achieved 43 new commitments, including becoming carbon neutral, sending no waste to landfill, 100% wild fish from the most sustainable sources available and bringing the 5,000th participant into our Marks & Start work experience programme. Since launching Plan A, we've received more than 100 sustainability awards, including the Queen's Award for Enterprise for Sustainable Development.
>
> This progress would not have been possible without the involvement and support of our customers on a range of social and environmental campaigns, our colleagues' actions on community, energy efficiency and recycling and our suppliers' help in developing new standards. Also, the vital support of partners including

Forum for the Future, Oxfam, WRAP, WWF, Business in the Community as well as many, many others.

CSR report: Various downloadable reports available from the company's website including 'Plan A' and 'How We Do Business'.

Exclusions

M&S stores are not able to support:

- Personal appeals on behalf of individual people, including overseas trips
- Advertising or goodwill messages
- Political parties
- Third party fundraising on behalf of a charity
- Religious bodies, except where the project provides non-denominational, non-sectarian support for the benefit of the general project
- Supplying clothing, other than in exceptional circumstances, as we already give clothes to BDF (Birth Defects Foundation) and Shelter

Applications

To stand any chance of success, check that your organisation can help to address key areas of the company's policy before applying.

Marsh Ltd

Insurance

Correspondent: Kathryn Pettifer, UK Community Relations Executive, Tower Place, Lower Thames Street, London EC3R 5BU (tel: 020 7357 1000; fax: 020 7929 2705; email: kathryn.s.pettifer@mmc.com; website: uk.marsh.com)

Directors: Peter Middleton, Chair; M. C. South, Chief Executive; N. C. Bacon; J. V. Barker; P. J. Box; M. C. Chessher; N. C. Frankland; J. C. Grogan; C. J. Lay; J. J. Nicholson; D. Pigot; R. I. White

Year end	31/12/2011
Turnover	£669,900,000
Pre-tax profit	£156,500,000

Nature of business: The company provides risk management, insurance and reinsurance broking services through its two principal businesses, Marsh and Guy Carpenter.

Company registration number: 1507274

Main locations: Liverpool, Birmingham, Edinburgh, Glasgow, Leeds, Bristol, Newcastle, London, Southampton

Membership: BITC

Charitable donations

UK cash (latest declared):	2011	£170,650
	2007	£319,000
	2006	£32,000
Total UK:	2011	£170,650
Total worldwide:	2011	£170,650
Cash worldwide:	2011	£170,650

Corporate social responsibility

CSR committee: The donation programme is administered centrally.

CSR policy: Information taken from Marsh and McLennan's website:

> Marsh has a well-established Corporate Social Responsibility programme which is supported at the most senior level.
>
> Through this programme we offer financial support and the time and skills of our employees to a wide variety of charities and community organisations in the cities and towns in which we operate, as well as an active environmental sustainability programme.

We were unable to determine the ratio of women to men on the board.

CSR report: There is an annual Sustainability report published by Marsh and McLennan.

Exclusions

Donations will not be made (other than in exceptional circumstances) to religious organisations or causes, political parties or causes, advertising in charity brochures, circular appeals, international crisis appeals, overseas causes, appeals for individuals' education, expeditions or recreation, animal welfare or sport.

Applications

For further information contact the correspondent.

Other information

In 2011 Marsh Ltd., gave £170,650 in UK charitable donations.

Information taken from the website of Marsh UK:

> Financial support and the time and skills of employees are given to a wide variety of charities and community organisations in the cities and towns in which it operates.
>
> The programme comprises the following:
>
> *National Charities*
>
> Marsh's donation programme is administered centrally. Under the theme of 'Helping People and Communities at Risk', the company has established a multi-year partnership with eight national UK charities who provide support and services in response to a broad range of human needs. The charities are: Addaction; The Bobby Moore Fund; Business in the Community; Friends of the Elderly; Great Ormond Street Hospital Charity; Kids Company; Mind; and Missing People.
>
> *Employee Volunteering*
>
> The employee volunteering policy entitles every employee to a minimum of one day per year to take part in a programme that supports the community. Activities range from one-day 'Team Challenges' to one-to-one mentoring.
>
> In addition, Marsh colleagues in the Bristol, Witham and London offices spend one lunchtime per week visiting local school children and helping them with their literacy and numeracy skills. In London, the company has had such a relationship with the Halley School since 1997.
>
> *Marsh MAGIC* (Matching and Giving for Involvement with Charities)
>
> Marsh matches the fundraising and volunteer efforts of employees, for the communities and charities of their choice, up to a ceiling of £300 per year.
>
> *Matched Funding*
>
> Marsh adds 10% to employees' payroll donations to charities of their choice via Give As You Earn.
>
> For more information on Marsh's community and charitable activities is in the UK, please contact Katy Pettifer on 020 7357 3033 or via email link on the company's website.

Marshall of Cambridge (Holdings) Ltd

Engineering

Correspondent: The Group Support Executive, Airport House, Newmarket Road, Cambridge CB5 8RX (tel: 01223 373737; fax: 01223 372472; website: marshallgroup.co.uk)

Directors: Sir Michael Marshall, Chair and Chief Executive; R. D. Marshall; P. Callaghan; W. C. M. Dastur; D. Gupta; J. D. Barker; S. Fitzgerald; J. C. G. Stancliffe; A. E. Cook; P. J. Harvey; Sir Ralph Robins; C. J. Sawyer; S. J. Sillars (women: 1; men: 12)

Year end	31/12/2010
Turnover	£883,974,000
Pre-tax profit	£5,197,000

Nature of business: The principal activities of the group are car and commercial vehicle sales, distribution, service, hire and associated activities, together with general engineering connected with aircraft and military systems.

Company registration number: 2051460

Main locations: Ipswich, Huntingdon, Cambridge, Croydon

Membership: Arts & Business

Charitable donations

UK cash (latest declared):	2010	£91,000
	2009	£110,000
	2008	£1,065,000
	2006	£195,000
	2005	£29,000
Total UK:	2010	£91,000
Total worldwide:	2010	£91,000
Cash worldwide:	2010	£91,000

Corporate social responsibility

CSR committee: There was no evidence of a separate CSR Committee.

CSR policy: This information was obtained from the company's annual report:

> We have a firm and long-standing commitment to the communities in which we live and work.
>
> Charitable donations are an important part of our community involvement and we direct this support primarily to causes with educational, engineering and scientific objectives, as well as social objectives connected with our business and place in the wider community.

CSR report: There was no evidence of a separate CSR report however two pages were dedicated to CSR in the annual report.

Exclusions

No support for advertising in charity brochures, animal welfare, appeals from individuals, fundraising events, overseas projects, political appeals, religious appeals, or local appeals not in areas of company presence.

Applications

In writing to the Group Support Executive.

Applications for the D G Marshall of Cambridge Trust should be addressed to the correspondent at the Trust c/o Airport House, Newmarket Road, Cambridge CB5 8RX.

Other information

In 2010 the company made charitable donations of £90,000 (2009: £110,000).

> *D G Marshall of Cambridge Trust*
>
> The charity will consider all applications for funding as received, provided the application is consistent with the charity's objects. There is no minimum or maximum donation.
>
> The group provides support to a number of schools and has 'sponsored' four Cambridge Schools, Teversham Church of England Primary School, Bottisham Village College, Coleridge Community College and the Fields Children's Centre, where dedicated members of staff assist with a wide range of projects, particularly those connected to science, technology, engineering and mathematics. The group also assists in a number of other schools where employees are involved with school management as governors.
>
> Senior directors and executives also take on a number of non-executive roles in business, charitable and community projects. The group also provides support to the Cambridge Air Training Corps Squadron.
>
> National projects which benefit from the encouragement and help of the group include: The Air League Educational Trust, the Air Training Corps, the RAF Benevolent Fund, the Duke of Edinburgh's Award Scheme and BEN, the charity of the Motor Industry.
>
> In conjunction with the World Land Trust, the group has successfully led the Cambridge Rainforest Appeal which raised over £200,000 towards the purchase and long-term protection of a corridor of rainforest in Borneo which links two sections of a wildlife sanctuary.

Payroll giving: The group encourages staff charitable donations under the Give As You Earn scheme.

Marston's plc

Brewers/distillers

Correspondent: Head Office Team, Marston's House, Brewery Road, Wolverhampton WV1 4JT (tel: 01902 711811; fax: 01902 429136; email: enquiries@marstons.co.uk; website: www.marstons.co.uk)

Directors: David Thompson, Chair; Ralph Findlay, Chief Executive; Andrew Andrea; Robin Hodgson; Rosalind Cuschieri; Anne-Marie Brennan; Robin Rowland; Neil Goulden; Peter Dalzell; Nick Backhouse (women: 2; men: 8)

Year end	29/09/2012
Turnover	£719,700,000
Pre-tax profit	(£135,500,000)

Nature of business: Brewers.

Company registration number: 31461

Brands include: Pedigree; Hobgoblin.

UK employees: 12289

Charitable donations

UK cash (latest declared):	2012	£10,244
	2009	£9,000
Total UK:	2012	£25,000

Corporate social responsibility

CSR report: There is a separate CSR report.

Applications

In writing to the correspondent.

Other information

According to the company's annual report for 2011/12, charitable donations during the period amounted to £10,244, all of which was given to the Responsible Gambling Trust. From information on the company's website (and quoted below), the company contribution slightly exceeds this amount, at least by the amount of match funding it provides.

The company's website states:

> Each year our licensed retail managers' pub staff and tenants raise significant amounts of money for many different charitable causes through local pub based activity and contributions from the Marston's Inns and Taverns Charitable Foundation. Donations from the foundation are funded directly from contributions made by employees within its' head office function, which are then matched by the Marston's Inns and Taverns division. [During 2012 the foundation donated £11,000 'to help support charitable activity' in Marston's pubs.]
>
> In addition to providing prizes and administrative support for the charitable activities of their tenants and lessees' Marston's Pub Company raises money for nominated charities and Marston's Beer Company makes hundreds of prize donations for charitable activities run by its Free Trade customers.
>
> Our employees also run their own Marston's Employee Charity Fund which we are proud to support. This fund is run by employees for employees and regularly makes donations to a range of good local causes nominated by our employees. In support of this the group runs Give As You Earn arrangements for employees enabling them to make tax-efficient donations to this or any other registered charity of their choice. The administration charges for running this scheme are borne by the group, thereby ensuring that employees' donations are given in their entirety to good causes.

Subsidiaries include: Marston's Trading Ltd; Marston's Property Developments Ltd; Marston's Pubs Ltd; Marston's Estates Ltd; Marston's Operating Ltd; Banks's Brewery Insurance Ltd.

Mascolo Ltd

Health/beauty products, personal care products

Correspondent: Krissy Sampy, 58–60 Stamford Street, LONDON SE1 9LX (tel: 020 7440 6660/020 7921 9091; fax: 020 7440 6668; email: charitablefoundation@toniandguy.co.uk; website: www.toniandguy.com)

Directors: G. T. Mascolo; S. M. Mascolo-Tarbuck; C. F. Mascolo; P. R. Mascolo; R. Staal

Year end	31/08/2011
Turnover	£11,145,000
Pre-tax profit	(£1,071,000)

Nature of business: Hairdressing and other beauty treatments.

Company registration number: 770236

Total employees: 294

Charitable donations

UK cash (latest declared):	2011	£28,500
	2009	£16,300
	2008	£143,000
Total UK:	2011	£28,500
Total worldwide:	2011	£28,500
Cash worldwide:	2011	£28,500

Corporate social responsibility

CSR committee: No information available.

CSR policy: None published.

It was not possible to determine the ratio of women to men on the board.

CSR report: None published.

Applications

In writing to the correspondent.

Other information

Mascolo Ltd is the parent company of the 200 or so TONI&GUY hair salons in the UK, some of which are franchised or partially-owned by the company. The company's charitable giving is directed through the TONI&GUY Charitable Foundation (Charity Commission no. 1095285). The company's accounts record that in 2010/11, the company made charitable donations of £28,500.

The TONI&GUY Charitable Foundation

The foundation is a UK registered charity established in 2003 by Toni Mascolo and his wife Pauline, with the aim of supporting a number of worthwhile charitable causes. Nominations for grants are generally elicited by informal means and include input from the Toni and Guy network of hairdressing salons.

The company's website states:

> We are currently funding a number of projects including: the renovation of the TONI&GUY Ward at the Variety Club Children's Hospital, London; Macmillan Cancer Support to help people in the UK living with cancer; Hair and Beauty Benevolent to support hair and beauty professionals that have fallen into financial difficulty; and Queen of the Angels Foundation in Italy, a refuge for young people.
>
> All grants made to charitable projects are fundraised through the generous support of TONI&GUY and essensuals staff, clients and business partners.

Bernard Matthews Ltd

Food manufacture

Correspondent: David Reger, Company Secretary, Great Witchingham Hall, Norwich NR9 5QD (tel: 01603 872611; fax: 01603 871118; website: www.bernardmatthews.com)

Directors: David McCall; Noel Bartram (women: 0; men: 2)

Year end	03/07/2011
Turnover	£470,844,000
Pre-tax profit	(£28,060,000)

Nature of business: The principal activities of the group are the production and marketing of turkey and red meat products, oven-ready turkeys, day-old turkeys, fish products and other poultry products.

Company registration number: 625299

Main locations: Norwich

Total employees: 3,489

Charitable donations

UK cash (latest declared):	2011	£85,000
	2009	£197,349
	2006	£197,349
	2005	£303,611
Total UK:	2011	£85,000
Total worldwide:	2011	£85,000
Cash worldwide:	2011	£85,000

Corporate social responsibility

CSR committee: No details found.

CSR policy: The company states on its website that it is:

> Working with our community to: educate people about food and in particular turkey; inspire people in our local community; and support our employees.

CSR report: There is a Corporate Responsibility Document on the website.

Exclusions

No support for political appeals.

Applications

In writing to the correspondent.

Other information

The death of Bernard Matthews, the founder of the company, was reported in the 2010/11 report and accounts.

During the year, the group made charitable contributions of £85,000 to a variety of national and local charities. The majority of these contributions were made to the Bernard Matthews Fund which is administered by the Norfolk Community Foundation which aims to support a wide range of charitable and community activities throughout Norfolk, North Suffolk and Lincolnshire.

The company is a founder charter member of the Duke of Edinburgh Scheme, supporting this charity for over 17 years.

Mazars LLP

Accountants

Correspondent: Company Secretary, Tower Bridge House, St Katherine's Way, London E1W 1DD (tel: 020 7063 4000; fax: 020 7063 4001; website: www.mazars.co.uk)

Directors: David Evans; David Herbinet; Glyn Williams; Philip Gregory (women: 0; men: 4)

Year end	31/08/2011
Turnover	£109,868,000
Pre-tax profit	£22,315,000

Nature of business: Accountants and Business Advisers.

Company registration number: 1485039

Main locations: London

Total employees: 1,041

Membership: BITC

Charitable donations

UK cash (latest declared):	2011	£224,000
	2009	£270,719
	2007	£244,000
	2005	£165,866
Total UK:	2011	£224,000
Total worldwide:	2011	£224,000
Cash worldwide:	2011	£224,000

Corporate social responsibility

CSR committee: Corporate Responsibility is led by Anthony Carey, a Partner in the business. A National Steering Group of people has been set up across the UK who have agreed to promote and manage CR activity at a regional level, and contribute to the national effort by reporting and sharing initiatives and best practice. See website for regional officers.

CSR policy: Policy on charitable giving is taken from the company's website: 'Charitable giving initiatives, including donating a proportion of our profits to a range of charities each year, as well as individual staff members fundraising through participation in events such as marathons, parachute jumps and swimathons.'

CSR report: No details found.

Exclusions

No support for political appeals, advertising in charity brochures, science/technology or sport.

The company will not permit a further application from a particular charity within a three year period of an earlier grant.

Applications

In writing to any partner or employee of the firm.

Any charity which would like to be considered as a Charity of the Year should contact: *christian.ball@mazars.co.uk*

For applications to the Trust contact: Bryan Rogers, 1 Cranleigh Gardens, South Croydon CR2 9LD. The trustees operate through a management committee which meets annually to consider applications for major grants. Some monies are allocated to six regional 'pot' holders who approve minor grant applications from within their own region.

Applicants for a national grant must be known to the team members of Mazars LLP. National and regional criteria are regularly reviewed but, in general, the trustees consider that the national grantmaking policy should avoid core funding and other activities that require funding over a number of years. Most national grants are therefore made towards one-off projects. Successful national applicants may not reapply within three years.

Other information

During 2010/11, Mazars LLP donated £224,000 to the Mazars Charitable Trust (Charity Commission no. 287735). The trust supports charities involved in the community/social welfare; enterprise/training; housing/homelessness; and poverty/social exclusion. A wide range of charities receive support from the trust in the form of time and money. Resources are committed almost entirely to charities known to the partners and employees of the firm. Charitable giving initiatives include a proportion of profits to the trust, as well as individual staff members fundraising through participation in events such as marathons, parachute jumps and swimathons.

The trust made donations in 2010 of £272,000.

Robert McAlpine Ltd

Building/construction

Correspondent: Brian Arter, Charity Administrator, Eaton Court, Maylands Avenue, Hemel Hempstead, Hertfordshire HP2 7TR (tel: 01442 233444; fax: 01422 230024; website: www.sir-robert-mcalpine.com)

Directors: David M. McAlpine; Ian M. McAlpine; Cullum McAlpine; Richard H. McAlpine; Andrew W. McAlpine; R. Edward McAlpine; Hector G. McAlpine; Anthony Aikenhead; Anthony W. Barratt; Vince Corrigan; Boyd McFee; Miles C. Shelley (women: 0; men: 12)

Year end	31/10/2011
Turnover	£749,255,000
Pre-tax profit	£25,636,000

Nature of business: The principal business of the group is that of civil engineering and building contractors and renewable energy.

Company registration number: 566823

Main locations: Hemel Hempstead

Total employees: 1,769

Charitable donations

UK cash (latest declared):	2011	£400,000
	2009	£340,000
	2007	£666,000
Total UK:	2011	£400,000
Total worldwide:	2011	£400,000
Cash worldwide:	2011	£400,000

Corporate social responsibility

CSR committee: Composed of staff from a variety of disciplines, the CSR Group reviews performance across the business. Led by a company director, it considers and identifies CSR issues, and reports directly to the Construction Board. The Group also ensures objectives and performance are publicised widely within the company.

CSR policy: Taken from the company's website:

> We aim to operate a successful, sustainable and socially responsible business which makes a positive contribution to the communities and environments in which we work.
>
> We review our objectives annually and set realistic, deliverable long-term targets across six strategic areas that are fundamental to our operations and stakeholders:
> - Environment
> - Community
> - Staff
> - Health and safety
> - Clients
> - Supply chain
>
> Our robust approach to measuring and reporting enables us to effectively evaluate our systems and the impact of initiatives undertaken to improve performance. In this way we are able to identify, adapt and implement measures which improve our operations and the services we provide clients.

Charitable support is given through the Robert McAlpine Foundation.

CSR report: There is an annual CSR report.

Exclusions

No support for local appeals not in areas of company presence.

Applications

In writing to the correspondent.

Other information

In 2010/11 The Robert McAlpine Foundation received £400,000 from the company. In turn it spent £492,500 in delivering grants to projects for the causes it supports.

The company has a preference for local charities in areas where it operates and charities in which a member of the company is involved. Preferred areas for support are children and youth, and education.

The Robert McAlpine Foundation (Charity Commission no. 226646)

The foundation generally supports causes concerned with children with disabilities, older people, medical research and social welfare. The trustees meet annually, normally in November. Successful applicants are informed at the end of the year. Applications should be addressed to the Secretary of the Trustees of the Robert McAlpine Foundation, at the company's address. The accounts for 2011 state: 'The policy of the trustees is to make grants to charitable institutions of amounts from £2,500 upwards in the specific categories of objectives which they support. A list of grants is produced separately and sent to the Charity Commission.'

The McAlpine Educational Endowment (Charity Commission no. 313156)

This trust is for 13- to 18-year-olds, who have sound academic ability, show leadership potential and are facing financial hardship. The trust favours ten particular schools, with referrals coming from the headmasters. Applications should be addressed to the Secretary to the Trustees of the McAlpine Educational Endowment, at the company's address.

McBride plc

Retail – miscellaneous

Correspondent: Corporate Social Responsibility Dept. (Community), Centre Point, 28th Floor, 103 New Oxford Street, London WC1A 1DD (tel: 020 7539 7850; email: enquiries@mcbride.co.uk; website: www.mcbride.co.uk)

Directors: Iain J. G. Napier, Chair; Chris Bull, Chief Executive; Richard Armitage, Group Finance Director; Colin Smith; Bob Lee; Christine A. Bogdanowicz-Bindert; Jeff Carr; Sandra Turner (women: 2; men: 6)

Year end	30/06/2011
Turnover	£812,400,000
Pre-tax profit	£19,400,000

Nature of business: Provider of Private Label Household and Personal Care products. The company develops, produces and sells its products to leading retailers primarily in the UK and across Continental Europe.

Company registration number: 2798634

Total employees: 5,421

Charitable donations

UK cash (latest declared):	2010	£1,500
	2009	£21,000
Total worldwide:	2011	£46,000
Cash worldwide:	2011	£11,000

Corporate social responsibility

CSR committee: The board has overall responsibility for maintaining and enhancing the group's CSR policies, guidelines and code of conduct which are published on the group's website at www.mcbride.co.uk. The Chief Executive is accountable for ensuring that the group operates in accordance with these policies. The group monitors the performance of its divisions through rigorous performance management systems and key performance indicators that enhance its ability to monitor and improve performance. Health, safety and environment managers are present at sites. Detailed reports are prepared by the HR Director and submitted to the group's executive directors who report any issues of major significance to the Board.

CSR policy: The following information is from the company's website: 'We work closely with the communities where we have our operations to make a positive contribution where possible, recognising there is economic interdependence between ourselves, local businesses and local government.'

CSR report: A CSR report is contained within the annual report of the company.

Applications

In writing to the correspondent.

Other information

The group made monetary donations to charities of £11,000 (2010: £1,500) during the year, mainly to small local community charities in the UK, Poland and Czech Republic, and to the Red Cross. Donations were also made to In Kind Direct of laundry and cleaning products with a value of approximately £35,000.

The following information is taken from the annual report:

> We make donations of laundry and dishwash products to In Kind Direct, which distributes goods to small, local charitable groups throughout the UK. In Kind Direct provides an easy way for manufacturers and retailers to donate surplus stock to voluntary groups, which can help them save money on their running costs and thus provide an enhanced service.
>
> The group is involved in a wide range of local community activities including undergraduate sponsorships and support of the UK SIFE programme, which works to mobilise university students to make a difference in their communities while developing the skills to become socially responsible business leaders. The group also provides support for the local statutory authorities via voluntary work and advice, sponsors specific educational awards, provides careers advice for students and school children provides mentoring support to assist ethnic minority students into employment, provides work experience placements, supports local charities, and hosts a wide range of factory visits for educational purposes or to exchange best practice.

McCain Foods (GB) Ltd

Food manufacture

Correspondent: Company Director, Marketing and Corporate Affairs, Havers Hill, Scarborough, North Yorkshire YO11 3BS (tel: 01723 584141; fax: 01723 581230; website: www.mccain.co.uk)

Directors: A. D. McCain; M. C. McCain; N. I. Vermont; W. A. Bartlett; G. Dent; R. A. Hunter; S. Jefferson; S. W. Herd; H. D. Snape; M. E. Millar; D. Stewart; A. R. Bridges; H. J. Priestly

Year end	30/06/2011
Turnover	£371,548,000
Pre-tax profit	£40,454,000

Nature of business: Manufacturer and supplier of frozen and ambient food products.

Company registration number: 733218

Main locations: Scarborough, Peterborough, Montrose, Wolverhampton, Teddington

UK employees: 1,418

Total employees: 1,418

Membership: BITC

Charitable donations

UK cash (latest declared):	2011	£21,000
	2009	£36,000
	2008	£39,000
	2007	£88,000
	2006	£69,000
Total UK:	2011	£21,000
Total worldwide:	2011	£21,000
Cash worldwide:	2011	£21,000

Corporate social responsibility

CSR committee: The Marketing and Corporate Affairs directors are responsible for community activities.

CSR policy: The following information is taken from the company's website:

> The interests of the local communities around our processing facilities and the broader communities we serve with our products are central to our operations. We rely on the goodwill of our communities, recruit our employees from them and supply our products to them. By supporting associations and charities at both local and national level, helping to address the issues surrounding healthy diet and lifestyle and by consulting and actively engaging with our communities on issues relating to our operations affecting them, we strive to build meaningful and lasting relationships of mutual benefit and trust.

Unable to determine the ratio of women to men on the board.

CSR report: No published CSR report.

Exclusions

Generally no support for: circular appeals; fundraising events; advertising in charity brochures; appeals from individuals; purely denominational (religious) appeals or local appeals not in areas of company presence.

Applications

In writing to the correspondent.

Other information

During 2010/11, the company made charitable donations in the UK of £21,000. We have no information regarding the beneficiaries but have been advised previously that support is only given to charities and organisations in the company's local area.

Additional support is provided through gifts in kind. The following information is taken from the company's website:

> McCain is a family company and understands the importance of the communities in which we operate. This is central to our operations and we actively support local schools, theatres, sports activities and charities financially.
>
> - By supporting associations and charities at both local and national level, and by actively engaging with them on issues relating to our operations, we strive to build meaningful and lasting relationships of mutual benefit and trust
> - We recognise our responsibility as a key member of the communities in which we operate and consult with local stakeholders on local issues wherever possible
> - We engage with community stakeholders on environmental issues with a view to developing effective and sustainable practices
> - We have contacted and polled the opinions of our various stakeholders, to establish shared issues which we can engage upon to resolve and identify common goals to achieve
> - We have an ongoing investment plan across all our UK sites in order to ensure the most up-to-date technology is in place to minimise any potential noise or odour emissions

The company partners:

- Fareshare
- Athletics4Life/UKA partnership/Track and Field/McCain Athletics Networks
- Royal Agricultural College/Harper Adams University College
- RSPB

McDonalds Restaurants Ltd

Retail – restaurants/fast food

Correspondent: Joe Zammuto, Corporate Affairs, 11–59 High Road, East Finchley, London N2 8AW (tel: 0870 241 3300; email: joe.zammuto@uk.mcd.com; website: www.mcdonalds.co.uk)

Directors: J. Tafani; B. Mullens; S. Easterbrook; G. McDonald; C. Hammer; R. Forte

Year end	31/12/2010
Turnover	£1,184,462,000
Pre-tax profit	£157,211,000

Nature of business: The activity of the company is quick service restaurants.

Company registration number: 1002769

Main locations: London

Total employees: 39,296

Membership: BITC

Charitable donations

UK cash (latest declared):	2010	£380,000
	2008	£357,000
	2007	£367,000
	2006	£385,000
	2005	£220,000
Total UK:	2010	£380,000
Total worldwide:	2010	£380,000
Cash worldwide:	2010	£380,000

Corporate social responsibility

CSR policy: No CSR information found.

We were unable to determine the ratio of women to men on the board.

Exclusions

No support for animal welfare charities, appeals from individuals, the arts, elderly people, medical research, overseas projects, political appeals, religious appeals, or science/technology.

Applications

In writing to the correspondent, preferably by email.

Other information

McDonald's Restaurants Ltd, made charitable donations in 2010 of £380,000 (2009: £371,000). The sole recipient was Ronald McDonald House Charities.

Ronald McDonald House Charities (Charity Commission no. 802047): All of the company's charitable donations are given to the charitable trust established in 1988. The bulk of the charity's work is the creation of 'home away from home' accommodation for the families of children requiring in-patient care in hospitals or hospices. RMHC UK is one of a network of RMHC 'chapters' operating in 52 countries throughout the world, providing services to support the wellbeing of children and families.

McDonald's Kick-Start Grants (Football Clubs)

The following information is taken from the company's website:

> You can apply for anything, which will help to support, grow or develop your players and the community. You can apply for one-off grants of between £500 to £2500 including VAT for a single project.
>
> Examples of things McDonald's will support include, but are not limited to: club facilities, grounds-keeping tools, training courses, pitch hire, mini-vans and washing machines; whatever your club and team could significantly benefit from.
>
> Examples of things McDonald's will not support include: advertising and promotions, fundraisers, kit/team wear, club trips/tours, holiday training camps and club personnel wages/expenses e.g. fuel.
>
> For the avoidance of doubt, an application must be submitted and approved prior to the project commencing for it to be considered eligible for a grant. No grant will be awarded for work that has already been completed prior to an application being submitted and approved. For more information see: www.mcdonalds.co.uk/ukhome/Sport/Football/Investment/small-grant.

Volunteering

McDonald's has an employee volunteering scheme and allows staff company time off in which to carry out charitable activities. Note, however, that staff are encouraged to participant in fundraising events for the company's own charity.

Sponsorship: the company supports a football coaching qualification provided by the national football associations of England, Northern Ireland, Scotland and Wales.

Medtronic Ltd

Healthcare, information technology

Correspondent: Company Secretary, Medtronic Ltd, Building 9, Croxley Green Business Park, Hatters Lane, Watford, Hertfordshire WD18 8WW (tel: 01923 212213; fax: 01923 241004; website: www.medtronic.co.uk)

Directors: S. Hamilton; A. Pleijsier; J. G. Fielding; M. Dovell

Year end	29/04/2011
Turnover	£57,571,000
Pre-tax profit	£4,913,000

Nature of business: The sale and marketing of medical technology to treat and manage conditions such as heart disease, neurological disorders, vascular illnesses and diabetes.

Company registration number: 1070807

Main locations: Watford

Total employees: 404

Charitable donations

UK cash (latest declared):	2010	£231,000
	2006	£231,000
	2005	£170,842
Total worldwide:	2011	£67,000
Cash worldwide:	2011	£67,000

Corporate social responsibility

CSR policy: No information for CSR within Medtronic Ltd annual report and accounts.

Unable to determine the ratio of women to men on the board.

Exclusions

No support for individuals, religious groups for religious purposes, fundraising events or activities, social events or goodwill advertising, reimbursable medical treatment, scientific research, lobbying, or political or fraternal activities.

Applications

Organisations from outside of the United States wishing to apply firstly need to select the grant programme of interest. You will then be directed to complete a letter of inquiry and instructed on where to send it.

Decisions can take up to three months.

Other information

In 2010/11 Medtronic Ltd donated £67,000 to predominantly medical research causes. It is not clear from the accounts whether this amount was awarded solely within the UK.

Meggitt plc

Engineering

Correspondent: Company Secretary, Atlantic House, Aviation Park West, Bournemouth International Airport, Christchurch, Dorset BH23 6EW (tel: 01202 597597; website: www.meggitt.com)

Directors: Sir Colin Terry, Chair; Terry Twigger, Chief Executive; Philip Green; Brenda Reichelderfer; David Robins; David Williams; Paul Heiden; Stephen Young, Group Finance Director (women: 1; men: 7)

Year end	30/12/2011
Turnover	£1,455,300,000
Pre-tax profit	£226,000,000

Nature of business: Meggitt plc is a global engineering group specialising in extreme environment components and sub-systems for aerospace, defence and energy markets

Company registration number: 432989

UK employees: 2,283

Total employees: 10,538

Charitable donations

UK cash (latest declared):	2011	£115,000
	2009	£4,000
Total UK:	2011	£115,000
Total worldwide:	2011	£115,000
Cash worldwide:	2011	£115,000

Corporate social responsibility

CSR committee: Taken from the CSR report:

> CR is overseen by our Group Corporate Affairs Director. HSE matters, trade compliance and ethics and business conduct are managed by a highly experienced team of functional specialists. The Board has appointed an Ethics and Trade Compliance Committee to ensure that we have effective programmes in these areas and to oversee their management. The Board reviews HSE at each of its meetings and receives a quarterly written report from the Vice-President, Health, Safety and Environment. Divisional presidents and site directors are responsible for implementing our policies at a local level.

CSR policy: Taken from the CSR report:

> Meggitt is committed to:

- Upholding sound corporate governance principles
- Providing a supportive, rewarding and safe working environment
- Conducting business relationships in an ethical manner
- Minimising the environmental impact of products and processes
- Acting as a responsible supplier and encouraging our contractors and suppliers to do the same
- Supporting our local communities

CSR report: The CSR report is contained within the annual report of the group.

Exclusions

No support for:

- Individuals
- Statutory organisations (such as schools)
- Trips abroad
- Mini buses
- Building costs or adaptations

Applications

In writing to the correspondent.

Other information

During the year, the group made charitable donations of £100,000 (2010: £100,000), principally to local charities serving the communities in which the group operates. The company made charitable donations of £15,000 (2010: £8,000).

Individual Meggitt sites work with the local community and support charities at their discretion. Yearly reports to the board detail the efforts of employees who give time and money to a wide range of national and local initiatives. Education Business Partnerships and the UK Government's STEM (Science, Technology, Engineering and Mathematics) initiative were supported locally by sites. Meggitt's headquarters, based in Dorset, UK, continued to sponsor the Arkwright Scholarship Trust, the Institute of Mechanical Engineers' Schools Aerospace Challenge, the local Community Foundation and the Poole Hospital Staff Excellence Awards.

According to the accounts for the Community Foundation for Bournemouth, Dorset and Poole, income received from Meggitt's was £2,500 and was applied for the purposes of The Meggitt Fund (see details given below).

The Meggitt Fund

This fund is managed on behalf of Meggitt plc based at Bournemouth International Airport. The company, in partnership with the Community Foundation for Bournemouth, Dorset and Poole seeks to support small voluntary/community groups working to benefit local people and address community need in the Bournemouth, Poole and/or Dorset area.

Grants of between £50 and £500 are available. However, this fund is very popular so it will be looking to make grants of between £50 and £200.

Who can apply

Constituted local community groups e.g. charities, voluntary organisations, not-for-profit organisations and social enterprise groups may be eligible to apply. Priority will be given to small, local and under-funded community groups.

You can apply for a grant by making an online application at: www.localgiving4dorset.org.uk. If you require a paper application ring 01202 292255.

For any further information or an informal chat call Kathy Boston-Mammah on 01202 292255 or email: kathy@cfbdp.org

Melrose plc

Business services

Correspondent: Company Secretary, Leconfield House, Curzon Street, London W1J 5JA (tel: 020 7647 4500; fax: 020 7647 4501; website: www.melroseplc.net)

Directors: Christopher Miller, Chair; David Roper, Chief Executive; Simon Peckham; Geoffrey Martin, Group Finance Director; Miles Templeman; Perry Crosthwaite; John Grant; Justin Dowley (women: 0; men: 8)

Year end	31/12/2011
Turnover	£1,153,900,000
Pre-tax profit	£97,400,000

Nature of business: Melrose, which is listed on the London Stock Exchange, seeks to acquire businesses, improve them, realise the value created and return it to shareholders.

Company registration number: 4763064

Total employees: 8,123

Charitable donations

UK cash (latest declared):	2009	£8,750
	2008	£8,750
Total worldwide:	2011	£50,000
Cash worldwide:	2011	£50,000

Corporate social responsibility

CSR committee: See 'CSR Policy' above.

CSR policy: The following statement is taken from the company's 2011 annual report:

> Due to the heavy industrial nature of some of the group activities, the directors recognise that its operations will potentially impact on a wide variety of stakeholders in terms of social, environmental and ethical matters, including employees, customers, suppliers and local communities.
>
> Many of the group's businesses have social and ethical policies, with responsibility for communication and implementation resting with relevant senior divisional managers. Such policies apply and extend to local law and standards and as a minimum include equal opportunities and anti-discrimination policies.

CSR report: No report published.

Applications

In writing to the correspondent.

Other information

The group paid £50,000 (2010: £21,550) to charities during the year. The majority of the businesses provided community support during the year with efforts ranging from charitable donations to voluntary assistance and fundraising.

John Menzies plc

Distribution, logistics

Correspondent: Gordon McVinnie, Charity Fund Administrator, 108 Princes Street, Edinburgh EH2 3AA (tel: 01312 258555; fax: 01312 201491; website: www.johnmenziesplc.com)

Directors: Iain Napier, Chair; Eric Born; Paul Dollman; Ian Harley; Ian Harrison; Dermot Jenkinson; David McIntosh; Octavia Morley; Craig Smyth; John Geddes (women: 1; men: 9)

Year end	31/12/2010
Turnover	£1,899,700,000
Pre-tax profit	£48,500,000

Nature of business: Logistics support services group.

Company registration number: SC4970

UK employees: 12,657

Total employees: 21,015

Charitable donations

UK cash (latest declared):	2010	£50,000
	2009	£57,000
	2007	£86,000
	2006	£112,000
	2005	£125,000
Total UK:	2010	£50,000
Total worldwide:	2010	£50,000
Cash worldwide:	2010	£50,000

Corporate social responsibility

CSR committee: There was no evidence of a CSR Committee.

CSR policy: This information was obtained from the company's CSR Report:

> We believe that our business conduct, policies and guidelines which we have in place concerning ethics, sound business practices and wider governance issues will not only enhance our standing in the community, but also provide a better business for all our stakeholders.
>
> In addition to supporting local causes where Menzies employees are involved, we aim to provide significant levels of support to a small number of charities nominated by each operating division each year.

CSR report: A full CSR report was available from the company's website.

Exclusions

No support for animal welfare, appeals from individuals, enterprise/training, overseas projects, political appeals, religious appeals, or science/technology.

Applications

Unsolicited applications are not considered.

Other information

Charitable donations totalling £50,000 were made during 2010.

The John M Menzies Community Fund

Donations requests received from employees are supported through the John M Menzies Community Fund. The group employs more than 19,000 people in 27 countries all around the world, many of whom participate in various forms of charitable, voluntary and other community-related work.

The John M Menzies Community Fund makes individual cash awards of up to £350 per employee, or £700 per team of employees, undertaking a charitable or community project. During 2010, some 30 applications were supported by this fund to a total of £8,150.

The Charities Fund

The fund is set each year by the group board which nominates charities to receive donations and in 2010 over £42,000 was donated to a small number of selected organisations. Beneficiaries included: Newstraid Benevolent Fund; Parikrma Humanity Foundation and Make A Wish Foundation.

Merck Sharp and Dohme Ltd

Pharmaceuticals

Correspondent: R Robinski, Company Secretary, Hertford Road, Hoddesdon, Hertfordshire EN11 9BU (tel: 01992 467272; fax: 01992 467270; website: www.msd-uk.com)

Directors: D. K. Khanna; M. A. C. McDowell; R. J. Armitage

Year end	31/12/2010
Turnover	£559,258,000
Pre-tax profit	£84,963,000

Nature of business: MSD is the UK subsidiary of Merck, a leading healthcare company that discovers, develops, manufactures and markets a wide range of innovative pharmaceutical products to improve human health.

MSD has committed substantial investment to research and manufacturing in the UK because of the unrivalled scientific excellence and skills base available here. It has two sites in the UK:

- Headquarters and pharmaceutical research and development laboratories in Hoddesdon, Hertfordshire
- Manufacturing at Cramlington in Northumberland

Company registration number: 820771

Main locations: Hoddesdon, Cramlington

Total employees: 1,113

Charitable donations

UK cash (latest declared):	2010	£7,000
	2008	£0
	2006	£32,000
	2005	£51,000
	2004	£70,000
Total UK:	2010	£7,000
Total worldwide:	2010	£7,000
Cash worldwide:	2010	£7,000

Corporate social responsibility

CSR committee: Taken from the group's 2011 CSR report:

> The Office of Corporate Responsibility coordinates the development, implementation and communication of Merck's global corporate responsibility approach and, with the Public Policy and Responsibility Council, for reporting on Merck's corporate responsibility performance. The Office of Corporate Responsibility works with business units and functional areas to integrate Merck's corporate responsibility principles into business policies, strategies and practices and brings the voice of external stakeholders into decision-making processes.

CSR policy: Taken from the Responsibility section of the group's website:

> We contribute to our communities in three key ways:
>
> - Direct and indirect economic contributions, such as employment, training, support of local suppliers and local R&D, and paying taxes
> - Managing our community impacts – for example, by ensuring confidence in environmental and safety performance and respecting human rights
> - Addressing community needs through philanthropy and community involvement

We were unable to determine the ratio of women to men on the board.

CSR report: Published annually on the group's website with further information in its annual report and accounts.

Other information

In 2010 the company gave £7,000 in charitable donations. We have no details of beneficiaries.

Information taken from the group's 2011 CSR report:

> In a variety of ways, Merck's philanthropic and employee volunteer programs address local community needs, support environmental stewardship, respond in times of emergency, and enable our employees to contribute to the well-being of their communities. Community giving is managed jointly by the Office of Corporate Philanthropy and regional and local management, supported by regional and local committees engaged with community stakeholders in identifying relevant community needs.

Merck's global community giving appears to be focused on overseas projects.

The Mersey Docks and Harbour Company

Transport and communications

Correspondent: C R Marrison Gill, Company Secretary, Maritime Centre, Port of Liverpool, Liverpool L21 1LA (tel: 01519 496000; fax: 01519 496300; website: www.merseydocks.co.uk)

Directors: J. Whittaker, Chair; T. E. Allison; G. E. Hodgson; S. Underwood; M. Whitworth

Year end	31/03/2011
Turnover	£117,592,000
Pre-tax profit	£49,223,000

Nature of business: The principal activities of the group are the operation and maintenance of port facilities on the Rivers Mersey and Medway, provision of cargo handling and associated services, and the conservancy and pilotage of the Ports of Liverpool and Medway and their approaches and the development of their respective dock estates.

Company registration number: 7438262

Main locations: Sheerness, Liverpool, Heysham, Birkenhead

Charitable donations

UK cash (latest declared):	2011	£50,000
	2009	£152,594
	2008	£162,511
	2007	£168,458
	2006	£150,773
Total UK:	2011	£50,000
Total worldwide:	2011	£50,000
Cash worldwide:	2011	£50,000

Corporate social responsibility

CSR policy: No CSR details available.

We were unable to determine the ratio of women to men on the board.

Exclusions

No support for political appeals.

Applications

In writing to the correspondent.

Other information

During 2010/11, the company made charitable donations totalling £50,000 (2009/10: £50,000). The company appears to make its donations to The Mersey Docks and Harbour Charitable Fund.

The Mersey Docks and Harbour Charitable Fund (Charity Commission no: 206913)

The fund gives grants annually to certain local charities. The trust was set up with three objectives:

- Reward of people assisting in the preservation of the life of the crew of any ship wrecked in the port of Liverpool or in the preservation of the ship or cargo or in the preserving or endeavouring to preserve people from drowning
- Relief of sick, disabled or superannuated men in the dock service or the families of such men who were killed in service
- Benefit of charities in the town or port of Liverpool

In 2010, the fund made donations totalling £44,000. Beneficiaries of the funds charitable donations include: Community Foundation for Merseyside (£23,750); The Mersey Mission to Seafarers (£10,000); Plaza Community Cinema (£3,000); National Museums Merseyside (£2,350); and St Joseph's Hospice (£1,000).

Metaswitch Networks Ltd

Information technology

Correspondent: Company Secretary, 100 Church Street, Enfield, Middlesex EN2 6BQ (tel: 020 8366 1177; fax: 020 8363 1468; website: www.metaswitch.com)

Directors: John Lazar, Chief Executive Officer; William Coughran; Ian Ferguson; Benjamin Ball; James Goetz; Deep Shah; Kevin DeNuccio; Jeffry Allen; Graeme MacArthur (women: 0; men: 9)

Year end	31/08/2011
Turnover	£94,888,000
Pre-tax profit	£5,282,620

Nature of business: Providers of communication and telephony software and hardware technology to major parts of the world's computer industry, to service providers and to large enterprises.

Formerly known as Data Connections Ltd.

Company registration number: 1578918

Main locations: Enfield

Total employees: 628

Charitable donations

UK cash (latest declared):	2008	£147,500
	2007	£101,400
	2006	£91,000
	2005	£18,000
Total worldwide:	2011	£89,000
Cash worldwide:	2011	£89,000

Corporate social responsibility

CSR policy: No CSR information found.

Applications

In writing to the correspondent.

Other information

In 2010/11 the company made charitable donations of £89,000. Details of beneficiaries were not available and no relevant community giving information could be found on the group's website.

Michelin Tyre plc

Motors and accessories

Correspondent: Christine Reynolds, Corporate Image Specialist, Campbell Road, Stoke-on-Trent ST4 4EY (tel: 01782 402000; fax: 01782 402011; email: christine.reynolds@uk.michelin.com; website: www.michelin.co.uk)

Directors: E. Le Corre; P. Benther; P. Verneuil; K. Shepherd; G. Alderman; T. Haines; M. Scovell

Year end	31/12/2011
Turnover	£962,497,000
Pre-tax profit	£39,232,000

Nature of business: The manufacture and sale of tyres, tubes, wheels and accessories, maps and guides, and mobility support services.

Company registration number: 84559

Main locations: Ballymena, Stoke-on-Trent, Dundee

Total employees: 2,677

Membership: BITC, LBG

Charitable donations

UK cash (latest declared):	2011	£83,500
	2009	£125,000
	2007	£125,000
Total UK:	2011	£83,500
Total worldwide:	2011	£83,500
Cash worldwide:	2011	£83,500

Corporate social responsibility

CSR committee: No details published.

> **CSR policy:** The following five core values today form the basis of our Corporate Social Responsibility Charter, known as 'Performance and Responsibility Michelin':
>
> - Respect for people
> - Respect for customers
> - Respect for shareholders
> - Respect for the environment
> - Respect for facts
>
> As part of its value 'respect for people', Michelin plays an active role in the communities local to its activities.

Unable to determine the ratio of women to men on the board.

CSR report: None available from website.

Exclusions

Michelin Tyre plc's Community Involvement Programme does not support requests which relate to:

- Organisations that do not have tax-exempt status
- Individuals
- Political organisations, candidates or lobby organisations
- Organisations with a limited constituency or membership
- Travel costs for groups or individuals
- Advertising
- Organisations outside the United Kingdom
- Activities that are not in line with Michelin's corporate values and image

Applications

Contacts

- Ballymena Ballymena-PRM@uk.michelin.com
- Dundee deborah.richardson@uk.michelin.com
- National christine.reynolds@uk.michelin.com
- Stoke-on-Trent michelin.requests@uk.michelin.com

Note: the 'National' contact should only be used for organisations that have a national presence or work on a national basis.

Application procedure

- All applications must be supported by a completed application form which can be downloaded from www.michelinrespectforcommunities.com/about-prm.aspx
- Make sure you meet the criteria outlined in 'Other information' before applying
- Add any supporting evidence, and email the correspondent concerned

Other information

During the year the company gave £83,500 in charitable donations. The following information is taken from the company's website:

> Our Aim is:
>
> - To enrich the quality of life in the communities where we live and work
> - To engage our employees in opportunities to positively contribute to the communities where we live and work
> - To enhance education, the environment and safety within our local communities
>
> Achieved through charitable donations and employee activities.
>
> *Focus Areas:*
>
> *Education*
>
> We are committed to developing creative thinkers for tomorrow's workplace. We foster and support programmes that build reading, literacy and numeracy skills within local schools. We also promote scientific and technical professions and encourage youth development through sport and culture. We believe these

programmes nurture creativity and develop important life and work skills.

Mobility Safety & Environment
We are committed to support programmes that reduce the impact of our activities on the environment. In addition, we look to support programmes that sustain our natural environment and promote green mobility. We work to educate, raise awareness of and sustain better mobility through road safety initiatives.

Community Enhancement
We are committed to supporting programmes that enrich the quality of life for individuals and our communities as a whole. Providing support in Health & Human services should be considered and we also believe the arts and our heritage are a powerful way to expose people to different cultures and celebrate the diversity of all people.

Getting support
If you would like to submit a request for support the company's website advises:

Michelin strives to build relationships with organisations that seek to benefit our local communities. We give the highest priority to organisations in our core focus areas of education, mobility safety and environment. Prior to submitting a request for support, the organisation should determine whether it falls within one of the core focus areas and meets our support guidelines. [See 'Applications' for information on how to apply.]

Support guidelines
Eligibility

- Michelin Tyre plc only provides support to charities, educational establishments and 'not for profit' entities. Support is generally awarded for specific activities, not general operating costs, however some operating costs may be allocated for the administration of a project
- Michelin seeks to support worthwhile initiatives in the communities *local* to its manufacturing operations at Stoke-On-Trent, Dundee and Ballymena

Payroll giving: The Give As You Earn scheme is operated by the company.

Micro Focus International plc

Business services

Correspondent: Company Secretary, The Lawn, 22–30 Old Bath Road, Newbury, Berkshire RG14 1QN (tel: 01635 32646; website: www.microfocus.com)

Directors: Kevin Loosemore, Chair; Mike Phillips, Chief Financial Officer; David Maloney; Paul Pester; Tom Skelton; Karen Slatford (women: 1; men: 5)

Year end	30/04/2011
Turnover	£270,095,000
Pre-tax profit	£70,935,000

Nature of business: 'Micro Focus, a member of the FTSE 250, provides innovative software that allows companies to dramatically improve the business value of their enterprise applications.'

Company registration number: 5134647

Total employees: 1,434

Charitable donations

UK cash (latest declared):	2011	£35,000
	2010	£46,900
	2009	£17,100
Total UK:	2011	£35,000
Total worldwide:	2011	£35,000
Cash worldwide:	2011	£35,000

Corporate social responsibility

CSR committee: CSR policies at Micro Focus are reviewed and monitored at board level on a six monthly basis, with non-executive director involvement in the CSR committee, which meets regularly to agree priorities and progress activities. During the year to 30 April 2011, the CSR committee met six times.

CSR policy: The following extracts are taken from the annual report and accounts:

The board, management team and employees are committed to operating the group in accordance with best practice in corporate social responsibility. Employees, shareholders, customers, business partners, suppliers and local communities all play a part in the structure and development of the Micro Focus CSR programme, as part of a broader commitment to effective corporate governance for the group. In this context, Micro Focus seeks to integrate CSR considerations into all aspects of its day-to-day operations.

CSR report: CSR is reported on within the company's annual report and accounts.

Applications

In writing to the correspondent.

Other information

In 2011 the group made charitable donations of around £35,000 to a number of local and national charities and other local organisations.

The company has a gift programme that matches employee donations. It also has a policy in place to encourage employees to volunteer a certain number of hours to assist local organisations.

The following extract is taken from the company's annual report 2011:

Community and charity work
Micro Focus' impact on the community has grown in line with its corporate expansion. The group is now active in 29 countries and serves more than 11,000 customers, independent software vendors and partners together with many more end users. Employees proactively support their local communities and Micro Focus encourages these initiatives. Corporate support is provided on a funds-matching basis and a number of man-days per month for team and national activities which directly benefit a charity. Policies are designed to select charities and causes that demonstrate strong educational and local impact. Project grants are offered throughout the year, with allocations limited so that charity and community initiatives are spread evenly over time, after approval by local country charity committees.

A team in Sofia, Bulgaria donated clothing and books, and set up an IT suite in a local orphanage. In Newbury, UK, employees gave money to fund a Christmas lunch for 50 local elderly residents who had no family nearby. In Mountain View, USA, employees provided 15 backpacks filled with school supplies for needy children.

In addition to community and charitable work, Micro Focus runs the Academic ConnecTIONs Program to support Enterprise IT skills development in academic institutions. The technology industry is one of the fastest growing industries in the world, and Micro Focus recognises the value in nurturing and encouraging the skills required to sustain the pace and breadth of the growing technology industry. The ACTION program is designed to promote the teaching of COBOL and modernization technologies in universities worldwide with free software downloads for students and the provision of materials to help colleges develop relevant courses in application modernisation technologies.

Microsoft Ltd

Computer software

Correspondent: Harsha Gadhvi, UK Community Affairs Manager, Microsoft Campus, Thames Valley Park, Reading RG6 1WG (tel: 0870 601 0100; fax: 08706020 100; email: ukcharity@microsoft.com; website: www.microsoft.com/en-gb)

Directors: Michel Van der Bel; Andy Hart; Barry Ridgway; Colin Brown; Chris Parker; John Jester; Mark Taylor; Neil Thompson; Dr Nicola Hodson; Theresa McHenry; Scott Dodds (women: 2; men: 9)

Year end	30/06/2011
Turnover	£663,198,000
Pre-tax profit	£66,538,000

Nature of business: Microsoft Ltd. is a subsidiary company of Microsoft Corporation – based in Redmond, Washington State – USA. It provides marketing and support to other group companies. Globally, a computer software manufacturer and supplier.

Company registration number: 1624297

Main locations: Edinburgh, London, Manchester, Reading

UK employees: 2,500

Total employees: 2,500

Membership: BITC

Charitable donations

UK cash (latest declared):	2011	£312,000
	2009	£425,000
	2008	£286,000
	2007	£258,200
	2006	£188,000
Total UK:	2011	£312,000
Total worldwide:	2011	£540,000,000
Cash worldwide:	2011	£30,000,000

Corporate social responsibility

CSR committee: No specific details found.

CSR policy: This information was obtained from the group's website:

> Microsoft partners with a number of charity and community organisations to help deliver the powerful benefits of technology to the widest possible constituency.
>
> Our partners include organisations that work in disability and accessibility, employment and training, education, health and provision of low-cost technology solutions to disadvantaged families and individuals.
>
> From cash and in kind donations to the many thousands of hours volunteered by our employees, we are proud to play an active and positive role in the communities we serve.

CSR report: A CSR report was available from the company's website.

Exclusions

Microsoft is only able to donate cash to selected major charity projects. They support a scheme to recycle PC's. No support is given, in any form, for political, religious or racially motivated projects.

Applications

In writing to the correspondent.

Other information

During 2010/11 the company Microsoft Ltd declared charitable donations of just under £312,000 (2009/10: £251,000). Although it is likely that the UK received much more than this from the global company, we have no geographical breakdown to determine the amount, either for cash donations or in kind contributions.

Microsoft's community affairs website contains extensive information on, and examples of, its community support in the UK and abroad and the following information regarding Microsoft's community support in the UK is taken from its website.

> *Charities:*
> Microsoft is involved in community projects right across the UK – both directly and through a series of effective partnerships which target help and resources where they are needed most. Technology helps nonprofits reduce costs, boost productivity, raise funds, and deliver new and improved services to their local communities. Microsoft has a longstanding commitment to ensuring that technology is accessible to nonprofits around the world, bringing the benefits of technology to local communities.
>
> **Donating software:** In 2011 we donated more than £540 million in software to 46,886 non-profits in 113 countries/ regions.
>
> *Education*
> Microsoft programs have a focus on helping youth and young adults around the world obtain the skills that they need, connect them to opportunities, and support them in pursuing their dreams. We have the unique ability through technology and partnerships to make education and learning more accessible and more engaging for them.
>
> The company has continued its efforts to help 250 million students and teachers around the world through the Partners in Learning programme which is set to be completed by 2013. The programme aims to help teachers build their skills, share best practices with one another, and innovate in their classrooms.
>
> *Fostering Innovation*
> The Microsoft Imagine Cup supports innovation from young people across the world to showcase their talent and inspire the next generation.
>
> In the UK, Microsoft works with and through charity partnerships to deliver the Unlimited Potential programme. All of our UK partners share our passion for the contribution that IT and IT skills can make to disadvantaged individuals and groups and through their networks we are able to reach out to those in greatest need.
>
> *Unlimited Potential*
> Launched in 2003 Unlimited Potential is a Microsoft global community investment programme, focused on improving lifelong learning for disadvantaged young people and adults by providing access to IT training and skills.
>
> The Microsoft Giving programme provides in kind support to charities and community groups each year by donating software for use in fundraising or helping to run voluntary organisations.
>
> *Volunteering:*
> At Microsoft we like to enhance our support by giving the community what we value most – the time and skills of our employees. With that in mind we introduced a formalised Employee Volunteering Programme in 2003. The UK programme enables employees to get involved in a way that suits them – whether they would like to spend a couple of hours helping out on a one-off key skills workshop or make a long-term commitment to mentor a young person.
>
> Our volunteering is delivered through a number of external partners – Leonard Cheshire Disability, Central Berkshire Education Business Partnership, IT4Communities and The Prince's Scottish Youth Business Trust amongst others.

Matching: 'Microsoft runs a matched giving scheme to encourage individual fundraising activities. The scheme matches staff fundraising up to £7,500 per annum, per employee. With employee contributions and the corporate match, we contributed a £60 million.'

Payroll giving: 'By signing up to GAYE, employees can choose to donate to a charity directly from their salary pre tax. Employees can choose any cause they wish to receive monthly donations.'

For more information on Microsoft's community investment, visit its website: www.microsoft.com/uk/citizenship

The Midcounties Co-operative

Financial services, retail – supermarkets

Correspondent: Social Responsibility Manager, Co-operative House, Warwick Technology Park, Warwick CV34 6DA (tel: 01865 249241; website: www.midcounties.coop)

Directors: Patrick Gray, President; John Boot; Helen Wiseman; Sheila Allen; Steve Allsopp; Olivia Birch; Isobel Burbridge; Bernadette Connor; Ruth Fitzjohn; Roy Frodsham; Margaret Jarvis; Donald Morrison; Jean Nunn-Price; Trish Poole; George Waddell; Vivien Woodell (women: 9; men: 7)

Year end	28/01/2012
Turnover	£641,131,000
Pre-tax profit	£12,379,000

Nature of business: The society has a number of diverse trading activities covering food, motor, property, travel childcare and funeral services.

Company registration number: IP19025R

Main locations: Gloucester, Oxford, Swindon

UK employees: 8,500

Total employees: 8,500

Membership: BITC

Charitable donations

UK cash (latest declared):	2012	£1,524,000
	2010	£260,000
	2008	£203,790
	2006	£150,000
Total UK:	2012	£2,800,000
Total worldwide:	2012	£2,800,000
Cash worldwide:	2012	£1,524,000

Community involvement

Information is taken from the company's 2011/12 annual report and accounts.

> Through fundraising, grant giving and projects we have supported 1,525 organisations during the year and given the equivalent of more than £2.8 million back to our local communities. Included in

this figure is £1.5 million of our new £2 million Community Fund, which distributes grants twice a year to support grassroots community groups. This £1.5 million comes from dormant share accounts with additional funding sourced through the Community Foundation Network.

Our two year charity partnership with *Women's Aid*, the national coordinating body for a network of domestic violence charities, began in February 2011. We raised £170,000 during the year which will really help make a difference. We were also proud to be shortlisted as an Example of National Excellence by Business in the Community for our work with the Oxfordshire Primary Care Trust in improving the dental health of young people.

Charity Partner: Women's Aid has been the company's charity partner for the past few years, and the company states that it is not looking for another charity partner until 2015.

Corporate giving

In 2011/12 investment in community and co-operative initiatives totalled more than £2.8 million (2010/11: £1.2 million). This figure includes the money given out as grants, the value of volunteering work and the annual investment in co-operative initiatives.

Employee-led support

Colleagues donated more than 32,500 volunteer hours to community activity (2010: 26,000 hours) and 1,950 colleagues took part in a volunteer project for the first time (2010: 1,600). Participation in community volunteering has risen from 38.3% of colleagues to 51.1% and our colleague volunteering has been valued at more than £472,000 (2010: £376,000).

Corporate social responsibility

CSR committee: During 2010 Midcounties appointed a Social Responsibility Manager, reporting in to the Executive, to co-ordinate the Society's social responsibility strategy. This is supported by a structure that reaches deep into the organisation – from the Board of Directors to focus groups and key management colleagues.

CSR policy: Information on CSR taken from the 2011 CSR report:

Our board has carried out a thorough review of our social goals and ways to address the commitments we have made. Using Business in the Community's Corporate Responsibility (CR) Index framework as a guide we have selected the following key areas for our social responsibility agenda:

- Energy and environment
- Community
- Member engagement
- Managing the supply chain
- Colleague engagement and development
- Health and safety
- Diversity

CSR report: Published annually and available from the website.

Exclusions

Applications from outside the operating area of the Midcounties Co-operative Society, i.e. Oxfordshire, Gloucestershire, Swindon, parts of Buckinghamshire and the West Midlands.

Midcounties Co-operative is also unable to help with funding for individuals, businesses and funding for overseas projects.

Applications

Applicants for Co-operative Community Funding must apply online – www.midcounties.coop/community/co-operative-community-funding.

Miller Group Ltd

Building/construction, property

Correspondent: Pamela Smyth, Company Secretary, Miller House, 2 Lochside View, Edinburgh Park, Edinburgh EH12 9DH (tel: 0870 336 5000; fax: 0870 336 5002; website: www.miller.co.uk)

Directors: Michael Whitman, Chair; Keith Miller, Group Chief Executive; John Richards, Group Finance Director; Mark Brown (women: 0; men: 4)

Year end	31/12/2011
Turnover	£587,600,000
Pre-tax profit	(£92,800,000)

Nature of business: Housing, property development, construction and mining.

Company registration number: SC018135

Main locations: Glasgow

UK employees: 1,117

Total employees: 1,117

Membership: BITC

Charitable donations

UK cash (latest declared):	2011	£115,000
	2009	£88,000
	2007	£177,000
Total UK:	2011	£115,000
Total worldwide:	2011	£115,000
Cash worldwide:	2011	£115,000

Corporate social responsibility

CSR committee: No specific committee details published.

CSR policy: The following statement is taken from the 2011 annual report and accounts.

A focus on people and communities

People lie at the heart of everything we do within The Miller Group. It is people, our own dedicated and highly trained staff members, who successfully complete our projects and, of course, we carry out our work for people. During 2011, we continued to review our CR programme to ensure that the resources available became more focused than ever on people. We were delighted to achieve silver accreditation from Investors in People (2010) across our businesses and we are looking to both maintain and improve our position as an employer of choice. We aim to be considerate in everything we do, from the construction of buildings, homes and developments we create to the employment opportunities we extend to our staff, and the care and support we offer the communities where we work. By combining these elements in all our projects, we hope to demonstrate our credentials as a good employer and a good neighbour.

CSR report: Review of CSR activities and performance is contained within the annual report and accounts.

Applications

In writing to the correspondent.

Other information

During 2011, the company made charitable contributions totalling £90,000 (2010: £63,000).

We actively encourage our employees to nominate charities which they believe deserve to receive a donation through our employee nominated charities initiative. In 2011, the charities chosen by our employees were The Anthony Nolan Trust, BLISS and Guide Dogs for the Blind Association. During the year, focus moved from supporting professional sports people to community-based activities and the arts. Beneficiaries include: Teenage Cancer Trust; the Young Persons Unit of The Royal Edinburgh Hospital; a theatre workshop for Drummond High School in Edinburgh; Place 2 be; Bliss; Anthony Nolan Trust; Guide Dogs for the Blind.

Sponsorship: The company worked with Macmillan Cancer Support sponsoring its annual Edinburgh Macmillan Art Show, which raised £46,500.

Matched funding: The company operates a Matched Funding Scheme. During 2011, employee fundraising efforts were matched through the scheme and made the company made further charitable donations totalling £25,000.

Mitchells and Butlers plc

Retail – restaurants/fast food

Correspondent: Doug Evans, Company Secretary and General Counsel, 27 Fleet Street, Birmingham B3 1JP (tel: 0870 609 3000; fax: 01212 332246; website: www.mbplc.com)

Directors: Ron Robson; Bob Ivell, Chair; Tim Jones, Finance Director; Douglas McMahon (women: 0; men: 5)

Year end	24/09/2011
Turnover	£1,796,000,000
Pre-tax profit	£132,000,000

Nature of business: Operator of managed pubs and pub restaurants.

Company registration number: 4551498

Main locations: Birmingham

Total employees: 40,728

Charitable donations

UK cash (latest declared):	2011	£65,000
	2009	£215,000
	2007	£215,000
	2006	£200,000
	2005	£143,000
Total UK:	2011	£65,000
Total worldwide:	2011	£65,000
Cash worldwide:	2011	£65,000

Corporate social responsibility

CSR committee: No information found.

CSR policy: Statement taken from the 2011 CSR review:

> For Mitchells & Butlers social responsibility means many things: providing our customers with quality, tasty food; making a positive difference to the communities in which we trade; the retailing of alcohol responsibly; investing in our employees' training and career development; understanding our environmental impact.

CSR report: Published annually.

Exclusions

The company will not support advertising space, political causes, sporting events, and religious appeals.

Applications

In writing to the correspondent.

Applicants must meet company criteria, which can be found on the company's website under 'Community and charity support'.

Other information

In 2010/11 around £65,000 has been donated to a variety of causes. This includes a £25,000 donation to the company's partner charity Marie Curie Cancer Care, and £40,000 of donations (ranging from approximately £100 to £500 in each case) to over 80 local and national charities covering a wide range of charitable purposes, including County Air Ambulance and the MS Society.

The company operates a community awards scheme which supports donations via their employees by supporting charities of their choosing to encourage fundraising. Many of the company's pubs have been involved with this scheme and have managed to raise money for organisations such as Cancer Research UK; Help for Heroes; the Alzheimer Society; and Great Ormond Street Hospital. Around £200,000 was given for charitable purposes in total, the majority of this was raised by employees and guests.

Charity partner: Marie Curie Cancer Care.

MITIE Group plc

Business services

Correspondent: Corporate Responsibility Team, 8 Monarch Court, The Brooms, Emersons Green, Bristol BS16 7FH (tel: 01179 708800; fax: 01173 026743; website: www.mitie.com)

Directors: Roger Matthews, Chair; Ian Stewart; Ruby McGregor-Smith, Chief Executive; Suzanne Baxter; Bill Robson; Larry Hirst; David Jenkins; Terry Morgan; Graeme Potts (women: 2; men: 7)

Year end	31/03/2011
Turnover	£1,891,400,000
Pre-tax profit	£86,800,000

Nature of business: The company provides facilities, property and asset management for public and private sector businesses.

Company registration number: SC 19230

Total employees: 58,860

Membership: BITC

Charitable donations

UK cash (latest declared):	2011	£191,000
	2010	£110,500
	2009	£184,000
Total UK:	2011	£191,000
Total worldwide:	2011	£543,000
Cash worldwide:	2011	£191,000

Corporate social responsibility

CSR committee: Corporate Responsibility Team.

CSR policy: See 'Other information' for community policy.

CSR report: Sustainability Review contained within the annual report and accounts.

Applications

In writing to the correspondent.

Other information

Donations to charity and community projects made during the year amounted to £191,000 (2010: £110,500). The total value of community investment was £543,000 (2010: £392,000)].

The company has recently (September 2012) established **The Mitie Foundation** (Charity Commission no. 1148858). The foundation has general charitable purposes and can give grants to individuals or organisations in the UK and anywhere in the world.

The following information is taken from the company's website and relates to its corporate responsibility policy:

> There are so many demands on businesses from charities and community groups for financial and in kind support and MITIE prioritises these demands by implementing a community strategy that:
>
> - Principally provides financial and in kind support for six employee nominated charities over a two/three year partnership
> - Supports our existing Construction and Facilities Management Skills Centre schools
> - Supports other charities that are local or relevant to our business operations
> - Internationally, supports the Bansang Hospital Appeal Charity in Gambia
> - Operates an employee volunteer programme to provide pro bono expertise for 'World of Work', 'Community Challenge' and 'Environmental Action' events; and
> - Supports organisations, including Prince's Trust and Business in the Community that promote employability opportunities for disadvantaged communities

The company has formed a close relationship with Veteran Aid, the UK charity for veterans in crisis. Having worked with the charity for just over a year, it has delivered a second mentoring programme that helps ex-service personnel in their efforts to return to the workplace.

Moneysupermarket.com Group plc

Miscellaneous

Correspondent: Corporate Social Responsibility Team, Community, Moneysupermarket House, St David's Park, Ewloe, Chester CH5 3UZ (tel: 01244 665700; fax: 01244 398753; website: corporate.moneysupermarket.com)

Directors: Gerald Corbett, Chair; Peter Plumb, Chief Executive Officer; Simon Nixon; Paul Doughty, Chief Financial Officer; David Osborne; Graham Donoghue; Michael Wemms; Rob Rowley; Bruce Carnegie-Brown; Darren Drabble (women: 0; men: 10)

Year end	31/12/2011
Turnover	£181,048,000
Pre-tax profit	£24,282,000

Nature of business: Comparison websites.

Company registration number: 6160943

Total employees: 430

Charitable donations

UK cash (latest declared):	2011	£37,500
	2009	£33,000
	2008	£25,000
Total UK:	2011	£37,500
Total worldwide:	2011	£37,500
Cash worldwide:	2011	£37,500

Corporate social responsibility

CSR committee: No specific committee.

CSR policy: The following statement is taken from the company's annual report and accounts:

> The group operates with an underlying awareness of its wider responsibilities to society.

Communities and charities
The group's community initiative was launched in 2008 and has continued to develop during 2011. The initiative is focused on providing support to charities located within a few miles of the group's offices in Ewloe and so support is targeted primarily in Flintshire and Cheshire.

CSR report: Contained within the annual report and accounts.

Applications

In writing to the correspondent.

Other information

During the financial year ended 31 December 2011, the group made charitable donations of £37,500 (2010: £30,000). The following information is taken from the CSR report published in the 2011 report and accounts:

> A volunteer group of employees meets each month to review requests for donations from charities and to allocate funds according to agreed donation guidelines. Employees are also active in researching and seeking out local good causes that the group can help support. The initiative has been effective at harnessing the energy and enthusiasm of the group's employees to benefit the communities in which it operates. In 2011 the group made £2,000 per month available for the Community initiative. This funding has been channelled via the Charities Aid Foundation, enabling the group to make gross donations to registered charities.
>
> Over the course of the year the group has supported 43 charities including: Relate North Wales; Marie Curie Cancer Care; Flintshire Disability Forum; North Wales Super Kids; Age UK Cheshire; and Flintshire Deaf Children's Society
>
> In addition to the Community initiative, the group and its employees continue to select and support a charity on an annual basis. Over the course of the year the group's employees raised £13,500 for Wales Air Ambulance with the group match funding the same amount.
>
> The group launched in October 2011 a volunteering scheme through which the group is supporting a total of 60 volunteering days per year to help those who are less fortunate and thereby make a valuable contribution to our local community.

Charity of the Year 2011/12: Alzheimer's Society.

Morgan Advanced Materials plc (formerly Morgan Crucible Company plc)

Manufacturing

Correspondent: Paul Bolton, Company Secretary, Quadrant, 55–57 High Street, Windsor, Berkshire SL4 1LP (tel: 01753 837000; fax: 01753 850872; email: info@morganplc.com; website: www.morganadvancedmaterials.com)

Directors: Tim Stevenson, Chair; Mark Robertshaw, Chief Executive; Kevin Dangerfield; Andrew Hosty; Martin Flower; Andrew Given; Paul Bolton; Don Klas; Simon Heale; Peter Blausten (women: 0; men: 10)

Year end	01/01/2012
Turnover	£1,100,000,000
Pre-tax profit	£111,400,000

Nature of business: The company employs over 10,000 people around the world and has operating sites in 34 countries serving customers in over 100 countries. Its three Divisions have leading positions in their target niches in the aerospace, defence and protection, power generation, medical, petrochemical and iron and steel markets.

Company registration number: 286773

UK employees: 1,552

Total employees: 10,028

Charitable donations

UK cash (latest declared):	2011	£195,000
	2009	£90,000
	2008	£90,000
	2007	£87,000
	2006	£93,000
Total UK:	2011	£195,000
Total worldwide:	2012	£195,000
Cash worldwide:	2012	£195,000

Corporate social responsibility

CSR committee: There was no evidence of a separate CSR Committee.

CSR policy: This information was obtained from the company's annual report:

> The group's practice is to engage with local communities in relation to matter of mutual interest and concern.

CSR report: A CSR report was available within the group's annual report.

Exclusions

No support for: animal welfare; appeals from individuals; overseas projects; political appeals; religious appeals; science/technology; or sport.

Applications

In writing to the correspondent. Grant decisions are made by a donations committee which meets quarterly.

Other information

During the year, the company's donations totalled £195,000 (2009: £235,000). Time is also given and donations made by the company's employees around the world.

The company's annual report for 2011 states:

> During 2011, Morgan Crucible supported a number of initiatives at Group, Divisional and site level. The main emphasis of this support is to help disadvantaged young people and sponsor local community projects which can also engage and involve employees. Example initiatives include:
>
> - The group continued its three-year, £60,000 programme to support the Army Cadet Force Association (ACFA) Outreach Project
> - Morgan Crucible continues to support the joint Barnardo's/Outward Bound initiative which provides opportunities for young people to develop life skills at a centre in Ullswater, UK
> - The group also supported the British Heart Foundation and a number of other sports and health-related charities and appeals

J. P. Morgan Chase

Financial services

Correspondent: The Corporate Social Responsibility Committee, 10 Aldermanbury, London EC2V 7RF (website: www.jpmorgan.com)

Directors: Jamie Dimon, Chair and Chief Executive; James A. Bell; Crandall C. Bowles; Stephen B. Burke; David M. Cote; James S. Crown; Ellen V. Futter; William H. Gray III; Laban P. Jackson Jr; David C. Novak; Lee R. Raymond; William C. Weldon (women: 1; men: 11)

Year end	31/12/2011
Turnover	£61,980,000,000
Pre-tax profit	£17,050,700,000

Nature of business: Financial services organisation.

Company registration number: 288553

Main locations: London

Total employees: 260157

Charitable donations

UK cash (latest declared):	2008	£50,000
	2007	£209,000
	2006	£241,000
Total worldwide:	2011	£127,400,500
Cash worldwide:	2011	£127,400,500

Corporate social responsibility

CSR committee: There was evidence of a separate CSR Committee.

CSR policy: This information was obtained from the company's website:

> J.P. Morgan is committed to building vibrant communities, preserving our environment and promoting an inclusive culture across the globe that benefits people not only today, but for generations to come.

CSR report: The 2010 CSR report was available on the website.

Applications

In writing to the correspondent.

Other information

The company used to make its donations through the J P Morgan Foundation, however this charity has since been removed from the central register of charities.

The company states that in 2011 it donated £127 million and 370,000 hours to charity.

Morgan Stanley International Ltd

Financial services

Correspondent: Anish Shah, Morgan Stanley International Foundation, 20 Bank Street, London E14 4AD (tel: 020 7425 8000/020 7425 1302; fax: 020 7425 8984; email: communityaffairslondon@morganstanley.com; website: www.morganstanley.co.uk)

Directors: C. D. S. Bryce; F. R. Petitgas; C. E. Woodman; P. Bailas; T. C. Kelleher, Chair; I. Plenderleith; R. Rooney; D. A. Russell

Year end	31/12/2011
Turnover	£2,577,456,078
Pre-tax profit	£516,367,475

Nature of business: Principal activities: the provision of financial services to corporations, governments, financial institutions and individual investors.

Company registration number: 3584019

Main locations: London

UK employees: 5,000

Membership: BITC

Charitable donations

UK cash (latest declared):	2011	£990,000
	2008	£3,300,000
	2007	£5,603,000
	2005	£2,610,000
Total UK:	2011	£990,000
Total worldwide:	2011	£990,000
Cash worldwide:	2011	£990,000

Community involvement

Almost all the company's charitable giving in the UK appears to be through the **Morgan Stanley International Foundation** (Charity Commission no. 1042671).

The following information is taken from the report of the trustees in the 2011 annual report and accounts:

> The principal objective of the foundation is to be a proactive, leading charitable institution that works in partnership with the private, public and voluntary sectors to make a real difference to the communities in which we are located. The foundation achieves this through financial contributions and, more importantly, acting as a catalyst for firm commitment to, and employee involvement with, our local communities. In addition, the foundation seeks to be a leader in best practice in our industry in these activities.

Education and employment

The foundation works with registered charities and state-funded schools that provide benefit to communities across EMEA. The foundation seeks to work with organisations that can increase access and opportunity to young people aged 4–21. The programmes the foundation supports are based predominantly in educational institutions and specifically address academic achievement, raising inspiration, aspiration and enhancing employability skills.

Children's health

The foundation invests in innovations in children's health and development, working with charitable organisations, hospitals and community based initiatives, supporting young people aged 0–18. The foundation strives to ensure that more children have access to healthcare and innovative health programmes that will either save a child's life, or through prevention ensure their lifespan is increased enabling them to have a healthier and more meaningful life.

> ***Grants policy***
>
> The foundation gives grants through two different channels: direct charitable grants and employee matching grants. Direct charitable grants are made across the Europe, Middle East and Africa ('EMEA') region. Applications are invited for funding of projects in this region, and are reviewed at quarterly trustees' meetings against specific grant objectives. Multi-year grants are monitored on an annual basis to ensure the grant criteria continue to be met.
>
> The second area of grant making focuses on creating incentives for Morgan Stanley's employees' fundraising and volunteering efforts, as follows:
>
> The foundation currently matches any contribution raised by an employee for a charitable organisation, to a maximum of £2,000 per employee per event. In addition, the foundation invites applications from employees for matching of their time in volunteering, and the size of the grant is dependent on the employee's length of service with both Morgan Stanley and the charitable organisation.

Charity of the Year: Kids Company (2011/12).

Corporate giving

In 2011, Morgan Stanley made charitable donations of £900,000 (2010: £900,000) to the Morgan Stanley International Foundation.

Morgan Stanley International Foundation

In 2011, the foundation had total funds of £2.2 million and an income of £1.3 million. Just over £1.11 million was distributed in grants.

The largest grant of £717,600 was made to the firm's 'Charity of the Year' – Kids Company. Other beneficiaries receiving grants of £2,000 or more included: Isle of Dogs Community Association (£68,800); MEND (£60,000); East London Business Alliance (£55,000); Community Links (£50,000); Tower Hamlets Education Business Partnership (£25,000); School Home Support (£23,500); George Green's School and Skateco UK Ltd (£15,000 each); Old Ford Primary School and Young Enterprise Scotland (£10,000 each); Charjoe (£4,000); A Little Gesture (£3,300); Oxfam (£3,200); NSPCC (£2,900); and Action for Children (2,500).

In kind support

Morgan Stanley's Global Volunteer Month is a worldwide service initiative that encourages employees to give back to their communities. Held each June, the campaign engages employees in teams and individually on local service projects, serving as a springboard for year-round volunteer engagement. In 2011, over 20,000 employees volunteered on nearly 1,000 projects, contributing over 170,000 hours of service and benefiting over 500 nonprofit organisations.

As part of Morgan Stanley's community outreach, in June 2011 a record 27%of EMEA employees took part in the firm's Global Volunteer Month campaign. During this period EMEA employees logged 15,524 hours of volunteering, 50% more than the 2010 total.

Employee-led support

'Employee engagement in the community is a cornerstone of Morgan Stanley's culture and the foundation of our charitable efforts. The firm encourages, recognises and rewards employee generosity through extensive grants, matching initiatives and coordinated volunteer efforts.'

Matched funding: The company operates a matched funding scheme.

Corporate social responsibility

CSR committee: There is a community affairs department in the London branch.

CSR policy: The company's website states: 'Our global citizenship is a direct reflection of the firm's core values and enhances our ability to provide superior service to our clients, our employees and our communities.'

We were unable to determine the ratio of women to men on the board.

CSR report: There is an annual Sustainability report published but this contains very little information on UK charitable/community giving.

Exclusions

The company's website states:

MSI Foundation does not make contributions to organisations that fall within the following criteria:

- Organisations which are not registered as a non profit organisation with the appropriate regulatory agencies in their country (unless a state funded school).
- National or International charities which do not operate in the regions we are located.
- Grants will not be made to either political or religious organisations, 'pressure groups' or individuals outside the Firm who are seeking sponsorship either for themselves (e.g. to help pay for education) or for onward transmission to a charitable organisation.
- Programmes that do not include opportunities for employee volunteer engagement

Applications

All initial funding enquiries should be directed to the correspondent.

T. J. Morris Ltd

Retail – department and variety stores

Correspondent: G P McLoughlin, Company Secretary, Axis Business Park, East Lancs Road, Gillmoss, Liverpool L11 0JA (tel: 01515 302920; website: www.homebargains.co.uk)

Directors: T. J. Morris; J. Morris

Year end	30/06/2011
Turnover	£721,359,000
Pre-tax profit	£59,453,000

Nature of business: The principal activity of the company during the year was wholesale distribution and retailing of toiletries, cosmetics and other household products.

Company registration number: 1505036

Total employees: 6,912

Charitable donations

UK cash (latest declared):	2011	£113,300
	2009	£350,483
	2008	£33,846
	2007	£184,280
	2006	£44,614
Total UK:	2011	£113,300
Total worldwide:	2011	£113,300
Cash worldwide:	2011	£113,300

Corporate social responsibility

CSR committee: No details found.

CSR policy: We were unable to determine the ratio of women to men on the board.

CSR report: None published. The website has details of the group's community involvement.

Exclusions

No support for political appeals.

Applications

In writing to the correspondent.

Other information

In 2010/11, the company made charitable donations of £113,300 (2009/10: £120,000). We have no details of the beneficiaries.

Sponsorship includes: The Skylight Gallery in the Museum of Liverpool and Woolton's 2010 entry for the Britain-in-Bloom contest.

W. Morrison Supermarkets plc

Retail – supermarkets

Correspondent: Nigel Robertson, Director – Corporate Compliance and Responsibility, Hillmore House, Gain Lane, Bradford BD3 7DL (tel: 0845 611 5000; website: www.morrisons.co.uk)

Directors: Sir Ian Gibson, Chair; Dalton Philips, Chief Executive; Richard Pennycock; Nigel Robertson; Philip Cox; Penny Hughes; Johanna Waterous (women: 2; men: 5)

Year end	29/01/2012
Turnover	£18,000,000,000
Pre-tax profit	£947,000,000

Nature of business: Retail distribution of goods through the medium of supermarkets.

Company registration number: 358949

Main locations: Bradford

UK employees: 131,207

Total employees: 131,207

Membership: Arts & Business, BITC

Charitable donations

UK cash (latest declared):	2012	£100,000
	2009	£100,000
	2008	£100,000
	2007	£300,000
	2006	£200,000
Total UK:	2012	£2,400,000
Total worldwide:	2012	£2,400,000
Cash worldwide:	2012	£100,000

Corporate social responsibility

CSR committee: There was evidence of a Corporate Compliance and Responsibility Committee.

CSR policy: This information was obtained from the company's website:

> Annually we provide support to thousands of charities, fund-raisers and good causes, both nationally and in the communities which are home to our stores. A key focus for charitable giving is the fundraising we undertake with our main corporate charity partner, which is chosen by our colleagues.

CSR report: A CSR report was available from the company's website.

Exclusions

No response to circular appeals or support for the arts, overseas projects, or political appeals.

Applications

In writing to the correspondent.

Other information

During the period to end of January 2012, the Group made charitable donations amounting to £100,000 (2010: £100,000). The donations were mainly small donations to support local communities. In addition the Group supported a variety of charitable activities, community initiatives and national events, which totalled £2.3 million.

The company's Charity of the Year is Save The Children until the end of the 2013/14 financial year; however, this relationship may be extended beyond that as the company has done in previous years.

Mothercare plc

Catalogue shopping, retail – department and variety stores

Correspondent: Charity Administrator, The Mothercare Charitable Foundation, Cherry Tree Road, Watford, Hertfordshire WD24 6SH (tel: 01923 241000/01923 206077; email: debra.barnes@mothercare.co.uk; website: www.mothercare.com)

Directors: Ian Peacock, Chair; Ben Gordon, Chief Executive; Neil Harrington, Finance Director; Bernard Cragg; David Williams; Amanda McKenzie; Richard Rivers (women: 1; men: 6)

Year end	26/03/2011
Turnover	£793,600,000
Pre-tax profit	£8,800,000

Nature of business: Principal activities: selling, by retail and mail order, clothing, household goods, furniture and furnishing. The company operates mainly in the UK, US and Europe.

Company registration number: 1950509

Total employees: 7,440

Charitable donations

UK cash (latest declared):	2011	£282,000
	2009	£125,000
	2008	£100,000
	2007	£100,000
	2006	£100,000
Total UK:	2011	£282,000
Total worldwide:	2011	£548,000
Cash worldwide:	2011	£548,000

Corporate social responsibility

CSR committee: The corporate responsibility steering committee is chaired jointly by Tim Ashby, the group general counsel and company secretary and Gillian Berkmen, the group brand commercial director. The steering committee reports directly to the plc board and is supported by a small central team and external experts.

CSR policy: Statement taken from the 2010/11 annual report:

> Corporate responsibility underpins our core relationships, those we depend on today and in the future:
> - Communities – parents and children
> - The people who work for us
> - Our suppliers who make and distribute our products
> - The environment

CSR report: Published annually.

Exclusions

Previous information stated that unsolicited appeals are unlikely to be successful. No response to circular appeals. Support is not given to: animal welfare, appeals from individuals, the arts, elderly people, environment/heritage, religious appeals, political appeals, or sport.

Applications

The company's website (in April 2012) has the following information: Regrettably, the foundation is not accepting funding applications at present, although this situation may change in the future.

Other information

In 2010/11 the group made charitable donations in the UK totalling £282,000. Gifts in kind totalled £266,000 and were clothing and shoes which were sent on to Pakistan following the floods there. Mothercare's total direct giving to charity last year was £548,000. The largest donation made was to the Mothercare Group Foundation, with further substantial gifts to the Foundation for the Study of Infant Death and Cancer Research UK. Employees raised £100,600.

> In October we announced a three-year global partnership with Save the Children. Called 'Born to Care', it aims to raise £1.75 million over three years, to support Save the Children's EVERY ONE Campaign to improve newborn and child survival around the world and its work to eliminate childhood poverty in the UK. To start the partnership Mothercare made an initial donation of £50,000, to help fund a Save the Children project aiming to improve health care for migrant mothers and their children in China. In the UK, Born to Care will help to fund Save the Children 'Families and Schools Together' projects, where parents and children take part in an eight-week programme to strengthen family bonds, and build relationships with the school, other parents and their community.

The **Mothercare Group Foundation** is an independent charity (Charity Commission no. 1104386) with the following objectives:

- Ensuring the good health and well-being of mums-to-be, new mums and their children
- Special baby-care needs and premature births; and
- Other parenting initiatives relating to family well-being

In 2010/11 the company donated £103,000 directly to the foundation. In the same year the foundation made awards totalling £219,000. The main grants were:

Wellbeing of Women (£51,000); Royal College of Midwives' Alliance Programme (£50,000); The Stroke Association (£41,500); and The University of Cambridge Foundation (Baby Growth Study) (£40,000).

Mott MacDonald Ltd

Consulting engineers

Correspondent: Philip Gregory, Company Secretary, Mott MacDonald House, 8–10 Sydenham Road, Croydon CR0 2EE (tel: 020 8774 2000; fax: 020 8681 5706; email: marketing@mottmac.com; website: www.mottmac.com)

Directors: Keith Howells, Chair; Richard Williams, Managing Director; Mike Barker; Marian Brooks; Chris Davis; Kevin Dixon; Guy Leonard; Kevin Stovell; Chris Trinder (women: 1; men: 8)

Year end	31/12/2011
Turnover	£531,425,000
Pre-tax profit	£12,744,000

Nature of business: International engineering, management and development consultancies.

Company registration number: 1243967

Main locations: Aberdeen, Belfast, Colwyn Bay, Glasgow, Liverpool, Preston

Total employees: 5,510

Membership: BITC

Charitable donations

UK cash (latest declared):	2009	£330,000
	2007	£303,000
Total worldwide:	2011	£490,000
Cash worldwide:	2011	£340,000

Corporate social responsibility

CSR committee: Each part of our business has its own corporate responsibility strategy, reflecting local community needs and the concerns that are of uppermost importance to its staff.

CSR policy: Information taken from the company's website:

> Mott MacDonald seeks to make a positive contribution to the well-being of our staff and the environment, communities and marketplaces in which we operate. Being an employee-owned company we are free to pursue a fully integrated corporate responsibility approach – one that encapsulates our values of PRIDE (progress, respect, integrity, drive, excellence). We believe in acting ethically and responsibly in serving our customers and in carrying out our operations on a clear basis to regularise the economic, environmental and social impacts of our activities on society.

CSR report: Published annually and available on the company's website and contained within the annual report and accounts. 'Each part of our business has its own corporate responsibility strategy, reflecting local community needs and the concerns that are of uppermost importance to its staff.'

Applications

In writing to the correspondent.

Other information

Figures for charitable giving were for 2010. In 2010, direct charitable giving was £340,000. The value of gifts in kind was over £150,000.

A significant proportion of the company's financial support for charitable activities is channelled through the **Mott McDonald Charitable Trust** (Charity Commission no. 275040). The trust provides financial assistance to individuals engaged in education in the fields of civil, structural, mechanical, electrical and allied engineering.

The company's community support programme was started in 2008 and supports up to three projects at any one time, each receiving a possible total of £30,000 over three years. In November 2011 the first Community Support Programme projects, a dual purpose school and cyclone shelter in Titkata, Bangladesh, was opened. The group has maintained support for charities and schools through direct giving, support for staff and contributions in kind.

Support and sponsorship is given to several disaster relief organisations including Engineers against Poverty and WaterAid. The company also sponsors the UK Institution of Civil Engineers' Henry Palmer Award, a national competition that promotes civil engineering in creative and practical ways to educational establishments. **Women into Science and Engineering** is also supported by the company.

The Community Awards Scheme has been running since 2006 and celebrates the voluntary work of staff.

Muir Group plc

Property

Correspondent: Company Secretary, Muir House, Belleknowes Industrial Estate, Inverkeithing, Fife KY11 1HY (tel: 01383 416191; website: www.muirgroup.co.uk)

Directors: J. W. Muir; C. Muir; R. W. Muir; I. M. Muir; J. S. H. Watt; A. C. Muir

Year end		31/01/2011
Turnover		£72,929,000
Pre-tax profit		£2,594,000

Nature of business: The principal activity of the association is the provision of affordable housing to people in housing need, either by way of rent or by sale on a shared ownership basis

Company registration number: SC215392

Total employees: 312

Charitable donations

UK cash (latest declared):	2011	£8,000
	2010	£46,000
	2009	£41,000
	2008	£98,000
Total UK:	2011	£8,000
Total worldwide:	2011	£8,000
Cash worldwide:	2011	£8,000

Corporate social responsibility

CSR policy: No information available on CSR.

Unable to determine the ratio of women to men on the board.

Applications

Applications are open to:

- Any individual Muir resident
- Any resident group or community group operating in an area where Muir Group residents live
- Any organisation or partnership that benefits an area where Muir Group operates

A grant application form and application guidance notes are downloadable from the group's website.

Applications can be made by writing to the correspondent at: Friends of Muir Group, Mere's Edge, Helsby, Cheshire WA6 0DJ. Alternatively, you can apply by telephone (01925 790624); by fax (01244 404026); or, by email (fomg@muir.org.uk).

Other information

In 2010/11 the company made donations totalling £8,000. Details of beneficiaries were not available. Previous research on donations identified that funding was spent on arts and sports, health, education and the environment.

National Express Group plc

Transport and communications

Correspondent: The Charity Panel, 7 Triton Square, London NW1 3HG (tel: 0845 013 0130; fax: 020 7506 4320; email: info@nationalexpress.com; website: www.nationalexpressgroup.com)

Directors: John Devaney, Chair; Dean Finch, Group Chief Executive; Jez Maiden, Group Finance Director; Joaquín Ayuso; Miranda Curtis; Andrew Foster; Tim Score; Jorge Cosmen; Chris Muntwyler; Lee Sander (women: 1; men: 9)

Year end		31/12/2011
Turnover		£2,238,000,000
Pre-tax profit		£180,200,000

Nature of business: Principally the provision of passenger transport services in coaches, buses, airports and trains in the UK, USA and Australia.

Company registration number: 2590560

Main locations: London

Total employees: 38,921

Membership: Arts & Business

Charitable donations

UK cash (latest declared):	2011	£228,000
	2009	£187,000
	2008	£386,000
	2007	£374,000
	2006	£296,000
Total UK:	2011	£228,000
Total worldwide:	2011	£228,000
Cash worldwide:	2011	£228,000

Corporate social responsibility

CSR committee: No evidence of this.

CSR policy: The business review section of the company's website states: 'National Express is an international business, and takes its community responsibilities seriously wherever it operates. Across the group, more than 100 community organisations and charities were supported, either through a donation or support in kind.'

CSR report: Included in the company's business review webpages.

Exclusions

The group does not support political or religious organisations and is unlikely to provide corporate assistance to high profile charities with significant existing corporate support.

Applications

Ten members of staff representing different areas of the business meet four times a year to allocate funding for charitable projects and events.

Other information

Charitable donations made during the year totalled £228,000 (2010: £151,000).

In 2009, the National Express Charity Panel was launched. Ten members of staff representing different areas of the business meet four times a year to allocate funding for charitable projects and events.

The company provides arts and good-cause sponsorship and supports its staff in their charitable activities where practical. It also matches employee fundraising to an amount which varies.

Payroll giving: A payroll giving scheme is in operation.

The National Farmers Union Mutual Insurance Society Ltd

Insurance

Correspondent: James Damian Creechan, NFU Mutual Charitable Trust, Tiddington Road, Stratford upon Avon, Warwickshire CV37 7BJ (tel: 01789 204211; email: nfu_mutual_charitable_trust@nfumutual.co.uk; website: www.nfumutual.co.uk)

Directors: Richard Percy, Chair; Lindsay Sinclair, Group Chief Executive; John Elliot; Chris Stooke; Jim McLaren; David Anderson; Kim Arif, Finance Director; Steve Bower; Chris Ide; Ian Leech; Eileen McCusker; Mark Tinsley (women: 2; men: 10)

Year end		31/12/2011
Pre-tax profit		(£47,000,000)

Nature of business: Insurers.

Company registration number: 111982

Total employees: 3,721

Membership: BITC

Charitable donations

UK cash (latest declared):	2011	£572,000
	2009	£256,000
	2008	£257,000
	2007	£262,000
	2006	£207,000
Total UK:	2011	£572,000
Total worldwide:	2011	£572,000
Cash worldwide:	2011	£572,000

Community involvement

The NFU Mutual Charitable Trust

(Charity Commission no. 1073064), was set up in 1998 with the objectives of promoting and supporting charitable purposes in the areas of agriculture, rural development and insurance in the United Kingdom – including education, the relief of poverty, social welfare and research and any other charitable purposes. Beneficiaries of support during 2011 included: Nuffield Farming Scholarship Trust; Farms for City Children; ARC-Addington Fund; Farm Crisis Network; Farming and Countryside Education; and The National Federation of Young Farmers Clubs.

The trustees' approach to these objectives has been to adopt a policy of supporting, through one-off donations and grants, charitable initiatives connected with agriculture and the countryside and with the insurance industry.

Community Giving Fund

This fund was set up in 2005 to support local initiatives and charitable events within the communities in which NFU Mutual operates. During 2011 the fund helped 57 community groups and charities including: The Royal British Legion, Macmillan Cancer Support; British Heart Foundation; Alzheimer's Research UK, Cancer Research; Asthma UK and numerous hospices, schools and sports clubs.

Corporate giving

During 2011 the company donated £322,000 to the **NFU Mutual Charitable Trust**, £240,000 to the Make A Wish Foundation and £10,000 to the Community Giving Fund.

Employee-led support

Charity partner: In 2009, the company engaged on a three year programme to support the UK children's charity Make-A-Wish Foundation UK. The company will support their staff and agents in fundraising activities. 'Make-A-Wish is an ideal charity partner for NFU Mutual and means we can make a real difference to the lives of the children for whom we help grant wishes. Working with Make-A-Wish also brings us many benefits from a corporate perspective such as developing teamwork as well as a tremendous sense of achievement.'

Corporate social responsibility

CSR committee: No details found.

CSR policy: 2011 was the second year of NFU Mutual's three year CSR programme entitled 'Making A Real Difference' focusing on three areas: community, corporate charity and the environment.

The programme looks at NFU Mutual's impact on its members, the environment and the communities in which it operates, aiming to benefit all stakeholders under these headings.

CSR report: Community, Charity and Environment pages contained within the annual report and accounts.

Applications

Applications to the NFU Mutual Charitable Trust should be made to the correspondent and include:

- The project, initiative or organisation for which funding is sought
- An indication of the amount of the donation requested
- Any business plans
- Details of any other funding sought and or obtained
- Any recognition which would be given to the Trust in recognition of its support
- Confirmation of whether or not the applicant is a registered charity

NFU Mutual's website states:

> Following a recent strategic review, the Trustees have indicated that in future, the Trust will focus on providing funding to larger initiatives, which would have a significant impact on the rural community. The Trustees are particularly interested in initiatives in the areas of education of young people in rural areas and relief of poverty within rural areas.

The trustees meet twice a year to consider applications received. These meetings are currently held in June and December.

National Grid Holdings One plc

Electricity

Correspondent: Julian Buttery, Head of UK Community Relations, National Grid House, Warwick Technology Park, Gallows Hill, Warwick CV34 6DA (01926 655278; email: julian.buttery@uk.ngrid.com; website: www.nationalgrid.com/uk)

Directors: A. J. Agg; A. R. J. Bonfield; M. C. Cooper; M. A. D. Flawn; S. J. Holliday; G. Holroyd; A. M. Lewis; M. J. Sellars; C. J. Walters

Year end	31/03/2011
Turnover	£5,565,000,000
Pre-tax profit	£1,821,000,000

Nature of business: The principal operations of the company are the ownership and operation of regulated electricity and gas infrastructure networks in the UK and the US.

Company registration number: 2367004

Main locations: Warwick

Total employees: 9,953

Membership: BITC, LBG

Charitable donations

UK cash (latest declared):	2011	£100,000
	2009	£1,100,000
	2008	£1,400,000
	2007	£2,900,000
	2005	£1,352,000
Total UK:	2011	£8,300,000
Total worldwide:	2011	£8,300,000
Cash worldwide:	2011	£100,000

Community involvement

The company, on its website states:

> We are involved in a wide range of community programmes in the UK and the US which fit into three themes: developing skills in the next generation; managing energy resources and the environment; and, being an active citizen in our local communities.
>
> National Grid has pioneered business involvement in the rehabilitation of offenders. Over 2,000 offenders have now gone through the Young Offender Programme. The Chancellor of the Exchequer in his budget statement 2003 asked National Grid to lead the expansion of the programme across all industries in the UK and we now lead in a partnership with over 80 companies engaged in this Programme.
>
> The re-offending rate is only 7%, compared with the national average of over 70%, resulting in a significant saving to taxpayers in the United Kingdom. It costs approximately £40,000 to keep a person in prison for one year and there are currently over 86,000 people in prison.
>
> The Programme is engaged with over 22 prisons both adult and young offender establishments.

Corporate giving

The company's annual report for 2010/11 states:

> During 2010/11 approximately £8.3 million (2009/10: £6.2 million) was invested in support of community initiatives and relationships in the UK. The London Benchmarking Group model was used to assess this overall community investment. Direct donations to charitable organisations amounted to £100,000 (2009/10: £1.4 million). In addition to our charitable donations, financial support was provided for our affordable warmth programme, education programme, university research and our Young Offenders Programme.

Employee-led support

The 'Working with our communities' section of the website states:

> We are committed to City Year, one of the leading youth-service organisations in the US. It is an inspiring programme where teams of young people who have just left education give a year of service to their community by acting as mentors to young people at risk of dropping out of education. Not only do we help fund the scheme, our employees also support teams of young people, 'mentoring the mentors'. In September 2010, we extended our support of City Year to London.

Commercially-led support

Taken from the company's website:

> This year marked a major landmark with the opening of our new energy education centre in, Willesden, which has been developed in parallel with the London power tunnels project. The tunnels are not due to be fully operational until 2018 but, once completed, they will have created ten new 400 kV circuits in London's transmission system and cost up to £900 million.
>
> The education centre gives local schools and visitors first-hand experience of what the new cable tunnels will look like. But it is also designed to help visitors understand the future energy challenge: how can we balance affordability with sustainability and the role we will play in making sure we have energy security in the future.
>
> New interactive tools, specially designed games and on site experts aim to inspire today's school children to choose science and engineering careers, helping to ensure we have the specialist skills needed to operate our energy systems into the future.

Corporate social responsibility

> **CSR committee:** Our Board Risk & Responsibility Committee monitors and reviews the Company's non-financial risks and interfaces with the Audit Committee.

> In relation to non-financial risks only, it is responsible for reviewing the strategies, policies, targets and performance of the Company.
>
> In September 2012, the Risk & Responsibility Committee will be replaced by a new committee, to be chaired by Philip, Aiken, which will focus on safety, environmental and health matters
>
> **CSR policy:** We are committed to being a responsible and sustainable business. This commitment is driven by our Framework for Responsible Business, underpinned by our Standards of Ethical Business Conduct, our suite of policies, procedures, public position statements and well-defined internal control processes.

Unable to determine from the accounts the ratio of women to men on the board.

CSR report: report published in Responsibility section of website and refers to both UK and US activities.

Exclusions

Support is not given to circular appeals, advertising in charity brochures, appeals from individuals, overseas projects, political appeals, religious appeals, and local appeals not in areas of company presence.

Applications

In writing to the correspondent. For innovative grants, applications must be submitted on a form by a senior manager of one of the group's businesses rather than the applicant charity.

Information available: A leaflet on National Grid's sponsorship and donations policy is available on request.

National Magazine Co. Ltd

Media

Correspondent: Team Secretary, MD's Office, National Magazine House, 72 Broadwick Street, London W1F 9EP (tel: 020 7439 5000; website: www.natmags.co.uk)

Directors: J. D. Edwards; S. Horne; F. A. Bennack; E. A. Kershaw; J. P. Loughlin; G. C. Maurer; M. Clinton; A. de Puyfontaine

Year end	31/12/2010
Turnover	£309,631,000
Pre-tax profit	£9,558,000

Nature of business: The main activities are the publishing and distribution of magazines and periodicals. The National Magazine Co. Ltd is a wholly owned subsidiary of Hearst Holdings Inc.

Company registration number: 112955

Main locations: London

Total employees: 954

Charitable donations

UK cash (latest declared):	2010	£100
	2008	£2,600
	2007	£16,000
	2006	£12,000
	2005	£45,000
Total UK:	2010	£100
Total worldwide:	2010	£100
Cash worldwide:	2010	£100

Corporate social responsibility

CSR committee: No details.

CSR policy: Webpage includes information on support for Catch 22.

We were unable to determine the ratio of women to men on the board.

CSR report: None published.

Exclusions

Local appeals not in areas of company presence.

Applications

In writing to the correspondent.

Other information

In 2010 the company's charitable donations dropped to only £100.

The company's website states:

> The company has become a supporter of London-based social enterprise, Catch 22. Run by Director Tokunbo Ajasa-Oluwa, Catch 22 (C22) works to engage, train and champion excluded young talent in journalism. It achieves this through three methods – a journalism training academy, youth culture magazine and a communications agency. The C22 Academy is run in conjunction with the London College of Communication (LCC) and trains young people in its 'introduction to magazine journalism programme'. Catch 22 aims to run the course four times a year. C22's prime target beneficiaries are excluded young talent aged 18 – 30 years old, based in London, who for numerous reasons, have not pursued the conventional academic pathway. They are likely to be from ethnic communities, not in education, employment or training (NEET), and in need of a break. In the long-term C22 aspires to be the prime source for employment-ready media talent from untraditional backgrounds and is seeking investment support from the industry. NatMag has agreed to provide financial and practical support to Catch 22 for the next three years as part of its corporate social responsibility.

It is not clear if the support for Catch 22 is in addition to the £100 cash donation.

The company has in the past supported the work of the Soho Family Centre and made small donations to groups near its Soho offices.

The company has previously stated that it supports employees' volunteering/charitable activities with financial help.

Nationwide Building Society

Building society

Correspondent: Jean Trace, CR Assistant, Nationwide House, Pipers Way, Swindon SN38 2SN (tel: 01793 656145/01793 656145; email: corporate.responsibility@nationwide.co.uk; website: www.nationwide.co.uk)

Directors: Geoffrey Howe, Chair; Graham Beale, Chief Executive; Chris Rhodes; Suzanna Taverne; Alan Dickinson; Robert Walther; Mitchel Lenson; Matthew Wyles; Tony Prestedge; Lynne Peacock; Mark Rennison; Roger Perkin; Michael Jary (women: 2; men: 11)

Year end	05/04/2011
Turnover	£5,390,000,000
Pre-tax profit	£229,000,000

Nature of business: The group provides a comprehensive range of personal financial services. The Cheshire, Derbyshire and Dunfermline Building Societies are Nationwide's regional brands.

FSA registration number: 106078

Main locations: Swindon

UK employees: 17,451

Total employees: 17,451

Membership: BITC, LBG

Charitable donations

UK cash (latest declared):	2011	£1,500,000
	2009	£4,474,000
	2008	£2,448,191
	2007	£2,380,565
	2006	£2,324,287
Total UK:	2011	£1,500,000
Total worldwide:	2011	£1,500,000
Cash worldwide:	2011	£1,500,000

Community involvement

The society has made the following statement:

> Nationwide has a strong history of involvement in community projects and is firmly committed to supporting the communities from which it has grown. Through sponsorship, fundraising and other activities, Nationwide supports hundreds of events and initiatives across the country each year.
>
> The Community Affairs team is responsible for co-ordinating charitable activity and making decisions on requests for sponsorship and funding made to Nationwide.
>
> The majority of the group donations are made through the **Nationwide Foundation** (Charity Commission no. 1065552). As a separate legal entity the foundation is not part of the Nationwide Group and is controlled by an independent board of trustees which determines the policies.

The Nationwide Foundation

The Nationwide Foundation was set up in 1998 by the society from which, as its main benefactor, it receives an annual donation. Over the past 10 years, the foundation's funding criteria have encompassed a number of diverse themes.

The strategy incorporates two grants programmes, the **Small Grants Programme** and the **Investor Programme**. The Small Grants Programme offers one-off grants of up to £5,000 to registered charities with an income of under £500,000. The Investor Programme is designed to offer long-term flexible support and core funding to a selected number of charities, over three years, while encouraging and funding partnership working among them.

NB The Nationwide Foundation's current strategy will draw to a close in 2012/13. Its board of trustees has commenced a strategic review to develop a new three year grant making strategy for implementation in 2012/13. The Financial Inclusion Centre has been engaged to independently review the UK's housing and finance sectors on behalf of the Board, to help identify key areas where The Nationwide Foundation's future grants could achieve maximum impact in the areas of housing and financial inclusion.

For more information and to keep up to date with the foundation's criteria, see its website (www.nationwidefoundation.org.uk).

Corporate giving

In 2010/11 charitable donations of £1.5 million (2009/10: £2.7 million) were made, including £700,000 (2009/10: £1 million) to **The Nationwide Foundation** (Charity Commission no. 1065552). The annual report and accounts refers to UK only charities in its giving and we have therefore taken the figure of £1.5 million as the UK cash donation figure.

The Foundation's three year strategy for 2009–12: Money Matters, Homes Matter, Families Matter has the following aims:

Money Matters: To tackle financial exclusion affecting disadvantaged groups across the UK.

Homes Matter: To address housing issues and homelessness among vulnerable groups in the UK.

Families Matter: To support families and help prevent family breakdown and its causes.

The **Small Grants Programme** comprises the following elements:

- Grants of up to £5,000; one-off payments
- Grants made to registered charities with annual income not exceeding £500,000
- Brief application forms
- Quick decision time e.g. Two months

The **Investor Programme** comprises:

- Research used to identify objectives to meet the aims (Money Matters, Homes Matter, Families Matter; preference given to overlap)
- Large three-year grants: for research, projects and/or awareness raising
- Partnership
- Building Resilience
- Leverage/links with NBS
- Evaluation
- Special Reserve
- End event

A partnership element is maintained within this strategy as well as many new features for strengthening the infrastructure, capacity and robustness of charities. This includes funding financial planning, strategy reviews, risk assessments and training for trustees and staff in order to improve and sustain the effectiveness of their work in the present economic climate and beyond the period of the foundation's grant.

The 2010/11 annual report states: The 'Money Matters, Homes Matter, Families Matter' strategy, incorporates the **Small Grants Programme** and the **Investor Programme**, both of which provide grants to charities across the UK in accordance with the strategic aims and objectives. During the year, the Small Grants Programme made grants of up to £5,000 to over 100 charities, in support of over 2,300 people in need. The Investor Programme supported ten charities, each with three year grants of £300,000, which aim to support thousands of people in need. The charities supported are: Age UK Camden; Age UK Wirral; Centre for Policy on Ageing; Centre for Sustainable Energy; The Haven, Wolverhampton; Money Advice Plus Services (maps); Rowan Alba; Runnymede Trust; Rural Media Company; and Thanet Citizens Advice.

The Investor Programme was designed to provide charities with a legacy of support which extends beyond the grant and so encompasses additional support, including independent evaluation, consultancy and training to help build the organisational resilience of the charities funded.

Email: enquiries@nationwidefoundation.org.uk; website: www.nationwidefoundation.org.uk

In kind support

Non-cash support in the form of equipment, consultancy, furniture, prizes/merchandise, and print/design is provided.

Employee-led support

Taken from the 2011/12 CR report:

We have always been supportive of our employees' involvement in their local communities, and in October 2010 we launched our employee volunteering programme offering them up to two days paid leave each year. In the last year the percentage of employees volunteering has more than tripled to 5.9%.

Payroll giving: Nationwide operates the Give As You Earn payroll giving scheme and supports employee fundraising in various ways.

Commercially-led support

Sponsorship

Information taken from the company's 2011/12 annual report and accounts:

Supporting local partners

Our Community Champions programme, launched mid 2011, is a network of over 100 employees promoting citizenship and driving local community activity across Nationwide.

Since 2003, the Derbyshire Building Society has sponsored the annual Derby 10k run. The 2011 race had 3,500 entrants. As well as bringing together the local community, it is an essential fundraising activity for the charity organiser, Sporting Futures. They seek to reduce the risk of crime and antisocial behaviour in Derbyshire's communities by encouraging targeted young people to join in physical recreation.

The Prospect Hospice in Swindon's annual Starlight Walk has been supported by Nationwide since 2008. This year 629 women took part and raised almost £87,000 for the hospice. Our catering supplier, Aramark, donated refreshments and provided volunteers to serve them.

Through our principal sponsorship of Bournemouth Symphony Orchestra (BSO), we now sponsor their Community Musician, Andy Baker, and work with the orchestra on a number of key community projects including BSO Resonate and its Rusty Musicians Project.

Supporting sporting opportunities for disabled people Disability Sport Events (DSE) is part of the English Federation of Disability Sport – the strategic lead for disabled people in sport throughout England. The events programme is world renowned, organising Championships in a variety of sports. Swimming and athletics are the highest participation sports for disabled people in the UK and our sponsorship allows DSE to provide opportunities from regional through to international level. The Nationwide programme helps DSE to engage over 500 swimmers at a national level and 1,000 swimmers in regional competition. In athletics, 400 athletes compete at national level, 2,000 take part at regional level.

Corporate social responsibility

CSR committee: Corporate Responsibility is owned by all our employees, but overall responsibility lies with the board of directors.

Purpose of the CR committee:

- To define and govern the Nationwide CR strategy

- To take ownership of the CR agenda and promote an integrated approach. To escalate issues to board level
- To measure the impact of CR, to celebrate successes and commit to continuous improvement

CSR policy: Taken from the company's website:

> *Mission statement*
>
> As an organisation, we embrace our responsibilities to our members, our employees and the communities we serve.
>
> Everything we do is underpinned by our core values of transparency, fairness and security. These are the foundations which enable us to maintain our financial strength and deliver long-term good value.

The company's CR strategy focuses on four areas: finance, environment, housing and community.

CSR report: Contained within the annual report and accounts. There is also a corporate responsibility page on the company's website.

Exclusions

No response to circular appeals. No support for advertising in charity brochures, animal welfare, appeals from individuals, medical research, overseas projects, political appeals, religious appeals, or for commercial (as opposed to community related) sponsorship.

Applications

Applications to the company for donations or sponsorship should be sent to the correspondent.

For applications to the Nationwide Foundation, further information can be obtained from the foundation's website (www.nationwidefoundation.org.uk).

On a local basis, giving depends on the local area managers, who have small budgets for local community projects.

Nestlé Holdings (UK) plc

Drinks manufacture, food manufacture

Correspondent: Nestlé in the Community, Nestlé UK Ltd, St Georges House, Croydon, Surrey CR9 1NR (tel: 020 8686 3333; website: www.nestle.co.uk)

Directors: P. Grimwood; M. Jones; E. Legge; P. Hagmann

Year end	31/12/2011
Turnover	£22,786,000
Pre-tax profit	£22,908,000

Nature of business: Holding company of some of the interests of Nestlé SA businesses operating in the UK. Nestlé manufacture and sale of food products and associated activities.

Company registration number: 462438

Brands include: Nestlé, Kit Kat, Smarties, Aero, Rowntree's, Quality Street, Nescafé, Herta, Ski, Perrier, Buxton, Vittel, Friskies.

Main locations: Hayes, Castleford, Croydon, Dalston, Fawdon, Girvan, Halifax, York, Tutbury

Membership: BITC, LBG

Charitable donations

UK cash (latest declared):	2011	£570,000
	2009	£700,000
	2007	£1,005,954
	2006	£1,200,000
	2005	£1,700,000
Total UK:	2011	£570,000
Total worldwide:	2011	£570,000
Cash worldwide:	2011	£570,000

Community involvement

Nestlé provided the following information regarding its community support in the UK:

> Nestlé has a very long history of community activities and support of charitable projects throughout the world. It is part of our company culture and principles that we act responsibly in the communities in which we operate. We support projects in the community that focus on our company strategies of nutrition, health and wellness and sustainability. We want to ensure that all the community work undertaken by Nestlé has a consistent approach and that our activities ultimately make a difference to the communities in which we have offices and factories.

Charity of the Year: Alzheimer's Society

Corporate giving

In 2011, the company made charitable donations totalling £570,000. Details of the specific amounts given to the company's key partners and/or other organisations were not available.

In kind support

Nestlé's main area of non-cash support is gifts in kind – the company providing product, furniture and equipment donations to local good causes.

Employee-led support

The 'Community' part of the company's website states:

> In 2011 our UK employees also took park in fundraising activities for our Charity of the Year, Alzheimer's Society, raising over £400,000 in just nine months. Employees in Ireland committed to raise €30,000 in 2011 for Irish charity The Jack and Jill Foundation. In 2011, in addition to our Charity of the Year, we continued our support for the Make Space for Health and PhunkyFoods initiatives, which are helping young people across the UK to learn about the benefits of good nutrition and healthy lifestyles.

The York site has their own employee charitable trust, which raises funds from employees and is donated in small grants to local organisations in which employees hold an interest. The trust is **The Nestlé Rowntree York Employees Community Fund Trust** (Charity Commission no. 516702). Contact the Chair of the Trust for further information at Haxby Road, York YO91 1XY. Tel: 01904 604808.

Payroll giving: A scheme is operated through an internal company community fund.

Corporate social responsibility

CSR committee: No details found.

CSR policy: Taken from the company's website:

> It is part of our company culture and principles that we act responsibly in the communities in which we operate. We support projects in the community that focus on our company strategies of nutrition, health and wellness and sustainability. We want to ensure that all the community work undertaken by Nestlé has a consistent approach and that our activities ultimately make a difference to the communities in which we have offices and factories.

CSR report: None specific to the UK published.

Exclusions

No support is given towards student expeditions, individuals, political causes, third-party fundraising events or the purchase of advertising space in charity programmes.

Applications

Applications should be made to nearest local site. Few national financial donations are given.

Network Rail Infrastructure Ltd

Engineering, transportation

Correspondent: Sustainable Development Improvement Group, Kings Place, 90 York Way, London N1 9AG (tel: 020 3356 9595; fax: 020 3356 9245; website: www.networkrail.co.uk)

Directors: David Higgins, Chief Executive; Patrick Butcher, Group Finance Director; Robin Gisby; Simon Kirby; Mike Firth; Graham Eccles; Lawrie Haynes; Paul Plummer; Peter Henderson; Rick Haythornthwaite, Chair; Richard Parry Jones; Malcolm Brinded (women: 0; men: 12)

Year end	31/03/2012
Turnover	£6,004,000,000
Pre-tax profit	£471,000,000

Nature of business: Network Rail owns operates and maintains Britain's rail network.

Company registration number: 2904587

Total employees: 35,253

Membership: BITC, LBG

Charitable donations

UK cash (latest declared):	2012	£589,000
	2009	£763,000
	2008	£785,000
	2007	£793,000
	2006	£973,000
Total UK:	2012	£2,222,660
Total worldwide:	2012	£2,222,660
Cash worldwide:	2012	£589,000

Community involvement

The following information is taken from the company's 2011/12 annual report:

> We support charities large and small, right across Britain, focusing on those which align most with our business objectives. Many of our people actively support our charity partners, making a real difference in the community. We believe that encouraging charitable giving can also increase employee engagement and productivity.
>
> *Charity of Choice*
>
> Network Rail supports a Charity of Choice, chosen by employees. In 2010/11, a two-year charity of choice was launched – *Cancer Research UK* (CRUK). During 2010/11, £885,000 was contributed to CRUK through employee fundraising, payroll giving, gifts in kind (including high profile advertising space at London Bridge station), volunteering time, and corporate donations.
>
> Following an employee vote in early 2012 in which almost 40 per cent of employees participated, Network Rail's new Charity of Choice for 2012 to 2014 will be *Action for Children*.
>
> *Partnership*
>
> In 2010, we launched a groundbreaking five-year partnership with *Samaritans* with the aim of reducing incidents of suicide on the railway by 20 per cent by 2015.
>
> *Our partners across Britain*
>
> At the start of 2010/11, we reviewed our 30 regional charity partnerships, and chose to continue to fund the 14 partners we believed were most closely aligned to our business and where we saw the greatest impact for us, for the charity and for the community. We continue to provide them with financial contributions and wider support such as employee volunteering time.
>
> Our key areas of focus for 2011/12 [were]:
>
> - Reviewing and relaunching our volunteer leave policy with the aim of increasing participation
> - Exceeding our £1 million partnership target with Cancer Research UK before March 2012
> - Relaunching our regional charity partnership scheme with a greater focus on engagement from local teams within our business
> - Improving data collection for charitable giving.

Corporate giving

During the year 2011/12 Network Rail donated £589,000 to charitable organisations (2010/11: £635,000) and leveraged a further £1.8 million through gifts in kind, employee fundraising and other initiatives, totalling £2.4 million. As the company's charitable contributions are linked with the corporate objectives, we have assumed that all giving is within the UK. We have been unable to accurately determine the exact corporate contribution but have taken the amount of £2.4 million as the total contribution figure and then deducted the staff fundraising we have figures for.

Employee-led support

The following extract is from the 2010/11 CR report:

> Getting involved: to increase participation in charitable activities this year, we made it easier to find information on our policies and how to apply for volunteer leave, matched giving and payroll giving on our Company intranet. *Volunteer leave:* we offer up to five days' paid volunteer leave per year to all employees. This can be used with any registered charity within a set of broad categories that align to our business (such as social inclusion and the environment). In 2010/11, we widened the scope of these categories to encourage greater use of volunteer leave. This contributed to an increase, with 193 employees volunteering (2009/10: 86) for a combined total of 496 days (2009/10: 233). We believe that even more volunteer activities took place without being officially recorded, so capturing accurate and robust data will be an area of focus for the coming year. (This differs from the previously published figure of 144 for 2009/10 because a historic data error was found and rectified during the reporting year. This had not been established at the time of our last report.
>
> *Matched giving:* During 2010/11, Network Rail matched employee fundraising contributions to the total of £150,000 (2009/10: £100,000) and donated this amount to Cancer Research UK.
>
> *Payroll giving:* As of 31 March 2011, 3.71% of our workforce was signed up to our Payroll Giving scheme (31 March 2010: 1.68%). In the month of March 2011, our people donated a combined total of £22,340 direct to charity out of their pay. Since August 2010, 'Payroll Giving in Action' has visited our workplaces on 117 occasions to promote the Payroll Giving scheme to our staff, signing up 821 of our people to give to a charity through their payroll.

Commercially-led support

Information taken from the 2010 CR report:

> **Engaging with our communities**: During 2010/11, our team of dedicated regional community safety managers continued to work in communities nationwide, primarily engaging in 'hotspot' areas which represent the greatest risk to railway users and to the infrastructure. They work with a variety of organisations including local police, sports clubs, schools and local councils to raise awareness of the dangers of taking risks on the tracks and to get young people involved in more fun activities.
>
> In 2010/11, we changed the way we collect community safety information. As a result, this year we do not have data that is comparable to that which has been reported in previous years. Establishing a new and robust baseline of community safety data will be a focus for 2011/12.

Corporate social responsibility

CSR committee: Taken from the company's 2011 annual report:

> Changes to our governance structure for sustainable development have also been made during 2011/12. This year has seen the end of our Corporate Responsibility Group (CRG), which provided strategic leadership on emerging issues in the area of sustainability and corporate responsibility. The group, which met four times in 2011/12, was chaired by the Chief Executive and included a combination of senior team members, functional representatives, area specialists and an employee representative.
>
> The role of the CRG will be incorporated into the new governance structure for the S&SD function during 2012, specifically within the Sustainable Development Improvement Group.

CSR policy: Taken from the 2011 CR report:

> *Communities:*
>
> There are lots of ways we engage with our communities. We run programmes to tackle level crossing misuse, as well as crime and anti-social behaviour on and around our network. We actively encourage our people to get involved with charities and the communities in which we work. And we work with community rail partnerships to support the rural and local railways that are important to the communities they serve.

CSR report: CR report published annually. Information will in future be published in the company's Sustainability report which will be available on its website.

Exclusions

Circulars, general appeals, individuals and political appeals are not supported.

Applications

In writing to the correspondent.

Newcastle Building Society

Building society

Correspondent: Gillian Tiplady, Head of Corporate Social Responsibility, Portland House, New Bridge Street, Newcastle upon Tyne NE1 8AL (tel: 01912 442000; website: www.newcastle.co.uk)

Directors: David Holborn, Chair; Jim Willens, Chief Executive; Ron

McCormick; Angela Russell, Finance Director; John Warden; Gillian Tiplady; John Morris; Richard Mayland; Catherine Vine-Lott; Phil Moorhouse; David Buffham (women: 3; men: 8)

Year end	31/12/2011
Turnover	£103,700,000
Pre-tax profit	£300,000

Nature of business: Building Society.

FSA registration number: 156058

UK employees: 855

Total employees: 855

Charitable donations

UK cash (latest declared):	2011	£58,000
	2009	£40,000
	2008	£83,000
	2007	£100,000
	2006	£100,000
Total UK:	2011	£58,000
Total worldwide:	2011	£58,000
Cash worldwide:	2011	£58,000

Corporate social responsibility

CSR committee: The contact is head of CSR.

CSR policy: As a mutual building society we aim to be a good social citizen. We are committed to supporting local causes within our Heartland and aim to assist grassroots charities with a special focus on social care and the elderly. These often include groups and associations proposed by both our customers and our staff

CSR report: Dedicated page on website.

Exclusions

No grants for: sponsorship and fundraising events; small contributions to major appeals; large capital projects; endowments; political or religious groups; or work which should be funded by health and local authorities, or government grant aid.

Applications

Applications to the Newcastle Building Society Community Fund should be made using an application form available from The Community Foundation serving Tyne and Wear and Northumberland, Cale Cross, 156 Pilgrim Street, Newcastle upon Tyne NE1 6SU (01912 220945; email: grants@communityfoundation.org.uk, website: www.communityfoundation.org.uk).

Applications should include background information and a full explanation of how any grant will be used. Applications can be received at any time and are acknowledged.

Full grant guidelines can be obtained from the society's website.

Other information

In 2011 the society made charitable donations of £58,000. The society has also established the Newcastle Building Society Community Fund. Considerable in kind support is also given.

Charitable projects that have received a grant include the Cricket Foundation's Chance to Shine at Gateshead Fell Cricket Club, which will receive £25,000 over five years to pay for extra coaching sessions in schools. We have also donated £13,000 so far to The Children Foundation's Whoops! Project, which aims to stamp out bullying in local schools.

The Newcastle Building Society wants to avoid disruption to its business caused by speculators. As a result all new customers opening share accounts are required to agree to assign any windfall benefits to which they might become entitled on a future conversion or take-over of the Society. The assignment will be in favour of the Community Foundation, one of the leading community foundations in the UK. The agreement is for a period of five years.

The Newcastle Building Society Community Fund

The society supports community groups and organisations through their sponsorship programmes and its community fund. The Community Foundation serving Tyne and Wear and Northumberland (Charity Commission no.: 700510) manages the Newcastle Building Society Community Fund. There is a strong focus on projects that help improve the community, nurture talent and support education. Grants are mainly of £1,000 or less. To date the Society has donated over £800,000 to over 800 good causes via the Community Foundation. Groups that have benefited from our donations include the Tynemouth Volunteer Life Brigade, Stepney Bank Stables, Chester Le Street Rowing Club, Gateshead Crossroads and Cargo Fleet Football Team, Middlesbrough.

Charity of the Year Scheme:

In 2008 Newcastle Building Society introduced a Charity of the Year Scheme which challenges staff to raise money for a local cause. For the 2012/13 fundraising year the Newcastle's staff voted to support **Help for Heroes**. As well as raising funds for this, the Society also supports other events including Children In Need, Red Nose Day and the national Macmillan Coffee Morning, in addition to local charities in and around our branch network.

The Members' Community Fund

In 2003 the society launched The Members' Community Fund which allows members to make an annual donation from one of their Newcastle Building Society savings accounts. The society selects three charitable themes aimed at covering a wide cross section of people and activities, including children's education, adult literacy and numeracy and IT schemes for the over 55s. The money raised is then divided among these themes so that if 30% of respondents choose to support children's education, 30% of the funds will go to causes related to this. As with the community fund, the funds are also held and distributed by The Community Foundation serving Tyne and Wear and Northumberland.

In addition to charitable donations, support is given through gifts in kind, joint promotions, and advice and mentoring.

News International Ltd

Media

Correspondent: The Community Affairs Manager, 1 Virginia Street, London E98 1XY (tel: 020 7782 6000; website: www.newscorp.com)

Directors: Rupert Murdoch, Chair and Chief Executive; Jose Maria Aznar; Natalie Bancroft; Peter L. Barnes; James W. Breyer; Chase Carey; David F. DeVoe; Viet Dinh; Sir Roderick I. Eddington; Joel I. Klein; Andrew SB. Knight; James R. Murdoch; Lachlan K. Murdoch; Arthur M. Siskind; John L. Thornton; Stanley S. Shuman (women: 1; men: 15)

Year end	30/06/2011
Turnover	£34,000,000,000
Pre-tax profit	£4,200,000,000

Nature of business: Investment company within the Newscorp Investments group.

Company registration number: 81701

Main locations: Glasgow, Knowsley, London, Peterborough

Total employees: 51,000

Charitable donations

UK cash (latest declared):	2009	£500,000
	2008	£900,000
	2007	£900,000
	2006	£1,200,000
	2005	£1,200,000

Corporate social responsibility

CSR committee: There was no evidence of a separate CSR Committee.

CSR policy: Information regarding the company's CSR policy was unavailable.

CSR report: There was no evidence of a separate CSR report.

Exclusions

No support for advertising in charity brochures, appeals from individuals, fundraising events, medical research, overseas projects, religious/political appeals, science/technology, sport or local appeals not in areas of company presence. As a general rule the company does not make contributions to capital building projects.

Applications

In writing to the correspondent. A charities committee meets regularly. Unsuccessful applicants are given reasons and the corporate policy is explained.

Appeals to subsidiary companies should be made to managing directors, managing editors or editors.

Other information

Information regarding charitable contributions for the year was unavailable (2008: £500,000). No details of the beneficiaries were available.

Previously, we were advised that there is a preference for supporting charities in which a member of staff is involved. Staff are encouraged to become volunteers in their own time and to become school governors.

Local appeals are dealt with by the company's plants in Glasgow, Knowsley, and Peterborough which are encouraged to pursue their own community affairs programmes. Unfortunately, no details were available regarding what this might cover.

Payroll giving: A scheme is operated by the company.

Next plc

Retail – clothing and footwear

Correspondent: Corporate Responsibility Manager, Legislation and Environment Department – Phase 2, Next plc, Desford Road, Enderby, Leicester LE19 4AT (tel: 0845 456 7777; website: www.next.co.uk)

Directors: John Barton, Chair; Lord Wolfson of Aspley Guise, Chief Executive; Christos Angelides; David Keens, Group Finance Director; Andrew Varley; Jonathan Dawson; Steve Barber; Christine Cross; Francis Salway (women: 1; men: 8)

Year end	28/01/2011
Turnover	£3,441,100,000
Pre-tax profit	£579,500,000

Nature of business: The principal activities of the group are high-street retailing, home shopping, customer services management and financial services.

Company registration number: 4521150

Main locations: Bradford, Leeds, Leicester

UK employees: 24,514

Total employees: 37,220

Membership: BITC

Charitable donations

UK cash (latest declared):	2011	£1,141,500
	2010	£996,623
	2008	£499,000
	2007	£383,000
	2006	£350,000
Total UK:	2011	£2,265,500
Total worldwide:	2011	£2,265,500
Cash worldwide:	2011	£1,141,500

Community involvement

The following information is taken from the company's Corporate Responsibility report for 2011:

> *Our Approach*
>
> With 525 stores in the United Kingdom and Ireland, we offer support to a wide range of charities and organisations of all sizes, by working to offer them donations that are of most benefit to them and their particular cause, whether it be a financial donation, or the offer of products that can be used to realise additional funding. Our aim is to make a difference, so we do not support a single 'Charity of the Year', as we believe we are able to make a greater impact by working with a wider group of charities and organisations. As well as supporting individual charity requests, we also agree to support some charities for an agreed number of years with a specified donation. This commitment helps the charities to be able to plan their work with confidence.
>
> *Our priorities are to:*
>
> - Focus our resources on projects that support the communities in which we operate
> - Offer support to charities and organisations of all sizes with a donation that is of most benefit to them
> - Work to identify and develop new relationships with charities and organisations
>
> To ensure we can measure and monitor our overall community investment, we calculate the value of our non-financial contributions gained from products donated from within the business. This figure is added to our financial contributions, to arrive at the total sum contributed for the year.
>
> Our charity and sponsorship programme is made up of donations to:
>
> **Registered charities** – we have offered support to over 350 charities of all sizes during 2010 who have asked for contributions to support their work in the areas of children, care for the sick and people with disabilities, healthcare and medical research and community support.
>
> **Individual requests/local and national groups and organisations** – we are able to help groups and organisations who do not have charitable status through these donations.
>
> **Commercial sponsorship** – we offer commercial sponsorship to a small number of sporting organisations, which provides Next with the benefit of raising awareness of our brand. We also support local sporting teams of all ages, especially where there is direct employee involvement with the team.
>
> *Our Challenges and Targets*
>
> - Work with charitable organisations to identify value they are able to realise from products Next can no longer use. This initiative supports both our community focus and our environment targets of waste reduction and landfill diversion
> - Work to encourage employee engagement with charitable causes

Corporate giving

During 2010/11, Next plc has offered financial support to: registered charities amounting to £857,400; individual requests, local and national groups and organisations amounting to £68,500 and commercial support and sponsorship amounting to £74,000.

Financial support has been complemented with the following fundraising activities to generate additional funds for registered charities, individuals, groups or organisations: Next charity events £215,500; Gifts in kind – donations of products £1.1 million; Charity link sales £287,500; Employee fundraising £19,200.

The figures we use for the company's UK and worldwide contributions do not include commercial sponsorship, charity link sales and employee fundraising as is our usual practice, however, they are noted here to provide full information.

Employee-led support

This information is taken from the 2011 Corporate Responsibility report:

> Next is enabling employees at Head Office to sign up to 'Oxfam Collects at Work' a scheme which enables employees to donate their unwanted goods to Oxfam whilst at work. We believe it provides employees with an opportunity to get involved in corporate citizenship in a simple, but sophisticated way, by donating unwanted items that Oxfam is able to create value from, to support its global work worldwide. Launched at Next in July 2010 Oxfam has raised over £7,000 from our employees' donations. Our aim is to work with the Oxfam Collects team to provide this scheme within other areas of our business

There is a **PAYE** scheme in operation throughout the company.

Commercially-led support

Next offers commercial support and sponsorship to a small number of sporting organisations, which provides Next with the benefit of raising awareness of its brand. It also supports local sporting teams of all ages, especially where there is direct employee involvement with the team.

Corporate social responsibility

CSR committee: There is a Corporate Responsibility Manager at the Legislation and Environment department of the company.

CSR policy: Statement taken from the CSR report for 2011:

> For Next, corporate responsibility (CR) means addressing key business-related social, ethical and environmental impacts in a way that aims to bring value to all our stakeholders, including our shareholders. Continuous improvement lies at the heart of our business and we are constantly looking for ways to ensure we run our business in a responsible way.
>
> *Community*: We work to deliver support through our charitable contributions to charities and community organisations.

CSR report: An annual CR report is published.

Exclusions

No support is given to political causes.

Applications

In writing to the correspondent.

Nike (UK) Ltd

Sports clothing

Correspondent: See 'Applications', One Victory Way, Doxford International Business Park, Sunderland, Tyne and Wear SR3 3XF (tel: 01913 355200; website: www.nike.com)

Directors: J. van Pappelendam; A. Maden

Year end	31/05/2011
Turnover	£70,355,000
Pre-tax profit	£10,859,000

Nature of business: Multi-national manufacturer of sports clothing and equipment.

Company registration number: 1887016

Main locations: Sunderland

Total employees: 247

Charitable donations

UK cash (latest declared):	2011	£0

Corporate social responsibility

CSR policy: No CSR information found for the UK company.

We were unable to determine the ratio of women to men on the board.

Exclusions

Only registered charities can be supported. No grants are made to individuals, sports teams, non-registered charities, for-profit groups, religious groups, capital campaigns, endowment funds, memorials or political activities.

Applications

At this time, Nike only supports product donation requests. Nike does not accept unsolicited cash proposals.

If you are a non-profit organisation **outside of the US or the Netherlands**, send your request to Consumer.Services@nike.com

You might also consider applying to your local Nike retail or office branch.

Other information

No charitable donations are declared in Nike UK Ltd's annual accounts for 2010/11. Nike's corporate responsibility globally is however considerable and its aims and achievements are detailed in the informative corporate responsibility report which you can find on its website. Unfortunately, there would appear to be very little (if anything) available from Nike Inc., for charitable or community organisations within the UK.

The following is taken from the company's website:

> We will invest a minimum of $315 million in grants product donations and in kind support through 2011 to give excluded youth greater access to sport programs designed to unleash human potential.
>
> Nike's approach to community investments is pro-active and focused. A significant majority of our investments are targeted toward our community work. The remainder goes to support local organisations in our backyards of Portland, Oregon; Memphis, Tennessee; Hilversum, Holland; Laakdal, Belgium and other corporate offices around the world. *In addition, we make local grants through our retail organisations*.
>
> We pro-actively seek out key strategic partners around the world to help us drive a three pronged strategy of:
>
> 1 Innovation – we selectively support grassroots programming that demonstrates innovation in leveraging sport as a vehicle for social change
> 2 Skills transfer – we seek out social innovators and social entrepreneurs that are thinking of new models to develop sustained grassroots programming and take best practice to scale. Our goal is to provide them with Nike's business acumen and build their capacity to succeed
> 3 Scale – we seek partners that will join with us in advocating for shifts in public policy and open up new channels of funding and other resources for programming and grassroots activities
>
> Because of this strategy of proactive, long-term engagement, it is rare that we will accept unsolicited requests.

Northern and Shell Network Ltd

Media

Correspondent: R Sanderson, Company Secretary, The Northern and Shell Building, Number 10 Lower Thames Street, London EC3R 6EN (tel: 08714341010; website: www.northernandshell.co.uk/community)

Directors: Richard C. Desmond, Chair; S. Myerson; R. Sanderson; M. S. Ellice; P. Ashford (women: 0; men: 5)

Year end	31/12/2011
Turnover	£713,618,000
Pre-tax profit	£4,979,000

Nature of business: Holding company in the Northern and Shell group of companies principally engaged in newspaper publishing and printing, magazine publishing and television broadcasting.

Company registration number: 4086475

Total employees: 1,347

Charitable donations

UK cash (latest declared):	2011	£518,000
	2008	£554,000
	2007	£547,000
	2006	£868,000
Total UK:	2011	£518,000
Total worldwide:	2011	£790,000
Cash worldwide:	2011	£790,000

Community involvement

RD Crusaders Foundation (Charity Commission no.: 1014352).

In recent years the foundation has focused its awards on children and young people's charities in the UK and has contributed extensively to further the wellbeing of disadvantaged sections of society. However larger charities have also benefited extensively with donations to schools, hospitals, old people's homes, carer organisations, hospices and a wide range of medical support groups.

Children's charities remain the focus of the foundation but consideration is given by the trustees to worthy causes outside this area, so long as the funds awarded can make a difference.

Corporate giving

During the year 2011, the Group made contributions of £790,000 (2010: £551,000) including £518,000 to the **RD Crusaders Foundation**.

In 2011 the foundation awarded £589,000 in grants. Beneficiaries included: Fight for Sight (£50,000); Elton John Aids Foundation (£35,000); Guys and St Thomas' Charity (£26,000); National Communities Resource Centre, Outward Bound Trust and RNIB (£10,000 each); Chai Cancer Care and Disability Challengers (£5,000 each); and Holocaust Centre, Juvenile Diabetes Research and Prospect Hospice (£1,000) each. Other grants of less than £1,000 totalled £11,000.

Corporate social responsibility

CSR committee: No details found.

CSR policy: No CSR statement but the following is taken from the company's website:

> Charitable giving lies at the heart of Northern & Shell. As a responsible business we are constantly on the lookout for opportunities to support a diverse range of good causes in every possible way. As our network has grown, so has

our commitment to working in the community.

CSR report: No details found.

Exclusions

No support for political appeals.

Applications

Applications for donations from the company should be made to the company secretary at the address given.

Applications to the *foundation* should be made in writing and sent to: Allison Racher, The RD Crusaders Foundation, Northern and Shell Building, Number 10 Lower Thames Street, London EC3R 6EN. (Tel: 08715207760; Email: allison.racher@express.co.uk).

Northern Foods Ltd

Food manufacture

Correspondent: Carol Williams, Company Secretary, 2180 Century Way, Thorpe Park, Leeds LS15 8ZB (tel: 01133 900110; website: www.northern-foods.co.uk)

Directors: R. S. Boparan; B. K. Boparan; K. Derry; S. Henderson; G. Hunter; K. Kular; V. Patel; J. Silk

Year end	02/04/2011
Turnover	£934,900,000
Pre-tax profit	(£12,300,000)

Nature of business: A leading supplier of high-quality chilled foods under the own labels of the major multiple retailers, with strong brands of its own in premium quality biscuits, fresh chilled dairy products, frozen food and savoury pastry products. The company has a strong operating presence in Nottingham, Sheffield, Greater Manchester, Batley and Lancashire.

Company registration number: 471864

Main locations: Accrington, Bolton, Batley, Sheffield, Nottingham, Oldham, Market Drayton, Manchester, Worksop, Wakefield, Corby, Carlisle, Hull

Total employees: 9,034

Charitable donations

UK cash (latest declared):	2011	£100,000
	2009	£93,900
	2008	£60,000
	2007	£59,600
	2006	£89,000
Total UK:	2011	£100,000
Total worldwide:	2011	£100,000
Cash worldwide:	2011	£100,000

Corporate social responsibility

CSR policy: No CSR information found.

We were unable to determine the ratio of women to men on the board.

Exclusions

No support for political or religious appeals.

Applications

In writing to the correspondent.

Other information

In 2010/11 the company made charitable donations totalling £100,000. We have no details of beneficiaries.

The company set up **The Northern Foods Foundation for Science and Technology**, (this is not a registered charity), which sponsors 30 new post-A-Level students a year throughout their degree course at Leeds, Nottingham and Reading universities. The company supports students wishing to study food science by awarding grants of £1,000.

Give As You Earn

The company operates a scheme.

Northern Powergrid Holdings Company (formerly CE Electric)

Electricity

Correspondent: J Elliot, Company Secretary, Lloyds Court, 78 Grey Street, Newcastle upon Tyne NE1 6AF (tel: 0800 668 877; website: www.northernpowergrid.com)

Directors: G. E. Abel; D. L. Anderson; R. Dixon; J. M. France; P. J. Goodman; P. A. Jones; J. N. Reynolds

Year end	31/12/2010
Turnover	£605,674,000
Pre-tax profit	£256,435,000

Nature of business: The company is responsible for delivering electricity to over 3.8 million properties across the North East of England, Yorkshire and northern Lincolnshire, operating through its subsidiary companies Northern Electric Distribution (NEDL) in the North East and North Yorkshire and Yorkshire Electricity Distribution (YEDL) in South and East Yorkshire and northern Lincolnshire.

Company registration number: 3476201

Charitable donations

UK cash (latest declared):	2010	£56,800
	2009	£100,600
	2008	£69,000
	2006	£57,000
	2005	£54,500
Total UK:	2010	£56,800
Total worldwide:	2010	£56,800
Cash worldwide:	2010	£56,800

Corporate social responsibility

CSR committee: There is no evidence of a separate CSR committee.

CSR policy: This information was obtained from the company's website: 'Northern Powergrid plays an active role in social, environmental and safety initiatives with communities across Yorkshire and the Northeast.'

Unable to determine the ratio of women to men on the Board.

CSR report: There is no evidence of a separate CSR report.

Exclusions

No support for circular appeals, advertising in national charity brochures, animal welfare, appeals from individuals, the arts, fundraising events, heritage, medical research, overseas projects, political or religious appeals, science/technology, sickness/disability, or a 'Charity of the Year'.

Applications

In writing to the correspondent.

Other information

During 2010, Northern Powergrid, formerly known as CE Electric, made charitable donations of £56,800 (2009: £100,600), principally to local charities serving the communities where the group has a presence.

Northern Rock (Asset Management) plc

Financial services

Correspondent: Paul Hopkinson, Company Secretary, Northern Rock House, Gosforth, Newcastle upon Tyne NE3 4PL (tel: 01912 857191; fax: 01912 848470; website: www.virgin.com/company/virgin-money-uk)

Directors: Richard Pym; Kent Atkinson; Richard Banks; Michael Buckley; Sue Langley; Philip McLelland; Keith Morgan; Louise Patten; John Tattershall (women: 2; men: 7)

Year end	31/12/2011
Turnover	£1,264,000,000
Pre-tax profit	£789,900,000

Nature of business: The following announcement has been made by Northern Rock (Asset Management) plc.

> The legal and capital restructure of the former Northern Rock was successfully completed on 1 January 2010. This resulted in the creation of two separate entities: Northern Rock (Asset Management) plc, *the existing company renamed* and a new bank, Northern Rock plc.
>
> - **Northern Rock (Asset Management) plc**, the existing company renamed, which held approximately £50 billion of residential mortgages and unsecured loans of £3.9 billion immediately post-restructure. Northern Rock (Asset Management) plc holds the government loan plus Northern Rock's non-deposit wholesale and secured funding instruments. Northern Rock (Asset Management) plc does not hold any retail deposits and does not offer any new mortgage lending
> - **Northern Rock plc**, a savings and mortgage bank that holds and services

> all customer savings accounts and a mortgage book which includes approximately £10 billion of mortgages transferred from the former Northern Rock at the start of 2010. The new bank is regulated as a deposit taker and mortgage lender by the FSA. It offers new savings products and new mortgage lending to increase mortgage supply and help sustain a competitive market. Northern Rock plc also holds certain wholesale deposits.

On 12 October 2012 Northern Rock plc was renamed Virgin Money plc, and Virgin Money Ltd was renamed Northern Rock Ltd.

Company registration number: 3273685

Subsidiaries include: Indemnity Company Ltd

Main locations: Newcastle upon Tyne

Total employees: 1,332

Charitable donations

UK cash (latest declared):	2011	£11,640
	2010	£15,000,000
	2009	£15,000,000
	2008	£15,000,000
	2007	£14,300,000
Total UK:	2011	£11,640
Total worldwide:	2011	£11,640
Cash worldwide:	2011	£11,640

Community involvement

The conversion of Northern Rock Building Society into a public company was completed on 1 October 1997. An integral part of this was the formation of a charitable body, the Northern Rock Foundation (Charity Commission no. 1063906). This was launched in January 1998 and is entitled to receive a covenant of about five % of annual pre-tax profits of Northern Rock plc.

In February 2008, Northern Rock was taken into temporary public ownership. As part of this arrangement the Chancellor announced that the foundation would receive a minimum of £15 million a year in 2008, 2009 and 2010 from Northern Rock.

The Northern Rock Foundation
(Charity Commission no. 1063906)
An independent charity, the foundation aims to tackle disadvantage and improve the quality of life in the North East and Cumbria. A board of trustees representing a wide range of interests in the community makes all decisions on governance, finance and policy.

The following information is taken from the charity's 2011 annual report and accounts:

> As a large and engaged grant-maker with a wide range of interests, the Foundation has had numerous grant-making programmes and special initiatives, a set of policies for delivering them and detailed guidance for applicants. Currently the Foundation operates five main grants programmes: Managing Money, Having a Home, Enabling Independence and Choice, Safety and Justice for Victims of Abuse and Changing Lives. Funding for training and development as well as for research and commissions, also continued.
>
> During 2011 the Foundation also piloted a new grant programme, the Fresh Ideas Fund, to provide funding for early stage development of new business ideas to help charities to grow in size, increase their impact and improve their long-term sustainability.

Detailed and helpful information regarding the foundation's activities and procedures can be found on its website: www.nr-foundation.org.uk, which was reviewed and updated in 2011.

Corporate giving

In November 2011 it was announced that Virgin Money would become the new owners of Northern Rock plc, and this acquisition took place on 1 January 2012. The funding agreement with Northern Rock plc to provide 1% of pre-tax profits to the **Northern Rock Foundation** has been renewed by Virgin Money until December 2013. A review of the foundation's strategy will be carried out in 2012, in the light of ongoing discussions with Virgin Money on future support and funding for the foundation.

We have retained this entry for readers because of the association of names between the company and the foundation. Financial information is taken from the annual report and accounts for 2011 of Northern Rock (Asset Management) plc.

The only charitable contributions we could determine from NRAM itself-was in the form of support for staff fundraising activities by way of matched funding and matching employee donations through a payroll-giving programme. During the year, NRAM matched employee fundraising to the total of £6,420 and payroll-giving totalled £5,220.

The company has also given gifts in kind in the form of staff's volunteering their skills, but we have no valuation for this contribution.

The Northern Rock Foundation
The main grant programmes for 2011 were: Managing Money, Having a Home, Enabling Independence and Choice, Safety and Justice for Victims of Abuse and Changing Lives. Funding for training and development as well as for research and commissions, was also available.

During the year, the foundation awarded 166 grants totalling £7.4 million under its grant programmes. 27% of the amount awarded was to projects within Tyne and Wear and 3% to projects benefiting the whole of the North East and Cumbria. Of the 166 grants awarded in 2011, 71% were for amounts below £60,000 and 10% were for amounts of £100,000 or more.

Beneficiaries included: Derwentside Domestic Abuse Service (£44,000); Cornerstone Supported Housing (£18,500); Humanah Community Consortium CIC (£15,000); The Octopus Collective (£10,000); and Northumbria Coalition Against Crime (£2,500).

There is a detailed entry for The Northern Rock Foundation in DSC's The Guide to Major Trusts Volume 1.

Employee-led support

Matched funding: The Staff Matched Giving Scheme supports individual colleagues who wish to raise money for, or give money to, UK registered charities or to exempt and excepted charities. The trustees have set an annual limit of £1,000 per person per year and £250,000 for the scheme in total.

Payroll giving: The Give As You Earn scheme is in operation.

Corporate social responsibility

CSR policy: No CSR information available.

Exclusions

The following information is from the *Grant programmes Guidance for Applicants*, which is available at the foundation's website:

> There are certain organisations, projects and proposals that we will **not** consider for grants. You should be aware that it costs the equivalent of several small grants to administer ineligible applications each year. If your organisation or your project falls into one of the categories below please **do not apply** to us for a grant.
>
> - Activities which are not recognised as charitable in law
> - Applications for under £1,000
> - Charities which appear to us to have excessive unrestricted or free reserves (up to 12 months expenditure is normally acceptable), or are in serious deficit
> - National charities which do not have a regional office or other representation in North East England or Cumbria
> - Grant-making bodies seeking to distribute grants on our behalf
> - Open-ended funding agreements
> - General appeals, sponsorship and marketing appeals
> - Corporate applications for founder membership of a charity
> - Retrospective grants
> - Replacement of statutory funding
> - Activities primarily the responsibility of central or local government or health authorities
> - Individuals and organisations that distribute funds to individuals
> - Animal welfare
> - Mainstream educational activity, schools and educational establishments
> - Medical research, hospitals, hospices and medical centres

- Medical treatments and therapies including art therapy
- Fabric appeals for places of worship
- Promotion of religion
- Expeditions or overseas travel
- Minibuses, other vehicles and transport schemes except where they are a small and integral part of a larger scheme
- Holidays and outings
- Playgrounds and play equipment
- Private clubs or those with such restricted membership as to make them not charitable
- Capital bids purely towards compliance with the Disability Discrimination Act
- Amateur arts organisations
- Musical instruments
- Sports kit and equipment

Applications

The following information is taken from the Northern Rock Foundation's website:

> The Foundation's trustees are reviewing the priorities for our grant programmes for 2013 to 2015 and plan to tighten further the focus of the grant programmes. Full details will be announced in January 2013.
>
> Any organisation planning to apply to the Foundation should contact the relevant Programme Manager before preparing an application. Potential applicants should be aware that the Foundation now concentrates on organisations it currently has a relationship with.
>
> The Foundation is currently funding its grant programmes from its reserves, which are expected to be fully expended in 2015. However, the Foundation remains in discussion with Virgin Money regarding future arrangements.
>
> If you have not applied to the Foundation previously please contact us before applying.
>
> Please read both the guidelines for applicants and completing an application for a grant before applying to us.
>
> If you are applying for salary costs please read the additional guidance on employing people.

Northern Trust Group Ltd

Leisure, property

Correspondent: The Corporate Responsiblity Committee, Lynton House, Ackhurst Business Park, Foxhole Road, Chorley PR7 1NY (tel: 01257 269400; fax: 01257 269997; website: www.northerntrust.com)

Directors: Frederick H. Waddell, Chair and Chief Executive; William L. Morrison; Sherry S. Barrat; Jeffrey D. Cohodes; Steven L. Fradkin; Timothy P. Moen; Michael G. O'Grady; Stephen N. Potter; Jana R. Schreuder; Joyce M. St Clair; Kelly R. Welsh (women: 4; men: 7)

Year end	31/12/2010
Turnover	£2,440,000,000
Pre-tax profit	£25,000,000

Nature of business: Property, leisure and investment.

Company registration number: 2776907

Total employees: 14,100

Charitable donations

UK cash (latest declared):	2010	£2,500
	2009	£37,000
	2008	£1,050,000
	2007	£25,000
	2006	£63,000
Total UK:	2010	£2,500
Total worldwide:	2010	£2,500
Cash worldwide:	2010	£2,500

Corporate social responsibility

CSR committee: There was evidence of a separate CSR Committee.

CSR policy: This information was obtained from the company's CSR Report:

> We are dedicated not only to meeting the needs of our clients and shareholders, but also serving as a responsible corporate citizen through support for the diverse communities and environments in which we live and work.
>
> Northern Trust supports organisations working in three core areas: education, social welfare, and arts and culture.
>
> We are committed to supporting education organisations that bring innovative, comprehensive and exemplary programs to students. Through our efforts to augment the priorities and goals of local education organisations, students in our global locations gain additional tools to strengthen their academic achievement and leadership development.
>
> We support effective organisations working to measurably improve the quality of life in our focus communities. Health, basic human needs and community development programs provide invaluable support to people who face obstacles that impede their full participation in society.
>
> And, we support organisations that bring opportunities to our communities, in order to create forums for social interaction that celebrate all of our diversity and heritage.

CSR report: There was evidence of a separate CSR report.

Exclusions

None known.

Applications

In writing to the correspondent.

Other information

The company donated £2,500 to the UK. The sole beneficiary was BBC Children in Need.

Northumbrian Water Group

Water

Correspondent: The Community Relations Manager, Abbey Road, Pity Me, Durham DH1 5FJ (tel: 0870 608 4820; website: www.nwl.co.uk)

Directors: Andrew John Hunter, Chair; Heidi Mottram, Chief Executive; Chris Green; Graham Neave; Ceri Jones; Duncan Nicholas Macrae; Tak Chuen Edmond; Hing Lam Kam; Martin Negre; Dr Simon Lyster; Margaret Fay; Paul Rew; Frank Frame; Martin Parker (women: 3; men: 11)

Year end	31/03/2011
Turnover	£738,100,000
Pre-tax profit	£304,200,000

Nature of business: Northumbrian Water Group plc is one of the UK's ten water and sewerage businesses. The company and its subsidiaries work in three related areas: the supply of water and waste water services within the UK; international water management; and a range of supporting technical and consultancy services.

Company registration number: 2560626

Main locations: Durham

UK employees: 3,031

Total employees: 3,031

Membership: BITC

Charitable donations

UK cash (latest declared):	2011	£152,000
	2009	£134,000
	2008	£135,000
	2007	£129,000
	2006	£122,000
Total UK:	2011	£152,000
Total worldwide:	2011	£152,000
Cash worldwide:	2011	£152,000

Corporate social responsibility

CSR committee: A CSR Committee was present. The CSR Committee consists of non-executive directors, NWL directors and senior managers who oversee all aspects of the company's CSR policy.

CSR policy: This information was obtained from the company's website:

> Communities are important to us and we want to build strong relationships with the communities we serve. We will ensure that corporate responsibility is embedded in performance management and that we benchmark ourselves against the best companies.

CSR report: This information was obtained from the company's website:

> In previous years we reported on corporate responsibility as a separate report. From 2011, in line with our vision and values, and reflecting the importance of sustainability to our business and how deeply it is embedded, we believe we should report sustainability issues

alongside our core business activities. We have done this throughout our annual report.

Exclusions

No support for circular appeals, local appeals not in areas of company presence, large national appeals or overseas projects (other than support for WaterAid).

Applications

In writing to the correspondent.

Other information

During 2010/11 the company made charitable donations of £152,000.

The following information is taken from the company's website:

> An employee volunteering scheme launched in 2002, *Just an Hour*, encourages employees to spend an hour of work time a month providing support to community or environmental initiatives. 27% of employees participate in the *Just an Hour* volunteering scheme and last year gave over 7,600 hours to the community.
>
> The *Care for Safety* scheme, which encourages employees to reduce accidents and associated lost time, has triggered payments totalling almost £16,000 (2008/09: £50,000) for nominated charities including: Great North Air Ambulance Service, Royal National Lifeboat Institution and Zoe's Place.
>
> The company gives additional support through gifts in kind, joint promotions and encouraging employee volunteering.
>
> **Sponsorship:** *The arts* – in recent years the company has sponsored the RSC.
>
> NWG gives not only money but also time and facilities to help its communities. These activities are mainly targeted to support projects which make the areas served better places in which to live, work or invest. The key elements of the programme include:
>
> - An extensive community involvement programme supporting the work of community foundations and encouraging voluntary time through the 'Just an hour' scheme and funding through 'Cheque it out
> - Health and environmental campaigning, including our innovative 'Water for health' initiative
> - Educational programmes which range from curriculum support to 'Back to Business' where NWL is a lead partner in a pilot scheme to link schools and businesses
> - Environmental partnerships and campaigns where, as well as being a member of many environmental organisations, NWL has developed some key partnerships to help the conservation and biodiversity of our sites, for example, with the Essex Wildlife Trust at Hanningfield
> - Regional support for local community organisations and support for our adopted charity, WaterAid

Nottingham Building Society

Building society

Correspondent: Anna Croasdale, Public Relations Manager, 5–13 Upper Parliament Street, Nottingham NG1 2BX (tel: 01159 481444; email: anna.croasdale@thenottingham.com; website: www.thenottingham.com)

Directors: David Marlow, Chief Executive; David Thompson, Chair; Robert Marchant; John Edwards; Richard Fiddis; Jane Kibbey; Mahomed Ashraf Piranie; Simon Taylor; Keith Whitesides (women: 1; men: 8)

Year end	31/12/2011
Turnover	£144,000,000
Pre-tax profit	£7,200,000

Nature of business: Independent building society offering a range of financial products and services.

FSA registration number: 200785

Main locations: Nottingham

UK employees: 401

Total employees: 401

Charitable donations

UK cash (latest declared):	2011	£49,000
	2009	£0
	2007	£22,720
	2005	£45,630
	2003	£55,538
Total UK:	2011	£49,000
Total worldwide:	2011	£49,000
Cash worldwide:	2011	£49,000

Corporate social responsibility

CSR committee: There was no evidence of a separate CSR Committee.

CSR policy: The group aims to help people with basic needs; education, housing, employment and personal finance management so that they can support themselves whilst also building strong, thriving communities.

CSR report: A separate CSR report was unavailable; however, information was available in the group's company accounts.

Exclusions

No support for advertising in charity brochures, appeals from individuals, children/youth, education, elderly people enterprise/training, overseas projects, political appeals, part funding of a larger project, travel expenses, rent or property maintenance, staffing costs or projects which are the responsibility of statutory organisations.

Applications

Application forms are available from the society or from local branches.

Other information

The group made charitable donations of £49,000 in 2011.

During 2010, a decision was taken that the group would take a more active role in supporting the local community. In early 2011, the group's community investment programme 'Doing Good Together' was launched, consisting of three key elements; fundraising, community grants and volunteering, with activity during 2011 focused on the themes of homelessness, financial education and employability.

With the assistance of the Nottinghamshire Community Foundation, the group have given community grants totalling £16,790 to ten charitable groups. At the end of 2011, the group has also put aside additional sums for the Nottinghamshire Community Foundation.

The group also assisted its funding charity partner, Framework, in a variety of initiatives with donations totalling £7,000.

The group continued its support of Nottingham Forest Football Club's Youth Academy through its Nottingham Forest Saver Account.

Employee volunteering/fundraising is also encouraged and the company will match fund monies raised up to £300 per event.

Novae Group plc

Insurance

Correspondent: Charities Committee, 71 Fenchurch Street, London EC3M 4HH (tel: 020 7903 7300; fax: 020 7903 7333; email: enquiries@novae.com; website: www.novae.com)

Directors: John Hastings-Bass, Chair; Matthew Fosh, Group Chief Executive; Oliver Corbett, Chief Financial Officer; Jeremy Adams; Laurie Adams; Bryan Carsberg; David Henderson; David Pye (women: 0; men: 8)

Year end	31/12/2011
Turnover	£606,400,000
Pre-tax profit	(£6,300,000)

Nature of business: Novae Group plc is the holding company of a group that carries on insurance business and associated financial activities.

Company registration number: 5673306

Total employees: 268

Charitable donations

UK cash (latest declared):	2011	£213,000
	2009	£47,000
	2008	£37,000
	2007	£25,000
	2006	£10,000
Total UK:	2011	£213,000
Total worldwide:	2011	£213,000
Cash worldwide:	2011	£213,000

Corporate social responsibility

CSR committee: There is a Charities Committee.

CSR policy: Taken from the company's website:

> Novae's long-term commercial success depends upon ethical treatment of its investors, clients, staff and suppliers; on its relationship with the community in which it operates; and on its approach to environmental issues. Novae's policies in these areas, which have been built on a stakeholder review conducted in 2007, are therefore central to its business practice.

CSR report: CSR is reported on within the annual report and accounts.

Applications

In writing to the correspondent.

Other information

Total donations to charities in 2011 amounted to £213,000 (£121,000 in 2010). In addition in 2011 Novae contributed £25,000 to Team GB for London 2012, complementing its contribution of £25,000 in 2010.

The company's 2011 annual report states:

> Novae acknowledges that its ability to achieve its strategic and operational goals is facilitated by its active engagement in the community and by its support of social and charitable initiatives. Novae actively supports staff involvement in programmes that contribute positively to society and the community in which the Group operates by providing financial and other support for initiatives inside and outside the workplace that directly and indirectly reinforce corporate policies and practices. Novae also promotes payroll giving and has a Payroll Giving Quality Mark from the Charities Trust.
>
> The group's Charities Committee has an annual budget of £10,000. In the year under review staff participated in sponsored events raising funds for charities in which they have a particular interest. Subject to a cap, Novae has matched the funds raised. Some funding is given following staff nominations of charities and there is a particular emphasis on the support of smaller charities for which the group's contribution will make a difference. Specific examples include Willen Hospice, The Newman Trust and The Red and White Appeal.
>
> Novae also supports staff who give their time to the Lloyd's Community Programme.
>
> At a corporate level, Novae has continued to support The Prince's Trust. As patrons the group contributed £174,000 in 2011 (£116,659 in 2010), comprising £161,000 of corporate support and a further £13,000 through fundraising events in which the group's staff participated. The most significant event which Novae sponsored in the year (for the second year running) was The Prince's Trust Rock Gala. Novae is particularly pleased to continue to support The Prince's Trust's work focused on mentoring support for the young to secure goals in employment, education and training.

Ocado Group Ltd

Food services

Correspondent: Charity Committee, Titan Court, 3 Bishop Square, Hatfield Business Park, Hatfield, Hertfordshire AL10 9NE (tel: 01707 227800; fax: 01707 227999; email: company.secretary@ocado.com; website: www.ocadogroup.com)

Directors: Michael Grade, Chair; Tim Steiner, Chief Executive Officer; Neill Abrams; David Grigson; Ruth Anderson; Robert Gorrie; Andrew Bracey, Chief Financial Officer; Jason Gissing; Mark Richardson; David Young; Jörn Rausing; Douglas McCallum (women: 1; men: 11)

Year end	27/11/2011
Turnover	£598,309,000
Pre-tax profit	(£2,423,000)

Nature of business: Online grocer operating home delivery.

Company registration number: 3875000

Total employees: 5,180

Charitable donations

UK cash (latest declared):	2009	£2,000
Total worldwide:	2011	£29,250
Cash worldwide:	2011	£29,250

Corporate social responsibility

CSR committee: In 2010 Ocado established a charity committee made up of eight employees, which increased to twelve employees in April 2011.

> **CSR policy:** Operating our business in a responsible way is fundamental both to the way we operate and to delivering sustainable profits and long-term value for our shareholders. The corporate social responsibility report explains how the group carries out its responsibilities with respect to the environment, employment practices and the community.

CSR report: Contained within the annual report and accounts.

Applications

In writing to the correspondent.

Other information

The following information is taken from the 2010/11 annual report and accounts:

> Ocado made charitable donations during the period 2010/11 of £29,250 (2009/10: £14,000) which includes £20,000 to Peace Winds (described below), £5,000 sponsorship of a visit from Lech Walesa, the former first president of Poland, for Migrant at Home Magazine as well as donations (of less than £2,000) to Peace One Day, CTT, Credit Action, the PwC Partners Charity Walk and various charity events.
>
> *Japan Appeal*: Ocado established an appeal to raise money for a Japanese charity called Peace Winds, who were helping over 300,000 people affected by the Japan tsunami and earthquake and subsequent Fukushima power plant evacuation in March 2011 by providing emergency food and blankets. Ocado appealed to its customers and staff for donations and promised to match the first £20,000 raised. The Ocado appeal raised over £250,000 for Peace Winds.
>
> *Peace One Day*: Peace One Day is a non-profit organisation which has established a ceasefire and non-violence day that occurs on 21 September each year. They are committed to raising global awareness of the 'peace day' through education and encouraging the global community to take action. Ocado is supporting this organisation by funding Peace One Day's 'UK citizenship resource pack' for secondary schools. Ocado funded a full time out-reach coordinator for three months to help schools use these resources; which were delivered to 31,500 students. In the next year, Ocado intends to support the creation by Peace One Day of a new resource for primary school children.
>
> *Christmas food donations*: Each Christmas, Ocado donates food for hampers to charities helping impoverished communities across the country. In the period, Ocado donated food to DENS, a charity based in Hemel Hempstead, SHOC based in Reading and Action for Children in Bristol.
>
> *Re-Wrap*: Ocado is currently producing canvas tote bags for customers with Re-Wrap. Re-Wrap is a not-for-profit organisation which works with disadvantaged families in India who produce the bags. The materials used are sustainable and recycled textiles and eco-friendly dyes. Re-Wrap are also a member of the World Fair Trade Organisation. By working with Re-Wrap, Ocado is helping to sustain disadvantaged families in India, retaining traditional Indian craft and supporting fair trade practices.
>
> JAMI: Ocado donated a significant number of desktop computers to the registered mental health charity, JAMI. The desktop computers were being replaced as part of the upgrades to the Ocado customer call centre.

Old Mutual plc

Financial services

Correspondent: Responsible Business Committee, 5th Floor, Old Mutual Place, 2 Lambeth Hill, London EC4V 4GG (tel: 020 7002 7000; website: www.oldmutual.com)

Directors: Patrick O'Sullivan, Chair; Julian Roberts, Group Chief Executive; Philip Broadley, Group Finance Director; Miles Arnold; Eva Castillo; Russell Edey; Alan Gillespie; Reuel Khoza; Roger Marshall; Bongani Nqwababa; Nku

Nyembezi-Heita; Lars Otterbeck (women: 2)

Year end	31/12/2011
Turnover	£9,784,000,000
Pre-tax profit	£994,000,000

Nature of business: Provision of financial services.

Company registration number: 3591559

Main locations: London

UK employees: 10

Total employees: 57,430

Charitable donations

UK cash (latest declared):	2009	£195,000
	2008	£672,000
	2007	£352,000
	2006	£359,000
	2005	£382,000
Total worldwide:	2011	£11,600,000
Cash worldwide:	2011	£216,000

Corporate social responsibility

CSR committee: There is a Responsible Business Committee which appears to be responsible for all CSR issues.

CSR policy: Taken from the Responsible Business Report for 2011:

> At a group level, we have adopted a more strategic approach to our community investment, focusing on financial education, enterprise and skills development and local community development. This ensures that the time and resources we commit are aligned to our core business objectives, and aligned to the skills and experience of our people.

CSR report: Annual report on responsible business entitled: 'Investing in the Future'.

Exclusions

No grants towards: sports; religious organisations; capital projects; non-registered charities; organisations without published, audited accounts for the last three years; or organisations whose total administrative and marketing expenses exceed 12% of the income.

Applications

In writing to the correspondent.

Other information

The company, its subsidiaries in the UK, and the Old Mutual Bermuda Foundation collectively made charitable donations of £216,000 during the year (2010: £191,000).

The company states in its 2011 Sustainable Business Report that:

> Community investment is delivered by individual business units through our five Old Mutual Foundations, the Nedbank Foundation and budgets focused on social investment. Our commitment usually extends beyond direct funding and often includes gifts in kind, such as the supply of venues, printed materials for projects and research support. Employees also share their time, skills and experience through volunteering programmes.
>
> *The Old Mutual Foundations*
>
> Of the total £11.6 million invested in communities by Old Mutual, £2.9 million was donated by the five foundations for the UK, Zimbabwe, South Africa, Malawi and Namibian businesses. The foundations primarily fund programmes aligned to the group's community investment approach focusing on financial education, enterprise and skills development and local community development. Most of the employee volunteering programmes are supported through the work of the Foundations to ensure Old Mutual's resources create maximum positive impact in society.

The majority of the company's community investment is overseas and there is little mention of giving within the UK, however we do know that the group head office continued to support financial education in London through the Young Enterprise Scheme, reaching over 4,000 young people.

Oracle Corporation UK Ltd

Information technology

Correspondent: Corporate/Community Senior Director, Oracle Parkway, Thames Valley Park, Reading, Berkshire RG6 1RA (tel: 01189 240000/01189 246468; fax: 01189 243000; website: www.oracle.com/uk)

Directors: D. Hudson; S. Allison; E. Courtney; J. Cleary

Year end	31/05/2011
Turnover	£26,820,000,000

Nature of business: Producer of IT solutions and database software.

Company registration number: 1782505

Main locations: Manchester, London, Reading, Edinburgh, Bristol, Birmingham, Belfast

UK employees: 4,544

Total employees: 104,569

Membership: BITC

Charitable donations

UK cash (latest declared):	2011	£0
Total UK:	2011	£0
Total worldwide:	2011	£1,415,000,000
Cash worldwide:	2011	£5,500,000

Corporate social responsibility

CSR committee: No UK details.

CSR policy: The following information is taken from the Corporate Citizenship Report for 2010:

> We continue to support K-12 and higher education institutions with technology education programs that reach 1.5 million students each year. Working to reduce our environmental footprint, we manage our facilities and business operations with an eye toward sustainability. We also donate millions of dollars to nonprofit organisations that share our goal of enriching community life globally.

No UK specific CSR information could be found.

We were unable to determine the ratio of women to men on the board.

CSR report: The group produces a corporate citizenship report which provides detailed information on its global, corporate contribution and can be obtained from its website.

Applications

In writing to the correspondent.

Other information

During 2010/11 the UK company declared nil charitable donations in its annual report and accounts. There seems to be little information available regarding the group's UK community investment but as a member of Business in the Community we believe the company still provides in kind support to charities in the UK focusing on advancing education, protecting the environment and enriching the community.

Data for this listing is taken from the from the group's Corporate Citizenship Report 2010. The directors listed are those for the UK company.

The company has helped Berkshire schools create materials to enhance financial coursework in business studies programmes and has established a number of resources, such as Think.com and Oracle Internet Academy, which provide free educational information for teachers and students alike.

Almost all of the group's charitable investment appears to be made overseas although the UK is included as a beneficiary of the Teach for All programme.

Teach For All: Oracle's grant expands the Teach For All network – which currently includes organisations in the US, UK, India, Australia, Argentina, Chile, Peru, Germany, Estonia, Latvia, and Lebanon – to 12 additional countries. The group's donation funds global infrastructure development, and the recruitment and training of 3,000 teachers in 23 countries.

Worldwide giving

The 2010 Corporate Citizenship Report states: 'In 2010, Oracle donated more than US$9 million [£5.5 million] in cash to nonprofit organisations and more than US$2.3 billion [£1.4 billion] in in kind resources to educational institutions.'

Volunteering

In 2010, Oracle employees logged 47,000 volunteer hours in 47 countries.

Organix Brands Ltd

Food manufacture, food services

Correspondent: Company Secretary, The Greenhouse, 120–122 Commercial Road, Bournemouth, Dorset BH2 5LT (tel: 0800 393 511; website: www.organix.com)

Directors: A. Rosier; A. Lawson; R. Baenziger

Year end	31/12/2010
Turnover	£33,954,000
Pre-tax profit	£2,190,000

Nature of business: The supply of baby and children's organic food to retailers for sale to the public.

Company registration number: 2716145

Total employees: 44

Charitable donations

UK cash (latest declared):	2010	£120,000
	2009	£120,000
Total UK:	2010	£120,000
Total worldwide:	2010	£120,000
Cash worldwide:	2010	£120,000

Corporate social responsibility

CSR committee: No information available.

CSR policy: We do not know the ratio of women to men on the board.

CSR report: None published.

Applications

In writing to the correspondent for requests from the company and to the correspondent of the company's foundation for grants.

Other information

In 2010 the company gave £120,000 in charitable donations. It would appear that this amount was given to The Organix Foundation (Charity Commission no. 1127780). The main activities of the charity in 2010/11 were to provide donations amounting to £202,460 (2010: £109,576) to aid research and included payments to the Food Commission and a number of Universities.

The Organix Foundation

This foundation has been established to advance education in food, nutrition and health, including undertaking and publishing research, for the benefit of young people and children. The foundation also makes grants. Further information can be found at: www.organixfoundation.org

The foundation's correspondent is Elizabeth Vann Thrasher, The Saxon Centre, Bargates, Christchurch BH23 1PZ. email: admin@organixfoundation.org telephone: 01202 486245.

Osborne and Little Ltd

Household, textiles

Correspondent: Human Resources, Riverside House, 26 Osiers Road, London SW18 1NH (tel: 020 8812 3000; fax: 020 8877 7500; email: oand@osborneandlittle.com; website: www.osborneandlittle.com)

Directors: Peter George Osborne; Peter Soar; Peter Worsfold; Graham John Noakes; Felicity Alexandra Osborne (women: 1; men: 4)

Year end	31/03/2011
Turnover	£22,914,000
Pre-tax profit	(£739,000)

Nature of business: The design and distribution of fine furnishing fabrics and wallpapers.

Company registration number: 923748

Main locations: London

Total employees: 141

Charitable donations

UK cash (latest declared):	2009	£11,200
	2008	£16,200
	2007	£16,000
	2006	£21,000
Total worldwide:	2011	£19,100
Cash worldwide:	2011	£19,100

Corporate social responsibility

CSR committee: No details found.

CSR policy: None published.

CSR report: None published.

Exclusions

The company does not advertise in charity brochures.

Applications

In writing to the correspondent.

Other information

In 2010/11 the company gave £19,100 in charitable donations. We have been told previously that education, the arts and children's organisations are preferred, but unfortunately, we have no details of the beneficiaries for this year.

Page Group (formerly Michael Page International)

Professional support services

Correspondent: Corporate Social Responsibility Team, Page House, 1 Dashwood Lang Road, Addlestone, Weybridge, Surrey KT15 2QW (website: www.page.com)

Directors: Robert Buchanan, Chair; Steve Ingham, Chief Executive; Andrew Bracey, Chief Financial Officer; Charles-Henri Dumon; Ruby McGregor-Smith; Tim Miller; Stephen Puckett; Hubert Reid; Reg Sindall (women: 1; men: 8)

Year end	31/12/2011
Turnover	£1,019,087,000
Pre-tax profit	£86,147,000

Nature of business: The group's business is in professional services recruitment.

Company registration number: 3310225

Total employees: 5,060

Charitable donations

UK cash (latest declared):	2009	£190,000
	2008	£153,400
Total worldwide:	2011	£299,000
Cash worldwide:	2011	£299,000

Corporate social responsibility

CSR committee: No specific details found.

CSR policy: Taken from the 2011 CSR report:

> Throughout the world, we seek to work closely with local communities, looking to give something back to the societies we operate in. To achieve this, we encourage our staff to be proactive in seeking projects within their own communities and to make a telling contribution. Around the world projects include consultants going into schools and giving CV and interview advice, as well as volunteers helping out on community or environmental projects in places such as hospitals, care homes, social centres and wildlife sanctuaries.

CSR report: Published annually and available online.

Applications

In writing to the correspondent.

Other information

The group made charitable donations of £299,000 during the year (2010: £181,000).

The following information is taken from the company's CSR report for 2011.

> *Volunteering*
>
> The UK's More Giving scheme allows each employee to have one day per year to help make a difference in the local community, or to a support a charity. In 2011, many used this day to help Macmillan cancer patients with garden tidy projects. Beneficiaries of these projects are often patients who have always been keen gardeners but are now unable to maintain their gardens themselves due to illness.

Charity of the Year: Macmillan Cancer Support

In the UK, Michael Page has a track record of partnering with one charity for a period of two years. In 2011, it announced the start of a new partnership with Macmillan Cancer Support and pledged to fund four Macmillan cancer nurse specialists who operate within major UK cities.

Palmer and Harvey McLane Ltd

Distribution

Correspondent: Charities Administrator, P&H House, 106–112 Davigdor Road, Hove, East Sussex BN3 1RE (tel: 01273 222100; fax: 01273 222101; website: www.palmerharvey.co.uk)

Directors: Jonathan Moxon; Christopher Etherington (women: 0; men: 2)

Year end	02/04/2011
Pre-tax profit	(£2,417,000)

Nature of business: The main activity of the company is tobacco and confectionery distribution.

Company registration number: 2274812

Main locations: Tonbridge, Coventry, Hove, Haydock

Total employees: 9

Charitable donations

UK cash (latest declared):	2011	£2,000
	2010	£22,000
	2009	£55,000
	2004	£40,000
Total UK:	2011	£2,000
Total worldwide:	2011	£2,000
Cash worldwide:	2011	£2,000

Corporate social responsibility

CSR committee: No details found.

CSR policy: None published.

CSR report: None published.

Applications

In writing to the correspondent. Previous research suggested the company provides no support for local appeals outside areas of company presence.

Other information

In 2010/11 the company made charitable donations totalling £2,000. Information on beneficiaries was not available. Previous research suggested that other than support for certain trade charities, the company has no set policy, although it prefers to support 'people charities' local to its branches.

Paragon Group of Companies plc

Property

Correspondent: Corporate Social Responsibility Department, St Catherine's Road, Herbert Court, Solihull, West Midlands B91 3QE (tel: 01217 122323; email: michael.clarke@paragon-group.co.uk; website: www.paragon-group.co.uk)

Directors: Bob Dench, Chair; Nigel Terrington, Chief Executive; Nicholas Keen, Finance Director; John A. Heron; Terence C. Eccles; Edward A. Tilly; Alan K. Fletcher; Peter J. N. Harthill (women: 0; men: 8)

Year end	30/09/2011
Turnover	£258,000,000
Pre-tax profit	£80,800,000

Nature of business: Paragon is a leading UK independent buy-to-let specialist, with more than 40,000 landlord customers.

Company registration number: 2336032

Total employees: 691

Charitable donations

UK cash (latest declared):	2011	£22,600
	2009	£51,000
	2008	£62,000
Total UK:	2011	£22,600
Total worldwide:	2011	£22,600
Cash worldwide:	2011	£22,600

Corporate social responsibility

CSR committee: None specified.

CSR policy: Information taken from the company's 2011 annual report and accounts:

> The group believes that the long-term interests of shareholders, employees and customers are best served by acting in a socially responsible manner. As such, the group ensures that a high standard of corporate governance is maintained.

CSR report: Contained within the annual report and accounts.

Applications

In writing to the correspondent.

Other information

The following information is taken from the company's website:

> The group contributes to registered charities relating to financial services or serving the local communities in which it operates. Included in the charitable contributions shown in the Directors' Report are contributions of £22,600 (2010: £46,400) made by the group to the work of the foundation for credit counselling which operates the Consumer Credit Counselling Service. The group has also contributed to charities throughout the year by way of single donations.
>
> The group's main objective is to support children's and local charities, although no charity request is overlooked. During the last year the group has helped many and varied charities and causes such as: Handicapped Children's Action Group, Rotary Club of St Alphege – Sponsorship of Youth Speaks for Solihull Schools, Royal Marsden Cancer Care, Pathway Project, Disability Law Service, Zoe's Place Baby Hospice, Action for Sick Children, 3H Fund, Second Chance, Shelter, Special Needs Adventure Playground – Kenilworth, Kids Out, Life & Hope, County Air Ambulance Trust, Happy Days, Reality Adventure Works, NSPCC, Children with Leukaemia, Orchid, Marie Curie Solihull, Muscle Help Foundation, the One Foundation, Little Angels Day Nursery, Guys & St Thomas Hospital for Sick Children, Brainwave, Chicks and the Lowe Syndrome Trust.
>
> The group also supports Paragon's Charity Committee, consisting of volunteer employees, which organises a variety of fundraising activities throughout the year, raising in the region of £9,000 for the employees' chosen charity. All employees are given the opportunity to nominate a charity and a vote is carried out to select the beneficiary of the year's fundraising.

Pearson plc

Media

Correspondent: Corporate Responsibility Team, 80 Strand, London WC2R 0RL (tel: 020 7010 2000; fax: 020 7010 6060; website: www.pearson.com)

Directors: Glen Moreno, Chair; Marjorie Scardino, Chief Executive; David Arculus; John Makinson; Rona Fairhead; Robin Freestone; Will Ethridge; Patrick Cescau; Vivienne Cox; Susan Fuhrman; Ken Hydon; John Lewis (women: 4; men: 8)

Year end	31/12/2011
Turnover	£5,862,000,000
Pre-tax profit	£1,155,000,000

Nature of business: The company is an international media group.

Company registration number: 53723

Subsidiaries include: Pearson Education, The Penguin Group, Financial Times Group Ltd

Main locations: London

Total employees: 41,521

Membership: BITC, LBG

Charitable donations

UK cash (latest declared):	2008	£7,700,000
	2007	£7,200,000
	2006	£3,600,000
	2003	£605,000
	2002	£868,000
Total worldwide:	2011	£11,500,000
Cash worldwide:	2011	£9,775,000

Community involvement

The following is taken from the 2011 CR report:

> Our company purpose is to help people of all ages to progress through their lives through learning. This is both a social purpose and our core business. Our commercial success provides the investment capacity for us to continue to innovate and expand into new geographic markets and new kinds of learning. We recognise that not-for-profit partners can help us extend our reach and impact in ways that have a real impact on learning – especially for the most disadvantaged – and are complementary to our business objectives.
>
> We also believe that our stakeholders expect and value our efforts to work in partnership with charitable organisations. We therefore partner and fund a number

of charitable organisations and the Pearson Foundation is the largest of these.

The Pearson Foundation plays an important role for Pearson. It is our preferred charity partner and has a remit within Pearson to look to unlock company assets – cash, products and services and employee time – for charitable purposes, particularly to benefit organisations and individuals who would not otherwise be able to access them.

We are proud of what the Pearson Foundation has achieved and will continue to support its mission to innovate around new models for learning. It plays an invaluable role to explore, demonstrate, and influence the future shape of statutory and commercial provision.

Partnerships with others

Taken from the 2011 annual report and accounts:

> A parent reading aloud with their children is one of the most powerful ways to boost vocabulary and language development, according to research we commissioned as part of our Booktime programme. Access to books providing opportunities for shared reading is vitally important. This year, we have brought together a range of initiatives to give books to promote reading under the *We Give Books* banner.
>
> 2011 saw us achieve some important milestones. We gave our six millionth book under our Booktime programme, which sees every child in England starting school receive a book pack containing two free books from Penguin and Pearson Primary to take home, read and keep. And we are about to give our one millionth book to *Book Aid,* the charity that supports the development of libraries in schools and local communities in sub-Saharan Africa. One in five of the books donated to Book Aid came from Pearson, helping benefit more than 2,000 libraries last year.

Corporate giving

In 2011 the company's worldwide community investment spend totalled £11.5 million. Pearson is the major (but not the only) funder of The Pearson Foundation which runs a wide range of innovative, philanthropic programmes in the US and around the world, designed to encourage people to read, to support teachers and to share insight into best practice in education. In addition Pearson also provides in kind support such as books, publishing expertise, advertising space and staff time. In 2011, Pearson's community investment was divided three ways. It gave £5.98 million to the foundation, £3.8 million in cash and £1.7 million in donated books.

The 2011 CR report states:

> Our 2011 community investment is lower than in 2010 reflecting that some of the 2011 projects undertaken by the Pearson Foundation were funded in 2010. In addition, Pearson volunteers donate time and Pearson has people in the business dedicated to managing our community partnerships. We do not include these contributions in our community spend figure.

In 2011, almost 2 million books were donated by the company.

In kind support

The operating companies respond to trade and local causes through in kind donations. The main area of non-cash support is via gifts in kind.

Employee-led support

Employee-led support:

Wherever possible, employees are encouraged to become involved in charitable work in their local communities.

Payroll giving:

The company runs and matches the Give As You Earn scheme.

Commercially-led support

Sponsorship: Support of the arts is undertaken.

Corporate social responsibility

CSR committee: Taken from the 2011 CR report:

> Corporate responsibility cannot be separated from our financial performance and reputation. As such, our board of directors has ultimate responsibility for considering issues of business responsibility in setting business strategy. The board reviewed corporate responsibility progress at the April 2011 meeting. The Pearson management committee drives implementation of business strategy including our response to the key issues and opportunities we face.
>
> Pearson's corporate responsibility steering group oversees the development of our corporate responsibility strategy on behalf of the board. It is chaired by Robin Freestone, the board member responsible for corporate responsibility. The group meets quarterly, with a remit to support and challenge the operating divisions both to grasp relevant commercial opportunities and to mitigate the risks inherent in the issues we track as part of our responsible business practice framework.

CSR policy: Taken from the company's 2011 CR report:

> Last year, we set out a new responsibility framework for Pearson:
>
> 1 We start with our company strategy and purpose. Pearson is a commercial organisation with a social purpose: to help people make progress in their lives through learning. We believe our commercial goals and our social purpose are mutually reinforcing and that our financial strength provides the means for us to invest and innovate
> 2 We focus on three key issues of social and economic importance where we believe Pearson can make a unique contribution. They are literacy, learning outcomes and competitiveness
> 3 Beyond those three issues, we have a wider agenda for responsible business practice that covers our interest in nurturing diversity, investment in community partnerships, supply chain management and environmental responsibility
> 4 We recognise that our approach to responsible business is grounded in our company values, ethics and behaviour

CSR report: A CR report is published annually.

Exclusions

No support for advertising in charity brochures, animal welfare, appeals from individuals, enterprise/training, environment/heritage, fundraising events, medical research, political/religious appeals, science/technology, sickness/disability charities, social welfare or sport.

Applications

Appeals should be addressed to the correspondent. Local and trade appeals should be sent directly to the relevant subsidiary company.

Pennon Group plc

Water

Correspondent: Ms Lorna Shearman, Communications Manager, Peninsula House, Rydon Lane, Exeter EX2 7HR (tel: 01392 446688/1392443022; fax: 01392 434966; email: lshearman@southwestwater.co.uk; website: www.pennon-group.co.uk)

Directors: Kenneth Harvey, Chair; Colin Drummond, Chief Executive, Viridor Ltd; Kenneth Woodier, Group General Counsel and Company Secretary; Martin Angle; Gerard Connell; David Dupont, Group Director of Finance; Christopher Loughlin; Dinah Nichols (women: 1; men: 7)

Year end	31/03/2012
Turnover	£1,233,100,000
Pre-tax profit	£200,500,000

Nature of business: Business is carried out through:

South West Water – the provider of water and sewerage services for Devon, Cornwall and parts of Dorset and Somerset.

Viridor Ltd – one of the leading UK recycling, renewable energy and waste management businesses.

Company registration number: 2366640

Main locations: Exeter

Total employees: 4,529

Charitable donations

UK cash (latest declared):	2012	£74,000
	2010	£132,000
	2009	£113,000
	2007	£183,000
	2006	£131,000
Total UK:	2012	£74,000
Total worldwide:	2012	£74,000
Cash worldwide:	2012	£74,000

Corporate social responsibility

CSR policy: Information taken from the group's website: 'Pennon Group is committed to exemplary engagement with society and to the conservation and enhancement of the natural environment. Our social and environmental policy ensures that these activities are pursued.' For the full policy, visit the website.

CSR report: Annual Corporate Sustainability report published and available online.

Exclusions

No support for circular appeals, medical research, political appeals, religious appeals, local appeals not in areas of company presence or overseas projects.

Applications

In writing to the correspondent.

Information available: The company produces an annual social responsibility report which is available online.

Other information

South West Water's support focuses on water, the environment and youth education in the South West. A small proportion of its support also goes to Water Aid, which assists water projects in developing countries.

Viridor's business is UK wide. Its community support focuses on environmental and science education, and on engagement with the communities in which it operates.

The group's financial involvement in the community is channelled through a number of initiatives:

- Charitable donations (Pennon)
- Community sponsorship programme (South West Water and Viridor Waste)
- Landfill Tax Credit Scheme (Viridor Waste)
- Environmental fund committee (Pennon)

Examples of beneficiaries in 2011/12 included: Cornwall Wildlife Trust's Your Shore Project; Devon Wildlife Trust's Nature Reserve publication; South West Tourism Awards; and Surf Life Saving GB Nipper Championships.

Community engagement

South West Water is actively involved with local community projects, including educational schemes co-ordinated in partnership with local schools, colleges and universities. During 2011/12 our educational support included:

- Providing work experience placements to school and university students
- Five gap-year student placements offered as part of the 'Year in Industry' programme
- Sponsorship for STEM (Science, Technology, Engineering and Maths) days in partnership with The Smallpiece Trust

Sponsorship: The company undertakes good-cause sponsorships. From 2011–2013 South West Water is sponsoring Keep Britain Tidy's Beach Care initiative. The programme involves beach cleaning, community engagement, volunteering, and the promotion of local ownership of beach related issues.

Pentland Group plc

Clothing manufacture, footwear manufacture

Correspondent: Community Involvement Officer, The Pentland Centre, Lakeside, Squires Lane, London N3 2QL (tel: 020 8346 2600; website: www.pentland.com)

Directors: R. S. Rubin, Chair; T. J. Hockings; A. J. Mosheim; B. A. Mosheim; A. K. Rubin; A. S. Rubin; C. L. Rubin; P. C. Leach; J. D. Morgan

Year end	31/12/2011
Turnover	£1,592,200,000
Pre-tax profit	£113,600,000

Nature of business: The main activities of the subsidiary companies are footwear, clothing and sports, consumer products and international trading.

Company registration number: 793577

Main locations: Sunderland, London, Nottingham

Total employees: 15,468

Membership: Arts & Business

Charitable donations

UK cash (latest declared):	2009	£209,000
	2008	£1,000,000
Total worldwide:	2011	£544,000
Cash worldwide:	2011	£544,000

Corporate social responsibility

CSR committee: The central CR team is based in London, Hong Kong and mainland China, and is available as a resource to all Pentland brands and employees.

CSR policy: CR statements taken from the group's website:

> We are committed to supporting appropriate local charities and communities, through product and financial donations and other in kind support. Some of our contributions are Pentland-wide and coordinated by our London head office. We also give our global offices and brands the flexibility to support causes that are most relevant to them.

We were unable to determine the ratio of women to men on the board.

CSR report: There is a CSR section on the group's website.

Exclusions

No support for local appeals not in areas of company presence.

Applications

In writing to the Community Involvement Officer for requests to the company. For requests to the Foundation contact: The Charity Correspondent, The Rubin Foundation, The Pentland Centre, Lakeside House, Squires Lane, London N3 2QL. Telephone: 020 8346 2600

Other information

The group's accounts for the year ending 31 December 2011 declare charitable donations of £544,000 (2010: £296,000). We have no details of specific beneficiary organisations or where the money was given and have taken the figure as the worldwide cash contribution.

The Rubin Foundation (Charity Commission no. 327062) is closely linked to the company, which it primarily relies on for its income.

For the period ending 5 April 2011, the foundation had an income of just £13,000, (2010: £21,000), with a total expenditure of £543,000. Previous beneficiaries have included: The United Jewish Israel Appeal and The Prince's Trust (£10,000 each); The Jewish Museum and Community Security Trust (£50,000 each); Student Partnership Worldwide (£24,000); Board of Deputies of British Jews, Crimestoppers Trust and In Kind Direct (£10,000 each); and The Public Memorial Appeal, Yad Vashem UK and Kemble Charitable Trust (£1,000 each).

The Pentland Group's website lists a number of UK charities it has supported including:

- People – The Prince's Trust; and Crimestoppers
- Health – British Lung Foundation; Dementia Relief Trust; Leuka; North London Hospice; and Teenage Cancer Trust
- Environment – Earth Charter
- Education – Barnet Educational Bursaries Partnership; Holocaust Education Trust; and Trialogue Education Trust
- Arts – Arts and Business; Donmar Warehouse; Royal Festival Hall; Royal Opera House Foundation; and Royal National Theatre
- Sport – British Wheelchair Sports Foundation; Pentathlon Foundation; Greenhouse Schools Project; and Peace and Sport

Employee volunteering

The Pentland website states:

> Employees at our Glover warehouse in the north of England volunteer at the nearby Washington Wetland Centre, for example helping to conserve an area of meadow by cutting grass and removing hay. Meanwhile, staff at our London headquarters volunteer as mentors at local schools.

PepsiCo International

Food manufacture

Correspondent: PepsiCo Consumer Care Team, 1600 Arlington Business Park, Theale, Reading, Berkshire RG7 4SA (0800 980 8235; website: www.pepsico.co.uk)

Directors: J. K. Averis; A. J. Macleod; A. J. Williams; L. C. Ten Cate

Year end	31/12/2010
Turnover	£103,201,000
Pre-tax profit	£1,262,000

Nature of business: Provision of management services to other group companies.

Company registration number: 1521219

Main locations: Reading, East Durham, Warrington, Leicester

UK employees: 359

Total employees: 359

Charitable donations

UK cash (latest declared):	2010	£1,500
	2009	£400
	2008	£2,800
Total UK:	2010	£1,500
Total worldwide:	2010	£1,500
Cash worldwide:	2010	£1,500

Corporate social responsibility

CSR committee: No details found.

CSR policy: The company's website states: 'Our commitment is to deliver sustained growth, through empowered people, acting with responsibility and building trust.'

We were unable to determine the ratio of women to men on the board.

CSR report: None published.

Applications

It is unclear whether this company accepts unsolicited applications from charities. However, with over thirteen sites around the UK, more success may be had at a local level.

Other information

Although charitable cash donations declared in the 2010 annual report of this company are minimal at the moment, it does contribute to its communities particularly regarding the health and welfare of children and young people and education.

The PepsiCo Inc. annual report covers PepsiCo's global business. The latest report is available at pepsico.com.

For information on PepsiCo UK, visit: www.pepsico.co.uk/any-questions

Persimmon plc

Building/construction

Correspondent: Neil Francis, Company Secretary, Persimmon House, Fulford, York YO19 4FE (tel: 01904 642199; fax: 01904 610014; website: www.persimmonhomes.com)

Directors: Nicholas Wrigley, Chair; Mike Farley, Group Chief Executive; Mike Killoran, Group Finance Director; Jeff Fairburn; David Thompson; Richard Pennycook; Neil Davidson; Jonathan Davie; Mark Preston (women: 0; men: 9)

Year end	31/12/2011
Turnover	£1,558,500,000
Pre-tax profit	£147,200,000

Nature of business: Principal activities: residential building and development. Persimmon Homes is based in Anglia, Midlands, North East, North West, Scotland, South Coast, South East, South West, Thames Valley, Wales, Wessex, and Yorkshire.

Company registration number: 1818486

Main locations: Leicester, Peterborough, Exeter, Fareham (Hampshire), Hamilton, York, Weybridge, Northampton, Llantrisant (Mid-Glamorgan), Lowestoft, Malmesbury (Wiltshire), Newcastle, Doncaster, Bristol, Lancaster, Leeds, Maidenhead, Warrington, Wolverhampton

Total employees: 142

Charitable donations

UK cash (latest declared):	2011	£94,000
	2009	£795,000
	2007	£210,000
	2006	£251,000
	2005	£203,000
Total UK:	2011	£94,000
Total worldwide:	2011	£94,000
Cash worldwide:	2011	£94,000

Corporate giving

In 2011, charitable donations of £94,000 were made by the company. The following statement is taken from the company's 2011 Sustainability Report:

> During 2011, we continued to support *Leukaemia & Lymphoma Research* as our charity of the year. Through this and our support of York Minster and other local charities and community groups, we donated £94,000. We also enabled our staff to hold fund raising events in support of our nominated charities.

In kind support

Extract from the 2011 Sustainability Report:

> We run an annual 'grow your own vegetable' scheme with local schools which has helped us to develop better relationships with them, as well as teaching children about their local environment and healthy eating. Other initiatives have included reading days and inviting pupils to our sites to promote safety.

Employee-led support

During 2011 staff raised £91,000 for charitable organisations.

Corporate social responsibility

CSR committee: No details found.

CSR policy: Taken from the company's 2011 Sustainability Report:

> As market conditions, stakeholder attitudes and legislation change we respond and adapt accordingly, but at the heart of our approach are six responsibilities. These are the foundations of what we do:
>
> Putting customers first; prioritising health and safety; building sustainable homes; operating efficiently and responsibly; investing in our communities; and investing in our people.

CSR report: Published annually.

Applications

In writing to the correspondent.

Personal Group Holdings plc

Insurance

Correspondent: Dr J Barber, Trustee PACT, John Ormond House, 899 Silbury Boulevard, Central Milton Keynes MK9 3XL (tel: 01908 605000/01908 440908; fax: 01908 201711; email: jbarber@personal-group.com; website: www.personal-group.com)

Directors: C. J. Curling, Chair; M. W. Scanion, Chief Executive; J. P. Barber; K. W. Rooney; H. H. Driver; R. M. Green; C. W. T. Johnston

Year end	31/12/2011
Turnover	£28,000,000
Pre-tax profit	£10,000,000

Nature of business: The provision of accident and health insurance, employee benefits, financial advice, and personal insurance and reinsurance broking services.

Company registration number: 3194991

Total employees: 164

Charitable donations

UK cash (latest declared):	2011	£100,000
	2009	£80,000
	2008	£80,000
Total UK:	2011	£100,000
Total worldwide:	2011	£100,000
Cash worldwide:	2011	£100,000

Corporate social responsibility

CSR committee: There was no evidence of a separate CSR Committee.

CSR policy: This information was obtained from the company's website: 'We believe a good business is not only about profitability and growth, but also a responsible approach to the environment and our local communities.'

CSR report: There was no evidence of a separate CSR report.

Exclusions

Individuals or groups who are not policyholders with, or employees of, Personal Insurance plc.

Applications

If you are a Personal Assurance policyholder and would like to nominate a charity to receive assistance from PACT, send an email to: pact@personal.com

Alternatively, you may complete the online PACT nomination form and post-it to the relevant party.

Other information

In 2011 the group made charitable donations of £100,000.

Personal Insurance Charitable Trust (PACT)

The trust was set up in 1993 to provide a source of funds for good causes from the revenues generated by the company.

Personal's corporate social responsibility policy states:

> The group is committed to ensuring that the way in which its business is conducted has a positive impact on its employees and on the communities in which it operates. Its activity in this respect includes a charitable fund to which Personal Assurance plc presently contributes approximately half of one percent of premium income. The group supports a range of voluntary sector and community activities, primarily where its own employees or employees of host companies from whom the group derives its business are actively involved.

Only Personal Assurance policyholders can nominate a charity or charitable purpose for the trustees to consider a donation.

July 2011 saw the launch of 'Personal Group Charity of the Year'. Voted for by employees, charities of the year have included Willen Hospice and the Little Lives appeal, both in Milton Keynes.

Pfizer Ltd

Chemicals and plastics, agriculture, healthcare

Correspondent: External Affairs, Walton Oaks, Dorking Road, Tadworth, Surrey KT20 7NS (tel: 01737 330713; fax: 01737 332526; website: www.pfizer.co.uk)

Directors: C. M. Seller; I. E. Franklin; R. M. McKernan; R. A. Coles; D. G. Bevan; R. M. Day; S. M. Poulton; J. M. Hanley; I. Gill; J. C. Emms; J. R. Smith

Year end	30/11/2011
Turnover	£1,831,528,000
Pre-tax profit	(£759,700,000)

Nature of business: The principal activities of the company are the discovery, development, manufacture, marketing and sale of pharmaceutical and animal health products.

Company registration number: 526209

Subsidiaries include: Howmedica International Ltd, Unicliffe Ltd, Shiley Ltd

Main locations: Sandwich, Tadworth

Total employees: 4,134

Charitable donations

UK cash (latest declared):	2011	£1,000,000
	2009	£1,000,000
	2008	£1,000,000
	2007	£1,845,528
	2006	£338,000
Total UK:	2011	£1,000,000
Total worldwide:	2011	£1,000,000
Cash worldwide:	2011	£1,000,000

Community involvement

Pfizer's sites in the UK are at Sandwich, Kent and Walton Oaks, Surrey. Both seek to work closely with many diverse charitable, local organisations and statutory agencies using two main mechanisms for their corporate giving:

- Pfizer UK Foundation – a national initiative which supports organisations across the UK working at community level to deliver projects which address local health inequalities
- Community funds – relevant to Pfizer sites, these are available to organisations local to the Sandwich (East Kent) and Walton Oaks (East Surrey) facilities

The Pfizer UK Foundation

Applications are welcomed from organisations that:

- Are based in Scotland, Northern Ireland, Wales or England
- Are charities, community-led organisations, PCTs, local health boards, local authorities and academic bodies
- Clearly address a defined health inequality
- Are based in a deprived or marginalized community, targeting a specific local area
- Can demonstrate a tangible impact on a defined group of people
- Require funding of between £3,000 and £50,000
- Intend to use the grant within a calendar year of payment

The foundation helps pilot projects that have historically been regarded as high risk and therefore more likely to be rejected from normal funding streams. The foundation's support enables them to pilot new approaches and test new thinking.

Community funds

In addition to health spending, Pfizer actively supports personal and social education and welfare through local sports and community groups.

Walton Oaks – established in 2008, the fund supports projects that:

- Align with Local Community Action Plans (LCAP)
- Supports local health needs (outside statutory funding), specifically, healthy living initiatives
- Directly respond to the local community's priority

Corporate giving

Whilst no charitable giving is declared in the company's annual accounts, we have confirmed with The Pfizer UK Foundation that it receives £1 million from the company over the course of a financial year. Since its inception, the foundation has supported 226 projects, reaching 565,000 beneficiaries and providing funding totalling £7.3 million.

The Pfizer UK Foundation (not a registered charity), donates around £1 million each year to organisations in England, Scotland, Wales and Northern Ireland. It was established in 2005, to work with individuals and organisations across the UK in the fight against health inequalities. The foundation's report for 2012 states that:

> This is because despite a huge amount of coordinated activity in recent years, there remain areas of the country and groups of people whose health suffers purely because of where they live, who they are and what their circumstances are. As a healthcare company, we feel that we have not only a duty and responsibility to help, but have the resources and experience to make a difference. Our medicines make a huge difference to the health of people in the UK. So does the Pfizer UK Foundation.
>
> Since its inception, the Pfizer UK Foundation has supported organisations and communities across the length and breadth of the UK across a wide range of health issues. We are proud that we have been able to play a part and remain committed to playing our part in improving the health and well-being of people in the UK. It is the people in the organisations we support who are at the heart of our success. Their projects make a difference because they are experts at knowing the needs of their communities and because they are best placed to understand what will work best to help meet those needs.

In kind support

Gifts in kind include: the use of premises, including the use of equipment, e.g. use of projector and/or screens and photocopying; staff secondments; and, training schemes.

Employee-led support

Pfizer gives the following information on employee-led support:

> Engaging colleagues in community activities is a core tenant of Pfizer's policy. In addition, Pfizer encourages its employees to share their skills and expertise with local voluntary organisations. Pfizer's 'Health Relief' (Walton Oaks) volunteering programme allows employees to take up to five days paid leave a year to work with a range of community projects.
>
> The company runs an annual Thinkathon dedicated group volunteering days when Pfizer colleagues nationwide support charities with specific business challenges they need help with. The first Thinkathon in 2010, involved 300 colleagues working with 12 local charities across the UK over the course of one week. In 2011 more than 280 colleagues worked with 15 new charities over a two-week period.
>
> *If you work for a community organisation or charity that could benefit from the time and skills of our colleagues, please contact us at* healthrelief@pfizer.com
>
> The **Health Relief Mentors** programme allows Pfizer colleagues to volunteer their time and skills to support an individual charity worker by mentoring them on an on-going basis. This programme allows us to offer more individual support to people working in UK charities and non-governmental organisations (NGOs) in the developing world. Colleagues donate around an hour of their time per week to share their skills via telephone, email or a secure social networking website, developing the mentoring relationship from their desk. The aim is to overcome the constraints of geography, cost and time and enable people to volunteer with an organisation over a longer period of time.
>
> Pfizer UK has partnered with three international development NGOs – VSO, Merlin and the West African College of Physicians – whose work is committed to improving the health outcomes of hundreds of thousands of people living in developing countries.
>
> Pfizer also has a global volunteering programme called **Global Health Fellows** in which UK colleagues are encouraged to participate. Launched in 2003, Global Health Fellows calls on talented, committed and trained employees to work in Africa, Asia, Eastern Europe and Latin America for three to six month periods. Fellows include Pfizer physicians, nurses, epidemiologists, laboratory technicians, marketing managers, financial administrators and health educators.
>
> During their assignments, colleagues train and support their local counterparts, transferring skills so that the important contributions they make are sustainable over time.
>
> More than 270 Pfizer colleagues, five of whom are UK based, have worked as Global Health Fellows with 40 partner organisations (NGOs) across 40 countries to deliver healthcare and health system support to those in need around the world. Participants come from all levels of management to share experience and expand the availability of healthcare services in some of the hardest to reach areas.
>
> For more information please visit: www.pfizer.com/ghf.

Payroll giving: The company operates a payroll giving scheme, where it matches employee individual donations to a maximum of £100 per calendar month.

Matched funding: Supporting colleagues in their fundraising, the company provides support up to £150 for an individual and £350 for teams.

Partners: *British Red Cross*

Commercially-led support

Sponsorship: Neither arts nor good-cause sponsorship are undertaken.

Corporate social responsibility

CSR committee: No details available.

CSR policy: Information taken from the Responsibility page of the company's website:

> *Supporting UK Communities*
> As a pharmaceutical company operating in the UK, it is important that we make investments to support the health of people in local communities. Pfizer's activities to support health and well-being programmes include financial grants, in kind support and the time and business skills of its colleagues through volunteering programmes. Pfizer offers additional support to the communities close to its facilities and offices.

We were unable to determine the ratio of women to men on the board.

CSR report: None published.

Exclusions

These programmes cannot support applications from organisations that:

- Are sectarian or political
- Are ex-service, fraternal, trade unions or professional societies
- Represent personal appeals by, or on behalf of, an individual
- Are seeking core funding i.e. building, equipment or ongoing staff costs
- Represent research projects

Applications

Pfizer UK Foundation

Full details of the foundation's application requirements can be found on the company's website.

The foundation's board meets three times a year (February, June and October) to consider submissions, assess applications against the key criteria and make funding decisions. There are four deadline dates during the course of a year.

Community funds

Walton Oaks – for further information on applying to this local fund for assistance, write to External Affairs at the company's address, telephone them on 01737 330713, or send a fax to 01737 332526.

Sandwich – for further information on applying to this local fund, write to Community Liaison, Ramsgate Road, Sandwich, Kent CT13 9NJ. Alternatively you can telephone them on 01304 616161.

Note: local appeals outside of these two areas will not be considered.

Philips Electronics UK Ltd

Electronics/computers

Correspondent: Martin Armstrong, Company Secretary, Philips Centre, Guildford Business Park, Guildford, Surrey GU2 8HX (tel: 01293 815000; website: www.philips.co.uk)

Directors: Callum Petrie, Director; P. Maskell; H. Vivash; M. Armstrong

Year end	31/12/2011
Turnover	£750,500,000
Pre-tax profit	£15,500,000

Nature of business: The manufacture and supply of electrical and electronic equipment, supported by a research and development activity. The company is a subsidiary of Koninklije Philips NV, incorporated in the Netherlands.

Company registration number: 446897

Main locations: Guildford, Reigate, Redhill, Manchester, Colchester, Hamilton – Lanarkshire

Total employees: 2,058

Charitable donations

UK cash (latest declared):	2011	£19,100
	2008	£36,600
	2007	£53,200
	2006	£125,515
	2005	£35,476
Total UK:	2011	£19,100
Total worldwide:	2011	£19,100
Cash worldwide:	2011	£19,100

Corporate social responsibility

CSR committee: No details of a UK committee found.

CSR policy: Information taken from the company's website:

> *Social Commitment*
> Living up to our heritage of social commitment we use our capabilities to enhance the lives of our employees and society at large. We believe our responsibility extends to the full value chain and view supplier sustainability as a matter of taking care of the environment and of workers' lives.

We were unable to determine the ratio of women to men on the board.

CSR report: There is a global Sustainability report available from the group website.

Applications

If you are a registered charity, or seeking sponsorship that meets the listed criteria, write to Philips with details about your charity, what participation you are seeking, and the objectives you are planning to achieve by working with Philips.

Other information

In 2011, the company declared charitable donations in the UK of £19,100 (2010: £13,000). We have no details of the beneficiaries. Philips has made the following statement regarding sustainability and responsibility:

> In the UK, Philips operates a social sponsorship programme that focuses on supporting activity that improves individuals' health and their quality of life.
>
> Our current policy is to concentrate our activities in three main areas:
>
> - Working with a national charity that places emphasis on improving the health and well-being of individuals
> - Sponsoring a range of projects in the Guildford area that support improving the health and quality of lives for the underprivileged
> - Working with the Surrey Community Foundation as a founder sponsor to support their work in providing grants that make a genuine difference to the lives of people in Surrey
>
> Philips receives a high number of requests for support and in order to have a proposal reviewed it must meet the objectives of the Philips social sponsorship programme. If it has been successful then Philips will contact the applicant directly to discuss this in more detail. Unfortunately we are unable to respond to every request.

Pilkington Group Ltd

Glass

Correspondent: Maria White, Public Relations, Alexandra Business Park, Prescot Road, St Helens, Merseyside WA10 3TT (tel: 01744 28882; fax: 01744 692660; email: maria.white@nsg.com; website: www.pilkington.com)

Directors: Katsuji Fujimoto, Chair; Tomoaki Abe; Craig Naylor; Mark Lyons; Mike Fallon; Keiji Yoshikawa; Clemens Miller; George Olcott; Sumitaka Fujita; Seiichi Asaka; Hiroshi Komiya (women: 0; men: 11)

Year end	30/03/2011
Turnover	£4,700,000,000
Pre-tax profit	£27,000,000

Nature of business: Producer of glass and related products worldwide.

Company registration number: 41495

Main locations: Doncaster

Total employees: 29,340

Charitable donations

UK cash (latest declared):	2009	£181,000
	2008	£181,000
	2005	£199,000

Corporate social responsibility

CSR committee: There was no evidence of a separate CSR Committee.

CSR policy: This information was obtained from the company's website:

> We believe that good corporate governance contributes to sustainable development by enhancing the performance of companies and increasing their access to outside sources of capital. We aim to maintain high levels of accountability and transparency, disclosing to all our stakeholders business goals and guidelines that clearly demonstrate a responsible management approach.

CSR report: There was no evidence of a separate CSR report.

Exclusions

No support for appeals from individuals, enterprise/training, overseas projects, political appeals or religious appeals.

Applications

In writing to the correspondent.

Other information

There was no information regarding charitable donations for 2010/11.

PKF (UK) LLP

Accountants

Correspondent: The Press Office, Farringdon Place, 20 Farringdon Road, London EC1M 3AP (tel: 020 7065 0000; fax: 020 7065 0650; website: www.pkf.co.uk)

Directors: I. E. Mills; M. R. Goodchild; R. S. Bint; C. L. Hardaker; R. F. McNaughton; C. W. Stewart; N. M. Whitaker

Year end	31/03/2011
Turnover	£108,000,000
Pre-tax profit	£16,000,000

Nature of business: Principal activities: chartered accountants and management consultants.

Company registration number: OC310487

Main locations: Bristol, Cardiff, Coatbridge, Derby, Lancaster, Ipswich, Leeds, Leicester, Edinburgh, Glasgow, Great Yarmouth, Sheffield, St Asaph, Liverpool, London, Northampton, Manchester, Lowestoft, Nottingham, Norwich, Stoke, Birmingham

Total employees: 1,324

Corporate social responsibility

CSR committee: There was no evidence of a separate CSR Committee.

CSR policy: This information was obtained from the company's website:

> The firm plays an active role in contributing to society through both financial support and through enabling our people to take part in activities organised by the firm as well as supporting them in their own initiatives.

Unable to determine the ratio of women to men on the board.

CSR report: There was no evidence of a separate CSR report.

Exclusions

No support for circular appeals, fundraising events, advertising in charity brochures, individuals, purely denominational (religious) appeals, local appeals not in areas of company presence, large national appeals or overseas projects.

Applications

In writing to the correspondent.

Other information

As with all professional firms, there is no legal obligation on PKF to make publicly known any charitable donations they may have made. For this reason we are unable to provide a figure for 2010/11. The following information regarding the firm's community giving is taken from its brochure, available from its website:

> All of PKF's people are encouraged to take part in charitable and voluntary activities in recognition that this strengthens our bond with the communities in which we work. These range from activities arranged by individuals in our local offices such as Easter and Christmas collections and themed dress-down days to the firm's membership of Business in the Community (BITC).
>
> Skillshare involves PKF representatives setting aside several days a year to advise social entrepreneurs on business ideas and startups. In this way, small social organisations can draw on expertise that they might not otherwise afford.
>
> PKF also participates in ProHelp, where professional firms provide free advice and support to local community groups and voluntary organisations. This allows not-for-profit enterprises to benefit from the same standard of advice and service enjoyed by commercial businesses.

Premier Farnell plc

Electronics/computers, engineering

Correspondent: Steven Webb, Company Secretary, 25/28 Old Burlington Street, London W1S 3AN (tel: 020 7851 4100; fax: 020 7851 4110; email: information@premierfarnell.com; website: www.premierfarnell.com)

Directors: Val Gooding, Chair; Harriet Green, Chief Executive Officer; Laurence

Bain; Nicholas Cadbury, Chief Financial Officer; Paul Withers; Dennis Millard; Andrew Dougal; Thomas Reddin; Steven Webb (women: 2; men: 7)

Year end	29/01/2012
Turnover	£973,100,000
Pre-tax profit	£104,600,000

Nature of business: Premier Farnell plc is a multi-channel, high service distributor of products, information, software and technology solutions to electronic design engineers, maintenance and repair engineers and purchasing professionals.

The group distributes its products and services throughout Europe, North America and Asia Pacific, supported by a global supply chain of suppliers.

Company registration number: 876412

Total employees: 88

Membership: BITC

Charitable donations

UK cash (latest declared):	2011	£59,000
	2010	£47,000
Total UK:	2011	£160,000
Total worldwide:	2012	£160,000
Cash worldwide:	2012	£59,000

Corporate social responsibility

CSR committee: The Board has overall responsibility for establishing the Group's Sustainability policies and the Group Chief Executive is accountable for ensuring that the Group operates in accordance with these policies. Reporting of our performance is led by the Company Secretary.

CSR policy: CSR information taken from the group's website:

> Our vision is to become the world's most sustainable provider of products and services to Electronic Design Engineers by 2020
>
> Premier Farnell believes that the stakeholders for its approach to sustainability are:
>
> - The employees of the Premier Farnell Group
> - Potential future employees
> - Customers and suppliers of all Premier Farnell Group companies
> - Members of the local communities in which we operate
> - Premier Farnell plc shareholders and the investment community at large

CSR report: The board receives a full report on the group's sustainability performance at least every six months. Periodic updates will be provided on the company's website and a formal report appears each year in the company's annual report and accounts and a separate, online Sustainability report. Quarterly reports focusing primarily on environmental affairs are presented to regional senior leadership, including a summary of other regional sustainability activity. The Premier Farnell Leadership Council of global senior leaders is updated twice annually on the programme as a part of the group's global strategy and engagement plans.

Exclusions

> The following requests will not be met by the Charitable Giving policy, as the company will not support a cause which conflicts with its Code of Ethics, does not support its Community Investment Strategy or puts human life at risk:
>
> - Educational institutions that are not existing community partner organisations
> - Political or religious causes
> - Activities which are the subject of public controversy or that are not clearly within the confines of local and national law
> - Activity which is potentially dangerous, including extreme or high risk sports activities
> - Activity which could damage the environment
> - Aid corporate marketing activity in charity publications that is: not related to our community strategy goals; and, not directly related to a formal community partner organisation
>
> All of the above are at the discretion of the regional senior executive responsible for the policy.

Applications

In writing to the correspondent.

Note that individuals or groups with no direct connection to the company will only be considered at the discretion of the regional senior executive responsible for the Charity Giving policy.

Other information

During the year 2011, the group made charitable donations in cash of £59,000. The following information is taken from the group's 2011 annual report and accounts:

> Our Community Investment Policy was reviewed and updated in 2011 and is available on our corporate website. We record all money donated and raised by employees during normal working hours and also time volunteered during those hours by employees.
>
> In 2011, total donations from Premier Farnell plc were £59,000. Stock donated totalled £53,000. Non-stock goods donated by employees totalled £9,000 and cash raised by employees was £56,000. Total hours volunteered were 3,072 with a value to the company of £48,000.

We understand that the group will only support good causes which are registered charities. Appropriateness of the cause is judged by the senior executive responsible for the policy regionally with the exclusions listed. Requests can be made for a cash donation, matched funds, goods in kind and volunteering hours in company time.

Premier Foods plc

Food manufacture

Correspondent: The Company Secretary, Premier House, Centrium Business Park, Griffiths Way, St Albans AL1 2RE (tel: 01727 815850; website: www.premierfoods.co.uk)

Directors: Ronnie Bell, Chair; Michael Clarke, Chief Executive; Mark Moran; Charles Miller Smith; David Beever; Ian McHoul; Louise Makin; David Wild (women: 0; men: 8)

Year end	31/12/2011
Turnover	£1,999,500,000
Pre-tax profit	(£259,100,000)

Nature of business: Premier's principal products are bread, shelf stable groceries and chilled foods.

Company registration number: 5160050

Brands include: Ambrosia, Batchelors, Bisto, Branston, Campbell's, Dufrais, Fray Bentos, Lyons, Mr Kipling, McDougall's, Paxo, Sarsons, Sharwoods

Charitable donations

UK cash (latest declared):	2011	£86,000
	2009	£167,000
	2008	£287,000
	2007	£158,000
	2006	£52,000
Total UK:	2011	£86,000
Total worldwide:	2011	£86,000
Cash worldwide:	2011	£86,000

Corporate social responsibility

CSR committee: There was no evidence of a separate CSR Committee.

CSR policy: This information was obtained from the company's website:

> Our support for charities and local communities are linked to common themes that celebrate the best of being British.
>
> Being a sustainable business not only means producing products in a sustainable way, it also means being a sustainable part of the communities in which we operate.
>
> As Britain's leading branded food company, we consider the UK to be our national community. We consequently aim to build two-year national partnerships with charities that have a strong British heritage and link. In 2011, the charity partner chosen by our employees is Help for Heroes who provide critical support for Britain's wounded armed forces.

CSR report: There was no evidence of a separate CSR report.

Exclusions

No support for local appeals not in areas of company presence; or, political appeals.

Applications

Requests for a donation should simply be addressed to the company as they will be passed to the appropriate person for consideration. Put '(Fundraising)' after the company name in the address.

Other information

In 2011, the group made charitable donations in the UK totalling £86,000 (2009: £167,000). We have no details of the beneficiaries.

Pricewaterhouse-Coopers LLP

Accountants

Correspondent: Community Affairs Manager, 1 Embankment Place, London WC2N 6RH (tel: 020 7583 5000/020 7212 3164; fax: 020 7822 4652; email: community.affairs@uk.pwc.com; website: www.pwc.co.uk)

Directors: Kevin Ellis; Owen Jonathan; Kevin Nicholson; Richard Sexton; Ian Powell, Chair and Senior Partner; Richard Collier-Keywood, Managing Partner; Keith Tilson, Chief Financial Officer; Gaenor Bagley; Richard Oldfield; Stephanie Hyde; James Chalmers (women: 2; men: 9)

Year end	30/06/2011
Turnover	£2,461,000,000
Pre-tax profit	£667,000,000

Nature of business: Professional services firm.

Company registration number: OC303525

Main locations: Leeds, Bristol, Southampton, Manchester, London, Birmingham

Total employees: 17,079

Membership: Arts & Business, BITC, LBG

Charitable donations

UK cash (latest declared):	2010	£1,782,000
	2009	£1,738,000
	2006	£1,500,000
	2004	£1,107,914
Total UK:	2010	£10,300,000
Total worldwide:	2011	£10,300,000

Community involvement

The following statement is taken from the firm's 2011 Corporate Sustainability report:

> *Next generation community affairs*
>
> This year, we've redefined our priorities so that we can make our programmes as relevant and impactful as possible. We're focusing on addressing the challenge of unemployment in disadvantaged groups, and we're supporting social entrepreneurs to try new ways of tackling pressing issues in our communities across the UK. Our next generation community affairs programme includes the creation of a hub for social change (The Fire Station), the opening of our own social enterprise bistro and bar (Brigade), and the launch of a knowledge exchange (the Centre for Social Impact).
>
> Located in a renovated fire station near our office in London Bridge, the lower floors will house Brigade, a joint venture social enterprise spanning the private, public and not-for-profit sectors and bringing the complementary skills of PwC, De Vere Venues, The Homes and Communities Agency and a social entrepreneur to tackle unemployment in Southwark. The upper floors will host our community affairs programmes, and be a new home for our main strategic community partner, the School for Social Entrepreneurs, as well as Social Enterprise UK. We hope that by concentrating skills and resources in this way we'll get better at sharing what we know and learn for the benefit of all the social entrepreneurs we support across the UK.
>
> Many not-for-profit organisations have limited resources, and welcome help in addressing their strategic or operational challenges. As a professional services business, our people are ideally positioned to work individually or in small teams to help find viable solutions.
>
> Our community and our learning and development teams collaborate to develop leadership programmes that encourage our people to share their skills with the third sector.

Corporate giving

Total community contributions in the UK in 2010, including cash, time and in kind support were £10.3 million (2010: £8.1 million). Whilst the firm is a member of LBG and measures its community contributions based on that model, the breakdown of cash, time and in kind support, in terms of financial value, is not published within the annual Corporate Sustainability report. The only figure we have for cash donations is that given for the matched giving programme.

Previous beneficiaries have included the Prince's Trust, Shakespeare's Globe, several local Community Foundations and Wings of Hope, which offers support to orphaned and poor children by providing free education.

In kind support

The firm runs a secondment programme for a small number of staff each year.

Employee-led support

In 2011, 4,226 staff were supported in their volunteering activities in working hours contributing more than 50,200 hours in total. This is a 34% increase over a four year period. Cancer-related charities received 25% of donations.

> The **PwC Pantomime** is an important part of the PwC in the Community programme in the UK. It is supported financially by the PwC Executive Board and the fundraising efforts of the PwC Pantomime Production team.
>
> The PwC Pantomime aims to bring joy to children everywhere, particularly to children from inner-city schools and charities. The show also provides children from inner city schools and charities with the chance to see a theatrical production at a professional theatre and aspires to nurture a life-long love of the performing arts.
>
> During 2011's show, 'Pinocchio', PwC gave away almost 8000 tickets to disadvantaged children from inner city schools and charities in addition to providing free transportation to the show and a goody bag, courtesy of our generous sponsors. Special performances were signed for hearing impaired children and described for visually impaired children respectively. The latter were also given a chance to interact with props, musical instruments and costumes before the show as part of our annual 'touch tour'. In addition, a performance was broadcast live to 7 hospitals across the UK to bring a smile to children who are ill and away from their parents.
>
> In addition to meeting some of the firm's corporate sustainability objectives, the PwC Pantomime also provides PwC employees with a means of developing skills they can apply on the job such as teamwork, leadership, communication, planning and time management, and is a great example of the firm doing the right thing for our clients, our people and our communities.

Matched giving programme: Almost 900 staff applied to the programme this year and the firm contributed more than £188,000 to 256 UK charities and voluntary organisations.

Payroll giving: The Give As You Earn scheme is operated with all administration costs paid for by the firm.

Commercially-led support

Partnerships: Projects include Our Theatre, a partnership with Shakespeare's Globe and Southwark Council that has involved students from Southwark schools since 1997; the School for Social Entrepreneurs; and the firm's employee volunteering work with The Harris Federation of South London Schools where staff have mentored school governors, headteachers, other teachers and the children themselves.

The firm is a Principal member of Arts and Business.

Corporate social responsibility

CSR committee: There is a Community Affairs department and a Charities Group which offers audit, assurance, tax and advisory services 'in a way that's affordable to charities'.

CSR policy: The following information is taken from the firm's 2011 Corporate Sustainability Report:

> Our PwC in the Community programme is designed to make the biggest possible impact on behalf of our most significant community stakeholders, using the skills that are uniquely ours and which fit with our business aims. These aims are to:

- Tackle current UK issues
- Use our extensive networks for the mutual benefit of our community partners and our people
- Use our regional network and share our knowledge to amplify our impact
- Apply our unique impact measurement skills to our community work

We focus on developing long-term relationships, where possible, so that we can make a lasting difference. And we offer a portfolio of support which includes financial donations, pro bono and discounted work and the skills or volunteering of our people.

CSR report: Annual Corporate Sustainability report published and available from the firm's website.

Exclusions

No support for circular appeals, advertising in charity brochures, animal welfare, appeals from individuals, the arts, elderly people, environment/heritage, fundraising events, medical research, overseas projects, political or religious appeals, science/technology, sickness/disability, social welfare, sport, or local appeals not in areas of company presence.

Applications

In writing to the correspondent. Donations are approved after consideration by a charities committee.

Principality Building Society

Building society, financial services

Correspondent: The Corporate Communications Manager, PO Box 89, Principality Buildings, Queen Street, Cardiff CF10 1UA (tel: 02920 382000; website: www.principality.co.uk)

Directors: Dyfrig D. J. John, Chair; Peter L. Griffiths, Chief Executive; W. G. Thomas, Group Finance Director; Gordon MacLean; Christopher Jones; Langley Davies; Keith Brooks; Graham H. Yorston; Joanne Kenrick (women: 1; men: 8)

Year end	31/12/2011
Turnover	£235,400,000
Pre-tax profit	£24,500,000

Nature of business: The provision of housing finance and a range of insurance and financial services.

FSA registration number: 155998

Main locations: Cardiff

UK employees: 1,173

Total employees: 1,173

Membership: BITC

Charitable donations

UK cash (latest declared):	2011	£20,000
	2009	£45,000
	2008	£45,000
	2007	£25,000
	2005	£11,000
Total UK:	2011	£20,000
Total worldwide:	2011	£20,000
Cash worldwide:	2011	£20,000

Corporate social responsibility

CSR committee: No details found.

CSR policy: CSR policy: 'Being close to our communities is at the very heart of our society. That's why we like to get involved.' Principality's corporate responsibility focuses on the environment, employees and community.

CSR report: None published. An update is contained within the annual report and accounts.

Applications

In writing to the correspondent.

Local branch managers should be contacted to find out more about the branch sponsorship programme.

Other information

In 2011 a total of £20,000 was given in charitable contributions. As well as sponsoring a number of national projects, Principality's branch network is involved in local level sponsorships through its local branches based throughout Wales and the borders, to support local schools, groups and community projects.

Sponsorship:

We receive many requests for sponsorship so we need to have strict policies and guidelines in place to ensure that we lend our support to initiatives that reflect our brand values. Sponsorship requests are looked at on an individual basis but please note that we cannot commit our support to:

- Political causes
- Projects promoting or supporting specific religions
- Projects run by companies for profit on behalf of charities
- Causes outside of the regions where we have branches
- Development or running costs for projects
- Individual fundraising

For more information about sponsorship, please contact Pat Ashman, Sponsorship and Events Manager, on 02920 773318, or email: pat.ashman@principality.co.uk

Staff volunteering

The following information is taken from the society's website:

We are delighted to have won the 'Community Service Award for Small to Medium Lenders' in the Mortgage Finance Gazette Awards 2011. And to have been highly commended in the Business in the Community Awards 2010 as 'Wales Responsible Company of the Year.

Thanks to the dedication of our staff, over the years, we have supported hundreds of community projects, such as:

- Painting and decorating – from village halls to school classrooms
- Digging gardens and building rockeries
- Setting up community groups to give all ages access to arts and music
- Supporting young sports stars
- Making it possible for small communities to put up Christmas lights
- Entertaining senior citizen groups

We also regularly take part in community events, such as:

- Flower festivals
- Agricultural shows
- Concerts and carol services
- Fashion shows
- Drama productions

If you are planning a community event and are looking for support, let your local Principality branch manager know.

Charity of the Year: In 2012, staff supported Cancer Research Wales. Founded in 1966, Cancer Research Wales have raised millions of pounds for research into the treatment and diagnosis of cancer which has benefitted people in Wales and all over the world.

Private Equity Foundation

Financial services

Correspondent: Shacks Ghosh, Chief Executive Officer, 2 Bath Place, Rivington Street, London EC2A 3DB (tel: 0845 838 7330; fax: 020 7749 5129; email: info@privateequityfoundation.org; website: www.privateequityfoundation.org)

Directors: J. Huth, Chair; T. Attwood; J. Barratta; D. Barker; D. Blitzer; C. Green; C. Parker; S. Patel; K. Peterson; D. Poler; R. Sousou; N. Stathopoulos; T. Walker

Year end	31/12/2011

Nature of business: The Private Equity Foundation (PEF) is a leading venture philanthropy fund which works with carefully selected charities to empower young people to reach their full potential. Its investments address the NEET (young people not in education, employment or training) issue and include not just money but also pro bono expertise from the private equity community.

Company registration number: 5882818

Main locations: Shoreditch

Total employees: 12

Charitable donations

UK cash (latest declared):	2011	£3,859,650
	2009	£2,535,000
	2008	£3,900,000
	2007	£4,028,606
Total UK:	2011	£3,859,650
Total worldwide:	2011	£3,859,650
Cash worldwide:	2011	£3,859,650

Community involvement

Established in 2006, the Private Equity Foundation (PEF) is both a private company limited by guarantee and a registered charity (Charity Commission no. 1116139). It is included here because it is funded by over 70 private equity firms and their advisors, including banks, law firms, accountancy firms, consultants and search firms. The directors are the trustees of the foundation. Its aims are as follows:

> PEF is committed to enabling disadvantaged children and young people to reach their full potential. By identifying the most effective interventions and supporting the charities to deliver them more efficiently and effectively, more young people can reach their potential. PEF matches the business skills of the private equity community to charities in order to enable them to achieve scale and become more efficient and effective in their work. As a result, PEF makes an invaluable contribution to the portfolio of charities and to the lives of thousands of young people. PEF's unique model of venture philanthropy is helping charities to reach their potential and helping to change the lives of individuals and communities.
>
> PEF envisions a world in which every individual achieves their full potential. Our mission is to empower children and young people to achieve this and to enable the private equity industry to reach its potential and give something back to the community. In order to achieve this, PEF has developed the following strategy:
>
> - To work with disadvantaged children and young people, helping them to engage with society and fulfil their potential
> - To enable charities to increase their social impact and demonstrate clear and measurable outcomes
> - To make the private equity industry leaders in venture philanthropy
> - To become a leading expert on the issues affecting children and young people by pursuing a rigorous and innovative research and political engagement programme
> - To establish a reputation for rigour and high impact social investments
> - To develop a model for sustainable revenue
> - To develop a highly skilled, expert, flexible, focused and results driven team

In addition to financial support, the foundation's backers may also provide pro bono and volunteer help.

Note: *Private Equity Foundation 1 Inc.* is the Private Equity Foundation's independent non-profit sister organisation in the USA. PEF 1 shares the charitable goals and charitable investment approach of PEF and supports its charity portfolio.

Corporate giving

In 2011 the foundation had an income of £4.8 million, of which £3.8 million came from donations. The trustees estimate that £173,500 (included in the donations figure), was given in services. Grants totalled £2.3 million. The accounts cover a 17 month period in order to bring them into line with most of the foundation's donors' accounting year end (31 December).

During the year £801,000 was given to UK organisations; £316,700 to research organisations; £88,500 to European organisations and £16,000 was spent on charitable programme costs.

In 2011, beneficiary organisations included: SWT/Think Forward (£428,000); School-Home Support (£150,000); Big Brother Big Sister – Germany (£88,500); Every Child a Chance Trust (£50,000); Community Links (£38,500); Place2Be (£32,300); City Year Skill Force (£20,280); Cranfield Trust Work Foundation (£14,400); and Rayne Foundation (£5,000).

In kind support

Goods and services are provided including pro bono work.

Corporate social responsibility

CSR policy: No specific CSR details found – this is a private limited company limited by guarantee and a registered charity funded by over 70 business firms.

We were unable to determine the ratio of women to men on the board.

Applications

Private Equity Foundation has its own charity selection process. It makes information available on its website when it is seeking new charities to join its portfolio. Criteria for selection can change depending on the grant round and applicants should check the website.

Procter and Gamble UK

Healthcare, household

Correspondent: Co-ordinator, Community Matters UK and Ireland, The Heights, Brooklands, Weybridge, Surrey KT13 0XP (tel: 01932 896073; fax: 01932 896233; website: www.pg.com/en_UK)

Directors: Angela Braly; Kenneth Chenault; Scott Cook; Susan Desmond-Hellmann; Robert McDonald; James McNerney, Jr; Johnathan Rodgers; Margaret Whitman; Mary Agnes Wilderotter; Patricia Woertz; Ernesto Zedillo (women: 4; men: 7)

Year end	30/06/2011
Turnover	£82,559,000,000

Nature of business: Procter and Gamble UK is a wholly owned subsidiary of The Procter and Gamble Company, USA. The principal activities of the company and its subsidiaries are the manufacture and marketing of innovative consumer products, with associated research and development services.

Company registration number: 83758

Main locations: Seaton Delaval, Skelmersdale, Weybridge, Manchester, Newcastle upon Tyne, West Thurrock, Egham, Harrogate, Bournemouth

Membership: BITC, LBG

Charitable donations

Total UK:	£4,700,000

Corporate social responsibility

CSR committee: There was no evidence of a separate CSR Committee.

CSR policy: This information was obtained from the company's website:

> For more than 80 years, P&G brands and people have touched and improved consumers' lives. Our commitment extends to our social investments. Our people and our brands are our greatest assets and together, they are a tremendous force that can make an impact that matters.

CSR report: There was no evidence of a separate CSR report.

Exclusions

No support is given to circular appeals, advertising in charity brochures, appeals from individuals, fundraising events, medical research, overseas projects, political or religious appeals, or local appeals not in areas of company presence.

Applications

Applications should be by letter only and addressed to the correspondent.

For financial grants in Tyne and Wear, and Northumberland only, call the 'P&G Fund' at The Community Foundation (01912 220945). Applications should be made on the standard foundation form.

Information available: The company produces a social responsibility report and provides policy guidelines for applicants. The company also produces a newsletter entitled 'Community Matters'.

Other information

Procter and Gamble Ltd, the UK holding company, declares no charitable donations in 2011.

Community Matters

Through its UK and Ireland Community Matters programme, P&G's chosen area of support is primarily assisting with the development of children in need, from birth to 13 years – in line with its corporate cause Live, Learn and Thrive. The company also aims to support educational; health and hygiene and strategically aligned projects to its local communities.

P&G helps local communities by providing:

- People involvement
- Funding, where appropriate
- Product donations
- Time and expertise
- Business skills and resources

P&G also encourages its employees to pursue their own voluntary activities and to share their time and expertise to help establish sustainable benefits to their local communities.

Further information about P&G's UK and Ireland Community Matters programme, including objectives, strategy, principles and guidelines, can be downloaded from their website.

P&G Fund

The Community Foundation for Tyne and Wear and Northumberland manages the above fund on behalf of Procter and Gamble to support the company's charitable giving. Procter and Gamble have pledged to build a £1 million fund over ten years to support charitable groups in the North East.

Applications are welcomed:

- From charitable groups in Tyne and Wear and Northumberland
- From projects requiring £500–£5,000 with the majority of grants around £1,000
- For capital purposes for equipment, or revenue support for running costs

Procter and Gamble aims to improve the quality of life for local people and grants are made in a broad field of activity to spread support across the community. Support is offered to organisations which deliver sustained benefit to the community in areas of education, cultural and leisure amenities, and social well-being. Procter and Gamble will target support at those groups which can demonstrate a sustained and long-term benefit to the communities they work with.

Globally, Procter and Gamble makes a significant contribution to health related matters. The following information is taken from its website:

> ***P&G Live, Learn and Thrive – Corporate Signature Program***
>
> P&G Live, Learn and Thrive comes to life through programs in our communities around the world. There are more than 100 Live, Learn and Thrive programs taking place in over 60 countries every day. From providing life-saving vaccinations and safe water in Africa, to safe homes across Europe, to educational opportunities in Asia, to essential nutrition in North America, to early childhood development in Latin America [. . .] P&G aims to improve life for children and youth around the world.
>
> We believe companies can be a force for good in the world, and this is who we are as a global corporate citizen. Live, Learn and Thrive is woven into our philanthropy, cause marketing, product donations, disaster relief, and employee engagement. The cause is a reflection of our Purpose, and it embodies our goal of being closer to consumers from all walks of life and in touch with the needs of communities around the world.
>
> Every year, thousands of P&G employees worldwide personally commit to helping children and youth live, learn and thrive in their communities and beyond. Many employees volunteer their time or work in groups on team-building projects such as building playgrounds for children, teaching the importance of safe hygiene, or mentoring tweens and teens. And millions of dollars have been donated by employees with the goal of improving life for children and youth.

For examples of the group's global community contribution, visit its website: www.pg.com.

Provident Financial plc

Insurance

Correspondent: Rob Lawson, Corporate Responsibility Manager, No. 1 Godwin Street, Bradford BD1 2SU (tel: 01274 351135; email: corporateresponsibility@providentfinancial.com; website: www.providentfinancial.com)

Directors: Peter Crook, Chief Executive; John van Kuffeler, Chair; Ken Mullen; Chris Gillespie; Robert Hough; Rob Anderson; Manjit Wolstenholme; Andrew Fisher, Finance Director (women: 1; men: 7)

Year end	31/12/2010
Turnover	£866,400,000
Pre-tax profit	£142,000,000

Nature of business: Personal credit and insurance.

Company registration number: 668987

Subsidiaries include: Greenwood Personal Credit Ltd

Main locations: Bradford

Total employees: 3,683

Membership: Arts & Business, BITC, LBG

Charitable donations

UK cash (latest declared):	2010	£1,237,000
	2009	£1,330,400
	2008	£507,000
	2007	£776,751
	2005	£677,751
Total UK:	2010	£1,542,000
Total worldwide:	2010	£1,542,000
Cash worldwide:	2010	£1,237,000

Community involvement

The company's 2010 CR report states:

> We have a long history of investing in the many communities we serve. This is built into both our mission statement and into the strategy that guides how our business operates. It is not an add-on or afterthought but an integral part of our business strategy and our overall CR programme. Our community investment applies to all areas of our business and takes the form of funding, sponsorship, charitable giving and employee volunteering activities.
>
> The strategy behind our community involvement activities is simple and has stood the test of time for the past ten years or so. It comprises two strands:
>
> - Helping to address the social inclusion needs of people who live in deprived communities
> - Working with the money advice sector on issues such as such as financial education
>
> ***Good Neighbour programme***
>
> The vast majority of our community involvement activities are delivered through our Good Neighbour programme. Good Neighbour was established in 2009 as our flagship community programme, and delivers activities in three ways:
>
> *Local community project support* – We identify and support projects for one or three years through our offices and employees across the country, which address issues that are relevant to the needs of the community.
>
> *Employee volunteering* – We encourage our employees to take part in a range of company-led volunteering initiatives.
>
> *Employee matched-giving.* Employees can apply for funding and volunteering grants to match the fundraising and volunteering activities they undertake outside work.
>
> ***Active Community Programme***
>
> In addition, Vanquis Bank runs its 'Active Community Programme' which delivers activities at a local, national, and international level. The local and national elements of the programme mirror the approach taken by Good Neighbour – supporting local communities and encouraging employees to take part in volunteering initiatives.
>
> At the international level, Vanquis works with the charity '*Teach Africa*', (Charity Commission no. 1112423), which provides poor children in Nairobi, Kenya with an opportunity to attend secondary school. Each year five employees are selected through an interview process to travel to Nairobi along with employees selected in previous years to help administer the scholarship programme.
>
> During 2010, we established twelve new, three-year projects across our operating divisions. This brings the total number of three-year projects to 22, addressing a wide range of social inclusion issues. The new three-year projects include:
>
> *The Venchie Children and Young People's Project* serves the Craigmillar area of Edinburgh and runs activities based

> around play, recreation and issue-based youth work. Our funding will support the continued delivery of their breakfast club. The club provides schoolchildren, who have been referred to the programme by school home liaison workers, with a pick up service, a healthy meal to start the day and last minute help with homework. The programme will help improve attendance records and levels of educational attainment of children from hard to reach families.
>
> *REACH Across* aims to create cross-community contact between young people aged 14–17 from Londonderry, Tyrone, and Fermanagh through personal development training, residential camps, weekly group meetings and international exchanges. Our funding will support a contact programme that will include courses on first aid, art and drama; a personal development programme; and an international exchange project.
>
> *The Door* is a Christian-based youth project working with young people aged 11–25. In 2009, we provided one-off funding to support the 'Light at The Door' mentoring programme which supported young people through difficult times by helping them with anger management and self-esteem issues, and giving them practical help to find employment. Our funding will support a programme of family mentoring, parenting courses and counselling.

One-off funding has also been provided to a range of projects across the UK and Ireland, including:

- *the African Caribbean Leadership Council* to support its 'Post-Code Wars' project which is designed to give young people from Tottenham, Wood Green and Hornsey skills in film-making
- *Keighley and Ilkley Voluntary and Community Action Initiative* to fund the purchase of new office equipment and furniture
- *The Veronica House Project* to support its 'Breaking The Cycle' initiative which will deliver therapeutic sessions to children who have been seriously affected by domestic abuse.

Corporate giving

During the year 2010, the company made cash donations for charitable purposes of just over £1.2 million (2009: £1.1 million). The value of employee time was £74,000 (2009: £58,000). Total contributions to charities and community projects was £1.5 million (2009: £1.1 million).

Employee-led support

Taken from the company's 2010 CR report:

> Through Good Neighbour and Vanquis' Active Community Programme, we encourage our employees to participate in their communities and offer them volunteering opportunities and matched funding. Employees are able to participate in team challenges which seek to address local community needs, a reading scheme to provide one-to-one support to children in need of additional reading assistance, and other volunteering initiatives in their community. During 2010, 615 (2009: 604) employees from across the group got involved in volunteering initiatives. 447 hours were volunteered by Provident employees during work hours

Employee matched-giving: Employees can apply for funding and volunteering grants to match the fundraising and volunteering activities they undertake outside work.

Corporate social responsibility

CSR committee: Information taken from the company's website:

> Our board is accountable for the way we manage the CR issues that are material to our business activities. Chief Executive Peter Crook is responsible for our overall, group-wide CR programme.
>
> Reports, which include CR and community affairs sections, are presented at every board meeting and enable the board to assess the materiality of environmental, social and governance (ESG) matters to the group.
>
> The management committee oversees the group's CR programme on behalf of the board. Since its formation in July 2007, the committee's role has been to ensure that within day-to-day operations our businesses manage the risks and respond to the opportunities which are presented by a group-wide issue such as CR.
>
> Three key working groups have been established to address the ESG issues that are material to our operations, products and services
>
> - The Responsible Lending group puts in place a framework to manage the issue of responsible lending for both the Consumer Credit Division and Vanquis Bank.
> - Environmental working groups at both the Consumer Credit Division and Vanquis Bank contribute to the development and delivery of our environmental management programme.
> - The Corporate Responsibility working group guarantees that human resources and supply chain management issues are factored into our CR programme.

CSR policy: Taken from the company's website:

> The key to our CR strategy is to focus on the social, environmental and economic issues that are material to our activities. We do this by making regular use of employee opinion surveys, focus groups and customer satisfaction surveys, as well as annual stakeholder roundtable sessions.
>
> Based on the feedback we receive we have developed a strategic approach organised around six key themes:
>
> - Governance and management
> - People
> - Customers
> - Supply chain
> - Environment
> - Community
>
> This approach also reflects the values that underpin our business – acting in a fair manner, conducting our business dealings responsibly, delivering accessible products to our customers, operating in a straightforward way and being progressive.

CSR report: CR report published annually.

Exclusions

No support for appeals from individuals, heritage, medical research, overseas projects, political appeals, or religious appeals.

Applications

In writing to the correspondent.

Prudential plc

Financial services, insurance

Correspondent: Group Responsibility Committee, Community Forum, Laurence Pountney Hill, London EC4R 0HH (tel: 020 7220 7588; fax: 020 7548 3528; website: www.prudential.co.uk)

Directors: Michael Garrett; Barry Stowe; Keki Dadiseth; Rob Devey; Harvey McGrath, Chair; Tidjane Thiam, Chief Executive; Nic Nicandrou, Chief Financial Officer; John Foley; Michael Wells; Howard Davies; Ann Godbehere; Alexander Johnston; Paul Manduca; Michael McLintock (women: 1; men: 13)

Year end	31/12/2011
Turnover	£36,506,000,000
Pre-tax profit	£1,926,000,000

Nature of business: Prudential plc, through its businesses in Europe, the US and Asia, provides retail financial products and services.

Company registration number: 1397169

Subsidiaries include: Scottish Amicable Life plc, M&G Investment Management Ltd, Jackson National Life

Brands include: M&G

Main locations: Belfast, Chelmsford, Reading, Nottingham, London, Stirling

UK employees: 4,628

Total employees: 25,414

Membership: Arts & Business, BITC, LBG

Charitable donations

UK cash (latest declared):	2011	£2,800,000
	2009	£2,700,000
	2006	£3,150,000
	2005	£3,500,000
	2003	£2,800,000
Total UK:	2011	£2,800,000
Total worldwide:	2011	£9,100,000
Cash worldwide:	2011	£7,200,000

Community involvement

Prudential's corporate community involvement is part of its wider commitment to corporate social responsibility. Each business within the group has its own community investment plan in place. However, identified as a key issue across all locations, is the need to improve financial literacy within communities. This is therefore dealt with at group level.

The following extract is taken from the 2011 CR report:

> *Our communities*
>
> Being a long-term business means supporting the long-term well-being of the communities in which we operate. All our businesses have community investment programmes in place, consisting of a mix of charitable donations, employee volunteering schemes and charity partnerships. We establish long-term relationships with our charity partners to ensure that the projects we support are sustainable, and we work closely with our partners to make sure that our programmes continuously improve.
>
> This year is a milestone in Prudential UK's involvement with Citizens Advice. It is the tenth year in which Prudential has provided financial support to the organisation, which offers free, confidential information and advice to individuals with financial, legal, consumer and other problems. Prudential's funding – and the contributions it in turn has triggered – has enabled Citizens Advice to dramatically increase the availability of financial education at its locations around the country. From Prudential's perspective, the relationship with Citizens Advice is one part of a broad commitment to financial education, alongside Adding up to a Lifetime – a schools programme funded by Prudential which provides 25 hours of material to teachers – and a new project with Age UK aimed at helping older people deal with their finances.
>
> In 2011, the Group continued to be a partner of Save the Children through support for its Children's Emergency Fund. As one of their Emergency Response Partners we are able to support communities around the world when a disaster strikes. We also support projects that encourage people from low income backgrounds into leading educational institutions.
>
> M&G has a longstanding relationship with the Social Mobility Foundation – www.socialmobility.org.uk – which helps high-achieving young people from low-income backgrounds to get into top universities and professions. The Social Mobility Foundation is supported through charitable donations, formal internships and mentors drawn from senior employees, who are matched with students to provide guidance and support.
>
> The charity Springboard for Children also received assistance from M&G in 2011, supporting literacy programmes in schools.
>
> Our intention for the future is to increase the level of support we provide to education. Especially in the UK, where the difficult economic conditions mean that youth unemployment is a growing problem, there is an increasing need for initiatives that can drive educational improvement and help get people into work. As part of that ambition, in 2012 we plan to increase our commitment to apprenticeship schemes in the UK, as well as establishing further long-term partnerships with charities working in education.

National (UK) and local charities are supported in areas where the company has offices.

Corporate giving

In 2011, the total cash donations and cash equivalent for in kind contributions (based on the London Benchmarking Group metric) amounted to £9.1 million, of which the direct cash donations were £7.2 million. UK and Europe (charitable cash donations) £2.8 million; Asia and US (charitable cash donations) £4.4 million; and in kind donations across the Group were £1.9 million. The cash contribution to charitable organisations from the EU operations is broken down as follows: social and welfare (£1.4 million); education (£1.2 million); staff volunteering £93,000; cultural £74,000; and environment and regeneration £27,000.

Previously, beneficiaries included: Citizens Advice; Specialist Schools and Academies Trust; National Institute of Adult Continuing Education; and, Personal Finance Education Group.

In kind support

A range of in kind support is offered to organisations on a local basis. This includes employees' time and skills, office space, meeting rooms, computers and office furniture.

Employee-led support

Information taken from annual report for 2011:

> Across all our businesses we encourage employee volunteering to support charitable organisations. We recognise that employee volunteering not only brings advantages to the charities we support but also provides development opportunities for our employees. Many of our employees volunteer through our Group-wide volunteering programme, the Chairman's Challenge, now in its seventh year.
>
> As part of Prudential plc's broad commitment to education, Prudential UK is making a lasting impact with a long-term programme to help some of the schools in the most deprived areas in Britain. Prudential is one of just four national Business Class champions, which, in conjunction with Business in the Community (BITC), are supporting young people from disadvantaged communities. The overall aim of Business Class is to help slow the decline in school performance in the UK, as highlighted in international league tables. BITC also says there is also a clear correlation between poverty and educational underachievement, with stark implications for future social mobility.
>
> A partnership between Prudential and Prestasi Junior Indonesia to allow more than 200 street children in Jakarta to benefit from facilities at a safe house was chosen by Prudential employees as the winner of the 2011 Chairman's Challenge.
>
> In 2011, 7,209 employees across the Group volunteered in their communities – an increase of nearly 21 per cent compared with 2010. At Prudential UK alone, 40 per cent of employees took part in volunteering during 2011, with 65 employees dedicating 1,884 hours to Age UK's Call in Time programme, which supports over 500 isolated older people.
>
> More than £250,000 was donated to the group's global charity partners. This includes the additional cash sums awarded to the winning projects, voted for by colleagues across the Group. The 2009 winning project was Plan International, Thailand. This project, supported by 368 volunteers in Thailand, aims to make a sustainable improvement to the lives of children and communities living in poverty.

Payroll giving: The company operates the Give As You Earn scheme.

Commercially-led support

Prudential is a Principal member of Arts and Business.

Corporate social responsibility

CSR committee: During 2011, the group's CR activities continued to be guided by the chair, Harvey McGrath. The board discusses the group's CR performance at least once a year and also reviews and approves the group CR report and strategy on an annual basis.

Below the board, the Responsibility Committee – comprising senior representatives from group functions and each of our core businesses – is responsible for monitoring the group's CR activities and reviewing CR policies. The Group's CR team is responsible for: collating data and information for internal and external reporting; publishing the annual CR report; external monitoring and horizon scanning; overseeing CR risk and issues management processes; and benchmarking.

CSR policy: CR information taken from the 2011 CR report:

> Across the group we focus on four global CR themes: customers; people; environment; communities. These themes demonstrate our commitments and principles to our stakeholders and provide

clarity to our businesses on where they should focus their CR efforts and resources in the context of their individual markets.

CSR report: Published annually.

Exclusions

No support for appeals for sponsorship of individuals or groups, fundraising events, advertising in charity brochures, circular appeals, political organisations, purely denominational (religious) appeals, local arts or drama groups, animal welfare, heritage and building projects, medical research, or science/technology.

Applications

Further information can be sought from the Corporate Responsibility team at the address/telephone number given here.

Psion plc

Electronics/computers

Correspondent: Group Communications, Alexander House, 85 Frampton Street, London NW8 8NQ (tel: 020 7535 4253; fax: 020 7535 4226; website: www.psionteklogix.com)

Directors: John Hawkins, Chair; John Conoley, Chief Executive Officer; Adrian Colman, Chief Financial Officer; Ross Graham; Mike O'Leary; Stuart Cruickshank; Peter Bertram; Gotthard Haug (women: 0; men: 8)

Year end	31/12/2011
Turnover	£176,000,000
Pre-tax profit	£100,000

Nature of business: Development, manufacture and supply of mobile, digital communication and computing technology. Psion analyses and manages its operations in three geographical sectors: Europe, Middle East and Africa (EMEA); Americas; and Asia Pacific.

Company registration number: 1520131

Main locations: Milton Keynes, London

Total employees: 895

Charitable donations

UK cash (latest declared):	2011	£27,000
	2009	£22,000
	2008	£17,000
	2007	£18,000
	2006	£13,000
Total UK:	2011	£27,000
Total worldwide:	2011	£27,000
Cash worldwide:	2011	£27,000

Corporate social responsibility

CSR committee: No details found.

CSR policy: The following statement is taken from the CSR report for 2011:

> We believe that our activities should generate economic benefits and opportunities for an enhanced quality of life for those whom our business impacts. We also believe that our conduct should be a positive influence, that our relationships should be honest and open and that we should be held accountable for our actions.

CSR report: CSR report contained within the annual report and accounts.

Exclusions

No support for appeals from individuals or local appeals not in areas of company presence. The company does not provide support for political parties.

Applications

In writing to the correspondent.

Other information

In 2011, Psion made charitable donations totalling £27,000 (2010: £16,000). Donations are made to charities close to the company's facilities or to which the group has a connection, for example, through the voluntary work of an employee. The company is a patron member of The Prince's Trust Technology Leadership Group which helps disadvantaged and socially excluded young people by offering them the financial and practical support they need to get into training, further education or a job.

Punch Taverns plc

Retail – restaurants/fast food

Correspondent: Company Secretary, Jubilee House, Second Avenue, Burton upon Trent, Staffordshire DE14 2WF (tel: 01283 501600; fax: 01283 501601; email: enquiries@punchtaverns.com; website: www.punchtaverns.com)

Directors: Roger Whiteside, Chief Executive Officer; Ian Fraser; Mark Pain; Steve Dando, Chief Finance Officer; Ian Dyson; Stephen Billingham, Chair (women: 0; men: 6)

Year end	20/08/2011
Turnover	£607,200,000
Pre-tax profit	(£335,400,000)

Nature of business: Punch Taverns is a pub group.

Company registration number: 3752645

Total employees: 651

Charitable donations

UK cash (latest declared):	2011	£18,000
	2009	£19,400
	2008	£12,000
Total UK:	2011	£18,000
Total worldwide:	2011	£18,000
Cash worldwide:	2011	£18,000

Corporate social responsibility

CSR committee: No details found.

CSR policy: Statement taken from the company's website:

> Corporate Social Responsibility has been embedded across many elements of our business, from corporate fundraising to responsible retailing. Our CSR strategy seeks to involve our employees and Partners in making our business, and in turn, their businesses more ethical and environmentally friendly.

CSR report: None published.

Applications

In writing to the correspondent.

Other information

In 2010/11 the group made charitable donations of £18,000. The sole beneficiary was Licensed Trade Support and Care, which is part of the Licensed Trade Charity, which provides support to people in crisis who are working or retired from the licensed drinks trade.

Punch Community Promise has been set up at the group's support centre in Burton. This will involve donating time and money to local causes, such as renovation projects. To qualify charities or causes must be located within a 15 mile radius of the group's offices in Burton on Trent. Priority will be given to requests from employees. To qualify for support from the Punch Community Promise, your request must fulfil the following criteria:

- Local not national causes supported (although national causes with a local focus will be considered)
- Area covered is ten miles radius of Burton, but will consider up to 15 miles
- No third party fundraising
- No funding towards running costs of projects
- No individual sponsorship

Application forms can be downloaded from the company's website.

QinetiQ Group plc

Defence, aerospace, marine, security services, telecommunications

Correspondent: Corporate Responsibility Team, Cody Technology Park, Ively Road, Farnborough, Hampshire GU14 0LX (website: www.qinetiq.com)

Directors: Mark Elliot, Chair; Leo Quinn, Chief Executive Officer; David Mellors, Chief Financial Officer; Michael Harper; Colin Balmer; Noreen Doyle; James Burnell-Nugent; Paul Murray (women: 1; men: 7)

Year end	31/03/2012
Turnover	£1,469,600,000
Pre-tax profit	£331,600,000

Nature of business: The group's principal activity is the supply of scientific and technical solutions and services.

Company registration number: 4586941

Main locations: Farnborough

Total employees: 10,637

Membership: Arts & Business

Charitable donations

UK cash (latest declared):	2010	£114,100
	2009	£133,500
	2008	£184,000
	2007	£19,000
	2006	£54,000
Total worldwide:	2012	£108,400
Cash worldwide:	2012	£108,400

Corporate social responsibility

CSR committee: At Board level, the Compliance Committee oversees the Group's Corporate Responsibility and Sustainability (CR&S) strategy, and receives progress updates.

At an Executive level, the Safety, Assurance and Sustainability Committee, which reports into the Group's Executive Team, meets quarterly to review progress.

The CR&S strategy and programmes are overseen by the Head of Corporate Responsibility and Sustainability, who works with the assurance and audit functions to monitor and evaluate programmes.

CSR policy: The company's Corporate Responsibility and Sustainability report states: 'Our vision encompasses more than financial success. We continue to focus on business ethics, our people, excellent environmental stewardship and being a good neighbour.'

CSR report: Corporate Responsibility and Sustainability report is contained within the annual report and accounts.

Applications

In writing to the correspondent.

Other information

Charitable donations during the year 2011/12 across the group amounted to £108,400 (2010/11: £196,900). The following information is taken from the 2011/12 annual report and accounts:

> *Community investment*
>
> Across the Group, employees support their communities by volunteering their time and professional skills. In the UK, we have introduced a new Employee Volunteering Scheme to build on a range of ad-hoc programmes and make it easier to monitor and measure success. Employees continued to focus on work with schools, through programmes such as the STEM (Science, Technology, Engineering, Maths) Academy and the QinetiQ Powerboat Challenge, with the aim of inspiring the next generation of scientists and engineers. Employees are also using their professional skills, such as our involvement in the Young Enterprise programme and with local charities. We continue to promote this programme to benefit communities in which we operate as well as to develop our people.
>
> Engineers in our Science for Society programme have provided technical advice to non-government organisations working in Laos on the disposal of unexploded ordnance (UXO), for the past six years. During a recent visit to Mahaxy district in Khammouane province, the team provided advice on sustainable technologies and training.
>
> QNA also recognises the importance of young people pursuing STEM careers and so supports initiatives, such as robot challenges. They also support a range of fundraising activities for military and health charities.
>
> **Matched funding**: In the UK, employees have chosen new charities to support (Cancer Research UK, RNLI and Help for Heroes) and these will continue to receive matched funding for any activities. UK employees also raised a further £54,000 through fundraising and payroll giving.

RAB Capital plc

Financial services

Correspondent: Ian Johnson, Company Secretary, 1 Adam Street, London WC2N 6LE (tel: 020 7389 7000/020 7389 0962; email: ian.johnson@rabcap.com; website: www.rabcap.com)

Directors: Charles Kirwan-Taylor, Chief Executive; Christopher de Mattos; Philip Richards; Adam Grant, Finance Director and Chief Operating Officer; Michael Alan Buckley, Chair; Xavier Coirbay; Rt Hon Lord Lamont of Lerwick; Derek Riches; Philip Moore (women: 0; men: 9)

Year end	31/12/2010
Turnover	£11,897,000
Pre-tax profit	(£20,196,000)

Nature of business: The company is a listed alternative asset manager which specialises in managing absolute return funds (often referred to as 'hedge' funds).

Company registration number: 3694213

Total employees: 103

Charitable donations

UK cash (latest declared):	2009	£900,000
	2008	£4,300,000
	2007	£5,260,000
	2006	£2,400,000
Total worldwide:	2010	£180,000
Cash worldwide:	2010	£180,000

Community involvement

The company in its 2010 report advocates the use of Sharegift. This is a charity share-donation scheme, which accepts donations of small parcels of shares where their value makes them uneconomic to sell. For more information visit www.sharegift.org or telephone: 020 7930 3737.

Corporate giving

The company's 2010 annual report states: 'Charitable payments made during the year amounted to £180,000 (2009: £900,000). This includes an amount of £110,000 (2009: £770,000) paid in 2010 by the company from emoluments for 2009 waived by directors and employees, none of which related to the highest paid director (2009: £nil)'. We have no details of the beneficiaries, or whether the donations were made within the UK, but believe there may be some preference for Christian causes.

Corporate social responsibility

CSR policy: No information on CSR was available.

Applications

In writing to the correspondent.

The Rank Group plc

Leisure

Correspondent: Frances Bingham, Company Secretary, Statesman House, Stafferton Way, Maidenhead SL6 1AY (tel: 01628 604000; fax: 01628 504042; website: www.rank.com)

Directors: Peter Johnson, Chair; Richard Greenhalgh; Owen O'Donnell; Tim Scoble; Bill Shannon; Mike Smith; John Warren; Ian Burke; Paddy Gallagher; Frances Bingham (women: 1; men: 9)

Year end	31/12/2010
Turnover	£567,800,000
Pre-tax profit	£73,500,000

Nature of business: The Rank Group is a leisure and entertainment company and an international provider of services to the film industry. Leisure and entertainment activities include casinos, bingo clubs, pub restaurants and holiday resorts.

Company registration number: 3140769

Main locations: London

Total employees: 8,937

Charitable donations

UK cash (latest declared):	2010	£360,000
	2009	£315,000
	2008	£264,000
	2007	£236,000
	2006	£244,000
Total UK:	2010	£360,000
Total worldwide:	2010	£594,000
Cash worldwide:	2010	£594,000

Corporate social responsibility

CSR committee: No details found.

CSR policy: Taken from the company's website: 'The Rank Group will attempt to make a positive difference to the lives of people in the locations where we operate through local engagement, community involvement and economic contribution.'

CSR report: None published.

Applications

In writing to the correspondent.

Other information

In 2010 the company made charitable donations in the UK of £360,000 (2009: £315,000), of which the largest was £306,000 (2009: £267,000) to The GREaT Foundation. Worldwide contributions were £594,000.

Rathbone Brothers plc

Financial services

Correspondent: Social and Environmental Committee, 159 New Bond Street, London W1S 2UD (tel: 020 7399 0000; email: marketing@rathbones.com; website: www.rathbones.com)

Directors: Paul Stockton; Mark Nicholls, Chair; Andy Pomfret, Chief Executive; Ian Buckley; Paul Chavasse; Richard Lanyon; Andrew Morris; Richard Smeeton; David Harrel; Kate Avery; Caroline Burton; Oliver Corbett; Kathryn Matthews (women: 3; men: 10)

Year end	31/12/2011
Turnover	£11,259,000
Pre-tax profit	£39,152,000

Nature of business: Independent provider of investment and wealth management services for private investors, charities and trustees.

Company registration number: 1000403

Total employees: 746

Charitable donations

UK cash (latest declared):	2011	£196,000
	2009	£174,000
Total UK:	2011	£196,000
Total worldwide:	2011	£196,000
Cash worldwide:	2011	£196,000

Corporate social responsibility

CSR committee: Taken from 2011 annual report:

> The SEC is responsible for ensuring that Rathbones effectively manages its sustainability issues. It is formed by members of staff from key functions such as facilities management, personnel, marketing, IT and investment management. It meets on a quarterly basis and reports directly to the group executive committee of the Board.

CSR policy: Information taken from the 2011 annual report:

> Rathbones' corporate responsibility strategy can be summarised as follows:
>
> *Environment*
>
> Actively manage our environmental impact, reduce our carbon footprint by the efficient use of resources and offset unavoidable emissions.
>
> *Clients and investments*
>
> Maintain and develop the relationships we have with our clients, treat them fairly and continue to meet their needs. Consider corporate responsibility and governance issues in the companies in which we invest on behalf of our clients.
>
> *Employees*
>
> Manage the health, well-being and development of our employees.
>
> *Communities*
>
> Engage in the communities in which we operate.

CSR report: Annual corporate responsibility report of the social and environmental committee (SEC) is contained within the annual report and accounts.

Applications

In writing to the correspondent.

Other information

During the year, the group made total charitable donations of £196,000, representing 0.5% of Group pre-tax profits (2010: £162,000, representing 0.54% of Group pre-tax profits).

Give As You Earn: Employees are encouraged to donate to charity in a tax efficient manner through the Give As You Earn (GAYE) payroll giving scheme. In 2011, Rathbone employees made payments totalling £189,000 (2010: £107,000) through this scheme, which is administered by the Charities Aid Foundation. The company matched staff donations of up to £200 per month made through Give As You Earn and in 2011 donated £108,000 (2010: £85,000) to causes chosen by employees through this method.

Employee volunteering: During the year, Rathbone employees have undertaken a wide variety of community and fundraising events.

Corporate sponsorship: Rathbones also provides support in the form of sponsorship, advertising and attendance at events organised by charities and arts organisations.

Charities of the year: In **2010**, Children with Cancer UK and The Anthony Nolan Trust were selected by an employee ballot as the charities to be supported for 2010 and 2011. During 2011, £17,000 has been raised by employees for these two charities.

For **2012 and 2013**, employees voted to support the **Claire House Children's Hospice** and **The Oliver King Foundation.**

Ravensale Ltd

Property

Correspondent: Bruce G Jarvis, Charity Correspondent, The Joron Foundation, 115 Wembley Commercial Centre, East Lane, North Wembley, Middlesex HA9 7UR (tel: 020 8908 4655)

Directors: B. D. G. Jarvis; J. R. Jarvis (women: 0; men: 2)

Year end	30/06/2011
Turnover	£3,272,046
Pre-tax profit	(£371,557)

Nature of business: The principal activity of Ravensale Ltd is property development and investment, and the design and manufacture of ballpoint pen components.

Company registration number: 1476675

Charitable donations

UK cash (latest declared):	2011	£2,104,500
	2009	£1,558,000
	2008	£785,000
	2007	£1,795,000
	2006	£1,893,000
Total UK:	2011	£2,104,500
Total worldwide:	2011	£2,104,500
Cash worldwide:	2011	£2,104,500

Community involvement

Ravensale Ltd directs all its charitable giving, which is substantial, through the registered charity, The Joron Charitable Trust (Charity Commission no. 1062547) of which two of the directors are trustees. The trust is established for general charitable purposes and makes grants to registered charities in various fields where it can be demonstrated that the grants will be used effectively.

There is no formal grant application procedure and the trustees retain the services of a charitable grants advisor and take advice when deciding on grants.

Corporate giving

In 2010/11 the company donated just over £2.1 million (2009/10: £2.8 million) to The Joron Charitable Trust (Charity Commission no. 1062547). The trust was established for general charitable purposes in 1997 and derives almost all of its income from Ravensale Ltd. The charity's policy is to make grants to registered charities in the fields of education, medical research and other charities.

Thirteen grants and donations were made totalling almost £3.5 million (2010: £1.7 million). The beneficiaries included: The Roan Charitable Trust (£2.9 million); The Princess Royal Trust for Carers (£150,000); The Wilderness Foundation (£131,000); Child's Dream Foundation (£126,000); NSPCC (£5,000); and The Honeypot Charity (£2,500).

Corporate social responsibility

CSR committee: None specified.

CSR policy: None published.

CSR report: None published. However, the company's charitable donation and its application are detailed in the charity accounts for The Joron Charitable Trust.

Exclusions

No support for political organisations.

Applications

There is no formal grant application procedure. Apply to the contact in writing at the company's address.

Reckitt Benckiser Group plc

Household, pharmaceuticals

Correspondent: The Corporate Communications Department, 103–105 Bath Road, Slough, Berkshire SL1 3UH (tel: 01753 217800; website: www.rb.com)

Directors: Adrian Bellamy, Chair; Liz Doherty, Chief Financial Officer; Richard Cousins; Peter Harf; Kenneth Hydon; Rakesh Kapoor, Chief Executive Officer; André Lacroix; Graham Mackay; Judith Sprieser; Warren Tucker (women: 2; men: 8)

Year end	31/12/2011
Turnover	£9,485,000,000
Pre-tax profit	£2,376,000,000

Nature of business: Principal activities: The manufacture and sale of household and healthcare products.

Company registration number: 527217

Brands include: Subsidiaries include: Propack.

Main locations: Derby, Hull, Slough, Windsor, Swindon

UK employees: 3,500

Total employees: 37,800

Charitable donations

UK cash (latest declared):	2009	£568,000
	2008	£704,000
Total UK:	2009	£535,000
Total worldwide:	2011	£535,000

Corporate social responsibility

CSR committee: The board is responsible for the overall Stewardship of the Company, including sustainability and corporate responsibility. The Chief Executive Officer (CEO) is the board member with specific responsibility for the Company's sustainability policies and performance.

> Our Director of Global Sustainability, Environment, Health and Safety coordinates the sustainability programme on a day-to-day basis. Our Senior Vice President (SVP) of Corporate Communications and Affairs is secretary to the Executive Committee. She is responsible for our community involvement and much of our stakeholder engagement.

CSR policy: Information taken from the group's Sustainability Report 2011:

> Success depends on operating ethically and making positive contributions from growing the business while reducing negative impacts, especially on the environment. Environmental issues are a key focus because our most significant sustainability impact is the greenhouse gas emissions that contribute to climate change. Our sustainability strategy also addresses three other important dimensions: marketplace, workplace and community.

CSR report: Sustainability report published annually.

Exclusions

No grants for animal welfare charities, the arts, elderly people, political appeals, religious appeals, science/technology, sickness/disability or sport.

Applications

In writing to the correspondent. Applications are considered by the Community Involvement Committee which meets four times a year. In addition to authorising donations, the committee is concerned with the implementation of policy relating to the company's community programme.

Other information

The group has continued its strategy of focusing on the group's nominated global charity, *Save the Children*. During the year, donations in the UK amounted to £1.6 million (2010: £774,000) of which £977,800 (2010: £610,000) was donated to Save the Children. The total donated to Save the Children was £2 million (2010: £1.6 million) including funds raised by Reckitt Benckiser companies and employees around the world. Unfortunately, no breakdown is given of what the company contributed and what staff raised.

The group's Sustainability Report for 2011 states that £535,000 was donated in cash and products to support Save the Children's emergency work in 2011 and we have taken that figure as the worldwide community contribution. This figure is also given as the UK total contribution as the charity is registered in the UK.

The company matches employee fundraising and its four UK offices each support local family, children's and health charities like Home-Start and Prospect Hospice.

Substantial support is given in the form of donated products.

Redrow Group plc

Property

Correspondent: Alan Jackson, Chair, Corporate Responsibility Committee, Redrow House, St David's Park, Flintshire CH5 3RX (tel: 01244 520044; fax: 01244 520720; website: www.redrowplc.co.uk)

Directors: Steve Morgan, Chair; John Tutte, Group Managing Director; Barbara Richmond, Group Finance Director; Alan Jackson; Debbie Hewitt; Paul Hampden Smith; Graham Cope, Company Secretary (women: 2; men: 5)

Year end	30/06/2011
Turnover	£452,700,000
Pre-tax profit	£25,300,000

Nature of business: The principal activity of the Group is residential development which includes mixed use development. Redrow plc is a public listed company, listed on the London Stock Exchange and domiciled in the UK.

Company registration number: 2877315

Main locations: Barnsley, Bexhill on Sea, Liverpool, Flintshire, Leek, Falkirk, Aberdare, Preston Brook, High Wycombe, Leigh, Cardiff, Launceston

UK employees: 933

Total employees: 933

Charitable donations

UK cash (latest declared):	2011	£568,000
	2009	£178,000
	2008	£281,000
	2007	£334,000
	2006	£304,000
Total UK:	2011	£568,000
Total worldwide:	2011	£568,000
Cash worldwide:	2011	£568,000

Corporate giving

In 2010/11, £568,000 was given in charitable donations – £565,000 in respect of national charities and £3,000 in support of local charities. The group and its employees are actively involved in fundraising activities for specific charities. The group made a £564,000 donation during the year to the Morgan Foundation, a UK registered charity of which Steve Morgan is a trustee. This is included within the charitable donations in respect of national charities noted above.

Employee-led support

The company's website provides the following information:

> We at Redrow are proud of our support for charitable causes and our divisions are encouraged to do so. For example our South Wales division has recently been involved in a number of activities associated with The Joshua Foundation (TJF), a Cardiff based national charity, created in September 1998 to provide holidays and experiences for children aged between birth and 19 with terminal cancer, and their families.
>
> In the South West at Chippenham, the after school club at St Nicholas School was saved from closure after Redrow employees from our South West Division raised £23,000 through a series of events including a golf day, annual dinner dance, car wash, five a side football tournament, casual clothes days and staff socials. Redrow staff have pledged continued support for the school for children and young people, aged four to nineteen, who

have severe, complex or profound and multiple learning disabilities.

Corporate social responsibility

CSR committee: Current Members of the Corporate Responsibility Committee

- Alan Jackson, Chair of the Corporate Responsibility Committee
- Nigel Smith, Redrow Research and Sustainability Director

The Corporate Responsibility Committee's terms of reference are kept under regular review being last reviewed in February 2011 and are published on the Group's website.

CSR policy: Taken from the company's website:

> As one of the UK's leading residential and commercial developers, Redrow is committed to the delivery of quality, sustainable communities.
>
> We achieve this through our focus on continuous improvement, innovation and good design, sympathetic to the locality and through recognition of our responsibility to our stakeholders, employees, customers, suppliers, subcontractors and shareholders as well as our obligation to respect the natural environment

CSR report: Published within the annual report and accounts.

Exclusions

No support for circular appeals, advertising in charity brochures, purely denominational (religious) appeals, large national appeals, overseas projects or local appeals not in areas of company presence.

Applications

In writing to the correspondent, or, via email to: foundation@redrow.co.uk. You will then be informed of the foundation's full criteria, together with the next date when the trustees are to meet to discuss the merits of each submission.

In considering each request, the trustees will be looking for evidence of leverage on the funds. State, therefore, how you intend to match or increase any donation you may receive in your application.

Rentokil Initial plc

Business services

Correspondent: Paul Griffiths, Company Secretary, 12th Floor, Portland House, Bressenden Place, London SW1E 5BH (tel: 020 7592 2700; website: www.rentokil-initial.com)

Directors: John McAdam, Chair; Alan Brown, Chief Executive; Peter Bamford; Richard Burrows; Alan Giles; Peter Long; Andy Ransom; William Rucker; Duncan Tatton-Brown; Jeremy Townsend (women: 0; men: 10)

Year end	31/12/2011
Turnover	£2,544,300,000
Pre-tax profit	(£50,500,000)

Nature of business: Principal activity: international company providing services to businesses including, pest control, package delivery, interior landscaping, catering, electronic security, cleaning.

Company registration number: 5393279

Main locations: East Grinstead, Orpington

Total employees: 66,470

Membership: BITC

Charitable donations

UK cash (latest declared):	2011	£58,000
	2009	£61,000
	2008	£142,000
	2007	£107,000
	2006	£198,000
Total UK:	2011	£58,000
Total worldwide:	2011	£135,000
Cash worldwide:	2011	£135,000

Corporate social responsibility

CSR committee: No details found.

CSR policy: Taken from the company's website:

> At the heart of Rentokil Initial's approach to corporate responsibility is a focus on doing what's right for colleagues and customers, and the vision and values which underpin the company. It emphasises local action to match the needs of individual businesses, while ensuring compliance with group-wide policies in areas such as health and safety, conduct, environment and product management.

CSR report: Published annually.

Exclusions

Consideration will not be given to any charity or sponsorship related proposal from any organisation unless a company employee or employees are involved.

Applications

In writing to the correspondent.

Other information

In 2011, charitable cash donations amounted to £135,000. Of this, £58,000 was given in the UK and £77,000 overseas. This excludes value in kind donations or management time. Rentokil Initial's community engagement consists of three separate approaches: charitable cash donations (often linked to employees' initiatives); community support; and community investment.

The following is taken from the CSR report for 2011:

> In several instances individual businesses have used cause-related marketing techniques to achieve business objectives with both internal and external audiences. Rentokil made donations to 'Malaria No More' for every Your Voice Counts questionnaire completed by its colleagues and donated nearly £8,000. City Link had a similar initiative, although in this case, the donations (over £3,000) went to the business's charity of the year, Make-A-Wish Foundation. Other divisions are conducting more traditional, customer focused, cause-related marketing. For every Christmas tree sold in 2011, Ambius donated £5 to Greenfingers, a charity creating gardens for children's hospices.

Matched giving: Helping Hands was introduced in 2011 and will be rolled out worldwide in 2012. Charities supported by this matched giving scheme in 2011 include: Macmillan Cancer Support, Age UK, Marie Curie Cancer Care, CLIC Sargent, British Red Cross, Devon Air Ambulance, National Autistic Society, Pancreatic Cancer Research Fund, Cancer Research UK, Alzheimer's Society, Ovarian Cancer Action, Make a Wish and Birmingham Children's Hospital.

Rexam plc

Engineering, print/paper/packaging

Correspondent: Company Secretary, 4 Millbank, London SW1P 3XR (tel: 020 7227 4100; fax: 020 7227 4109; website: www.rexam.com)

Directors: Noreen Doyle; John Langston; Wolfgang Meusburger; David Gibson; Peter Ellwood, Chair; Stuart Chambers; Graham Chipchase, Chief Executive; David Robbie, Finance Director; Leo Oosterveer; Jean-Pierre Rodier (women: 1; men: 9)

Year end	31/12/2011
Turnover	£4,734,000,000
Pre-tax profit	£431,000,000

Nature of business: Rexam plc is an international consumer packaging company and beverage can maker.

Company registration number: 191285

Main locations: Stevenage, Wakefield, Milton Keynes, Deeside, Luton, London, Tonbridge

Total employees: 19,000

Charitable donations

UK cash (latest declared):	2011	£55,000
	2009	£38,000
	2008	£61,000
	2007	£48,000
	2006	£61,000
Total UK:	2011	£55,000
Total worldwide:	2011	£497,000
Cash worldwide:	2011	£458,000

Corporate social responsibility

CSR committee: No specific committee details published.

CSR policy: Extract taken from the company's website:

> *Sustainability*: We believe that running our business sustainably is essential to near term success and long-term prosperity. Our Group vision is to be the best global consumer packaging company and this

includes our actions in and around sustainability, encompassing products, operations and people.

Our approach has been to identify realistic goals that our customers can depend upon as they seek to reduce the environmental impacts of the products they commercialise and to assure an ethical supply chain.

CSR report: Published within the annual report and accounts.

Applications

In writing to the correspondent.

Other information

Rexam's total charitable cash donations and community activities (including in kind community and charitable support in the form of time, facilities and products but excluding employees' dedicated fundraising during 2011 amounted to some £497,000 (2010: £480,000). Cash donations were £458,000 (£55,000 given in the UK).

The following extract is taken from the 2011 annual report:

> Rexam is a committed partner in the communities in which we operate, and as part of this commitment many of our plants and sites work closely with local charities and groups to make a positive impact.
>
> In January 2011, Rio de Janeiro suffered from a series of destructive floods and mudslides. Our employees raised almost US$60,000 within 15 days, and we provided a lorry to help clear up and reconstruct the area. We also pride ourselves on being an ambassador for recycling, dedicating a large amount of effort in promoting and encouraging it. Our North American beverage can operations' involvement in the annual 'America Recycles Day' included a six week recycling contest. They collected a total of 1,836 metric tonnes of aluminium cans; this great result saw Rexam win first place for the fifth year in a row. Our 'Community Can Challenge' was launched in 2011 and involved 12 plants across nine European countries. It raised over £15,000 for the plants' chosen charities and helped promote recycling and can collection. Over the 10 weeks, employees collected nearly 400,000 cans (over 6.5 tonnes of metal), equating to 58 tonnes of CO2.
>
> In Brazil, through Abralatas, we sponsored and supported can collection activities during the Carnival season. The Rexam Academy is a leadership training programme that is run by the Rexam Business School. Each year around 25 of our employees are selected from across our global operations to participate in this investment in our people. As part of the programme, participants are involved in a leadership challenge, and this year the group hosted a charity dinner for UNICEF's East Africa Children's Crisis Appeal. Our employees also donated money to the fund and our South American beverage can operations carried out local fundraising. In total, the event raised over £41,000 for UNICEF.
>
> We monitor how many of our sites are involved in some form of community programme, and in the long term we are targeting that 100% of our sites will be involved in at least one local community programme (2011: 59%).

Richer Sounds plc

Retail – electrical

Correspondent: Fiona Brown, The Persula Foundation, Unit 3/4, Richer House, Gallery Court, Hankey Place, London SE1 4BB (tel: 020 7357 9298/ 2075515360; fax: 020 7357 8685; email: info@persula.org; website: www.persula.com)

Directors: Julian Richer; D. Robinson; J. Currier (women: 0; men: 3)

Year end	30/04/2012
Turnover	£138,419,000
Pre-tax profit	£4,100,000

Nature of business: Retailer and e-tailer of hi-fi, home cinema and flat screen TV equipment.

Company registration number: 1402643

Main locations: London

UK employees: 460

Total employees: 460

Charitable donations

UK cash (latest declared):	2012	£779,000
	2011	£818,000
	2009	£515,000
	2008	£410,000
	2005	£216,500
Total UK:	2012	£779,000
Total worldwide:	2012	£779,000
Cash worldwide:	2012	£779,000

Community involvement

The Persula Foundation (Charity Commission no. 1044174), was established in 1994 as an independent grant-giving foundation. The foundation supports any cause which the trustees feel strongly about. Whilst always researching new projects and charities to support, it does have core interests, e.g. animal welfare, disabilities, human welfare and human rights.

Corporate giving

The company is an unlisted plc which is 100% owned by Julian Richer, the founder and managing director of the company. Support for charitable causes is routed through the **Persula Foundation** which was initiated by Julian Richer. During 2011/12 the company gave £779,000 to various charities.

In 2010/11, the foundation had an income of £849,000 and spent £900,000 in grants to various charities including: RSPCA (£60,000); Amnesty International, Liberty and Prison Reform Trust (£25,000) and Tapesense (£21,000).

In kind support

The Persula Foundation has access to many resources from the company, such as marketing, design and strategic consultation. It prefers to use these resources to provide an added value aspect to its collaboration with organisations. It also offers support in the form of time and resources.

Employee-led support

The company supports employee volunteering, allowing paid time off work to volunteers.

Matched funding: The company has a scheme in place to match employees' fundraising.

Commercially-led support

Tapesense, the foundation's mail-order service, offers subsidised, brand new blank audio cassettes, and popular hi-fi accessories to blind and visually impaired people.

Corporate social responsibility

CSR policy: No CSR details.

Exclusions

No support for circular appeals, advertising in charity brochures, appeals from individuals, the arts, education, enterprise/training, fundraising events, medical research, overseas projects, political/religious appeals, science/ technology, sport or large national appeals.

Money for core costs, buildings/building work or to statutory bodies is not given.

Sponsorship is not undertaken.

Applications

The charity considers applications from a variety of charitable organisations for funding. Applications are reviewed and levels of grants payable are decided by the Trustees.

Ridgesave Ltd

Property

Correspondent: Zelda Weiss, 141b Upper Clapton Road, London E5 9DB

Directors: Joseph Leib Weiss; E. Englander; Zelda Weiss (women: 1; men: 2)

Year end	31/03/2011
Turnover	£351,441

Nature of business: Property investment and trading.

Ridgesave Ltd is a registered charity with two non-charitable operating subsidiaries: Bullion Properties Ltd and Doxit Company Ltd.

Company registration number: 1745720

Charitable donations

UK cash (latest declared):	2011	£1,343,700
	2009	£1,900,000
	2008	£1,700,000
	2007	£1,100,000
	2006	£944,000
Total UK:	2011	£1,343,700
Cash worldwide:	2011	£1,343,700

Community involvement

This is a somewhat unusual entry in the context of our research into company giving. Ridgesave, although registered as a company limited by guarantee, is also a registered charity (Charity Commission no. 288020).

We have decided to include them here because it has two non-charitable operating subsidiaries – Bullion Properties Ltd (property trading) and Doxit Co. Limited (property investment). In addition, the bulk of the charity's income is derived from four other companies of which some of the trustees of the charity are also directors. These companies are: Islehurst Ltd; Shirestates Ltd; Urbanhold Ltd; and Halastar Ltd.

Corporate giving

During 2010/11, the charitable company has continued its philanthropic activities and has maintained its support of organisations engaging in education, advancement of religion, and the giving of philanthropic aid. The charity had an unusually low income of £351,000 and grants for the year totalled £1.3 million.

Corporate social responsibility

CSR policy: No CSR details available.

Applications

In writing to the correspondent.

Rio Tinto plc

Mining

Correspondent: Community Relations Team, Legal and External Affairs, 2 Eastbourne Terrace, London W2 6LG (tel: 020 7781 2000; fax: 020 7781 1800; website: www.riotinto.com)

Directors: Andrew Gould; Guy Elliott; Vivienne Cox; Richard Goodmanson; Ann Godbehere; Lord Kerr of Kinlochard; Paul Tellier; Michael Fitzpatrick; Sam Walsh; Robert Brown; Jan du Plessis, Chair; Tom Albanese, Chief Executive; Chris Lynch; John Varley (women: 2; men: 12)

Year end	21/02/2011
Turnover	£38,092,726,230
Pre-tax profit	£4,263,148,490

Nature of business: Rio Tinto is one of the world's largest mining companies. Based in the UK, Rio Tinto has substantial worldwide interests in metals and industrial minerals with major assets in Australia, South America, Asia, Europe and Southern Africa.

Company registration number: 719885

Subsidiaries include: Anglesey Aluminium Ltd

Main locations: London

Total employees: 68,000

Charitable donations

UK cash (latest declared):	2011	£400,000
	2009	£1,800,000
	2008	£1,900,000
	2007	£1,800,000
	2006	£2,500,000
Total UK:	2011	£400,000

Community involvement

Rio Tinto group companies around the world give active support to their local communities, both directly and through independently managed foundations. The company in its 'Communities Factsheet' available from the website, states the following with regard to its community support:

> Community engagement and planning leads us to develop programmes that respond to both business and community priorities. These help us to optimise the effects of our activities on our host communities' livelihoods and the overall economy. Community programmes include enterprise development, training, employment, community-based health, and social and cultural heritage initiatives. The programmes are designed to make a contribution to local socioeconomic development, and they must promote self-sufficiency and avoid dependency. Eventually, responsibility for specific initiatives should devolve to community members or institutions.

There is very little information regarding the company's charitable giving in the UK.

Corporate giving

The following information is taken from the company's annual report: 'During 2011, the group spent US$294 million (£184 million) on community assistance programmes and payments into receiving trusts set up in directly negotiated community impact benefit agreements. Donations in the UK during 2011 amounted to £400,000.' We have no details of the UK beneficiary groups.

As the group's global community assistance programmes involve much more than charitable or community giving and are tied up with the group's impact on the communities which it affects, we have not used this figure as a global community contribution.

Corporate social responsibility

CSR committee: There is a Sustainability Committee.

CSR policy: The following is taken from the company's website:

> *Communities*
>
> Good community relations are as necessary for our business success as the effective management of our operations. This belief is at the heart of our overall approach to communities work and is why we build good quality relationships with the people in the areas where we operate. We seek to understand the social, environmental and economic implications of our activities so we can optimise benefits and reduce negative impacts, both for local communities and for regional and national economies. We accept that we cannot meet everybody's concerns and expectations, but wherever we operate we seek to do so with broad-based community support.

CSR report: There is an annual sustainability report available from the company's website but no reference is made to UK charitable giving.

Exclusions

No support is given, directly or indirectly, to any sectarian, religious or political activity. No funding is provided for building projects or general running costs, nor for advertising in charity brochures. Support is not given to individuals, animal welfare or any sporting events.

RM plc

Computer software, electronics/computers

Correspondent: H R Director, New Mill House, 183 Milton Park, Abingdon, Oxfordshire OX14 4SE (tel: 01235 826000; fax: 01235 826999; website: www.rm.com)

Directors: Iain McIntosh, Chief Financial Officer; Sir Bryan Carsberg; Jo Connell; Sir Mike Tomlinson; Martyn Ratcliffe, Chair; Deena Mattar; Lord Andrew Adonis (women: 2; men: 5)

Year end	30/11/2011
Turnover	£350,785,000
Pre-tax profit	(£23,380,000)

Nature of business: The principal activities of the group are the supply of educational products and services to schools, colleges and universities, local government and central government departments and agencies.

Company registration number: 1148594

Main locations: Glasgow, Cheadle, Otley, Sheffield, Leeds, Wrexham, Abingdon

Total employees: 2,864

Charitable donations

UK cash (latest declared):	2011	£88,000
	2010	£23,000
	2009	£112,000
	2008	£98,000
	2007	£74,000
Total UK:	2011	£138,000

Corporate social responsibility

CSR committee: No details found.

Applications

In writing to the correspondent.

Other information

During the year 2010/11, the group made various charitable donations totalling £126,000, which included £50,000 to Tipton RSA Academy 'to enable it to utilise the Academy for marketing purposes'. A further £12,000 was given to locally based community support projects.

Unfortunately there are no further details of the company's charitable activities in the 2010/11 accounts, unlike previous years, beyond information on sponsorship arrangements with organisations connected to directors of the company.

Roche Products Ltd

Pharmaceuticals

Correspondent: Corporate Affairs, Hexagon Place, 6 Falcon Way, Shire Park, Welwyn Garden City, Hertfordshire AL7 1TW (tel: 01707 366000; fax: 01707 338297; email: welwyn.corporate_affairs@roche.com; website: www.roche.co.uk)

Directors: J. Melville; A. Brabeck-Letmathe; J. van den Boer (women: 0; men: 3)

Year end	31/12/2010
Turnover	£837,253,000
Pre-tax profit	£74,491,000

Nature of business: Principal activity: the manufacture and sale of pharmaceutical products used in health care.

Company registration number: 100674

Main locations: Welwyn Garden City, Burgess Hill

Total employees: 1,376

Charitable donations

UK cash (latest declared):	2009	£187,000
	2008	£119,000
	2007	£101,000
	2006	£155,000
	2005	£61,000
Total worldwide:	2010	£397,000
Cash worldwide:	2010	£397,000

Corporate social responsibility

CSR committee: No committee details published.

CSR policy: The company's website states:

> Our UK companies are committed to being good corporate citizens. We take very seriously our responsibilities to patients, our employees, to the communities in which we operate and to the environment around us. We are dedicated to maintaining the highest standards in science and business.

CSR report: No report published but information available from the company's website.

Applications

In writing to the correspondent.

Other information

In the year 2010 the company donated £397,000 for charitable purposes (2009: £353,000).

The following information is taken from the company's Corporate Responsibility pages on its website:

> An important contribution to Roche's success around the world is its involvement with the communities in which it operates. We focus our resources on a small number of selected projects where our contribution can make a real difference and with which we are able to act as a long-term partner. We also align our support to charitable organisations linked to education, health and science.
>
> In recognition of this commitment, Roche's pharmaceutical business in Welwyn Garden City is forging strong links with a local school which has achieved science academy status. Employees are encouraged to share their expertise and skills to the benefit of the students.
>
> Each year, Welwyn employees nominate and support a Charity of the Year for which, through a programme of fundraising activities, they actively raise funds for the cause. Age UK [was] Roche's Charity of the Year for 2012.
>
> With an emphasis on unlocking the potential in people through innovative projects, a diverse range of charities and organisations are supported by Roche at Welwyn. These include Setpoint Hertfordshire, an organisation that encourages scientific study in schools; the Mixed Group, an initiative that provides a wonderful Christmas Day for the lonely and elderly in the local area who otherwise would have been alone, and the London School of Pharmacy.
>
> As a long-term business resident of Sussex, Roche's diagnostics business continues to grow its involvement with charities and its commitment to the county. Our aim is to build strong community partnerships and, at a local level, support important health causes, scientific education and youth activity.
>
> Roche appreciates that sport not only improves health and increases self-confidence, but also acts as a focus for young people, thereby improving community links.
>
> Furthermore, making science interesting to young people is critical for developing the next generation of scientists upon whom advances in healthcare will depend. Roche is therefore proud to support educational initiatives such as the Brighton Science Festival and local schools' programmes.
>
> Every year, our employees across the UK contribute to Roche's global humanitarian efforts by taking part in the Roche Employee Children's Walk, an event which helps to fund projects that support children in Malawi who have been orphaned as a result of HIV/AIDS with a matched-donation given to a local charity that supports vulnerable children here in the UK. In 2011 Roche employees voted that the Great Ormond Street Hospital Charity should benefit from the matched donation.

Charity of the Year: No information for 2013 at the time of writing (January 2013).

Rolls–Royce plc

Engineering

Correspondent: Health and Safety and Environment Committee, 65 Buckingham Gate, London SW1E 6AT (tel: 020 7222 9020; website: www.rolls-royce.com)

Directors: James M. Guyette; Peter J. Byrom; Colin Smith, Director; Prof. Peter Gregson; Helen Alexander; Iain Conn; Mike Terrett; John Neill; Ian Strachan; Lewis Booth; Simon Robertson, Chair; John Rishton, Chief Executive; Frank Chapman; John McAdam; Mark Morris (women: 1; men: 14)

Year end	31/12/2011
Turnover	£11,124,000,000
Pre-tax profit	£1,105,000,000

Nature of business: Rolls-Royce is a global company providing power on land, sea and air.

Company registration number: 1003142

Subsidiaries include: Vickers plc, NEI Overseas Holdings Ltd, Vickers Engineering plc, Sourcerer Ltd

Main locations: Bristol, Derby, Dounreay, East Kilbride, Hucknall, Hillington, Newcastle, London, Sunderland, Barnoldswick, Ansty

UK employees: 21,600

Total employees: 40,400

Membership: Arts & Business, BITC, LBG

Charitable donations

UK cash (latest declared):	2011	£2,100,000
	2009	£1,500,000
	2007	£1,100,000
	2006	£728,000
	2005	£671,000
Total UK:	2011	£2,100,000
Total worldwide:	2011	£4,800,000
Cash worldwide:	2011	£3,700,000

Community involvement

The following information is taken from the company's annual Sustainability Report:

> *Community investment*
>
> Rolls-Royce has a firm, long-standing commitment to the communities in which we operate around the world. During

2011, the group's total contributions (including money, employee time and gifts in kind) were £7.1 million. Our community investment activities support the group's strategy and future success, particularly in the areas of: recruitment and employee retention, employee engagement, professional development and the group's reputation in the community. During the year, the group approved a new global charitable contributions and social sponsorships policy and procedure, confirming our major areas of support as:

- Education and skills, particularly in the areas of STEM which are key to our future success
- Environment, adding value to the Group's environment strategy
- Social investment, making a positive difference to the communities in which we operate
- Arts and culture, contributing to the cultural vibrancy in geographic areas in which we operate
- Requests relating to the group's business such as armed services related, engineering and aviation

The new policy and procedure also sets out a clear structure for global governance, ensuring consistency of approach and global visibility of contributions.

Corporate giving

In 2011 the group's charitable donations and 'social sponsorships' amounted to £3.7 million, of which £2.1 million were made in the UK. Total worldwide contributions were £7.1 million. The table below gives a useful breakdown of the company's global giving.

Charitable contributions and social sponsorships – UK	£2.1 million
Charitable contributions and social sponsorships – Worldwide	£1.6 million
Commercial sponsorship	£700,000
Employee time	£2.6 million
Gifts in kind	£100,000
Payroll giving UK	£500,000
Payroll giving North America	£300,000

In kind support

The group offers support in kind to local initiatives including providing places on in-house training programmes; donating surplus computer equipment and furniture; the loan of engines and components; and offering the free use of meeting rooms and premises.

Employee-led support

The company supports employees' volunteering/charitable activities by allowing time off in which to volunteer and through financial support. Employee time contributed during 2011 is estimated at a value of £2.6 million, with employees participating in activities such as community projects and team-building activities with societal benefits. These projects are recognised at the group's Global Learning and Development Awards.

Payroll giving: In addition to the group's own contributions, Rolls-Royce finances the administration of a Payroll Giving Scheme for UK employees, enabling them to make tax-free donations to their chosen charities. In the UK during 2011, employees gave £500,000. In North America, £300,000 was donated.

Commercially-led support

Sponsorship: In addition to charitable donations, contributions of £2.1 million were made towards sponsorships and educational programmes.

Rolls Royce Science Awards: Established in 2004, the Rolls-Royce Science Prize is part of the company's commitment to promote science and engineering in schools by rewarding inspirational teaching. Since this time, over £800,000 in prize money has been distributed to 300 schools across the UK. In addition, Rolls-Royce has contributed £1 million to Project ENTHUSE, a partnership between business and Government dedicated to training and inspiring STEM subject teachers.

Corporate social responsibility

CSR committee: Charitable and community giving is contained within the group's Sustainability Report. Health and Safety and Environment data from all wholly owned operations and majority owned joint ventures worldwide is reported to the Corporate HS&E centre based in Derby, UK, and covers a wide range of pertinent key performance indicators (KPIs).

CSR policy: Statement taken from the 2011 Sustainability Report:

> We remain committed to working with all our stakeholders to develop new approaches and technologies that will help provide solutions to sustainable economic growth. We are striving to power a better world and recognise that we have a key part to play. We will continue to invest for the long-term; we have a strong track record of innovation, and a long-standing commitment to research and development. Our sustainability programmes address: the environment; our people; and, the communities in which we operate.
>
> NB: In September 2011, we issued our response to the Davies Report on women on boards confirming our support for the development of a diverse workforce. We govern this through our Global Diversity and Inclusion Steering Group, the membership of which includes main board directors and senior executives. The nominations committee discusses this topic regularly and expects to make demonstrable progress in this area by 2015.

CSR report: Sustainability report contained within the annual report and accounts.

Exclusions

No support for advertising in charity brochures, political appeals, religious appeals, or local appeals not in areas of company presence.

Applications

In writing to the correspondent.

N. M. Rothschild and Sons Ltd

Banking

Correspondent: Annette Shepherd, Secretary to the Charities Committee, New Court, St Swithin's Lane, London EC4P 4DU (tel: 020 7280 5000; website: www.rothschild.com)

Directors: David de Rothschild, Chair; Anthony Alt, Deputy Chair; Andrew Didham; Anthony Salz; Daniel Bouton; Mark Evans; Eric de Rothschild; Leopold de Rothschild; Peter Smith (women: 0; men: 9)

Year end	31/03/2011
Turnover	£28,000,000
Pre-tax profit	£45,900,000

Nature of business: The company and its subsidiaries carry on the business of merchants and bankers. The parent company is Rothschild Continuation Ltd and the ultimate holding company is Rothschild Concordia A G, incorporated in Switzerland.

Company registration number: 925279

Main locations: London, Manchester, Leeds, Birmingham

Total employees: 1,185

Membership: BITC, LBG

Charitable donations

UK cash (latest declared):	2011	£546,000
	2009	£439,000
	2008	£624,000
	2007	£817,000
	2006	£709,000
Total UK:	2011	£546,000
Total worldwide:	2011	£546,000
Cash worldwide:	2011	£546,000

Community involvement

The group supports charities both in the areas in which it operates and those in the wider community. The Charities Committee was established in 1975 to consider the requests received every year from charities seeking financial support.

Typical beneficiaries continue to include organisations concerned with elderly people, healthcare, social welfare and education. Requests for support from staff in respect of charitable causes with which they are associated, or have an involvement, are actively encouraged. Applications from small, local charities are particularly welcomed.

The company's subsidiaries around the world support causes in their areas of operation.

Corporate giving

The sum of £546,000 (2010: £439,000) was charged against the profits of the group during the year in respect of gifts for charitable purposes.

Rothschild has supported approximately 250 charities during the 2010/11 financial year including: Action for Sick Children; Age UK; Brainwave; Chance to Shine; Deafblind UK; The English Musical Festival; Future Talent; Gavriel Mier Trust; Help for Heroes; Jane Tomlinson Appeal; Kith and Kids; Little Hearts Matter; Macmillan Trust; National Autistic Society; Orphaids UK; Plan UK; Queen Alexandra College; Red Balloon; Tower Hamlets Friends and Neighbours; SADS UK; Tommy's; Vision Charity; WaterAid; Yellow Submarine Respite Holidays and Zimbabwe Benefit Foundation.

Employee-led support

Apart from making financial donations, the Group is committed to engaging in long-term relationships with local schools, charities and community organisations through the Rothschild in the Community volunteering programme.

Requests for support from staff in respect of charitable causes with which they are associated, or have an involvement, are actively encouraged.

Payroll giving: The Give As You Earn scheme is in operation.

Charity of the Year: Cancer Research UK. The Charity of the Year is chosen by staff in January each year.

Corporate social responsibility

CSR committee: In the UK the Rothschild Charities Committee meets quarterly to consider applications.

CSR policy: This information was obtained from the company's website:

> The Rothschild Group considers requests for financial support, particularly from charities working in the fields of social welfare, young people and healthcare.

CSR report: There was no evidence of a separate CSR report.

Exclusions

No response to circular appeals. No grants for advertising in charity brochures; animal welfare; appeals from individuals; fundraising events; overseas projects; political appeals; religious appeals or sport.

Applications

In writing to the Secretary to the Charities Committee, which meets quarterly to make grant decisions.

Rotork plc

Engineering

Correspondent: The Secretary, Charity Committee, Brassmill Lane, Bath BA1 3JQ (tel: 01225 733200; fax: 01225 333467; email: mail@rotork.co.uk; website: www.rotork.com)

Directors: Graham Ogden; Ian King; John Nicholas; Peter France, Chief Executive; Roger Lockwood, Chair; Jonathan Davis, Finance Director; Bob Arnold; Gary Bullard (women: 0; men: 8)

Year end	31/12/2011
Turnover	£447,833,000
Pre-tax profit	£112,550,000

Nature of business: Designers and builders of actuators.

Company registration number: 578327

Total employees: 2,500

Charitable donations

UK cash (latest declared):	2011	£90,000
	2009	£87,000
	2008	£71,000
Total UK:	2011	£90,000
Total worldwide:	2011	£163,000
Cash worldwide:	2011	£163,000

Corporate social responsibility

CSR committee: Information taken from the CSR pages of the company's website states:

> The Group Chief Executive chairs the Corporate Social Responsibility Committee ('CSR') which reports to the Rotork Management Board and through the Group Chief Executive to the Board of Rotork plc. The CSR has four sub-committees:
> - Ethics Committee (chaired by the Group Legal Director)
> - Health & Safety Committee (chaired by the Group Operations Director)
> - Social Issues Committee (chaired by the Group Human Resources Director)
> - Environmental Committee (chaired by the Group Operations Director)

CSR policy: The company's mission statement states that it will 'be a good corporate citizen, supporting the local community, acting with integrity and honesty whilst always considering ways of improving our operational impact on the environment'.

CSR report: Contained within the annual report and accounts.

Applications

In writing to the charity committee.

Other information

During the year 2011 the company made charitable donations of £94,000 (2010: £87,000) which was part of the total group contribution of £163,000 (2010: £144,000).

The following information is taken from the company's website:

> In 2011, Rotork has held and participated in numerous fundraising events for its nominated charity, WaterAid. Highlights over the last year include:
> - All Rotork Sweden employees donated cash in lieu of the annual Christmas gift from Rotork
> - Rotork Malaysia sold t-shirts
> - Rotork Italy held a charity lottery and a charity football match
> - A team of UK employees took part in Coast Along, a 10km trail around Cardiff Bay, Wales
>
> The Group donated £90,000 to WaterAid and a further £19,000 was raised from employee fundraising. The Group will continue to support WaterAid in 2012 and sponsor its Jeldu Woreda Solar Powered water project in Ethiopia, which will improve access to clean drinking water, provide education and promote good sanitation practices. In addition, in 2012, Rotork is looking to set up its own global charity initiatives.
>
> Rotork also believes it is important to be a good neighbour by working in the community. We regard this as part of our ongoing responsibilities as a corporate entity and seek to be regarded as a good corporate citizen. One of the ways the Group does this is by having local Charity Committees at each of its sites which donate to local charities. This empowers local employees to decide how to distribute the funds in their local communities. During 2011, £70,000 was donated by the local Charity Committees. For example, Rotork Milwaukee, USA donated school supplies to fill 50 rucksacks to be distributed to children from the Silver Spring Neighborhood Center, a non-profit social service agency which supports Wisconsin's largest low-income housing development as well as surrounding communities.
>
> *Education:*
>
> Rotork has forged links with local universities, colleges and schools in a number of the locations where it operates. It also sponsors students to go into higher education in India in addition to sponsoring a school there. Rotork is the industry member of the Bath Education Trust, which has as its objectives educational advancement in local schools and the promotion of community cohesion. The Bath Education Trust has provided Rotork with an opportunity to further develop local links. Staff hold sessions for students providing experience through courses intended to develop skills such as negotiating, presenting, project management, conducting meetings and financial management.
>
> Rotork has a representative who is a member of the Industrial Advisory Board for the Mechanical Engineering Department of Bath University. Rotork is also a member of an initiative of the Engineering Development Trust and sponsors a science project currently being undertaken by pupils in the sixth form of a local Bath school.

Matched funding: Individual employees or groups of employees also engage in community activities and the Charity Committee normally matches monies raised by employees who undertake charitable events personally.

The Royal Bank of Scotland Group plc

Financial services, insurance, banking

Correspondent: Sustainability Team, Business House F, PO Box 1000, Gogarburn, Edinburgh, United Kingdom EH12 1 HQ (tel: 01316 263660; fax: 01316 263074; website: www.rbs.com/sustainability.html)

Directors: Aileen Taylor; Joseph P. McHale; Bruce Van Saun, Group Finance Director; Sandy Crombie; Penny Hughes; John McFarlane; Arthur Ryan; Philip Scott; Philip Hampton, Chair; Stephen Hester, Chief Executive; Alison Davis; Tony Di Iorio; Brendan Nelson; Baroness Noakes (women: 4; men: 10)

Year end	31/12/2011
Turnover	£21,410,000,000
Pre-tax profit	(£766,000,000)

Nature of business: The Royal Bank of Scotland Group plc is the holding company of a large global banking and financial services group. Headquartered in Edinburgh, the group operates in the United Kingdom, the United States and internationally through its two principal subsidiaries, the Royal Bank and NatWest.

Company registration number: SC045551

Subsidiaries include: Direct Line Insurance Group, RBS Insurance Group Ltd, NatWest Bank plc, Ulster Bank plc

Brands include: NatWest; Coutts and Co.; Direct Line; Citizens Bank.

Main locations: Edinburgh

UK employees: 90,600

Total employees: 142,600

Membership: BITC, LBG

Charitable donations

UK cash (latest declared):	2009	£34,700,000
	2008	£24,800,000
	2007	£32,173,000
	2006	£25,411,000
	2005	£24,278,000
Total worldwide:	2011	£39,100,000
Cash worldwide:	2011	£39,100,000

Community involvement

The following information is taken from the annual report and accounts for 2011:

To ensure it makes its community investments as effective as possible, the group's policy is to focus its resources on a small number of substantial strategic programmes. These are issues most relevant to a financial institution and relate broadly to financial education, supporting enterprise and microfinance and the charitable endeavours of employees.

Community programmes

Supporting enterprise

The Supporting Enterprise programme focuses on two streams of activity. First, the group works with partners to support potential entrepreneurs directly, through training and mentoring, to help them overcome their particular barriers to entry. Second, the group helps build the capability of alternative means of finance and support for would-be entrepreneurs who would not normally qualify for direct support from banks.

In the UK, RBS group is the largest corporate supporter of The Prince's Trust Enterprise Programme, which has helped over 70,000 young people since its inception. This programme offers young entrepreneurs from disadvantaged backgrounds loan funding, advice and the support of a business mentor (including our own employees) when starting up in business.

In Scotland, the group works closely with The Prince's Scottish Youth Business Trust (PSYBT) to help them achieve their goals of promoting and supporting of self-employment and business creation amongst young people.

MoneySense for Schools

The RBS group has committed to educating young people about money management through its MoneySense for Schools programme. MoneySense for Schools is the RBS group's financial education programme. Since 2005 it has reached 70% of secondary schools in Britain, and taught over 2.5 million young people how to manage their money and prepare for the financial decisions in life.

Teachers can deliver the lessons supported by a dedicated team of RBS and NatWest employees and volunteers from across the group. To keep the MoneySense for Schools programme as relevant as possible, over the last five years, over 50,000 of Britain's 12–19 year olds have been asked how much they know about money management. This is the fifth and final year of the MoneySense Research Panel and its findings can be viewed at: www.rbs.com/sustainability/community-programmes/moneysense.

Local Chief Executive Officers (Local CEOs)

In 2011 the group restructured its Branch Banking model to respond to the demand for a more local level of service. This included the creation of a network of Local CEOs, empowered to make decisions and encouraged to take an active role in the wider success of their local community.

CommunityForce

2011 also saw the launch of CommunityForce, a project designed to support local communities by enabling customers, staff and the wider public to vote for the causes that matter most to them, and offer their time as volunteers. Each of the 158 Local CEOs awarded three charities or projects in their communities with a share of the £3 million fund, thereby keeping the benefit at a local level. This initiative received over 450,000 votes for the 6,800 charities and projects nominated across the UK.

Divisional community initiatives

As well as the tailored group community programmes, there is also a wider range of community initiatives that are led from within the different businesses across the organisation. In 2011:

Ulster Bank continued to expand their MoneySense programme, providing financial education to more people in Ireland than ever before. Over 30 schools are also participating in the Ulster Bank QuickStart initiative which provides school children with the opportunity to learn about setting up their own enterprise.

Markets & International Banking (M&IB) focus their activities on helping children and young people in a variety of ways: More than 3,500 employees volunteered in 2011, supporting 21,000 disadvantaged young people.

400 employees acted as business advisors, coaches and mentors and hosted workplace visits to raise the aspirations and employability skills of local young people.

Over 3,000 employees took part in initiatives to improve access to play facilities for disadvantaged children and their families. This included 1,000 UK employees, who rebuilt and improved two London-based adventure play areas for young people with disabilities.

In addition, M&IB have strong links with schools in the UK, US and Hong Kong where employees help primary school children develop their numeracy and literacy skills.

M&IB employees also support disaster relief efforts through volunteering. For example 40 employees in Japan volunteered time to help rebuild Minamisanriku-cho, a town that had been hard hit by the tsunami.

Citizens Financial Group, the group's business in the US, focuses on three areas:

- Human services (food and nutrition, family support, domestic violence protection and community healthcare)
- Housing development
- Economic development, including financial literacy

During the year, Citizens invested more than $16 million through charitable giving and community sponsorships to support more than 1,200 non-profit organisations.

Citizens also launched the TruFit Good Citizen Scholarship programme, offering 20 scholarships totalling $50,000 to students whose volunteer efforts have made a difference in their communities.

The Citizens Charitable Foundation invested $1.5 million in financial education, training adults and young people in basic banking, budgeting, credit, home ownership, debt management, and retirement planning.

Coutts

Coutts support clients who would like to use their wealth towards a social cause. It is one of the few private banks in the UK that has an established and dedicated philanthropy team. Coutts offers families and individuals bespoke advice as well as practical guides to ensure their philanthropy is as effective as possible.

Coutts have also been supporting entrepreneurs for a number of years through bursary programmes, and have been promoting enterprise through sharing knowledge and experience amongst the entrepreneur community.

In 2011 Coutts sponsored: London Fashion Week; the London Design Festival; MADE, the entrepreneur festival in Sheffield. Coutts was also heavily involved with the Global Entrepreneurship Week in the UK in 2011.

UK Retail

As part of the group's UK Retail Customer Charter, CommunityForce was launched in 2011 to help support local community projects.

Corporate giving

Group community programmes are broadly focused around supporting enterprise, community engagement and MoneySense, the group's financial education programme. In addition, the business divisions have tailored initiatives that respond to the local needs of their communities and employees. The group sponsorship approach also focuses on benefitting the local community.

In 2011, the group states it invested £72 million in communities through these programmes, through both cash and in kind donations, as well as employee time.

The total amount given for charitable purposes by the company and its subsidiary undertakings during the year ended 31 December 2011 was £39.1 million (2010: £29.6 million). It is not known how much of this support was for the benefit of UK-based organisations.

In kind support

In 2011, over 50,000 employees volunteered a total of 236,600 hours in supporting charities across the globe.

Employee-led support

Employee and Community Engagement Programme

The employee and community engagement programme operates in the communities where employees live and work and staff are encouraged to get involved. They are supported in this in a number of ways:

- The employee volunteering programme was launched in 2010. This programme gives staff paid time off to volunteer in their community. In 2011, nearly 56,000 employees were given over 235,000 hours off to volunteer
- Community Cashback gives further support to employees who fundraise and volunteer in their own time. In 2011 cash grants were given to over 3,000 charities and community groups across the world
- Payroll Giving allows employees in the UK, Ireland, India and US to donate to the charity of their choice via their salary. The company matches this donation
- Community Stars is an employee recognition programme for those who achieved 'fantastic results' for the good causes that matter most to them. Employees are given a chance to win a financial award for the charity they supported

RBS and NatWest Retail Banking staff gave over 16,000 days in 2011 to volunteer and fundraise in their local communities. In addition to a number of nationwide partner charities who offer the group's employees various opportunities for one day volunteering, over 600 CommunityForce projects have registered an interest in support from the wider public and employees and local staff will be introduced to these charities.

Commercially-led support

Sponsorship: The following information is taken from the group's website:

> *Community sponsorship*
>
> Over the past two years we have refocused our approach to sponsorship, making it much more centred on supporting communities.
>
> - Through our RBS 'RugbyForce' initiative the facilities of over 400 local rugby clubs were improved in 2011
> - NatWest CricketForce brought together around 85,000 volunteers who helped to improve more than 1,500 cricket clubs in the UK
> - Citizens' sponsorship of the Philadelphia Phillies in the US includes support of an initiative to help feed those in need in the greater Philadelphia area
> - In 2011 we created 'Set4Sport' with Andy, Jamie and Judy Murray – a programme designed to encourage parents and younger children to get involved in sport and healthy lifestyles

Submit all requests for sponsorship via the RBS Group online at: www.rbs.com/about/sponsorship.html

> *Local and National Sponsorship*
>
> Although we are committed to many local and national initiatives, we are unable to support every sponsorship opportunity. As a general rule, we're unlikely to be able to sponsor clubs or societies, teams, venues, fundraising events, publications, videos, films, recordings or website development.

Corporate social responsibility

CSR committee: The Group Sustainability Committee is responsible for reviewing the group's overall sustainability strategy, values and policies and aligning the group's approach to ethical, social and environmental issues.

CSR policy: Statement taken from the 2011 annual report and accounts:

> *RBS in the community*
>
> Being a good corporate citizen is also about supporting the communities in which we operate. Our group community programmes are mainly focused around supporting enterprise, financial education and employee engagement.

CSR report: No CSR report published but the website has useful information on RBS in the community and the annual report and accounts has information on the group's community contributions.

Exclusions

Sponsorship

Before completing the online sponsorship application form, be aware that in line with current strategic policy, RBS Group cannot consider new sponsorship applications to support the following:

- Motorsports
- Extreme danger/combat sports
- Political or religious groups/events
- Individual clubs or teams
- Funding for individuals (e.g. training, equipment or travel expenses), outwith the RBS Ambassadors programme or a wider national or international initiative
- Local or regional events (e.g. community festivals) without a wider national or international programme

Employee activities

In backing the fundraising and volunteer efforts of employees the group does not support charities direct with grants, general funding contributions, core costs, charity advertising, sponsorships of events in aid of charity, individuals/team fundraising for charities.

Applications

Charitable requests should be directed to the Sustainability Team who manages RBS Group's relationships with charitable organisations.

The Royal London Mutual Insurance Society Ltd

Insurance

Correspondent: Corporate Responsibility Team, Royal London House, Alderley Road, Wilmslow SK9 1PF (tel: 0845 050 2020; fax: 01625 605406; email: corporate.responsibility@royallondongroup.co.uk; website: www.royallondongroup.co.uk)

Directors: Tim Melville-Ross, Chair; Phil Loney, Group Chief Executive; Stephen Shone, Group Finance Director; Kerr Luscombe; Andy Carter; David Williams; Andrew Palmer; Duncan Ferguson; Kathryn Matthews; Jane Platt; David Weymouth (women: 2; men: 9)

Year end	31/12/2011
Turnover	£2,341,000,000
Pre-tax profit	£64,000,000

Nature of business: Principal activities: the group's businesses offer pensions, life assurance, savings and investment products, protection insurance and provide investment management.

Company registration number: 99064

Main locations: Wilmslow, Edinburgh, Douglas

Total employees: 2,692

Membership: BITC

Charitable donations

UK cash (latest declared):	2011	£67,000
	2009	£65,000
	2008	£65,000
	2007	£65,000
	2006	£63,000
Total UK:	2011	£67,000
Total worldwide:	2011	£67,000
Cash worldwide:	2011	£67,000

Corporate social responsibility

CSR committee: There is a CR team.

CSR policy: The following statement is taken from the company's Community Strategy Update of October 2011:

> ***Royal London Community Strategy***
>
> Since its inception, over 150 years ago, Royal London has played an important part in the local community, helping people to help themselves. Over time our role in the Community has evolved with our business model but we still firmly believe that we should be active citizens and share our skills and resources to make a positive impact on the wider community.
>
> Our Community Investment Strategy and the associated Community policy cover four core themes and have been developed to guide the ways in which we can maximize this impact on the community whilst simultaneously engaging our employees and members. The core themes are:
>
> - Charitable giving
> - Community investment
> - Employer supported volunteering
> - Commercial initiatives

CSR report: Published within the annual report and accounts.

Exclusions

No support for advertising in charity brochures, animal welfare, appeals from individuals, environment/heritage, overseas projects, political appeals, or religious appeals.

Applications

In writing to the correspondent to whom sponsorship proposals should also be addressed. Further information on the company's donations policy and how to apply are available upon request.

Other information

In 2011, grants worth £67,000 were awarded. This includes £25,000 to the first beneficiaries of the Degge and Ridge Award, (see The Royal London Foundation details below) and the Tea Time Club operated by the Corstorphine Dementia Project in North West Edinburgh. (In 2012, Royal London will make a donation of £75,000 to the Leukaemia and Lymphoma Research charity and £75,000 to the Juvenile Diabetes Research Foundation.)

The following information is taken from the company's Community Strategy Update of October 2011:

> ***The Royal London Foundation***
>
> We want to support the communities that Royal London's members live and work in and so in April 2011, we launched The Royal London Foundation in honour of our founders Henry Ridge and Joseph Degge and the principles with which they set up Royal London. The Foundation focuses on three core areas which we believe encompass issues relevant to our members and UK communities:
>
> *Education*: causes which support the education of people of all ages, including skills to help those seeking employment.
>
> *Elderly*: causes which help older generations who require assistance in their daily lives.
>
> *Health*: causes that provide health and fitness activities to those who might not otherwise have access to such facilities.
>
> Each year we will also grant a £25,000 award, the 'Degge and Ridge Award', to one deserving cause under one of the three themes.

The company's volunteer programme, Stepforward, encourages people to take two days per year of company time to volunteer in the community. In 2010, 458 people took part in projects, which equates to over 3,650 hours. These included participating in the Number and Reading Partners programme, which aims to boost the learning skills of primary schoolchildren in Edinburgh.

Gifts in kind: Wherever possible Royal London supports giving in kind through the provision of resources and facilities to charities and community organisations which are based in the locality of its offices.

Matched funding: The company will match funds raised by an individual up to £250 and by a team up to £1,000

Charity partner (2012): Alzheimer's Research Trust

Royal Mail Group plc

Miscellaneous

Correspondent: The Charities Committee, 100 Victoria Embankment, London EC4Y 0HQ (tel: 020 7250 2888; website: www.royalmailgroup.com)

Directors: Mark Higson; Paul Murray; Les Owen; Nick Horler; Donald Brydon, Chair; Moya Greene, Chief Executive; Orna Ni-Chionna; Matthew Lester, Chief Finance Officer; Paula Vennells; David Currie; Cath Keers (women: 4; men: 7)

Year end	25/03/2012
Turnover	£9,352,000,000
Pre-tax profit	£263,000,000

Nature of business: This is the parent company of Royal Mail, Parcelforce and the Post-Office.

Company registration number: 4074919

Brands include: Parcel Force Worldwide, Post-Office, Royal Mail, GLS.

Main locations: London

UK employees: 159,000

Total employees: 159,000

Membership: BITC

Charitable donations

UK cash (latest declared):	2012	£5,200,000
	2011	£2,100,000
	2010	£1,700,000
	2009	£2,000,000
	2008	£1,800,000
Total UK:	2012	£5,200,000
Total worldwide:	2012	£5,200,000
Cash worldwide:	2012	£5,200,000

Community involvement

The following information is taken from the 'Community' section of the Royal Mail website:

> Our support for communities starts with the services we provide and our direct economic impact as an employer and purchaser of goods and services. This is supported by our active investment in communities and our charitable giving programme.
>
> - Each year, Royal Mail invests more than £10 million directly in UK communities, including support for our colleagues' fundraising and volunteering activities
> - We hold the Guinness World Record for payroll giving, with more than 975 charities benefiting. Royal Mail employees account for six percent of all payroll giving donors in the UK

- We provide a free delivery service for blind and visually impaired people, worth around £5 million a year
- Our colleagues raised £2.6 million for our previous Charity of the Year partner, Barnardo's
- We support a charitable fund, the Rowland Hill Benevolent Fund, dedicated to helping Royal Mail employees, pensioners and their families during times of need
- More than one million pupils across the UK benefit from our educational support materials

Charity of the Year: *Prostate Cancer UK* (formally known as The Prostate Cancer Charity) is the UK's leading charity helping more men survive prostate cancer and enjoy a better quality of life. The charity provides support for men and their families, runs awareness programmes and funds vital research into the disease.

The group's two year partnership, which began in July 2012, aims to raise at least £2 million for the charity. This will fund up to 50 specialist prostate cancer nurses, based at the heart of communities, helping around 44,000 more men across the country.

Agreement is reached with the group's Charity of the Year partner as to how the money will be used, and then collaborates on a dedicated fundraising programme, staff teams working with the charity to develop exciting ideas. The charity also co-ordinates its own activities and events – treks, bike rides, fun runs and quiz nights have been supported by staff.

Corporate giving

During the year Royal Mail Group made charitable contributions of £5.2 million directly to charities and good causes across the UK, compared to £2.1 million during 2010/11. The company were unable to give further information as to beneficiaries of the donations and we were referred to The Charities Trust in Liverpool – tel: 01514 752002.

In kind support

Education: Royal Mail publishes a magazine called Teacher's Post-three times a year aimed at supporting teachers in the classroom. The magazine is distributed to 26,000 schools in the UK. Also published is a range of educational material aimed at primary and secondary school teachers and children, and also for children with learning difficulties.

The Communications Workers Union also has its own charity. **Communications Workers Union Humanitarian Aid** (CWUHA) helps vulnerable children in the UK and around the world. Staff have participated directly in its projects, and transport convoys have delivered thousands of tonnes of aid to hundreds of orphanages, foster and adoption centres, hospitals and families in Africa and Eastern Europe.

The group donates its decommissioned bicycles to the charities **Re-Cycle** and **The Krizevac Project** which ship them to Africa. Royal Mail bikes are highly prized as they are strong and able to carry heavy loads. Nearly 3,000 have been donated so far.

Employee-led support

Staff are encouraged to volunteer and employees are available for secondments. The group supports colleagues' fundraising for any charity or worthwhile cause.

Payroll giving: The company operates a scheme managed on its behalf by the **Charities Trust**. Over 40,000 employees take part. The biggest beneficiaries among the charities supported by the scheme include Barnardo's, County Air Ambulance Trust, Help the Hospices, Macmillan Cancer Support and the Rowland Hill Benevolent Fund. Employees have donated over £45 million through payroll giving since 1989, supporting 1,000 charities across the UK.

Matched funding: In 2011/12, employees claimed over £180,000 in matched funding. For the first time, Royal Mail has committed to matching funds raised by colleagues, penny for penny, up to £1 million a year for each of the two years of the partnership with **Prostate Cancer UK.** Once colleagues and Royal Mail have raised £2 million for the charity, any funds colleagues raise for either Alzheimer's Society, Prostate Cancer UK or Whizz-Kidz will also be matched by Royal Mail, up to further £1 million.

Apart from the Charity of the Year 'Matched Giving' scheme, there is also a 'Community Support Matched Giving' scheme which provides up to £200 per year per person, towards the money they raise for all other registered charities and good causes. To help the company's fundraisers, there is also a £200 fundraising grant available to cover start-up costs for their planned charity event.

Commercially-led support

The group provides placements for work experience and apprenticeships and supports schools' literacy and numeracy curriculums.

Corporate social responsibility

CSR committee: Our management of CR issues is integrated within Royal Mail's overall governance structures. This ensures that our responsibilities to our customer, colleagues and communities are high on the senior management agenda. 'The Group's board reviews the corporate responsibility and community investment strategies on a regular basis. Major corporate responsibility initiatives now come under the scrutiny of our Chief Executive's Committee.'

CSR policy: CSR information is taken from the group's website:

> Our CR strategy, which is regularly reviewed, focuses on:
>
> - Securing the sustainability of the Universal Service to deliver economic and social benefit to the UK
> - Making commerce happen: linking customers, companies and communities for the same price across the UK
> - Delivering our modernisation programme in a way which brings our people with us and drives environmental efficiencies
> - Communicating openly and transparently with stakeholders about our performance, our contribution to the UK and our future plans.

Exclusions

The company does not consider circulars, political or general appeals, or applications from religious groups or individuals.

Applications

In writing to the correspondent. It appears that local organisations can also apply directly to their regional office for support.

RPS Group plc

Marine, oil and gas/fuel, water

Correspondent: PA to Company Secretary, Centurion Court, 85 Milton Park, Abingdon, Oxfordshire OX14 4RY (tel: 01235 438151; fax: 01235 438188; email: rpsmp@rpsgroup.com; website: www.rpsgroup.com)

Directors: J. Bennett; B. Land, Chair; A. Hearne, Chief Executive; G. Young; P. Williams; R. Miller-Bakewell; Louise Charlton; Tracey Graham (women: 2; men: 6)

Year end	31/12/2011
Turnover	£528,710,000
Pre-tax profit	£40,451,000

Nature of business: RPS Britain is separated into three business segments: planning and development; environmental management; and energy.

Company registration number: 2087786

Total employees: 4,686

Membership: BITC

Charitable donations

UK cash (latest declared):	2009	£480,000
Total worldwide:	2011	£316,000
Cash worldwide:	2011	£316,000

Corporate social responsibility

CSR committee: Corporate Governance Committee.

CSR policy: Taken from the 2011 annual report and accounts:

> *Corporate Responsibility*
> Commitment: the group's corporate governance policies provide a framework within which it can look to achieve attractive levels of return for its shareholders whilst striking a balance between this objective and recognition of its obligations to its employees, clients and society in general. The Corporate Governance Committee exercises general oversight in relation to environmental, social and governance (ESG) matters although in the normal course of business the board and the executive committee assess the risks and opportunities to which such issues give rise. In the board's view it has adequate information to enable the proper assessment of these issues.

CSR report: Information on CSR contained within the annual report and accounts.

Applications

In writing to the correspondent.

Other information

During the year the group made charitable donations in cash of £206,000. The following statement is taken from the 2011 annual report:

> *Community Involvement*
> RPS has supported a range of community and charitable initiatives with gifts in kind and financial contributions throughout the year, mostly at office level. In 2011 the group and its staff gave or raised £438,000 in charitable contributions (2010: £472,000). Taking into account the £250,000 spent on academic bursaries and educational initiatives (2010: £188,000), the total contribution of the group and its employees to the communities in which it operates was £688,000 (2010: £660,000).
>
> *Corporate Sponsorship: Tree Aid*
> The group has for a number of years been an active supporter of Tree Aid and its programme of education, tree planting and woodland conservation programmes in Sub-Saharan Africa. This support has been sustained over several years through charitable contributions, fund raising and gifts in kind. In 2011 RPS was again acknowledged as the leading corporate sponsor of Tree Aid. The group has agreed to focus its charitable contribution on Tree Aid by sponsoring two additional projects in Ghana and Mali for which funding of around £330,000 over a three year period commencing in 2012 will be provided together with appropriate technical support from employees within the group. We are proud to have further developed our association with this award winning work that assists some of Africa's poorest rural communities to succeed in the fight against poverty and the effects of climate change.

We have unfortunately been unable to separate corporate donations from staff fundraising in our totals for UK and worldwide giving. We have used the cash figure of £206,000 given by the group and added the £110,000 a year due to Tree Aid for three years.

RSA Insurance Group plc (formerly Royal and Sun Alliance Insurance Group plc)

Insurance

Correspondent: The Corporate Responsibility Manager, 9th Floor, One Plantation Place, 30 Fenchurch Street, London EC3M 3BD (email: corporate.responsibility@gcc.rsagroup.com; website: www.rsagroup.com/rsagroup/en/corporate-responsibility)

Directors: Edward Lea; George Culmer, Group Financial Officer; John Maxwell; Noel Harwerth; Simon Lee, Group Chief Executive; Johanna Waterous; Malcolm le May; John Napier, Chair; Adrian Brown, Chief Executive UK; Alastair Barber; Joseph Streppel (women: 2; men: 9)

Year end	31/12/2011
Turnover	£8,735,000,000
Pre-tax profit	£613,000,000

Nature of business: The company's principal activity is the transaction of personal and commercial general insurance business.

Company registration number: 2339826

Subsidiaries include: Phoenix Assurance plc, Royal Insurance Holdings plc, Swinton (Holdings) Ltd, RSA E-Holdings Ltd, The Marine Insurance Co. Ltd, Sun Insurance Office Ltd, Legal Protection Group Holdings Ltd, FirstAssist Group Ltd, Royal International Insurance Holdings Ltd, The Globe Insurance Co. Ltd

Brands include: Brands include: Answer; Codan; Link4; More Th>n; RSA.

Main locations: Belfast, Birmingham, Glasgow, Horsham, Leeds, Bristol, Manchester, Liverpool, London

UK employees: 8,671

Total employees: 23,240

Membership: BITC, LBG

Charitable donations

UK cash (latest declared):	2011	£700,000
	2009	£1,500,000
	2008	£2,200,000
	2007	£2,278,660
	2005	£530,000
Total UK:	2011	£700,000
Total worldwide:	2011	£2,600,000
Cash worldwide:	2011	£2,600,000

Community involvement

The following information is taken from the 2011 Corporate Responsibility Report:

> Our approach to Corporate Responsibility remains practical and focused on three key themes:
> - The environment – Our partnership with WWF continued to focus on key business relevant issues. As a leading marine insurer we are a member of the Sustainable Shipping Initiative (SSI), an alliance of global companies and NGOs working to deliver a vision of a sustainable industry. Our Global Renewable Energy business is a leading insurer of wind, solar and other low carbon technologies and we published research with WWF on how to overcome the barriers preventing the widespread adoption of renewable energy. In our own operations we have increased the use of renewable energy, improved energy efficiency in our offices and are building a strong environmental culture among our employees
> - Safety – In 2011, we extended our work on road safety around the world. This included a new eyesight campaign in the UK, encouraging stronger regulation around eyesight tests for driving licence renewals. Our Scandinavian programme continued to grow with more than 170,000 high visibility vests and reflectors being handed out in the winter months to protect members of the public
> - Social inclusion – We launched a Global Charitable Programme in 2011 to support employees and local communities. Employees anywhere within RSA can now apply for matched funding, a charitable grant, or up to a three month charitable secondment. The programme aims to help improve employee engagement even further, support local community organisations and promote RSA in the community

Local charitable committees engage with communities to identify partners and channel support.

Charity partner: World Wildlife Fund.

Corporate giving

In 2011, the company and its subsidiaries worldwide made charitable donations of £2.6 million (2010: £2.4 million) during the year, of which £700,000 (2010: £1.2 million) related to donations made to UK based charities.

In kind support

Non-cash support includes staff involvement, gifts in kind, training schemes, nod use of resources (premises and equipment).

Employee-led support

In 2011, the company launched its Global Charitable Programme to support employees who help in their local communities. Employees anywhere within RSA can now apply for matched funding, a charitable grant or a charitable secondment for up to three months. The programme is aimed at helping improve employee engagement, supporting local charitable organisations and promoting RSA in the community. In 2011, over 17,000 volunteer hours (2010: 58,000) were donated by around 5,200 volunteers (2010: 13,160). (2010 included a significant increase in volunteer numbers and volunteer hours due to the group's 300 years birthday celebrations.)

A highlight of 2011 was the launch of the Arctic Challenge with WWF. It encouraged more than 60% of employees to actively participate in reducing their carbon footprint, develop the best business green idea and fundraise for WWF or other green charities. 'The campaign increased awareness of the partnership with WWF and the role insurers can play in combating climate change.'

In the UK, more than 100 employees singed up to help mentor teenagers from under-privileged backgrounds aspiring to pursue careers in business.

Payroll giving: Through the company payroll, the Give As You Earn scheme enables staff and pensioners to make tax-efficient donations to any charity of their choice.

Matched funding: The company matches employee donations to registered charities up to a maximum value of £250 for individuals and up to £1,000 for teams of three or more. The company has a 2012 target to double the amount of money available for matched funding.

Commercially-led support

WWF Partnership

For the past three years, the partnership with WWF has operated across the UK, Canada, Sweden, Denmark and China focusing on the insurance risks of environmental change. RSA has supported conservation projects relevant to its business including a marine protection project in Canada to help safeguard the long-term future of the fishing industry, a renewable energy project in China and a flood defence project in the UK.

Corporate social responsibility

CSR committee: The group executive committee acts as the CR Steering Committee, supported by a group CR team. The Steering Committee meets twice a year to oversee development, implementation and progress of the CR strategy and monitor compliance with our global CR, environmental, human rights and community policies. It provides a common reference point for regional businesses, where CR managers or coordinators are in place in all operating countries. Country and site-based community and environment committees determine and respond to local priorities.

CSR policy: CSR information taken from the 2011 CR report:

> The group CR policy applies to all operations, including wholly or majority-owned subsidiaries and associated companies where RSA has management control. The policy sets out commitments to:
>
> - Improve our environmental performance reducing our direct and indirect impacts
> - Support employees who want to contribute to their communities
> - Uphold human rights in our operations and supply chain
> - Provide excellent customer service and products that contribute to society
> - Work with suppliers to improve their social and environmental impacts
> - Engage with relevant stakeholders, including our peers and business partners, and contribute to public policy debates to encourage more responsible behaviour
> - Regularly review our CR strategy, approach and performance with the group executive committee and board
> - Provide an annual, independently verified report of our CR performance
>
> Focus is on three main themes: safety, inclusion and the environment.

CSR report: There is an informative and comprehensive annual CR report.

Exclusions

There are few circumstances in which the company is able to provide support outside its policy framework. Therefore, applicants such as political, religious appeals, social or animal welfare, overseas projects or heritage are not considered, nor can charities whose work mainly benefits people overseas or individuals seeking personal or professional sponsorship. Requests received by circular are not actioned.

Applications

Generally applications should be in writing to the correspondent.

Saga Group Ltd

Financial services, leisure

Correspondent: John Davies, Director Saga Charitable Foundation, Saga Building, Enbrook Park, Sandgate, Folkestone, Kent CT20 3SE (tel: 01303 771766/01303 771199; website: www.saga.co.uk)

Directors: J. A. Goodsell; S. M. Howard

Year end	31/01/2011
Turnover	£85,500,000
Pre-tax profit	£66,673,000

Nature of business: Travel, financial services, health and lifestyle.

Company registration number: 638891

Total employees: 513

Membership: BITC

Charitable donations

UK cash (latest declared):	2011	£280,600
	2008	£274,000
	2007	£143,000
Total UK:	2011	£280,600
Total worldwide:	2011	£280,600
Cash worldwide:	2011	£280,600

Corporate social responsibility

CSR policy: No CSR information found.

We were unable to determine the ratio of women to men on the board.

CSR report: No CSR report but there is a 'Charity' website page.

Exclusions

No support for advertising in charity brochures; animal welfare; the arts; enterprise/training; fundraising events; medical research; political appeals; religious appeals; science/technology; or sport.

Applications

For further information apply in writing to the correspondent.

Other information

The company's donations to its charities do not appear to be recorded in its annual report and accounts. However, we have used the income information provided in each of the company's associated charities as a fair estimate of the amount available for charitable purposes. The company's website invites donations and so it's unclear whether the money comes from the general public or the company itself.

The **Saga Charitable Foundation** (Charity Commission no. 1147124), was set up in 2012 to be the principal umbrella for all of Saga's charitable activities.

The foundation raises funds for Saga's existing charities – The Saga Charitable Trust, which helps underprivileged communities in developing countries, and the Saga Respite for Carers Charitable Trust which provides breaks for family carers living in the UK.

In addition, the foundation commissions and undertakes research into the lives of the over 50s, examining issues such as income, employment and inflation, as well as focusing on quality of life, health and well-being of the nation's over 50s. Through the promotion and publication of this research, the foundation aims to help educate opinion formers so they take issues affecting the over 50s into account when making public policy decisions. The foundation also aims to help advise and inform over 50s on a variety of public policy matters and, by doing so, benefit the lives of Britain's 21 million people aged 50 and over.

As this is a newly established charity, no accounts were required or received by the Charity Commission at the time of writing (August 2012).

Saga Charitable Trust (Charity Commission no. 291991)
Founded by Saga Holidays, the Saga Charitable Trust's mission is to benefit underprivileged communities at destinations in developing countries that host Saga holidaymakers. It does this by supporting projects that deliver health and welfare benefits, and by providing the skills and opportunities for communities to become self-sufficient and ultimately to help break the cycle of poverty.

The Saga Charitable Trust funds four key areas – education, training, healthcare and income generation. The trust works closely with local communities to identify programmes, and by directly targeting local needs it is able to make a real and sustainable difference. Income from the company for the year was £140,560.

Saga Respite for Carers Trust (Charity Commission no. 1124709)
Saga Respite for Carers Trust was established to give unpaid carers a much needed break, by providing hundreds of free holidays every year for the carer and a travelling companion, whilst ensuring continuity of care for their loved ones in the form of paid respite.

Care funding in the UK is in crisis and more and more families are forced into providing care for their loved ones within their own homes. Family carers save our economy billions each and every year, but despite suffering from seven of the top ten workplace stresses, they often receive little to no funding or support. Government has repeatedly claimed to boost funding for respite breaks for carers, but their failure to ring-fence additional money has left many providing care 24 hours a day, 365 days a year without a break from their caring responsibilities. Income from the company for the year was £140,000.

J Sainsbury plc

Retail – supermarkets

Correspondent: Sainsbury's Community Affairs, 33 Holborn, London EC1N 2HT (tel: 020 7695 6000; fax: 020 7695 7610; website: www.j-sainsbury.co.uk/cr)

Directors: Darren Shapland; Mike Coupe; Val Gooding; Gary Hughes; Bob Stack; John McAdam; Anna Ford; Mary Harris; Matt Brittin; John Rogers, Chief Financial Officer; David Tyler, Chair; Justin King, Chief Executive (women: 3; men: 9)

Year end	19/03/2011
Turnover	£21,102,000,000
Pre-tax profit	£827,000,000

Nature of business: The group's principal activities are food retailing, financial services and property development. The group is composed of Sainsbury's Supermarkets, Shaws Supermarkets and Sainsbury's Bank.

Company registration number: 185647

Main locations: London

Total employees: 148,000

Membership: BITC, LBG

Charitable donations

UK cash (latest declared):	2010	£1,900,000
	2009	£5,700,000
	2005	£2,340,000
	2004	£1,600,000
	2002	£5,000,000
Total UK:	2010	£2,100,000
Total worldwide:	2011	£2,100,000

Community involvement

J Sainsbury's community investment focuses on two areas: support for charities and other organisations promoting healthy eating and active living, particularly with children, and donating food to homeless hostels and other charities to provide nutritious meals for people in need, e.g. the Salvation Army, FareShare, Betel of Britain and animal charities. The company supports many charitable organisations and community projects through either donating cash, making in kind donations or through colleague volunteering.

The following is taken from the company's CR report 2011:

> There has been much talk of the Government's 'Big Society' initiative over the past year. Whilst we feel that, as a responsible retailer, we have been doing Big Society for years, we have identified an area that we can further develop to support the communities in which we operate. This year we have worked in partnership with the Government, the voluntary sector, Business in the Community and other stakeholders to develop the concept of Business Connectors, and to look at how we can further contribute to local communities. As part of this, we have committed to second a number of our senior colleagues to help businesses and the voluntary sector work together more closely.
>
> To support local good causes, we work with local charities and community groups. We also support larger nationwide charities, including Comic Relief, the Royal British Legion and the Scouts. In 2010, with the support of our customers, we donated over £3.3 million to the Royal British Legion's Poppy Appeal campaign: approximately 10 per cent of the total raised across the country. We also act on our concern for some of today's social problems, such as childhood obesity and supporting disadvantaged groups.

Future targets
The 2011 annual report states:

- We will support community based fundraising and colleague volunteering, encouraging our customers and colleagues to make a positive difference in the local community
- We will offer local groups and charities space in our stores to support community activities and events, helping bring the community together

Corporate giving

During the year 2010/11, cash and in kind donations totalled £2.1 million (2009/10: £1.9 million). No breakdown between cash and in kind donations was available. Sainsbury's colleagues, customers and suppliers raised £22.9 million (2009/10: £15.7 million) for charities through events supported by the company, including Sport Relief.

> *Active Kids:*
> To help tackle childhood obesity, our Active Kids scheme aims to encourage children to eat more healthily and take more exercise. We know there is no quick and simple answer to this problem, but as long as it remains a serious concern in the UK, we will continue to promote the importance of getting the right balance between energy-in and energy-out. Through the scheme, customers receive vouchers that schools and other organisations can exchange for sports, cooking and gardening equipment, and active experiences. We have donated over £100 million worth of equipment and experiences to date, with more than 40,000 schools, nurseries, sports clubs, and Scout and Guide groups registered with Active Kids. Our Active Kids Get Cooking scheme is also available to UK schools, helping teach children about cooking and healthy eating. The Active Kids Get Cooking scheme is a partnership between Sainsbury's, the Design and Technology Association, and the British Nutrition Foundation and now has over 14,000 schools registered. There's more information at www.activekidsgetcooking.org.uk.

Local Charity: The company's 'Local Charity' scheme encourages colleagues and customers select a local charity to support each year. Nominations are taken in the store, and local Colleague Councils select three charities that they feel address local needs. One charity is then selected from these three by the councils. Sainsbury's is running the scheme for the third year in 2011 encouraging staff to become more involved through volunteering and fundraising.

So far, more than 800 local charities have received support through this scheme and all stores and depots are a part of it. Over the year 2010/11, over £1.5 million has been raised for charity and staff have volunteered more over 6,500 days between them.

More than a store

We pride ourselves on providing efficient, well-run supermarkets with everything local people need for their weekly shop. This in itself has a positive effect on our communities, but in many places, our stores are also genuine community facilities.

Our Salford store is working in partnership with Salford City Council and the Education Authority to support a local learning development group by turning its old smoking room into a classroom. The development group uses the store as a training centre five days a week, giving people with learning disabilities experience and support in a working environment. The scheme, which is supported by three teachers and currently has ten students using the facility, is run with a view to employing some of them in the store.

The scheme offers valuable opportunities to learn basic work skills in real working conditions, and to find local employment. The classroom involvement also generates confidence for individuals who have previously lacked social skills, self confidence and were afraid of working environments. Our Salford store has now employed two of the students and is actively supporting others in obtaining employment in the local area.

The London 2012 Paralympic Games:

We have set up a Paralympic Legacy Fund, which will support Paralympic athletes beyond the Paralympic Games. We will raise money for this through initiatives such as our Paralympic Games bag, a specially designed reusable shopping bag, with a proportion of profits from sales going to the fund.

Comic Relief:

Having donated nearly £60 million to Comic Relief since 1999, we are the charity's largest corporate partner. We have also been its official supermarket sponsor for 12 years. In March 2011, our cheque for more than £10 million was the biggest donation ever received on the night of Red Nose Day, making it our best yet. Our final donation to Comic Relief this year was a massive £11.4 million.

In kind support

Sainsbury provides in kind support in a number of ways, including:

Food donations – Sainsbury's has been donating surplus food to local charities since 1998, and in the last year alone 300 stores gave over £1.5 million worth to a network of organisations across the UK. The company endeavours to work with local charities but when it is not possible works with FareShare, a national charity set up to relieve food poverty. FareShare takes on the distribution of food that is past its sell-by date, but within its use-by date. This initiative makes a positive difference – not only helping people in need, but also reducing the waste sent to landfill, building stronger relationships with local charities and helping colleagues get a better understanding of some of the issues in their community. Sainsbury's is also encouraging its suppliers to adopt this initiative.

Make the Difference Days

This year, colleague suggestions have inspired our Make the Difference Day programme, ensuring our customers and colleagues are the driving force behind the social and environmental issues we champion. Each Make the Difference Day shows people how a small shift in behaviour can add up to a significant change. A good example of this is our August 2010 Make the Difference Day, when we introduced phone charger recycling banks at the entrances to all our stores over a four-week period. In an industry first, we collected more than 35,000 chargers, which may otherwise have been sent to landfill. This was a great way of raising awareness about recycling and being environmentally responsible, using an appliance our customers may not have even realised they could recycle.

Another simple idea with a big impact was our May Make the Difference Day on packaging reductions. Milk bags use 75 per cent less packaging than the equivalent plastic bottles – so, to support customers who wanted to make the change from bottles to bags, we gave away around 300,000 Jugit milk jugs.

Charity donation boxes – All stores have a charity donation box for customers' 'loose change', with the money being given to local registered charities.

Store door collections – Registered charities can hold cash collections outside company stores by applying in writing to the Store Manager.

Gift vouchers – Stores are allocated small budgets for charitable donations. These are usually in the form of gift vouchers for local groups and charities for use as raffle prizes. The vouchers can be used as a prize themselves or exchanged at any Sainsbury's for suitable goods.

Employee-led support

Local heroes: Sainsbury's Local Heroes scheme, recognises and rewards the charitable activities of its staff (colleagues). Those who volunteer on a regular basis, or who fundraise for charity, can claim up to £700 through the matched funding scheme. Over the past year, 2010/11, colleagues' contributions have been matched to the value of over £200,000 – a total of over £1 million since the scheme began.

Payroll giving: The company operates the Give As You Earn payroll giving scheme.

Commercially-led support

Sponsorship: Corporate sponsorship requests should also be addressed to Sainsbury's Marketing Department.

Cause-related marketing: 'Active Kids' is a nationwide initiative launched in 2005 to encourage schoolchildren to take more exercise through non-traditional activities. Customers earn one 'Active Kids' voucher for every £10 spent. These are then collected and redeemed by schools for activity and sports equipment.

Sainsbury's continues to be the national retail partner for Comic Relief's Red Nose Day and is committed to continue its support until at least 2011. Money is raised by selling Red Noses in its stores and through Sainsbury's to You (online shopping). It also works with suppliers to stock products that promote the campaign and include a donation in their price.

Sainsbury's has been the official supermarket sponsor of Comic Relief for 11 years now and is also their largest corporate partner, having donated over £48 million since 1999. The Sainsbury's Sport Relief Mile 2010 was the biggest ever, attracting more than 175,000 participants in more than 330 mile events up and down the country. 90 tonnes of Fairtrade certified cotton was ordered by Sainsbury's to produce the Sport Relief merchandise, which included a range of t-shirts exclusively designed. Colleagues raised over £1.8 million, which contributed towards the total of more than £5.4 million donated to Sport Relief this year.

Corporate social responsibility

CSR committee: Justin King, our CEO, and Anna Ford, the chair of our Corporate Responsibility Committee and Non-Executive Director, conduct five formal meetings each year – one for each of our five values. We use these to check whether we are pursuing the right strategy on certain issues, and ask for advice if we are not.

CSR policy: Taken from the company's 2011 CR report: 'Our Approach'

> For Sainsbury's, corporate responsibility means many things. It is about providing our customers with the widest choice of quality food, at fair prices. But also about paying our suppliers a fair price and providing the reassurance of knowing that they have a buyer for their products on reasonable terms. It means enriching our communities through employment and career development opportunities, while growing our business profitably for our shareholders. And it means making the most effective use of our valuable resources like water and electricity, and respecting the local environment.

CSR report: The company publishes its social report on the Responsibility section of its website. Progress on CR initiatives is published quarterly alongside the financial updates.

Exclusions

No response to circulars. No support for advertising in charity brochures, individuals, enterprise/training, environment/heritage, medical research, science/technology, social welfare, restoration/fabric of buildings, National Health projects, overseas projects, local appeals not in areas of company presence, political or religious causes, core or pump priming.

Applications

Appeals to head office should be addressed to the correspondent. Applications can be received at any time, and should include details of aims and objectives, target audience and PR opportunities. Local appeals should be sent to local stores who will then approach the donations committee. This meets quarterly, but a subcommittee meets as and when necessary.

A separate budget exists for small donations to local charities/voluntary groups, administered at store level, in the form of vouchers.

There are also a number of Sainsbury Family Trusts with major grantmaking programmes. These are administered separately (see *The Guide to the Major Trusts, also published by DSC*), although close contact is maintained with the company's donations programme.

Advice to applicants: Sainsbury's advises applicants to try to avoid stereotyped circulars.

Samsung Electronics (UK) Ltd

Electronics/computers

Correspondent: G C Song, Company Secretary, 1000 Hillswood Drive, Chertsey, Surrey KT16 0PS (tel: 01932 455000; fax: 01932 455400; website: www.samsung.com/uk)

Directors: I. G. Hong; S. P. Kim; G. C. Song; A. R. Griffiths; J. Y. Kim

Year end	31/12/2011
Turnover	£2,142,251,000
Pre-tax profit	£39,940,000

Nature of business: Samsung Electronics (UK) Ltd's principal activities are: Importers and distributors of electronic and electrical goods; Samsung's European head office; the purchase and sale of components and capital equipment; the provision of research and development services to the ultimate parent company; and importers and distributors of telecommunications systems.

Company registration number: 3086621

Main locations: Yateley, London, Telford, Chertsey, Wynard

UK employees: 917

Total employees: 917

Membership: BITC

Charitable donations

UK cash (latest declared):	2011	£29,400
	2009	£26,000
	2008	£7,300
Total UK:	2011	£29,400
Total worldwide:	2011	£29,400
Cash worldwide:	2011	£29,400

Corporate social responsibility

CSR committee: No committee details relevant to the UK.

CSR policy: The group's website states:

> Samsung Electronics implements diverse local community engagement programs responsive to the respective needs and sentiments of eight overseas business areas. In particular, we strive to improve the educational conditions in underdeveloped countries through our partnerships with The Korean National Commission for UNESCO and Samsung UNESCO Education Fund.

We were unable to determine the ratio of women to men on the board.

CSR report: A Social Contributions report is published online.

Applications

In writing to the correspondent.

Other information

In 2011, Samsung Electronics (UK) Ltd made charitable donations totalling £29,400 (2010: £47,800). These figures do not reflect Samsung's worldwide giving but the cash donations given by the UK Ltd company within the UK. Globally Samsung gives mainly outside of the UK although there is reference in the Social Contributions Report for 2011 of support for an anti-obesity program in partnership with the European Olympic committees. Samsung also provided support for its Pink Ribbon Campaign across Europe.

Beneficiaries of the £29,400 cash included: Philharmonia Orchestra (£15,000); Korean Resident Society in the UK (£6,000); Jamie Oliver Foundation (£5,000); and Korea Sports Council in the UK (£2,000).

Santander UK

Banking

Correspondent: Sharon Squire, Head of CSR, 2 Triton Square, Regent's Place, London NW1 3AN (tel: 0870 607 6000; website: www.santander.co.uk)

Directors: Lord Burns, Chair; Ana Botin, Chief Executive Officer; José María Nus; Steve Pateman; Stephen Jones, Chief Financial Officer; Juan Rodríguez Inciarte; Roy Brown; José María Carballo; José María Fuster; Rosemary Thorne (women: 2; men: 8)

Year end	31/12/2011
Turnover	£7,618,000,000
Pre-tax profit	£1,261,000,000

Nature of business: Provision of an extensive range of personal financial services. Large scale operations throughout Europe, Latin America and the USA.

In 2010 Abbey, the savings business of Bradford and Bingley, and the Alliance and Leicester were united under the single brand of Santander. The company also announced its agreement to acquire (subject to certain conditions) bank branches and business

banking centres and associated assets and liabilities from the Royal Bank of Scotland group.

Company registration number: 2294747

Subsidiaries include: Scottish Mutual Assurance plc, Carfax Insurance Ltd, Cater Allen International Ltd, Scottish Mutual Investment Managers Ltd, Scottish Provident Ltd, Scottish Mutual Pension Funds Investments Ltd

Main locations: Glasgow, Milton Keynes, London, Sheffield, Bradford, Leicester, Bootle, Teesside, Belfast

Total employees: 26,194

Membership: BITC, LBG

Charitable donations

UK cash (latest declared):	2011	£14,000,000
	2009	£3,626,000
	2008	£3,047,000
	2007	£1,950,000
	2005	£1,557,000
Total UK:	2011	£14,000,000
Total worldwide:	2011	£14,000,000
Cash worldwide:	2011	£14,000,000

Community involvement

Community Relations

Santander has combined elements of the community initiatives from Abbey, Alliance and Leicester and Bradford and Bingley savings business into a single integrated programme.

Santander's community relations programme encompasses five areas of activity:

- Corporate donations
- Universities
- Volunteering
- Fundraising
- Sponsorship/social partnerships

The following statement is taken from the company's website:

> ***Communities***
>
> With a business focused on retail banking and SMEs, our community investment is focused on local organisations, reflecting our local footprint.
>
> We provide charitable grants through the Santander Foundation, support students via Santander Universities and under Santander Breakthrough facilitate SMEs to grow. In 2011 we contributed over £14 million to good causes in the UK supporting education, employment and enterprise.

Corporate donations are made through:

The Santander UK Foundation Ltd (Santander Foundation)
The company's charitable support is given mainly through Santander Foundation (Charity Commission no. 803655). This foundation was originally set up with a donation from the then Abbey National plc of £5 million following the sale of shares unclaimed since the company's flotation. This endowment fund received a further £750,000 from Abbey Housing Association Ltd, increasing the endowment fund to £5.75 million.

The foundation is committed to supporting local communities and disadvantaged people, particularly in areas where Santander has a significant presence. Its priorities are:

- Education and training
- Financial advice to help with money management

For details of the foundation's 2011 giving, see 'Corporate Giving' and for further information about the foundation go to: www.santanderfoundation.org.uk which provides very detailed information and guidance for those seeking funding.

Santander Universities
Santander Universities, launched in 1997, aims to contribute to the development and prosperity of society by providing support to the higher education sector. Since its creation, over £500 million has been donated via scholarships, travel grants, support for special projects, academic and non-academic awards. Santander Universities was launched in the UK in 2007 and in four years over 55 universities have become partners of the programme. Currently, over 1,000 universities around the world are part of the Santander Universities network and the group has committed to providing 500\ million euros of funding to the sector over the next five years.

For further information on the Universities programme see the company's 2011 corporate social responsibility report available from its website.

Charity of the Year
Charities wishing to be considered as the Santander Charity of the Year must be a large registered UK charity. They must be able to provide a dedicated account manager to work with Santander to deliver innovative fundraising campaigns for its 26,000 UK staff across its network of around 1,400 branches and head office sites across the UK. Santander looks to offer its employees the opportunity to take part in a full range of activities; including overseas treks, national events, physical challenges, corporate events, and smaller scale fundraising, as well as pin badge campaigns. For more details on Santander's Charity of the Year criteria and how to apply, charities should visit: www.aboutsantander.co.uk/csr/communities. The deadline for applications is 5pm on 30 June.

The company's Charity of the Year for 2013 is CLIC Sargent.

Corporate giving

Historically the majority of community support has been through charitable grants made by the Santander Foundation and support for students via Santander Universities, together equating to some £8 million a year. Reflecting the company's strategy to increase giving as part of the 'CSR three year plan', Santander invested over £14 million in 2011 in community projects, 'the majority through cash donations', an increase of 39% compared to 2010. This figure includes monies paid under the Santander Breakthrough programme and it has not been possible to distinguish the amount given to non-charitable social enterprises. Santander Universities Global Division provides support to higher education through a range of programmes including scholarships, mobility awards for students to carry out their studies overseas and funding for entrepreneurial activities. In 2011 this saw £4.9 million contributed to the sector in the UK.

The following is a breakdown of the company's total community investment:

Education and training	£7.5 million
Communities and SME's	£2.5 million
Relief of suffering	£1.6 million
Financial capability	£1.2 million
Other causes	£428,500

In 2011, Santander, (the company), donated over £3.6 million to the Santander Foundation and in turn, the foundation made grants totalling £3.9 million, broken down as follows:

Education and training	444	£1.68 million
Relief of suffering	1,160	£1.28 million
Financial capability	66	£592,000
Other	278	£364,000

In 2011 beneficiaries of grants from the foundation of £10,000 and over included: British Trust for Conservation Volunteers, Citizens Advice, Garden Organic, Gingerbread; Housing Associations Charitable Trust and MIND (£50,000 each); Alzheimer's Society (£46,500); Age UK Leicestershire and Rutland and Sunderland AFC Foundation (£30,000); and Autism Centre for Supported Employment, Carers Milton Keynes, Chesterfield Law Centre, Eden Trust, Engineering Development Trust Eva Women's Aid, Headway Belfast, Helping Hands Community Trust, Rainbow Project, St Mungo Community Housing Association and Voluntary Action Leicester (£10,000 each).

Bank Workers Charity
There is an annual donation to the Bank Workers Charity, the charity for banking employees and retirees. The charity provides services in three areas: wellbeing, home and money.

In kind support

In 2011 the company contributed gifts in kind to the Santander Foundation of £100,000. The value of volunteering time in 2011 was £147,000.

Employee-led support

Staff volunteering: In 2011 the number of staff volunteers increase by 51% from 2010. Staff took part in a varied range of activities including schools volunteering, delivering business skills and career days around the company's main sites in Belfast, Milton Keynes, Leicester, Glasgow and London.

Matched funding: Employees at Santander raised significant amounts of money during the year for charities across the UK, and in 2011, over £1.8 million was donated through their efforts and matched by Santander.

Santander also supports staff volunteering through a matched time scheme where we give up to 35 hours a year of paid work time to enable employees to help their favourite causes. Through our Community Days scheme, staff are encouraged to take a day out from the office to volunteer with a local cause. In 2011, over 1,500 employees supported 120 projects around the UK, providing over 11,000 hours of volunteering time to good causes such as working on conservation and regeneration projects and educational schemes with schools.

Charity of the Year 2013: To support and encourage employee activities, the company runs a Charity of the Year scheme and Santander staff have chosen **CLIC Sargent,** the UK's leading cancer charity for children and young people, as its new Charity of the Year partner. The year-long partnership, which begins on 1 January, has a fundraising target of £800,000 which will help to fund CLIC Sargent's eight Homes from Home across the UK for an entire year. Previous charity partners have included Great Ormond Street Hospital, the Alzheimer's Society and Marie Curie Cancer Care.

Payroll giving: Santander also participates in the Payroll Giving scheme to enable employees to make a monthly donation to charity directly from their salary.

Partnerships: The company has a long-term partnership with **British Heart Foundation**, supporting the charity's cycling events programme to encourage people to improve their health and raise funds for vital research into heart disease.

Commercially-led support

Santander Breakthrough

In 2011 Santander launched the Breakthrough programme aimed at helping fast-growing small and medium-sized enterprises, to boost economic recovery and the creation of local employment.

Breakthrough offers mezzanine-type debt finance to high growth SMEs in the UK with a turnover of between £500,000 and £10 million through a £200 million Growth Capital Fund. In addition to finance, Santander provides fast-growth companies with the resources and knowledge they need to achieve the next level of growth through live events, masterclasses, overseas trade missions and internships.

In addition to supporting mainstream SMEs, Santander has created the Social Enterprise Development Awards to provide finance and support to growing social businesses. In 2012 a prize fund of £2.3 million will be distributed to over 70 social enterprises around the UK to help them increase their social impact.

Early in Career

This new initiative launched in 2011 supports school leavers in accessing qualifications through a structured development programme, provides roles for graduates and internship positions. The company also signed up to the government's Business Compact, committing it to proactively supporting people from all areas of society in joining the workforce.

Sponsorship

Sporting links

Reflecting Santander's links with Lewis Hamilton, Jenson Button and Rory McIlroy, the bank provides support to up and coming sporting talent through the Santander Sporting Heroes programme. The scheme features a Hall of Fame for employees who are involved in competitive sports, and for those who are at international level and representing their country there is the **Sporting Heroes Elite**. In 2011 seven employees joined the Elite and received £1,000 in sponsorship to help with their equipment and training costs.

Through **Sporting Heroes Grassroots** staff can also nominate local community sports clubs and groups to receive free training kit and equipment and in 2011, 370 sports groups benefitted from this scheme.

Corporate social responsibility

CSR committee: There is a CSR team that has responsibility for defining the content for the annual CSR report and it works with representatives from around the business for the five CSR stakeholder groups in order to prepare the material. The head of CSR is Sharon Squire – see 'Contact details'.

CSR policy: Statement taken from the company's website:

> With a business focused on retail banking and SMEs, our community investment is focused on local organisations, reflecting our local footprint.
>
> We provide charitable grants through the Santander Foundation, support students via Santander Universities and under Santander Breakthrough facilitate SMEs to grow.

CSR report: Excellent CSR report published annually.

Exclusions

The company cannot make donations which:

- Are for statutory duties
- Are for part of a major capital appeal
- Support a specific individual (this includes Gap Year funding, overseas travel, medical treatment or holidays)
- Are for bursaries
- Support lobbying or political parties
- Have a restricted benefit to a single religious or single ethnic group
- Help causes outside the UK
- Help to gain specialist school status
- Are for commercial sponsorship or for fundraising events, conferences or advertising

Applications

The correspondent of the foundation is: Alan Eagle, Santander UK Foundation Manager, Santander Foundation, 201 Grafton Gate East, Milton Keynes MK9 1AN. Tel: 01908 343224 Email: alan.eagle@santander.co.uk

Detailed and helpful information on the application process is provided on the foundation's website. Applicants should bear in mind that rejected applications are often those which do not contain the required information which has been provided by the foundation. **Note:** Start by checking the sections on 'What we fund' and 'How to apply' which cover the questions asked most often. The best way to contact the foundation if you still have a question is by email to grants@santander.co.uk.

If you do not have access to email write to us at the address above. The following further tips were provided by Santander's Foundation Manager on the foundation's website:

> The successful applications are the ones that clearly address each of the points that we have set out in the section 'How to Apply'. The applications that are most likely to succeed are the ones which rather than simply assert that 'there is a need for this project' show me evidence of how they know that there is a need because they have consulted their service users or clients. All funders give a donation in order to change things for the better and it is the applications that convince me of the long-term difference that our funding will achieve, backed up with some evidence, that succeed. Whereas applications that use phrases such as 'we hope' or 'believe that we will achieve' without providing some evidence to back up these aspirations are the ones that fail.
>
> Applications for revenue costs need to share their funding strategy with us because we know that it can take at least nine months to secure replacement funding. Judging whether these projects are likely to pick up future funding strongly influences our decision to fund.
>
> Are there any common mistakes that applicants can avoid?
>
> - Don't make assumptions
> - Don't use jargon
> - Get someone else to read it – they are sure to spot any mistakes or anything that may not be clear
> - Check that you've signed the application and enclosed everything (such as a simple budget or a self-addressed postcard if you want us to acknowledge safe receipt)
> - Check that you have used the correct postage (nearly every day we receive a large envelope with the insufficient postage).

The Head of CSR at Santander UK is Sharon Squire and community investment enquiries, other than those relating to the foundation, should be addressed to her at the address given under 'Correspondent'.

Savills plc

Property

Correspondent: Corporate Responsibility Working Group, 20 Grosvenor Hill, Berkeley Square, London W1K 3HQ (tel: 020 7499 8644; fax: 020 7495 3773; website: www.savills.co.uk)

Directors: P. Smith, Chair; M. Angle; T. Ingram; C. McVeigh; J. Helsby; S. Shaw (women: 0; men: 6)

Year end	31/12/2010
Turnover	£677,000,000
Pre-tax profit	£47,300,000

Nature of business: Savills is a global real estate service provider. Savills plc is a holding company. Its principal subsidiaries' activities are advising on matters affecting commercial, agricultural and residential property, and providing corporate finance advice, property and venture capital funding and a range of property related financial services.

Company registration number: 2122174

Main locations: Banbury, Birmingham, Bishop's Stortford, Bath, Perth, Salisbury, Solihull, Sevenoaks, Stamford, Southampton, Windsor, Winchester,

Wimbourne, Wilmslow, Esher, Harpenden, Cirencester, Canford Cliffs, Beaconsfield, York, London, Manchester, Oxford, Norwich, Nottingham, Chelmsford, Cranbrook, Bristol, Brechin, Cambridge, Telford, Ipswich, Henley, Lincoln, Glasgow, Exeter, Farnham, Edinburgh, Guildford, Sunningdale

UK employees: 3,222

Total employees: 21,588

Charitable donations

UK cash (latest declared):	2009	£0
	2006	£59,500
	2005	£64,000

Corporate social responsibility

CSR committee: CSR is the responsibility of the Board of Directors. There is a CR working group which is responsible for co-ordinating activity to deliver agreed goals and monitoring progress and performance. Operational forums, reporting to the CR working group are established as necessary to develop and deliver initiatives at business level.

CSR policy: Taken from the 2010 annual report and accounts:

> Our definition of corporate responsibility remains unchanged – it is our commitment to the positive impact that our business, through our people, can make on the stakeholders and communities with whom we interface. Four critical areas of CR are people, clients, environment and community.

CSR report: Information contained within the annual report and accounts.

Applications

In writing to the correspondent. Local appeals should be addressed to the nearest Savills office, not the head office.

Other information

No figures could be found for the company's community contributions. The company's website stated the following in January 2013:

> Our offices and our people are actively involved in their communities, and in the UK, 61% of our offices actively support local community initiatives. At the national level, we have developed a series of community engagement programmes to ensure that Savills is firmly engaged with the communities we serve.
>
> In the UK, we support two major charities – Land Aid and Honeypot. LandAid is the charity of the UK's property sector. It helps homeless people. Honeypot provides respite holidays and support to young carers and at-risk children.
>
> Both charities are involved in areas – homelessness and vulnerable young people – that our UK staff care about.
>
> In line with our ethos of recruiting and retaining the best people, we've made community engagement an integral part of our graduate training programme. As well as delivering social benefits, we believe greater community engagement increases employee commitment and provides real-life development opportunities.

Schroders plc

Financial services

Correspondent: Giles Neville, Charity Co-ordinator, 31 Gresham Street, London EC2V 7QA (tel: 020 7658 6000/ 020 7658 6676; fax: 020 7658 6965; email: giles.neville@schroders.com; website: www.schroders.com)

Directors: Michael Miles, Chair; Michael Dobson, Chief Executive; Alan Brown; Philip Mallinckrodt; Kevin Parry; Massimo Tosato; Ashley Almanza; Andrew Beeson; Luc Bertrand; Robin Buchanan; Lord Howard of Penrith; Merlyn Lowther; Bruno Schroder (women: 1; men: 12)

Year end	31/12/2011
Turnover	£1,502,000,000
Pre-tax profit	£410,000,000

Nature of business: Schroders plc is the holding company of an international asset management group. The group is organised into three principal operating divisions on a worldwide basis: Institutional, Retail/Unit Trusts and Private Banking.

Company registration number: 637264

Charitable donations

UK cash (latest declared):	2011	£1,200,000
	2009	£600,000
	2008	£1,100,000
	2007	£1,252,090
	2006	£616,000
Total UK:	2011	£1,200,000
Total worldwide:	2011	£1,200,000
Cash worldwide:	2011	£1,200,000

Corporate giving

In 2011, the company made charitable donations of £1.2 million (2009: £600,000), including discretionary, one-off donations totalling £300,000, to charities involved with social welfare in the UK. Its charitable giving is focused on employee choice, with the group matching employee donations and sponsorship.

Previous beneficiaries have included: Childs Dream; Farleigh Hospice; Muscular Dystrophy Campaign; Western Parishes Youth Community Centre Trust; and, Whizz- Kidz.

Employee-led support

Employees are encouraged to volunteer, with financial rewards being given to the charity they are involved with. Every employee has been given the opportunity to take up to 15 hours paid leave per year to provide volunteer services to the community. In 2011, staff took part in voluntary schemes across the globe, including Down Syndrome Education International; Doctors With Africa; and The Island Foundation.

Schroders is a significant corporate supporter of the Hackney Schools Mentoring Programme, with its staff continuing to help mentor 14 and 15 year old students in the London borough.

Matched funding: The company matches employee fundraising and employee giving (subject to set maximum amounts).

Payroll giving: The 'Community' section of the company's website states:

> Payroll-giving schemes are operated in a number of our offices. In the UK, 25 per cent of employees opted to give in this way, and charitable 'matching' donations by the firm of £250,000 (2010: £220,000) were made. We again received the Payroll Giving Quality Mark Gold Award from the Charities Aid Foundation.

Corporate social responsibility

CSR committee: This Committee oversees employee, environmental and community involvement issues and is responsible for the development of policies on corporate responsibility and their implementation throughout the Group.

CSR policy: This information was obtained from the company's annual report: 'Corporate responsibility is important to Schroders and we have policies and schemes in place to ensure that the group acts in a socially responsible way in its day-to-day operations.'

CSR report: A CSR report was available from the company's website.

Exclusions

No support for advertising in charity brochures, animal welfare, appeals from individuals, the arts, children/youth, elderly people, environment, fundraising events, heritage, medical research, political appeals, religious appeals, science/technology, sickness/disability, social welfare, or sport.

Applications for 'Charity of the Year' status are not considered.

Applications

In writing to the correspondent.

Information available: The company can provide policy guidelines to those seeking support. It also produces an annual corporate responsibility report.

Scott Bader Company Ltd

Chemicals and plastics

Correspondent: Sue Carter, Commonwealth Secretary, Wollaston Hall, Wollaston, Wellingborough, Northamptonshire NN29 7RL (tel: 01933 663100/01933 663676; fax: 01933 666608; email: sue.carter@scottbader.com; website: www.scottbader.com)

Directors: Richard Stillwell, Chair; Agne Bengtsson; Philip Bruce; Dean Bugg; Andrew Forrester; Peter Hartill; Liyaqatali Khan; Calvin O'Connor; Malcolm Forsyth (women: 0; men: 9)

Year end	31/12/2011
Turnover	£200,830,000
Pre-tax profit	£2,090,000

Nature of business: The company manufactures and distributes synthetic resins and chemical intermediates.

Company registration number: 189141

Main locations: Fareham, Brierley Hill, Leeds, Stockport, Plymouth, Wollaston

UK employees: 276

Total employees: 612

Charitable donations

UK cash (latest declared):	2011	£203,500
	2009	£30,600
	2008	£134,000
	2007	£123,000
	2006	£125,000
Total UK:	2011	£203,500
Total worldwide:	2011	£203,500
Cash worldwide:	2011	£203,500

Corporate social responsibility

CSR committee: Scott Bader Commonwealth Ltd is a registered charity administered and managed by trustees. This charity is responsible for the company's charitable contribution in the UK and worldwide.

CSR policy: Taken from the company's website:

> Scott Bader has a clear set of ethical, social, charitable and environmental values and guiding principles handed down by the founder, Ernest Bader. In 1951 he gave the company to the workforce who became Commonwealth members, to own collectively for the common good. All employees can become Commonwealth members, by committing to and upholding our ethics. Scott Bader has been actively practising corporate social responsibility for over 40 years.
>
> Ernest Bader's aim was to create a company whose governance and well-being is entrusted to those who work in it, with democratic involvement, thereby incorporating Scott Bader into the local and wider community. This allows the business to better understand its effects and influences on its stakeholders and the world.

CSR report: Report produced of projects supported by the company's charity. Charity accounts available from the Charity Commission.

Exclusions

There is no support available for individuals in need, animal welfare, travel and adventure schemes, construction, renovation or maintenance of buildings, advertising, medical research or equipment, arts projects or sports. Political, religious or general appeals or sponsorship proposals will not be considered.

Applications

There is a process for applications and the dates of the various stages can be found on the company's website. To find out more about the company's assessment criteria or to download an application form, visit the website: www.scottbader.com/global-corporate-charities.aspx

Applications accepted by email: commonwealth_office@scottbader.com or by post.

Other information

Scott Bader has been a Common Trusteeship Company for 60 years, with no external shareholders. Its shares are held by Scott Bader Commonwealth Ltd, (SBCL), a company limited by guarantee and a registered charity. The company was given into common ownership by its founder Ernest Bader in 1951 and is now a leading member of the common ownership movement. Its large philanthropic expenditure reflects the ethos of the company. A key element of the company is the constitutional requirement regarding the use of profit. A minimum of 60% has to be retained within the business for investment and development. Of the remaining 40% a maximum of 20% can be paid as bonus to staff, with an equal or greater amount given to charity.

Global Charity Fund

The Scott Bader Global Charity Fund aims to annually provide grants to charitable organisations around the world whose purposes support our charitable objects e.g. to help young or disadvantaged people, especially anyone suffering deprivation and discrimination, such as poor, homeless and vulnerable women and children, minority communities, particularly where people are affected by: poverty, a lack of education, malnutrition and disease. Only UK registered charities are supported. The Global Charity Fund is divided into two categories.

Local Funds

Funds are made available to all the companies in the Scott Bader Group (proportionate to the number of people employed at each location) for them to submit applications to the charity trustees for charities they wish to support. Usually this will be to support the work of charities situated near to or associated with each company i.e. in Northamptonshire in the UK, Co. Meath in Eire, Amiens in France, Falkenberg in Sweden, Barcelona in Spain, Liberec in the Czech Republic, Zagreb in Croatia, Dubai, Cape Town in South Africa, Ohio in the USA or Shanghai in China.

Central Fund

The central fund annually supports two large, community based, environmental or educational projects to the value of £25,000 each. These can be located anywhere in the world and should benefit young or disadvantaged people or a particular community project.

A small fund of £5,000 has been set up to provide small grants of £500–£2,000 to support international projects that do not fit the criteria of the local or central fund described above.

In 2011 donations from Scott Bader Company Ltd., to Scott Bader Commonwealth Ltd., were £203,500.

The company supports projects which respond to the needs of those who are most underprivileged. They aim to help people to help themselves based on community based projects. National and local charities are supported, with preference being given to those within a 25-mile radius of Scott Bader locations in the UK.

The criteria for funding are very specific and detailed and applicants are advised to refer to the details set out on the company's website.

Volunteering among staff is encouraged and Scott Bader matches employees' fundraising to a maximum amount.

Sponsorship is not undertaken.

ScottishPower plc

Electricity

Correspondent: Kathryn Bennett, Community Liaison Manager (CSR), 1 Atlantic Key, Glasgow C2 8ST (tel: 01412 488200; email: enquires@energypeopletrust.co.uk; website: www.scottishpower.com)

Directors: José Ignacio Sánchez Galán, Chair; Amparo Moraleda; Fernando Becker Zuazua; José Luis San Pedro Gerenabarrena; José Miguel Alcolea Cantos; José Sainz Armada; Juan Carlos Rebollo; Lord Macdonald of Tradeston; Lord Kerr of Kinlochard; Tom Farmer (women: 0; men: 10)

Year end	31/12/2011
Turnover	£299,600,000
Pre-tax profit	£155,800,000

Nature of business: In 1995 Manweb and ScottishPower merged, and combined they provide 2.5 million homes in the UK with power.

ScottishPower has been part of the Iberdrola Group since April 2007, and is one of the UK's largest energy companies employing more than eight thousand people across Generation; Transmission; Distribution and Retail sectors.

Company registration number: 2366937

Main locations: Warrington, Glasgow, Rhostylien

Total employees: 7,530

Membership: BITC, LBG

Charitable donations

UK cash (latest declared):	2011	£1,300,000
	2006	£2,610,000
	2002	£3,500,000
Total UK:	2011	£2,500,000
Total worldwide:	2011	£2,500,000
Cash worldwide:	2011	£1,300,000

Community involvement

The company's community investment strategy reflects its culture and the main areas of investment are:

- Education and training (including public safety)
- Environment
- Social welfare
- Arts, culture and other

The majority of community investment programmes are directed at improving the lives and prospects of young people and tackling fuel poverty.

Education and Training

A wide-ranging education and training programme is supported, with the principal aim of encouraging young people to acquire the skills necessary for a career in the power sector.

Public safety initiatives include:

Crucial Crew

Crucial Crew is a national programme where children take part in a range of fast-paced scenarios designed to raise awareness of the dangers of electricity and other common hazards and give children the knowledge they need to prevent accidents. In 2011, approximately 11,745 children in the final stages of primary school education attended eight Crucial Crew events, at which staff from the company's Networks business presented the potential dangers of electricity. Over the course of the year, this equated to 106 employee work days.

Educational events

As well as schools, Energy Networks provides electrical safety information and educational events to the public, including high-risk industrial sectors, such as construction and agriculture. In 2011 the company supported an Agricultural Safety and Health Awareness Day in Ayrshire promoting essential safety messages about working in the vicinity of overhead power lines to around 100 delegates.

Three seminars for Welsh Water on working safely near overhead powerlines and underground cables were conducted. These were attended by approximately 70 design and construction staff.

A safety presentation was given for 30 volunteers from Cheshire Search and Rescue, providing vital information on how to safely approach a rescue at an incident involving equipment on the electricity network.

Environment

Green Energy Trust (Scottish Charity No. SC030104)

ScottishPower established the Green Energy Trust as an independent charity, in 1998. It supports the development of new renewable sources in the UK, helping to reduce our reliance on fossil fuels and combat climate change.

In 2011 the Green Energy Trust committed funding of £105,445 to nine small-scale renewable energy projects at community level that may not otherwise have been developed. These projects, including biomass, solar and hydro schemes, save CO2 emissions, reduce fuel bills and help to educate the public about renewable energy.

Projects funded in 2011 included a water powered windmill at a Royal Society for the Protection of Birds centre, a biomass project at Glasgow School of Art and a solar thermal scheme at an historic Roman site on the Isle of Wight. The trust also awarded a grant of £11,280 to Glasgow Building Preservation Trust to help fund a wood pellet stove boiler at Pollokshaws West Station, which is set to become home to a community cycle repair and resource centre in 2012, run by South West Community Cycles.

To date the Green Energy Trust has funded 137 projects with a total amount of £1,469,800.

For further information, visit the trust's website: www.scottishpowergreentrust.co.uk

ScottishPower continued to invest in environmental projects with community benefits during 2011.

Countryside Rangers

The company continued its co-sponsorship of five countryside rangers at its sites, in association with local authorities and the Scottish Wildlife Trust.

Social welfare

ScottishPower supported a wide range of humanitarian causes and projects in 2011, ranging from major investments, such as funding for the ScottishPower Energy People Trust (see community contributions section), an independently administered charity that provides grants to not-for-profit groups that work at grass roots level to alleviate fuel poverty, to many small donations to local community charities that operate close to the company's major sites.

Other community investments include Longannet Power Station's ongoing sponsorship of a community police vehicle, which operates in the local community, and the Your Champions and Community Heroes award schemes that recognise examples of outstanding citizenship in North-west England and North Wales.

Arts and culture

ScottishPower is a long-term supporter of the Edinburgh International Book Festival, which in 2011 was attended by 800 authors and 190,000 visitors.

In parallel with the festival, the company ran the ScottishPower Story Swap Shop, a competition that encourages primary schoolchildren to read, pass on their books to others and raise money for the Aberlour Children's Trust.

For further information on the company's considerable community involvement, visit its website.

Corporate giving

During 2011, ScottishPower's businesses contributed £3.3 million in community support activity of which £2.6 million was contributed to registered charitable organisations.

The £3.3 million total incorporated £1.3 million categorised as charitable gifts, £1.2 million categorised as community investment and £0.8 million categorised as commercial initiatives, given in cash, through staff time and in kind donations.

Much of ScottishPower's community contribution is delivered through its grantmaking charity:

Scottish Power Energy People Trust (Scottish Charity No. SC0036980)

In 2010 the trust awarded almost £1.65 million in 77 grants of between £300 and £68,000 to charitable organisations. Since the trust was established in November 2005, it has awarded over £9 million to 185 projects, which have helped more than 1.5 million people in around 1.2 million households throughout Britain.

The trust is administered by, but makes decisions independently of, ScottishPower and is part the ScottishPower Fuel Poverty Programme, which also includes measures such as energy efficiency and a social tariff.

The trust was established in November 2005 to provide much-needed funding to not-for-profit organisations for projects which combat fuel poverty through investment in four categories: crisis funding, income maximisation, energy efficiency and research. In many cases funding is awarded to projects spanning two or three of these categories.

Examples of projects funded by the trust are:

North Ayrshire Women's Aid which received a grant for its Staywarm project which seeks to empower women through increased awareness of energy efficiency and income maximisation, thereby helping to ensure affordable warmth for women and their families in refuge and when they are re-housed. Assistance will include information, advocacy, practical and crisis support.

West Lothian Credit Union Forum which received funding for its Energy Advice Programme to help lift young people and families with young children out of fuel poverty.

Beneficiary organisations also included: Renewable Energy Foundation (£79,000); Festival Housing (£61,000); Age Concern Blackpool and District (£47,500); Localise West Midlands (£24,000); and Starter Packs Dundee (£15,000).

Further information about ScottishPower's range of community investment, including the annual reports of the trust, is available on its website.

Employee-led support

Power stations support hundreds of local charities, good causes and community events each year. In addition staff raise many thousands of pounds for charities supporting community causes and national charities such as Help for Heroes and Children in Need. The company matches fundraising by employees and employee giving.

Matched funding

Staff fundraising efforts are matched up to a maximum of £300. In 2010, the company paid out just under £30,000 under this scheme.

Charity partner: Cancer Research UK.

Payroll giving: The company operates the Give As You Earn scheme in the UK.

Commercially-led support

Sponsorship: The Arts

ScottishPower has a long tradition of supporting the arts within and for local communities. Examples are: **Celtic Connections** – a three-year sponsorship of Scotland's international traditional music festival which now attracts renowned artists from all over the world; **ScottishPower Piper Band** – the company's award winning pipe band continues to be among the top ten in the world. Over the years the band has won European and British titles, and twice achieved second place in the World Championship; **Transform** allows schools and creative communities to transform their approaches to learning. By bringing together cutting edge theatre professionals, communities and groups of local primary schools, the partnerships produce a high impact theatre event that uses the local environment as a backdrop to tell compelling stories. Schools in Ayrshire, Fife and East Lothian have benefited to date. ScottishPower has sponsored the venue for these events, **National Theatre of Scotland.**

The company also undertakes good cause sponsorship.

Corporate social responsibility

CSR committee: ScottishPower's Corporate Social Responsibility (CSR) team is responsible for the production of CSR TV and the ScottishPower Sustainability Summary, and maintains strong links with communities in which the company operates.

For useful contact information visit: www.scottishpowercsrannualreview.com/contact/

CSR policy: Statement taken from the company's website:

> Our principal aim in our relationships with communities is to be a good neighbour to those around us by conducting our business responsibly – and making a positive contribution to society and community life.

CSR report: CSR Annual Review and Annual Sustainability Review are both published online.

Exclusions

No support is given to appeals from individuals, national charities (unless the fund is used solely for a local project), expeditions, political or military organisations, circular appeals, advertising in charity brochures, animal welfare charities, religious appeals, local appeals not in areas of company presence or overseas projects.

Sponsorship for sporting events and advertisements in publications, etc., will normally only be considered commercially, in terms of potential advertising benefits.

Applications

For applications to either ScottishPower, for awards from the company, or the ScottishPower Energy People Trust, apply in writing to the correspondent. For regional contacts, visit: www.scottishpowercsrannualreview.com/contact/.

SDL International plc

Distribution, manufacturing

Correspondent: Alastair Gordon, SDL Foundation, 64 Tastelnau, London SW13 9EX.

Company address: Globe House, Clivemont Road, Maidenhead, Berkshire SL6 7DY (tel: 01628 410100; fax: 01628 410150; email: sdlfoundation@sdl.com; website: www.sdl.com)

Directors: J. Hunter, Chief Executive Officer; M. Lancaster, Chair; M. Gradden; J. Matthews; C. Batterham; J. Campbell; J. Thompson; D. Clayton; M. Knight, Chief Financial Officer (women: 2; men: 7)

Year end	31/12/2011
Turnover	£229,001,000
Pre-tax profit	£33,761,000

Nature of business: Provision of technology and services to allow companies to trade effectively in global markets.

Company registration number: 3021207

Total employees: 2,278

Charitable donations

UK cash (latest declared):	2011	£262,000
	2009	£250,000
Total UK:	2011	£262,000
Total worldwide:	2011	£262,000
Cash worldwide:	2011	£262,000

Corporate social responsibility

CSR committee: No information regarding a CSR committee.

CSR policy: Information taken from the 2011 annual report:

> Our corporate social responsibility framework continues to target three primary areas of employment and employee engagement, the environment and community involvement. Community activities are wide ranging and, through our registered charity, the SDL Foundation, include support for educational projects, infrastructure regeneration and charitable giving.

CSR report: CSR information contained within the annual report.

Exclusions

Taken from the company's website:

> The SDL Foundation has a strict independency policy and will not support causes where Trustees or SDL employees will receive direct benefit from donations of the SDL Foundation. The SDL Foundation will not support activities which could in anyway be seen as Political or discriminatory. Neither will they support causes which are recognized as being large or well-known national or international charities or international appeals. Only causes supported and sponsored by SDL employees will be considered by the SDL Foundation.

Applications

SDL Employees create regional groups in SDL's worldwide offices to provide support for the SDL Foundation. Regional Foundation groups provide: regular forum for brainstorming; focus and momentum; supply of applications. All projects supported by the SDL Foundation have been presented by an SDL Employee sponsor who is actively involved in the charitable cause and who is responsible, along with an SDL Executive sponsor, for the success of the initiative.

The company will not support causes which are recognized as being large or well-known national or international charities or international appeals. **Only causes supported and sponsored by SDL employees will be considered by the SDL Foundation.**

Other information

Charitable donations amounting to £2,000 were made to external charities and £260,000 was donated to **The SDL Foundation**, a UK charity (Charity Commission no. 1127138), managed by an independent trustee committee, and chaired by ex SDL CFO, Alastair Gordon. To show its commitment to the SDL Foundation, the SDL Board has resolved to donate a percentage of the group's pre-tax profits to the SDL Foundation each year.

The SDL Foundation is committed to supporting sustainable development for communities across the globe. 'We achieve this by providing financial grants for programs which are aligned with our primary focus of: building physical and economic infrastructures; assisting community advancements; and promoting self-sufficiency.'

SEGRO plc

Property

Correspondent: Manager External Affairs, 234 Bath Road, Slough, Berkshire SL1 4EE (tel: 01753 537171; fax: 01753 820585; website: www.segro.com)

Directors: Nigel Rich, Chair; David Sleith, Chief Executive Officer; Justin Read, Finance Officer; Andrew Palmer; Chris Peacock; Thom Wernink; Doug Webb; Mark Robertshaw (women: 0; men: 8)

Year end	31/12/2011
Turnover	£400,100,000
Pre-tax profit	(£53,600,000)

Nature of business: Industrial and commercial property development, construction and investment, supply of utility services and the provision of services associated with such activities.

Company registration number: 167591

Main locations: Birmingham, Heathrow, Portsmouth, Slough

Total employees: 276

Membership: Arts & Business, BITC

Charitable donations

UK cash (latest declared):	2009	£200,000
	2007	£363,000
	2006	£617,000
	2005	£628,000
Total worldwide:	2011	£1,700,000

Corporate social responsibility

CSR committee: No specific committee details found.

CSR policy: Taken from the company's website: 'Objective: To make a positive contribution to communities where SEGRO has a presence.'

CSR report: An annual sustainability report is published within the annual report and accounts.

Exclusions

No grants for non-charities, circular appeals, local appeals not in areas of company presence, appeals from individuals, or overseas projects.

Applications

Decisions are made by a committee which meets quarterly.

Other information

In 2011 the company states it gave over £1.7 million in good causes, through money, time and business space. The company invested in local communities around four of its largest business locations in the UK; Park Royal, Slough, Heathrow and Enfield. We do not have figures for the company's cash donations and it would appear that the major part of the contribution was given in kind, i.e. business space.

Statement taken from the company's 2011 annual report and accounts:

> We are in the process of implementing and maintaining structured community engagement plans. In 2011 we began programmes in Hounslow, Ealing and Hillingdon in the UK. During 2012, a structured approach to community engagement for Continental Europe will be established with our operations teams in Paris and Düsseldorf.
>
> During 2011 we actively increased our engagement in the communities in which we operate, supporting 80 charities and community groups compared with 52 in 2010. We continue to offer a wide variety of support to local and national organisations to help ensure their needs are met, including the provision of free commercial space, business advice and guidance and donating much needed cash and equipment. As well as maintaining and developing links with many charities, such as Berkshire East and South Bucks Women's Aid, new and exciting partnerships have been formed. In October 2010, we teamed up with Alexander Devine Children's Hospice Trust to work towards building Berkshire's very own children's hospice for local families by helping the trust to establish new fundraising headquarters on the Slough Trading Estate.
>
> SEGRO made a number of cash donations in 2011. We continued our popular community bursary scheme in Heywood, through which seven charities received funding, and we made new donations to community centres in Slough, Hounslow and Ealing to support the development of young people from deprived backgrounds. SEGRO will continue to work with these community centres throughout 2012. For the fourth consecutive year, we supported The Outward Bound Trust, which provides residential courses to help young people from challenging backgrounds to develop new skills and confidence.

In 2011, employees spent 1,052 hours on fundraising, and managing community initiatives with a total value of £38,000. SEGRO actively supports volunteering by giving employees one work day each year to volunteer in the local community or to work on behalf of a charity.

Other areas of involvement included a SEGRO team tree planting at Haymill Valley Nature Reserve in Berkshire, through the Proud to be Slough group, the SEGRO Young Artists Programme for schools in the South East of England, Scout Groups and school Governorships.

> ***Charity of the Year:***
> Every other year, SEGRO runs a Charity of the Year programme which sees employees actively involved in fundraising for its chosen charity partner, with the company matching the money raised, to a maximum of £50,000. Since 2005, over £410,000 has been donated to four charities; Macmillan Cancer Relief, Barnardo's, Dogs for the disabled and ActionAid.
>
> For the programme, employees select the charity partner though two ballots – the first to decide the charity sector, the second to select a charity within that sector.

Senior plc

Aerospace

Correspondent: The Corporate Social Responsibility Committee, 59–61 High Street, Rickmansworth, Hertfordshire WD3 1RH (tel: 01923 775547; fax: 01923 775583; email: companysecretary@seniorplc.com; website: www.seniorplc.com)

Directors: Charles Berry, Chair; David Best; Andy Hamment; Mark E. Vernon; Ian Much; Mark Rollins, Group Chief Executive; Simon Nicholls, Group Finance Director (women: 0; men: 7)

Year end	31/12/2011
Turnover	£640,700,000
Pre-tax profit	£72,700,000

Nature of business: Senior is an international manufacturing group with operations in 11 countries. Senior designs, manufactures and markets high technology components and systems for the principal original equipment producers in the worldwide aerospace, defence, land vehicle and energy markets.

Company registration number: 282772

UK employees: 1,070

Total employees: 5,374

Charitable donations

UK cash (latest declared):	2011	£113,000
	2009	£43,000
	2008	£35,000
Total UK:	2011	£113,000
Total worldwide:	2011	£113,000
Cash worldwide:	2011	£113,000

Corporate social responsibility

CSR committee: Information taken from the 2011 CSR report:

> To lead and oversee the Group's safety and environmental objectives, Senior operates a Health, Safety and Environment Committee which meets quarterly. The Committee is chaired by the Group Chief Executive, who leads the Board's efforts in improving the Group's ethical, social, health, safety and environmental performance and is also responsible for external stakeholder issues. The chief executives of the Group's three divisions also sit on the Committee.

CSR policy: Taken from the company's CSR report 2011:

> The group's approach to corporate social responsibility is focused broadly on three key areas of activity: developing employees by creating a working environment that attracts and retains the best people; operating with integrity by acting in an ethical and responsible manner; and ensuring safe working conditions and reducing the group's environmental footprint by continuously improving the management of health, safety and the environment.
>
> *Contributing to communities*
>
> The group's operations are encouraged to involve themselves in their local communities and to support local charities. These relationships are normally managed at a local level, where the employees typically select non-profit-making organisations and charitable interests active within their community. These are often long-standing relationships and involve employees volunteering their time, making financial donations and raising funds to help those in need of support within their local communities.

CSR report: Contained within the annual report and accounts.

Applications

In writing to the correspondent.

Other information

During the year, the group made charitable donations amounting to £113,000 (2010: £138,000), principally to local charities serving the communities in which it operates – Bury, Congleton, Crumlin, Macclesfield and Hertfordshire.

Serco Group plc

Business services

Correspondent: Joanne Roberts, Company Secretary, Serco House, 16 Bartley Wood Business Park, Bartley Way, Hook, Hampshire RG27 9UY (tel: 01256 745900; fax: 01256 744111; website: www.serco.com)

Directors: Alastair Lyons, Chair; Christopher Rajendran Hyman, Chief Executive; Andrew Mark Jenner, Finance Director; Angie Risley; David Richardson; Leonard V. Broese van Groenou; Ralph D. Crosby (women: 1; men: 6)

Year end	31/12/2011
Turnover	£4,646,400,000
Pre-tax profit	£283,300,000

Nature of business: The provision of a range of facilities management and systems engineering services.

Company registration number: 2048608

Main locations: London, Oldbury, Sunbury-on-Thames, Southampton, Wolverhampton, Hook, Glasgow, Lincoln, Leicester

Total employees: 76,670

Membership: BITC

Charitable donations

UK cash (latest declared):	2009	£643,000
	2007	£556,000
	2005	£586,324
Total worldwide:	2011	£1,826,000
Cash worldwide:	2011	£717,000

Corporate social responsibility

CSR committee: Overseen by the Corporate Assurance Group, which reports directly to the Group Board and takes an integrated view of all aspects of corporate governance, risk management, health and safety, and social responsibility.

CSR policy: CSR information taken from the company's website:

> Social responsibility (community engagement) has always been important to us. It underpins our culture and values, which are unique to Serco and help distinguish us in our markets. It is not an add-on: we've embedded it in the way we do business as part of our Serco Management System, which shapes the way we run our business.

CSR report: Annual CSR report published.

Applications

In writing to the correspondent.

Other information

The following information was taken from the company's 2011 annual report:

> The group continues to encourage all staff to participate in their local communities and has a process to assess both the value and type of investment on a worldwide basis. This measure is based upon the Business in The Community reporting format. The value of this investment in 2011 at £2.5 million (2010: £2.3 million) represents 1.06% of the group's pre-tax profit.

The CSR report for 2011 states: 'Our work serves many diverse communities – of which we are also part. We encourage local community engagement to develop strong relationships, building trust and understanding.' Support is by way of donations, assets, gifts in kind and employee time and is broken down as follows: cash donations (£717,000); gifts in kind (£448,000); and 'expertise and volunteering' (£661,000). Unfortunately there is no breakdown of the amounts spent solely in the UK and so we have taken these as the worldwide figures. Management costs of £706,000 are excluded from the totals in line with our policy. The report also states:

> In the UK, the government's drive to reduce youth unemployment has seen the launch of a new work experience scheme aimed at 18–24 year olds. The scheme targets the creation of 100,000 work experience placements of two to eight weeks in length over the next two years. Serco has committed to offering 1,000 placements and 500 apprenticeships.
>
> Serco is also taking part in an industry-led initiative, supported by the UK government, to develop an online careers platform for young people. This will provide a single starting point for young people to explore their work ambitions and to plan how to achieve them. The website will be launched in 2012.

The company prefers to support local appeals relevant to the business. Support is given with a preference for children and youth, education, and sport. Following a review in 2003 of its charitable giving policy, Serco decided to place more of an emphasis on supporting local charities and communities.

On 12 December 2012, Serco announced the proposed establishment of **The Serco Foundation**. The press release states that:

> The foundation will work with charities and NGOs, within the regions where Serco operates, to capitalise on the passion of its people to do good and to make donations that will significantly benefit the campaigns of the charities it chooses to work with. It will also seek to work with large scale foundations and NGOs to help them consider how to

> improve the delivery outcomes they seek to achieve.
>
> The foundation will be independent of Serco and will operate on a not-for-profit basis. To ensure that the foundation will have a long-term future it will be established with a one-off endowment of £5 million from Serco. In addition Serco is planning to make small regular donations to the Foundation comprising cash donations and secondments.

The foundation was registered on 3 January 2013 with the Charity Commission no. 1150338; contact: John Hickey, Palm Court, 4 Heron Square, Richmond, Surrey TW9 1EW; tel: 01256 745900.

Severn Trent plc

Water

Correspondent: Community Affairs Manager, 2297 Coventry Road, Birmingham B26 3PU (tel: 01217 224000/01217 224000; fax: 01217 224800; email: corporateresponsibilty@stplc.com; website: www.severntrent.com)

Directors: Tony Ballance; Bernard Bulkin; Richard Davey; Martin Lamb; Michael McKeon; Sheila Noakes; Andrew Duff, Chair; Gordon Fryett; Tony Wray, Chief Executive Officer; Andy Smith; Martin Kane (women: 1; men: 10)

Year end	31/03/2012
Turnover	£1,770,600,000
Pre-tax profit	£156,700,000

Nature of business: The group's principal activities are the supply of water and sewerage services, waste management and the provision of environmental services.

Company registration number: 2366619

Main locations: Birmingham

Total employees: 8,051

Membership: LBG

Charitable donations

UK cash (latest declared):	2012	£3,607,000
	2010	£2,326,000
	2009	£2,352,000
	2008	£413,000
	2007	£278,000
Total UK:	2012	£3,607,000
Total worldwide:	2012	£3,607,000
Cash worldwide:	2012	£3,607,000

Community involvement

Severn Trent Trust Fund

Taken from the Trust Funds' 2011 annual report:

> The independent trustees have adopted a policy of giving grants to individuals and families to (a) help them overcome immediate crisis and (b) to encourage financial stability. The majority of grants provide help toward insurmountable water debt but, in addition, help is given with other priority urgent bills and household needs. The trust supports money advice and debt counselling work and has funded advice work in agencies spread throughout the region. All the donations received by the trust in the year were from Severn Trent Water plc. This is the thirteenth year of informing potential beneficiaries of help available in addition to providing grants where applicable.
>
> *Help for individuals*
>
> In pursuit of charitable objectives the trust was able to award grants toward water and other costs. It is the policy of the trustees that w here a grant is given to assist with outstanding debt, then wherever possible, it will be paid to the person or organisation owed. During the year the Trust received 10,219 (2010 – 13,884) applications and was able to provide grants to 4,921 (2010 – 7,487) individuals or families amounting to £3 million.
>
> *Debt counselling*
>
> In pursuit of charitable objectives, the trust was able to provide debt counselling. Recognising the value of long-term help and support to individuals of professional money advice services, the trustees adopted a policy of making grants available to organisations that provide free debt advice and debt counselling services. [Almost £370,000 has been given for this purpose during the year.]

The company is also committed to supporting WaterAid, the UK's only major charity dedicated to improving access to safe water, hygiene and sanitation in the world's poorest countries.

Corporate giving

Donations to charitable organisations during the year amounted to £107,000 (2010/11: £182,000). Donations are given to charities whose projects align closely with the company's aim to promote the responsible use of water resources and waste water services which provide the opportunity for longer term partnerships. Additionally, each year the company donates to The Severn Trent Trust Fund (Charity Commission no. 1108278), which distributes money to people who are finding it difficult to pay their bills. In 2011/12 the company donated £3.5 million.

Employee-led support

During 2011/12, the Severn Trent WaterAid committee helped to raise over £335,000 for WaterAid through various fundraising events and projects.

A matched funding scheme is in operation.

Corporate social responsibility

CSR committee: The committee provides guidance and direction to the group's Corporate Responsibility (CR) programme, reviews the group's key non-financial risks and opportunities and monitors progress. The terms of reference for the committee can be found on the company's website (www.severntrent.com) and are also available from the Company Secretary.

CSR policy: Information on CSR taken from the 2011/12 annual report and accounts:

> The structure for our CR policy and framework has been based around the four areas of Workplace, Marketplace, Environment and Community. This provides a common framework for both our businesses – regulated and non-regulated. We will continue to review the framework as we integrate corporate responsibility into our core business operations for both Severn Trent Water and Severn Trent Services.

CSR report: Information regarding CSR achievements is published on the company's website.

Exclusions

No support for advertising in charity brochures, appeals from individuals, local appeals not in areas of company presence, medical research, fundraising events, political or religious appeals, expeditions, study tours and cultural exchanges or third party organisations fundraising on behalf of national charities.

Applications

In writing to the correspondent. Your application to the company should include:

- A summary of the aims and objectives of your charity
- A summary of the project for which the donation is required
- An explanation of how the money will be spent
- A copy of your latest annual report and accounts

For more information on how to apply to the **Severn Trust Fund** website, visit www.sttf.org.uk.

Shaftesbury plc

Property

Correspondent: Corporate Responsibility Team, Community Engagement, Pegasus House, 37–43 Sackville Street, London W1S 3DL (tel: 020 7333 8118; fax: 020 7333 0660; email: shaftesbury@shaftesbury.co.uk; website: www.shaftesbury.co.uk)

Directors: Brian Bickell, Chief Executive; P. J. Manser, Chair; Simon J. Quayle; Thomas J. C. Welton; Christopher P. A. Ward; Jonathan S. Lane; W. Gordon McQueen; Jill C. Little; Oliver J. D. Marriott; Hilary S. Riva; John R. K. Emly (women: 2; men: 9)

Year end	30/09/2011
Turnover	£81,400,000
Pre-tax profit	£115,700,000

Nature of business: Property Investors. Shaftesbury owns a portfolio of over 450 properties in London's West End (Carnaby and Chinatown) and Covent Garden.

Company registration number: 1999238

UK employees: 19

Total employees: 19

Membership: LBG

Charitable donations

UK cash (latest declared):	2011	£48,000
	2009	£97,000
	2008	£108,000
Total UK:	2011	£356,000
Total worldwide:	2011	£356,000
Cash worldwide:	2011	£48,000

Corporate social responsibility

CSR committee: There is a CSR committee in place.

CSR policy: Information taken from the company's website:

> Throughout its activities, Shaftesbury is committed to sustainability and by the re-use and careful management of existing buildings, it supports government and local policies for sustainable development.
>
> The policy is reviewed on an annual basis by the board and forms the framework for updating objectives and targets during 2011/12 against which the Group will monitor and report publicly on its performance at the financial year-end. As a measure of the company's commitment the remuneration of all staff includes key performance indicators take from the corporate responsibility objectives and targets.

CSR report: Reporting on CSR published on the company's website.

Applications

In writing to the correspondent.

Other information

During the year, the group made charitable donations in cash amounting to £48,000 (2010: £46,000). The group measures its community investment in line with the London Benchmarking Group guidance. For the year ended 30 September 2011 this was assessed as £356,000. Voluntary contributions to public realm works are excluded from this figure.

The group has stated that it will continue to support local community groups by providing financial help and advice to local community groups and charities operating within Carnaby, Covent Garden and Chinatown including:

- The London branch of the Samaritans (located in Carnaby)
- The Hungerford Drugs Rehabilitation Project
- The Soho Family Centre
- The Soho Green Charity
- The Chinatown Stakeholders Group
- The Seven Dials Trust

Community Engagement

In addition to funding particular projects, Shaftesbury also recognises the importance of engagement with the local community through the provision of advice and resources. To this end Shaftesbury will continue to:

- Invite local groups and charities including representatives of local authorities to visit Shaftesbury to obtain a better understanding of the group's business and its corporate responsibility objectives
- Encourage Shaftesbury's employees to be involved in the work of these and other charities and identify any additional assistance that the group may be able to provide or procure

The 'Community Investment Initiatives' section of the company's website states:

> We also provide space on very flexible terms to enable charitable, community and educational events to take place during the year. We provide subsidised accommodation for a number of these organisations including the Association of British Orchestras, Make Justice Work, Stage One, National Campaign for the Arts, Yellow Earth Theatre Company, London Chinatown Association and Chinatown Arts Space.

Shanks Group plc

Waste management

Correspondent: Corporate Social Responsibility Team, Dunedin House, Auckland Park, Mount Farm, Milton Keynes, Buckinghamshire MK1 1BU (tel: 01908 650580; fax: 01908 650651; email: info@shanksplc.co.uk; website: www.shanksplc.co.uk)

Directors: Adrian Auer, Chair; Tom Drury, Group Chief Executive; Chris Surch, Group Finance Director; Eric van Amerongen; Stephen Riley; Jacques Petry; Peter Johnson (women: 0; men: 7)

Year end	31/03/2011
Turnover	£717,300,000
Pre-tax profit	£21,200,000

Nature of business: Waste Management.

Company registration number: SC077438

UK employees: 792

Total employees: 4,246

Membership: BITC

Charitable donations

UK cash (latest declared):	2011	£19,000
	2010	£552,000
Total UK:	2011	£19,000
Total worldwide:	2011	£19,000
Cash worldwide:	2011	£19,000

Corporate social responsibility

CSR committee: Taken from the 2010/11 annual report and accounts: 'To co-ordinate improvement, Shanks has established a dedicated Group Corporate Responsibility Committee comprising senior persons from across its operations. This Committee reports directly to the Group Executive Committee.'

CSR policy: Information taken from the company's website:

> Our CR policy is aimed at both providing a structure for and an umbrella under which future specific corporate responsibility systems and policies can be developed and implemented and to state formally the standards, all Shanks employees are required to abide by. The policy includes sections on:
>
> - Organisation, reporting, communication and objectives
> - Responsibility
>   - Principles and policy standards for all employees, including on the environment, people, labour practices and human rights, community involvement, customer and consumer issues, shareholder issues, supply chain issues and business ethics and fair operating practices
> - Feedback including whistle-blowing
> - Monitoring

CSR report: An annual Corporate Responsibility report is published.

Applications

In writing to the correspondent.

Other information

During the financial year donations made by the group for charitable purposes amounted to £19,000 (2010: £2,000). Included within this total the board are pleased to report their support for the UK youth charity, the Prince's Trust, with a funding commitment of £15,000 per annum for the next three years. The board will also look for opportunities to support similar charities in the Netherlands and Belgium.

In the UK, through the Landfill Communities Fund, the group has applied £546,000 (2010: £552,000) via not-for-profit organisations to undertake projects such as disused land restoration, public park maintenance and habitat conservation.

In addition, staff at individual group businesses have organised various fundraising events to support local and national charities.

Shell

Oil and gas/fuel

Correspondent: Sally Gold, Head of Social Investment, Shell Centre, York Road, Waterloo, London SE1 7NA (tel: 020 7934 1234/020 7934 3199; email: sally.gold@shell.com; website: www.shell.co.uk)

Directors: A. F. Hand; G. Cayley; G. R. van't Hoff, Chair; P. Milliken;

R. J. Henderson; S. A. Constant-Glemas; T. Baker

Year end	31/12/2011
Turnover	£11,811,000,000
Pre-tax profit	£405,000,000

Nature of business: Shell is a global group of energy and petrochemicals companies. Most people know Shell for its retail stations, and its exploration and production of oil and natural gas. However, its activities also include: marketing, transporting and trading oil and gas; generating electricity (including wind power); providing oil products for industrial uses; producing petrochemicals used for plastics, coatings and detergents; and developing technology for hydrogen vehicles.

Company registration number: 140141

Main locations: Aberdeen, Fife, Ellesmere Port, London, Lowestoft, Stanlow (Merseyside), Wythenshawe

Total employees: 90,000

Membership: BITC, LBG

Charitable donations

UK cash (latest declared):	2011	£6,828,800
	2009	£15,525,000
	2007	£13,000,000
	2005	£7,730,000
Total UK:	2011	£6,828,800
Total worldwide:	2011	£77,600,000

Community involvement

The following information is taken from Shell's 2011 Sustainability Report:

> We invest in community programmes in which our expertise can provide a positive, lasting impact. We focus our social investments on projects linked to road safety, local enterprise development, and securing safe and reliable access to energy for the communities around us. For example, we work hard to reduce road incidents through road safety awareness programmes. Programmes such as *Shell LiveWIRE* encourage the development of local enterprises by offering business advice to young entrepreneurs.
>
> Through our support for the *Global Alliance for Clean Cookstoves* – a coalition of public and private organisations including the independent charity Shell Foundation – we help provide access to a cleaner and safer way of cooking to communities in developing countries.
>
> Shell's community contributions in the UK are channelled in two ways.
>
> Firstly, Shell provides support through its regional offices by way of small grants, volunteering and gifts-in kind, for causes in the communities that neighbour its places of operation. An example of activities supported at this level include *The Connection at St Martin's*, (a place of safety and opportunity for people who are homeless or at risk of homelessness). Support is also given to local projects at engineering training colleges, arts events, schools (mentoring and literacy schemes) and business mentoring amongst others.
>
> Secondly, Shell manages and delivers its own nationwide social investment programmes. These focus on entrepreneurship, skills and training, science education and innovation:
>
> - *Shell Education Service* – provides practical, interactive science workshops to over 60,000 children and teachers in 600 primary schools every year, in addition to after-school science clubs and family science days
> - *Shell LiveWIRE* – offers year-round help and advice to young entrepreneurs and runs a web service to provide them with information and support. It also offers 5 x £1,000 *Grand Ideas Awards* each month
> - *Shell Technology Enterprise Programme (STEP)* – matches over 600 penultimate year university students each summer with SMEs for a managed eight week project placement, for the benefit of both the student and the company
> - *Shell Springboard* – a national competition offering a no-strings payment of £40,000 to 8 companies that are commercially viable and have a product or service that reduces carbon emissions

Charity of the Year: UK plants and offices each select their own Charity of the Year.

The Shell Foundation (Charity Commission no. 1080999) is established and registered in the UK but operates overseas in South America, Africa, India, Mauritius, Netherlands, Pakistan, Turkey and the United States. The foundation's annual grant programmes are funded by distributions from its endowment fund. Shell Group donated US$6 million (£3.7 million) in 2011, approved some funding for 2012, and agreed 'in principle' to some funding in 2013 in the event that the endowment does not generate sufficient income for the charity to achieve its objectives and maintain impact.

Corporate giving

In the UK, Shell companies and subsidiaries (including Shell UK Ltd) donated $11 million in 2011 (£6.8 million) to charitable causes and sponsorships. This included donations to: The Big Bang, the UK's largest single science and engineering fair for young people; a climate science gallery at the Science Museum, London; the Shell Classic International, a series of international concerts held at the Royal Festival Hall, London; and the Shell Foundation, an independent charity established in 2000 that applies business thinking to global development challenges. We have been unable to determine a figure for UK community contributions which would include cash donations and gifts in kind. Neither have we been able to discover the amount of cash given worldwide but there is a figure of £77.6 million for total social investment.

The 2011 Sustainability Report, which covers all Shell group's companies and subsidiaries states: We aim to make our social investment projects beneficial to society in measurable ways and to be sustainable beyond Shell's involvement. In 2011, we spent around $125 million (£77.6 million) on voluntary social investments worldwide. We estimate that $45 million (£27.9 million) of our spend in 2011, was in countries that according to the UNDP Human Development Index 2010 have a gross domestic product of less than $15,000 (£9,300) a year per person.

The National Maritime Museum
Shell is continuing to support The National Maritime Museum, which comprises three sites: the Maritime Galleries, the Royal Observatory and the Queen's House. Together these constitute one museum working to illustrate for everyone the importance of the sea, ships, time and the stars and their relationship with people.

The Connection at St Martin-in-the-Fields
Shell supports The Connection at St Martin's, a place of safety and opportunity for people who are homeless or at risk of homelessness. They help people to recover self-esteem, overcome the barriers they face, and to re-skill and find work.

In kind support

Shell in the UK offers its facilities at key UK plants and offices to community organisations by prior arrangement. Contact your nearest local community relations team to discuss this.

Employee-led support

Shell employees and pensioners in the UK are very active in their local communities. Many employees get involved in local community activities through initiatives run by local Shell sites. For example, Shell's North West plant runs the Save 'n' Score scheme, linking safe workplace operations by employees to the size of a monthly grant to local good causes. While in London, Shell employees take part in volunteer reading and mentoring at local secondary schools.

Shell supports its employees and pensioners in their work with local organisations by making small grants available. Support is given to a wide range of causes, from local schools and technical colleges to environmental groups through to arts and sports organisations.

Employees offer their own time to support a range of good causes, from parent-teacher associations to mentoring schemes for the local homeless. Shell encourages them by supporting time out and offering small grants for projects they are involved in. A number of volunteering trips overseas are also possible, through the *Project Better World* scheme.

Shell matches employee fundraising up to a maximum of £500 per person per year.

Payroll giving: Shell operates the Give As You Earn scheme.

Commercially-led support

Shell Springboard: provides a financial boost to UK enterprises with innovative and commercially viable business ideas that contribute to the low-carbon economy. Shell Springboard aims to find the UK's next big idea in low carbon enterprise and innovation. Every year, Shell awards £330,000 to innovative and commercially viable business ideas that aim to reduce greenhouse gas emissions.

Scholarships and Prizes: Shell is engaged in a list of joint research work and has well-established relationships to support recruitment. For example, a small number of scholarships are offered in partnership with universities (Masters in Chemical or Mechanical Engineering, Geophysics or Geology). Shell also supports the Royal Anniversary Trust Prizes, recognising outstanding achievements by UK universities and colleges.

Globally, with a number of UK (and Dutch) universities, Shell also jointly funds scholarships for postgraduate students from developing countries. The aim of the Shell Centenary Scholarship Fund is for students to gain skills that will make a long-term contribution to the further development of their countries.

National Theatre: Shell is continuing to support its neighbour on London's South Bank by sponsoring The Shell Series: Classic Drama at the National Theatre.

Southbank Centre: The Shell Classic International concert series is part of Shell's major sponsorship of Southbank Centre's recent Transformation

The Mayor's Thames Festival: The festival is a celebration of London and its river and has become a key highlight in the city's cultural life. Shell's support has enabled hundreds of Year 8 students at a local secondary school to be involved in creative workshops.

Corporate social responsibility

CSR committee: The Corporate and Social Responsibility Committee (CSRC) of the Board of Royal Dutch Shell plc reviews policies and performance with respect to the Shell General Business Principles, Code of Conduct, HSSE & SP standards and issues of public concern on behalf of the Board. In addition to regular meetings, members of the CSRC visit facilities to become more familiar with our operations and the views of local people. They also meet with the External Review Committee of the Shell Sustainability Report to hear its views on our approach to sustainability.

CSR policy: Statement from the group's website: 'The energy we supply helps to support economic growth and development. At our operations we aim to address social concerns and work to benefit local communities, protecting our reputation as we do business.'

We were unable to determine the ratio of women to men on the board of directors.

CSR report: The Shell group publishes a comprehensive annual Sustainability report.

Exclusions

Shell is unable to support animal welfare appeals.

Applications

In writing to the community relations teams at Shell plants or offices for enquiries about local support.

Shell does not award grants outside neighbourhoods surrounding Shell plants and offices, but if you have an enquiry not appropriate for local sites, you should address it to: UK Social Investment, Shell Centre, York Road, London SE1 7NA.

Shepherd Building Group Ltd

Building/construction

Correspondent: The Company Secretary, Huntington House, Jockey Lane, York YO32 9XW (tel: 01904 650700; fax: 01904 650701; website: www.shepherd-group.com)

Directors: Alan Thomas Fletcher, Chair; Patrick Michael Shepherd; Martin Clark; Mark Perkins; Stephen Price; Alastair Mark Shepherd; Terence Smith (women: 0; men: 7)

Year end	30/06/2011
Turnover	£611,000,000
Pre-tax profit	£31,500,000

Nature of business: The company is a holding company with subsidiaries engaged in building and ancillary activities.

Company registration number: 653663

Main locations: York, Manchester, London, Northampton, Langley, Leeds, Darlington, Birmingham

Total employees: 3,187

Membership: BITC

Charitable donations

UK cash (latest declared):	2011	£87,000
	2009	£134,000
	2008	£157,000
	2007	£195,000
	2005	£98,000
Total UK:	2011	£87,000
Total worldwide:	2011	£87,000
Cash worldwide:	2011	£87,000

Corporate social responsibility

CSR committee: No details published.

CSR policy: Taken from the company's website:

> The Shepherd Group's Corporate Social Responsibility programme is a tangible and practical demonstration of our commitment to ensuring our operations are carried out with the highest regard for our people, customers, business partners, suppliers and the local communities where we undertake our work.

CSR report: The company publishes a community support newsletter.

Exclusions

No support for political appeals.

Applications

In writing to the correspondent.

Other information

During 2010/11, the company made charitable donations of £87,000 (2009/10: £120,000). Beneficiaries have included: Action Medical Research; Alzheimer's Society; Ancient Society of York Florists; Heworth Cricket Club; Hearing Dogs for the Deaf; Huntington Primary School; Macmillan Cancer Support; Norton District Lions Club Charity; Muscular Dystrophy – York.

The company's website states:

> Shepherd Group is a substantial family-owned business with its headquarters and a high proportion of its shareholders and staff based in and around York. The group benefits from being based in a healthy local environment for business, and is keen to put something back into the community.
>
> Shepherd has a flexible Community Support Policy that directs available resources to support people and organisations mainly where the business operates.
>
> Support is principally given in the York area, but initiatives that relate to the group's operations and staff elsewhere are also considered.
>
> The extent and high profile of the group's operations prompts a large number of requests for help, more than available resources allow. Support is, therefore, weighted towards initiatives that fulfil one or more criteria that have been a feature of the group's practice for many years successful requests tend to relate to the following:
>
> - Education and training
> - Healthcare
> - The arts
> - Sport

- Backing local business, inward investment and employment
- Employee involvement

Charitable and non-profit making organisations are given priority.

One of the latest charities to be supported by Shepherd is Lifelites. This seeks to provide and maintain computer technology in children's hospices, to enable children with life threatening conditions to learn and to have fun, and therefore to improve their often limited quality of life.

Shire Pharmaceuticals plc

Pharmaceuticals

Correspondent: Tatjana May, Company Secretary, Hampshire International Business Park, Chineham, Basingstoke, Hampshire RG24 8EP (tel: 01256 894000; fax: 01256 894708; email: shirecorporateresponsibility@shire.com; website: www.shire.com)

Directors: Matthew Emmens, Chair; Angus Russell, Chief Executive; Graham Hetherington, Chief Financial Officer; David Kappler; William Burns; Dr David Ginsburg; Susan Gilsby; Anne Minto; Patrick Langlois; Dr Jeffrey Leiden; David Stout (women: 2; men: 9)

Year end	31/12/2011
Turnover	£2,645,439,819
Pre-tax profit	(£54,790,152)

Nature of business: Speciality pharmaceutical company.

Company registration number: 2883758

Main locations: Basingstoke

Total employees: 5,000

Membership: BITC

Charitable donations

UK cash (latest declared):	2011	£496,400
	2009	£1,300,000
	2007	£243,000
	2006	£303,000
	2005	£154,933
Total UK:	2011	£496,400
Total worldwide:	2011	£3,102,500
Cash worldwide:	2011	£3,102,500

Community involvement

The following information was taken from the company's helpful and informative website:

> We care about who we are and the legacy we leave behind. Through our many community initiatives, we're making a difference by supporting programs ranging from the education of young scientists to helping vulnerable young people. Responsibility means having a long-term commitment to patients and to the conditions our medicines and devices treat, as well as the communities in which we live and work. The company will make donations (to include both cash and in kind giving) to local, national or international organisations that support Shire's community and/or relieving disease in its therapeutic focus area.
>
> Shire's corporate giving through sponsorships and donations are driven by local sites and businesses. These activities – and the employee volunteerism that often accompanies them – are an important aspect of Shire's role in the communities where our employees live and work. We care about neighborhoods we call home, and we take an active role in helping to support initiatives that benefit the community at large. We accomplish this in several ways, including involvement with chambers of commerce, local councils and interest groups that have a particular focus on health and life sciences.

Corporate giving

During the year 2011, donations to charities (including matching of funds raised by employees), not-for-profit organisations and entities supporting medical education amounting to $5 million (£3.1 million) were made of which $800,000 (£496,400) were made in the UK. Beneficiaries included: MPS Society, Amersham (£50,000); European Gaucher Alliance (£21,400); Action on Addiction, Salisbury (£15,000); Ensham Charity, Andover (£10,000); and St Bartholomew's Hospital, London (£1,000). Unfortunately, we could find no total figure for in kind contributions.

The company's website provides detailed information on funding given: 'In keeping with our commitment to ensuring responsible business practices, Shire believes transparency in our funding decisions is vital to building and maintaining trust with our stakeholders.' To learn more about the funding provided by Shire to charities, patients' groups, and US-based independent medical education organisations, visit: www.shire.com/shireplc/en/resp/communities/groups.

In kind support

Since 2001, Shire has been working with AmeriCares to donate specialty medicines that have supported much needed treatment for patients in 48 countries. In 2012, AmeriCares and Shire expanded their partnership to provide needed charitable access to rare disease patients suffering from Fabry disease, Gaucher disease and Hunter syndrome (MPS II).

Annual nominated charity – Shire does not send seasonal greetings cards to customers or suppliers. Instead, a group of employees at each site nominates a not-for-profit beneficiary and a one-off donation is made. This organisation is then publicised via Shire's outgoing emails during the month of December.

> Our Lexington site recently donated over $35,000 in retired manufacturing and laboratory equipment to two technical schools in Massachusetts and Rhode Island, US. While outdated in Shire's rapidly changing high-tech world, the schools tell us they are delighted with the equipment, which they find enhances their laboratory capacities and career development programs.
>
> We are currently liaising with other schools about further equipment donations. If this is something that would be of interest to your school, please email: shirecorporateresponsibility@shire.com

Employee-led support

The following information is taken from the company's website:

> All Shire employees are provided one full day annually to volunteer with a community organisation of their choice. This is done on an individual basis and as team-building activities too. Volunteering at a food bank, at community gardens, as a mentor at a local school, and cooking meals at a local homeless shelter are just a few examples of Shire employees in action. In some instances where employees are actively engaged through community volunteerism, Shire may provide financial support for those events and projects.

Shire operates a 'Give As You Earn' scheme and matches money raised by employees for charity.

Commercially-led support

The company has a long-term partnership with Kids Company, starting with a funding grant and sponsorship of a research program at Great Ormond Street Hospital in London.

The company has also been working with the Royal Society of Chemistry since 2007, on a five-year project to encourage young people to choose a career in science. Each year they invest £50,000 in a prize for the best chemistry students in the UK.

Corporate social responsibility

CSR committee: There is a dedicated Responsibility Team with named individuals – details given on the company's website.

CSR policy: Taken from the company's corporate responsibility policy document:

> Shire's leadership as a global biopharmaceutical company extends beyond researching and developing medicines that enable people to lead better lives. It includes taking an active role in supporting the therapeutic and geographic communities aligned with our mission, purpose, values and brave culture.
>
> Connecting with our communities is part of our core responsibility initiatives. We define our communities broadly, as the neighborhoods where significant numbers of our employees live and work, and as the organisations aligned with our primary therapeutic areas which may be patient

advocacy organisations, charitable institutions, or healthcare research organisations. Ultimately, the objective of all our community activities is to assist us in meeting our strategic goals and to benefit the development of our employees and our business. We are guided by several factors including:

- Our obligations to our stakeholders: patients and their families; physicians, caregivers and healthcare providers; employees and business partners; investors and shareholders; payors; regulators; therapeutically-aligned patient advocacy and research organisations; and communities where our employees live and work
- Maintaining the highest professional and ethical standards
- Galvanizing the entire company around growing our business
- Executing our strategy
- Fostering a rewarding and enjoyable workplace for our employees

CSR report: There is an annual Responsibility Highlights report.

Exclusions

No support for political appeals.

Applications

Full details of how to apply for funding is provided on the company's helpful website.

Use of charitable contribution funds is unrestricted, which means Shire does not control the recipient's use of the funds; use is at the sole discretion of the recipient.

The company aims to acknowledge all approaches in writing, including refusals.

Shoe Zone Ltd

Retail – clothing and footwear

Correspondent: Michael John Smith, Correspondent – Shoe Zone Trust, Shoe Zone, Haramead Business Centre, Humberstone Road, Leicester LE1 2LH (tel: 01162 223000/01162 223007; fax: 01162 223001; email: info@shoezone.net; website: www.shoezone.com)

Directors: M. J. Smith; A. E. P. Smith; J. C. P. Smith; C. A. Howes; J. Davis; S. D. Orr; N. T. Shefford; C. R. Bloor

Year end	01/01/2011
Turnover	£185,608,000
Pre-tax profit	£10,543,000

Nature of business: Footwear retailer.

Company registration number: 148038

Total employees: 4,376

Charitable donations

UK cash (latest declared):	2010	£150,000
	2009	£70,000
	2008	£0
	2007	£100,000
	2006	£80,000
Total UK:	2010	£150,000
Total worldwide:	2011	£150,000
Cash worldwide:	2011	£150,000

Corporate social responsibility

CSR committee: No committee.

CSR policy: The following statement is published within the 2010/11 accounts: 'The company is committed to responsible growth. By putting customers first and through its relationship with its employees, the company has developed effective ways of making positive contributions to society and the environment.'

The ratio of women to men on the board is unknown.

CSR report: No report published.

Applications

In writing to the correspondent.

Other information

In 2010 the company made charitable donations in the UK of £150,000 (2009: £70,000), all of which went to the Shoe Zone Trust. The company committed a further £100,000 in 2011.

Shoe Zone Trust (Charity Commission no. 1112972)

> The objects of the charity are to make grants and donations to other charities to relieve financial hardship and poverty and/ or advancement of education, mainly for children and young persons under age 18 particularly in Leicestershire and Rutland and for certain charities operating in the Philippines and other countries.

In addition, Shoe Zone staff are encouraged in their volunteering and fundraising activities by the company and in 2010 raised £50,000 which was allocated to various charities.

Support is also given to local charities and community groups and schools in the Leicestershire area.

Siemens plc

Electronics/computers

Correspondent: Head of Sustainability, Ian Bowman, Sir William Siemens Square, Frimley, Camberley, Surrey GU16 8QD (tel: 01276 696000; website: www.siemens.co.uk)

Directors: H. O. G. Dombrowe; A. J. Goss; R. Jaksch; G. T. Gent

Year end	30/09/2011
Turnover	£2,564,360,000
Pre-tax profit	£59,604,000

Nature of business: Siemen's principal activities in the UK cover: information and communication, automation and control, transportation, power, and medical businesses. The company are also engaged in the supply of lighting, commercial research and development, and financial services.

Company registration number: 727817

Main locations: Birmingham, Banbury, Basildon, Frimley, Swindon, Telford, Wellingborough, Worcester, Congelton, Cirencester, Manchester, London, Newcastle, Milton Keynes, Nottingham, Oxford, Reading, Poole, Harrogate, Harrow, Ipswich, Hayes, Langley, Hitchin, Hinckley, Lincoln, Crawley, Staines, Ramsey, Walton on Thames

Total employees: 7,468

Membership: BITC, LBG

Charitable donations

UK cash (latest declared):	2011	£270,000
	2009	£62,516
	2007	£62,516
	2006	£90,970
Total UK:	2011	£1,900,000
Total worldwide:	2011	£1,900,000
Cash worldwide:	2011	£270,000

Corporate social responsibility

CSR committee: Siemens global sustainability organisation is led by Chief Sustainability Officer and Global Board Director; Barbara Kux. In the UK, sustainability responsibility sits with the Chief Executive Officer and the Executive Management Board. Co-ordination of UK operations is the responsibility of Head of Sustainability; Ian Bowman.

CSR policy: Information taken from the UK website: 'Siemens in the UK follows three areas of sustainable development as defined by Siemens globally and managed by the UK team: environment; business and society.'

We were unable to determine the ratio of women to men on the board.

CSR report: Annual Sustainability report and update.

Applications

In writing to the correspondent.

Other information

In 2010/11 charitable donations declared in the accounts, in the UK totalled £270,000 (2009/10: £230,000). The company supports local charitable organisations involved in education; young/vulnerable people; the environment; and disaster relief. Siemens has also developed two programmes – Siemens Generation21, which is committed to education and Siemens Caring Hands, which aims to create stronger communities.

The group Sustainability Update for the UK in 2011 states:

> Measure modified in 2009 to use the London Benchmark Group standard. Siemens plans by 2011 to ensure that all sites use LBG to monitor staff involvement with an aim of reach 1% of profits reinvested through donations in cash, kind and time by 2015. Siemens currently donates £1.9 million to education and community groups through cash, gifts in kind and employee volunteering and in 2011 there were 1,612 volunteer days (0.13 days/employee) relating to

education and 845 volunteer days (0.07 Days/employee) relating to community.

Our Sustainability KPIs reflect Siemens most significant and relevant sustainability issues (2008 – 2011). These are measured annually against a rolling three year target. The measures reflect Siemens UK's requirements and are coordinated with Siemens global reporting. For more information on Siemens global sustainability reporting go to: www.siemens.com/sustainability.

We do not know the split between education and community groups and have used the £1.9 million as the worldwide contributions figure.

SIG plc

Building materials, distribution

Correspondent: Charities Committee, Corporate office, Signet House, 17 Europa View, Sheffield Business Park, Sheffield S9 1XH (tel: 01142 856300; fax: 01142 856349; email: info@sigplc.co.uk; website: www.sigplc.co.uk)

Directors: Leslie Van de Walle, Chair; Chris Davies, Chief Executive; Doug Robertson; Chris Geoghegan; Jonathan Nicholls; Janet Ashdown; Mel Ewell (women: 1; men: 6)

Year end	31/12/2011
Turnover	£2,745,000,000
Pre-tax profit	£7,500,000

Nature of business: The principal activity of the Group is the supply of specialist products to construction and related markets in the UK, Ireland and Mainland Europe. The main products supplied are Insulation and Energy Management, Exteriors and Interiors.

Company registration number: 998314

Main locations: Sheffield, Southampton, Barking, Littleborough, Leominster, Leicester, London, Maidstone, Crawley, Cardiff, Wednesbury, Hyde, St Ives

Total employees: 10,600

Membership: BITC

Charitable donations

UK cash (latest declared):	2011	£145,000
	2009	£138,000
	2008	£169,000
	2007	£162,000
	2006	£100,000
Total UK:	2011	£145,000
Total worldwide:	2011	£145,000
Cash worldwide:	2011	£145,000

Corporate social responsibility

CSR committee: There is a Charities Committee. The Group Chief Executive has lead responsibility for policy implementation within the Group and this policy is signed by the CEO to demonstrate the Board's commitment.

CSR policy: The company's website states:

SIG recognises its corporate and social responsibilities to its Shareholders, customers, suppliers, employees and other stakeholders and is committed to conducting business in a manner which achieves sustainable growth whilst fulfilling legal and moral obligations.

We aim to achieve our business objectives in a caring and responsible manner recognising the economic, social and environmental impacts of our activities.

Business Principles and Code of Ethics

We are committed to ensuring that our business is conducted in all respects according to the highest ethical and professional standards, taking into account legislation and customs in the countries and regions we operate in.

Community: We endeavour to contribute to the communities in which we operate, particularly those neighbouring our sites, through the support of community initiatives and local charities. Each business unit is encouraged to develop programmes, which address the needs of their local community alongside the contributions that SIG plc makes annually to its partner charities.

For further information see the SIG Ethics, Whistleblowing and Anti Competitive Trading Policies.

CSR report: Contained within the annual report and accounts.

Exclusions

No support for political appeals.

Applications

In writing to the correspondent.

Other information

During the year the group made donations of £145,000 (2010: £117,000). The following is taken from the annual report and accounts for 2011:

The group reviewed its Charitable Donations Policy in 2011. As a result SIG introduced a new initiative to use funds to provide matched donations in respect of monies raised by the group's employees for charitable causes. SIG employees can apply for a matched donation (up to a maximum of £500 or local equivalent).

A Charities Committee has been set up to approve applications and to ensure that they are in line with SIG's Charitable Donations Policy. Matched donations from employee applications in 2011 were made to various charities and community projects including: the Alpe d'Huez Foundation in Benelux, Macmillan Cancer Support, Cancer Research UK, Tommy's, Breast Cancer Campaign, BBC Children in Need and local community football teams for children and adults.

The group's particular focus of support is for charities that enhance SIG's engagement in the communities in which it operates, assist in managing the sustainability of the local environment or educate young people and assist disadvantaged groups.

In addition to matched funding, in 2011 SIG gave its support to the following charities:

- *Action For Kids* – A donation was made to the '12 Trikes for Xmas Appeal' to help provide 12 tricycles for 12 disabled children from the UK. Action For Kids is a national charity working to create independence, provide opportunities and offer support to disabled children, young people and their families all around the UK. Action For Kids was partnered by SIG for a 3 year period ending in 2010
- *LivLife* – A donation to build an outreach centre in Tanzania. LivLife works in Northern Tanzania with some of the world's most disadvantaged people, many of whom live in desperate poverty, without the chance to go to school, learn skills or find employment – many have had no education at all. LivLife Centres provide the relevant opportunities for people to get themselves out of poverty through learning and employment. The education centres are sustainable, locally-run and locally-relevant. Crucially they are entirely free to use, thereby giving everyone in the communities the opportunity to live their life, and to do so on their own terms
- *St Wilfrid's Centre (Sheffield UK)* – Donation towards a new residential centre for homeless people. This is a charity which supports the homeless, the vulnerable and those who are socially excluded by providing a safe environment where they can learn life skills. St Wilfrid's has its own printing, pottery and woodwork centre staffed by homeless volunteers who craft goods for sale in the shop located in the Centre. The residential centre will help educate homeless people in how to take care of themselves in social accommodation with the end goal of breaking the cycle of homelessness

Donations were also made to *Myeloma UK & Alzheimer's* in memory of our respected colleague, Jon Hudson, who sadly passed away in 2011.

The group has in place a **Payroll Giving Scheme**, which is available to all UK employees. Employees are free to choose any charity of their choice. Donations of £22,000 were made through the scheme in 2011.

Employees also undertake personal fundraising endeavours for a wide range of charities. The UK intranet, which is available at each location, has a dedicated forum for employees to highlight their fundraising efforts and receive support from their colleagues.

Simmons and Simmons LLP

Legal

Correspondent: Vickie Chamberlain, Employee Relations and CR Manager, CityPoint, One Ropemaker Street, London EC2Y 9SS (tel: 020 7628 4274; fax: 020 7628 2070; email: vickie.chamberlain@simmons-simmons.com; website: www.simmons-simmons.com)

Directors: David Dickinson; Jeremy Hoyland; Marco Franzini; Paul Li; Richard Perry; Leo Verhoeff; Patrick Wallace; Sarah Bowles; Rodger Hughes; Pamela Kirby; David McLaughlin (women: 2; men: 9)

Year end	30/04/2011
Turnover	£240,000,000
Pre-tax profit	£52,000,000

Nature of business: Law firm.

Company registration number: OC352713

Main locations: London

Total employees: 1,447

Charitable donations

UK cash (latest declared):	2011	£80,000
	2010	£80,000
Total UK:	2011	£2,260,000
Total worldwide:	2011	£2,260,000
Cash worldwide:	2011	£80,000

Corporate social responsibility

CSR committee: A CSR Committee was present.

CSR policy: This information was obtained from the company's CSR report:

> At Simmons & Simmons, our CR strategy focuses on taking a sustainable approach to our activities and initiatives so that we achieve long-term and credible outcomes. Pro bono work is at the heart of this, providing quality legal expertise to support innovative projects. We have also been developing partnerships with clients to increase the scale and impact of our pro bono projects.

CSR report: A CSR report was available from the company's website.

Applications

In writing to the correspondent.

Other information

In 2010/11 the firm donated £80,000 to its Charity of the Year Scope. According to its website the firm has conducted 7,700 hours of pro bono and community engagement hours during 2010/11 amounting to £2.2 million.

Pro bono work: Beneficiaries of this support have included The Big Issue. The firm runs a weekly evening surgery at Battersea Legal Advice Centre in London offering free legal advice to the local community.

Payroll giving: In addition to raising funds for their Charity of the Year, the firm supports and actively promotes payroll giving.

> **Charity of the Year:** Each year the firm identifies a charity that will be supported by the London office. Our international offices each support their own choice of local charities. In 2010/11 the charity is Scope, a national disability charity and was decided upon via an online poll of partners and employees. Previous charities of the year have included The Royal Marsden Cancer Campaign (2009); Kids Company (2008); The Royal National Institute of the Blind (RNIB) (2007); and World Wildlife Fund (WWF) (2006).
>
> **Mentoring schemes:** In London the company is involved in five mentoring schemes which include reading schemes with primary school children, language mentoring with GCSE students and mentoring of college and university students. Primary school schemes provide younger children with an opportunity to experience the joy of reading and improve their skills, particularly where English is not their first language. Secondary school, college and university mentoring schemes focus on providing career advice and guidance to older students thinking about further education or their choice of career. The company's mentoring scheme at Tower Hamlets College has been so successful that it has been extended for the duration of the students' degrees, and offered an annual contribution towards their university fees and legal work experience placements.
>
> **Twist Partnership:** Simmons & Simmons has joined the Twist Partnership to support a pioneering youth inclusion programme, 'Step Up'. This project aims to empower young people from Tower Hamlets who are at risk of offending or exclusion from school by giving them the responsibility to organise and execute a large project, supported by members of the firm, and the opportunity of work experience placements across the business services departments.

The company is also involved in international community work in locations where it is based including Hong Kong; Shanghai; The Netherlands and The Middle East.

Slaughter and May

Legal

Correspondent: Kate Hursthouse, Correspondent, Slaughter and May Charitable Trust, Company address (tel: 020 7600 1200/020 7090 3433; fax: 020 7090 5000; website: www.slaughterandmay.com)

Directors: Chris Saul, Senior Partner, Chair; Paul Olney, Practice Partner, Managing Director; Graham White, Executive Partner (women: 0; men: 3)

Year end	13/02/2011

Nature of business: Law firm, regulated by the Solicitors Regulation Authority.

Law Society ID: 55388

Total employees: 1,370

Charitable donations

UK cash (latest declared):	2011	£351,400
	2009	£461,000
	2008	£333,000
Total UK:	2011	£351,400
Total worldwide:	2011	£351,400
Cash worldwide:	2011	£351,400

Corporate social responsibility

CSR committee: Community activities are directed by the Community Affairs Committee and funded by the Slaughter and May Charitable Trust.

CSR policy: The firm's website states:

> We work as hard at making a positive impact on the world around us as we do at providing the best service to our clients. We do this by continually investing in our local community and preserving our environment.
>
> We aim to be an example of best practice in all of our Community and Environment activities – the full backing of the firm's partnership enables us to achieve this.

CSR report: No specific report was available. Trust accounts available from the Charity Commission.

Applications

The company's Community Affairs Committee meets periodically to review issues relating to its community affairs strategy. The company are proactive in their support of charitable groups and state that unfortunately, they are unable to accept unsolicited funding applications from schools, charities or individuals.

Other information

The company's charitable donations are made through its own charity, The Slaughter and May Charitable Trust (Charity Commission no. 1082765). In 2011 the trust received £351,400 in donations from the firm, and gave £262,600 in grants. The trust was established for general charitable purposes and during 2011 made grants including those to: Princess Royal Trust for Carers (£84,000); City Solicitors' Educational Trust (£60,000); Islington Law Centre (£35,000); Legal Advice Centre and South West London Law Centres (£15,000 each); London Symphony Orchestra and Volunteer Services Overseas (£10,000 each); Marie Curie Cancer Care and Young Enterprise (£5,000 each); and Prisoners' Education Trust, Rape and Sexual Abuse Support Centre and Saint Francis Hospice (£1,000 each).

The company is proactive in its support for charitable/good causes. Its website states:

We focus on a small number of charities to ensure that each receives the level of support it needs. That support is given in the form of legal and strategic expertise, volunteer participation, annual donations and in kind assistance such as hosting meetings and events.

Our two key charity partners, the National Literacy Trust and Carers Trust, were chosen because of their outstanding reputations and our ability to support them effectively. We also work with St Luke's Community Centre and our volunteers are involved in projects that support local residents.

30% of our London employees regularly volunteer. The neighbourhood surrounding our office is one of the most deprived in London and, for this reason, our community investment is focused here.

We work to improve the educational experience of students at three of our local primary schools – Prior Weston School, St Luke's Primary School and Moreland School – and a local secondary school, Central Foundation Boys' School.

Our volunteers work with young people on literacy, employability and enterprise projects. The volunteers find these projects incredibly rewarding, and the young people gain confidence and develop essential skills.

We are proud to be a founding member of PRIME, a sector-wide initiative to provide fair access to quality work experience. Our new flagship social mobility project at Central Foundation Boys' School will ensure we meet our commitment to PRIME

Our community activities are directed by our Community Affairs Committee and funded by the Slaughter and May Charitable Trust. We help the community on our doorstep and do this by developing long-term, strategic partnerships with local schools and charities. Our approach reflects our client-facing values of excellence, innovation and exceptional service.

Our community programme enables our legal and non-legal staff to give their time and skills to a wide range of volunteering and pro bono opportunities. We also develop collaborative projects with clients and fellow law firms.

We have a long history of providing free legal advice to charities and individuals.

Our pro bono work falls into two categories:

- Law centre volunteering – every week we provide teams of volunteer advisers to staff two London law centres: the University House Legal Advice Centre in Bethnal Green and Islington Law Centre, and an additional team of qualified litigators serve as Honorary Legal Advisers at the RCJ Advice Bureau
- Charity clients – we provide our charity partners with pro bono support whenever it is required and actively seek ways in which our legal expertise might be used to support their causes

We are a member of a number of pro bono referral organisations, including LawWorks A4ID and TrustLaw, which enable us to reach many different types of charities and community groups, locally and globally.

We have no figures for in kind support such as pro bono work or volunteering although this appears to be at a substantial cost to the firm.

Smith and Nephew plc

Healthcare

Correspondent: Don Young, Corporate Sustainability Team, Smith and Nephew, 1450 Brooks Road, Memphis, TN 38116 (tel: 020 7401 7646; fax: 020 7960 2350; email: sustainability@smith-nephew.com; website: www.smith-nephew.com)

Directors: John Buchanan, Chair; Olivier Buhuon, Chief Executive; Adrian Hennah, Chief Financial Officer; Ian Barlow; Richard De Schutter; Pamela Kirby; Brian Larcombe; Joseph Papa; Ajay Piramal; Virginia Bottomley; Susan Swabey (women: 3; men: 9)

Year end	31/12/2011
Turnover	£2,699,109,900
Pre-tax profit	£532,289,600

Nature of business: A global medical devices company manufacturing and marketing clinical products principally in orthopaedics, endoscopy, wound management and rehabilitation.

Company registration number: 324357

Main locations: Cambridge, Hull, Huntingdon, Gilberdyke, York

UK employees: 1,670

Total employees: 10,743

Membership: Arts & Business

Charitable donations

UK cash (latest declared):	2009	£258,000
	2007	£250,000
	2005	£325,000
Total worldwide:	2011	£8,543,500
Cash worldwide:	2011	£5,712,700

Corporate social responsibility

CSR committee: There appears to be a Sustainability Committee.

CSR policy: The following is taken from the company's website:

> Smith & Nephew's new sustainability strategy is true to our mission of improving people's live. It will consistently align our environmental, social and economic imperatives across the entire business. It will raise standards across a multi-year timeframe and bring benefits to bear wherever we operative and live.

CSR report: There is an annual Sustainability report published and available online.

Exclusions

No support for political appeals.

Applications

In writing to the correspondent.

Other information

In 2011, Smith and Nephew made total cash contributions worldwide of £5.7 million. UK contributions were not specified, however the company continues to support the communities in which it operates, particularly Hull, where the group was founded. As part of a new strategy, disaster relief and donations to countries where medical care is less accessible are also being supported. Smith and Nephew offer in kind donations (usually of medical products), volunteer time, cash donations and sponsorship. The company is currently sponsoring The Prince's Trust Development Awards. Smith and Nephew aims to contribute more than 1% of adjusted pre-tax profit annually towards corporate citizenship/ philanthropy up to and throughout 2015.

Corporate volunteering programmes: According to the 2011 CSR report 'a formal volunteering programme will be instituted to allow employees to engage in community service.'

Matched Funding: A formal match funding policy is available to staff when fundraising, however no further details are given.

Partnerships:
International Health Partners.

D. S. Smith Holdings plc

Print/paper/packaging

Correspondent: Group Communications Manager, Beech House, Whitebrook Park, 68 Lower Cookham Road, Maidenhead, Berkshire SL6 8XY (tel: 01628 583400; website: www.dssmith.uk.com)

Directors: Peter Johnson, Chair; Miles Roberts, Chief Executive; Steve Dryden, Finance Director; Christopher Bunker; Gareth Davis; Philippe Mellier; Jonathan Nicholls (women: 0; men: 7)

Year end	30/04/2011
Turnover	£2,474,500,000
Pre-tax profit	£102,200,000

Nature of business: Production of corrugated and plastic packaging, primarily from recycled waste, and the distribution of office products.

Company registration number: 1377658

UK employees: 6,231

Total employees: 12,301

Charitable donations

UK cash (latest declared):	2011	£76,000
	2009	£78,000
	2008	£72,000
	2007	£71,000
	2006	£84,000
Total UK:	2011	£76,000
Total worldwide:	2011	£76,000
Cash worldwide:	2011	£76,000

Corporate social responsibility

CSR committee: No specific committee is responsible for CSR.

CSR policy: In relation to its communities DS Smith seeks to focus its charitable activity on projects local to operations that foster engagement with and between its employees and communities.

CSR report: The group's policies and performance on the key areas of corporate responsibility are described in the Corporate Responsibility Review in the group's annual report.

Exclusions

No support for advertising in charity brochures, animal welfare, appeals from individuals, the arts, fundraising events, overseas projects, political or religious appeals.

Applications

In writing to the correspondent.

Other information

The group contributed £76,000 (2009/10: £72,000) to charities in the UK. Donations were made by operating divisions to support their local communities. The group also supported a number of other charities across a range of causes. The company's 2010/11 annual report states:

> We seek to develop and maintain good relations in the local communities in which we operate; this is particularly important as in many of the locations where we operate we are one of the largest employers. As well as providing significant employment opportunities, we aim to make positive contributions to our communities and build a reputation as a good neighbour and employer. Our businesses work closely with local schools and colleges providing training, mentoring, work experience placements and other opportunities for pupils to learn about industry and business. The Group is involved in a wide range of other local community activities including sponsorship of community projects or sports teams and provision of adult skills training.

Unfortunately there has been no calculation made on these community contributions and we have therefore used the cash donation quoted in the annual report – £76,000.

WH Smith plc

Retail – miscellaneous

Correspondent: Sarah Heath, Head of Communications, Greenbridge Road, Swindon, Wiltshire SN3 3RX (tel: 01793 616161; fax: 01793 562560; email: corporate.responsibility@whsmith.co.uk; website: www.whsmithplc.co.uk)

Directors: Walker Boyd, Chair; Kate Swann, Chief Executive; Robert Moorhead; Steve Clarke; Mike Ellis; Drummond Hall; Henry Staunton; Jeff Harris; Ian Houghton (women: 1; men: 8)

Year end	31/08/2011
Turnover	£1,273,000,000
Pre-tax profit	£93,000,000

Nature of business: The group's principal activities are the retail, publishing and news distribution.

Company registration number: 471941

Total employees: 16,273

Membership: BITC

Charitable donations

UK cash (latest declared):	2011	£313,000
	2009	£343,800
	2008	£399,250
	2007	£600,300
	2005	£781,000
Total UK:	2011	£933,000
Total worldwide:	2011	£933,000
Cash worldwide:	2011	£313,000

Corporate social responsibility

CSR committee: There was no evidence of a CSR Committee.

CSR policy: This information was obtained from the company's website:

> WHSmith is a valued member of communities across the UK, and we are committed to making a positive impact wherever we operate our stores. Through our work to champion literacy and support good causes, our community programme enables us to contribute to local areas.

CSR report: A separate CSR report was available via the company's website.

Exclusions

Unsolicited requests are not supported. No support for advertising in charity brochures, animal welfare, appeals from individuals, the arts, older people, enterprise/training, environment/heritage, fundraising events, medical research, overseas projects, political appeals, religious appeals, science/technology, sickness/disability, social welfare or sport.

Applications

The group is proactive in identifying potential partners for its community programme. Unsolicited requests, therefore, are not considered.

Other information

Charitable donations during the year ended 31 August 2011 totalled £162,000 (2009: £89,700). In addition, the company facilitated the sale of charitable products which gave rise to further donations of £151,000 (2009: £254,000).

This information was obtained from the company's annual report:

> The WHSmith Group Charitable Trust, an independent registered charity, actively supports employees that are involved with charitable organisations in their local community. In addition, we recognise employee involvement in the community through our annual Community Awards. Supporting our literacy objectives, the group has been working with the WHSmith Trust and with the National Literacy Trust for the past four years to fund the WHSmith Summer Read. This programme aims to foster a love of reading in children and encourage them to keep reading during their summer holidays.
>
> We also raise funds for charities and good causes through the promotion and sale of tailored products in our stores, such as charity cards and calendars and our Adopt an Animal range.
>
> Promoting literacy is at the heart of our community engagement programmes. We are working with the National Literacy Trust to provide courses for parents who want to develop skills to support their children's literacy development.

The company regularly engages with organisations, such as the Woodland Trust, the Employers Forum on Disability and the Ethical Trading Initiative to improve its performance regarding CSR.

Smiths Group plc

Aerospace, engineering

Correspondent: Charitable Donations Committee, 2nd Floor, Cardinal Place, 80 Victoria Street, London SW1E 5JL (tel: 020 7808 5500; fax: 020 7808 5533; website: www.smiths.com)

Directors: Donald Brydon, Chair; Philip Bowman, Chief Executive; Peter Turner, Finance Director; David Challen; Stuart Chambers; Anne Quinn; Kevin Tebbit; Bruno Angelici (women: 1; men: 7)

Year end	31/07/2011
Turnover	£2,842,000,000
Pre-tax profit	£397,900,000

Nature of business: The company is involved in the medical, industrial, aerospace and sealing solutions industries.

Company registration number: 137013

Main locations: Birmingham, Dundee, Eastleigh, Gloucester, Hounslow, Burnley, Crawley, Tewkesbury, Watford, Croydon, Glasgow, Wolverhampton, Hythe, Ilford, Orpington, Nelson,

Onchan, Newmarket, Newbury, Manchester, Luton, Slough, Southampton, Christchurch

Total employees: 22,900

Charitable donations

UK cash (latest declared):	2011	£300,000
	2009	£504,000
	2007	£389,000
	2005	£625,000
Total UK:	2011	£300,000
Total worldwide:	2011	£482,000
Cash worldwide:	2011	£482,000

Corporate social responsibility

CSR committee: There is a charitable donations committee.

CSR policy: Chief executive's statement from the 2011 CSR report: 'Promoting a culture of responsibility throughout the business is one of our fundamental values and an important part of our strategy. We strive to behave ethically, work safely, reduce our environmental impact and contribute to our communities.'

CSR report: There is an annual CSR report published.

Exclusions

No support for advertising in charity brochures, animal welfare, appeals from individuals, the arts, fundraising events, overseas projects, political appeals, religious appeals or sport.

Applications

If your organisation and proposed funding initiative fit the criteria complete the application form from the website and email it to cr@smiths.com. Postal applications will not be responded to.

Other information

During the financial year 2010/11, the company made donations of £482,000 for charitable purposes. This comprised payments totalling £300,000 to the Institute of Child Health, in sponsorship of the Smiths Medical Professor of Anaesthesia and Critical Care and the Portex Anaesthesia, Intensive Care and Respiratory Unit and other donations made by the company and its businesses worldwide. The Group supports charities working in the areas of health; education and wellbeing; and the environment. We have used the £300,000 figure as the UK cash contribution as we know this went to a UK registered charity.

The following information is taken from the company's website:

Community

Smiths contributes positively to the communities in which we operate. In addition to providing employment opportunities and playing a beneficial role in local economies, we support community involvement through charitable giving and education initiatives.

This activity is primarily managed at a divisional level. However, Smiths does offer some support to community and charitable organisations from a central budget. Consideration is given to charities and organisations that demonstrate how a donation will enhance the well-being of people through improved education, health and welfare or environment. Projects local to our operational facilities or connected to the industries in which we operate are the primary focus of Smiths support.

Education is a major recipient of our support. For example together with the Royal Academy of Engineering in the UK, the Smiths Technology Education Programme (STEP) is now in its fifth year. STEP assists able students from any background, facing economic or social barriers, into a career in technology.

Through the programme, school students are offered the opportunity to participate in summer school courses in engineering and technology. Those students who then go on to take an engineering or technology degree course at university are eligible to receive Smiths bursaries.

Charitable giving policy

Smiths seeks to contribute to the communities in which we live and work in a number of ways. In addition to providing employment opportunities and minimising our environmental impact, we support a variety of local community initiatives. Our charitable donations and community initiatives facilitate projects around the globe that, like our products, seek to help make the world a safer, healthier and more productive place.

Smiths Group and its operating divisions – John Crane, Smiths Medical, Smiths Detection, Smiths Interconnect and Flex-Tek – support organisations that promote the advancement or wellbeing of people through a range of health and education initiatives. Each division is responsible for agreeing and administering its own charitable donations budget. To apply to these funds, please download a form from the website and email cr@smiths.com.

In addition to this, Smiths Group has a limited corporate budget for charitable donations that make a positive impact in the community in and around the area near to its head office in London or to the sectors we operate in.

We support: The Smiths Group corporate charitable donations fund focuses on small charitable organisations that:

- Work in the community close to our Head Office (London, UK) and/or
- Have connections to the industries in which we operate

Grant sizes: Donations from the corporate fund are generally less than £1,000.

We fund: We consider applications from charities and non-profit organisations that demonstrate how a donation will enhance the well-being of people through improved education, health/welfare or environment.

Your organisation does not need to be a registered charity, but it should be charitable.

Organisations must be working in:

- Health
- Education and wellbeing
- Environment
- Based or working in or around London

Some examples of organisations that could be funded by Smiths Group include hospices, school projects, community initiatives, homeless charities and hospitals.

Payroll giving: A number of schemes are operated by the company.

Sodexo Ltd

Catering services, food services

Correspondent: Thomas Jelley, Corporate Citizenship Manager, Communications Department, Capital House, 2nd Floor, 25 Chapel Street, London NW1 5DH (tel: 020 7535 7400; fax: 020 7535 7401; email: thomas.jelley@sodexo.com; website: uk.sodexo.com)

Directors: P. Hooper; A. D. Leach; J. Bristow; M. P. Hanson; C. J. John; W. S. Scrivens; N. Bickford; K. Fitzpatrick; V. Sharma; N. D. Murray; P. R. Andrew; A. L. Leech

Year end	31/08/2011
Turnover	£950,555,000
Pre-tax profit	£66,823,000

Nature of business: The provision of catering management services to clients in commercial, industrial, educational, healthcare and other establishments. Activities also include catering at special events, sporting, leisure and public locations, vending services, supply of catering equipment, facilities management, design and allied services.

Company registration number: 842846

Main locations: Hitchin, Abertillery, Aberdeen, Alperton, Aldershot

Total employees: 28,318

Membership: BITC

Charitable donations

UK cash (latest declared):	2011	£89,000
	2009	£23,500
	2008	£16,500
	2007	£34,000
	2006	£40,000
Total UK:	2011	£89,000
Total worldwide:	2011	£89,000
Cash worldwide:	2011	£89,000

Corporate social responsibility

CSR committee: There is a Corporate Citizen Team.

CSR policy: CSR information taken from the group website:

Corporate citizenship, which to us means integrating economic, social and environmental factors into our everyday

> business practice, is fundamental to the way Sodexo operates. By addressing the issues that affect our stakeholders, and therefore our success, our approach to corporate citizenship aims to ensure a better quality of life for present and future generations through sustainable business practice.
>
> We are deploying a sustainability strategy to 2020, the Better Tomorrow Plan, which was launched in 2009 and focuses on the sustainability issues that are material to our business.

We were unable to determine the ratio of women to men on the board.

CSR report: Corporate Citizenship report published annually.

Applications

In writing to the correspondent.

Note: In addition to supporting FareShare and a number of smaller charities that meet the STOP Hunger objectives, the trustees receive from time to time requests from employees to support a local cause. In such cases the following policy applies:

- Requests should be submitted by employees and should relate to a project or cause with which they are personally involved
- Such grants are limited to a maximum of £500 per applicant
- Such grants are only made to registered charities

Other information

In 2010/11 the company declared £89,000 in UK charitable donations.

The company has established the **Sodexo Foundation** (Charity Commission no. 1110266). Its objectives are to educate and provide relief from financial hardship in relation to health, nutrition and well-being through the provision of grants, goods and services. In 2011, the foundation had an income of almost £363,000. Grants awarded totalled £169,000, and beneficiaries included: Breast Cancer Haven, Community Foundation for Ireland, Council for Homelessness, Outward Bound Trust, SSAFA, Training for Life and The Prince's Trust.

In 2005, the company launched the STOP Hunger campaign in the UK and Ireland, with clear aims to both combat poor nutrition in our local communities and provide a central focus for community related activities. The campaign is managed through the foundation. It supports a number of charities but is insistent that each are involved in one or more of the following activities:

- Healthy eating and healthy lifestyle education
- Healthy food provision to those in need
- Basic life skills education to those in need, for example cooking on a budget, basic cooking skills, basic food hygiene and health and safety

Charity Partner: Sodexo partnered with The Prince's Trust to provide a two-week hospitality programme for unemployed young people in North Wales. The programme, which was held at Deeside College in Flintshire, helped nine people aged under 25 to improve their knowledge of the industry and gave them the opportunity to take part in valuable work experience.

- Week one: courses on food hygiene, health and safety and customer care; Sodexo's Spirit of Inclusion training, which looks at diversity and inclusion from an individual, team and business perspective
- Week two: real work experience in various foodservice areas at the college, which are all provided by Sodexo

The Sodexo Foundation donated £17,000 to support the programme, which was delivered on behalf of The Prince's Trust with further significant in kind support from Sodexo Education.

Sodexo employees are involved in the following three ways; financial donations through employee fundraising, employee volunteering and the sharing of Sodexo knowledge and expertise with charity partners (beneficiary charities).

Payroll giving: The company operates a giving scheme.

Sony Europe Ltd

Electronics/computers

Correspondent: The Company Secretary, The Heights, Brooklands, Weybridge, Surrey KT13 0XW (tel: 01932 816000; fax: 01932 817000; website: www.sony.net)

Directors: F. Nishida; M. Tamagawa; K. Takeda; S. Foucher; G. Pelhet; R. Londema

Year end	31/03/2012
Turnover	£4,762,928,000
Pre-tax profit	£589,792,530

Nature of business: The company is the distributor in the United Kingdom of Sony branded products which are principally electronic goods for the domestic, leisure, business and professional markets. The company distributes Sony branded video and audio systems for commercial and professional use, and computer peripheral and component products, including semiconductor products, for use throughout Europe, Africa and the Middle East. Sony colour televisions, television tubes and other key components for the domestic and export markets are manufactured at factories which are operated by the company in South Wales.

Company registration number: 2422874

Main locations: Bridgend, Thatcham, Pencoed, Weybridge, Basingstoke

UK employees: 1,368

Total employees: 5,062

Charitable donations

UK cash (latest declared):	2011	£121,825
	2009	£125,000
	2008	£121,000
	2007	£84,000
	2006	£71,000
Total UK:	2011	£121,825
Total worldwide:	2012	£31,689,000

Corporate social responsibility

CSR committee: No details relevant to the UK found.

CSR policy: The group website states that: 'Sony defines its community engagement policy as 'Undertaking activities in fields where Sony is best able to do so, to help address the needs of communities.'

We were unable to determine the ratio of women to men on the board.

CSR report: Published within the annual report and accounts.

Applications

Appeals should be addressed to the correspondent.

Other information

In 2011/12 donations to charitable organisations made by Sony Europe Ltd totalled £243,650. A list of beneficiaries was not available, however the company accounts state that donations were made in support of: Community (76%) and Sport (24%).

From previous research we know that in the UK, Sony prefers to support local charities in areas of company presence (Weybridge, Basingstoke, Thatcham, Pencoed and Bridgend), appeals relevant to company business, and charities in which a member of staff is involved.

Globally, Sony donated £31.6 million which included 'sponsorships and independent program expenses (including facility operation expenses), this amount includes the market prices of products donated'. Europe received 3% of this investment but we have no breakdown of what was given in the UK or what was given in cash or in kind, and so have taken the UK cash figure to be 50% of that declared in the company's accounts.

Southern Co-operatives Ltd

Retail – miscellaneous, retail – supermarkets

Correspondent: Clerk to the Trustees, Southern Co-operatives Foundation, 1000 Lakeside, Western Road, Portsmouth, Hampshire PO6 3FE (tel: 02392 222500; fax: 02392 222650; website: www.southern.coop)

Directors: David Blowe, Chair; Pauline Lympany; Amber Vincent-Prior; Fran Hobson; Silena Dominy; Tom Blair; Steve Toone; Neil Blanchard; Glenn Heath; Mike Hastilow (women: 4; men: 6)

Year end	28/01/2012
Turnover	£309,057,000
Pre-tax profit	£9,826,000

Nature of business: Independent consumer co-operative society.

Company registration number: IP01591R

UK employees: 3,525

Total employees: 3,525

Charitable donations

UK cash (latest declared):	2009	£119,000
	2008	£69,000
	2007	£77,000
Total UK:	2009	£676,000
Total worldwide:	2012	£676,000

Corporate social responsibility

CSR report: Annual Review available from the website.

Applications

The Co-operatives website contains full details of how to apply to each of the schemes available. For example, for major grants guidance notes are provided on how to complete the required application form.

Other information

In 2011/12, the total community support strategy expenditure, excluding expenses, was £676,000 (£407,000 in 2010/11). We have no breakdown of cash or in kind contributions but the company states that the total represents 6.88% (4.47% in 2010/11) of pre-tax profit.

The company works with partners across the areas in which it trades. Two of the key partners are the Hampshire and Isle of Wight Wildlife Trust and the Sussex Wildlife Trust. It also supports The Greening Campaign which endeavours to make community environments greener. Support has also been given to Portsmouth Festivities, Express FM, the local community radio station and Hampshire Fare.

Community Support Card

This scheme is designed to raise funds for local good causes, as chosen by a panel of members from that community. The Southern Co-operative makes a donation to the fund every time a member has their special community card swiped. The scheme now operates in 24 communities across the south of England. In 2011/12, £230,000 has been given to 30 local causes.

Charity of the Year: Canine Partners (2012/13)

Full details of the company's CSR activities can be found in its Annual Review.

Spar (UK) Ltd

Retail – supermarkets

Correspondent: Marketing Director, Mezzanine Floor, Hygeia Building, 66–68 College Road, Harrow HA3 1BE (tel: 020 8426 3700; fax: 020 8426 3701; website: www.spar.co.uk)

Directors: S. Blackmore; S. Darbyshire; R. R. Hill; M. Keeley; C. Lewis; P. W. Marchant; D. M. Robinson

Year end	30/04/2011
Turnover	£61,700,000
Pre-tax profit	£400,000

Nature of business: Independently-owned nationwide convenience stores operating under the SPAR banner.

Company registration number: 634226

UK employees: 50,000

Total employees: 50,000

Membership: BITC

Charitable donations

UK cash (latest declared):	2011	£55,500
	2009	£90,500
Total UK:	2011	£55,500
Total worldwide:	2011	£55,500
Cash worldwide:	2011	£55,500

Corporate social responsibility

CSR policy: No specific CSR details found.

Exclusions

No support for political or religious causes.

Applications

Contact your local store manager.

For applications to the Spar Charitable Fund, contact P W Marchant, Correspondent, Spar Charitable Fund at the company's address.

Other information

SPAR sees its role within the community as an integral part of the way it does business and because of this is a subscribed member of Business in the Community (BITC). In addition, national organisations can also receive support with those involved with children and sport being particularly favoured. The company's chosen charities are the NSPCC and its sister organisation in Scotland, CHILDREN 1ST. Spar is also the official sponsor of United Kingdom Athletics.

SPAR also has an associated charity:

The SPAR Charitable Fund (Charity Commission no. 236252)
The Spar Charitable Fund with the support and assistance of the Spar Benevolent Fund seeks to provide charitable assistance to independent Spar retailers who face adverse problems and difficulties with health, bereavement, and social issues. The charitable fund also supports retail industry charitable organisations One major objective of the Spar charitable fund is to provide a vehicle to enable the Spar organisation through its 2,600 stores across the UK to engage with the public to raise awareness of public charitable needs and raise funding in a wide variety of ways. Income for the year was £55,500 and grants paid totalled £93,000. Beneficiaries included: NSPCC (£70,500); Business in the Community (£12,500); and Caravan (£10,000).

We have used the figure of £55,500 as the company's UK charitable giving contribution as no other figures were available.

Charity partner

Branches of the NSPCC local to SPAR stores.

Spectris plc

Engineering

Correspondent: Corporate Social Responsibility Team, Station Road, Egham, Surrey TW20 9NP (tel: 01784 470470; fax: 01784 470848; email: headoffice@spectris.com; website: www.spectris.com)

Directors: John Hughes, Chair; John O'Higgins, Chief Executive; Clive Watson, Group Finance Director; Jim Webster; Peter Chambré; Russell King; John Warren; Roger Stephens (women: 0; men: 8)

Year end	31/12/2011
Turnover	£1,106,200,000
Pre-tax profit	£166,000,000

Nature of business: Develops and markets precision instrumentation and controls.

Company registration number: 2025003

Total employees: 6,447

Charitable donations

UK cash (latest declared):	2011	£11,000
	2009	£6,000
	2008	£22,400
Total UK:	2011	£11,000
Total worldwide:	2011	£76,500
Cash worldwide:	2011	£76,500

Corporate social responsibility

CSR committee: Overall responsibility for developing corporate policies on environmental, social, ethical and health and safety matters, and for reviewing their effectiveness, lies with the Spectris board of directors. These policies are mandated across all business units and applied within each particular business, taking account of local legislation and regulation. All policies are reviewed periodically and any updates are communicated to the operating companies.

CSR policy: The following extract is taken from the company's website:

> Spectris is committed to creating business growth through adding value for its customers whilst ensuring that its impact on the environment is minimised. Spectris operates from 160 offices in 29 countries around the world. The companies' products are used to monitor and control processes in many industries, helping customers to improve efficiency and minimise their impact on the environment by reducing raw material consumption, waste or energy use. In turn, Spectris companies themselves actively seek to minimise their impact on the environment by designing products which are more energy-efficient and avoid the use of harmful substances

CSR report: Published annually and contained within the annual report and accounts.

Applications

In writing to the correspondent.

Other information

Total donations to charities and community causes in 2011 were £76,500, of which £11,000 were in the UK (2010: £27,500 of which £8,300 in UK). This included donations to the Red Cross in response to the tsunami and earthquake in Japan and the East Africa crisis, and to other charities and local schools and colleges. The company also makes contributions in kind to a number of projects but unfortunately this has not been costed by them.

Spectris companies worldwide participate in a range of local activities and educational initiatives in support of their local communities. Educational initiatives include providing apprenticeships and work placements for students, working with local schools and colleges on science projects, and sponsorship of scientists attending key scientific conferences.

Spirax Sarco Engineering plc

Engineering

Correspondent: W G Stebbings, Company Secretary and Solicitor, Charlton House, Cirencester Road, Cheltenham, Gloucestershire GL53 8ER (tel: 01242 521361; fax: 01242 581470; website: www.spiraxsarcoengineering.com)

Directors: Bill Whiteley, Chair; Mark E. Vernon, Chief Executive; Gareth Bullock; Neil Daws; David Meredith; Krishnamurthy Rajagopal; Clive Watson (women: 0; men: 7)

Year end	31/12/2011
Turnover	£644,000,000

Nature of business: The supply of engineered solutions for the efficient design, maintenance and operation of industrial and commercial steam systems.

Company registration number: 596337

Charitable donations

UK cash (latest declared):	2011	£132,000
	2009	£86,000
	2008	£81,000
	2007	£72,000
	2006	£62,000
Total UK:	2011	£132,000
Total worldwide:	2011	£132,000
Cash worldwide:	2011	£132,000

Corporate social responsibility

CSR committee: There was no evidence of a separate CSR Committee.

CSR policy: This information was obtained from the company's annual report:

> The group takes seriously its corporate social responsibility to all of its stakeholders in safeguarding the performance of the business in an environmentally friendly way. We encourage our local operating companies to support local charities and organise their own activities.

CSR report: There was no evidence of a separate CSR report, however information was available from the company's interactive annual report.

Exclusions

Previous information collated suggested that the company will make no response to circular appeals, and no grants for advertising in charity brochures, religious appeals, local appeals not in areas of company presence and large national appeals.

Applications

In writing to the correspondent.

Other information

During 2011, the Group made £132,000 in donations, primarily through the Spirax-Sarco Engineering plc Group Charitable Trust (Charity Commission no. 1082534) which benefits charities both in the UK and abroad.

The operating companies in the Group are encouraged to provide support to local communities through company donations, employee organised charitable activities, donation of equipment no longer required and through provision of information. Spirax-Sarco Ltd continues to support the National Star College in Cheltenham.

In India, the group's Associate company gives priority to improving education and women's health. One of the initiatives teaches English and life skills to children at three after-school centres.

Spirent plc

Electronics/computers

Correspondent: The Company Secretary, Spirent Communications plc, Northwood Park, Gatwick Road, Crawley, West Sussex RH10 9XN (tel: 01293 767676; fax: 01293 767677; website: www.spirent.com)

Directors: Ian Brindle; Sue Swenson; Duncan Lewis; Eric Hutchinson, Chief Financial Officer; Alex Walker, Chair; Tom Maxwell; Bill Burns, Chief Executive Officer (women: 1; men: 6)

Year end	31/12/2011
Turnover	£335,988,020
Pre-tax profit	£78,431,130

Nature of business: An international technology group focused on the design, development, manufacture and marketing of specialist electronic products.

Company registration number: 470893

Main locations: Crawley, Devon, Bedfordshire

Total employees: 1,540

Charitable donations

UK cash (latest declared):	2009	£91,000
	2008	£52,000
	2007	£40,000
	2006	£32,000
	2005	£96,000
Total worldwide:	2011	£70,600
Cash worldwide:	2011	£70,600

Corporate social responsibility

CSR committee: See 'CSR Policy'.

CSR policy: Taken from the CSR report in the 2011 annual report and accounts:

> The board takes ultimate responsibility for CSR with a fundamental commitment to create and sustain long-term value for shareholders, recognising that acting responsibly and sustainably creates value.
>
> Spirent's CSR strategy covers our accountability to all of our stakeholders, this includes striving for the highest ethical standards of business practice; how we support, develop and reward our employees; how we minimise our impact

on the environment; and how we support and engage in the communities in which we operate. Community Spirent aims to build stronger and healthier global communities through education, charitable donations and support of non-profit agencies in the communities in which we operate. Working with established non-profit organisations maximises the impact of our community building initiatives.

CSR report: Published in the annual report and accounts.

Applications

In writing to the correspondent.

Other information

In 2011 the Group made charitable donations totalling £70,600. Details of beneficiaries were not available.

The company encourages its employees to support particular needs to their local community by contributing to local charities and participating in community initiatives. Support takes the form of employee time and skills, gifts in kind and cash donations.

Sportech plc

Gaming

Correspondent: Richard Boardley, Director of Corporate Affairs, 101 Wigmore Street, London W1U 1QU (tel: 020 7268 2400/020 7268 2400; email: cr@sportechplc.com; website: www.sportechplc.com)

Directors: Michael John Barnes; Steve Cunliffe, Finance Director; Roger Withers, Chair; Ian Penrose, Chief Executive; Ian Hogg; Brooks Pierce; Peter Williams; Lorne Weil; Mor Weizer (women: 0; men: 9)

Year end	31/12/2011
Turnover	£118,200,000
Pre-tax profit	£8,000,000

Nature of business: The principal activities of the Group are those of Football Gaming and e-Gaming.

Company registration number: SC69140

Main locations: Liverpool, London

Total employees: 849

Charitable donations

UK cash (latest declared):	2011	£800,000
	2009	£1,000,000
	2008	£1,000,000
	2007	£1,300,000
	2006	£1,300,000
Total UK:	2011	£800,000
Total worldwide:	2011	£800,000
Cash worldwide:	2011	£800,000

Community involvement

In 2008, the group launched 'The New Football Pools' and established The Football Pools Trust which addresses the needs of community football.

The group was for many years the sole funder of the Foundation for Sport and the Arts, which closed in 2012.

Disability football

The Football Pools presented Blackpool Football Club Community Trust with £20,000 at the home game against Coventry City as the club announces an exciting new scheme that will grow disability football across the region. Blackpool is the 48th Football League Club to join the Every Player Counts scheme, which is designed to grow disability provision across the UK.

Corporate giving

The 2011 annual report states that around £800,000 a year is generated for charitable use in the UK through Sportech's management and operation of society lottery products.

The following information is taken from the group's CSR report of 2011:

> In 2007, the Group changed the focus of its charitable donations specifically towards football charities and signed a deed with the four English and Scottish professional football leagues to direct donations of £5.9 million towards football-related charities in the period up to June 2011. Of the committed monies:
>
> £1.6 million has been allocated to Premier League Health, a joint initiative between the group and the premier league, launched in February 2009. This initiative sees 17 premier league clubs working with local health agencies such as primary care trusts to engage with over 4,000 men. The project aims to tackle issues as diverse as depression linked to unemployment, obesity and general poor physical health, as well as alcohol and drug addiction.
>
> In addition, a scheme to use the power of football to assist unemployed people back into work, training or education has been supported with a donation of £206,000, used to trial this scheme with four premier league clubs – Chelsea, Everton, Portsmouth and Sunderland.
>
> £2.6 million has been donated to the Football League Trust for a scheme that will grow football provision for people who have disabilities, across England and Wales. The three-year, pan-disability scheme will develop football opportunities at 39 football league clubs.
>
> Just under £1.2 million has been donated to the Scottish football league in a multi-channelled scheme that will tackle serious issues within the game, such as young people's heart screening, alcohol awareness training for under 16s and under 19s, as well as the donation of a defibrillator to every football club across the leagues. All 30 clubs are involved.
>
> With an award of £294,000, the Scottish Premier League is running the Football Fans in Training scheme across all twelve clubs. This emulates the current Premier League Health scheme using the power of football and club brands to encourage men to get fit and healthy.

Employee-led support

'The group encourages employees to raise funds for local charities and supports those efforts where appropriate.'

Corporate social responsibility

CSR committee: No specific details found.

CSR policy: Statement from the 2011 CSR report:

> Corporate social responsibility is about behaving responsibly towards employees, customers and society in general. The group takes its responsibilities extremely seriously and is justifiably proud of its record in maintaining the highest ethical standards of corporate social responsibility in respect of all those who come into contact with our business.

CSR report: Annual CSR report published and available from the group's website.

Applications

Applications should be made in writing to the correspondent.

Sportingbet plc

Gaming

Correspondent: Corporate Responsibility Team, 4th Floor, 45 Moorfields, London EC2Y 9AE (tel: 020 7184 1800; fax: 020 7184 1810; email: info@sportingbet.com; website: www.sportingbetplc.com)

Directors: Andrew McIver, Group Chief Executive; Peter Dicks, Chair; Jim Wilkinson, Group Finance Director; Brian Harris; Rory Macnamara; Chris Moss (women: 0; men: 6)

Year end	31/07/2011
Turnover	£206,300,000
Pre-tax profit	£23,800,000

Nature of business: Online gaming company.

Company registration number: 3534726

Total employees: 630

Charitable donations

UK cash (latest declared):	2011	£240,000
	2010	£229,600
Total UK:	2011	£240,000
Total worldwide:	2011	£240,000
Cash worldwide:	2011	£240,000

Corporate social responsibility

CSR committee: Yes, see 'Policy'.

CSR policy: Extract taken from the company's website:

> We have always sought to exhibit responsible and ethical practices. Our culture was formalised in 2000 in a series of written statements – our Code of Conduct and Customer Charter. These statements illustrate our social responsibility to our customers, to our shareholders, to our employees and to the

governments of markets in which we operate.

Our objective is to provide a protected entertainments environment, in which our customer care programmes give responsible adults the confidence of knowing that their money is safe, whilst providing Sportingbet with the confidence that all reasonable steps are being taken to protect the vulnerable. We also appoint a Social Responsibility Committee to review corporate social responsibility policies and to stimulate group wide best practice on matters including age verification, fraud, money laundering, responsible gaming, self-exclusion and privacy.

CSR report: Published in the annual report and accounts.

Applications

In writing to the correspondent.

Other information

During the year, the group donated approximately £240,000 to a number of charities. This figure includes donations to the GREaT Foundation (formerly the Responsibility in Gambling Trust), the Island Academy International School, Antigua, HEROS (Homing Ex-Racehorses Organisation Scheme). Included in this total was a donation of £16,500 to the Friends of Israel Sport Centre for the Disabled, of which Brian Harris is the founder.

The company's website states:

> Recognising that some customers may be affected by gambling dependency, we have continued to provide funding in the UK to the GREaT Foundation (formally known as Responsibility in Gambling Trust) which raises funds through voluntary donations to support research, education and treatment of problem gambling.
>
> We also support many charitable organisations that are not linked to the online gaming industry:
>
> - HEROS (Homing Ex-Racehorses Organisation Scheme)
> - Injured Jockeys Fund
> - Bishop Simeon Trust in South Africa
> - Headway in Guernsey
> - Friends of Israel Sport Centre for the Disabled
> - The Dan Maskell Tennis Trust
> - Bury St Edmunds Theatre
>
> *Community Liaison*
>
> In order to encourage a socially-integrated work environment, we place an emphasis on investing in the local communities in which we operate.
>
> In Guernsey, where our primary licence and operations are based, we have invested a significant amount of time and money into the local community, including the sponsorships of Heather Watson, the UK's number one seeded and world number 13 tanked junior tennis player, the Channel Islands Athletics Club, and local events like the Sportingbet Guernsey Marathon and the Sportingbet Channel Island's Sports Personality of the Year awards.
>
> In Antigua, where we have held sports betting and gaming licences for many years, we have donated a significant sum of money to fund both the building of a library at the Island Academy International School and bursaries for a number of less privileged local children. The Antiguan Girl's High School has benefitted from a donation to provide desks and other key furniture, as part of the school's commitment to update its resources.
>
> In the United Kingdom, Sportingbet supports the Home Office funded scheme, Tackling Knives Action Programme. In the West Midlands, this programme has been implemented through Braveheart – a scheme which takes youth leaders, policemen, former gang members and community workers into the Scottish Islands for a week to improve their leadership skills, self reliance and confidence. In conjunction with the Wolverhampton Wanderers FC Community Trust, Sportingbet has sponsored three of its employees to act as members and to join youth leaders on this scheme, and is working with West Midlands police and community groups in the area to encourage other companies to join the 'Braveheart' programme.

Sportingbet sponsored four employees from across its global workforce, and two Non-Executive Directors to climb Mount Kilimanjaro in February 2010. The team, along with ten external people who will be joining the climb, will be raising money for Breast Cancer Care, Haven and the Injured Jockeys Fund.

Sports Direct International plc

Retail – clothing and footwear

Correspondent: Company Secretary, Unit A, Brook Park East, Shirebrook, Derbyshire NG20 8RY (tel: 0845 129 9200; email: info@sports-world.com; website: www.sports-direct-international.com)

Directors: Keith Hellawell, Chair; David Forsey, Chief Executive; Michael Ashley; Robert Mellors, Group Finance Director; Simon Bentley; David Singleton; Charles McCreevy; Claire Jenkins (women: 1; men: 7)

Year end	24/04/2011
Turnover	£1,599,237,000
Pre-tax profit	£118,789,000

Nature of business: Sports retailer.

Company registration number: 6035106

UK employees: 16,166

Total employees: 18,210

Charitable donations

UK cash (latest declared):	2010	£4,000
	2009	£50,000
Total worldwide:	2011	£449,600
Cash worldwide:	2011	£20,900

Corporate social responsibility

CSR committee: The board is responsible for CSR policy and procedure. No details of a UK based committee.

CSR policy: Statement taken from the 2011 annual report:

> The board recognises the importance of balancing the interests of all its key stakeholders, including customers, employees, shareholders, suppliers and the communities in which it operates. A formal corporate responsibility policy was adopted and the Board is committed to applying and developing this policy at every level of the business.

The focus of the group's corporate responsibility activities are in five key areas; employees, health and safety, customers, the environment and the community.

CSR report: CSR reporting is published within the annual report and accounts.

Applications

In writing to the correspondent.

Other information

During the year, the group made charitable cash donations of £20,896 (2010: £4,000) to the Retail Trust in the UK and to various small charities within the USA and additional non-cash items which are listed in the Corporate Responsibility Report.

The group supports the participation in a wide range of sporting activities primarily for children that would not normally have access to the expertise or equipment needed for the sport. For full details of the group's support for sporting achievement, view its corporate responsibility report published in the annual report and accounts.

Slazenger donated equipment to the value of £170,000 to the UK cricket development programme, 'Chance to Shine', which is run through the English Cricket Board's charitable arm, the Cricket Foundation. 'Chance to Shine' is a national campaign delivered through individual projects throughout England and Wales.

Dunlop also donated in the region of £100,000 of equipment during the year to the International Tennis Federation. Dunlop works in conjunction with its sponsored professional golfers, to supply clothing to their respective junior player development schemes also known as their 'Golf Schools' which provide qualified coaching and mentoring to youngsters from across the UK. Over £10,000 worth of clothing has been donated to the schemes so far.

These and other items of equipment listed in the CSR report amounted to £428,700 and we have used this figure together with the cash donation of £20,900 as the worldwide contribution.

SSE plc (formerly Scottish and Southern Energy plc)

Electricity

Correspondent: Lynn Prophet, Inveralmond House, 200 Dunkeld Road, Perth PH1 3AQ (tel: 01738 456000/ 01738 456112; email: info@sse.com; website: www.sse.com)

Directors: Rene Medori; Alistair Phillips-Davies; Richard Gillingwater; Robert Smith, Chair; Ian Marchant, Chief Executive; Susan Rice; George Alexander, Finance Director; Thomas Thune Anderson; Jeremy Beeton; Katie Bickerstaffe (women: 2; men: 8)

Year end	31/03/2012
Turnover	£31,723,900,000
Pre-tax profit	£268,500,000

Nature of business: The group's main business is the generation, transmission, distribution and supply of electricity to industrial, commercial and domestic customers; electrical and utility contracting; and gas marketing.

Company registration number: SC117119

Subsidiaries include: Scottish Hydro Electricity, SSE Services plc, Airtricity Holdings Ltd, Keadby Generation Ltd, SSE Generation Ltd, Southern Electric Contracting Ltd, Medway Power Ltd, Neos, hienergyshop, SSE Telecom

Main locations: Perth

UK employees: 19,647

Total employees: 19,647

Charitable donations

UK cash (latest declared):	2012	£6,100,000
	2010	£1,410,000
	2009	£1,001,000
	2008	£873,000
	2007	£685,000
Total UK:	2012	£6,100,000
Total worldwide:	2012	£6,100,000
Cash worldwide:	2012	£6,100,000

Community involvement

Information taken from the 2011/12 annual report:

> In support of its core values such as Service, Sustainability and Teamwork, SSE has a wide-ranging programme of community based activities. With its origins in the north of Scotland and central southern England, and with over 19,000 employees throughout the UK and Ireland, SSE can make a positive impact to hundreds of communities. The programme has four principal features:
>
> Employee volunteering, under which employees are given one day of leave to support community programmes. During 2011/12, 6,216 volunteer days were given to 570 projects in the UK and Ireland;
>
> Visitor facilities in Dorset, Cheshire and Perthshire. During 2011/12 a fundamental review of the facilities was undertaken, with opportunities for future development being identified;
>
> Financial support for community programmes near wind farm developments and in the wider regions where wind farms are developed; and
>
> Support for the work of schools through Eco Schools programmes.

The following is taken from the group's website:

> *Community funds*
>
> SSE's renewable energy projects are already bringing a range of community benefits in addition to generating clean and sustainable energy. These include increased job opportunities and improvements to the built and natural environment. In addition we have, for a number of years, established local funds as our way of saying thank you to the communities which host our wind farms and other renewable energy schemes.
>
> The time has come where we want to do even more to ensure more specific benefits from our renewable energy programme are delivered to the people and economy of Great Britain. We have therefore established a new community investment policy and, if our planned wind farms get the go-ahead, during their lifetime we expect to invest a total of over £240 million in local and regional community projects.
>
> Our current policy for wind generation in Great Britain is to invest £5,000 per megawatt of installed capacity. This is shared between a local community fund (£2,500) and a regional fund for large projects typically benefitting the local region.

For information on specific area community funds visit: www.sse.com/ Community/Funds

Advice line

There is a dedicated advice line for vulnerable customers. Careline is a free priority service that includes a team of specially trained advisers and specialist services for registered customers.

Corporate giving

During 2011/12, SSE made payments of £6.1 million to charitable and community programmes in the UK and Ireland.

The Scottish Hydro-Electric Community Trust (Scottish Registered Charity Number SC027243)

The Scottish Hydro Electric Community Trust established in 1998, is an independent charitable trust. Through it the group offers help to customers faced with high charges for an electricity connection within the Scottish Hydro Electric Power Distribution area, particularly those in rural areas. The trustees award grants to offset high connection costs in deserving individual domestic cases and for special community projects. Although not allowed to differentiate between customers or to cross-subsidise customer connection, the company is aware of the problems caused by high connection charges in rural communities.

How to apply

First you should obtain a quotation for the electricity supply from the local Scottish Hydro Electric depot. The supply must be for a domestic property or a community project. It can be for a new property or to upgrade an existing supply. Application forms are available from the company's website.

Award conditions

- The property can be for domestic use or a community project which is not profit-making
- Domestic properties must be the sole residence of the applicant
- Planning permission, where required, should have been applied for
- Applicants should be a member of the local community. Applications for holiday or second homes will not be considered
- Applicants are required to provide information on the costs, funding and purpose of their project

Levels of award

The level of award granted will be at the sole discretion of the trustees. However, the normal level of assistance when granted is 30% of the connection costs.

In kind support

The following information is from SSE's Corporate Responsibility Policy Statement:

> SSE supports educational initiatives through the provision of materials aimed at 7–11 year-olds. These comprise a comic and associated activity sheet, and an interactive website which cover topics including safety and energy efficiency. SSE also has a Museum of Electricity in Christchurch, Dorset, and Visitors' Centres at its Fiddler's Ferry Power Station and at Pitlochry Dam and Power Station in Perthshire. Entry to both these facilities is free.

Employee-led support

The group's website gives the following information:

> *Volunteering*
>
> Community at Heart' supports initiatives that are happening on our doorsteps. It's an opportunity for us to actively make a difference to things we're passionate about outside of work. Although our organisation stretches across the UK, we work locally. And supporting the communities around us is something that's important to us. The great thing is the project has few restrictions. From DIY and clean-up tasks to projects that

involve strategic planning, we can help. We've many talents across the company so we hope we'll be able to offer lots of different help to lots of different people.

Can we help you?

SSE employees are already out and about in the community helping organisations like yours to achieve their goals. Can we help you? Tell us how you could benefit from Community at Heart by downloading and completing our Volunteer request form. When you have completed the form, scan it if you can, and email it to: volunteering@sse.com; or post it to: SSE Community at Heart, Corporate Affairs, 55 Vastern Road, Reading RG1 8BU.

Commercially-led support

Sponsorship

The group's sponsorship strategy is to support community based initiatives in the areas it serves. A number of initiatives are sponsored through various brands.

Scottish Hydro

- The Hydro
- Team Scottish Hydro
- Scottish Hydro Challenge
- Scottish Hydro Camanachd Cup
- St Johnstone
- Glasgow Comedy Festival
- Royal Highland Show
- Edinburgh Military Tattoo

Southern Electric

- Southern Electric Premier Cricket League

SWALEC

- Welsh Rugby Union
- Glamorgan County Cricket Club
- SWALEC Stadium
- SWALEC Cricket Development Fund
- ISPS Handa Wales Open

SSE

- Weymouth and Portland National Sailing Academy
- Rugby Football Union
- Glasgow 2014 Commonwealth Games
- SSE Scottish Senior Golf Open

Corporate social responsibility

CSR committee: No details of a dedicated CSR committee found.

CSR policy: The following statement is taken from the group's website:

> We are committed to eight principles of corporate responsibility, focused on issues of particular significance to the company and the sectors in which we operate.
>
> The principles adopted reflect four impact areas defined by Business in the Community: workplace; environment; marketplace; and community. They have also been selected on the basis that there are clear and measurable performance indicators.
>
> ***Our principles of corporate responsibility are:***
>
> - Achieving the highest standards of health and safety performance
> - Providing opportunities for employees to be shareholders in the company
> - Being actively responsible by complying with and exceeding, where appropriate, all statutory and regulatory environmental requirements
> - Prioritising, and continually improving, environmental performance across all activities
> - Working to ensure that the quality of service delivered to customers is sector-leading
> - Responding effectively to any customer concerns about products and services
> - Ensuring that the communities which we serve have a safe and reliable supply of electricity
> - Encouraging employees to be good citizens in the communities in which they live and work

CSR report: No CSR report found but details of community contribution provided on the website.

Exclusions

The company does not support individuals, teams or organisations which have political affiliations. It also excludes advertising in charity brochures, research projects including medical research, overseas projects, animal welfare and religious appeals.

Applications

In writing to the correspondent.

Application forms for The Scottish Hydro-Electric Community Trust can be downloaded from the company's website.

St James's Place plc

Financial services

Correspondent: Mark Longbottom, The Secretary, St James's Place Foundation, 1 Tetbury Road, Cirencester, Gloucestershire GL7 1FP (tel: 01285 640302/01285 878562; email: mark.longbottom@sjp.co.uk; website: www.sjp.co.uk)

Directors: Andrew Croft, Chief Financial Officer; Ian Gascoigne; Sarah Bates; Steve Colsell; Charles Gregson, Chair; Mike Power; David Lamb; Roger Walsom; David Bellamy, Chief Executive; Vivian Bazalgette; Iain Cornish (women: 1; men: 10)

Year end	31/12/2011
Turnover	£371,500,000
Pre-tax profit	£190,800,000

Nature of business: St James's Place plc is a financial services group involved in the provision of wealth management services. Lloyds Banking Group plc now owns an approximate 60% shareholding in St James's Place. However, St James's Place operates independently of LBG and the relationship is conducted on an arm's length basis. There is currently one LBG appointed non-executive director on the St James's Place Board.

Company registration number: 3183415

Subsidiaries include: J Rothschild Assurance plc

Main locations: London

Total employees: 746

Membership: BITC

Charitable donations

UK cash (latest declared):	2011	£1,500,000
	2009	£1,333,000
	2008	£1,041,000
	2007	£1,200,000
	2006	£950,000
Total UK:	2011	£1,500,000
Total worldwide:	2011	£1,500,000
Cash worldwide:	2011	£1,500,000

Community involvement

St James's Place channels almost all of its cash contributions to charity through the **St James's Place Foundation** (Charity Commission no.1144606) established in 1992. All administrative and management costs are met by St James's Place plc. The foundation is a grantmaking charity which relies on the support it receives from the entire SJP community, including employees, partners, suppliers, fund managers and other third parties connected to the group. Over 80% of all the partners and employees make regular monthly donations out of their income or salary to the foundation and also help to raise funds from events and sponsored activities.

The St James's Place Foundation funds hundreds of projects each year and to ensure its needs can be supported it relies heavily on the generosity and actions of partners and staff to raise vital funds. Since its inception £24 million has been raised.

The foundation supports charities under the following themes:

- Cherishing the Children
- Combating Cancer
- Supporting Hospices

Since the outset, the foundation has been keen to support small to medium-sized charities that can benefit substantially from relatively small grants. The rapid growth in the funds raised has meant that the foundation has been able to extend its support in recent years through a Major Grants Programme, donating anything from £10,000 to (exceptionally) in excess of £1 million to medium-sized charities.

The vast majority of the awards made by the foundation are donated to good causes which fit in with the giving priorities chosen by the SJP community. In 2011, these themes were helping children and young people who have special needs or who are disadvantaged, supporting the hospice movement and people affected by cancer.

Cherishing the Children
The main giving theme is 'Cherishing the Children' which provides support to projects for children and young people up to the age of 25 who have a physical or mental disability or who have a life-threatening or degenerative illness. The foundation also considers applications from charities supporting children who are marginalised or disadvantaged. In 2011, a total of £2.3 million was donated to fund projects assisting children with disabilities, illness or life limiting conditions as well as those who are disadvantaged either socially or economically or are struggling to reach their full potential.

Combating Cancer
The Foundation will support projects that provide directly for people with cancer. Where organisations include other groups, 75% of beneficiaries must fit these parameters.

Supporting Hospices
Grants of up to £10,000 for items such as equipment or a contribution towards the cost of specialist nursing care or therapies are made by the foundation. The foundation assists hospices to improve the quality of care they offer people in their care and their families. If you are a UK registered charity or special needs school, you can find out more about applying for a grant on the company's website.

Corporate giving

St James's Place plc matches, on a pound for pound basis, all the money raised by the foundation. In 2011, the foundation raised in excess of £3 million and in turn donated £3.4 million to UK registered charities operating both in the UK and abroad. In addition, the foundation has conditionally committed a further £2.9 million to various charities in 2012 to 2014. We have given the corporate figure as half of the money raised by the foundation (£1.5 million).

Funds donated and raised come from the following sources: company match funding (£1.3 million); fundraising, donations and event income (£1 million); regular monthly donations from partners and employees (£600,000); Gift Aid and interest (£200,000).

Two examples of charities supported through the Cherishing the Children theme are set out below:

The National Star College is an independent specialist college working with young people who have physical, sensory or learning disabilities from across the UK. In September 2011, the new student residence at the college was officially opened. The foundation donated a total of £656,000 towards this project following on from the previous grant of £10,000 for a multi-sensory room in 2007.

Hope and Homes for Children is a UK charity operating in some of the poorest parts of the world, helping children and young people who have been orphaned or abandoned. The foundation has supported the charity over the last ten years, donating in excess of £4 million in this time. In 2011, the foundation committed £850,000 to assist Hope and Homes for Children to close an outdated orphanage in Makiriv (near Kiev). The brand new social services centre called Ray of Hope, a small family home and a mother and baby unit all provide holistic support services to hundreds of children and their families. Overall the project will impact on the lives of over 600 children and young people and their families.

Employee-led support

As well as giving regularly by covenant, many partners and employees also raise significant sums by taking part in organised events or by creating their own fundraising events, from walks and cycle rides to mountain treks, triathlons, talent competitions and quiz nights. The funds raised through their activities are then match-funded by the company.

Commercially-led support

Sponsorship:
Loughborough University Swimming Programme

Corporate social responsibility

CSR committee: St James's Place's CSR programme is overseen by the executive committee of the board, comprising the four executive directors, who in turn, delegate the management of some of the group's CSR activities to specialist subcommittees, comprising senior employees and partners from across the business. The group's charitable activities are assisted by the foundation committee.

CSR policy: Statement taken from the 2011 CSR report:

> St James's Place is committed to growing the business in a way that considers the economic, social and environmental impacts of what we do. We understand that responsible management is increasingly important to all our stakeholders – shareholders, clients, partners, employees, suppliers and the communities in which we operate.

CSR report: An informative and detailed CSR report is published within the annual report and accounts.

Exclusions

Charities with reserves of over 50% of income, administrative costs, activities primarily the responsibility of statutory agencies, replacement of lost statutory funding, research, events, advertising, holidays, contributions to large capital appeals, single faith charities, charities that are raising funds on behalf of another charity. No response to circular appeals, and no grants for advertising in charity brochures sponsorship or individuals.

Applications

The foundation will only consider applications from established charities or special needs schools for projects that meet the funding criteria.

The management committee of the St James's Place Foundation considers applications at its quarterly meetings. Application forms can be requested from the secretary.

St Modwen Properties plc

Property

Correspondent: Corporate Social Responsibility Team, Sir Stanley Clarke House, 7 Ridgeway, Quinton Business Park, Quinton, Birmingham B32 1AF (tel: 01212 229400; fax: 01212 229401; website: www.stmodwen.co.uk)

Directors: Bill Shannon, Chair; Bill Oliver, Chief Executive; Michael Dunn, Group Finance Director; David Garman; Steve Burke; Lesley James; Katherine Innes Ker; John Salmon; Simon Clarke (women: 2; men: 7)

Year end	30/11/2011
Turnover	£109,600,000
Pre-tax profit	£50,400,000

Nature of business: Property development – regeneration specialists.

Company registration number: 349201

UK employees: 234

Total employees: 234

Charitable donations

UK cash (latest declared):	2011	£11,000
	2009	£14,000
	2008	£7,000
Total UK:	2011	£11,000
Total worldwide:	2011	£11,000
Cash worldwide:	2011	£11,000

Corporate social responsibility

CSR committee: There is a CSR team.

CSR policy: The following statement is taken from the company's website:

> St Modwen takes Corporate Social Responsibility ('CSR') very seriously and as a result, ensures that it forms an integral part of everything the company does. CSR activities are grouped into three specific areas: sustainability and the environment; community and economy; St Modwen Environmental Trust.

CSR report: The company's CSR report is contained within the annual report and accounts.

Applications

In writing to the correspondent.

Other information

Direct charitable donations during the year, excluding donations made by the St Modwen Environmental Trust totalled £11,000 (2010: £12,000). The following is taken from the company's website:

> *Communities and social inclusion*
>
> Many of the projects undertaken by the company – often in partnership with local authorities and other public sector bodies – are in areas of significant deprivation. We are therefore often at the forefront of attempts to address issues of social exclusion, by providing local jobs and improving local amenities, infrastructure and affordable housing stocks. Outstanding examples in the last year included: the completion of a £27 million state-of-the-art new leisure centre at Edmonton Green (in partnership with Enfield Borough Council); and the launch of a major speculative programme for small and medium enterprises in the city of Stoke-on-Trent involving 83 units totalling 287,000 sq ft. Once a project is under way, active participation in local community activities is a key feature of the company's approach. We deploy a combination of initiatives to encourage local communities to share in the improvements brought about by its regeneration schemes, including:
>
> - Encouraging the employment of local people.
> - Incorporating opportunities for local traders in markets or small units in our retail schemes at sustainable levels of rent.
> - Subsidising local initiatives such as a Credit Union, local radio stations and community wardens.
> - Encouraging community participation in our developments. At Trentham Gardens we have a team of 46 volunteers, 6 from special needs groups, and 7 from groups supporting the rehabilitation of the long-term unemployed (including the Prince's Trust).
> - Incorporating non-intrusive, but high levels of security facilities in our schemes to reassure and protect the vulnerable.
> - Sponsoring local sport, leisure and charitable activities, including the Trentham Water Sports Association that provides access to water sports for universities, schools, disabled groups and local community initiatives, and the Dursley Bowls Club for whom we provided new changing rooms, kitchen and other clubhouse
>
> At a number of our sites, we provide free, or heavily subsidised, space and facilities for the use of local charities. These include: free use of our Trentham Gardens site for a number of charities including the Race for Life, the Donna Louise Trust, and the Douglas Macmillan Hospice, which together raised £750,000 from Trentham events; and the provision in our Edmonton Green Shopping Centre of 10,000 sq ft of heavily subsidised accommodation for an integrated network of training and employment charities and not for profit organisations, together with 15,000 sq ft of community theatre and arts-related facilities.

St Modwen Environmental Trust

Affiliated to the Government's Landfill Tax Credit Scheme and regulated by ENTRUST, it seeks to support projects where alternative funding is unlikely to be available, targeting not-for-profit organisations such as community groups and charities. In 2011, over £100,000 was committed to 11 projects across the country.

Stagecoach Group plc

Transport and communications

Correspondent: Director of Corporate Communications, 10 Dunkeld Road, Perth PH1 5TW (tel: 01738 442111/ 01738 442111; fax: 01738 643648; website: www.stagecoach.com)

Directors: Brian Souter, Chief Executive; Martin Griffiths, Finance Director; George Mathewson; Ewan Brown; Ann Gloag; Gary Watts; Helen Mahy; Phil White; Will Whitehorn (women: 2; men: 7)

Year end	30/04/2012
Turnover	£2,590,700,000
Pre-tax profit	£239,800,000

Nature of business: Principal activity: The provision of public transport services in the UK and North America.

Company registration number: SC100764

Main locations: Ilford, Chichester, Isle of Wight, Exeter, Gwent, Northampton, Perth, Sheffield, Rugby, Sunderland, Oxford, Manchester, London, Liverpool, Cowdenbeath, Cambridge, Chesterfield, Carlisle, Gloucester, Ayr

UK employees: 29,200

Total employees: 32,700

Charitable donations

UK cash (latest declared):	2012	£500,000
	2011	£600,000
	2009	£700,000
	2008	£700,000
	2007	£700,000
Total UK:	2012	£500,000
Total worldwide:	2012	£500,000
Cash worldwide:	2012	£500,000

Corporate social responsibility

CSR committee: No specific details found.

CSR policy: Statement taken from the annual report and accounts for 2011/12:

> Responsible business remains central to what we do every day – from the principles that underpin our business, to the way we support our employees and the steps we take to engage with our stakeholders.
>
> The group has published separate documents outlining its sustainability strategy and its approach to corporate social responsibility. These documents and additional information and case studies are provided on our website at: www.stagecoach.com.

CSR focuses mainly on sustainability and green issues.

CSR report: Sustainability report is published annually and available from the website. CSR is reported on within the Financial Review of the annual report and accounts.

Applications

In writing to the Stagecoach Group Community Fund.

Other information

Group companies made charitable donations of £500,000 (2010/11: £600,000) during the year to fund the work of local, national and international charities including many health charities and local community projects.

The group has provided financial support to the Eden Project in Cornwall, London's Air Ambulance and to the road safety charity, Brake. The charity, the Railway Children, which works for runaway and abandoned children who live in or around the world's railway stations, has also received support. Funding has also been given to the National Rail Chaplaincy Service, whose welfare support is available to all current and retired rail staff members, their families and the travelling public.

During the year, Stagecoach announced a new three-year partnership with businessdynamics, part of the Enterprise Education Trust, to help change young people's perception of business, and build their skills and confidence.

Stagecoach has provided backing for dozens of smaller initiatives, as well as offering match funding to complement many fundraising activities by employees for national campaigns or local good causes. Significant in kind support has been given by donating free transport and assisting with employee secondments to charitable projects.

Give As You Earn is in operation for the company's employees and the company operates a secondment programme.

Standard Chartered plc

Financial services, banking

Correspondent: The Community Relations Manager, 1 Basinghall Avenue, London EC2V 5DD (tel: 020 7885 8888; website: www.standardchartered.co.uk)

Directors: Val Gooding; Mike Rees; John Paynter; Paul Skinner; Rudy Markham; Ruth Markland; Dr Han Seung-soo; Jamie Dundas; Simon Lowth; Jaspal

Bindra; Steve Bertamini; Richard Delbridge; Annmarie Durbin; Oliver Stocken; John Pearce, Chair; Peter Sands, Group Chief Executive; Richard Meddings, Group Finance Director; V. Shankar (women: 3; men: 15)

Year end	31/12/2011
Turnover	£10,245,595,200
Pre-tax profit	£4,185,595,000

Nature of business: The group's principal activity is the provision of banking and other financial services.

Company registration number: 966425

Main locations: London

Total employees: 86,865

Membership: LBG

Charitable donations

UK cash (latest declared):	2009	£760,000
	2007	£2,250,000
	2005	£71,000
	2003	£780,000
Total worldwide:	2011	£23,292,000
Cash worldwide:	2011	£10,991,500

Community involvement

The group's donations policy is focused on those countries in Asia, Africa, the Middle East and Latin America where it has operations.

In addition to many initiatives at a global, regional and local level the group operates four major programmes; Living with HIV, Seeing is Believing, Nets for Life and Goal. These programmes are underpinned by employee volunteering activities. The following information is taken from the annual report for 2011:

> ***Community investment***
>
> Since 2003, we have reached more than 25 million people through our global campaign to tackle avoidable blindness.
>
> In 2011 we renewed our commitment to Seeing is Believing, announcing a new fundraising target of $100 million by 2020. This pledge underscores our determination to take a long-term, strategic approach to community investment.
>
> Launched by Standard Chartered in 2006, Goal uses sport, life skills and financial education to help transform the lives of adolescent girls. Operating in cities across China, India, Jordan, Nigeria and Zambia, by the end of 2011 Goal had reached 18,865 girls.
>
> In 2010 we met our Clinton Global Initiative commitment to educate one million people on HIV and AIDS – through Living with HIV, our workplace education programme, and by working with partners across the public, private and NGO sectors. This year, our dedicated network of staff volunteers have continued to help deliver education on HIV and AIDS, supporting our partner organisations and sharing our HIV education materials with others free of charge.
>
> In 2006 we joined forces with five other donors to launch Nets for Life with the aim of distributing malaria-preventing nets across 15 African countries. In 2011 we reached a total of 6.6 million nets distributed.

For further information visit www.standardchartered.com

Note: Although some support is given to UK registered charities, this is only given to those focusing on supporting work outside the United Kingdom.

Corporate giving

In 2011, a total investment of $54.4 million (£33.6 million) to charities, community organisations and causes across our footprint during the year. This sum included direct financial support of $17.8 million (£10.9 million) and indirect contributions, such as employees' time, the donation of non-monetary goods and donations worth $37.8 million (£23.3 million) raised by employees. The money raised by employees has been deducted from the global figure as is our usual practice.

The 2011 annual report states: 'In 2010 an online data collection tool was introduced, along with some standard charity on-boarding guidelines across all markets in order to collate quality-assured data about the types of initiatives we are involved in.'

It has not been possible to determine the amount given to fund the work of registered charities in the UK (given to support their work outside the UK).

In kind support

The company also supports a range of fundraising events, provides advice, secondments and scholarships.

Employee-led support

Standard Chartered encourages its people to become involved in the communities in which they work. Many participate in a wide range of charitable and community support programmes. Staff are given two days a year to take part in volunteering activities.

In 2011, globally staff were given 65,880 days of volunteering leave.

Corporate social responsibility

CSR committee: No details found.

CSR policy: CSR information taken from the 2011 Sustainability Report: 'Our community investment strategy **promotes sustainable socio-economic development** within local communities and at the same time delivers long-term value to our shareholders.'

CSR report: Sustainability report published annually.

Exclusions

Generally no support for charities working to the benefit of communities in the UK, circular appeals, advertising in charity brochures, appeals from individuals, purely denominational (religious) appeals, local appeals not in areas of company presence or large national appeals. Donations are not made to political parties.

Applications

We have been advised that applicants should note the following points:

- Ensure that the project for which you are seeking support fits the criteria set out
- Write a short summary of the project (not more than one page of A4 paper). It should then be sent to the Standard Chartered corporate affairs manager of the country where the project is taking place. Should the group then be able to consider supporting the project a more detailed proposal will be required. The company has operations in over 40 countries in Africa, Asia, the Middle East, and Latin America
- As donation plans for the year are usually agreed at the end of the year, it is advisable to submit a proposal no later than the third quarter of a given year
- It is group practice to support a limited number of charities and, where possible, to support them for a period of up to three years. The opportunity for involvement of Standard Chartered and direct support by our people is a key element in gaining funding

Standard Life

Insurance, banking

Correspondent: Gerry Grimstone, Chair, Corporate Responsibility Committee, Standard Life House, 30 Lothian Road, Edinburgh EH1 2DH (tel: 01312 252552; website: www.standardlife.com)

Directors: Gerry Grimstone, Chair; David Nish, Chief Executive; Jackie Hunt, Chief Financial Officer; Lord Blackwell; Colin Buchan; Pierre Danon; Crawford Gillies; David Grigson; Baroness McDonagh; John Paynter; Keith Skeoch; Sheelagh Whittaker (women: 3; men: 9)

Year end	31/12/2011
Turnover	£3,343,000,000
Pre-tax profit	£595,000,000

Nature of business: Life assurance, pensions, health insurance, investment management and banking.

Company registration number: SC286832

Main locations: Edinburgh

UK employees: 4,029

Total employees: 8,789

Membership: LBG

Charitable donations

UK cash (latest declared):	2011	£195,000
	2009	£343,000
	2007	£263,000
	2005	£342,000
Total UK:	2011	£195,000
Total worldwide:	2011	£1,840,000
Cash worldwide:	2011	£195,000

Corporate social responsibility

CSR committee: There is a CSR committee. Full details contained within the Corporate Governance pages of the annual report and accounts.

CSR policy: Extract taken from the group's website: CCI is making an outstanding contribution through our Community and Education programmes in each of the communities in which we operate. This policy is in place to ensure that all group companies work within the guiding principles set out in the CCI framework, focus on societal issues and objectives related to our business and the wider community, which support the three key areas of CCI focus:

- Financial capability
- Employability
- Engagement

For the full policy visit: www.standardlife.com.

CSR report: Sustainability report published online.

Exclusions

Political or religious activities, animal welfare, buildings and heritage, or sports clubs.

Applications

In writing to the correspondent.

Other information

During 2011 the company gave a total of £195,000 (2010: £259,000) in charitable contributions of which £182,000 (2010: £198,000) was given to Cancer Research UK and Alzheimer's Scotland – Action on Dementia.

The group run workshops in skills for life and during 2011 employees led 245 Step up in Life and 88 Skills for Life workshops attended by nearly 8,000 secondary school pupils.

The following is taken from the 2011 Sustainability Report:

> *2011 Highlights*
> - We invested £1.84 million in the communities we work in
> - We raised £453,310 by group-wide charity fundraising
> - Cash value of in kind contributions totalled £223,380

The group uses the LBG model to calculate its giving. Unfortunately no breakdown of the £1.84 million community investment could be found.

Standard Life Charitable Trust (SLCT) (Scottish Charity no. SC040877) is an independent charity established by Standard Live in 2009.

At first, SLCT will help people most in need of support to develop the skills they need to manage their finances. SLCT will initially focus on the following groups: young people, lone parents, young offenders and the Armed Forces. The Trust aims to support initiatives and programmes that make lasting and sustainable changes. In 2011 support was given to the Royal British Legion, Shelter and Grand Central Savings.

Sponsorship: Standard Life undertakes sponsorship including in 2011 the Royal National Institute for the Blind. It has also sponsored the printing of publicity materials and helped to publicise events.

Payroll giving: The Give As You Earn scheme is in operation.

Starbucks Coffee Company (UK) Ltd

Retail – miscellaneous

Correspondent: A Thurston, Company Secretary, Chiswick Park, 566 Chiswick High Road, London W4 5YE (tel: 020 8834 5000; website: www.starbucks.co.uk)

Directors: N. Williams; D. Calcutt; P. Engskov

Year end	02/10/2011
Turnover	£397,716,000
Pre-tax profit	(£32,854,000)

Nature of business: The retail and wholesale of gourmet coffee, tea and related products in the United Kingdom.

Company registration number: 2959325

Main locations: London

Total employees: 8,763

Membership: BITC

Charitable donations

UK cash (latest declared):	2009	£60,000
	2006	£60,000

Corporate social responsibility

CSR committee: No details found.

CSR policy: Information taken from the group's website:

> We are committed to doing business responsibly and conducting ourselves in ways that earn the trust and respect of our customers, partners and neighbors. We call this Starbucks Shared Planet – our commitment to doing business responsibly.
>
> Community Involvement: From the neighborhoods where our stores are located to the ones where our coffee is grown – we believe in being involved in the communities we're a part of. Bringing people together, inspiring change and making a difference in people's lives – it's all part of being a good neighbor. By 2015, we plan to contribute one million volunteer hours each year to our communities.

We were unable to determine the ratio of women to men on the board.

CSR report: No details found.

Applications

In writing to the correspondent, or contact your local cafe.

Other information

There is no reference to cash charitable donations or the value of community contributions either in the company's annual report and accounts or on the website, though it is clear that various community contributions are made at a cost to the company.

In 2008, Starbucks announced a five year partnership with The Prince's Trust and have raised and donated over £250,000 through work placements, employee support and fundraising. As well as working with The Prince's Trust, Starbucks began a new five year partnership with The National Literacy Trust (NLT) with the aim of making a difference to disadvantaged young people and local communities. The following information is taken from the company's website:

> ***Starbucks and the Prince's Trust***
>
> Starbucks is a platinum sponsor of the Prince's Trust Team Programme, a 12 week life skills course for at risk young people. We also have partners who volunteer to run CV workshops, host mock interviews and in over 100 of our stores we provide work experience placements. Our partners also regularly get involved with awareness and fundraising events for the Prince's Trust, both in our stores and beyond them.
>
> Recently 6 partners raised £5,000 for the Trust through the Wild Adventure Challenge – covering 100 miles in three days of hiking, biking and kayaking from Minehead to Exmouth.
>
> ***Youth Action***
>
> This programme inspires and empowers young people from across the UK and Ireland to make a difference in their communities by applying to Starbucks Youth Action for seed funding and volunteer hours from Starbucks partners. As well as supporting the young people to bring to life the projects that mean the most to them, we also offer training to young people on managing a budget, working with volunteers and project management. At the end of the first year we are supporting over 50 youth-led projects in 10 cities in the UK and Ireland. Whether it is introducing bee-hives to an inner-city park in Manchester, tackling cyber-bullying in Cardiff or supporting cheer-leaders in Kensington we are committed to supporting young people to make their communities better places to be.

Good Neighbours
We're inspiring partners (employees) and customers alike to get involved in their communities through innovative volunteer programs. For further information on how Starbucks might help your organisation, visit the website.

Stemcor Holdings Ltd

Metals

Correspondent: The Charity Committee, Level 27, CityPoint, 1 Ropemaker Street, London EC2Y 9ST (tel: 020 7775 3600; fax: 020 7775 3679; email: groupenquiries@stemcor.com; website: www.stemcor.com)

Directors: Ralph Oppenheimer, Chair; Michael Broom, Chief Financial Officer; Gerry Craggs; Graham Donnell; Philip Edmonds; David Faktor; Steve Graf; Ron Harvey; Colin Heritage; David Paul; Chris Rocker; Matthew Stock; Julian Verden; Paul Whitehead (women: 0; men: 14)

Year end	31/12/2011
Turnover	£6,253,537,000
Pre-tax profit	£65,203,000

Nature of business: The principal activity of the group is international trading in both steel products and raw materials for the production of steel.

Company registration number: 1038435

Total employees: 1,860

Charitable donations

UK cash (latest declared):	2009	£573,000
	2008	£514,000
	2007	£650,000
	2006	£464,000
Total worldwide:	2011	£905,000
Cash worldwide:	2011	£905,000

Corporate social responsibility

CSR committee: Information taken from the CR report in the 2011 annual report and accounts:

> *Responsibility for policies, systems, performance and monitoring*
> - Stemcor's executive chairman is ultimately responsible for the group's CR performance
> - The corporate affairs director, supported by the board, is responsible for developing CR policies and systems and subsequently promulgating them throughout the group
> - Individual business units are responsible for the implementation of policies and systems, and for reporting back to head office in a timely and complete fashion

CSR policy: Taken from the 2011 annual report and accounts:

> We are committed to working within the law, not only providing a healthy and fair working environment for our own employees and contractors but also extending this ethos throughout our supply chain. We strive to promote internationally accepted standards within the regions and cultures where we do business, especially as regards the education and welfare of children living in poverty.
>
> Stemcor aims to be a good neighbour in all our locations, as our licence to operate is dependent on good relations with local communities and authorities.
>
> The group is expanding in developing economies, particularly in its mining activities. As such, we will face certain expectations and requirements regarding our social investment and will build on our experiences gained in India.
>
> Our group's work with socially focused organisations is themed on education, health, housing, disaster relief and the environment and is designed to achieve far-reaching impact in the areas in which we operate.
>
> We aim to address issues that can have an impact in areas related to our core business objectives and seek measurable progress reports regarding these projects. At our locations in India we have, since day one, had an active involvement with local stakeholders and are committed to regular and constructive dialogue.

CSR report: A Corporate Responsibility report is published within the annual report and accounts.

Applications

In writing to the correspondent.

Other information

The following extract is taken from the company's annual report and accounts for the year 2011:

> It is the group's policy to set aside a percentage of its profits for charitable and social investment purposes. Education, health, community support, disaster relief and the environment are the group's key charitable objectives. During 2011 the group allocated approximately £905,000 (2010: £900,000) to carefully selected charitable partners. Major funding included supporting the following initiatives:
> - Sponsorship of a maternal literacy and early childhood development programme in Cairo, Egypt
> - A Literacy Boost programme in Timor, Indonesia, focused on assessments, teacher training and community action to significantly improve children's core reading skills
> - The first year of a three year commitment to an Early Steps to School Success (ESSS) programme in poor rural communities in southern states of the USA. ESSS provides education services to children from birth to age five, support to parents and ongoing training to community educators
> - Sponsorship of science students from low-income families in the UK, via the Ironmongers' Foundation
> - A Girls Education project in Odisha, India, sponsored by CARE. The group's three years of past support has established a solid level of sustainability, allowing for an expansion of this initiative for which the group is providing two more years of major funding
> - Support for Magic Bus in creating equal opportunities for children and youth living in some of the most vulnerable circumstances in India
> - Emergency relief funding for the outstanding work that Medecins Sans Frontieres does, often in hazardous areas of the world

Many smaller donations were also made, including matching grants for the individual fundraising efforts of Stemcor staff around the world. Unfortunately it has not been possible to determine how much was given in the UK alone.

Steria Ltd

Computer software

Correspondent: Company Secretary, Three Cherry Trees Lane, Hemel Hempstead, Hertfordshire HP2 7AH (tel: 0845 601 8877; fax: 01442 884335; website: www.steria.com/uk)

Directors: J. P. Torrie; D. S. Ahluwaha; L. P. C. Lemaire; J. J. Moran; Mme S. C. M. Dangu (women: 1; men: 4)

Year end	31/12/2011
Turnover	£484,733,000
Pre-tax profit	£35,017,000

Nature of business: Formerly trading as the Xansa Group, the company is now part of the Steria Group. Principal activities are as an outsourcing and technology company.

Company registration number: 4077975

Main locations: Bedford, Manchester, Northampton, Southampton, Reading, Edinburgh, Holborn

Total employees: 3,538

Charitable donations

UK cash (latest declared):	2011	£86,000
	2009	£74,105
	2007	£74,105
	2006	£68,307
	2005	£102,882
Total UK:	2011	£86,000
Total worldwide:	2011	£86,000
Cash worldwide:	2011	£86,000

Corporate social responsibility

CSR committee: No details.

CSR policy: No specific policy for Steria Ltd.

CSR report: No published report.

Applications

In writing to the correspondent.

Other information

In 2011, £86,000 was donated to charities. We do not have any details of the beneficiaries. We do know that in the past the company had a partnership with Scope and that support is offered to a range of charitable organisations involved in the community/social welfare; youth/children; computing and education.

Matched funds are also given to support employee fundraising efforts.

SThree plc

Business services

Correspondent: Corporate Social Responsibility Team – Communities, 5th Floor, GPS House, 215–227 Great Portland Street, London W1W 5PN (tel: 020 7268 6000; fax: 020 7268 6001; email: investor-enquiries@sthree.com; website: www.sthree.com)

Directors: Russell Clements, Chief Executive Officer; Gary Elden; Alex Smith, Chief Financial Officer; Steve Hornbuckle, Company Secretary; Clay Brendish, Chair; Tony Ward; Alicja Lesniak; Paul Bowtell; Nadhim Zahawi (women: 1; men: 8)

Year end	27/11/2011
Turnover	£542,450,000
Pre-tax profit	£30,299,000

Nature of business: SThree is a specialist permanent and contract staffing business.

Company registration number: 3805979

UK employees: 1,017

Total employees: 3,059

Charitable donations

UK cash (latest declared):	2009	£51,000
	2008	£81,000
Total worldwide:	2011	£48,000
Cash worldwide:	2011	£48,000

Corporate social responsibility

CSR committee: Taken from the annual report and accounts for 2011:

> The board pays due regard to environmental, health and safety and employment responsibilities and devotes appropriate resources to monitoring compliance with and improving standards. The chief executive officer has responsibility for these areas at board level, ensuring that the group's policies are upheld and providing the necessary resources. Further information is contained in the Corporate Responsibility Report, whilst information on employee share plans and share ownership is contained in the directors' Remuneration Report.

CSR policy: The following statement is taken from the company's website:

> ***CSR – Strategy***
>
> Recognising and developing talent is at the heart of everything we do. Corporate responsibility is no exception. By concentrating on what we do best, we can contribute more.
>
> Day in, day out, we match skilled individuals to unique business needs. By doing so, we help society by fostering economic sustainability and growth.
>
> Our basic environmental and social responsibilities include helping to tackle climate change and treating all our stakeholders – candidates, clients, employees, shareholders, suppliers – with due respect and courtesy. The more we concentrate on hiring and training the right people the better we will be able to meet these responsibilities.
>
> Last, but not least, by encouraging our people to volunteer their skills and enthusiasm, we believe we can help more than just the communities in which we live and work. We also help our employees develop their own talents by working with people from different backgrounds in new and unfamiliar circumstances.

CSR report: An annual report is published.

Applications

In writing to the correspondent.

Other information

During the period the group made charitable donations of £48,000 (2010: £65,000). We have no details of beneficiary groups. The following information is provided by the company:

> Building on our previous work with young people who are not in education, employment or training, we made 'Employability and Raising Aspiration' a central focus for our community engagement in 2011.
>
> ***Activities span the following areas:***
>
> *Volunteering*
>
> We continued to work closely with Time & Talents for Westminster, and commenced new relationships with City Action and East London Business Alliance (ELBA) to support our volunteering goals in London.
>
> *Corporate giving and fundraising*
>
> For the past three years, we have supported SOS Children's Villages, an orphan and abandoned children's charity that works in over 120 countries. Our contribution in 2011 brought the three-year total to over £200,000. This has funded projects in Africa, China, Haiti, India and Syria.
>
> A particular 2012 highlight saw one of our employees run five marathons within the year to raise money for SOS Children's Villages and become their Supporter of the Month.
>
> *University Scholarships*
>
> In line with our aspiration to support Science, Technology, Engineering and Maths (STEM) talent pipelines, we are funding four scholarships at the University of Birmingham, and two at the University of Manchester. All six young people are being supported through Access programmes for students from disadvantaged backgrounds.

Charity partner: SOS Children's Villages.

J Stobart and Sons Ltd

Transport and communications

Correspondent: (See 'Applications'), Newlands Mill, Hesket Newmarket, Wigton, Cumbria CA7 8HP (tel: 01697 478261)

Directors: R. J. Stobart; R. A. Stobart; P. J. Stobart; L. E. Rigg (women: 1; men: 3)

Year end	31/12/2010
Turnover	£14,251,520
Pre-tax profit	£560,453

Nature of business: The manufacture and retail of animal feeding stuffs.

Company registration number: 783738

Main locations: Carlisle

Total employees: 20

Charitable donations

UK cash (latest declared):	2010	£625,000
	2008	£890,000
	2007	£785,000
	2006	£700,000
	2005	£700,000
Total UK:	2010	£625,000
Total worldwide:	2010	£625,000
Cash worldwide:	2010	£625,000

Community involvement

The company channels its support through **The Stobart Newlands Charitable Trust** (Charity Commission no. 328464)

The objective of the trust is to make grants to charities and charitable purposes with funds provided by the company. It aims to provide financial support mainly to Christian religious and missionary bodies. It has a policy of supporting various charities on an annual basis but has not entered into any guarantees or commitments.

The trust relies solely on donations from its trustees and J. Stobart and Sons Ltd to fund its objective and does not engage in external fundraising.

The trust also owns a chapel building which it leases to the Hesket New Market Free Church Trust whose charitable object is to promote the Christian religion.

Corporate giving

In 2010 the company made charitable donations of £625,000, all of which went to the associated family trust of which the directors of the company are also trustees.

The Stobart Newlands Charitable Trust

For the year ended 31 December 2010, the trust made 28 grants of £1,000 or more to various charities totalling over £864,000, the majority to Christian, religious and missionary bodies. Major beneficiaries were: World Vision

(£250,000); Operation Mobilisation (£175,000); and London City Mission and Open Air Mission (£26,000 each).

Corporate social responsibility

CSR committee: No details.

CSR policy: None published.

CSR report: None published.

Exclusions

No grants for individuals.

Applications

In writing to: Mr Ronnie Stobart, The Stobart Newlands Charitable Trust, Mill Croft, Newlands, Hesket Newmarket, Wigton, Cumbria CA7 8HP. Note, however, that unsolicited causes are unlikely to succeed.

Stobart Group

Logistics

Correspondent: Sponsorship and Charitable Donations, Stobart Group, Solway Business Centre, Carlisle, Cumbria CA6 4BY (tel: 01925 605400; email: charity@stobartgroup.com; website: www.stobartgroup.co.uk)

Directors: Andrew Tinkler, Chief Executive Officer; Rodney Baker-Bates, Chair; Michael Kayser; Jesper Kjaedegaard; Ben Whawell, Chief Financial Officer; Richard Butcher; Alan Kelsey; Paul Orchard-Lisle; David Beever (women: 0; men: 9)

Year end	29/02/2012
Turnover	£551,921,000
Pre-tax profit	£30,546,000

Nature of business: Stobart Group has an airport operating business, a biomass products supply business, a transport and distribution business, a property investment and development business and an infrastructure and civil engineering business.

Company registration number: 39117

Total employees: 5,615

Charitable donations

UK cash (latest declared):	2012	£223,000
	2010	£30,000
Total UK:	2012	£223,000
Total worldwide:	2012	£223,000
Cash worldwide:	2012	£223,000

Corporate social responsibility

CSR committee: Chief Financial Officer, Ben Whawell takes board level responsibility for developing and implementing the group's policy and approach for corporate responsibility. This includes its arrangements for matters relating to people, society and the environment.

CSR policy: Policy statement taken from the group's website:

> Stobart Group is committed to continuing with annual charitable donations and to encouraging staff and business units to support and develop initiatives within the communities in which they operate. The Group will support the requirements of the community in the local areas of its business, alongside the donations that the group makes annually to its chosen charity.

CSR report: An annual CSR report is published online.

Exclusions

The Group states:

> We do not regularly support the following:
> - Requests from external parties
> - Funding for overseas visits or trips
> - Funding for arts/media projects e.g. student films, exhibitions etc
> - Projects that only benefit one person

Applications

In writing to the correspondent. Due to the volume of applications the group receives staff will only respond to successful applications.

Other information

During the year 2011/12 the company gave £223,000 in cash donations to various charities including: sponsorship of the Emeralds and Ivy Ball supporting Cancer Research UK; Carlisle Youth Zone (£50,000); and £23,000 in matched funding for various charities including Alzheimer's Society, Air Ambulances, Kidscape and Movember.

The company supports its local communities and national good causes, through sponsorship, donations and direct involvement. There is a varied programme in place, supporting worthwhile charities such as local hospices and larger, national charities.

> *Charitable giving and sponsorship*
> Annually Stobart Group provides support to a large number of charities, fundraisers and good causes. On a daily basis Stobart receives many requests for sponsorship, transport, vehicle, monetary and raffle prize donations from equally deserving causes but unfortunately we cannot offer help to all. Below are some of the guidelines that we follow.
>
> *Charity of the year*
> A key focus for charitable giving is the support we give to our charity of the year. Each year we enter into a partnership to support a chosen charity.
>
> Cancer Research UK is Stobart Group's chosen charity.
>
> To be considered as Stobart charity of the year please submit a short written application to the address below. Proposals will be considered during the latter part of each year.
>
> *Sponsorship and donation*
> Stobart Group prefers to support local community groups and charitable activity. As a result of the Group having a number of depots across the UK and Ireland, we choose to do this by supporting charities via our employees. This also encourages employees to become involved in local charities and their community.

Directors William Stobart and Andrew Tinkler are involved with Ronan Keating's annual 'Emeralds and Ivy Ball' which is held in association with Cancer Research UK; Stobart Group's Charity of the Year in 2011. The group's involvement resulted in £120,000 in total donations from individuals to be included on a specially liveried unit with the addition of £150,000 direct sponsorship for the event. William and Andrew are also responsible for an annual donation to Carlisle Youth Zone of £50,000. The project provides social opportunities for the young people of Cumbria.

Stobart Group has been an avid sponsor of various charitable events in 2011, including the support of The Lesters awards which raises money for the Injured Jockeys' Fund. The glittering Hilton Birmingham Metropole awards ceremony which celebrated the achievements of jockeys around the globe, took place in front of over 400 sporting stars, celebrities and guests. As sponsor of The Lesters, Stobart Group displayed two cabs in the awards room on the night and guests took part in a raffle for the coveted chance to name them. All the proceeds from the evening went to the Injured Jockeys Fund.

In kind giving:
Donations of prizes and sponsored tables at Chico's Rainbow Child Foundation Ball assisted in the raising of £27,000 at the event which was held in November at Manchester's prestigious Lowry Hotel. The Rainbow Child Foundation aims to provide self-sustaining, eco-friendly Rainbow Child villages for under-privileged children around the world.

Staff volunteering:
Stobart Group actively promotes employee engagement in its charitable giving, and all staff are entitled to apply for a company donation for their chosen cause. In 2011 alone more than £23,000 was donated through this scheme, covering a wide range of charities supporting the Alzheimer's Society, Air Ambulances, Kidscape, Movember and many more.

Campaigns:
Stobart Group have supported the Madeleine McCann Campaign by creating awareness of the campaign through the livery on one of the trailers 'tramping' around the UK.

Professorship:
A Stobart Professor of Logistics has been created through a partnership with the University of Cumbria, launching a groundbreaking national project for logistics and transport.

Levi Strauss (UK) Ltd

Clothing manufacture

Correspondent: The Company Secretary, Swann Valley, Northampton NN4 9BA (tel: 01604 581501; fax: 01604 599815; website: www.levistrauss.com)

Directors: Stephen Neal, Chair; Charles Bergh, Chief Executive; Robert Haas; Fernando Aguirre; Vanessa Castagna; Robert Eckert; Peter Haas; Leon Level; Patricia Salas Pineda; Blake Jorgensen; Anne Rohosy; Aaron Beng-Keong Boey (women: 3; men: 9)

Year end	27/11/2011
Turnover	£3,100,000,000
Pre-tax profit	£128,000,000

Nature of business: Clothing marketing and sales under the Levi's brand.

Company registration number: 892419

Main locations: Northampton

Total employees: 17,000

Charitable donations

UK cash (latest declared):	2009	£2,800
	2007	£465
	2006	£560
	2005	£161,300

Corporate social responsibility

CSR committee: There was no evidence of a separate CSR Committee.

CSR policy: This information was obtained from the company's annual report:

> In the spirit of our founder, Levi Strauss & Co. has been giving back to communities for more than 150 years through employee volunteering, corporate sponsorship and the Levi Strauss Foundation. Our employee volunteer and corporate sponsorship programs mobilize resources and create authentic partnerships in communities around the globe to address HIV/AIDS, equality and sustainability. These efforts create positive impact in communities where we work, and also help to increase our reputation and build value for our brands. In addition to our corporate giving efforts, the Levi Strauss Foundation, founded in 1952, is driving pioneering social change that brings our values courage, empathy, originality and integrity to life in communities around the world.
>
> The foundation focuses on making a difference in three issues Asset Building, Workers' Rights and HIV/AIDS, while also supporting programs that advance the fields of philanthropy and human rights.

CSR report: There was no evidence of a separate CSR report.

Exclusions

No support is given to: individuals; capital or endowment campaigns; building work; sports teams or competitions; advertising; event sponsorship; sectarian or religious activities; or political campaigns or causes.

Applications

Due to the proactive stance taken by the Levi Strauss Foundation in finding organisations to support, unsolicited grant requests, product donation requests or charitable sponsorship requests are not accepted.

Other information

No definitive figure was found for charitable donations for this financial year.

Philanthropic support is given by Levi Strauss and Co. through its two foundations:

Levi Strauss Foundation

The Levi Strauss Foundation is focused on making a difference on three issues, all of which are rooted in the values of Levi Strauss and Co.:

- HIV/AIDS
- Asset Building
- Workers Rights

During 2010/11, fundraising efforts included:

- Following the devastating earthquake in Haiti, the Levi Strauss Foundation provided $100,000 in grant support to three organisations working on immediate relief, Oxfam, Partners in Health and the Global Fund for Women. Employees globally supported relief efforts through the company's matching gift program
- Following heavy rains in Indonesia and the failure of the Situ Gintung dam, which devastated the local community, employees led a month-long fundraising campaign that ultimately raised approximately $3,000 to aid recovery efforts
- The Levi Strauss Foundation also provided a $50,000 grant to the United Nations High Commissioner for Refugees

The Red Tab Foundation

From emergency aid to financial literacy and asset building to scholarship programs, *the Red Tab Foundation* provides support to Levi Strauss and Co. employees, retirees and their families around the world.

The substantial contribution made by Levi Strauss and Co. through its American foundations is detailed at: www.levistrauss.com/about/foundations.

The company may occasionally make some of their products (jeans) available to charitable organisations. Donations of furniture, machines, and the like that are no longer in use may also be made to support the work of an organisation.

Staff are allowed one company day off for activity of community benefit and encouraged to become volunteers in their own time. The company operates a matching scheme for employee fundraising.

STV Group plc

Media

Correspondent: Jane E A Tames, Secretary, Pacific Quay, Glasgow G51 1PQ (tel: 01413 003670; website: www.stvplc.tv)

Directors: Richard Findlay, Chair; Rob Woodward, Chief Executive; George Watt; David Shearer; Vasa Babic; Jamie Matheson; Michael Jackson (women: 0; men: 7)

Year end	31/12/2011
Turnover	£102,000,000
Pre-tax profit	£14,000,000

Nature of business: Formerly Scottish Media Group plc, STV Group plc is a Scottish media company.

Company registration number: SC042391

Brands include: Grampian TV, Primesight, Virgin Radio

Main locations: Glasgow

UK employees: 387

Charitable donations

UK cash (latest declared):	2011	£93,000
	2009	£19,000
	2008	£15,000
	2007	£29,000
Total UK:	2011	£93,000
Total worldwide:	2011	£93,000
Cash worldwide:	2011	£93,000

Corporate social responsibility

CSR committee: There was no evidence of a separate CSR Committee.

CSR policy: The STV Group aim to use its media presence in Scotland for the common good. The group recognises the need to give something positive back to the communities in which it operates.

CSR report: There was no evidence of a separate CSR report.

Exclusions

Sponsorship is not undertaken. No support for fundraising events, advertising in charity brochures, purely denominational (religious) appeals, local appeals not in areas of company presence, large national appeals or overseas projects.

Applications

In writing to the correspondent.

Other information

In 2011, STV gave nearly £93,000 in charitable donations.

STV collaborated with The Hunter Foundation to launch STV Appeal 2011. Through a dedicated campaign, engaging with corporate Scotland, the Scottish government and STV viewers, over £1.2 million was raised for children and young people affected by poverty in Scotland. The company worked closely with Arbelour; Action for Children; Barnardo's Scotland; Children 1st; Save the Children Scotland; and One Parent Families Scotland to create long-term sustainable change.

STV has also worked with pupils from high schools in Ullapool, Galrioch, Plockton and Portree as part of NESTA's Idiscover educational programme. The programme aims to develop the skills and talents of young people for their future growth.

The company also continued its work with STV Local- a network of hyper-local news and information websites for communities across Scotland. STV Local works closely with individuals, groups and organisations in the towns which they serve. It offers charities and organisations their own dedicated page on the website, giving these groups a way to effectively communicate with their hometown.

Swann-Morton Ltd

Manufacturing

Correspondent: Company Secretary, Owlerton Green, Sheffield S6 2BJ (tel: 01142 344231; fax: 01142 314966; website: www.swann-morton.com)

Directors: M. I. Hirst; R. J. Whiteley; C. L. Taylor

Year end	31/10/2011
Turnover	£18,139,916
Pre-tax profit	£368,534

Nature of business: The manufacture of fine edge blades for both surgical and industrial purposes.

Company registration number: 696744

UK employees: 318

Total employees: 318

Charitable donations

UK cash (latest declared):	2011	£4,300
	2009	£45,000
	2008	£45,800
	2007	£53,600
Total UK:	2011	£4,300
Total worldwide:	2011	£4,300
Cash worldwide:	2011	£4,300

Corporate social responsibility

CSR committee: There does not appear to be a CSR committee.

CSR policy: None published.

We were unable to determine the ratio of women to men on the board.

CSR report: None published.

Applications

In writing to the correspondent.

Other information

In 2010/11, the company made charitable donations totalling £4,300. The company's foundation received £40,000 in gift aid.

Swann-Morton Foundation (Charity Commission no. 271925)

The aims and objectives of the foundation are as follows:

- The purchase of medical instruments or equipment for the use by or for patients with infirmity
- The promotion of education and research in medicine and surgery aimed at the relief of suffering or handicap
- For the encouragement of scholarship at schools, colleges and universities

In 2010/11 the foundation had an income of £50,600 and made grants totalling £53,000. Beneficiaries included: Sheffield Children's Hospital and St Luke's Hospice (£3,500 each); and Charles Clifford Dental Hospital, Jessop Hospital for Women and Northern General Hospital (£3,000 each).

John Swire and Sons Ltd

Marine, aviation, property

Correspondent: J L Farmery, Company Secretary, Swire House, 59 Buckingham Gate, London SW1E 6AJ (tel: 020 7834 7717; fax: 020763003; website: www.swire.com)

Directors: J. W. J. Hughes-Hallett; Baroness Dunn; N. A. H. Fenwick; B. N. Swire; J. S. Swire; M. B. Swire; W. J. Wemyss; R. B. Woods

Year end	31/12/2010
Turnover	£5,183,000,000
Pre-tax profit	£1,396,000,000

Nature of business: Principal activities: marine including ship-owning and operating, aviation (via Cathay Pacific Airways), cold storage and road transport, industrial and trading activities, plantations and property. The company owns a stake in the tea trader, James Finlay.

Company registration number: 133143

Main locations: London

Total employees: 73,021

Charitable donations

UK cash (latest declared):	2010	£602,000
	2008	£805,000
	2007	£635,000
	2006	£634,000
	2005	£508,000
Total UK:	2010	£602,000
Total worldwide:	2010	£5,261,000
Cash worldwide:	2010	£5,261,000

Corporate giving

In 2010, the company made charitable donations in the UK of £602,000 (2009: £594,000). The annual report states: The Swire Group and certain charitable trusts made contributions for world-wide charitable and educational purposes of £5,261,000. We have no details of the organisations which received support directly from the company.

Although there are several trusts with connections to the company – John Swire (1989) Charitable Trust (Charity Commission no. 802142), the Swire Educational Trust (Charity Commission no. 328366) and the Swire Charitable Trust (Charity Commission no. 270726) – as the latter receives almost all of its income from the company it is to this that we refer.

The Swire Charitable Trust

The trust makes grants for charitable purposes in the UK and in 2010 made awards totalling over £561,000. Beneficiary groups included: National Maritime Museum (£52,500); Fields in Trust, King James Bible Trust, Marine Society and Sea Cadets (£25,000 each); Cancer Vaccine Institute, Marine Stewardship Council and Multiple Sclerosis (£10,000 each); Children in Crisis and Mobile Art School in Kenya (£5,000 each); British Heart Foundation and International Spinal Research Trust (£2,500 each), and London's Air Ambulance (£1,000).

Corporate social responsibility

CSR committee: The company's Sustainable Development Policy section on the website states:

> Given the wide diversity of the group's business portfolio, implementation of the policy is handled on a company-by-company basis and is overseen by the directors appointed to the company by Swire; this is a core responsibility of each company's management team.

CSR policy: The Sustainable Development Policy section continues:

> The Swire group's Sustainable Development Policy commits the group to working on the environmental, health and safety, employment, supply chain and community issues that our operations affect, and to working with other parties to promote sustainable development in the industries in which we operate.

For information on the specific actions taken by individual companies to implement Swire's Sustainable Development Policy, see: www.swirepacific.com.

The following extract is from the *John Swire and Sons Sustainability Report 2011*: 'As members of the community, we endeavour to understand the needs of others through dialogue with stakeholders. Ultimately, we want to make a positive contribution, and add value in the way that we run our business.'

Much of the company's community contribution is aimed at minimising the impact of the company's operations.

Unable to determine the ratio of women to men on the board.

CSR report: The major operating companies within the Swire group annually publish their own Sustainable Development reports. Details can be found on the group's website.

Applications

In writing to the correspondent saying how the funds could be used and what would be achieved.

Synergy Health plc

Healthcare

Correspondent: Corporate Social Responsibility Team, Ground Floor Stella, Windmill Hill Business Park, Whitehill Way, Swindon, Wiltshire SN5 6NX (tel: 01772 299900; fax: 01772 299901; email: enquiries@synergyhealthplc.com; website: www.synergyhealthplc.com)

Directors: Robert Lerwill, Chair; Richard Steeves, Group Chief Executive; Gavin Hill, Group Finance Director; Duncan K. Nichol; Constance Baroudel (women: 1; men: 4)

Year end	03/04/2011
Turnover	£287,314,000
Pre-tax profit	£36,733,000

Nature of business: Synergy Health delivers a range of specialist outsourced services to healthcare providers and other customers concerned with health management.

Company registration number: 3355631

Total employees: 4,301

Charitable donations

UK cash (latest declared):	2011	£17,000
	2010	£5,000
	2009	£8,000
Total UK:	2011	£17,000
Total worldwide:	2011	£17,000
Cash worldwide:	2011	£17,000

Corporate social responsibility

CSR committee: The following information is from the company's 2011 annual report:

> In early 2011, we developed a group CEO-led team to implement a CSR Programme, which consists of representatives from different areas of our business. To ensure the standards are cascaded effectively throughout our business, the plc and senior executive boards are updated on progress within the programme on a regular basis. In the past year, a second team has worked on a project to link Synergy's core values to its brand, with the objective of creating a sustainable culture and leadership environment.

CSR policy: Information taken from the company's CSR report:

> Synergy is expanding its engagement with issues of CSR, recognising the importance of managing day-to-day activities in a responsible way, being accountable for the impact of all operational activities on the environment and our local communities, and creating a working environment in which our colleagues can flourish. CSR is a business approach that creates value by embracing opportunities and managing risks deriving from economic, environmental and social developments whilst maintaining global competitiveness and brand reputation.
>
> *Senior leadership*
>
> This year we welcomed Constance Baroudel to the plc board as the first of two appointments that will see a more appropriate balance between men and women on the board. Within our Senior Leadership Community, which represents our top global 65 leaders, women represent just 17% of the community. Whilst we are not intending to set targets per se, we are putting in place support networks to ensure that all of our people who have senior leadership potential are given adequate support and to ensure that there are not artificial barriers that would impede their career development within Synergy. We take a similar view towards ethnicity, where we believe we would benefit from a much more diverse population of senior leaders.

CSR report: Contained within the annual report and accounts.

Applications

In writing to the correspondent.

Other information

During the period the group made charitable donations totalling £17,000 (2010: £5,000).The following information is taken from the company's CSR report contained within the 2010/11 annual report and accounts:

> *Community relationships*
>
> There are many examples of Synergy's employees organising charitable events internally. The Company has also supported charitable activities such as donating funds for important healthcare equipment. There is scope for further development within this area, which will start by the implementation of a company charity to be chosen by employees. To ensure the partnership is effective, the company is donating employee time for charitable activities. Even though there will be a designated company charity, we will continue to support employees who are involved in other fundraising exercises. In the past individual facilities have arranged fundraising events and we are encouraging this to continue in the future.

Synthomer plc (formerly Yule and Catto Co.)

Building/construction, chemicals and plastics, pharmaceuticals

Correspondent: Richard Atkinson, Company Secretary, Central Road, Temple Fields, Harlow, Essex CM20 2BH (tel: 01279 442791; fax: 01279 641360; email: info@synthomer.com; website: www.synthomer.com)

Directors: N. A. Johnson, Chair; A. M. Whitfield, Chief Executive; D. C. Blackwood; The Hon. A. G. Catto; Dr J. Jansz; I. Macpherson; Dato' Lee Hau Hian; J. K. Maiden; J. Chen (women: 0; men: 9)

Year end	31/12/2011
Turnover	£1,060,000,000
Pre-tax profit	£85,000,000

Nature of business: The principal activities of the company are in the areas of speciality chemicals, pharmaceuticals and building products.

Company registration number: 98381

Main locations: Harlow

Total employees: 2,539

Charitable donations

UK cash (latest declared):	2011	£54,000
	2009	£56,000
	2008	£51,500
	2007	£54,000
	2006	£92,000
Total UK:	2011	£54,000
Total worldwide:	2011	£54,000
Cash worldwide:	2011	£54,000

Corporate social responsibility

CSR committee: There was no evidence of a separate CSR Committee.

CSR policy: There was limited information available regarding CSR Policy.

CSR report: There was no evidence of a separate CSR report.

Exclusions

No support for overseas projects, political appeals, or religious appeals.

Applications

In writing to the correspondent, but note that as the company has charities which it supports regularly, unsolicited applications are unlikely to be successful.

Other information

In 2011, the company made cash donations of £54,000. No details of recipients could be found but support has been given in the past to: Harlow Community Trust, St Clare Hospice Care Trust, Help the Aged, Age Concern – England, and Barnardo's.

The company supports an established list of charities, mainly in the fields of children and youth, elderly people, medical research, and sickness/disability charities. Both local and national charities (in the Harlow area) are supported.

Tata Steel Europe Ltd

Metals

Correspondent: Company Secretary, 30 Millbank, London SW1P 4WY (tel: 020 7717 4444; fax: 020 7717 4455; website: www.tatasteeleurope.com)

Directors: B. Muthuraman; K. Chatterjee; I. Hussain; K. Köehler, Chief Executive; A. Robb, Chair; F. Royle; N. K. Misra; J. Schraven; H. Nerurkar

Year end	31/03/2012
Turnover	£10,111,000,000
Pre-tax profit	(£846,000,000)

Nature of business: The manufacture and sale of steel.

Company registration number: 5957565

Main locations: York, Wolverhampton, Rotherham, Port Talbot, Newport

Charitable donations

UK cash (latest declared):	2012	£550,000
Total UK:	2012	£550,000
Total worldwide:	2012	£550,000
Cash worldwide:	2012	£550,000

Community involvement

Support in the UK is given for cultural, social, educational and sporting activities that contribute to the well-being of residents, both in the immediate vicinity of plants and elsewhere.

Tata's information on its significant worldwide community involvement can be found at: www.tatasteel.com/corporate-citizenship/community.asp

Charity Partnership: The Tata group has been a corporate partner for the British Triathlon since 2006.

Corporate giving

In 2010/11 the group gave £550,000 in charitable donations within the UK. The most significant support during this year was for the Queen Elizabeth Prize for Engineering Foundation.

Employee-led support

Tata Kids of Steel: This is run over the summer months at locations all around the UK, enabling children to experience the three sports of swimming, cycling and running. Since 2007 more than 35,000 children from almost 400 schools have had the opportunity to experience triathlon.

The group supports a number of sports clubs in the UK and the Netherlands to encourage participation, and to help employees maintain and improve their health. These include 'Start to Run' workshops organised by the Tata Steel Runners Club.

Through voluntary work, employees also apply their skills in practical ways for the community.

Individual fundraising activities are encouraged.

Corporate social responsibility

CSR committee: No details relevant to the UK.

CSR policy: The group's website states: 'Every major business has an impact on the communities and societies in which it operates. In all its operations throughout the world, Tata Steel contributes to local and regional economic and social development in myriad ways.'

We were unable to determine the ratio of women to men on the board.

CSR report: An annual CSR report is published online.

Exclusions

No support for purely denominational appeals, small purely local appeals not in areas of company presence, appeals from individuals, fundraising events or circulars.

Applications

Applications (including sponsorships) should be made in writing to the correspondent, although local appeals should be made through local offices.

Tate and Lyle plc

Sugar refiners

Correspondent: The Corporate Responsibility Manager, 1 Kingsway, London WC2B 6AT (tel: 020 7257 2100; website: www.twww.tateandlyle.com)

Directors: Peter Gershon, Chair; Javed Ahmed, Chief Executive; Tim Lodge, Chief Financial Officer; Liz Alrey; William Camp; Evert Henkes; Douglas Hurt; Ajal Puri; Robert Walker; Robert Gibber (women: 1; men: 9)

Year end	31/03/2012
Turnover	£3,088,000,000
Pre-tax profit	£379,000,000

Nature of business: Principal activities are: the processing of carbohydrates to provide a range of sweetener and starch products and animal feed; and bulk storage. The company's UK sugar refinery is in London.

Company registration number: 76535

Total employees: 4,636

Charitable donations

UK cash (latest declared):	2012	£6,000
	2011	£19,000
	2009	£699,000
	2008	£642,000
	2007	£687,000
Total UK:	2012	£6,000
Total worldwide:	2012	£308,000
Cash worldwide:	2012	£308,000

Corporate social responsibility

CSR policy: The company's website gives the following information regarding its community involvement outlook:

> We have just completed a review of our community involvement objectives and programme. We have looked at our community work of recent years – talking to colleagues who have been involved in it across the business from the United States, through Europe, to Asia – and asking how we can do more to help our communities around the world. We have also taken some expert, external advice on this matter.
>
> The result is that going forward we shall be implementing a revitalised community involvement programme – Tate & Lyle in the Community – building on our work to date and focusing on specific objectives in the areas of education, well-being and environment. We will:
>
> - Achieve a wider geographical reach across our global business;
> - Develop international as well as local community programmes; and
> - Make a larger financial commitment to this important area
>
> Tate & Lyle recognises that being a responsible corporate citizen includes having a strong and forward-looking community involvement programme.

CSR report: The CSR report is published within the annual report and accounts.

Exclusions

No support is given to circular appeals, advertising in charity brochures, individuals, purely denominational (religious) appeals, local appeals not in areas of company presence, animal welfare, political appeals, sport or large national appeals.

Applications

In writing to the correspondent.

Other information

In the year ended 31 March 2012 charitable donations were £308,000 (2011: £346,000) of which £6,000 (2011: £19,000) was donated within the UK. The website states: 'The year-on-year decrease was a key item in the review of our community involvement programme. In the year to 31 March 2013 we will make a significant increase in our financial commitment to community work.'

In the UK support is given to health and well-being charities.

Taylor Wimpey plc

Building/construction

Correspondent: Charity Committee, Gate House, Turnpike Road, High Wycombe, Buckinghamshire HP12 3NR (tel: 01494 558323; fax: 01494 885663; email: twplc@taylorwimpey.com; website: plc.taylorwimpey.co.uk)

Directors: Kevin Beeston, Chair; Pete Redfern, Chief Executive; Ryan Mangold, Group Finance Director; James Jordan; Robert Rowley; Brenda Dean; Anthony Reading; Mike Hussey; Kate Barker (women: 2; men: 7)

Year end	31/12/2011
Turnover	£1,808,000,000
Pre-tax profit	£78,600,000

Nature of business: Homebuilding company with operations in the UK, North America, Spain and Gibraltar.

Company registration number: 296805

UK employees: 3,464

Total employees: 3,529

Membership: BITC

Charitable donations

UK cash (latest declared):	2011	£211,000
	2009	£55,000
	2008	£132,000
	2007	£13,000
	2006	£9,000
Total UK:	2011	£211,000
Total worldwide:	2011	£211,000
Cash worldwide:	2011	£211,000

Corporate social responsibility

CSR committee: There is a charity committee responsible to the CSR Committee.

CSR policy: The following extract is taken from the CSR report for 2011:

> We aim to be a good neighbour, particularly in the way that we build and in how we interact with local people. We are focused on making our community consultation and engagement process increasingly transparent, accessible and consistent across our business and the development lifetime of our schemes. We seek to communicate effectively and to work in genuine partnership with local authorities, communities and other local stakeholders to fully understand their needs and concerns.

CSR report: There is an annual CSR report available from the website.

Exclusions

No support for appeals from individuals, fundraising events, political or religious appeals.

Applications

In writing to the correspondent.

Other information

Taylor Wimpey was formed through the merger of George Wimpey and Taylor Woodrow on 3 July 2007. Both businesses have a history dating 80 years or more with George Wimpey dating back to the 1880's and Taylor Woodrow to the 1920's.

In 2011 the company gave £211,000 in donations which appear to be for registered UK charities.

During 2009, the company reinstated its Charity Committee, which reports to the Corporate Responsibility Committee. The charity committee's aims are to monitor and review charitable donations made by regional businesses and to assess and administer some larger donations centrally.

The following is taken from the group's CSR report for 2011:

> We try to support local community organisations when we can. A team of our employees, contractors and suppliers provided a much needed new car park, street lighting and road repairs for a local hospice in Paisley in 2011. We also contribute to local communities in the areas in which we build through a wide range of charitable and community activities and we actively encourage our employees to take part and help fundraise.
>
> We are increasingly trying to get more involved with charities and community organisations and to give them practical assistance through volunteering labour, advice and materials wherever possible.
>
> Each year we nominate one main national charity and we are supporting Centrepoint in 2011 and 2012.
>
> Taylor Wimpey is a patron of CRASH, the construction and property industries' charity for homeless people and we provide funding as well as helping the charity with various projects and initiatives. We also support CRISIS, the national charity for single homeless people and our chief executive is now a trustee of the charity.

The group's donations policy is available at plc.taylorwimpeyplc.co.uk/ CorporateResponsibility/Policies/

Sponsorship

Various local groups are sponsored by the group including: Coalville Town Ravenettes; Wath-upon-Dearne Rugby Union Football Club First XV; and Upper Haugh Cricket Club.

TelecityGroup

Information management and communication

Correspondent: Corporate Social Responsibility Team, Suite 8.01, 2 Harbour Exchange Square, London E14 9GE (tel: 020 7001 0000; fax: 020 7001 0001; website: www.telecitygroup.com)

Directors: John Hughes, Chair; Michael Tobin, Chief Executive Officer; Brian McArthur-Muscroft, Chief Finance Director; Simon Batey; Maurizio Carli; Sahar Elhabashi; John O'Reilly (women: 1; men: 6)

Year end	31/12/2011
Turnover	£239,818,000
Pre-tax profit	£66,987

Nature of business: 'Telecity Group is the industry-leading pan-European operator of network independent data centres offering a range of highly flexible, scalable data centre and related managed services to a wide range of organisations.'

Company registration number: 5603875

Total employees: 527,000

Charitable donations

UK cash (latest declared):	2009	£81,000
	2008	£52,000
Total UK:	2009	£150,000
Total worldwide:	2011	£150,000

Corporate social responsibility

CSR committee: Board level CSR committee.

CSR policy: Information taken from the company's website:

> We are committed to responsible business with minimal impact on the environment. We recognise that being a major international business presents opportunities for us to have a positive impact on the wider society. Therefore we are committed to doing business responsibly and managing our relationships with stakeholders with integrity and transparency. We want to maximise our positive impact while taking steps to minimise any adverse consequences our operations may cause. We are an active participant in our marketplace and build strong and mutually beneficial relationships with customers, suppliers and the wider industry. In line with our corporate values of efficiency, entrepreneurship, integrity, innovation and stakeholder return, we have identified our CSR priorities as workplace, marketplace, environment and community with a focus on children and youth care, education and opportunity.

CSR report: Information taken from the 2011 annual report and accounts:

> The shift towards reporting on business-critical corporate responsibility issues means that, in future annual reports, data on some of the group's activities such as community investment and charitable partnerships will only feature in the corporate responsibility section of the group website at: www.telecity.com.

Applications

In writing to the correspondent.

Other information

During the year the business made cash and in kind donations of over £150,000 to a range of (mainly UK) charities including the NSPCC, Make-A-Wish Foundation, the Prince's Trust and Action for Children. In addition, the group became a patron of the Prince's Trust Technology Leadership Group.

The group focuses its community investment activities on providing education and opportunities for disadvantaged children and young people in local and international communities. The nature of the business means the company also seeks to promote responsible behaviour within internet communities.

Employees across the group have been involved in a number of fundraising and volunteering activities including, Byte Night's annual sleep out (the board of which Michael Tobin is a member) for Action for Children, and The Prince's Trust 'Palace to Palace' bike ride.

Telefonica UK Ltd

Telecommunications

Correspondent: See 'Applications', 260 Bath Road, Slough, Berkshire SL1 4DX (tel: 01132 722000; website: www.o2.com)

Directors: Ronan Dunne; Mark Evans; Robert Harwood; Edward Smith; Paul Whelan (women: 0; men: 5)

Year end	31/12/2011
Turnover	£5,968,000,000
Pre-tax profit	£794,000,000

Nature of business: The principal activities of the company were the operation of a cellular communications network, and the sale of fixed and mobile, voice and data services.

Company registration number: 1743099

Brands include: giffgaff.

Main locations: Braddan, Bury, Hammersmith, Douglas, Leeds, Runcorn, Slough

Total employees: 10,532

Membership: BITC

Charitable donations

UK cash (latest declared):	2011	£1,435,400
	2009	£750,000
	2007	£675,000
	2006	£264,000
	2005	£636,000
Total UK:	2011	£1,435,400
Total worldwide:	2011	£115,266,230
Cash worldwide:	2011	£112,261,880

Community involvement

Telefonica's community involvement is focused mainly where it the company has its biggest presence, Spain and Latin America. The following information is available regarding giving in the UK:

Think Big

The Think Big programme was launched in Europe during 2010 to support young people in their transition to an independent and responsible adult life. Think Big was set up with backing from Fundación Telefónica. Its aim is to provide financial support and training so that young people can demonstrate their talent to the wider community, make a positive impact and drive forward their role as agents of social change, inspiring and celebrating their successes as they take the lead in their own projects.

The programme is committed to a positive view of youth and was launched in the UK under the slogan 'We believe in young people'. The website collects proposals for projects ranging from the struggle against youth crime to improving community spaces or teaching music to other young people. Think Big is now up and running in the UK, Germany, Ireland, the Czech Republic and Slovakia, and supported more than 500 projects and trained nearly 1,600 young people in 2011. Activities are programmed in cooperation with various leading NGOs (such as, in the UK, the National Youth Agency and UK Youth).

The young participants receive appropriate project funding, training, the chance to call on a mentor chosen by themselves from among the Telefónica Volunteers network and support from the company to give their projects national visibility. The programme also includes activities aimed at persuading customers to take an active part in the projects being pitched and developed by the youngsters.

Child protection

It's vital that our customers can use our services with confidence, especially in terms of security and privacy. Safeguarding children is particularly important, which is why O2 in the UK and Europe has adopted a common child protection strategy.

For full information on Telefonica's initiatives on child protection issues, visit: www.o2.co.uk/thinkbig/people/childprotection

People with disabilities

Telefónica's activities, particularly those of Fundación Telefónica, in the area of disabilities include a substantial R&D effort aimed at making it easier for people with disabilities to access information, communication, training and employment, improving healthcare and support for those who are old, sick, incapacitated or vulnerable, and helping with health education and preventative approaches to dealing with various illnesses and disabilities.

Corporate giving

In 2011, £1.4 million was donated by the company to UK registered charities. We do not have details of the beneficiaries. Globally, Telefónica set aside €143.26 million (£115.26 million) for community investment, an 8.6% increase on the previous year. £112.26 million (97.4%) of this was in cash; £1.41 million in employee time; £954,000 gifts in kind; and almost £627,000 was in management costs.

Employee-led support

Volunteers at Telefónica

Fundación Telefónica runs a multicultural network of volunteers from Telefónica Group, which supports social and collaborative projects by employees. The volunteers undertake charity work either as part of Fundación Telefónica's own programmes or in partnership with other foundations.

The programme runs in all 19 countries where Telefónica group is active, and in 2011 some 26,000 volunteers took an active part in the 1,459 volunteering initiatives on offer, providing almost 113,000 hours and directly benefitting 268,660 people.

Commercially-led support

Music sponsorship

The group sponsors the *Nordoff-Robins Silver Clef Awards*, which raise money for the charity. 'The Nordoff Robbins O2 Silver Clef Awards recognise outstanding talent across the industry, and are an opportunity for us to give something back to the music industry who support us so generously throughout the year.' David Munns, Chair, Nordoff Robbins

Telefónica Europe will not consider commercial sponsorships for funding unless the key objective is to address a charitable or social cause. The marketing teams within the Telefónica Europe operating businesses deal with commercial sponsorships (such as sports, art or cultural projects). Enquiries can be made through the Interactive Partnerships department: sponsorship@o2.com.

Initiatives for people with disabilities

Telefónica O2 UK offers a wide range of services for persons with disability, including bills in Braille, accessible customer care and dedication corners of the corporate website ('Access for all') containing information of interest. One of O2 UK's new projects was a pilot test intended to form a group of experts in its stores known as 'Gurus' on accessibility issues so that they can advise customers with disabilities on how to get the most from their phones and show them how to use the latest accessible mobile applications targeted at the disabled.

Corporate social responsibility

CSR committee: The corporate responsibility governance section of the O2 website states:

Our overall corporate responsibility activities, our policies, practices and strategic objectives, are overseen by the board. Reviews are carried out both through an annual conference and at regular board meetings.

Individual directors take responsibility for different aspects of our programme and act as Champions for the business, led by the chief executive who has responsibility for all aspects of our social, environmental and ethical activities. Directors are closely supported in this role by our Corporate Responsibility Forum.

CSR policy: The community investment section of the O2 website states:

> At Telefónica Europe we believe that companies who respond to the needs of communities are most likely to thrive and survive.
>
> As a provider of mobile communications to consumers and businesses, we want to harness our services, skills and the active involvement of our employees to help others and to enrich lives.
>
> We talk to and work with various charities and community bodies in the countries where we operate and we offer support, know-how and technology. Many of our employees are involved in mentoring and volunteering.

CSR report: There is an annual Corporate Sustainability report covering Telefonica's global CSR activities available online.

Exclusions

The O2 Think Big website outlines the following exclusions:

> *Think Big*
> - Think Big will not support projects that aim to convert people to a religion
> - You can't apply if your project is something you do for a living
> - It's not for promoting political parties
> - It cannot involve anything dangerous
>
> And you cannot apply directly for £2,500, you must do your £300 project first, and only if everything is going really well might you get invited to apply for more.

Applications

Full details of how to apply for 'Think Big' are available at: www.o2thinkbig.co.uk/Start-a-project/.

Telegraph Media Group Ltd

Media

Correspondent: Company Secretary, 111 Buckingham Palace Road, London SW1W 0DT (tel: 020 7931 5000; website: www.telegraph.co.uk)

Directors: A. S. Barclay, Chair; M. MacLennan, Chief Executive Officer; F. P. Ronayne, Chief Financial Officer; H. M. Barclay; D. Cobley; R. K. Mowatt; P. L. Peters; M. Seal; L. Twohill

Year end	01/01/2012
Turnover	£331,000,000
Pre-tax profit	£54,500,000

Nature of business: Publication of national newspapers.

Company registration number: 451593

Main locations: London

Total employees: 1,055

Charitable donations

UK cash (latest declared):	2011	£126,000
	2009	£58,000
	2008	£52,000
	2007	£116,000
	2006	£76,000
Total UK:	2011	£126,000
Total worldwide:	2012	£126,000
Cash worldwide:	2012	£126,000

Corporate social responsibility

CSR policy: No CSR details found.

We were unable to determine the ratio of women to men on the board.

Applications

We would suggest in writing to the correspondent although it should be noted that support for organisations unconnected with the newspaper industry appears to be very limited.

Other information

In 2011, charitable donations were made by the group of £126,000 (2010: £103,400), principally to charities associated with the newspapers and their employees.

Payroll giving: The Give As You Earn scheme is operated by the company.

Tesco plc

Retail – supermarkets

Correspondent: Lucy Neville-Rolfe, CSR Director, Tesco House, Delamare Road, Cheshunt, Hertfordshire EN8 9SL (tel: 01992 632222; website: www.tescoplc.com)

Directors: A. T. Higginson; D. T. Potts; Patrick Cescau; Stuart Chambers; Ken Hydon; Lucy Neville-Rolfe; R. Brasher; Gareth Bullock; Tim Mason; Karen Cook; Jonathan Lloyd; Laurie McIlwee; Ken Hanna, Director; Jacqueline Tammenoms Bakker; Richard Broadbent, Chair; Philip Clarke, Group Chief Executive (women: 4; men: 11)

Year end	25/02/2012
Turnover	£64,539,000,000
Pre-tax profit	£3,835,000,000

Nature of business: The principal activity of the group is retailing and associated activities in the UK, China, the Czech Republic, Hungary, the Republic of Ireland, India, Japan, Malaysia, Poland, Slovakia, South Korea, Thailand, Turkey and the US. The Group also provides retail banking and insurance services through its subsidiary, Tesco Bank.

Company registration number: 445790

Subsidiaries include: Spen Hill Properties Ltd

Main locations: Cheshunt

UK employees: 300,373

Total employees: 519,671

Membership: BITC

Charitable donations

UK cash (latest declared):	2012	£25,600,000
	2009	£28,278,867
	2008	£22,655,173
	2007	£17,698,393
	2006	£15,047,768
Total UK:	2012	£25,600,000
Total worldwide:	2012	£74,589,000
Cash worldwide:	2012	£25,646,000

Community involvement

Tesco's community involvement varies from country to country, but typically support is given to environmental action, healthy lifestyles, children and the nominated 'Charity of the Year'. The latter becomes the main focus for staff fundraising and receives a 20% 'top up' from the Tesco Charity Trust, (Charity Commission no. 297126), as does Cancer Research UK's Race for Life yearly run.

There is a central committee team in head office who manage national charity and sponsorship activity and set the guidelines for the company's community support. There are 669 'Tesco Community Champions' across the group (China, the Czech Republic, Hungary, Ireland, Malaysia, Slovakia, South Korea and the UK) working specifically to support local charities and organisations. The following information is taken from the 2010/11 CSR report:

> Our in-store Community Champions help us communicate effectively with local communities. By giving our employees the time and tools to work with their neighbourhood, we make a real difference. Community Champions are paid to spend 18 hours a week working with their local community. For example:
> - Giving store tours to local schoolchildren or going into the local primary school to talk about healthy eating
> - Organising collections or bag packing for a local charity
> - Meeting the fire service or local charities to find out how we can help them
> - Getting our staff and customers involved in events such as Race for Life

The company differentiates between donations and sponsorship (although not between donations and cause-related marketing). The former are made through the Tesco Charity Trust, which supports registered charities only, or organisations recognised by the Inland Revenue as having charitable status.

Community Fairs

The Fairs, held up and down the UK, provided an opportunity for local charities to sign up new volunteers and for local suppliers to showcase their products. There are now 100 Community Fairs with over 10,000 new volunteers signing up in 2011 for local projects.

Charity of the Year: Diabetes UK (2013).

Corporate giving

In 2011/12 cash donations to charities amounted to £25.6 million (2010/11: £15.6 million). Total contributions to community projects including cash, cause-related marketing, gifts-in kind, staff time and management costs amounted to £74.6 million (2010/11: £64.3 million). The Corporate Responsibility Manager confirmed that Tesco 'don't publically disclose this breakdown at a more nuanced level'. According to the 2010/11 Tesco Charity Trust accounts, it 'received £2 million from Tesco Stores Ltd' and we have used this figure as the company's UK cash donations figure although it is likely that the true figure is substantially more.

Tesco Charity Trust

The Tesco Charity Trust (Charity Commission no. 297126) was set up on 1 June 1987 to support national, local and international community charities, and to add a 20% top up to staff fundraising. It is run by a board of trustees recommended by the main board of Tesco plc. The trust supports charitable activities on a local, national and international basis and its main income comes from donations made by Tesco plc, Tesco Stores Ltd and staff fundraising. Donations under the company's Give As You Earn scheme are managed by the trust.

The Tesco Charity Trust runs two funding schemes – the Community Awards and the Larger Grants.

Community Awards

The Tesco Charity Trust Community Awards Scheme provides one-off donations of between £500 and £4,000 to local projects that support children and their education and welfare, elderly people, and adults and children with disabilities.

There are four rounds of funding each year and a copy of the criteria and application deadlines can be downloaded from the company's website. Applications should be made via the online application form. You may also want to view a copy of the application questions before filling out the application form.

In the year ended February 2012, the Tesco Charity Trust had an income of £6.9 million and made cash grants of almost £5.3 million to charities, including £2.2 million to the Alzheimer's Society.

For Community Awards criteria and application form, go to www.tescocharitytrustcommunityawards-applications.co.uk. You should look at the 'Questions' before completing the form online.

Guidelines for the Tesco Charity Trust Community Award Scheme can be downloaded from the company's website, or obtained by writing to Tesco Charity Trust, Tesco Stores Ltd.

Larger Grant Awards

The Tesco Charity Trust's trustees also consider grant applications at their tri-annual meetings. These grants range between £4,000 and £25,000 and are to support local, national or international projects in areas where the Group operates.

In 2011/12 the trust's beneficiaries also included: CLIC Sargent (£984,000); Barking Badgers (£20,000); and Muscular Dystrophy Campaign (£2,000).

Guidelines are available on the company's website. If you would like to apply for a grant send details of your project to Michelina Filocco, Tesco Charity Trust, New Tesco House, Delamare Road, Cheshunt, Herts EN8 9SL, or alternatively email Michelina Filocco at: Michelina.Filocco@uk.tesco.com Ensure you clearly mark your correspondence, 'For the Trustees Meeting – Grants'.

If you require any support when completing the application, you are advised to call the company's helpline on: 0845 612 3575.

Community vouchers

In addition to the above, stores receive an allocation of community vouchers to support requests for raffle prizes and so on. The vouchers may be redeemed at checkouts in the store. A maximum donation of £50 can be made to local organisations through this scheme.

Employee-led support

Staff and customers raised £10.1 million for charity in 2011/12.

Payroll giving: The company operates the Give As You Earn and Sharing the Caring payroll giving schemes.

Commercially-led support

The company's CSR report gives the following information:

> ***Sponsorship:***
> In the UK, our 2010 Great School Run involved over one million primary school children, and over 700,000 staff and customers took part in Cancer Research UK's Race for Life and Run 10k. Since 2002, nearly two-thirds of our staff have taken part in or supported our races, raising a total of £7.1 million.

Cause-related marketing: – Through Tesco for Schools and Clubs, UK customers can collect and redeem vouchers for equipment for schools. In 2010/11, the company donated £9.3 million of equipment to 41,000 schools and clubs, bringing the total to more than £170 million in the last 20 years. For more information, visit: www.tescoforschoolsandclubs.com.

Corporate social responsibility

CSR committee: The Corporate Responsibility Committee comprises four independent non-executive directors, including the non-executive chair.

CSR policy: The following statement is taken from the company's CSR report:

> Our core purpose and values are the foundation of the management tool which drives our day-to-day approach and prioritises the key issues for the business. This is called our Steering Wheel, and consists of five segments: Community, Operations, People, Finance and Customer.
>
> *Tesco Community Promises*
> Our values are reflected in the five pillars of our corporate responsibility strategy, which we call Community Promises.
>
> 1 Buying and selling our products responsibly
> 2 Caring for the environment
> 3 Actively supporting local communities
> 4 Providing customers with healthy choices
> 5 Creating good jobs and careers. Corporate responsibility plays an important part in our commercial decisions
>
> Thanks to the Steering Wheel, looking after communities is not a specialist function at Tesco – it is part of everyone's job. In each of our markets we build annual Community Plans which focus and target local and national activities. These plans reflect both group targets and local and national priorities, ensuring local ownership of specific issues.

CSR report: CSR report published annually.

Exclusions

No support for circular appeals, advertising in charity brochures, animal welfare, appeals from individuals, the arts, enterprise/training, environment/heritage, fundraising events, medical research, overseas projects (outside of help given through the British Red Cross), political appeals, religious appeals, or science/technology.

The trust will not give grants to other trusts or charities acting as intermediaries.

Applications

In writing to the correspondent and also see 'Community Contributions' section of this entry.

Other information: The company's Retired Staff Association maintains links with retired employees and through it can offer support and assistance to those in retirement who need it.

Thales UK Ltd

Telecommunications

Correspondent: Mike Seabrook, Thales Charitable Trust, 2 Dashwood Lang Road, The Bourne Business Park, Addlestone, Surrey KT15 2NX (tel: 01932 824800; fax: 01932 824887; email: mike.seabrook@thalesgroup.com; website: www.thalesgroup.co.uk)

Directors: Jean-Bernard Lévy, Chair and Chief Executive; Oliver Bourges; Charles Edelstenne; Yannick d'Escatha; Dominique Floch; Stève Gentili; Philippe Lépinay; Didier Lombard; Bruno Parent; Jeanne-Marie Prost; Martine Saunier; Loïk Segalen; Amaury de Sèze; Anne-Claire Taittinger; Ann Taylor; Eric Trappier

Year end	31/12/2011
Turnover	£342,054,000
Pre-tax profit	(£46,350,000)

Nature of business: Principal activities: The design, manufacture and sale of defence electronic products, encompassing electronic warfare, radar, displays, defence radio and command information systems.

Company registration number: 868273

Main locations: Belfast, Birmingham, Bury St Edmunds, Glasgow, Doncaster, Stockport, Addlestone

Total employees: 2,003

Membership: BITC

Charitable donations

UK cash (latest declared):	2011	£150,000
	2010	£150,000
	2008	£150,000
	2007	£166,000
	2006	£167,070
Total UK:	2011	£150,000
Total worldwide:	2011	£150,000
Cash worldwide:	2011	£150,000

Corporate social responsibility

CSR committee: The group has an Ethics and Corporate Responsibility Department. Email: ethics.cr@thalesgroup.com

CSR policy: Taken from the group's website:

> *Our CR Mission:*
> To be committed to a better future for our people, our communities, our environment and our business.
>
> *Our CR Policy:*
> Thales UK intends to create a better future for our people, communities, environment and business by acting in a corporately responsible manner, in all our activities and relationships and in doing so achieve business growth.
>
> *Our CR Principles:*
> Thales UK has CR Principles across our four 'CR Pillars' of Business, People, Community and Environment which include the following:
>
> - Our Business: In all dealings and at all times, we will act in a legal, ethical manner and with integrity
> - Our People: We uphold the need for equal opportunities and a diverse workforce
> - Our Communities: We are dedicated to supporting local and national causes particularly for causes related to youth, technology and education
> - Our Environment: We are committed to reducing our impact on the environment by identifying energy efficiency opportunities and reducing consumption

Unable to determine the ratio of women to men on the board.

CSR report: Group's CSR report is published annually.

Applications

All appeals for charitable donations should be sent in writing to the correspondent.

Other information

In 2011 the company's charitable trust had an income of £150,000. The trust's accounts state that it relies entirely on funds coming from the Thales group of companies.

Thales Charitable Trust (Charity Commission no: 1000162)

Donations are given to charities in line with current themes of youth, technology and education and care for permanent or terminal conditions operating on a national basis.

The following is taken from the CSR report for 2011:

> Employees in the United Kingdom, have been active in supporting charities for several years, promoting causes in various ways and providing significant financial support. A total of £500,000, for example, has been donated to Marie Curie Cancer Care over a five-year period through sports events and other fundraising projects.
>
> Through its charitable trust, Thales UK continued to support Youthnet, an organisation dedicated to providing young people aged 16 to 24 with the information they need to make informed career choices. The company has a partnership with The Railway Children, a charity that provides shelter, clothes and meals to homeless children. Thales also participated in the development of the Talk, Don't Walk website, a service dedicated to dissuading children from running away from home and providing services to help families overcome relationship problems.

Thomas Cook Group plc

Leisure

Correspondent: Health Safety and Environment Committee – Communities, The Thomas Cook Business Park, Coningsby Road, Peterborough PE3 8SB (tel: 01733 417100; website: www.thomascookgroup.com)

Directors: Paul Hollingworth, Group Chief Financial Officer; Sam Weihagen, Group Chief Executive Officer; David Allvey; Roger Burnell; Bo Lerenins; Peter Middleton; Dawn Airey; Frank Meysman, Chair; Peter Marks; Martine Verluyten (women: 2; men: 8)

Year end	30/09/2011
Turnover	£9,808,900,000
Pre-tax profit	(£398,200,000)

Nature of business: Thomas Cook Group is one of the world's leading leisure travel groups. Operating under six geographic segments in 22 countries.

Company registration number: 742748

Main locations: Rochdale

UK employees: 17,227

Membership: LBG

Charitable donations

UK cash (latest declared):	2011	£36,300
	2009	£0
	2005	£15,000
Total UK:	2011	£357,580
Total worldwide:	2011	£465,550
Cash worldwide:	2011	£186,060

Corporate social responsibility

CSR committee: Information taken from the 2011 annual report:

> The board, through the Health, Safety & Environmental Committee and Group Executive Board, sets the group's sustainability strategy. Robust management systems and policies support the implementation of our sustainability strategy.
>
> Over 2010/11, we made good progress in embedding sustainability further into the business and continued to refine our key issues within the four strategic areas. We set up our Group Working Party on Sustainability ('GWPS'), in 2010 for strategic decision-making. Over 2011, we made progress in developing a global approach to sustainability, encouraging sustainability leadership across the Group and sharing best practice across our operations internationally.
>
> Across the group, we communicate on sustainability to our people using the intranet, emails, employee magazines and newsletters. We also have networks of sustainability champions across the group, who take a leadership role in shaping the sustainability focus of their business.

CSR policy: Taken from the annual report 2011:

> We believe that the success of our business rests on our commitment to be economically, environmentally and socially sustainable. Our approach is to maximise the benefits that our business brings, while minimising the adverse impacts of our operations.
>
> Our sustainability strategy is centred on the key areas which we believe contribute to a sustainable business model: people, marketplace (encompassing customers and suppliers),environment and communities.

CSR report: Annual Sustainability report published.

Applications

In writing to the correspondent.

Other information

During 2010/11 the company gave £465,500 in total community contributions.

Cash contributions for the UK were £36,300 with a total of £186,000 worldwide. In kind contributions were £321,700 in the UK and £523,000 worldwide. Management costs are included in these totals.

The following extract is taken from the 2011 Sustainability Report:

In January 2011, Thomas Cook joined the London Benchmarking Group (LBG), which enabled us to embed a process by which all our community engagement activity can be tracked and outcomes measured on a consistent basis. Developing our 2020 sustainability aims was a key achievement for us this year. These were developed in line with the Key issues that our Group Working Party on Sustainability identified as most important to our business. Our aims are ambitious and provide us with greater focus and direction for our sustainability efforts over the medium to long-term.

Our communities

Vision

To build relationships and partnerships with the communities in all the places where our customers visit and where our people live and work.

Aims

- Develop and implement a child protection policy for the group and all segments by 2013
- Prioritise local sourcing of food and beverages at all group-owned hotels by 2014
- All segments to implement a charitable strategy for home and destination communities by 2014
- Measure and improve the contribution our holidays bring to communities and the local economy by 2020

In 2011, the Group Working Party on Sustainability agreed that our aim was to refine our group charitable giving and community activity to focus on three areas: children and education; health; and environment. Here are examples of our support in some of those areas:

Children and education

In Sweden, we support Mentor Sweden – a charity promoting health and preventing drug abuse among young people. We have had four volunteers lecturing in schools in 2011 and have held lunchtime seminars with representatives from the charity presenting sessions for 80 employees on drugs and parenting support.

Health

Thomas Cook India supports Jeevan Jyot Centre – a strategic support centre for people affected by sexually transmitted diseases, primarily AIDS. We sponsor the premises for the centre, career guidance counselling and alternative therapy.

Environment

Thomas Cook UK supported The Travel Foundation on a successful project focused on working with more than 20 hotels in Cyprus to look at ways of reducing plastic consumption.

Charitable giving

We have a strong tradition of charitable giving and fundraising, dating back to our founder who was a passionate philanthropist. Through a mixture of donations and fundraising activities, we continue to support charities and local community projects. Group-wide cash donations totalled £186,000 for the year. The group has donated £25,000 to the charity, Just a Drop, which is committed to providing safe water in developing countries around the world in order to reduce child mortality rates. Our donation will fund a sustainable water and sanitation project in villages in Uganda.

In the UK, our people can support charities of their choice through a payroll giving scheme. During the year, we were delighted to be awarded the Charities Aid Foundation (CAF) Bronze Payroll Giving Quality Mark, recognising our commitment to charitable causes by encouraging our workforce to actively donate through their salaries. Total participation in 2010/11 was just under 5% of the workforce who raised £40,000 for charities in the UK. We are now working towards the Silver Mark, which requires a minimum 5% participation.

Thomas Cook Children's Charity Set up in 2009, the Thomas Cook Children's Charity is a registered charitable trust, which aims to make dreams come true for sick and disadvantaged children, both in the UK and overseas. Thomas Cook UK pays for the charity's running costs, so all donations go directly to the children. We offer customers the Buying local produce and supporting local communities in Turkey.

Charities Aid Foundation (CAF) awarded Thomas Cook UK & Ireland the Bronze Payroll Giving Quality Mark.

For us, supporting our communities is about much more than donating financially. We encourage our people to get involved in activities not only to benefit local communities, but also so they can develop new skills.

Thomas Cook UK and Ireland's Flight of Dreams organised by the Children's Charity opportunity to donate when they book a holiday and we also collect unwanted coins in store and on return Thomas Cook Airlines flights to the UK.

Customers and employees of Thomas Cook UK have raised over £2.3 million to date for the charity. In 2010/11, funds raised from customer donations and employee fundraising totalled £1.2 million. Projects that the trustees of the Children's Charity granted funds to include:

- Royal Manchester Children's Hospital – the paediatric hydrotherapy unit has recently been refurbished thanks to a £150,000 donation. Young visitors to this facility are taken on a holiday-themed journey, changing facilities have been themed as beach huts and the pool area now offers a whole new underwater experience. It is hoped that the design will put children at ease as they enter the facility and also allow them to focus on the many images that are around them, seeing something different at each visit
- SE1 United – a youth-led organisation in Waterloo received a grant from the Children's Charity for a mentoring scheme in which over 800 young people were helped to realise their ambitions while reducing crime rates
- Flight of Dreams – an annual Christmas event running from major UK airports for sick and disadvantaged children. Volunteers dressed as elves and accompanied more than 500 children on Thomas Cook UK airline flights, with Santa handing out presents mid-flight. This enabled over 500 school children from deprived areas to enjoy a flight with Santa

Thomas Cook UK & Ireland [was] the official provider of short breaks to the London 2012 Games, and in 2011 the Thomas Cook Children's Charity joined forces with Sport England, the government agency responsible for creating a world-class community sport environment. The trustees agreed to allocate up to £500,000 to improve sporting opportunities for disadvantaged young people across England.

Volunteering

2010/11 was a successful year for volunteering in the UK, with over 200 staff volunteering over 3,500 hours of support. Looking forward, we aim to finalise a formal UK volunteering policy to encourage more employee participation. This will also enable our people to take time during working hours to participate in worthwhile causes in our local and destination communities and in line with our corporate strategy.

Thomson Reuters plc

Media

Correspondent: Corporate Responsibility Team, The Thomson Reuters Building, 30 South Colonnade, Canary Wharf, London E14 5EP (tel: 020 7542 8599; email: foundation@reuters.com; website: www.thomsonreuters.com)

Directors: James C. Smith, President and CEO; Stephane Bello, Chief Financial Officer; David Craig; Chris Kibarian; Shanker Ramamurthy; Mike Suchsland (women: 0; men: 7)

Year end	31/12/2011
Turnover	£8,891,708,000
Pre-tax profit	£718,704,000

Nature of business: Reuters Ltd supplies the global business community and news media with a wide range of products including real-time financial data, transaction systems, information management systems, access to numeric and textual databases, news and news pictures.

Company registration number: 145516

Main locations: London, Edinburgh

Total employees: 60,500

Charitable donations

UK cash (latest declared):	2011	£4,260,000
	2009	£3,330,000
	2008	£1,100,000
Total UK:	2011	£5,232,800
Total worldwide:	2011	£7,600,800
Cash worldwide:	2011	£6,627,900

Community involvement

In April 2008, The Thomson Corporation and Reuters Group plc combined to form Thomson Reuters. The following information is taken from Reuters' 2011 Corporate Responsibility Report:

> Our CR approach encompasses a proud heritage of community giving by both The Thomson Corporation and Reuters Group plc and established policies around business ethics, employee wellbeing and environmental management. Over the last few years we have taken these strong foundations and built on them to shape a robust company-wide CR program for Thomson Reuters, structured around four focus areas: Marketplace, Workplace, Community and Environment. Within each area we manage a wide range of impacts and activities, which we discuss in this report.
>
> We are constantly working to improve our CR program and achieve best practice. This year we focused on revising several of our core CR policies and reviewing a number of key systems and processes. We created a more joined-up CR function, bringing together key individuals from different locations into a single virtual team, led by our Global Head of CR. And we established a CR Roundtable, made up of representatives from across the business, to provide governance for the CR function, build support across the business and help embed changes. These developments are part of our ongoing journey towards a CR approach that is fit for the future and aligned with our core business.
>
> Looking ahead In the coming year, we will be focusing on:
>
> - Embedding our new governance structure
> - Implementing a number of work streams that will help shape our new CR approach, including developing and communicating a new CR strategy
> - Developing capabilities and systems to enable us to better measure and report on our performance and shape our program going forward
> - Supporting the relevant business units to set clear goals and concrete targets in each of our key areas
> - Doing more to lead our sector in key CR-related areas where our knowledge or expertise can benefit the wider industry or society
>
> *Community*
>
> As a global organisation we actively support the communities in which we operate by providing assistance and services directly as a business and through our charity the Thomson Reuters Foundation. We also recognize that it is important to support employees who want to make a contribution either by giving their time, their professional skills and expertise or by charitable donations. Our policies support and facilitate these activities.
>
> In 2011 we responded to employee feedback to ensure that our programs are as engaging and, above all, as practical as possible, for our people. Our Community Support Policy outlines the different community programs we have in place across the business. By having a defined policy, we are able to focus our community investments to have the greatest impact. The policy was refreshed in 2011 to better reflect the needs of our communities and the passions of our employees.
>
> Throughout 2012 we will continue to develop new programs and create opportunities for all Thomson Reuters employees.

For detailed information on Reuters' corporate responsibility programmes, visit www.thomsonreuters.com.

Thomas Reuters Foundation (Charity Commission no. 1082139)

Established in 1982, the Thomson Reuters Foundation is the charitable arm of Thomson Reuters. A registered charity in the US and UK, the foundation is committed to empowering people in need around the world with trusted information and free legal assistance.

> The Thomson Reuters Foundation is a catalytic foundation which shares the skills and experiences of our business across a wider landscape to increase access to valuable information in the most needed areas. Operating across flagship programs, 2011 was a year of growth for our Foundation building on the successes already in place and developing our offer to stakeholders through the following services:
>
> - TrustLaw – a global center for free legal assistance and anti-corruption news. Its aim is to empower people in need by providing trusted information and leveraging professional expertise
> - AlertNet – a free news service covering humanitarian crises worldwide providing trusted information on natural disasters, wars, hunger, diseases and climate change
> - TrustMedia – a leader in international journalism training and a key provider of media training. Offering 60 courses worldwide each year, over 9,000 journalists have received this hands-on training
>
> In 2011, the Foundation successfully launched TrustLaw Woman, a hub for news and information on women's rights, and YouTrust.org, a social media platform that enables our community to easily share multimedia information and create their own campaigns.
>
> *Social Investment*
>
> The *New York City Investment Fund41* and *Social Business Trust42* in the UK are two of the ways in which we identify and support the growth of social enterprises, offering financial and practical support alongside networks of other global businesses to help build a stronger and more diversified local economy.
>
> *Corporate grants and donations*
>
> Cash grants are given to local causes wherever the company has a large number of employees. Often championed at an executive level, these grants support local community projects and charitable groups, making a lasting impact for communities in many regions of the world. In 2011 over US $2 million was donated to such causes in a few of the company's larger locations.

Corporate giving

Thomson Reuters Foundation

A substantial proportion of the donations received by the foundation are made up of an annual grant from Reuters Ltd, a wholly owned subsidiary of Thomson Reuters Group. In 2010, this grant was £3.2 million (2009: £3.3 million). Gifts in kind of £973,000 were also received from Reuters (2009: £728,000). In 2009, £5.77 million was spent on charitable activities.

Charitable funds were spent in the following proportions – 2010 figures in brackets: Journalism – 41% (60%); Humanitarian Aid – 28% (40%); Legal – 31% (0%).

Beneficiaries of grant funding included: Oxford University (£1.6 million over three years); Tsinghua University – China (£34,000); Mona Megalli Fellowship – Oxford University (£9,000); and Haiti Earthquake (£8,300).

Note that Thomson Reuters Foundation does not consider unsolicited requests for support.

In kind support

In kind support is given to the Thomas Reuters Foundation. In 2010 the amount recorded in the accounts was £973,000.

Employee-led support

Community Champion Awards

The annual Community Champion Awards program celebrates the personal volunteer commitments of employees. Winners receive a substantial donation for the cause of their choice. Since its launch in 2001 the program has donated US $1 million to not-for-profit groups across the world. In 2011 the awards recognised the outstanding volunteer work of 45 individual employees and groups from across the business. The winners received cash grants for their chosen groups totalling US $150,000. The winning entries not only demonstrated a personal commitment to volunteering but also highlighted the skills and talents required to give long-term support to deserving communities and groups. The top winners for 2011 each received US $25,000 for their chosen charities – Children at Risk, based in Houston, Texas and Urban Synergy Mentoring, in Greenwich, East London.

Dollars for Doers

This programme, open to all regular employees, makes a US $1,000 donation to a chosen not-for-profit on behalf of staff who have volunteered for the same organisation for more than 40 hours over six months, either during or out of working hours. Following employee feedback, the company will be making this programme more flexible in 2012 by rewarding 20-hours' service with a US $500 donation, up to a maximum of US $1,000.

Employee-Giving Campaigns

The Employee-Giving program is available to employees in specific locations, enabling them to make a one-off charitable donation from their pay. 'This system is now firmly embedded in our corporate culture, reflecting its popularity and success.'

Matched Funding

Employees charitable donations to registered charities are matched up to US$1,000 a year. The Executive Committee members and their direct staff also have access to a bespoke matching programme with an annual limit of US$10,000 and US$5,000 respectively.

Volunteering

Staff are encouraged to volunteer and offered a day a year with pay if volunteering for a registered charity. In 2011, 20,675 hours were worked.

> The Volunteer Action Network (VAN) promotes community investment and provides opportunities for employees to get involved at designated office locations across the globe. Teams of champions drive employee engagement by promoting collaborative events each quarter around four focus areas: Education; Environment; Youth and Hunger. Employees participate in volunteering, fundraising and collections, and promoting awareness for each of these themes.
>
> Our Corporate Responsibility (CR) Champions are an integral part of our community story at Thomson Reuters. Employee groups and networks in a wide variety of locations have established partnerships with their local communities where they participate in volunteering activities and support programs local to their offices.
>
> Both the VAN and the CR Champions drive local initiatives in addition to their regular day-jobs. During 2012 we will be looking at strengthening the networks that are already in place, aligning their aims and ensuring that as a business we are investing fully in our local communities.

Commercially-led support

Sponsorship

Taken from the CR report for 2011:

> Sponsorship can be a useful marketing tool, enabling our brand to reach the right audiences in an increasingly crowded marketplace. But as well as the commercial benefits, we also leverage our resources and network to help generate publicity and funds for causes and people we believe in. In 2011 we sponsored a wide range of these kinds of projects – from hosting a Girl Scouts Careers Day in New York, USA to the ongoing supply of professional trading equipment for *Cass Business School,* London, UK. The common thread to this activity is that we pick projects and issues where our skills and resources are relevant.
>
> Our sponsorships vary in scale, from long-term international partnerships such as our relationship with golf Masters winner Mike Weir and his charitable foundation to activities organized locally over short durations such as the *Atlantic Cup* where our sponsorship helped to raise funds for the *Boomer Esiason Foundation* and cystic fibrosis.

Corporate social responsibility

CSR committee: In place. The committee oversees the review and updating of key CR policies and seeks to ensure a common approach across Thomson Reuters. For more detailed information see 'Community Involvement'.

CSR policy: Taken from the annual report for 2011:

> Corporate Responsibility (CR) is an integral part of the way we do business. We have a CR policy that describes how we manage our impact in four areas: the community (the places and societies in which we operate), our workplace (employees), the environment and the marketplace (customers, suppliers and investors). By articulating focus areas, we are able to define our responses to global standards and charters in ways that are meaningful to our business.
>
> In 2011, we began developing a new approach to CR that is more reflective of our business and more responsive to the needs and expectations of our stakeholders. We created a CR governance committee comprised of representatives from across our business.

CSR report: Published annually.

Applications

Thomson Reuters Foundation does not consider unsolicited requests for support.

Daniel Thwaites plc

Brewers/distillers

Correspondent: Chief Executive Officer, Penny Street, Star Brewery, Blackburn, Lancashire BB1 6HL (tel: 01254 686868; fax: 01254 681439; website: www.thwaites.co.uk)

Directors: R. A. J. Bailey, Chief Executive Officer; Ann Yerburgh, Chair; K. D. Wood, Group Finance Director; A. H. Spencer, Managing Director – Hotels and Inns; P. A. Boddy; R. G. R. Thompson; A. M. R. Yerburgh (women: 1; men: 6)

Year end	31/03/2011
Turnover	£126,700,000
Pre-tax profit	£7,000,000

Nature of business: Principal activities are the brewing and canning of beer, the distribution of wines and spirits and the operation of hotels and public houses.

Company registration number: 51702

Main locations: Blackburn

UK employees: 1,470

Total employees: 1,470

Charitable donations

UK cash (latest declared):	2011	£25,000
	2009	£29,200
	2008	£16,600
	2006	£27,000
	2005	£28,000
Total UK:	2011	£25,000
Total worldwide:	2011	£25,000
Cash worldwide:	2011	£25,000

Corporate social responsibility

CSR policy: No CSR information published.

Applications

In writing to the correspondent.

Other information

In 2010/11 the company gave £25,000 in charitable donations. We have no information on where the £25,000 was given or for what purposes. The following is taken from the 2010/11 annual report but there is no information on what the 'support' referred to was:

> The communities in which we operate are vitally important to us, particularly in our North West heartland. During the year we were delighted to join with other local businesses to support the development of the Blackburn Youth Zone. This will be a superb facility for youngsters from the Blackburn area to meet and develop their sporting and social skills in a safe and supportive environment and has been very successfully piloted in other communities in the North West.

The Daniel Thwaites Charitable Trust (Charity Commission no. 1038097) which has previously benefited from the company's annual charitable donation was established in 1994. The trust states that 'emphasis is placed on giving tangible, physical help, be that wheelchairs, computers, musical instruments, beds or other specialist equipment for helping improve interaction, or items such as bingo machines and televisions that improve the quality of life for groups of people'. Support is given across the UK, although there is a preference for appeals from within a 50 mile radius of Blackburn. The trust has had no income or expenditure since 2009 although it remains on the Central Register of Charities.

TJX UK (formerly TK Maxx)

Retail – clothing and footwear

Correspondent: Marketing Department, 50 Clarendon Road, Watford, Hertfordshire WD17 1TX (tel: 01923 473000; website: www.tkmaxx.com)

Directors: Alfred Appel; Jeffrey Naylor; Paul Sweetenham; Mary Blier Reynolds; Joseph Wilmot (women: 1; men: 4)

Year end	29/01/2011
Turnover	£128,694,400
Pre-tax profit	£92,035,900

Nature of business: A nationwide chain of stores selling clothing, gifts and homeware below recommended retail prices.

Company registration number: 3094828

Brands include: TK Maxx; Homesense.

Main locations: Watford

UK employees: 15,066

Total employees: 15,066

Charitable donations

UK cash (latest declared):	2011	£879,000
	2009	£931,000
	2007	£897,520
	2006	£750,824
	2005	£590,161
Total UK:	2011	£879,000
Total worldwide:	2011	£879,000
Cash worldwide:	2011	£879,000

Community involvement

Although a name change took place in 2007, the company still trades under the TK Maxx brand. The information contained here relates to the UK company TJX UK.

The majority of the company's giving is to support its six partner charities but it also supports local charities. The following information is taken from its website:

> Our Community Fund helps us support smaller charitable organisations that might be low key on a national level but are very important for our associates and customers – either through personal experiences or due to the support they give in local communities.
>
> Since the Community Fund was created in 2008, we have supported over 150 local charities for a wide range of reasons. Here are just a few of the people and organisations that have benefitted from the Community Fund to date:
>
> - Bury Hospice, which works to provide end of life and palliative care to people who have been diagnosed with a life limiting disease
> - CHICKS, which provides free respite breaks for vulnerable children aged between 8–15 who may be in care, poverty or suffering due to illness or bereavement
> - The Brain Research Trust, which funds vital basic and clinical research into the causes, treatments, prevention and cure of neurological diseases
> - Julia's House Children's Hospice, which is based in Dorset, and cares for children with life limiting illnesses, the majority of which won't live past the age of 16

Corporate giving

In 2010/11 the company gave £879,000 in cash donations to its five nominated charities – Action for Children, Cancer Research UK, Comic Relief, The Woodland Trust and Uganda Classroom Fund (working with Save the Children).

Employee-led support

Significant fundraising is carried out by the company's employees and in 2010/11, £644,000 was generated through fundraising.

Commercially-led support

During the year, the company began raising funds for charity through the sale of carrier bags and over £376,600 was raised by this initiative. This will be donated to The Woodland trust and Uganda Classroom Project. Other commercially led support includes initiatives with its other charity partners.

Charity Partners:

Action for Children, Cancer Research UK, Comic Relief, Enable Ireland The Woodland Trust and Uganda Classroom Fund (working with Save the Children).

Corporate social responsibility

CSR committee: No details found of a UK committee.

CSR policy: Taken from the group's website:

> At TK Maxx we are passionate about conducting our business with integrity and being a responsible retailer. But what does that actually mean? It means supporting the local communities where we live and work. It means taking a responsible and ethical approach to the way we do business. And last but definitely not least, it means doing our bit for the environment too.

CSR report: CSR annual report covers the group's global programme.

Applications

In writing to the correspondent.

TNT UK Ltd

Logistics, transport and shipping services

Correspondent: Alistair Cochrane, Managing Director, Express Services UK and Ireland, TNT Express House, Holly Lane, Atherstone, Warwickshire CV9 2RY (tel: 01827 303030; fax: 01827 720215; website: www.tnt.co.uk)

Directors: J. C. Downing; S. E. Barnes; A. D. J. Cochraine; R. M. Judge

Year end	31/12/2011
Turnover	£791,107,000
Pre-tax profit	£3,490,000

Nature of business: Transportation and logistics holding company.

Company registration number: 1628530

Main locations: Atherstone, Bury, Stubbins

Total employees: 10,227

Charitable donations

UK cash (latest declared):	2011	£35,000
	2009	£529,000
	2007	£529,000
	2005	£160,000
Total UK:	2011	£35,000
Total worldwide:	2011	£35,000
Cash worldwide:	2011	£35,000

Corporate social responsibility

CSR committee: Information taken from the company's website:

> Corporate responsibility is an integral part of TNT's strategy and daily operations. Alistair Cochrane, Managing Director, TNT Express Services UK & Ireland is responsible for implementing TNT's corporate responsibility policies and the

CR performance of the UK & Ireland business unit.

CSR policy: Statement taken from the 2011 CSR report:

> TNT believes the management of corporate responsibility is not only the right thing to do, it also makes good business sense. TNT aims to achieve standards of responsible care across a number of key areas including: customers, health and safety, the environment, employees and the community in which we operate.

And from the company's website:

> TNT is committed to managing its business in a socially responsible manner – one that seeks to make a positive contribution to the communities in which it works and yet has a minimum impact on the environment in which it operates.

We were unable to determine the ratio of women to men on the Board.

CSR report: Published annually.

Exclusions

No support for political and religious appeals.

Applications

In writing to the correspondent.

Other information

TNT UK Ltd declared charitable donations of £6,000 (2010: £18,000).

TNT Express is a major supporter of the Wooden Spoon, a charity that funds projects for children and young people who are physically, mentally or socially disadvantaged within the UK and since adopting the Wooden Spoon as its chosen charity in 1997, TNT has raised in excess of £3 million. The company also supports the World Food Programme and in 2011 the UK business donated £35,000 to WFP. As it is not clear how much the company itself-has donated, as opposed to staff fundraising efforts, and as we were not able to find a value for in kind giving, we have taken the business figure of £35,000 as the total contributions figure.

In addition to the Wooden Spoon and the World Food Programme, TNT people support other selected charities. Every year TNT transforms one of its customer contact centres into a Children in Need call centre where employees from throughout the country give up their time to man the phones. Last year, at TNT's Lount centre, the company took a record £176,000 in donations and pledges for the BBC charity.

TNT staff dedicate at least one day every year to Wear it Pink Day in aid of Breast Cancer Campaign for whom, in 2011, more than £17,000 was raised.
Employees also heavily support Comic Relief, Sport Relief and numerous other local charities.

Tomkins Ltd

Manufacturing

Correspondent: Charitable Fund Administrator, East Putney House, 84 Upper Richmond Road, London SW15 2ST (tel: 020 8871 4544; fax: 020 8877 5055; website: www.tomkins.co.uk)

Directors: James Nicol, Chief Executive; John Zimmerman; Al Power; Terry O'Halloran (women: 0; men: 4)

Turnover	£1,289,200,000
Pre-tax profit	(£303,100,000)

Nature of business: Tomkins plc is an international engineering business. The company is organised into two business segments – Industrial and Automotive and Building Products, consisting of various business areas which operate in a variety of end markets.

Company registration number: 203531

Main locations: London

UK employees: 1,799

Total employees: 28,182

Charitable donations

UK cash (latest declared):	2009	£61,000
	2008	£202,000
	2007	£98,000
	2006	£156,000
	2005	£165,000

Corporate social responsibility

CSR committee: There was no evidence of a separate CSR Committee.

CSR policy: There was no information regarding CSR Policy.

CSR report: There was no evidence of a separate CSR report.

Exclusions

No support for overseas projects.

Applications

Applications should be made in writing to the correspondent.

Other information

There was no information available regarding charitable donations.

Tomkins provided the following statement regarding its community support policy:

> Tomkins has well-established guidelines that determine the nature of organisations to which support is given. The charities given assistance cover a wide range of activities including health and welfare, education, civic and community projects, culture and the arts. Tomkins prefers to spread its charitable giving across many smaller local charities that usually do not have the organisation, structure or resources to compete with the marketing skills of the larger, high-profile charitable bodies. Tomkins makes further donations through advertising, products for prizes and volunteers or other in kind support.
>
> In the UK, applications are normally made to Tomkins' corporate office in London. Requests for donations are made from a variety of charities and Tomkins tries to respond positively to as many requests as possible, provided they come from smaller local charities and are registered with the Charity Commission.
>
> Each year, upon the initiative of the board of Tomkins, consideration is given to making a single donation to a registered charity of an amount exceptional to Tomkins' normal level of giving. Normally, such single donations are made in response to an appeal with a special purpose and the board, in its absolute discretion, determines whether or not such appeal is eligible for consideration and the amount of the donation.

Topps Tiles plc

Retail – miscellaneous

Correspondent: Janet Burgess, jburgess@toppstiles.co.uk, Thorpe Way, Grove Park, Enderby, Leicestershire LE19 1SU (tel: 01162 828000; fax: 01162 828178; website: www.toppstiles.co.uk)

Directors: Michael Jack, Chair; Matthew Williams, Chief Executive Officer; Robert Parker, Finance Director; Nicholas Ounstead; Alan White (women: 0; men: 5)

Year end	01/10/2011
Turnover	£175,525,000
Pre-tax profit	£7,908,000

Nature of business: The principal activity of the company is the retail and wholesale distribution of ceramic tiles, wood flooring and related products.

Company registration number: 3213782

Main locations: Enderby

Total employees: 1,661,000

Charitable donations

UK cash (latest declared):	2009	£10,000
	2008	£10,000
	2007	£10,000
	2006	£10,000
	2005	£20,000
Cash worldwide:	2011	£0

Corporate social responsibility

CSR committee: No details of a dedicated committee found.

CSR policy: The following is taken from the company's website:

> Taking responsibility for our impact on society is important to us as a business and we have been developing our corporate social responsibility agenda since 2004. Over the past eight years we have evolved and enhanced our programme to ensure we are an active member within the communities we work, that we work in an environmentally conscious manner, and we ensure our employees feel supported, developed and engaged.

We are proud of our achievements in this area and focus our attention across 3 primary areas:

- Community and Charity
- Environment
- Our People

CSR report: Published within the annual report and accounts.

Exclusions

The company does not make political contributions.

Applications

Applications for support of cash or in kind should be made in writing to the correspondent.

Other information

During the period 2011, the group made no charitable donations (2010: £10,000 to Help for Heroes).

Usually, support is given to a particular cause and appeals from areas in which the company has a presence. Only a limited number of appeals can be assisted in any one year.

Charity of the Year: During 2011 the company continued to support Help for Heroes as the group's Charity of the Year.

Sponsorship: *Sport* – Topps provides new kits and equipment to junior teams local to its stores. Whenever a new store is opened, a local team is selected for support. The company considers this to be a simple and effective way of reaching out to the local community wherever it trades. Topps is one of the biggest supporters of youth football in the UK and currently supports over 300 teams.

Mosaics – The third key area of community support is Topps sponsorship of two major competitions designed to showcase the work of novice mosaic artists.

Toshiba Information Systems (UK) Ltd

Electronics/computers, telecommunications

Correspondent: P Whelan, The Company Secretary, Toshiba Court, Weybridge Business Park, Addlestone Road, Weybridge, Surrey KT15 2UL (tel: 01932 841600; fax: 01932 847240; website: www.toshiba.co.uk)

Directors: A. Thompson; A. Bass; K. Matsuda

Year end	31/03/2012
Turnover	£511,216,530
Pre-tax profit	£11,221,663

Nature of business: The sale, marketing and distribution of computers and telephone systems, consumer products and mobile phones.

Company registration number: 918861

Main locations: Weybridge

Total employees: 254

Charitable donations

UK cash (latest declared):	2012	£18,850
	2009	£21,600
	2008	£47,000
Total UK:	2012	£18,850
Total worldwide:	2012	£18,850
Cash worldwide:	2012	£18,850

Corporate social responsibility

CSR committee: No committee relevant to the UK.

CSR policy: The Toshiba Corporation states:

> Toshiba Group's Corporate Philosophy emphasises respect for people, creation of new value, and contribution to society. The group slogan – 'Committed to People, Committed to the Future' – expresses the essence of our corporate philosophy. We recognize that it is our corporate social responsibility (CSR) to put our philosophy and slogan into practice in our day-to-day business activities. In doing so, we accord the highest priority to human life and safety and to compliance.

The Corporation's CSR community investment does not include the UK.

We were unable to determine the ratio of women to men on the board.

CSR report: There is an annual CSR report published on the website but has no information regarding UK community giving.

Applications

In writing to the correspondent.

Other information

In 2011/12 the company made charitable donations totalling £18,850 which included a number of small donations to local charities and £8,000 to Reed School Cobham for disadvantaged children. This information relates to Toshiba Information Systems (UK) Ltd and not the Toshiba Corporation which gives mainly to organisations in 'developing countries'.

Total UK Ltd

Oil and gas/fuel

Correspondent: Claire Elliot, Corporate Communications Manager, 40 Clarendon Road, Watford, Hertfordshire WD17 1TQ (tel: 01923 694000; fax: 01923 694400; website: www.total.co.uk)

Year end	31/12/2011
Turnover	£4,411,000,000
Pre-tax profit	£11,000,000

Nature of business: The refining, distribution and sale of petroleum products and lubricants. The company was formed through the merger of Total, Petrofina and Elf.

Company registration number: 553535

Main locations: Milford Haven, London, Watford, Redhill, Immingham, Stalybridge, Aberdeen

UK employees: 3000

Total employees: 96100

Membership: BITC

Charitable donations

UK cash (latest declared):	2011	£112,000
	2008	£370,000
	2007	£540,000
	2006	£536,000
	2005	£280,000
Total worldwide:	2011	£22,518,300

Corporate social responsibility

CSR committee: No committee

CSR policy: Chief executive's statement on corporate responsibility: 'We make a real effort to be involved in and assist the communities where we operate. Young people, education and the environment are three common themes in our community involvement and all three are exemplified in our Total Green School Awards project.'

We were unable to determine the ratio of women to men on the board.

CSR report: A Corporate Social Responsibility report is available at the company's website.

Exclusions

No support for circular appeals, advertising in charity brochures, animal welfare, appeals from individuals, elderly people, fundraising events, overseas projects, political appeals, religious appeals, sickness/disability, social welfare or sport.

Applications

In writing only to the correspondent for those organisations located near to Total refining and marketing facilities (refer to the list of 'preferred locations'). For organisations based near to Total's exploration and production facilities in Aberdeen, contact: Sandra McIntosh, Public Affairs and Corporate Communication Department, Total E&P plc, Crawpeel Road, Altens, Aberdeen AB12 3FG (Tel: 01224 297000).

Other information

Charitable donations in 2011 amounted to £211,000. Beneficiaries included: the Dacorum Community Trust; Watford Peace Hospice and Watford Mencap. The national charity CLIC Sargent appears to receive yearly support from the company. At a local level, regional offices, refineries and service stations hold 'fun days', raising thousands of pounds for charities in their area.

We were previously advised that the company had a preference for local charities in areas of company presence (i.e. Aberdeen, Watford, Immingham,

Milford Haven, Redhill and Stalybridge), appeals relevant to company business, or those which have a member of company staff involved. Preferred areas of support are: the arts, youth, education, enterprise/training, environment/ heritage, medical research and science/ technology.

Environment: The following is taken from the company's UK CSR report:

> Young people, education and the environment are at the heart of our community activities, with the Total Green School Awards, our national initiative for primary school children, now established as a flagship project. Run by the Young People's Trust for the Environment in partnership with Total, the awards aim to generate interest in the environment and raise awareness of the need for sustainable energy sources.
>
> Well over 120,000 children from all parts of Britain have so far taken part in the awards since they began six years ago. Strong links have been forged between our various Total locations, the children and staff of neighbouring schools and with our other stakeholders. The awards are specifically designed to assist and encourage cross-curricular work on the environment among children aged from five to 11. The 2011 awards attracted entries from 21,343 young people across the UK.

Prizes range from £100 to £5,000.

Education: 'Education also remained at the core of Total UK's community involvement and once again the long-standing support for Watford Football Club Sports and Community Sports and Education Trust featured strongly.' The company also provide mentoring and work experience schemes for local students.

Payroll giving: The company operates the Give As You Earn Scheme.

Sponsorship: Sponsorship is undertaken for organisations involved in health, education, sports and community projects.

Match funding: Staff raised more than £26,250 through their individual initiatives and matching funds from the company.

Volunteering: The company holds an annual 'Volunteer 2Day Scheme'.

Toyota Motor Manufacturing (UK) Ltd

Motors and accessories

Correspondent: The External Affairs Department Team, External Affairs Department, Burnaston, Derbyshire DE1 9TA (tel: 01332 282121; website: www.toyotauk.com)

Directors: T. Kawabata; H. Ochiai; T. Kubo; K. Kokima; A. Walker; Y. Hiraoka; T. Karasawa

Year end	31/03/2011
Turnover	£1,865,189,000
Pre-tax profit	(£109,260,000)

Nature of business: Car and engine manufacture.

Company registration number: 2352348

Main locations: Burnaston, Deeside

Total employees: 3,338

Membership: BITC

Charitable donations

UK cash (latest declared):	2011	£645,000
	2009	£541,000
	2008	£350,000
	2007	£257,000
Total UK:	2011	£645,000
Total worldwide:	2011	£645,000
Cash worldwide:	2011	£645,000

Community involvement

Toyota Manufacturing UK provides grants of up to £1,000 for successful projects in the fields of the environment, children, education and health within its local communities. These grants are intended for the purchase of long-term tangible equipment and resources up to the value of £1,000.

In June 2008 the **Toyota Manufacturing UK Charitable Trust** was established (Charity Commission no. 1124678). The funds are raised by members of the company and in this year, 2010/11, £99,000 was distributed by the trust.

Corporate giving

In 2010/11, the company donated £645,000 for charitable purposes (2009/10: £238,500). These donations comprised:

- £38,500 to charities involved in conserving the environment and promoting environmental preservation and awareness
- £89,000 to charities involved in medical research; and
- £518,000 was donated to local charities involved in a range of activities in the communities surrounding Burnaston and Deeside

In kind support

Local charitable events are regularly supported through the donation of raffle prizes and vehicles.

Employee-led support

Employee involvement in the community is encouraged and, where suitable, financial support given.

Matched funding: Employee fundraising efforts are matched by the company up to a maximum of £250 per activity.

Payroll giving: A payroll giving scheme is in operation.

Corporate social responsibility

CSR committee: None.

CSR policy: Environmental policy relating to car emissions and waste.

We were unable to determine the ratio of women to men on the board.

CSR report: Update on environment policy published within the annual report and accounts.

Exclusions

No support for advertising in charity brochures, animal welfare, appeals from individuals, the arts, enterprise/training, fundraising events, overseas projects, political or religious appeals, science/ technology, social welfare, sport, or local appeals not in areas of company presence. No response to circular appeals.

Applications

A self-screening eligibility form and an application form are posted on the company's website. If your organisation meets the eligibility criteria, forward your completed application form to the correspondent.

Travelex Holdings Ltd

Financial services

Correspondent: PA to the Chair, 65 Kingsway, London WC2B 6TD (tel: 020 7400 4000/020 7400 4000; fax: 020 7400 4001; website: www.travelex.co.uk)

Directors: Lloyd Dorfman; Peter Jackson; Lord John Stevens; Stephen Grabiner; Michael Ball; Gavin Laws; Phil Hodkinson; James Ruane; Michael Phillips; Sylvain Pignet (women: 0; men: 10)

Year end	31/12/2010
Turnover	£695,600,000
Pre-tax profit	(£74,000,000)

Nature of business: The provision of travel money services, funds transfer services, issuance of travellers' cheques, dealing in foreign bank notes and the provision of other travel and financial related services. The Group operates through its subsidiaries in the United Kingdom, North America, Asia Pacific, Continental Europe and Africa.

Company registration number: 5356574

Total employees: 7,098

Charitable donations

UK cash (latest declared):	2009	£25,000
	2008	£26,000
	2007	£17,000
	2006	£85,000
Total worldwide:	2010	£25,000
Cash worldwide:	2010	£25,000

Corporate social responsibility

CSR committee: No details found.

CSR policy: See 'Other information'.

Unable to determine the ratio of women to men on the board.

CSR report: Very brief report contained within the annual report and accounts.

Exclusions

No support for advertising in charity brochures, local appeals not in areas of company presence.

Applications

In writing to the correspondent.

Other information

Over the past few years charitable donations have been in the region of around £25,000. Previously the company has supported cancer research, the development of young people, and the arts.

The annual report states that the company operates through a wide global network and CSR activity is currently managed locally so to remain close to the communities in which it operates. The global Christmas card fund is donated to an appropriate appeal and this year the company supported Shelter – no details were given of the amount.

The UK company sponsors The National Theatre providing cut price tickets to customers.

Travis Perkins plc

Building/construction

Correspondent: Marketing Director, Lodge Way House, Harlestone Road, Northampton NN5 7UG (tel: 01604 752424; fax: 01604 758718; website: www.travisperkins.co.uk)

Directors: Robert Walker, Chair; Geoff Cooper, Chief Executive; Paul Hampden Smith, Finance Director; John Carter; Ruth Anderson; Philip Jansen; Chris Bunker; Andrew Simon; John Coleman (women: 1; men: 8)

Year end	31/12/2011
Turnover	£4,779,100,000
Pre-tax profit	£269,600,000

Nature of business: The marketing and distribution of timber, building and plumbing materials and the hiring of tools to the building trade and industry generally.

Company registration number: 824821

Brands include: BSS Industrial, PTS, Keyline, City Plumbing Supplies, CCF, Wickes, Benchmarx, Tile Giant and Toolstation.

Main locations: Northampton

UK employees: 22,000

Total employees: 22,000

Charitable donations

UK cash (latest declared):	2011	£146,200
	2009	£211,000
	2008	£211,000
	2007	£154,000
	2006	£203,000
Total UK:	2011	£146,200
Total worldwide:	2011	£146,200
Cash worldwide:	2011	£146,200

Corporate social responsibility

CSR committee: No specific committee.

CSR policy: Information on CSR taken from the company's annual report and accounts: 'Corporate social responsibility is the responsibility of the individual businesses particularly when it comes to charitable fundraising and community programmes.'

CSR report: The company has not produced a separate CR statement in the report and accounts since it believes these matters are sufficiently important to receive the personal attention of individual directors rather than risking less focus through the exercise of collective responsibility. Full details of those areas normally covered by such a report are contained in the reports of the directors responsible for such matters. For further information see 2010/11 annual report and the chief executive's review of the year.

Exclusions

No support for advertising in charity brochures, animal welfare, appeals from individuals, the arts, children/youth, education, elderly people, enterprise/ training, environment, heritage, medical research, overseas projects, political appeals, religious appeals science/ technology, sickness/disability, social welfare, sport, local appeals not in areas of company presence or large national appeals.

Applications

In writing to the correspondent.

Travis Perkins reviews its supported charities every two years. If you are looking for charitable support contact the Internal Communications Manager on 01604 752424.

Other information

The chief executive's review of the year for 2011 states that 'through the efforts of the group's employees, ably supported by customers and suppliers, £1.9 million was raised for worthy causes including £146,200 contributed by the group'. We have therefore taken the figure of £146,200 as the company's UK charitable contribution as we have no way of estimating any volunteering or fundraising time, gifts in kind etc., made by the group for these activities.

Further information regarding employees' fundraising efforts taken from the website:

Four charities benefit from the fundraising activities of Travis Perkins:

Breast Cancer Campaign

Breast Cancer Campaign's mission is to beat breast cancer by funding innovative world-class research to understand how breast cancer develops, leading to improved diagnosis, treatment, prevention and cure.

Together for Short Lives

Together for Short Lives is the national charity that gives voice and support to all children's hospice services. Its vision is for every child and young person who is not expected to reach adulthood – and their family – to have awareness of, and access to, the highest standards of care and support close to or in the home.

WNAA – Warwickshire and Northamptonshire Air Ambulance

WNAA service routinely carries senior Doctors and Consultants to the scene of incidents in just minutes, providing lifesaving treatment and medication at the scene and en-route to hospital. In essence, they take the hospital to the patient, providing the best possible chance of a full recovery.

Keech Hospice Care for Children

Keech children's hospice service supports families from across Bedfordshire, Hertfordshire and Milton Keynes with a child or young person diagnosed with a life-limiting condition. Their staff offer medical and social care, emotional support and friendship to the whole family, throughout the child's illness and after their death, for as long as it is needed. This care is available in-house at the charity's bright and comfortable children's hospice near Luton, or via our community nursing team at the family home.

Travis Perkins reviews its supported Charities every 2 years. If you are looking for charitable support please contact our Internal Communications Manager on 01604 752424.

A charity committee helps to steer a variety of fundraising activities at branches nationwide and Travis Perkins head office throughout the year. Past events have included parachute jumps, marathons and fun runs, auctions, charity balls, '3 Peaks' and 'Beat the Moon' challenges, car washes and much more.

To celebrate the new charity partnership with Breast Cancer Campaign, Travis Perkins adopted a pink theme, and began by re-spraying 4 of its delivery trucks bright pink. Branches across the country are taking it in turn to use the trucks in their local area when they are fundraising, so look out for a pink Travis Perkins truck near you!

Travis Perkins plc also operates Payroll Giving, enabling its employees to donate to charity directly from their salary. Travis Perkins plc matches any donation made by colleagues to its nominated charities. The company also runs a colleague lottery and salary sacrifice scheme called 'Small Change, Big Difference', where employees donate the 'spare' pennies from their monthly salary to the company's nominated charities.

Trinity Mirror plc

Media

Correspondent: Paul Vickers, Group Secretary and Legal Director, One Canada Square, Canary Wharf, London E14 5AP (tel: 020 7293 3000; fax: 020 7510 3405; email: paul.vickers@trinitymirror.com; website: www.trinitymirror.com)

Directors: Sir Ian Gibson, Chair; Sly Bailey, Chief Executive; David Grigson; Gary Hoffman; Jane Lighting; Kathleen O'Donovan; Donal Smith; Vijay Vaghela; Paul Vickers; Laura Wade-Gery; Nick Fullagar; Georgina Harvey; Mark Hollinshead; Tony Pusey (women: 5; men: 9)

Year end	31/12/2011
Turnover	£750,000,000
Pre-tax profit	£92,000,000

Nature of business: The main activity of the group is the publication and printing of newspapers both in the UK and overseas.

Company registration number: 82548

Charitable donations

UK cash (latest declared):	2011	£75,000
	2009	£84,000
	2008	£84,000
	2007	£80,000
	2005	£60,000
Total UK:	2011	£75,000
Total worldwide:	2011	£75,000
Cash worldwide:	2011	£75,000

Corporate social responsibility

CSR committee: There was no evidence of a separate CSR Committee.

CSR policy: This information was obtained from the company's website:

> Trinity Mirror believes that it can best support charities through the pages of its newspapers. This support will either be through appeals to readers for donations or through editorial content, describing the aims and activities of various charities. In every case the decision as to whether or not to support a charity appeal or whether to run editorial comment will be one for the editor of each newspaper.

CSR report: There was no evidence of a separate CSR report.

Exclusions

No support for local appeals not in areas of company presence.

Applications

Applications at group level should be made in writing to the correspondent, but only where one of the following applies:

- Charities connected with or associated with the newspaper, printing or advertising industries
- Charities operating in the communities immediately surrounding Trinity Mirror's offices and print sites
- Legitimate and supportable causes falling outside the above two criteria, but with a demonstrable business/commercial reason why such support should be given

Applications at regional level should be addressed to the editor or manager of the newspaper/print site based in your community. Prior agreement of the relevant managing director will be required before a donation can be made.

Other information

During the year contributions for charitable purposes totalled £75,000, principally to various charities connected or associated with the newspaper, printing or advertising industries and local charities serving the communities in which the company operates.

The company's policy with regard to charitable donations and other such payments is as follows as outlined in its annual report:

> Trinity Mirror plc will make direct cash donations to charities in certain limited circumstances. The company will, at a group level, support various charities connected with or associated with the newspaper, printing or advertising industries. A second category of direct cash support will be to charities operating in the communities immediately surrounding the group's offices and print sites. The charities that are likely to receive support are smaller community based charities where a modest donation will make a big impact. It is unlikely that a major national charity that just happens to be based very close to one of our offices would receive a donation.
>
> There will be a further limited general pool of funds out of which donations will be made to legitimate and supportable causes that fall outside the above two criteria. There will, however, need in each case to be a demonstrable business or commercial reason why such support should be given. Each of our regional newspaper companies have a small budget out of which they will make direct cash donations to charities working in the community in which the newspaper is based. Scottish Daily Record and Sunday Mail Ltd will similarly make a number of donations to appropriate charities based in Scotland.
>
> The national titles of the Daily Mirror, Sunday Mirror and The People are most unlikely to make direct cash donations. They will do so only where they are asked to make a payment to a charity in lieu of a fee for an interview or some form of support.
>
> In addition to cash donations, the company is active in making donations in kind, in the form of used computer equipment, furniture, books and so on. Through its community involvement programmes the company makes available members of its staff for volunteering and mentoring programmes. The company has an established employee volunteering policy which enables all of its employees to volunteer to work for a day to support a good cause in their area. This is backed up with unspecified financial support.

TT Electronics plc

Engineering

Correspondent: The Company Secretary, Clive House, 12–18 Queens Road, Weybridge, Surrey KT13 9XB (tel: 01932 841310; fax: 01932 836450; website: www.ttelectronics.com)

Directors: Sean Watson, Chair; Geraint Anderson, Chief Executive; Shatish Dasani; Tim Roberts; John Shakeshaft; Michael Baunton; Stephen King; Wendy Sharp (women: 0; men: 8)

Year end	31/12/2011
Turnover	£590,000,000
Pre-tax profit	£32,000,000

Nature of business: The main activities of the company are in two business divisions: electronic components and industrial engineering.

Company registration number: 87249

Main locations: Havant, Edenbridge, Gravesend, Filey, Letchworth, Hinckley, Haverhill, Lancing, Cardiff, Cowes, Colnbrook, Coalville, Cleckheaton, Chester-le-Street, Tipton, Swindon, Wolverhampton, Mountain Ash, Newport, Manchester, Skelmersdale, Sevenoaks, Scarborough, Rotherham, Romford, Ramsbottom, Bedlington, Ashford, Blyth, Bootle

Total employees: 6,215

Charitable donations

UK cash (latest declared):	2009	£53,000
	2007	£50,000
	2006	£50,000
	2005	£50,000
	2004	£50,000
Total worldwide:	2011	£58,000
Cash worldwide:	2011	£58,000

Corporate social responsibility

CSR committee: There was evidence of a separate CSR Committee.

CSR policy: This information was taken from the company's latest annual report:

> We are committed to understanding, monitoring and managing our social, environmental and economic impact to enable us to contribute to society's wider goal of sustainable development. We aim to demonstrate these responsibilities through our actions and within our corporate policies.

CSR report: There was no evidence of a separate CSR report.

Exclusions

The company does not make political contributions, or respond to circulars or general appeals.

Applications

In writing to the correspondent.

Other information

In 2011 the company donated £58,000 to charitable causes. Its annual report states that in addition to the cash amount there was giving-in kind through employee time. 'During 2011, we actively encouraged employees to become involved in worthwhile community activities, in partnership with community organisations.'

TUI Travel plc

Transport and communications

Correspondent: The Company Secretary, TUI Travel House, Crawley Business Quarter, Fleming Way, Crawley, West Sussex RH10 9QL (tel: 01293 645700; website: www.tuitravelplc.com)

Directors: Michael Frenzel, Chair; Michael Hodgkinson; Peter Long, Chief Executive; William Waggott, Chief Financial Officer; Johan Lundgren; Volker Böttcher; Horst Baier; Tony Campbell; Clare Chapman; Bill Dalton; Rainer Feuerhake; Harold Sher; Albert Schunk; Erhard Schipporeit; Minnow Powell; Coline McConville (women: 2; men: 14)

Year end	30/09/2011
Turnover	£14,687,000,000
Pre-tax profit	£87,000,000

Nature of business: The principal activities of the company comprise the provision of inclusive holidays and the sale of other related travel services, including the sale of foreign currencies.

Company registration number: 6072876

Main locations: London

Total employees: 53,247

Charitable donations

UK cash (latest declared):	2009	£291,000
	2008	£236,000
Total worldwide:	2011	£380,700
Cash worldwide:	2011	£380,700

Corporate social responsibility

CSR committee: No dedicated CSR committee.

CSR policy: No specific CSR policy. The company focuses on its sustainability initiatives.

CSR report: There is an annual sustainability report published in the annual report and accounts. Charitable giving is included in the report.

Applications

In writing to the correspondent.

Other information

During the year, the group made charitable donations of £380,700 (2010: £475,300). We have no information regarding the beneficiaries of this.

The following information is taken from the company's Sustainability Report published in the 2010/11 annual report and accounts:

> In the last year, our businesses supported many source market and destination charities. Our group-wide charity policy and guidelines help businesses to ensure transparency, report annual monies collected and manage charity relationships. Key achievements in 2010/11 include:
>
> - We are the largest corporate sponsor of the Family Holiday Association a charity that provides holidays to disadvantaged children and their families. Since 2009 we have donated more than £1 million
> - Street Child World Cup has been selected as the Specialist & Activity Sector's chosen charity for the next three years. Colleagues will be involved in raising as much money as possible for millions of vulnerable children living on the streets around the world
> - Many TUI Travel businesses support the Travel Foundation, a charity which helps the travel industry understand, manage and take effective action on sustainable tourism. To date we have donated more than £2.8 million

Tullis Russell Group Ltd

Print/paper/packaging, professional support services

Correspondent: G D Miller, Company Secretary, Rothersfield, Markinch Glenrothes, Fife KY7 6PB (tel: 01592 753311; fax: 01592 755872; website: www.tullisrussell.com)

Directors: F. A. W. Bowden; T. J. Bowdler; B. M. Jackson; G. D. Miller; C. A. G. Parr; A. Scott

Year end	31/03/2011
Turnover	£177,524,000
Pre-tax profit	£2,416,000

Nature of business: Tullis Russell Group Ltd is an employee-owned industrial holding company, providing management services. The principal subsidiary companies are involved in the manufacture of papers and boards for clients world-wide.

Company registration number: SC150075

Main locations: Bollington, Hanley, Glenrothes

Total employees: 763

Charitable donations

UK cash (latest declared):	2011	£349,000
	2009	£39,000
	2008	£17,000
	2007	£18,000
	2006	£29,000
Total UK:	2011	£349,000
Total worldwide:	2011	£349,000
Cash worldwide:	2011	£349,000

Corporate social responsibility

CSR policy: No CSR information found.

We were unable to determine the ratio of women to men on the board.

Exclusions

No grants for local appeals not in areas of company presence, large national appeals, enterprise/training, medical research, overseas projects, political appeals, science/technology or sport.

Applications

In writing to the correspondent.

Other information

During the year 2010/11 the group gave charitable donations of £349,000 (2009/10: £32,000). The donations were all made to local charitable organisations in order to support the community, including £330,000 to the Tullis Russell Eco Centre.

UBS

Banking

Correspondent: Nick Wright, Managing Director, Community Affairs, 100 Liverpool Street, London EC2M 2RH (tel: 020 7568 2365; fax: 020 7567 3364; website: www.ubs.com)

Directors: Rainer-Marc Frey; Ann F. Godbehere; Helmut Panke; William G. Parrett; Kaspar Villiger, Chair; Michel Demaré; David Sidwell; Bruno Gehrig; Axel P. Lehmann; Wolfgang Mayrhuber; Joseph Yam (women: 1; men: 10)

Year end	31/12/2011
Turnover	£18,587,612,000
Pre-tax profit	£3,578,657,000

Nature of business: International banking.

Company registration number: 2035362

Main locations: Taunton, Brighton, Edinburgh, Manchester, London, Newcastle, Edinburgh, Birmingham

Total employees: 64,820

Membership: BITC, LBG

Charitable donations

UK cash (latest declared):	2009	£2,000,000
	2005	£2,000,000
Total worldwide:	2011	£20,800,000
Cash worldwide:	2011	£20,800,000

Community involvement

The following information is from UBS's CR report:

We are continuing with our well-established tradition of supporting the advancement and empowerment of organisations and individuals within the communities in which we do business. Our initial focus was centered on direct cash donations, but we have progressed to a position where our community investment program encompasses employee volunteering, matched-giving schemes, in kind donations, disaster relief efforts and partnerships with community groups, educational institutions and cultural organisations in all of our business regions.

Throughout the region, we continue to support educational and entrepreneurial activities, particularly in areas close to where we conduct our business. We now have active Community Affairs programs in the UK, France, Italy, South Africa, Poland, UAE, Russia, Ireland and Jersey.

The regional flagship program is our partnership with the Bridge Academy, a mixed, non-denominational school for 11–18 year olds in Hackney, one of the most deprived boroughs in London and adjacent to UBS's London base.

Client Foundation (UBS Optimus Foundation)

Charitable organisations and projects across the globe – usually in regions where we do not maintain a business presence – also benefit from the support of the UBS Optimus Foundation. The UBS Optimus Foundation is one of Switzerland's largest charitable foundations. It is a not-for-profit organisation which offers UBS clients a broad range of opportunities to improve the lives of children around the globe.

Corporate giving

In 2011, UBS and affiliated foundations made direct cash donations totalling of CHF 31.1 million [£20.8 million] to carefully selected not-for-profit partner organisations and charities. These donations were directed primarily towards achieving our Community Affairs key themes of 'education' and 'entrepreneurship'. Unfortunately, we have been unable to determine what proportion of this community support was given in the UK. Contributions were also made to other activities, in particular disaster relief, including CHF 3.2 million in Japan.

Client foundation

Since its foundation in 2000, the foundation has contributed over CHF 118 million to 250 projects in 73 countries. Employing a sophisticated funding strategy, it plays a key role in bringing about positive social change in the areas including healthcare, education and child protection. As UBS bears all the administrative costs related to the UBS Optimus Foundation, clients can be sure that 100% of every donation goes directly to the project.

In kind support

Support to those in need is sometimes given in kind, especially through the recycling of unwanted goods such as mobile phones, business clothes, foreign coins, spectacles, office equipment and toys.

Employee-led support

Across all business regions, employees play an active role in the company's community investment efforts, in particular through their volunteering activities. In 2011, 11,678 employees spent 105,000 hours volunteering. Staff are supported in their commitment by the company which offers up to two working days a year for volunteering efforts, and also matches employee donations to selected charities.

In Switzerland, our community investment efforts are also advanced by the UBS Culture Foundation, the UBS Foundation for Social Issues and Education, and the association A Helping Hand from UBS Employees. In 2011, these organisations have again made valuable contributions to important social causes, including fostering the humanities and the creative arts, supporting communities in need, and helping disabled and disadvantaged people.

Payroll giving: The Give As You Earn scheme is in operation, which in most instances is matched by the company pound for pound.

Commercially-led support

Sponsorship: *The arts* – UBS supports the London Symphony Orchestra through its Soundscapes collaboration.

Corporate social responsibility

CSR committee: There is a Corporate Responsibility Committee.

CSR policy: Statement taken from the 2011 annual CR report:

In 2011, we continued working towards meeting the demanding societal goals and commitments we have set ourselves, guided by our Code of Business Conduct and Ethics. While we undoubtedly faced significant challenges in 2011, this has only served to strengthen our resolve to ensure that all our people at every level follow the code unreservedly both in letter and spirit. By adhering to the code, we demonstrate our desire to be a responsible corporate institution and to act with integrity in all our interactions with our stakeholders.

CSR report: There is an annual corporate responsibility report published online.

Applications

In writing to the correspondent.

UIA (Insurance) Ltd

Insurance

Correspondent: Andrew Gay, Company Secretary, Kings Court, London Road, Stevenage, Hertfordshire SG1 2TP (tel: 01438 761761; fax: 01438 761762; email: charitable.foundation@uia.co.uk; website: www.uia.co.uk)

Directors: Ian Templeton; Ian Cracknell; Gerry Gallagher; Peter Dodd; Malcolm Cantello; Bob Newton; Marion Saunders; Andrew Wainwright-Brown (women: 1; men: 7)

Year end	31/12/2011
Turnover	£22,000,000
Pre-tax profit	£990,000

Nature of business: Insurance company.

Company registration number: AC000532

Main locations: Stevenage

UK employees: 144

Total employees: 144

Charitable donations

UK cash (latest declared):	2011	£50,000
	2009	£48,600
	2008	£12,500
	2007	£23,000
	2006	£30,000
Total UK:	2011	£50,000
Total worldwide:	2011	£50,000
Cash worldwide:	2011	£50,000

Corporate social responsibility

CSR committee: There was no evidence of a separate CSR Committee.

CSR policy: The company's community support programme is directed through a charitable foundation set up in 1999 for the 'disadvantaged in society'. The foundation is funded entirely by donations from UIA (Insurance) Ltd, UNISON's insurance company, and focuses its support on lesser known groups that take positive action on important social issues that might not otherwise be addressed.

CSR report: There was no evidence of a separate CSR report.

Exclusions

The foundation does not make grants for the following:

- Organisations that are not registered charities or formally constituted voluntary organisations
- Organisations that are not based in the UK
- Charities whose combined grant-related support costs and governance costs are greater than 10% of their turnover
- Work that we believe should be, or is, publicly funded
- National charities that have an established constituency of supporters
- Funding for information/advice-giving or newsletters

- Conferences or training courses
- Personal support of individuals
- The arts
- Work in mainstream education, including schools, nurseries, playschools, 'out of hours' clubs and academic research
- Environment, conservation, animal welfare, heritage or sporting projects
- Work with a bias towards a particular religion

This list may be amended at any time.

Applications

Committee meetings are usually held twice a year, in March and September. The trustees will only consider applications submitted on the foundation's application form and operate on a first come first served basis. In order to keep costs down and avoid postage, applicants are asked to download the form from this website and post-eight copies and their annual accounts to the named correspondent. Applications should reach the company no later than the beginning of February or August, but note that receipt of an application does not guarantee that it will be considered at the next meeting.

Other information

During the year to December 2011, the company made a donation of £50,000 to the UIA Charitable Foundation, (double the figure for the previous year).

UIA Charitable Foundation (Charity Commission no. 1079982)

Support is given to small organisations or groups where a modest grant (generally under £1,000), will make a real difference and which deal with:

- Victims of domestic abuse
- Victims of drug and alcohol addiction
- Rehabilitation of offenders
- Third World poverty
- Third World human rights

UK Coal plc

Mining

Correspondent: Company Secretary, Harworth Park, Blyth Road, Harworth, Doncaster, South Yorkshire DN11 8DB (tel: 01302 751751; fax: 01302 752420; website: www.ukcoal.com)

Directors: Jonson Cox, Chair; David Brocksom, Finance Director; Gareth Williams; Owen Michaelson; Peter Hickson; Lisa Clement; Keith Heller; Steven Underwood (women: 1; men: 6)

Year end	31/12/2011
Turnover	£488,216,000
Pre-tax profit	£57,983,000

Nature of business: The principal activities of the group are coal mining, opencast and underground, and associated activities.

Company registration number: 2649340

Main locations: Doncaster

Total employees: 2,605

Membership: BITC

Charitable donations

UK cash (latest declared):	2011	£0
	2009	£51,500
	2008	£45,000
	2007	£24,200
	2006	£5,300
Total UK:	2011	£0
Total worldwide:	2011	£0
Cash worldwide:	2011	£0

Corporate social responsibility

CSR committee: No information found.

> **CSR policy:** UK Coal believes in supporting suitable community projects around its surface and deep mines and work with suppliers and customers to restore former coal mining sites by investing in sustainable land regeneration projects and renewable technologies. We consistently measure the impact of our mining and development activities to help mitigate risks associated with our operations and meet environmental and safety standards.

CSR report: Published within the annual report and accounts.

Exclusions

No support for local appeals outside areas of company presence.

Applications

In writing to the correspondent.

Other information

During the year 2011 the company made no charitable contributions (2010: £39,000). The following statement is taken from the 2011 annual report:

> UK Coal is committed to working with its employees, customers, suppliers and contractors to promote responsible working and trading practices. It also provides assistance to the wider community by way of financial support for charitable and other local causes.
>
> Over the years UK Coal has invested millions of pounds in projects as diverse as schools, sports clubs and the creation of green spaces. All have benefitted from substantial funds provided by the extraction of indigenously mined coal. UK Coal's surface mine restoration team has won further awards in the last 12 months for their work on land rehabilitation. Close collaboration between UK Coal, Leeds City Council and the RSPB has resulted in a former mine site, St Aidan's near Leeds, being transformed over 10 years into an area of international wildlife importance.

Ultra Electronics Holdings plc

Defence, electronics/computers, security services, transport and communications

Correspondent: The Charities Committee, 417 Bridport Road, Greenford, Middlesex UB6 8UA (tel: 020 8813 4321; fax: 020 8813 4322; email: information@ultra-electronics.com; website: www.ultra-electronics.com)

Directors: Douglas Caster, Chair; Rakesh Sharma, Chief Executive; Paul Dean, Finance Director; Christopher Bailey; Ian Griffiths; Robert Walmsley; Andy Hamment (women: 0; men: 7)

Year end	31/12/2011
Turnover	£731,733,000
Pre-tax profit	£91,179,000

Nature of business: Ultra Electronics is an internationally successful defence, security, transport and energy company.

Company registration number: 2830397

Total employees: 4,206

Charitable donations

UK cash (latest declared):	2009	£60,000
	2008	£66,000
Total worldwide:	2011	£58,000
Cash worldwide:	2011	£58,000

Corporate social responsibility

CSR committee: Previous research identified a charities committee.

CSR policy: Information taken from CR pages of annual report:

> Ultra believes that it should at all times be a responsible corporate citizen and as such the group complies with all applicable legislation in the countries in which it operates. Ultra's policies relating to its corporate responsibility are generally established by the board, with the individual businesses taking a major role in their implementation.

No information relating specifically to community could be found.

CSR report: Corporate Responsibility pages contained within annual report.

Applications

In writing to the correspondent.

Other information

In 2011, the group contributed £58,000 (2010: £70,000) to charities. We have no details of beneficiaries. Donations are decided by a Charities Committee.

Staff are actively encouraged to take part in community and fundraising events.

Unilever UK

Food manufacture, household

Correspondent: Community Affairs Team, Unilever House, Springfield Drive, Leatherhead KT22 7GR (tel: 01372 945000; website: www.unilever.co.uk)

Directors: Michael Treschow, Chair; Paul Polman, Chief Executive; Kees Storm; Jean-Marc Huet; Louise Fresco; Ann Fudge; Charles Golden; Byron Grote; Sunil B. Mittal; Hixonia Nyasulu; Sir Malcolm Rifkind; Paul Walsh (women: 3; men: 9)

Year end	31/12/2011
Turnover	£4,650,000,000
Pre-tax profit	£630,000,000

Nature of business: Unilever is one of the world's leading suppliers of fast moving consumer goods in foods, household and personal care products.

Unilever UK is based in a number of sites around the UK. The head office is in Walton on Thames, and it is from here that UK Community Involvement is managed.

Company registration number: 41424

Subsidiaries include: Diversey Lever, Ben and Jerry's Ice Cream, Birds Eye Wall's, Lever Fabergé, Slimfast, Unipath

Brands include: Ben and Jerry's, Bird's Eye, Carte d'Or, Cif, Coleman's, Comfort, Domestos, Dove, Flora, Hellmann's, Impulse, Knorr, Lynx, MARMITE, Olivio, Organics, Persil, PG Tips, Physio Sport, Pot Noodle, Slim Fast, Sure, Surf, Timotei, Wall's

Main locations: Bedford, Walton on Thames, Lowestoft, Purfleet, London, Manchester, Port Sunlight, Windsor, Kingston on Thames, Burton on Trent, Crumlin, Bebington, Warrington, Crawley, Leeds, Hull, Ipswich, Gloucester

Membership: BITC, LBG

Charitable donations

UK cash (latest declared):	2008	£700,000
	2007	£1,000,000
	2005	£2,800,000
	2003	£7,600,000
Total worldwide:	2011	£2,670,000
Cash worldwide:	2011	£360,000

Corporate social responsibility

CSR committee: There was evidence of a separate CSR Committee.

CSR policy: Unilever endorses the concept of 'doing well by doing good' and maintains that these values 'will never be compromised, no matter how difficult the economic conditions become, and nor will the group's commitment to help tackle deep-seated global issues in such areas as nutrition and hygiene.' In pursuit of these objectives the group continues to work closely alongside agencies like the World Food Programme (WFP) and UNICEF.

Locally, Unilever has a number of local sites around the UK. Each of these sites is encouraged to develop partnerships with key local organisations to address local issues. Again, many of these partnerships are with long-term established community partners. Decisions about local programmes are made locally at the relevant site.

CSR report: There was no evidence of a separate CSR report.

Exclusions

Support is not given to political parties or to organisations with primarily political aims. Unilever makes a declaration to this effect in the Annual Report and Accounts that binds Unilever and all its operating units. Support is not given to churches or denominational charities. This does not exclude support for charities with a religious connection whose work is ecumenical. Support is not given to individuals to undertake studies, gap year trips, social work or for any other purposes.

Applications

Projects supported by Unilever's community investment programme are mostly researched and identified by its in-house community investment team. Unsolicited applications are not therefore encouraged as less than 1% of unsolicited applications sent to the UK head office generally receive support.

Unilever asks that you use the 'Contact Us' section of the Unilever UK website to ensure that your request is directed to the correct person.

Information Available: Unilever UK has an internet site www.unilever.co.uk which contains information about its community involvement activities as well as more general information on its approach to managing corporate responsibility issues.

Requests for product donations, advertising or brand sponsorship (e.g. Flora London Marathon) should be addressed directly to the brand concerned at the following address: Freepost-RRHS-XXKK-LKAE, Consumerlink Unilever, London W4 5QB. Alternatively, email: sponsorshipenquiries@unileverconsumerlink.co.uk.

Other information

Unilever collates the cost of its community involvement activities using the London Benchmarking Group model. The model recommends the separation of charitable donations, community investment, commercial initiatives in the community and management costs relating to the programme of activity.

During 2011 UK group companies made a total contribution of £2.67 million, broken down as:

- Charitable donations: £360,000
- Community investment: £1.56 million
- Commercial initiatives in the community: £750,000

Information taken from the company's latest accounts available at the time of writing:

> The company's community involvement takes many forms, from direct funding for national projects to employee volunteering support for local community initiatives.
>
> Unilever is increasingly focusing on longer term partnerships, in some cases lasting up to 25 years. This means that while Unilever invests a great deal in community involvement, budgets are often fully committed years in advance, with funding for major projects only becoming available when an existing project comes to an end.
>
> In order to maximise the impact of Unilever UK's community investment programme its efforts are focused on the following key areas:
>
> - Education – in the form of school governance and leadership
> - Sustainable development – in the areas of water, agriculture and fisheries
> - The arts – focused on visual arts
> - Health – focused on nutrition and healthy lifestyles
>
> Unilever maintains the Platinum standard in the UK's Business in the Community Corporate Responsibility Index and can boast 10 years as sector leader of the Dow Jones Sustainability Index.
>
> The main areas of non-cash support are secondments, employee time and occasional donations of stock.

Education: Education is a key area of support, particularly for employee volunteering, and a number of sites participate in reading and number partner schemes. Unilever has moved away from the funding and provision of curriculum based educational resources, although selected resources such as From Field to Fork (a KS 3 and 4 resource focused on plant science, nutrition and sustainability) continue to be funded on an ongoing basis.

Sustainable development: Unilever is committed to sustainable development and this is reflected in the UK by the significant support provided to a number of key organisations and campaigns. Unilever has a 25 year commitment to providing support to the Mersey Basin Campaign and is a Foundation Corporate Partner of the Forum for the Future, the UK's leading sustainable development charity.

Health and nutrition: Unilever provides significant funding to both the British Nutrition Foundation and the British Skin Foundation. It has also worked with the Anaphylaxis Campaign to raise the awareness of food allergy issues.

Many Unilever employees give time in assisting local schoolchildren with their reading and writing skills and through the Unilever Governors' network, support has been given to employees who volunteer to be school governors.

Payroll giving: The company operates the Give As You Earn scheme.

Sponsorship: *The arts* – The company sponsors 'The Unilever Series at Tate Modern'. Unilever began this sponsorship in 2000 and has extended its support to 2012.

Unipart Group of Companies Ltd

Instrumentation, motors and accessories

Correspondent: Communications Department, CSR Team, Unipart House, Garsington Road, Cowley, Oxford OX4 2PG (tel: 01865 778966; website: www.unipart.co.uk)

Directors: Lord Shepherd, Chair; John M. Neill, Chief Executive; Anthony J. Mourgue, Chief Financial Officer; John Clayton; Frank Burns; Fred Vinton; Steve Johnson (women: 0; men: 7)

Year end	31/12/2010
Turnover	£1,129,900,000
Pre-tax profit	£6,900,000

Nature of business: Unipart develops, implements and operates supply chain solutions in the logistics market in partnership with its customers in a wide range of automotive technology, rail retail and consumer industries.

Company registration number: 1994997

Membership: BITC

Charitable donations

UK cash (latest declared):	2010	£23,200
	2009	£15,900
	2008	£19,200
Total UK:	2010	£191,000
Total worldwide:	2010	£191,000
Cash worldwide:	2010	£23,200

Corporate social responsibility

CSR committee: There are local CSR teams.

CSR policy: Information taken from the 2010 annual report and accounts:

> Across the group thousands of people are involved in initiatives to reduce energy consumption, assist in local community projects and work both up and down our supply chain to improve value for our customers in a socially responsible manner. In 2010 the group was awarded platinum status in the BitC CR index.

CSR report: CSR report published in 2010.

Exclusions

Unipart will not support an activity whose purpose is to benefit a political or morally corrupt cause.

Applications

In writing to the correspondent. Local sites can also be approached.

Other information

In 2010 the group supported charities with donations of £23,200 of which £12,900 was for health and well-being purposes, £3,200 in respect of child welfare and youth development and £7,100 to other charitable purposes. Total community investment in 2010 was £191,000 (2009: £158,000) an increase of 21% on the previous year. This included cash donations, employee time and gifts in kind.

Information taken from the CSR report 2010:

> Investments in our 5 key target areas of Education, Employability, Environment, Health and Economic Development represented around 80% of our community activities. We are aiming to develop longer term relationships with community partners in these areas.
>
> A major investment area across Unipart sites is relationships with local schools, and working with them to stimulate an interest in developing business skills (particularly engineering and Lean), to generate enthusiasm for a career in business. InspirED is an organisation which provides a learning environment for pupils who have been excluded from normal schooling. As well as providing premises and facilities for InspirED over several years, we have recently worked with them to set up 'Project Dig', an opportunity for students to set up their own allotment on our premises, with Unipart providing horticultural input, and use of simple Unipart Way tools to control the activities.
>
> ***Employee-led activities***
>
> Local sites and CSR teams are encouraged to support health charities and generally do so through a variety of fund raising activities. Unipart Technology Logistics executives took part in a gruelling '5 Peaks challenge' and raised £30,000 for Macmillan Cancer in the process.

Unisys Ltd

Electronics/computers

Correspondent: Human Resources Department, Bakers Court, Bakers Road, Uxbridge UB8 1RG (tel: 01895 237137; fax: 01895 862093; website: www.unisys.co.uk)

Directors: R. Chapman; M. Gould; M. Piercy; F. Mallia; M. Godfrey

Year end	31/12/2010
Turnover	£158,658,000
Pre-tax profit	(£50,391,000)

Nature of business: The development, manufacture, supply and maintenance of information technology systems and related services and supplies.

Company registration number: 103709

Main locations: Altrincham, Birmingham, Bristol, Glasgow, Leeds, Slough, Milton Keynes, Liverpool, Uxbridge

UK employees: 71

Total employees: 71

Charitable donations

UK cash (latest declared):	2010	£16,000
	2008	£22,000
	2007	£48,400
	2006	£32,400
	2005	£101,000
Total UK:	2010	£16,000
Total worldwide:	2010	£16,000
Cash worldwide:	2010	£16,000

Corporate social responsibility

CSR committee: No details found.

CSR policy: Taken from the global website:

> As a company that strives to be a good corporate citizen, Unisys invests in the communities where it does business and where its employees and their families live. These investments take the form of leadership, expertise and contributions in the areas of Technology and Business Education, Health and Human Services, and Global Diversity.

We were unable to determine the ratio of women to men on the Board.

CSR report: None found.

Exclusions

Charitable causes operating outside of community focused employee-led initiatives.

Applications

In writing to the correspondent, but in view of support being directed towards matching employee fundraising initiatives, unsolicited applications are unlikely to be successful.

Other information

In 2010, Unisys Ltd made cash donations to charitable organisations amounting to £16,000. We have no details of the beneficiaries, but were previously advised that the company no longer makes cash donations directly to charitable organisations. Instead, it channels financial help towards supporting employee initiatives. It prefers to invest in those communities in which it has a presence. These investments take the form of:

- Technology and business education
- Health and human services
- Arts, cultural and civic organisations
- Global diversity

UNITE Group plc

Property

Correspondent: Andrew Reid, Correspondent, The Unite Foundation, The Core, 40 St Thomas Street, Bristol BS1 6JX (tel: 01173 027000/01173 027116; email: info@unite-group.co.uk; website: www.unite-group.co.uk)

Directors: Phil White, Chair; Mark Allan, Chief Executive; Joe Lister, Chief Financial Officer; Richard Simpson; Richard Smith; Tim Wilson; Manjit Wolstenholme; Stuart Beevor; Nigel Hall; Richard Walker (women: 1; men: 9)

Year end	31/12/2011
Turnover	£94,900,000
Pre-tax profit	£4,700,000

Nature of business: Developers and co-managers of student accommodation.

Company registration number: 3199160

Total employees: 977

Charitable donations

UK cash (latest declared):	2011	£21,000
	2009	£30,000
	2008	£20,000
Total UK:	2011	£21,000
Total worldwide:	2011	£21,000
Cash worldwide:	2011	£21,000

Corporate social responsibility

CSR committee: No specific committee referred to in annual report.

CSR policy: Information taken from the 2011 annual report and accounts:

> We believe that UNITE should act professionally and responsibly at all times, and that we should have a positive impact on the communities in which we work, as well as society more broadly. We also understand that it is important that we limit the impact of our business activities on the environment, find ways to use resources more efficiently, and help educate customers, partners and suppliers to do the same. We are involved in a variety of programmes which aim to ensure we are a good corporate citizen. We encourage our employees to understand and support these programmes, work with causes they are passionate about, engage with local community projects which are aligned with our CSR policy, and benefit from and contribute to an exceptional working environment.

CSR report: Published within the annual report and accounts.

Applications

In writing to the correspondent of The Unite Foundation.

Other information

The following information is taken from the 2011 annual report and accounts:

> At a corporate level our strategy is to support a small number of charitable causes which make a significant difference to two overarching objectives:
>
> - Widening access to higher education
> - Integrating students within local communities
>
> We work closely with Students in Free Enterprise (SIFE), an international organisation that mobilises University students around the world to make a difference in their communities, while developing their skills to become socially responsible business leaders. This year we donated £15,000 (2010: £15,000) to SIFE and our employees offered practical support by providing business advice, and sitting on judging panels for SIFE's UK Region Award scheme.
>
> At an individual level, we offer UNITE employees a charity match scheme in which up to £250 is paid to the individual's charity of choice to match the amount they raise. In 2011, UNITE contributed £5,848 (2010: £6,669) in matched donations to charities across the UK.
>
> In January 2012 we launched The UNITE Foundation, [Charity Commission no. 1147344], through which we will channel our corporate donations, going forward. It will have two main areas of activity:
>
> - UNITE Bursaries that cover living expenses and provide free accommodation for students from poorer backgrounds wishing to go to University. This scheme will replace the donations we made in previous years to the UNIAID Foundation
> - Donations to a small number of organisations that support the aims of the Foundation make up the other major strand of activity
>
> Initial beneficiaries will be IntoUniversity and SIFE.
>
> In celebration of our 21st birthday, 21 students from the University of Bristol, the University of Edinburgh, King's College London and Sheffield Hallam University will benefit from bursaries in 2012/13 which include free accommodation in a UNITE property for the duration of their study and £3,000 per year towards living expenses (£4,000 in London). A number of the bursaries will give priority to students who have been looked after in local authority care, a group that is particularly under-represented in Higher Education.

As The Unite Foundation is a newly registered charity, accounts were not required or received by the Charity Commission. We do not know how much was donated by the company in establishing the charity.

United Biscuits Ltd

Food manufacture

Correspondent: Communications Department, Hayes Park, Hayes End Road, Hayes, Middlesex UB4 8EE (tel: 020 8234 5000; fax: 020 8234 5555; website: www.unitedbiscuits.co.uk)

Directors: David Fish, Chair; Jeff van der Eems, Chief Financial Officer; Benoit Testard, Group Chief Executive; Kevin McGurk (women: 0; men: 4)

Year end	31/12/2011
Turnover	£1,333,600,000
Pre-tax profit	£88,600,000

Nature of business: The principal activity of the group is the manufacture and sale of a wide range of food products, including biscuits and savoury snacks.

Company registration number: 3877866

Main locations: Glasgow, Harlesden, Halifax, Hayes, High Wycombe, Carlisle, Manchester, Liverpool, Consett, Rotherham, Ashby-de-la-Zouch

Total employees: 8,156

Membership: BITC

Charitable donations

UK cash (latest declared):	2009	£106,000
	2008	£72,000
	2007	£40,000
	2005	£50,000

Corporate social responsibility

CSR committee: No details found.

CSR policy: The following is taken from the company's website:

> We have set ourselves a wide ranging set of community goals from supporting fund raising and providing additional time off for community activities, to supporting students, schools and colleges. We are also extending the development opportunities for employees and improving health and well- being. Finally we are not forgetting that we want our sites to be enjoyable places to work and so we want to have some fun along the way.

CSR report: Community progress report published annually.

Exclusions

No response to circular appeals. No grants for animal charities, political appeals, or religious appeals.

Applications

In writing to the correspondent.

Other information

The following information is taken from the company's Community progress report for 2011:

> With our employees we have donated over £275,000 in funds or product and have granted 186 days leave for our employees to do volunteer work in their communities. Some sites offer practical help in a different way. For example, two of our factories provided a day of mock interviews to members of the charity CRISIS, which helps to support homeless people.

Of the £275,000, WWF received a donation of £100,000.

As there is no breakdown of what was raised by employees and given by the company, we are unable to give a donations figure.

United Business Media Ltd

Media

Correspondent: Anne Siddell, Company Secretary, United Business Media Ltd, Ludgate House, 245 Blackfriars Road, London SE1 9UY (tel: 020 7921 5000; fax: 020 7928 2728; website: www.ubm.com)

Directors: John Botts, Chair; David Levin, Chief Executive; Robert Gray, Chief Financial Officer; Jonathan Newcomb; Pradeep Kar; Karen Thomson; Alan Gillespie; Terry Neill; Greg Lock (women: 1; men: 8)

Year end	31/12/2011
Turnover	£972,300,000
Pre-tax profit	£139,700,000

Nature of business: UBM is an international media and business information company.

Company registration number: 152298

Main locations: London

UK employees: 1,329

Total employees: 6,565

Charitable donations

UK cash (latest declared):	2009	£560,000
	2007	£543,372
	2006	£600,138
	2005	£434,300
Total worldwide:	2011	£270,000
Cash worldwide:	2011	£270,000

Corporate social responsibility

CSR committee: No details found.

CSR policy: The majority of UBM's community investment is outside of the UK. The following statement is taken from the company's annual report and accounts for 2011: 'We continue to focus on using our events management skills to support key community initiatives reflected in the expansion of our NGO Events series to include a new event in the UK.'

CSR report: Sustainability report is published annually.

Exclusions

The company will not support political appeals.

Applications

In writing to the correspondent.

Other information

In 2011 the group donated £270,000 to charitable organisations (2010: £438,000). There was no separate donations figure for UK giving nor value given for employees volunteering initiatives.

Payroll giving: UBM operates a payroll giving scheme in the UK, whereby regular donations by employees are matched by the company. A separate matched giving scheme through which fundraising efforts by UBM's employees are matched on a one-off basis also exists.

United Utilities Group plc

Electricity, oil and gas/fuel, water

Correspondent: Corporate Responsibility Panel, Haweswater House, Lingley Mere Business Park, Great Sankey, Warrington WA5 3LP (tel: 01925 237000; fax: 01925 237066; website: www.unitedutilities.com)

Directors: John McAdam, Chair; Steve Mogford, Chief Executive; Russ Houlden, Chief Financial Officer; Catherine Bell; Paul Heiden; David Jones; Nick Salmon (women: 1; men: 6)

Year end	31/03/2011
Turnover	£1,513,300,000
Pre-tax profit	£327,100,000

Nature of business: United Utilities plc is the intermediate holding company of the UK's largest listed water business. The group owns and manages the regulated water and wastewater network in the North West of England, through its subsidiary United Utilities Water plc (UUW), which constitutes the vast majority of the group's assets and profit. The group also applies its utility skills to manage and operate other utility infrastructure.

Company registration number: 2366616

Main locations: Warrington

Total employees: 4,735

Membership: BITC, LBG

Charitable donations

UK cash (latest declared):	2011	£3,200,000
	2010	£5,000,000
	2009	£3,670,000
	2008	£3,790,569
	2007	£3,080,070
Total UK:	2011	£5,194,000
Total worldwide:	2011	£5,194,000
Cash worldwide:	2011	£3,200,000

Community involvement

In 2010/11, there were 19 bespoke community projects delivered through the United Futures Partnership with Groundwork UK. Over £250,000 was invested 'and leveraged' in a further £687,000 from other sources. These projects included:

- Transforming a local community centre in Liverpool
- Creating wildlife gardens for schools in Preston and Lowton
- Pond clearance work in Penketh
- An environmental educational programme (which is ongoing) across a number of schools in Blackburn

The company's 2011 CSR report states:

> We have also innovated to develop and trial delivery routes in addition to United Futures. To this end we successfully implemented a community grant scheme in Penrith, in which local community groups were invited to apply for small scale grants to support good works. So we have directly contributed to grassroots community activities in areas impacted by one of our projects.
>
> The results of this trial have been very encouraging, in terms of:
>
> - The impacts of the financial grants themselves
> - The positive stakeholder engagement in support of the capital project
> - The wider opportunities afforded for connecting with the community in Penrith
>
> Over the next year we will extend this trial to six other capital schemes across the region. We plan to assess further its merits as a very efficient, effective and scalable community investment solution.
>
> *Partners*
>
> *Our partnerships*
>
> We regularly review our existing community programme to ensure alignment with our strategy and to ensure that we can measure the benefits and impacts using an agreed measurement tool. All community partnerships that have entered a new agreement have been approved by our stringent governance approach. Our partnerships continue to be managed and reviewed by the in-house team. Partnerships on-going the last year have included:
>
> - United Futures
> - Royal Society for the Protection of Birds (RSPB)
> - Cumbria Woodlands
> - Green Partnership Awards
> - Young Enterprise
> - Start
> - WaterAid
>
> We continually look for new opportunities for partnerships that offer mutual benefit. We believe that working in this way gives something back to the community while meeting a business objective, ranging from operational performance through to employee engagement In 2011 we have also entered into a number of new partnerships such as Street League, UTV Media and Beachcare.
>
> We hope to expand our portfolio of community partnerships in 2012 to provide more opportunities for our employees and communities alike where it makes business and community sense to do so.

For more detailed information on the company's work with its partners, visit: www.unitedutilities.com.

United Utilities Trust Fund (Charity Commission no. 1108296)

The grantmaking trust was established in 2005 to help people out of poverty and debt. Funded by United Utilities, the day to day management and administration is carried out by Auriga Services Ltd in line with the policy set by the trustees. As with similar trusts established by other utility companies, the people it primarily assists are customers who are unable to pay their water bills. The following statement is taken from the 2010/11 annual report:

> We recognise that we need to maintain the affordability of customer bills, in what continues to be a tough economic environment, and we continue to fund our charitable trust, providing £5 million per year to help customers who are struggling to pay their water bills.

Corporate giving

The company's annual report and accounts state: 'charitable donations by the group in the year amounted to £5.2 million (2010: £5.25 million) in support of charitable causes in the local communities in which it operates and those of interest to its employees.'

Confusingly, the company's CSR report states:

> Each year we collect the amount of cash, time and in kind help given to charities and community groups using the LBG model. [Unfortunately, we could not find the breakdown of figures in the company's reports.] Over the last year we are proud to say we invested around £2 million in the communities that have been impacted by our operations, through the activities of our employees (including our education and catchment teams) and through work with partners such as Groundwork, RSPB and WaterAid. This investment has also enabled other organisations to raise over £3 million for their causes.
>
> Support for charitable causes went towards supporting the company's official community partners; Groundwork, RSPB, WaterAid, Youth Sport Trust, Hope Through Action, Still Waters and Mersey Basin Campaign.

We have used the figure quoted in the annual report and accounts as the company's total UK and worldwide contribution which includes cash and in kind contributions.

Employee-led support

The following is taken from the 2011 CSR report:

> We recognise that a positive workforce is a productive workforce and that many of our people take part in community-based activities. Volunteering is about giving time to do something positive. It can be a great way to meet new people, learn new skills and gain useful experience. The time employees spend volunteering directly contributes to our community commitment, which we account for and report on an annual basis. Working with the local community is a great opportunity to develop vocational skills.
>
> This year we launched a community learning scheme where our employees can meet personal development needs through volunteering with one of our community partners. This provides an alternative to traditional training courses and ensures our employees gain skills in a way which benefits them and people in the community. We believe that this kind of company support sends a clear signal that we are interested in the communities we serve, and this will translate to day-to-day operations, to operational performance and customer service. At a very local level, volunteering can help connect our people with their communities, improving mutual understanding.
>
> *Community learning*
>
> As a responsible business, we play an active role in the communities where we operate. Our approach includes our community partnership programme, where we work with selected charities and organisations for mutual benefit. Community learning is about providing individuals, teams or business areas with learning and development opportunities through working with our community partners. These volunteering opportunities develop skills such as mentoring, presentation and communication. Our current community providers are:
>
> - RSPB (Royal Society for the Protection of Birds)
> - WaterAid
> - Young Enterprise
> - Groundwork

Matched funding: United Utilities match funds employees fundraising efforts on behalf of charitable organisations up to a maximum of £250 per application.

Payroll giving: The company offers its employees the Charities Trust payroll giving scheme.

Corporate social responsibility

CSR committee: Taken from the company's website:

> We reviewed our CR governance last year. As a result the former Community Investment Committee has evolved into the Corporate Responsibility Committee. The key changes are that the CR Committee should:
>
> - Scrutinise the work of the business in implementing the commitments set out in the CR policy
> - Keep under review the group's overall approach to CR
> - Review CR issues and objectives material to the group's stakeholders
> - Identify and monitor the extent to which issues and objectives are reflected in group strategies, plans and policies
> - Submit an annual report to the board on how effective UU management has been in implementing the CR policy, ensuring alignment with the group strategy
> - If appropriate, recommend amendments to such policies to the board

CSR policy: The following policy statement is taken from the company's website:

> The panel oversees policy co-ordination, management and reporting of key areas of impact to stakeholders within the defined areas of:
>
> - Environment
> - Workplace
> - Customers
> - Community impacts
>
> *Community Engagement*
>
> We work in partnership for mutual benefit and to enrich the lives of the communities where we operate taking into account traditions and cultures. We will:
>
> - Recognise and support corporate responsibility in the regions in which we operate by working with relevant organisations and local communities; and
> - Invest in selected community partnerships and in a community education programme which support our corporate responsibility commitments and add value to our operations

CSR report: An annual CSR report is published – 145 pages long and published exclusively online. Not much information within the report on community giving.

Exclusions

No support for appeals from individuals, religious appeals or political appeals.

Applications

In writing to the correspondent.

Unum

Insurance

Correspondent: Inderpal Sokhy, Head of Community Affairs, Milton Court, Dorking, Surrey RH4 3LZ (tel: 01306 887766 Txt Tel: 01306 887784; fax: 01306 881394; email: inderpal.sokhy@unum.co.uk; website: www.unum.co.uk)

Directors: Thomas Watjen, Chair; Peter Hales; Edward Langston; Malcolm McCaig; Ian Owen (women: 0; men: 5)

Year end	31/12/2011
Turnover	£629,801,000
Pre-tax profit	£39,909,000

Nature of business: Income protection insurance.

Company registration number: 4661006

Main locations: Dorking

Charitable donations

UK cash (latest declared):	2009	£168,000
	2008	£578,000
	2007	£921,400
	2006	£704,700
	2005	£400,000
Total UK:	2009	£247,000
Total worldwide:	2011	£247,000

Corporate social responsibility

CSR committee: There is a Community Affairs department but no mention of a specific CSR committee.

CSR policy: Taken from the company's website: 'Unum takes corporate responsibility very seriously. We have a number of internal policies in place in relation to this area and our practices are largely based on a structure developed by Business in the Community.'

CSR report: No published report. There is a dedicated page on the company's website.

Exclusions

No support for advertising in charity brochures, animal welfare, appeals from individuals, enterprise/training, local appeals outside areas of company presence, medical research, overseas projects, political/religious appeals, or science/technology.

Applications

In writing to the correspondent.

Other information

Total donations made by the company during the year 2011 for charitable purposes were £247,000 (2010: £212,000). The notional salary costs of the 899 (2010: 768) volunteering days undertaken by staff during the year are included in these amounts. We do not have the actual figures for the 'cost' of volunteer days and so have been unable to calculate the actual cash donated to charitable organisations.

The company's charitable donations are focused around disability and rehabilitation. Gifts in kind may be given in support of appropriate causes. Employees are encouraged and supported in their volunteering activities.

The following information is taken from the company's website and relates to the preceding year (2010):

> In 2010 Unum continued to base our financial donations policy around the themes of Disability and Rehabilitation. We continued to support national issues related to all aspects of disability through the membership of the Employer's Forum on Disability. At a local level we have helped around 60 smaller organisations and other charities with monetary donations.
>
> Despite the demanding business climate in 2010, Unum staff achieved 768 equivalent working days of volunteering and helped 97 community partners in local areas:
>
> - Unum's flagship charity event in 2010 was our annual sponsored run, 'Site2Site' covering 164 miles between the main UK office sites. Over 200 staff took part in the event, raising more than £31,000 for Unum's main charity partner for 2010, Vitalise – a national charity providing respite care for the disabled, visually impaired people and their carers.
> - Staff took part in a wide range of volunteering and fundraising projects throughout 2010, such as working with young people in a number of schools, youth organisations and sports teams in various UK locations.
> - There were also many gardening and maintenance type projects for local charities
>
> For the first time in March 2010 Unum UK also participated in a Unum Group-wide 'Food Drive' and collected both food and financial donations which were presented to a number of charities.

Payroll giving: A scheme is in operation.

UPS

Logistics, transportation

Correspondent: Marketing and Communications, Forest Road, Feltham, Middlesex TW13 7DY (tel: 0845 787 7877; fax: 020 8844 2815; email: marketinguk@ups.com; website: www.ups.com)

Directors: D. Scott Davis, Chair and Chief Executive; F. Duane Ackerman; Michael J. Burns; Stuart E. Eizenstat; Michael L. Eskew; William R. Johnson; Candace Kendle; Ann M. Livermore; Rudy HP. Markham; Clark T. Randt, Jr; John W. Thompson; Carol B. Tome (women: 3; men: 9)

Year end	31/12/2011
Turnover	£34,000,000,000
Pre-tax profit	£3,700,000,000

Nature of business: Carrier and package delivery company providing specialist transportation, logistics, capital and e-commerce services.

Company registration number: 1933173

Main locations: Feltham

Total employees: 398000

Charitable donations

UK cash (latest declared):	2011	£150,000
	2009	£150,000
	2008	£150,000
	2007	£148,500
Total UK:	2011	£150,000
Total worldwide:	2011	£62,000,000

Corporate social responsibility

CSR committee: There was evidence of a separate CSR Committee.

CSR policy: This information was obtained from the company's annual report:

> We believe that strong communities are vital to the success of our company. By combining our philanthropy with the volunteer time and talents of our employees, UPS helps drive positive change for organisations and communities in need across the globe.

CSR report: An up to date sustainability report was available from the company's website.

Exclusions

The UPS Foundation does not award grants to individuals, religious organisations or theological functions, or church-sponsored programmes limited to church members.

Grants supporting capital campaigns, endowments or operating expenses are seldom approved.

Applications

As of 1 June 2007, The UPS Foundation no longer accepts or responds to unsolicited proposals.

Information available: UPS's sustainability report can be accessed at: www.sustainability.ups.com

Further information about its community support programme is available at: www.community.ups.com.

Other information

The following information is taken from the UPS foundation's website:

> At UPS, we have long believed that we grow not only by investing in our business, but also in our people and our communities. We believe the best way to give back is to draw upon our company's unique business assets: linking philanthropic dollars with our logistics expertise, transportation assets and the skills and passions of our global employees.
>
> The UPS Foundation was established by UPS founder Jim Casey in 1951, Today, we lead UPS's corporate citizenship efforts, investing nearly $100 million each year and more than 1.4 million hours of UPSers' volunteer time into our global communities each year.

The UPS Foundation directs its giving through four global giving strategies. These strategies leverage all of UPS' resources – financial, human and knowledge.

The foundation makes donations in the UK totalling £150,000 per year. Previous beneficiaries are: RNID; RNIB; 1st Bury St Edmunds Scout Troop; Children's Adventure Farm Trust; and, Business Dynamics.

Grants in the UK are made through the US-based UPS Foundation (Federal Tax ID No. 13–6099176). However, these are initiated by the company proactively seeking potential beneficiaries whose work ties in with the interests of the foundation. National and local charities UK wide can be supported.

The foundation has four focus areas, namely: Diversity; Community Safety (within this focus are the Humanitarian Relief Program and Road Safety); Environment; and Volunteerism.

Valero Energy Ltd (Chevron Ltd)

Oil and gas/fuel

Correspondent: Company Secretary, 1 Westferry Circus, Canary Wharf, London E14 4HA (tel: 020 7719 3000; website: www.chevron.com)

Directors: J. W. Fraser; J. W. Gorder; M. E. Loeber; N. E. V. Roberts; E. M. Tomp

Year end	31/07/2011
Turnover	£5,851,600,000
Pre-tax profit	(£109,300,000)

Nature of business: Principal activities of the company are the refining, distribution, transport and marketing of petroleum products.

In August 2011, Valero Energy Corporation, through Valero Energy Ltd, acquired the network of more than 1,000 Texaco branded wholesale sites – the largest branded network in the UK – from Chevron Ltd. Valero has continued with the Texaco brand in the market.

Company registration number: 145197

Main locations: Pembroke, Aberdeen

Total employees: 1,222

Charitable donations

UK cash (latest declared):	2011	£163,500
	2009	£422,000
	2006	£400,000
	2005	£300,000
Total UK:	2011	£163,500
Total worldwide:	2011	£163,500
Cash worldwide:	2011	£163,500

Corporate social responsibility

CSR policy: No CSR information for this company found.

We were unable to determine the ratio of women to men on the board.

Exclusions

No support for circular appeals, individuals, local appeals not in areas of company presence, large national appeals or overseas projects.

Applications

In writing to the correspondent. Normally a decision will be made within three weeks of receiving an application. Decisions cannot be discussed over the telephone.

Other information

In 2010/11 charitable donations amounted to £163,500 (2009/10: £168,000). Donations were made to support various charities and causes local to the Pembroke refinery in support of the surrounding community. These covered music, arts and community, sports, education and youth services and other charitable causes. The company was gold sponsor of the Duke of Edinburgh Awards in Wales and also supported the Pembroke Dock Sunderland Trust, The Tour of Pembrokeshire and various other organisations.

Victrex plc

Chemicals and plastics

Correspondent: Staff Committee (Charity Donations), Victrex Technology Centre, Hillhouse International, Thornton Cleveleys, Lancashire FY5 4QD (tel: 01253 897700; fax: 01253 897701; website: www.victrex.com)

Directors: Anita Frew, Chair; David Hummel, Chief Executive; Steve Barrow, Finance Director; Giles Kerr; Patrick De Smedt; Lawrence Pentz; Pamela Kirby (women: 2; men: 5)

Year end	30/09/2011
Turnover	£215,800,000
Pre-tax profit	£94,200,000

Nature of business: Victrex plc, a leading global manufacturer of high performance polymers, comprises two divisions: Victrex Polymer Solutions that focuses on transport, industrial and the electronics markets and Invibio Biomaterial Solutions that focuses on providing specialist solutions for medical device manufacturers.

Company registration number: 2793780

Total employees: 552

Charitable donations

UK cash (latest declared):	2011	£1,800
	2009	£4,100
	2008	£15,500
Total UK:	2011	£1,800
Total worldwide:	2011	£6,300
Cash worldwide:	2011	£6,300

Corporate social responsibility

CSR committee: Staff committees distribute money to charities nominated by employees.

CSR policy: Policy contained within the 2010/11 annual report and accounts.

CSR report: No specific reporting on CSR.

Applications

In writing to the correspondent.

Other information

The group made charitable donations of £6,300 during the year 2010/11, of which £1,800 were in the UK. In addition, old computer equipment is given to either local schools or charities chosen by the staff committee.

The following extract is taken from the company's 2010/11 annual report:

> The group participates in a range of activities within the local communities where we operate, from charitable giving, offering apprenticeships and supporting science education and awareness in schools, to sponsorship of undergraduates and the advancement of research work at universities.
>
> In the UK, a proportion of the charitable donations budget is distributed by the staff committee mainly to local charities chosen from nominations made by employees. National or overseas charities are supported where there is strong employee involvement.

Virgin Atlantic Ltd

Aviation

Correspondent: See 'Applications', Company Secretariat, The Office Manor Roay, Crawley, West Sussex RH10 9NU (tel: 01293 562345; website: www.virgin.com)

Directors: Richard Branson, President; Stephen Murphy, Chair; David Baxby; Chan Hon Chew; Timothy Livett; Ng Chin Hwee; Mark Poole; Stephen Ridgway; Julie Southern; Paul Tan Wah Liang; Tan Pee Teck; Yeoh Phee Teik (women: 1; men: 11)

Year end	28/02/2011
Turnover	£2,744,900,000
Pre-tax profit	(£80,200,000)

Nature of business: Virgin is a leading international investment group. Conceived in 1970 by Richard Branson, the Virgin Group has gone on to grow successful businesses in sectors ranging from mobile telephony, travel, financial services, leisure, music, holidays and health and wellness. Across its companies, Virgin employs approximately 50,000 people, in 34 countries and global branded revenues in 2011 were around £13bn ($21bn).

Virgin Atlantic Ltd is an operator of air services for the carriage of passengers, freight and tour operating.

Company registration number: 3552500

Total employees: 9,301

Membership: BITC

Charitable donations

UK cash (latest declared):	2011	£5,842,000
Total UK:	2011	£6,092,000
Total worldwide:	2011	£6,092,000
Cash worldwide:	2011	£5,842,000

Community involvement

The Virgin Foundation known as Virgin Unite (Charity Commission no. 297540)

In 1987 Virgin founded Unite, a UK registered charity,

> to unite people to tackle tough social and environmental problems in an entrepreneurial way. The aim is to help revolutionise the way that governments, businesses and the social sector work together, in order to address the scale and urgency of the challenges facing the world today.

There are three core areas to Unite's work: business action; incubating global leadership initiatives; and working with the company's global community. The charity seeks to implement programmes and campaigns around issues such as health, economic empowerment, conservation and climate change.

Much of Virgin Atlantic's giving is focused on its charity partner, **Free the Children**, and sourced by the generosity of its customers and the fundraising activities of its staff.

The following information is taken from Virgin Atlantic's Sustainability Report for 2012:

> *Free the Children*
> Virgin Atlantic raises funds through staff fundraising activities as well as passenger donations. Those funds are used by Free the Children (FTC) to support projects in some of our destinations, as well as in the UK. Since the partnership began we've donated well over £2 million to FTC.
>
> FTC was founded in Canada in 1995, by 12 year old Craig Kielburger, who read about child labour in developing countries and was so moved he decided to take action. The organisation has since grown into the world's largest network of children helping children through education, with more than one million young people involved in their innovative education and development programmes in 45 countries.
>
> *Free the Children – UK Schools programme*
> Virgin Atlantic funds this programme aimed at children aged between 7–18 years. At the end of its second successful year (2011–12), it has surpassed our objectives in engaging UK young people to make a positive difference to their own and others' lives. Existing schools have been supported and new schools engaged. The school programme has two parts. A motivational speech in assembly to the entire school (heard by 16,000 students each year) followed by a 'Leadership and Entrepreneurship training workshop' for around 30 students selected by the school (2,340 in year 2011–12). In this workshop, the young people debate social and environmental entrepreneurship. FTC's staff work as mentors with the students, thus reducing teacher workloads and supporting existing curriculum objectives.
>
> Youth in Action Groups (YIAGs) are then formed bringing together exceptional students from different schools along with their teachers to learn how to bring change to their local and global communities. The participants also have an opportunity to hear inspirational speeches from FTC speakers and come away with new friendships, connections and memories to inspire them on their path to making a difference. FTC use social media to connect with young people and keep them informed.
>
> *Scholarships*
> In the 2010–11 school year, 30 students were awarded international scholarships to visit FTC communities in Kenya, and another 28 scholarships have been awarded for 2011–12.
>
> Young people fundraising for FTC's 'Adopt a Village' international development programme are able to have their donations matched pound for pound, up to £2,500 per project, from a £150,000 'Matching Fund.
>
> *Virgin Atlantic staff engagement*
> An exciting part of the UK school programme is that there are lots of opportunities for our colleagues to be involved, for example through assisting in facilitating discussions, bringing their enthusiasm for the FTC programme directly to young people. Staff have combined their own passion and interests to support FTC in the UK in other ways too. For example, the Virgin Atlantic HR team are providing mentorship to FTC staff on best practices including hiring, recruitment and retention.
>
> *We Day*
> The FTC programme originated in Canada. Since 2007, over 160,000 Canadian 11–18 year olds have attended We Day – these are annual events organised by FTC, held in stadiums, featuring inspirational speakers and popular artists, attended by thousands of children from FTC-participating schools. The events help focus young people's energy and passion to be change-makers, showing them they're not alone in their journey to make a difference.
>
> FTC plan to host over 5,500 young people from FTC participating schools across the UK, and are working with local education authorities, teacher associations and the Cabinet Office to form educational partnerships and link the event with government initiatives. Young people will be involved in the planning from the outset.

Overseas

Full details of Virgin Atlantic's considerable involvement in projects overseas are included in the Sustainability Report for 2012 from which the following information is taken:

> Our international development projects with FTC are focused on delivering real and sustainable improvements on environmental and social justice issues in some of our destinations. With the funds raised through our onboard donations and colleague fundraising activities, Virgin Atlantic supports communities in India, China and Kenya. We are also now developing a new programme with FTC in Ghana. We are committed to creating opportunities for children and families living in remote rural areas to escape the cycle of poverty and preventing mass migration to the cities.

Virgin Blue's 'Red Jet' charity foundation is currently focusing on 'Indigenous Communities and Natural Environments' in Australia. The foundation has provided assistance to several projects including a residential energy efficiency programme in Alice Springs and a savannah fire management project in Arnhem Land.

Virgin America works with the California State Parks Foundation and selects California-based carbon offset projects via its partnership with www.carbonfund.org. Virgin America also hosts regular e-waste collection events to clean-up local beaches and parks.

Virgin Atlantic s 2012 Sustainability Report states:

> *Emergency relief funding*
> Virgin Atlantic continues to provide emergency relief funding in response to various international crises, such as the Japanese earthquake and tsunami, and the drought and associated famine in East Africa. Over the last two years, we've given over £250,000 in funding to disaster relief projects as well as offering cargo space to Shelterbox and UNICEF to send vital equipment overseas.

Corporate giving

Because of the very many companies registered under the Virgin brand name, we have used the financial information declared in the annual report and accounts for Virgin Atlantic Ltd, company no. 3552500. CSR information is taken from the company's 2012 Sustainability Report. We have focused on Virgin Atlantic's community and charitable involvement as we believe it represents the philosophy behind the Virgin brand and offers good examples of activities undertaken by staff and the involvement of the company's customers.

Due to Virgin's active involvement with its customers in fundraising for charitable and community causes, it has not been possible to differentiate between what the individual companies have contributed and what has been donated by generous staff and customers. We do know however, from the accounts of Virgin's charitable foundation, Unite, that the 'Virgin Group' gave £3.1 million to the foundation and Richard Branson donated his speaking fees at various events through the year totalling £2.7 million. We have used these amounts as the UK and worldwide cash contributions figures although the company has probably given substantially more both in cash and in kind.

Virgin Unite

In 2010/11 the foundation made grants totalling £4.2 million. There were 23 grants of over £25,000 and beneficiaries included: Carbon War Room (£1.4 million); Free the Children (£412,300); Eva, Initiatives (£388,100);

Kids Company (£187,700); Youth at Risk (£119,900); Make IT right Foundation (£96,000); War Child (£63,200); Charles Darwin University Foundation (£30,600); and Reuben Foundation (£81,550).

In kind support

In 2011, the company has supported additional UK charities by donating over 100 flight tickets to good causes helping children and young people, such as Help a London Child, Great Ormond Street, children's hospices and others, so they can auction them to help raise valuable funds. The company also offers help, when possible, to fly children to other countries for life-saving medical treatment.

In kind donations from Virgin Atlantic were £250,000.

Employee-led support

Virgin Atlantic s 2012 Sustainability Report gives the following information:

> ***Charity Partner**: Free the Children*
> Virgin Atlantic raises funds through staff fundraising activities as well as passenger donations. Those funds are used by FTC to support projects in some of our destinations, as well as in the UK. Since the partnership began we've donated well over £2 million to FTC. The long-term impact this is having is phenomenal, as our colleagues and passengers are seeing first hand. Simply by asking passengers to donate their loose change in charity envelopes in their amenity packs, Virgin Atlantic's Change for Children appeal raises approximately £50,000 a month. In 2011 it raised £643,000 – a 7% increase on 2010. And August 2012 was a record-buster month: our passengers donated nearly £70,000 in that month alone.

In 2011, passengers donated more than 4 million of their accumulated Flying Club miles, which enabled young people from the UK to participate in FTC's international volunteer trips to China, India and Kenya.

Also in 2011, 195 staff raised a total of £230,000 through various fundraising activities and volunteering time was calculated at £83,500.

Corporate social responsibility

CSR committee: There is a Corporate Responsibility and Sustainable Development Team.

CSR policy: Taken from the company's Sustainability Document 2010 which covers all Virgin companies:

> ***Managing Corporate Responsibility and Sustainable Development Across the Group***
> We have interpreted this definition of sustainable development into four main challenges which we believe businesses need to meet in the 21st century:
> - Emit minimal carbon and other greenhouse gases
> - Learn to use the planet's finite resources responsibly
> - Strive towards poverty alleviation and the fair treatment of all individuals
> - Offer products and services that enhance emotional and physical wellbeing.

CSR report: There is an annual Sustainability report published online.

Applications

The Virgin Foundation known as Virgin Unite: Contact the correspondent – Alistair McGregor, Virgin Unite, The School House, 50 Brook Green, Hammersmith, London W6 7BJ. Tel: 020 3126 3709. Email: contact@virginunite.co.uk

Virgin companies: There is not one source to which applications for funding can be made. Applicants should refer to Virgin's individual companies' websites.

Vodafone Group plc

Telecommunications

Correspondent: Andrew Dunnett, Director of Vodafone UK Foundation, Vodafone House, The Connection, Newbury, Berkshire RG14 2FN (tel: 01635 674478; fax: 01635 45713; email: groupfoundation@vodafone.com; website: www.vodafone.com)

Directors: John Buchanan; Andy Halford; Alan Jebson; Nick Land; Anne Lauvergeon; Samuel Jonah; Luc Vandevelde; Tony Watson; Philip Yea; Michael Combes; Stephen Pusey; Renee James; Gerard Kleisterlee; John Bond, Chair; Vittorio Colao, Chief Executive (women: 2; men: 13)

Year end	31/03/2011
Turnover	£45,884,000,000
Pre-tax profit	£9,498,000,000

Nature of business: Mobile telecommunications.

Company registration number: 1833679

Main locations: Banbury, Gloucester, Warrington, Welwyn Garden City, Theale, Trowbridge, Croydon, Newbury, Abingdon

UK employees: 8,174

Total employees: 83,862

Membership: BITC, LBG

Charitable donations

UK cash (latest declared):	2011	£21,000,000
	2010	£2,838,440
	2008	£6,743,199
	2006	£5,390,000
Total UK:	2011	£21,000,000
Total worldwide:	2011	£44,400,000
Cash worldwide:	2011	£44,400,000

Community involvement

The company supports good causes nationally, globally and in the communities around its offices. Much of its support in the UK is given through the **Vodafone Foundation** (Charity Commission no. 1089625).

The Vodafone Foundation

The majority of the foundation funds are distributed in grants through operating company foundations to a variety of local charitable organisations meeting the needs of the communities in which they operate. The foundation's strategy has four major themes:

World of Difference

The World of Difference programme – which is open to anyone in the UK – enables people to take paid time to work for a charitable purpose of their choice in their own community or in a developing country.

Mobiles for Good

Through using mobile communication technologies the foundation funds projects which address some of the world's most pressing humanitarian challenges.

Red Alert

Through the SIMS giving programme Red Alert, and with the support of partners such as the World Food Programme and Telecoms Sans Frontieres, the foundation supports the preparation for and execution of rapid humanitarian response to crises and disasters.

In-Country Grants

Through its partnerships with the 27 local and independent Vodafone foundations, the foundation gives financial support to good causes that benefit local communities in significant and timely ways. Each of the foundations is financed by an annual contribution from the Vodafone Foundation as well as additional funds from the local operating company.

Foundation's UK programmes

Lifetracks

Lifetracks is a UK programme funded by the foundation that aims to empower 16–25 year olds to make informed choices about their work, study and training and reflects their commitment to supporting young disadvantaged people. Run through a consortium with Youthnet, Foyer, Skill, and Rathbone, the VF UK is investing over £4 million into this project. Supported by teams that reach young offenders and disadvantaged young people on the streets, it includes workshops, helplines, a website and Vodafone volunteers. Following a strategic review of the partnership, the trustees approved a refreshed programme with a strong focus on enabling Youthnet to use funds to enhance its ICT platforms.

Take A Chance

A mentoring scheme in schools, Take a Chance in the UK completed its third full year in 2010 with over 70 volunteer Vodafone 'buddies' helping students in their mid-teens in nine local schools and colleges. The initiative, in which the foundation is investing £400,000, aims to motivate and inspire students while providing core business skills through workshops and talent coaching.

Small grants

Each year £500,000 is set aside by the foundation to run a small grants programme which was launched in 2007. Projects supported are those which the trustees consider to be outside their core grants programme, but which merit support.

The company's annual report for 2011 states:

> We have continued to fund the good work of the Vodafone Foundation. Through the Vodafone Foundation and our network of national affiliate foundations we support communities and societies in the countries in which we operate. In this financial year we invested a total of £50 million in foundation programmes and social causes. Our World of Difference programme is now in 20 countries and has so far enabled 1,500 people to take paid time to work for a charitable purpose of their choice in their own community or in a developing country. Our Mobiles for Good programme, combining our technology with our giving, saw the launch of Instant Network, a partnership with Telecoms Sans Frontieres which enables a network to be deployed from three suitcases, covering 10 sq km for usage of up to 12,000 people. Field trials are currently underway.

During 2011/12 the foundation built on its progress to date by:

- Expanding the Mobiles for Good programme, increasing the funds available from the foundation for this programme
- Scaling up the World of Difference programme and launching the Grahame Maher Award for the World of Difference alumni
- Developing the foundations' fundraising capacity with a roll-out of JustTextGiving in the UK and in other countries
- Celebrating the 20th anniversary of the Vodafone Foundation and sharing best practice/project learnings across the group

Across the group, text giving is promoted, enabling customers to give money simply and free of charge to support charitable appeals following disasters.

Full details of the Vodafone Group Charitable Donations Policy can be found on its website (www.vodafonefoundation.org).

Corporate giving

The 2011 Annual Report for the company states:

> The Vodafone Foundation and its network of 27 local foundations continue to invest in the communities in which Vodafone operates. Specific initiatives include Mobiles for Good projects which include the piloting of handsets for women at risk of domestic violence and an instant network which provides rapid network coverage for emergencies, Red Alert SMS fundraising services for emergency appeals and its World of Difference programme which enables individuals to take paid time to work for a charity of their choice for up to a year. We make grants to a variety of local charitable organisations meeting the needs of their communities. Total donations for the year were £49.6 million and included donations of £5.2 million towards foundation operating costs.

The foundation's annual review for 2010/11 gives full and detailed information regarding its giving. It declares an income of £22 million with Vodafone Group plc donating £19 million, Vodafone UK donating £2 million and 'donated services and facilities' at £1 million. Donated services and facilities represents the estimated financial cost borne by Vodafone Group plc in providing seconded staff and other management and administrative services. In 2010/11 the foundation distributed £19.8 million to charities. We have used the information detailed in the review, as far as possible, to determine the amounts given here for both cash donations and community contributions.

Employee-led support

Payroll giving: Vodafone employees in the UK are able to donate through this method if they choose to do so.

Matched funding: The Vodafone Foundation gives financial support to UK-based Vodafone employees or teams who fundraise in their own time. This is processed through matched funding of up to £350 per employee, per event and for up to four events per year. In 2010/11 the VF allocated £363,000 towards the fundraising efforts of Vodafone employees.

Corporate social responsibility

CSR committee: The Executive Committee receives a formal update on CR twice a year and the Board receives an annual presentation on CR. A CR management structure is established in each local operating company and CR performance is closely monitored and reported at most local operating company boards on a regular basis. CR is also integrated into risk management processes, such as the formal annual confirmation provided by each local operating company detailing the operation of their controls system.

CSR policy: Taken from the group's website:

> Our approach to Corporate Responsibility ('CR') is to engage with stakeholders to understand their expectations on the issues most important to them and respond with appropriate targets, programmes and reports on progress. We understand that responsible behaviour is key to building and maintaining trust in our brand.
>
> *Strategy*
>
> There is increasing interest in how businesses are addressing the challenges of sustainability. Our licences to operate are granted by governments that seek evidence of responsible business practices. Our research shows that consumers are becoming more concerned about sustainability. Ethical investors and non-government organisations remain focused on issues, such as supply chain standards and privacy, and our corporate customers seek information on our performance through questionnaires and meetings.
>
> CR is relevant across all aspects of our activities and therefore we seek integration into all key business processes. The CR strategy focuses on CR issues material to the Group and has the following main strands:
>
> - To capture the potential of mobile communications to bring socio-economic value in both emerging economies and developed markets through broadening access to communications to all sections of society;
> - To deliver against stakeholder expectations on the key areas of climate change, a safe and responsible internet experience and sustainable products and services; and
> - To ensure our business practices are implemented responsibly, underpinned by our business principles.

The Annual Report for 2011 states:

> The board welcomed the publication of the Davies Review on Women on Boards in February 2011. It is our aspiration to have a minimum of 25% female representation on the board by 2015. Subject to securing suitable candidates, we intend to effect the changes required to the board's composition by recruiting additional directors and/or filling vacancies which arise when directors do not seek re-election, by appointing new directors who fit the skills criteria and gender balance which would meet the Board's aspirations. The FRC is currently consulting on changes to the UK Corporate Governance Code which may result in the code including a recommendation that companies adopt a boardroom diversity policy; we expect to comply with any such recommendation. The board recognises the importance of gender balance throughout the group and continues to support Vittorio Colao in his efforts to build a diverse organisation. Further information, including the proportions of women in senior management and within the organisation overall, is contained in our 2011 sustainability report at: www.vodafone.com/sustainability.

Currently: 2 women: 13 men on the board.

CSR report: There is a CSR report published annually.

Exclusions

The company does not support political appeals, religion, individuals, advertising in charity brochures, local appeals not in the company's areas of operation, or non-charities.

Applications

An application form can be downloaded from The Vodafone Foundation's website (www.vodafonefoundation.org). Alternatively, email a proposal to groupfoundation@vodafone.co.uk.

Warburtons Ltd

Food manufacture

Correspondent: Corporate Responsibility Team, Back o'th Bank House, Hereford Road, Bolton, Lancashire BL1 8HJ (tel: 01204 531004; fax: 01204 523361; website: www.warburtons.co.uk)

Directors: Jonathan Warburton, Chair; Brett Warburton; W. Ross Warburton; Robert Higginson; Angela Megson; Nigel Dunlop (women: 1; men: 5)

Year end	24/09/2011
Turnover	£495,465,000
Pre-tax profit	£19,553,000

Nature of business: The production and distribution of bakery products.

Company registration number: 178711

Main locations: Wakefield, Bolton, Enfield, North London

Total employees: 4,659

Membership: BITC

Charitable donations

UK cash (latest declared):	2011	£254,000
	2009	£183,000
	2008	£219,000
	2007	£191,000
	2006	£232,000
Total UK:	2011	£254,000
Total worldwide:	2011	£254,000
Cash worldwide:	2011	£254,000

Corporate social responsibility

CSR committee: There is a community responsibility team contactable via the website. Every Warburtons bakery has a community champion who represents the community giving programme, managing funds and exploring local needs.

CSR policy: Information on CSR taken from the company's website:

> Warburtons supports charities and the community in three ways: with financial support, product donations and the personal involvement of individual people – both Warburton family members and employees.
>
> Our main focus is on grass roots activities that have a positive effect on the aspirations, education, skills and employability of young people, as well as projects that are centred on family life, promoting healthier lifestyles and contributing to improvements in the local community.

CSR report: Corporate responsibility section on website.

Exclusions

No support for those associated with addiction, criminal rehabilitation, religion or politics, animal welfare (except assistance dogs), professional sports, individual academic fees or third party fundraisers.

Applications

Applications should be made via the online form.

Note: Where a financial donation is being applied for, the company requests that the money is used to fund a specific need or project. Financial support will not be awarded to assist ongoing fundraising activity.

Other information

During 2010/11 Warburtons made charitable donations totalling £254,000 to community projects and charities. Warburtons supports charities and the community in three ways: with financial support, product donations and the personal involvement of individual people – both Warburton family members and employees.

The main focus is on grass roots activities that have a positive effect on the aspirations, education, skills and employability of young people, as well as projects that are centred on family life, promoting healthier lifestyles and contributing to improvements in the local community.

The following statement written by Jill Kippax, Corporate Affairs Manager at Warburtons, is taken from the company's website:

> We have a long tradition of charitable giving and helping support the communities we serve. This is led by members of my family and focuses on charities, organisations and initiatives that aim to improve the quality of family life.
>
> You can read about our guidelines for giving and the kind of support we provide here, apply for funding online, product donations and also contact us for details about our long-running National School Visitor Programme.
>
> Last year, we committed 1% of our pre-tax profit to community focused causes and projects.

The company run a scheme where funds raised by their people for charities and projects they are interested in personally can be matched by equal amounts from the company.

Wates Group Ltd

Building/construction

Correspondent: Huw Davies, Chief Financial Officer and Company Secretary, Wates House, Station Approach, Leatherhead, Surrey KT22 7SW (tel: 01372 861000; website: www.wates.co.uk)

Directors: Paul Drechsler, Chair and Chief Executive; Jonathan Wates; Nicholas MacAndrew; James Wates; Timothy Wates; David Smith; Charles Wates; Friedrich Ternofsky; Andrew Wates; Peter Johnson; Graeme McFaull; Huw Davies, Chief Financial Officer and Company Secretary (women: 0; men: 12)

Year end	31/12/2011
Turnover	£1,117,000,000
Pre-tax profit	£40,100,000

Nature of business: Construction services and residential development.

Company registration number: 1824828

Total employees: 2,500

Membership: BITC

Charitable donations

UK cash (latest declared):	2011	£1,400,000
	2009	£45,000
	2007	£58,000
Total UK:	2011	£1,400,000
Total worldwide:	2011	£1,400,000
Cash worldwide:	2011	£1,400,000

Community involvement

Wates Family Enterprise Trust (Charity Commission no. 1126007)

Wates Giving is the grants programme of the Wates family's independent charity, the Wates Family Enterprise Trust. Its aim is to invest in projects that benefit communities for the long-term, by bringing together the philanthropy of the family with the drive, professionalism and enthusiasm of Wates' employees.

The following is an extract from the company's website:

> Wates is a family owned business that has been working at the heart of communities like yours for over 114 years. Our regional offices throughout the UK have strong ties with the local communities they serve and seek to use their experience, expertise, funding and connections to help support people in these areas.
>
> ***Our commitment to communities is at the heart of our values.***
>
> - We work alongside a network of community partners to deliver an effective programme of community engagement
> - Our people are involved in local community activity through charity fundraising events and our annual Community Day, which this year saw over 2,000 people contributing 12,886 hours of work to local projects
> - Community activity ranges from supporting local companies,

commitment to employing local people on our projects, appointing social enterprises, engagement with schools and employee volunteering
- Over £1.2 million was committed by Wates Giving, our charitable funding vehicle, to local community projects
- Wates provides employees with time off for volunteering in their local communities

Charity partner: Barnardo's
Wates are proud to be working in partnership to support Barnardo's in delivering their vision of building better lives for children. We are clear we can support across a wide remit and therefore have developed the partnership into a true strategic role focused on four key areas:
- Funding
- Time Giving
- Gift-in kind
- Education and employment opportunities

Corporate giving

During the year 2011 the group made charitable donations to the Wates Family Enterprise Trust totalling £1.4 million.

From December 2008 to January 2012, Wates Giving has committed over £5 million to good causes across five areas: education, training and employment; community building; social enterprise; environment and energy sustainability; and thought leadership

The trust's income arises from a formal agreement with the Wates Group in accordance with the wishes of Family-owners and shareholders of the Wates businesses. In 2011 this amounted to £1.4 million.

In the year the trust made new awards to the value of £1 million. By programme, this is made up of 35 major awards totalling £634,000; 24 Community awards at £124,000; 26 Family awards at £183,000; four new sponsorships valued at £19,000 and match funding and Give As You Earn awards at £43,500. A new Supply Chain Fund was created in the year and made one award of £500.

Employee-led support

The annual Community Day brings together employees, customers and supply chain partners to carry out a wide range of projects. In 2011, employees, customers and supply chain partners worked on 112 projects, donating 12,886 hours across the UK.

In addition, the company's Lend A Hand scheme enables staff to undertake 16 hours of paid voluntary activity per year during work time.

Corporate social responsibility

CSR committee: No specific details found.

CSR policy: Statement taken from the company's website:

> A deep commitment to social action is shared by all in Wates, and is embedded in our business at every level. Our priority is to accelerate progress in creating more sustainable communities by raising educational aspirations, improving skills and creating employment. To achieve this we understand the value of working with partners.
>
> Our thought leadership on communities and our many community projects across the country have a huge impact. They are testament to the powerful role businesses can play in society.
>
> The Wates family see themselves as stewards of the Company for their children. Our aim is to pass on a bigger, better and more sustainable business to the next generation. For us, sustainability is more about who we are than what we do. It links closely to our core value 'Respect for People and Communities.
>
> In 2010, three mainstream programmes aligned our CR activity with customers' interests and provided a framework for investment and action: Transforming Communities, Minimising Waste and Reducing our carbon footprint.

CSR report: Information contained within the annual report and accounts.

Applications

In writing to the correspondent.

Weetabix Ltd

Food manufacture

Correspondent: Marketing Department, Weetabix Mills, Burton Latimer, Kettering, Northamptonshire NN15 5JR (tel: 01536 722181; fax: 01536 726148; website: www.weetabix.co.uk)

Directors: L. Lea; R. Darwent; D. Halstenberg; A. Rosen

Year end	01/01/2011
Turnover	£422,857,000
Pre-tax profit	£20,423,000

Nature of business: The manufacture, marketing and sale of ready to eat cereal foods.

Company registration number: 267687

Main locations: Hastings, Corby

UK employees: 1,344

Total employees: 1,849

Charitable donations

UK cash (latest declared):	2010	£123,000
	2009	£130,000
	2008	£96,000
	2007	£87,000
	2006	£159,000
Total UK:	2010	£123,000
Total worldwide:	2011	£123,000
Cash worldwide:	2011	£123,000

Corporate social responsibility

CSR committee: No details found.

CSR policy: CSR policy is confined to environmental and sustainability issues.

We were unable to determine the ratio of women to men on the board.

CSR report: None published but achievements listed within the CSR policy published on the website.

Exclusions

No support for local appeals not in areas of company presence, or appeals from individuals.

Applications

In writing to the correspondent.

Other information

Charitable donations made during 2010 were £123,000 (2009: £130,000). These consisted mainly of amounts paid to the National Grocers Benevolent Fund and local charities. Charitable giving was in the past both direct to local groups and through Weetabix Charitable Trust, (Charity Commission no. 1044949), although it is not clear whether the trust's income is still derived from the company. During this year (2010), the trust's income was only £1,100. Expenditure was £31,000 but we have no details of beneficiary groups supported.

Weetabix Ltd is now wholly owned by the Latimer Group Ltd, a company incorporated by Lion Capital. The financial information contained herein refers to the Latimer Group.

The Weir Group plc

Engineering

Correspondent: Group Executive Committee, Clydesdale Bank Exchange, 20 Waterloo Street, Glasgow G2 6DB (tel: 01416 377111; fax: 01412 219789; website: www.weir.co.uk)

Directors: Lord Smith of Kelvin, Chair; Keith Cochrane, Chief Executive; Jon Stanton, Finance Officer; Lord Robertson of Port Ellen (George); Michael Deardon; Stephen King; Alan Ferguson; Melanie Gee; Richard Menell; John Mogford; Alan Mitchelson (women: 1; men: 10)

Year end	31/12/2011
Turnover	£2,292,000,000
Pre-tax profit	£391,500,000

Nature of business: Principal activities: engineering services and specialist engineering products.

Company registration number: SC002934

Main locations: Aylestone, Altens, Bristol, Cathcart, Glasgow, Newton Heath, Huddersfield, Stockton on Tees, South Gyle, Petersfield

Total employees: 11,669

Charitable donations

UK cash (latest declared):	2009	£252,000
	2008	£234,000
	2007	£252,227
	2006	£169,218
	2005	£101,757
Total worldwide:	2011	£422,300
Cash worldwide:	2011	£422,300

Corporate social responsibility

CSR committee: Responsibility with the group's executive committee.

CSR policy: Information taken from the annual report for 2011:

> The group considers sustainability a key part of its strategy and recognises its importance in delivering shareholder value. Our sustainability approach is embedded in our business through six key areas: environment; health and safety; employees; communities; products and technologies; and ethics.
>
> *Communities*: Weir respects the communities in which it operates and during 2011 a number of new and existing projects worldwide recognised our ongoing obligation to minimise our environmental impact and invest in local communities. As a global company doing business in more than 70 countries, we have a consistent framework in place to guide our community investment activities.

CSR report: Sustainability report published annually within the annual report and accounts.

Exclusions

No support for political appeals.

Applications

In writing to the correspondent.

Other information

In 2011, worldwide charitable donations (being specifically for health, educational and community purposes) totalled £422,300 (2010: £333,900). We have no details of the beneficiaries. Key themes for community investment are education and health. These are priorities for communities worldwide and focused investment, whether at early years or adult level.

Wessex Water Services Ltd

Water

Correspondent: Group Head of Public and Community Relations, Claverton Down Road, Claverton Down, Bath BA2 7WW (tel: 01225 526000; fax: 01225 528000; email: info@wessexwater.co.uk; website: www.wessexwater.co.uk)

Directors: Colin Skellett, Chair; Julian Dennis; Sean Cater; Dave Elliott; Mark Watts; David Barclay; Gillian Camm; Peter Costain; Jonathon Porritt; Francis Yeoh; Hong Yeoh; Mark Yeoh; Kathleen Chew (women: 2; men: 11)

Year end	31/03/2011
Turnover	£444,900,000
Pre-tax profit	£149,900,000

Nature of business: Water and sewerage services.

Company registration number: 2366633

Main locations: Bath

UK employees: 1,595

Total employees: 1,595

Membership: Arts & Business

Charitable donations

UK cash (latest declared):	2011	£360,000
	2008	£150,000
	2007	£93,000
	2005	£56,000
Total UK:	2011	£360,000
Total worldwide:	2011	£360,000
Cash worldwide:	2011	£360,000

Corporate social responsibility

CSR committee: There is a Community Involvement Committee.

CSR policy: The company's main focus is on education and the environment.

CSR report: A Sustainability report with a page devoted to community matters was available from the company's website.

Exclusions

No support for national charities, advertising in charity brochures, animal welfare, the arts, enterprise/training, political appeals, religious appeals or science/technology.

Applications

In writing to the correspondent. The community involvement committee meets monthly.

Other information

In 2010/11 the company donated a total of £360,000 to UK charitable and community groups.

Launched in 1993, Wessex Watermark is a grant scheme set up by the company to help fund environmental projects in the region. Organised by the Conservation Foundation, grants from £100 to £2,500 are awarded to numerous environmental projects throughout the region.

Local charities based within the region also receive support through the company's Community Involvement Committee which awards small grants every month.

Since its creation in 1981, Wessex Water has supported WaterAid, the international water and sanitation charity by organising fundraising events and raising money through customers and staff. In 2008, in recognition of the UN international year of sanitation, Wessex Water launched a new campaign working with WaterAid called Wessex for West Africa.

Education: Wessex Water offers an education service catering for 5 to 15 year olds. There are now nine education centres in the Wessex Water region. Services include:

- Primary and secondary education packs
- Education advisers
- Visits to schools
- Tailor-made lessons (water cycle, river and pond studies, WaterAid and practical sessions)
- Education centres (nine in total – details on website)
- Site visits

Special needs: Customer Care Plus is a special programme for those customers with special needs, including those who are older and/or have disabilities. A register of such customers is held, in order that the company can identify and respond to their requirements. Help includes: a text telephone service for people with impaired hearing; Braille or audio bills; a doorstep security password system; and advance warning of interruptions to water supply.

Grants are given to registered charities operating in the area administered by Wessex Water, i.e. South Gloucestershire, Wiltshire, Dorset, and Somerset.

Conservation grants are available through the Watermark Award. In kind support is mainly given in connection with schools education programmes.

Sponsorship: *The environment* – The company sponsors local, environmental and water-related activities.

Payroll giving: The company operates the Give As You Earn scheme.

West Bromwich Building Society

Building society

Correspondent: PA to the Company Secretary, 374 High Street, West Bromwich, West Midlands B70 8LR (tel: 0845 330 0611; fax: 01215 005961; website: www.westbrom.co.uk)

Directors: Mark Nicholls, Chair; Jonathan Westhoff, Chief Executive; John Ainley; Huw Davies; Mark Gibbard; Lesley James; Andrew Jones; Mark Preston; Martin Ritchley; Richard Sommers (women: 1; men: 9)

Year end	31/03/2011
Turnover	£31,200,000
Pre-tax profit	(£5,900,000)

Nature of business: Building society.

FSA registration number: 104877

Main locations: West Bromwich

UK employees: 747

Total employees: 747

Corporate social responsibility

CSR committee: No specific details found.

CSR policy: Taken from the 2011 annual report and accounts:

> Creating and fostering supportive relationships with the various communities we serve is a significant principle for the Society. This commitment, whether to members, staff, business partners and local communities, is influenced by a concern to conduct our social and environmental responsibilities in an ethically consistent way.

CSR report: Published within the annual report and accounts.

Applications

In writing to the correspondent.

Other information

The 2010/11 annual report states that during the year the society did not make any charitable donations. The society did, however, raise significant sums through its community programme, affinity accounts and voluntary staff initiatives. Such support encompasses a wide range of community and charitable causes, notably: corporate support – structured sponsorship and financial assistance programmes; organising or participating in fundraising activities; and staff involvement in community projects with the society's endorsement, for example the partnership with the Diocese of Lichfield (the Mercian Trust Partnership).

Nominated Charity: Each year, staff organise and take part in fundraising activities on behalf of the society's nominated charity, which is chosen by them. In the last year, over £15,000 was raised for Macmillan Cancer Support, which helps people living with cancer.

Educational and Recreational Funding: Working with the organisations such as West Bromwich Albion, Walsall and Shrewsbury Town Football Clubs, the society has funded programmes geared to giving educational and recreational opportunities for young people, particularly in disadvantaged communities.

Affinity accounts: Beneficiaries have included Warwickshire County Cricket Club and Severn Valley Railway, and an alliance account with Birmingham Children's Hospital.

It has not been possible to determine the value of the support given by the society and no overall amount could be found of its total community contributions.

Western Power Distribution

Electricity

Correspondent: Sharon Cross, Corporate Communications, Avonbank, Feeder Road, Bristol BS2 0TB (tel: 01179 332005/01179 332005; fax: 01179 332001; email: scross@westernpower.co.uk; website: www.westernpower.co.uk)

Directors: R. A. Symmons, Chief Executive; D. G. Harris; D. C. S. Oosthuizen, Finance Director; R. L. Klingensmith; M. E. Fletcher

Year end	31/03/2012
Turnover	£323,300,000
Pre-tax profit	£124,000,000

Nature of business: Distribution of electricity.

Company registration number: OC303753

Main locations: Bristol

Total employees: 1,517

Charitable donations

UK cash (latest declared):	2012	£15,000
	2009	£56,000
	2008	£154,000
	2006	£55,000
Total UK:	2012	£15,000
Total worldwide:	2012	£15,000
Cash worldwide:	2012	£15,000

Corporate social responsibility

CSR committee: No details found.

CSR policy: The following statement is taken from the 2011/12 annual report and accounts:

> WPD's Community Support Policy is reviewed annually by WPD's executive and endorsed by our chief executive officer. We identify areas where business issues link to social issues, and determine criteria that all community support projects must meet. We work in partnership with local community groups to deliver a wide range of projects. Our key themes of education, safety and the environment form the bedrock of our support activity and continued to guide our community support policy throughout 2011/12.

We were unable to determine the ratio of women to men on the Board.

CSR report: None published.

Exclusions

No support for local appeals not in areas of company presence, advertising in charity brochures, animal welfare, appeals from individuals, overseas appeals, religious appeals, political appeals, or sport.

Applications

In writing to the correspondent.

Other information

During the year ended 31 March 2012, donations of £56,000 were made by the company to community organisations, of which £15,000 was donated to charities. The company's Community Support Policy sponsors a range of projects that relate to education, safety and the environment.

The company has a charitable foundation, established in 1996, that supports registered charities and other voluntary organisations. The foundation was set up with a £1 million donation and, in May 2001, an affiliate donated a further £1 million.

The foundation made donations of £54,000 to organisations in the South West in 2011/12. The foundation is administered by the Charities Aid Foundation and so does not appear to have its own Charity Commission registration number. For enquiries relating to the foundation, contact the correspondent.

The annual report and accounts of the company gives the following information:

> During the year WPD supported over 200 separate charitable and non-charitable organisations. Highlights included:
>
> Continuation of the partnership with the Centre for Sustainable Energy, a UK-wide independent charity specialising in fuel poverty and carbon reduction issues. Together, we are providing energy-saving grants to community buildings and village halls which are run by trusts or non-profit making groups and/or communities. The grants support initiatives like heating and lighting upgrades and insulation, energy monitors and door and window draft excluding.
>
> Environmentally, we continued to develop our tree planting partnerships with the British Trust for Conservation Volunteers and the Silvanus Trust (over 7,000 trees planted), while our 'keen to be green' brand was used to develop links with a range of organisations. We extended our existing tree scheme to include the planting of orchards during 2011. Following a direct request from the daily newspaper in Exeter, which is familiar with our scheme, we donated £2,000 to enable schools to plant an orchard in Topsham. This involved 10 schools who have equal responsibility for managing the site which is owned by the City Council. Our aim is to help children understand how reducing food miles can contribute to sustainable living as well as giving a sense of responsibility to those involved.
>
> The continued promotion of WPD's free 0800 contact number for the elderly using information literature and fridge magnets displaying our Freephone number. New initiatives have also been formed with cancer charities Tenovus and Breast Cancer Care designed to educate people in terms of prevention, awareness and coping strategies.

The company encourages its employees to support their communities in practical as well as monetary terms. This may be through the Leading Lights initiative – an employee volunteer scheme – or by fundraising for their favourite charity, which WPD acknowledges by matching the funds raised pound for pound.

Sponsorship: Good cause sponsorship may be undertaken.

Note in 2010/11 annual report and accounts:

> Western Power Distribution (South West) plc is an integral part of a larger UK group. The structure of the group is such that the financial statements of Western Power Distribution (South West) plc must be read in conjunction with the group financial statements of PPL WW Holdings Ltd to gain a full understanding of the group results for the year and the related cash flows, together with the financial position of the group as at 31 March.

J. D. Wetherspoon plc

Leisure, retail – restaurants/ fast food

Correspondent: Alex Bull, abull@jdwetherspoon.co.uk, Wetherspoon House, Central Park, Reeds Crescent, Watford WD24 4QL (tel: 01923 477777; fax: 01923 219810; website: www.jdwetherspoon.co.uk)

Directors: Tim Martin, Chair; John Hutson, Chief Executive; Kirk Davis; Su Cacioppo; John Herring; Elizabeth McMeikan; Debra van Gene; Sir Richard Beckett (women: 3; men: 5)

Year end	24/07/2011
Turnover	£1,072,014,000
Pre-tax profit	£66,781,000

Nature of business: The development and management of public houses.

Company registration number: 1709784

UK employees: 24,067

Total employees: 24,067

Membership: BITC

Charitable donations

UK cash (latest declared):	2011	£0
	2009	£69,000
	2008	£61,500
	2007	£46,000
	2006	£44,000
Total UK:	2011	£0
Total worldwide:	2011	£0
Cash worldwide:	2011	£0

Corporate social responsibility

CSR committee: There was no evidence of a separate CSR Committee.

CSR policy: This information was obtained from the company's annual report:

> The company aims to be an important part of the local communities in which it trades, managing its responsibilities from both corporate and social perspectives. The company's corporate social responsibility plan identifies four areas: people; responsible retailing; community and charity; the environment.

CSR report: There was no evidence of a separate CSR report; however a section of the annual report was devoted to CSR.

Applications

In writing to the correspondent.

Other information

No charitable contributions were made in 2010/11.

> The company is the largest single corporate fundraiser for the CLIC Sargent charity (caring for children with cancer and their families), a partnership now in its eighth consecutive year, raising over £4.6 million to date, with a pledge to raise a further £1 million annually. During the past financial year Wetherspoons has raised £1.1 million.

Whitbread plc

Hotels, leisure, retail – restaurants/fast food

Correspondent: Simon Barratt, Counsel and Company Secretary, Whitbread Court, Houghton Hall Business Park, Porz Avenue, Dunstable LU5 5XE (tel: 01582 424200; website: www.whitbread.co.uk)

Directors: Anthony Habgood, Chair; Patrick Dempsey; Christopher Rogers, Finance Director; Richard Baker; Andy Harrison, Chief Executive; Stephen Williams; Wendy Becker; Susan Hooper; Ian Cheshire; Simon Melliss; Susan Taylor Martin (women: 3; men: 8)

Year end	01/03/2012
Turnover	£1,778,000,000
Pre-tax profit	£320,100,000

Nature of business: The company's principal activities are the operation of hotels, restaurants and racquets, health and fitness clubs.

Company registration number: 29423

Main locations: London

Total employees: 30,484

Membership: BITC

Charitable donations

UK cash (latest declared):	2012	£578,000
Total UK:	2012	£1,210,000
Total worldwide:	2012	£1,210,000
Cash worldwide:	2012	£578,000

Community involvement

£750,000 was raised by staff and customers for the **Costa Foundation** (Charity Commission no. 1147400).

The foundation's aims are to relieve poverty, advance education and the health and environment of coffee-growing communities around the world. The foundation's work follows on from the support Costa has provided for many years via funds donated to the Charities Trust, also a registered charity. Those funds have improved the social and economic welfare of coffee-growing communities in countries such as Colombia, Costa Rica, Ethiopia, Guatemala, Uganda and Vietnam.

Good Together

The Chief Executive states: This [corporate responsibility] is a fundamental part of our company strategy, which focuses on the three key stakeholder areas of Team Engagement, Customer Heartbeat and Profitable Growth. This year we more closely aligned our Good Together programme to reflect these areas and we now have three key pillars of activity around 'Team and Community', 'Customer Wellbeing' and 'Environment'.

Corporate giving

The 2011/12 annual report states:

> No direct charitable donations have been made by the company. Costa Ltd, a subsidiary of the company, made a direct donation of £368,000 to the Costa Foundation. In addition, the company organised and supported a number of charitable events and a number of its employees carried out charitable activities during working hours. The value of these activities has not been quantified.

Charitable cash giving: This would seem to be mainly contributed by customers as opposed to the company itself. We have used the amount of £368,000 together with the matched funding (see Employee-led section) as the company's cash contribution and added the in kind valuation of £1 million to this to give the total community contribution.

In kind support

Working with our supply chain and waste management teams, a process is in place to donate duvet covers and pillows which are no longer required within our business to the Salvation Army. In 2011 this equated 333 thousand duvets and 55 thousand pillows with a value of £1 million.

Employee-led support

Team and Community is one of the three purposes of the **Good Together Programme**. The company includes the development of its workforce and job opportunities under this heading.

Payroll Giving: Give and Match is Whitbread's payroll giving scheme.

Match funding: The *Whitbread Raise and Match Scheme* is one of Whitbread's ways of recognising and supporting its team members who volunteer in their own personal time to raise funds for charities or good causes. Raise and Match enables Whitbread team members to apply for match funding, whereby Whitbread will match funds raised pound for pound within specified matching limits.

In 2010/11 £421,000 was raised across Whitbread through these two schemes. We have taken Whitbread's company cash contribution as half of this amount as no breakdown has been given.

Corporate social responsibility

CSR policy: Chief Executive's statement on Corporate Responsibility:

> Good Together is a fundamental part of our company strategy, which focuses on the three key stakeholder areas of Team Engagement, Customer Heartbeat and Profitable Growth. This year we more closely aligned our Good Together programme to reflect these areas and we now have 3 key pillars of activity around 'Team and Community', 'Customer Wellbeing' and 'Environment.

CSR report: Information is published within the annual report and accounts and there is a CSR section on the website.

Applications

In writing to the correspondent.

Wilkinson Hardware Stores Ltd

Household, retail – DIY/ furniture

Correspondent: See 'Community involvement' and 'Commercially-led support' for details.

Company address: J K House, Roebuck Way, Manton Wood, Worksop, Nottinghamshire S80 3YY (tel: 01909 505505; fax: 01909 505777; website: corporate.wilkinsonplus.com)

Directors: L. J. Wilkinson; K. L. Swann

Year end	28/01/2011
Turnover	£1,559,384,000
Pre-tax profit	£60,824,000

Nature of business: Principal activity: sale of domestic hardware and other related goods.

Company registration number: 365335

Main locations: Worksop

Total employees: 23,063

Membership: BITC

Charitable donations

UK cash (latest declared):	2011	£800,000
	2009	£462,000
	2008	£400,000
	2007	£367,000
	2005	£565,000
Total UK:	2011	£800,000
Total worldwide:	2011	£800,000
Cash worldwide:	2011	£800,000

Community involvement

The following information is taken from the company's website:

> *Helping Hands*
>
> Helping the local community which we serve and being a good neighbour is really important to us. If you're a local charity or community group in need of a Helping Hand, please visit your local Wilkinson store to pick up an application form.
>
> Every Wilkinson store has a small budget to help their local community to do great things. We want our donations to improve the lives of as many local people as possible and can make a big difference to lots of good causes. Whether you need a small raffle prize or pot of paint or even something a little bigger, come along to your local Wilkinson store to see if we can help you.
>
> To apply for a donation from the Helping Hands budget you need to visit your local store and pick up an application form. These forms can be found at the customer service desk or please ask a Wilkinson's' Team Member who will be more than happy to help you.
>
> Where you can, please give us as much notice as possible as we receive lots of application forms and our team members will meet once a month to review your request and get in contact with you as quickly as they can.
>
> Please direct any Helping Hands application forms to your local store. If any letters requesting a donation are sent to Head Office we will endeavour to send them to the appropriate local store where possible. Alternatively please download a Helping Hands application form from the website to complete and take to your local store.

Corporate giving

In 2010/11 'payments of a charitable nature' totalled £800,000 (2009/10: £350,000). We have no details of specific beneficiaries but there is a list of supported charities by store given on the company's website.

Employee-led support

As well as supporting local charities, staff give their support through fundraising to national charities such as BBC Children in Need, Comic Relief and the Royal British Legion.

Charity of the Year: Anthony Nolan Trust. Staff and suppliers raised over £1 million for this charity.

Commercially-led support

> *Sponsorship:*
>
> *Local Stars*
>
> Through sponsorship, we help as many of life's big achievers from right across the UK as we can. Whether they've got a special talent, have overcome personal difficulties or benefited others in their community – they're all winners in our eyes. If you or someone you know deserves to be recognised, then we'd love to hear all about it.
>
> We sponsor big achievers in our communities to help them fulfil their dreams – from Olympic hopefuls to future Broadway stars.
>
> If you feel you fit the criteria above and wish to apply to be one of our local stars you need to visit your local store and pick up an application form. This then needs posting to the Charity Department, Local Stars Wilkinson's at the company's address.
>
> Your application will then be considered by the Charity Committee. Only completed Local Stars application forms will be considered please do not write in separately to the Local Stars Scheme.
>
> You can find a copy of our Local Stars information leaflet and application form on the website.

Corporate social responsibility

CSR committee: No details found.

CSR policy: The following statement is taken from the company's website:

> *Community*
>
> It is so important for Wilkinson to support and to be part of the communities that we serve. We aim to help our communities by supporting local registered charities that share our family values, culture and business heritage. We want to build sustainable local relationships through supporting charity, community initiatives and volunteering our time.

We were unable to determine the ratio of women to men on the board.

CSR report: None published but some information contained within the annual report and accounts.

Exclusions

No support for local appeals not in areas of company presence.

Applications

See 'Community involvement' and 'Commercially-led support'.

Willmott Dixon Holdings plc

Building/construction

Correspondent: Group Chief Executive, Spirella 2, Icknield Way, Letchworth, Hertfordshire SG6 4GY (tel: 01462 671852; fax: 01462 681852; website: www.www.willmottdixongroup.co.uk)

Directors: Colin Enticknap, Chair; Rick Willmott, Group Chief Executive; Chris Durkin; John Frankiewicz; Andrew Telfer; Jonathan Porritt; Christopher Sheridan (women: 0; men: 7)

Year end	31/12/2011
Turnover	£1,052,137,000
Pre-tax profit	£21,148,000

Nature of business: The provision of major capital works construction to non-housing clients, including building fabric maintenance and care, interior design and fit-out, plus sustainable consultancy.

Company registration number: 198032

Main locations: Letchworth

Total employees: 2,845

Membership: BITC

Charitable donations

UK cash (latest declared):	2009	£23,000
	2008	£5,000
	2007	£23,000
	2006	£18,000
	2005	£53,000
Total UK:	2009	£338,000
Total worldwide:	2011	£338,000

Corporate social responsibility

CSR committee: No details available.

CSR policy: The company's website states: 'In working towards sustainable development our approach is focused in four key areas: Putting People First; Climate Change and Energy Efficiency; Smarter Use of Natural Resources; and Responsible Business.'

CSR report: An annual Sustainability Review is published and can be found at the company's website.

Exclusions

General and unsolicited appeals are not considered. No grants for local appeals not in areas of company presence or for overseas projects.

Applications

In writing to the correspondent.

Other information

In 2011, £338,000 was donated in staff time and donations for good causes.

Previous information has suggested that strong emphasis is placed on involvement by staff with their favoured charities, coupled with a commitment to support clients' preferred causes wherever possible. We have been informed that the directors choose one charity per year to donate to.

Robert Wiseman Dairies plc

Dairy products

Correspondent: Wiseman in the Community Team, 159 Glasgow Road, East Kilbride, Glasgow G74 4PA (tel: 01355 244261; fax: 01355 230352; email: care@muller-wiseman.co.uk; website: www.muller-wiseman.co.uk)

Directors: Robert Wiseman, Chair; William Keane, Managing Director; Gerard Sweeney; Norman Murray; Martyn Mulcahy; Jack Perry; Ernest Finch; David Dobbins (women: 0; men: 8)

Year end	02/04/2011
Turnover	£917,491,000
Pre-tax profit	£34,357,000

Nature of business: The processing and distribution of milk and associated products.

Company registration number: SC146494

Main locations: Glasgow

UK employees: 4,861

Total employees: 4,861

Charitable donations

UK cash (latest declared):	2011	£28,000
	2009	£9,000
	2008	£12,000
	2007	£0
	2006	£10,000
Total UK:	2011	£623,000
Total worldwide:	2011	£623,000
Cash worldwide:	2011	£28,000

Corporate social responsibility

CSR committee: A group of staff from across the UK meet to discuss Wiseman in the Community.

CSR policy: CSR falls under three headings: Employee engagement and development; Supplier relationships; and Wiseman in the Community.

CSR report: A report is published within the annual report and accounts.

Exclusions

Local appeals not in areas of company presence. No support for appeals from individuals. In writing to the correspondent.

Other information

In 2010/11, the company declared UK cash donations of £28,000 and total community spend of £623,000 principally for the benefit of local charities serving the communities in which it operates. This amount includes in kind gifts, sponsorship, staff and company fundraising and cash.

The company's website states:

> With the growth of the company our community focus is becoming more and more national and as such we identified a need to overhaul our approach to community involvement, and have established Wiseman in the Community.
>
> There are five Wiseman in the Community groups, each centred on a dairy. The members of each group represent a cross section of all staff from the sites around the dairy. The groups are autonomous and are responsible for getting Wiseman involved in the local community, through events and fundraising initiatives.

Designated charity

In 2009, Robert Wiseman Dairies launched their partnership with Help the Hospices by unveiling the first of a fleet of 14 vehicles displaying the Help the Hospices logo and sunflowers. Employees are encouraged to fundraise on behalf of the company's designated charity. Staff within the company continue to work with Help the Hospices and their local hospices to develop fundraising initiatives at a local and national level.

Cause-related marketing

The company also uses its products to support numerous events and good causes throughout the year via on pack promotions, this has included Macmillan Cancer Support's World's Biggest Coffee Morning fundraiser, and the My Heroes schools project, a competition on milk packs offering prizes of farm visits to winning classes. The company also has supported the charity Mercy Ships.

Application for support should be made in writing to the contact.

Wolseley plc

Building material merchants

Correspondent: See 'Applications'., 26 New Street, St Helier, Jersey, JE2 3RA, Channel Islands (website: www.wolseley.com/responsibility)

Directors: Gareth Davis, Chair; Ian Meakins, Group Chief Executive; John Martin, Chief Financial Officer; Frank Roach; Andrew Duff; Michael Wareing; Michael Clarke; Tessa Bamford; Richard Shoylekov (women: 1; men: 8)

Year end	31/07/2012
Turnover	£13,421,000,000
Pre-tax profit	£198,000,000

Nature of business: Wolseley is a trade distributor of plumbing and heating products and a leading supplier of building materials.

Company registration number: 106605

Brands include: Brands include: Plumb Center, Parts Center, Pipe Center, Drain Center, Climate Center, William Wilson.

UK employees: 7,018

Total employees: 43,170

Membership: Arts & Business

Charitable donations

Total worldwide:	2012	£1,400,000
Cash worldwide:	2012	£1,400,000

Corporate social responsibility

CSR committee: Taken from the 2011/12 annual report:

> Community engagement is, by its very nature, a local activity and our corporate head offices and individual businesses manage their own activities in this area to suit their own preferences and locations.
>
> The overall CR programme is agreed by the board and reviewed annually to ensure its on-going relevance to business strategy, stakeholder expectations and broader national and international sustainability agendas.

CSR policy: Taken from the 2011/12 annual report:

> Our Corporate Responsibility (CR) programme is intrinsically linked to the long-term, profitable growth of the Company. For example, reducing the number of days lost through injury improves productivity. A well-trained and motivated workforce delivers exceptional customer service and strengthens the Company's market share. Reduced fuel

and energy consumption lowers our cost base and expands our margins.

CSR report: An annual CR report is published within the annual report and accounts.

Applications

In writing to your nearest local business.

Other information

The group's charitable donations in 2011/12 totalled nearly £1.4 million (2010/11: £1.4 million). 'Donations to charitable organisations from the businesses across the group range from small to substantial amounts.' Unfortunately, we could find no geographical breakdown of the awards made, nor who benefitted, other than Impetus Trust and the Prince's Foundation for Building Community.

Information taken from the group's website:

> Our businesses seek to be contributing members to the communities in which they operate. We also support a number of charitable organisations both at a Group and a business unit level. Our principal areas for charitable support continue to be the alleviation of homelessness, the provision of training for the homeless or marginalised in order to allow them to return to work, and the improvement of the quality of the built environment. Our businesses have also supported numerous other charitable causes, including support for neglected and vulnerable children and provision of care for sufferers of cancer or other illnesses.

Staff volunteering

Wolseley encourages volunteering by its staff. For example, in 2011, the Ripon team formed a 'volunteering partnership' with the community and now offer help with social action work in the area by supplying small teams to assist with projects. Since launch they have completed five volunteering projects in the community and supplied a total of 134 volunteers (offering more than 1,000 man hours). In addition to the Volunteering Partnership the Ripon office have also raised over £10,000 for both local and national charities via various fundraising activities during the financial year.

Partnerships: Impetus Trust and the Prince's Foundation for Building Community.

John Wood Group

Engineering

Correspondent: Carolyn Smith, John Wood House, Greenwell Road, East Tullos, Aberdeen AB12 3AX (tel: 01224 851000/01224 851099; fax: 01224 851474; email: carolyn.smith@woodgroup.com; website: www.woodgroup.com)

Directors: Sir Ian Wood, Chair; Allister Langlands, Chief Executive; Alan Semple; Bob Keiller; Mark Papworth; Mike Straughen; Les Thomas; Ian Marchant; Michel Contie; Dr Christopher Masters; John Morgan; Neil Smith; Jeremy Wilson; David Woodward (women: 0; men: 14)

Year end	31/12/2011
Turnover	£358,060,000
Pre-tax profit	£254,100,000

Nature of business: Engineering services to the oil and gas, petrochemical and power-related industries.

Company registration number: SC036219

Total employees: 27,848

Charitable donations

UK cash (latest declared):	2009	£596,500
	2008	£568,700
	2007	£395,000
	2006	£320,000
	2005	£184,000
Total worldwide:	2011	£467,400
Cash worldwide:	2011	£467,400

Corporate social responsibility

CSR committee: There was no evidence of a CSR Committee.

CSR policy: This information was obtained from the company's annual report:

> Being socially responsible is integral to the way we operate, it means doing the right thing for the right reasons, not just because it enhances our reputation. We nurture local businesses and skills to encourage sustainable community development. We believe in making a positive difference in the communities in which our businesses operate. We support an extensive range of local and international charities and causes spanning health, education, the arts, medical research and the prevention and reduction of poverty. We have a well-established Employee Community Fund supporting charities and fundraising efforts involving our employees.

CSR report: There was no evidence of a CSR report.

Exclusions

The following causes are not likely to receive support: specific religious groups, political organisations, sports organisations with no Wood Group employee involvement, and organisations without charitable status.

Applications

In writing to the correspondent. All requests for donations are reviewed monthly by the charity and community relations committee.

Other information

During the year the group made charitable donations amounting to £464,700 (2009: £596,500). This sum relates to cash donations and does not recognise donations of time or other resources which have been made during 2011.

During 2011 the company has supported the North East of Scotland final of the national K'NEX Young Engineers Challenge, the Aberdeen International Youth Festival, Glencraft and the Aberdeen University Word Festival.

> In the UK, we have an active community programme including sponsorship of the North East Scotland final of the national Junior Engineer for Britain K'NEX challenge, a programme designed to introduce primary school children to engineering. We are a long-term supporter of the annual Aberdeen International Youth Festival, the world's premier participatory youth arts festival. Wood Group is also a long-term supporter of the Grampian-Houston exchange which provides opportunities for student nurses to experience health care in the UK and US.

WPP Group plc

Advertising/marketing, information management and communication

Correspondent: Janet Smith, Executive PA, 27 Farm Street, London W1J 5RJ (tel: 020 7408 2204; fax: 020 7493 6819; email: jsmith@wpp.com; website: www.wpp.com)

Directors: Christopher Mackenzie; David Komansky; Esther Dyson; Jeffrey Rosen; John Quelch; Koichiro Naganuma; Orit Gadiesh; Paul Richardson; Paul Spencer; Mark Read; Colin Day; Stanley Morten; Lubna Olayan; Timothy Shriver

Year end	31/12/2011
Turnover	£997,237,250
Pre-tax profit	£99,911,555

Nature of business: Principal activity: the provision of communications services worldwide.

Company registration number: 1003653

Subsidiaries include: The Gepetto Group, Banner MacBride, Goldfarb Consultants, IMRB International, PRISM Group, Tempus Group plc, Carl Byoir and Associates, The Food Group, Management Ventures, A Eicoff and Co., Mando Marketing, The Farm, RTCdirect, Walker Group/CNI, MindShare, Coley Porter Bell, Millward Brown, SCPF, Pace, The Henley Centre, Portland Outdoor, BDG McColl, International Presentations, The Market Segment Group, Lambie-Nairn, Buchanan Communications, EWA, Addison, P Four Consultancy, The Grass Roots Group, Ogilvy Public Relations, CommonHealth, RMG International, The Wexler Group, Y and R Advertising, Clever Media, Research International,

Shire Hall Group, Savatar, Einson Freeman, J Walter Thompson, The Media Partnership, Timmons and Company, Ogilvy and Mather, Oakley Young, Metro Group, Media Insight/ Maximize, Brierley and Partners, Chime Communications plc, ROCQM, Equus, Quadra Advisory, Enterprise IG

Main locations: London

UK employees: 907

Total employees: 4,732

Membership: BITC

Charitable donations

UK cash (latest declared):	2011	£4,800,000
	2009	£4,100,000
	2007	£3,500,000
	2006	£3,900,000
	2005	£3,400,000
Total UK:	2011	£15,300,000
Total worldwide:	2011	£15,300,000
Cash worldwide:	2011	£4,800,000

Community involvement

The company's social investment includes pro bono work, in kind and cash donations to charity and employee volunteering. Pro bono projects are agreed between WPP companies and the charities concerned. The companies often have long-standing relationships with their pro bono partners. WPP, the parent company, helps to co-ordinate pro bono projects involving multiple WPP companies or cross-group collaborations.

The following policy relates to donations and support provided by the UK parent company:

The company focuses its support on education, the arts and young people. Other areas supported included health, local community, environment and drugs/alcohol. No geographical area is given preference; each application is considered on merit.

Support is also provided by the operating companies.

Corporate giving

In 2011, the total value of the company's social investment was £15.3 million (2010: £14.3 million). This is equivalent to 1.5% of reported profit before tax and includes direct cash donations to charities of £4.8 million and £10.5 million worth of pro bono work. These figures are based on fees the organisations would have paid for work.

Although we do not know what proportion of this contribution went to UK organisations, the company stated in its 2011 annual report and accounts that WPP, the parent company, supports a range of charities and non-profit organisations, with a particular focus on education, the arts and young people. As previous beneficiary organisations have in the main been registered in the UK, we have taken the £4.8 million as the UK cash contribution. Previous beneficiaries include:

- NABS, a charity which offers financial, practical and emotional support to those in the advertising industry
- The London Business School
- The National Portrait Gallery
- The Natural History Museum
- The Paley Centre for Media
- University of Oxford

In kind support

Assistance may be given in the form of gifts in kind, joint promotions and pro bono marketing and communication support.

Statement taken from the website: 'Pro bono work also benefits WPP by showcasing our creative skills and ability to create compelling communications on a wide range of social and environmental issues. Our people gain a breadth of experience and the chance to contribute to their communities.'

Employee-led support

This varies between operating companies.

Commercially-led support

Sponsorship: *Arts and education* – sponsorship is undertaken. In the UK, WWP sponsorship support includes that to Charles Edward Brooke Girls' School, which specialises in media arts; the Royal College of Art; and two bursary awards for D&AD, the professional association for design and advertising. The company is the corporate patron of the National Portrait Gallery in London.

Corporate social responsibility

CSR committee: No details found.

CSR policy: The following statement is taken from the group's website:

> *Sustainability at WPP*
> WPP aims to make a positive contribution to society and the environment. We work hard to reduce our impact on the environment, to manage any ethical issues associated with our work, to support and engage our people and to help good causes through our pro bono work.

CSR report: Sustainability report published within the annual report and accounts.

Applications

In writing to the correspondent.

Wragge and Co. LLP

Legal

Correspondent: Corporate Responsibility Team, 55 Colmore Row, Birmingham B3 2AS (tel: 01219 031000; fax: 01219 041099; website: www.wragge.com)

Directors: Quentin Poole; I. R. Metcalfe

Year end	30/04/2011
Turnover	£112,979,000
Pre-tax profit	£28,058,000

Nature of business: Legal firm.

Company registration number: OC304378

Main locations: London, Birmingham

UK employees: 958

Total employees: 958

Membership: BITC, LBG

Charitable donations

UK cash (latest declared):	2011	£67,000
	2009	£20,000
	2007	£45,000
	2004	£64,000
Total UK:	2011	£782,500
Total worldwide:	2011	£782,500
Cash worldwide:	2011	£67,000

Corporate social responsibility

CSR committee: There is a CSR committee.

CSR policy: The website is clear about what CR means to the company:

> Yup, there's a lot said about corporate responsibility.
>
> But while all the talking is going on, we get on with it!
>
> So what do we mean by that? Something we get asked a lot! For us, corporate responsibility is all about being a good neighbour, a good employer, a good citizen and a good partner. In practice, this means:
>
> - **Community investment** – this is all about pro bono, volunteering and charitable donations. Our priorities are homelessness, education and mentoring, and inner city needs.
> - **Our people** – it's vital that we attract and retain the very best. Our people give a lot to the business, that's why our diversity and well-being programmes are so important to us.
> - **Environment** – reduce, reuse and recycle; that's our daily mantra...
> - **External partners** – to extend the reach of our CR activities we involve other people. We talk to our suppliers, our clients and other community partners so we can share our experiences, learn and most importantly, encourage others to adopt responsible business practices

17% of partners are female. The firm produces comprehensive diversity figures – visit: www.wragge.com/diversity_statistics.

CSR report: Published annually and available on the website.

Exclusions

No grants for individuals or for local appeals not in the area of company presence.

Applications

For the trust, applications should be made in writing to the correspondent, enclosing a copy of the most recent accounts.

Other information

In 2010/11 Wragge's total investment in corporate responsibility activity was £857,000 made up of £67,000 cash donations, £143,000 of staff volunteering time, £573,000 in kind contributions including pro bono work and management costs of almost £75,000.

Wragge stated on its website that, 'Free legal advice is at the heart of our community work. Pro bono clients range from large non-governmental organisations (NGOs) to small charities and community organisations.' Support is also given, for example, to homeless people to help them back into employment. This includes the use of staff skills around drafting CVs, preparing for interviews and giving homeless people practical work experience. Many of the firm's staff are reading partners to primary schoolchildren in some of the more deprived areas of Birmingham and London and some also act as mentors to law students in local universities. As at 31 October 2011, 456 employees had been involved in community investment activity, which is 44% of UK employees. 4,483 hours of pro bono work were given by staff at a cost to the business of £564,594.

The Wragge and Co. Charitable Trust

Most of the firm's cash support appears to be channelled through The Wragge and Co. Charitable Trust (Charity Commission no. 803009) which receives a gift aid donation each year. Support is given across the West Midlands and nationally to registered charities only, with some preference for health related issues. The firm does not have a strict grantmaking policy and supports many diverse local and national charities with small grants, usually under £1,000.

In 2010/11 the firm provided the trust with a total income from gift aid donations, (including tax repayable and interest) of £26,000 and the trust in turn made grants amounting to £18,000.

The following examples of Wragge s initiatives are taken from the 2011 CSR report.

Wragge and LGBT

In 2011, Wragge & Co. extended its diversity work to sexual orientation. We joined Stonewall's Diversity Champions programme. Promoting good practice regarding sexual orientation in the workplace, the programme is the UK's fastest growing diversity employers' forum.

As part of this relationship, we took part in Stonewall's Workplace Equality Index, a tool we can use to evaluate our workplace practices on sexual orientation equality. We asked our lesbian, gay and transgender (LGBT) people to complete an anonymous survey and we are working with Stonewall to progress our activities based on feedback from the survey.

As well as promoting LGBT events – Out of Office, InterLaw Diversity Forum, Pride and Halcyon – we formed our own in-house LGBT network. Following a launch networking event, this group is now focusing on ways in which it can support the firm in areas like recruitment and business development.

Despite the fact that it is a breach of international law to criminalise someone's sexuality, homosexuality is a crime in 82 countries around the world. The Human Dignity Trust is using the legal expertise and influence of solicitors and barristers to change these laws.

This year, Wragge & Co. accepted an invitation to join this international pro bono initiative. Chosen for the quality of our litigation practice, we are one of a select group of law firms that have been invited to join the Trust's new Litigation Steering Group.

Wragge and Domestic Violence

This year, we became a member of the 'Corporate Alliance Against Domestic Violence (CAADV)'. CAADV is a group of companies working collectively to raise awareness of the impact of domestic violence and to provide assistance and resources for employees.

Wragge & Co's head of corporate responsibility is an ambassador for CAADV. Since joining CAADV, we have provided specialist training to our HR advisers and undertaken an internal communications campaign to raise awareness of the issues and provide support to our people.

Charity of the Year:

Each calendar year our people nominate and then vote for the firm's charity of the year. As this report covers the financial year from 1 May to 30 April, two charities feature. Our last report focused on the 2010 charity of the year, Over The Wall, for which we raised more than £15,000.

2011's charity of the year was Macmillan Cancer Support. To help us gather ideas and funds we introduced charity champions. These eight volunteers from around the firm helped ensure a bumper fundraising year, in which we raised £35,000. We also hosted a number of one-off fundraising activities, which helped us to reach this fantastic total.

WSP Group plc

Professional support services

Correspondent: Graham Bisset, Group Secretary, WSP House, 70 Chancery Lane, London WC2A 1AF (tel: 020 7314 5000; fax: 020 7314 5111; email: info@wspgroup.com; website: www.wspgroup.com)

Directors: Ian Barlow, Chair; Christopher Cole, Chief Executive; Peter Gill; Rikard Appelgren; Paul Dollin; Stuart McLachlan; Christopher Stephens; Mark Rollins; Anders Karlsson; Huw Davies (women: 0; men: 10)

Year end	31/12/2011
Turnover	£720,000,000
Pre-tax profit	£19,000,000

Nature of business: An international business supplying specialist management and integrated services in the built and natural environment.

Company registration number: 2136404

Main locations: London

Total employees: 8,882

Membership: BITC

Charitable donations

UK cash (latest declared):	2011	£24,000
	2009	£7,029
	2008	£35,180
	2007	£26,902
	2006	£12,232
Total UK:	2011	£24,000
Total worldwide:	2011	£170,000
Cash worldwide:	2011	£170,000

Corporate social responsibility

CSR committee: There was no evidence of a separate CSR Committee.

CSR policy: The group's CSR aims were unavailable.

CSR report: There was no evidence of a separate CSR report.

Exclusions

No support for general or circular appeals, individuals, political or religious causes, or local appeals not in areas of company presence.

Applications

In writing to the correspondent.

Other information

During the year the group made charitable donations of £169,000 (2010: £103,000) principally to local charities and foundations serving the communities in which the group operates. Included in this figure was £24,000 (2010: £7,000) donated in the UK. **Note:** these figures do not include pro bono and volunteering contributions. The company's policy is to contribute to the economic, social and sustainable development of the communities in which it operates. On an informal basis the company makes donations to support charities with which its staff are involved.

Payroll giving: A wider reaching Give As You Earn scheme was rolled out in April 2008.

Xchanging plc

Business services

Correspondent: CSR Committee, 13 Hanover Square, London W1S 1HN (tel: 020 7780 6999; fax: 020 7499 0169; website: www.xchanging.com)

Directors: Geoff Unwin, Chair; Ken Lever, Chief Executive; David Bauernfeind, Chief Financial Officer; Dennis Millard; Pat O'Driscoll; Michel Paulin; Bill Thomas (women: 1; men: 6)

Year end	31/12/2011
Turnover	£288,800,000

Nature of business: Xchanging is one of the largest business processors, with a wide range of multinational customers in 42 countries and employing almost 8,000 people.

Company registration number: 5819018

Total employees: 7,930

Charitable donations

UK cash (latest declared):	2009	£36,000
	2008	£25,000
Total worldwide:	2011	£53,000
Cash worldwide:	2011	£53,000

Corporate social responsibility

CSR committee: Dedicated CSR committee. Names of members published in annual report and accounts.

CSR policy: Corporate social responsibility is fundamental to the way we plan and run our business, and is closely aligned with our values. We divide CSR into four categories: people; environment; communities; marketplace.

CSR report: Published within the annual report and accounts.

Applications

In writing to the correspondent.

Other information

Donations towards various international, national and local charities amounted to £53,000 during the year. The following information is taken from the 2011 annual report and accounts:

Communities

We support the communities in which we operate, with an approach aligned to our people value of creating value and being empowered to make a difference, and our Integrity Value of being dependable, responsible and committed to being open, transparent, honest and direct in all our activities. This means that we look to create long-term sustainable relationships with our communities, and focus on projects linked to youth and education. For example, our partnership with Vinoba Vidyalaya, a school in Shimoga, India, has a direct and positive impact on the Shimoga community. In 2011, Xchanging employees raised £12,000 for Vinoba Vidyalaya.

Each of our sites supports local charities, as well as national partners including Children in Need. In 2011, we donated our call centre facilities to the BBC and over 100 of our employees volunteered their time to take calls.

We are primarily focused on supporting youth and education and in 2011 we supported 24 charities worldwide. In the UK we continued to support our local educational charity partners, working with schools and colleges to introduce students studying business, IT or finance related A-levels or equivalents to the world of work. Our volunteering programme has seen 1,563 hours donated by employees in activities based around our commitment to youth and education, the local community and the environment.

We believe that all of our employees have the skills and experience to make a real difference and that this is also an excellent opportunity for personal development.

Xerox (UK) Ltd

Print/paper/packaging

Correspondent: Cheryl Walsh, Correspondent, The Xerox UK Trust (tel: 01895 251133/01895 251133; fax: 01895 254095; website: www.xerox.com)

Directors: A. P. Charnley, Managing Director; J. Hopwood; F. J. Mooney; M. C. O'Driscoll; M. E. Richards

Year end	31/12/2010
Turnover	£470,500,000
Pre-tax profit	£27,800,000

Nature of business: The principal activity of the group during the year was the marketing and financing of xerographic and electronic printing equipment, document managing systems and ancillary supplies in the UK.

Company registration number: 330754

Main locations: Mitcheldean, Cambridge, Welwyn Garden City

Total employees: 2,648

Charitable donations

UK cash (latest declared):	2010	£30,000
	2009	£0
	2008	£60,000
Total UK:	2010	£30,000
Total worldwide:	2010	£30,000
Cash worldwide:	2010	£30,000

Corporate social responsibility

CSR committee: No evidence of a CSR committee for the UK company.

CSR policy: The UK company's CSR policy is in line with the group's policy and states that the company is committed to reducing its impact on the environment, reducing waste and minimising energy consumption.

We could not determine the ration of women to men on the board.

CSR report: Not for UK.

Exclusions

Strictly no support for non-registered charities, or charities concerned with 'non-UK' activities or causes.

Applications

In writing to the correspondent.

Other information

Charitable donations made by the company are through its associated charitable trust, Xerox (UK) Trust (Charity Commission no. 284698), which supports a range of causes including: arts, sports, animal welfare, people with disabilities, education and training, health and community purposes. The company accounts for Xerox (UK) Ltd show £30,000 paid to the trust in 2010.

Yattendon Group plc (formerly Yattendon Investment Trust plc)

Media

Correspondent: George Bremner, The Iliffe Family Charitable Trust, Barn Close, Yattendon, Berkshire RG18 0UX (tel: 01635 203929; fax: 01635 203921; website: www.yattendongroup.co.uk)

Directors: Lord Iliffe, Chair; Francois Austin; David Fordham; Lisa Gordon; Simon Gray; Edward Iliffe; Michael Lawrence; Michael Spencer; Catherine Fleming (women: 2; men: 7)

Year end	31/12/2011
Turnover	£102,918,000
Pre-tax profit	£3,780,000

Nature of business: Yattendon Investment Trust is a private company owned by the Iliffe family, with operations in the UK and Canada, and interests in newspaper publishing, television, electronic media, marinas and property.

Company registration number: 288238

Main locations: Thatcham

Total employees: 1,021

Charitable donations

UK cash (latest declared):	2011	£350,000
	2009	£150,000
	2008	£150,000
	2007	£150,000
	2006	£150,000
Total UK:	2011	£350,000
Total worldwide:	2011	£350,000
Cash worldwide:	2011	£350,000

Corporate social responsibility

CSR policy: No CSR information available.

We were unable to determine the ratio of women to men on the board.

Applications

The trust is administered from the same address as the company. Applications should be addressed to the charity correspondent, G A Bremner. Only successful applications are acknowledged.

Other information

Charitable giving is made through The Iliffe Family Charitable Trust (Charity Commission no. 273437). The trust was established in February 1977 for 'such exclusively charitable objects and purposes in the United Kingdom or in any other part of the world as the trustees think fit'. The trust generally, however, donates funds to charities operating in the areas of education, medicine, welfare, religion, conservation and heritage.

In 2011, The Iliffe Family Charitable Trust received £350,000 gift-aided by the company. Whilst we are not sure whether this was gifted by employees or family members, we have used this figure as the company's charitable cash donation. Grants by the trust were awarded totalling £211,500. Some of the donations listed include: Marine Society and Sea Cadets (£30,500 each); Royal Shakespeare Company and Mary Rose Trust (£20,000 each); Cystic Fibrosis Trust (£10,000); Sea Change Sailing Trust (5,000); and Ronnie Bowker Foundation (£500).

Yorkshire Building Society

Building society

Correspondent: Mrs A L Fitzpatrick, Trust Secretary, Yorkshire House, Yorkshire Drive, Bradford BD5 8LJ (tel: 01274 472512; email: charitable@ybs.co.uk; website: www.ybs.co.uk)

Directors: Ed Anderson, Chair; Kate Barker; Roger Burden; Lynne Charlesworth; Richard Davey; Philip Johnson; David Paige; Simon Turner; Chris Pilling, Chief Executive; Andy Caton; Robin Churchouse, Finance Director (women: 2; men: 10)

Year end	31/12/2011
Turnover	£155,600,000
Pre-tax profit	£106,200,000

Nature of business: Building Society.

FSA registration number: 106085

Total employees: 3,266

Charitable donations

UK cash (latest declared):	2011	£45,250
	2009	£75,000
	2008	£75,000
	2007	£50,000
	2006	£75,000
Total UK:	2011	£45,250
Total worldwide:	2011	£45,250
Cash worldwide:	2011	£45,250

Corporate social responsibility

CSR committee: No specific details found.

CSR policy: Taken from the society's website:

> Rooted in the ethos of a mutual building society is a deep commitment to its local communities and here at the Yorkshire we take that commitment very seriously, whilst embracing our values of fun, fairness, passion and people working together. Our programme covers all the community, charity and volunteering activities for the society's brands; Yorkshire, Barnsley, Chelsea and Norwich & Peterborough building societies, and Egg – hence 'Societies Together'. Our Societies Together vision is to have a community programme that inspires, motivates and engages our members, staff and local communities to get involved in our community activities.

CSR report: A CSR report is contained within the annual report and accounts.

Exclusions

The society does not support any activity which is not carried out by a registered charity or which does not otherwise count as being a good cause. Additionally, there may be projects or activities which could be considered as registered charities or good causes but which the society feels do not fall within its priorities or meet other criteria. Examples of these are:

- Fundraising for the purposes of pursuing political or propagandist activities
- The support of religious activities or the advancement of religion (although this would not prevent consideration for support to members of a group or community that was otherwise in need)
- Any fundraising or activity under which those organising the fundraising activity would or could have a personal benefit
- Provision of support for a person or people who do not come within the priority of the foundation or are not in genuine need
- Applications from national charitable organisations for general ongoing funding (although this would not prevent consideration of specific items for local initiatives/branches)
- Any organisation considered to be illegal or which may act illegally, or where funds are raised from, or for immoral purposes
- Provision of sport generally or seeking to achieve excellence or professionalism in sport. For example this would exclude any sponsorship activities, or the provision of equipment for sports teams. The only exception to this would be, for example, some sporting activity for children who are in need, or disabled people, or other people suffering hardship
- Support for individuals or groups engaged in expeditions or projects requiring them to raise funds to enable them to participate
- Proposals which are purely concerned with raising funds for other organisations or charities and/or where such funds are likely to go to the administration expenses of such organisations e.g. provision of sponsorship to an individual or individuals participating in another charitable or good cause event
- Carnivals or shows which are concerned with mainly entertaining the public and where there is no control over the eventual destination of funds raised
- Any purposes concerned with the promotion of friendship or international friendship e.g. town twining associations
- Support for a person or persons who do not come within the priority of the Foundation, or are not thought to be in genuine need
- Support of activities in or equipment for mainstream schools. The only exception to this would be activities or equipment to help children with special needs
- Provision of equipment for hospitals or other health establishments which are the responsibility of a statutory body. Equipment to be provided by a charity or good cause supporting a hospital/establishment may be considered

Applications

Applications are usually received from members of the society or through the society's branches or head office departments. This helps ensure support is given to local charities and good causes in areas important to members and staff.

To apply, contact your local branch to discuss your application. Staff there will be pleased to help and provide you with a copy of the foundation guidelines. If you don't have a local branch, apply in writing to the above named correspondent.

Other information

In 2011, the donation from the Yorkshire Building Society to its charitable foundation was £45,250. Other income was received from staff fundraising and customer contributions.

The following information is taken from the society's annual report and accounts for 2011:

Yorkshire Building Society Charitable Foundation (Charity Commission no. 1069082)
The foundation's focus, in addition to its annual campaigns, is on providing grants to charities nominated by the society's members and causes that staff have a personal interest in.

In 2011 over £462,000 was donated to over 2,000 causes – 90% of which were nominated by our members. Our unique Small Change, Big Difference scheme provides a large proportion of the foundation's funding – over £2 million since 2000. Through the scheme members donate their pennies of interest every year to the foundation – an average of less than 50p per account, per year – demonstrating that the small change really can make a big difference to the lives of others in our local communities.

Small Change, Big Difference
Since July 2011 new and existing Chelsea members have been able to join the Small Change, Big Difference scheme. To celebrate this launch, the foundation donated £1,000 to a charity nominated by every Chelsea branch. The charities included; Streatham Youth and Community Trust, The Chelsea Pensioners Appeal and Harrow Carers. This resulted in a total of £35,000 being donated to 35 good causes in areas where our Chelsea members and staff live and work.

The YBS enjoys major contributions from its staff in supporting charitable activities. Information taken from the company's annual report for 2011 states that these include the following:

- Charity of the Year – staff raised over £85,000 and, with a donation from the Yorkshire Building Society Charitable Foundation, the Alzheimer's Society received £175,000 [in 2011]
- Yorkshire Building Society Charitable Foundation donated over £462,000 to more than 2,000 charities, of which 90% were member nominated
- Make a Difference Week received over 1,600 nominations for donations to local causes that are important to our members
- Successful launch of Small Change, Big Difference scheme to members who joined the Group as a result of our merger with Chelsea – 11% of these members have already signed up
- Over 177,000 accounts joined Small Change, Big Difference scheme in 2011; resulting in just under 800,000 members now participating in the scheme
- Over 3,500 volunteer hours were completed by staff working on around 60 projects in our local communities

Charity of the Year: RNLI (2012)

Zurich Financial Services (UKISA) Ltd

Life assurance

Correspondent: Pam Webb, Community Affairs Team, PO Box 1288, Swindon, Wiltshire SN1 1FL (tel: 01793 514514/ 01793 502450; email: communityaffairs@ uk.zurich.com; website: www.zurich.co. uk)

Directors: E. U. Angehrn; D. J. Pender; S. Lewis; O. C. Tengtio; P. Sutton; J. R. Dyke

Year end	31/12/2011

Nature of business: Zurich Financial Services (UKISA) is a holding company and part of the Zurich Financial Services Group and comprises the group's operations in the UK, Ireland and South Africa.

Company registration number: 1860680

Main locations: Swindon

Total employees: 60,000

Membership: BITC, LBG

Charitable donations

UK cash (latest declared):	2011	£2,670,000
	2008	£2,655,000
	2007	£1,900,000
	2006	£1,900,000
	2005	£1,900,000
Total UK:	2011	£3,255,250
Total worldwide:	2011	£3,255,250
Cash worldwide:	2011	£2,670,000

Community involvement

Zurich Community Trust (Charity Commission no. 266983)

Zurich states that it is: 'Committed to be good corporate citizens, and in doing so to encourage and support its employees to do their part to make a better world'. In striving to achieve this goal, the Zurich Community Trust provides the umbrella for all the company's community work in the UK.

The main objective of the trust is to give money, skills and time donated from Zurich together with money and time leveraged from employees of Zurich and advisors and employees of Openwork to help disadvantaged people achieve an independent future for themselves.

The focus is on disadvantaged local communities, on issues that are often overlooked and where we can have the biggest impact.

The trust fulfils this objective through:

- Long-term transformation programmes focusing on particular areas of social need
- Charity partnerships and grant programmes through the Zurich Cares programme
- Charity partnerships and grant programmes through the Openwork Foundation
- An employee volunteering programme through the Zurich Cares programme

As well as making charitable grants, a significant amount of Zurich staff time is committed to the community through working in partnership with charity partners and by brokering the volunteering needs of the voluntary sector with time and skills available from employees within the Zurich business.

There are two strands to the Zurich Community Trust.

Transformation programmes
These work in partnership with charities to deliver transformational change over a minimum five year period. The current programmes are focusing on:

- Helping non-governmental organisations (NGO's) in Southern India build their capacity ('India Programme')
- Supporting vulnerable older people ('Call In Time')
- Breaking the generational cycle of drug misuse ('Breaking The Cycle')
- Supporting young people experiencing mental health issues and their families. ('Mental Health and Families Programme')

Zurich only accepts applications from those who are invited to apply.

The 'Zurich Cares' employee involvement programme
The trust uses some of the financial donation from the Zurich UK business to match the financial donations from Zurich employees. Zurich also provides business time to enable employees to volunteer in the community and get involved in organising and managing fundraising events, volunteering schemes and local grant programmes. A great deal of employee personal time is also leveraged through this programme. This is all managed by members of the Zurich Community Trust Team.

The Openwork Foundation
This fund administered within the overall charity is funded by advisors and employees of Openwork. The objective of this foundation is to help disadvantaged children under the theme 'Cares 4 Kids'.

The Openwork Foundation also supports other charities working with disadvantaged children through a regional grant programme, via sponsored application, and a small discretionary grant programme where advisors and employees of Openwork can recommend charities for support.

During 2011 a donation of £100,000 was made to the Openwork Foundation by an Openwork client to support disadvantaged young people in the West Midlands area. This donation coupled with the Gift Aid is supporting projects with the Warwickshire Association of Youth Clubs, helping young people leaving care, The Prince's Trust Fairbridge programme, helping young people recovering from mental health issues and will support Doorway Nuneaton and Bedworth, Warwickshire helping young homeless people.

Charity partners: In September 2012, the Alzheimer's Society joined CLIC Sargent and Hope and Homes for Children as Zurich Community Trust's third national charity partner.

Corporate giving

In 2011, Zurich UK businesses donated £2.67 million (2010: £1.88 million) to the **Zurich Community Trust**; we have used this figure as the company's UK cash contribution. Zurich employees and advisors donated a further £1 million.

In total, grants totalling £1.1 million were made through the Zurich Cares programme; £609,000 through the trust's Transformation programmes and £249,000 was donated through the Openwork Foundation. Grants were broken down as follows:

Transformation and Trust	
Young People's Mental Health	£346,000
India programme	£105,000
Call in Time (Age UK)	£88,000
Breaking the Cycle (Addaction)	£70,000
Zurich Cares (long-term community partners)	
Marie Curie Cancer Care	£50,000
Calvert Trust	£25,000
Hope and Homes for Children	£50,000
Canine Partners	£25,000
CLIC Sargent	£50,000
Various local partners	£28,000
Local grants	£552,000
Employee nominated grants	£271,000
Overseas grants	£70,000
Openwork Foundation	
Philippine Community Trust	£50,000
Children's Hospices UK	£13,000
Together for Short Lives	£12,000
Regional grants	£170,000
Discretionary grants	£4,000

In kind support

In kind support is provided including assistance from Zurich employees in supporting the Zurich Community Trust's activities.

Employee-led support

Zurich Community Trust – Employee involvement

Over 25% of Zurich employees give regularly. Over £1 million was donated by employees and advisers to the trust in 2011 which was also matched by the business. The trust also 'leverages' around 41,000 hours of volunteer time each year through its active employee volunteer programme.

Staff are encouraged to support charitable causes through contributions of time as well as money. Two funds exist to facilitate this:

Zurich Cares

In 2011 over £520,000 was donated together with over 5,900 days of volunteering.

Supported by staff of the UK businesses, Zurich Cares encourages them in sharing time and money with local communities. They do this through:

- Payroll giving scheme
- Active volunteering
- Challenge programmes
- Matching schemes for staff and their children for fundraising for charity (50% to £500 maximum per event)
- Donation of gifts – for example, at Christmas and Easter time
- Partnerships with local, national and overseas voluntary organisations
- Being school governors or charity trustees in their community, (Zurich supports employees in this initiative by awarding the organisation with £200 grant award)
- A local grant programme awarding grants to local and overseas projects – all selected by employees

Local grant programmes are active in Wiltshire, Hampshire, Gloucestershire and a few other locations where Zurich has large offices. Grants range from £100 – £10,000 and support disadvantaged people to live a more independent lifestyle. Support has also been given for carers, special needs children, people with disabilities, counselling, homeless people, teenage pregnancy, and people from 'ethnic minorities'.

Grants are sometimes given for core costs such as salaries, premises, transport and food costs, whilst a number of one-off purchases e.g. IT equipment, training, access and equipment for people with disabilities, have also been made.

Openwork Foundation

This is funded by employees and members of Openwork. The objective of the Openwork Foundation is to help disadvantaged children.

Payroll giving: The company runs the Give As You Earn scheme. Employees' giving is matched in full by the company, without limit.

Commercially-led support

My Community Starter: is a website that helps people who want to get involved in organising smaller, straightforward community activities to help people understand and overcome potential barriers to volunteering in the local community. The website will help the public to understand some of the legal, health and safety, planning issues and insurance considerations of whatever they are involved in. It is free and available for individuals and groups.

Arson Combated Together (ACT): is an initiative developed by the company together with the Fire and Rescue Services and other arson-related organisations. Its aim is to teach children about the risk and consequences of arson. In addition the company states that its lobbying was instrumental in persuading the government to ensure that all new school buildings include sprinkler systems.

Sponsorship: Arts and good-cause sponsorship is undertaken.

Partnerships: Marie Curie; Hope and Homes for Children; CLIC Sargent; Calvert Trust and Canine Partners.

Corporate social responsibility

CSR committee: There is a Corporate Responsibility Council in the UK.

CSR policy: Statement taken from the Zurich UK website:

> At Zurich, corporate responsibility is an integral part of how we do business. Being a responsible company is fundamental to our long-term sustainability. We are committed to creating sustainable value for our shareholders, our customers, our employees and the communities in which we live and work. In the UK, we demonstrate our commitment to Corporate Responsibility with numerous Zurich initiatives and the dedication of both time and money.

We were unable to determine the ratio of women to men on the board.

CSR report: An annual CSR report is published and available from the company's website. The report outlines the company's priority areas in the UK, which are:

- Workplace
- Marketplace
- Environment
- Communities.

Exclusions

No grants to individuals, research, animal welfare, emergency or disaster appeals or to political, religious or mainstream educational institutions – unless directly benefiting people with disabilities, political or religious organisations.

Applications

Trust programmes – potential partners are researched, identified and selected by the Community Affairs team.

Arts & Business

Arts & Business, now a part of Business in the Community, aims to build the knowledge and capacity of the arts and cultural sectors by supporting organisations to engage with the private sector and to stimulate personal philanthropy. In the organisation's own words: 'We connect companies, communities and individuals to cultural organisations and provide the delivery, expertise and insight for their relationships to thrive, for their mutual benefit and that of the wider community.'

The organisation's principal focus is within the areas of not-for-profit performing and visual arts, but it also actively supports the activities of museums, libraries, archives, and literary and heritage organisations. Within this, Arts & Business's priorities, which it asks companies to take action on, are: education and young people; enterprise and culture; workplace and employees; tackling unemployment; and marketplace sustainability. To achieve its aims, Arts & Business works in partnership with stakeholders across the UK, including Arts Council England and the governments of Scotland, Wales and Northern Ireland.

If you are an arts or cultural organisation based in England, Scotland, Wales or Northern Ireland and would like information about building your fundraising potential or recruiting members for your board from the business sector, visit the website of the appropriate regional Arts & Business office listed below.

Arts & Business produces a number of resources giving advice on topics such as sponsorship and tax. These are available at: www.artsandbusiness.bitc.org.uk

Contacts

Arts & Business Head Office (London)

137 Shepherdess Walk
London
N1 7RQ

Tel: 020 7566 6650
Email: Contactus@artsandbusiness.org.uk

Birmingham

Business in the Community
c/o Kraft foods
83 Bournville Lane
Birmingham B30 2HP

Tel: 01214 512227

Manchester

Business in the Community
2nd Floor Amazon House
3 Brazil Street
Manchester M1 3PJ

Tel: 01214 512227

Northern Ireland

Bridge House
Paulett Avenue
Belfast
BT5 4HD
Northern Ireland

Tel: 02890 735150
Email: info@artsandbusinessni.org.uk

Scotland

11 Abercromby Place
Edinburgh
EH3 6LB

Tel: 01315 563353
Email: contactus@aandbscotland.org.uk

Wales (north)

Room 40
The Town Hall
Lloyd Street
Llandudno
LL30 2UP

Tel: 01492 574003
Email: contactus@aandbcymru.org.uk

Wales (south)

16 Museum Place
Cardiff
CF10 3BH

Tel: 02920 303023
Email: contactus@aandbcymru.org.uk

Corporate Principal Members

England

Bank of America
Bloomberg
BP
The Co-operative
Ernst & Young
GlaxoSmithKline
Jaguar/LandRover
JTI
Northern Trust
PricewaterhouseCoopers
Prudential
Sky Arts
Corporate Members
Northern ireland
Abbey Bond Lovis
AES
Allianz
Arthur Cox
Arup
Barclays
Belfast Harbour Commissioners
Belfast Media Group
Bombardier Aerospace
Botanic Inns Ltd
BT
Burke Shipping Group
Business First
Carson McDowell
Cathy Law Communications
Census Financial Planning

Clear Partnership, Belfast
Cleaver, Fulton & Rankin
Coca Cola Bottlers (Ulster)
Co-operative Group
Cunningham Coates Stockbrokers
Danske Bank
Diageo Northern Ireland
Donnelly Neary & Donnelly
Edwards & Co. Solicitors
Everglades Hotel
Gentle Dental
Harbinson Mulholland
Harrison Photography
Hill Business Growth Consultants
Image Zoo
Irwin, Donaghy, Stockman
JTI
James Street South
KBC Bank
KPMG
McKenna Gallery
Marsh UK Ltd
Maze Long Kesh Corporation
Pinsent Masons
McKinty and Wright, Solicitors
Millar McCall Wylie Solicitors
Nicholson & Bass Limited
Northgate Managed Services
Osborne King
Origin Partners
The Outlet, Banbridge
PricewaterhouseCoopers
Smarts Communicate
Stratagem
Titanic Quarter
Translink
U105 Ltd
Ulster Bank Ltd
Ulster Journals Ltd
University of Ulster, Jordanstown
Whitenoise
WJR Consulting
Willis and Company (Insurance Brokers) Ltd

Scotland

Aberdeen and Grampian Chamber of Commerce
Aberdeen City Council
Aberdeenshire Council
Accenture Scotland
Allander Print
Anderson Strathern
Ashleybank Investments
Audrey McIntosh
Baillie Gifford Investment Managers
Baker Tilly
Barefoot Wine
Benromach Whisky
Black Light
BP
CB Richard Ellis
City of Edinburgh Council
Chevron Upstream Europe
Clydesdale Bank
Cowan & Partners
Cutty Sark
Dundee & Angus Chamber of Commerce
Dundee City Council
Edinburgh Chamber of Commerce, Edinburgh
Eskmills
First ScotRail
Freight Design
Front Page
Glasgow Chamber of Commerce
Glasgow Life / Glasgow City Council
Great Circle Communications
Heineken UK
Henzteeth
Institute of Directors Scotland
Inverness Chamber of Commerce
James Law
J Thomson Colour Printers
Keegan & Pennykid
Kynesis
Liddell Thomson
The List
Lloyds Banking Group
Maersk Oil North Sea UK
Malcom Cannon
Material Marketing and Communications
McFadden Associates
Murray Beith Murray
Perth & Kinross Council
Pinsent Masons
Prudential
Quality Scotland
Royal Institution of Chartered Surveyors
Scottish Business in the Community
Scottish Council for Development & Industry
Scottish Friendly Assurance
Scottish Government
ScottishPower
Scottish Retail Consortium
Shell UK
Skypark Unit Trust
Studio Norse
Talisman Energy (UK)
TAQA Bratani
TESCO Bank
Total E&P UK
The Town House Company
Turcan Connell
Whitespace
William Grant & Sons Distillers
Wolffe

Wales

Admiral Group
Amcen Cyfyngedig
Ancre Hill Vineyard
Arup
The Angel Hotel
Bangor University
BBC Cymru Wales
Blackhorse
Broomfield & Alexander
Cardiff Marriott Hotel
Cardiff School of Art & Design
Carmarthenshire County Council
Carrick Creative
CBI Wales
Ceidiog Communication
Civitas Law
Coastal Housing Group Ltd
Confused.com
Conwy County Borough Council
The Creative Work Place
Daily Post
Dischromatics
Dwr Cymru Welsh Water
Eversheds
Everything Everywhere
Fulcrum Direct
Gamlins Solicitors
Geldards
Glyndwr University
G W Consulting
Hospital Innovations
Hugh James Solicitors
John Lewis
Legal & General Ltd
Manorhaus
Maskreys Ltd
Milford Haven Port Authority
Newport City Council
Peninsula Home Improvements
Park Plaza Cardiff
Pendine Park Care Homes
Pobol
Principality Building Society
Radisson Blu Hotel Cardiff
Redrow Homes
Research Institute for Arts & Humanities at Swansea University
Royal Oak Hotel
S4C
Salisbury Accountants
ScottishPower
Smoke Control Services (SCS Group)
Spindogs
Swayne Johnson Solicitors
University of Wales
University of Wales Newport
Unity Trust Bank
Valero
Wales & West Utilities
West Coast Energy
Willmott Dixon Construction
Zeffa

Business in the Community

Business in the Community aims to make community involvement a natural part of successful business practice, and to increase the quality and extent of business activity in the community. It exists to work with companies to mobilise resources (skills, expertise, influence, products and profits) to promote social and economic regeneration. ProHelp (see page 354) is an initiative of Business in the Community.

Contacts

Business in the Community Head Office (covering London and South East)

137 Shepherdess Walk
London
N1 7RQ

Tel: 020 7566 8650
Email: information@bitc.org.uk
Web: www.bitc.org.uk

Northern Ireland

Belfast

Bridge House
Paulett Avenue
Belfast
BT5 4HD

Tel: 02890 460606
Email: info@bitcni.org.uk

Northern Ireland

North West

BEAM Social Enterprise Centre
Invista House
Maydown Works
Derry/Londonderry
BT47 6TH

Tel: 02871 861550
Email info@bitcni.org.uk

Wales

Cardiff

2nd Floor, Riverside House
31 Cathedral Road
Cardiff
CF11 9HB

Tel: 02920 780050
Email: wales@bitc.org.uk

Mold

St. Andrews Park
Queens Lane
Mold
CH7 1XB

Tel: 01745 817325
Email: wales@bitc.org.uk

North East

c/o The Sage Group
North Park
Newcastle upon Tyne
NE13 9AA

Tel: 01912 946033
Email: northeast@bitc.org.uk

England

North West

Manchester

2nd Floor
Amazon House
3 Brazil Street
Manchester
M1 3PJ

Tel: 01612 337750
Email: northwest@bitc.org.uk

North West

Merseyside

Suite 322a
The Cotton Exchange
Old Hall Street
Liverpool
L3 9LQ

Tel: 01516 003560

Yorkshire & Humberside

Leeds

44–60 Richardshaw Lane
Pudsey
Leeds
West Yorkshire
LS28 7UR

Tel: 01132 058200
Email: yorkshire@bitc.org.uk

Sheffield

c/o Yorkshire Water
Newton Chambers Road
Thorncliffe
Sheffield
S35 2PQ

Tel: 01142 013307

Hull

c/o Arco Ltd
Henry Boot Way
Hull
HU4 7DY

Tel: 01482 351609

East Midlands

3rd Floor
30–34 Hounds Gate
Nottingham
NG1 7AB

Tel: 01159 247400
Email: eastmidlands@bitc.org.uk

West Midlands
83 Bournville Lane
Birmingham
B30 2HP
Tel: 01214 512227
Email: westmidlands@bitc.org.uk

West Midlands
Black Country
c/o Blakemore Wholesale
Wolverhampton Science Park
Coxwell Avenue
Wolverhampton
WV10 9RT
Tel: 01902 717491
Email: westmidlands@bitc.org.uk

West Midlands
Coventry & Warwickshire
c/o Jaguar Cars Limited
B/7/006 Browns Lane
Coventry
CV5 9DR
Tel: 02476 401056
Email: westmidlands@bitc.org.uk

East
Office 4, Rookery House
The Guineas
Newmarket
Suffolk
CB8 8EQ
Tel: 01638 663272
Email: eastern@bitc.org.uk

South East
c/o Systems Technology Park
Elettra Avenue
Waterlooville
Hampshire
PO7 7XS
Tel: 02392 230692
Email: Southeast@bitc.org.uk

South West
Bristol
Portwall Place
Portwall Lane
Bristol
BS99 7UD
Tel: 01179 309380
Email: southwest@bitc.org.uk

South West
Plymouth
c/o Shekinah Mission
Bath Street
Plymouth
PL1 3LT
Tel: 01752 203484
Email: southwest@bitc.org.uk

Members

12/8 Group
2 Sisters Food Group
3i Group
3M UK
A4e Ltd
AB Glass Ltd
ABB Ltd.
Abbott Mead Vickers
Aberdeen Asset Management
Accenture
Access Bank
Addison Lee Plc
Addleshaw Goddard
ADI Group
Adnams Plc
AESSEAL plc
AF Blakemore & Son Ltd
Affinity Sutton Group
AIMIA
Aircelle Ltd
Allen & Overy
Alliance Boots
Alumet Systems (UK) Ltd
American Express Services Europe
AmicusHorizon
Anglian Water Group
Anglo American
Anglo Beef Processors
APCO
APCOA Parking (UK) Limited
API Laminates Ltd
APS Group
Aramark
Archant
Arco
Ardmore Group
Argent Group
Arora Hotels
ASDA Stores Ltd
ASDAN Education
Aspall
Associated British Foods
Audi UK
Avios
Aviva plc
Avox Ltd
AWE
AXA UK
Axis Europe
Azzurri Communications
BAE SYSTEMS MARITIME SERVICES
Bain & Company
Baker Tilly
Balfour Beatty
BAM
Bank of America Merrill Lynch
Bank of New York Mellon
Banks Group
Barclays
Barques Design
Barratt Developments
BaxterStorey
BBC
BCSC
BDR Thermea
Bentley Motors Limited
Bettys & Taylors Group Ltd
Bevan Brittan LLP
BHP Billiton
Biffa Waste Services
Bird & Bird LLP
Birmingham Airport
Birmingham City University
Birmingham Metropolitan College
BlackBerry
Blackstone Group International
Bloomberg
Bluestone Resorts Limited
BNP Paribas
Bolton at Home
Bombardier Transportation UK
Bouygues UK
BP
Bradford College
Brakes
Bray Leino
Bristol Zoo Gardens
British Airways
British American Tobacco
British Horseracing Authority
British Land Company
Britvic Soft Drinks
Broadridge Financial Solutions Ltd
Brother Industries UK (Wales)
Bruntwood
BSkyB
BT
Bupa
Business in the Community
Buy as You View Ltd
Cadbury
Calico Housing
Calor Gas
Cambridge University Press
Camden Glass Ltd
Camelot Group Plc
Campbell McCleave
Canary Wharf Group
Capgemini
Capital One
Capital Shopping Centres Group plc
Cardiac Services
Cardiff Airport
Cardiff City Transport Services
Carecall
Carillion Plc
Carson McDowell Solicitors
Castle Leisure
Castleoak Holdings
Catlin Group

Cavanagh Kelly
CE Electric UK
CEMEX
Central YMCA
Centrica
Channel 4 Television
Chapelfield
Chesapeake
Chime Communications
Chiswick Park Estate Management
Cinven
Circe Ltd
Cirque du Soleil
CISCO Systems
Citi Citi
City & Guilds
City of Bradford Metropolitan District Council
City of Bristol College
City of London
CityWest Homes
Clancy Group (Clancy Docwra Limited)
Clanmil Housing Association
Clarehill Plastics
Clarendon Executive
Cleaver Fulton Rankin
Cleone Foods Limited
Clifford Chance
Cluttons
Clydesdale & Yorkshire Bank
CMG Solicitors
Cobham
Coca Cola
Coca Cola Bottlers (Ulster)
Coffey International Limited
Colt Technology Services Compass Group
Compass Group
Connswater Homes
Connswater Shopping Centre
Consarc Design Group Ltd
Cooper Parry Copeland
Costain Group
Council for the Curriculum Examinations & Assessment (CCEA)
Crane Stockham Valve Ltd
Credit Suisse
Crossrail
Credit360
Croda International plc
CSC Computer Sciences
Crown Estate, The
Crystal Collections Ltd
Currencies Direct
CSR Plc
Cummins Engine Company
Cushman & Wakefield
Danone UK Ltd
Dairy Crest Group
Debenhams Retail
Davy
DCC Energy (NI) Ltd
Deloitte
Decora Blind Systems
Delap & Waller
Department for Communities and Local Government
Deloitte (NI)
Delta Print & Packaging Ltd
Department of Justice
Department for Work and Pensions
Department of Health
Derry City Council
DePuy UK
Derby College
Diageo
DFC
DHL Aviation (UK)
Diageo (NI)
DLA Piper UK
Dillon Bass Ltd
Direct Rail Services Limited
Drax Power
Dolmans Solicitors
Domino's Pizza Group Ltd
Duchy of Cornwall
Driver and Vehicle Agency DTZ
DWF LLP
Dunbia
Dunhills (Pontefract) plc
Dwr Cymru Welsh Water
E&I Engineering
E H Booth & Co
Eaga
E.ON UK
e2v technologies (UK)
Ecclesiastical Insurance Group
East Coast Mainline Company Ltd.
East Midlands Airport
Elior UK
EDF Energy
Eircom UK Ltd
Enterprise Employers For Childcare
Energia
Equiniti ICS
Enterprise Rent-A-Car
Ernst & Young LLP
Equiniti ICS
Eric Wright Group Ltd
Eversheds
ESB Independent
Energy Esh Group
Experian
Everything Everywhere
Evron Foods Ltd
ExxonMobil
F&C Asset Management
Fabrick Housing Group
FGS McClure Watters
Fairwood Trust
FG Wilson (Engineering) Ltd
Findel Education
Fidessa Group
Financial Services Authority
Firmus Energy
Findus Group
Finlay Communications
Firstsource
First Trust Bank
FirstGroup
Fold Housing Association
Flint Bishop
Flybe
FPM Chartered Accountants
Ford
Foyle Food Group
Freshfields Bruckhaus Deringer
Francis Hanna & Co
FremantleMedia
Fujitsu Friends Provident
Fujitsu
Futures (NI)
G4S Funeral Services NI Ltd
Gallaher Limited – A member of the JTI group of Companies
G4S
Gala Coral Group
Gallions Housing Association
GAM Fund Management
Gateshead College
GEDA Construction
General Electric
General Trading Company (Mayfair) Ltd
Genesis Breads
Gentoo Group
GeoPost UK
George Best Belfast City Airport
GF Tomlinson Birmingham Ltd
GF Tomlinson Group Ltd.
Gilbert-Ash N.I. Limited
GlaxoSmithKline
Gleeds
GMI Construction Group plc
Goldblatt McGuigan
Goldman Sachs International
Golf Holdings
Golley Slater & Partners
Good Relations Wales
Grafton Group
Graham
Graham & Brown Ltd
Grainger Building Services
Grant Thornton
Greater Manchester Fire and Rescue Service
Greencore Direct to Store
Greggs Grimsby Institute of Further & Higher Education
Grosvenor
Groupama Insurances
GSS Architecture
Guardian Media Group
H & J Martin Ltd
Habinteg Housing Association

Hadley Group
Hafod Housing Association
Halcrow Group
Haldane Fisher Ltd
Halfords
Hallmark Cards
Hammerson
Hammonds
Harper Adams University College
Hays Specialist Recruitment
HCL Insurance BPO Services Ltd
Heathrow Airport Limited
Heineken UK
Helm Housing Association
Henry Brothers (Magherafelt) Ltd
Hill & Smith Holdings HLN
Architects
HM Revenue and Customs
HML
Hogan Lovells LLP
Holder Mathias Architects
Home Retail Group
House of Fraser
HRG
HSBC Bank
HSBC plc Trade Services
Huhtamaki (UK) Ltd
Hutchinson Homes
IBM UK
Identity and Passport Service
IEB Software
IKEA
ILEX Urban Regeneration Company
Impact Development Training
Imperial Tobacco Group
Intellectual Property Office
International Nuclear Services
Invest NI
Intercontinental Hotels Group
Ipsos MORI
INVISTA Textiles (UK) Limited
Iron Mountain
Irwin Mitchell
Irish News Ltd
Isles of Scilly Steamship Group
ISS UK
ISG
ITV
J D Wetherspoon
J J Kelly & Co
J Sainsbury
J P Corry Group Limited
Jackson Graham Associates
Jaguar Land Rover
Jackel International Ltd.
JN Bentley
Jobsite UK
James Hall & Co. (Southport) Ltd.
John Lewis Partnership
John Thompson and Sons Ltd
John Laing
Johnston Campbell Partnership
Jones Lang LaSalle
Johnson Matthey
KCOM Group plc
Keepmoat
Kaplan Altior
Kelly Fuels
Kennedy Group
Kelda Group
Kier Group
Kilwaughter Chemical Company Ltd
Kerry Foods
Kingfisher plc
Kingspan Group
King Sturge
KPMG in Ireland
Knight Frank
L E Pritchitt & Co
Ltd Lafarge Cement (NI)
Kraft Foods
Lagan Holdings
Laing O'Rourke
Lafarge Cement UK
Lancaster University
Land Registry
Lakehouse Contracts
Langford Lodge Engineering
Larne Harbour Ltd
Land Securities
Lavendon Group plc
LBM Latens
Leckpatrick Foods
Leeds Metropolitan University
Leadership & Management Wales
Legal & General Group
Lend Lease
Leeds University Business School
Linc-Cymru Housing Association
Lincolnshire Co-operative
Leo Burnett
Linklaters
Liverpool City Council
Linden Foods
Lloyds Banking Group
Lloyds of London
Liverpool John Moores University
Londonderry Port & Harbour
Commissioners
Loughborough University
London Clubs International
Lubrizol Mace
LSI Architects LLP
Man Group
Manchester Airport
Magnox North
Marks & Spencer (NI)
Mars UK
Marks & Spencer
Marshalls
Masterlease UK
Masternaut (UK)
Martineau
Maydown Precision Engineering Ltd
Mazars
May Gurney
McCain Foods (GB) Ltd
McDonald's Restaurants
McAvoy Group Ltd
McKinsey & Co UK
McLaughlin & Harvey Construction
McGrigors
Media Wales
MediCare Pharmacy Group
McMullen Architectural Systems Ltd
Merseytravel
Met Office
Merlin Entertainments Group
Michelmores
Microsoft
Michelin Tyre
Midas Group
Midland Heart
Microsoft (NI)
Mills & Reeve Solicitors
Mills Selig
MITIE Group
Mivan
Ministry of Defence
Moat
Montupet (UK) Ltd
MJM Group
Morgan Sindall plc
Morgan Stanley
Moody's Investors Service
Morrow Contracts Ltd
Mott
MacDonald Group
Morrison Facilities Services
Muller Dairy (UK)
Multi Development (NI)
Moy Park Ltd
Munster Simms Ltd
Murdock Group Ltd
Munro & Forster
Musgrave Retail Partners GB
MWH UK
Musgrave Retail Partners GB
National Grid
National House-Building Council
NACCO Materials Handling Ltd
Nationwide Building Society
National House-Building Council
Navigators
NEC Group
NATS
Network Rail
New World Solar
Nestle Holdings UK
NFT Distribution
NFU Mutual Insurance Co
Next
NI Housing Executive
Nicholls (Fuel Oils) Ltd
NI Assembly
NIjobs.com

Nitec Solutions
nichols plc
Nomura International
Norfolk & Waveney Mental Health
NHS Foundation Trust
Nominet
Norse Commercial Services
NORTEL NI
Norfolkline
North West Regional College
Northern Bank Ltd
North Midland Construction plc
Northern Health & Social Services Board
Northern Ireland Ambulance Service
Health & Social Services
Northern Foods Trust
Northern Ireland Blood Transfusion Service
Northern Ireland Chamber of Commerce & Industry
Northern Ireland Water
Northgate Information Solutions
Northern Rail Ltd.
Northumbrian Water Ltd
Northwest Regional Development Agency
Northstone (NI) Limited
Nottingham Forest Football Club
Nottingham Trent University
Norton Rose
NP Aerospace
NPS Group Property Consultants
Novosco
Nutricia
O'Neill & Brady Ltd. OCS Group
Office for National Statistics
Old Bushmills Distillery Co Ltd
Odyssey Trust Company
Oracle Corporation UK
Ordnance Survey
Optima Legal Services Ltd
Osborne
Parker Green International
Patton Group
Paymex Group
Peabody Trust
Pause
Peel Holdings
Pennine Healthcare
Pearson
Permira Advisers
Petrofac Services
PepsiCo UK and Ireland
PHP Architects
PHS Group
Phoenix Natural Gas
Pilkington NSG
Pinsent Masons
Pickfords
Places for People
Police Service of Northern Ireland
PKF (UK)
Positive Futures
Precision Cleaning Group
Port of Tyne Authority
Premier Farnell
PricewaterhouseCoopers
Precision Industrial Services Ltd
Principality Building Society
Priory Group
PricewaterhouseCoopers
Procter & Gamble UK
Produce World
Probation Board for Northern Ireland
Progressive Building Society
Property Consortium
Prudential UK & Europe
PZ Cussons (UK) Ltd.
Provident Financial
Quadrant PR
Queen's University Belfast
QinetiQ Group
Real Radio
Red Sky Group
RCT Homes
Reed in Partnership
Reed Smith
Reed Elsevier
Rentokil Initial
Rhondda Housing Association
Remploy
Ridgeons Right Management
Ricoh UK
Ringway Group
Rio Tinto
right4staff group
RKCR/Y&R
Robinson & McIlwaine
Riverside Group
Rok Group
Rolls-Royce Plc
Rockwool
Royal Bank of Scotland
Royal London Group
Rothschild
Royal Mail Group
RPS Consulting Engineers (NI)
Royal Mail Group
RSA Insurance Group
RSK Group
RSA Insurance Group
RWE npower
S A Brain & Co
SABMiller
Sage UK
Saica Packaging UK Ltd
Saga Group
Sanctuary Group
Santander UK
Samworth Brothers (Holdings)
SAS Software
Schlumberger SAP
ScottishPower
SDC Trailers Ltd
Scottish and Southern Energy (SSE)
Seddon Property Services Ltd
SEGRO
Seagate Technology (Ireland) Ltd
Serco
Serco Ireland
Sellafield Ltd.
SHAW TRUST
Sheffield Business School
Severn Trent
Shields Environmental Plc
Shine Group
Shell UK
Shoosmiths
SHS Group Ltd
Shire Pharmaceuticals Group
SIG plc
Simons
Siemens plc
SITA UK
SJ Berwin
Singularity
Social Security Agency
Societe Generale
Smarts
Sodexo
South Eastern Health and Social Care Trust
South Wales Police
Southampton Solent University
South Eastern Regional College
SP McCaffrey & Co Accountants
SPAR
Southern Health and Social Care Trust
Spice
Sports Council for Northern Ireland
Speedy Hire plc
St Brendan's Irish Cream Liquer
St David's Park Hotel
Springfields Fuels
St James's Place
Standard Life
St George Regeneration
Starbucks Coffee Company
State Street
Staples Advantage
Stradform
Stratagem (NI) Ltd
Stevenson Munn
Stream Ltd
Styles & Wood
Strategic Investment Board Limited
Supreme Creations
T-Mobile (UK)
Tal Ltd
Tata Consultancy Services
Tate & Lyle Plc
Targetfollow Group
TD Waterhouse
Telefonica O2

Taylor Wimpey
Tesco
Teletech UK Ltd
Thames Water
The Apollo Group
Thales Group
The Bio Group
The Body Shop UK
The Baird Group
The Capita Group plc
The BSS Group
The Co-operative Group
The Care Circle Group
The Henderson Group
The Hyde Group
The Football League Trust
The Karl Group
The Law Society
The Karl Group
The Orchardville Society
The Wrigley Company
The Midcounties Co-operative
Thomas Vale Construction
Thomson Reuters Group
The Writer
Titanic Quarter Ltd
TLT Solicitors T
Thorntons
Topaz Energy Ireland (previously Shell Northern Tolent Construction Ireland)
Tower Hotel
Towers Watson
Toyota Motor Manufacturing (UK)
TR Group
Trafford Housing Trust
Trainline.com Ltd
Translink
Triangle Housing Association
Tribal Group
Trinity Mirror
TT Electronics
Tughan Solicitors
UBS
UCAS
UES
UffindellWest
UK Coal plc
Ulster Bank Limited
Ulster Carpets
Ulster Stores Ltd
Unilever
Unipart Group
United Biscuits
United Business Media
United Dairy Farmers Ltd
United Utilities
United Welsh Housing Association
University College of St Mark & St John
University of Bradford
University of Central Lancashire
University of Derby
University of East Anglia
University of Glamorgan
University of Hertfordshire
University of Hull Business School
University of Nottingham
University of Plymouth
University of Portsmouth
University of Sheffield Management School
University of Sunderland
University of Ulster
University of Wales Institute, Cardiff
University of Wales Newport
University of Warwick
University of Winchester
USEL
UTV Media
Valuation Office Agency
Veolia Environnement Group
Vielife
Vinci
Virgin Media
Viridian Group plc
Visa Europe
Vision Capital
VocaLink
Vodafone (NI)
Volker Fitzpatrick
VT Group
W5
Wales and West Utilities
Walt Disney Company
Warburtons
Ward Hadaway
Warner Estate Holdings
Warrenpoint Harbour Authority
Wates Group
Welsh Contact Centre Forum
Wessex Water
West Yorkshire Police
Western Health & Social Care Trust
Westmorland
WH Stephens & Sons
Whitbread Group
White Young Green (NI)
Whitemountain Quarries Ltd
WHSmith Retail
Wilkinson
Williams Medical Supplies Ltd
Willmott Dixon
Wincanton
Wolseley plc
Working Links
Workspace Group
Worthington Solicitors
WPP Group
Wragge & Co
Wrightbus Ltd
WS Atkins Consultants Ltd
WSP Group
WYG
Yell Group
Your Homes Newcastle
Zolfo Cooper
Zurich Financial Services

Scottish Business in the Community

Scottish Business in the Community (SBC) acts as a broker between business and communities, providing support and advice as well as channelling resources to deliver sustainable community investment. It states:

> *We provide opportunities for organisations of all sizes and sectors to improve their Triple Bottom Line of; Society, the Environment and the Economy. Through our extensive range of projects and programmes, themed events and training and advisory services we provide the practical solutions necessary to embed sustainable and responsible business practices into the core of your organisation.*
>
> *We provide unique networking opportunities and our wide range of events, workshops and seminars provide an ideal platform for discussion and debate allowing you to address the issues that affect you and your community most.*
>
> *We work with you to position your business as a leader in sustainable and responsible business practices through awards, communications and tendering support.*

SBC promotes CSR as a mark of sound business practice. This is achieved through an integrated mix of national programmes and contributions to genuine, effective local partnerships.

SBC's programmes and activities are designed to offer companies a practical means of engaging in community investment.

Scottish Business in the Community
Account Management Team
Livingstone House
First Floor (East)
43a Discovery Terrace
Heriott-Watt Research Park
Edinburgh, EH14 4AP

Tel: 0131 451 1100
Fax: 0131 451 1127
Email: info@sbcscot.com
Web: www.sbcscot.com

Members (as of March 2013)

Aberdeen City Council
Alliance Boots
Amey
Anderson Strathern
ARAMARK Ltd.
Arts & Business Scotland
Asda Stores Ltd
BAA Edinburgh Airport
Baker Tilly
BEAR Scotland
BP plc
BSkyB
BT Scotland
Buro Happold Ltd
Capita plc
City of Edinburgh Council
DC Thomson & Co Ltd
Diageo plc
DLA Piper UK LLP
Edinburgh Napier University Business School
Enterprise
Enterprise Rent-A-Car
GlaxoSmithKline
Halcrow
Haven Products Ltd
Highlands & Islands Airports Limited
Intelligent Storage Solutions
John Lewis Partnership
John Wood Group plc
Johnson & Johnson Medical Ltd
Johnston Carmichael
Kingdom Shopping Centre
Langler Investments
LifeScan Scotland
Lloyds Banking Group
Lothian Buses Plc
Maersk Oil
Marks & Spencer plc

Maxxium UK Ltd
McGrigors LLP Edinburgh
Michael Page International
Mitie
Morrison Plc MPC
Nairns Oatcakes
National Australia Group (Clydesdale Bank)
Network Rail
North Highland Initiative
Oracle
People's Postcode Lottery
Pinsent Masons LLP
PricewaterhouseCoopers
Prudential Corporation Plc
Quality Scotland
Rabbie's Trail Burners Ltd
Recruitment Zone
Redeem Plc
Royal Bank of Scotland
Royal Edinburgh Military Tattoo
Royal London Group
Scottish Enterprise
Scottish Gas
Scottish Power
Scottish Water
SERCO
Sew Good Curtains & Blinds
Shell U.K. Limited
Shepherd and Wedderburn
Skills Development Scotland
Sodexo
Sopra
SQA
SSE Plc
Standard Life
State Street
TAQA Bratani Limited
The Caves
Total E&PUK Limited
Town House Collection
Virgin Money
Weir Group
Wolffe

Business in the Community's CommunityMark

Business in the Community aims to make community involvement a natural part of successful business practice, and to increase the quality and extent of business activity in the community. It states that:

> *CommunityMark companies take a holistic approach to community investment, which means they are good from the inside, out. The CommunityMark is not an award – it is an independent, 360-degree, rigorous assessment process that defines innovators and leaders in community investment.*
>
> *Open to companies in the UK of all sizes and sectors, this national standard has been developed by Business in the Community in consultation with the private, public and voluntary sector bodies. The CommunityMark challenges companies to minimise their negative and maximise their positive impact on society through an assessment process that recognises milestones on the way to achieving long term sustainable benefits to both business and the community.*
>
> *The questions in the survey are built around the five principles of community investment excellence.*

There are 46 companies that have achieved the CommunityMark since its launch. Of these, 38 are currently recognised as upholding this standard of excellence, and are listed below.

Anglo American
Axis
Barclays
Boots UK
Brentford Football Club
British Gas
BSkyB
Capital Shopping Centres plc
Contract Scotland
Deloitte
East Midlands Airport
E.ON UK
Ernst & Young
Heart of Midlothian Football Club
Heineken UK
Hogan Lovells
Jaguar Land Rover
John Laing
KPMG
Lend Lease
Linklaters LLP
Liverpool Football Club
LSI Architects
Lloyds Banking Group
Manchester Airport
Marks and Spencer
Microsoft (UK)
The Midcounties Co-operative
Nationwide Building Society
Octink
PriceWaterhouseCoopers
Prudential
RWE npower
Sainsbury's
TD Direct
Thinktastic
Zurich UK

ProHelp

What is ProHelp?

A Business in the Community initiative, ProHelp is a national network of over 400 professional firms committed to making a difference in their local community by providing free advice and professional support. Collectively, ProHelp is the largest national provider of pro bono support in England, Wales and Northern Ireland.

Participating professional firms include lawyers, accountants, IT consultants, architects, surveyors, marketing specialists and engineers. Community groups that receive support from ProHelp are non-profit-making, locally based and cannot afford to pay for professional services. Firms can contribute towards a single project or give longer-term strategic support such as becoming a trustee.

What help can it provide?

The professional firms undertake short assignments which include feasibility studies, structural surveys, marketing and business plans, legal and accountancy advice and property valuations.

Will my project be eligible?

You must be a community-based not-for-profit organisation working for the social and economic regeneration of your local area and fit within the following criteria:

- you must have a track record of working successfully with the local community;
- you must not have the funding for the specific piece of work to be done nor be retaining paid advisors to do the work;
- if you are a branch of a national organisation, you must be locally constituted and prove that neither the expertise nor the funding to pay for the work is available centrally;
- your project must be realistic and viable; and
- your governing body must authorise the involvement of ProHelp.

When will a project not qualify?

- applications for assistance with litigation will not be considered;
- help is generally not given to animal welfare organisations, nor to those whose primary focus is overseas aid; and
- assistance to religious groups will only be offered if the project benefits the wider community.

What do I do now?

If you have a project in mind which could benefit from support from ProHelp, please get in touch with the relevant regional contact listed below.

What happens next?

Your completed application form will be checked by the local ProHelp Manager once it is received. They will contact you if they have any questions or need to discuss the application. Sometimes it may be necessary for you to meet with a representative from ProHelp to develop a fuller brief for the project assignment.

A summary of your request will then be taken to ProHelp members to consider and where possible match. If a firm is able to help, a meeting will then be arranged with you to take things further.

BITC is not always able to help with every project request but will always communicate this to you and where possible make alternative suggestions for organisations that may be able to help.

It can take a couple of weeks or often much longer to match a project; the local ProHelp Manager will give you an indication of timescales.

What will happen then?

If your project is appropriate, you will be asked to fill in a standard questionnaire. It may also be necessary for you to meet with a representative from ProHelp to develop a fuller brief for the assignment. A summary of your project will then be taken to a group who will decide whether or not your project meets the eligibility criteria and if there is a firm available to do the work. A meeting will then be arranged between your and the interested professional firm.

For more information, please visit the ProHelp website: www.bitc.org.uk/programmes/prohelp

Company activity listing

This section classifies the companies included in the guide according to their main activities. It should enable charities to target companies for specific appeals or services. Companies which fall into two or more categories are listed under each one, except in the more obvious cases. For example, building companies and property companies, where the categories have been cross-referenced. Retailers have been split into further categories due to the variety covered.

Accountants

Accenture UK Ltd
Caledonia Investments
Cooper-Parry LLP
Deloitte
KPMG LLP
Mazars LLP
PKF (UK) LLP
PricewaterhouseCoopers LLP

Advertising/marketing

Abbott Mead Vickers – BBDO Ltd
DDB UK Ltd
Hibu (formerly Yell Group plc)
WPP Group plc

Aerospace

BAE Systems
Cobham plc
QinetiQ Group plc
Senior plc
Smiths Group plc

Agriculture

Alan Hudson Ltd
Man Group plc
Pfizer Ltd

Airports

Birmingham International Airport Ltd
East Midlands Airport
Heathrow Airport Holdings Ltd (formerly BAA Ltd)
Manchester Airport Group plc

Aviation

British Airways plc
easyJet plc
John Swire & Sons Ltd
Virgin Atlantic Ltd

Banking

Bank of England
Barclays plc
CIBC World Markets plc
Close Brothers Group plc
Clydesdale Bank plc
Co-operative Group Ltd
Coutts & Co
Credit Suisse
Deutsche Bank
Goldman Sachs International
HFC Bank Ltd
Julian Hodge Bank Ltd
HSBC Holdings plc
Investec plc
Lazard & Co. Ltd
Lloyds Banking Group plc
N M Rothschild & Sons Ltd
The Royal Bank of Scotland Group plc
Santander UK
Standard Chartered plc
Standard Life
UBS

Brewers/distillers

Adnams plc
Diageo plc
Greene King plc
Heineken UK Ltd
Marston's plc
Daniel Thwaites plc

Building/construction

AMEC plc
Barratt Developments plc
Bellway plc
Berkeley Group plc
Carillion plc
CEMEX UK Operations
Costain Group plc
Esh Group
Gladedale Group Holdings Ltd
Keepmoat Ltd
Kier Group plc
Robert McAlpine Ltd
Miller Group Ltd
Persimmon plc
Shepherd Building Group Ltd
Synthomer plc (formerly Yule Catto & Co.)
Taylor Wimpey plc
Travis Perkins plc
Wates Group Ltd
Willmott Dixon Holdings plc

Building material merchants

Wolseley plc

Building materials

SIG plc

Building societies

Bradford & Bingley plc
Chelsea Building Society
Cheshire Building Society
Coventry Building Society
Derbyshire Building Society
Leeds Building Society
Nationwide Building Society
Newcastle Building Society
Nottingham Building Society
Principality Building Society
West Bromwich Building Society
Yorkshire Building Society

Business services

Ashmore Group plc
Autonomous Research LLP

Balfour Beatty plc
BlueBay Asset Management plc
Canon UK Ltd
Colt Group
Domino Printing Sciences plc
Economist Newspaper Ltd
ERM Group Holdings Ltd
Fidessa Group plc
Halma plc
Hibu (formerly Yell Group plc)
Informa plc
Logica plc
Melrose plc
Micro Focus International plc
MITIE Group plc
Rentokil Initial plc
Serco Group plc
SThree plc
Xchanging plc

Cash 'n carry

Bestway (Holdings) Ltd
Booker Group plc
Dhamecha Group Ltd

Catalogue shopping

Findel plc
Mothercare plc

Catering services

ARAMARK Ltd
Sodexo Ltd

Chemicals and plastics

3M United Kingdom plc
Akzo Nobel UK Ltd
BASF plc
Bayer plc
Croda International plc
Dow Chemical Company Ltd
Dow Corning Ltd
Elementis plc
Fenner plc
Huntsman/Tioxide Europe Ltd
Kodak Ltd
Low & Bonar plc
Pfizer Ltd
Scott Bader Company Ltd
Synthomer plc (formerly Yule Catto & Co.)
Victrex plc

Clothing manufacture

GAP (UK) Ltd
Levi Strauss (UK) Ltd
Pentland Group plc

Commodity traders

Cargill plc
Glencore UK Ltd

Computer software

Adobe Systems Europe Ltd
CA plc
The Game Group plc
Microsoft Ltd
RM plc
Steria Ltd

Confectionery

Cadbury plc
Lofthouse of Fleetwood Ltd

Consultancy

Bain & Company Inc. United Kingdom

Consulting engineers

Arup Group Ltd
Mott MacDonald Ltd

Dairy products

Dairy Crest Group plc
Robert Wiseman Dairies plc

Defence systems

Avon Rubber plc
BAE Systems
HESCO Bastion Ltd
QinetiQ Group plc
Ultra Electronics Holdings plc

Distribution

Bunzl plc
Cargill plc
Electrocomponents plc
John Menzies plc
Palmer & Harvey McLane Ltd
SDL International plc
SIG plc

Domestic appliances

Dyson Ltd
Hoover Ltd

Drinks manufacture

A G Barr plc
Britvic Soft Drinks plc
Coca-Cola Great Britain
Innocent Drinks
Nestlé Holdings (UK) plc

Electricity

Drax Group plc
E.ON UK plc
EDF Energy plc
National Grid Holdings One plc
Northern Powergrid Holdings Company (formerly C E Electricity UK Funding Company)
Scottish and Southern Energy plc
ScottishPower plc
United Utilities plc
Western Power Distribution

Electronics/computers

CEF Holdings Ltd
Cobham plc
Filtronic plc
Hewlett-Packard Ltd
IBM United Kingdom Ltd
Philips Electronics UK Ltd
Premier Farnell plc
Psion plc
RM plc
Samsung Electronics (UK) Ltd
Siemens plc
Sony Europe Ltd
Spirent plc
Toshiba Information Systems (UK) Ltd
Ultra Electronics Holdings plc
Unisys Ltd

Engineering

Aggreko plc
AMEC plc
BBA Aviation plc
Biwater Holdings Ltd
Bodycote plc
Cummins Ltd
Dyson Ltd
GKN plc
IMI plc
Keller Group plc
The Laird Group plc
Marshall of Cambridge (Holdings) Ltd
Meggitt plc
Network Rail Infrastructure Ltd
Premier Farnell plc
Rexam plc
Rolls–Royce plc
Rotork plc
Smiths Group plc
Spectris plc
Spirax Sarco Engineering plc
TT Electronics plc
The Weir Group plc
John Wood Group

Exploration

Hunting plc

Financial services

3i Group plc
Aberdeen Asset Management
Apax Partners LLP
Aurum Funds Ltd
Bank of Ireland UK Financial Services Ltd
BC Partners Ltd
BGC International LP
BlackRock Investment Management (UK) Ltd
Boyer Allan Investment Investment Management LLP
The British Land Company plc
Caledonia Investments
Capital One Holdings Ltd
Capital Shopping Centres Group plc
Cattles plc
Citibank International plc
Close Brothers Group plc
Doughty Hanson & Co. Managers Ltd

Ernst & Young LLP
Execution Ltd
F&C Asset Management plc
Family Assurance Friendly Society Ltd
Fidelity Investment Management Ltd
Financial Services Authority
Henderson Group plc
HSBC Holdings plc
ICAP plc
International Personal Finance
Investec plc
Legal & General plc
Liverpool Victoria
Lloyds Banking Group
Man Group plc
Marks and Spencer Group plc
The Midcounties Co-operative
J P Morgan Chase
Morgan Stanley International Ltd
Northern Rock (Asset Management) plc
Old Mutual plc
Principality Building Society
Private Equity Foundation
Prudential plc
RAB Capital plc
Rathbone Brothers plc
The Royal Bank of Scotland Group plc
Saga Group Ltd
Schroders plc
St James's Place plc
Standard Chartered plc
Travelex Holdings Ltd

Food manufacture

Arla Foods Ltd
Associated British Foods plc
Baxters Food Group Ltd
Devro plc
Diageo plc
Duchy Originals Ltd
Greencore Group UK
Greggs plc
H J Heinz Co. Ltd
Kellogg Company of Great Britain Ltd
Kraft Foods UK Ltd
Bernard Matthews Ltd
McCain Foods (GB) Ltd
Nestlé Holdings (UK) plc
Northern Foods Ltd
Organix Brands Ltd
PepsiCo International
Premier Foods plc
Unilever UK
United Biscuits Ltd
Warburtons Ltd
Weetabix Ltd

Food services

Cargill plc
Ocado Group Ltd
Organix Brands Ltd
Sodexo Ltd

Footwear

Pentland Group plc

Furniture manufacture

Cadogan Group Ltd
Howden Joinery Group plc

Gaming

Betfair Group Ltd
bwin.party
Camelot Group plc
Genting UK plc
William Hill plc
IG Group Holdings plc
Ladbrokes plc
Sportech plc
Sportingbet plc

Glass

Pilkington Group Ltd

Health/beauty products

Avon Cosmetics Ltd
Lush Cosmetics Ltd
Mascolo Ltd

Healthcare

AXA UK plc
Baxter Healthcare Ltd
Boots
BUPA Ltd
GE Healthcare
GlaxoSmithKline plc
Medtronic Ltd
Pfizer Ltd
Procter & Gamble UK
Smith & Nephew plc
Synergy Health plc

Hotels

Adnams plc
Intercontinental Hotels Group plc
Ladbrokes plc
Whitbread plc

Household

P Z Cussons plc
S C Johnson Ltd
Osborne & Little Ltd
Procter & Gamble UK
Reckitt Benckiser plc
Unilever UK
Wilkinson Hardware Stores Ltd

Industrial products/services

Ashtead Group plc
Du Pont (UK) Ltd

Information management

AEA Technology plc
Communisis plc
Informa plc
TelecityGroup
WPP Group plc

Information technology

AEA Technology plc
Agilent Technologies UK Ltd
AOL UK Ltd
W S Atkins plc
Autonomy Corporation plc
Aveva Group plc
CA plc
Colt Group
Computacenter plc
Doughty Hanson & Co. Managers Ltd
Fujitsu Services Holdings plc
HP Enterprise Services UK Ltd
Lockheed Martin UK Ltd
Medtronic Ltd
Metaswitch Networks Ltd
Oracle Corporation UK Ltd

Instrumentation

Invensys plc
Unipart Group of Companies Ltd

Insurance

Admiral Group plc
Aegon (Scottish Equitable plc)
Ageas Insurance Ltd (formerly Fortis Insurance Ltd)
Allianz Insurance plc
Amlin plc
Aviva plc
AXA UK plc
Beazley plc
Brit Insurance Holdings plc
BUPA Ltd
Catlin Group Ltd
Congregational & General Insurance plc
Cooper Gay (Holdings) Ltd
Ecclesiastical Insurance Group plc
Friends Life FPL Ltd
Hiscox plc
Jardine Lloyd Thompson Group plc
Lancashire Holdings Ltd
Liverpool Victoria
Lloyd's
Marsh Ltd
The National Farmers Union Mutual Insurance Society Ltd
Novae Group plc
Personal Group Holdings plc
Provident Financial plc
Prudential plc
Royal & Sun Alliance Insurance Group plc
The Royal Bank of Scotland Group plc
The Royal London Mutual Insurance Society Ltd
Standard Life
UIA (Insurance) Ltd
Unum

Legal

Addleshaw Goddard
Allen & Overy LLP

Freshfields Bruuckhaus Deringer LLP
Herbert Smith Freehills LLP
Linklaters
Simmons & Simmons LLP
Slaughter and May
Wragge & Co. LLP

Leisure

Caledonia Investments
Center Parcs Ltd
Deep Sea Leisure plc
William Hill plc
Ladbrokes plc
Northern Trust Group Ltd
The Rank Group plc
Saga Group Ltd
Thomas Cook Group plc
J D Wetherspoon plc
Whitbread plc

Life assurance

Zurich Financial Services (UKISA) Ltd

Logistics

Geopost UK Ltd
John Menzies plc
Stobart Group
TNT UK Ltd
UPS

Manufacturing

Caparo Group Ltd
Cookson Group plc
Euro Packaging Ltd
Imagination Technologies Group plc
The Morgan Crucible Company plc
SDL International plc
Swann-Morton Ltd
Tomkins Ltd

Marine

Babcock International Group plc
Forth Ports plc
QinetiQ Group plc
RPS Group plc
John Swire & Sons Ltd

Media

Aegis Group plc
AOL UK Ltd
Archant
Bloomsbury Publishing plc
British Sky Broadcasting Group plc
Chrysalis Group Ltd
Daily Mail and General Trust plc
Economist Newspaper Ltd
Future plc
Guardian Media Group plc
IPC Media Ltd
ITV plc
Johnston Press plc
National Magazine Co. Ltd
News International Ltd
Northern & Shell Network Ltd
Pearson plc
STV Group plc
Telegraph Media Group Ltd
Thomson Reuters plc
Trinity Mirror plc
United Business Media Ltd
Yattendon Investment Trust plc

Metals

Alcoa UK Holdings Ltd
Anglesey Aluminium Metals Ltd
Johnson Matthey plc
Stemcor Holdings Ltd
Tata Steel Europe Ltd

Mining

Anglo American plc
The Banks Group
BHP Billiton plc
Celtic Energy Ltd
Lonmin plc
Rio Tinto plc
UK Coal plc

Miscellaneous

Amey UK plc
eaga plc
Johnson Service Group plc
Moneysupermarket.com Group plc
Royal Mail Group plc

Motors & accessories

Arriva plc
Avon Rubber plc
BMW UK Ltd
Citroen UK Ltd
Ford Motor Company Ltd
General Motors UK Ltd
Honda of the UK Manufacturing Ltd
Inchcape plc
Jaguar Cars Ltd
Kwik-Fit Group
Michelin Tyre plc
Toyota Motor Manufacturing (UK) Ltd
Unipart Group of Companies Ltd

Music

EMI Group Ltd

Oil & gas/fuel

Air Products Group Ltd
BP plc
Calor Gas Ltd
Centrica plc
Dana Petroleum plc
E.ON UK plc
Esso UK Group Ltd
Hess Ltd
RPS Group plc
Shell
Total UK Ltd
United Utilities Group plc
Valero Energy Ltd (Chevron Ltd)

Personal care

Colgate-Palmolive UK Ltd
Mascolo Ltd

Pharmaceuticals

AstraZeneca
Boots
Bristol-Myers Squibb Pharmaceuticals Ltd
BTG International Ltd
Co-operative Group Ltd
P Z Cussons plc
Eli Lilly and Company Ltd
GlaxoSmithKline plc
Hikma Pharmaceuticals plc
Merck Sharp & Dohme Ltd
Reckitt Benckiser plc
Roche Products Ltd
Shire Pharmaceuticals plc
Synthomer plc (formerly Yule Catto & Co.)

Plant equipment

J C Bamford Excavators Ltd

Print/paper/packaging

Bunzl plc
De La Rue plc
LINPAC Group Ltd
Low & Bonar plc
Rexam plc
D S Smith Holdings plc
Tullis Russell Group Ltd
Xerox (UK) Ltd

Professional support services

Capita Group plc
Michael Page International
Tullis Russell Group Ltd
WSP Group plc

Property

AMEC plc
Berkeley Group plc
The British Land Company plc
Broadland Properties Ltd
Bruntwood Ltd
Cadogan Group Ltd
Caledonia Investments
Canary Wharf Group plc
Crest Nicholson plc
Daejan Holdings plc
Dhamecha Holdings Ltd
Doughty Hanson & Co. Managers Ltd
Evans Property Group Ltd
Gladedale Group Holdings Ltd
Grainger plc
Great Portland Estates plc
Grosvenor Group
Hammerson plc
Helical bar plc
Jones Lang LaSalle Ltd
Kingfisher plc
Land Securities Group plc

Miller Group Ltd
Muir Group plc
Northern Trust Group Ltd
Paragon Group of Companies plc
Ravensale Ltd
Redrow Group plc
Ridgesave Ltd
Savills plc
SEGRO plc
Shaftesbury plc
St Modwen Properties plc
John Swire & Sons Ltd
UNITE Group plc

Quarrying

Aggregate Industries Ltd
Lafarge Aggregates Ltd

Retail – clothing and footwear

Dunelm Group plc
GAP (UK) Ltd
JD Sports Fashion plc
JJB Sports plc
Marks and Spencer Group plc
Next plc
Shoe Zone Ltd
Sports Direct International plc
TJX UK (formerly TK Maxx)

Retail – department stores

Anglia Regional Co-operative Society Ltd
Co-operative Group Ltd
Debenhams plc
Dunelm Group plc
Fenwick Ltd
House of Fraser (Stores) Ltd
John Lewis Partnership plc
Littlewoods Shop Direct Home Shopping Ltd
T.J. Morris Ltd
Mothercare plc

Retail – DIY

Howden Joinery Group plc
Kingfisher plc
Wilkinson Hardware Stores Ltd

Retail – electrical

DSG International plc
Kesa Electricals plc
Richer Sounds plc

Retail – miscellaneous

The Body Shop International plc
Boodle & Dunthorne Ltd
N Brown Group plc
The Carphone Warehouse Group plc
Clinton Cards plc
Greggs plc
Halfords Group plc
McBride plc
WH Smith plc
Southern Co-operatives Ltd
Starbucks Coffee Company (UK) Ltd
Topps Tiles plc

Retail – restaurants/fast food

Compass Group plc
Diageo plc
McDonalds Restaurants Ltd
Mitchells & Butlers plc
Punch Taverns plc
J D Wetherspoon plc
Whitbread plc

Retail – supermarkets

Anglia Regional Co-operative Society Ltd
ASDA Stores Ltd
Co-operative Group Ltd
Costcutter Supermarkets Group Ltd
John Lewis Partnership plc
The Midcounties Co-operative
W Morrison Supermarkets plc
J Sainsbury plc
Southern Co-operatives Ltd
Spar (UK) Ltd
Tesco plc

Securities/shares

BGC International LP
Goldman Sachs International

Security services

QinetiQ Group plc
Ultra Electronics Holdings plc

Services

Aggreko plc
Big Yellow Group plc
eaga plc
HomeServe plc

Shipping

Cargill plc

Sports clothing

adidas (UK) Ltd
JJB Sports plc
Nike (UK) Ltd

Sugar refiners

British Sugar plc
Tate & Lyle plc

Telecommunications

AT&T (UK) Ltd
BT Group plc
Cable & Wireless Worldwide plc
Cable & Wireless Communications plc
The Carphone Warehouse Group plc
Channel 4 Television Corporation
Everything Everywhere Ltd (formerly T-Mobile (UK) Ltd)
QinetiQ Group plc
Telefonica UK Ltd
Thales UK Ltd
Toshiba Information Systems (UK) Ltd
Vodafone Group plc

Textiles

Coats plc
Osborne & Little Ltd

Tobacco

British American Tobacco plc
Imperial Tobacco Group plc

Toy manufacture and distribution

Hasbro UK Ltd

Transportation and communication

BBA Aviation plc
First plc
G4S plc
The Go Ahead Group plc
The Mersey Docks and Harbour Company
National Express Group plc
Stagecoach Group plc
J Stobart and Sons Ltd
TUI Travel plc
Ultra Electronics Holdings plc

Transport and shipping services

ABPA Holdings Ltd
TNT UK Ltd

Transportation

Babcock International Group plc
Network Rail Infrastructure Ltd
UPS

Waste management

Biwater Holdings Ltd
Shanks Group plc

Water

Anglian Water
Dwr Cymru Welsh Water
Kelda Group Ltd
Northumbrian Water Group
Pennon Group plc
RPS Group plc
Severn Trent plc
United Utilities Group plc
Wessex Water Services Ltd

Wholesale

Booker Group plc

Geographical listing of head offices

This geographical index is based on the head office address given at the start of each company entry. While it is generally the case that companies give some preference to charities local to their operating sites, including the head office, this is not always so. Once this index has been used to produce a preliminary list of potential companies to approach, the individual entries for each company should be read carefully to determine whether or not your particular project falls within the company's criteria.

England

Bedfordshire

easyJet plc
General Motors UK Ltd
Kier Group plc
Whitbread plc

Berkshire

3M United Kingdom plc
Agilent Technologies UK Ltd
Baxter Healthcare Ltd
Bayer plc
BMW UK Ltd
CA plc
Cable & Wireless Worldwide plc
Centrica plc
Citroen UK Ltd
Costain Group plc
Fujitsu Services Holdings plc
Hewlett-Packard Ltd
Hibu (formerly Yell Group plc)
HP Enterprise Services UK Ltd
Logica plc
Micro Focus International plc
Microsoft Ltd
The Morgan Crucible Company plc
Oracle Corporation UK Ltd
PepsiCo International
The Rank Group plc
Reckitt Benckiser plc
SDL International plc
SEGRO plc
D S Smith Holdings plc
Telefonica UK Ltd
Vodafone Group plc
Yattendon Investment Trust plc

Bristol

Bank of Ireland UK Financial Services Ltd
MITIE Group plc
UNITE Group plc
Western Power Distribution

Buckinghamshire

Halma plc
Intercontinental Hotels Group plc
Personal Group Holdings plc
Shanks Group plc
Taylor Wimpey plc

Cambridgeshire

Anglian Water
Autonomy Corporation plc
Aveva Group plc
Domino Printing Sciences plc
Alan Hudson Ltd
Marshall of Cambridge (Holdings) Ltd

Cheshire

BASF plc
Bodycote plc
Cheshire Building Society
Findel plc
Johnson Service Group plc
Moneysupermarket.com Group plc
The Royal London Mutual Insurance Society Ltd
United Utilities Group plc

County Durham

The Banks Group
Esh Group
Huntsman/Tioxide Europe Ltd
Northumbrian Water Group

Cumbria

eaga plc
J Stobart and Sons Ltd
Stobart Group

Derbyshire

Cooper-Parry LLP
Derbyshire Building Society
East Midlands Airport
Greencore Group UK
Sports Direct International plc
Toyota Motor Manufacturing (UK) Ltd

Devon

Pennon Group plc

Dorset

Cobham plc
Liverpool Victoria
Lush Cosmetics Ltd
Meggitt plc
Organix Brands Ltd

East Sussex

Family Assurance Friendly Society Ltd
Palmer & Harvey McLane Ltd

East Yorkshire

Croda International plc
Fenner plc

Essex

Britvic Soft Drinks plc
Clinton Cards plc
Ford Motor Company Ltd
Synthomer plc (formerly Yule & Catto Co.)

Gloucestershire

Chelsea Building Society
Ecclesiastical Insurance Group plc
Kraft Foods UK Ltd
Spirax Sarco Engineering plc
St James's Place plc

Greater Manchester
adidas (UK) Ltd
Balfour Beatty plc
A G Barr plc
N Brown Group plc
Bruntwood Ltd
Co-operative Group Ltd
P Z Cussons plc
Kellogg Company of Great Britain Ltd
Kwik-Fit Group
Manchester Airport Group plc

Hampshire
Ageas Insurance Ltd (formerly Fortis Insurance Ltd)
BAE Systems
De La Rue plc
Eli Lilly and Company Ltd
The Game Group plc
IBM United Kingdom Ltd
QinetiQ Group plc
Serco Group plc
Shire Pharmaceuticals plc
Southern Co-operatives Ltd

Hertfordshire
Camelot Group plc
DSG International plc
Du Pont (UK) Ltd
Everything Everywhere Ltd (formerly T-Mobile (UK) Ltd)
Imagination Technologies Group plc
Kodak Ltd
Robert McAlpine Ltd
Medtronic Ltd
Merck Sharp & Dohme Ltd
Mothercare plc
Ocado Group Ltd
Premier Foods plc
Roche Products Ltd
Senior plc
Steria Ltd
Tesco plc
TJX UK (formerly TK Maxx)
Total UK Ltd
UIA (Insurance) Ltd
J D Wetherspoon plc
Willmott Dixon Holdings plc

Kent
Fidelity Investment Management Ltd
Saga Group Ltd

Lancashire
JD Sports Fashion plc
JJB Sports plc
Lofthouse of Fleetwood Ltd
Northern Trust Group Ltd
Daniel Thwaites plc
Victrex plc
Warburtons Ltd

Leicestershire
Aggregate Industries Ltd
Barratt Developments plc
Dunelm Group plc
Lafarge Aggregates Ltd
Next plc
Shoe Zone Ltd
Topps Tiles plc

London
3i Group plc
Abbott Mead Vickers – BBDO Ltd
ABPA Holdings Ltd
Accenture UK Ltd
Addleshaw Goddard
AEA Technology plc
Aegis Group plc
Akzo Nobel UK Ltd
Allen & Overy LLP
AMEC plc
Amlin plc
Anglo American plc
AOL UK Ltd
Apax Partners LLP
ARAMARK Ltd
Arup Group Ltd
Ashmore Group plc
Ashtead Group plc
Associated British Foods plc
AstraZeneca
Aurum Funds Ltd
Autonomous Research LLP
Aviva plc
AXA UK plc
Babcock International Group plc
Bain & Company Inc. United Kingdom
Bank of England
Barclays plc
BBA Aviation plc
BC Partners Ltd
Beazley plc
Bestway (Holdings) Ltd
Betfair Group Ltd
BGC International LP
BHP Billiton plc
BlackRock Investment Management (UK) Ltd
Bloomsbury Publishing plc
BlueBay Asset Management plc
Boyer Allan Investment Investment Management LLP
BP plc
Bristol-Myers Squibb Pharmaceuticals Ltd
Brit Insurance Holdings plc
British Airways plc
British American Tobacco plc
The British Land Company plc
British Sky Broadcasting Group plc
BT Group plc
BTG International Ltd
Bunzl plc
BUPA Ltd
Cable & Wireless Communications plc
Cadbury plc (now Kraft)
Cadogan Group Ltd
Caledonia Investments
Canary Wharf Group plc
Caparo Group Ltd
Capita Group plc
Capital Shopping Centres Group plc
The Carphone Warehouse Group plc
Catlin Group Ltd
Channel 4 Television Corporation
Chrysalis Group Ltd
CIBC World Markets plc
Citibank International plc
Close Brothers Group plc
Coats plc
Coca-Cola Great Britain
Colt Group
Compass Group plc
Computacenter plc
Cookson Group plc
Cooper Gay (Holdings) Ltd
Coutts & Co
Credit Suisse
Cummins Ltd
Daejan Holdings plc
Daily Mail and General Trust plc
DDB UK Ltd
Debenhams plc
Deloitte
Deutsche Bank
Dhamecha Holdings Ltd
Diageo plc
Doughty Hanson & Co. Managers Ltd
Dow Chemical Company Ltd
Duchy Originals Ltd
Economist Newspaper Ltd
EDF Energy plc
Elementis plc
EMI Group Ltd
ERM Group Holdings Ltd
Ernst & Young LLP
Execution Ltd
F&C Asset Management plc
Fidessa Group plc
Financial Services Authority
Freshfields Bruuckhaus Deringer LLP
GlaxoSmithKline plc
Glencore UK Ltd
Goldman Sachs International
Grainger plc
Great Portland Estates plc
Grosvenor Group
Guardian Media Group plc
Hammerson plc
Hasbro UK Ltd
Heathrow Airport Holdings Ltd (formerly BAA Ltd)
H J Heinz Co. Ltd

Helical bar plc
Henderson Group plc
Herbert Smith Freehills LLP
Hess Ltd
Hikma Pharmaceuticals plc
William Hill plc
Hiscox plc
Howden Joinery Group plc
HSBC Holdings plc
Hunting plc
ICAP plc
IG Group Holdings plc
Inchcape plc
Informa plc
Innocent Drinks
Invensys plc
IPC Media Ltd
Jardine Lloyd Thompson Group plc
Johnson Matthey plc
Jones Lang LaSalle Ltd
Keller Group plc
Kesa Electricals plc
Kingfisher plc
KPMG LLP
Ladbrokes plc
The Laird Group plc
Land Securities Group plc
Lazard & Co. Ltd
Legal & General plc
John Lewis Partnership plc
Linklaters
Lloyd's
Lloyds Banking Group
Lockheed Martin UK Ltd
Lonmin plc
Low & Bonar plc
Man Group plc
Marks and Spencer Group plc
Marsh Ltd
Mascolo Ltd
Mazars LLP
McBride plc
McDonalds Restaurants Ltd
Melrose plc
Metaswitch Networks Ltd
J P Morgan Chase
Morgan Stanley International Ltd
National Express Group plc
National Magazine Co. Ltd
Network Rail Infrastructure Ltd
News International Ltd
Northern & Shell Network Ltd
Novae Group plc
Old Mutual plc
Osborne & Little Ltd
Pearson plc
Pentland Group plc
PKF (UK) LLP
Premier Farnell plc
PricewaterhouseCoopers LLP
Private Equity Foundation
Prudential plc
Psion plc
RAB Capital plc
Rathbone Brothers plc
Ravensale Ltd
Rentokil Initial plc
Rexam plc
Richer Sounds plc
Ridgesave Ltd
Rio Tinto plc
Rolls–Royce plc
N M Rothschild & Sons Ltd
Royal & Sun Alliance Insurance Group plc
Royal Mail Group plc
J Sainsbury plc
Santander UK
Savills plc
Schroders plc
Shaftesbury plc
Shell
Simmons & Simmons LLP
Slaughter and May
Smith & Nephew plc
Smiths Group plc
Sodexo Ltd
Spar (UK) Ltd
Sportech plc
Sportingbet plc
Standard Chartered plc
Starbucks Coffee Company (UK) Ltd
Stemcor Holdings Ltd
SThree plc
John Swire & Sons Ltd
Tata Steel Europe Ltd
Tate & Lyle plc
TelecityGroup
Telegraph Media Group Ltd
Thomson Reuters plc
Tomkins Ltd
Travelex Holdings Ltd
Trinity Mirror plc
UBS
Ultra Electronics Holdings plc
Unisys Ltd
United Biscuits Ltd
United Business Media Ltd
UPS
Valero Energy Ltd (Chevron Ltd)
WPP Group plc
WSP Group plc
Xchanging plc
Xerox (UK) Ltd

Merseyside

Boodle & Dunthorne Ltd
Littlewoods Shop Direct Home Shopping Ltd
The Mersey Docks and Harbour Company
T.J. Morris Ltd
Pilkington Group Ltd

Norfolk

Archant
Bernard Matthews Ltd

North Lincolnshire

Costcutter Supermarkets Group Ltd

North Yorkshire

Broadland Properties Ltd
Drax Group plc
McCain Foods (GB) Ltd
Persimmon plc
Shepherd Building Group Ltd

Northamptonshire

Avon Cosmetics Ltd
Booker Group plc
Scott Bader Company Ltd
Levi Strauss (UK) Ltd
Travis Perkins plc
Weetabix Ltd

Nottinghamshire

Boots
Capital One Holdings Ltd
Center Parcs Ltd
Nottingham Building Society
Wilkinson Hardware Stores Ltd

Oxfordshire

Amey UK plc
Electrocomponents plc
RM plc
RPS Group plc
Unipart Group of Companies Ltd

Peterborough

Anglia Regional Co-operative Society Ltd
British Sugar plc
Thomas Cook Group plc

Somerset

Future plc
Imperial Tobacco Group plc
Rotork plc
Wessex Water Services Ltd

South Yorkshire

Keepmoat Ltd
SIG plc
Swann-Morton Ltd
UK Coal plc

Staffordshire

J C Bamford Excavators Ltd
Michelin Tyre plc
Punch Taverns plc

Suffolk

Adnams plc
Adobe Systems Europe Ltd
Greene King plc

Surrey

Air Products Group Ltd
Allianz Insurance plc

W S Atkins plc
Berkeley Group plc
Big Yellow Group plc
Biwater Holdings Ltd
Canon UK Ltd
Cargill plc
CEMEX UK Operations
Colgate-Palmolive UK Ltd
Crest Nicholson plc
Dairy Crest Group plc
Esso UK Group Ltd
Friends Life FPL Ltd
Gladedale Group Holdings Ltd
S C Johnson Ltd
Mott MacDonald Ltd
Nestlé Holdings (UK) plc
Michael Page International
Pfizer Ltd
Philips Electronics UK Ltd
Procter & Gamble UK
Samsung Electronics (UK) Ltd
Siemens plc
Sony Europe Ltd
Spectris plc
Thales UK Ltd
Toshiba Information Systems (UK) Ltd
TT Electronics plc
Unilever UK
Unum
Wates Group Ltd

Tyne & Wear

Arriva plc
Bellway plc
C E Electric UK Funding Company
Fenwick Ltd
The Go Ahead Group plc
Greggs plc
Newcastle Building Society
Nike (UK) Ltd
Northern Rock (Asset Management) plc

Warwickshire

Calor Gas Ltd
CEF Holdings Ltd
Coventry Building Society
E.ON UK plc
GAP (UK) Ltd
GE Healthcare
Jaguar Cars Ltd
The Midcounties Co-operative
The National Farmers Union Mutual Insurance Society Ltd
National Grid Holdings One plc
TNT UK Ltd

West Midlands

Birmingham International Airport Ltd
Carillion plc
Euro Packaging Ltd
Genting UK plc
Geopost UK Ltd
HFC Bank Ltd
HomeServe plc
IMI plc
LINPAC Group Ltd
Marston's plc
Mitchells & Butlers plc
Paragon Group of Companies plc
Severn Trent plc
St Modwen Properties plc
West Bromwich Building Society
Wragge & Co. LLP

West Sussex

The Body Shop International plc
G4S plc
Spirent plc
TUI Travel plc
Virgin Atlantic Ltd

West Yorkshire

Alcoa UK Holdings Ltd
Arla Foods Ltd
ASDA Stores Ltd
Bradford & Bingley plc
Cattles plc
Communisis plc
Congregational & General Insurance plc
Evans Property Group Ltd
Filtronic plc
HESCO Bastion Ltd
International Personal Finance
ITV plc
Kelda Group Ltd
Leeds Building Society
W Morrison Supermarkets plc
Northern Foods Ltd
Provident Financial plc
Yorkshire Building Society

Wiltshire

Avon Rubber plc
Dyson Ltd
Honda of the UK Manufacturing Ltd
Nationwide Building Society
WH Smith plc
Synergy Health plc
Zurich Financial Services (UKISA) Ltd

Worcestershire

AT&T (UK) Ltd
GKN plc
Halfords Group plc

Scotland

Aberdeen

Aberdeen Asset Management
Dana Petroleum plc
First plc
John Wood Group

Edinburgh

Aegon (Scottish Equitable plc)
Forth Ports plc
Heineken UK Ltd
Johnston Press plc
John Menzies plc
Miller Group Ltd
The Royal Bank of Scotland Group plc
Standard Life

Fife

Deep Sea Leisure plc
Muir Group plc
Tullis Russell Group Ltd

Glasgow

Aggreko plc
Clydesdale Bank plc
Devro plc
House of Fraser (Stores) Ltd
ScottishPower plc
STV Group plc
The Weir Group plc
Robert Wiseman Dairies plc

Moray

Baxters Food Group Ltd

Perth

Scottish and Southern Energy plc
Stagecoach Group plc

Wales

Caerphilly

Celtic Energy Ltd

Cardiff

Admiral Group plc
Julian Hodge Bank Ltd
Principality Building Society

Flintshire

Redrow Group plc

Gwynedd

Anglesey Aluminium Metals Ltd

Merthyr Tydfil

Dwr Cymru Welsh Water
Hoover Ltd

Vale of Glamorgan

Dow Corning Ltd

Overseas

Bermuda

Lancashire Holdings Ltd

Channel Islands

Wolseley plc

Gibraltar

bwin.party

South Africa

Investec plc

Useful contacts

In this section we list national agencies which may be helpful in the context of company giving, under the general headings: employees, sponsorship, enterprise and training, education, donations, promoting good practice, media, general and informal contacts.

Employees/ professional advice

Business in the Community

137 Shepherdess Walk
London
N1 7RQ

Tel: 020 7566 8650
Web: www.bitc.org.uk

Chartered Surveyors Voluntary Service

Most large towns and rural areas in the UK are covered by CSVS (registered charity no. 1043479). If you feel that the CSVS could benefit you they can be contacted through your Citizens Advice Bureau (CAB) and other advice agencies.

Tel: 0870 333 1600
Fax: 0207 334 3811
Email: csvs@rics.org

Community Service Volunteers (CSV)

237 Pentonville Road
London
N1 9NJ

Tel: 020 7278 6601
Web: www.csv.org.uk

Life Academy

Beechwood House
Christchurch Road
Newport
NP19 8AJ

Tel: 01633 548026
Web: www.life-academy.co.uk

ProHelp

c/o Business in the Community
137 Shepherdess Walk
London
N1 7RQ

Tel: 020 7566 8650
Web: www.bitc.org.uk

REACH (Retired Executives Action Clearing House)

89 Albert Embankment
London
SE1 7TP

Tel: 020 7582 6543
Web: www.reachskills.org.uk

The Retirement Trust

Silton Cottage
Chantlers Hill
Paddock Wood
Tonbridge
Kent
TN12 6LX

Tel: 01892 838474
Web: www.theretirementtrust.org.uk

Volunteering England

Society Building
8 All Saints Street
London
N1 9RL

Tel: 020 7520 8900
Web: www.volunteering.org.uk

Sponsorship

Arts and Business

c/o Business in the Community
137 Shepherdess Walk
London
N1 7RQ

Tel: 020 7566 8650
Web: artsandbusiness.bitc.org.uk

Community Links

Canning Town Public Hall
105 Barking Road
Canning Town
London
E16 4HQ

Tel: 020 7473 2270
Web: www.community-links.org

Groundwork UK

Lockside
5 Scotland Street
Birmingham
B1 2RR

Tel: 0121 236 8565
Web: www.groundwork.org.uk

Enterprise & Training

Common Purpose UK

Common Purpose
Discovery House
28–42 Banner Street
London
EC1Y 8QE

Tel: 020 7608 8118
Web: www.commonpurpose.org.uk

There are regional offices throughout the UK.

Community Development Foundation (CDF)
Headquarters
Unit 5, Angel Gate
320–326 City Road
London
EC1V 2PT

Tel: 020 7833 1772
Web: www.cdf.org.uk

National Federation of Enterprise Agencies
12 Stephenson Court
Fraser Road
Priory Business Park
Bedford
MK44 3WJ

Tel: 01234 831623
Web: www.nfea.com

Education

Confederation of British Industry (CBI)
Centre Point
103 New Oxford Street
London
WC1A 1DU

Tel: 020 7379 7400
Web: www.cbi.org.uk

Council for Industry and Higher Education (CIHE)
Studio 11
Tiger House
Burton Street
London
WC1H 9BY

Tel: 020 7383 7667
Web: www.cihe-uk.com

The Work Foundation
The Work Foundation
21 Palmer Street
London
SW1H 0AD

Tel: 020 7976 3565
Web: www.theworkfoundation.com

Donations

CAF (Charities Aid Foundation)
25 Kings Hill Avenue
Kings Hill
West Malling
Kent
ME19 4TA

Tel: 03000 123 000
Web: www.cafonline.org

Charities Trust
Suite 22
Century Building
Brunswick Business Park
Tower Street
Liverpool
L3 4BJ

Tel: 0151 286 5129
Web: www.charitiestrust.org

Charity Commission

London
2nd Floor
One Drummond Gate
Victoria
London
SW1V 2QQ

Liverpool
12 Princes Dock
Princes Parade
Liverpool
L3 1DE

Taunton
Woodfield House
Tangier
Taunton
Somerset
TA1 4BL

Newport
8th Floor
Clarence House
Clarence Place
Newport
South Wales
NP19 7AA

In Kind Direct
62–64 Cornhill
London
EC3V 3PL

Tel: 020 7398 5510
Web: www.inkinddirect.org

ShareGift
17 Carlton House Terrace
London
SW1Y 5AH

Tel: 020 7930 3737
Web: www.sharegift.org

Workplace Giving UK
2nd Floor
Cavendish House
369 Burnt Oak Broadway
Edgware
Middlesex
HA8 5AW

Tel: 020 8731 5125
Web: www.workplacegiving-uk.co.uk

Promoting good practice

Business in the Community
137 Shepherdess Walk
London
N1 7RQ

Tel: 020 7566 8650
Web: www.bitc.org.uk

Scottish Business in the Community
Livingstone House
First Floor (East)
43a Discovery Terrace
Heriott-Watt Research Park
Edinburgh
EH14 4AP

Tel 0131 451 1100
Web: www.sbcscot.com

Charities Tax Group (CTG)
Church House
Great Smith Street
London
SW1P 3AZ

Tel: 020 7222 1265
Web: www.ctrg.org.uk

Corporate Citizenship
5th Floor Holborn Gate
330 High Holborn
London
WC1V 7QG

Tel: 020 7861 1616
Web: www.corporate-citizenship.com

The Corporate Responsibility Group

4th Floor
Samuel House
6 St Alban's Street
London
SW1Y 4SQ

Tel: 020 7148 4383
Web: www.crguk.org

Directory of Social Change

London
24 Stephenson Way
London
NW1 2DP

Tel: 08450 77 77 07

Liverpool
1st Floor
Federation House
Hope Street
Liverpool
L1 9BW

Research: 0151 708 0136
Training: 0151 708 0117

International Business Leaders Forum (IBLF)

3rd Floor
60 Gray's Inn Road
London
WC1X 8AQ

Tel: 020 7467 3600
Web: www.iblf.org

LBG

c/o Corporate Citizenship
5th Floor Holborn Gate
330 High Holborn
London
WC1V 7QG

Tel: 020 7861 1616
Web: www.corporate-citizenship.com

Media

BBC Charity Appeals Office

Room 4225
White City
201 Wood Lane
London
W12 7TS

Tel: 020 8008 1198
Web: www.bbc.co.uk/charityappeals

Campaign for Press & Broadcasting Freedom

2nd Floor
Vi & Garner Smith House
23 Orford Road
Walthamstow
London
E17 9NL

Tel: 020 8521 5932
Web: www.cpbf.org.uk

Channel Four Television Company

Channel 4 Enquiries
PO Box 1058
Belfast
BT1 9DU

Tel: 0845 076 0191
Web: www.channel4.com

CSV Action Network

237 Pentonville Road
London
N1 9NJ

Tel: 020 7833 5689
Web: http://www.csv.org.uk/Services/social-action-media

ITV Network Centre

200 Gray's Inn Road
London
WC1X 8HF

Tel: 020 7156 6000
Web: www.itv.com

Media Trust

4th Floor
Block A, Centre House
Wood Lane
London
W12 7SB

Tel: 020 7871 5600
Web: www.mediatrust.org

General company information

Companies House

Crown Way
Maindy
Cardiff
CF 14 3UZ

Tel: 0303 1234 500
Web: www.companieshouse.gov.uk

Co-operative and Community Finance

Brunswick Court
Brunswick Square
Bristol
BS2 8PE

Tel: 01179 166750
Web: www.icof.co.uk

British Urban Regeneration Association

4th Floor
63–66 Hatton Garden
London
EC1N 8LE

Tel: 020 7539 4030
Web: www.bura.org.uk

Trades Union Congress (TUC)

Congress House
Great Russell Street
London
WC1B 3LS

Tel: 020 7636 4030
Web: www.tuc.org.uk

URBED (Urbanism Environment Design)

The Building Centre
26 Store Street
London
WC1E 7BT

Tel: 07714 979 956
Web: www.urbed.com

Young Enterprise UK

Peterley House
Peterley Road
Oxford
OX4 2TZ

Tel. 01865 776 845
Web: www.young-enterprise.org.uk

Index

3i: 3i Group plc 1
3M: 3M United Kingdom PLC 1
Abbott: Abbott Mead Vickers – BBDO Ltd 1
Aberdeen: Aberdeen Asset Management 2
ABPA: ABPA Holdings Ltd 2
Accenture: Accenture UK Ltd 3
Addleshaw: Addleshaw Goddard 4
adidas: adidas (UK) Limited 4
Admiral: Admiral Group plc 4
Adnams: Adnams plc 5
Adobe: Adobe Systems Europe Limited 6
AEA: AEA Technology plc 6
Aegis: Aegis Group Plc 7
Aegon: Aegon (Scottish Equitable plc) 7
Ageas: Ageas Insurance Limited (formerly Fortis Insurance Limited) 8
Aggregate: Aggregate Industries Ltd 8
Aggreko: Aggreko plc 8
Agilent: Agilent Technologies UK Ltd 9
Air: Air Products Group Ltd 9
Akzo: Akzo Nobel UK Ltd 10
Alcoa: Alcoa UK Holdings Limited 10
Allen: Allen and Overy LLP 11
Allianz: Allianz Insurance plc 12
AMEC: AMEC plc 12
Amey: Amey UK plc 12
Amlin: Amlin plc 13
Anglesey: Anglesey Aluminium Metals Ltd 13
Anglia: Anglia Regional Co-operative Society Limited 14
Anglian: Anglian Water 14
Anglo: Anglo American plc 15
AOL: AOL UK Ltd 16
Apax: Apax Partners LLP 16
ARAMARK: ARAMARK Limited 17
Archant: Archant 18
Arla: Arla Foods Ltd 18
Arriva: Arriva plc 19
Arup: Arup Group Ltd 19
ASDA: ASDA Stores Ltd 20
Ashmore: Ashmore Group plc 21
Ashtead: Ashtead Group plc 21
Associated: Associated British Foods plc 22
AstraZeneca: AstraZeneca 23
ATandT: ATandT (UK) Ltd 24
Atkins: W. S. Atkins plc 24
Aurum: Aurum Funds Ltd 24
Autonomous: Autonomous Research LLP 25
Autonomy: Autonomy Corporation plc 25
Aveva: Aveva Group plc 26
Aviva: Aviva plc 26
Avon: Avon Cosmetics Ltd 28
Avon Rubber plc 28
AXA: AXA UK plc 29
Babcock: Babcock International Group plc 29
BAE: BAE Systems 30
Bain: Bain and Company Inc. United Kingdom 31
Balfour: Balfour Beatty plc 31
Bamford: J. C. Bamford Excavators Ltd 32
Bank: Bank of England 33
Bank of Ireland UK Financial Services Ltd 33
Banks: The Banks Group 34
Barclays: Barclays PLC 34
Barr: A. G. Barr plc 36
Barratt: Barratt Developments plc 36
BASF: BASF plc 36
Baxter: Baxter Healthcare Limited 37
Baxters: Baxters Food Group Limited 37
Bayer: Bayer plc 37
BBA: BBA Aviation plc 38
BC: BC Partners Limited 39
Beazley: Beazley plc 39
Bellway: Bellway plc 39
Berkeley: Berkeley Group plc 40
Bestway: Bestway (Holdings) Ltd 40
Betfair: Betfair Group Ltd 41
BGC: BGC International LP 41
BHP: BHP Billiton Plc 41
Big: Big Yellow Group plc 42
Birmingham: Birmingham International Airport Ltd 42
Biwater: Biwater Holdings Ltd 43
BlackRock: BlackRock Investment Management (UK) Limited 44
Bloomsbury: Bloomsbury Publishing plc 44
BlueBay: BlueBay Asset Management plc 44
BMW: BMW UK Ltd 45
Body: The Body Shop International PLC 45
Bodycote: Bodycote plc 47
Boodle: Boodle and Dunthorne Ltd 47
Booker: Booker Group plc 47
Boots: Boots 48
Boyer: Boyer Allan Investment Investment Management LLP 50
BP: BP Plc 51
Bradford: Bradford and Bingley plc 51
Bristol-Myers: Bristol-Myers Squibb Pharmaceuticals Ltd 52
Brit: Brit Insurance Holdings plc 52
British: British Airways plc 53
British American Tobacco plc 54
The British Land Company plc 54
British Sky Broadcasting Group plc 55
British Sugar plc 57
Britvic: Britvic Soft Drinks plc 57
Broadland: Broadland Properties Ltd 58
Brown: N. Brown Group plc 58
Bruntwood: Bruntwood Limited 58
BT: BT Group plc 59
BTG: BTG International Ltd 61
Bunzl: Bunzl plc 61
BUPA: BUPA Ltd 61
bwin.party: bwin.party 62
CA: CA plc 63
Cable: Cable and Wireless Worldwide plc 63
Cable and Wireless plc 64
Cadbury: Cadbury plc (now Kraft) 64
Cadogan: Cadogan Group Ltd 65
Caledonia: Caledonia Investments 65
Calor: Calor Gas Ltd 66
Camelot: Camelot Group plc 66
Canary: Canary Wharf Group plc 67
Canon: Canon UK Ltd 67
Caparo: Caparo Group Ltd 68
Capita: Capita Group plc 68
Capital: Capital One Holdings Ltd 69
Capital Shopping Centres Group PLC 70
Cargill: Cargill plc 70
Carillion: Carillion plc 71

Carphone: The Carphone Warehouse Group PLC 72
Catlin: Catlin Group Ltd 73
Cattles: Cattles plc 73
CEF: CEF Holdings Ltd 74
Celtic: Celtic Energy Ltd 74
CEMEX: CEMEX UK Operations 75
Center: Center Parcs Ltd 75
Centrica: Centrica plc 76
Channel: Channel 4 Television Corporation 77
Chelsea: Chelsea Building Society 78
Cheshire: Cheshire Building Society 78
Chrysalis: Chrysalis Group Limited 79
CIBC: CIBC World Markets plc 79
Citibank: Citibank International plc 79
Citroen: Citroen UK Ltd 81
Clinton: Clinton Cards plc 81
Close: Close Brothers Group plc 81
Clydesdale: Clydesdale Bank plc 82
Coats: Coats plc 83
Cobham: Cobham plc 84
Coca-Cola: Coca-Cola Great Britain 84
Colgate-Palmolive: Colgate-Palmolive UK Ltd 85
Colt: Colt Group 85
Communisis: Communisis plc 85
Compass: Compass Group plc 86
Computacenter: Computacenter plc 87
Congregational: Congregational and General Insurance plc 87
Cookson: Cookson Group plc 87
Cooper: Cooper Gay (Holdings) Ltd 88
Co-operative: Co-operative Group Limited 88
Cooper-Parry: Cooper-Parry LLP 91
Costain: Costain Group plc 91
Costcutter: Costcutter Supermarkets Group Ltd 92
Coutts: Coutts and Co 92
Coventry: Coventry Building Society 93
Credit: Credit Suisse 94
Crest: Crest Nicholson PLC 95
Croda: Croda International plc 95
Cummins: Cummins Ltd 95
Cussons: P. Z. Cussons plc 96
Daejan: Daejan Holdings plc 96
Daily: Daily Mail and General Trust plc 96
Dairy: Dairy Crest Group plc 97
Dana: Dana Petroleum plc 98
Darty: Darty plc (formerly Kesa Electricals plc) 99
DDB: DDB UK Ltd 99
De: De La Rue plc 99
Debenhams: Debenhams plc 100
Deep: Deep Sea Leisure plc 101
Deloitte: Deloitte 101
Derbyshire: Derbyshire Building Society 102
Deutsche: Deutsche Bank 102
Devro: Devro plc 104
Dhamecha: Dhamecha Holdings Ltd 104
Diageo: Diageo plc 105
Domino: Domino Printing Sciences plc 106
Doughty: Doughty Hanson and Co. Managers Ltd 107
Dow: Dow Chemical Company Ltd 107
Dow Corning Ltd 108
Drax: Drax Group plc 109
DSG: DSG International plc 109
Du: Du Pont (UK) Ltd 110
Duchy: Duchy Originals Ltd 111
Dunelm: Dunelm Group plc 111
Dŵr: Dŵr Cymru Welsh Water 111
Dyson: Dyson Limited 112
E.ON: E.ON UK plc 113
Eaga: Eaga plc 113
East: East Midlands Airport 114
easyJet: easyJet plc 114
Ecclesiastical: Ecclesiastical Insurance Group plc 115
Economist: Economist Newspaper Ltd 116
EDF: EDF Energy PLC 116
Electrocomponents: Electrocomponents plc 118
Elementis: Elementis plc 119
Eli: Eli Lilly and Company Limited 119
EMI: EMI Group Limited 120
ERM: ERM Group Holdings Ltd 121
Ernst: Ernst and Young LLP 121
Esh: Esh Group 122
Esso: Esso UK Group Ltd 123
Euro: Euro Packaging Limited 123
Evans: Evans Property Group Limited 124
Everything: Everything Everywhere Limited (formerly T-Mobile (UK) Ltd) 124
Execution: Execution Limited 125
FandC: FandC Asset Management plc 125
Family: Family Assurance Friendly Society Limited 126
Fenner: Fenner PLC 126
Fenwick: Fenwick Ltd 127
Fidelity: Fidelity Investment Management Limited 127
Fidessa: Fidessa Group plc 128
Filtronic: Filtronic plc 129
Financial: Financial Services Authority 129
Findel: Findel plc 130
First: First plc 130
Ford: Ford Motor Company Ltd 131
Forth: Forth Ports plc 132
Freshfields: Freshfields Bruuckhaus Deringer LLP 132
Friends: Friends Life FPL Limited 133
Fujitsu: Fujitsu Services Holdings PLC 134
Future: Future plc 134
G4S: G4S plc 135
Game: The Game Group plc 135
GAP: GAP (UK) Ltd 136
GE: GE Healthcare 136
General: General Motors UK Ltd 137
Genting: Genting UK plc 137
Geopost: Geopost UK Limited 137
GKN: GKN plc 138
Gladedale: Gladedale Group Holdings Ltd 138
GlaxoSmithKline: GlaxoSmithKline plc 138
Glencore: Glencore UK Ltd 140
Go: The Go Ahead Group plc 140
Goldman: Goldman Sachs International 141
Grainger: Grainger plc 143
Great: Great Portland Estates plc 143
Greencore: Greencore Group UK 143
Greene: Greene King plc 144
Greggs: Greggs plc 145
Grosvenor: Grosvenor Group 146
Guardian: Guardian Media Group plc 147
Halfords: Halfords Group plc 147
Halma: Halma plc 148
Hammerson: Hammerson plc 148
Hasbro: Hasbro UK Limited 148
Heathrow: Heathrow Airport Holdings Limited (formerly BAA Limited) 149
Heineken: Heineken UK Ltd 150
Heinz: H. J. Heinz Co. Ltd 150
Helical: Helical bar plc 151
Henderson: Henderson Group plc 151
Herbert: Herbert Smith Freehills LLP 152
HESCO: HESCO Bastion Limited 152
Hess: Hess Ltd 153
Hewlett-Packard: Hewlett-Packard Ltd 154
HFC: HFC Bank Ltd 154
Hibu: Hibu (formerly Yell Group plc) 155
Hikma: Hikma Pharmaceuticals PLC 155
Hill: William Hill Plc 156
Hiscox: Hiscox plc 156
Hodge: Julian Hodge Bank Ltd 157
HomeServe: HomeServe plc 157
Honda: Honda of the UK Manufacturing Limited 158
Hoover: Hoover Ltd 158
House: House of Fraser (Stores) Limited 158
Howden: Howden Joinery Group Plc 159

HP: HP Enterprise Services UK Limited 159
HSBC: HSBC Holdings plc 160
Hudson: Alan Hudson Ltd 161
Hunting: Hunting plc 161
Huntsman: Huntsman / Tioxide Europe Ltd 162
IBM: IBM United Kingdom Ltd 162
ICAP: ICAP plc 163
IG: IG Group Holdings plc 164
Imagination: Imagination Technologies Group plc 164
IMI: IMI plc 165
Imperial: Imperial Tobacco Group PLC 165
Inchcape: Inchcape plc 166
Informa: Informa plc 167
Innocent: Innocent Drinks 167
Intercontinental: Intercontinental Hotels Group plc 167
International: International Personal Finance 168
Invensys: Invensys plc 169
Investec: Investec plc 169
IPC: IPC Media Limited 170
ITV: ITV PLC 171
Jaguar: Jaguar Cars Ltd 172
Jardine: Jardine Lloyd Thompson Group plc 173
JD: JD Sports Fashion plc 173
JJB: JJB Sports plc 173
Johnson: S. C. Johnson Ltd 174
Johnson Matthey plc 174
Johnson Service Group plc 175
Johnston: Johnston Press plc 175
Jones: Jones Lang LaSalle Ltd 176
Keepmoat: Keepmoat Ltd 176
Kelda: Kelda Group Ltd 177
Keller: Keller Group plc 177
Kellogg: Kellogg Company of Great Britain Limited 178
Kier: Kier Group plc 179
Kingfisher: Kingfisher plc 179
Kodak: Kodak Ltd 180
KPMG: KPMG LLP 180
Kraft: Kraft Foods UK Ltd 181
Kwik-Fit: Kwik-Fit Group 182
Ladbrokes: Ladbrokes PLC 182
Lafarge: Lafarge Aggregates Ltd 183
Laird: The Laird Group plc 183
Lancashire: Lancashire Holdings Limited 184
Land: Land Securities Group PLC 184
Lazard: Lazard and Co. Ltd 185
Leeds: Leeds Building Society 185
Legal: Legal and General plc 185
Lewis: John Lewis Partnership plc 186
Linklaters: Linklaters 187
LINPAC: LINPAC Group Limited 189
Littlewoods: Littlewoods Shop Direct Home Shopping Ltd 189
Liverpool: Liverpool Victoria 190
Lloyd's: Lloyd's 190
Lloyds: Lloyds Banking Group 191
Lockheed: Lockheed Martin UK Ltd 193
Lofthouse: Lofthouse of Fleetwood Ltd 194
Logica: Logica plc 194
Lonmin: Lonmin plc 195
Low: Low and Bonar plc 195
Lush: Lush Cosmetics Limited 195
Man: Man Group plc 196
Manchester: Manchester Airport Group plc 197
Marks: Marks and Spencer Group plc 198
Marsh: Marsh Ltd 199
Marshall: Marshall of Cambridge (Holdings) Ltd 199
Marston's: Marston's plc 200
Mascolo: Mascolo Ltd 200
Matthews: Bernard Matthews Ltd 201
Mazars: Mazars LLP 201
McAlpine: Robert McAlpine Ltd 202
McBride: McBride plc 202
McCain: McCain Foods (GB) Ltd 203
McDonalds: McDonalds Restaurants Ltd 203
Medtronic: Medtronic Ltd 204
Meggitt: Meggitt PLC 204
Melrose: Melrose plc 205
Menzies: John Menzies plc 205
Merck: Merck Sharp and Dohme Ltd 206
Mersey: The Mersey Docks and Harbour Company 206
Metaswitch: Metaswitch Networks Limited 207
Michelin: Michelin Tyre plc 207
Micro: Micro Focus International plc 208
Microsoft: Microsoft Ltd 208
Midcounties: The Midcounties Co-operative 209
Miller: Miller Group Limited 210
Mitchells: Mitchells and Butlers plc 210
MITIE: MITIE Group plc 211
Moneysupermarket.com: Moneysupermarket.com Group plc 211
Morgan: Morgan Advanced Materials plc (formerly Morgan Crucible Company plc) 212
J. P. Morgan Chase 212
Morgan Stanley International Limited 213
Morris: T. J. Morris Limited 214
Morrison: W. Morrison Supermarkets plc 214
Mothercare: Mothercare plc 214
Mott: Mott MacDonald Ltd 215
Muir: Muir Group plc 215
National: National Express Group plc 216
The National Farmers Union Mutual Insurance Society Ltd 216
National Grid Holdings One plc 217
National Magazine Co. Ltd 218
Nationwide: Nationwide Building Society 218
Nestlé: Nestlé Holdings (UK) plc 220
Network: Network Rail Infrastructure Limited 220
Newcastle: Newcastle Building Society 221
News: News International Ltd 222
Next: Next plc 223
Nike: Nike (UK) Ltd 224
Northern: Northern and Shell Network Limited 224
Northern Foods Limited 225
Northern Powergrid Holdings Company (formerly CE Electric) 225
Northern Rock (Asset Management) plc 225
Northern Trust Group Ltd 227
Northumbrian: Northumbrian Water Group 227
Nottingham: Nottingham Building Society 228
Novae: Novae Group plc 228
Ocado: Ocado Group Ltd 229
Old: Old Mutual plc 229
Oracle: Oracle Corporation UK Ltd 230
Organix: Organix Brands Ltd 231
Osborne: Osborne and Little Ltd 231
Page: Page Group (formerly Michael Page International) 231
Palmer: Palmer and Harvey McLane Ltd 232
Paragon: Paragon Group of Companies plc 232
Pearson: Pearson plc 232
Pennon: Pennon Group plc 233
Pentland: Pentland Group plc 234
PepsiCo: PepsiCo International 235
Persimmon: Persimmon plc 235
Personal: Personal Group Holdings plc 235
Pfizer: Pfizer Limited 236
Philips: Philips Electronics UK Ltd 237
Pilkington: Pilkington Group Ltd 238
PKF: PKF (UK) LLP 238
Premier: Premier Farnell plc 238
Premier Foods plc 239
PricewaterhouseCoopers: PricewaterhouseCoopers LLP 240
Principality: Principality Building Society 241
Private: Private Equity Foundation 241
Procter: Procter and Gamble UK 242
Provident: Provident Financial plc 243
Prudential: Prudential plc 244
Psion: Psion plc 246
Punch: Punch Taverns plc 246

QinetiQ: QinetiQ Group plc 246
RAB: RAB Capital plc 247
Rank: The Rank Group plc 247
Rathbone: Rathbone Brothers Plc 248
Ravensale: Ravensale Ltd 248
Reckitt: Reckitt Benckiser Group plc 249
Redrow: Redrow Group plc 249
Rentokil: Rentokil Initial plc 250
Rexam: Rexam PLC 250
Richer: Richer Sounds plc 251
Ridgesave: Ridgesave Limited 251
Rio: Rio Tinto plc 252
RM: RM plc 252
Roche: Roche Products Ltd 253
Rolls–Royce: Rolls–Royce plc 253
Rothschild: N. M. Rothschild and Sons Ltd 254
Rotork: Rotork plc 255
Royal: The Royal Bank of Scotland Group plc 256
The Royal London Mutual Insurance Society Ltd 258
Royal Mail Group plc 258
RPS: RPS Group Plc 259
RSA: RSA Insurance Group plc (formerly Royal and Sun Alliance Insurance Group plc) 260
Saga: Saga Group Ltd 261
Sainsbury: J. Sainsbury plc 262
Samsung: Samsung Electronics (UK) Ltd 264
Santander: Santander UK 264
Savills: Savills plc 266
Schroders: Schroders plc 267
Scott: Scott Bader Company Ltd 268
ScottishPower: ScottishPower plc 268
SDL: SDL International plc 270
SEGRO: SEGRO plc 271
Senior: Senior plc 271
Serco: Serco Group plc 272
Severn: Severn Trent plc 273
Shaftesbury: Shaftesbury plc 273
Shanks: Shanks Group plc 274
Shell: Shell 274
Shepherd: Shepherd Building Group Ltd 276
Shire: Shire Pharmaceuticals plc 277
Shoe: Shoe Zone Ltd 278
Siemens: Siemens plc 278
SIG: SIG plc 279
Simmons: Simmons and Simmons LLP 280
Slaughter: Slaughter and May 280
Smith: Smith and Nephew plc 281
D. S. Smith Holdings plc 281
W. H. Smith plc 282
Smiths: Smiths Group plc 282
Sodexo: Sodexo Ltd 283
Sony: Sony Europe Limited 284
Southern: Southern Co-operatives Ltd 285
Spar: Spar (UK) Ltd 285
Spectris: Spectris plc 285
Spirax: Spirax Sarco Engineering plc 286
Spirent: Spirent plc 286
Sportech: Sportech PLC 287
Sportingbet: Sportingbet plc 287
Sports: Sports Direct International plc 288
SSE: SSE plc (formerly Scottish and Southern Energy plc) 289
Saint: St James's Place plc 290
St Modwen Properties plc 291
Stagecoach: Stagecoach Group plc 292
Standard: Standard Chartered plc 292
Standard Life 293
Starbucks: Starbucks Coffee Company (UK) Ltd 294
Stemcor: Stemcor Holdings Ltd 295
Steria: Steria Limited 295
SThree: SThree plc 296
Stobart: J. Stobart and Sons Ltd 296
Stobart Group 297
Strauss: Levi Strauss (UK) Ltd 298
STV: STV Group plc 298
Swann-Morton: Swann-Morton Ltd 299
Swire: John Swire and Sons Ltd 299
Synergy: Synergy Health plc 300
Synthomer: Synthomer plc (formerly Yule and Catto Co.) 300
Tata: Tata Steel Europe Limited 301
Tate: Tate and Lyle plc 301
Taylor: Taylor Wimpey plc 302
TelecityGroup: TelecityGroup 302
Telefonica: Telefonica UK Limited 303
Telegraph: Telegraph Media Group Ltd 304
Tesco: Tesco plc 304
Thales: Thales UK Limited 306
Thomas: Thomas Cook Group plc 306
Thomson: Thomson Reuters PLC 308
Thwaites: Daniel Thwaites plc 309
TJX: TJX UK (formerly TK Maxx) 310
TNT: TNT UK Limited 310
Tomkins: Tomkins Ltd 311
Topps: Topps Tiles plc 311
Toshiba: Toshiba Information Systems (UK) Ltd 312
Total: Total UK Ltd 312
Toyota: Toyota Motor Manufacturing (UK) Ltd 313
Travelex: Travelex Holdings Ltd 313
Travis: Travis Perkins plc 314
Trinity: Trinity Mirror plc 315
TT: TT Electronics plc 315
TUI: TUI Travel plc 316
Tullis: Tullis Russell Group Ltd 316
UBS: UBS 316
UIA: UIA (Insurance) Ltd 317
UK: UK Coal plc 318
Ultra: Ultra Electronics Holdings plc 318
Unilever: Unilever UK 319
Unipart: Unipart Group of Companies Ltd 320
Unisys: Unisys Ltd 320
UNITE: UNITE Group plc 321
United: United Biscuits Ltd 321
United Business Media Limited 322
United Utilities Group PLC 322
Unum: Unum 323
UPS: UPS 324
Valero: Valero Energy Limited (Chevron Ltd) 325
Victrex: Victrex plc 325
Virgin: Virgin Atlantic Limited 325
Vodafone: Vodafone Group plc 327
Warburtons: Warburtons Ltd 329
Wates: Wates Group Ltd 329
Weetabix: Weetabix Ltd 330
Weir: The Weir Group PLC 330
Wessex: Wessex Water Services Ltd 331
West: West Bromwich Building Society 331
Western: Western Power Distribution 332
Wetherspoon: J. D. Wetherspoon plc 333
Whitbread: Whitbread PLC 333
Wilkinson: Wilkinson Hardware Stores Ltd 334
Willmott: Willmott Dixon Holdings plc 334
Wiseman: Robert Wiseman Dairies plc 335
Wolseley: Wolseley plc 335
Wood: John Wood Group 336
WPP: WPP Group plc 336
Wragge: Wragge and Co. LLP 337
WSP: WSP Group plc 338
Xchanging: Xchanging plc 339
Xerox: Xerox (UK) Ltd 339
Yattendon: Yattendon Group plc (formerly Yattendon Investment Trust plc) 339
Yorkshire: Yorkshire Building Society 340
Zurich: Zurich Financial Services (UKISA) Ltd 341

What else can DSC do for you?

Let us help you to be the best corporate fundraiser that you can possibly be. DSC can equip you with expert skills and information centred around raising money from companies. With the latest techniques, best practice and funding resources all brought to you by our team of experts, you will not only boost your corporate income but also exceed your expectations.

Publications

More than 60 fundraising titles covering thousands of funding sources and the latest in fundraising techniques.

Training

The voluntary sector's best-selling fundraising training – 28 courses covering every type of fundraising, including cororate support and funding.

In-house Training

Our courses, your premises

Expert trainers and facilitators working closely with you on your premises, offering coaching, consultancy, mentoring and support.

Conferences and Fairs

DSC conferences are a fantastic way to network with voluntary sector professionals whilst taking part in intensive practical training workshops.

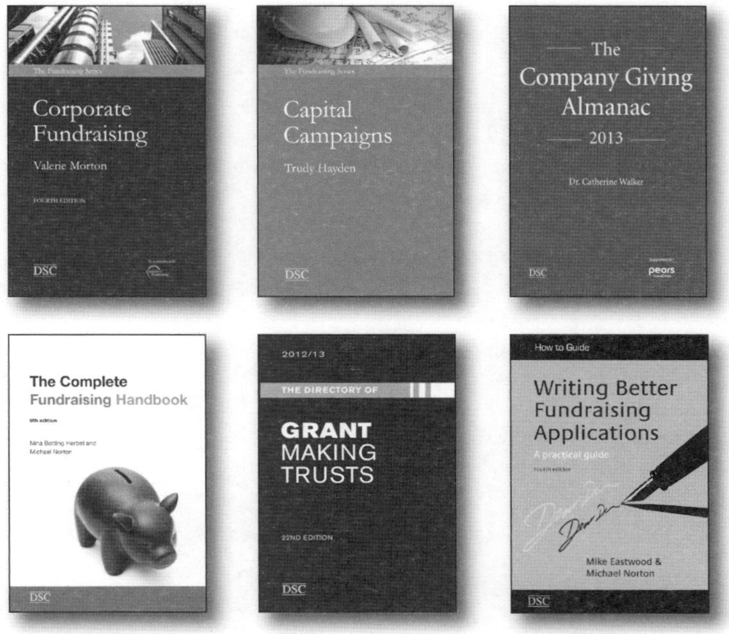

Funding Websites

*DSC's funding websites provide access to thousands of trusts, grants, statutory funds and corporate donations. You won't get more funders, commentary and analysis anywhere else. Demo one of our sites **free** today.*

Trust**funding**.org.uk
Government**funding**.org.uk
Company**giving**.org.uk
Grantsfor**individuals**.org.uk

Visit our website today and see what we can do for you:

www.**dsc.org.uk**

Or contact us directly: publications@dsc.org.uk

@DSC_Charity
For top tips and special offers

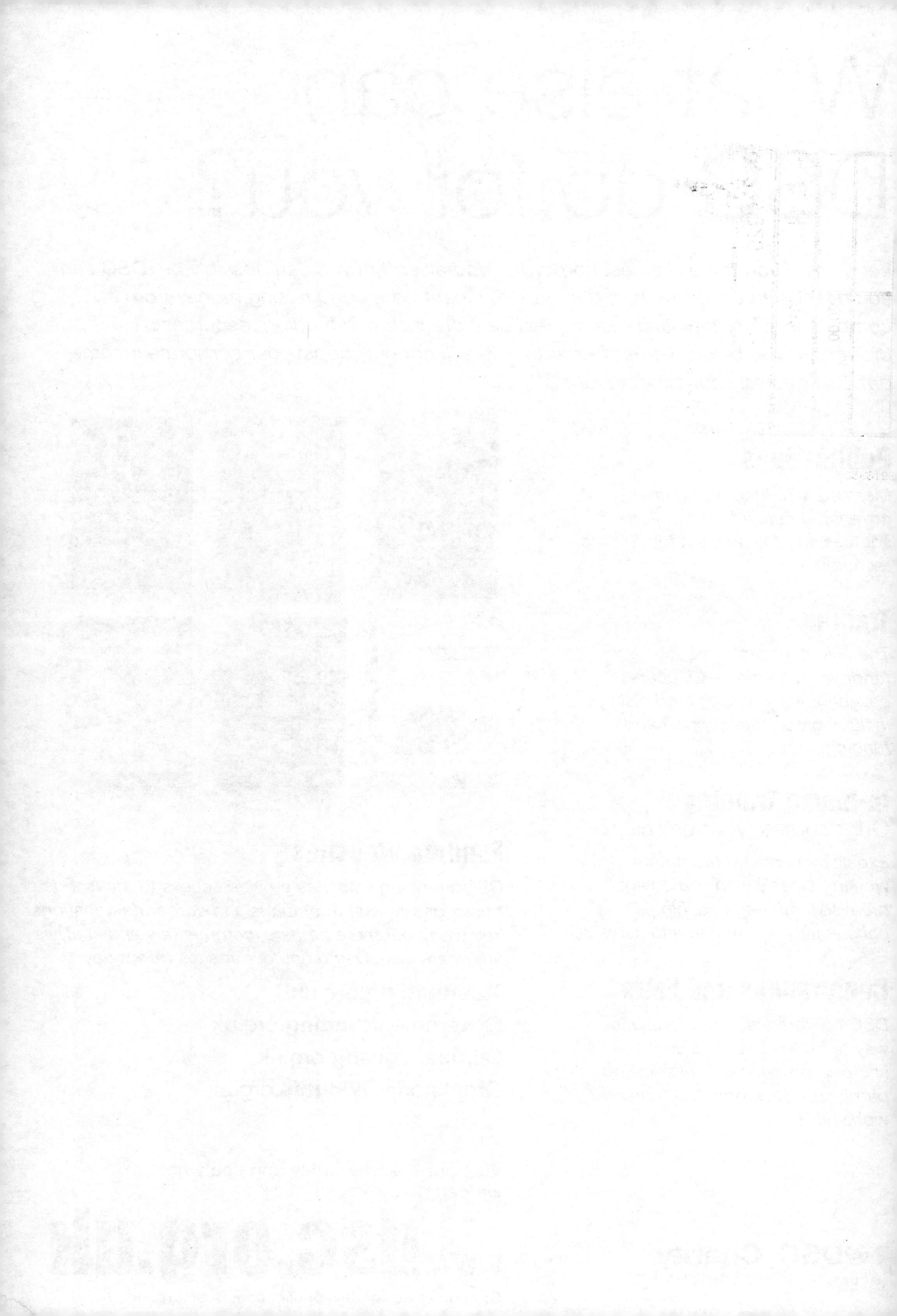